BARRON'S

HOW TO PREPARE FOR THE GED

HIGH SCHOOL EQUIVALENCY EXAM

10TH EDITION

Murray Rockowitz, Ph.D.
Former Chairman, Board of Examiners,
New York City Board of Education
Former Principal,
John Philip Sousa Junior High School,
New York City
Former Chairman, English Department,
Charles Evans Hughes High School,
New York City

Samuel C. Brownstein
Former Chairman, Biology Department,
Wingate High School, Brooklyn, New York

Max Peters
Former Chairman, Mathematics Department,
Wingate High School, Brooklyn, New York

Ira K. Wolf, Ph.D.
Teacher of Mathematics
Benjamin N. Cardozo High School
Bayside, New York

Johanna M. Bolton
Instructor, Adult High School Program
Daytona Beach Community College
Daytona Beach, Florida

All inquiries should be addressed to:
Barron's Educational Series, Inc.
250 Wireless Boulevard
Hauppauge, New York 11788
http://www.barronseduc.com

Library of Congress Catalog No. 98-27424

International Standard Book No. (without computer disks) 0-7641-0433-0
International Standard Book No. (with computer disks) 0-7641-7205-0

Library of Congress Cataloging-in-Publication Data

How to prepare for the GED High School Equivalency Examination /
Murray Rockowitz . . . [et al.]. — 10th ed.
p. cm.
Rev. ed. of: How to prepare for the GED High School Equivalency Examination / Murray Rockowitz, Samuel C. Brownstein, Max Peters. 9th ed. c1995.
ISBN 0-7641-0433-0 (book). — ISBN 0-7641-7205-0 (book/disk pkg.)
1. General educational development tests—Study guides.
2. High school equivalency examinations—Study guides.
I. Rockowitz, Murray.
LB3060.33.G45R63 1998
373.126'2—dc21
98-27424
CIP

PRINTED IN THE UNITED STATES OF AMERICA
9 8 7 6

CONTENTS

PREFACE

This edition includes the most recent changes in the content and format of the tests of General Educational Development (GED) required to qualify for a High School Equivalency Diploma. The authors, all specialists in various areas of the high school curriculum, have developed practice exercises and tests that reflect these changes and provide extensive preparation for the GED Examination.

TO THE READER

"Until recently, all we asked of job applicants was that they be able to sign their names and find their way to the time clock. Now they've got to have a high school diploma." These words of an electronics manufacturer are a warning to the student and jobseeker of today.

IF you want an interesting job—one that does not lead to a dead end;
IF you want to be accepted into a good company's apprenticeship program;
IF you want to advance on the job from a one-operation task to the technician or troubleshooting level;
IF you want to continue your studies at a technical school;
IF you want to get a technical or junior professional Civil Service position;
IF you want to be accepted in a specialized assignment in the Armed Forces;

you must have a high school diploma.

If you have not yet completed high school, this book will help you earn that precious diploma by passing a High School Equivalency Examination. All fifty states, the District of Columbia, many U.S. territories, and most Canadian provinces have programs that enable you to do this.

To help you,

we have carefully analyzed the latest GED tests, and, on the basis of that analysis, have prepared materials that provide:

- explanations of key ideas,
- concise summaries of each topic,
- thorough drill exercises,
- realistic practice tests.

All you need add is the determination to use these materials according to the schedule we have suggested. If you do, you will gain the confidence and knowledge you need to pass the High School Equivalency Examination and earn your high school diploma.

TO THE INSTRUCTOR

If you are using this book in a class preparing for the High School Equivalency Examination, please note that:

- all necessary background materials have been included;
- after every principle, appropriate illustrations may be found;
- after each topic and subtopic, there are ample drill exercises;
- sample reading selections have been thoroughly analyzed;
- answers for all exercises have been included and, in most cases, explanations for the correct answer are given.

You will *not* have to go to any other sources for additional materials. We have included more than enough practice and drill for any student in your class who seeks the High School Equivalency Diploma.

ACKNOWLEDGMENTS

The authors gratefully acknowledge the kindness of all organizations concerned with the granting of permission to reprint passages, charts, graphs, and outlines. The test directions used in our diagnostic and practice examinations were adapted with permission from the "Official GED Practice Test" published by the GED Testing Service of the American Council on Education.

We are indebted to Scholastic Magazines, Inc. for their kind permission to reproduce passages from *Senior Scholastic* that formed the basis for original questions interpreting items to be analyzed in social studies. Sources and permissions for charts and graphs appear on the appropriate pages throughout the book through the courtesy of the following organizations: U.S. Department of Agriculture; U.S. Department of Health, Education and Welfare—Office of Education; U.S. Bureau of the Budget; Social Security Administration.

The copyright holders and publishers of quoted materials are listed below.

Page 34, Graph for Questions 39–40: Frederick S. Mattson, reprinted by permission of CDM and Associates, Arlington, Virginia.

Page 39, Cartoon for Questions 62–63: from *The Times Union*, July 1991.

Pages 55–56, Passage for Questions 11–15: Excerpt from ALL GOD'S CHILDREN NEED TRAVELING SHOES by Maya Angelou, Copyright © 1986 by Maya Angelou. Reprinted by permission of Random House, Inc.

Page 57, Poem for Questions 21–25: from "Elegy for Jane" by Theodore Roethke, Copyright © 1950 by Theodore Roethke, in COLLECTED POEMS OF THEODORE ROETHKE. Reprinted by permission of Doubleday & Co., Inc.

Pages 58–59, Passage for Questions 26–30: from *A Raisin in the Sun*, by Lorraine Hansberry. Copyright © 1958 by Robert Nemiroff, as an unpublished work. Copyright © 1959, 1966, 1984 by Robert Nemiroff. Reprinted by permission of Random House, Inc.

Pages 59–60, Passage for Questions 31–35 from "Memoirs of Chief Red Fox." Copyright © McGraw-Hill 1997.

Page 233, Passage from *Paths to the Present*, by Arthur M. Schlesinger, Sr. Reprinted by permission of Arthur Schlesinger, Jr.

Page 237, Passage from Arthur H. Doerr and J.L. Guernsey, *Principles of Geography—Physical and Cultural*, Second Edition Revised. Copyright © 1975 Barron's Educational Series, Inc.

Page 240, Passage 2 from "Cultural Differences" in *Global Studies, Vol. 1*, 2nd Edition. Copyright © 1993 Barron's Educational Series, Inc.

Page 245, Pie Graph from *Annual Energy Review*. Copyright © 1995 *Energy Information Review*.

Page 246, Line Graph adapted from Klose and Lader, *College Review: United States History*, Vol. 2 Copyright © 1994 Barron's Educational Series, Inc.

Page 258, Table for Questions 38–40: from *Let's Review Global Studies*, 2nd Edition. Copyright © 1994 Barron's Educational Series, Inc.

Pages 300–301, Passage for Questions 13–15: from a speech by Jonathan Kozol, Boston College, May 1969.

Pages 302–303, Passage for Questions 22–25: from "What It Is Like To Be Underdeveloped" in *Global Studies, Vol. I*, 2nd Edition. Copyright © 1993 Barron's Educational Series, Inc.

Pages 303–304, Passage for Questions 26–28: from "Apologies to the Iroquois" by Edmund Wilson, Copyright © 1992. Reprinted by permission of Syracuse University Press.

Page 305, Passage for Questions 35–37: from "Indians" in *The Reader's Companion to American History*. Copyright © 1991 Houghton Mifflin.

Page 307, Passage for Questions 44–46: from Erwin Rosenfeld and Harriet Geller, *Afro-Asian Culture Studies*, Second Revised Edition. Copyright © 1976 Barron's Educational Series, Inc.

Page 308, Map and Passage for Questions 47–49: from Erwin Rosenfeld and Harriet Geller, *Afro-Asian Culture Studies*, Second Revised Edition. Copyright © 1976 Barron's Educational Series, Inc.

Page 309, Passage for Questions 50–52: from "Conservation and Environmental Movements" in *The Reader's Companion to American History*. Copyright © 1991 Houghton Mifflin.

Pages 309–310, Passage for Questions 53–55: from "Women and the Work Force" in *The Reader's Companion to American History*. Copyright © 1991 Houghton Mifflin.

Page 311, Passage for Questions 62–64: Gordon H. Bower, "How to . . . Uh . . . Remember!" reprinted with permission from *Psychology Today Magazine*. Copyright © 1973.

Page 353–354, Passage for Questions 37–39: adapted from Carl P. Swanson, *The Cell*, Second Edition, Copyright © 1964, p. 23. Reprinted by permission of Prentice-Hall, Inc., Englewood Cliffs, New Jersey.

Pages 409–410, Article from *Investor's Business Daily*, December 1, 1997.

Page 420, Passage for Questions 31–35: from *The Adventures of Augie March* by Saul Bellow. Copyright © 1949, 1951, 1952, 1953 Saul Bellow. Used by permission of Viking Penguin, a division of Penguin Books USA Inc.

Page 421, Poem for Questions 36–40: from "Along" by Maya Angelou in *Poems*. Copyright © Random House 1986.

Page 422, Poem for Questions 41–45: from "Old Photograph of the Future" by Robert Penn Warren. Copyright © 1979 Random House.

Page 423, Passage for Questions 46–50: from *Ordinary People* by Judith Guest, filmscript Paramount Pictures.

Page 431, Passage for Questions 86–90: from "The Mother" in *Television Plays* by Paddy Chayevsky. Copyright © 1955 by Simon and Schuster.

Page 432, Passage for Questions 91–95: from "Destruction Men" by Michael Goldstein in *New York Magazine*, May 28, 1994, pp. 63–64.

Page 433, Passage for Questions 96–100: from "The Shakespeare Nobody Knows" by Leo Rosten in *Reader's Digest*, October 1986, pp. 38–40.

Page 434, Passage for Questions 101–105: from *America as a Civilization*, by Max Lerner. Copyright © 1957, 1985 by Max Lerner. Reprinted by permission of Simon & Schuster, Inc.

Pages 434–435, Passage for Questions 106–110: from "Hollywood's John Ford" by Charles Oliver in *Investor's Business Daily*, April 21, 1994, pp. 1–2.

Page 591, Cartoon for Question 9: from *The Pittsburgh Post Gazette*, 1994.

Page 600, Passage for Questions 46 and 47: excerpted with permission from "Don't Be Afraid to Let Your Feelings Show," by John Kord Lagamann, in *Reader's Digest*, May 1976, pp. 205–210. Copyright © 1976 by the Reader's Digest Association, Inc.

Page 623, Passage for Questions 6–10: from "Literary Cavalcade" by Leonel I. Castillo. Copyright © December 1986 Scholastic, Inc.

Page 625, Poem for Questions 21–25: from "To A Photographer" by Barton Braley. Copyright © 1965 Barton Braley.

Page 626, Passage for Questions 26–30: from Howard Lindsay and Russell Crouse, *State of the Union*. Copyright © 1946 Random House.

Page 690, Passage for Questions 27 and 28: from Arthur H. Doerr and J.L. Guernsey, *Principles of Geography—Physical and Cultural*, Second Edition Revised. Copyright © 1975 Barron's Educational Series, Inc.

Page 694, Passage for Questions 44–46: excerpted with permission from "Making it More Intimate," by Alice Fleming, in *Reader's Digest*, October 1976, pp. 155–158. Copyright © 1976 by the Reader's Digest Association, Inc.

Page 697, Cartoon for Question 58: from *The Miami Herald*. Copyright © 1990 Morin.

Page 699, Cartoon for Question 64: from *The Los Angeles Times Syndicate*. Copyright © 1990 Danziger.

Page 715, Passage for Questions 1–5: from "Magnificent Hybrid: A Rockefeller Aerie" by Paul Goldberger in *The New York Times*, May 6, 1994, p. C 30.

Page 716, Passage for Questions 6–10: from "Green Seal of Approval" by Michael Lipske in *National Wildlife*, June–July 1994, pp. 22–23.

Page 720, Passage for Questions 26–30: from Arthur Miller, *Death of a Salesman*. Copyright © 1949 The Viking Press.

Page 722, Passage for Questions 36–40: from "Willa Cather: Voice of the Frontier," by William Howarth. Copyright © 1982 by National Geographic Society.

Page 723, Passage for Questions 41–45: excerpted with permission from "Oscar: Little Statue of Dreams," by John Culhane in *Reader's Digest*, March 1987. Copyright © 1987 by the Reader's Digest Association, Inc.

UNIT I

INTRODUCTION TO THE GED EXAMINATION

Preparing for the GED Examination

The Importance of the GED Examination

The General Education Development or GED Examination offers anyone who has not completed his or her high school diploma a way to earn a High School Equivalency Certificate. This is the equivalent of a high school diploma, and it is necessary for those who want to continue their education in college or another career-oriented program. Having a high school diploma today is also very important if you want a good job.

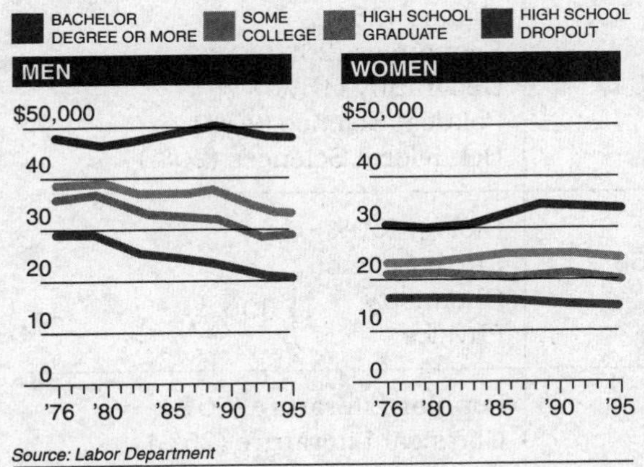

Source: Labor Department

Study these graphs briefly. Note that the black line indicates the average annual earnings of high school graduates aged 25 to 64. The bottom gray line represents the average annual earnings of high school dropouts of similar age. Compare the two lines for 1995. You see that high school graduates earned much more than high school dropouts. Men earned nearly $10,000 a year more; women earned over $5,000 a year more. Over the span of years from age 25 to age 64, a male high school graduate earns about $400,000 more than a high school dropout; the woman graduate earns over $200,000 more. *It pays to have a high school diploma.*

This book has been written to help you prepare to take the GED Examination. It contains reviews of the subject material, practice exercises, and even practice tests, all of which will familiarize you with the content and format of the actual examination. Nearly two million people have already used this book to help them pass the GED Examination. You can too!

The Five GED Test Areas

The GED Examination is divided into five tests:

1. Writing Skills
2. Social Studies
3. Science
4. Literature and the Arts
5. Mathematics

The five tests are designed to measure the knowledge and skills that a student should have acquired after four years in high school. One important thing about the tests is that, even though the questions may involve a specific area of study such as science, you don't have to memorize specific facts, details, dates, or even exact definitions. Much of this information is given to you in the test itself. You have to be able to read and understand the material that is presented and then to answer questions about it.

With the exception of the essay part of the Writing Skills test, all of the questions in the GED Examination are multiple-choice. You will be given a brief statement, short passage, map, table, or diagram, and then you will have to answer one or more multiple-choice questions about this material. This book will help you learn how to analyze and use information presented in these various ways.

Commonly Asked Questions About the GED Tests

1. ***Who can take the GED tests?*** Adults who meet the eligibility requirements established by their state, territorial, or provincial departments of education can take the GED tests.
2. ***Where are the GED tests given?*** The address of your state, territorial, or provincial administrator can be obtained from your local high school. Write to that office for the location of the GED testing center nearest your home.

TIMETABLE OF A HIGH SCHOOL EQUIVALENCY EXAMINATION
TOTAL: 7 HOURS, 35 MINUTES

	Section	Time Allowed*	Number of Test Items*	Description
Test 1	The Writing Skills Test Part I	75 minutes	55	Sentence Structure (35%) Usage (35%) Mechanics (spelling, punctuation, capitalization) (30%)
	Part II	45 minutes		Essay on a given topic
Test 2	The Social Studies Test	85 minutes	64	History (25%) Economics (20%) Geography (15%) Political Science (20%) Behavioral Sciences (20%)
Test 3	The Science Test	95 minutes	66	Biology (50%) Earth Science, Chemistry, Physics } 50%
Test 4	The Interpreting Literature and the Arts Test	65 minutes	45	Popular Literature (50%) Classical Literature (25%) Commentary About Literature and the Arts (25%)
Test 5	The Mathematics Test	90 minutes	56	Arithmetic (50%) Algebra (30%) Geometry (20%)

3. ***What score is required to earn a High School Equivalency Diploma?*** The standard score requirements vary for each state, territory, or province. You will find that in some states a candidate must earn a minimum score of 40 on each of the five test areas or a minimum average score of 45 for the five tests. The majority of states require a minimum average score of 45 and no individual test score below 35 or 40.
4. ***What types of questions are on the GED tests?*** Part II of the Writing Skills test requires a written essay. For the other test questions, you will be given information in the form of a written passage, graph, diagram, map, or table, and asked to answer one or more multiple-choice questions based on the information presented. Five answer choices are given for each question.
5. ***How can experience outside the classroom help me pass the GED tests?*** Many people worry about the difficulty of taking the GED Examination, especially if they've been out of school for a long time. What you should realize is that learning continues after you leave school. You read newspapers and follow political events; you travel and talk to many different people; you listen to the radio, watch television, and go to the movies. All of these experiences are forms of learning and add to your educational background.
6. ***Why are maturity and motivation strong assets?*** More mature students have experiences that will help them visualize or understand situations that may be involved in a problem on the GED Examination. Also, older students understand the need for good study habits and have the self-discipline to work regularly in this book. With the mature decision to study for the GED tests, half the battle is over. Many educators know that motivation, the desire to learn, is the first step toward success.
7. ***When are you ready to take the GED Examination?*** After reviewing and doing the practice exercises, take the practice tests in Unit VIII, and score your results. If your scores are in the category Good or Excellent, you are probably ready to walk into the examination room with confidence. If, however, you did not attain such scores, do not apply for the GED Examination until you have studied further. Concentrate on the areas in which you are weak. This chapter includes a thirty-session study schedule (see page 8).

Organizing Your Plan of Study

SOME STUDY HINTS

Educators agree that, for learning to be efficient, certain steps must be followed. As a mature person, you will probably appreciate the value of carefully following these ten tips for successful study.

1. **Physical conditions.** Find a quiet place. Tolerate no distraction—noise or music. Do not work in an overheated room.
2. **Timing.** You will learn faster and remember longer if you study in several short sessions rather than in one long session. Do not attempt to study for an entire weekend. Fatigue will set in after a few hours. It is wiser to spend some time each day rather than to "cram" your work into one or two days.
3. **Schedule for study.** A study schedule must be workable, realistic, practical, and, above all, suited to you and your other obligations. Decide which days and hours you can spare for study. Make a schedule, and stick to it.
4. **Using odd moments.** Put spare time and wasted moments to work. Riding on the bus or train may be a good time to memorize troublesome spelling words and to study rules of grammar or definitions of unfamiliar terms.
5. **Efficiency.** Most people find that learning occurs faster in the early part of the day. Perhaps you can work into your schedule some time for study before your day's work begins or on weekend mornings. Certainly you should not schedule study in the later hours of the evening.
6. **Review periods.** On certain days, plan to review. Take stock of yourself in these study periods. This review will serve at least two purposes. It will definitely reinforce the learning, and the gratification of knowing that you have acquired new

material will stimulate you to learn more.

7. **Writing while you learn.** Wherever possible, write what you are studying. Spelling can best be learned by writing. Get into the habit of writing down key ideas of the passages you read. This writing will focus attention on your learning, will help you avoid distractions that may cause your mind to wander, and will provide an opportunity to check up on yourself. Also, educators believe that the more senses employed while studying, the more effective the learning will be.
8. **Reading.** The best way to improve reading comprehension is by practicing reading. You will find that a great part of the test involves the interpretation of reading material. Read your newspaper very carefully. Make it a habit to read the editorials. If possible, engage a member of your family or a friend in frequent discussions of the ideas presented in your newspaper. Of course, this book has specific reading exercises on the various phases of the test. But remember: there is no substitute for general reading.
9. **The dictionary.** The most important single book, in addition to this one, that can help you prepare for the High School Equivalency Examination is the dictionary. It is important to have one nearby as you study. A suggested inexpensive dictionary is the pocket-size paperback edition of *Webster's New World Dictionary of the American Language*.
10. **S Q 3R.** A popular way to remember the five important steps needed to study effectively is the S Q 3R method.
    - S stands for survey. You examine the material to be learned to get a general idea of the content.
    - Q stands for question. You turn the topic, the title of the section you are studying, into a question or questions. For example, if the title of the section is "Drawing Conclusions," you turn it into a challenging question: "How do I draw conclusions from what I read?"
    - The first of the three R's stands for read. You use the reading skills that are taught in this book, such as locating the main idea, finding details, reading critically, detecting propaganda, determining cause and effect, and comparing and contrasting ideas.
    - The second R stands for recite. You close the book and speak aloud from memory. Include especially the main ideas you have located and any name, word, or fact you find difficult to remember.
    - The third R stands for review, which literally means to "view" or see again. You look over your notes, the lines you have highlighted, or the outline you have made. Do this again until you are sure you have mastered the material, for example, spelling words that trouble you or a rule of punctuation you find hard to remember.

    This is a summary of the S Q 3R method of study:

    S urvey
    Q uestion
    R ead
    R ecite
    R eview

BEFORE THE TEST DATE

1. **Use this book wisely.** It can help you achieve your goal—the High School Equivalency Diploma. After you take the Diagnostic Test, you will discover your specific weaknesses and can concentrate your review on these areas. Study the examination strategies, and apply them when you do the exercises and take the practice tests.
2. **Practice reading and writing.** Besides using the material in this book, spend more time reading. Read the local newspaper and some magazines. Also practice writing. Write letters to friends and relatives. Instead of using the telephone, use your pen.
3. **Don't rush to take the tests.** Don't be in too big a hurry to apply for the GED Examination. First be sure that you are prepared by taking the exercises and tests in this book. Even though most states will let you retake the tests after a waiting period, a notice that you failed the first time is unpleasant and may even discourage you from trying again. Instead of rushing into the examination and trusting to

good fortune for a passing grade, it's better to wait until you know that you're ready. Also, don't procrastinate and cram all your study into the last few days. This rarely works. It's much better to set a realistic study schedule that gives you enough time to prepare.

4. **Know what to expect.** By the time you finish the preparation material in this book, you will be familiar with all the kinds of questions you will encounter on the GED tests. The exercises and practice test questions in this book are very similar to the actual test questions. Knowing what to expect will relieve some of your anxiety about taking the exam.
5. **Be relaxed.** It's a good idea to relax the evening before you take the GED Examination. A good night's sleep will help you to think logically; you'll be well rested and alert. Also, do not eat a heavy meal, which will make you feel dull and sleepy, before you take the test.

Tactics and Strategies in the Examination Room

1. **Allow plenty of time to get to the test site.** Taking a test is pressure enough. You don't need the extra tension that comes from worrying about whether you will get there on time.
2. **Read all directions and questions carefully.** Answer the question given, not one you expected. Look for key words, such as *except*, *exactly*, and *not*. Carefully examine tables, graphs, and diagrams so you don't miss important information.
3. **Don't expect trick questions.** A straightforward presentation is used in all test sections.
4. **When you have difficulty finding an answer, eliminate choices that are definitely wrong.** Then consider the remaining choices.
5. **Don't let one or two challenging questions upset you.** Some questions are definitely harder than others. Remember you do not have to get 100 percent on this examination. No one does.
6. **Don't get bogged down on any one question.** If a question is taking too much time, circle it and make a guess. Then, if you have time at the end of the examination, go back and review the circled questions.
7. **Change answers only if you have a good reason for doing so.** Don't change your answer on a hunch or a whim. Most often the first judgment that you make is correct.
8. **Check answer order frequently.** Make sure you are putting your answers in the right spaces.
9. **Use your time wisely.** After taking the practice tests in this book, you will be familiar with the proper pace needed to complete each test.
10. **Be careful not to make stray pencil marks on the answer sheet.** These may interfere with the rating of your performance. If you wish to change an answer, be sure to erase your first mark completely. The rating machine will automatically mark an answer wrong if more than one choice is made. Also, do not fold or crease the answer sheet.
11. **Answer all questions, even if you have to guess.** Your score will be determined by the number of correct answers; no points are deducted for wrong answers. For this reason it is better to guess at an answer than to not respond at all. Of course, wherever possible, eliminate as many wrong answers as you can before guessing. Every answer you eliminate improves your chance of guessing correctly.
12. **Remain as calm as possible.** If you consider yourself a person who "goes to pieces" on tests, cheer up! Psychologists claim that more than 90 percent of us think we don't perform well on tests *of any kind.* Nobody likes tests. But more than 80 percent of the people who have taken the High School Equivalency tests in the New York area, for example, have passed them. They must be doing something right. And so can you—with the right attitude and careful preparation.

A Suggested Study Schedule

The task of reading this book and learning the material may seem impossible—after all, it's a big book! If, however, you divide everything up into thirty lessons, the job suddenly becomes much easier. The teachers who prepared this material for you have done just that—they have arranged everything into small lesson "bites." Another benefit is that, if you follow their plan, you will not have the problem of jumping from one subject to another and being worried that you may be missing something important.

If you find that you cannot manage the time necessary for the thirty-lesson plan outlined below, you can easily divide the work into sixty sessions. In any case, if you follow this plan and check off each task as it is accomplished, when you are finished, you will be prepared to walk into the GED Examination with confidence.

1. Read Chapter 1 to familiarize yourself with the GED Examination. Analyze the Examination Timetable. Examine the general study hints, tactics, and strategies in this chapter. Plan a schedule for study. Refer to the table of contents of this book to become acquainted with your "self-tutor."
2. In Chapter 2, take the Writing Skills test and the Social Studies test (Diagnostic Examination). Study the analyses of correct answers. Make a note of your weaknesses.
3. In Chapter 2, take the Science test and the Interpreting Literature and the Arts test (Diagnostic Examination). Study the analyses of correct answers. Make a note of your weaknesses.
4. In Chapter 2, take the Mathematics test (Diagnostic Examination). Analyze your errors, and note the topics on which you committed the most errors.
5. In Chapters 3 and 4, study the sections on sentence structure and usage. Do the practice exercises. Check the answers and the answer analyses.
6. In Chapters 5 and 6, study the sections on mechanics and additional writing skills. Do the practice exercises. Check the answers and the answer analyses.
7. In Chapter 7, study and do all practice exercises on the sample paragraphs. Check the answers and the answer analyses.
8. Study and do all practice exercises in Chapter 8. Write several essays using suggested topics.
9. Now it is time to take the Writing Skills test, Parts I and II (Practice Examination One) in Unit VIII. Check your answers. Analyze your errors. Study the analyses of the correct answers.
10. In Chapter 9, study the analyzed passages on the basics in social studies.
11. In Chapter 9, study the basics for interpreting tables, graphs, and maps. Do the practice exercises.
12. Study the "Glossary of Social Studies Terms" in Chapter 10. In Chapter 11, do the concept questions as well as the reading passage questions, and analyze your errors.
13. Now it is time to take the Social Studies test (Practice Examination One) in Unit VIII. Check your answers. Analyze your errors.
14. In Chapters 12 and 13, read about the Science test. Study the sample questions. Check your areas of weakness. Study the "Glossary of Scientific Terms." Check any terms that are unfamiliar.
15. In Chapter 14, do the practice exercises in biology. Refer to the glossary in Chapter 13 for troublesome terms.
16. In Chapter 14, do the practice exercises in earth science. Refer to the glossary in Chapter 13 for troublesome terms.
17. In Chapter 14, do the practice exercises in chemistry and physics. Refer to the glossary in Chapter 13 for troublesome terms.
18. Now it is time to take the Science test (Practice Examination One) in Unit VIII. Check your answers. Analyze your errors. Study the analyses of correct answers.
19. In Chapter 15, study the material on reading skills and skills in interpreting classical and popular literature. Study the material on commentary about literature and the arts.
20. In Chapter 16, do the practice exercises on classical and popular literature and commentary.

21. Now it is time to take the Interpreting Literature and the Arts test (Practice Examination One) in Unit VIII. Check your answers. Analyze your errors. Study the analyses of correct answers.
22. In Chapter 17, study the material on how to read and solve verbal math problems. Read the testing tactics in mathematics.
23. In Chapters 18 and 19, review the sections on arithmetic and algebra. Do the practice exercises. Check your answers.
24. In Chapters 20, 21 and 22, review the sections on geometry, graphs, and measures. Do the exercises. Check your answers.
25. Take the three practice mathematics tests in Chapter 23. Check your answers.
26. Now it is time to take the Mathematics test (Practice Examination One) in Unit VIII. Check your answers. Analyze your errors.
27. You are now ready to take Practice Examination Two in Unit VIII. Take the Writing Skills test, Parts I and II. Check your answers. Analyze your errors. Study the analyses of correct answers.
28. Take the Social Studies test (Practice Examination Two). Check your answers. Analyze your errors. Study the analyses of correct answers.
29. Take the Science test and the Interpreting Literature and the Arts test (Practice Examination Two). Check your answers. Analyze your errors. Study the analyses of correct answers.
30. Take the Mathematics test (Practice Examination Two). Check your answers. Analyze your errors. Study the analyses of correct answers.

A WORD ABOUT TIME

Don't try to learn everything or take every practice test in one session. Work at your own speed and in your own way. A book can't be completely flexible—but we urge you to be flexible. Use this book to suit your individual needs. If you need review in math but feel pretty confident about English, concentrate on math. If you want to try the exams first and skip a study section, do so. Remember that High School Equivalency Examinations are given frequently. Remember also that in most states you can take one test at a time—or two, or three, or all five. Remember especially that, if you fail one test, you can take another...and another. However, you will probably take all five tests and pass them all the first time you try. That is what this book aims to help you do.

2

A Diagnostic Examination

The direction sheets, mathematics formulas,* and question formats of this examination are constructed like the actual test you will take. The examination consists of five parts.

	Tests	Questions	Time Allowance
Test 1:	The Writing Skills Test, Part I	55	1 hour, 15 minutes
	The Writing Skills Test, Part II	Essay	45 minutes
Test 2:	The Social Studies Test	64	1 hour, 25 minutes
Test 3:	The Science Test	66	1 hour, 35 minutes
Test 4:	The Interpreting Literature and the Arts Test	45	1 hour, 5 minutes
Test 5:	The Mathematics Test	56	1 hour, 30 minutes
		Total:	7 hours, 35 minutes

For this examination, we have included an answer sheet and a self-appraisal chart. Mark yourself on each test, checking your answers against the answer key. Read the answer explanations to be sure you understand the correct answer choices. After you have calculated the scores for all five tests, refer to the self-appraisal materials to determine your subject area strengths and weaknesses as well as your total GED score.

The main purpose of the test is to help you discover your strengths and your weaknesses. IMPORTANT: You should spend more time studying those chapters that deal with the tests in which you are weakest. In that way, you will improve your score when you take the two practice examinations at the end of this book.

SIMULATE TEST CONDITIONS

To make conditions similar to those on the actual examination, do not take more time than that allowed for each test.

*Directions and mathematics formulas are reprinted by permission of the GED Testing Service of the American Council on Education.

Answer Sheet for the Diagnostic Examination

TEST 1: THE WRITING SKILLS TEST

1. ① ② ③ ④ ⑤
2. ① ② ③ ④ ⑤
3. ① ② ③ ④ ⑤
4. ① ② ③ ④ ⑤
5. ① ② ③ ④ ⑤
6. ① ② ③ ④ ⑤
7. ① ② ③ ④ ⑤
8. ① ② ③ ④ ⑤
9. ① ② ③ ④ ⑤
10. ① ② ③ ④ ⑤
11. ① ② ③ ④ ⑤
12. ① ② ③ ④ ⑤
13. ① ② ③ ④ ⑤
14. ① ② ③ ④ ⑤
15. ① ② ③ ④ ⑤
16. ① ② ③ ④ ⑤
17. ① ② ③ ④ ⑤
18. ① ② ③ ④ ⑤
19. ① ② ③ ④ ⑤
20. ① ② ③ ④ ⑤
21. ① ② ③ ④ ⑤
22. ① ② ③ ④ ⑤
23. ① ② ③ ④ ⑤
24. ① ② ③ ④ ⑤
25. ① ② ③ ④ ⑤
26. ① ② ③ ④ ⑤
27. ① ② ③ ④ ⑤
28. ① ② ③ ④ ⑤
29. ① ② ③ ④ ⑤
30. ① ② ③ ④ ⑤
31. ① ② ③ ④ ⑤
32. ① ② ③ ④ ⑤
33. ① ② ③ ④ ⑤
34. ① ② ③ ④ ⑤
35. ① ② ③ ④ ⑤
36. ① ② ③ ④ ⑤
37. ① ② ③ ④ ⑤
38. ① ② ③ ④ ⑤
39. ① ② ③ ④ ⑤
40. ① ② ③ ④ ⑤
41. ① ② ③ ④ ⑤
42. ① ② ③ ④ ⑤
43. ① ② ③ ④ ⑤
44. ① ② ③ ④ ⑤
45. ① ② ③ ④ ⑤
46. ① ② ③ ④ ⑤
47. ① ② ③ ④ ⑤
48. ① ② ③ ④ ⑤
49. ① ② ③ ④ ⑤
50. ① ② ③ ④ ⑤
51. ① ② ③ ④ ⑤
52. ① ② ③ ④ ⑤
53. ① ② ③ ④ ⑤
54. ① ② ③ ④ ⑤
55. ① ② ③ ④ ⑤

TEST 2: THE SOCIAL STUDIES TEST

1. ① ② ③ ④ ⑤
2. ① ② ③ ④ ⑤
3. ① ② ③ ④ ⑤
4. ① ② ③ ④ ⑤
5. ① ② ③ ④ ⑤
6. ① ② ③ ④ ⑤
7. ① ② ③ ④ ⑤
8. ① ② ③ ④ ⑤
9. ① ② ③ ④ ⑤
10. ① ② ③ ④ ⑤
11. ① ② ③ ④ ⑤
12. ① ② ③ ④ ⑤
13. ① ② ③ ④ ⑤
14. ① ② ③ ④ ⑤
15. ① ② ③ ④ ⑤
16. ① ② ③ ④ ⑤
17. ① ② ③ ④ ⑤
18. ① ② ③ ④ ⑤
19. ① ② ③ ④ ⑤
20. ① ② ③ ④ ⑤
21. ① ② ③ ④ ⑤
22. ① ② ③ ④ ⑤
23. ① ② ③ ④ ⑤
24. ① ② ③ ④ ⑤
25. ① ② ③ ④ ⑤
26. ① ② ③ ④ ⑤
27. ① ② ③ ④ ⑤
28. ① ② ③ ④ ⑤
29. ① ② ③ ④ ⑤
30. ① ② ③ ④ ⑤
31. ① ② ③ ④ ⑤
32. ① ② ③ ④ ⑤
33. ① ② ③ ④ ⑤
34. ① ② ③ ④ ⑤
35. ① ② ③ ④ ⑤
36. ① ② ③ ④ ⑤
37. ① ② ③ ④ ⑤
38. ① ② ③ ④ ⑤
39. ① ② ③ ④ ⑤
40. ① ② ③ ④ ⑤
41. ① ② ③ ④ ⑤
42. ① ② ③ ④ ⑤
43. ① ② ③ ④ ⑤
44. ① ② ③ ④ ⑤
45. ① ② ③ ④ ⑤
46. ① ② ③ ④ ⑤
47. ① ② ③ ④ ⑤
48. ① ② ③ ④ ⑤
49. ① ② ③ ④ ⑤
50. ① ② ③ ④ ⑤
51. ① ② ③ ④ ⑤
52. ① ② ③ ④ ⑤
53. ① ② ③ ④ ⑤
54. ① ② ③ ④ ⑤
55. ① ② ③ ④ ⑤
56. ① ② ③ ④ ⑤
57. ① ② ③ ④ ⑤
58. ① ② ③ ④ ⑤
59. ① ② ③ ④ ⑤
60. ① ② ③ ④ ⑤
61. ① ② ③ ④ ⑤
62. ① ② ③ ④ ⑤
63. ① ② ③ ④ ⑤
64. ① ② ③ ④ ⑤

TEST 3: THE SCIENCE TEST

1. ① ② ③ ④ ⑤
2. ① ② ③ ④ ⑤
3. ① ② ③ ④ ⑤
4. ① ② ③ ④ ⑤
5. ① ② ③ ④ ⑤
6. ① ② ③ ④ ⑤
7. ① ② ③ ④ ⑤
8. ① ② ③ ④ ⑤
9. ① ② ③ ④ ⑤
10. ① ② ③ ④ ⑤
11. ① ② ③ ④ ⑤
12. ① ② ③ ④ ⑤
13. ① ② ③ ④ ⑤
14. ① ② ③ ④ ⑤
15. ① ② ③ ④ ⑤
16. ① ② ③ ④ ⑤
17. ① ② ③ ④ ⑤
18. ① ② ③ ④ ⑤
19. ① ② ③ ④ ⑤
20. ① ② ③ ④ ⑤
21. ① ② ③ ④ ⑤
22. ① ② ③ ④ ⑤
23. ① ② ③ ④ ⑤
24. ① ② ③ ④ ⑤
25. ① ② ③ ④ ⑤
26. ① ② ③ ④ ⑤
27. ① ② ③ ④ ⑤
28. ① ② ③ ④ ⑤
29. ① ② ③ ④ ⑤
30. ① ② ③ ④ ⑤
31. ① ② ③ ④ ⑤
32. ① ② ③ ④ ⑤
33. ① ② ③ ④ ⑤
34. ① ② ③ ④ ⑤
35. ① ② ③ ④ ⑤
36. ① ② ③ ④ ⑤
37. ① ② ③ ④ ⑤
38. ① ② ③ ④ ⑤
39. ① ② ③ ④ ⑤
40. ① ② ③ ④ ⑤
41. ① ② ③ ④ ⑤
42. ① ② ③ ④ ⑤
43. ① ② ③ ④ ⑤
44. ① ② ③ ④ ⑤
45. ① ② ③ ④ ⑤
46. ① ② ③ ④ ⑤
47. ① ② ③ ④ ⑤
48. ① ② ③ ④ ⑤
49. ① ② ③ ④ ⑤
50. ① ② ③ ④ ⑤
51. ① ② ③ ④ ⑤
52. ① ② ③ ④ ⑤
53. ① ② ③ ④ ⑤
54. ① ② ③ ④ ⑤
55. ① ② ③ ④ ⑤
56. ① ② ③ ④ ⑤
57. ① ② ③ ④ ⑤
58. ① ② ③ ④ ⑤
59. ① ② ③ ④ ⑤
60. ① ② ③ ④ ⑤
61. ① ② ③ ④ ⑤
62. ① ② ③ ④ ⑤
63. ① ② ③ ④ ⑤
64. ① ② ③ ④ ⑤
65. ① ② ③ ④ ⑤
66. ① ② ③ ④ ⑤

TEST 4: THE INTERPRETING LITERATURE AND THE ARTS TEST

1. ① ② ③ ④ ⑤
2. ① ② ③ ④ ⑤
3. ① ② ③ ④ ⑤
4. ① ② ③ ④ ⑤
5. ① ② ③ ④ ⑤
6. ① ② ③ ④ ⑤
7. ① ② ③ ④ ⑤
8. ① ② ③ ④ ⑤
9. ① ② ③ ④ ⑤
10. ① ② ③ ④ ⑤
11. ① ② ③ ④ ⑤
12. ① ② ③ ④ ⑤
13. ① ② ③ ④ ⑤
14. ① ② ③ ④ ⑤
15. ① ② ③ ④ ⑤
16. ① ② ③ ④ ⑤
17. ① ② ③ ④ ⑤
18. ① ② ③ ④ ⑤
19. ① ② ③ ④ ⑤
20. ① ② ③ ④ ⑤
21. ① ② ③ ④ ⑤
22. ① ② ③ ④ ⑤
23. ① ② ③ ④ ⑤
24. ① ② ③ ④ ⑤
25. ① ② ③ ④ ⑤
26. ① ② ③ ④ ⑤
27. ① ② ③ ④ ⑤
28. ① ② ③ ④ ⑤
29. ① ② ③ ④ ⑤
30. ① ② ③ ④ ⑤
31. ① ② ③ ④ ⑤
32. ① ② ③ ④ ⑤
33. ① ② ③ ④ ⑤
34. ① ② ③ ④ ⑤
35. ① ② ③ ④ ⑤
36. ① ② ③ ④ ⑤
37. ① ② ③ ④ ⑤
38. ① ② ③ ④ ⑤
39. ① ② ③ ④ ⑤
40. ① ② ③ ④ ⑤
41. ① ② ③ ④ ⑤
42. ① ② ③ ④ ⑤
43. ① ② ③ ④ ⑤
44. ① ② ③ ④ ⑤
45. ① ② ③ ④ ⑤

TEST 5: THE MATHEMATICS TEST

1. ① ② ③ ④ ⑤
2. ① ② ③ ④ ⑤
3. ① ② ③ ④ ⑤
4. ① ② ③ ④ ⑤
5. ① ② ③ ④ ⑤
6. ① ② ③ ④ ⑤
7. ① ② ③ ④ ⑤
8. ① ② ③ ④ ⑤
9. ① ② ③ ④ ⑤
10. ① ② ③ ④ ⑤
11. ① ② ③ ④ ⑤
12. ① ② ③ ④ ⑤
13. ① ② ③ ④ ⑤
14. ① ② ③ ④ ⑤
15. ① ② ③ ④ ⑤
16. ① ② ③ ④ ⑤
17. ① ② ③ ④ ⑤
18. ① ② ③ ④ ⑤
19. ① ② ③ ④ ⑤
20. ① ② ③ ④ ⑤
21. ① ② ③ ④ ⑤
22. ① ② ③ ④ ⑤
23. ① ② ③ ④ ⑤
24. ① ② ③ ④ ⑤
25. ① ② ③ ④ ⑤
26. ① ② ③ ④ ⑤
27. ① ② ③ ④ ⑤
28. ① ② ③ ④ ⑤
29. ① ② ③ ④ ⑤
30. ① ② ③ ④ ⑤
31. ① ② ③ ④ ⑤
32. ① ② ③ ④ ⑤
33. ① ② ③ ④ ⑤
34. ① ② ③ ④ ⑤
35. ① ② ③ ④ ⑤
36. ① ② ③ ④ ⑤
37. ① ② ③ ④ ⑤
38. ① ② ③ ④ ⑤
39. ① ② ③ ④ ⑤
40. ① ② ③ ④ ⑤
41. ① ② ③ ④ ⑤
42. ① ② ③ ④ ⑤
43. ① ② ③ ④ ⑤
44. ① ② ③ ④ ⑤
45. ① ② ③ ④ ⑤
46. ① ② ③ ④ ⑤
47. ① ② ③ ④ ⑤
48. ① ② ③ ④ ⑤
49. ① ② ③ ④ ⑤
50. ① ② ③ ④ ⑤
51. ① ② ③ ④ ⑤
52. ① ② ③ ④ ⑤
53. ① ② ③ ④ ⑤
54. ① ② ③ ④ ⑤
55. ① ② ③ ④ ⑤
56. ① ② ③ ④ ⑤

DIAGNOSTIC EXAMINATION

TEST 1: WRITING SKILLS, PART I

Directions

The Writing Skills test is intended to measure your ability to use clear and effective English. It is a test of English as it should be written, not as it might be spoken. This test includes both multiple-choice questions and an essay. These directions apply only to the multiple-choice section; a separate set of directions is given for the essay.

The multiple-choice section consists of paragraphs with numbered sentences. Some of the sentences contain errors in sentence structure, usage, or mechanics (spelling, punctuation, and capitalization). After reading the numbered sentences, answer the multiple-choice questions that follow. Some questions refer to sentences that are correct as written. The best answer for these questions is the one that leaves the sentence as originally written. The best answer for some questions is the one that produces a sentence that is consistent with the verb tense and point of view used throughout the paragraph.

You should spend no more than 75 minutes on the multiple-choice questions and 45 minutes on your essay. Work carefully, but do not spend too much time on any one question. You may begin working on the essay part of this test as soon as you complete the multiple-choice section.

To record your answers, mark the numbered space on the answer sheet beside the number that corresponds to the question in the test.

FOR EXAMPLE:

Sentence 1: **We were all honored to meet governor Phillips.**

What correction should be made to this sentence?

(1) insert a comma after <u>honored</u>
(2) change the spelling of <u>honored</u> to <u>honered</u>
(3) change <u>governor</u> to <u>Governor</u>
(4) replace <u>were</u> with <u>was</u>
(5) no correction is necessary

① ② ● ④ ⑤

In this example, the word "governor" should be capitalized; therefore, answer space 3 would be marked on the answer sheet.

GO ON TO THE NEXT PAGE

TEST 1: WRITING SKILLS, PART I

Questions 1 to 9 refer to the following paragraph.

(1) A combination of attributes make vegetable gardening a national hobby with both young and old. (2) For an ever-increasing number of individuals seed catalogs and the thoughts of spring gardening provide a happy escape from the winter doldrums. (3) Vegetable gardeners unanimously agree that many home-grown vegetables picked at their peak of maturity have quality. seldom found in vegetables purchased from commercial markets. (4) From Spring to late Fall, a well-planned and maintained garden can provide a supply of fresh vegetables, thus increasing the nutritional value of the family diet. (5) Freezers make it possible to preserve some of the surplus vegetables to be enjoyed at a later date other vegetables can be stored for a few months in a cool area. (6) Not to be overlooked is the finger-tip convenience of having vegetables in the backyard; this in itself justifies home gardening for many individuals. (7) In addition, vegetable gardening provides excercise and recreation for both urban and suburban families. (8) Although your initial dollar investment for gardening may be nominal, one cannot escape the fact that gardening requires manual labor and time. (9) Neglecting jobs that should be performed on a regular basis may result in failure and a negative feeling toward gardening.

1. Sentence 1: **A combination of attributes make vegetable gardening a national hobby with both young and old.**

   What correction should be made to this sentence?

   (1) insert a comma after attributes
   (2) change make to makes
   (3) capitalize vegetable gardening
   (4) reverse with and both
   (5) no correction is necessary

2. Sentence 2: **For an ever-increasing number of individuals seed catalogs and the thoughts of spring gardening provide a happy escape from the winter doldrums.**

   What correction should be made to this sentence?

   (1) remove the hyphen from ever-increasing
   (2) change number to amount
   (3) insert a comma after individuals
   (4) insert a comma after catalogs
   (5) no correction is necessary

3. Sentence 3: **Vegetable gardeners unanimously agree that many home-grown vegetables picked at their peak of maturity have quality. seldom found in vegetables purchased from commercial markets.**

   Which of the following is the best way to write the underlined portion of this sentence? If you think the original is the best way, choose option (1).

   (1) quality. seldom
   (2) quality. Seldom
   (3) quality seldom
   (4) quality; seldom
   (5) quality, seldom

4. Sentence 4: **From Spring to late Fall, a well-planned and maintained garden can provide a supply of fresh vegetables, thus increasing the nutritional value of the family diet.**

   What correction should be made to this sentence?

   (1) remove capitals from Spring and Fall
   (2) remove the hyphen from well-planned
   (3) remove the comma after vegetables
   (4) change thus to however
   (5) no correction is necessary

GO ON TO THE NEXT PAGE

TEST 1: WRITING SKILLS, PART I

5. Sentence 5: **Freezers make it possible to preserve some of the surplus vegetables to be enjoyed at a later date other vegetables can be stored for a few months in a cool area.**

   Which of the following is the best way to write the underlined portion of this sentence? If you think the original is the best way, choose option (1).

   (1) date other
   (2) date, other
   (3) date. Other
   (4) date, while other
   (5) date; while other

6. Sentence 6: **Not to be overlooked is the finger-tip convenience of having vegetables in the backyard; this in itself justifies home gardening for many individuals.**

   What correction should be made to this sentence?

   (1) insert a comma after overlooked
   (2) change the spelling of vegetables to vegtables
   (3) replace the semicolon after backyard with a comma
   (4) change the spelling of gardening to gardning
   (5) no correction is necessary

7. Sentence 7: **In addition, vegetable gardening provides excercise and recreation for both urban and suburban families.**

   What correction should be made to this sentence?

   (1) remove the comma after addition
   (2) change the spelling of excercise to exercise
   (3) insert a comma after recreation
   (4) change for both to both for
   (5) no correction is necessary

8. Sentence 8: **Although your initial dollar investment for gardening may be nominal, one cannot escape the fact that gardening requires manual labor and time.**

   What correction should be made to this sentence?

   (1) change Although to Because
   (2) remove the comma after nominal
   (3) change one to you
   (4) change requires to require
   (5) no correction is necessary

9. Sentence 9: **Neglecting jobs that should be performed on a regular basis may result in failure and a negative feeling toward gardening.**

   What correction should be made to this sentence?

   (1) insert a comma after jobs
   (2) insert a comma after basis
   (3) change may result to results
   (4) change and to despite
   (5) no correction is necessary

Questions 10 to 19 refer to the following paragraph.

(1) In coming years, families will need to learn to turn to their computers for assistence. (2) With the increasing amounts of information a family is required to process, the home computer will become a necessity for both decision making and family record storage and retrieval. (3) A home communications revolution is predicted with the arrival of the home computer. It will serve as a source and processor of information. (4) A virtually infinite amount of information from many sources will be at the instantaneous disposal of the family for more efficient decision making. (5) The computer will plan meals, turn lights on at appropriate times keep track of family members' schedules, calculate budget information, and oversee credit, spending, and bank accounts. (6) Just as home equiptment frees the homemaker from the labor of housekeeping, the computer releases family members from some repetitious managerial

GO ON TO THE NEXT PAGE

TEST 1: WRITING SKILLS, PART I

duties. (7) The home terminal may serve as a home education center for children's homework and part of the lifelong learning program of parents and elderly family members. (8) The change that will have the most immediate effect on family decision making will be increased discretionary time. (9) For economic reasons, many families will decide to use they're "free" time to hold a second job. (10) With the increasing interest in personal development, a segment of the time might be allotted by some to develop alternative interests through lifelong educational programs that will facilitate career changes, to increase skills for effective citizenship, and learning new skills to enhance their family living.

10. Sentence 1: **In coming years, families will need to learn to turn to their computers for assistence.**

    What correction should be made to this sentence?

    (1) remove the comma after years
    (2) change will need to need
    (3) change the spelling of their to they're
    (4) change the spelling of assistence to assistance
    (5) no correction is necessary

11. Sentence 2: **With the increasing amounts of information a family is required to process, the home computer will become a necessity for both decision making and family record storage and retrieval.**

    What correction should be made to this sentence?

    (1) change With the to Despite
    (2) change is to are
    (3) remove the comma after process
    (4) change the spelling of necessity to neccesity
    (5) no correction is necessary

12. Sentence 3: **A home communications revolution is predicted with the arrival of the home computer. It will serve as a source and processor of information.**

    Which of the following is the best way to write the underlined portion of the sentence? If you think the original is the best way, choose option (1).

    (1) computer. It
    (2) computer, It
    (3) computer, it
    (4) computer it
    (5) computer; It

13. Sentence 4: **A virtually infinite amount of information from many sources will be at the instantaneous disposal of the family for more efficient decision making.**

    What correction should be made to this sentence?

    (1) insert a comma after information
    (2) insert a comma after sources
    (3) insert a comma after family
    (4) change the spelling of efficient to eficient
    (5) no correction is necessary

14. Sentence 5: **The computer will plan meals, turn lights on at appropriate times keep track of family members' schedules, calculate budget information, and oversee credit, spending, and bank accounts.**

    What correction should be made to this sentence?

    (1) remove comma after meals
    (2) insert comma after times
    (3) change members' to member's
    (4) change the spelling of schedules to skedules
    (5) no correction is necessary

GO ON TO THE NEXT PAGE

TEST 1: WRITING SKILLS, PART I

15. Sentence 6: **Just as home equiptment frees the homemaker from the labor of housekeeping, the computer releases family members from some repetitious managerial duties.**

    What correction should be made to this sentence?

    (1) change Just as to Although
    (2) change the spelling of equiptment to equipment
    (3) remove the comma after housekeeping
    (4) change releases to will have released
    (5) no correction is necessary

16. Sentence 7: **The home terminal may serve as a home education center for children's homework and part of the lifelong learning program of parents and elderly family members.**

    If you rewrote sentence 7 beginning with

    Children's homework and part of the lifelong learning program of parents and elderly family members

    the next words should be

    (1) are served
    (2) may serve
    (3) may be served
    (4) serve
    (5) will serve

17. Sentence 8: **The change that will have the most immediate effect on family decision making will be increased discretionary time.**

    What correction should be made to this sentence?

    (1) change will have to having
    (2) change the spelling of effect to affect
    (3) change family to family's
    (4) change will be to is
    (5) no correction is necessary

18. Sentence 9: **For economic reasons, many families will decide to use they're "free" time to hold a second job.**

    What correction should be made to this sentence?

    (1) remove the comma after reasons
    (2) change the spelling of families to familys
    (3) change the spelling of they're to their
    (4) change to to and
    (5) no correction is necessary

19. Sentence 10: **With the increasing interest in personal development, a segment of the time might be allotted by some to develop alternative interests through lifelong educational programs that will facilitate career changes, to increase skills for effective citizenship, and learning new skills to enhance their family living.**

    What correction should be made to this sentence?

    (1) change the spelling of development to developement
    (2) change the spelling of through to thorough
    (3) remove the comma after changes
    (4) change learning to to learn
    (5) no correction is necessary

Questions 20 to 28 refer to the following paragraphs.

(1) To lessen the threat of faulty car repair work or repair frauds, they're a number of constructive steps you can take. (2) While these measures can't offer full protection they are wise insurance against dented pocketbooks and expanded time schedules.

(3) First, never wait until a small problem becomes a big and costly one. (4) Always take your car in for a check at the first sign of trouble.

(5) But before you take the car in, make a list of all problems and "symptoms" so you are prepared to describe the trouble as accurately and specifically as possible.

(6) Don't just ask to have the car put in "working order," (7) that kind of general

GO ON TO THE NEXT PAGE

TEST 1: WRITING SKILLS, PART I

statement can lead directly to unnecessary work.

(8) On your initial visit, make certain you get a copy of the work authorization that you sign or a general estimate of the total cost of the repairs. (9) Don't leave until you do.

(10) Ask the repair garage to telephone you when the exact work to be done has been determinned. (11) When you recieve the call, say you now want to return to the station to obtain another work order itemizing the cost of each repair to be made.

20. Sentence 1: **To lessen the threat of faulty car repair work or repair frauds, they're a number of constructive steps you can take.**

    What correction should be made to this sentence?

    (1) change lessen to lesson
    (2) remove the comma after frauds
    (3) change the spelling of they're to there are
    (4) change can to might
    (5) no correction is necessary

21. Sentence 2: **While these measures can't offer full protection they are wise insurance against dented pocketbooks and expanded time schedules.**

    What correction should be made to this sentence?

    (1) change while to nevertheless
    (2) insert a comma after protection
    (3) change insurance to insurence
    (4) insert a hyphen in pocketbooks
    (5) no correction is necessary

22. Sentence 3: **First, never wait until a small problem becomes a big and costly one.**

    What correction should be made to this sentence?

    (1) change first to firstly
    (2) remove the comma after first
    (3) change the spelling of until to untill
    (4) change becomes to will become
    (5) no correction is necessary

23. Sentence 4: **Always take your car in for a check at the first sign of trouble.**

    What correction should be made to this sentence?

    (1) change always to allways
    (2) change take to you should take
    (3) change your to your'e
    (4) insert a comma after check
    (5) no correction is necessary

24. Sentence 5: **But before you take the car in, make a list of all problems and "symptoms" so you are prepared to describe the trouble as accurately and specifically as possible.**

    What correction should be made to this sentence?

    (1) change take to will take
    (2) remove the comma after in
    (3) change are to will be
    (4) change the spelling of specifically to specificaly
    (5) no correction is necessary

25. Sentences 6 and 7: **Don't just ask to have the car put in "working order," that kind of general statement can lead directly to unnecessary work.**

    Which of the following is the best way to write the underlined portion of these sentences? If you think the original is the best way, choose option (1).

    (1) order," that
    (2) order" that
    (3) order": that
    (4) order". that
    (5) order." That

GO ON TO THE NEXT PAGE

TEST 1: WRITING SKILLS, PART I

26. Sentence 8: **On your initial visit, make certain you get a copy of the work authorization that you sign or a general estimate of the total cost of the repairs.**

    What correction should be made to this sentence?

    (1) change the spelling of <u>initial</u> to <u>initail</u>
    (2) remove the comma after <u>visit</u>
    (3) insert a comma after <u>sign</u>
    (4) change the spelling of <u>estimate</u> to <u>estemate</u>
    (5) no correction is necessary

27. Sentence 10: **Ask the repair garage to telephone you when the exact work to be done has been determinned.**

    What correction should be made to this sentence?

    (1) insert a comma after <u>you</u>
    (2) change <u>when</u> to <u>while</u>
    (3) change <u>has</u> <u>been</u> to <u>will have been</u>
    (4) change the spelling of <u>determinned</u> to <u>determined</u>
    (5) no correction is necessary

28. Sentence 11: **When you recieve the call, say you now want to return to the station to obtain another work order itemizing the cost of each repair to be made.**

    What correction should be made to this sentence?

    (1) change the spelling of <u>recieve</u> to <u>receive</u>
    (2) remove the comma after <u>call</u>
    (3) insert a comma after <u>order</u>
    (4) change <u>to be made</u> to <u>that will have been made</u>
    (5) no correction is necessary

<u>Questions 29 to 37</u> refer to the following paragraphs.

(1) Total dollars available, family tastes storage and preparation facilities, end use, and item cost all affect a buying decision. (2) Unit pricing can help by taking the guesswork out of the price factor and simplifying cost comparisons.

(3) Unit price is just what its name implies—the price per unit. (4) To be more specific, unit pricing gives you the cost per ounce or per pound or per 100 or per square foot. (5) This price per unit enables you to readily find the best buy dollarwise among several items in different size packages with different total prices.

(6) Thousands of retail food chain stores now have unit pricing programs. (7) Such programs are required by local laws in several areas, but generally the programs are voluntary.

(8) Stores that offer unit pricing generally use a shelf tag system—a label on the shelf edge below the item gives the name of the item, the size, the total price, and the unit price.

(9) When unit pricing was first introduced there were some problems with the shelf tag system since just keeping the tags on the shelves in the right location can be difficult. (10) But as unit pricing has gained acceptance, some of these mechanical problems have been overcome, and the label information has become more usable from the shoppers standpoint.

29. Sentence 1: **Total dollars available, family tastes storage and preparation facilities, end use, and item cost all affect a buying decision.**

    What correction should be made to this sentence?

    (1) insert a comma after <u>tastes</u>
    (2) change <u>all</u> to <u>each</u>
    (3) change <u>affect</u> to <u>effect</u>
    (4) change the spelling of <u>buying</u> to <u>bying</u>
    (5) no correction is necessary

GO ON TO THE NEXT PAGE

TEST 1: WRITING SKILLS, PART I

30. Sentence 1: **Total dollars available, family tastes storage and preparation facilities, end use, and item cost all affect a buying decision.**

If you rewrote sentence 1 beginning with

A buying decision is affected

the next words should be

(1) because of
(2) by
(3) depending on
(4) however
(5) therefore

31. Sentence 2: **Unit pricing can help by taking the guesswork out of the price factor and simplifying cost comparisons.**

What correction should be made to this sentence?

(1) change can to could
(2) change by taking to to take
(3) insert a hyphen in guesswork
(4) insert a comma after factor
(5) no correction is necessary

32. Sentences 3 and 4: **Unit price is just what its name implies—the price per unit. To be more specific, unit pricing gives you the cost per ounce or per pound or per 100 or per square foot.**

Which of the following is the best way to write the underlined portion of these sentences? If you think the original is the best way, choose option (1).

(1) . To be more specific
(2) , To be more specific
(3) ; To be more specific
(4) : To be more specific
(5) —To be more specific

33. Sentence 5: **This price per unit enables you to readily find the best buy dollarwise among several items in different size packages with different total prices.**

What correction should be made to this sentence?

(1) change you to one
(2) insert comma before and after dollarwise
(3) change among to between
(4) change size to sized
(5) no correction is necessary

34. Sentences 6 and 7: **Thousands of retail food chain stores now have unit pricing programs. Such programs are required by local laws in several areas, but generally the programs are voluntary.**

The most effective combination of sentences 6 and 7 would include which of the following groups of words?

(1) and such programs
(2) although such programs
(3) whereas such programs
(4) programs that are
(5) programs some being

35. Sentence 8: **Stores that offer unit pricing generally use a shelf tag system—a label on the shelf edge below the item gives the name of the item, the size, the total price, and the unit price.**

Which of the following is the best way to write the underlined portion of this sentence? If you think the original is the best way, choose option (1).

(1) system—a label
(2) system. a label
(3) system; a label
(4) system: a label
(5) system, a label

GO ON TO THE NEXT PAGE

TEST 1: WRITING SKILLS, PART I

36. Sentence 9: **When unit pricing was first introduced there were some problems with the shelf tag system since just keeping the tags on the shelves in the right location can be difficult.**

What correction should be made to this sentence?

(1) change was to had been
(2) insert a comma after introduced
(3) change there to their
(4) insert commas before and after in the right location
(5) no correction is necessary

37. Sentence 10: **But as unit pricing has gained acceptance, some of these mechanical problems have been overcome, and the label information has become more usable from the shoppers standpoint.**

What correction should be made to this sentence?

(1) change the spelling of acceptance to acceptence
(2) remove the comma after acceptance
(3) change the spelling of usable to useable
(4) add an apostrophe after shoppers
(5) no correction is necessary

Questions 38 to 47 refer to the following paragraphs.

(1) You are going to move. (2) That statement will ring true for most Americans. (3) You will be the exception if you maintain your present residence for the rest of your life. (4) About one in five persons moves each year, put another way, the average person moves once every five years.

(5) Again dealing in averages most moves of household goods are completed without difficulty, although some are not. (6) The moving experience can be uneventful, but it should be recognized that many of the factors involved can lead to frustrations uncertainties, and expected courses of action that suddenly must be changed.

(7) Most moves involve fulfilment of a positive development. (8) A promotion has come through, (9) or perhaps an opportunity to move to a better climate. (10) Maybe there's a long-sought chance to be closer to the home folks or the grandchildren.

(11) On the other side of the coin, a familar neighborhood is being left behind. (12) The personal effort that must be put into a move can leave family members exhausted just at the time when they need to be at their sharpest.

38. Sentences 1 and 2: **You are going to move. That statement will ring true for most Americans.**

The most effective combination of sentences 1 and 2 would include which of the following groups of words.

(1) would be a statement that will ring
(2) is a statement that will ring
(3) might be a statement that will ring
(4) being a statement that will ring
(5) will be a statement that will ring

39. Sentence 3: **You will be the exception if you maintain your present residence for the rest of your life.**

What correction should be made to this sentence?

(1) change will be to are
(2) change the spelling of exception to exeption
(3) insert a comma after exception
(4) change your to you're
(5) no correction is necessary

40. Sentence 4: **About one in five persons moves each year, put another way, the average person moves once every five years.**

Which of the following is the best way to write the underlined portion of this sentence? If you think the original is the best way, choose option (1).

(1) year, put
(2) year, although put
(3) year, and put
(4) year, because put
(5) year, or put

GO ON TO THE NEXT PAGE

TEST 1: WRITING SKILLS, PART I

41. Sentence 5: **Again dealing in averages most moves of household goods are completed without difficulty, although some are not.**

What correction should be made to this sentence?

(1) insert a comma after averages
(2) insert a hyphen in household
(3) change the spelling of difficulty to dificulty
(4) remove the comma after difficulty
(5) no correction is necessary

42. Sentence 6: **The moving experience can be uneventful, but it should be recognized that many of the factors involved can lead to frustrations uncertainties, and expected courses of action that suddenly must be changed.**

What correction should be made to this sentence?

(1) change the spelling of experience to experiance
(2) remove the comma after uneventful
(3) change but to and
(4) insert a comma after frustrations
(5) no correction is necessary

43. Sentence 7: **Most moves involve fulfilment of a positive development.**

What correction should be made to this sentence?

(1) change most moves to most every move
(2) change involve to could involve
(3) change the spelling of fulfilment to fulfillment
(4) change the spelling of development to developement
(5) no correction is necessary

44. Sentences 8 and 9: **A promotion has come through, or perhaps an opportunity to move to a better climate.**

Which of the following is the best way to write the underlined portion of these sentences? If you think the original is the best way, choose option (1).

(1) through, or
(2) through. or
(3) through : or
(4) through ; or
(5) through—or

45. Sentence 10: **Maybe there's a long-sought chance to be closer to the home folks or the grandchildren.**

What correction should be made to this sentence?

(1) change there's to they're is
(2) remove the hyphen from long-sought
(3) add an apostrophe to folks
(4) change the spelling of grandchildren to grandchildern
(5) no correction is necessary

46. Sentence 11: **On the other side of the coin, a familar neighborhood is being left behind.**

What correction should be made to this sentence?

(1) remove the comma after coin
(2) change the spelling of familar to familiar
(3) change the spelling of neighborhood to nieghborhood
(4) change is being to has been
(5) no correction is necessary

GO ON TO THE NEXT PAGE

TEST 1: WRITING SKILLS, PART I

47. Sentence 12: **The personal effort that must be put into a move can leave family members exhausted just at the time when they need to be at their sharpest.**

    What correction should be made to this sentence?

    (1) insert commas around that must be put into a move
    (2) change can to could
    (3) change the spelling of exhausted to exausted
    (4) insert a comma after time
    (5) no correction is necessary

Questions 48 to 55 refer to the following paragraphs.

(1) In fishing, the first step for the angler is to upgrade his equipment so that the availible range of lures, line weights, distances, etc., is substantially increased. (2) Usually a spinning reel and rod are selected as the next phase in advancement.

(3) The spinning reel consists of a stationery spool carrying a length of monofilament line, a bail or pickup device to direct the line onto the reel and a crank that rotates the pickup device restoring the line to the spool.

(4) In operation, the lure, attached to the monofilament line and dangling several inches beyond the rod tip is cast by swinging the rod from a position slightly behind the shoulder through a forward arc to a position in front at approximately eye level.

(5) Proper timing of the finger pressure on the line as it leaves the reel, combined with the rod acceleration, control the distance the lure will travel.

(6) Lures as light as a sixteenth of an ounce with two-pound test monofilament line will provide enjoyable sport with any of the panfish, heavier lures and lines will more than adequately subdue far larger fish.

(7) Lures are available in a near infinite range of weights, sizes, shapes, and colors and include such items as spoons, spinners, jogs, plugs, and bugs as well as natural baits.

(8) With adequate spinning gear, anyone is prepared to pursue the fascinating and challenging game fish. (9) This category includes the world-famous and aristocratic salmon, the trout, the chars, the grayling, the basses, and the pike family.

48. Sentence 1: **In fishing, the first step for the angler is to upgrade his equipment so that the availible range of lures, line weights, distances, etc., is substantially increased.**

    What correction should be made to this sentence?

    (1) change the spelling of availible to available
    (2) remove the comma after lures
    (3) remove the period after etc.
    (4) change the spelling of substantially to substantialy
    (5) no correction is necessary

49. Sentence 2: **Usually a spinning reel and rod are selected as the next phase in advancement.**

    If you rewrote sentence 2 beginning with

    The next phase in advancement

    the next words would be

    (1) are selected a spinning
    (2) are selecting a spinning
    (3) selects a spinning
    (4) is the selection of a spinning
    (5) will be selecting a

50. Sentence 3: **The spinning reel consists of a stationery spool carrying a length of monofilament line, a bail or pickup device to direct the line onto the reel, and a crank that rotates the pick-up device restoring the line to the spool.**

    What correction should be made to this sentence?

    (1) change the spelling of stationery to stationary
    (2) change the spelling of length to lenth
    (3) remove the comma after line
    (4) insert a comma after device
    (5) no correction is necessary

GO ON TO THE NEXT PAGE

TEST 1: WRITING SKILLS, PART I

51. Sentence 4: **In operation, the lure, attached to the monofilament line and dangling several inches beyond the rod tip is cast by swinging the rod from a position slightly behind the shoulder through a forward arc to a position in front at approximately eye level.**

    What correction should be made to this sentence?

    (1) change the spelling of attached to attatched
    (2) insert a comma after tip
    (3) insert a comma after shoulder
    (4) change the spelling of approximately to approximatly
    (5) no correction is necessary

52. Sentence 5: **Proper timing of the finger pressure on the line as it leaves the reel, combined with the rod acceleration, control the distance the lure will travel.**

    What correction should be made to this sentence?

    (1) insert a comma after pressure
    (2) insert a comma after line
    (3) insert commas before and after reel
    (4) change control to controls
    (5) no correction is necessary

53. Sentence 6: **Lures as light as a sixteenth of an ounce with two-pound test monofilament line will provide enjoyable sport with any of the panfish, heavier lures and lines will more than adequately subdue far larger fish.**

    Which of the following is the best way to write the underlined portion of this sentence? If you think the original is the best way, choose option (1).

    (1) panfish, heavier
    (2) panfish: heavier
    (3) panfish; heavier
    (4) panfish. heavier
    (5) panfish. Heavier

54. Sentence 7: **Lures are available in a near infinite range of weights, sizes, shapes, and colors and include such items as spoons, spinners, jogs, plugs, and bugs as well as natural baits.**

    What correction should be made to this sentence?

    (1) change near to nearly
    (2) change the spelling of infinite to infinate
    (3) remove the comma after shapes
    (4) remove the comma after plugs
    (5) no correction is necessary

55. Sentences 8 and 9: **With adequate spinning gear, anyone is prepared to pursue the fascinating and challenging game fish. This category includes the world-famous and aristocratic salmon, the trout, the chars, the grayling, the basses, and the pike family.**

    The most effective combination of sentences 8 and 9 would include which of the following groups of words?

    (1) and this category includes
    (2) since this category includes
    (3) which category includes
    (4) which include
    (5) and including

GO ON TO THE NEXT PAGE

TEST 1: WRITING SKILLS, PART II

Directions

This part of the Writing Skills test is intended to determine how well you write. You are asked to write an essay that explains something or presents an opinion on an issue. In preparing your essay, you should take the following steps:

1. Read carefully the directions and the essay topic given below.
2. Plan your essay carefully before you write.
3. Use scratch paper to make any notes.
4. Write your essay on the lined pages of a separate answer sheet.
5. Read carefully what you have written and make any changes that will improve your essay.
6. Check your paragraphs, sentence structure, spelling, punctuation, capitalization, and usage, and make any necessary corrections.

You will have 45 minutes to write on the topic below.

Many Americans feel that the current state of world affairs requires continued involvement of the United States as a world superpower. Others feel that America should concentrate on domestic problems and limit alliances and political relations with foreign nations.

Write a composition of about 200 words in which you indicate your views on this issue. Give appropriate reasons to support your position.

END OF EXAMINATION

TEST 2: SOCIAL STUDIES

Directions

The Social Studies test consists of multiple-choice questions intended to measure general social studies concepts. Most questions are based on short readings that often include a graph, chart, or figure. Study the information given and then answer the question(s) following it. Refer to the information as often as necessary in answering the questions.

You should spend no more than 85 minutes answering the questions. Work carefully, but do not spend too much time on any one question. Be sure you answer every question. You will not be penalized for incorrect answers.

To record your answers, mark the numbered space on the answer sheet beside the number that corresponds to the question in the test.

FOR EXAMPLE:

Early colonists of North America looked for settlement sites that had adequate water supplies and were accessible by ship. For this reason, many early towns were built near

(1) mountains ① ② ● ④ ⑤
(2) prairies
(3) rivers
(4) glaciers
(5) plateaus

The correct answer is "rivers"; therefore, answer space 3 would be marked on the answer sheet.

GO ON TO THE NEXT PAGE

TEST 2: SOCIAL STUDIES

Questions 1 to 3 are based on the following passage.

The governor is empowered to veto single items of the budget bill, appending to each a message, and to return the same to the legislature if it is still in session. Such items can be enacted over his veto. This authority, not possessed by the president of the United States, lays a heavy responsibility on the governor for the integrity of the budget in all its parts.

All bills passed within the last ten days of a legislative session fall under what is called the "30-day" rule. None can become a law unless within 30 days (Sundays included) it has been signed by the governor.

The veto power is not used sparingly. More than one out of four bills falls to the deadly stroke of the executive pen.

1. The passage indicates that the governor

   (1) vetoes about one fourth of the bills
   (2) vetoes about three fourths of the bills
   (3) vetoes all bills during the legislative session
   (4) vetoes no bills during the legislative session
   (5) uses the veto power very sparingly

2. The "30-day" rule applies to

   (1) the time limit for exercising the veto
   (2) the pocket veto
   (3) the amount of time in which to appeal the governor's action
   (4) bills passed within the last ten days of a legislative session
   (5) the limitation on passing a law over the governor's veto

3. The governor's veto power is greater than that of the president in that the governor has the ability to

   (1) take as much time as he wishes before signing a bill
   (2) veto a bill in less than 10 days
   (3) ignore all bills during the last month of the legislature
   (4) veto single items of the budget bill
   (5) override the two-thirds vote of the legislature

Questions 4 to 6 are based on the following passage.

The consumer's first line of defense is information. Before you buy any product—especially before you make a major purchase of any kind—get all the information you can about the manufacturer's guarantee or warranty provisions.

Remember, a guarantee is a statement by the manufacturer or vendor that he stands behind his product or service. Guarantees and warranties usually have limitations or conditions, so get all promises in writing.

Before you buy any product or service covered by a guarantee or warranty, make sure you resolve these questions:

—What, exactly, is covered?

—Whom should you call when you need repairs under the warranty?

—Must repairs be made at the factory or by an "authorized service representative" to keep the warranty in effect?

—Who pays for parts, for labor, for shipping charges?

—How long does the warranty last?

—If pro rata reimbursement is provided, what is the basis for it?

—If the warranty provides for reimbursement, is it in cash or credit toward a replacement?

Keep the warranty and sales receipt for future reference.

4. The advice given to the consumer in this passage deals chiefly with

   (1) business ethics
   (2) unconditional guarantees
   (3) product safety
   (4) unwarranted promises
   (5) pre-purchase information

5. Guarantees and warranties, the passage implies, should be

   (1) conditional
   (2) in writing
   (3) made by the salesman
   (4) cancelable
   (5) dependent on the use of the product

GO ON TO THE NEXT PAGE

TEST 2: SOCIAL STUDIES

6. Warranties usually include all of the following EXCEPT

   (1) what is covered
   (2) who does the repairs
   (3) where the repairs are made
   (4) who pays for expenses incurred in doing the repairs
   (5) return of monies paid

Questions 7 and 8 are based on the following chart.

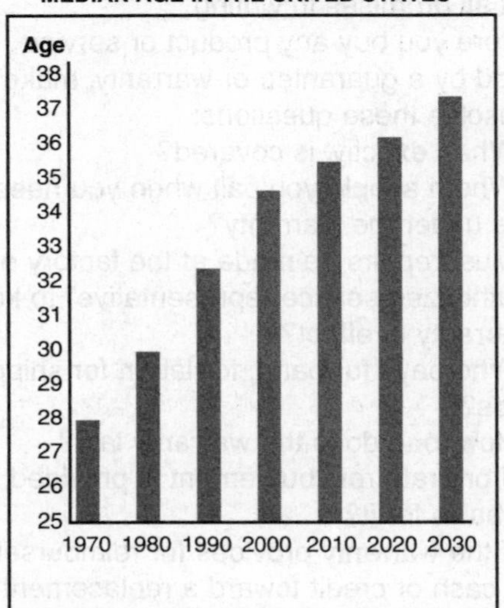

7. Which situation will be most likely to occur after the period shown in the graph?

   (1) Advertisers will increase their emphasis on youth.
   (2) The size of the average family will increase.
   (3) School districts will build more elementary schools.
   (4) The cost of the Social Security program will rise.
   (5) Population will begin to decline.

8. Which factor would most likely reverse the direction of the trend indicated by the graph?

   (1) development of a cure for cancer
   (2) a large increase in the birth rate
   (3) a prolonged period of economic depression
   (4) an increase in infant mortality
   (5) pollution control

9. Government policies designed to foster economic growth by encouraging greater consumption would probably meet with the greatest opposition from which group?

   (1) labor leaders
   (2) business executives
   (3) military leaders
   (4) environmentalists
   (5) individual entrepreneurs

Questions 10 and 11 are based on the following cartoon.

10. What is the main idea of the cartoon?

    (1) The world lacks sufficient energy resources to survive much longer.
    (2) Concerns of environmentalists have had little impact on the actions of industrialists.
    (3) The struggle between energy and the environment cannot be resolved.
    (4) The need to produce energy comes into conflict with the need to preserve the environment.
    (5) A stalemate has been arrived at between industrialists and environmentalists.

GO ON TO THE NEXT PAGE

TEST 2: SOCIAL STUDIES

11. In dealing with the situation referred to in the cartoon during the late 1970s, the United States federal government generally followed a policy that

(1) gave priority to energy demands over environmental concerns
(2) sided with environmentalists against corporations
(3) sought new energy sources outside the United States
(4) attempted to divert national attention to other issues
(5) dealt evenhandedly with industrialists and environmentalists

12. The presidents of the United States from the time of World War II to the present have been most influential in the area of

(1) civil rights
(2) urban affairs
(3) foreign affairs
(4) states rights
(5) human rights

Questions 13 and 14 are based on the following passage.

American industry in general, and America's highest paid industries in particular, export more goods to other markets than any other nation; and command our own market here in the United States.

Given this strength, accompanied by increasing productivity and wages in the rest of the world, there is less need to be concerned over the level of wages in the low-wage countries. These levels, moreover, are already on the rise, and we would hope, will continue to narrow the current wage gap, encouraged by appropriate consultations on an international basis.

This philosophy of the free market—the wider economic choice for men and nations—is as old as freedom itself. It is not a partisan philosophy. For many years our trade legislation has enjoyed bipartisan backing from those members of both parties who recognized how essential trade is to our basic security abroad and our economic health at home. This is even more true today.

—John F. Kennedy

13. In this passage, President Kennedy is emphasizing the need for

(1) the free market
(2) increasing our imports
(3) reducing our tariffs
(4) increasing our exports
(5) American industrial efficiency

14. The immediate purpose of President Kennedy's message was to

(1) try to restrict foreign competition
(2) increase benefits for the American worker
(3) close the wage gap between the United States and other countries
(4) gain congressional support for trade legislation
(5) decrease American imports

Questions 15 and 16 are based on the following passage.

Fourscore and seven years ago our fathers brought forth on this continent a new nation, conceived in liberty, and dedicated to the proposition that all men are created equal.

Now we are engaged in a great civil war, testing whether that nation, or any nation so conceived and so dedicated, can long endure. We are met on a great battlefield of that war. We have come to dedicate a portion of that field as a final resting-place for those who here gave their lives that that nation might live. It is altogether fitting and proper that we should do this.

But, in a larger sense, we cannot dedicate—we cannot consecrate—we cannot hallow—this ground. The brave men, living and dead, who struggled here, have consecrated it far above our poor power to add or detract.

—Abraham Lincoln

15. In the first paragraph, the speaker refers to

(1) the Declaration of Independence
(2) the Articles of Confederation
(3) the United States Constitution
(4) the Northwest Ordinance
(5) the Monroe Doctrine

16. The purpose of the speech was to

(1) commemorate a battle
(2) remember the founding of our nation
(3) dedicate a cemetery
(4) deplore civil war
(5) seek political support in an election

GO ON TO THE NEXT PAGE

TEST 2: SOCIAL STUDIES

Questions 17 to 19 are based on the following chart, which lists some characteristics of Nations *A* and *B*.

Factors of Production	*Nation A*
Land (natural resources)	Relative scarcity
Labor	Relative abundance
Capital	Relative abundance
Business management	Relative abundance

Factors of Production	*Nation B*
Land (natural resources)	Relative abundance
Labor	Relative abundance
Capital	Relative scarcity
Business management	Relative scarcity

17. Which economic decision would most probably be in the best interests of Nation *A*?
    (1) permitting an unfavorable balance of payments
    (2) seeking foreign markets
    (3) attracting investments from foreign nations
    (4) encouraging immigration
    (5) increasing imports

18. During the early 19th century, which nation most nearly resembled Nation *A*?
    (1) the United States
    (2) Great Britain
    (3) Russia
    (4) Turkey
    (5) China

19. If Nation *B* wishes to industrialize, how can it best encourage its own citizens to invest their capital in domestic industries?
    (1) by permitting an unfavorable balance of payments and seeking colonies
    (2) by permitting an unfavorable balance of payments and encouraging immigration
    (3) by attracting investments from foreign nations and encouraging immigration
    (4) by instituting high protective tariffs and giving tax concessions to business
    (5) by lowering taxes on imports

20. "Our policy in regard to Europe . . . is not to interfere in the internal concerns of any of its powers"—President Monroe, 1823

    "It must be the policy of the United States to support free peoples who are resisting attempted subjugation by armed minorities or by outside pressures."—President Truman, 1947

    The most valid conclusion to be drawn from these statements is that
    (1) President Truman followed President Monroe's theory of foreign relations
    (2) during the 19th and 20th centuries, the United States was not interested in international affairs
    (3) during the 19th century, events in Europe did not affect the United States
    (4) President Truman changed the policy of President Monroe
    (5) conditions were different in 1947 from those in 1823

Questions 21 and 22 are based on the following graphs.

Of all women with children under 6 and living with their husbands, how many work?

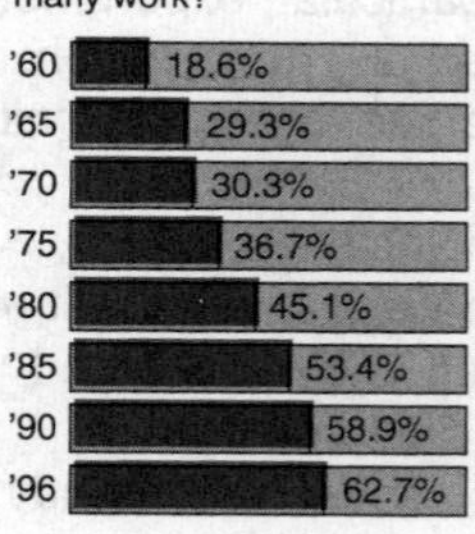

Of all woman who work, how many have children under 6 years old?

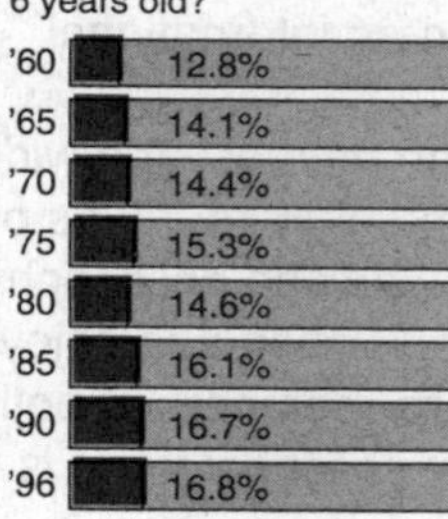

Of all working women with children under 6 and living with their husbands, how many work...

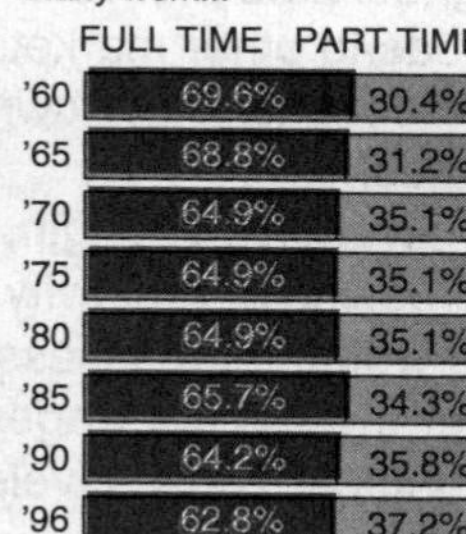

Source: Bureau of Labor Statistics

GO ON TO THE NEXT PAGE

TEST 2: SOCIAL STUDIES

21. The period with the greatest increase in the percentage of working women having children under 6 and living with their husbands was

(1) '60–'65
(2) '70–'75
(3) '80–'85
(4) '85–'90
(5) '90–'96

22. The percentage of women working part time remained steadiest between

(1) '60 and '70
(2) '70 and '80
(3) '75 and '85
(4) '80 and '90
(5) '90 and '96

---

23. Ethnocentrism is a belief that one's own ethnic group, nation, or culture is inherently superior to all others. An example of ethnocentrism is

(1) the use of the word *barbarian* to describe people of differing backgrounds
(2) the singing of a country's national anthem at sports events
(3) Japanese acceptance and imitation of Western culture
(4) the spread of Chinese culture to Southeast Asia
(5) a liberal immigration policy

Question 24 is based on the following diagram.

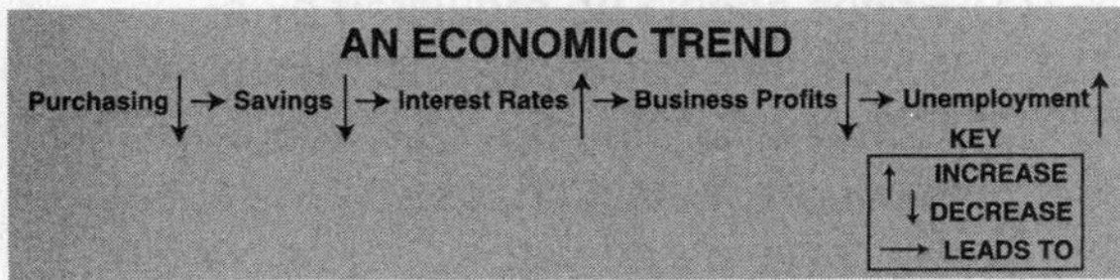

24. Which is occurring in the economy illustrated above?

(1) increase in real income
(2) devaluation of currency
(3) growth
(4) recession
(5) recovery

---

25. "All forms of life developed from earlier forms. In every case the fittest survived and the weak died out. It is the same for people and nations."

This passage expresses a view most often found in

(1) fundamentalism
(2) social Darwinism
(3) liberalism
(4) utopian socialism
(5) egalitarianism

Questions 26 to 28 are based on the following passage.

The problems we face in conserving natural resources are laborious and complex. The preservation of even small bits of marshlands or woods representing the last strands of irreplaceable biotic communities is interwoven with the red tape of law, conflicting local interests, the overlapping jurisdiction of governmental and private conservation bodies, and an intricate tangle of economic and social considerations. During the time spent in resolving these factors, it often happens that the area to be preserved is swallowed up. Even more formidable is the broad-scale conservation problem raised by the spread of urban belts in such places as the northeastern part of the United States. The pressures of human growth are so acute in such instances that they raise issues that would tax the wisdom of Solomon.

26. The author of this passage is primarily concerned with

(1) biotic communities
(2) legal red tape
(3) obstacles to conservation
(4) private conservation organizations
(5) encroaching suburbs

27. The most perplexing problem of conservationists is the one involving

(1) population growth
(2) public indifference
(3) favorable legislation
(4) division of authority
(5) increased taxes

GO ON TO THE NEXT PAGE

TEST 2: SOCIAL STUDIES

28. The author's attitude toward the situation he describes is
    (1) optimistic
    (2) realistic
    (3) apathetic
    (4) illogical
    (5) combative

Questions 29 to 31 are based on the following passage.

We must pursue a course designed not merely to reduce the number of delinquents. We must increase the chances for young people to lead productive lives.

For these delinquent and potentially delinquent youth, we must offer a New Start. We must insure that the special resources and skills essential for their treatment and rehabilitation are available. Because many of these young men and women live in broken families, burdened with financial and psychological problems, a successful rehabilitation program must include family counseling, vocational guidance, education and health services. It must strengthen the family and the schools. It must offer courts an alternative to placing young delinquents in penal institutions.

I recommend the Juvenile Delinquency Prevention Act of 1967.

—Lyndon B. Johnson

29. The emphasis in this speech is on
    (1) diagnosis and research
    (2) prevention and rehabilitation
    (3) rehabilitation and research
    (4) treatment and diagnosis
    (5) research and diagnosis

30. The main purpose of this speech is to
    (1) provide federal financial aid
    (2) give advice to broken families
    (3) support research and experimentation
    (4) praise "halfway houses"
    (5) advocate legislation to combat juvenile delinquency

31. The passage implies that
    (1) delinquents cannot lead productive lives
    (2) detention of delinquents is unnecessary
    (3) delinquency is caused by family problems
    (4) the federal government must assume responsibility for preventing juvenile delinquency
    (5) courts must place young delinquents in the proper penal institutions

Questions 32 and 33 are based on the following cartoon.

32. Which statement best summarizes the main idea of the cartoon?
    (1) Prices should be regulated by a committee of private business people.
    (2) Competition among major industries has led to economic chaos.
    (3) Strict price-and-wage controls would assure a stable economy.
    (4) Government has been unable to deal effectively with a major economic problem.
    (5) Deregulation leads to lower prices.

GO ON TO THE NEXT PAGE

TEST 2: SOCIAL STUDIES

33. A likely response to the problem referred to in the cartoon would be an increase in the

(1) interest rates on bank loans
(2) amount of government spending
(3) amount of money in circulation
(4) number of loans approved by banks
(5) number of housing starts

34. Humanism as an intellectual and cultural movement stressed human values and welfare rather than religious interests.

The statement most in agreement with the humanist view is

(1) Life on earth is only a preparation for another life.
(2) Individuals are important and should be treated with dignity.
(3) Degree of faith is an accurate measure of a person's worth.
(4) The best education comes from a thorough understanding of religious doctrines and values.
(5) Man does not have the free will to determine his own destiny.

<u>Questions 35 to 37</u> are based on the following quotation.

"...American social development has been continually beginning over again on the frontier. This perennial rebirth, this fluidity of American life, this expansion westward with its new opportunities, its continuous touch with the simplicity of primitive society, furnish the forces dominating American character. The true point of view in the history of this nation is not the Atlantic coast, it is the Great West. The frontier is the line of most rapid and effective Americanization. The wilderness masters the colonists."

—Frederick Jackson Turner,
"The Significance of the Frontier in American History"—1893

35. According to Frederick Jackson Turner, the culture of the United States was primarily the result of the

(1) dependence of each generation upon its predecessors
(2) Western settlers' experience in adjusting to new surroundings
(3) pioneers' ability to maintain contact with the settled areas back East
(4) influence of the frontier in making settlers more like Easterners
(5) original thirteen colonies

36. In this quotation Turner describes the frontier not only as an area but also as a

(1) process of developing culture
(2) preserver of traditions
(3) solution to European problems
(4) developer of economic systems
(5) refuge for colonists

37. Which characteristic of the West as described by Turner is most applicable to contemporary society in the United States?

(1) simplicity of life
(2) westward expansion
(3) new opportunities
(4) frontier environment
(5) urban redevelopment

38. A primary source is an eyewitness account of an event or events in a specific time period. Which would be an example of a primary source of information about life in the 18th-century American colonies?

(1) a diary of a colonial shopkeeper
(2) a painting of the colonial period by a 20th century artist
(3) a novel about the American Revolutionary War
(4) a reproduction of furniture used during the colonial period
(5) a social history of the period

GO ON TO THE NEXT PAGE

TEST 2: SOCIAL STUDIES

Questions 39 and 40 are based on the following graph.

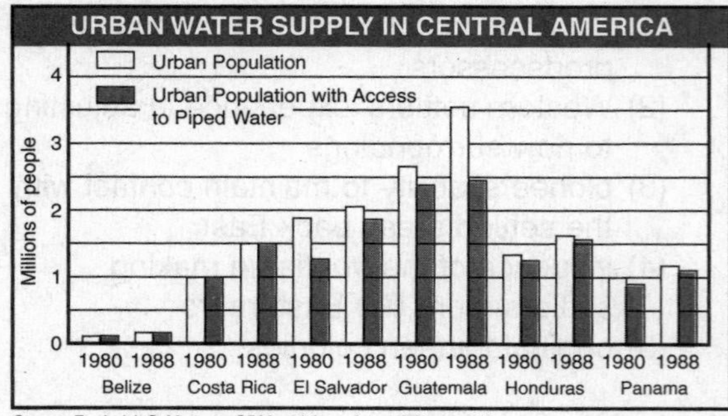

Source: Frederick S. Mattson, CDM and Associates, Arlington, VA

39. Which statement is best supported by the data in the graph?
    (1) The urban areas of Honduras and Panama require the largest supply of water in Central America.
    (2) Belize and Costa Rica are meeting the water needs of their urban population.
    (3) Urban water supplies are declining in many Central American countries.
    (4) Most Central American countries experienced a decrease in urban population between 1980 and 1988.
    (5) The supply of water increased in Central America between 1980 and 1988.

40. In 1988 the country with the largest urban population without access to piped water was
    (1) Costa Rica
    (2) El Salvador
    (3) Honduras
    (4) Panama
    (5) Guatemala

Questions 41 to 43 are based on the statements made by Speakers *A*, *B*, *C*, *D*, and *E*.

Speaker *A*: Government could not function very well without them. The flow of information they provide to Congress and the federal agencies is vital to the functioning of our democratic system.

Speaker *B*: Yes, but the secrecy under which they generally operate makes me suspicious that they are influencing lawmakers in improper ways.

Speaker *C*: Don't forget that they not only try to influence Washington opinion but also attempt to shape public opinion across the nation in order to create a favorable climate for their views.

Speaker *D*: That's true. Any politician who ignores 40,000 letters does so at great risk. We have to pay attention to them whether we accept their views or not.

Speaker *E*: I agree with Speaker *C*. Public opinion is essential to the functioning of our American way of life.

41. Which group are the speakers most likely discussing?
    (1) lawyers
    (2) reporters
    (3) government workers
    (4) media analysts
    (5) lobbyists

42. Which speaker is most concerned about the impact of the methods used by this group upon democratic government?
    (1) *A*
    (2) *B*
    (3) *C*
    (4) *D*
    (5) *E*

43. Which speaker implies that lawmakers frequently must deal with a great many issues about which they know very little?
    (1) *A*
    (2) *B*
    (3) *C*
    (4) *D*
    (5) *E*

GO ON TO THE NEXT PAGE

TEST 2: SOCIAL STUDIES

Question 44 is based on the following cartoon.

44. Which statement best summarizes the main point of the above cartoon?

    (1) The citizen's vote is a powerful means of influencing legislators seeking reelection.
    (2) Citizens are dependent upon the legislative branch of government for protection.
    (3) Federal and state legislators usually agree on major campaign issues.
    (4) The public generally does not favor consumer protection legislation.
    (5) Voters are easily fooled by politicians seeking votes.

Questions 45 to 47 are based on the following passage.

The people and groups that provide the stimulation and contact necessary for social development—the socializing agents—usually fall into two classes: (1) those people with authority over the individual, such as parents and teachers, and (2) those in positions of equality with him or her—age peers, such as playmates or a circle of friends. Since the family is the socializing agent during the critical first years of life, it naturally has had great influence. But because of the increased specialization of the functions of the family, the rapidity of social change that tends to divide the generations, and the high degree of mobility and social fluidity, the peer group is of growing importance in modern urban life.

45. Parents, teachers, and age peers share the role of

    (1) people with authority over the individual
    (2) peer group members
    (3) the friendly circle
    (4) the family circle
    (5) socializing agents

46. All of these reasons are given for the increased role of peers in an individual's social development EXCEPT

    (1) social mobility
    (2) social fluidity
    (3) generation gap
    (4) growing number of peers
    (5) specialization of family functions

47. The family, in modern urban life, is

    (1) exerting influence
    (2) growing in importance
    (3) being replaced by the peer group
    (4) filling a broadening role
    (5) influential only in the early years of life

Questions 48 and 49 refer to the following statements made by Speakers *A*, *B*, and *C*.

Speaker *A*: Increased contact among nations and peoples is characteristic of our times. A single decision by OPEC or a multinational corporation can send ripples of change throughout our global society.

Speaker *B*: If we are to survive, all passengers on our Spaceship Earth must participate in efforts to solve the issues that threaten humankind—poverty, resource depletion, pollution, violence, and war.

GO ON TO THE NEXT PAGE

TEST 2: SOCIAL STUDIES

Speaker *C*: We must understand that no single culture's view of the world is universally shared. Other people have different value systems and ways of thinking and acting. They will not see the world as we do.

48. Which concept is discussed by both Speakers *A* and *B*?

(1) self-determination
(2) nationalism
(3) conservation
(4) interdependence
(5) protectionism

49. Speaker *C* indicates a desire to reduce

(1) ethnocentrism
(2) globalism
(3) social mobility
(4) religious tolerance
(5) interdependence

Questions 50 and 51 are based on the following cartoon.

"Witnesses for the Prosecution"

50. The cartoon is concerned primarily with determining responsibility for which situation?

(1) use of poison gas during World War I
(2) slave labor camps in the Soviet Union during the Stalin era
(3) the Holocaust in Europe during the 1930s and 1940s
(4) apartheid practices in South Africa
(5) the blitzkrieg of World War II

51. The trial symbolized in the cartoon is significant because it was the first time that

(1) the United Nations International Court of Justice worked effectively
(2) individuals were prosecuted for crimes against humanity
(3) war guilt was applied to a whole nation
(4) international law was enforced
(5) the United States cooperated with the United Nations

Questions 52 to 54 are based on the following passage.

Organized economic studies date only from the 17th century. Since then, there have been a number of major schools of economic thought. They can be briefly identified as follows:

(1) mercantilism—advocates, in foreign trade, a surplus of exports over imports to accumulate gold and supports development of local industries protected by tariffs from foreign trade competition

(2) laissez-faire—opposes state intervention in economic affairs to allow free trade and competition

(3) Marxism—teaches that value created by labor and profit is surplus value skimmed off by the capitalist who owns the means of production, which should be eventually controlled by the proletariat or the industrial workers

(4) Keynes theory—focuses on the need to create demand by government spending and the curbing of excess demand by tight budget policies

(5) supply-side economics—supports stimulating production rather than demand by drastic tax reductions to increase business investment and advocates a cutback in government spending to eliminate deficits

GO ON TO THE NEXT PAGE

TEST 2: SOCIAL STUDIES

Each of the following describes an action or proposal relating to the economic policies described above. Indicate which school of economic thought would approve the action.

52. The president recommends drastic cuts in defense and nondefense spending.
    (1) mercantilism
    (2) laissez-faire
    (3) Marxism
    (4) Keynes theory
    (5) supply-side economics

53. Congress is considering a tariff on Japanese imports to protect the United States electronics industry.
    (1) mercantilism
    (2) laissez-faire
    (3) Marxism
    (4) Keynes theory
    (5) supply-side economics

54. A company is bought out by its employees.
    (1) mercantilism
    (2) laissez-faire
    (3) Marxism
    (4) Keynes theory
    (5) supply-side economics

---

55. Cultural diffusion is the spread of one culture to other areas of the world. An example is
    (1) an immigrant learning a new language
    (2) a child learning to walk
    (3) conflict between old and new cultures
    (4) the superiority of the United States' culture over all others
    (5) a Russian playing basketball

56. "Under a government which imprisons anyone unjustly, the true place for a just man is also a prison."
    —Henry David Thoreau

    Which does this quotation most strongly support?
    (1) social control
    (2) conformity
    (3) suspension of civil liberties
    (4) dictatorship
    (5) civil disobedience

Questions 57 and 58 are based on the following cartoon.

57. Which best states the main idea of the cartoon?
    (1) The United States establishes immigration policies that meet its specific needs.
    (2) There is a surplus of highly trained people in foreign countries.
    (3) Highly trained people will be able to pass literacy tests required to enter the United States.
    (4) The United States lags behind other nations in technological development.
    (5) Untrained people are not welcome in the United States.

GO ON TO THE NEXT PAGE

TEST 2: SOCIAL STUDIES

58. One similarity between immigration policy suggested in the cartoon and United States immigration policy in the 1920s is that both show a

    (1) reluctance to admit non-English speaking people
    (2) preference for certain groups
    (3) desire to encourage increased immigration
    (4) desire to adopt the values of international human rights organizations
    (5) desire to increase ethnic diversity

Question 59 is based on the following headline.

NIXON MUST SURRENDER TAPES, SUPREME COURT RULES, 8 TO 0; HE PLEDGES FULL COMPLIANCE

House Committee Begins Debate on Impeachment

59. Which feature of the United States constitutional system is best illustrated by the above headline?

    (1) checks and balances
    (2) executive privilege
    (3) power to grant pardons
    (4) federalism
    (5) the Bill of Rights

Questions 60 and 61 are based on the following graph.

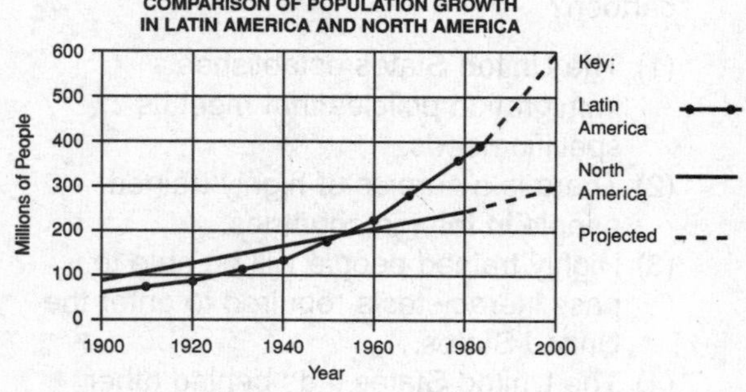

60. Based on the information in the graph, which is a valid conclusion about the populations of Latin America and North America?

    (1) There has always been a large difference in the population growth of Latin America and North America.
    (2) By the year 2000, the population of Latin America is expected to be approximately twice that of North America.
    (3) In 1900, the number of people in Latin America was equal to the number of people in North America.
    (4) In the early 1980s, the difference in population between the two regions was about 300 million.
    (5) The rate of population growth of Latin America has been steadier than that of North America.

61. Which best accounts for the situation shown in the graph?

    (1) decline in the standard of living in North America
    (2) growing trade surplus of most Latin American nations
    (3) improved nutrition and medical care in Latin America
    (4) increased death rate in North America due to contagious diseases
    (5) increase in democracy in Latin America

TEST 2: SOCIAL STUDIES

Questions 62 and 63 are based on the following cartoon.

IN AMERICA, WE SAY:
CHEESEBURGER DELUXE / ONION RINGS / THE PATE' WAS FLAT / I COULDN'T EAT ANOTHER THING / TRY THE LOBSTER / VEGGIES / I'VE HAD BETTER VEAL / EGGS BENEDICT / I'M STUFFED / WITH WHIPPED CREAM OF COURSE / CHOLESTEROL COUNT / WAITER, I SAID WITHOUT OLIVES / PASTA / CREAM SAUCE / OYSTERS ON THE HALF SHELL
IN BANGLADESH, IT'S:
—WATER

Source: The Times Union, July 1991

62. What is the main idea of the cartoon?

    (1) The people of developing nations have refused to ask for aid.
    (2) Relief workers have died trying to help suffering people in developing nations.
    (3) Industrialized nations have prevented starvation in developing nations.
    (4) People in some developing nations lack the basic necessities, while people in other nations have more than they need.
    (5) Prosperous nations are concerned with the problems of developing nations.

63. The cartoon implies that

    (1) Industrialized nations should help developing nations.
    (2) People in some countries are doomed to a life of poverty.
    (3) The problems of developing nations are no concern of America.
    (4) Americans exploit developing nations.
    (5) Some countries are overpopulated.

---

64. "I believe that it must be the policy of the United States to support free peoples who are resisting attempted subjugation by armed minorities or by outside pressures. I believe that we must assist free peoples to work out their own destinies in their own way. I believe that our help should be primarily through economic and financial aid...."

    —Harry S. Truman

    The recommendation made in this quotation resulted from a perception that the United States needed to

    (1) oppose Communist expansion just after World War II
    (2) prepare for World War I
    (3) fight Nazi aggression in 1941
    (4) justify the withdrawal of United States forces from Korea
    (5) return to a policy of isolationism

END OF EXAMINATION

TEST 3: SCIENCE

Directions

The Science test consists of multiple-choice questions intended to measure the general concepts in science. The questions are based on short readings that often include a graph, chart, or figure. Study the information given and then answer the question(s) following it. Refer to the information as often as necessary in answering the questions.

You will have 95 minutes to answer the questions. Work carefully, but do not spend too much time on any one question. Be sure you answer every question. You will not be penalized for incorrect answers.

To record your answers, mark the numbered space on the answer sheet beside the number that corresponds to the question in the test.

FOR EXAMPLE:

Which of the following is the smallest unit?

(1) solution
(2) element
(3) atom
(4) compound
(5) mixture

① ② ● ④ ⑤

The correct answer is "atom"; therefore, space 3 would be marked on the answer sheet.

GO ON TO THE NEXT PAGE

TEST 3: SCIENCE

<u>Questions 1 to 4</u> refer to the following article.

Scientists have different explanations of how evolution occurred, but they all agree that all living things evolved from other living things. Paleontologists have justified this conclusion from their studies of fossil remains. There is also evidence from other branches of science that there have been changes in organisms, and that these changes are still going on.

While archaeologists have been digging through the remains of ancient civilizations, adding their bit to knowledge, the origin of human beings has been the subject of study for the anthropologist. Anthropologists specialize in their areas of research. One may study the history of a language, while another investigates the various types of pottery that are unearthed. Physical anthropology is involved with the anatomy of various vertebrates. Of particular interest to physical anthropologists are primates, that is, the group of mammals that includes humans, apes, monkeys, and chimpanzees. With the aid of fossil records, comparisons can be made between the structures of animals from the past and present forms.

1. Which of the following terms includes all the others?

   (1) human
   (2) primate
   (3) monkey
   (4) ape
   (5) chimpanzee

2. Evolution is the biological process by which

   (1) fossils are produced in rocks
   (2) the anatomy of vertebrates is compared
   (3) ancient human life is studied
   (4) new kinds of living things arise
   (5) chimpanzees give rise to humans

3. Which of the following gives the most direct evidence that different forms of life existed in the past?

   (1) organic chemistry
   (2) fossils
   (3) comparative anatomy
   (4) archeology
   (5) laboratory experiments

4. Which of the following discoveries would suggest that the human species is still evolving?

   (1) The human brain is much larger than the brain of a gorilla.
   (2) In early stages of development, human embryos have a large tail.
   (3) There is a strong similarity between the chemistry of humans and that of chimpanzees.
   (4) The armor of medieval knights is too small for today's average man.
   (5) Tractors have replaced horses for farm work.

<u>Questions 5 to 8</u> are based on the following diagrams.

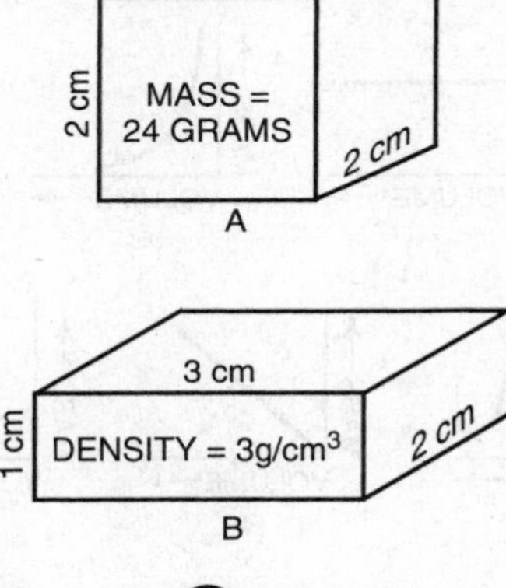

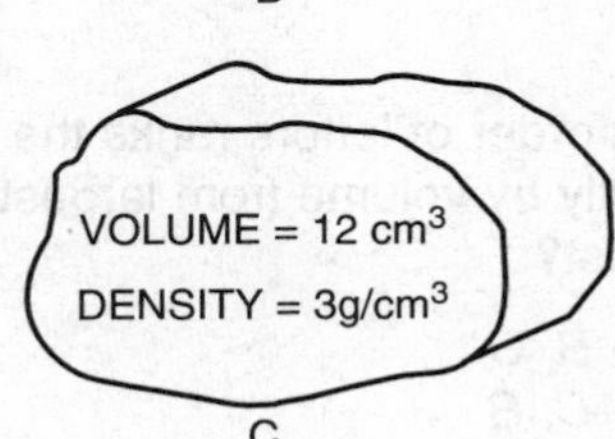

These diagrams, not drawn to scale, represent three samples of the same substance, each having a different size and shape. The following formulas are involved:

$$\text{Volume} = \text{length} \times \text{height} \times \text{width}$$

$$\text{Density} = \frac{\text{mass}}{\text{volume}}$$

GO ON TO THE NEXT PAGE

TEST 3: SCIENCE

5. What is the density of sample *A*?

(1) 0.33 g/cm^3
(2) 2.0 g/cm^3
(3) 3.0 g/cm^3
(4) 4.0 g/cm^3
(5) 8.0 g/cm^3

6. If sample *B* were split in half, what would be the density of each piece?

(1) 1.0 g/cm^3
(2) 1.5 g/cm^3
(3) 3.0 g/cm^3
(4) 6.0 g/cm^3
(5) 8.0 g/cm^3

7. Which graph best represents the relationship between the mass and the volume of the substance?

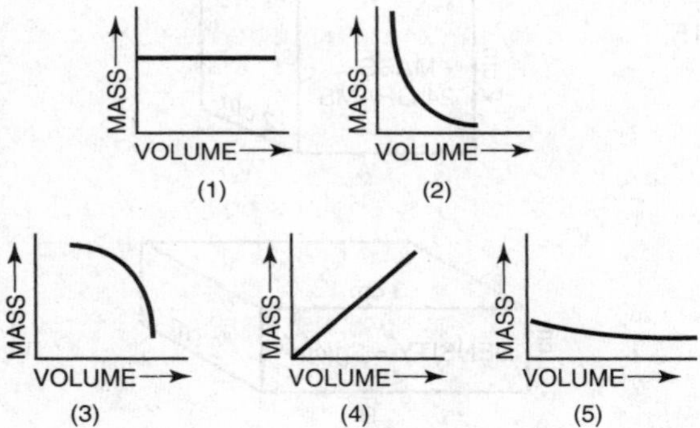

8. Which order of letters ranks the samples correctly by volume from largest to smallest?

(1) *A, B, C*
(2) *A, C, B*
(3) *B, C, A*
(4) *C, B, A*
(5) *C, A, B*

9. An island may form when material expelled by an undersea volcano gradually builds up and rises above the surface of the water. This has happened in numerous places in the Pacific Ocean. Over time, however, another island may begin to form some distance from the first. It is possible that chains of islands, such as the Hawaiian Islands, were formed in this way. One reason for this may be that

(1) the volcano moves along the bottom of the ocean
(2) the plates of earth and rock that cover the interior of planet Earth are slowly moving, taking the islands with them
(3) when the first island was finished, some leftover lava started another island
(4) volcanoes erupted in places where islands were going to be formed
(5) volcanic eruptions have had nothing to do with the formation of islands

10. The depth of a body of water can be measured by a method called sonar. Sonar is an acronym for *SO*und *NA*vigation *R*anging, and the method works on the same principle as radar. Sound waves (sonar beams) are aimed at the ocean floor, and the times when they bounce back are recorded. Since we know that the speed of sound in water is approximately 4,800 feet per second, the depth of the ocean can be determined by measuring how long it takes a beam to bounce off the ocean floor and return to the ship.

How far, in feet, would a sonar beam travel in 2½ seconds?

(1) 14,400
(2) 9,500
(3) 2,400
(4) 4,850
(5) 12,000

Questions 11 to 13 refer to the following article.

The ancient Greeks found that pieces of a certain iron ore attract or repel each other. These were early examples of natural magnets, and the effect that the Greeks observed is called magnetism. Like the planet Earth, which is itself a giant magnet, these smaller magnets have a north and a south pole. Like poles repel each other, while opposite poles attract.

Magnets are in common use today and can be found on almost any refrigerator. Some are shaped like a rod or bar; in others the rod is bent into a horseshoe shape.

Wrapping a piece of metal, such as a nail,

GO ON TO THE NEXT PAGE

TEST 3: SCIENCE

with wire can produce another kind of magnet, an electromagnet. When electricity is run through the wire, you get a magnetic field.

11. Magnets have many uses. Some are small enough to be used in the motor of a hair dryer, while others are large enough to lift enormous amounts of scrap metal that may once have been a car or truck. Since this kind of magnet can be turned on and off, it is probably

    (1) an electromagnet
    (2) a natural magnet
    (3) a magnetic ore
    (4) a horseshoe magnet
    (5) magnetite

12. The fact that the needle of a compass always points north is proof that

    (1) the point of the compass must be a north pole
    (2) many materials that occur in nature have a strong magnetic attraction
    (3) a compass is an important part of any navigator's equipment
    (4) Earth is itself a magnet and can exert a magnetic force
    (5) magnets have been used since ancient times

13. Lodestone is an ore used by ancient Chinese to make compasses. This use was possible only because lodestone was

    (1) very common in China
    (2) a neutral material capable of being magnetized
    (3) capable of being made into electromagnets
    (4) paramagnetic
    (5) a natural magnet

<u>Questions 14 to 16</u> refer to the following article.

In one kind of internal-combustion engine, a mixture of gasoline and air is compressed in a cylinder and then ignited by a spark from a spark plug. The German engineer Rudolf Diesel developed another type of engine that works without spark plugs. The intake stroke of this engine admits only air, which is strongly compressed in a cylinder, causing it to heat to a very high temperature. Heavy fuels, such as oil, are then injected into this hot, compressed air and are exploded by the heat.

Because diesel engines need such a strong compression stroke, they are heavy and require the strength of a thick-walled compression chamber to function. However, they get more energy out of the less expensive fuel they burn because they can operate at a much higher temperature than a gasoline engine.

14. What is true of the diesel engine but not of the gasoline engine?

    (1) It needs no air supply.
    (2) It has no cylinders.
    (3) It has no spark plugs.
    (4) It uses less expensive types of gasoline.
    (5) It has no pistons.

15. Why are diesel engines used on locomotives?

    (1) They can get more heat energy from a less expensive fuel.
    (2) Coal-burning engines pollute the air.
    (3) It is difficult to store large quantities of gasoline safely in the locomotive.
    (4) Electric power is not easily available in remote, rural areas.
    (5) Diesel fuel is available in remote, rural areas.

16. Why aren't diesel engines used in airplanes?

    (1) Diesel engines are heavy engines.
    (2) Diesel oil is very explosive.
    (3) Airplanes do not need the power of diesel engines.
    (4) Housing the cylinders would take up too much space.
    (5) Diesel oil produces more pollutants than other fuels.

<u>Questions 17 to 19</u> refer to the following article.

All nations agree that cooperative efforts are needed in research to study and predict earthquakes. In July 1956 the first World Conference on Earthquake Engineering was held in Tokyo. Its purpose was to share information

GO ON TO THE NEXT PAGE

TEST 3: SCIENCE

about the prediction of earthquakes and methods of constructing buildings and bridges that can withstand the shocks.

What causes earthquakes? The crust of the Earth is a broken mosaic of pieces, bounded by deep cracks called faults. When forces deep inside the Earth move these pieces, tremendous shock waves start from the faults. Shock waves in the crust, from whatever source, can be detected by seismographs all over the world. If the earthquake occurs beneath the ocean, it produces an enormous wave, called a tsunami, that can do much damage when it arrives at a shore.

17. What is the most frequent cause of major earthquakes?

    (1) movements within the Earth
    (2) folding
    (3) landslides
    (4) submarine currents
    (5) tsunamis

18. How can earthquake destruction be minimized?

    (1) more frequent use of seismographs
    (2) better construction of buildings
    (3) quicker methods of evacuation
    (4) early detection and warning
    (5) better control of tsunamis

19. Nuclear explosions can be detected by seismographs because they

    (1) cause tsunamis
    (2) occur on geologic faults
    (3) cause earthquakes
    (4) produce shock waves in the crust
    (5) compress the rock

Questions 20 to 23 refer to the following article.

All matter is made up of atoms. Atoms contain protons, which have positive charges; electrons, which have negative charges; and neutrons, which are neither positively nor negatively charged. Since the atom has the same number of protons and electrons, the atom as a whole is neutral.

The center of the atom, the nucleus, holds protons and neutrons, while the electrons move around in orbits called shells. Each shell has the capacity to hold a maximum number of electrons. The first shell can hold no more than two electrons, while the second shell is complete with eight electrons. The third shell can hold eighteen electrons, except when it happens to be the outer shell, in which case its capacity is only eight electrons. In some atoms, additional shells carry additional electrons.

An atom tends to complete the outer shell either by borrowing electrons, lending electrons, or sharing electrons. The number of electrons available for such action is called valence. For example, a valence of + 2 means an atom has two electrons to lend. An atom with a valence of –1 needs one electron to complete its outer ring. The borrowing, lending, and sharing of electrons gives rise to the formation of compounds.

The atomic mass of an atom is the sum of the total mass of its protons and neutrons. The proton has a mass of one atomic mass unit. The neutron also has a mass of one atomic mass unit, but the electron adds almost nothing to the mass of an atom and so does not have to be considered in calculating atomic mass. The atomic number tells you the number of protons in the atom.

20. The valence of calcium (Ca) is +2. The valence of chlorine (Cl) is –1. When these elements combine to form calcium chloride, the correct formula for this compound is

    (1) $CaCl$
    (2) Ca_2Cl
    (3) $CaCl_2$
    (4) Ca_2Cl_2
    (5) Ca_4Cl_2

21. Lithium has an atomic mass of 7 and an atomic number of 3. How many neutrons are there in the lithium atom?

    (1) none
    (2) two
    (3) three
    (4) four
    (5) ten

22. The atomic number of an atom is always equal to the total number of

    (1) neutrons in the nucleus
    (2) neutrons and protons in the atom
    (3) protons and electrons in the atom
    (4) electrons in the orbits
    (5) protons in the nucleus

GO ON TO THE NEXT PAGE

TEST 3: SCIENCE

23. What is the valence of an element that has 11 protons?

(1) +11
(2) −11
(3) +8
(4) +1
(5) −1

Questions 24 to 29 refer to the following article.

Photosynthesis is a complex process involving many steps. Water in the soil is absorbed by the roots of a plant, rises through veins called xylem, and moves through the stems and into a leaf. Carbon dioxide, diffused from the air through the stomata and into the leaf, comes into contact with the water and dissolves. The solution of carbon dioxide in water then diffuses through the cell walls and into the cells. Organelles within the cell, called chloroplasts, contain chlorophyll, a green pigment that captures light energy from the sun and transforms it into chemical energy. This chemical energy acts to decompose the carbon dioxide and water. The products of this decomposition are recombined into new compounds, then into other compounds. These compounds become more and more complex until finally a sugar is produced. Oxygen is given off as a by-product of the photosynthetic process.

24. Which plant structure is directly involved in the making of sugar?

(1) stoma
(2) xylem
(3) cell wall
(4) plasma membrane
(5) chloroplast

25. To carry on photosynthesis, the water of the soil must be transported to the leaf. Which structure conducts soil water to the leaf?

(1) chlorophyll
(2) stoma
(3) xylem
(4) phloem
(5) chloroplasts

26. Why is chemical energy needed for photosynthesis?

(1) to bring water to the leaf
(2) to decompose chlorophyll
(3) to decompose water
(4) to change the form of light energy
(5) to recombine the products of photosynthesis

27. Sugar is composed of carbon, hydrogen, and oxygen. In the process of photosynthesis, what is the source of these chemical elements?

(1) carbon dioxide alone
(2) water alone
(3) either the carbon dioxide or the water
(4) both the carbon dioxide and the water
(5) neither the carbon dioxide nor the water

28. What is the function of chlorophyll in photosynthesis?

(1) serves as a source of carbohydrate
(2) produces carbon dioxide
(3) changes light energy to chemical energy
(4) supplies chemical energy
(5) provides the green color

29. Carbon dioxide enters a plant by way of the

(1) roots
(2) xylem
(3) plasma membrane
(4) stomata
(5) intercellular spaces

---

30. In photosynthesis, green plants produce the carbohydrates that become the energy supply of the plants and of the animals that eat them. Photosynthesis can take place only when the plants are in sunlight.

Which statement below is a summary of this process?

(1) Light and chemical energy are used for growth.
(2) Chemical energy is converted to light energy.
(3) Light energy is used for growth.
(4) Chemical energy is used for growth.
(5) Light energy is converted to chemical energy.

GO ON TO THE NEXT PAGE

TEST 3: SCIENCE

31. Green plants, in sunlight, absorb carbon dioxide to produce glucose, releasing oxygen in the process. Which of the following would be most likely to increase the rate at which this process goes on?

(1) Increase the amount of oxygen in the air.
(2) Add glucose to the soil.
(3) Move the plants into the shade.
(4) Reduce the amount of carbon dioxide in the air.
(5) Increase the amount of carbon dioxide in the air.

Questions 32 to 34 refer to the following article.

In the process of evolution, organisms undergo certain physical changes so that they are better adapted to survive in their environment. These changes help them to find and eat their food, attract mates, or perhaps defeat or confuse their enemies.

A bird's bill usually defines the type of food that the bird eats. Some hunting birds have sharp hooked bills. Other birds have slender bills to extract nectar from flowers. The interesting bill of the South American toucan is huge and brightly colored and can be as long as half the length of the the bird's body. This bill is useful in picking fruit.

32. What is the probable reason that African hornbills closely resemble the South American toucan, even though the two species are unrelated?

(1) The resemblance is purely a coincidence.
(2) There has been an interchange of genetic material between the two species of birds.
(3) The two species of birds have evolved from a common ancestor.
(4) Both species of birds are fruit eaters in tropical rain forests.
(5) The toucans have migrated from Africa.

33. When the Industrial Revolution introduced great smoke-belching factories into England, a certain species of moth found itself threatened. These white moths lived on the bark of light-colored trees, where they were virtually invisible to predators. When smog from the factories turned everything in the area black with soot, the trunks of the trees were not immune. As time passed, the population of this moth dropped dramatically. The chief reason for the decline may have been that

(1) because the white moths were now visible against the sooty bark, they were easier for birds to catch
(2) the soot was poisonous to the moths
(3) the soot killed off the moth's primary source of food
(4) the soot destroyed the moth's eggs
(5) the moths had to find other trees because the old ones were now too dark

34. Snakes are solitary creatures. With a few exceptions, they crawl off to live alone after they hatch. Occasionally a female snake will lay a trail of a special scent called a pheromone. The reason for laying this trail is that the only life process a snake cannot carry on alone is

(1) respiration
(2) hibernation
(3) reproduction
(4) regulation
(5) locomotion

GO ON TO THE NEXT PAGE

TEST 3: SCIENCE

35. Potassium is receiving special attention as an important nutritional requirement. Potassium conducts an electric charge that is important in the transmission of nerve impulses and muscle contraction. Such foods as bananas and dried apricots are rich in potassium. These foods are recommended for persons who lose potassium because their medication causes the loss of body water. Why might the heart malfunction because of loss of potassium?

(1) The heart needs banana and apricot
(2) The heart absorbs much potassium
(3) High blood pressure can be treated
(4) Low blood pressure can be treated
(5) Contraction of heart muscles requires potassium

36. Oxides of carbon, sulfur, and nitrogen, which occur in the stack gases of coal-burning plants, react with atmospheric water to form acids. The pollution caused by stack gases may be responsible for all the following forms of environmental damage EXCEPT

(1) physical deformity of developing fish
(2) corrosion of buildings
(3) death of many forest trees
(4) damage to human lungs
(5) sewage contamination of water supplies

37. The laws that control recombination of genes seem to be much the same for all sexually reproducing organisms. These laws are studied by statistical analysis of large numbers of offspring for several generations. Which of the following organisms would be most useful in experiments to study the laws of recombination of genes?

(1) bacteria
(2) human beings
(3) mice
(4) dogs
(5) oak trees

38. The early atmosphere of the Earth had no oxygen. It was first produced when bacteria developed the green pigment that made photosynthesis possible. In which of the following groups is the sequence in which the organisms appeared on Earth presented correctly?

(1) animals, green bacteria, nongreen bacteria
(2) green bacteria, animals, nongreen bacteria
(3) animals, nongreen bacteria, green bacteria
(4) nongreen bacteria, green bacteria, animals
(5) nongreen bacteria, animals, green bacteria

39. The graph below shows the changes in the populations of wolves and moose in a northern forest for a period of 6 years. What is the most reasonable explanation of the facts shown?

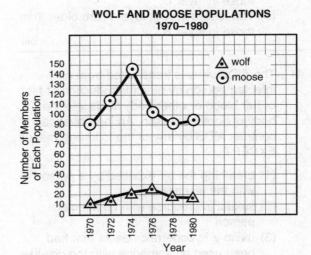

WOLF AND MOOSE POPULATIONS
1970–1980

(1) Moose produce more offspring when there are few wolves.
(2) When there are many moose, there are more recreational hunters.
(3) Wolves produce more offspring when there are many moose.
(4) Both wolf and moose populations vary according to the weather conditions.
(5) Wolf populations have no relationship to the availability of moose.

GO ON TO THE NEXT PAGE

TEST 3: SCIENCE

Question 40 is based on the following diagram.

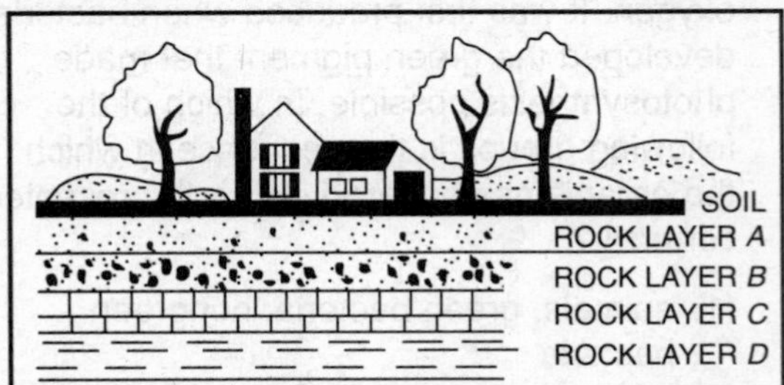

40. When sediments are deposited in the ocean, new layers form on top of preexisting layers. The sediments may eventually turn into fossil bearing rocks. What might a geologist conclude about fossils found in the rock layers shown in the diagram above?

(1) All the fossils are of the same age.
(2) The relative ages of the fossils cannot be determined.
(3) The fossils in rock layer *D* are older than those in layer *A*.
(4) The fossils in rock layer *B* are older than those in layer *C*.
(5) The fossils in rock layer *A* are older than those in layer *B*.

---

41. The AIDS virus is transmitted from an infected person by direct introduction of his or her blood or other body fluids into the body of another person. An individual can contract AIDS by any of the following means EXCEPT

(1) breathing the air expelled by a person with the disease
(2) sexual intercourse with an infected person
(3) using a hypodermic needle that had been used by someone with the disease
(4) receiving a blood transfusion from an infected person
(5) passage of the virus from a pregnant woman into the fetus she is carrying

42. Some corn plants may have genes that make them immune to the poisonous effects of herbicides. These genes can arise spontaneously by mutation, and will then be passed on to future generations. What might a plant breeder do to develop a line of corn that would not be killed by herbicides?

(1) Apply herbicides to cause mutations.
(2) Prevent mutations by careful control of environmental conditions.
(3) Find immune plants by applying herbicides and breeding the survivors.
(4) Withhold all fertilizers and breed the plants that survive.
(5) Withhold all herbicides and breed whichever plants mutate.

43. Since World War II, new varieties of rice have been developed that produce two or three times as much grain when they are grown with heavy doses of chemical fertilizers. A farmer should decide NOT to use these varieties if

(1) he or she is accustomed to growing more familiar varieties of rice
(2) he or she is cultivating only a small plot
(3) his or her farm is in an unusually wet climate
(4) there is no way he or she can obtain the seed of the new varieties
(5) the fertilizer needed costs more than the value of the extra grain

44. Why do you feel cool when you get out of the surf on a dry day?

(1) The water takes heat from your body as it evaporates from your wet skin.
(2) Evaporation produces heat.
(3) Condensation cools the body.
(4) The air is cooler than the surf water.
(5) Sea breezes make you feel cooler.

GO ON TO THE NEXT PAGE

TEST 3: SCIENCE

Questions 45 to 49 refer to the following article.

Today some plants are cloned to produce millions of offspring from a small piece of the original plant. Plant cloning is possible because each plant cell contains a complete blueprint, in the form of chromosomes, for reproducing itself. After a piece of the plant is placed in a growth medium, special plant growth hormones, called auxins and cytokinin, are added to stimulate the production of new plants. The new plants are genetically identical to the original plant and to each other.

The process and equipment for cloning are more expensive than those used for other forms of vegetative propagation. The advantage of cloning is that large numbers of plants are produced in a short period of time. For example, a million plants of a new variety can be cloned in about six months. This process is very useful for developing strains of disease resistant crops or plants that not only can survive in a difficult climate but also will produce a large harvest.

45. For which reason is cloning used to reproduce plants?

    (1) Plants with a large degree of genetic variability are produced.
    (2) Plants are produced more cheaply than by other vegetative methods.
    (3) Plants are produced by the sexual process, resulting in seeds.
    (4) A large number of plants are produced in a short period of time.
    (5) Plants with large degrees of variation are produced.

46. It is possible to clone plants that are identical to their parent plants because

    (1) scientists have developed blueprints to make so many different plants
    (2) every plant cell is the same
    (3) chromosomes carry blueprints from the parent plant
    (4) hormones are used to induce plants to reproduce
    (5) plants are easy to grow under the correct conditions

47. Which statement describes the hormones auxin and cytokinin?

    (1) They are forms of vegetative propagation.
    (2) They can develop into a zygote.
    (3) They stimulate the production of new plants.
    (4) They inhibit the production of new plants.
    (5) They are forms of asexual reproduction.

48. How is cloning defined?

    (1) a form of sexual reproduction
    (2) a form of vegetative propagation
    (3) an inorganic hormone
    (4) an inorganic component of the growing medium
    (5) an auxin

49. An important difference between plants produced by cloning and plants grown from seed is that

    (1) cloned plants are healthier
    (2) cloned plants are identical to the parent plant
    (3) plants grown from seed are identical to the parent plant
    (4) plants grown from seed are better adapted to the conditions in which the plants are grown
    (5) cloned plants do not need as much care

---

50. If particles are to be considered soluble, they must dissolve in water. In this case, the resulting solution will be clear. Sometimes, however, some of the substance will settle out of the solution, leaving a residue on the bottom of the container.

    Why do we find the instruction "Shake well before using" on the labels of some medicines?

    (1) The liquid is a solution.
    (2) The mixture is not a solution.
    (3) The particles are the size of molecules.
    (4) The particles are not visible.
    (5) Light goes through the solution.

GO ON TO THE NEXT PAGE

TEST 3: SCIENCE

Questions 51 to 53 refer to the following article.

Compounds known as bases are bitter to the taste and have a slippery feel. Acids taste sour. Litmus paper is used to determine whether a substance is acidic or basic; the paper turns blue in a base and red in an acid. If exactly correct quantities of an acid and a base are combined, they react chemically to produce a salt, which is neither acidic nor basic.

51. All of the following are acids EXCEPT

    (1) oranges
    (2) vinegar
    (3) sour cream
    (4) apples
    (5) butter

52. Which of the following would turn litmus paper blue?

    (1) alcohol
    (2) soap
    (3) grapefruit
    (4) pure water
    (5) cola

53. Either a base such as ammonia or an acid such as vinegar can clean accumulated dirt from glass. Knowing this, a housekeeper makes a mixture of ammonia and vinegar to clean windows. How will this work?

    (1) There is no way to predict how well the mixture will work.
    (2) The mixture will work better than either substance alone.
    (3) The ammonia will still be effective, but the vinegar will not improve the material.
    (4) The vinegar will still be effective, but the ammonia will not improve the material.
    (5) The mixture will probably not work well at all.

54. Which of the following general rules is the best explanation of the way an ice cube cools a drink?

    (1) Cold moves to objects of higher temperature.
    (2) Heat moves to objects of higher density.
    (3) Heat moves to objects of lower density.
    (4) Cold moves to objects of lower temperature.
    (5) Heat moves to objects of lower temperature.

Questions 55 to 58 are based on the following passage and diagram.

When air rises, it expands, and this change makes it cool down. Conversely, when air sinks, it is compressed and becomes warmer. As air cools down, its relative humidity rises; when the relative humidity reaches 100%, moisture condenses out of the air.

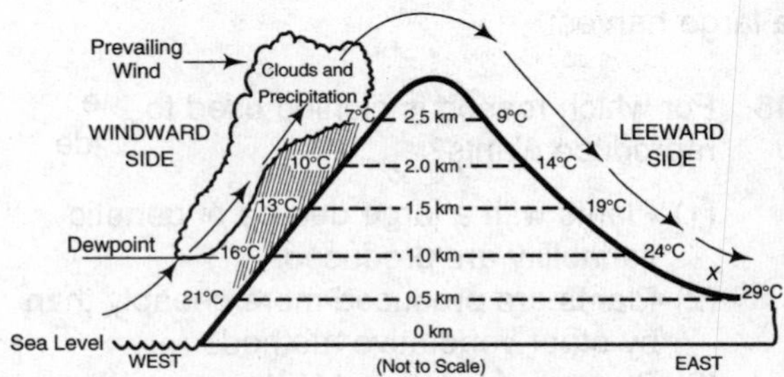

The diagram shows the prevailing wind directions and air temperatures at different elevations on both sides of a mountain.

55. What is the approximate air temperature at the top of the mountain?

    (1) 12°C
    (2) 10°C
    (3) 0°C
    (4) 7°C
    (5) 4°C

GO ON TO THE NEXT PAGE

TEST 3: SCIENCE

56. On which side of the mountain and at what elevation is the relative humidity probably 100%?

(1) on the windward side at 0.5 km
(2) on the windward side at 2.5 km
(3) on the leeward side at 1.0 km
(4) on the leeward side at 2.5 km
(5) on the leeward side at 1.5 km

57. How does the temperature of the air change as the air rises on the windward side of the mountain between sea level and 0.5 kilometer?

(1) The air is warming owing to compression of the air.
(2) The air is warming owing to expansion of the air.
(3) The air is cooling owing to compression of the air.
(4) The air is cooling owing to expansion of the air.
(5) The air is warmed and cooled owing to expansion of the air.

58. Which feature is probably located at the base of the mountain on the leeward side (location *X*)?

(1) a dry, desertlike region
(2) a jungle
(3) a glacier
(4) a large lake
(5) a river

---

59. Human activities produce or add all these pollutants EXCEPT

(1) sound
(2) pollen
(3) radiation
(4) smoke
(5) carbon oxides

Questions 60 and 61 are based on the following passage and diagram.

The block marked *A* is being pulled uphill at constant speed by the falling weight. Since the speed is constant, the force pulling the block uphill must be equal in magnitude to the force holding it back. This opposing force is called friction.

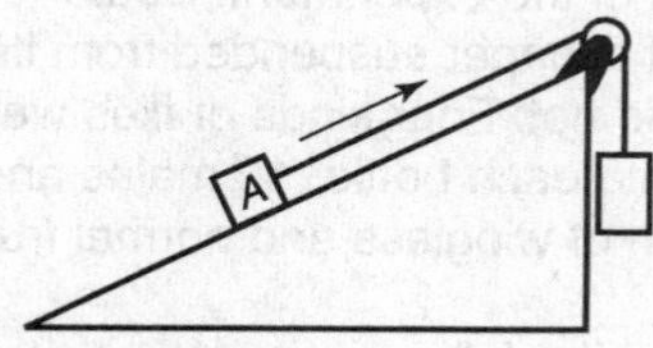

60. How would the situation change if a larger weight were used?

(1) Nothing would be different.
(2) Both the block and the weight would accelerate instead of going at a constant speed.
(3) Both the block and the weight would be going at a higher constant speed.
(4) The weight would accelerate, but the block would still travel at constant speed.
(5) Both the block and the weight would slow down.

61. While you are probably most familiar with animals that have an internal skeleton, called an endoskeleton, certain organisms have their skeletons on the outside of their bodies. This exoskeleton is an excellent means of support and protection, but as the animal grows, its skeleton does not. Because of this, the exoskeleton has to be shed or molted now and then.

Animals with an exoskeleton are called invertebrates. Of the animals listed below, which one is *not* an invertebrate?

(1) lobster
(2) turtle
(3) snail
(4) horseshoe crab
(5) spider

GO ON TO THE NEXT PAGE

TEST 3: SCIENCE

Questions 62 to 66 refer to the following information.

An experiment was performed to find out whether there are any circumstances in which an abnormal type of fruit fly has a selective advantage over the normal kind. Two culture bottles were prepared, using the same kind of food, and were kept next to each other for the entire period of the experiment. Bottle *A* had a small strip of flypaper suspended from its stopper; *B* did not. Four kinds of flies were introduced into each bottle: 10 males and 10 females each of wingless and normal fruit flies.

62. Which of the following is an important control in this experiment?
   (1) the use of both males and females
   (2) placing the flypaper in one bottle only
   (3) using the same kind of food in both bottles
   (4) putting both kinds of flies in each bottle
   (5) taking care that the bottles are well stoppered

63. What is the hypothesis being tested?
   (1) Male fruit flies have a better survival rate than females.
   (2) Flies with wings have a better survival rate than those without.
   (3) There are circumstances in which winglessness confers an advantage in survival.
   (4) Wingless flies have a better survival rate than those with wings.
   (5) All kinds of flies are equally likely to survive.

64. The experiment started with equal numbers of the four kinds of flies in each jar. This is
   (1) an irrelevant fact
   (2) a detail of experimental design
   (3) an assumption
   (4) a general law of nature
   (5) an experimental finding

65. It is known that winglessness in fruit flies sometimes arises by mutation. In the context of this experiment, this is
   (1) an assumption
   (2) a general law of nature
   (3) a hypothesis
   (4) a statement of the problem
   (5) an irrelevant fact

66. What general principle of nature would be explained by finding that most of the flies with wings died on the flypaper?
   (1) Flypaper is an effective means of control of insects.
   (2) Fruit flies exist in nature in many different forms.
   (3) Evolution favors the forms with the best survival values.
   (4) The survival value of a trait depends on the environment in which the organism lives.
   (5) Processes in natural ecosystems cannot be simulated in the laboratory.

END OF EXAMINATION

TEST 4: INTERPRETING LITERATURE AND THE ARTS

Directions

The Interpreting Literature and the Arts test consists of excerpts from classical and popular literature and articles about literature or the arts. Each excerpt is followed by multiple-choice questions about the reading material.

Read each excerpt first and then answer the questions following it. Refer to the reading material as often as necessary in answering the questions.

Each excerpt is preceded by a "purpose question." The purpose question gives a reason for reading the material. Use these purpose questions to help focus your reading. You are not required to answer these purpose questions. They are given only to help you concentrate on the ideas presented in the reading materials.

You should spend no more than 65 minutes answering the questions. Work carefully, but do not spend too much time on any one question. Be sure you answer every question. You will not be penalized for incorrect answers.

To record your answers, mark the numbered space on the answer sheet beside the number that corresponds to the question in the test.

FOR EXAMPLE:

It was Susan's dream machine. The metallic blue paint gleamed, and the sporty wheels were highly polished. Under the hood, the engine was no less carefully cleaned. Inside, flashy lights illuminated the instruments on the dashboard, and the seats were covered in rich leather upholstery.

The subject ("It") of this excerpt is most likely

(1) an airplane ① ② ● ④ ⑤
(2) a stereo system
(3) an automobile
(4) a boat
(5) a motorcycle

The correct answer is "an automobile"; therefore, answer space 3 would be marked on the answer sheet.

GO ON TO THE NEXT PAGE

TEST 4: INTERPRETING LITERATURE AND THE ARTS

Questions 1 to 5 refer to the following excerpt from a work of prose nonfiction.

WHAT WAS MARY WHITE'S LAST HOUR LIKE?

The last hour of Mary White's life was typical of its happiness. She came home from a day's work at school, topped off by a hard grind with the copy on the high school annual, and felt that a ride would refresh her. She climbed into her khakis, chattering to her mother about the work she was doing, and hurried to get her horse and be out on the dirt roads for the country air and the radiant green fields of the spring. As she rode through the town at an easy gallop, she kept waving at passersby. She knew everyone in town. For a decade the little figure with the long pigtail and the red hair ribbon had been familiar on the streets of Emporia, and she got in the way of speaking to those who nodded at her. She passed the Kerrs, walking the horse, in front of the Normal Library, and waved at them; passed another friend a few hundred feet farther on, and waved at her. The horse was walking, and as she turned into North Merchant Street, she took off her cowboy hat, and the horse swung into a lope. She passed the Tripletts and waved her cowboy hat at them, still moving gaily north on Merchant Street. A *Gazette* carrier passed—a high school boy friend—and she waved at him, but with her bridle hand; the horse veered quickly, plunged into the parking lot where a low-hanging limb faced her, and while she still looked back waving, the blow came. But she did not fall from the horse; she slipped off, dazed a bit, staggered, and fell in a faint. She never quite recovered consciousness.

—W.A. White

1. The passage gives details that create a picture of

   (1) a sad death
   (2) a bookish lady
   (3) an active girl
   (4) a boy-crazy kid
   (5) a pathetic child

2. Mary White was

   (1) small of stature
   (2) big-boned
   (3) tall
   (4) husky
   (5) pretty

3. The picture contains such details as

   (1) jeans, a green ribbon, a pigtail
   (2) riding clothes, sombrero, plait
   (3) overalls, cowboy hat, short hair
   (4) khakis, cowboy hat, red hair ribbon
   (5) bridle, saddle, spurs

4. The death of Mary White can be said to have been caused indirectly by her

   (1) poor horsemanship
   (2) small size
   (3) fast riding
   (4) friendliness
   (5) failure to take proper precautions

5. The main purpose of the author is to

   (1) report the tragic end of a happy life
   (2) stress that it was an accident that killed Mary White
   (3) inform us of the mistake she made in waving with the wrong hand
   (4) show Mary White's bravery in not falling from the horse
   (5) emphasize the unexpectedness of the fatal blow

Questions 6 to 10 refer to the following excerpt from a work of prose fiction.

WHAT CAN A BEREAVED FATHER DO?

Iona sees a hall porter with some sacking, and decides to talk to him.

"Friend, what sort of time is it?" he asks.

"Past nine. What are you standing here for? Move on."

Iona moves on a few steps, doubles up, and abandons himself to his grief. He gives a tug at the reins; he can bear it no longer. "The stables," he thinks, and the little horse, as if it understood, starts off at a trot.

One of the cabdrivers around the stove

GO ON TO THE NEXT PAGE

TEST 4: INTERPRETING LITERATURE AND THE ARTS

half gets up, grunts sleepily, and stretches toward a bucket of water.

"Do you want a drink?" Iona asks him.

"Don't I want a drink!"

"That's so? Your good health! But listen, mate—you know, my son is dead...Did you hear? This week, in the hospital...It's a long story."

Iona looks to see what effect his words have, but sees none—the young man is fast asleep again. Just as much as the young one wants to drink, the old man wants to talk. Is it nothing to tell?

"I'll go and look after my horse," thinks Iona; "there's always time to sleep. No fear of that!"

When he is alone, he dares not think of his son; he can speak about him to anyone, but to think of him, and picture him to himself, is unbearably painful.

"That's how it is, my old horse. There's no more Kuzma Ionitch. Now let's say, you had a foal, you were this foal's mother, and suddenly, let's say, that foal went out and left you to live after him. It would be sad, wouldn't it?"

The little horse munches, listens, and breathes over its master's hand...

Iona's feelings are too much for him, and he tells the little horse the whole story.

6. In this story it is ironic that
   (1) the cabdriver wants a drink
   (2) the hall porter tells Iona to move on
   (3) Iona tells his story to his horse
   (4) Iona has run out of food for his horse
   (5) the horse had a foal

7. Iona goes to take care of his horse. He does so most probably to
   (1) have something to do
   (2) protest the high cost of feed
   (3) show his great love for his horse
   (4) prove that he does not resent the cabdriver's action
   (5) remove his feelings of guilt

8. The setting for this story is probably a 19th-century
   (1) American city
   (2) eastern European city
   (3) northern European farm
   (4) American small town
   (5) English city

9. The author's purpose in using the present tense is most probably to
   (1) make the story seem modern
   (2) increase the length of the story
   (3) heighten the reader's sense of immediacy
   (4) write the story as consciously as possible
   (5) reinforce the first-person point of view

10. Iona's situation is brought home to the reader when he
    (1) asks the hall porter for the time
    (2) asks the cabdriver for a drink
    (3) talks to himself
    (4) fights off sleep
    (5) compares himself to a foal's mother

<u>Questions 11 to 15</u> refer to the following excerpt from a work of prose fiction.

HOW DID A MOTHER AND A SON REACT TO A TRAGEDY?

After living nearly two years in Cairo, I had brought my son Guy to enter the University of Ghana in Accra. Guy was seventeen and quick. I was thirty-three and determined. We were Black Americans in West Africa, where for the first time in our lives the color of our skin was accepted as correct and normal. The future was plump with promise. For two days Guy and I laughed. On the third day, Guy, on a pleasure outing, was injured in an automobile accident. One arm and one leg were fractured and his neck was broken.

July and August stretched out like fat men yawning after a sumptuous dinner. They had every right to gloat, for they had eaten me up. Gobbled me down. Consumed my spirit,

GO ON TO THE NEXT PAGE

TEST 4: INTERPRETING LITERATURE AND THE ARTS

not in a wild rush, but slowly, with the obscene patience of certain victors. I became a shadow walking in the white hot streets, and a dark spectre in the hospital.

Trying utterly, I could not match Guy's stoicism. He lay calm, in a prison of plaster from which only his face and one leg and arm were visible. His assurances that he would heal and be better than new drove me into a faithless silence.

Admittedly, Guy lived with the knowledge that an unexpected sneeze could force the fractured vertebrae against his spinal cord, and he would be paralyzed or die immediately, but he had only an infatuation with life. He hadn't lived long enough to fall in love with this brutally delicious experience. He could lightly waft away to another place, if there really was another place, where his youthful innocence would assure him wings, a harp, and an absence of nostalgic yearning. My wretchedness reminded me that, on the other hand, I would be rudderless. We had been each other's home and center for seventeen years. He could die if he wanted to and go off to wherever dead folks go, but I, I would be left without a home.

—Maya Angelou

11. The narrator notes that there are differences between herself and Guy in both age and

    (1) education
    (2) temperament
    (3) intelligence
    (4) agility
    (5) devotion

12. Which literary device is used in line 14?

    (1) understatement
    (2) hyperbole
    (3) simile
    (4) onomatopoeia
    (5) metaphor

13. The word *they*, as used in line 15, is intended to mean the

    (1) certain victors
    (2) days of July and August
    (3) fat men
    (4) narrator's thoughts
    (5) West Africans

14. The narrator portrays the delicate nature of her son's life with the words

    (1) "seventeen and quick"
    (2) "dark spectre"
    (3) "hadn't lived long"
    (4) "lightly waft away"
    (5) "infatuation with life"

15. What does the imagery in lines 19 and 21 convey about the narrator's situation?

    (1) Her sudden helplessness seemed unreal.
    (2) Her physical health had deteriorated.
    (3) She was a Black American walking freely in a once white-only area.
    (4) She was undefeated by the adversity of life.
    (5) She was uncertain about her future.

Questions 16 to 20 refer to the following poem.

WHAT IS IT LIKE WHEN ELECTRIC POLES REPLACE TREES?

On their sides, resembling fallen timbers without rough
Barks—a hundred feet apart—lie power poles.
Just yesterday, this road was edged
With eucalyptus; in aisles
Between rows of trees, seats for the aged.
Now tree odors hover in the air, residues of life.
The poles are erected. The frigid,
Passionless verticals
Strive
To fill the socket-shaped holes
Left by trees. Identical, cement-wedged
Below, parasitically fastened to live wires above,
Tree imposters, never to be budged

GO ON TO THE NEXT PAGE

TEST 4: INTERPRETING LITERATURE AND THE ARTS

From a telegraphic owl's
Knowitallness, they stand—rigid!
Sad children, wishing to climb, scan the miles
And miles of uninterrupted electric forests for leaves.

16. Which phrase best expresses the ideas of this poem?
    (1) the new trees
    (2) the promising verticals
    (3) improving the landscape
    (4) on climbing trees
    (5) tree odors

17. The poet seems to resent the power poles'
    (1) rough barks
    (2) new odors
    (3) lifelessness
    (4) expensiveness
    (5) electric charge

18. In this poem, the children are sad because
    (1) the poles are too slippery to climb
    (2) the poles are too rigid to climb
    (3) they have been forbidden to climb the poles
    (4) the poles have replaced the trees
    (5) they have grown to love the owls

19. The poet's point of view is expressed by the use of such phrases as
    (1) fallen timbers
    (2) power poles
    (3) passionless verticals
    (4) socket-shaped holes
    (5) live wires

20. An example of a poetic figure of speech is found in the words
    (1) tree odors
    (2) cement-wedged
    (3) tree imposters
    (4) sad children
    (5) scan the miles

<u>Questions 21 to 25</u> refer to the following poem.

WHAT IS THE REACTION OF A TEACHER TO HIS STUDENT'S DEATH?

I remember the neckcurls, limp and damp as tendrils;
And her quick look, a sidelong pickerel smile;
And how, once startled into talk, the light syllables leaped for her,
And she balanced in the delight of her thought,
A wren, happy, tail into the wind,
Her song trembling the twigs and small branches.
The shade sang with her;
The leaves, their whispers turned to kissing;
And the mold sang in the bleached valleys under the rose.

Oh, when she was sad, she cast herself down into such a pure depth,
Even a father could not find her:
Scraping her cheek against straw;
Stirring the clearest water.

My sparrow, you are not here,
Waiting like a fern, making a spiny shadow.
The sides of wet stones cannot console me,
Nor the moss, wound with the last light.

If only I could nudge you from this sleep,
My maimed darling, my skittery pigeon.
Over this damp grave I speak the words of my love:
I, with no rights in this matter,
Neither father nor lover.

—Theodore Roethke, "Elegy for Jane"

21. The poet wrote this poem mainly to
    (1) describe Jane
    (2) criticize Jane
    (3) mourn Jane
    (4) remember Jane
    (5) forget Jane

GO ON TO THE NEXT PAGE

TEST 4: INTERPRETING LITERATURE AND THE ARTS

22. The poet's feeling for Jane, as indicated in the poem, is one of

(1) awe
(2) reverence
(3) regret
(4) nostalgia
(5) love

23. To what does the poet repeatedly compare Jane?

(1) a flower
(2) a shooting star
(3) a bird
(4) a small pet
(5) a lovely song

24. The change that takes place in the poem starting on line 21 is that the poet

(1) becomes resigned
(2) recollects further details
(3) compares himself to a father
(4) talks directly to the dead student
(5) becomes more angry at his loss

25. The poem is powerful in its impact on the reader because the poet feels he

(1) is like a father to Jane
(2) is like a lover to Jane
(3) is like a teacher to Jane
(4) has no right to write the poem
(5) is responsible for her tragedy

Questions 26 to 30 refer to the following excerpt from a play.

HOW DOES THE FAMILY RESPOND TO LINDNER'S OFFER?

WALTER: I mean—I have worked as a chauffeur most of my life—and my wife here, she does domestic work in people's kitchens. So does my mother, I mean—we are plain people . . .

LINDNER: Yes, Mr. Younger—

WALTER: [*Really like a small boy, looking down at his shoes and then up at the man*] And—uh—well, my father, well, he was a laborer most of his life.

LINDNER: [*Absolutely confused*] Uh, yes—

WALTER: [*Looking down at his toes once again*] My father almost beat a man to death once because this man called him a bad name or something, you know what I mean?

LINDNER: No, I'm afraid I don't.

WALTER: [*Finally straightening up*] Well, what I means is that we come from people who had a lot of pride. I mean—we are very proud people. And that's my sister over there and she's going to be a doctor—and we are very proud—

LINDNER: Well—I am sure that is very nice, but—

WALTER: [*Starting to cry and facing the man eye to eye*] What I am telling you is that we called you over here to tell you that we are very proud and that this is—this is my son, who makes the sixth generation of our family in this country, and that we have all thought about your offer and we have decided to move into our house because my father—my father—he earned it. [MAMA *has her eyes closed and is rocking back and forth as though she were in church, with her head*

GO ON TO THE NEXT PAGE

TEST 4: INTERPRETING LITERATURE AND THE ARTS

nodding the amen yes] We don't want to make no trouble for nobody or fight no causes—but we will try to be good neighbors. That's all we got to say. [*He looks the man absolutely in the eyes*] We don't want your money. [*He turns and walks away from the man*]

LINDNER: [*Looking around at all of them*] I take it then that you have decided to occupy.

BENEATHA: That's what the man said.

LINDNER: [*To* MAMA *in her reverie*] Then I would like to appeal to you, Mrs. Younger. You are older and wiser and understand things better I am sure...

MAMA: [*Rising*] I am afraid you don't understand. My son said we was going to move and there ain't nothing left for me to say. [*Shaking her head with double meaning*] You know how these young folks is nowadays, mister. Can't do a thing with 'em. Good-bye.

LINDNER: [*Folding up his materials*] Well—if you are that final about it... There is nothing left for me to say. [*He finishes. He is almost ignored by the family who are concentrating on* WALTER LEE. *At the door* LINDNER *halts and looks around*] I sure hope you people know what you're doing. [*He shakes his head and exits*]

—Lorraine Hansberry, *A Raisin in the Sun*

26. The story Walter tells about his father almost beating a man to death for calling him a name is

(1) an anecdote
(2) a lie
(3) a warning
(4) a dream
(5) an allusion

27. From this point on, the family will

(1) stay in the ghetto
(2) try for a new life
(3) sell their house
(4) retreat to the South
(5) fight for causes

28. After this incident, the head of the house will be

(1) Travis
(2) Mama
(3) Walter
(4) Ruth
(5) Beneatha

29. Mr. Lindner

(1) understands the Youngers
(2) despises the Youngers
(3) is sympathetic to the Youngers
(4) is tolerant of the Youngers
(5) disagrees with the Youngers

30. The word that best describes Walter's family is

(1) plain
(2) vicious
(3) proud
(4) trouble-making
(5) uncooperative

Questions 31 to 35 refer to the following passage.

HOW DOES AN INDIAN CHIEF REMEMBER HIS CHILDHOOD?

I have acted in the movies and in Wild West shows, and served as an interpreter between the Indian and the White man. I have met presidents and kings, writers, scientists, and artists. I have had much joy and received many honors, but I have never forgotten my wild, free childhood when I lived in a tepee and heard the calling of the coyotes under the stars . . . when the night winds, the sun, and everything else in our primitive world reflected the wisdom and benevolence of the Great Spirit. I remember seeing my mother bending over an open fire toasting buffalo meat, and my father

GO ON TO THE NEXT PAGE

TEST 4: INTERPRETING LITERATURE AND THE ARTS

returning at night with an antelope on his shoulder. I remember playing with the other children on the banks of a clean river, and I shall never forget when my grandfather taught me how to make a bow and arrow from hard wood and flint, and a fishhook from the rib of a field mouse. I am not sentimental but memories haunt me as I review scenes from those days before I was old enough to understand that all Indian things would pass away.

The average American child of today would enjoy the privileges I had out there on the unspoiled prairie one hundred years ago. I was usually awake in time to see the sun rise. If the weather was warm, I went down to the river that flowed near our village and dipped water out of it with my hands for a drink, then plunged into it. The river came down out of the hills, ferrying leaves, blossoms, and driftwood. Fish could be seen in the pools formed near the rapids over which it rippled. Birds nested and flew among the banks, and occasionally I would see a coon or a fox in the brush. Hawks circled overhead, searching the ground for mice or other small animals for their breakfast, or to feed the young in their nests. There were never enough hours in a day to exhaust the pleasure of observing every living creature—from the orb spider spinning his magic and all but invisible web to the bald eagles on their bulky nests atop the tallest trees, teaching fledglings how to eject safely.

—Memoirs of Chief Red Fox

31. The mood of the selection is one of

(1) nostalgia
(2) bitterness
(3) resignation
(4) envy
(5) anticipation

32. One of the most important of the chief's memories is that of

(1) Wild West shows
(2) many honors
(3) meeting presidents and kings
(4) family members
(5) coyotes

33. The writer's primitive world was characterized by

(1) evidence of the Great Spirit
(2) fishhooks
(3) bow and arrow
(4) the call of the coyotes
(5) night winds

34. The writer's love of nature led him to

(1) observe it closely
(2) benefit from its warmth
(3) collect specimens
(4) search for small animals
(5) sleep late

35. Nature a hundred years ago was preferable to nature today because it was more

(1) varied
(2) wild
(3) magical
(4) friendly
(5) unspoiled

GO ON TO THE NEXT PAGE

TEST 4: INTERPRETING LITERATURE AND THE ARTS

Questions 36 to 40 refer to the following commentary on the plays *Romeo and Juliet* and *West Side Story*.

HOW DO *ROMEO AND JULIET* AND *WEST SIDE STORY* COMPARE?

What glorious verse falls from the lips of Shakespeare's boys and girls! True, there is a rollicking jazzy vigor in such songs of *West Side Story* as the one of Officer Krupke, but it pales alongside the pyrotechnical display of Mercurio's Queen Mab speech. There is tenderness in "Maria," but how relatively tongue-tied is the twentieth-century hero alongside the boy who cried, "He jests at scars that never felt a wound." "Hold my hand and we're halfway there," say Maria and Tony to each other, and the understatement touches us. But "Gallop apace, you fiery-footed steeds" and the lines that follow glow with a glory that never diminishes. The comparisons of language could be multiplied, and always, of course, Shakespeare is bound to win.

Without its great poetry *Romeo and Juliet* would not be a major tragedy. Possibly it is not, in any case; for as has frequently been remarked, Shakespeare's hero and heroine are a little too slender to carry the full weight of tragic grandeur. Their plight is more pathetic than tragic. If this is true of them, it is equally true of Tony and Maria: for them, too, pathos rather than tragedy. But there is tragedy implicit in the environmental situation of the contemporary couple, and this must not be overlooked or underestimated. Essentially, however, what we see is that all four young people strive to consummate the happiness at the threshold on which they stand and which they have tasted so briefly. All four are deprived of the opportunity to do so, the Renaissance couple by the caprice of fate, today's youngsters by the prejudice and hatred engendered around them. All four are courageous and lovable. All four arouse our compassion, even though they may not shake us with Aristotelian fear.

Poets and playwrights will continue to write of youthful lovers whom fate drives into and out of each other's lives. The spectacle will always trouble and move us.

36. The author of the selection implies that
    (1) the songs of *West Side Story* lack strength
    (2) the language of *West Side Story* leaves us cold
    (3) the language of *Romeo and Juliet* lacks the vigor of that of *West Side Story*
    (4) the poetry of *Romeo and Juliet* will prevail
    (5) the speech of *West Side Story* can compete with the verse of *Romeo and Juliet*

37. In comparing the language of *Romeo and Juliet* with that of *West Side Story* the author
    (1) takes no position
    (2) likes each equally
    (3) favors that of *Romeo and Juliet*
    (4) favors that of *West Side Story*
    (5) downplays the differences

38. Both plays share a common weakness. That weakness is
    (1) the stature of their heroes and heroines
    (2) the absence of deep emotion
    (3) their dramatic construction
    (4) the lack of substance of their themes
    (5) the lack of linguistic power

39. The couples in the two plays share all of the following EXCEPT
    (1) a pathetic situation
    (2) lack of opportunity to achieve happiness
    (3) courage
    (4) inability to instill fear in the reader
    (5) inability to arouse pity in the reader

40. The couples in the two plays differ in the nature of
    (1) their plight
    (2) their ultimate fate
    (3) the cause of their tragic situation
    (4) their attractiveness
    (5) their love for one another

GO ON TO THE NEXT PAGE

TEST 4: INTERPRETING LITERATURE AND THE ARTS

Questions 41 to 45 refer to the following article on art.

WHAT IS THE MESSAGE OF CHAGALL'S WORK?

"Your colors sing!" Chagall's teacher, Leon Bakst, had told him. Indeed, Chagall slapped on colors in bold, solid patches, often contrasting them with striking effects. His burning reds, juicy greens and the magic "Chagall blue" give an almost sensual gratification. Yet when I once asked, "How do you get your blues?" he replied with a typical pixie twinkle, "I buy them in a shop. They come in tubes."

When he entered his 60s, the painter's inventiveness began to run dry. He had become, in the words of one critic, "his own most faithful imitator." At this crucial point, inspiration struck. Chagall turned to stained glass. He spent days examining the gemlike windows in France's great medieval cathedrals, where plain bits of colored glass were turned into jewels by the sun. In 1957 he made two small windows, depicting angels, for a chapel in Savoy. The next year he met one of France's foremost stained-glass makers, Charles Marq. Chagall began spending up to 12 hours a day at the Marq workshop in the cathedral town of Reims.

Chagall's stained-glass creations, a staggering total of 11,000 square feet, include windows for churches, a synagogue in Jerusalem, and the General Assembly Building of the U.N. in New York. But when Chagall was approached in 1972 to do three windows in Reims's 13th-century cathedral, where more than 20 French kings were crowned, he was alarmed. "I adorn a national shrine? Unthinkable." Finally he complied, once more refusing pay.

On entering the dim Gothic nave of Reims Cathedral today, the first thing you perceive in the distance is the sapphire gleam of Chagall's stained-glass window, depicting, on the left, the sacrifice of Abraham and, on the right, Christ on the cross. In joining Old and New Testaments into a harmonious whole, Chagall reflected his own deep faith in the all-embracing message of Scripture—mankind's ascent through suffering to salvation.

41. The author writes approvingly of which of the following traits in Chagall's character?

    (1) his sensuality
    (2) his arrogance
    (3) his imitativeness
    (4) his impish humor
    (5) his materialism

42. The article is most concerned with Chagall's

    (1) paintings
    (2) pastels
    (3) murals
    (4) drawings
    (5) stained glass

43. In his paintings, Chagall used

    (1) contrasting colors
    (2) soft solid colors
    (3) Chagall reds
    (4) gemlike radiances
    (5) sapphire gleams

44. According to the article, Chagall believed deeply in

    (1) French kings
    (2) national shrines
    (3) mankind's salvation
    (4) the Old Testament only
    (5) the New Testament only

45. Chagall turned to the medium of stained glass because

    (1) it was more profitable
    (2) he met Charles Marq
    (3) he was invited to work in the Reims Cathedral
    (4) he had come to imitate his own work
    (5) he got magic blues

END OF EXAMINATION

TEST 5: MATHEMATICS

Directions

The Mathematics test consists of multiple-choice questions intended to measure general mathematics skills and problem-solving ability. The questions are based on short readings that often include a graph, chart, or figure.

You should spend no more than 90 minutes answering the questions. Work carefully, but do not spend too much time on any one question. Be sure you answer every question. You will not be penalized for incorrect answers.

Formulas you may need are given on page 64. Only some of the questions will require you to use a formula. Not all the formulas given will be needed.

Some questions contain more information than you will need to solve the problem. Other questions do not give enough information to solve the problem. If the question does not give enough information to solve the problem, the correct answer is "Not enough information is given."

The use of calculators is not allowed.

To record your answers, mark the numbered space on the answer sheet beside the number that corresponds to the question in the test.

FOR EXAMPLE:

If a grocery bill totaling $15.75 is paid with a $20.00 bill, how much change should be returned?

(1) $5.26
(2) $4.75
(3) $4.25
(4) $3.75
(5) $3.25

① ② ● ④ ⑤

The correct answer is "$4.25"; therefore, answer space 3 would be marked on the answer sheet.

GO ON TO THE NEXT PAGE

TEST 5: MATHEMATICS

FORMULAS

Description	Formula
AREA (*A*) of a:	
square	$A = s^2$; where s = side
rectangle	$A = lw$; where l = length, w = width
parallelogram	$A = bh$; where b = base, h = height
triangle	$A = \frac{1}{2}bh$; where b = base, h = height
circle	$A = \pi r^2$; where $\pi = 3.14$, r = radius
PERIMETER (*P*) of a:	
square	$P = 4s$; where s = side
rectangle	$P = 2l + 2w$; where l = length, w = width
triangle	$P = a + b + c$; where a, b, and c are the sides
circumference (*C*) of a circle	$C = \pi d$; where $\pi = 3.14$, d = diameter
VOLUME (*V*) of a:	
cube	$V = s^3$; where s = side
rectangular container	$V = lwh$; where l = length, w = width, h = height
cylinder	$V = \pi r^2 h$; where $\pi = 3.14$, r = radius, h = height
Pythagorean relationship	$c^2 = a^2 + b^2$; where c = hypotenuse, a and b are legs, of a right triangle
distance (*d*) between two points in a plane	$d = \sqrt{(x_2 - x_1)^2 + (y_2 - y_1)^2}$; where (x_1,y_1) and (x_2,y_2) are two points in a plane
slope of a line (*m*)	$m = \frac{y_2 - y_1}{x_2 - x_1}$; where (x_1,y_1) and (x_2,y_2) are two points in a plane
mean	mean = $\frac{x_1 + x_2 + \ldots + x_n}{n}$; where the x's are the values for which a mean is desired, and n = number of values in the series
median	median = the point in an ordered set of numbers at which half of the numbers are above and half of the numbers are below this value
simple interest (*i*)	$i = prt$; where p = principal, r = rate, t = time
distance (*d*) as function of rate and time	$d = rt$; where r = rate, t = time
total cost (*c*)	$c = nr$; where n = number of units, r = cost per unit

GO ON TO THE NEXT PAGE

TEST 5: MATHEMATICS

1. On 5 successive days a deliveryman listed his mileage as follows: 135, 162, 98, 117, 216. If his truck averages 14 miles for each gallon of gas used, how many gallons of gas did he use during these 5 days?

(1) 42

(2) 52

(3) 115

(4) 147

(5) 153

2. Parking meters in Springfield read: "12 minutes for 5¢. Maximum deposit 50¢." What is the maximum time, in hours, that a driver may be legally parked at one of these meters?

(1) 1

(2) 1.2

(3) 12

(4) 2

(5) Not enough information is given.

Question 3 is based on the following figure.

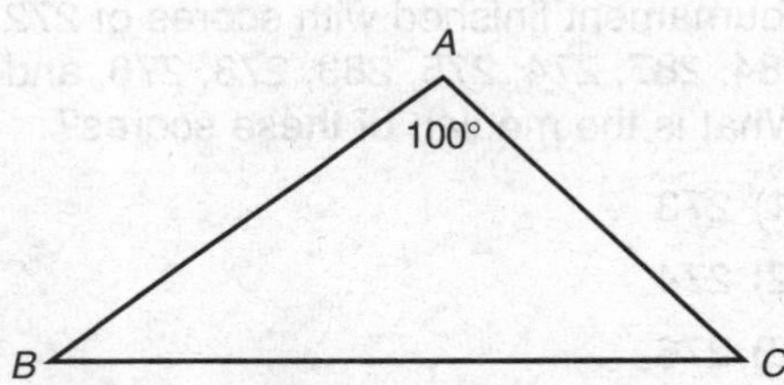

3. If $AB = AC$ and m $\angle A = 100°$, what is the measure of $\angle B$?

(1) 40°

(2) 45°

(3) 50°

(4) 60°

(5) 80°

4. The ABC Department Store had a special sale on shirts. One group sold at \$15 per shirt, and another group sold at \$18 per shirt. If 432 shirts were sold at \$15 each and 368 shirts were sold at \$18 each, the number of dollars taken in at the shirt sale may be represented as

(1) 800(15 + 18)

(2) (15)(368) + (18)(432)

(3) (15)(800) + (18)(800)

(4) 33(432 + 68)

(5) (15)(432) + (368)(18)

5. A hockey team won X games, lost Y games, and tied Z games. What fractional part of the games played were won?

(1) $\frac{X}{X+Y+Z}$

(2) $\frac{X}{XYZ}$

(3) $\frac{X}{XY}$

(4) $\frac{X}{X+Y}$

(5) $\frac{X}{X-Y-Z}$

GO ON TO THE NEXT PAGE

TEST 5: MATHEMATICS

6. One-half the students at Madison High School walk to school. One-fourth of the rest go to school by bicycle. What part of the school population travels by some other means?

(1) $\frac{1}{8}$

(2) $\frac{3}{8}$

(3) $\frac{3}{4}$

(4) $\frac{1}{4}$

(5) Not enough information is given.

7. Which of the following is a solution of the inequality $2x > 9$?

(1) 0

(2) 2

(3) 3

(4) 4

(5) 5

8. Which of the following units would be most appropriate to measure the distance between New York and San Francisco?

(1) meter

(2) kilometer

(3) kilogram

(4) liter

(5) centimeter

9. A flagpole casts a shadow 16 feet long. At the same time, a pole 9 feet high casts a shadow 6 feet long. What is the height, in feet, of the flagpole?

(1) 18

(2) 19

(3) 20

(4) 24

(5) Not enough information is given.

10. Martin has a piece of lumber 9 feet 8 inches long. He wishes to cut it into 4 equal lengths. How far from the edge should he make the first cut?

(1) 2.5 ft.

(2) 2 ft. 5 in.

(3) 2.9 ft.

(4) 29 ft.

(5) 116 in.

11. A purse contains 6 nickels, 5 dimes, and 8 quarters. If one coin is drawn at random from the purse, what is the probability that the coin drawn is a dime?

(1) $\frac{5}{19}$

(2) $\frac{5}{14}$

(3) $\frac{5}{8}$

(4) $\frac{5}{6}$

(5) $\frac{19}{5}$

12. The leaders in the Peninsula Golf Tournament finished with scores of 272, 284, 287, 274, 275, 283, 278, 276, and 281. What is the median of these scores?

(1) 273

(2) 274

(3) 276

(4) 278

(5) 280

GO ON TO THE NEXT PAGE

TEST 5: MATHEMATICS

13. The cost of a dozen ballpoint pens and 8 pencils is \$4.60. If the cost of the pens is 3 for \$0.97, what is the cost, in cents, of 1 pencil?

(1) 6
(2) 8
(3) 8.5
(4) 9
(5) 9.5

14. The scale on a map is 1 inch = 150 miles. The cities of Benton and Dover are $3\frac{1}{2}$ inches apart on this map. What is the actual distance, in miles, between Benton and Dover?

(1) 525
(2) 545
(3) 580
(4) 625
(5) Not enough information is given.

<u>Question 15</u> is based on the following figure.

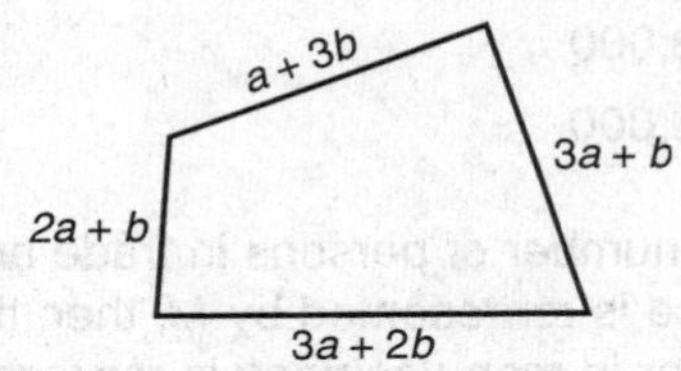

15. What is the perimeter of the figure?

(1) $8a + 5b$
(2) $9a + 7b$
(3) $7a + 5b$
(4) $6a + 6b$
(5) $8a + 6b$

<u>Question 16</u> is based on the following number line.

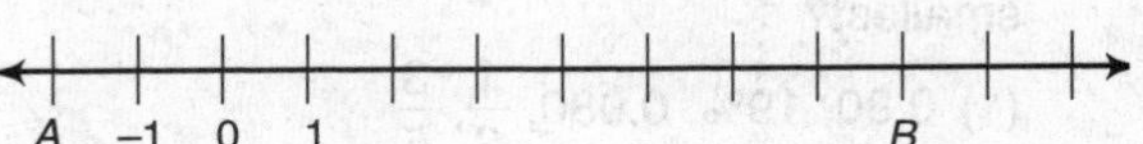

16. On the number line, what is the coordinate of the midpoint of $\overline{AB}$?

(1) –11
(2) 0
(3) 2
(4) 3
(5) 8

17. The Men's Shop advertised a spring sale. David Morris was especially interested in the following sale items.

ties: 3 for \$23
shirts: 3 for \$43
slacks: \$32.75 per pair
jackets: \$58.45 each

David bought 6 ties, 3 shirts, 2 pairs of slacks, and 1 jacket. What was his bill?

(1) \$157.20
(2) \$180.20
(3) \$189.95
(4) \$202.95
(5) \$212.95

GO ON TO THE NEXT PAGE

TEST 5: MATHEMATICS

18. In which of the following lists are the numbers written in order from greatest to smallest?

    (1) 0.80, 19%, 0.080, $\frac{1}{2}$, $\frac{3}{5}$

    (2) 0.80, $\frac{1}{2}$, 0.080, $\frac{3}{5}$, 19%

    (3) 0.80, $\frac{3}{5}$, $\frac{1}{2}$, 19%, 0.080

    (4) $\frac{1}{2}$, 0.80, $\frac{3}{5}$, 19%, 0.080

    (5) $\frac{3}{5}$, $\frac{1}{2}$, 19%, 0.080, 0.80

19. If an airplane completes its flight of 1,364 miles in 5 hours and 30 minutes, what is its average speed, in miles per hour?

    (1) 240
    (2) 244
    (3) 248
    (4) 250
    (5) 260

20. The distance between two heavenly bodies is 85,000,000,000 miles. This number, written in scientific notation, is

    (1) 8.5×10^{-10}
    (2) 8.5×10^{10}
    (3) 85×10^{9}
    (4) 0.85×10^{-9}
    (5) 850×10^{7}

21. What is the value of $3ab - x^2y$ if $a = 4$, $b = 5$, $y = 3$, and $x = 2$?

    (1) 18
    (2) 24
    (3) 48
    (4) 54
    (5) 72

Questions 22 and 23 are based on the following graph.

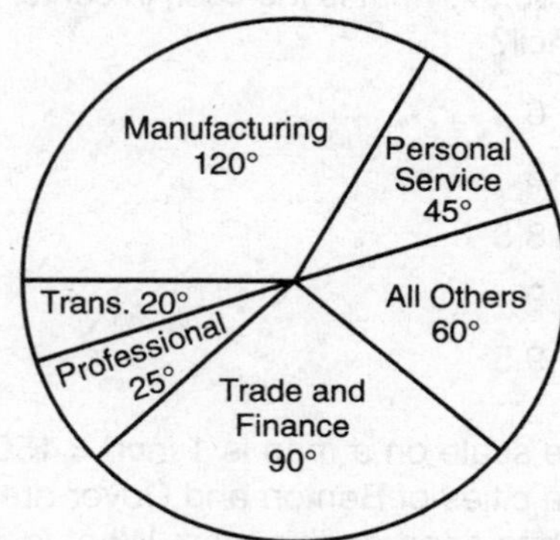

This circle graph shows how 180,000 wage earners in a certain city earned their livings during a given period.

22. The number of persons engaged in transportation in the city during this period was

    (1) 3,600
    (2) 9,000
    (3) 10,000
    (4) 18,000
    (5) 36,000

23. If the number of persons in trade and finance is represented by M, then the number in manufacturing is represented as

    (1) $\frac{M}{3}$
    (2) $M + 3$
    (3) $30M$
    (4) $\frac{4M}{3}$
    (5) Not enough information is given.

GO ON TO THE NEXT PAGE

TEST 5: MATHEMATICS

Question 24 is based on the following figure.

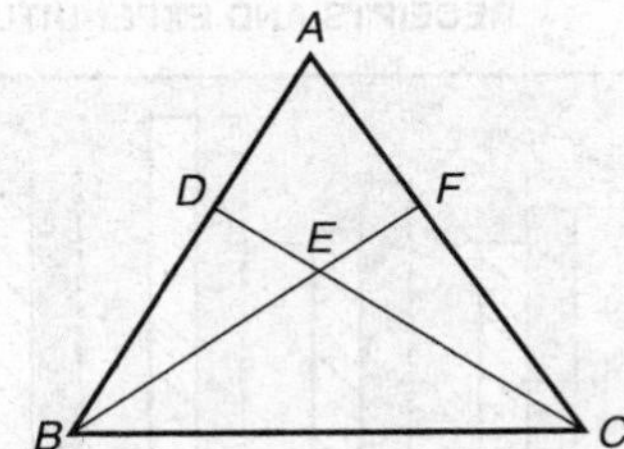

24. If $\overline{BF}$ bisects $\angle ABC$, $\overline{CD}$ bisects $\angle ACB$, $m\angle ABC = 68°$, and $m\angle ACB = 72°$, then $m\angle BEC =$

(1) 90°

(2) 98°

(3) 100°

(4) 110°

(5) 120°

---

25. Bill has \$5 more than Jack, and Jack has \$3 less than Frank. If Frank has \$30, how much money does Bill have?

(1) \$30

(2) \$27

(3) \$32

(4) \$36

(5) Not enough information is given.

26. John Davis weighed 192 pounds. His doctor put him on a diet, which enabled him to lose at least 4 pounds per month. What was John's weight after 6 months on the diet?

(1) 160 lb.

(2) 165 lb.

(3) 167 lb.

(4) 168 lb.

(5) Not enough information is given.

27. Mr. Ames bought a bond for \$10,000. The bond yields interest at $8\frac{1}{2}$ % annually. If the interest is paid every 6 months, how much is each interest payment?

(1) \$400

(2) \$425

(3) \$475

(4) \$500

(5) \$850

28. An aquarium is in the form of a rectangular solid. The aquarium is 3 feet long, 1 foot 8 inches wide, and 1 foot 6 inches high. What is the volume, in cubic feet, of the aquarium?

(1) 6.16

(2) 6.4

(3) 7.5

(4) 7.875

(5) 8.64

29. The ratio of men to women at a professional meeting was 9:2. If there were 12 women at the meeting, how many men were at the meeting?

(1) 33

(2) 44

(3) 54

(4) 66

(5) Not enough information is given.

30. What is the slope of the line that passes through point A (2,1) and point B (4,7)?

(1) $\frac{1}{3}$

(2) $\frac{2}{3}$

(3) $\frac{3}{2}$

(4) 2

(5) 3

GO ON TO THE NEXT PAGE

TEST 5: MATHEMATICS

31. In a basketball game Bill scored three times as many points as Jim. Together they scored 56 points. How many points did Bill score?

    (1) 14
    (2) 28
    (3) 42
    (4) 48
    (5) Not enough information is given.

Question 32 is based on the following graph.

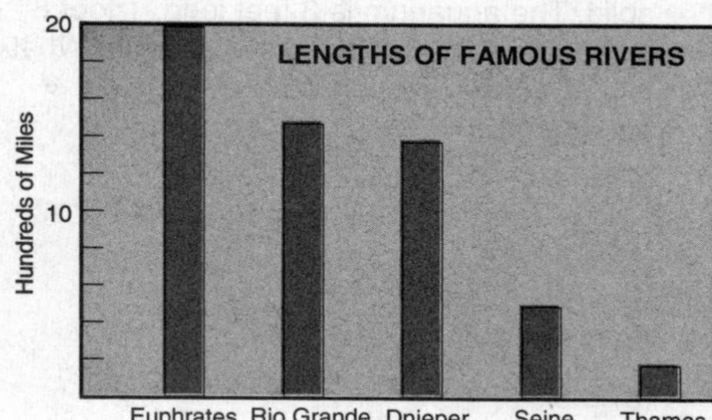

32. The graph shows the lengths of some famous rivers correct to the nearest hundred miles. Which one of the following statements is correct?

    (1) The Thames is more than one-half as long as the Seine.
    (2) The Dnieper is 1,200 miles long.
    (3) The Euphrates is about 250 miles longer than the Rio Grande.
    (4) The Rio Grande is about 1,000 miles longer than the Seine.
    (5) The Thames is about 100 miles long.

Question 33 is based on the following graph.

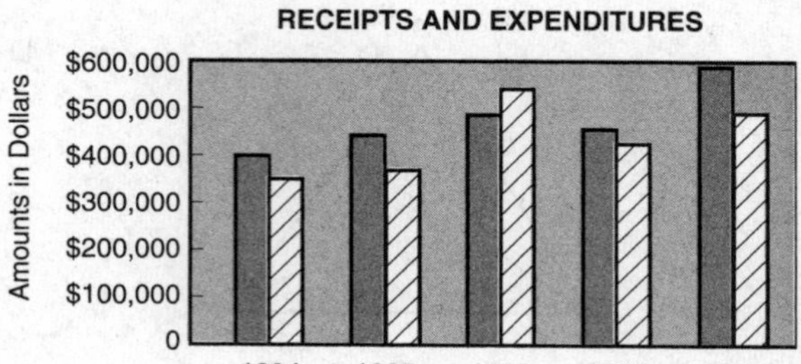

33. The graph shows receipts and expenses for the years indicated. The receipts are designated by shaded bars and the expenses by striped bars. The year in which receipts exceeded expenses by $100,000 was

    (1) 1984
    (2) 1985
    (3) 1986
    (4) 1987
    (5) 1988

---

34. If 1 pencil costs y cents, then 6 pencils will cost, in cents,

    (1) $6y$
    (2) $\frac{y}{6}$
    (3) $\frac{6}{y}$
    (4) $y + 6$
    (5) $\frac{y}{2}$

TEST 5: MATHEMATICS

35. Mr. Martin earns $12 per hour. One week Mr. Martin worked 42 hours; the following week he worked 37 hours. Which of the following indicates the number of dollars Mr. Martin earned for the 2 weeks?

(1) $12 \times 2 + 37$

(2) $12 \times 42 + 42 \times 37$

(3) $12 \times 37 + 42$

(4) $12 + 42 \times 37$

(5) $12(42 + 37)$

36. The enrollment of a college is distributed as follows:

360 freshmen
300 sophomores
280 juniors
260 seniors

The freshman class makes up what percent of the total enrollment?

(1) 18%

(2) 20%

(3) 25%

(4) 30%

(5) Not enough information is given.

<u>Question 37</u> is based on the following figure.

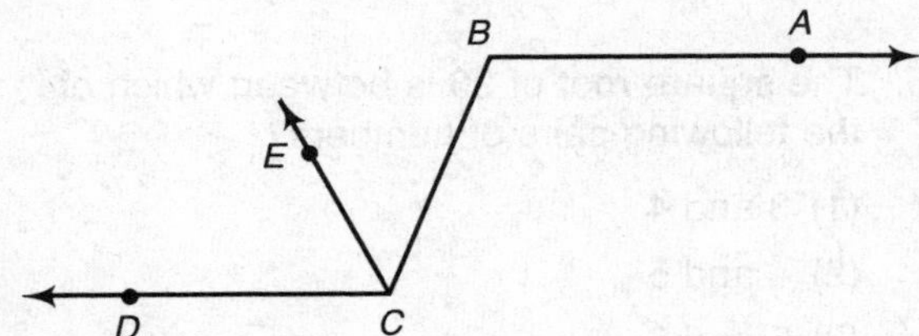

37. In the figure $\overleftrightarrow{AB} \parallel \overleftrightarrow{CD}$, $\overleftrightarrow{CE}$ bisects $\angle BCD$, and $m\angle ABC = 112°$. Find $m\angle ECD$.

(1) 45°

(2) 50°

(3) 56°

(4) 60°

(5) Not enough information is given.

38. Mrs. Garvin buys a bolt of cloth 22 feet 4 inches in length. She cuts the bolt into four equal pieces to make drapes. What is the length of each piece?

(1) 5 ft.

(2) 5 ft. 7 in.

(3) 5 ft. 9 in.

(4) 6 ft. 7 in.

(5) Not enough information is given.

<u>Questions 39 and 40</u> are based on the following graph.

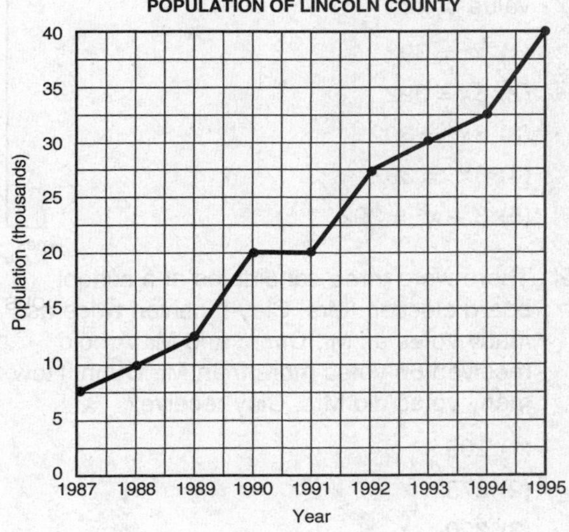

The graph shows the growth in population in Lincoln County between the years 1987 and 1995.

39. What was the population of Lincoln County in the year 1992?

(1) 20,000

(2) 25,000

(3) 26,000

(4) 27,500

(5) 30,000

GO ON TO THE NEXT PAGE

TEST 5: MATHEMATICS

40. The population of Lincoln County did not change between the years

(1) 1988 and 1989
(2) 1989 and 1990
(3) 1990 and 1991
(4) 1991 and 1992
(5) 1992 and 1993

---

41. A box is in the form of a rectangular solid with a square base of side x units in length and a height of 8 units. The volume of the box is 392 cubic units. Which of the following equations may be used to find the value of x?

(1) $x^2 = 392$
(2) $8x = 392$
(3) $8x^3 = 392$
(4) $8x^2 = 392$
(5) $8 + x^2 = 392$

42. There were three candidates at a school board election. Mrs. Clay received twice as many votes as Mr. Dunn, and Mr. Arnold received 66 votes more than Mr. Dunn. How many votes did Mrs. Clay receive?

(1) 209
(2) 275
(3) 320
(4) 402
(5) Not enough information is given.

<u>Question 43</u> is based on the following figure.

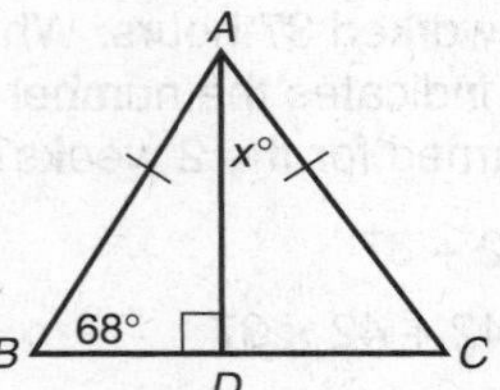

43. If $AB = AC$, $\overline{AD} \perp \overline{BC}$, and $m\angle B = 68°$, what is the value of x?

(1) 12°
(2) 22°
(3) 32°
(4) 44°
(5) 68°

---

44. A hiker walks 12 miles due north. Then he turns and walks 16 miles due east. At this point, how many miles is the hiker from his starting point?

(1) 12
(2) 16
(3) 18
(4) 20
(5) Not enough information is given.

45. The square root of 30 is between which of the following pairs of numbers?

(1) 3 and 4
(2) 4 and 5
(3) 5 and 6
(4) 6 and 7
(5) 15 and 16

GO ON TO THE NEXT PAGE

TEST 5: MATHEMATICS

Question 46 is based on the following figure.

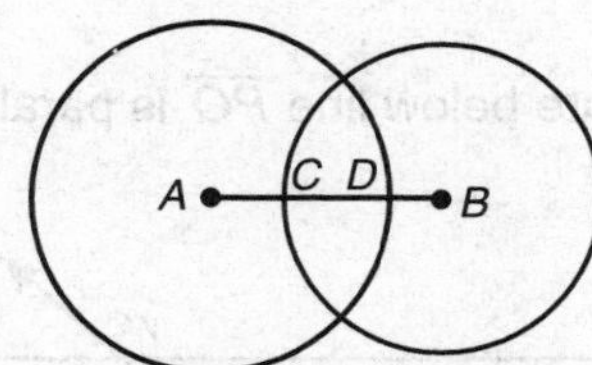

46. The radius of circle A measures 20 inches, and the radius of circle B measures 8 inches. If $CD = 6$ inches, find AB, in inches.

(1) 22
(2) 24
(3) 25
(4) 28
(5) Not enough information is given.

Question 47 is based on the following figure.

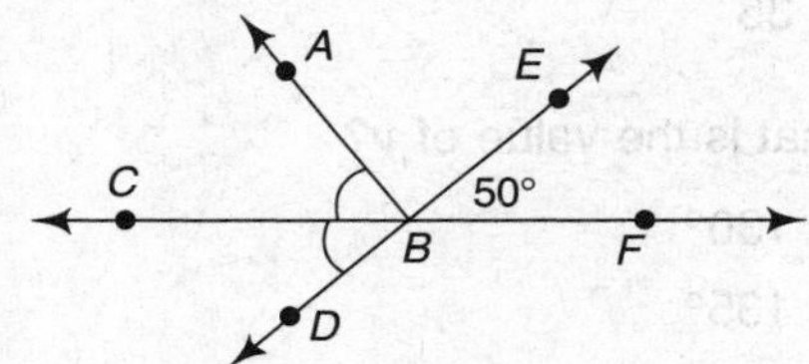

47. $\overleftrightarrow{CF}$ and $\overleftrightarrow{ED}$ intersect at B, $m\angle EBF = 50°$ and $\overleftrightarrow{CB}$ bisects $\angle ABD$. Find $m\angle ABC$.

(1) 30°
(2) 32°
(3) 40°
(4) 50°
(5) 60°

48. A woman buys n pounds of sugar at c cents a pound. She gives the clerk a \$1.00 bill. The change she receives, in cents, is

(1) $nc - 100$
(2) $n + c - 100$
(3) $100 - (n + c)$
(4) $100 - nc$
(5) Not enough information is given.

49. Of a high school graduating class, 85% planned to go to college. If 170 graduates planned to go to college, how many students were in the graduating class?

(1) 200
(2) 250
(3) 340
(4) 400
(5) 500

Question 50 is based on the following figure.

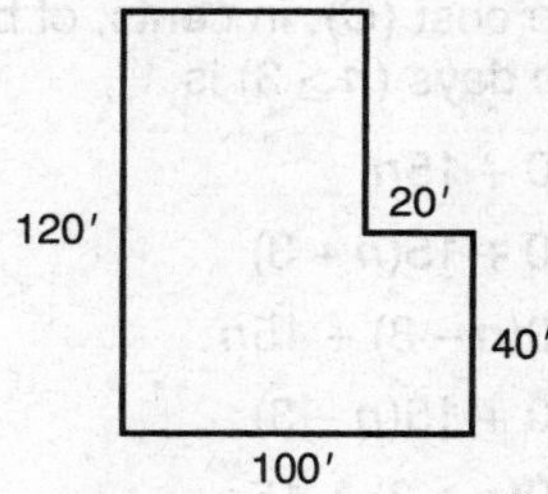

50. Mr. Denby planned to build a house on the plot of ground shown. What is the area, in square feet, of this plot of ground?

(1) 10,000
(2) 10,400
(3) 10,800
(4) 12,000
(5) 104,000

GO ON TO THE NEXT PAGE

TEST 5: MATHEMATICS

51. If $x = 10$, each of the following is true **EXCEPT**

(1) $3x + 1 > 12$
(2) $2x - 3 < 25$
(3) $x^2 + 1 > x^2 - 1$
(4) $4x - 1 = 39$
(5) $2x - 7 < 7 - 2x$

52. In a right triangle the measure of one acute angle is 4 times as great as the measure of the other acute angle. What is the measure of the larger acute angle?

(1) 18°
(2) 36°
(3) 40°
(4) 65°
(5) 72°

53. The cost of borrowing a book from a circulating library is $0.50 for the first 3 days and $0.15 per day thereafter. A formula for finding the cost (C), in cents, of borrowing a book for n days ($n \geq 3$) is

(1) $C = 50 + 15n$
(2) $C = 50 + 15(n + 3)$
(3) $C = 50(n - 3) + 15n$
(4) $C = 50 + 15(n - 3)$
(5) $C = 50(n + 3) + 15n$

<u>Questions 54 and 55</u> are based on the following information.

In the figure below line $\overleftrightarrow{PQ}$ is parallel to line $\overleftrightarrow{RS}$.

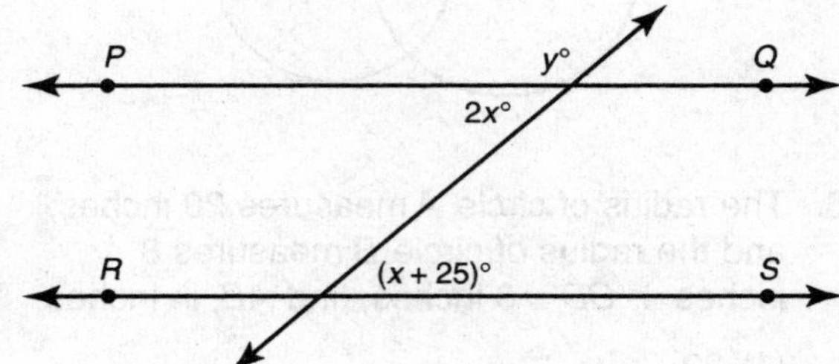

54. What is the value of x?

(1) 15
(2) 20
(3) 25
(4) 30
(5) 35

55. What is the value of y?

(1) 130°
(2) 135°
(3) 140°
(4) 145°
(5) Not enough information is given.

56. Given the equation $x^2 - x - 12 = 0$, which of the following give(s) a complete solution of the equation?

(1) 4 only
(2) –4 only
(3) 3 and 4
(4) –3 and 4
(5) –4 and 3

END OF EXAMINATION

Answer Keys, Summaries of Results, and Self-Appraisal Charts

TEST 1: WRITING SKILLS, PART I/PAGE 13

I. CHECK YOUR ANSWERS, using the following answer key:

1. **2**	11. **5**	20. **3**	29. **2**	38. **2**	47. **5**
2. **3**	12. **1**	21. **2**	30. **1**	39. **5**	48. **1**
3. **3**	13. **5**	22. **5**	31. **5**	40. **5**	49. **4**
4. **1**	14. **2**	23. **5**	32. **1**	41. **1**	50. **1**
5. **4**	15. **2**	24. **3**	33. **2**	42. **4**	51. **2**
6. **5**	16. **3**	25. **5**	34. **4**	43. **3**	52. **4**
7. **2**	17. **5**	26. **5**	35. **3**	44. **1**	53. **5**
8. **3**	18. **3**	27. **4**	36. **2**	45. **5**	54. **1**
9. **5**	19. **4**	28. **1**	37. **4**	46. **2**	55. **4**
10. **4**					

II. SCORE YOURSELF:

Number correct:

Excellent ______ 50–55

Good ______ 44–49

Fair ______ 36–43

III. EVALUATE YOUR SCORE: Did you get at least 38 correct answers? If not, you need more practice for the Writing Skills, Part I test. In any event, you can improve your performance to Excellent or Good by analyzing your errors.

IV. ANALYZE YOUR ERRORS: To determine your areas of weakness, list the number of correct answers you had under each of the following categories (which correspond to the content areas of the Writing Skills, Part I test), and compare your score with the average scores specified in the right-hand column. Review the answer analysis section beginning on page 81 for each of the questions you got wrong, and give yourself more practice in your weak areas with the appropriate material in Unit II before attempting Practice Examination One.

Content Areas	Items	Your Score	Average Score
Sentence Structure	3, 5, 12, 16, 25, 29, 32, 34, 38, 40, 44, 49, 53, 55		10
Usage	1, 8, 19, 20, 24, 52, 54		5
Spelling	7, 10, 15, 18, 27–28, 43, 46, 48, 50		7
Punctuation	2, 4, 14, 21, 30, 33, 35–37, 41–42, 51		9
Capitalization	4		1
No correction	6, 9, 11, 13, 17, 22–23, 26, 31, 39, 45, 47		8

Total ______

TEST 2: SOCIAL STUDIES/PAGE 26

I. CHECK YOUR ANSWERS, using the following answer key:

1. **1**	12. **3**	23. **1**	34. **2**	45. **5**	56. **5**
2. **4**	13. **1**	24. **4**	35. **2**	46. **4**	57. **1**
3. **4**	14. **4**	25. **2**	36. **1**	47. **1**	58. **2**
4. **5**	15. **1**	26. **3**	37. **3**	48. **4**	59. **1**
5. **2**	16. **3**	27. **1**	38. **1**	49. **1**	60. **2**
6. **5**	17. **2**	28. **2**	39. **2**	50. **3**	61. **3**
7. **4**	18. **2**	29. **2**	40. **5**	51. **2**	62. **4**
8. **2**	19. **4**	30. **5**	41. **5**	52. **5**	63. **1**
9. **4**	20. **4**	31. **3**	42. **2**	53. **1**	64. **1**
10. **4**	21. **1**	32. **4**	43. **1**	54. **3**	
11. **1**	22. **2**	33. **1**	44. **1**	55. **5**	

II. SCORE YOURSELF:

	Number correct:
Excellent	______ 57–64
Good	______ 51–56
Fair	______ 45–50

III. EVALUATE YOUR SCORE: Did you get at least 45 correct answers? If not, you need more practice for the Social Studies test. In any event, you can improve your performance to Excellent or Good by analyzing your errors.

II. ANALYZE YOUR ERRORS: To determine your specific weaknesses, list the number of correct answers you had under each of the following categories (which correspond to the content areas of the Social Studies test), and compare your score with the average scores specified in the right-hand column. Review the answer analysis section beginning on page 83 for each of the questions you got wrong, and give yourself more practice in your weak area with the appropriate material in Unit IV (including the "Glossary of Social Studies Terms") before attempting Practice Examination One.

Content Areas	Items	Your Score	Average Score
Political Science	1–3, 12, 41–44, 56, 59		8
Economics	4–6, 9, 13–14, 17–19, 21–22, 24, 32–33, 48, 52–54		13
History	15–16, 20, 25, 34–38 50–51, 57–58, 62–64		12
Geography	7–8, 10–11, 26–28, 39–40, 60–61		9
Behavioral Science	23, 29–31, 45–47, 49, 55		6

Total ______

TEST 3: SCIENCE/PAGE 40

I. CHECK YOUR ANSWERS, using the following answer key:

1. **2**	12. **4**	23. **4**	34. **3**	45. **4**	56. **2**
2. **4**	13. **5**	24. **5**	35. **5**	46. **3**	57. **4**
3. **2**	14. **3**	25. **3**	36. **5**	47. **3**	58. **1**
4. **4**	15. **1**	26. **3**	37. **3**	48. **2**	59. **2**
5. **3**	16. **1**	27. **4**	38. **4**	49. **2**	60. **2**
6. **3**	17. **1**	28. **3**	39. **3**	50. **2**	61. **2**
7. **4**	18. **2**	29. **4**	40. **3**	51. **5**	62. **3**
8. **5**	19. **4**	30. **5**	41. **1**	52. **2**	63. **3**
9. **2**	20. **3**	31. **5**	42. **3**	53. **5**	64. **2**
10. **5**	21. **4**	32. **4**	43. **5**	54. **5**	65. **5**
11. **1**	22. **5**	33. **1**	44. **1**	55. **5**	66. **4**

II. SCORE YOURSELF:

Number correct:

Excellent ______
60–66

Good ______
49–59

Fair ______
40–48

III. EVALUATE YOUR SCORE: Did you get at least 40 correct answers? If not, you need more practice for the Science test. In any event, you can improve your performance to Excellent or Good by analyzing your errors.

IV. ANALYZE YOUR ERRORS: To determine your specific weaknesses, encircle the number of each question that you got wrong. This will reveal the specific science area that needs emphasis in planning your study program. After studying the answer analysis section beginning on page 87 for each of the questions you got wrong, list the terms that you feel need further explanation and study them in the "Glossary of Scientific Terms." Then give yourself more practice in your weak areas with the appropriate material in Unit V before attempting Practice Examination One.

Content Areas	Items	Your Score	Average Score
Biology	1–4, 24–39, 41–43, 45–49, 59, 61–66		24
Earth Science	9–13, 17–19, 40, 44, 55–58		7
Chemistry	20–23, 44, 50–52		6
Physics	5–8, 14–16, 53–54, 60		7

Total ______

TEST 4: INTERPRETING LITERATURE AND ARTS/PAGE 53

I. CHECK YOUR ANSWERS, using the following answer key:

1. **3**	9. **3**	17. **3**	25. **4**	32. **4**	39. **4**
2. **1**	10. **5**	18. **4**	26. **3**	33. **1**	40. **3**
3. **4**	11. **2**	19. **3**	27. **2**	34. **1**	41. **4**
4. **4**	12. **3**	20. **3**	28. **3**	35. **5**	42. **5**
5. **1**	13. **2**	21. **3**	29. **5**	36. **4**	43. **1**
6. **3**	14. **4**	22. **5**	30. **3**	37. **3**	44. **3**
7. **1**	15. **1**	23. **3**	31. **1**	38. **1**	45. **4**
8. **2**	16. **1**	24. **4**			

II. SCORE YOURSELF:

Number correct:

Excellent ______
41–45

Good ______
36–40

Fair ______
31–35

III. EVALUATE YOUR SCORE: Did you get at least 31 correct answers? If not, you need more practice for the test on Interpreting Literature and the Arts. In any event, you can improve your performance to Excellent or Good by analyzing your errors.

IV. ANALYZE YOUR ERRORS: To determine your specific weaknesses, first list the number of correct answers you had under each of the following categories and compare your score with the average scores specified in the right-hand column. After studying the answer analysis section beginning on page 90 for each of the questions you got wrong, study the material in the section *Basic Reading Skills* and the section *Reading Prose, Poetry, and Drama* in Unit VI as well as the "Glossary of Literary Terms" to strengthen your weak areas before attempting Practice Examination One.

Reading Skills	Items	Your Score	Average Score
Locating the Main Idea	5, 16, 21, 44		3
Finding Details	2, 3, 12, 18, 23–24, 32–33, 38–45		11
Inferring Meaning	13–15, 19–20, 22, 34–35		5
Making Inferences	1, 4, 7, 10, 25, 36–37		5
Determining Tone and Mood	6, 9, 17, 26–27, 31		4
Inferring Character	11, 28–30		3
Inferring Setting	8		1

Total ______

Now, to see how your scores in the content areas of Interpreting Literature and the Arts test compare with the average scores in the right-hand column, list your score for each of the following:

Content Areas	Items	Your Score	Average Score
Popular Literature	6–10, 16–35		17
Classical Literature	1-5, 11–15		7
Commentary	36–45		7

Total _____

Literary Forms	Items	Your Score	Average Score
Prose Fiction	6–15		7
Prose Nonfiction	1-5, 31–35		7
Prose Nonfiction (Commentary)	36–45		7
Poetry	16–25		7
Drama	26–30		3

Total _____

Note: While Commentary on the Arts is a content area in itself, the commentary, as written, is in the form of prose nonfiction.

TEST 5: MATHEMATICS/PAGE 63

I. CHECK YOUR ANSWERS, using the following answer key:

1. **2**	11. **1**	21. **3**	30. **5**	39. **4**	48. **4**
2. **4**	12. **4**	22. **3**	31. **3**	40. **3**	49. **1**
3. **1**	13. **4**	23. **4**	32. **4**	41. **4**	50. **2**
4. **5**	14. **1**	24. **4**	33. **5**	42. **5**	51. **5**
5. **1**	15. **2**	25. **3**	34. **1**	43. **2**	52. **5**
6. **2**	16. **4**	26. **5**	35. **5**	44. **4**	53. **4**
7. **5**	17. **5**	27. **2**	36. **4**	45. **3**	54. **3**
8. **2**	18. **3**	28. **3**	37. **3**	46. **1**	55. **1**
9. **4**	19. **3**	29. **3**	38. **2**	47. **4**	56. **4**
10. **2**	20. **2**				

II. SCORE YOURSELF:

Number correct:

Excellent ______
51–56

Good ______
44–50

Fair ______
38–43

III. EVALUATE YOUR SCORE: Did you get at least 38 correct answers? If not, you need more practice for the Mathematics test. In any event, you can improve your performance to Excellent or Good by analyzing your errors.

IV. ANALYZE YOUR ERRORS: To determine your specific weakness, list the number of correct answers you had under each of the following skill areas, and compare your score with the average scores specified in the right-hand column. After studying the answer analysis section beginning on page 91 for each of the questions you got wrong, give yourself more practice in your weak areas with the appropriate material in Unit VII before attempting Practice Examination One.

Content Areas	Items	Your Score	Average Score
Arithmetic	1–2, 4, 6, 8, 10–14, 16–20, 22–23, 25–27, 32–33, 35–36, 38–40, 45		18
Algebra	5, 7, 15, 21, 28–29, 31, 34, 41–42, 48–49, 51–53, 55–56		11
Geometry	3, 9, 24, 30, 37, 43–44, 46–47, 50, 54		7

Total ______

YOUR TOTAL GED SCORE

The Writing Skills Test ______

The Social Studies Test ______

The Science Test ______

The Interpreting Literature and the Arts Test ______

The Mathematics Test ______

Total ______

Answer Analysis

TEST 1: WRITING SKILLS, PART I/PAGE 13

1. **2** There is an error in usage. The subject of the sentence is *combination*, which is singular. A singular verb, *makes*, is required for agreement.
2. **3** The error is in punctuation. A comma is needed to set off an introductory phrase.
3. **3** There is a sentence fragment beginning with *seldom*. This is corrected by removing the period and joining the fragment to the rest of the sentence.
4. **1** There is an error in capitalization. Seasons are *not* capitalized.
5. **4** The run-on sentence can be corrected by subordinating the second idea to the first. *Some...vegetables* can be frozen...while *other vegetables can be stored...in a cool area.*
6. **5** No correction is necessary.
7. **2** The correct spelling is *exercise*.
8. **3** The usage error is in the shift in person in two pronouns that refer to the same person. The second-person pronoun *your* in the introductory clause requires a continuation of the second person, *you*, in the main clause.
9. **5** No change is necessary.
10. **4** The correct spelling is *assistance*.
11. **5** No correction is necessary.
12. **1** The original is correct. Two sentences are needed.
13. **5** No correction is necessary.
14. **2** A comma is required to set off items in a series.
15. **2** *Equipment* is the correct spelling.
16. **3** The meaning of the sentence requires *may be served*.
17. **5** No correction is necessary.
18. **3** The correct spelling is *their* rather than *they're*, which is a contraction of *they are*.
19. **4** There is an error in usage. Parallel structure requires the use of infinitives: *to develop, to increase, to learn* (rather than *learning*).
20. **3** The sentence requires the use of *there are* rather than *they are (they're)*. *They are a number of...steps* doesn't make sense.
21. **2** A comma is required after the introductory clause "While...protection."
22. **5** No correction is necessary.
23. **5** No correction is necessary.
24. **3** The future tense should be used for an action taking place in the future, that is, when you take the car in.
25. **5** Two sentences are necessary to correct the run-on sentence. To accomplish this, a period after *order* and a capitalized *That* are needed.
26. **5** No correction is necessary.
27. **4** The correct spelling is *determined.*
28. **1** The correct spelling is *receive.*
29. **1** A comma is needed to set off items in a series.
30. **2** The rewritten sentence should read "A buying decision is affected by total dollars...."
31. **5** No correction is necessary.
32. **1** The original way is the best among the choices offered.
33. **2** Commas are used to set off words or phrases that interrupt the normal word order of the sentence.
34. **4** The relative pronoun *that* avoids the unnecessary use of the words *such programs*.
35. **3** A semicolon is used to separate independent clauses in a sentence.
36. **2** A comma is used after an introductory clause.
37. **4** An apostrophe must be added after the plural noun *shoppers'* to show possession.
38. **2** Making "You are going to move" the subject of the verb *is* eliminates the need for "That statement" and effectively combines the two sentences.
39. **5** No correction is necessary
40. **5** *Or* is correct because "another way" to state the fact is given.
41. **1** A comma is used after an introductory phrase.
42. **4** A comma is used to set off items in a series.

43. 3 The correct spelling is *fulfillment*.
44. 1 The original is correct because *or* connects two independent clauses (*has come through* is understood after *an opportunity to move to a better climate*).
45. 5 No correction is necessary.
46. 2 The correct spelling is *familiar*.
47. 5 No correction is necessary.
48. 1 The correct spelling is *available*.
49. 4 Rewriting the sentence with *The next phase* as the subject requires a singular verb, *is*, in the present tense.
50. 1 The correct spelling is *stationary* when the reference is to a nonmoving object.
51. 2 A phrase inserted in a sentence is set off by commas. Here the second comma should be inserted after *tip*.
52. 4 The subject, *timing*, is singular and the verb *controls* must agree in number with the subject.
53. 5 This is necessary to correct the run-on sentence.
54. 1 An adverb, *nearly*, is necessary when the word modified is an adjective.
55. 4 The sentences can be combined by using an adjective clause, beginning with *which include*, to describe the noun *game fish*.

TEST 1: WRITING SKILLS, PART II/PAGE 25

SAMPLE ESSAYS

For involvement

Americans who believe, as I do, that we should intervene in the problems of the world cite a number of reasons for their view.

The world, they claim, has been made so small by modern technology that countries are interrelated. Thanks to television, we are present when wars break out anywhere in the world. Leaders of foreign nations can communicate directly with us through radio and television. Foreign correspondents bring foreign affairs to our doorstep daily. What happens in Europe, Asia, Africa, and Latin America affects us directly.

Since our foreign markets are essential to us, if we help other nations, we help ourselves. Trading partners throughout the world are essential to our economy since many of our largest corporations are multinational.

Stable governments abroad are in our own best interest. If we support democracies, they are likely to support us if conflict breaks out.

There is also the American tradition of helping the less fortunate. After World War 11, the United States helped rebuild Europe to everyone's benefit. We have been in the forefront of such programs as CARE and the Peace Corps. Many Americans have adopted children living in poor nations. We should continue this tradition of national outreach.

These are the reasons why the United States should remain involved in world affairs.

Summary of reasons for involvement:

1. In our time, the entire world is interrelated.
2. The world has been made small by technology.
3. By helping other nations and their economies, we help our own.
4. Promoting stable foreign governments is in our own best interest.
5. Helping the less fortunate is an American tradition.

Against involvement

> *Many Americans believe, as I do, that we should not be involved with other nations' problems. They feel that we should help ourselves first. The needs of our own homeless, poor, and unemployed should receive priority. Our resources should be used for domestic purposes before we help foreign nations.*
>
> *Also, foreign aid often does not reach the people who need it most. Food and medical supplies fall into the hands of the military and others who profit from their distribution. Many foreign nations are under the rule of dictatorships, and aid is used to enrich the people in power and to keep them in office.*
>
> *The United States contributes over a billion dollars to such organizations as the United Nations and NATO and over 15 billion dollars in aid to foreign military programs, including the cost of maintaining 1.5 million military personnel abroad. Thus we shoulder a disproportionate amount of the foreign aid burden. Nations in Europe and Asia should contribute their fair share.*
>
> *Many Americans feel that they are overtaxed in order to pay for the millions in aid that is sent abroad.*
>
> *For these reasons, we should solve our own problems before taking on the world's.*

Summary of reasons <u>against</u> involvement:

1. We should solve our own domestic problems first.
2. Foreign aid does not reach the people who need it.
3. In some instances, foreign aid keeps dictatorships in power.
4. The United States pays a disproportionate amount of foreign aid and contributes more military personnel than other nations.
5. American citizens are overtaxed at present and should not have to bear the additional taxes needed for foreign involvement.

TEST 2: SOCIAL STUDIES/PAGE 26

1. **1** The last paragraph of the passage states clearly that the governor's veto power is not used sparingly, and that more than one out of four bills fails to receive approval.
2. **4** The second paragraph of the selection deals with the "30 day" rule. The first sentence of this paragraph states that all bills passed within the last ten days of the legislative session are covered by this rule.
3. **4** The first sentence of the first paragraph states that the governor has the power to veto single items of the budget bill. This is an authority not possessed by the president of the United States.
4. **5** Nearly all of the selection deals with a plan of action for use before the consumer buys. See the second sentence and also the first words of the third paragraph.
5. **2** The consumer is advised to get all promises in writing.
6. **5** It is specifically mentioned that pro rata (or partial) return of moneys and credit toward a replacement may be part of a warranty.
7. **4** By 2030, increasing numbers of Americans will reach the age that makes them eligible for Social Security benefits.
8. **2** A large increase in the birth rate would cause the average age to become lower since the many babies added to the population would counteract the older Americans.
9. **4** Persons concerned with the natural environment fear that an emphasis on greater production and consumption will mean further pollution of the air (by factory smokestacks and apartment house incinerators) and of rivers, lakes, and

streams (by industrial wastes and sewage disposal); and increased problems of solid waste disposal and rising noise levels.

10. **4** There is no movement toward a solution to the energy problem as long as the two cyclists representing energy and environment keep pedaling in different directions.

11. **1** A fivefold increase in the price of imported crude oil from 1973 to 1980 severely affected the U.S. economy and forced a search for alternative domestic sources of energy, despite possible immediate negative effects on the environment.

12. **3** This is directly related to the big change from isolationism to internationalism in U.S. foreign policy. From 1920 to 1940 we had no political or military ties to non-American countries, and we never joined the League of Nations. Since World War II, which ended in 1945, the United States has pursued policies of collective security. President F. D. Roosevelt called for the United Nations, of which we are a charter member. President Truman committed U.S. aid to Europe through the Marshall Plan, the Truman Doctrine, and NATO. Subsequent presidents have continued economic aid to Asia and Africa, military assistance to Middle East and Asian nations, and commitments to Korea and Vietnam. President Kennedy started the Peace Corps, and President Nixon tried to negotiate peace in Vietnam and in Israel. Each of the other choices involves areas in which the Congress, the Supreme Court, and the states have been more influential than the president.

13. **1** The passage stresses the ability of the United States to compete with other countries in a free market.

14. **4** In the final paragraph, President Kennedy mentioned the need for bipartisan support (by both houses of Congress) for his trade legislation.

15. **1** The Gettysburg Address was delivered in 1863. Fourscore and seven years earlier—that is, 87 years earlier—the Declaration of Independence had been signed. It declared the liberty of the thirteen colonies and stated that all men are created equal.

16. **3** The speech was delivered at the Gettsyburg cemetery. In the second paragraph, Lincoln states that this is the purpose of the occasion.

17. **2** Lacking land for agriculture, Nation *A* will use its abundant labor, capital, and management skills to develop industry. The resulting products can be sold to domestic and foreign markets.

18. **2** In the 1800s, Great Britain led the world in manufactures and resembled Nation *A* in factors of production.

19. **4** Nation *B*, with its natural resources and labor, must encourage new industries by protectionist tariffs and by tax concessions to attract capital investment.

20. **4** The purpose of the Truman Doctrine, as opposed to President Monroe's policy of noninterference, was to support the governments of Greece and Turkey against direct and indirect Communist aggression. In 1947 Greece was in especially weakened condition following Nazi occupation during World War II, and was under attack by Communist guerrilla bands.

21. **1** From '60 to '65, the increase was 29.3% minus 18.6%, or 10.7%, greater than for any other interval.

22. **2** Between '70 and '80, the percentage of women working part time remained unchanged at 35.1%.

23. **1** The Chinese of the Middle Kingdom and the ancient Greeks held the belief that their cultures were superior to those of any other group. The word *barbarian* comes from the term used by the Greeks of antiquity to describe foreigners who did not speak Greek.

24. **4** A recession takes place in the economy when purchasing, saving, and business profits go down. The result is an increase in unemployment and a period of reduced economic activity—a recession.

25. **2** Social Darwinism became popular in the second half of the 19th century. It applied Darwin's theory of natural

selection to people and nations, attempting thereby to justify the widening gap between the rich and the poor in the United States.

26. **3** The focus of the paragraph is the "problems we face in conserving natural resources."

27. **1** "The pressures of human growth" are identified in the passage as being "acute."

28. **2** The author recognizes the problems realistically and does not minimize them.

29. **2** The purpose of this speech by President Lyndon Johnson was to help troubled young people lead productive lives. In dealing with delinquent and potentially delinquent youth, he was concerned first about preventing them from getting into trouble; then, if they did, in helping them to become useful citizens. These ideas are stated in the first two paragraphs.

30. **5** President Johnson states that he recommends the Juvenile Delinquency Prevention Act of 1967.

31. **3** Family counseling is recommended because so many delinquents "live in broken families, burdened with...problems."

32. **4** Economic controls tried by government have been unable to slow down or catch up with the greased pig of runaway price inflation.

33. **1** Higher interest rates discourage bank loans by business owners and consumers, thereby decreasing the amount of money in circulation and reducing the rate of inflation.

34. **2** Humanists stressed human concerns rather than problems of the next world.

35. **2** The writer states that the frontier experience was the unique element in the development of American culture and values.

36. **1** American social development on the frontier is noted in the first sentence of the passage.

37. **3** Such new opportunities as space exploration and computerization are an important part of contemporary American society.

38. **1** A primary source is an eyewitness account of an event, such as a description in a diary, or an artifact constructed in a specific time period.

39. **2** The data support the conclusion that Belize and Costa Rica are meeting the water needs of their urban populations. In 1980 and 1988, all of the urban population of both nations had access to piped water.

40. **5** The bars for urban population and urban population with access to piped water in 1988 are almost the same height for all countries except Guatemala and El Salvador. The disparity is greatest, however, for Guatemala, where over a million urban-dwelling people have no access to piped water.

41. **5** Lobbyists are representatives of special-interest groups who attempt to influence congressmen by providing information, preparing bills, and testifying at hearings.

42. **2** (*B*) Lobbyists sometimes use undesirable ways of influencing legislation by giving gifts and campaign contributions. The laws they sponsor may not benefit the general public.

43. **1** (*A*) Thousands of bills in many areas are introduced during each session of Congress. These must be handled by standing committees who try to bring expertise to each subject.

44. **1** Out of concern for their own reelection, legislators (the Boy Scouts in the cartoon) introduce consumer protection bills during an election year.

45. **5** Parents, teachers, and age peers are mentioned in the two classes of socializing agents.

46. **4** In the last sentence, all of the reasons are mentioned except the *number* of peers. The group is mentioned as being of increasing importance.

47. **1** The passage, in the second sentence, refers to the great influence of the family.

48. **4** Speaker *A* is talking about a world made smaller by modern technology. Speaker *B* agrees and adds that the problems of any area now become the problems of all humankind. Both feel that, as the world becomes one

community, interdependence is a factor in world survival.

49. **1** Ethnocentrism is the view that one's own culture is superior to all others. Speaker *C* is calling for the appreciation of other people's value systems and ways of life.

50. **3** The extermination of over six million people, nearly all Jews, by the Nazi regime in Germany is called the Holocaust.

51. **2** The Nuremberg Trials after World War II, conducted by the Allies against Germany and Japan, established the principle that individuals are responsible to a higher law than that of individual nations. Acts against humanity could not be defended on the grounds of having to follow orders from a superior.

52. **5** A supply-side economist would welcome cutbacks in government spending to eliminate deficits. An action by the president that sought to cut spending would be supported by a supply-side economist.

53. **1** Mercantilism advocates tariffs to protect local industries from foreign competition.

54. **3** A company is bought out by its employees. This action would be in the direction of the Marxist belief that the means of production should be controlled by the workers.

55. **5** Basketball is a part of U.S. culture that has been adopted by the Russians through the process of cultural diffusion.

56. **5** Thoreau urged his followers to refuse to obey unjust laws, and he himself disobeyed laws that he considered unjust; in other words, he practiced civil disobedience.

57. **1** The Immigration Act of 1965 established occupation as a basic factor in selecting immigrants according to current needs, particularly in technology.

58. **2** Both the immigration policy suggested in the cartoon and the U.S. immigration policy in the 1920s show a preference for certain groups, be they specific nationalities (as in the 1920s) or programmers and electrical engineers (as in the cartoon.)

59. **1** President Nixon refused to turn the Watergate tapes over to Congress until the Supreme Court told him that his continued refusal would be an unconstitutional act. This check by the judiciary on the powers of the executive branch of government is an illustration of the system of checks and balances.

60. **2** The graph shows a projected Latin American population of about 600 million people by the year 2000, as opposed to an estimated 300 million for North America (the United States and Canada).

61. **3** Improved nutrition and medical care help account for an increase in the growth rate of the Latin American population.

62. **4** The cartoon shows that people in underdeveloped nations lack basic necessities, whereas people in developed nations have more than they need. The point is made by showing a child in Bangladesh, one of the poorest, most overpopulated nations, who is unable to find drinkable water while an American can choose from an abundance and variety of food.

63. **1** The stark contrast in diet for Americans and Bangladeshi is designed by the cartoonist to arouse our pity for the underfed and to motivate us to do something about the situation.

64. **1** This quotation from a speech on March 12, 1947, has come to be known as the Truman Doctrine. Truman asked for and got $400 million in economic and financial aid to Greece and Turkey to help them resist the "outside pressures" of communism.

TEST 3: SCIENCE/PAGE 40

1. **2** Human, monkey, ape, and chimpanzee all belong to the primate group of mammals.
2. **4** Evolution is a process in all of life, not just humans or chimpanzees. Fossils and anatomy provide some of the evidence for evolution.
3. **2** Fossils are the remains of actual living things of the past, so they give the most direct evidence that different forms of life existed.
4. **4** The discovery that today's men are different in size from those of only a few hundred years ago suggests that evolution has not stopped.
5. **3** Use the formula:

$$\text{Density} = \frac{\text{mass}}{\text{volume}}$$

$$\frac{24\text{ g}}{8\text{ cm}^3} = 3\text{ g / cm}^3$$

6. **3** The diagram indicates that the density of sample *B* is 3 g/cm^3. If the sample were split in half, the density would remain the same. The density of a sample is the ratio of its mass to its volume. When the sample is cut in half, both the mass and the volume of the sample are also reduced by half. As a result, the density remains the same.
7. **4** The mass and volume for different samples of a given substance are directly proportional. This relationship is illustrated by graph 4, which shows a direct relationship between mass and volume. As mass increases, volume increases proportionally.
8. **5** To answer this question, the volumes of samples *A* and *B* must first be calculated.

   Volume = length × width × height

   For *A*: Volume = 2 cm × 2 cm × 2 cm = 8 cm^3

   For *B*: Volume = 3 cm × 2 cm × 1 cm = 6 cm^3

   The volume for sample *C* is given as 12 cm^3. Sample *C* therefore has the largest volume, and sample *B* has the smallest volume.
9. **2** According to the theory of continental drift and plate tectonics, the surface of the Earth is moving. The undersea volcanic vent, however, opens deep into the center of the Earth and is stable. One theory about the formation of the Hawaiian Islands suggests that a section of the Earth moves over the volcanic vent, which spews forth enough material to form an island; then, as a new section of Earth moves over the vent, another island is formed.
10. **5** 2.5 × 4,800 ft./sec. = 12,000 ft.
11. **1** An electromagnet is the only type of magnet that can be turned on and off.
12. **4** That Earth is a magnet is proved by the fact that the planet can exert a magnetic force.
13. **5** Lodestone is a well-known natural magnet.
14. **3** In diesel engines the tight-fitting pistons compress air and thus cause the temperature to rise above the kindling temperature of the heavy fuels used. This serves the same purpose as the spark plugs in the gasoline engine.
15. **1** Locomotives can easily carry the heavy diesel engine and thus take advantage of using a less expensive fuel.
16. **1** Because of the strong compression stroke, diesel engines are very heavy and therefore not suitable for airplanes.
17. **1** Earthquakes are the result of the movement of rock masses below the Earth's surface, resulting in breaking rock layers and displacement (fault) of segments of the layer at the breaking point. The folding of rock layers results from the action of lesser forces acting over a longer period of time. The forces produced by landslides are too small to create an earthquake.
18. **2** The 1989 earthquake in San Francisco killed many people because older buildings and roadways were not built to withstand such a severe shock. The more modern buildings stood.
19. **4** It is shock waves in the crust that a seismograph detects, whether they are produced by earthquakes or by nuclear explosions.

20. **3** A calcium atom with a valence of +2 has two electrons in its outer ring. Chlorine with a valence of –1 needs one electron to complete its outer ring. Two chlorine atoms can combine with one atom of calcium to form calcium chloride ($CaCl_2$).
21. **4** Atomic mass (number of protons plus number of neutrons) minus atomic number (number of protons) equals number of neutrons. For lithium, $7 - 3 = 4$.
22. **5** The atomic number is equal to the number of protons.
23. **4** This element, sodium, which has 11 protons, must have 11 electrons in its shells. The first shell holds 2, and the second shell holds 8, leaving 1 electron in its outer shell. Since it can lend this electron to another atom, it has a valence of +1.
24. **5** Many parts of the plant are involved, but it is in the chloroplasts that the actual chemical process takes place.
25. **3** Water from the soil is conducted through the xylem.
26. **3** Chemical energy is needed to split water into H^+ (combined in the glucose) and O_2.
27. **4** Hydrogen and carbon dioxide are successively built up into sugars.
28. **3** Chlorophyll in the chloroplasts of the cells transforms the energy of light into chemical energy.
29. **4** The stomata are openings through which carbon dioxide enters the leaf.
30. **5** The energy that enters the plant is in the form of light; the output is the chemical energy stored in the carbohydrates. The passage says nothing about growth.
31. **5** Since carbon dioxide is used in photosynthesis, increasing the supply would speed up the process.
32. **4** The birds have come to resemble each other because they have evolved to adapt to the same lifestyle. Choices 2, 3, and 5 contradict the statement that the birds are unrelated.
33. **1** According to the information, the white moths were invisible to predators against the light-colored bark. When the trees were darkened by soot, however, the moths were very easy to see.
34. **3** The only life process that a snake cannot perform alone is reproduction.
35. **5** Since the heart is a muscle with nerves that conduct impulses, potassium is an important nutrient. Many prescription drugs that heart patients take have a tendency to remove excess water. Dissolved potassium is thus lost.
36. **5** Stack gases combine with atmospheric water to produce acid rain, which can damage embryos, buildings, trees, and lungs.
37. **3** Mice have many offspring, with a short time between generations. Choice 1 is wrong because bacteria do not reproduce sexually. Choices 2 and 4 are wrong because dogs and humans, while of great practical interest, are not as prolific as mice. Oak trees are extremely prolific, but they have to grow for many years before they produce acorns.
38. **4** The passage implies that green bacteria evolved from nongreen forms, which must have been on earth first. Animal life requires oxygen, so it must have come after the green bacteria changed the atmosphere.
39. **3** The wolf population peaked a year after the peak of the moose population, so many wolves must have been born when the moose population was at its highest.
40. **3** The fossils in rock layer *D* are older than those in layer *A*. Fossils are found in sedimentary rocks. Sedimentary rocks are formed as layer upon layer of material is deposited. The oldest sediment layer *D* was laid down first and appears at the bottom. The youngest layer is at the top.
41. **1** Breathing air is not a form of direct transmission of body fluids. In sexual intercourse, each person has intimate contact with the body fluids of the other, so Choice 2 is wrong. Choices 3, 4 and 5 all involve transmission of blood from person to person.
42. **3** The breeder's problem is to locate the immune plants, which will be those that survive when herbicides are applied.
43. **5** Choice 1 is wrong; a farmer might follow this practice, but it is not what

he *should* do. Choice 4 is wrong because you are asked the basis on which he should decide. There is no reason to suspect that Choices 2 and 3 are relevant.

44. 1 When evaporation occurs, heat is required to change a liquid (here, water) to a gas. Evaporation is a cooling process.

45. 4 Cloning is used to produce a large number of plants in a short period of time. According to the passage, one million plants can be cloned in about 6 months.

46. 3 According to the passage, each cell contains chromosomes, a complete blueprint for reproducing itself.

47. 3 The hormones auxin and cytokinin stimulate the production of new plants. Hormones are substances that regulate the growth and reproduction of organisms.

48. 2 Cloning is defined as a form of vegetative propagation. Vegetative propagation is a form of asexual reproduction; that is, only one parent is required.

49. 2 Sexual reproduction processes mix the heredities of the two parents, and produce offspring different from both. In cloning and other vegetative methods, there is no change in the genotype.

50. 2 The medicine is a suspension, not a solution. All incorrect choices are characteristic of solutions.

51. 5 All other choices have a sour taste, so they are acid.

52. 2 The slippery feel of soap indicates that it is a base.

53. 5 Mixing an acid and a base would produce a product that is neither.

54. 5 Heat is a form of energy that moves spontaneously from regions of higher temperatures to lower. Cold is not a thing; the word here is used as an adjective.

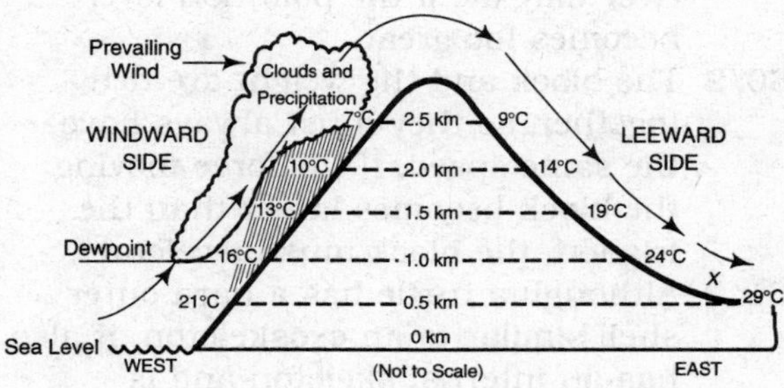

55. 5 On the west side of the mountain, the temperature is dropping 3°C for each 0.5 km. At 2.5 km the temperature is 7°C. At the top it is 3° less, or 4°C. The same results would be obtained by using data from the east side of the mountain, where the temperature is dropping 5°C for each 0.5 km.

56. 2 When precipitation occurs, the relative humidity is 100%. In the diagram, precipitation is occurring on the windward side of the mountain at an elevation of 2.5 km.

57. 4 As the air rises, it expands. When it expands, it cools. You may have noticed that the air rushing out of a tire feels cool. This is because the air is expanding.

58. 1 As the air descends on the leeward side of the mountain, it becomes warmer. As a result, there will rarely be precipitation there. The lack of precipitation will produce an arid region. The deserts in the southwestern part of the United States are located on the leeward sides of mountain ranges.

59. 2 Some plants release pollen to the atmosphere. Human activity does not greatly affect the amount of pollen in the atmosphere. Substances are usually considered pollutants when they are added to the environment by human activity. Any portion of the environment can become polluted, including the atmosphere, the hydrosphere, or the lithosphere. The environment is said to be polluted when more of some substance is added than would normally be present. If, for example, large amounts of waste are dumped into a river, the water becomes polluted.

Fish and other living organisms in the river may die if the pollution level becomes too great.

60. **2** The block and the weight are tied together, so they must always have the same speed. If the force moving the block becomes larger than the friction, the block must accelerate.

61. **2** Although a turtle has a hard outer shell similar to an exoskeleton, it also has an internal skeleton and is classified as a vertebrate.

62. **3** If the experiment is to test the effect of the flypaper, there must be no other difference between the two bottles; all properties that are the same in both are controls.

63. **3** The investigator is clearly using flypaper in the bottle because it will trap flies that can fly, but not the others.

64. **2** The experimenter must decide in advance what to put in the bottles in order that the outcome will give a meaningful answer to the question.

65. **5** The source of winglessness has nothing to do with the experimental problem.

66. **4** In most circumstances in nature, it must be expected that wings are useful. This experiment sets up an artificial environment in which the survival values are reversed. Some such environment might well exist in nature.

TEST 4: INTERPRETING LITERATURE AND THE ARTS/PAGE 53

1. **3** Mary's activities included school work, volunteer editorial work, and riding.

2. **1** Mary is referred to as a "little figure."

3. **4** All three are mentioned: she wore khakis and a red hair ribbon, and waved her cowboy hat.

4. **4** Because she waved to a friend with the wrong hand, the horse veered.

5. **1** The topic sentence refers to Mary White's last hour as being typical of her happiness.

6. **3** Only an animal is awake to listen to Iona.

7. **1** Iona feels he must do something since he can always sleep later.

8. **2** The name of Iona's son, Kuzma Ionitch, is a clue to an eastern European setting.

9. **3** The present tense gives a feeling that the events described are happening now.

10. **5** Iona asks the horse to put herself in the position of a foal's mother who loses her foal.

11. **2** Guy is "quick," and the narrator is "determined." There is a contrast also, in their reactions to the accident and the possibility of death.

12. **3** A simile is a direct comparison that uses the word *like* or *as*.

13. **2** The pronoun *they* refers to the subjects of the preceding sentence, July and August.

14. **4** If the narrator's son were to die, he would "lightly waft" or float away.

15. **1** The narrator became a shadow and a spectre, a ghost, both of which are intangible or unreal.

16. **1** The power poles are replacing the eucalyptus and thus are, in a sense, new trees.

17. **3** The poet calls the power poles "frigid" and "passionless."

18. **4** The children realize they cannot climb the "new trees" and miss the old ones.

19. **3** The poet considers the electric poles incapable of feeling ("passionless verticals") since they are not like trees, which are members of the Plant Kingdom and draw life from the earth.

20. **3** "Tree imposters" is a metaphor in which the poles are compared to false-pretending people.

21. **3** Line 25 states that the poet cannot be consoled. He wishes he could wake Jane from "this sleep"—death.

22. **5** In line 28, he speaks of "my love."

23. **3** Jane is referred to as "a wren," "my sparrow," and "my skittery pigeon."

24. **4** The poet goes from "she" to "her" to "you."

25. **4** In line 29, he indicates he has "no rights in this matter."

26. **3** Walter indirectly indicates that Lindner can expect the same treatment if Lindner insults him.

27. **2** It can be inferred that a better home will be part of a new life.

28. 3 Mama says, "My son said we was going to move," so Walter will be the head of the house.
29. 5 As he leaves, Lindner shakes his head in disagreement.
30. 3 Walter says, "We are very proud people."
31. 1 The author repeats "I remember" and says he has "never forgotten" and "shall never forget."
32. 4 The chief remembers his mother cooking, his father returning from hunting, his grandfather teaching him.
33. 1 The writer says his world reflected the wisdom and benevolence of the Great Spirit.
34. 1 The author writes, "There were never enough hours in a day to exhaust the pleasure of observing every living creature."
35. 5 The author describes the privileges he had on the "unspoiled prairie one hundred years ago."
36. 4 The author says that, in comparisons of language, Shakespeare is bound to win.
37. 3 The author says, among other unfavorable comparisons, that the songs of *West Side Story* pale next to the speech of Mercutio.
38. 1 The passage states that Romeo and Juliet "are a little too slender" to carry the play and this is "equally true of Tony and Maria."
39. 4 The passage observes that the heroes and heroines do "not shake us with...fear."
40. 3 Romeo and Juliet suffer from "the caprice of fate," while Tony and Maria suffer from prejudice and hatred.
41. 4 The author reports that Chagall plays down the "almost sensual gratification" of his colors with a "typical pixie twinkle."
42. 5 Only the first paragraph is concerned with painting. The rest of the article deals with stained glass.
43. 1 The article states that Chagall "slapped on colors . . ., often contrasting them."
44. 3 The conclusion of the article stresses Chagall's faith in mankind's ascent through suffering to salvation.
45. 4 A critic is quoted as saying that Chagall became "his own most faithful imitator."

TEST 5: MATHEMATICS/PAGE 63

1. 2 First find the total mileage.

$$135 + 162 + 98 + 117 + 216 = 728 \text{ mi.}$$

Divide the total mileage (728) by the number of miles covered for each gallon of gas used (14) to find the number of gallons of gas needed.

$$728 \div 14 = 52 \text{ gal.}$$

2. 4 Since 5¢ will pay for 12 min. $0.50 will pay for 10 × 12 = 120 min. 120 min. = 2 hr.

3. 1 If $AB = AC$, then $\angle ABC$ is an isosceles triangle and base angles B and C have equal measures: $m\angle B = m\angle C$.
Let $x = m\angle B = m\angle C$.

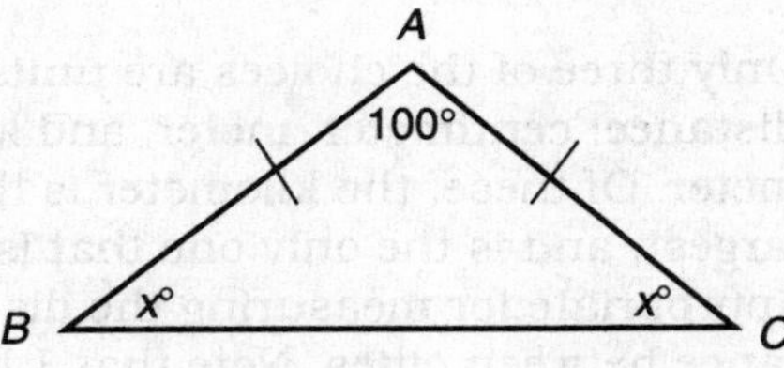

The sum of the measures of the angles of a triangle is 180°, so

$$\begin{aligned} x + x + 100 &= 180 \\ 2x + 100 &= 180 \\ 2x &= 180 - 100 = 80 \\ x &= 40 \end{aligned}$$

4. 5 Since 432 shirts were sold at $15 each, the number of dollars taken in was 15 × 432.
Since 368 shirts were sold at $18 each, the number of dollars taken in was 18 × 368.

The total amount taken in was $15 \times 432 + 18 \times 368$, which may be written as

$$(15)(432) + (368)(18).$$

5. **1** The total number of games played was $X + Y + Z$.
The number of games won was X.
The fractional part of the games won was $\frac{X}{X+Y+Z}$

6. **2** $\frac{1}{2}$ of the pupils walk to school.
$\frac{1}{4}$ of the other $\frac{1}{2} = \frac{1}{4} \times \frac{1}{2} = \frac{1}{8}$ use bicycles.
$$\frac{1}{2} + \frac{1}{8} = \frac{4}{8} + \frac{1}{8} = \frac{5}{8}$$
of the pupils either walk or use bicycles.
Therefore, $1 - \frac{5}{8} = \frac{3}{8}$ use other means.

7. **5** Since $2x > 9$, then
$$x > \frac{9}{2} = 4\frac{1}{2}.$$
The only choice that is greater than $4\frac{1}{2}$ is 5.
An alternative method is to replace x by each of the choices given. The only choice that makes the inequality true is $x = 5$.

8. **2** Only three of the choices are units of distance: centimeter, meter, and kilometer. Of these, the kilometer is the largest, and is the only one that is appropriate for measuring the distance between cities. Note that 1 km is approximately $\frac{5}{8}$ mi.

9. **4** Let x = height of flagpole. The two poles and their shadows can be represented by two triangles.

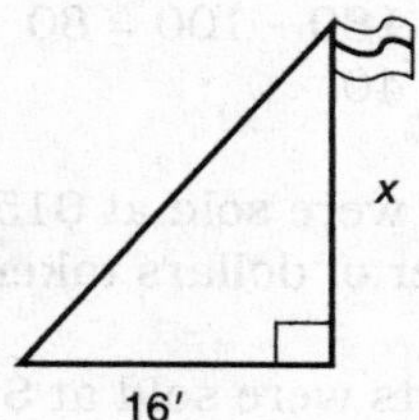

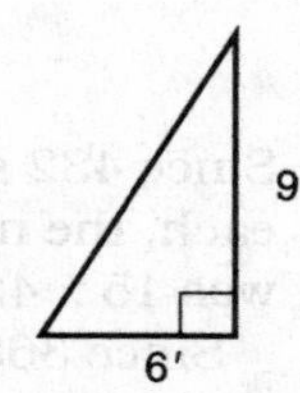

Since the triangles are similar, the lengths of corresponding sides are in proportion.
Set up the proportion:
$$\frac{h\text{ (flagpole)}}{h\text{ (pole)}} = \frac{l\text{ (flagpole shadow)}}{l\text{ (pole shadow)}}$$
$$\frac{x}{9} = \frac{16}{6}$$
$$6x = 9 \times 16 = 144$$
$$x = \frac{144}{6} = 24$$

10. **2** 1 ft. = 12 in.
9 ft. 8 in. = $9 \times 12 + 8 = 116$ in.
$116 \div 4 = 29$ in. = 2 ft. 5 in.

11. **1** The purse contains $6 + 5 + 8 = 19$ coins, 5 of which are dimes.
Therefore, the probability of drawing a dime is $\frac{5}{19}$.

12. **4** When an odd number of scores are arranged in increasing order, the median is the middle number. In this case, there are 9 numbers, so the median is the fifth number.

272, 274, 275, 276, 278, 281, 283, 284, 287
↓
median

13. **4** The pens cost 3 for $0.97.
Cost of 1 dozen pens = 4($0.97) = $3.88.
Cost of 8 pencils = $4.60 − 3.88 = $0.72.
Cost of 1 pencil = $0.72 ÷ 8 = 9 cents.

14. **1** Since 1 in. on the map represents 150 mi., 3 in. represents 3(150) = 450 mi., and $\frac{1}{2}$ in. represents $\frac{1}{2}(150) = 75$ mi.
Then $3\frac{1}{2}$ in. represents
$450 + 75 = 525$ mi.

15. **2** To find the perimeter of the figure, find the sum of the lengths of the four sides:
$2a + b + a + 3b + 3a + b + 3a + 2b$
$= 9a + 7b.$

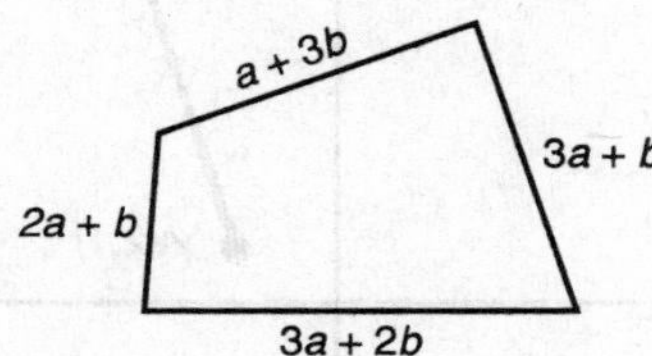

16. **4** The distance between point *A* and point *B* is 10 units. Thus, the midpoint of $\overline{AB}$ is located at 5 units to the right of point *A*.
The coordinate of the midpoint of $\overline{AB}$ is 3.

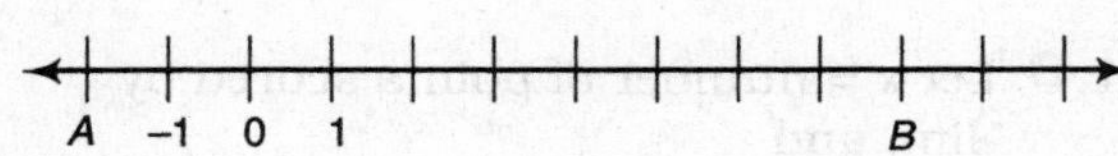

17. **5** Since 3 ties sold for \$23,
6 ties cost 2(\$23) = \$46.
3 shirts cost \$43.
Since slacks sold for \$32.75 per pair,
2 pairs of slacks cost
2(\$32.75) = \$65.50.
1 jacket cost for \$58.45.
\$46 + \$43 + \$65.50 + \$58.45
= \$212.95

18. **3** Write all the numbers as decimals, so that it is easier to arrange the numbers in order of size.
19% = 0.19,
$\frac{1}{2} = 0.50$, and $\frac{3}{5} = 60$.
The correct order from greatest to smallest is
0.80, 0.60, 0.50, 0.19, 0.080
or 0.80, $\frac{3}{5}$, $\frac{1}{2}$, 19%, 0.080
The correct choice is (3).

19. **3** To find the average speed, in miles per hour, divide the distance, in miles, by the time, in hours. Since 5 hr. and 30 min. is $5\frac{1}{2}$, or 5.5 hr., divide 1,364 by 5.5: $1364 \div 5.5 = 248$.

20. **2** To write a number in scientific notation, write it as the product of a number between 1 and 10 and a power of 10. In this case, the number between 1 and 10 is 8.5. In going from 8.5 to 85,000,000,000, you move the decimal point 10 places to the right. Therefore 85,000,000,000 = 8.5×10^{10}.

21. **3** $3ab - x^2y = 3(4)(5) - (2)(2)(3)$
$= 60 \quad - 12 = 48$

22. **3** The sum of the measures of the angles around the center of the circle is 360°. The fraction that represents the part of the total number of workers engaged in transportation is $\frac{20}{360} = \frac{1}{18}$.
$\frac{1}{18}$ of $180{,}000 = \frac{180{,}000}{18} = 10{,}000$

23. **4** *M* = number of persons in trade and finance
Let *x* = number of persons in manufacturing
Set up a proportion:
$\frac{90}{M} = \frac{120}{x}$
$90x = 120M$
$x = \frac{120M}{90} = \frac{4M}{3}$

24. **4** Since m∠*ABC* = 68° and $\overline{BF}$ bisects ∠*ABC*, then m∠*EBC* = $\frac{1}{2}(68) = 34°$.
Since m∠*ACB* = 72° and $\overline{CD}$ bisects ∠*ACB*, then m∠*ECB* = $\frac{1}{2}(72) = 36°$.

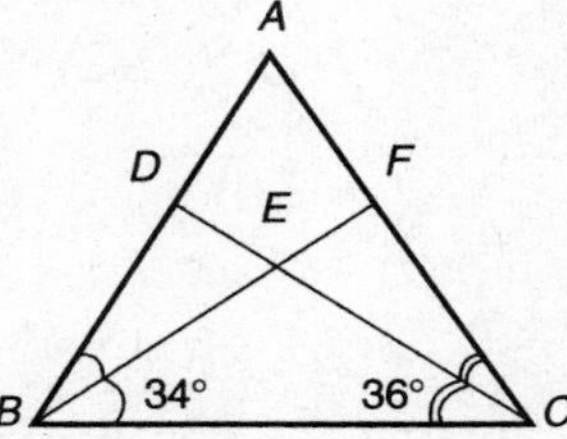

Since the sum of the measure of the angles of a triangle is 180°,

m∠*EBC* + m∠*ECB* + m∠*BEC* = 180°
34 + 36 + m∠*BEC* = 180°
70 + m∠*BEC* = 180°
m∠*BEC* = 180 – 70 = 110°

25. **3** Frank has \$30.
Jack has \$30 − \$3 = \$27.
Bill has \$27 + \$5 = \$32.

26. **5** You know that John Davis lost *at least* 4 lb. each month. But he may have lost much more. Not enough information is given to determine his exact weight after the 6-month period.

27. **2** The annual interest on \$10,000 at $8\frac{1}{2}$% is \$10,000 × 0.085 = \$850.
Thus, every 6 months Mr. Ames receives $\frac{1}{2}$ of \$850 = \$425.

28. **3** Since the aquarium is in the shape of a rectangular solid, its volume is given by the formula $V = lwh$. To find the volume in cubic feet, express each of l, w, and h in feet.

Length, l, is 3 ft.
Width, w = 1 ft. 8 in. = $1\frac{2}{3}$ ft. = $\frac{5}{3}$ ft.
Height, h, is 1 ft. 6 in. = $1\frac{1}{2}$ ft. = $\frac{3}{2}$ ft.

$$V = 3 \times \frac{5}{3} \times \frac{3}{3} = \frac{15}{2} = 7.5 \text{ cu. ft.}$$

29. **3** Let $9x$ = number of men at the meeting, and
$2x$ = number of women at the meeting.

Since $2x = 12$, $x = 6$.
Then $9x = 9(6) = 54$.

30. **5** Slope of $\overleftrightarrow{AB}$ $= \dfrac{\text{change in } y\text{-coordinates}}{\text{change in } x\text{-coordinates}}$

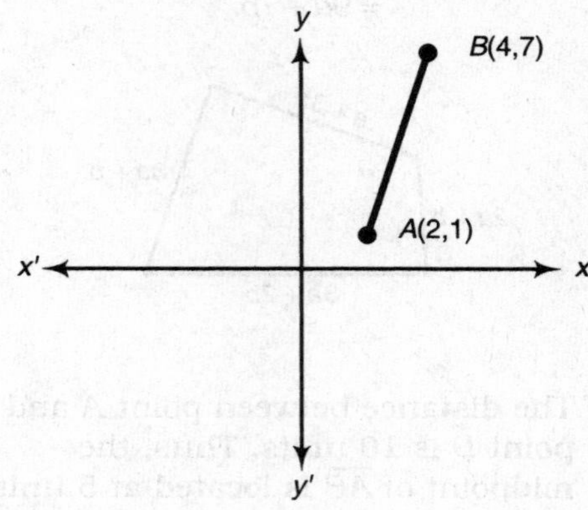

Slope of $\overleftrightarrow{AB} = \frac{7-1}{4-2} = \frac{6}{2} = 3$

31. **3** Let x = number of points scored by Jim, and
$3x$ = number of points scored by Bill.

$$x + 3x = 56$$
$$4x = 56$$
$$x = 56 \div 4 = 14$$
$$3x = 3(14) = 42$$

32. **4** Note that each subdivision line on the vertical axis represents 200 mi. The Rio Grande is about 1,500 mi. long, and the Seine is about 500 mi. long. Therefore, the Rio Grande is about 1,000 mi. longer than the Seine.

33. **5** In 1988, the receipts were \$600,000 and the expenses were \$500,000. In 1988, receipts exceeded expenses by \$100,000.

34. **1** Six pencils will cost 6 times as much as 1 pencil. Since y is the cost of 1 pencil, the cost of 6 pencils is 6 times $y = 6y$.

35. **5** In 2 weeks Mr. Martin worked a total of (42 + 37) hr. and earned \$12 for each hour. Therefore, the total number of dollars he earned was 12(42 + 37).

36. **4** The total enrollment is

$$360 + 300 + 280 + 260 = 1{,}200$$

The part of the total enrollment that represents the freshmen is

$$\frac{360}{1{,}200} = \frac{36}{120} = \frac{3}{10} = 30\%.$$

37. **3** Since pairs of alternate interior angles of parallel lines have equal measures, $m\angle BCD = m\angle ABC$. Thus $m\angle BCD = 112°$.

$$m\angle ECD = \frac{1}{2} m\angle BCD$$
$$= \frac{1}{2}(112°) = 56°$$

38. **2** 22 ft. 4 in. = 22(12) + 4 = 268 in.

$268 \div 4 = 67$ in. per piece

$$\frac{67}{12} = 5\frac{7}{12}$$

Each piece is 5 ft. 7 in. in length.

39. **4** According to the graph, the population in 1992 was midway between 25,000 and 30,000.

$$25{,}000 + 30{,}000 = 55{,}000$$
$$55{,}000 \div 2 = 27{,}500$$

40. **3** According to the graph, the population in 1990 was 20,000 and in 1991 it was also 20,000.

There was no change in population between 1990 and 1991.

41. **4** Use the formula $V = lwh$ to represent the volume of the rectangular solid.

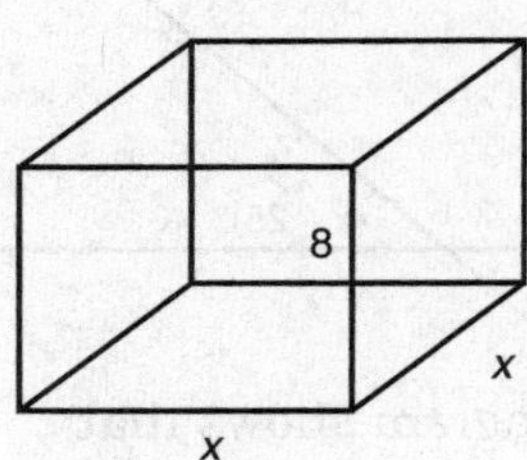

$$V = x \cdot x \cdot 8 = 8x^2$$
$$8x^2 = 392$$

42. **5** Since the total number of votes cast is not given, an equation to solve the problem cannot be set up.

43. **2** If $\overline{AB} = \overline{AC}$, $m\angle C = m\angle B = 68°$. Since $\overline{AD} \perp \overline{BC}$, $m\angle ADC = 90°$.

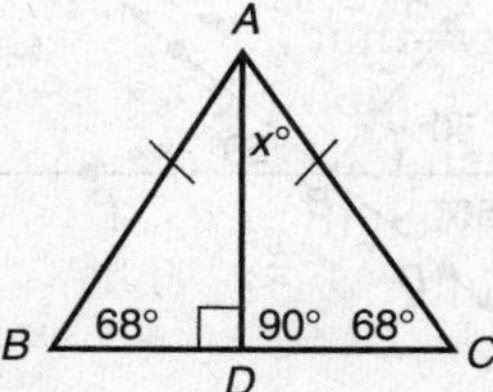

Since the sum of the measures of the angles of a triangle is 180°:

$$68 + 90 + m\angle x = 180$$
$$158 + m\angle x = 180$$
$$m\angle x = 180 - 158 = 22°$$

44. **4** In the right triangle use the Pythagorean theorem.

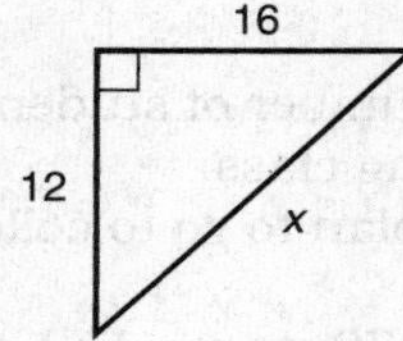

$$x^2 = (12)^2 + (16)^2$$
$$= 144 + 256 = 400$$
$$x = \sqrt{400} = 20$$

45. **3** Since $5^2 = 25$ and $6^2 = 36$, $\sqrt{30}$ is between 5 and 6.

46. **1** AD = radius of large circle = 20 in. BC = radius of small circle = 8 in.

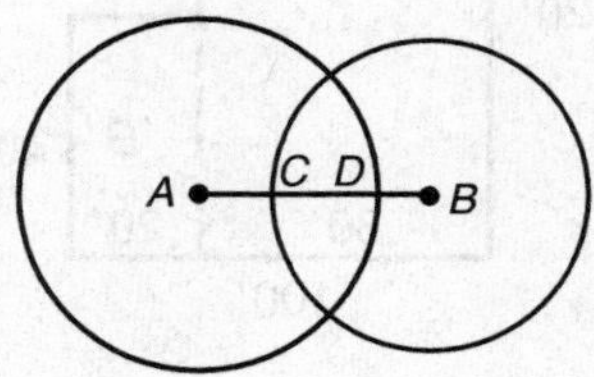

$$CD = 6$$
$$DB = BC - CD = 8 - 6 = 2$$
$$AB = AD + DB = 20 + 2 = 22 \text{ in.}$$

47. **4** m∠EBF = m∠CBD = 50° since vertical angles have equal measures.

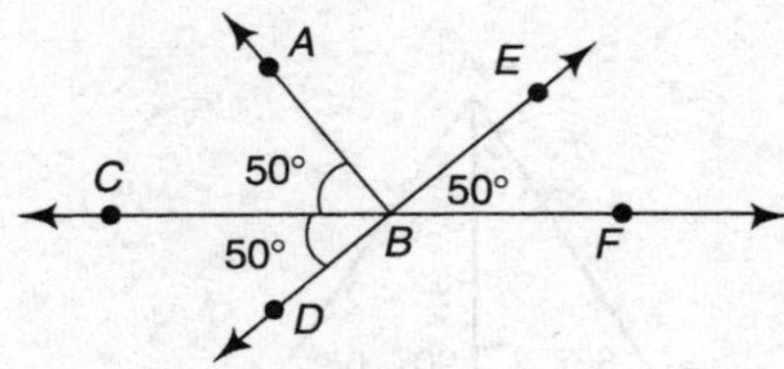

Since $\overleftrightarrow{CB}$ bisects ∠ABD, m∠ABC = m∠CBD.

Thus, m∠ABC = 50°.

48. **4** To find the cost of n lb. of sugar at c cents per pound, multiply n by c to obtain nc.

To find the change received subtract nc cents from 100 cents. The result is $100 - nc$.

49. **1** Let x = number of students in the graduating class.

$0.85x$ plan to go to college

$0.85x = 170$, so $x = 170 \div 0.85$

$0.85\overline{)170.00}$ = 200

50. **2** Divide the given figure into two rectangles by drawing a dotted line.

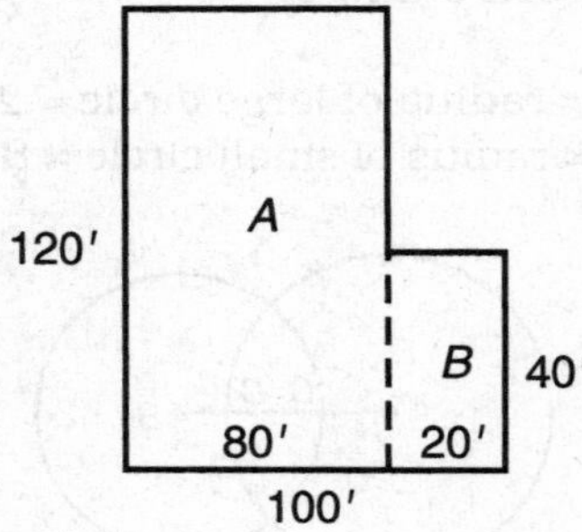

Width of rectangle A =
$100 - 20 = 80$
Length of rectangle A = 120
Area of rectangle A =
(80)(120) = 9,600 sq. ft.
Area of rectangle B =
40×20 = 800 sq. ft.
Area of figure = 9,600 + 800 =
10,400 sq. ft.

51. **5** Check each inequality or equation in turn.
(1) $3(10) + 1 > 12$, $30 + 1 > 12$. True
(2) $2(10) - 3 < 25$, $20 - 3 < 25$. True
(3) $10^2 + 1 > 10^2 - 1$,
$100 + 1 > 100 - 1$. True
(4) $4(10) - 1 = 39$, $40 - 1 = 39$. True
(5) $2(10) - 7 > 7 - 2(10)$,
$20 - 7 < 7 - 20$. Not true
The correct choice is (5).

52. **5** Let x = measure of smaller acute angle, and
$4x$ = measure of larger acute angle.

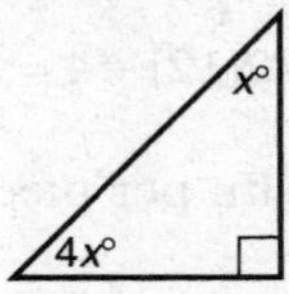

$$\begin{aligned} x + 4x &= 90° \\ 5x &= 90° \\ x &= 90 \div 5 = 18° \\ 4x &= 4(18) = 72° \end{aligned}$$

53. **4** The borrower pays 50 cents for the first 3 days plus 15 cents for each of the $(n - 3)$ days after the third day.

Thus, the correct formula is
$C = 50 + 15(n - 3)$.

54. **3** Since PQ is parallel to RS, alternate interior angles are equal: $2x = x + 25$. Subtracting x from each side yields $x = 25$.

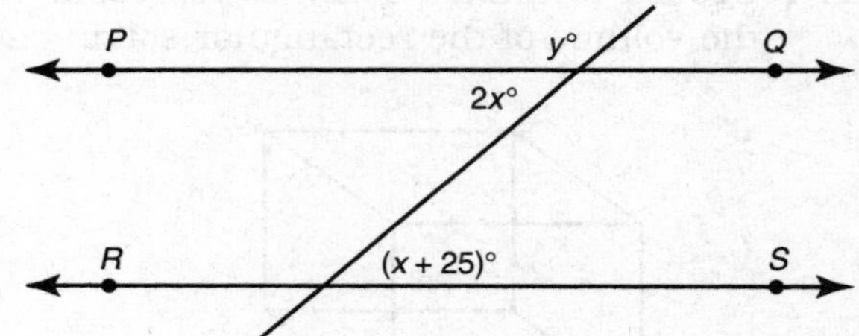

55. **1** The diagram shows that $2x + y = 180°$. In question 55 it was determined that $x = 25°$. Then $180 = 2(25) + y = 50 + y$, so $y = 130°$.

56. **4** Factor the left-hand side of
$x^2 - x - 12 = 0$:
$(x - 4)(x + 3) = 0$,
$x - 4 = 0$ **or** $x + 3 = 0$
$x = 4$ **or** $x = -3$

UNIT II

WRITING SKILLS

TEST 1, PART I

CHAPTER 3: Sentence Structure

We identify *seven* kinds of run-on sentences and *six* kinds of sentence fragments. Parallel structure, misplaced modifiers, and writing correct sentences are thoroughly covered.

CHAPTER 4: Usage

Key areas of usage are limited to agreement, case of nouns and pronouns, and errors in verb form and tense. A glossary defines over a hundred usage terms and provides examples of each.

CHAPTER 5: Mechanics

Fifteen basic rules of capitalization are listed. Basic rules are presented for each of the *nine* major punctuation marks. *Thirteen* helpful spelling rules follow the *three* basic skills of a good speller. The spelling words in *three* graded lists complete coverage of mechanics.

CHAPTER 6: Additional Writing Skills

You will learn the importance of context, the difference between denotation and connotation, and the differences between 30 pairs of words frequently confused or misused. A Basic 750-Word Vocabulary is presented. Tone and styles of writing are described. *Five* kinds of wordiness are demonstrated. Idioms are listed.

CHAPTER 7: Practice with Sample Test Paragraphs

We have provided sample paragraphs and questions based on them, similar to those on the GED. These contain, with explanations, examples of the sentence correction, sentence revision, and construction shift items on the GED and will thus give you experience with the kind of materials you will face on the examination.

3 Sentence Structure

A sentence is the basic means of communicating an idea.

A sentence may be defined as a group of words having a subject and a predicate and expressing a complete thought. Each sentence should be separated from the one that follows it by some form of end punctuation such as a period, a question mark, or an exclamation point.

Run-On Sentences

In one important group of errors, you may fail to separate two or more sentences by using the proper punctuation. Instead, you may either use no punctuation at all or incorrectly use a comma. The general term for this group of errors is the *run-on sentence* or, if a comma is incorrectly used, the *comma splice*.

Here are frequently made errors and the ways in which they may be corrected.

Note: Types are indicated by number for easy reference in the answer analysis section.

Type 1

This type can result from an incorrectly used or omitted conjunction or adverb.

EXAMPLE

WRONG:

Joe was elected class president *x* he is very popular.

CORRECT:

Joe was elected class president *because* he is very popular.

"Joe was elected class president" and "he is very popular" are both independent sentences. The two sentences have been run together because there is no end punctuation between them. This error can be corrected by simply placing a period between the two sentences. A better way to correct this error, however, is to look for a relationship between the two sentences. The first sentence, "Joe was elected class president," is a result of the second, "he is very popular." It is, therefore, possible to join the two sentences using the conjunction *because*. Joe was elected president *because* he is very popular.

EXAMPLES

WRONG:

Joe is very popular *x* therefore he was elected class president.

Joe is very popular *x* so he was elected class president.

CORRECT:

Joe is very popular and, as a result, he was elected class president.

Joe is very popular. Therefore, he was elected class president.

Joe is very popular; therefore, he was elected class president.

To correct this type of error, you must substitute a conjunction for the adverbs *therefore* and *so* or break the run-on sentence at the point marked *x* with either a period or a semicolon.

PRACTICE

Some of these sentences have errors; others are correct. Rewrite correctly the sentences that contain errors. Write "correct" for those that have no errors.

1. Hector studied very hard. So he passed the test.
2. Maria was very beautiful therefore she was chosen queen of the prom.
3. Avital has lots of friends she is very good-natured.

Answers

1. Correct.
2. Maria was very beautiful. Therefore, she was chosen queen of the prom.
3. Avital is very good-natured and, as a result, she has lots of friends.

Type 2

EXAMPLES

WRONG:

Joe worked hard *x* he was bound to succeed.

CORRECT:

Joe worked *so* hard *that* he was bound to succeed.

WRONG:

Joe worked hard *x* consequently he was bound to succeed.

CORRECT:

Joe worked hard. *Consequently*, he was bound to succeed.

CORRECT:

Since Joe worked hard, he was bound to succeed.

Practice

1. Since the employer required a high school diploma, I had to pass the GED test.
2. Helena was a good shopper she saved lots of money.

Answers

1. Correct.
2. Helena was a good shopper. Consequently, she saved lots of money.

Type 3

EXAMPLES

WRONG:

Joe disliked English *x* he got a good mark anyhow.

CORRECT:

Joe disliked English, *but* he got a good mark anyhow.

WRONG:

Joe disliked English *x* nevertheless he got a good mark.

CORRECT:

Joe disliked English. *Nevertheless*, he got a good mark.

Although Joe disliked English, he got a good mark.

WRONG:

Joe disliked English *x* however he got a good mark.

CORRECT:

Joe disliked English. *However*, he got a good mark.

Practice

1. The politician did not do much campaigning nevertheless he was elected.
2. Although the team rallied, it lost the game.

Answers

1. The politician did not do much campaigning. Nevertheless, he was elected.
2. Correct

Type 4

EXAMPLES

WRONG:

Joe is excellent in mathematics *x* he is also good in English.

CORRECT:

Joe is excellent in mathematics *and* he is also good in English.

WRONG:

Joe is excellent in mathematics *x* furthermore he is good in English.

CORRECT:

Joe is excellent in mathematics. *Furthermore*, he is good in English.

WRONG:

Joe is excellent in mathematics *x* besides he is good in English.

CORRECT:

Joe is excellent in mathematics. He is *also* good in English.

Joe is excellent in mathematics. *Besides*, he is good in English.

PRACTICE

1. Fernando is an excellent violinist he is a fine violist as well.
2. The telecast raised much money for muscular dystrophy research, furthermore it was very entertaining.

ANSWERS

1. Fernando is an excellent violinist; he is a fine violist as well.
   or
   Fernando is an excellent violinist. Besides, he is a fine violist.
2. The telecast raised much money for muscular dystrophy research. Furthermore, it was very entertaining.

Type 5

EXAMPLE

WRONG:
Joe is always imitating the coach, he respects him greatly.

CORRECT:
Joe is always imitating the coach *whom* he respects greatly.

In the above example, *coach* is the word (noun) described and *whom he respects greatly* is the descriptive clause.

PRACTICE

1. The class elected Juan president of the class they liked him best of all the candidates.
2. Anna was the best student the class admired her.

ANSWERS

1. The class elected Juan, whom they liked best of all the candidates, president of the class.
2. Anna, whom the class admired, was the best student.

Type 6

EXAMPLE

WRONG:
Did Joe win *x* he was the best candidate.

CORRECT:
Did Joe win? He was the best candidate.

"Did Joe win?" is an interrogative sentence. "He was the best candidate" is a declarative sentence. Often students combine, in error, the question and the answer given to it.

PRACTICE

1. Is Conchita home? I have to speak to her.
2. Did you go to see the play it was very entertaining.

ANSWERS

1. Correct.
2. Did you go to see the play? It was very entertaining.

Type 7

This type of run-on sentence error involves the punctuation of quotations. Therefore, refer to "Basic Rules of Punctuation" beginning on page 143.

EXAMPLE

WRONG:
"Joe won," he said, "I thought he was the best runner."

CORRECT:
"Joe won," he said. "I thought he was the best runner."

"Joe won." He said, "I thought he was the best runner."

PRACTICE

1. "Come in," said the hostess, "I'm happy to see you."
2. "Study hard," advised the teacher. "You'll pass the test."

ANSWERS

1. "Come in," said the hostess. "I'm happy to see you."
2. Correct.

Sentence Fragments

In another important group of errors, you may fail to complete the sentence. (You will remember that a sentence is defined as a group of words having a subject and a predicate and expressing a complete thought.) In the kind of error called a *sentence fragment*, either the subject is left out, so that a predicate is left standing by itself (e.g., "Wish you were here.") or a part of the predicate is broken off from the sentence and made to stand by itself (e.g., "Walking down the street.").

Type 1

EXAMPLE

WRONG:

Am having a wonderful time. Wish you were here.

CORRECT:

I am having a wonderful time. *I* wish you were here.

In each case, without the subject it is impossible to know *who* is doing the action indicated in the predicate.

PRACTICE

1. Miss you. Will be home tomorrow.
2. Great idea. Wish you luck.

ANSWERS

1. We miss you. We'll be home tomorrow.
   or
   I miss you. I'll be home tomorrow.
   or
   They miss you. They'll be home tomorrow.
2. That's a great idea. I (We) wish you luck.

Type 2

EXAMPLE

WRONG:

Joe studied hard. Passed all his tests and was graduated.

CORRECT:

Joe studied hard, passed all his tests, and was graduated.

Note that *studied hard*, *passed all his tests*, and *was graduated* are all parts of the predicate, and they all tell us something about Joe.

PRACTICE

1. Don collected baseball cards. Played the piano and excelled in sports.
2. Donna went to school. Worked as a babysitter.

ANSWERS

1. Don collected baseball cards, played the piano, and excelled in sports.
2. While Donna went to school, she worked as a babysitter.

Type 3

EXAMPLES

WRONG:

Joe got a good mark in English. Although he doesn't like the subject. [Adverbial clause]

CORRECT:

Joe got a good mark in English, although he doesn't like the subject.

WRONG:

Joe has an English teacher. Whom he likes very much. [Adjective clause]

CORRECT:

Joe has an English teacher whom he likes very much.

PRACTICE

1. Fern is popular. Because she is considerate.
2. I enjoy being with Jill. Who is very amusing.

ANSWERS

1. Fern is popular, because she is considerate.
2. I enjoy being with Jill, who is very amusing.

Type 4

EXAMPLES

WRONG:

Joe got up early. To go to school. [Infinitive phrase]

CORRECT:

Joe got up early to go to school.

WRONG:

Joe worked hard. Studying his lessons. [Participial phrase]

CORRECT:

Joe worked hard studying his lessons.

WRONG:

Walking down the street. Joe thought about his job. [Participial phrase]

CORRECT:

Walking down the street, Joe thought about his job.

> **IMPORTANT NOTE:**
>
> A clause and a phrase can be detached in error either at the *beginning* or at the *end* of the sentence.

EXAMPLES

WRONG:

Joe went to the movies. With his friend.

CORRECT:

Joe went to the movies with his friend.

WRONG:

Joe enjoyed himself. At the movies.

CORRECT:

Joe enjoyed himself at the movies.

PRACTICE

1. Looking around the room. Cynthia saw her friend.
2. Frances practiced daily, doing her exercises on the piano.
3. I was too tired. To go to the supermarket.

ANSWERS

1. Looking around the room, Cynthia saw her friend.
2. Correct.
3. I was too tired to go to the supermarket.

Type 5

EXAMPLE

WRONG:

Joe enjoys all sports. Baseball, football and swimming.

CORRECT:

Joe enjoys all sports: baseball, football, and swimming.

Sports is the object; baseball, football, and swimming are nouns in apposition. Note that the colon is used to introduce listings. See the section "Basic Rules of Punctuation" beginning on page 143.

EXAMPLE

WRONG:

Joe admires the captain of the team. Ron Jones.

CORRECT:

Joe admires the captain of the team, Ron Jones.

PRACTICE

1. Miguel collects antiques. Stamps and coins.
2. Dick met his fiancee's mother, Mrs. Ellis.

ANSWERS

1. Miguel collects antiques, stamps, and coins.
2. Correct.

Type 6

EXAMPLE

WRONG:

Joe has excelled in his studies. Also in sports and extracurricular activities.

CORRECT:

Joe has excelled in his studies, in sports, and in extracurricular activities.

PRACTICE

1. Noel spent his spare time at the movies. Also at the pool and at the gym.
2. Sheila helped at home, in school, and at church.

ANSWERS

1. Noel spent his spare time at the movies, the pool, and the gym.
2. Correct.

PRACTICE WITH RUN-ON SENTENCES AND SENTENCE FRAGMENTS

Beneath each sentence you will find five ways of writing the underlined part. Choose the answer that makes the best sentence. Answer 1 is always the same as the underlined part and is sometimes the right answer. This is the sentence revision type of multiple-choice item.

1. Yolanda had a passion for fruits; melons, pineapples, grapefruits, and pears.

   (1) fruits; melons,
   (2) fruits. melons,
   (3) fruits, melons,
   (4) fruits: melons,
   (5) fruits. Melons,

2. "Take your umbrella," suggested the boy's mother. "It might rain."

   (1) mother. "It
   (2) mother," it
   (3) mother,". It
   (4) mother: "It
   (5) mother:" it

3. "Why he didn't come home on time." stated the parent, "is beyond me."

   (1) time." stated
   (2) time? "stated
   (3) time"? stated
   (4) time, "Stated
   (5) time," stated

4. The teacher told her student to bring his books to class every day.

   (1) student to bring his
   (2) student that he should bring his
   (3) student he should bring his
   (4) student: bring your
   (5) student—bring your

5. Arnold studied hard he wanted to make the honor roll.

   (1) hard he
   (2) hard because he
   (3) hard: He
   (4) hard, he
   (5) hard. since he

6. Have you been to the museum it has an excellent exhibition.

   (1) museum it
   (2) museum, it
   (3) museum? it
   (4) museum? It
   (5) museum which

7. "The Red Sox won the pennant," said the sportscaster, "I thought they were the best team."

   (1) pennant," said the sportscaster, "I
   (2) pennant." said the sportscaster, "I
   (3) pennant", said the sportscaster, "I
   (4) pennant," said the sportscaster. "I
   (5) pennant." said the sportscaster. "I

8. The student replied that he is living here for the last three years.

   (1) that he is
   (2) that "He is
   (3) that, "He is
   (4) that he was
   (5) that he has been

9. I should agree to the proposal if I were in your situation.

   (1) I should agree to the proposal if I were
   (2) I would agree to the proposal if I would be
   (3) I would agree to the proposal if I was
   (4) I would agree to the proposal, if I was
   (5) I would agree to the proposal; if I were

10. The employer refused the worker the raise besides, he threatened to fire him.

    (1) raise besides,
    (2) raise, besides,
    (3) raise: besides.
    (4) raise. besides
    (5) raise. Besides,

11. Studying hard. Miss you. Write.

    (1) Studying hard. Miss you. Write.
    (2) I am studying hard. Miss you. Write.
    (3) I am studying hard. I miss you. Write.
    (4) Studying hard; miss you; write.
    (5) Studying hard: miss you. Write.

12. To succeed in school: Juan attended regularly, did his homework, and studied hard.

    (1) school: Juan
    (2) school. Juan
    (3) school, Juan
    (4) school—Juan
    (5) school Juan

13. Why didn't you come I waited for hours for your arrival.

    (1) come I
    (2) come, I
    (3) come; I
    (4) come: I
    (5) come? I

14. Joanne didn't like to study she passed the examination anyhow.

    (1) study she
    (2) study and she
    (3) study, and she
    (4) study: but she
    (5) study, but she

15. They objected to me staying. Nevertheless, I remained at the gathering.

    (1) me staying. Nevertheless, I
    (2) me staying, nevertheless I
    (3) my staying, nevertheless, I
    (4) my staying. Nevertheless I
    (5) my staying. Nevertheless, I

16. Can't be at your wedding send all our love.

    (1) Can't be at your wedding send
    (2) Can't be at your wedding; send
    (3) Can't be at your wedding; we send
    (4) Can't be at your wedding, we send
    (5) We can't be at your wedding, but we send

17. Although Vincent and Giuseppe, buddies during the Vietnam War, hadn't met for over five years.

    (1) Giuseppe, buddies during the Vietnam War, hadn't met
    (2) Giuseppe buddies during the Vietnam War hadn't met
    (3) Giuseppe, buddies during the Vietnam War, didn't meet
    (4) Giuseppe were buddies during the Vietnam War yet hadn't met
    (5) Giuseppe were buddies during the Vietnam War, they hadn't met

18. Will you come to my party I'd be happy to have you there.

    (1) party I'd
    (2) party. I'd
    (3) party; I'd
    (4) party: I'd
    (5) party? I'd

19. "This is most unusual," said Jorge," the mail has never come late before."

    (1) Jorge, "the
    (2) Jorge, "The
    (3) Jorge. "The
    (4) Jorge; "The
    (5) Jorge: "The

ANSWER KEY

1. **4**	5. **2**	9. **1**	13. **5**	17. **5**
2. **1**	6. **4**	10. **5**	14. **5**	18. **5**
3. **5**	7. **4**	11. **3**	15. **5**	19. **3**
4. **1**	8. **5**	12. **3**	16. **5**	

WHAT'S YOUR SCORE?

_______ right, _______ wrong

Excellent	18–19
Good	15–17
Fair	12–14

If you scored lower, study the kinds of run-on sentences and sentence fragments illustrated in this section.

ANSWER ANALYSIS

1. **4** See Type 5 under "Sentence Fragments." The nouns in apposition with *fruits* should be preceded by a colon. See Rule 1 under "The Colon" (page 146).
2. **1** No error.
3. **5** See Rule 7 under "The Comma" (page 144), as it refers to the divided quotation where commas are used to set off the speaker.
4. **1** No error.
5. **2** See Type 1 under "Run-on Sentences" (page 99). A cause for Arnold's studying hard is needed to bring the two sentences together.
6. **4** See Type 6 under "Run-on Sentences" (page 101). Two sentences of different kinds are improperly run together.
7. **4** See Type 7 under "Run-on Sentences" (page 101). The two sentences are improperly run together because there is a divided quotation.
8. **5** The present perfect tense is required since the student has been living here up to the present time.
9. **1** Correct as is.
10. **5** See Type 4 under "Run-on Sentences" (page 100). In this run-on sentence, an additional idea is incorrectly connected to the first idea.
11. **3** See Type 1 under "Sentence Fragments" (page 102). The subjects of the first two sentences are improperly left out. In *Write*, the subject *you* is understood.
12. **3** See Type 4 under "Sentence Fragments" (page 103). The Important Note mentions that a phrase may, in error, be detached at the beginning of the sentence. Here, it is "To succeed in school." The colon detaches the phrase; the comma connects it to the sentence. (Also, see Rule 4 under "The Comma," page 144).
13. **5** Two sentences of different kinds are incorrectly run together.
14. **5** See Type 3 under "Run-on Sentences" (page 100). A conflicting idea is incorrectly connected to the idea it apparently contradicts.
15. **5** See Problem 3 under "Some Special Problems" of "Case of Nouns and Pronouns" (page 127).
16. **5** See Type 1 under "Sentence Fragments" (page 102). The subject of the sentence is improperly left out. In addition, see Type 3 under "Run-on Sentences" (page 100). A conflicting idea is incorrectly connected to the idea it apparently contradicts.
17. **5** See Type 4 under "Sentence Fragments" (particularly **Important Note**, page 103). This is an example of a detached clause at the beginning of the sentence.
18. **5** See Type 6 under "Run-on Sentences" (page 101). Two sentences of different kinds are incorrectly run together. "Will you come to my party?" is an interrogative sentence; "I'd be happy to have you there" is a declarative sentence.
19. **3** See Type 7 under "Run-on Sentences" (page 101). Two different sentences are run together improperly because there is a divided quotation.

Parallel Structure

A major error in structure is failure to keep elements of the sentence that perform the *same purpose* in the *same form*. This is called an error in parallel structure.

Here is an example of such an error.

WRONG:
Joe likes *swimming*, *fishing*, and, if he has the time, *to take* a long walk.

The sentence tells us three things Joe likes. They are related to us by words that are the objects of the verb *likes*, and they serve the same purpose. But are their forms alike? Let us line them up vertically.

Joe likes swimming
fishing
to take a long walk

No, they are not. *Swimming* and *fishing* are gerunds (verbs used, in the *-ing* form, as nouns). *To take,* however, is an infinitive. Words having the same function should have the same form. Then, the sentence has parallel in structure. The sentence should read:

Joe likes swimming
fishing
taking a long walk

CORRECT:

Joe likes *swimming, fishing,* and, if he has the time, *taking a long walk.*

PRACTICE

1. Irene enjoys baking, cooking, and to prepare meals.
2. Julie excels at embroidering, crocheting, and hooking rugs.

ANSWERS

1. Irene enjoys baking, cooking, and preparing meals.
2. Correct.

Here is another example of lack of parallel structure.

WRONG:

Jane and Jim took part *in* baseball games, *in* swimming *contests,* and *in learning* about golf.

The sentence tells us three things in which Jane and Jim took part. All three are objects of the preposition *in.* They serve the same purpose, yet the form of one of them is different.

Jane and Jim took part
in baseball *games*
in swimming *contests*
in *learning* about golf

Two are nouns; the third is a gerund (a verb used, in the *-ing* form, as a noun). To maintain parallel structure, the third must also be a noun.

Jane and Jim took part
in baseball *games*
in swimming *contests*
in *golf lessons*

Lessons is a noun. The structure of the items in the sentence is now parallel.

CORRECT:

Jane and Jim took part *in* baseball *games, in* swimming *contests,* and *in* golf *lessons.*

PRACTICE

1. Ben took courses in computers, in mathematics, and in learning about fine arts.
2. Jesse couldn't decide on a career in education, in business, or becoming a doctor.

ANSWERS

1. Ben took courses in computers, in mathematics, and in fine arts.
2. Jesse couldn't decide on a career in education, in business, or in medicine.

Here is another type of error in parallel structure.

WRONG:

The backers failed to realize *the success of the show* or *how long it would run.*

Two things were realized: both are objects of the infinitive *to realize.* Yet one is a noun, *success;* the other a noun clause, *how long it would run.* Since both fill the same purpose in the sentence, they should have the same form. Either both should be nouns or both should be noun clauses. You may correct this sentence in either of two ways to achieve parallel structure.

CORRECT:

The backers failed to realize the *success* of the show or the *length* of its run. [Two nouns]

The backers failed to realize *how successful the show would be* or *how long it would run.* [Two noun clauses]

PRACTICE

1. Jane needed financial support and being encouraged.
2. Arnold was not aware of his strength or how good-looking he was.
3. The movie was entertaining and it instructed us as well.

Answers

1. Jane needed financial support and encouragement.
2. Arnold was not aware of how strong or how good-looking he was.
3. The movie was entertaining and instructive.

Here is another type of error in parallel structure.

Note: Certain pairs of words in the English language are called correlatives. They connect parts of a sentence which are equal in importance—*parallel elements*. You are familiar with a number of them:

both...and
either...or
neither...nor
not only...but also
whether...or

Remember to use these *immediately before* the parallel element each accompanies.

A few examples will make this point clear.

WRONG:
Chiquita was *both* asked to work the switchboard *and* to address envelopes.

Note that only one of the correlatives, *and*, precedes an infinitive, *to address*. Both correlatives should precede the infinitives, *to work* and *to address*.

Chiquita was asked *both* to work
and to address

CORRECT:
Chiquita was asked *both* to work the switchboard *and* to address envelopes.

Here is another example.

WRONG:
The basketball star *not only* was popular *but also* modest.

The basketball star was
not only popular
but also modest

CORRECT:
The basketball star was *not only* popular *but also* modest.

Practice

1. Carmen was interested neither in sports nor in books.
2. He was not only smart but also handsome.

Answers

1. Correct.
2. Correct.

If you want to remember the idea behind parallel structure, here are two examples—one simple, one profound.

Something *old*
Something *new*
Something *borrowed*
Something *blue*

Note that *Something* is followed by four different adjectives.

Finally, here is a splendid example from Abraham Lincoln's Second Inaugural Address. (The parallel elements are underlined.) "With malice toward none, with charity for all, with firmness in the right as God gives us to see the right, let us finish the work we are in, to bind up the nation's wounds, to care for him who shall have borne the battle and for his widow and his orphan, to do all which may achieve and cherish a just and a lasting peace among ourselves and with all nations."

Practice with Parallel Structure

Beneath each sentence you will find five ways of writing the underlined part. Choose the answer that makes the best sentence. Answer 1 is always the same as the underlined part and is sometimes the right answer. These are included in the sentence correction type of multiple-choice item.

1. To strive for perfection, to serve one's fellow man, to help the needy are ideals all should try to follow.

   (1) To strive for perfection, to serve one's fellow man, to help

(2) To strive for perfection, serving one's fellow man, helping
(3) Striving for perfection, serving one's fellow man, and to help
(4) Striving for perfection, to serve one's fellow man, helping
(5) To strive for perfection. To serve one's fellow man. To help

2. Jones, the president of the union and who is also a member of the community group, will be in charge of the negotiations.

(1) who is also a member of the community group,
(2) since he is a member of the community group
(3) a member of the community group
(4) also being a member of the community group
(5) , in addition, who is a member of the community group

3. Marie is good-looking, with intelligence, and has youth.

(1) with intelligence, and has youth
(2) intelligent, and has youth
(3) intelligent, and is youthful
(4) , with intelligence, and youthful
(5) intelligent, and youthful

4. The instructor told the student to hold the club lightly, keeping his eye on the ball and drawing the club back quickly, but too much force should not be used on the downward stroke.

(1) to hold the club lightly, keeping his eye on the ball and drawing the club back quickly, but too much force should not be used
(2) to hold the club lightly, keep his eye on the ball, and drawing the club back quickly, and too much force should not be used
(3) to hold the club lightly, keep his eye on the ball, draw the club back quickly and not use too much force
(4) to hold the club lightly, keep his eye on the ball, draw the club back quickly and too much force should not be used
(5) he should hold the club lightly, keeping his eye on the ball, drawing the club back quickly, and not using too much force

5. He is rude, gruff, and doesn't think of the feelings of others or of showing consideration to others.

(1) and doesn't think of the feelings of others or of showing consideration to
(2) and doesn't think of or show consideration to
(3) thoughtless, and inconsiderate of
(4) thoughtless of others and of showing consideration to
(5) thoughtless of others' feelings, and lacking in consideration to

Answer Key

1\. 1 2. 3 3. 5 4. 3 5. 3

WHAT'S YOUR SCORE?

_______ right,	_______ wrong
Excellent	5
Good	4
Fair	3

If you scored lower, review this section and study the examples of correct parallel structure.

Answer Analysis

1\. 1 No error.

2\. 3 The nouns in apposition must be parallel to one another. "Jones, the *president*...and a *member*...."

3\. 5 This is a case of parallel structure involving three adjectives.

4\. 3 Four infinitives in parallel form are much clearer than the mixture of an infinitive (*to hold*), two participles (*keeping* and *drawing*), and a clause (*too much force should not be used*).

5\. 3 Parallel structure requires the use of four adjectives (*rude, gruff, thoughtless,* and *inconsiderate*) instead of two adjectives (*rude, gruff*) and two phrases (*of the feelings..., of showing...*) following the unnecessary verb *doesn't think*.

Misplaced Modifiers

A modifier is a word or a group of words that help describe another word or group of words by giving a more exact meaning. The modifier may be an adjective (a *big* house) or an adverb (walk *slowly*), an adjective clause (the man *who came to dinner*) or an adjective phrase (Jeanie *with the light brown hair*), an adverbial clause (he arrived *when the clock struck twelve*) or an adverbial phrase (he arrived *on time*). Very often, confusion in meaning takes place when a modifier is used incorrectly.

A modifier that is misplaced in a sentence may cause confusion in meaning.

EXAMPLE

WRONG:
Fred cut himself while shaving *badly*.

The word *badly* is a misplaced modifier. It is an adverb that modifies the meaning of the verb *cut* and, therefore, should be placed where there is no doubt about what it modifies. (It certainly isn't intended to modify *shaving*.)

CORRECT:
Fred cut himself *badly* while shaving.

The meaning is completely changed by the placement of the modifier. Now the sentence means what the writer intended to say.

EXAMPLE

WRONG:
The fire was put out before any damage was done *by the firefighters*.

The phrase *by the firefighters* is a misplaced modifier. It is an adverbial phrase that modifies the verb *put out* and, therefore, should be placed near the verb it modifies. The writer certainly did not mean to say that the firefighters did any damage, yet this is the message conveyed. Once again, the misplaced modifier completely confuses the meaning.

CORRECT:
The fire was put out *by the firefighters* before any damage was done.

EXAMPLE

WRONG:
What do you think of Bill Clinton *as a foreign diplomat*?

The adjective phrase *as a foreign diplomat* is obviously not intended to modify Bill Clinton, who cannot possibly be one. It should be placed near the word it modifies, *you*.

CORRECT:
As a foreign diplomat, what do you think of Bill Clinton?

What do you, *as a foreign diplomat*, think of Bill Clinton?

By now, you may have figured out the rule that will save you from misplacing modifiers. *Always place the modifier, be it a word or a group of words, as near as possible to the word it modifies* so that the reader will not be in any doubt about the meaning of the sentence.

Here's a humorous example of a misplaced modifier to help you remember the rule.

WRONG:
They were *almost* married for five years.

To save the couple from gossip, you must place the modifier, *almost*, near the word it modifies, *five*.

CORRECT:
They were married for *almost* five years.

PRACTICE

1. Julia almost won all the prizes that were awarded.
2. The girl was dancing with her boyfriend in the red dress.
3. What do you think of Shakespeare as an English teacher?

ANSWERS

1. Julia won almost all the prizes that were awarded.
2. The girl in the red dress was dancing with her boyfriend.
3. As an English teacher, what do you think of Shakespeare?

DANGLING MODIFIERS

In the preceding examples, the modifier was misplaced. It should have been placed clearly and unmistakably near the word or words it modified. At least, though, there was a word in the sentence with which the modifier belonged. In the case of the *dangling modifier,* the problem is that there is no word or words to which the modifier clearly refers.

Here are some examples.

EXAMPLE 1

WRONG:

Standing on the corner, *the car* passed me by.

It is important to note that merely turning the incorrect sentence around will not keep the modifier from dangling.

WRONG:

The car passed me by, *standing* on the corner.

The sentence has to be rewritten to read:

CORRECT:

While I was *standing* on the corner, the car passed me by.

Standing is now part of the verb in the subordinate clause and is no longer dangling.

EXAMPLE 2

WRONG:

Speeding down the track at ninety miles an hour, *the stalled car* was demolished by the train.

The stalled car obviously can't be speeding. The dangling modifier, *speeding*, can refer only to the train. This is an easy one to correct.

CORRECT:

Speeding down the track at ninety miles an hour, *the train* demolished the stalled car.

EXAMPLE 3

WRONG:

At ten, my parents took me on a trip to California.

The phrase *at ten* is dangling since it does not have a noun it clearly modifies. Who was ten? Surely not the parents. The phrase has to be converted into a clause to correct the error.

CORRECT:

When I was ten, my parents took me on a trip to California.

HOW CAN DANGLING MODIFIERS BE AVOIDED?

Dangling modifiers can be avoided by following an introductory phrase immediately with the word it modifies. Note that the dangling modifier need not be a particular grammatical form. It can be

—a prepositional phrase
—an infinitive phrase
—a gerund phrase
—a participial phrase
—a clause

Note the following examples.

EXAMPLE 4 (Infinitive phrase)

WRONG:

To get good grades, *lessons* must be prepared carefully.

CORRECT:

To get good grades, *you* must prepare your lessons carefully.

EXAMPLE 5 (Gerund phrase)

WRONG:

After graduating from school, my father got me a good job.

CORRECT:

After I was graduated from school, my father got me a good job.

EXAMPLE 6 (Participial phrase)

WRONG:

Watching the baseball game, the frankfurters tasted delicious.

CORRECT:

Watching the baseball game, I ate delicious frankfurters.

EXAMPLE 7 (Clause)

WRONG:

His leg was injured *while playing* tennis.

CORRECT:

He injured his leg *while playing* tennis.

EXAMPLE 8 (A humorous one)

WRONG:

Walking around in the zoo, my eye was caught by the gorilla.

Did you ever see an eye walking?

CORRECT:

As *I* was *walking around in the zoo,* the gorilla caught my eye.

PRACTICE

1. Sightseeing in Washington, D.C., the White House was my first stop.
2. Struggling in the water, the lifeguard saw me.
3. To earn an equivalency diploma, the GED test must be passed.

ANSWERS

1. When I was sightseeing in Washington, D.C., the White House was my first stop.
2. The lifeguard saw me while I was struggling in the water.
3. To earn an equivalency diploma, you must pass the GED test.

Now we come to the case of the modifier that can modify, not one, but two words or phrases.

Here's an example.

EXAMPLE 1

WRONG:

Does a man live here with a wife and a child *named Johnny?*

Who is named Johnny, the man or the child? The sentence is unclear as it stands. If the man is named Johnny, then this is how the question should have been written.

CORRECT:

Does a man *named Johnny* live here with a wife and a child?

If, however the child is named Johnny, the sentence has to be changed to put *Johnny* in apposition with *child,* thus making them equivalent.

CORRECT:

Does a man live here with a wife and a child, *Johnny?*

Here are some other two-way modifiers.

EXAMPLE 2

WRONG:

Plans for withdrawing troops *gradually* were drawn up by the government.

There are two possible meanings here: that the troops will be withdrawn gradually *or* that the plans were drawn up gradually. The writer probably meant:

CORRECT:

Plans for the gradual withdrawal of troops were drawn up by the government.

EXAMPLE 3

WRONG:

Because we studied hard *for a week* we were ready for the examination.

Did we study hard for a week, or were we ready for the examination for a week? It is not clear from the sentence what the writer intended. A comma, put in the right place, will help get rid of the two-way modifier.

CORRECT:

Because we studied hard for a week, we were ready for the examination.

PRACTICE

1. Because we had no classes for a week we were on vacation.
2. After I passed the GED test with the help of the teacher I got a job.
3. Hopes for recovering from the operation quickly were dashed by the doctor.

Answers

1. Because we had no classes, for a week we were on vacation.
   or
   Because we had no classes for a week, we were on vacation.
2. After I passed the GED test, with the help of the teacher I got a job.
   or
   After I passed the GED test with the help of the teacher, I got a job.
3. Hopes for recovering quickly from the operation were dashed by the doctor.
   or
   Hopes for recovering from the operation were quickly dashed by the doctor.

Practice with Modifiers

Beneath each sentence you will find five ways of writing the underlined part. Choose the answer that makes the best sentence. Answer 1 is always the same as the underlined part and is sometimes the right answer.

1. Turning the corner, my eye caught sight of the house where I used to live.
   (1) Turning
   (2) After turning
   (3) Having turned
   (4) When turning
   (5) When I turned

2. The horse, ridden by the experienced jockey with the broken leg, had to be destroyed.
   (1) horse, ridden by the experienced jockey with the broken leg, had
   (2) horse ridden by the experienced jockey with the broken leg had
   (3) horse with the broken leg ridden by the experienced jockey had
   (4) horse with the broken leg ridden by the experienced jockey, had
   (5) horse with the broken leg, ridden by the experienced jockey, had

3. The interviewee was asked, "What is your opinion of Elizabeth Taylor as a movie critic?"
   (1) asked, "What is your opinion of Elizabeth Taylor as a movie critic?"
   (2) asked his opinion of Elizabeth Taylor as a movie critic.
   (3) asked "What his opinion was of Elizabeth Taylor as a movie critic?"
   (4) asked, "As a movie critic, what is your opinion of Elizabeth Taylor?"
   (5) asked as a movie critic "What is your opinion of Elizabeth Taylor?"

4. Wagging its tail, the dog food was quickly consumed by the happy puppy.
   (1) Wagging its tail, the dog food was quickly consumed by the happy puppy.
   (2) Wagging it's tail, the dog food was quickly consumed by the happy puppy.
   (3) The happy puppy quickly consumed the dog food wagging its tail.
   (4) Wagging its tail, the happy puppy quickly consumed the dog food.
   (5) The dog food was quickly consumed by the happy puppy wagging it's tail.

5. At the age of ten, my parents took me to Disneyland.
   (1) At the age of ten, my parents took me
   (2) At the age of ten my parents took me
   (3) My parents took me at the age of ten
   (4) My parents took me aged ten
   (5) At the age of ten, I was taken by my parents

6. The secretary located the picture of Gerald Ford looking through the files.
   (1) The secretary located the picture of Gerald Ford looking through the files.
   (2) The secretary located Gerald Ford's picture looking through the files.
   (3) Looking through the files, Gerald Ford's picture was located by the secretary.
   (4) Looking through the files, the secretary located the picture of Gerald Ford.
   (5) Looking through the files the picture of Gerald Ford was located by the secretary.

7. The Smiths were almost married ten years before they had their first child.
   (1) were almost married
   (2) were married almost
   (3) almost were married
   (4) had been almost married
   (5) had been married almost

8. We finally agreed on a price for the picture of the ship that hung in the balcony.
   (1) picture of the ship that hung
   (2) picture of the ship that was hung
   (3) picture of the ship that hanged
   (4) ship's picture that hung
   (5) ship's picture that hanged

9. Our guest let us know that he would be arriving next week in his last letter.
   (1) that he would be arriving next week in his last letter
   (2) that he was arriving next week in his last letter
   (3) that he will arrive next week in his last letter
   (4) in his last letter that he would be arriving next week
   (5) in his last letter that he was arriving next week

10. My mother lives in the house on the hill that she just bought.
   (1) house on the hill that she just bought
   (2) house on the hill she just bought
   (3) house she just bought on the hill
   (4) house on the hill which she just bought
   (5) house, she just bought, on the hill

ANSWER KEY

1. **5**	3. **4**	5. **5**	7. **5**	9. **4**
2. **5**	4. **4**	6. **4**	8. **4**	10. **3**

WHAT'S YOUR SCORE?

_______ right, _______ wrong

Excellent	9–10
Good	8
Fair	7

If you scored lower, review the corrected examples in this section

ANSWER ANALYSIS

1. **5** The way the sentence reads with the dangling modifier, the *eye* is *turning the corner.*
2. **5** *With the broken leg* is a misplaced modifier. Also see Rule 8 under "The Comma" (page 145). In this sentence, commas are required to set off the phrase *ridden...jockey*.
3. **4** Again there is a misplaced modifier. *Movie critic* should be placed near the word it modifies—*interviewee.*
4. **4** The dangling modifier gives the impression that the *dog food was wagging its tail.* The possessive pronoun *its* does not have an apostrophe.
5. **5** The dangling modifier, *At the age of ten,* erroneously modifies *parents.*
6. **4** The dangling modifier *looking through the files* gives the mistaken impression that *the picture* was doing the looking.

7. 5 The modifier, *almost*, is misplaced. It should be near *ten years*, which it modifies. Also see "Misplaced Modifiers" (page 110). The past perfect tense, *had been married*, is needed because the years of marriage in the past *preceded* the birth of the child, also in the past.
8. 4 The modifier, *that hung in the balcony*, should be near the noun, *picture*, which it modifies. See "Misplaced Modifiers" (page 110). The past tense of *hang* (an object) is *hung*.
9. 4 The misplaced modifier, *in his last letter*, gives the mistaken impression that the guest would be arriving *in* the letter. The phrase should be near *know*, which it modifies.
10. 3 *She just bought* modifies *house* and should be placed next to it.

Writing Correct Sentences

Poorly constructed or awkward sentences are often confusing because they fail to finish what they start.

EXAMPLE

WRONG:

A depression is *x* when there is widespread unemployment, falling prices and wages, and a lessening of business activity.

The reader expects to find out *what* a depression is, not *when*. The sentence is incomplete because a word is missing (technically, a predicate nominative) that is the equivalent of the subject *depression*. Why is an equivalent necessary? Because the verb *is* requires it. Words are omitted where the *x* appears.

CORRECT:

A *depression* is an economic *condition* characterized by widespread unemployment, falling prices and wages, and a lessening of business activity.

Another example of an awkward sentence that results from an illogical complement (predicate) is the following:

EXAMPLE

WRONG:

The most unusual food I ever ate was when I had a dish of enchiladas.

Again the sentence requires a word that is the equivalent of the word *food*, and the reader expects that word to follow immediately after the verb *was*.

CORRECT:

The most unusual *food* I ever ate was *enchiladas*.

Here are some additional awkward sentences.

EXAMPLE

WRONG:

The main reason I quit my job is *x* the work was long and uninteresting.

In this sentence, the subject *reason* has been made equal to the complement *work* when clearly the two are not equivalent. There is an incompleteness at the point indicated by the *x*. The reason for quitting is really the long and uninteresting work. One way to correct this sentence is to make the whole complement the reason.

CORRECT:

The main *reason* I quit my job is *that the work was long and uninteresting.*

EXAMPLE

WRONG:

I was successful in business is the reason I left school.

In this sentence, the same error is made but this time the omission is at the start of the sentence.

CORRECT:

The fact that I was successful in business is the *reason* I left school.

EXAMPLE

WRONG:

Before I was graduated from school, everything I learned about life was studying books.

This sentence is somewhat different. Here, the subject *everything* is equated with *studying books*. Logically, though, everything that was learned was not *studying books* but the information that was contained in the books.

There are a number of ways to correct this error. Here are two.

CORRECT:

Before I was graduated from school, everything I learned about life I learned from the books I studied.

Before I was graduated from school, everything I learned about life was learned from the books I studied.

To avoid these kinds of awkwardness, always be certain that the statement about the subject of the sentence is completed. If a subject is said to be something, that something should be indicated.

PRACTICE

1. An error is when the fielder doesn't handle the ball properly.
2. Because I didn't study hard, I passed the test.

ANSWERS

1. An error is made when the fielder doesn't handle the ball properly.
2. Although I didn't study hard, I passed the test.

Poorly written sentences result when necessary words are omitted

Let us look at some omissions that take place when comparisons are made.

1. *Omission of* ***than*** *or* ***as*** *in a comparison.*

EXAMPLE

WRONG:

Deborah is as bright *x* if not brighter than her sister.

If the words *if not brighter than* are temporarily removed from the sentence, the sentence reads "Deborah is as bright... *x* her sister," clearly a sentence that makes no sense. If *as* is added at the point indicated, however, the sentence makes sense.

CORRECT:

Deborah is as bright as, if not brighter than, her sister.

OR BETTER STILL

Deborah is as bright as her sister, if not brighter.

2. *Omission of one part of the comparison.*

EXAMPLE

WRONG:

I like Mary better than *x* Suzy *x*.

This omission causes a confusion in meaning. Do you mean that you prefer Mary to Suzy? Or do you mean that you like Mary more than Suzy likes her?

CORRECT:

I like Mary better than I like Suzy. (First *x*)

OR

CORRECT:

I like Mary better than Suzy does. (Second *x*)

3. *Omission of the part of the comparison to which another person or object is being compared.*

EXAMPLE

WRONG:

The Yankees played better baseball last year *x*.

Better than who? You must indicate what the Yankees are being compared to. A possible correction is:

CORRECT:

The Yankees played better baseball last year than any other team in the American League.

4. *Omission of* ***other*** *after* ***than*** *or* ***as*** *in comparing two things or groups of things in the same category.*

In the correct sentence above dealing with the Yankees, notice the inclusion of the word *other*. If *other* is omitted, the meaning is changed.

EXAMPLE

WRONG:

The Yankees played better baseball last year than any team in the American League.

Since the Yankees *are* in the American League, this sentence indicates that the Yankees played better baseball than themselves!

5. *Omission of words that prevent a false or impossible comparison.*

EXAMPLE

WRONG:

According to Ray, the legal profession is better than a doctor.

You cannot compare a profession with a person. You can only compare a profession with a profession, or a person with a person.

CORRECT:

According to Ray, the legal profession is better than the medical profession.

According to Ray, being a lawyer is better than being a doctor.

Other kinds of omissions do not involve comparisons.

1. *Omission of a noun necessary to complete the meaning of the sentence.*

EXAMPLE

WRONG:

Some people consider him one of the best *x*, if not the best athlete, in the world.

One of the best athlete or athletes? Clearly something is missing. You must supply the suitable noun after the first "best."

CORRECT:

Some people consider him one of the best *athletes*, if not the best athlete, in the world.

2. *Omission of a preposition necessary to complete the meaning of the sentence.*

EXAMPLE

WRONG:

Americans should show their faith *x* and loyalty to the democratic way of life.

As the sentence reads, the noun *faith* is followed by the preposition *to*, a preposition with which it does not belong. One has faith *in* something. The sentence should read:

CORRECT:

Americans should show their faith *in* and loyalty *to* the democratic way of life.

3. *Omission of part of a verb necessary to complete the meaning of a sentence.*

EXAMPLE

WRONG:

We always have *x* and always will try to do our best.

Two ideas are contained in the sentence, but one of them is indicated incompletely.

We always *have tried* to do our best.

We always *will try* to do our best.

You will notice that *will* is properly followed by *try* but *have* is followed by nothing in the incorrect sentence. The word *tried*, the past participle, must be added.

CORRECT:

We always *have tried* and always *will try* to do our best.

Here's another example.

EXAMPLE

WRONG:

As children, we were happy and *x* brought up strictly.

The word *were* should be added before *brought* because the first *were* is a verb in itself and the word *brought* is only part of the verb *were brought*.

CORRECT:

As children, we *were* happy and *were* brought up strictly.

4. *Omission of other parts of speech necessary to complete the meaning of the sentence.*

EXAMPLE

WRONG:

He asked both the secretary and *x* treasurer to stand.

As written, the secretary and treasurer is one person. If they are actually two people, as the word *both* implies, the article the must be repeated.

CORRECT:

He asked both the secretary and *the* treasurer to stand.

Poorly written sentences result when you needlessly shift the construction of your sentences or your point of view. This happens in a number of ways.

1. *The subject may be unnecessarily shifted when the writer moves from the main clause to a coordinate or subordinate clause.*

EXAMPLE

WRONG:

Jim was a loyal friend, but self-discipline was lacking in him.

In this sentence, the subject of the main clause is Jim. For some reason, the writer chose to shift to another subject in the coordinate clause although it was not necessary to do so.

CORRECT:

Jim was a loyal friend, but he lacked self-discipline.

EXAMPLE

WRONG:

We traveled in Israel, where archeological sites interested us.

Here, again, there is an unnecessary shift, this time from the subject of the main clause to the subject of the subordinate clause.

CORRECT:

We traveled in Israel, where we were interested in archeological sites.

2. *The verb may be shifted unnecessarily from the active to the passive voice, from the imperative mood to the indicative mood, or from one tense to another.*

EXAMPLE

WRONG:

Alice enjoyed the movies, and television was also enjoyed by her.

Wherever possible, the active verb should be used in preference to the passive because it expresses an idea more effectively. Having correctly started with an active verb, it is simply illogical to shift to the passive voice. In the first sentence, Alice *enjoyed* movies actively in the main clause, but then television was *enjoyed* (the passive verb) in the coordinate clause.

CORRECT:

Alice enjoyed movies and also television.

EXAMPLE

WRONG:

First do the required homework, and then you should try to do the optional assignment.

In this sentence, the imperative mood (command) *do* is used in the main clause, but then there is a shift to the indicative mood (statement) *you should try*. Actually, the words *you should* are unnecessary and both parts of the sentence will be in the imperative if they are dropped.

CORRECT:

First do the require homework, and then try to do the optional assignment.

EXAMPLE

WRONG:

When her son did not return for hours after the agreed-on time, the mother begins to get worried and then she called the police.

In this sentence, the mother *begins* to worry (present tense) and then she *called* the police (past tense). If you are telling what happened, you must use tense consistently.

CORRECT:

..., the mother *began* to worry and then she *called* the police.

Another shift in verb tense is shown in this sentence.

EXAMPLE

WRONG:

I told my fiancée I will call for her at six.

Here the tenses for direct and indirect conversation are being confused. There is a shift from *told* to *will*.

CORRECT:

I told my fiancée I would call for her at six.

I told my fiancée, "I will call for you at six."

Sometimes indirect and direct conversation are mixed.

EXAMPLE

WRONG:

Frank asked whether I knew Lola and will she come to the party.

To correct this shift, use either indirect or direct discourse throughout.

CORRECT:

Frank asked whether I knew Lola and whether she would come to the party. [Indirect conversation is used in both clauses.]

Frank asked, "Do you know Lola? Will she come to the party?" [Direct conversation is used in both clauses.]

3. *The number and person of the pronoun may be shifted unnecessarily.*

EXAMPLE

WRONG:

If one wishes to succeed, they should work hard.

In this sentence, there is a shift in number from the singular pronoun *one* to the plural pronoun *they*. The number of the pronoun should be kept consistent.

CORRECT:

If *one* wishes to succeed, *one* should work hard.

OR

If *they* wish to succeed, *they* should work hard.

4 Usage

Agreement

SUBJECT AND VERB

A common error is failure to provide agreement between subject and verb. The basic rule is:

THE VERB MUST AGREE WITH ITS SUBJECT IN *NUMBER* AND IN *PERSON*.

Number

1. If the subject is *singular* (there is only one person or thing spoken about), the verb must be *singular*.
2. If the subject is *plural* (there is more than one person or thing spoken about), the verb must be *plural*.

Person

The verb must agree with the subject in *person.*

EXAMPLE

Singular	
I study	–First Person
You study	–Second Person
He / She / It } studies	–Third Person
Plural	
We study	–First Person
You study	–Second Person
They study	–Third Person

(See the "Glossary of Usage" (page 136) for a complete definition of *person.*)

There are two difficulties to overcome.

1. ***What is the subject?***

Ask yourself, "What is spoken about?" Ordinarily, you should have no trouble. Sometimes, however, the *subject and the verb are separated* by a number of intervening words.

EXAMPLE

Joe, despite the fact that he was a newcomer, *was* elected president.
[*Joe* is still the subject—singular.]

The intervening words may contain a plural.

EXAMPLE

Joe, together with all his friends, *was* welcomed warmly.
[*Joe* is still the subject—singular.]

2. ***Is the subject singular or plural?***

EXAMPLE

A *box* of chocolates *is* on the table.
[*Box*, the subject, is singular.]

Most of the time, *pronouns* will be involved in this type of error. Some pronouns that can cause confusion are:

Singular Pronouns		**Singular or Plural Pronouns**
anybody	neither	any
anyone	nobody	all
each	no one	more
either	one	most
everybody	somebody	none
everyone	someone	some

However, *compound subjects* may also be involved. When a subject has more than one part and the parts are connected by *and* or by a word or groups of words similar in meaning to *and*, it is considered a *compound subject* and is plural. A compound subject can consist of more than one group of words, more than one phrase, or more than one clause.

EXAMPLES

Joe *and* his friend *are* here.

To study hard, to play hard, to enjoy life are desirable aims.

Her outstanding contribution to school athletics, her service as class officer, and her excellent scholastic record qualify her for the position of president.

EXCEPTION

A compound subject that consists of two singular subjects connected by *either...or*, or *neither...nor* is considered a singular subject.

EXAMPLE

Neither Joe nor his friend *is* here.

> **NOTE:**
>
> Agreement is always with the number of the part of the subject nearest the verb.
>
> **EXAMPLE**
>
> Neither Joe nor I *am* voting for Frank.

Sometimes the subject comes after the verb. It is still the subject and may be singular or plural.

EXAMPLE

Pasted in the upper right-hand corner of the envelope were two ten-cent stamps.

[*Stamps* is the subject, even though it is the last word in the sentence. The verb is plural because the subject, *stamps,* is plural.]

SOME SPECIAL PROBLEMS

1. Agreement of subject and certain irregular verbs

The addition of the negative contraction *n't*, should not result in an error you would not make if the *n't* were omitted.

EXAMPLE

WRONG:
It don't matter.

CORRECT:
It doesn't matter.

You would never say, "It do matter." You would say, "It does matter."

Sometimes the reversal of subject and verb in a question causes an error that would not be made in a declarative sentence.

EXAMPLE

WRONG:
Was you there?

CORRECT:
Were you there?

2. Use of singular or plural after *there* at the opening of a sentence

The use of *is* or *are* depends on the *noun or pronoun that follows* the verb.

EXAMPLE

WRONG:
There's many ways to show you care.

CORRECT:
There are many ways to show you care.

3. Subjects that are plural in form but singular in meaning

The mere fact that a noun ends in *s* doesn't make it plural.

> **NOUNS WITH SINGULAR MEANINGS**
>
> economics, mathematics, measles, mumps, news, physics

4. Subjects that are singular in form but plural in meaning

Despite what you might think, these subjects take a *singular* verb when the group involved is thought of as a single unit.

NOUNS WITH PLURAL MEANINGS

army	group
class	orchestra
club	team
crowd	

EXAMPLE

The crowd *was* dispersed by the police.

PRACTICE

1. Economics is my most difficult subject.
2. The group of students are gathering at the office.
3. Neither Jules nor I are coming to the meeting.
4. There's a great many problems to be solved.
5. The teacher, together with her students, are going to the theater.

ANSWERS

1. Correct.
2. The group of students is gathering at the office.
3. Neither Jules nor I am coming to the meeting.
4. There are a great many problems to be solved.
5. The teacher, together with her students, is going to the theater.

PRONOUN AND ANTECEDENT

Another common error is failure to provide agreement between a pronoun and the noun it is replacing, its *antecedent*. The basic rule is:

A PRONOUN MUST AGREE WITH ITS ANTECEDENT IN *NUMBER, GENDER,* AND *PERSON.*

Number

If the antecedent is singular, the pronoun replacing it is singular.

EXAMPLE

Joe does *his* homework.
[The pronoun *his* takes the place of Joe. *Joe* is singular (one person); therefore, the pronoun is singular]

Gender

If the antecedent is masculine, the pronoun replacing it is masculine. If the antecedent is feminine, the pronoun replacing it is feminine.

EXAMPLE

Susan does *her* homework.

Person

Note above that both *Joe* and *Susan* are in the third person. Therefore, the pronouns replacing each must be in the third person—*his, her*.

How do you find the antecedent? Sometimes it is not easy to determine what noun the pronoun is replacing. The *antecedent may be separated from the pronoun* that takes its place by a number of words or by a phrase.

EXAMPLES

Joe is a *boy* who does *his* work.
[*boy*—antecedent; *his*—pronoun]

One of the boys who walked to school was late to *his* class.
[*one*—antecedent; *his*—pronoun]

The same procedure should be used to *determine the number of the pronoun when it replaces a compound subject.*

EXAMPLE

Joe and his *friend* brought *their* books.

When *either...or* or *neither...nor* connects singular subjects, the pronoun is singular.

EXAMPLE

Neither Joe *nor* his friend brought *his* book.

However, a pronoun that refers to a singular and a plural antecedent connected by *or* or *nor* agrees in number with the closer antecedent.

EXAMPLE

Either Kathy *or* the boys should explain *their* reasons.

SOME SPECIAL PROBLEMS

1. Pronouns that appear to be plural but are, in fact, singular

Some pronouns appear to refer to more than one person, but they never refer to more than one person *at a time*. Others may be either singular or plural.

Singular Pronouns		Singular or Plural Pronouns
anybody	neither	any
anyone	nobody	all
each	no one	more
either	one	most
everybody	somebody	none
everyone	someone	some

The following sentence may sound a little strange to you, but it is correct.

EXAMPLE

Every student must do *his* homework every day.

2. Pronouns that refer to nouns that appear to be plural but are singular in form

These pronouns require a verb in the singular.

EXAMPLE

The team continued *its* winning streak.

3. Pronouns with indefinite antecedents

The antecedent must be clear or the sentence rephrased.

EXAMPLE

WRONG:

Frank told Joe to take *his* books to school.

[To whom does *his* refer—to Frank or to Joe? The sentence must be rewritten to clear up this confusion.]

CORRECT:

Frank told Joe to take Frank's books to school for him.

OR BETTER

Frank said to Joe: "Take my books to school for me."

PRACTICE

1. Will everyone who has the right answer raise their hands?
2. Every participant must do his best.
3. The mother told her daughter to take her laundry to the laundromat.
4. One of my friends who went to school with me lost his mother.
5. Either the workers or the foreman are expected to attend.

ANSWERS

1. Will everyone who has the right answer raise his hand?
2. Correct.
3. The mother told her daughter, "Take my laundry to the laundromat."
4. Correct.
5. Either the workers or the foreman is expected to attend.

PRACTICE IN AGREEMENT

In each sentence, five parts are underlined and numbered. Where there is an error in agreement, choose the number of the underlined part that contains the error. If there is no error, choose answer 5. No sentence contains more than one error. These are included in the sentence correction type of multiple-choice item.

1. Luis, accompanied by his (1) friend are (2) waiting to see whether you and I (3) are (4) joining them. No error (5)

2. There (1), Mr. Chairman, is (2) all the reports that the committee prepared in its (3) work as well as the notes that (4) were taken. No error (5)

3. There's (1) several ways for the city to solve its (2) fiscal problems, but one (3) of them is not to lose its (4) integrity. No error (5)

4. News from abroad is (1) that each country is supporting its (2) own policies despite the fact that ours (3) are (4) superior to theirs. No error (5)

5. Let everyone who agrees (1) raise his (2) hand so that neither George nor I am (3) in doubt about what the majority opinion is. (4) No error (5)

6. Margaret asked Rosa to take her (1) clothes to the cleaners and to make certain that none (2) of them (3) were (4) in need of repair. No error (5)

7. Watching our (1) game were (2) Fred and his father and his mother, together with their (3) other children and their (4) neighbors. No error (5)

8. Each (1) American must ask himself (2): "Don't (3) it matter if we pollute our (4) environment?" No error (5)

9. "Neither I (1) nor they (2) are (3) attending the game," we said to its (4) promoter. No error (5)

10. Everyone (1) gave her (2) opinion that a blue and white suit was (3) the best choice for Liz to wear although there were (4) exceptions. No error (5)

Answer Key

1. **2**	3. **1**	5. **5**	7. **5**	9. **5**
2. **2**	4. **5**	6. **1**	8. **3**	10. **5**

WHAT'S YOUR SCORE?

_______right,	_______wrong
Excellent	9–10
Good	8
Fair	7

If you scored lower, restudy this section, concentrating on the rules and examples.

Answer Analysis

1. **2** Luis, the subject of the sentence, is singular, so the verb should be singular: *is* instead of *are*.
2. **2** The subject of the sentence, *reports*, follows the verb. Since the subject is plural, the verb should be plural: *are*, not *is*.
3. **1** The subject is *ways*, which follows the verb. The verb must be plural to agree with the plural subject. *There's* should be *There are*.
4. **5** No error.
5. **5** No error.
6. **1** The antecedent of *her* is not clear. Is it Margaret or Rosa? Depending on the answer, *her* should be changed to *Margaret's* or *Rosa's*.
7. **5** No error.
8. **3** The correct form of the third person singular of the verb *do* is *does*. *Doesn't it*...is correct.
9. **5** No error.
10. **5** No error.

Case of Nouns and Pronouns

NOUNS

In English, the form of a noun rarely changes because of its case (its relation to other words in the sentence). Only in the *possessive case* do the forms of most nouns change.

Nominative Case

EXAMPLE

Frank hit Joe.
[*Frank* is the subject.]

Objective Case

EXAMPLES

Joe hit *Frank*.
[*Frank* is the object.]

Ellen ate the *salad*.
[*Salad* is the object.]

Possessive Case

EXAMPLE

Cesar's friend went away.
[A noun requires an apostrophe to indicate possession.]

PRONOUNS

Nearly all pronouns have different forms in the nominative, objective, and possessive cases. Only the pronoun forms *you* and *it* do NOT change when the case changes from *nominative* to *objective* or vice versa.

Nominative Case (for subjects)	Possessive Case	Objective Case (for objects)
I	my, mine	me
you	your, yours	you
he	his	him
she	her, hers	her
it	its	it
we	our, ours	us
they	their, theirs	them
who	whose	whom
whoever	–	whomever

BASIC RULES FOR THE CASE OF PRONOUNS

Nominative

1. The subject of a verb (a noun or a pronoun) is in the nominative case. This is true whether the subject is singular or compound.

   EXAMPLE

   WRONG: Me and Frank are good friends.
   CORRECT: Frank and *I* are good friends.

2. A predicate pronoun, whether singular or plural, is in the nominative case.

   EXAMPLES

   They thought that the visitor was *he*.

   Frank and Joe knocked on the door. "It is *they*," Sue said.

3. Pronouns in apposition with nouns in the nominative case are also in the nominative case.

   EXAMPLE

   The two *contestants, she* and *I*, were tied for first place.

Objective

4. The object of a verb (a noun or pronoun) is in the objective case. This is true whether the object is singular or compound.

   EXAMPLE

   They applauded *him* and *her*.

   Did they face Frank and *us* in the contest?

5. The object of a proposition is in the objective case. This is true whether the object is singular or compound.

   EXAMPLES

   Everyone but *her* did the homework.

   Between *you* and *me*, Sue is my best friend.

6. Pronouns in apposition with nouns in the objective case are also in the objective case.

   EXAMPLES

   They gave the prizes to the *winners, her and me.*

   For *us amateurs*, it is fun to watch professionals perform.

7. The subject of an infinitive is in the objective case; the same is true for the object of an infinitive.

   EXAMPLES

   We asked *him* to go.

   We wanted him to ask *them* to come along.

Possessive

8. Pronouns in the possessive case, unlike nouns in the possessive case, *never* have an apostrophe.

   EXAMPLES

   The dog wagged *its* tail.

   We have met the enemy and they are *ours*.

   She has *hers;* they have *theirs*.

SOME SPECIAL PROBLEMS

1. The case of pronouns coming after a comparison involving *than* or *as*

EXAMPLE

Joe received more votes than *I*.

The problem of deciding the case, and therefore the form, of the pronoun is complicated by the fact that the verb following *I* is understood.

Joe received more votes than I (did).

This is, therefore, a special instance of Rule 1 (page 125): The subject of a verb is in the nominative case. This rule is true even if the verb is understood.

2. The case of the relative pronoun *who* or *whom*

Determine whether the relative pronoun is the subject or the object in its clause, and don't be fooled by words that come between the subject and the verb.

EXAMPLES

Who do you think *was elected* president?
[*Who* is the subject of *was elected* and is therefore in the nominative case.]

Whom did you invite to the party?
[*Whom* is the object of *did invite* and is therefore in the objective case.]

The same rule applies to *whoever* and *whomever*.

EXAMPLES

Give the book to *whoever asks* for it.
[*Whoever* is the subject of *asks* and is in the nominative case.]

He impressed *whomever he approached.*
[*Whomever* is the object of *approached* and is in the objective case.]

3. The case of pronouns (or nouns) coming before verbs ending in *-ing* and used as nouns

EXAMPLE

I do not object to *his* going with me.

Going is a verb form ending in *-ing* and used as a noun—object of the preposition *to*. The possessive case, *his*, must be used. This is a fine point, but it often appears on tests.

Here are several more examples:

EXAMPLES

Fatigue was the cause of *Frank's* falling asleep at the wheel.

My going to school daily helped my work.

The television program interfered with *Sue's* and *Joe's* doing their homework.

4. The case of shift in pronoun reference

Unnecessary shift in pronoun reference is another common error. This involves pronouns that refer to the same person in the same sentence.

EXAMPLE

WRONG:

If *one* has a good sense of humor, *you* will probably be popular.

CORRECT:

If *one* has a good sense of humor, *one* will probably be popular.

If *you* have a good sense of humor, *you* will probably be popular.

Remember to be consistent in your use of pronouns. Do not shift from a pronoun in one person (*one* is in the third person) to another pronoun in another person (*you* is in the second person) unless the two pronouns refer to different people.

PRACTICE

1. Dolores was prettier than her.
2. Juana didn't like us asking her all those questions.
3. Who can you trust with your money these days?
4. Whoever thought of this idea is a genius.
5. Who do you feel deserves the prize?
6. When one works hard, he feels he deserves a raise.

ANSWERS

1. Dolores was prettier than she.
2. Juana didn't like our asking her all those questions.

3. Whom can you trust with your money these days?
4. Correct.
5. Correct.
6. When one works hard, one feels one deserves a raise.

Practice with Nouns and Pronouns

In each sentence, five parts are underlined and numbered. Where there is an error in case, choose the number of the underlined part that contains the error. If there is no error, choose answer 5. No sentence contains more than one error.

1. If I (1) were she (2), I would not exchange hers (3) for mine (4). No error (5)

2. Whom (1), do you think, should be asked to send his (3) regrets to them (4) and me (5)? No error (5)

3. It is they (1) whom (2) we invited, not him (3) and her (4). No error (5)

4. She (1) and I (2) decided to give ours (3) to whoever (4) we pleased. No error (5)

5. They (1) and I (2) gave the prize to the winners, him (3) and her (4). No error (5)

6. The winners, he (1) and she (2), were welcomed to the society by us (3) and them (4). No error (5)

7. Did Joe and him (1) meet John and her (2) in the finals when they eliminated their (3) opponents and ours (4)? No error (5)

8. Between you (1) and I (2), it's (3) their problem, not ours (4). No error (5)

9. Whose (1) going to get more votes than I, he (3) or she (4)? No error (5)

10. For us (1) newcomers, his (2) going upset us (3), me (4) particularly. No error (5)

Answer Key

1. **5**	3. **5**	5. **5**	7. **1**	9. **1**
2. **1**	4. **4**	6. **5**	8. **2**	10. **5**

WHAT'S YOUR SCORE?

______right,	______wrong
Excellent	9–10
Good	8
Fair	7

If you scored lower, restudy this section, concentrating on the rules and examples.

Answer Analysis

1. **5** No error.
2. **1** The relative pronoun that begins the sentence is the subject of *should be asked* and should therefore be in the nominative case, *who.*
3. **5** No error.
4. **4** This word is the object of the preposition *to*, so it should be in the objective case. *Whomever* is correct.
5. **5** No error.
6. **5** No error.
7. **1** This word is part of the subject and should be in the nominative case. *He* is correct.

8. **2** *Me* is correct since the objective case is required for the object of the preposition *between.*
9. **1** A subject and verb are required, not a possessive pronoun. *Who's* (or *who is*) is correct.
10. **5** No error.

Verbs

The *verb*, the part of the sentence that indicates the action carried out by the subject, *also indicates* when the action was carried out. It does so by its tense.

TENSE

The most widely used tenses are the

present,
past, and
future.

Two additional tenses, less frequently used, sometimes cause difficulty. These are the

present perfect and
past perfect.

Both of the perfect tenses require the use of a helping verb (*have, had*) and the past participle of the verb.

Verb: *to live*	
Present tense:	live
Past tense:	lived
Future tense:	shall live
Present perfect tense:	have lived
Past perfect tense:	had lived

Examples of the use of tense:

Note the way in which the rest of each sentence is affected.

Present tense:	I *live* in New York *now.*
Past tense:	I *lived* in New York *last year.*
Future tense:	I *shall live* in New York *next year.*
Present perfect tense:	I *have lived* in New York for *five years.*

VERB FORMS

The principal parts of *to live, to see, to do,* and *to lie* are:

Verb	Past	Past Participle
live	lived	lived
see	saw	seen
do	did	done
lie	lay	lain

Many of the difficulties you have with verbs involve the *irregular verbs.* These change form in either the past or the past participle or in both. The most frequent error is the use of the wrong part of the verb, most often the past participle for the simple past.

EXAMPLES

WRONG:
I seen him do it.

CORRECT:
I *saw* him do it.

WRONG:
I done it.

CORRECT:
I *did* it.

Note: The present perfect tense is formed with *have* plus the past participle; the past perfect tense is formed with *had* plus the past participle.

EXAMPLE

I *had seen* enough; I was glad to leave.

Study the following lists of most frequently confused verbs.

FREQUENTLY USED IRREGULAR VERBS

Verb	Past Tense	Present Perfect Tense
be	I was	I have been
beat	I beat	I have beaten
become	I became	I have become
begin	I began	I have begun
bite	I bit	I have bitten
blow	I blew	I have blown
break	I broke	I have broken
bring	I brought	I have brought
buy	I bought	I have bought
catch	I caught	I have caught
choose	I chose	I have chosen
come	I came	I have come
dig	I dug	I have dug
do	I did	I have done
draw	I drew	I have drawn
drink	I drank	I have drunk
eat	I ate	I have eaten
fall	I fell	I have fallen
fly	I flew	I have flown
freeze	I froze	I have frozen
get	I got	I have got *or* gotten
give	I gave	I have given
go	I went	I have gone
grow	I grew	I have grown
have	I had	I have had
know	I knew	I have known
lay	I laid (place)	I have laid
lead	I led	I have led
lie	I lay (recline)	I have lain
lose	I lost	I have lost
make	I made	I have made
ride	I rode	I have ridden
ring	I rang	I have rung
rise	I rose	I have risen
run	I ran	I have run
say	I said	I have said
see	I saw	I have seen
shake	I shook	I have shaken
sink	I sank	I have sunk
speak	I spoke	I have spoken
swim	I swam	I have swum
swing	I swung	I have swung
take	I took	I have taken
teach	I taught	I have taught
tear	I tore	I have torn
think	I thought	I have thought
throw	I threw	I have thrown
win	I won	I have won
write	I wrote	I have written

50 OTHER IRREGULAR VERBS

Verb	Past Tense	Present Perfect Tense
arise	I arose	I have arisen
awake	I awaked *or* awoke	I have awaked *or* awoke
bear	I bore	I have borne *or* born
bend	I bent	I have bent
bind	I bound	I have bound
build	I built	I have built
creep	I crept	I have crept
deal	I dealt	I have dealt
dive	I dived, dove	I have dived
drive	I drove	I have driven
drown	I drowned	I have drowned
feed	I fed	I have fed
feel	I felt	I have felt
fight	I fought	I have fought
find	I found	I have found
flee	I fled	I have fled
forget	I forgot	I have forgotten
forgive	I forgave	I have forgiven
hang (an object)	I hung	I have hung
hang (a person)	I hanged	I have hanged
hide	I hid	I have hidden
hold	I held	I have held
kneel	I knelt	I have knelt
leave	I left	I have left
lend	I lent	I have lent
meet	I met	I have met
mistake	I mistook	I have mistaken
pay	I paid	I have paid
prove	I proved	I have proved *or* proven
seek	I sought	I have sought
sell	I sold	I have sold
send	I sent	I have sent
sew	I sewed	I have sewed *or* sewn
shine	I shone	I have shone
shrink	I shrank	I have shrunk
sing	I sang	I have sung
slay	I slew	I have slain
slide	I slid	I have slid
sleep	I slept	I have slept
spend	I spent	I have spent
spring	I sprang	I have sprung
steal	I stole	I have stolen
strike	I struck	I have struck
swear	I swore	I have sworn
sweep	I swept	I have swept
swing	I swung	I have swung
wake	I waked *or* awoke	I have waked *or* woken
wear	I wore	I have worn
weep	I wept	I have wept
wind	I wound	I have wound

Practice

1. They begun to improve after much practice.
2. Aaron brung the book I needed to school.
3. My friends had drunk all the lemonade at the party.
4. The valise that had lain out in the rain was soaked.
5. The batter swang the bat at the wild pitch.
6. The hostess had laid out the cookies beautifully on the table.
7. The oarsman almost drownded when the winds blew up.
8. The choir sung all the songs on the program.
9. The sun shined all day.
10. The guest awoked before I did.

Answers

1. They began to improve after much practice.
2. Aaron brought the book I needed to school.
3. Correct.
4. Correct.
5. The batter swung the bat at the wild pitch.
6. Correct.
7. The oarsman almost drowned when the winds blew up.
8. The choir sang all the songs on the program.
9. The sun shone all day.
10. The guest awoke before I did.

A SPECIAL PROBLEM

The irregular verbs you have just studied present difficulties when used in simple sentences. Even more difficult are complex sentences (see the "Glossary of Usage" on page 136). In these sentences, you have to figure out the time (or tense) relationship between the verbs in the two clauses.

What is the proper sequence of tenses for verbs in the main and dependent clauses of a complex sentence?

This can vary, but some common sequences follow.

VERB SEQUENCES

Main Clause	Dependent Clause
Present tense: I *gain* weight	**Present tense:** when I *eat* too much.
Present tense: I *believe*	**Past tense:** that he *studied* for the examination.
Past tense: The audience *applauded*	**Past tense:** when the soloist *finished.*
Past tense: I *played* my first concert	**Past perfect tense:** after I *had studied* piano for three years.
Note: The action of the dependent clause (the studying) took place *before* the action in the main clause.	
Future tense: I *shall leave*	**Present tense:** when he *comes*.

Practice

1. After Patrick attended high school for four years, he earned a diploma.
2. If my father was here, he'd be proud of me.

Answers

1. After Patrick had attended high school for four years, he earned a diploma.
2. If my father were here, he'd be proud of me.

Practice with Verbs

In each sentence, five parts are underlined and numbered. Choose the number of the underlined part that contains the error. If there is no error, choose answer 5. No sentence contains more than one error.

1. He was suppose (1) to lay (2) the book on the table after he had brought (3) it home from the man from whom he had taken (4) it. No error (5)

2. After the pitcher had thrown (1) a fast ball, the batter swung (2) the bat and hit (3) the ball to left field, where it was caught (4). No error (5)

3. The child awoke (1) when the parent brung (2) the gift he had chosen (3) and gotten (4) into the bedroom. No error (5)

4. After he drunk (1) his milk, the athlete dived (2) into the pool and swam (3) ten laps more than he had said (4) he would. No error (5)

5. I lay (1) in bed dreaming of the places I had seen, (2) the friends I had not forgotten, (3) and the new friends I had met (4). No error (5)

6. After I had wrote (1) her that I wanted it done, (2) Rita hung (3) the picture that had lain (4) on the floor. No error (5)

7. The entertainer sung (1) the song I had sung (1) when you saw (2) me, and I was shaken (4) by the coincidence. No error (5)

8. He would have drownded, (1) had I not bent (2) the board which pinned him down and then broken (3) it with the tool I had found. (4) No error (5)

9. I arose; (1) I sprang (2) after the mugger; I struck (3) him; I threw (4) him to the ground. No error (5)

10. The suspect admitted: "I done (1) it. I crept (2) into the apartment. I fought (3) with the man. I tore (4) his clothes." No error (5)

Answer Key

1.	**1**	3.	**2**	5.	**5**	7.	**1**	9.	**5**
2.	**5**	4.	**1**	6.	**1**	8.	**1**	10.	**1**

WHAT'S YOUR SCORE?

______right,	______wrong
Excellent	9–10
Good	8
Fair	7

If you scored lower, restudy this section, concentrating on the rules and examples.

ANSWER ANALYSIS

1. **1** The past participle of *suppose* is *supposed.*
2. **5** No error.
3. **2** The past tense of *bring* is *brought.*
4. **1** The past tense of *drink* is *drank.*
5. **5** No error.
6. **1** The past participle of *write* is *written.*
7. **1** The past tense of *sing* is *sang.*
8. **1** The past participle of *drown* is *drowned.*
9. **5** No error.
10. **1** The past tense of *do* is *did.*

Adjectives and Adverbs

An ***adjective*** *is used to describe a noun or pronoun.*

EXAMPLE

He wore a *dark* hat.

An ***adverb*** *is used to modify a verb, an adjective, or another adverb.*

EXAMPLE

He played *very poorly.*
[*Poorly* modifies *played; very* modifies *poorly.*]

There are times, however, when adjectives and adverbs may be confused. This confusion can be caused by

Use of a verb that describes a condition, not an action

If the verb is not used as an action verb, or if the verb describes a condition, then an *adjective rather than an adverb* must follow it. Why? The reason is that the adjective really modifies the subject and not the verb.

VERBS THAT DESCRIBE A CONDITION

look	be
feel	am
taste	is
seem	are
become	was
smell	were
grow	has been
sound	had been

EXAMPLES

He looks *sick.*
[*Sick* describes *he.*]
I feel *good.*
[Good describes *I.*]
The fruit tastes *sweet.*
[*Sweet* describes *fruit.*]

Adjectives or adverbs that have the same form

ADJECTIVES AND ADVERBS WITH THE SAME FORM

fast	long
slow	ill
deep	sharp

EXAMPLES

He worked very *fast.*

He cut *deep* into the skin.

SOME SPECIAL PROBLEMS

1. Adjectives that indicate the degree to which they describe nouns

Degree is indicated in one of two ways:

- the adverb *more* or *most* is placed before the adjective;
- The suffix *-er* or *-est* is added to the adjective.

EXAMPLES

He was *more quiet* than she.

He was *quieter* than she.

He was the *most friendly* person there.

He was the *friendliest* person there.

What is the problem? It is that you must use the *more* or *-er* form when two and only two persons or things are involved. Similarly, you must use the *most* or *-est* form when three or more persons or things are involved. Never use *both* in the same sentence.

EXAMPLES

He was the *shyer* of the two.

He was the *most shy* among the three of them.

NOTE:

Some irregular adjectives do not follow these rules. The most frequently used are:

	Comparative (Comparison between two people or things)	***Superlative (Comparison among more than two people or things)***
bad	worse	worst
far	farther	farthest
good	better	best
many, much	more	most

2. Incorrect use of a negative adverb and a negative adjective in the same sentence

EXAMPLE

WRONG:

He does*n't* do *no* work.
[A negative adverb—*n't [not]* and a negative adjective—*no*]

CORRECT:

He doesn't do *any* work.

PRACTICE

1. The orchestra sounded superb.
2. Alfredo waited long for his reward.
3. Enrique was the noisiest student in the class.
4. Of the three children, the youngest was the worst.

ANSWERS

1. Correct.
2. Correct.
3. Correct.
4. Correct.

PRACTICE WITH ADJECTIVES AND ADVERBS

In each sentence, five parts are underlined and numbered. Choose the number of the underlined part that contains the error. If there is no error, choose answer space 5. <u>No sentence contains more than one error.</u>

1. Hardly <u>hadn't</u> (1) he <u>quietly</u> (2) and <u>painfully</u> (3) built the sand castle than it was <u>swiftly</u> (4) torn down. <u>No error</u> (5)

2. Although I feel <u>good</u> (1), I look <u>sick</u> (2) because I ate <u>sparingly</u> (3) and <u>improperly</u> (4). <u>No error</u> (5)

3. <u>Gladly</u> (1) I'll say that he <u>surely</u> (2) hit the ball <u>real</u> (3) <u>well</u> (4). <u>No error</u> (5)

4. Anita was the most (1) intelligent (2) girl although she didn't dress well (3) or act properly. (4) No error (5)

5. The lunch, which was lovingly (1) and carefully (2) prepared, tastes deliciously (3) and is healthful. (4) No error (5)

6. He worked fast; (1) I worked slow. (2) He rested frequently; (3) I worked continuously. (4) No error (5)

7. It doesn't seem right (1) that some flowers that look ugly (2) smell sweet (3) while others that look pretty smell bad. (4) No error (5)

8. Doesn't Chico succeed just as good (1) as Carlos though he isn't as hard-working, (2) serious, (3) and conscientious? (4) No error (5)

9. The worse (1) of the two storms ended as quickly (2) and suddenly (3) as it had begun, leaving us ill (4) with fear. No error (5)

10. He spoke deliberately (1) and chose his words carefully, (2) with the result that his speech cut deep (3) and he was the more (4) effective of the two speakers. No error (5)

Answer Key

1. **1**	3. **3**	5. **3**	7. **5**	9. **5**
2. **5**	4. **5**	6. **5**	8. **1**	10. **5**

WHAT'S YOUR SCORE?

______right,	______wrong
Excellent	9–10
Good	8
Fair	7

If you scored lower, restudy this section, concentrating on the rules and examples.

Answer Analysis

1. **1** To avoid a double negative, the correct word is *had.*
2. **5** No error.
3. **3** The word modifies the adverb *well,* so it should be an adverb—*really.*
4. **5** No error.
5. **3** The verb *tastes* requires a predicate adjective. *Delicious* is correct.
6. **5** No error.
7. **5** No error.
8. **1** This word modifies the verb *Does(n't) succeed,* so an adverb, *well,* is required.
9. **5** No error.
10. **5** No error.

Glossary of Usage

ACTIVE VERB Verb whose subject is the doer of the action that the verb is indicating. (The batter *hit* the ball.)

ADJECTIVE Part of speech that helps describe a noun or pronoun by giving it a more exact meaning. (*big* house; *many* friends; *this* pencil)

ADVERB Part of speech that helps describe a verb, an adjective, or another adverb by giving it a more exact meaning. (walks *slowly; very* pretty)

AGREEMENT This refers to parts of a sentence that are alike in gender, number, and person such as a subject and its verb and a pronoun and its antecedent. (*I study. He studies.* The *dog* wagged *its* tail.)

ANTECEDENT Noun that is replaced with a pronoun. (*EVERYONE* will please remove *his* hat. *WALKING* is *what* I like to do most.)

ANTONYM Word that is opposite in meaning to another word. (happy, sad)

APPOSITION Condition describing two nouns, next to each other in a sentence, that are equivalent in meaning. (my brother, Joe; Mrs. Brown, the secretary)

AUXILIARY VERB Verb that helps another word show voice or tense. (I *would have* forgotten. She *had* left.)

CASE Form of a noun or pronoun that shows its relation to the other words in a sentence.

Nominative case of pronouns has the forms *I, you, he, she, we, they, who,* and is used as the subject of a verb or as a predicate noun. (*They* go. It is *we.*)

Possessive case shows possession. In nouns, it is formed with the apostrophe: (Frank's). Possessive pronouns include *mine, yours, his, hers, its, ours, theirs, whose.* (*Note:* There is no apostrophe in any possessive pronoun.)

Objective case of pronouns has the forms *me, you, him, her, us, them, whom,* and is used as the object of a verb, object of a preposition, subject or object of an infinitive. (They hit *him*. They gave it to *him*. I want *him* to go. I want to hit *him*.)

CLAUSE Group of words in a sentence that contains a subject and a predicate.

Independent clauses can stand alone. (He played well.)

Dependent clauses (adverb, adjective, or noun clauses) cannot stand alone. (He played well *although he was hurt*. The book *that I read* was very interesting. *That he recovered* was a miracle.)

COMPARISON Change of form in adjectives and adverbs to show increase in amount or quality. (strong, strong*er*, strong*est*; good, bett*er*, be*st*)

Comparative refers to a greater degree in quality or quantity of one item or person with respect to another. (smart*er* of the two)

Superlative refers to a greater degree in the quality or quantity of one item or person with respect to two or more others. (larg*est* of the three)

COMPLEX SENTENCE Sentence that has one independent clause and at least one dependent clause. (We are happy *that you came.*)

COMPOUND-COMPLEX SENTENCE Sentence that has two independent clauses and at least one dependent clause. (*Joe sang* and *Joan played the song that she had been studying.*)

COMPOUND PREDICATE Two or more predicates usually joined by *and* or *or*. (He *goes to school by day* and *works at night.*)

COMPOUND SENTENCE Sentence that has two independent clauses. (*Joe sang* and *Joan played the piano.*)

COMPOUND SUBJECT Two or more subjects that take the same verb. (*Frank* and *I* will come.)

CONJUNCTION Part of speech that connects words, phrases, or clauses. (bread *and* butter; "to be *or* not to be"; She came *when* I left.)

CONSONANT Letter other than *a, e, i, o, u* (which are considered vowels) or *y* (which is considered a semivowel).

DASH Punctuation mark that shows a pause or break in a sentence. (He may not come—but why should I worry?)

DIRECT OBJECT Noun or pronoun that receives the action of the verb. (Jon struck *him*. Give *it* to Gerry.)

DIRECT QUOTATION Use of the exact words of the speaker. (The teacher said, "Do your homework.")

FIRST PERSON Pronoun and verb forms that refer to the person or persons speaking. (*I, we; my, our; me, us; am, are*)

FUTURE TENSE Time of verb that shows a happening yet to take place. (He *will retire* next year.)

GENDER Classification of nouns and pronouns into three groups: masculine, feminine, and neuter. A *masculine* pronoun is *he*; a *feminine* pronoun is *she*; a pronoun in the *neuter* gender is *it*.

GLOSSARY Listing of difficult or unusual words occurring in a book with their definitions. It is usually found in the back of the book. This glossary is at the end of the chapter to which it relates.

HOMONYM Word with the same sound as another word or words but with a different spelling and meaning. (to, too, two; pear, pair, pare)

HYPHEN Mark (-) used to form a compound adjective (two-faced), to join certain prefixes to words (ex-president) or to separate words into syllables (En-glish).

IDIOM Group of words that, taken together, differs in meaning from the individual words used separately. (once upon a time)

INDIRECT OBJECT Word that shows, without any preposition, to whom or for whom the action in the sentence is taking place. (He gave *me* a pen.)

INDIRECT QUOTATION Quotation that does not use the exact words of the speaker. (The candidate said [that] he would accept the nomination.)

INFINITIVE Verb form that is usually indicated by *to* before the verb. Sometimes *to* is understood. (I want *to go*. He made me *laugh.)*

INTERJECTION Independent word that expresses strong feeling. (ah!; oh!; alas!)

INTERROGATIVE SENTENCE Sentence that asks a question. (Did he leave?)

INTRANSITIVE VERB Verb that has no object. (He *stands*. I *sit.)*

MODIFIER Word or group of words that help describe another word or group of words by giving a more exact meaning. See ADJECTIVE, ADVERB.

NOMINATIVE CASE Form of the noun or pronound that is the subject or predicate noun in a sentence. *(She* is *president.)*

NOUN Part of speech that is the name of a person, place, or thing. (George Washington; New York; toy)

NUMBER Change in the form of a noun, pronoun, adjective, or verb to show whether there is one *(singular)* or more than one *(plural)* (man, men; he, they; this, these; is, are)

OBJECT Noun or pronoun that names the person or thing acted upon by the verb. (She brought the *book*. I admire *her*.)

OBJECTIVE CASE Form of the noun or pronoun that shows it is the person or thing that receives the action. (I hit *him*.)

OBJECT OF A PREPOSITION Noun or pronoun that follows a preposition that controls it. (with *me*; between *you* and *me*; among *him* and *them*)

PARALLELISM Two parts of a sentence that are given the same form, and therefore have the same importance, in the sentence. (He eats *both* meat *and* vegetables. *Not only* the relatives were invited *but also* the friends. Beth enjoys *jogging, skating*, and skiing.)

PARTICIPLE Form of a verb that is used both as an adjective and as part of a verb. (the *sleeping* child; am *going*; have *gone*)
present participle (going)
past participle (gone)

PART OF SPEECH One of eight categories into which words in a sentence are assigned: *noun, pronoun, verb, adjective, adverb, preposition, conjunction, interjection.*

PASSIVE Form of verb that is used when the subject of the sentence receives the action. (The watch *was given* to Joe. The man *was laid* to rest.)

PAST TENSE Time of verb that shows that an action has been completed. (He *went*. We *did go*.)

PERSON Form of pronoun or verb that tells whether the person (or persons) speaking is doing the action (*first person*); a person being spoken to is doing the action *(second person);* or the person spoken about is doing the action *(third person).* (*We* left for home. *You* stayed here. *They* arrived late.)

PHRASE Group of words without a subject and predicate, usually introduced by a preposition, that has a use in a sentence like that of a noun, adjective, or adverb. (*In the park* is where I like to sit. Jeannie *with the light brown hair.* He ran *to first base.)*

PLURAL Form of noun, pronoun, adjective, or verb that indicates that more than one person, place, or thing is being spoken about in the sentence. (boys; they; these; are)

POSSESSIVE Form of noun or pronoun that shows ownership. *(girl's* pencil; *ladies'* hats; *its* paw)

PREDICATE Part of the sentence that tells something about the subject (what the subject does, what is done to the subject, or what is true about the subject). (The boy *went home quickly.* This milk *tastes sour.*)

PREFIX Addition (usually a single syllable) to the beginning of a word that adds to or changes the meaning of the word. (*impossible*; *ex*-president; *re*view; *pre*fix)

PREPOSITION Part of speech that shows the relationship between a noun or pronoun that it controls (and which is its object) and some other word in the sentence. (Mary went *to* the library.)

PRESENT PERFECT TENSE Time of verb that shows an action that started in the past and is continuing or has just been completed in the present. It requires the use of an auxiliary verb in the present tense and the past participle. (He *has been* our friend for years.)

PRESENT TENSE Time of verb that shows an action that is going on now. There are three forms of this tense—he *says*, he *is saying*, he *does say*.

PRONOUN Part of speech that is used in place of a noun. (John came. *He* was welcome.) The four main kinds of pronouns are:
demonstrative (this, that, these, those);
personal (I, you, he, she, it, we, they);
possessive (mine, yours, his, hers, ours, theirs);
relative (that, what, who, which).

PROPER NOUN Noun that refers to an individual person, place, or thing. (George Washington; New York City; City Hall)

ROOT Basic part of a word, without prefixes or suffixes, that gives the main meaning of the word. (*cred*—believe; with prefix *in* and suffix *ible*—in *cred* ible—unbelievable)

RUN-ON (or COMMA SPLICE) SENTENCE Two sentences that are made into one by mistake. They are separated either by a comma or by no punctuation at all. (Wrong: Kay is class president, she is my friend. Correct: Kay is class president. She is my friend.)

SENTENCE Group of words containing a subject and a predicate and expressing an independently complete thought. (*He came early.*) Three chief kinds of sentences are:
declarative (makes a statement);
interrogative (asks a question);
imperative (gives a command).

SENTENCE FRAGMENT Group of words that may contain a subject and a predicate but that fails to express a complete thought and is, by error, punctuated as if it did. (Wrong: Hoping to hear from you. Correct: I am hoping to hear from you.)

SINGULAR Form of noun, pronoun, adjective, or verb that refers to one person, place, or thing in a sentence. (boy; he; this; is)

SUBJECT Part of the sentence that does the action or is spoken about. (*He* hit the ball. *The watch* was given to the man.)

SUFFIX Addition to the ending of a word that adds to or changes its meaning. (hand*ful*; quick*ly*; act*or*)

SYLLABLE Smallest group of sounds, consisting of a vowel sound, and one or more consonant sounds that are pronounced as a unit. (con-so-nant)

SYNONYM Word that is very similar in meaning to another word. (happy—glad)

TENSE Time of an action, indicated by the verb as *present, past, future, present perfect*, etc. These are the most widely used tenses in English.

USAGE Actual use of language by the people at large. *Good usage* is the actual use of language by educated persons and other persons in positions of importance.

VERB Part of speech that indicates the action carried out by the subject or that tells something about the subject. (He *hit* the ball. She *was* in the garden.)

VOWELS Letters representing the sounds *a, e, i, o, u*. The letter *y* is considered a semivowel, as in *slowly*.

5 Mechanics

Mechanics deals with capitalization, punctuation, and spelling.

Capitalization. Fifteen basic rules are provided with applications for each.

Punctuation. Basic rules and examples are given for each of the major punctuation marks: period, question mark, exclamation point, comma, semicolon, colon, apostrophe, parentheses and quotation marks.

Spelling. A total of 965 words has been broken down into three lists for you to study: "The Basic 100"; "200 Often Used Easy Words"; and "665 More Frequently Used Words," with the difficult parts underlined.

CAPITALIZATION

BASIC RULES OF CAPITALIZATION

1. Capitalize the first word of a sentence.

   EXAMPLE

   We went to the theater.

2. Capitalize the first word of a direct quotation.

   EXAMPLE

   He said, "Don't give up."

3. Capitalize the first word of a line of poetry.

   EXAMPLE

   "Poems are made by fools like me..."

4. Capitalize proper nouns (names of specific persons, places, or things).

   EXAMPLES

   Winston Churchill; Mr. James Jones; New York City; Main Street; City Hall

5. Capitalize proper adjectives (adjectives formed from proper nouns).

   EXAMPLES

   American; Shakespearean

6. Capitalize names of specific organizations or institutions.

EXAMPLES

Sousa Junior High School; Columbia University; American Red Cross; Federal Bureau of Investigation

7. Capitalize days of the week, months of the year, and holidays. (*Note:* Do *not* capitalize seasons, e.g., winter.)

EXAMPLES

Sunday; June; Thanksgiving

8. Capitalize languages. (*Note:* These are the *only* school subjects that are capitalized.)

EXAMPLES

French; Hebrew
I study English, Spanish, biology, mathematics, and social studies.

9. Capitalize races and religions.

EXAMPLES

Hindu; Christian

10. Capitalize references to the Deity and to the titles of holy books.

EXAMPLES

the Almighty; the Old Testament; the Koran

11. Capitalize titles of people when they are followed by a name, being careful to capitalize both the title and the name. (*Note:* If a specific person is meant, the name may, at times, be omitted.)

EXAMPLES

President Bill Clinton; Dr. Schweitzer; Her Majesty the Queen

12. Capitalize titles of works of literature, art, and music.

EXAMPLES

War and Peace (note that articles, short prepositions, and conjunctions such as *and* are not capitalized in titles); *American Gothic;* Beethoven's Fifth Symphony

13. The pronoun *I* is capitalized at all times.

EXAMPLES

I walked one mile south to the school.

14. Sections of the country are capitalized, but directions are not.

EXAMPLES

I lived in the South for five years.

We traveled south.

15. Capitalize specific places and addresses, but do not capitalize the second half of a hyphenated number.

EXAMPLE

Times Square; 25 Main Street; 65 West Thirty-third Street.

PRACTICE

1. Junior belongs to the Boy scouts.
2. My favorite subject in school is English.
3. New York City is about 250 miles south of Boston.
4. The bible is a holy book to millions.
5. Salt Lake city is in Utah.
6. My cousin shouted, "be careful!"
7. Donna's cat was named sandy.
8. My home is located near broadway.
9. Most inhabitants of Israel are jewish.
10. Labor day occurs in September.

ANSWERS

1. Junior belongs to the Boy Scouts.
2. Correct.
3. Correct.
4. The Bible is a holy book to millions.
5. Salt Lake City is in Utah.
6. My cousin shouted, "Be careful!"
7. Donna's cat was named Sandy.
8. My home is located near Broadway.
9. Most inhabitants of Israel are Jewish.
10. Labor Day occurs in September.

PRACTICE WITH CAPITALIZATION

The following sentences contain problems in capitalization. If there is an error, select the one underlined part that must be changed to make the sentence correct. If there is no error, choose answer 5. No sentence contains more than one error. These are included in the sentence correction type of multiple-choice item.

1. Peter Winkle of West Virginia (1), the last doubtful republican (2) name to be called on May (3) 16, was, like Ross (4), a "nobody." No error (5)

2. Most of our compound words beginning with Indian (1) can be traced to the white man's contact with these original Americans (2); thus we have Indian (3) summer, Indian (4) file and Indian giver. No error (5)

3. Her sons have used books in the way her father, the Hon. (1) John F. (2) Fitzgerald, mayor (3) of Boston, used Thanksgiving (4) turkeys as elaborate calling cards. No error (5)

4. As the 800-foot-long tanker *Houston* (1) passed beneath the Verrazano (2) Bridge (3), the captain (4) ordered its speed reduced. No error (5)

5. The English (1) teacher assigned the Poe (2) story "Murders (3) in The (4) Rue Morgue." No error (5)

6. He lived on Twenty- (1) First (2) Street (3), at the corner of Broadway (4). No error (5)

7. The Frick (1) Museum (2) is located East (3) of Central Park (4). No error (5)

8. He failed Chemistry (1) and French (2) but passed English (3) and Spanish (4). No error (5)

9. I attended Dawson (1) School (2) and Southern (3) University (4). No error (5)

10. Mr. (1) and Mrs. (2) Jones (3) and Family (4) invite you to a party at their home. No error (5)

Answer Key

1. **2**	3. **5**	5. **4**	7. **3**	9. **5**
2. **5**	4. **5**	6. **2**	8. **1**	10. **4**

Answer Analysis

1. **2** See Rule 6 on page 140. Capitalize names of specific organizations.
2. **5** No error.
3. **5** No error.
4. **5** No error.
5. **4** Unimportant words in the title of a literary work are not capitalized.
6. **2** In an address, the second part of a hyphenated number is not capitalized.
7. **3** Directions are not capitalized.
8. **1** Only languages, among school subjects, are capitalized.
9. **5** No error.
10. **4** This word refers to a general group and, therefore, is not capitalized.

WHAT'S YOUR SCORE?

______right,	______wrong
Excellent	9–10
Good	8
Fair	7

If you scored lower, restudy this section, concentrating on the rules and examples.

PUNCTUATION

BASIC RULES OF PUNCTUATION

***The Period** is used after*

1. a sentence that makes a statement;

   EXAMPLE

   He arrived on time.

2. a sentence that gives a command;

   EXAMPLE

   Sit up straight.

3. some abbreviations and contractions.

   EXAMPLES

   Mr., lb., A.M., etc.

***The Question Mark** is used after a sentence that asks a question.*

EXAMPLE

Did you like the game?

The Exclamation Point *is used after a sentence that emphasizes a command or that conveys strong feeling.*

EXAMPLES

Stop writing immediately!

What a pleasant surprise!

The Comma *is*

1. used to separate a word or words that indicate the person to whom a remark is addressed;

   EXAMPLES

   John, please come here.

   You may come, little friend, if you like.

2. used to separate a word or words that are in apposition with a noun; that is, add information about the noun;

   EXAMPLE

   Nancy, my secretary and receptionist, is very efficient.

3. used to set off expressions or phrases that are inserted in the sentence and that interrupt the normal word order.

   EXAMPLES

   Notre Dame, in my opinion, will win the championship.

   Joan, on the other hand, disagrees with us.

   Note: The next two rules (4 and 5) do not apply to short introductory phrases and clauses and short independent clauses.

4. used after introductory phrases and clauses, particularly when they are long or when the meaning may be temporarily confused if the comma is omitted;

   EXAMPLES

   When the dog jumped up, Darryl's parents became frightened.

   After a long but exciting trip through the Alps, Amy returned tired but happy.

   Springing into action, the police caught the bandit.

5. used to separate independent clauses of a compound sentence joined by a conjunction such as *and, but, for, nor, or, so,* or *yet;*

   EXAMPLE

   Joe decided to attend the game, but I remained at home.

   but

   Joe returned but I remained.

6. used to separate items in a series

   EXAMPLES

   The box contained books, toys, games, and tools.

   Jason, Meghan, and Sarah are going to the office today.
   [If the comma is omitted after "Meghan," it might seem that Jason was being told that Meghan and Sarah were going to the office]

   For breakfast he had juice, ham and eggs, and coffee.

7. used before the text of a quotation; in a divided quotation, commas are used to set off the speaker.

EXAMPLES

The teacher said, "Return to your seats."
"Return to your seats," said the teacher, "so we may continue the lesson."

8. used to set off clauses and phrases that are not essential to the meaning of the sentence. *(No commas are needed if the clause or phrase is essential to the meaning intended by the speaker or writer.)*

EXAMPLE

Jan, who was seated beside me, left early.
[Note that the clause "who was seated beside me" is not essential to the sentence, which, without it, would read, "Jan left early."]

but

The students who studied hard passed the test.
[The clause "who studied hard" is essential since only the students who studied hard passed. Without this clause the meaning intended by the writer—that students who did not study hard failed—would not be clear to the reader]

The comma also has a number of uses that are the result of custom:

9. after the salutation in a friendly letter;

EXAMPLE

Dear Dad,

10. after the complimentary close in all letters;

EXAMPLE

Very truly yours,

11. between the day of the month and the year in writing a date;

EXAMPLE

May 24, 1919

12. between the city and the state in writing an address.

EXAMPLE

Brooklyn, New York 11201

Note: **Do NOT** use a comma

—between a subject and its verb when the verb immediately follows the subject;

EXAMPLE

The boys on the team celebrated their victory.

—to separate parts of a compound predicate.

EXAMPLE

They enjoyed a good dinner and saw a play.

PRACTICE

1. Invite Constance my sister to the dance.
2. What nonsense!
3. Eli, if you ask me, is the smartest of them all.
4. After Ruth rested at home she felt better.

ANSWERS

1. Invite Constance, my sister, to the dance.
2. Correct.
3. Correct.
4. After Ruth rested at home, she felt better.

BASIC RULES OF PUNCTUATION (CONTINUED)

***The Semicolon** is used to*

1. separate independent clauses in a sentence; either a semicolon or a comma may be used when the clauses are short;

   EXAMPLE

   I came; I saw; I conquered. (*or* I came, I saw, I conquered.)

2. separate items in a series when these items contain commas.

   EXAMPLE

   The guests included William H. Rehnquist, Chief Justice of the United States; Madeleine Albright, Secretary of State; and Newt Gingrich, Speaker of the House.

***The Colon** is used*

1. to introduce a series or a list of items;

   EXAMPLE

   These items were included on the shopping list: fruit, vegetables, meat, fish, and ice cream.

2. before a restatement, an illustration, or an explanation of the main idea of the sentence;

   EXAMPLE

   I have but one rule of conduct: do unto others as you would be done by.

3. after the salutation of a business letter.

   EXAMPLE

   Dear Sir:

***The Apostrophe** is used to*

1. indicate possession:
   a. In general, to make a singular noun possessive, add an apostrophe and *s* ('s) to words not ending in *s*.

   EXAMPLE

   boy's hat

   b. To make a plural noun possessive, add an apostrophe if the noun ends in *s*. If it does not end in *s*, add an apostrophe and *s*.

   EXAMPLES

   ladies' hats

   men's coats

2. indicate that one or more letters have been omitted in a contraction;

   EXAMPLE

   He didn't come.

3. indicate the plural of letters or numbers

EXAMPLE

There are 4 *s*'s in Mississippi

Note: Before adding the apostrophe to make the possessive, first form the plural of the noun;

EXAMPLE

child—children—children's

—Do *not* break up a word by using the apostrophe. The apostrophe can be added only at the end of a word.

EXAMPLE

WRONG:
ladie's hats

CORRECT:
ladies' hats

Parentheses *are used to enclose any words that explain or add to an idea or ideas contained in a sentence. Parentheses are always used in pairs (that is, one opens and the other closes the included word or words).*

EXAMPLE

Frank Jones (author of *Ideas that Work*) has written many best sellers.

Quotation Marks *are used to*

1. indicate the titles of works that are *part* of a book; (*Note:* The title of a whole book is underlined to indicate that the title should be italicized in print.)

EXAMPLES

I particularly enjoyed Chapter 3, "Your Pet as a Companion."

"Trees" is a poem by Joyce Kilmer.

2. set off a direct quotation of the speaker or the writer. (*Note:* Only the speaker's or writer's exact wording may be used.) Indirect quotations, quotations that do not use the exact words of the speaker or writer, do *not* require quotation marks.

EXAMPLES

Nathan Hale said: "I regret that I have but one life to give for my country."

The boy said that he would be late.

but

The boy said, "I will be late."

Note: In almost every case, the comma and the period are enclosed *within* the quotation marks.

PRACTICE

1. The childrens' clothing department was well stocked.
2. Your country expects only one thing from you citizens; do your duty.
3. Present at the meeting were General Smith, Army Chief of Staff: Admiral Jones, Chief of Naval Operations: and General Gray, Commanding General of the Marine Corps.
4. Maria indicated that she wouldnt come.
5. My parents warned me, "Dont be late".

ANSWERS

1. The children's clothing department was well stocked.
2. Your country expects only one thing from you citizens: do your duty.
3. Present at the meeting were General Smith, Army Chief of Staff; Admiral Jones, Chief of Naval Operations; and General Gray, Commanding General of the Marine Corps.
4. Maria indicated that she wouldn't come.
5. My parents warned me, "Don't be late."

PRACTICE WITH PUNCTUATION

The following sentences contain problems in punctuation. Choose the number of the underlined part that must be changed to make the sentence correct. No sentence contains more than one error. If there is no error, choose answer 5. These are included in the sentence correction type of multiple-choice item.

1. Consider, for example, the widespread
   (1) (2)
   notion that a clean environment can
   be obtained by reducing our
   dependence on_"technology". No error
   (3) (4) (5)

2. However, we often get careless; we
   (1) (2)
   say, "It's close enough, or "Who cares
   (3)
   anyway." No error
   (4) (5)

3. Gasoline and whisky have much in
   common; they're both blended, both
   (1) (2) (3)
   distilled—and both have something of
   (4)
   a kick. No error
   (5)

4. The object_therefore, is to clean up
   (1) (2)
   the air; the higher the vapor
   (3)
   pressure, the more likely it is that
   (3)
   gasoline will evaporate. No error
   (5)

5. At 6 PM tomorrow, however, they will
   (1) (2) (3)
   be fed into a 12-inch diameter
   pipeline, each entering at a different
   (4)
   point. No error
   (5)

6. Woodrow Wilson, when he was
   (1)
   president of the United States, said
   (2)
   that _he made the world safe for
   (3)
   democracy. No error
   (4) (5)

7. Mr. James Smith, President
   (1)
   The Line Company_
   (2)
   16 Fifth Street_
   (3)
   Lansing, Arizona 47962
   Dear Mr. Smith,
   (4)
   No error
   (5)

8. 1413 Sixth Street_
   (1)
   Columbus_Florida_
   (2) (3)
   March 5, 1984
   (4)
   No error
   (5)

9. "Are you coming?" he asked.
   (1)
   "Yes."
   (2)
   "When?"
   (3)
   "Now."
   (4)
   No error
   (5)

10. "You take care of your problems,"
    (1)
    said those to whom we addressed our
    questions, "and we'll take care of
    (2)(3)
    ours". No error
    (4) (5)

ANSWER KEY

1. 4	3. 5	5. 1	7. 4	9. 5
2. 4	4. 1	6. 3	8. 2	10. 4

WHAT'S YOUR SCORE?

______right,	______wrong
Excellent	9–10
Good	8
Fair	7

If you scored lower, restudy this section, concentrating on the rules and examples.

ANSWER ANALYSIS

1. 4 At the end of a sentence, the period should be placed between the quotation marks and the word (*technology.*").
2. 4 The question mark is used after a sentence that asks a question.
3. 5 No error.
4. 1 See Rule 3 under "The Comma" (page 144). The comma is used to set off expressions or phrases that are inserted in the sentence and that interrupt the normal word order.
5. 1 See Rule 3 under "The Period" (page 143). The period is used after most abbreviations.
6. 3 See Rule 2 under "Quotation Marks" (page 147). Indirect quotations do not require quotation marks.
7. 4 A colon is required after the salutation of a business letter.
8. 2 In an address, a comma is used between the city and the state.
9. 5 No error.
10. 4 The period should be enclosed within the quotation marks.

Spelling

Modern educational research has made the job of becoming a good speller a lot easier than it used to be. We now know which words are used most frequently in print. In fact, thorough mastery of the words on the following lists will enable you to spell correctly approximately *two thirds* of the words you use in writing.

THE BASIC 100

The first list contains 100 basic words that you should know thoroughly.

ache	grammar	since
again	guess	some
always	half	straight
among	having	sugar
answer	hear	sure
any	heard	tear
been	here	their
beginning	hoarse	there
believe	hour	they
blue	instead	though
break	just	through
built	knew	tired
business	know	tonight
busy	laid	too
buy	loose	trouble
can't	lose	truly
choose	making	Tuesday
color	many	two
coming	meant	used
cough	minute	very
could	much	wear
country	none	Wednesday
dear	often	week
doctor	once	where
does	piece	whether
done	raise	which
don't	read	whole
early	ready	women
easy	said	won't
enough	Saturday	would
every	says	write
February	seems	writing
forty	separate	
friend	shoes	

How do you go about studying this list? One way involves the following steps.

1. Fold a sheet of paper into three parts, holding the paper sideways.
2. Fold the left third of the paper over so that it covers the center part.
3. Look at the word, noticing the difficult spot or spots. Say it aloud carefully.
4. Look at the word again, spelling it aloud by syllables. We'll help you with the problem of dividing words into syllables later on.
5. Spell the word aloud by syllables again, without looking at it this time.
6. Look at the word a third time, copying the letters on the folded part of the paper while you say them aloud by syllables.
7. Turn the fold back, this time writing the letters on the right-hand third of the paper while you again say them aloud by syllables.
8. Fold the left third of the paper over again so that you can compare the word you originally copied with the word you wrote from memory. If it is spelled correctly, turn the fold back and write the word twice more on the central third of the paper being careful to spell the word aloud by syllables each time. If you made an error, the word will require more study, particularly of the letter or syllable you misspelled.
9. Master this list before turning to the next list. This second word list contains 200 words that are somewhat more difficult than the basic 100, but that are still rated "Easy" by those who test spelling ability. The letters or parts of the words that cause difficulty are underlined.

200 OFTEN USED EASY WORDS

absence
accept
accident
address
adjourn
advice
advise
airplane
allowed
almost
already
altogether
American
amount
annual
anxious
around
aroused
arrival
article
asked
athletic
attacked
attention
author

because
before
brakes
breathe

careful
carrying
certain
changing
chief
children
choice
chosen
climbed
cloth
clothes
cloud
coarse
collar
common
conceal
confident
conquer
corner
course
crowd
curtain
customer

decided
delivery
destroy
determine
device
dictator
didn't
different
dining
discussed
divided
doesn't
dropped
due
dying

earliest
easily
effect
eighth
eliminate
English
entirely
envelope
etc.
everybody
evidently
excellent
expense
experience
extremely

fatigue
formerly
forth
forward
fourteen
fourth
future

generally
genius
gentlemen
good-bye
guard

handful
handle
handsome
hasn't
height
hoping
hundred
hungry
hurrying

interesting
invitation
its
it's

jealous

ladies
later
latter
led
library
losing
lying

magazine
merely
minutes
movable

neither
nevertheless
nickel
niece
ninety
ninth

o'clock
officer
operate
owing

paid
partner
passed
past
perform
perhaps
permanent
planning
politics
possible
presence
probably
prominent
promptly
proved
purpose

quarter
quiet
quite
quizzes

realize
really
receipt
received
recognize
reference

safety
salary
sandwich
scarcely
secretary
sentence
shining
shriek
speech
stopped
stories
strength
stretched
strictly
striking
studying
succeed
success
summer
surely
surround

terrible
than
they're
thorough
those
threw
together
toward
tries
twelfth

until
unusual
useful

varied

wasn't
weather
weird
welfare
whose
wonderful
wouldn't
written

you're
yours

665 MORE FREQUENTLY USED WORDS

This list contains 665 additional words that occur frequently in print. Each appears on several well-known spelling lists of words often misspelled by high school students. Each appears regularly on examinations.

a lot
ability
absolutely
abundance
acceptable
accidentally
accommodate
accompanied
accomplish
accordance
accordingly
accumulation
accurately
accuse
accustomed
achievement
acknowledge
acquainted
acquired
across
actually
additional
adequate
advantageous
advertisement
advisable
aerial
affectionately
against
aggravate
aggressive
agreement
aisle
allege
all right
although
amateur
analysis
analyze
angel
angle
another
antiseptic
apologize
apparatus
apparently
appearance
appetite
application
apply
appreciation
approaching
appropriate
approval
approximately
arctic
arguing
argument
arrangements
artificial
ascend
ascertain
assistance
assistant
association
attaching
attempt
attendance
audience
August
automobile
autumn
auxiliary
available
avenue
aviator
awful
awkward

bachelor
balance
balloon
bargain
basic
beautiful
become
beggar
being
benefited
between
bicycle
board
bored
borrow
bottle
bottom
boundary
breadth
brilliant
Britain
building
bulletin
bureau
buried
bushes

cafeteria
calculator
calendar
campaign
candidate
capital
capitol
captain
career
careless
carriage
category
ceiling
celebrity
cemetery
cereal
changeable
chaos
character
charity
chocolate
cigarette
circumstances
citizen
coffee
collect
college
colonel
column
comedy
comfortable
commission
commitment
committed
committee
communication
community
company
comparative
compel
competent
competition
complement
completely
compliment
conceit
conceivable
concentration
conception
condition
conference
congratulate
connection
conscience
conscientious
conscious
consequently
considerable
consideration
consistency
consul
continually
continuously
controlled
convenience
conversation
coolly
corporal
correspondence
corroborate
council
counselor
courageous
courteous
courtesy
criticism
crucial
crystal
curiosity
cylinder

daily
daughter
daybreak
death
deceive
December
deception
decision
decisively
deed
definite
delicious
dependent
deposit
derelict
descend
descent
description
desert
desirable
despair
desperate
dessert
destruction
develop

development
died
difficulty
dilemma
dinner
direction
disappeared
disappointed
disapproval
disastrous
discipline
discover
discriminate
disease
disposition
dissatisfied
dissection
dissipate
distance
distinction
division
dollar
doubt
dozen
duly

earnest
ecstasy
education
efficiency
either
eligible
embarrass
embarrassment
emergency
eminent
emphasize
enclosure
encouraging
endeavor
enemies
engineer
enormous
entrance
environment
equipment
equipped
especially
essentially
evening
exaggeration
examination
exceedingly
except
exceptional
excitement
exercise

exhausted
exhilaration
existence
exorbitant
experiment
explanation
extension

facility
factory
familiar
fascinating
finally
financial
financier
flourish
forcibly
forehead
foreign
foresee
formal
fortunate
freight
frequent
frightening
fugitive
fundamental
further

gallon
gardener
government
governor
grateful
great
grievance
grocery
guarantee
guardian
guidance

hammer
handkerchief
happiness
harassed
healthy
heavy
heroes
heroine
hideous
himself
holiday
hopeless
hospital
humorous
hurriedly

identity
ignorance
imaginary
imbecile
imitation
immediately
immigrant
incidentally
increase
indefinitely
independence
indispensable
individual
inevitable
influence
influential
ingenious
initiate
innocence
inoculate
inquiry
insistent
instinct
integrity
intellectual
intelligence
intercede
interfere
interpreted
interrupt
irrelevant
irresistible
irritable
island
itself

January
jewelry
journal
judgment

kindergarten
kitchen
knock
knowledge

laboratory
language
laugh
legible
leisure
length
lesson
license
lieutenant
lightning
likelihood

likely
literal
literature
livelihood
loaf
loneliness
loveliness
loyalty

maintenance
maneuver
marriage
married
match
material
mathematics
meanness
measure
medicine
memorandum
merchandise
million
miniature
minimum
miracle
miscellaneous
mischievous
misspelled
mistake
momentous
monkey
monotonous
moral
morale
mortgage
mountain
mournful
murmur
muscle
mutual
mysterious

narrative
naturally
necessary
needle
negligence
neighbor
newspaper
newsstand
noticeable

obedient
oblige
obstacle
occasion
occurred

ocean
offer
omission
omitted
opinion
opportunity
optimistic
organization
origin
original
oscillate
ought
ounce
overcoat

pamphlet
panicky
parallel
particular
pastime
patience
peaceable
pear
peculiar
pencil
people
perceive
perception
perfectly
performance
period
perpendicular
perseverance
persistent
personally
personnel
persuading
pertain
physically
picture
plain
playwright
pleasant
pleasure
pocket
poison
population
portrayed
positive
possesses
possibility
post office
potatoes
practically
prairie
preceding
precise
predictable
preference
preferred
prejudice
preparations
prescription
president
prevalent
primitive
principal
principle
privilege
procedure
proceeded
produce
professional
professor
profitable
promise
pronunciation
propeller
prophecy
prophesy
prophet
prospect
psychology
pursuing

quality
quantity
quarreling

realistic
reason
rebellion
recede
recipe
recommend
recuperate
referee
referred
refugee
regretting
rehearsal
repeat
repetition
replying
representative
requirements
resemblance
reservoir
resistance
resources
respectability
response
responsibility
restaurant
rhyme
rhythm
ridiculous
right
role
roommate

sacrifice
satisfactory
scene
schedule
scientific
scissors
season
seize
seminar
sergeant
service
several
severely
shepherd
sheriff
shoulder
siege
sight
signal
significance
similar
sincerely
site
skiing
soldier
solemn
sophomore
soul
source
souvenir
special
specified
specimen
stationary
stationery
statue
stockings
stomach
strenuous
substantial
suddenness
sufficient
suggestion
superintendent
suppress
surprise
suspense
sweat
sweet
syllable
symmetrical
synonym

technical
telegram
telephone
temperament
temperature
temporary
tenant
tendency
tenement
therefore
title
tobacco
tomorrow
tongue
tragedy
transferred
treasury
tremendous
twelve
typical
tyranny

undoubtedly
United States
university
unnecessary
unusually

vacuum
valley
valuable
vegetable
vein
vengeance
versatile
vicinity
vicious
view
village
villain
visitor
voice
volume

waist
weak
weight
while
wholly
woman
wretched

yield

MOST FREQUENTLY MADE ERRORS

Over sixty percent of all spelling errors are caused by either leaving out a letter that belongs in a word or substituting one letter for another (usually because of incorrect pronunciation of the word).

An example of a word misspelled because of a letter left out is *recognize*. Many students mispronounce the word by leaving out the "g"; they also, therefore, leave out the "g" when they spell the word.

An example of a word misspelled because one letter is substituted for another is *congratulations*. Many students mispronounce the word by substituting the voiced "d" sound for the unvoiced "t" sound; they also, therefore, substitute a "d" for the "t" when they spell the word.

Other words that are misspelled because of the omission or substitution of letters are:

accidentally	library
arctic	partner
candidate	postpone
chocolate	prejudice
diphtheria	probably
environment	surprise
escape	temperature
February	tragedy
government	tremendous
laboratory	usually

Over twenty percent of all errors are caused by either adding letters to a word or reversing two letters within the word.

An example of a word to which a letter is added is *equipment*. Some people incorrectly pronounce the word with a *t* after the *p*. As a result, they add a *t* to the word when they spell it.

An example of a reversal of letters within the word is the simple word *doesn't*. Very often, the letters *e* and *s* are reversed and the student spells the word incorrectly—"dosen't."

Other words that are misspelled because of the addition or reversal of letters are:

asparagus	*(not "gras")*
athletics	*(no e after the th)*
barbarous	*(no i after the second bar)*
chimney	*(no i after the m)*
disastrous	*(no e after the t)*
hundred	*(not "derd")*
introduce	*(not "ter")*
lightning	*(no e after the t)*
mischievous	*(no i after the v)*
modern	*(not "dren")*
percent	*(not "pre")*
performance	*(not "pre")*
perspire	*(not "pre")*
produce	*(not "per")*
profession	*(not "per")*
pronounce	*(not "per")*
protect	*(not "per")*
remembrance	*(no e after the b)*
secretary	*(not "er")*
umbrella	*(no e after the b)*

The next most common error is the confusion of two words having the same pronunciation but different spellings and meanings. These are called *homonyms.* In this humorous sentence—"A doctor must have lots of patients (patience)"—there is no way of our knowing which word the speaker means if the sentence is spoken. Therefore, we don't know how to spell the word. The words *patients* and *patience* are homonyms.

Forty of the most frequently used groups of homonyms follow. Be certain to check the meaning of each word in each group so that you can figure out the spelling from the meaning of the word as it is used in a sentence.

air; ere; heir	hour; our
ate; eight	knew; new
blew; blue	know; no
bough; bow	lead; led
brake; break	mail; male
buy; by	meat; meet
cent; scent; sent	pail; pale
coarse; course	pair; pare; pear
for; four	peace; piece
forth; fourth	principal; principle
grate; great	read; red
groan; grown	right; write
hear; here	road; rode
him; hymn	sew; so; sow
hole; whole	stationary; stationery

steal; steel	threw; through
straight; strait	to; too; two
some; sum	way; weigh
son; sun	wood; would
their; there; they're	your; you're

HOW TO BECOME A GOOD SPELLER

There are three things you can do to help eliminate the frequently made errors and to equip yourself with the skills you will need to become a good speller.

Learn how to syllabicate. Knowing how to syllabicate—divide a word into syllables—will help you avoid many kinds of errors. This skill is particularly helpful with words of more than average length. Here are some simple rules that will help you to syllabicate properly.

RULES ON HOW TO SYLLABICATE

1. When a word has more than one vowel sound, it is broken into parts or syllables.

   EXAMPLES

   strength *strength* [one syllable]
   metal *me/tal* [two syllables]

2. Every syllable contains a sounded vowel or a pair of vowels sounded as one vowel (digraph).

   EXAMPLES

   going *go/ing* [sounded vowel in each syllable]
   breakout *break/out* [pairs of vowels sounded as one vowel in each syllable]

3. Sometimes a sounded vowel forms a syllable by itself.

   EXAMPLE

   again *a/gain*

4. Double consonants usually are separated.

   EXAMPLES

   mitten *mit/ten*
   possesses *pos/ses/ses*

5. A consonant between two vowels usually is joined to the vowel that follows it.

   EXAMPLES

   local *lo/cal*
   final *fi/nal*

6. When the suffix "ed" is added to a word ending in "d" or "t," it forms a separate syllable.

   EXAMPLE

   added *add/ed*

Applying these rules to the words listed earlier will help you avoid many of the common types of errors, particularly in the omission and addition of letters.

EXAMPLES

ath / le / tics
chim / ney
um / brel / la
ac / ci / den / tal / ly

Learn the correct pronunciation of the word you must spell. Mispronunciation is known to be one of the most common causes of misspelling. Your best ally in learning the pronunciation of a word is the dictionary. Knowing the correct pronunciation will help you attack successfully such words as:

EXAMPLES

Feb / ru / a / ry
[The first *r* is often not pronounced.]

gov / ern / ment
[The first *n* is often not pronounced.]

choc / o / late
[The second *o* is often not pronounced.]

Learn the most helpful spelling rules, and know how to apply them.

BASIC RULES OF SPELLING

1. Plurals of most nouns are formed by adding *s* to the singulars.

EXAMPLE

house, hous<u>es</u>

2. When the noun ends in *s*, *x*, *ch*, or *sh*, the plural generally is formed by adding "*es*."

EXAMPLES

gas, gas<u>es</u>
box, box<u>es</u>
witch, witch<u>es</u>
dish, dish<u>es</u>

3. a. The plural of a noun ending in *y* preceded by a consonant is formed by changing *y* to *i* and adding *es*.

EXAMPLE

lady, lad<u>ies</u>

b. The plural of a noun ending in *y* preceded by a vowel does not change *y* to *i* EXCEPT for words ending in *quy*.

EXAMPLES

toy, toy<u>s</u>
but
soliloquy, soliloqu<u>ies</u>

4. a. A word that ends in *y* preceded by a consonant usually changes *y* to *i* before a suffix unless the suffix begins with *i*.

EXAMPLE

beauty, beaut<u>iful</u>

b. A word that ends in *y* preceded by a vowel usually keeps the *y* when a suffix is added.

EXAMPLE

coy, coy<u>er</u>

5. a. A word that ends in silent *e* generally keeps the *e* when a suffix beginning with a consonant is added.

EXAMPLE

care, care<u>ful</u>

b. A word that ends in silent *e* generally drops the *e* when a suffix beginning with a vowel is added.

EXAMPLES

believe, believ<u>able</u>
move, mov<u>ing</u>

6. **Exceptions to Rule 5.**
Words ending in *ce* and *ge* keep the letter *e* before *able* and *ous*.

EXAMPLES

notice, notic*eable*
change, chang*eable*
courage, courag*eous*

7. A one-syllable word that ends in one consonant following a short vowel generally doubles the consonant before a suffix that begins with a vowel.

EXAMPLES

big, big*gest*
thin, thin*ner*

8. A word of more than one syllable that ends in one consonant following one short vowel generally doubles the final consonant before a suffix beginning with a vowel *if* the accent is on the last syllable.

EXAMPLES

omít, omit [t]*ed*
regrét, regret [t]*ing*
allót, allot [t]*ed*

9. The letter "i" is generally used before "e" except after "c."

EXAMPLES

bel*ie*ve, rec*ei*ve

There are many exceptions, as:

either
neither
neighborhood
weigh
leisure

10. An apostrophe is used to show that a letter has been omitted in a contraction.

EXAMPLES

it is, it's
they are, they're

11. An abbreviation is always followed by a period.

EXAMPLE

etc.

12. Nouns of Latin origin ending
—in *us* become *i* in the plural,

EXAMPLE

rad*ius*, rad*ii*

—in *a* become *ae* in the plural,

EXAMPLE

formul*a*, formul*ae*

—in *um* become *a* in the plural,

EXAMPLE

medi<u>um</u>, medi<u>a</u>

—in *is* become *es* in the plural,

EXAMPLE

ax<u>is</u>, ax<u>es</u>

13. The suffix *ful* is spelled with a single *l*.

EXAMPLES

help<u>*ful*</u>
tablespoon<u>*ful*</u>

(*Note:* The word *full* itself is the only exception.)

PRACTICE WITH SPELLING

In each set of words, find the misspelled word if there is one. <u>No set has more than one misspelled word</u>. If there is no misspelled word, choose answer 5. This kind of error is included in the sentence correction type of multiple-choice item.

1. (1) rein
(2) conceited
(3) cheif
(4) shield
(5) no error

2. (1) greif
(2) wield
(3) relieve
(4) besiege
(5) no error

3. (1) proceed
(2) succeed
(3) preceed
(4) exceed
(5) no error

4. (1) illegal
(2) illegible
(3) unatural
(4) uncivilized
(5) no error

5. (1) prespective
(2) present
(3) proceed
(4) proposal
(5) no error

6. (1) combustible
(2) intelligible
(3) perceptable
(4) taxable
(5) no error

7. (1) tangible
(2) lamentible
(3) considerable
(4) separable
(5) no error

8. (1) logically
(2) typically
(3) verbally
(4) globally
(5) no error

9. (1) practically
(2) exceptionally
(3) significantly
(4) intelligently
(5) no error

10. (1) advantagous
(2) perilous
(3) desirous
(4) adventurous
(5) no error

11. (1) mischievious
(2) previous
(3) poisonous
(4) mountainous
(5) no error

12. (1) murderous
(2) slanderous
(3) grievous
(4) beauteous
(5) no error

13. (1) momentous
(2) marvelous
(3) outragous
(4) hazardous
(5) no error

14. (1) channal
(2) acquittal
(3) flannel
(4) kernel
(5) no error

15. (1) sparkle
(2) disciple
(3) thimbal
(4) clerical
(5) no error

16. (1) corpuscle
(2) muscle
(3) proposal
(4) morsel
(5) no error

17. (1) nickle
(2) pickle
(3) logical
(4) neutral
(5) no error

18. (1) signal
(2) medical
(3) swivel
(4) shuttel
(5) no error

19. (1) senator
(2) investigator
(3) inventer
(4) stenographer
(5) no error

20. (1) actor
(2) ancestor
(3) purchaser
(4) elevater
(5) no error

21. (1) begger
(2) bookkeeper
(3) regular
(4) singular
(5) no error

22. (1) calender
(2) passenger
(3) collar
(4) hangar
(5) no error

23. (1) spectator
(2) educator
(3) dollar
(4) receiver
(5) no error

24. (1) pendant
(2) brilliant
(3) superintendent
(4) permanent
(5) no error

25. (1) descendant
(2) repentant
(3) defendent
(4) president
(5) no error

26. (1) lieutenent
(2) sergeant
(3) resident
(4) tenant
(5) no error

27. (1) appearance
(2) endurance
(3) persistance
(4) remembrance
(5) no error

28. (1) presence
(2) absence
(3) hindrance
(4) attendance
(5) no error

29. (1) cemetary
(2) imaginary
(3) dictionary
(4) boundary
(5) no error

30. (1) stationary
(2) secondary
(3) elementery
(4) honorary
(5) no error

31. (1) revolutionary
(2) infirmary
(3) vocabulary
(4) voluntary
(5) no error

32. (1) advise
(2) capsize
(3) despise
(4) surprize
(5) no error

33. (1) supervise
(2) exercise
(3) disguize
(4) baptize
(5) no error

34. (1) hypnotize
(2) antagonize
(3) patronize
(4) authorize
(5) no error

35. (1) merchandise
(2) dramatise
(3) centralize
(4) neutralize
(5) no error

36. (1) specialize
(2) franchize
(3) arise
(4) enterprise
(5) no error

37. (1) realize
(2) recognize
(3) compromise
(4) advertise
(5) no error

38. (1) emphasise
(2) revise
(3) modernize
(4) fertilize
(5) no error

39. (1) agonize
(2) analyze
(3) generalize
(4) paralyze
(5) no error

40. (1) houses
(2) classes
(3) waltzs
(4) businesses
(5) no error

41. (1) sopranos
(2) torpedos
(3) vetoes
(4) echoes
(5) no error

42. (1) chiefs
(2) loaves
(3) beliefs
(4) handkerchieves
(5) no error

43. (1) rooves
(2) calves
(3) hoofs
(4) proofs
(5) no error

44. (1) thiefs
(2) briefs
(3) knives
(4) shelves
(5) no error

45. (1) radios
(2) tangos
(3) silos
(4) cameos
(5) no error

46. (1) valleys
(2) monkeys
(3) attorneys
(4) alleys
(5) no error

47. (1) allies
(2) journeys
(3) dormitorys
(4) armies
(5) no error

48. (1) spagheti
(2) ravioli
(3) confetti
(4) bacilli
(5) no error

49. (1) carrying
(2) hurrying
(3) tragedys
(4) chimneys
(5) no error

50. (1) desirable
(2) knowledgeable
(3) lovable
(4) advisable
(5) no error

51. (1) desirous
(2) advantageous
(3) porous
(4) courageous
(5) no error

52. (1) suddeness
(2) genuineness
(3) vagueness
(4) likeness
(5) no error

53. (1) pursuing
(2) relieving
(3) canoeing
(4) toeing
(5) no error

54. (1) truely
(2) carefully
(3) solemnly
(4) purely
(5) no error

55. (1) wholy
(2) duly
(3) sincerely
(4) freely
(5) no error

56. (1) agreeable
(2) noticeable
(3) changable
(4) serviceable
(5) no error

57. (1) vengence
(2) insurance
(3) manageable
(4) desirable
(5) no error

58. (1) occuring
(2) preferring
(3) conference
(4) admittance
(5) no error

59. (1) traveled
(2) controlled
(3) annulment
(4) compelled
(5) no error

60. (1) dinning
(2) committing
(3) equipping
(4) omitting
(5) no error

61. (1) regretable
(2) transferable
(3) comparable
(4) controllable
(5) no error

62. (1) beginning
(2) admitting
(3) benefiting
(4) rebeling
(5) no error

63. (1) awful
(2) beautiful
(3) hopefuly
(4) usefully
(5) no error

64. (1) its
(2) your's
(3) ours
(4) there's
(5) no error

65. (1) childrens'
(2) women's
(3) girls'
(4) mothers'
(5) no error

66. (1) alltogether
(2) all right
(3) already
(4) allot
(5) no error

67. (1) labratory
(2) licorice
(3) privilege
(4) diamond
(5) no error

68. (1) athletic
(2) February
(3) libary
(4) interesting
(5) no error

69. (1) Wednesday
(2) goverment
(3) kindergarten
(4) handkerchief
(5) no error

70. (1) arctic
(2) choclate
(3) environment
(4) partner
(5) no error

71. (1) probably
(2) usually
(3) temperture
(4) tragedy
(5) no error

72. (1) tremendous
(2) postpone
(3) diphtheria
(4) supprise
(5) no error

73. (1) performance
(2) perspire
(3) pertect
(4) percent
(5) no error

74. (1) mischievous
(2) lightning
(3) disastrous
(4) chimney
(5) no error

75. (1) hundred
(2) childern
(3) modern
(4) laundry
(5) no error

76. (1) Britain
(2) villian
(3) captain
(4) crucial
(5) no error

77. (1) fascinating
(2) ascertain
(3) discipline
(4) descent
(5) no error

78. (1) attendence
(2) audience
(3) assistance
(4) balance
(5) no error

79. (1) carriage
(2) marriage
(3) morgage
(4) college
(5) no error

80. (1) harass
(2) embarass
(3) across
(4) success
(5) no error

81. (1) arguement
(2) advertisement
(3) requirement
(4) agreement
(5) no error

82. (1) courtesy
(2) hypocrisy
(3) prophecy
(4) delinquent
(5) no error

83. (1) appreciate
(2) definate
(3) syndicate
(4) adequate
(5) no error

84. (1) aqueduct
(2) aquaintence
(3) acquire
(4) acknowledge
(5) no error

85. (1) accommodate
(2) recommend
(3) committee
(4) ammendment
(5) no error

86. (1) paralell
(2) unusual
(3) colonel
(4) additional
(5) no error

87. (1) allege
(2) knowlege
(3) oblige
(4) siege
(5) no error

88. (1) remedy
(2) medecine
(3) vegetable
(4) repetition
(5) no error

89. (1) doubt
(2) endeavor
(3) bureau
(4) amature
(5) no error

90. (1) foward
(2) forehead
(3) toward
(4) foresee
(5) no error

91. (1) familiar
(2) miniture
(3) religious
(4) similar
(5) no error

92. (1) tobacco
(2) accross
(3) macaroni
(4) occasion
(5) no error

93. (1) necesary
(2) professor
(3) possesses
(4) success
(5) no error

94. (1) develop
(2) envelope
(3) equiptment
(4) interrupt
(5) no error

95. (1) proceeded
(2) proceedure
(3) preceding
(4) precedent
(5) no error

96. (1) tenth
(2) lenth
(3) strength
(4) height
(5) no error

97. (1) attatched
(2) watched
(3) detached
(4) stomach
(5) no error

98. (1) studying
(2) lying
(3) hoping
(4) planning
(5) no error

99. (1) murmer
(2) gutter
(3) conquer
(4) neither
(5) no error

100. (1) mistake
(2) disease
(3) passtime
(4) dessert
(5) no error

ANSWER KEY

1. 3	21. 1	41. 2	61. 1	81. 1
2. 1	22. 1	42. 4	62. 4	82. 5
3. 3	23. 5	43. 1	63. 3	83. 2
4. 3	24. 5	44. 1	64. 2	84. 2
5. 1	25. 3	45. 5	65. 1	85. 4
6. 3	26. 1	46. 5	66. 1	86. 1
7. 2	27. 3	47. 3	67. 1	87. 2
8. 5	28. 5	48. 1	68. 3	88. 2
9. 5	29. 1	49. 3	69. 2	89. 4
10. 1	30. 3	50. 5	70. 2	90. 1
11. 1	31. 5	51. 5	71. 3	91. 2
12. 5	32. 4	52. 1	72. 4	92. 2
13. 3	33. 3	53. 5	73. 3	93. 1
14. 1	34. 5	54. 1	74. 5	94. 3
15. 3	35. 2	55. 1	75. 2	95. 2
16. 5	36. 2	56. 3	76. 2	96. 2
17. 1	37. 5	57. 1	77. 5	97. 1
18. 4	38. 1	58. 1	78. 1	98. 5
19. 3	39. 5	59. 5	79. 3	99. 1
20. 4	40. 3	60. 1	80. 2	100. 3

WHAT'S YOUR SCORE?

______right,	______wrong
Excellent	91–100
Good	81–90
Fair	71–80

If you scored lower, turn back to the section giving the rules that can help to make you a good speller. Then try the test again, possibly having someone dictate to you the words that you missed.

ANSWER ANALYSIS

1. **3** chief
2. **1** grief
3. **3** precede
4. **3** unnatural
5. **1** perspective
6. **3** perceptible
7. **2** lamentable
8. **5** no error
9. **5** no error
10. **1** advantageous
11. **1** mischievous
12. **5** no error
13. **3** outrageous
14. **1** channel
15. **3** thimble
16. **5** no error
17. **1** nickel
18. **4** shuttle
19. **3** inventor
20. **4** elevator
21. **1** beggar
22. **1** calendar
23. **5** no error
24. **5** no error
25. **3** defendant
26. **1** lieutenant
27. **3** persistence
28. **5** no error
29. **1** cemetery
30. **3** elementary
31. **5** no error
32. **4** surprise
33. **3** disguise
34. **5** no error
35. **2** dramatize
36. **2** franchise
37. **5** no error
38. **1** emphasize
39. **5** no error
40. **3** waltzes
41. **2** torpedoes
42. **4** handkerchiefs
43. **1** roofs
44. **1** thieves
45. **5** no error
46. **5** no error
47. **3** dormitories
48. **1** spaghetti
49. **3** tragedies
50. **5** no error
51. **5** no error
52. **1** suddenness
53. **5** no error
54. **1** truly
55. **1** wholly
56. **3** changeable
57. **1** vengeance
58. **1** occurring
59. **5** no error
60. **1** dining
61. **1** regrettable
62. **4** rebelling
63. **3** hopefully
64. **2** yours
65. **1** children's
66. **1** altogether
67. **1** laboratory
68. **3** library
69. **2** government
70. **2** chocolate
71. **3** temperature
72. **4** surprise
73. **3** protect
74. **5** no error
75. **2** children
76. **2** villain
77. **5** no error
78. **1** attendance
79. **3** mortgage
80. **2** embarrass
81. **1** argument
82. **5** no error
83. **2** definite
84. **2** acquaintance
85. **4** amendment
86. **1** parallel
87. **2** knowledge
88. **2** medicine
89. **4** amateur
90. **1** forward
91. **2** miniature
92. **2** across
93. **1** necessary
94. **3** equipment
95. **2** procedure
96. **2** length
97. **1** attached
98. **5** no error
99. **1** murmur
100. **3** pastime

6 Additional Writing Skills

Correct Use of Words

Here are thirty pairs of words that are frequently confused and misused. Study the distinctions between the words in each pair. An example of the correct use of each member of the pair is given.

ACCEPT, EXCEPT

The verb **accept** means "to receive something" or "to agree to something." **Except** is most frequently used as a preposition meaning "leaving out." The use of *except* as a verb meaning "to leave out" is rare.

EXAMPLES

He was chosen to *accept* the gift.

Everyone came *except* him.

AGGRAVATE, IRRITATE

The verb **aggravate** means "to make worse." The verb **irritate** means "to annoy." In general, a person is *irritated*; a situation or a condition is *aggravated*.

EXAMPLES

Constant rubbing tended to *aggravate* the already painful wound.

The behavior of the child *irritated* all the guests.

ALREADY, ALL READY

Already is an adverb of time meaning "previously." **All ready** means exactly what the two words indicate—all prepared.

EXAMPLES

When I arrived, he had *already* left.

When I arrived, I found them *all ready* for the meeting.

ALTOGETHER, ALL TOGETHER

Altogether is an adverb of degree meaning "completely." **All together** means exactly what the two words indicate—all the persons in a group.

EXAMPLES

He was *altogether* unprepared for the assignment.

We found the team *all together* in the locker room.

AMONG, BETWEEN

Among is used when more than two persons or things are involved. **Between** is used when only two persons or things are involved. (You needn't be concerned with the rare exceptions to these rules.)

EXAMPLES

Frank, Joe, and Ed shared the expenses *among* them.

Jane and Joan shared the expenses *between* them.

AMOUNT, NUMBER

Amount is used for things or ideas that cannot be counted, and is usually followed by a singular noun—*money, talent, courage*. **Number** is used for persons or things that can be counted.

EXAMPLES

Sue carried a large *amount* of cash.

The *number* of accidents this year is greater than we thought.

I needed a large *amount* of money.

I needed a large *number* of dollars to pay my bills.

In the third example, the word *money* is thought of as a single unit. In the fourth, the word *dollars* is thought of as individual items that can be counted.

AROUND, ABOUT

Around is correctly used to indicate direction in a circle around an object. **About** should be used when number or size is indicated.

EXAMPLES

They walked *around* the house.

There were *about* 50,000 fans in the stadium.

The rug was *about* nine feet wide.

AS, LIKE

Only **as** can introduce a clause. **Like** cannot serve as a conjunction to introduce a clause; it is most frequently used as a preposition meaning "similar to."

EXAMPLE

WRONG:

This cereal tastes good *like* a cereal should.

CORRECT:

This cereal tastes good *as* a cereal should.

CORRECT:

He wanted everyone to be *like* him.

BEAT, BET

Beat means "to defeat." **Bet** means "to wager," or "to gamble something of value," on the result of a game.

EXAMPLES

Frank *beat* Jack in straight sets in their tennis match.

I *bet* five dollars that Joan would outrun Jane.

BESIDE, BESIDES

Beside means "at the side of." **Besides** means "in addition."

EXAMPLES

He came over to sit *beside* me.

There were nine others present *besides* Joe.

BORROW, LEND

Borrow means that the borrower is on the taking end of the transaction. **Lend** means that the lender is on the giving end of the transaction.

EXAMPLES

Please let me *borrow* ten dollars from you.

I'll be glad to *lend* the ten dollars to you.

BOTH, EACH

Both refers to two objects or persons taken together. **Each** refers to one or more objects or persons taken individually.

EXAMPLES

Both my pens cost ten dollars.

(***Note: Don't*** use *both* in the above example if you mean that the cost of the two pens was twenty dollars. *Both* means the pair of pens.)

Each of my pens cost five dollars.

BRING, TAKE

Bring is used when the movement in the sentence is toward the speaker or the writer. **Take** is used when the movement in the sentence is away from the speaker or the writer.

EXAMPLES

Bring the pencils to me, please.

Take these books to the principal's office.

CAN, MAY

Can is used to indicate the ability to do

something. **May** is used when permission is sought to do something, most frequently in the form of a question.

EXAMPLES

I *can* tie a slip knot.

May I have the car tonight?

FEWER, LESS

The correct use of these words follows the same rules as those indicated for **amount** and **number**. **Fewer** is used for persons or things that can be counted. **Less** is used for things or ideas that cannot be counted. (Note that *less* is usually followed by a singular noun, *fewer* by a plural noun.)

EXAMPLES

The number of accidents this year is *fewer* than we thought.

We enjoyed *less* freedom this year than last.

HANGED, HUNG

Hanged refers to a specific kind of execution that has taken place. **Hung** refers to something that has been suspended from an object.

EXAMPLES

The murderer was *hanged.*

The picture was *hung* on the hook attached to the wall.

IMPLY, INFER

Imply is used to indicate that the speaker or the writer is making a hint or suggestion. **Infer** is used to indicate that the hint or suggestion made by the speaker was taken by the audience, which drew a conclusion from it.

EXAMPLES

I mean to *imply* that he didn't get the job done.

I *infer* from your remarks that he was lazy.

IN, INTO

In is used to indicate that something is already in a place. **Into** is used to indicate that someone or something is moving from the outside to the inside of a place.

EXAMPLES

The dog is *in* the living room.

The dog dashed *into* the living room from the kitchen.

LATEST, LAST

Latest means "the most recent in a series." **Last** means "final."

EXAMPLES

The popular candidate was seen talking with his *latest* rival.

He appeared on television for the *last* time before his retirement.

LEARN, TEACH

Learn is used to indicate that knowledge or behavior is being acquired. **Teach** is used to indicate that knowledge or behavior is being provided.

EXAMPLES

He tried to *learn* how to hang-glide.

I tried to *teach* him how to hang-glide.

MYSELF, ME

Myself may be used properly in one of two ways. It can be used for emphasis, or it can be used as the object of an action verb with *I* as the subject. (*Never* use *myself* when *I* or *me* is correct.)

EXAMPLES

I *myself* will attend to this matter.

I hit *myself* in the hand.

WRONG:

He gave the awards to Frank and myself.

CORRECT:

He gave the awards to Frank and me.

WRONG:

Frank and myself will get the awards.

CORRECT:

Frank and I will get the awards.

POUR, SPILL

Pour means "to cause a liquid to flow deliberately." **Spill** means "to cause a liquid to flow accidentally or unintentionally."

EXAMPLES

The hostess *poured* coffee for her guests.

The hostess was embarrassed when she *spilled* the coffee on her guest's dress.

PRECEDE, PROCEED

Precede means "to come or go before" something or someone. **Proceed** means "to go on," particularly after an interruption.

EXAMPLES

Jimmy Carter *preceded* Ronald Reagan as president of the United States.

The speaker *proceeded*, after he was interrupted by a heckler.

PRINCIPAL, PRINCIPLE

Principal may be used in two ways. It can denote the head of a school, or it can be used as an adjective meaning "the main" or "the most important." **Principle** is used to indicate a law or a rule of conduct.

EXAMPLES

The *principal* addressed the teachers and the parents.

He was the *principal* speaker at the graduation exercises.

We are dedicated to the *principle* that all men are created equal.

QUITE, QUIET

The adverb **quite** means "completely" or "very." The adjective **quiet** means "still" or "calm."

EXAMPLES

He was *quite* angry when he lost the game.

After his fit of temper, he became *quiet*.

RAISE, RISE

Raise means "to lift" or "to bring up" something or someone. **Rise** means "to get up" or "to go up"; it does *not* take an object.

EXAMPLES

The guard *raised* his rifle when he heard a sound.

He *rises* in the morning when the sun rises.

ROB, STEAL

One is said to **rob** a *person* or an *institution* such as a bank by taking property or valuables from it. One is said to **steal** *an object* such as personal property or valuables from someone or some institution.

EXAMPLE

The criminal was caught in the act of trying to *rob* the bank.

The criminal tried to *steal* the man's wallet.

SET, SIT

Set means "to put something in a certain place." **Sit** means "to be seated."

EXAMPLES

The delivery boy *set* the packages on the kitchen floor.

Please *sit* in this chair.

STAND, STAY

You **stand** when you are on your feet. (The past tense is *stood*.) You **stay** when you remain in a given place. (The past tense is *stayed*.)

EXAMPLES

He *stood* all the way home in the bus.

He *stayed* at the stadium until the game was over.

STATIONARY, STATIONERY

Stationary means "not moving" or "still." **Stationery** refers to writing paper, envelopes, and other office supplies.

EXAMPLES

The *stationary* animal provided an excellent target for the hunter.

The student bought his notebooks at the *stationery* store.

FREQUENT ERRORS IN WORD USE

1. **DON'T USE** the expression *being that.* Instead, use a conjunction such as *because* or *since.*

   WRONG:

   Being that he was first, he won the prize.

   CORRECT:

   Since he was first, he won the prize.

2. **DON'T USE** the expression *could of, should of,* or *would of.* Instead, use the correct expression (with *have*) for which any of these aural distortions is an incorrect substitute.

   WRONG:

   He could of been the winner if he had tried.

   CORRECT:

   He *could have* been the winner if he had tried.

3. **DON'T USE** the expression *different than.* Instead, use *different from.*

   WRONG:

   Playing baseball is different than playing softball.

   CORRECT:

   Playing baseball is *different from* playing softball.

4. **DON'T USE** incorrect prepositions.

   WRONG:

   May I borrow a dollar off you?

   CORRECT:

   May I borrow a dollar *from* you?

   WRONG:

   Come over our house for a party.

   CORRECT:

   Come *to* our house for a party.

5. **DON'T USE** *don't* in the third person singular. Use *doesn't,* which is the contraction of *does not.*

   WRONG:

   He don't belong here.

   CORRECT:

   He *doesn't* belong here.

6. **DON'T USE** any article after the expression *kind of* or *sort of.*

   WRONG:

   He's not the kind of a person I like.

   CORRECT:

   He's not the *kind of* person I like.

7. **DON'T USE** the expression *the reason is because.* Use *the reason is that* since the words *reason* and *because* have similar meanings; a *reason* is indeed a cause.

   WRONG:

   The *reason* he left is because he did not get a raise.

   CORRECT:

   The *reason* he left *is that* he did not get a raise.

8. **DON'T USE** *who's* when you mean *whose. Whose* should be used to show possession. *Who's* is a contraction of *who is.*

   WRONG:

   I know who's book this is.

   CORRECT:

   I know *whose* book this is.

PRACTICE WITH CONFUSED AND MISUSED WORDS

In each sentence, five parts are underlined and numbered. Choose the number of the underlined part that contains the error. If there are no errors, choose number 5. This kind of error is included in the sentence correction type of multiple-choice item.

1. The number of persons present this
   (1)
   time was much different than the
   (2) (3)
   number that came last time.
   (4)
   No error
   (5)

2. Fewer visitors were allowed in our
   (1) (2)
   hospital than yours. No error
   (3) (4) (5)

3. We were already to leave as we had
(1) (2)
been instructed had it not been for
him and her. No error
(3) (4) (5)

4. Bring this book to whoever you
(1) (2)
think is most deserving besides me.
(3) (4)
No error
(5)

5. He awoke to find less people at the
(1) (2)
party than he thought he
(3)
had invited. No error
(4) (5)

6. Geraldo and I asked Conchita and
(1)
him whether they'd except the gift.
(2) (3) (4)
No error
(5)

7. Of him and myself, he was the
(1) (2)
brighter and the more shy.
(3) (4)
No error
(5)

8. Anyone may ask a question about
(1)
any problem bothering him because
(2)
it's the kind of situation which is
(3)
most aggravating. No error
(4) (5)

9. Francesca is the kind of a person
(1)
whom everyone likes despite the
(2)
fact that it is she who is least
(3)
likely to do anyone a favor.
(4)
No error
(5)

10. Enclosed are checks that
(1) (2)
cover all the expenses except hers.
(3) (4)
No error
(5)

11. Give the book to whoever asks for
(1)
it despite the large number of
(2)
requests and say it is a gift from
him and myself. No error
(3) (4) (5)

12. She insists it is I who am
(1) (2)
mistaken about the effect of the
order on those who have less
(3)
responsibilities than I. No error
(4) (5)

13. He considered it altogether likely
(1) (2)
that less accidents would occur
(3)
this year than last since the speed
(4)
limit was changed. No error
(5)

14. Hector felt that, among the three of
(1)
us who ran for office, the number
(2)
of votes should have proven that
(3)
the winners were Enrique and
myself. No error
(4) (5)

15. Inside of the house, besides my
(1) (2)
brother and me, were two guests
(3) (4)
and a friend. No error
(5)

ANSWER KEY

1. 3	4. 1	7. 2	10. 5	13. 3
2. 2	5. 2	8. 4	11. 4	14. 4
3. 1	6. 4	9. 1	12. 3	15. 1

WHAT'S YOUR SCORE?

15 right, 0 wrong

Excellent	14–15
Good	11–13
Fair	9–10

If you scored lower, restudy this section, concentrating on the differences between the pairs of words and the ten errors in word use to avoid.

ANSWER ANALYSIS

1. 3 Use *different from* rather than *different than.*
2. 2 *Into* must be used to indicate that the visitors are moving from the outside to the inside of the hospital.
3. 1 *All ready* must be used in the meaning of *all* prepared.
4. 1 *Take* should be used when the movement in the sentence is away from the speaker or writer.
5. 2 *Fewer* is used for things or persons that can be counted.
6. 4 *Accept* is used to mean "to receive something."
7. 2 Never use *myself* when *me* is correct.
8. 4 The verb *irritate* should be used since the required meaning is "annoying."
9. 1 Don't use an article after the expression *kind of.*
10. 5 No error.
11. 4 Since neither emphasis nor an object of an action verb is required, *me* should be used.
12. 3 *Fewer* is correct since responsibilities can be counted.
13. 3 *Fewer* should be used since the accidents can be counted.
14. 4 Since neither emphasis nor an object of an action verb is needed in this sentence, *I* should be used.
15. 1 The word *of* is not needed.

Wordiness: The Problem of Too Many Words

Wordiness, the use of more words than is necessary, is a frequent weakness of many speakers and writers. It is particularly undesirable when it confuses the reader.

Some sentences contain words or phrases that are unnecessary.

EXAMPLE

My friend *he* is a baseball fan.

In this sentence, both the noun *friend* and the pronoun *he* are unnecessary when referring to the same person. A pronoun takes the place of a noun. The sentence should read:

"My friend is a baseball fan."

OR

"He is a baseball fan."

EXAMPLE

This *here* pen writes better than that *there* one.

Both *here* and *there* are not needed. *This* means nearer than another person or thing referred to as *that*.

EXAMPLE

Take your feet off *of* the table.

Off means "so as to be no longer on." The word *of* in the sentence is superfluous.

EXAMPLE

Whatever he does, he does *it* well.

The pronoun *it* isn't needed. In fact, the pronoun replaces nothing in the sentence and what *it* refers to isn't clear.

Some sentences contain words that are repetitive since they restate parts of the meaning of other words in the sentence.

EXAMPLE

I have a friend *of mine* who helps me with my housework.

In this sentence, *mine* means "belonging to me," and the idea is already contained in the words *I have*. Therefore, *of mine* should be eliminated from the sentence.

EXAMPLE

I have to be at work at 9 A.M. *in the morning.*

In this sentence, A.M. means "ante meridiem" or "before noon." It conveys the idea of *morning*. Therefore, the phrase *in the morning* isn't needed.

EXAMPLE

Congress has decided to refer the matter *back* to committee.

The word *refer*, contains a prefix (*re-*) which means "back." Therefore, the word *back* is unnecessary. A similar incorrect expression is "return back."

Some sentences contain words that unnecessarily repeat other words in the sentence.

EXAMPLE

We left after *the conclusion of* the concert.

After means "later than," so the words *the conclusion of* are unnecessary.

EXAMPLE

Helen Keller wrote an autobiography *of her life.*

An *autobiography* is the story of one's life; *of her life* should be omitted.

EXAMPLE

In my opinion, *I think* the criminal should be pardoned.

In this sentence, *think* means to "hold an opinion," so either *in my opinion* or *I think* can safely be dispensed with.

Some sentences express ideas clumsily because too many words are used.

This fault can be corrected by omitting unnecessary words, recasting the sentence, or substituting a single word for a phrase or clause.

EXAMPLE

The reason I joined the club was *on account of the fact* that I needed a place to go to in my spare time.

On account of the fact should be omitted, as it is unnecessary.

PRACTICE

1. That there book belongs to me.
2. Despite the rain, the umpires decided to continue on with the game.
3. Please refer back to page 12 in the book.
4. My parents they are completely devoted to me.
5. I usually go to bed at 11 P.M. at night.
6. Each and every student should pay attention.
7. Felicia doesn't want for you to date her anymore.
8. When I was eighteen years old, I was graduated from high school.

ANSWERS

1. That book belongs to me.
2. Despite the rain, the umpires decided to continue the game.
3. Please refer to page 12 in the book.
4. My parents are completely devoted to me.
5. I usually go to bed at 11 P.M.
6. Each student should pay attention. Every student should pay attention.
7. Felicia doesn't want you to date her anymore.
8. When I was eighteen, I was graduated from high school.

PRACTICE WITH WORDINESS

Beneath each sentence you will find five ways of writing the underlined part. Choose the answer that makes the best sentence. Answer 1 is always the same as the underlined part and is sometimes the right answer.

1. After the conclusion of the game, my friend, he decided to return back home.

   (1) After the conclusion of the game, my friend, he decided to return back
   (2) After the conclusion of the game, my friend decided to return back

(3) After the conclusion of the game, my friend decided to return
(4) After the game, my friend decided to return back
(5) After the game, my friend decided to return

2. At this point in time, type up five copies of this here contract.

(1) point in time, type up five copies of this here
(2) point in time, type five copies of this here
(3) time, type five copies of this
(4) time, type five copies of this here
(5) time, type up five copies of this

3. Because we cooperated together, we divided up the work on the report that was assigned.

(1) together, we divided up the work on the report that was assigned
(2) together, we divided the work on the report that was assigned
(3) , we divided up the work on the report that was assigned
(4) , we divided the work on the assigned report
(5) , we divided up the work on the assigned report

4. Write down each and every true fact.

(1) down each and every true fact
(2) down each true fact
(3) each true fact
(4) each fact
(5) down each fact

5. Mr. Steele, who was president of the company, repeated again what he had said while we were having dinner.

(1) who was president of the company, repeated again what he had said while we were having
(2) who was president of the company, repeated what he had said while we were having
(3) president of the company, repeated what he had said while we were having
(4) president of the company, repeated again what he had said during
(5) president of the company, repeated what he had said during

6. At 8:00 P.M. in the evening, he continued on his walk, which was enjoyable.

(1) in the evening, he continued on his walk, which was enjoyable
(2) he continued on his walk, which was enjoyable
(3) he continued on his enjoyable walk
(4) in the evening, he continued his enjoyable walk
(5) he continued his enjoyable walk

7. A large crowd of people waited outside of the building.

(1) A large crowd of people waited outside of
(2) A crowd waited outside
(3) A crowd waited outside of
(4) There was a large crowd of people who waited outside of
(5) There was a large crowd who waited outside of

8. I don't want for you to meet up with my friend until the time I tell you.

(1) for you to meet up with my friend until the time
(2) for you to meet my friend until the time
(3) for you to meet my friend until
(4) you to meet my friend until
(5) you to meet my friend until the time

9. The senator rose up to say that, in his opinion, he thought the bill should be referred back to committee.

(1) rose up to say that, in his opinion, he thought the bill should be referred back to
(2) rose up to say that he thought the bill should be referred back
(3) rose up to say that he thought the bill should be referred
(4) rose up to say that, in his opinion, the bill should be referred
(5) rose to say that he thought the bill should be referred

10. My wife wanted that I should return to school when I was thirty years of age.

(1) that I should return to school when I was thirty years of age
(2) that I should return back to school when I was thirty years of age
(3) me to return back to school when I was thirty years of age
(4) me to return to school when I was thirty years of age
(5) me to return to school when I was thirty

ANSWER KEY

1. 5	3. 4	5. 5	7. 2	9. 5
2. 3	4. 4	6. 5	8. 4	10. 5

WHAT'S YOUR SCORE?

10 right, 0 wrong

Excellent	9–10
Good	8
Fair	7

If you scored lower, review the four kinds of wordiness illustrated in this section.

ANSWER ANALYSIS

1. 5 *The conclusion of, he,* and *back* are all included in the meanings of other words in the sentence.
2. 3 *Point in, up,* and *here* are all included in the meanings of other words in the sentence.
3. 4 *Together* and *up* are included in the meanings of other words in the sentence. The adjective *assigned* is preferable stylistically to the adjective clause *that was assigned.*
4. 4 *Down, every,* and *true* are unnecessary.
5. 5 *Again* is unnecessary. The appositive, *president,* is preferable stylistically to the adjective clause *who was president.* The preposition *during* is preferable to the adverb clause *while we were having.*
6. 5 *In the evening* and *on* are included in the meanings of other words in the sentence. The adjective *enjoyable* is preferable to the adjective clause *which was enjoyable.*
7. 2 The words *large* and *of* are unnecessary. *That* is preferable to *who* when it refers to a neuter noun such as *crowd.*
8. 4 The words *up* and *the time* are included in the meanings of other words in the sentence. The word *for* is awkward and unnecesary.
9. 5 The words *up, in his opinion,* and *back* are unnecessary.
10. 5 The words *years of age* are unnecessary. The expression *that I should* is clumsy and can easily be replaced by the words *me to.*

A Basic 750-Word Vocabulary

Here is a list of 750 basic words to help you build your vocabulary. For each word, a definition is provided. You should use these lists together with a good dictionary such as *Webster's New World Dictionary of the American Language.*

200 USEFUL NOUNS

ACCESS (means of) approach or admittance (e.g., to records)
ACCORD agreement
AFFLUENCE abundance; wealth (e.g., age of ______)
AGENDA list of things to be done or discussed (e.g., at a meeting)
ALIAS assumed name (e.g., Fred Henry, ______ John Doe)
ANIMOSITY great hatred (e.g., toward strangers)
ANTHOLOGY collection of writings or other creative work such as songs
ATLAS book of maps
AUDACITY boldness
AVARICE greed for wealth
AWE feeling of respect and wonder (e.g., in ______ of someone's power)

BIGOTRY unwillingness to allow others to have different opinions and beliefs from one's own

BLEMISH defect (e.g., on one's record)
BONDAGE slavery
BOON benefit (e.g., a _____ to business)
BRAWL noisy fight
BREVITY shortness
BULWARK strong protection (e.g., a _____ against corruption)

CALIBER quality (e.g., a person of high _____)
CAMOUFLAGE disguise, usually in war, by changing the appearance of persons or material
CASTE social class or distinction
CATASTROPHE sudden disaster (e.g., an earthquake)
CHRONICLE historical record
CLAMOR uproar
CONDOLENCE expression of sympathy (e.g., extended _____ to a bereaved)
CONNOISSEUR expert judge (e.g., of paintings, food)
CONSENSUS general agreement
CONTEXT words or ideas just before or after a given word or idea (e.g., meaning of a word in a given _____)
CRITERION standard of judgment (e.g., good or poor by this _____)
CRUX the essential point (e.g., the _____ of the matter)

DATA known facts (e.g., _____ were found through research)
DEBUT first appearance before an audience (e.g., actor, pianist)
DELUGE great flood (e.g., rain or, in a special sense, mail)
DEPOT warehouse
DESTINY predetermined fate (e.g., it was his _____ to)
DIAGNOSIS determination of the nature of a disease or a situation
DILEMMA situation requiring a choice between two unpleasant courses of action (e.g., he was in a _____)
DIN loud, continuing noise
DISCORD disagreement
DISCREPANCY inconsistency (e.g., in accounts, in testimony)
DISSENT difference of opinion (e.g., from a decision)
DROUGHT long spell of dry weather

ELITE choice part or element (e.g., of society)
ENVIRONMENT surrounding influences or conditions
EPOCH period of time associated with an important person or event (e.g., the _____ of spaceflight)
ERA period of time marked by an important person or event (e.g., the Napoleonic _____)
ESSENCE basic nature (e.g., of the matter)
ETIQUETTE rules of social behavior that are generally accepted
EXCERPT passage from a book or a document
EXODUS departure, usually of large numbers

FALLACY mistaken idea; reasoning that contains an error
FANTASY imagination (e.g., he indulged in _____)
FEUD continued deadly hatred (e.g., between two families)
FIASCO complete, humiliating failure
FIEND inhumanly cruel person
FINALE last part or performance
FLAIR natural talent (e.g., for sports)
FLAW defect
FOCUS central point (e.g., of attention)
FOE enemy
FORMAT physical appearance or arrangement (e.g., of a book)
FORTITUDE steady courage (e.g., when in trouble)
FORUM a gathering for the discussion of public issues
FOYER entrance hall (e.g., to a building or dwelling)
FRAUD deliberate deception
FRICTION rubbing of the surface of one thing against the surface of another
FUNCTION purpose served by a person, object, or organization

GHETTO section of a city where members of a particular group (formerly religious, now usually racial) live
GIST essential content (e.g., of a speech or an article)
GLUTTON one who overeats or indulges in anything else to excess
GRIEVANCE complaint made against someone responsible for a situation believed to be unjust

HAVOC great damage and destruction (e.g., wreak _____ on)

HAZARD danger
HERITAGE inheritance either of real wealth or of a tradition
HOAX deliberate attempt to trick someone, done either with serious intent or as a joke
HORDE crowd
HORIZON limit (of knowledge, experience, or ambition)
HUE shade of color
HYSTERIA wild emotional outburst

IDIOM expression peculiar to a language that, as a whole, has a different meaning from the words that comprise it (e.g., hit the road)
ILLUSION idea or impression different from reality
IMAGE likeness or reflected impression of a person or object
INCENTIVE spur or motive to do something (e.g., profit ____)
INCUMBENT present holder of an office
INFLUX flowing in (e.g., of money into banks, tourists into a country)
INFRACTION violation of a rule or a law
INITIATIVE desire or ability to take the first step in carrying out some action (often a new plan or idea)
INNOVATION introduction of a new idea or method
INTEGRITY moral and intellectual honesty and uprightness
INTERIM meantime (e.g., in the ____)
INTERLUDE period of time between two events (e.g., ____ between the acts of a play)
INTRIGUE secret plot
INTUITION knowledge derived through instinct rather than thought
ITINERARY route followed on a trip, actual or planned

JEOPARDY risk of harm (e.g., put into ____)

KEYNOTE main theme (e.g., He sounded the ____ of the convention)

LARCENY theft (e.g., The jury couldn't decide whether the crime was grand or petty ____)
LAYPERSON one who is not a member of a particular profession (e.g., from the point of view of a ____)
LEGACY material or spiritual inheritance (e.g., from a parent)
LEGEND story passed on from generation to generation and often considered to be true
LORE body of traditional knowledge (e.g., nature ____)

MALADY disease (e.g., incurable ____)
MANEUVER skillful move (e.g., a clever ____)
MARATHON contest requiring endurance
MEDIA means of communication (e.g., ____ of radio and television)
MEMENTO object that serves as a reminder (e.g., a ____ of the war)
METROPOLIS main city of a state or region (or any large city)
MORALE state of mind as it affects possible future action (e.g., The troops had good ____)
MULTITUDE a large number
MYTH a story that is a traditional explanation of some occurrence, usually in nature (e.g., the ____ of Atlas holding up the heavens)

NICHE suitable and desirable place (e.g., He found his ____ in the business organization)
NOMAD wanderer
NOSTALGIA desire to return to past experiences or associations

ODYSSEY long journey
OMEN something that is believed to predict a future event (e.g., an evil ____)
OPTIMUM best possible quantity or quality (e.g., He participated to the ____)
OVATION enthusiastic reception usually accompanied by generous applause (e.g., He received a tumultuous ____)
OVERSIGHT failure to include something through carelessness (e.g., His name was omitted because of an ____)

PAGEANT public spectacle in the form of a stage performance or a parade (e.g., a historical ____)
PANORAMA clear view of a very broad area
PARADOX statement of a truth that appears to contradict itself (e.g., a 20-year-old who had only five birthdays because he was born on February 29)
PASTIME way of spending leisure time (e.g., He took up golf as a ____)
PAUPER very poor person
PEER an equal in age, social standing, ability, or other feature

PHENOMENON event that can be scientifically explained, such as the tides

PITFALL trap

PITTANCE very small sum of money (e.g., He survived on a ______)

PLATEAU area of level land located at a height

PLIGHT condition, usually unfavorable (e.g., the sorry ______ of the refugees)

POISE calm and controlled manner of behavior (e.g., He showed ______ in difficult situations)

PREDICAMENT unpleasant situation from which it is difficult to free oneself (e.g., He found himself in a ______)

PREFACE introductory statement to a book or speech

PRELUDE something that is preliminary to a more important act or work

PREMISE statement from which a conclusion is logically drawn (e.g., Granted the ______ that..., we may conclude...)

PREMIUM amount added to the usual payment or charge (e.g., He paid a ______ for the seats)

PRESTIGE respect achieved through rank, achievement, or reputation

PRETEXT reason given as a cover-up for the true purpose of an action (e.g., He gave as a ______ for stealing the ring, his sentimental attachment to it)

PRIORITY something that ranks before others in importance (e.g., He gave ______ to his studies)

PROCESS step-by-step system for accomplishing some purpose (e.g., the ______ of legislation)

PROSPECT outlook for the future (e.g., the ______ of peace)

PROXIMITY nearness

PSEUDONYM assumed name, usually by an author (e.g., Mark Twain, ______ of Samuel Clemens)

PUN play on words depending on two different meanings or sounds of the same word (e.g., Whether life is worth living depends on the *liver*)

QUANDARY uncertainty over a choice between two courses of action (e.g., He was in a ______ between the careers of law or medicine)

QUERY question

QUEST search (e.g., ______ for knowledge)

RARITY something not commonly found (e.g., A talent like his is a ______)

REFUGE place to which one can go for protection (e.g., He found ______ in the church)

REMNANT remaining part (e.g., ______ of the troops)

REMORSE deep feeling of guilt for some bad act (e.g., He felt ______ at having insulted his friend)

RENDEZVOUS a meeting or a place for meeting

REPLICA an exact copy (e.g., ______ of a painting)

REPRIMAND severe criticism in the form of a scolding (e.g., He received a ______ from his superior)

RESIDUE remainder

RESOURCES assets, either material or spiritual, that are available for use

RESPITE temporary break that brings relief (e.g., ______ from work)

RÉSUMÉ summary

REVERENCE feeling of great respect (e.g., ______ for life)

ROBOT one who acts mechanically or like a mechanical man

ROSTER list of names (e.g., ______ of guests)

SABOTAGE deliberate damage to vital services of production and supply, usually to those of an enemy in wartime

SAGA long tale, usually of heroic deeds

SALUTATION greeting, written or spoken (e.g., The ______ of a letter may be "Dear Sir")

SARCASM use of cutting remarks

SATIRE attack upon evil or foolish behavior by showing it to be ridiculous

SCAPEGOAT person who is blamed for the bad deeds of others

SCENT distinctive smell

SCOPE entire area of action or thought (e.g., the ______ of the plan)

SEGMENT part or section of a whole (e.g., ______ of a population)

SEQUEL something that follows from what happened or was written before (e.g., ______ to a novel)

SILHOUETTE outline drawing in black

SITE location of an object or an action (e.g., original ______ of a building)

SLANDER untruth spoken or spread about a person that damages his or her reputation

SLOGAN motto that is associated with an action or a cause (e.g., Pike's Peak or bust!)
SLOPE slant (e.g., ______ of a line)
SNARE trap
SOLACE comfort (e.g., She found ______ in work)
SPONSOR person or organization that endorses and supports an individual, an activity, or a cause
SPUR something that moves one to act (e.g., a ______ to sacrifice)
STAMINA ability to fight off physical difficulties such as fatigue and cold
STATURE height reached physically or morally (e.g., a man of great ______)
STATUS standing, social or professional
STIMULUS any encouragement to act
STRATEGY skillful planning and execution (e.g., the ______ in a battle)
STRIFE conflict (e.g., ______ between labor and management)
SUMMIT the highest point (e.g., the ______ of his career)
SUPPLEMENT amount added to complete something (e.g., ______ to a budget)
SURVEY broad study of a topic (e.g., a ______ of employment)
SUSPENSE tenseness brought about by uncertainty as to what will happen
SYMBOL something that is used to represent something else (e.g., Uncle Sam is a ______ of the United States)
SYMPTOM indication of something (e.g., ______ of disease)
SYNOPSIS brief summary

TACT ability to say and do the appropriate thing
TALLY record of a score or an account (e.g., the ______ of the receipts)
TECHNIQUE method or skill in doing work (e.g., the ______ of an artist)
TEMPERAMENT natural disposition, often to act in a contrary manner (e.g., He displayed a changeable ______)
TEMPO pace of activity (e.g., The ______ of life is increasing)
TENSION mental or emotional strain (e.g., She was under great ______)
THEME topic of a written work or a talk
THRESHOLD starting point (e.g., the ______ of a career)
TINT shade of color
TOKEN sign that stands for some object or feeling (e.g., a ______ of esteem)
TONIC something that is a source of energy or vigor
TRADITION body of customs and beliefs received by one generation from another
TRAIT distinguishing feature (e.g., ______ of character)
TRANSITION movement from one situation to another (e.g., ______ from dictatorship to democracy)
TRIBUTE display of respect or gratitude (e.g., He paid a ______ to his parents)
TURMOIL disturbance (e.g., great ______ at the meeting)
TUTOR private teacher

ULTIMATUM final ("Take it or leave it") offer
UNREST restless dissatisfaction
UPHEAVAL sudden overthrow, often violent
UTENSIL useful implement (e.g., a kitchen ______)
UTOPIA ideal place or society

VALOR courage
VENTURE undertaking that involves risk
VICINITY neighborhood
VICTOR winner
VIGOR vitality
VIM energy
VOW solemn pledge

WAGER bet
WHIM sudden notion or desire
WOE great sorrow (e.g., He brought ______ to his friends)
WRATH intense anger (e.g., He poured his ______ on his enemies)

ZEAL eager desire
ZEST keen enthusiasm (e.g., ______ for competition)

200 USEFUL VERBS

ABSOLVE free from guilt (e.g., for a crime)
ACCEDE agree to (e.g., a request)
ACCELERATE speed up
ADJOURN put off to a later time (e.g., a meeting)
ADVOCATE act in support of (e.g., revolution)
ALLEGE claim
ALLOT assign (e.g., a share)
ALLUDE refer to (e.g., a book)
ALTER change
ASSENT agree

ATONE make up for (e.g., a sin)
AUGMENT add to
AVERT prevent

BAN forbid
BAR exclude

CEDE give up (e.g., territory)
CHASTISE punish
CITE mention in order to prove something
COERCE force
COLLABORATE work with someone
COMMEND praise
CONCUR agree
CURTAIL cut short or reduce

DEDUCE draw a conclusion from given facts
DEEM consider
DEFER postpone
DELETE remove or erase (e.g., a word)
DEPLORE regret
DEPRIVE keep someone from having or getting something
DESPISE scorn
DETAIN delay temporarily
DETECT uncover something that is not obvious
DETEST hate
DETRACT take away from
DEVOUR eat greedily
DIGRESS depart from the subject under consideration
DILUTE weaken by adding something less strong (e.g., a mixture)
DISINTEGRATE fall apart
DISPEL drive away
DISPERSE scatter
DISRUPT break up
DISTORT present incorrectly (e.g., facts)
DIVERGE go in different directions
DIVULGE reveal

EJECT throw out
ENCOUNTER meet
ENDEAVOR try
ENHANCE increase the quality or value of
ENSUE follow as a result
ERR make a mistake
ERUPT break out
EVADE avoid or escape from someone or something
EXCEED surpass
EXTOL praise highly

FALTER stumble
FAMISH starve
FEIGN pretend
FLOURISH thrive
FOIL prevent
FORSAKE abandon
FRUSTRATE prevent someone from achieving a goal

GAUGE estimate

HARASS disturb constantly
HEAVE lift and throw
HEED pay attention to (e.g., advice)
HINDER keep back
HURL throw with force

IGNITE set fire to
IMMERSE plunge into a liquid
IMPAIR damage
IMPLY suggest
INCITE arouse
INFER come to a conclusion based on something known
INSTIGATE spur to action
INTERROGATE question
INTIMIDATE frighten by making threats
IRK annoy

JEER poke fun at (e.g., by sarcastic remarks)

LAMENT feel sorrow for
LAUNCH set in motion
LOP cut off
LURE tempt
LURK remain hidden, usually for an evil purpose

MAGNIFY enlarge
MAIM cripple
MIMIC imitate
MOCK ridicule
MOLEST annoy

NARRATE tell (e.g., a story)
NAVIGATE steer (e.g., a ship)
NEGATE deny

ORIENT adjust oneself or someone else to a situation or place
OUST expel

PEND remain undecided
PERFECT complete
PERPLEX puzzle
PERTAIN have reference to
PERTURB upset greatly

PERUSE read carefully
PRECLUDE prevent something from happening
PRESCRIBE order (e.g., for use or as a course of action)
PRESUME take for granted
PREVAIL win out over
PROBE investigate thoroughly
PROCURE obtain
PROSPER be successful
PROTRUDE project
PROVOKE arouse to action out of irritation
PRY look closely into

QUELL subdue

REBATE give back, usually part of an amount paid
REBUKE reprimand
RECEDE move backward
RECONCILE bring together by settling differences
RECTIFY correct
RECUR happen again
REFRAIN keep from
REIMBURSE pay back
REITERATE repeat
REJECT refuse to take
RELINQUISH give up
REMINISCE recall past happenings
REMUNERATE pay for work or other service done
RENOUNCE give up (e.g., a claim)
RENOVATE restore (e.g., a house)
REPENT regret (e.g., a sin)
REPOSE rest
REPROACH blame
REPULSE drive back (e.g., an attack)
RESTRAIN hold back
RETAIN keep
RETALIATE return in kind (e.g., a blow for a blow)
RETARD delay
RETRIEVE get back
REVERE have deep respect for

SCAN look at closely; look over quickly
SCOFF mock
SCORN treat with contempt
SCOUR clean thoroughly; move about widely in a search
SCOWL look angry
SEEP ooze
SEETHE boil
SEVER divide
SHED throw off (e.g., clothing)
SHIRK seek to avoid (e.g., duty or work)
SHUN avoid
SHUNT turn aside
SIFT sort out through careful examination (e.g., evidence)
SIGNIFY mean
SINGE burn slightly
SKIM read over quickly
SMITE hit hard
SNARL tangle
SOAR fly high in the air
SPURN reject scornfully
STARTLE surprise
STIFLE suppress (e.g., feelings)
STREW scatter
STRIVE try hard
STUN daze
SUBSIDE lessen in activity
SUCCUMB yield to
SUFFICE be enough
SURGE increase suddenly
SURMOUNT overcome (e.g., an obstacle)
SUSTAIN support
SWAY move back and forth

TAMPER meddle with
TARNISH discolor
TAUNT reproach mockingly
THAW melt
THRASH defeat thoroughly
THRIVE prosper
THROB beat insistently
THRUST push forcefully and suddenly
THWART prevent someone from achieving a goal
TINGE color slightly
TORMENT afflict with pain
TRANSFORM change the appearance of
TRANSMIT send along
TRUDGE walk slowly and wearily

UNDERGO experience
UNDO return to condition that existed before something was done
USURP seize power illegally
UTILIZE make use of
UTTER speak

VACATE make empty
VANQUISH conquer
VARY change
VEND sell
VERIFY prove the truth of
VEX annoy
VIBRATE move back and forth
VIOLATE break (e.g., a law)

VOUCH guarantee

WAIVE give up (e.g., a right or privilege)
WANE decrease in strength
WAVER sway back and forth
WHET sharpen
WIELD put to use (e.g., power or a tool such as a club)
WITHSTAND hold out against (e.g., pressure)
WREST pull violently

YEARN long for
YIELD give up

250 USEFUL ADJECTIVES

ADAMANT unyielding
ADEPT skilled
ADROIT skillful
AESTHETIC having to do with beauty
AGILE nimble
AMBIDEXTROUS equally skilled with both hands
AMENABLE disposed to follow (e.g., advice)
AMIABLE friendly
APT suitable
ARDENT passionate
ARROGANT over proud
ARTICULATE able to express oneself cleary (e.g., an ______ person)
ASTUTE shrewd
AUTHENTIC genuine

BARREN unfruitful
BIZARRE strange
BLAND gentle; soothing
BLATANT overloud
BOISTEROUS rambunctious
BRUSQUE rudely brief

CALLOUS unfeeling
CANDID honest
CASUAL offhand
CHIC stylish
CHRONIC continuing over a long period of time
CIVIC municipal
CIVIL courteous
COLOSSAL huge
COMPATIBLE capable of getting along together
CONCISE brief but complete
CRAFTY sly
CREDIBLE believable
CUMBERSOME bulky
CURT rudely brief

DEMURE modest; reserved
DEROGATORY belittling
DESOLATE lonely
DESTITUTE poverty-stricken
DETERGENT cleansing
DEVIOUS indirect
DEVOID completely free of (e.g., feeling)
DEVOUT very religious
DIMINUTIVE tiny
DIRE dreadful
DISCREET careful
DISINTERESTED impartial
DISMAL gloomy
DISTRAUGHT driven to distraction
DIVERSE varied
DOMESTIC having to do with the home
DOMINANT ruling
DORMANT sleeping
DRASTIC extreme (e.g., changes)
DREARY gloomy
DUBIOUS doubtful
DURABLE lasting
DYNAMIC energetic

EARNEST intensely serious
EBONY black
ECCENTRIC peculiar (e.g., behavior)
EDIBLE fit to be eaten
EERIE weird
ELEGANT tastefully fine
ELOQUENT powerfully fluent in writing or speech
ELUSIVE hard to get hold of
EMINENT distinguished (e.g., author)
EPIC heroic in size
ERRATIC not regular
ETERNAL everlasting
ETHNIC having to do with race
EXORBITANT unreasonable (e.g., price)
EXOTIC foreign
EXPLICIT clearly indicated
EXTEMPORANEOUS spoken or accomplished with little preparation
EXTENSIVE broad

FANATIC extremely enthusiastic
FEASIBLE possible to carry out (e.g., a ______ plan)
FEEBLE weak
FERTILE productive
FERVENT warmly felt
FESTIVE in the spirit of a holiday (e.g., celebration)

FICKLE changeable
FLAGRANT noticeably bad (e.g., violation)
FLEET swift
FLIMSY not strong (e.g., platform)
FLUENT smooth (e.g., speech)
FORMIDABLE fear-inspiring because of size or strength (e.g., enemy)
FRAGILE easily broken
FRAIL delicate
FRANK outspoken
FRATERNAL brotherly
FRIGID extremely cold
FRUGAL thrifty
FUTILE useless

GALA festive
GALLANT courteously brave (e.g., conduct)
GENIAL kindly
GIGANTIC huge
GLUM gloomy
GORY bloody
GRAPHIC vividly realistic
GRATIS free
GRIM sternly forbidding (e.g., future)
GROSS glaringly bad (e.g., injustice)
GRUESOME horrifying

HAPHAZARD chance
HARSH disagreeably rough
HEARTY friendly (e.g., welcome)
HECTIC feverish
HEINOUS outrageous (e.g., crime)
HIDEOUS extremely ugly
HILARIOUS very merry, mirthful
HOMOGENEOUS of like kind (e.g., group)
HORRENDOUS horrible
HOSTILE unfriendly (e.g., unwelcome)
HUMANE merciful
HUMBLE modest
HUMID damp

IMMACULATE spotlessly clean
IMMENSE very large
IMMINENT about to happen (e.g., storm)
IMPARTIAL unbiased
IMPERATIVE necessary
IMPERTINENT rude
IMPROMPTU without any preparation (e.g., remarks)
IMPUDENT rudely bold
INCESSANT uninterrupted
INCLEMENT rough (e.g., weather)
INCOHERENT not clearly connected
INDELIBLE unable to be erased
INDIFFERENT showing no interest
INDIGENT poor
INDIGNANT very angry
INDISPENSABLE absolutely necessary
INDUSTRIOUS hard-working
INEPT ineffective
INFAMOUS having a bad reputation
INFINITE endless
INFLEXIBLE unbending
INGENIOUS clever
INNATE inborn
INNOCUOUS harmless
INSOLENT boldly rude
INTENSIVE thorough (e.g., study)
INTERMITTENT starting and stopping (e.g., rain)
INTOLERANT unwilling or unable to respect others or their beliefs
INTRICATE complicated
INVINCIBLE unable to be conquered
IRATE angry
IRRATIONAL unreasonable

JOVIAL good-humored
JUBILANT joyous

LABORIOUS demanding a lot of work
LATENT hidden (e.g., talent)
LAVISH extremely generous (e.g., praise)
LAX loose (e.g., discipline)
LEGIBLE easily read (e.g., print)
LEGITIMATE lawful (e.g., claim)
LETHAL fatal
LOATH reluctant
LOFTY very high
LUCID clear
LUCRATIVE profitable (e.g., business)

MAJESTIC grand (e.g., building)
MALICIOUS spiteful
MALIGNANT harmful
MAMMOTH gigantic
MANUAL done by the hands (e.g., labor)
MARINE of the sea (e.g., life)
MARTIAL warlike
MASSIVE bulky and heavy
MEAGER scanty
MENIAL lowly (e.g., task)
METICULOUS extremely careful
MILITANT aggressive
MOBILE movable (e.g., home)
MUTUAL reciprocal (e.g., admiration)

NAIVE innocently simple

NAUSEOUS disgusting
NEGLIGENT neglectful
NEUROTIC describing the behavior of a person suffering from an emotional disorder
NIMBLE moving quickly and easily
NONCHALANT casual and unexcited
NOTABLE important (e.g., person)
NOTORIOUS well-known in an unfavorable way (e.g., criminal)
NULL having no effect

OBESE very fat
OBJECTIVE free from prejudice (e.g., analysis)
OBNOXIOUS extremely unpleasant (e.g., behavior)
OBSOLETE out-of-date (e.g., machine)
OBSTINATE stubborn
OMINOUS threatening (e.g., clouds)
OPPORTUNE timely
ORTHODOX usually approved (e.g., religious beliefs)
OUTRIGHT complete

PARAMOUNT chief (e.g., importance)
PASSIVE not active (e.g., participation)
PATHETIC pitiful
PERILOUS dangerous
PERTINENT relevant
PETTY relatively unimportant
PIOUS devoutly religious
PLACID calm (e.g., waters)
PLAUSIBLE apparently true (e.g., argument)
POIGNANT keenly painful to the emotions
POMPOUS self-important (e.g., person)
PORTABLE capable of being carried (e.g., radio)
POSTHUMOUS taking place after a person's death (e.g., award)
POTENT powerful (e.g., drug)
POTENTIAL possible (e.g., greatness)
PRECARIOUS risky
PRECISE exact
PREDOMINANT prevailing
PREPOSTEROUS ridiculous
PREVALENT widespread
PRIMARY fundamental (e.g., reason)
PRIME first in importance or quality
PRIMITIVE crude (e.g., tools)
PRIOR previous (e.g., appointment)
PRODIGIOUS extraordinary in size or amount (e.g., effort)
PROFICIENT skilled

PROSAIC ordinary
PRUDENT discreet (e.g., advice)
PUNY small in size or slight in strength (e.g., effort)
PUTRID rotten

QUAINT pleasantly odd (e.g., custom)

RAMPANT spreading unchecked (e.g., violence)
RANCID having the bad taste or smell of stale food (e.g., butter)
RANDOM decided by chance (e.g., choice)
RASH reckless
RAUCOUS harsh (e.g., sound)
REFLEX referring to an involuntary response (e.g., action)
REGAL royal
RELENTLESS persistent (e.g., chase)
RELEVANT pertinent
REMOTE far distant (e.g., time or place)
REPULSIVE disgusting
REPUTABLE respectable (e.g., doctor)
RESIGNED submitting passively to (e.g., one's fate)
RESOLUTE firmly determined
RETICENT speaking little (e.g., child)
RIGID stiff
ROBUST strong and healthy
ROWDY rough and disorderly (e.g., mob)
RUGGED rough
RUTHLESS pitiless (e.g., dictator)

SAGE wise (e.g., advice)
SALUTARY healthful (e.g., climate)
SANE mentally sound
SCANTY meager
SCHOLASTIC having to do with school and education (e.g., record)
SCRUPULOUS careful and honest (e.g., accounting)
SEDATE dignified
SERENE calm
SHEER very thin (e.g., stockings); utter (e.g., nonsense)
SHREWD clever in one's dealings (e.g., businessperson)
SIMULTANEOUS happening at the same time (e.g., events)
SINGULAR remarkable; strange (e.g., behavior)
SINISTER threatening evil
SKEPTICAL showing doubt (e.g., attitude)
SLENDER small in size or amount (e.g., contribution)
SLUGGISH slow-moving
SNUG comfortable
SOBER serious

SOLEMN grave (e.g., occasion)
SOLITARY lone
SOMBER dark and gloomy (e.g., outlook)
SOPHISTICATED wise in the ways of the world
SPARSE thinly scattered
SPIRITUAL referring to the spirit or soul
SPONTANEOUS happening as a result of natural impulse (e.g., reaction)
SPORADIC happening at irregular times (e.g., shooting)
SPRY nimble
STALWART robust
STARK bleak (e.g., outlook)
STATELY dignified
STATIC stationary
STATIONARY not moving
STEADFAST firm
STERN severe (e.g., look)
STOUT fat; firm (e.g., resistance)
STRAIGHTFORWARD honest (e.g., answer)
STRENUOUS demanding great energy (e.g., exercise)
STURDY strongly built
SUAVE smoothly polite (e.g., manner)
SUBLIME inspiring admiration because of noble quality (e.g., music)
SUBSIDIARY less important (e.g., rank)
SUBSTANTIAL having considerable numbers or size
SUBTLE suggested delicately (e.g., hint)
SULLEN resentful
SUMPTUOUS costly (e.g., meal)
SUNDRY various
SUPERB of a high degree of excellence
SUPERFICIAL not going beyond the obvious (e.g., examination)
SUPERFLUOUS beyond what is needed
SUPERLATIVE superior to all others (e.g., performance)
SUSCEPTIBLE easily affected by

TANGIBLE capable of being touched; actual (e.g., results)
TARDY late (e.g., student)
TART having a sharp taste (e.g., food)
TAUT tightly stretched (e.g., rope)
TEDIOUS long and tiresome (e.g., study)
TENACIOUS holding fast (e.g., grip)
TENTATIVE temporary for a period of trial (e.g., agreement)
TEPID lukewarm (e.g., water)
TERMINAL concluding
TERSE brief but expressive (e.g., comment)
TIDY neat (e.g., appearance)
TIMELY happening at a desirable time (e.g., arrival)
TIMID shy
TIRESOME tiring
TITANIC having enormous size or strength
TORRID intensely hot
TRANQUIL calm (e.g., waters)
TRANSIENT passing away after a brief time
TRIFLING having little importance
TRITE ordinary (e.g., remark)
TRIVIAL insignificant
TURBULENT agitated

ULTIMATE final (e.g., conclusion)
UNANIMOUS in complete agreement (e.g., decision)
UNASSUMING modest
UNCANNY unnatural (e.g., accuracy)
UNDAUNTED not discouraged
UNDERHAND sly
UNIQUE being the only one of its kind (e.g., specimen)
UNRULY disorderly (e.g., crowd)
UNWIELDY clumsy to use, usually because of size (e.g., implement)
UPRIGHT honest (e.g., citizen)
UTMOST most extreme (e.g., in distance, height or size)

VAIN futile (e.g., attempt); conceited (e.g., person)
VALIANT brave
VALID (legally) sound (e.g., argument)
VAST very large in extent or size (e.g., distances)
VEHEMENT violent in feeling (e.g., protest)
VERBATIM word for word (e.g., report)
VERSATILE able to perform many tasks well (e g., athlete)
VIGILANT watchful (e.g., sentry)
VILE highly disgusting (e.g., conduct)
VISIBLE able to be seen (e.g., object)
VITAL essential (e.g., contribution)
VIVACIOUS lively
VIVID bright (e.g., color)
VULNERABLE open to attack (e.g., position)

WARY cautious
WEARY tired
WEE very small
WEIGHTY important (e.g., decision)
WHOLESOME causing a feeling of well-being (e.g., entertainment)
WILY cunning (e.g., magician)
WITTY amusingly clever (e.g., remark)
WORDY using too many words (e.g., reply)
WORTHY deserving (e.g., choice)
WRETCHED miserable

7 Practice with Sample Test Paragraphs

This chapter presents a fully analyzed sample GED test paragraph and three additional paragraphs, with answers, for practice.

PRACTICE TEST PARAGRAPH 1

The following items are based on a paragraph that contains numbered sentences. Some of the sentences may contain errors in sentence structure, usage, or mechanics. <u>A few sentences, however, may be correct as written.</u> Read the paragraph and then answer the items based on it. For each item, choose the answer that would result in the most effective writing of the sentence or sentences. The best answer must be consistent with the meaning and tone of the rest of the paragraph.

(1) Savings have been refered to as the tool for accomplishing future goals. (2) After a family has decided on a savings plan the decision on how to invest wisely must be made. (3) Life insurance is a way to provide immediate financial protection for the loss of income through the death of the breadwinner. (4) Once children are expected, the need arises for life insurance. (5) Life insurance is purchased to cover the cost of the funeral, to pay the expenses of the last illness, and to provide income for the survivors. (6) When planning for this type of financial protection, be sure to consider all resources the survivors will have to use (earning ability as well as financial) the amount of income that will meet necessities, and finally the cost of such a program. (7) Concentrate insurance dollars on the breadwinner, and buy the type of insurance that will give the most protection for the cost. (8) A savings account is the second leg of the stool for a savings program. (9) It is here where a family keeps the money that it may need immediately or plans to use within the near future. (10) After the family will protect itself with insurance for the survivors and with a savings account, it is then ready to invest in other possible channels. (11) At this point a family needs to consider these channels in line with its distant goals and with the economy.

1. Sentence 1. **Savings have been refered to as the tool for accomplishing future goals.**

   What correction should be made to this sentence?

   (1) change <u>have</u> to <u>has</u>
   (2) change the spelling of <u>refered</u> to <u>referred</u>
   (3) insert a comma after <u>to</u>
   (4) change the spelling of <u>accomplishing</u> to <u>acomplishing</u>
   (5) no correction is necessary

2. Sentence 2. **After a family has decided on a savings plan the decision on how to invest wisely must be made.**

What correction should be made to this sentence?

(1) change has to have
(2) insert an apostrophe after savings
(3) insert a comma after plan
(4) change the spelling of decision to descision
(5) change how to invest to how to have invested

3. Sentence 3. **Life insurance is a way to provide immediate financial protection for the loss of income through the death of the breadwinner.**

Which of the following is the best way to write the underlined portion of this sentence? If you think the original is the best way, choose option (1).

(1) protection for the
(2) protection. For
(3) protection, for
(4) protection; for
(5) protection—for

4. Sentences 4 and 5. **Once children are expected, the need arises for life insurance. Life insurance is purchased to cover the cost of the funeral, to pay the expenses of the last illness, and to provide income for the survivors.**

The most effective combination of these sentences would include which of the following groups of words?

(1) insurance, life insurance is
(2) insurance that is purchased
(3) insurance, in fact life insurance
(4) insurance, that is to say life insurance
(5) insurance life insurance is then purchased

5. Sentence 6. **When planning for this type of financial protection, be sure to consider all resources the survivors will have to use (earning ability as well as financial) the amount of income that will meet necessities, and finally the cost of such a program.**

What correction should be made to this sentence?

(1) change when planning to having planned
(2) insert a comma after the second parenthesis
(3) substitute quotation marks for the parentheses
(4) change the spelling of necessities to neccessities
(5) remove the comma after necessities

6. Sentence 7. **Concentrate insurance dollars on the breadwinner, and buy the type of insurance that will give the most protection for the cost.**

What correction should be made to this sentence?

(1) capitalize breadwinner
(2) insert a hyphen between bread and winner
(3) change will give to gives
(4) remove the before most protection
(5) no correction is necessary

7. Sentences 8 and 9. **A savings account is the second leg of the stool for a savings program. It is here where a family keeps the money that it may need immediately or plans to use within the near future.**

The most effective combination of these sentences would include which of the following groups of words?

(1) program where a family
(2) program for which a family
(3) program here where a family
(4) program in which a family
(5) program to which a family

8. Sentence 10. **After the family will protect itself with insurance for the survivors and with a savings account, it is then ready to invest in other possible channels.**

   What correction should be made to this sentence?

   (1) change will protect to protects
   (2) insert a comma before and
   (3) remove the comma after account
   (4) change then to therefore
   (5) no correction is necessary

9. Sentences 10 and 11. **After the family will protect itself with insurance for the survivors and with a savings account, it is then ready to invest in other possible channels. At this point a family needs to consider these channels in line with its distant goals and with the economy.**

   The most effective combination of these sentences would include which of the following groups of words?

   (1) channels in line with
   (2) channels that are considered in line with
   (3) channels a family needs to consider in line with
   (4) channels at this point in line with
   (5) channels to be considered in line with

Answer Key

1. **2**	3. **1**	5. **2**	7. **1**	9. **1**
2. **3**	4. **2**	6. **5**	8. **1**	

Answer Analysis

1. **2** (1) is not correct because *savings* may be considered a plural noun. (2) is correct because "r" is doubled in *referred* because the accent is on the second syllable. See rule 8 on page 158. (3) is wrong because no comma is needed here. (4) is wrong because *accomplishing* is correctly spelled. (5) is wrong because a correction is necessary.

2. **3** (1) is not correct because *family* may be considered a collective noun in the singular. (2) is wrong because no apostrophe is necessary since the idea of possession is not involved. (3) is correct because a comma *is* necessary after an introductory clause. See rule 4 on page 143. (4) is incorrect because *decision* is spelled correctly. (5) is wrong because *to invest* is the correct tense since the investment has not yet taken place.

3. **1** This is so because the original is the best way. In (2), a period would result in a sentence fragment. In (3), (4), and (5), no punctuation is necessary after *protection.*

4. **2** In (1) the change would result in a run-on sentence. (2) is correct because *that is purchased* is an adjective clause describing *insurance.* In (3), (4), and (5), all the corrections would result in run-on sentences.

5. **2** In (1), the present tense is correct and should not be changed. In (2), a comma should be inserted in a series according to rule 6, page 143, so this is correct. (3) is wrong because no one is being quoted. (4) is incorrect because *necessities* is the correct spelling. In (5), the comma is needed to punctuate a series.

6. **5** This is so because no correction is necessary. (1) is incorrect because breadwinner is not a proper noun (see rule 4, page 140) and should not be capitalized. (2) is wrong because breadwinner is a single word that does not need a hyphen. In (3), *will give* is the correct tense because the future tense is required and, therefore, there should be no change. In (4), *the* is necessary because a definite article is needed. Therefore (5) is the correct answer.

7. **1** This is a tricky question because it calls for the *most effective combination.* (1) is the most effective combination because the adjective clause immediately follows the noun, *program*, that it describes. (2), (4), (5) are awkward and not as effective. (3) is incorrect because an adjective clause is required.

8. **1** The family protects itself in the *present* so the present tense, not the future tense, is needed. In (2), no comma is needed where only two items are involved: insurance and savings. In (3), the comma after *account* is necessary after an introductory clause. (4) is wrong because *then* is correct since it means "at that time." (5) is incorrect because there is an error in the sentence.
9. **1** Again the most effective combination is called for. In this case, an adverbial clause with the unnecessary words eliminated is best. That choice is (1), which eliminates ten unneeded words after *channels* in the first sentence. All the other choices have superfluous words that reduce the effectiveness of the combination.

Three Additional Sample Test Paragraphs with Answer Analyses

Refer to page 186 for directions in answering the questions based on these paragraphs.

Important: Do not answer any question until you have read and analyzed all the possible choices. You will have to draw on your knowledge of sentence structure, usage, and mechanics, all of which may be involved in a single question.

PRACTICE TEST PARAGRAPH 2

(1) To improve consumer choice use good buying strategies and tactics to carry out the basic plan. (2) Prices, quality, and conveniance can vary greatly in buying food, auto insurance, or dandruff treatments. (3) A watermelon is a better buy at certain times of the year because of transportation costs. (4) Air conditioning may be a good buy at other times. (5) A used car may be adequate for many purposes. (6) A turnip is nutritious. (7) The choice available makes your personal consumer decision process complex, but the potential savings and improvements is huge compared to poor results from not shopping harder. (8) A great deal of regret can be avoided by obtaining reliable information in consumer education courses consumer magazines, and numerous books and pamphlets. (9) Unfair and deceptive practices of a few buisneses would largely disappear, if consumers practiced self-defense. (10) Such defense means being well informed. (11) Consumers can assist in improving product safety, help to maintain reasonable prices, and raising the quality of goods not only by buying wisely, but by addressing themselves to economic and consumer problems. (12) Theres a mutual responsibility among consumers to seek and to improve the ways in which producers make and sell their products and services.

1. Sentence 1. **To improve consumer choice use good buying strategies and tactics to carry out the basic plan.**

   What correction should be made to this sentence?

   (1) insert a comma after <u>choice</u>
   (2) change <u>strategies</u> to <u>stratagies</u>
   (3) insert a comma after <u>strategies</u>
   (4) change <u>to</u> to <u>and</u>
   (5) no correction is necessary

2. Sentence 2. **Prices, quality, and conveniance can vary greatly in buying food, auto insurance, or dandruff treatments.**

   What correction should be made to this sentence?

   (1) remove the comma after <u>quality</u>
   (2) change the spelling of <u>conveniance</u> to <u>convenience</u>
   (3) change <u>can</u> to <u>could</u>
   (4) remove the comma after <u>food</u>
   (5) no correction is necessary

3. Sentences 3 and 4. **A watermelon is a better buy at certain times of the year because of transportation costs. Air conditioning may be a good buy at other times.**

   The most effective combination of sentences 3 and 4 would include which of the following words?

   (1) costs, although air
   (2) costs, and air
   (3) costs, but air
   (4) costs, however air
   (5) costs, whereas air

4. Sentence 7. **The choice available makes your personal consumer decision process complex, but the potential savings and improvements is huge compared to poor results from not shopping harder.**

   What correction should be made to this sentence?

   (1) change the spelling of available to availible
   (2) remove the comma after complex
   (3) change but to and
   (4) change is to are
   (5) no correction is necessary

5. Sentence 8. **A great deal of regret can be avoided by obtaining reliable information in consumer education courses consumer magazines, and numerous books and pamphlets.**

   What correction should be made to this sentence?

   (1) change can to could
   (2) change by obtaining to if you obtained
   (3) insert a comma after courses
   (4) remove the comma after magazines
   (5) no correction is necessary

6. Sentence 9. **Unfair and deceptive practices of a few businesses would largely disappear, if consumers practiced self-defense.**

   What correction should be made to this sentence?

   (1) change the spelling of busineses to businesses
   (2) change would to should
   (3) remove the comma after disappear
   (4) change the spelling of disappear to disapear
   (5) no correction is necessary

7. Sentences 9 and 10. **Unfair and deceptive practices of a few businesses would largely disappear, if consumers practiced self-defense. Such defense means being well-informed.**

   Which of the following is the best way to write the underlined portion of this sentence? If you think the original is the best way, choose option (1).

   (1) self-defense. Such
   (2) self-defense such
   (3) self-defense, such
   (4) self-defense; such
   (5) self-defense, nevertheless such

8. Sentence 11. **Consumers can assist in improving product safety, help to maintain reasonable prices, and raising the quality of goods not only by buying wisely, but by addressing themselves to economic and consumer problems.**

   What correction should be made to this sentence?

   (1) remove the comma after safety
   (2) change help to helping
   (3) change but to and
   (4) change the spelling of addressing to adressing
   (5) no correction is necessary

9. Sentence 12. **Theres a mutual responsibility among consumers to seek and to improve the ways in which producers make and sell their products and services.**

   What correction should be made to this sentence?

   (1) change the spelling of Theres to There's
   (2) change among to between
   (3) change to seek to and seek
   (4) change and to or
   (5) no correction is necessary

ANSWER KEY

1. **1**	3. **2**	5. **3**	7. **1**	9. **1**
2. **2**	4. **4**	6. **5**	8. **2**	

ANSWER ANALYSIS

1. **1** There is an error in punctuation. A comma is used after an introductory phrase.
2. **2** There is an error in spelling. *Convenience* is the correct spelling.

3. **2** A coordinating conjunction is required because the two independent clauses are equally important.
4. **4** There is an error in usage. A plural subject, *savings and improvement*, requires a plural verb, *are*.
5. **3** There is an error in punctuation. A comma is required to separate items in a series.
6. **5** No correction is necessary.
7. **1** The original is correct. All other choices result in run-on sentences.
8. **2** There is an error in usage. The use of the participle *helping* is required to parallel the participles *improving* and *raising*.
9. **1** There is an error in spelling. *There's* is a contraction of *there is*, the subject and verb needed to make this sentence.

PRACTICE TEST PARAGRAPH 3

(1) Household insects seem to have an incredible ability to escape extinction. (2) Cockroaches for example which have been on earth millions of years longer than human beings, can subsist on any kind of food. (3) They thrive in all parts of the world, some species prefer a human home to other habitats. (4) Once they enter it they use countless instinctive tricks to keep from being killed or evicted. (5) You can control household pests. (6) Do systematic house cleaning. (7) The best way to rid your home of practically all insect pests is by a combination of good housekeeping practices and proper use of the right insecticide. (8) It is easier to prevent pests from infesting your home than it is to get rid of them after they are established. (9) Household insects seek available food in places where they can hide and breath. (10) If one eliminates these attractions from your home, the insects will look elsewhere for them. (11) Keep storage cabinets, kitchen drawers, and washtubs clean. (12) Frequent scrubbings with hot water and soap will do the job.

1. Sentence 2. **Cockroaches for example which have been on earth millions of years longer than human beings, can subsist on any kind of food.**

   What correction should be made to this sentence?

   (1) insert commas before and after for example
   (2) change which to who
   (3) remove the comma after human beings
   (4) change can subsist to have subsisted
   (5) no correction is necessary

2. Sentence 3. **They thrive in all parts of the world, some species prefer a human home to other habitats.**

   Which of the following is the best way to write the underlined portion of this sentence? If you think the original is the best way, choose option (1).

   (1) world, some species
   (2) world. Some species
   (3) world some species
   (4) world but some species
   (5) world because some species

3. Sentence 4. **Once they enter it they use countless instinctive tricks to keep from being killed or evicted.**

   What correction should be made to this sentence?

   (1) change it to man's home
   (2) insert a comma after it
   (3) change being killed to having been killed
   (4) change or to and
   (5) no correction is necessary

4. Sentences 5 and 6. **You can control household pests. Do systematic house cleaning.**

   The most effective combination of sentences 5 and 6 would include which of the following groups of words?

   (1) pests and do
   (2) pests if they try to do
   (3) pests while doing
   (4) pests by doing
   (5) pests having done

5. Sentence 7. **The best way to rid your home of practically all insect pests is by a combination of good housekeeping practices and proper use of the right insecticide.**

   If you rewrote sentence 7 beginning with

   A combination of good housekeeping practices and proper use of the right insecticide is

   the next word(s) would be

   (1) indeed
   (2) therefore
   (3) furthermore
   (4) for example
   (5) however

6. Sentence 8. **It is easier to prevent pests from infesting your home than it is to get rid of them after they are established.**

   Which of the following is the best way to write the underlined portion of this sentence? If you think the original is the best way, choose option (1).

   (1) them after
   (2) them. After
   (3) them, after
   (4) them; after
   (5) them, and after

7. Sentence 9. **Household insects seek available food in places where they can hide and breath.**

   What correction should be made to this sentence?

   (1) change the spelling of available to availible
   (2) insert a comma after places
   (3) change can to could
   (4) change the spelling of breath to breathe
   (5) no correction is necessary

8. Sentence 10. **If one eliminates these attractions from your home, the insects will look elsewhere for them.**

   What correction should be made to this sentence?

   (1) change your to one's
   (2) remove the comma after home
   (3) change will to would
   (4) change elsewhere to somewhere else
   (5) no correction is necessary

9. Sentences 11 and 12. **Keep storage cabinets, kitchen drawers, and washtubs clean. Frequent scrubbings with hot water and soap will do the job.**

   The most effective combination of sentences 11 and 12 would include which of the following groups of words?

   (1) and frequent scrubbings
   (2) by frequent scrubbings
   (3) because frequent scrubbings
   (4) since frequent scrubbings
   (5) as a matter of fact frequent scrubbings

Answer Key

1. **1**	3. **2**	5. **5**	7. **4**	9. **2**
2. **2**	4. **4**	6. **1**	8. **1**	

Answer Analysis

1. **1** There is an error in punctuation. Commas are used to set off clauses that are inserted into a sentence.
2. **2** There is an error in sentence structure. As written, this is a run-on sentence. A period is needed to divide the two sentences, and the second sentence must start with a capital letter.
3. **2** There is an error in punctuation. A comma is needed to set off the introductory clause.
4. **4** The sentences are best combined by changing the second sentence into an adverbial phrase modifying the verb *control.*
5. **5** *However* is used when the idea in a sentence differs from the idea in the preceding sentence. In this case, the preceding sentence mentioned one method of control. This sentence refers to a combination of methods.

6. **1** The original is correct, since *after they are established* is an adverbial clause modifying *get rid of*.
7. **4** *Breathe* is the correct spelling of the verb that is needed here. *Breath* is a noun.
8. **1** There is an error in the use of the pronouns—a needless shift from the third person *one* to the second person *your*. If you use more than one pronoun to refer to the same person, you must be consistent. The words *If one eliminates* must be followed by *from one's home*.
9. **2** The best combination is *by frequent scrubbings*, which modifies the verb *keep* and makes the words *will do the job* unnecessary.

PRACTICE TEST PARAGRAPH 4

(1) Among your important records are a thorough household inventory. (2) Before this can be of much value, in case of fire or burglary, youll need to supply some details. (3) Be sure to list the item date bought, purchase price, model number if it applies, brand name, dealer's name. (4) And general description (color, size, style, electric or gas, etc.) (5) Don't forget to include a realistic lump sum in your list for clothes and jewelry if you don't itemize these. (6) This information serves a triple purpose. (7) It helps you to determine the value of your possessions so you can have adequate insurance protection. (8) It helps you if it becomes necessary for you to make an insurance claim. (9) Some families take pictures of their rooms to help identify posessions. (10) One copy of the household inventory should be put in your safe deposit box; you may wish to give a copy to your insurance company.

1. Sentence 1. **Among your important records are a thorough household inventory.**

   What correction should be made to this sentence?

   (1) change your to you're
   (2) change are to is
   (3) change thorough to through
   (4) change the spelling of inventory to inventary
   (5) no change is necessary

2. Sentence 2. **Before this can be of much value, in case of fire or burglary, youll need to supply some details.**

   What correction should be made to this sentence?

   (1) remove the comma after value
   (2) remove the comma after burglary
   (3) change youll to you'll
   (4) change to supply to to have supplied
   (5) no correction is necessary

3. Sentence 3. **Be sure to list the item date bought, purchase price, model number if it applies, brand name, dealer's name.**

   What correction should be made to this sentence?

   (1) insert a comma after item
   (2) capitalize date bought
   (3) remove the comma after applies
   (4) change dealer's to dealers
   (5) no correction is necessary

4. Sentences 3 and 4. **Be sure to list the item date bought, purchase price, model number if it applies, brand name, dealer's name. And general description (color, size, style, electric or gas, etc.)**

   Which is the best way to write the underlined portion of this sentence? If you think the original is the best way, choose option (1).

   (1) name. And
   (2) name. and
   (3) name and
   (4) name, and
   (5) name, And

5. Sentence 5. **Don't forget to include a realistic lump sum in your list for clothes and jewelry if you don't itemize these.**

   What correction should be made to this sentence?

   (1) change Don't to Dont
   (2) change the spelling of realistic to reelistic
   (3) insert a comma after sum
   (4) change the spelling of clothes to cloths
   (5) no correction is necessary

6. Sentences 6 and 7. **This information serves a triple purpose. It helps you to determine the value of your possessions so you can have adequate insurance protection.**

   Which of the following is the best way to write the underlined portion of this sentence? If you think the original is the best way, choose option (1).

   (1) purpose. It
   (2) purpose it
   (3) purpose It
   (4) purpose, so it
   (5) purpose although it

7. Sentence 8. **It helps you if it becomes necessary for you to make an insurance claim.**

   What correction should be made to this sentence?

   (1) insert a comma after you
   (2) change you to one
   (3) change becomes to will become
   (4) change the spelling of necessary to neccessary
   (5) no correction is necessary

8. Sentence 9. **Some families take pictures of their rooms to help identify posessions.**

   What correction should be made to this sentence?

   (1) change the spelling of their to they're
   (2) insert a comma after rooms
   (3) change to help to which helps
   (4) change the spelling of posessions to possessions
   (5) no correction is necessary

9. Sentence 10. **One copy of the household inventory should be put in your safe deposit box; you may wish to give a copy to your insurance company.**

   What correction should be made to this sentence?

   (1) change should be to is to be
   (2) change the semicolon after box to a colon
   (3) change may to might
   (4) capitalize insurance company
   (5) no correction is necessary

Answer Key

1. **2**	3. **1**	5. **5**	7. **5**	9. **5**
2. **3**	4. **4**	6. **1**	8. **4**	

Answer Analysis

1. **2** There is an error in usage. The subject of the sentence is *inventory*, which is singular. The verb, therefore, must also be singular, *is*, since subject and verb must agree in number.
2. **3** The error is in spelling. The proper contraction of *you will* is *you'll* with the apostrophe indicating that letters are omitted.
3. **1** There is a punctuation error. Commas are needed to set off items in a series.
4. **4** Inclusion of the phrase *and general description* in the previous sentence removes the sentence fragment. A comma is necessary because the phrase is one of a series of phrases.
5. **5** No correction is necessary.
6. **1** The original is correct. Two separate sentences are required.
7. **5** No correction is necessary
8. **4** There is a spelling error. *Possessions* is the correct spelling.
9. **5** No correction is necessary.

WHAT'S YOUR SCORE?

Total your score on the four practice test paragraphs (the analyzed paragraph and the three additional sample test paragraphs).

______ right,	______ wrong
Excellent	32–36
Good	27–31
Fair	22–26

UNIT III

WRITING SKILLS

TEST 1, PART II

CHAPTER 8: The Essay

The purpose of the GED Essay test is to test directly your ability to write. It does this by requiring you to write an essay of about 200 words in which you either present your opinion on an issue, a problem that has positive and negative sides, or explain a situation about which you have some general knowledge. The purpose is not to test *how much you know but* rather to assess *your ability to express in writing what you know* about the issue or situation presented. No specialized information is necessary to write on the topic. In this chapter, through examples and practice, you will learn the essential skills of writing *effective*, *interesting*, and *varied* sentences, ways to develop paragraphs, and how to plan the essay in the time allotted. You will also learn how to improve a satisfactory essay to a superior one.

8 The Essay

The Sentence: Examples and Practice

The basic unit of communication is the sentence. The *sentence* is a complete thought expressed in words. It must be independent of other words or groups of words. It must have a *subject*, the person or thing spoken about, and a *predicate* that makes a statement about the subject. The subject is a noun or pronoun that is stated or a noun or pronoun that is understood, as in a command. *Stop!* (*You* or the *name of the person addressed* may be understood.) The predicate must contain at least one verb form.

EXAMPLE

Pedro likes food.

Pedro is the subject, and the predicate makes a statement about Pedro—that he likes food. The predicate contains the verb—*likes*.

Sentences may serve many purposes. They may make a statement, as in the case of Pedro. Such a sentence is termed *declarative*. They may indicate a command—*Don't go*. This is an *imperative* sentence. The sentence may ask a question—*Does Pedro like food?* This is an example of an *interrogative* sentence. Finally, an *exclamatory* sentence may show extreme emotion—*I can't believe it!*

A sentence may be simple, with one main, independent clause.

EXAMPLE

Dahlia has many friends.

Or a sentence may be *compound*, with two or more main, independent clauses linked together.

EXAMPLE

I stayed home last night, and my brother helped me with my homework.

A sentence may also be *complex*, with one main clause and one or more dependent clauses, groups of words that cannot stand independently.

EXAMPLE

Consuela got a job after she graduated.

Consuela got a job is the independent clause, and after she graduated, which cannot stand by itself, is the dependent clause.

WRITING EFFECTIVE SENTENCES

A most important element of good sentence structure is the *ability to relate ideas to one another effectively*.

There are *two* ways to do this.

Relate an idea in one sentence to an idea in another sentence.

The word used depends, of course, on the nature of the relationship between the ideas. In general, there are *seven* different kinds of relationships.

1. *Add other ideas to an idea already expressed, using words or phrases that indicate addition.* Since more than one sentence may be involved, be careful not to commit a run-on sentence error (Review the section "Run-On Sentences" on page 99.)

WORDS AND PHRASES THAT INDICATE ADDITION

also	again
too	likewise
in addition	similarly
moreover	what's more
furthermore	

WORDS THAT EMPHASIZE OR CALL SPECIAL ATTENTION TO THE IDEA BEING ADDED

indeed	certainly
in fact	truly
as a matter of fact	

EXAMPLES

The work I do is interesting. *Moreover*, it pays well.

Mr. Jones was wealthy. In *addition*, he was generous to a fault.

The quarterback was an excellent passer. *In fact*, he was an all-round athlete.

2. *Illustrate an idea or explain it further.* This is considered a special case of addition.

WORDS THAT HELP ILLUSTRATE AN IDEA

for example	to illustrate
for instance	thus

WORDS THAT HELP EXPLAIN AN IDEA FURTHER

in other words	that is to say
as has been said	

EXAMPLES

Athletes in some sports earn huge sums of money. *For example*, the heavyweight boxing champion earns millions of dollars in one fight.

Politics often ignores ethics. *In other words*, political decisions are based on practical considerations rather than on principles of right or wrong.

3. *Establish an order, in either time or space, in the ideas expressed.*

WORDS THAT ESTABLISH TIME ORDER

first, second, etc.	later
next	previously
further	after
then	subsequently
then again	afterwards
finally	last

WORDS THAT ESTABLISH SPACE ORDER

above	in front
beyond	to the right
nearby	to the left
far off	

EXAMPLES

The father spanked his son for misbehaving. *Afterwards*, he felt sorry that he had.

Beyond the house stood the barn, and to *the left* was the silo.

4. *Contrast ideas or show how they differ from each other.* Be careful not to commit a run-on sentence error. (Review the section "Run-On Sentences" on page 99.)

WORDS THAT INDICATE CONTRAST

although	yet
but	however
nevertheless	rather
on the other hand	still
on the contrary	

EXAMPLES

My father is advanced in years. *Still*, he likes to participate actively in sports.

My son is independent in most respects where money is concerned. *On the other hand*, he comes to me for advice about clothes.

5. *Admit that an already expressed idea has some limitations.*

WORDS THAT INDICATE LIMITATION OF AN IDEA

of course	granted that
to be sure	I admit

EXAMPLE

Presidents in the United States are popularly elected. Gerald Ford, *of course*, was an exception.

6 *Show that one idea results from another.*

WORDS THAT INDICATE RESULTS

as a consequence	so
therefore	hence
consequently	accordingly
as a result	

EXAMPLES

At the baseball game, the fan ate too many hot dogs. *As a result*, he got an upset stomach.

The student prepared thoroughly. *Therefore*, he got a high grade.

7. *Summarize briefly ideas contained in a preceding sentence or preceding sentences.*

WORDS THAT SUMMARIZE

in brief	in short
in sum	to sum up
in summary	

EXAMPLES

The doctor recommended swimming, jogging, tennis, and handball. *In sum*, she preferred active sports.

PRACTICE

Use an appropriate word from one of the preceding boxes to join each pair of sentences. For each pair, the word (or words) in parentheses indicates the relationship.

1. (Contrast) I have a wealthy friend. His tastes are simple.
2. (Result) The athlete put in long hours of practice. He won the trophy.
3. (Summary) The teenager eats lots of potato chips, french fries, candy bars, and cookies. She likes junk foods.
4. (Time order) The child spoke disrespectfully to his parents. He felt sorry.
5. (Time order) The worker hurt his leg when he fell. The pain subsided.
6. (Example) Many handicapped persons achieve greatness. Helen Keller was a great writer.
7. (Emphasis) Frank Sinatra had a very broad repertoire. He could sing a wide variety of popular songs.
8. (Explain further) Our village is a microcosm. It is a miniature of the world.
9. (Addition) My parents are good parents. They are my friends.
10. (Contrast) My father spends little on himself. He is very generous to us children.

ANSWERS

There are several possible answers to each of the questions. Two are provided for each question, but others can be found in the same box from which these two are taken.

1. I have a wealthy friend, *but* his tastes are simple.
   I have a wealthy friend; *however* his tastes are simple. (Note important change in punctuation.)
2. The athlete put in long hours of practice. *Therefore*, he won the trophy.
   The athlete put in long hours of practice. *As a result*, he won the trophy.
3. The teenager eats lots of potato chips, french fries, candy bars, and cookies. *In brief*, she likes junk foods.
   The teenager eats lots of potato chips, french fries, candy bars, and cookies. *In sum*, she likes junk foods.
4. The child spoke disrespectfully to his parents. *After*, he felt sorry.
   The child spoke disrespectfully to his parents. *Then* he felt sorry.
5. The worker hurt his leg when he fell. *Later* the pain subsided.
   The worker hurt his leg when he fell. *Afterwards* the pain subsided.

6. Many handicapped persons achieve greatness. *For example*, Helen Keller was a great writer.
   Many handicapped persons achieve greatness. *For instance*, Helen Keller was a great writer.
7. Frank Sinatra had a very broad repertoire. *Indeed*, he could sing a wide variety of popular songs.
   Frank Sinatra had a very broad repertoire. *In fact*, he could sing a wide variety of popular songs.
8. Our village is a microcosm. *In other words*, it is a miniature of the world.
   Our village is a microcosm. *That is to say*, it is a miniature of the world.
9. My parents are good parents. *What's more*, they are my friends.
   My parents are good parents. *Furthermore*, they are my friends.
10. My father spends little on himself, *yet* he is very generous to us children.
    Although my father spends little on himself, he is very generous to us children.

PRACTICE

Here are some more pairs of sentences. Figure out the relationship between them and use one of the appropriate words from the preceding boxes to show that relationship. (In several cases, the pairs of sentences can be joined into a single sentence.)

1. In high school, I studied mathematics. I studied English.
2. The farm worker was very poor. He didn't know where his next meal was coming from.
3. Frank was slight of build and rather short. He was a fine athlete.
4. Deena was graduated from high school. She went on to college.
5. Mother recently underwent surgery. She feels extremely weak.
6. The nutritionist recommended dairy foods, fruits, cereals, and proteins. She advised a balanced diet.
7. Exercising regularly is important. Walking is healthful.
8. The baby had a fever. Her parents called the doctor.
9. My grandmother is over ninety years old. She is quite alert.
10. My car needs gas. It needs oil.

ANSWERS

There are several possible answers to the questions. Two are given for each.

1. In high school, I studied mathematics. I *also* studied English.
   In high school, I studied mathematics. *In addition*, I studied English.
2. The farm worker was very poor. *Indeed*, he didn't know where his next meal was coming from.
   The farm worker was very poor. *In fact*, he didn't know where his next meal was coming from.
3. Frank was slight of build and rather short; *yet* he was a fine athlete.
   Frank was slight of build and rather short. *Nevertheless*, he was a fine athlete.
4. *After* Deena was graduated from high school, she went on to college.
   Deena was graduated from high school. *Then* she went on to college.
5. Mother recently underwent surgery. *Hence* she feels extremely weak.
   Mother recently underwent surgery, *so* she feels extremely weak.
6. The nutritionist recommended dairy foods, fruits, cereals, and proteins. *To sum up*, she advised a balanced diet.
   The nutritionist recommended dairy foods, fruits, cereals, and proteins. *In short*, she advised a balanced diet.
7. Exercising regularly is important. *Thus* walking is healthful.
   Exercising regularly is important. *To illustrate*, walking is healthful.
8. The baby had a fever. *Therefore*, her parents called the doctor.
   The baby had a fever. *Consequently*, her parents called the doctor.
9. My grandmother is over ninety years old, *but* she is quite alert.
   My grandmother is over ninety years old. *However*, she is quite alert.
10. My car needs gas. It *also* needs oil.
    My car needs gas. *In addition* it needs oil.

Relate ideas within a single sentence.

There are a number of possible kinds of relationships.

1. *Connect two ideas of equal importance.*

CONNECTING WORDS	
and	nor
or	for
but	

EXAMPLES

I enjoy my work *and* look forward to each working day.

She does housework *or* goes shopping on the days she does not work.

2. *Combine two sentences by subordinating the less important action pertaining to a person or object described in a separate sentence.* This may be done by using a relative clause that is introduced by a relative pronoun.

RELATIVE PRONOUNS USED TO INTRODUCE RELATIVE CLAUSES			
who	whom	which	that

EXAMPLE

I married Mary. She is the girl I met at your house.

COMBINED:

I married Mary, *whom* I met at your house.

Whom I met is the relative clause that enables you to subordinate the idea of meeting (less important) to the idea of marrying (more important).

EXAMPLE

The children left their clothes strewn about the room. The mother had to pick them up.

COMBINED:

The mother had to pick up the clothes *that* the children left strewn about the room.

That the children left strewn is the relative clause that subordinates the idea of leaving about (less important) to the idea of picking up (more important).

At times you not only save unnecessary words in this manner, but also express your ideas more effectively by indicating their relative importance to the reader.

3. *Combine sentences by subordinating a less important action described in one sentence to a related more important action described in another, using a subordinate conjunction.*

SUBORDINATE CONJUNCTIONS

Showing Time Relationships

when	before
while	after

Showing Causal Relationships

because	since

Showing Opposite Relationships

although

Showing Dependent Relationships

if

A number of examples indicating these relationships follows. In each case, the second action is subordinate (less important) to the first.

EXAMPLE

ORIGINAL:

I was happy. I had a good job.

COMBINED:

(Time relationship)	I was happy *when* I had a good job.
	I was happy *while* I had a good job.
	I was happy *before* I had a good job.
	I was happy *after* I had a good job.
(Causal relationship)	I was happy *because* I had a good job.
	I was happy *since* I had a good job.
(Opposite relationship)	I was unhappy *although* I had a good job.
(Dependent relationship)	I was happy only *if* I had a good job.

4. *Combine sentences by using a phrase to subordinate a less important action described in one sentence to a related, more important action described in another.* In the following examples, note the italicized phrases. In each case, the idea expressed in the phrase is less important than the idea described in the sentence in which it appears.

EXAMPLES

ORIGINAL:

There are many famous home-run hitters in baseball. Babe Ruth is the most colorful.

COMBINED:

Of the many famous home-run hitters in baseball, Babe Ruth is the most colorful.

ORIGINAL:

I took the baby out of the stroller. I entered the supermarket to shop.

COMBINED:

Taking the baby out of the stroller, I entered the supermarket to shop.

ORIGINAL:

The Careys decided to hire a housekeeper. She had to take care of the baby while they were at work.

COMBINED:

To take care of the baby while they were at work, the Careys decided to hire a housekeeper.

5. *Combine sentences by substituting a word or words for an entire subordinate (less important) sentence that describes a related action.* In the following examples, note the italicized words.

EXAMPLES

ORIGINAL:

The student prepared his lesson. He did so, however, in a way that showed he wasn't careful.

COMBINED:

The student prepared his lesson *carelessly*.

ORIGINAL:

The young lady caught my eye. She was an extraordinary beauty.

COMBINED:

The *extraordinarily beautiful* young lady caught my eye.

ORIGINAL:

He had one important quality. It was that he was extremely intelligent.

COMBINED:

Extreme intelligence was his one important quality.

6. *Combine sentences by placing a description of a person or object in one sentence in apposition (see "Glossary of Usage" on page 136) with the word identifying that person in another.* In the following examples, the words in apposition are italicized.

EXAMPLE

ORIGINAL:

My mother is very active in community affairs. She is president of the Parents' Association.

COMBINED:

My mother, *president of the Parents' Association*, is very active in community affairs.

EXAMPLES

My mother, *who is president of* the Parents' Association, is very active in community affairs.

BECOMES

My mother, *president* of the Parents' Association, is very active in community affairs.

Note: In each example, the subordinate or less important idea is first in the sentence, with the more important idea kept for last.

Important note: With the exception of item 1 on page 201—to "connect two ideas of equal importance"—it is also possible to use *phrases* instead of clauses and sentences.

Jet airplanes, *which are a twentieth-century phenomenon,* have brought the world's nations closer together.

BECOMES

Jet airplanes, *a twentieth-century phenomenon,* have brought the world's nations closer together.

Practice

Combine into a single sentence the ideas contained in the following pairs of sentences.

1. Claudia introduced me to Fred. He is the president of the club.
2. I had few responsibilities. I was young.
3. José could go to college. He had saved enough money.
4. The actor gave a magnificent performance. He was handsome.
5. Celia likes to swim. She likes to play tennis.
6. Sue and Joe got married. They met at a party.
7. Jennifer failed the test. She had studied very hard.
8. Dwight was given a diploma. It was well earned.
9. Let me introduce Shira. I spoke to you about her.
10. Many women do not like housework. They do not like marketing.

Answers

1. Claudia introduced me to Fred, *who is* the president of the club.
   Claudia introduced me to Fred, the president of the club.
2. I had few responsibilities *when* I was young.
3. *Because* José had saved enough money, he could go to college.
4. The *handsome* actor gave a magnificent performance.
5. Celia likes to swim *and* play tennis.
   Celia likes to swim, *and* she likes to play tennis.
6. Sue and Joe got married *after* they met at a party.
7. *Although* she had studied very hard, Jennifer failed the test.
8. Dwight was given a *well-earned* diploma.
9. Let me introduce Shira, about *whom* I spoke to you.
10. Many women like *neither* housework *nor* marketing.

WAYS TO IDENTIFY AN IMPORTANT THOUGHT

• Use certain words or phrases to emphasize the idea:

mainly	above all
principally	in the main
chiefly	most important
mostly	foremost

• Use the word *first* to indicate that a particular idea is of primary importance.

• Use superlatives of adjectives to indicate importance, for example:

biggest
most significant

• State that an idea is important, for example:

I think it most important that...
...is most significant.
...should be emphasized.

These are your ways of conveying what is most important to you, the writer. They are signals that say "Pay close attention. This is important."

WRITING INTERESTING SENTENCES

There are a number of additional ways to make your sentences, and, therefore, your essay, more interesting.

Use personal pronouns where possible.

You will recall that the personal pronouns are:

Singular	Plural
I	we
you	you
he	they
she	
it	

Using these pronouns, where appropriate, instead of the more formal nouns, creates interest.

EXAMPLE

The reader will find this book helpful in studying for the examination.

How much better is the simple, direct "*You* will find...." *You* replaces the more formal *The reader*.

EXAMPLE

It is expected that you...

IS MORE FORMAL THAN

You are expected to...

The writer feels that...

IS LESS INTERESTING THAN

I feel that...

Use active verbs in preference to passive verbs.

Active verbs, verbs that usually take objects, add power to your writing.

EXAMPLE

PASSIVE:

The examination was passed by me. [weak]

ACTIVE:

I passed the examination. [much stronger]

PASSIVE:

Diane *is loved by everyone*.

HAS LESS POWER THAN

ACTIVE:

Everyone loves Diane.

Not only are passive verbs weaker, but also, because they require two or more words where one will do, they result in longer sentences.

Use conversation wherever it belongs naturally in your writing.

You know how you feel when you see unbroken pages of print. Conversation breaks up the printed page and makes what you have to say more interesting.

Compare these two passages.

I told my friend, John, that I was going to the ball game. I asked if he would come along. He answered, thanking me for the invitation, but he added that he would have to check to see if he was needed at home by his mother.

"John, I'm going to the ball game. Would you like to come along?"

"Thanks for the invitation, but I have to check to see if my mother needs me at home."

There is no doubt that the passage with the direct conversation is far more interesting (and easier to read) than the passage with the wordier indirect conversation.

PRACTICE

Rewrite the following sentences using personal pronouns and/or active verbs.

1. All the food served to me was eaten by me.
2. The book was enjoyed by my father.
3. It is certain that you will be invited.
4. The writer of this letter wishes to comfort you.
5. Roberto was admired by his classmates.

ANSWERS

1. *I ate* all the food *I* was served.
2. My father *enjoyed* the book.
3. *You* are certain to be invited.
4. *I wish* to comfort you.
5. His classmates *admired* Roberto.

WRITING VARIED SENTENCES

WAYS TO ACHIEVE SENTENCE VARIETY

Vary the types of sentences within a paragraph.

Sentences may be simple, compound, complex, and compound-complex.

1. A *simple sentence* contains one independent clause and no dependent clauses.

   EXAMPLE

   Joan played the piano.

2. A *compound sentence* contains two independent clauses.

EXAMPLE

Joan played the piano and John sang.
[The clauses are joined by the coordinating conjunction *and.*]

3. A *complex sentence* contains one independent and at least one dependent clause.

EXAMPLE

Joan played the piano while John sang.
[The second clause is dependent.]

4. A *compound-complex sentence* contains two independent clauses and at least one dependent clause.

EXAMPLE

Joan played the piano, and Joe sang the song that recalled their meeting.
[The last clause is dependent.]

Sentence variety can be achieved by mixing these types of sentences in a paragraph.

EXAMPLE

I like hero sandwiches.
[Simple sentence]

Although I like all kinds, a cold meat sandwich is my favorite.
[Complex sentence]

My brother, Frank, likes eggplant with Parmesan cheese, and my sister likes meatballs that are drowned in tomato sauce. [Compound-complex sentence]

Vary the purpose of the sentences.

Most sentences are statements. "I got up at 7:00 A.M. I had breakfast..."

A series of statements can become very boring. *Why not vary the purpose of one or more of the sentences?* You can do this in a number of ways.

1. *Ask a question.* We asked you a question in the preceding paragraph. This technique has the advantage of making the reader think of an answer. Indeed, the author can also proceed to answer the question.

2. *Give a command.* This is another way to vary sentences.

EXAMPLE

"Don't give up the ship."

The command may be phrased, "Let us..."

EXAMPLE

"Let us look at the problem from a different angle."

3. *Make an exclamation.* The exclamation adds variety and life when interspersed once in a while in a group of sentences that make statements.

EXAMPLE

"I got up at 7:00 A.M. I had my usual breakfast. *What a dull way to start the day!...*"

4. *Use a direct quotation.* Instead of an indirect quotation, use a direct one. It adds variety and is much more interesting. Compare these two sentences:

EXAMPLE

My brother said that it was a good idea and that he would join us at the party.

AND

My brother said, "That's a good idea. I'll join you at the party."

Vary the sentence length.

A short sentence of two or three words following a more lengthy one is an effective way to get sentence variety.

EXAMPLE

After a long flight from Los Angeles, the soldier on leave dashed through the airport terminal anxiously searching the crowd for his fiancée. At the end of the long corridor, standing impatiently at the information desk, was the object of his search. *It was Anna.*

The short, three-word sentence at the end not only serves to vary the sentence length (the first two sentences are 23 words and 19 words long, respectively) but also focuses the reader's attention on the subject of the paragraph, the soldier's fiancée, Anna.

The Paragraph: Examples and Practice

A paragraph is a group of related sentences that develop a single central idea or a single important aspect of a central topic. Its purpose is to help your reader follow the organization of your thoughts.

At its simplest, a paragraph may be considered a visual device to help your reader follow and understand your ideas. Mechanically, a paragraph is set off from the rest of the printed page by an indentation of its first sentence and perhaps by some extra space between it and the preceding and succeeding paragraphs.

Depending on the topic and its difficulty, the kind of reader, and the purpose of the writing, the number of paragraphs in an essay will vary.

HOW THE PARAGRAPH IS CONSTRUCTED

Each paragraph contains a *topic sentence* that states the main idea or unifying thought.

Here are some examples of typical topic sentences:

> Many television programs contain too much violence. [Which?]
>
> There is a great deal of humor in everyday life. [When and where?]
>
> Jogging is a good way to keep fit. [Why?]
>
> Sewing is quite different from knitting. [How?]
>
> Thomas Jefferson was an all-round American. [For example?]

Each of these topics contains a main thought that can be developed in a suitable way to answer the question that follows it.

A topic sentence focuses on the main point you wish the reader to understand.

Where should the topic sentence be placed? Most often, it should be at the *beginning of the paragraph*, but not necessarily so. For example, the sentence "Sewing is quite different from knitting" can come in the *middle of the paragraph* after sewing has been discussed and before knitting is described. Frequently, you may wish to withhold the topic sentence until the very *end of the paragraph* in order to hammer home your main idea.

EXAMPLE

> If you enjoy the strategy of games, tic-tac-toe, backgammon, or poker; if you like to solve codes and ciphers or are interested in crossword puzzles; if you like to fool around with numbers—then you will enjoy logic. Those who take up logic, you should be warned, join a fanatical sect. On the other hand, they have a good time. Theirs is one of the most lasting, interesting, and inexpensive pleasures. Logic is fun.

The brief *final* sentence of the paragraph is the *topic sentence*.

How can a topic sentence be created from an essay question? Let us assume that you are asked to write an essay on computers indicating your views on the ways they have affected our lives.

The best way to turn the essay topic into a topic sentence is to make "computers" (or whatever topic you are given) the subject of the topic sentence and to make a general statement that tells how you feel about it.

EXAMPLE

GENERAL:

> Computers have greatly affected our lives.

MORE SPECIFIC:

> Computers have had a positive (or negative) influence on our lives.

Or, if the essay assigned deals with nuclear energy, these topic sentences can be used.

EXAMPLE

GENERAL:

> Nuclear energy has greatly affected our lives.

MORE SPECIFIC:

> Nuclear energy has been a boon (or bane) to civilization.

These topic sentences give unity to the essay that follows.

Having written a good topic sentence, you must next select the best way to develop the topic sentence into a paragraph.

WAYS TO DEVELOP PARAGRAPHS

The paragraph may be developed by details.

The most frequent method of paragraph development is the use of details. In the paragraph that follows, details help produce a picture of a famous adventurer.

EXAMPLE

> Who is that short, sturdy, plainly dressed man who stands with legs a little apart, hands behind his back, looking up with keen gray eyes into the face of each speaker? His cap is in his hands, so you can see the bullet head of crisp brown hair and the wrinkled forehead, as well as the high cheekbones, the short square face, the broad temples, the thick lips, which are set firm as granite. A coarse plebeian stamp of a man: yet the whole figure and attitude are that of boundless determination, self-possession, energy; and when at last he speaks a few blunt words, all eyes turn respectfully to him. He is *Sir Francis Drake*.

In a dozen and a half details, the author, Charles Kingsley, has created a paragraph word picture of the man who traveled around the globe in the sixteenth century and led the English fleet in its defeat of the Spanish Armada in 1588.

The paragraph may be developed by illustration and example.

A paragraph's topic sentence may be developed by means of examples or typical instances.

EXAMPLE

> Even before the war, French had borrowed generously from English. It had adopted *baby, bridge, club, sandwich, film*, and *wagon*. Then came such words as *gangster, steak* (used in place of the older loan-word *bifteck*), *des shorts, un bikini, boyfriend, bestseller, groggy, racket, covergirl*.

Be certain that the examples you choose are accurate and are actual illustrations of the statement in the topic sentence.

The paragraph may be developed by defining or explaining something or some idea.

A definition answers the question: What is meant by this? A paragraph that tries to define something explains what it is and what makes it different from other similar or different things.

How important is definition? It is really the basis for any discussion dealing with a challenging subject. How can you talk about democracy unless you define what it is? Here is one such definition.

> The term *democracy* refers primarily to a form of government by the many as opposed to government by the one—government by the people as opposed to government by a dictator or an absolute monarch.

This general definition serves as a basis for a discussion. It tells what democracy is so that the reader understands the term at the start, before the discussion begins.

What makes a definition a definition? Every definition has two parts: a classification or kind and a distinguishing characteristic. The term *democracy* refers primarily to a *form of government*; this is the classification to which democracy belongs. What distinguishes this form of government from others? The distinguishing characteristic is that it is run by *many* as distinguished from governments that are run by *one person*.

Here are some brief definitions. Find the classification and distinguishing characteristic of each term that is defined.

> A child is someone who passes through your life and then disappears into an adult.

> Kindness is a language that the deaf can hear and the blind can see.

> The most powerful weapon on earth is the human soul when it is on fire.

The classifications are: child-someone; kindness-language; weapon-soul. The rest of the sentences give the distinguishing characteristics.

The paragraph may be developed by classifying persons or objects.

Once the terms to be used in a discussion or a piece of writing have been logically defined, the writer frequently goes on to classify the terms involved. For example, after defining democracy, he or she may describe different kinds of democracies. The topic sentence in the next paragraph might read: "There are three different kinds of democracies functioning today." Or, following the definition of leadership, there may be a paragraph beginning, "There are three different kinds of leaders—democratic, authoritarian, and laissez-faire."

Classification is important because it groups ideas and makes them easier for your reader to grasp; people remember better if they can put things into categories or classifications. There are a number of things to keep in mind when classifying:

1. *Select one basis for your classification.* In the leadership example, the classification is by kind of leadership.
2. *Make bases for classification mutually exclusive.* What falls into one category should not fall into another. A democratic leader cannot be confused with an autocratic (dictatorial) one.
3. *Make these bases for classification complete.* Try to fit all possible kinds of leaders into as few categories as possible. A leader involves the people he or she leads in deciding what to do (*democratic*), tells them what to do (*authoritarian*), or takes no part in the decision-making process, leaving them to do as they choose (*laissez-faire*). These three bases include all leaders.

Another way to define classification is to say that it is a logical way of dividing persons or things into a complete system of categories that do not overlap.

The paragraph may be developed by comparison and contrast.

After two or more ideas have been defined and/or divided into subcategories, the writer may wish to compare or contrast them. In *comparison*, similarities between two or more things are pointed out. In *contrast*, differences between two or more things are noted.

Why do we compare or contrast?

1. We may want to compare an unknown idea or object with a known one in order to help the reader understand it better. In describing a game of skill like Scrabble, the writer might compare it with checkers, with which most readers are more familiar.
2. We may want to help the reader understand some quality of two objects or two persons that is not known in relation to a well-known idea that applies to both. For example, we might compare and contrast family life in two societies in distant lands with our own.
3. Finally, taking the second reason a step further, we may want to compare or contrast several ideas or persons to arrive at some general principle. For example, we can compare Michael Jordan, Ken Griffey, Jr., and Tiger Woods to determine the qualities that make an outstanding athlete.

Basically, there are two ways to organize a paragraph that compares or contrasts two items. One is to describe the first item thoroughly and then turn to the second, indicating similarities and differences between them. The second is to move back and forth from one to the other, comparing or contrasting specific aspects of each.

Both methods are effective, but each must be used consistently.

The paragraph may be developed by reasons and proof.

Very often we write not only to explain (by details, by examples, by definition, by classification, by comparison and contrast), but also to persuade, to convince the reader of our point of view.

Daily we make statements of either fact or opinion that we have to justify. A six-year-old girl will try to convince her parents to let her stay up late. A worker will try to persuade the boss to give him or her a raise. A wife or husband will try to convince a tired spouse to go out for the evening.

In *argument*, you try to win someone over to a belief or opinion; in *persuasion*, you present arguments to bring about some action you want someone to take. *How do you do this?*

In *argument*, you start with a proposition, something you will attempt to prove. How do you prove a proposition? Like a lawyer, you have to present evidence that will convince others of the validity of your position. You may cite facts; you may bring in the opinion of authorities; you may bring to bear beliefs that are widely held. In this manner, you establish your proof—proof being a string of related reasons as to why some position or proposition is valid. Here are some propositions to be argued:

Women deserve equal rights with men.

Wealth does not bring happiness.

Education is essential in a democracy.

The United Nations has failed to prevent war.

Urban living is preferable to rural living.

In *persuasion*, you continue from the proposition you have established to an action you want to convince someone to take. Here are some actions that people might be persuaded to take:

All people should stop smoking cigarettes.

All citizens should vote in national and local elections.

Education through college should be compulsory.

Drivers should be reexamined periodically and relicensed.

Juvenile felons should be treated in the same way as other offenders.

In these instances, reasons must be given to persuade either positive or negative courses of action: smoking may cause cancer or other diseases; therefore, people should stop smoking; voting is important; therefore, people should vote.

WRITING EFFECTIVE PARAGRAPHS

1. ***Vary the types of sentences in the paragraph.*** Mix simple, compound, complex, and compound-complex sentences. See page 204.
2. ***Vary the purposes of the sentences in the paragraph.*** Ask questions. Use commands. Make exclamations. Do not hesitate to use direct quotations. See page 205.
3. ***Vary the length of the sentences in the paragraph.*** Throw in a two- or three-word sentence to break up a series of longer ones, particularly if you have an idea you wish to emphasize.
4. ***Vary paragraph length.*** One of the most effective means of drawing the reader's attention to a key idea is the single-sentence paragraph, but this device must not be overused.
5. ***Organize the paragraph carefully to emphasize the most important idea.*** You have a choice between starting the paragraph with a sentence that contains the main idea to be developed in the paragraph (the topic sentence) or building up to the main idea. (See page 206.) Either method can be effective.

A word about summary sentences. Although the summary sentence may seem to be repetitive, more often than not it is better to have one.

If your paragraph has dealt with the United Nations, it helps to have a summary sentence such as "The United Nations has indeed had (failed to have) great influence on the world we live in."

Summary sentences reinforce for the reader what you set out to do in your essay, what views you wanted to get across.

PRACTICE

Of the ways to develop paragraphs, several are most likely to be used on the actual GED test because they allow you to present your views. Here are some topics for paragraphs and suggested ways to develop them.

1. (By illustration) Computers: Magicians or Monsters
2. (By reasons and proof) The Changing Role of Women in the Family
3. (By reasons and proof) It Pays to Dress Well

ANSWERS

Possible sample paragraphs are presented for each of the three topics given.

1. Computers: Magicians or Monsters

   Computers are the latest and the most effective tool mankind has developed to make this world a better one. Consider how and where computers are used. Our supply of electricity is controlled by a computer. The type in our daily newspaper is set by computer. The automobile we drive is the product of computer machinery. Our banking services rely on the computer, which issues checks and reviews them. Most of our bankbook transactions are handled by computers, including the withdrawal and deposit of money by using a plastic card.

Note: The above paragraph is developed by illustration.

2. The Changing Role of Women in the Family

   The role of women in the family is changing rapidly in today's society. Many women are rediscovering great personal satisfaction in the wife-mother role in the family. This role is taking on greater economic significance as society begins to place dollar value on family functions such as caring for children and providing services for family members. The contribution by women is becoming more important and complex because of the information they need for decision making and the knowledge that the health and productivity of family members depend upon the quality of the choices they make.

Note: The above paragraph is developed by reasons and proof.

3. It Pays to Dress Well

   At every stage of your life, clothes can help you establish your identity for yourself and for those with whom you interact. Many roles in life can't be carried off successfully without the aid of the props of costume. The degree to which you choose effectively the clothes that fit a role will affect your performance in that role. Clothes are, moreover, an important factor in developing your feelings of self-confidence and self-respect. When you look good, you feel good.

Note: The above paragraph is developed by reasons and proof.

You have reviewed the basics of writing—the sentence and the paragraph. Now you are ready to tackle the writing of the essay.

The Essay: Examples and Practice

Opening the test booklet, you see, under Writing Skills, Part II, the following essay topic:

> Television plays a very important part in American life. As an entertainment and educational medium, it has brought the world into the average home. It has its advantages and disadvantages.
>
> Write an essay of about 200 words giving your views on television, indicating its positive effects, its negative effects, or both. Support your views by giving specific examples.

This topic requires you to *present your opinion and defend it.* How do you go about doing this?

BEFORE YOU BEGIN

Note the following important facts:

1. The essay must be *about 200 words*, or a minimum of 25 lines for the average writer.
2. You are allowed 45 minutes to write the essay.
3. You must write your essay legibly in ink, on the answer sheet provided.

Read the instructions carefully. You will learn additional important information, including advice on how to take the test.

Essentially there are three major steps:

1. Planning the essay
2. Writing the essay
3. Revising the essay

You are advised to (1) plan carefully, (2) write your essay, and (3) revise your essay to improve what you have written before handing in your paper.

Finally, you are told how your essay will be rated. Two evaluators will read it, judging how clearly you express your opinions, how well you support your opinions by examples and/or arguments, and how effectively and correctly you write.

PLANNING THE ESSAY

The first step is to

1. ***Allot your time.*** Remembering that you have a 45-minute maximum, allow the following amounts of time:

   1. For reading the instructions: 3 minutes
   2. For reading the topic and planning the outline: 7 minutes
   3. For writing the 200-word essay: 20–25 minutes
   4. For reading and revising the essay: 5–10 minutes

   These limits are not compulsory, but they will prevent you from failing to finish your essay (and be penalized) or from handing in a paper containing errors you did not have time to correct.

2. ***Plan your essay.*** It is essential to read the topic carefully and to write on the given topic. *Your essay will receive a failing grade if you write on a topic different from the one you are given.*

Let us return to our sample topic: television. Reread the topic carefully, noting on your scrap paper what is required. You are asked to do two things: *give your opinions and support them by specific examples and proof.* (See page 208.) You are given a choice of the aspects of television on which you will write: *its good points, its bad points, or both.* You must plan your essay accordingly.

Think through the topic, briefly jotting down your ideas. Your *notes* might look like this.

TV is entertaining.
Too much violence
Public TV is educational.
Sitcoms
Informative news programs
Cost of programs
Reruns waste time.
Overdone game shows
"Sesame Street"
Baseball, football, and other sports

To organize your notes into an *outline* or *plan*, combine ideas that belong together and eliminate those that don't fit in.

The notes *TV is entertaining, Public TV is educational, Informative news programs, "Sesame Street," and Baseball, football, and other sports* might be positive examples of programming. *Too much violence, Reruns waste time,* and *Overdone game shows* are negative aspects of programming. *Cost of programs* is irrelevant to the other notes, so drop it.

After you have gathered related ideas from your notes, combine them into a paragraph that has a suitable topic sentence (see page 206). Simple sentences like "Television has many good points" and "Television has its bad points" can serve as headings under which to put your related notes.

Warning: Notes are just that—notes. Your outline or plan should be *written in full sentences* so you can go directly from the outline into your essay. A sample plan from the notes looks like this.

SAMPLE PLAN

1. Television affects the lives of all Americans. It has its good points and its bad points. (*Restatement of the given topic can serve as a topic sentence.* You have chosen to deal with the positive *and* negative aspects of television.)
2. Television has many good points.
   a. There are educational programs on public TV.
   b. There are informative news programs.
   c. There are entertaining comedies, adventures, and mysteries.
   d. There are exciting sports events.
3. Television also has its bad points.
   a. It often portrays violence.
   b. Its situations are unrealistic.
   c. Its programs are often a waste of time.
4. Despite its good/bad points, television enriches/impoverishes our lives. (You may choose either conclusion *to serve as a summary sentence.*)

WRITING THE ESSAY

This plan can easily be expanded into an essay of about 200 words. All you need to do is:

1. ***Give more reasons.*** Television brings good movies into the home; it provides excellent programs for children; it features important sports events. Or, negatively, there are too many and too annoying commercials; there are too many reruns of movies; its dramas are tasteless. (Review Ways to Develop Paragraphs page 207.)
2. ***Give more examples.*** Under 2 of the Sample Plan above, you can give examples of nature programs (National Geographic specials), politics (election coverage), theater (Shakespeare), and music (Metropolitan Opera). (Review Ways to Develop Paragraphs, page 207.)

Here is a sample essay in which you present your opinion and defend it.

TELEVISION: A FORCE FOR GOOD OR EVIL

Television affects the lives of all Americans. It has its good points and its bad points.

Television programming has much to recommend it. It features excellent educational programs on public television as well as on certain commercial stations. Well-known programs include "Masterpiece Theater," which presents dramas, the National Geographic specials featuring natural history, "Great Performances" of music and ballet, and educational children's programs such as "Sesame Street." News programs keep us well informed. Nightly newscasts include international and local news, and programs like "Meet the Press" bring us face to face with newsmakers. Entertainment is provided by comedies such as "Friends," dramas such as "ER," and quiz shows such as "Jeopardy." On many sports specials, the television viewer has a front seat.

Unfortunately, however, television programming also has a negative side. It often portrays violence in its ugliest forms. Viewing is often a waste of time when tasteless dramas, overdone reruns of sitcoms, and poor movies are presented. Viewers may be frustrated and envious when they see game-show participants win huge prizes.

(There are two possible endings depending on your own feelings.)

Despite its bad points, television can be a powerful force for enriching our lives, since its faults can be improved if the public insists.

OR

Despite its good points, television's weaknesses make this medium an evil influence on the viewing public. The American public would be better off without it.

WRITING A SUPERIOR ESSAY

Although this sample essay would receive a good grade, the reasons and examples deal only with programming. Television, however, has deeper effects on American life. *If you treat these less obvious but more important aspects of the topic, you will get a superior grade.*

Television affects the use of our leisure time. If we watch television as *spectators*, we cannot be *participants* in other activities. We have less time for reading, less time for physical activity, and less time for conversation and other socialization. These are some of the negative sociological effects of television.

On the other hand, television can have deeper positive effects. Those who must endure long periods of forced inactivity such as shut-ins or the frail elderly, have, because of television, an entertaining and sometimes constructive way to use their time. Furthermore, viewers can experience many things that they cannot know firsthand, such as faraway places, underwater and space exploration, and scientific discoveries.

These kinds of reasons are more mature than discussions dealing merely with programming. Therefore, this kind of essay will receive a higher grade.

EXPLANATORY TOPICS

Another kind of topic you might be given is an explanatory topic. This requires you to explain something. There are four major kinds of explanatory topics and we shall analyze each of these in turn. One might be a *process* (example, How to Prepare a Budget); another might be a *term to be defined* (example, Being a Good Citizen). Still another might be a *comparison*, explaining similarities (example, Big Cities Are All Alike), *or* differences, explaining *a contrast* (example, Urban and Suburban Ways of Life). Finally, the topic might call for *classification* (example, The Basic Four of a Good Diet).

1. ***Explaining a process.*** This involves a series of steps each of which is a part of a total process. These steps must be presented in order, so that an exact sequence is followed. For the explanation to be clear, each paragraph must be developed in a definite time sequence.

   Note that the four steps of the budget process are presented in a definite order. All must be included and one step must follow the other in time sequence.

Here is a sample essay that explains a process.

HOW TO PREPARE A BUDGET

Preparing a budget involves a definite series of steps.

First, determine the total amount of money you have available to spend. It can be a single amount, money from a single wage earner, or it can be money earned by both husband and wife. It can include wages, dividends, and interest from bank accounts or investments.

After you have determined your income, list your necessary expenditures. These fall into several categories. Most important are food, rent, clothing, health care, transportation, entertainment, education, insurance, and miscellaneous. Some of these expenses are daily (carfare); weekly (food marketing); monthly (rent or mortgage payments); quarterly (income tax payments), or yearly (insurance premiums). The miscellaneous category includes extraordinary expenses such as unusual medical expenses or automobile repair bills.

The next step is to allocate the proper percentage to each category, for example, 25% for shelter. These allocations fall into two categories. They are either necessary or optional expenditures. Food and lodging are necessities. Entertainment is an optional expenditure. It is also important not to forget savings, an important part of every budget.

Finally, total the expenditures and compare them with your income to make certain the budget is balanced and you are not spending more than is available. If you are, you must go back and revise the allocations you have made.

These are the essential steps in preparing a budget.

2. ***Defining a term.*** (See page 207.) The best way to write an essay that defines a term is to list the parts that make up the concept being defined and to give an example of each. For example, good citizenship may be explained by a number of behaviors that, taken together, make up a definition. A *sample outline* of this topic follows.

BEING A GOOD CITIZEN

1. Every American wants to be a good citizen. But what is good citizenship?
2. A good citizen is well informed. To be a good citizen, one must read newspapers and magazines, listen to radio newscasts and telecasts, and keep in touch with public officials.
3. A good citizen not only is well informed, but also acts on the information obtained. The good citizen votes and expresses his or her views to legislative representatives and the press.
4. A good citizen contributes his or her time, talents, and wealth to the public good. The good citizen is active in community organizations and contributes to worthy causes, thereby showing concern for fellow citizens.

5. A good citizen displays the personal qualities that make our democracy strong. Such a citizen is a good family member, is law-abiding, and is loyal to his or her country.
6. These are the qualities that make a good citizen. (Note this final summary sentence.)

You can expand this outline of 148 words to 200 words by adding examples to outline items 2, 3, 4, and 5. For instance, a good citizen expresses his or her views on pending legislation, does jury duty, pays taxes, serves in the armed forces when called upon, and supports such local service organizations as the police, the firefighters, and the public library.

3. ***Making a comparison or a contrast.*** (See page 208.) In a *comparison*, you discuss the similarities in two or more items. You can follow a simple outline such as this:

   1. Topic sentence: *Big cities are alike in many ways.*
   2. Similarity 1: *Big cities are crowded (have a high population density).*
   3. Similarity 2: *Big cities are burdened by traffic congestion.*
   4. Similarity 3: *Big cities have high crime rates.*
   5. Closing summary sentence: *These are some of the ways in which big cities are alike.*

   Sandwiched between a topic sentence and a closing summary sentence, the three paragraphs make up an essay that would, when expanded to 200 words, receive a passing grade.

   In making a *contrast* between two ideas or objects, use the same plan, but point out the differences. Your topic sentence might read: *Urban and suburban living differ in many ways.* Then these paragraphs indicating differences can follow.

One difference between urban and suburban living is population density. Suburbia is less crowded and, therefore, tends to have fewer problems caused by inner-city overcrowding. Although an automobile is more often a necessity in suburbia, traffic problems are less frequent. Crime, while it certainly exists, occurs at a much lower rate than in a big city.

In addition, inhabitants of suburbia tend to have higher incomes. They have more money to spend. Housing is generally more luxurious. Unemployment and poverty levels are lower than those of urban areas.

Finally, suburbia usually has few of the problems that industry brings to the city. Air pollution is lower, and problems of industrial waste are fewer.

It can safely be said that life in suburbia and in urban centers is vastly different.

Note: The final sentence is the concluding or summary sentence.

Urban living and rural living differ in many ways. Some people prefer city life because of its many career and cultural advantages. Others delight in country living because they feel the quality of life it offers is superior.

Write a composition of about 200 words in which you present the advantages of *both* types with appropriate reasons.

City dwellers prefer urban life because it makes many aspects of the good life readily available. More diverse educational institutions are at hand—colleges, technical schools, trade schools, music schools, and art schools. Also, there are more cultural offerings. Most cities have theaters for drama, opera, concerts, and dance, as well as sports stadiums. Residents can subscribe by purchasing season tickets.

The city also offers more conveniences and more services—medical centers, libraries, and financial institutions. The greater concentration of population provides more career opportunities in business and industry. Access to work and leisure activities is made possible by efficient internal transportation systems. And, for those who prefer it, there is more privacy, more anonymity.

Rural dwellers prefer suburbia or country life because it is more individualized. Being less crowded, people have more contact with each other. There is a greater sense of community.

Adults tend to belong to service organizations such as the Kiwanis and the Lions Club. Young people are active in scouting. There are many more community-sponsored activities such as picnics. Since country people generally have more space available, they tend to be closer to nature: they bicycle, they fish, they hike. In short, they lead more outdoor lives than their city cousins.

Also, life in rural areas tends to be slower paced and is not as rushed as in the big cities. Other advantages include less traffic, less air and noise pollution, less crime.

In weighing these considerations, it is up to each individual to choose the way of life he or she prefers.

ADDITIONAL ESSAYS

Study the following essays carefully. Note that each one is based on the arguments listed after it. Note also how each paragraph supports the opinion presented.

> Affirmative action is the use of racial, ethnic, or gender preference in allocating economic and social benefits: job hiring and promotion, admission to schools, and establishment of seniority.
>
> Some regard affirmative action as necessary because of historical discrimination. Others believe that it is undesirable because it results in reverse discrimination.
>
> Write a composition of about 200 words in which you present your view on this issue, giving reasons and examples to support your position.

FOR AFFIRMATIVE ACTION

For many generations, large numbers of Americans have suffered discrimination in many forms. People of color have not been hired because of race, and certain ethnic groups have been excluded from social benefits. Educational and job opportunities for women have been limited. Discrimination against the elderly continues to be widespread. Minorities and women do not have access in many instances to higher, better paid positions.

As a result, in the competition for jobs and admission to good schools, minorities, women, and the elderly are at a disadvantage.

Affirmative action is needed to compensate for this discrimination, which has led to illiteracy, poverty, and general second-class citizenship. Under affirmative action, minorities and women receive preference in hiring and in promotion. Places are set aside by colleges and professional schools for preferential admission. Compensatory programs provide additional training to level the field of competition. Scholarships help promising minority students and women who lack money for college or other training. Also, since past discrimination did not allow certain groups to gain seniority in the workplace, seniority is waived when firings are necessary.

All these benefits can be achieved by federal and state legislation and, if necessary, by court order.

Only by affirmative action programs can historical wrongs be righted and equality of opportunity provided for these long-suffering citizens.

Summary of reasons *for* affirmative action programs

1. Affirmative action programs correct past discrimination because of race and sex.
2. Affirmative action programs provide improved opportunity for minorities competing for jobs and admission to good schools.
3. Compensatory programs of training and scholarships enable all to compete fairly.
4. Legislation by government and orders by courts can result in affirmative action being taken.

AGAINST AFFIRMATIVE ACTION

Although in the past America has provided unequal opportunity to many of its citizens, affirmative action programs are not the way to remedy this situation.

Reverse discrimination results when racial and gender preferences determine who is to be hired. Qualified members of majorities are passed over in favor of minority-group members for available jobs. Women are favored over equally qualified men. In most instances, the individuals who were passed over were in no way responsible for the discrimination of the past. Instead of merit, race or gender has been substituted as the criterion for hiring. When this happens, quotas, that is, fixed numbers of jobs set aside for minorities, limit job opportunities for other, more qualified applicants.

Affirmative action hurts the U.S. economy. In many cases, to make jobs available to minorities, less qualified, less productive applicants are hired.

In addition, affirmative action often has a negative effect on the people who supposedly benefit from it because they feel that they did not achieve their goals on their own merits. As a result, minority-group members are split, with the qualified, who do not need preference, on one side and the less qualified, who need help, on the other.

For these reasons, affirmative action programs are unwise.

Summary of reasons *against* affirmative action programs

1. Affirmative action results in reverse discrimination against those who are not responsible for past wrongs.
2. Use of racial and gender preferences in hiring and in admission to schools replaces merit as the criterion, hurting performance.
3. Affirmative action leads to the establishment of quotas that limit opportunity for large numbers of Americans.
4. Affirmative action may have a negative effect on those who supposedly benefit most from it.

The issue of financing elections in the United States has received considerable attention. Some believe that elections for public office should be financed by the public; others think that the costs of campaigning should be borne by the candidates.

In a composition of about 200 words, present your views either in favor of public financing or against it. Support your positions with appropriate reasons.

FOR PUBLIC FINANCING

Many Americans feel that there should be public financing of campaigns for public office. They offer a number of reasons.

The costs of campaigning have risen to astronomical heights. In addition to necessary staffs for administrative purposes, there are the costs of setting up campaign trips and barnstorming through all fifty states by bus, train, and air. Stops have to be planned by front men, speeches must be written; publicity has to be arranged.

The single biggest expenditure, however, is for television advertising; thousands of dollars per minute must be spent. Also, advertisements in other media, such as newspapers and radio, have to be financed.

Most candidates do not have the wealth to pay for all this publicity. They must raise funds from business corporations, labor groups, public institutions, and wealthy individuals. In return, large donors will exert pressure on candidates to support their undertakings even if these are not in the public interest. Public financing would not only attract candidates who are not wealthy but would enable candidates to be independent of pressure from contributors.

Private financing disrupts the democratic process because small groups of individuals are able to exercise great political power. Public financing would enlarge each candidate's political base.

For these reasons, I feel that public financing is preferable to private financing.

Summary of reasons *for* public financing

1. A broader field of qualified candidates would be available since they would not need to be wealthy.
2. Dependence on pressure groups demanding favors would be reduced.
3. Public financing would prevent undermining of the democratic process.
4. Accountability of the candidates would be easier to establish.

AGAINST PUBLIC FINANCING

Many Americans are against public financing of campaigns for election to public office. They feel that the political process will be disrupted if candidates receive public money. Candidates of splinter parties with no chance of election will get valuable television time, for example, and thus distract attention from the candidates supported by the larger constituencies of voters in the country.

Majority rule will be undermined if the voting public can choose from an increased number of parties. As it is, few public candidates achieve a majority; most get only a plurality.

It is now possible for candidates to raise considerable financing privately on their own. They can appeal to public-minded citizens who agree with the platforms they are advocating. They can arrange fund-raising dinners. It is possible for candidates to appear on talk shows and on other programs that present diverse views on issues that will arise in the elections. Interviews with the press can be arranged. Service organizations such as Lions Clubs and Rotary International, women's groups, and veterans organizations offer opportunities to speak to large numbers of voters. The League of Women Voters has arranged programs of this type for many years.

For the American citizen, public financing will result in one more tax that will fall on many who cannot afford the additional burden. Also, there is a difficult question: "Who will decide how the public funds will be distributed?"

For these reasons, I feel that private financing is preferable to public financing of election campaigns.

Summary of reasons *against* public financing

1. The election process will be disrupted if a large number of candidates from small parties gain access to public money.
2. Majority rule will be undermined if many splinter parties gain votes.
3. Candidates can now raise big sums of money on their own.
4. Americans will have one more tax added to their already large burden.

Many states have instituted lotteries as a way of raising money for state programs. Many Americans advocate their use. Others oppose state-sponsored lotteries.

In a composition of 200 words, take a position on this issue and defend it with appropriate reasons.

FOR STATE-SPONSORED LOTTERIES

I favor state-sponsored lotteries for many reasons. Most important is the need of the states to raise additional revenues for important services. Chief among these is education. Education is primarily a state responsibility, and the revenues for it are raised by state income and property taxes. The burden on taxpayers and homeowners is very heavy. Setting aside a percentage of the income from lotteries eases this burden.

Participation in lotteries is purely voluntary. No one is forced to participate. Those who wish to buy tickets can do so for very small amounts of money, in many instances as little as a single dollar, so participation in lotteries does not drain individual budgets.

Lotteries are state-run and are run impartially. All aspects of the process, such as winning numbers and the amounts of prizes, are open to the public. Lotteries also divert those who wish to gamble from more expensive operations, which may fall under the control of gangsters. Betting on sports events, for example, has been found, in many instances, to be manipulated by bookmakers and mobsters.

Also, lotteries are democratic in that everyone who participates has an equal chance to win. Psychologically, lotteries offer excitement and potential wealth. In some instances, the dreams of a lifetime have been fulfilled.

For these reasons, I support state-sponsored lotteries.

Summary of reasons *for* state-sponsored lotteries.

1. A portion of the money raised through lotteries is used to provide and improve state services in such vital areas as education.
2. Participation is purely voluntary.
3. Participation does not require large outlays of money.
4. Lotteries are run fairly, with the winning numbers and the amount of winnings made public.
5. Those who participate add hope and excitement to their lives.

AGAINST STATE-SPONSORED LOTTERIES

I am opposed to state-sponsored lotteries for many reasons.

Although lotteries may be run fairly, they encourage those who can least afford it to gamble. Lines of working peole form at newspaper-store cash registers to buy tickets, especially if the prize climbs to many millions of dollars. The money spent on tickets could better be spent on such necessities as food and clothing.

Those who purchase tickets do not stop to think of the astronomic odds against their winning. For example, the possibility of getting the winning numbers in New York State with a one-dollar ticket and two chances are 13 million to 1.

Psychologically, lotteries offer excitement and potential wealth, but the odds of winning that wealth are so great that nearly every participant is doomed to disappointment. The floors of betting parlors are littered with tickets that have proved to be losers and been thrown away.

Even the winners face many problems. Federal income taxes on winnings are enormous. Often the get-rich-quick results are devastating to the family. We read daily in the newspapers of lawsuits between family members.

For these reasons, I feel that state-run lotteries are not in the public interest.

Summary of reasons *against* state-run lotteries.

1. Lotteries encourage those who can least afford it to gamble.
2. The odds against winning are astronomical.
3. Most participants are doomed to disappointment.
4. Winnings are heavily taxed.
5. Many winners cannot cope with their newly acquired wealth.

PRACTICE

For each of the following controversial topics: (1) build a composition from the arguments, for or against, presented; (2) use examples and fill in necessary details to arrive at a composition of about 200 words.

TOPIC—CAPITAL PUNISHMENT

The majority of the states in the United States have adopted capital punishment for murder in the first degree. Over a dozen states, however, have no death penalty.

Arguments *for* the death penalty.

1. The death penalty acts as a deterrent to those who plan to commit murder.
2. Since ancient times and in many places today, the practice of an eye for an eye and, therefore, a life for a life is followed.
3. Capital punishment prevents the possible release of potential murderers and their return, during parole, to their criminal ways.

Arguments *against* the death penalty.

1. Some feel that capital punishment is "cruel and unusual" punishment under the U.S. Constitution and that it is unfairly carried out.
2. Mistakes are made, and some accused murderers are innocent of any crime.
3. Capital punishment makes it impossible to rehabilitate criminals who might become productive members of society.

TOPIC—GUN CONTROL

The use of firearms in the United States is a problem for us all. Some believe that guns, particularly automatic weapons, should be strictly controlled. Others think that controls are unnecessary—that people, not guns, are responsible for killings.

Arguments *for* gun control.

1. Each year thousands of people are killed by guns in criminal acts and in accidental shootings.
2. Guns fall into the hands of those who do not know how to use them properly. Easy access to guns encourages crime.
3. Most Americans are for gun control measures. Only the well-financed National Rifle Association lobbies against it.

Arguments *against* gun control.

1. The U.S. Constitution guarantees the right of U.S. citizens to bear arms.
2. Guns are needed for self-defense against the criminal element in society.
3. Proper safeguards can be taken to prevent guns from falling into improper hands.

REVISING THE ESSAY

You read the directions and the topic carefully; you planned what you would say; you have written your essay. You may think you are finished, but in reality you are not.

It is essential that you read the essay you have written, revising it where necessary. You will recall that you left 5 to 10 minutes for revision when you planned your time.

What do you look for when you read your essay?

CHECKLIST FOR REVISION

Content

1. Are your ideas pertinent to the topic?
2. Are they clearly stated?
3. Are they properly organized?
4. Are they logically developed? Have you used the proper connecting and transitional words?
5. Is the purpose of your essay achieved? If you had to make a judgment, did you do so? Explain a process? Did you define a term? Did you make a comparison or contrast?

Organization

1. Does each paragraph have a good topic sentence?
2. Is each key idea developed in a separate paragraph?
3. Does each paragraph conclude with a clear summary sentence?

Correctness (Review Writing Skills Part I Unit)

1. Is your essay free of sentence errors (run-on sentences and sentence fragments)?
2. Are agreement, case of pronouns, and verb forms correct?
3. Have you punctuated and capitalized correctly?
4. Have you chosen your words with proper usage in mind?
5. Have you spelled them correctly?

Only after you have read and revised your essay can you feel you have completed the Writing Skills, Part II test. Don't hesitate to make changes or corrections on your paper. As long as *your writing is legible*, neatness is not a factor.

HOW THE ESSAY WILL BE RATED, WITH EXAMPLES

The GED testing service, which prepares the essay test, granted permission to include its GED Essay Scoring Guide. This will give you a good idea of how your essay will be graded.

GED ESSAY SCORING GUIDE

Papers will show *some or all* of the following characteristics.

Upper-half papers make clear a definite purpose, pursued with varying degrees of effectiveness. They also have a structure that shows evidence of some deliberate planning. The writer's control of English usage ranges from fairly reliable at 4 to confident and accomplished at 6.

6 Papers scored as a 6 tend to offer sophisticated ideas within an organizational framework that is clear and appropriate for the topic. The supporting statements are particularly effective because of their substance, specificity, or illustrative quality. The writing is vivid and precise, though it may contain an occasional flaw.

5 Papers scored as a 5 are clearly organized with effective support for each of the writer's major points. The writing offers substantive ideas, though the paper may lack the flair or grace of a 6 paper. The

surface features are consistently under control, despite an occasional lapse in usage.

4 Papers scored as a 4 show evidence of the writer's organizational plan. Support, though sufficient, tends to be less extensive or convincing than that found in papers scored as a 5 or 6. The writer generally observes the conventions of accepted English usage. Some errors are usually present, but they are not severe enough to interfere significantly with the writer's main purpose.

Lower-half papers either fail to convey a purpose sufficiently or lack one entirely. Consequently, their structure ranges from rudimentary at 3, to random at 2, to absent at 1. Control of the conventions of English usage tends to follow this same gradient.

3 Papers scored as a 3 usually show some evidence of planning or development. However, the organization is often limited to a simple listing or haphazard recitation of ideas about the topic, leaving an impression of insufficiency. The 3 papers often demonstrate repeated weaknesses in accepted English usage and are generally ineffective in accomplishing the writer's purpose.

2 Papers scored as a 2 are characterized by a marked lack of development or inadequate support for ideas. The level of thought apparent in the writing is frequently unsophisticated or superficial, often marked by a listing of unsupported generalizations. Instead of suggesting a clear purpose, these papers often present conflicting purposes. Errors in accepted English usage may seriously interfere with the overall effectiveness of these papers.

1 Papers scored as a 1 leave the impression that the writer has not only *not* accomplished a purpose, but has not made any purpose apparent. The dominant feature of these papers is the lack of control. The writer stumbles both in conveying a clear plan for the paper and in expressing ideas according to the conventions of accepted English usage.

0 The zero score is reserved for papers which are blank, illegible, or written on a topic other than the one assigned.

Now, keeping this scoring guide in mind, study the following treatments of the unfavorable effects on health of smoking.

Paper 1

The major effects of smoking include a shortened life span. Each year nearly half a million Americans die prematurely as a result of smoking. Smoking is responsible for 30 percent of all cancer deaths in the United States, including those from lung cancer.

Smoking weakens the heart's ability to function, leading to heart attacks and strokes. In addition, tens of thousands die from chronic lung disease linked to smoking.

Women who smoke during pregnancy are ten times more likely to have miscarriages. Also, the babies of smoking mothers tend to have lower birth weights.

Finally, there is the risk of death or severe illness for those who are exposed to second-hand smoke: lung cancer, emphysema, bronchitis, pneumonia, or heart disease.

Paper 2

Smoking has many unfavorable effects. It affects the health of the smoker in many ways. It results in shortness of breath. It causes tobacco stains.

Smoking becomes a habit that is hard to break smokers become addicted to cigarettes because of the nicotine.

Smoking is also very expensive three packs a day cost about $50 a week which could buy alot of food and necesities.

If you have a family, they are affected by second-hand smoke. Children learn to smoke by imitating there parents.

That's why you shouldn't smoke.

Paper 3

Smoking has bad affects. Millions of americans smoke they spend a great deal of money on cigarettes.

Smoking is bad for you. It destroys your health and causes Cancer. You may think its grown up to smoke but it really isnt.

Smoking also hurts the ones around you. Who inhale your smoke. Women who are pregnant might hurt they're babies.

Smokers pollute the air. And make it hard for others around them to breath.

This is why you should think twice before you light up.

Paper 1 has excellent organization of materials relating to the subject. Paragraphing is logical. Specific facts are presented, and everything relates directly to the topic. There are no errors in sentence structure, punctuation, or capitalization

Paper 2 has elements of organization. Each of the first four paragraphs makes a single argument.

This paper has two main weaknesses. First, the arguments are not backed up by any relevant facts. One of the effects mentioned (tobacco stains) is unimportant, while important effects on health are omitted. In addition, there are a number of errors. Paragraph two has a run-on sentence, as has paragraph three. *A lot* is misspelled as *alot*, and *necessities* as *necesities*; also, there should be a comma after *week*. In paragraph four, an incorrect pronoun refers to family—*they* instead of *it*, and *there* should be replaced by *their*. Although this paper has good organization, the errors would reduce the rating to a 4.

Paper 3, is poorly organized. Irrelevant material is included (money spent, grown-up feeling). Statements are repeated and not documented (causes cancer). Also, there are many errors in accepted English usage. There are sentence errors—a run-on sentence in the first paragraph, and sentence fragments in the third and fourth paragraphs. There are several spelling errors; *affects* should be *effects*; *its* should be *it's*; *isnt* should be *isn't*; *they're* should be *their*; *breath* should be *breathe*. *Americans*, not *americans*, and *cancer*, not *Cancer*, are correct. Sentences are very short, even childish.

There is no doubt that Paper 1 will receive a 5, but Paper 3 will receive a 2 or a 1.

UNIT IV

SOCIAL STUDIES

TEST 2

CHAPTER 9: Reading and Interpreting Social Studies Materials

The basic skills in reading social studies materials are thoroughly treated. A special section deals with basics in interpreting tables, graphs, and maps, and an additional section deals with interpreting political cartoons.

CHAPTER 10: Handling Social Studies Skills Questions

The four basic kinds of skills questions are analyzed with examples of each. Twenty questions offer practice in dealing with questions testing comprehension, application, analysis, and evaluation. An outline of study for all the social studies is included. The Glossary of Social Studies Terms is a mini-dictionary with clear and simple definitions.

CHAPTER 11: Social Studies Practice

The 64 questions based on passages, tables, and maps provide ample practice in reading and interpreting social studies materials.

9

Reading and Interpreting Social Studies Materials

How to Read Political Science, History, Economics, Geography, and Behavioral Science Passages

Reading in the social studies requires a number of skills that are common to all reading materials. When you read in any subject, you want to identify the *main ideas* of the writer. So, too, in social studies you need to get at the key thoughts being expressed.

LOCATING THE MAIN IDEA

If you read too slowly, you may miss the main point because you have gotten too involved in details. It is important, therefore, that you first read the selection through to the end rather quickly *before* you turn to the questions.

Where do you look for the main idea? Most often you will find it in the topic sentence, usually the first sentence in the passage. Sometimes, however, the writer will withhold the main idea until the last sentence, building up to it throughout the entire selection. At other times, the writer will include both a main idea and an important secondary (or subordinate) idea.

To train yourself in **locating the main idea**, ask yourself the same questions that will be asked of you on the examination.

1. What is the main idea of the passage?
2. What is the best title for the passage?
3. If I were choosing a suitable headline for the article in a newspaper, what headline would I choose?
4. What is the *topic sentence* of this paragraph or paragraphs; *that is, the sentence that includes the ideas contained in all the other sentences?*

FINDING DETAILS

After you have determined the main idea, the next step is to *locate the facts supporting the main idea or details* that flow from the main idea. If, for example, the main idea of a passage is that democracy is the best form of government, the author will undoubtedly provide facts or reasons to support this statement or include facts that show the superiority of democracy to other forms of government. If the main idea is a general conclusion that many persons with physical disabilities have overcome them and become famous, details would probably include such examples as Helen Keller and Franklin D. Roosevelt.

How do you locate a detail? You go back to the selection a second or third time to dig it out of the passage. It most frequently will come in the middle or toward the end of the selection. Sometimes clues in the passage steer you to the detail or fact in question. Clues for locating details may read:

An example is...

One reason is...

An argument in support of (or against)...is...

A reason for...is...

> To train yourself in **locating details**, ask yourself these questions:
>
> 1. What examples are given to illustrate the main point?
> 2. What reasons are offered to support the author's position?
> 3. What arguments for or against a proposal does the author present?
> 4. When, where, how did something happen?
> 5. What did someone do?
> 6. Why did he or she do it?

To find the proper detail, it will be necessary for you to *learn how to skim*, that is, to read rapidly to locate the piece of information you are seeking. You can do this only if you know specifically what you need to find in a given selection and limit your reading to finding only that fact.

DETERMINING ORGANIZATION

Note the manner in which the writer organizes his or her material. This will help you to follow the author's thoughts effectively. The writer may organize his or her material chronologically, that is, in the order in which a series of events happened. Alternatively, the writer may organize the material logically by presenting the arguments *for* a position in one paragraph and the arguments *against* in another. Or the writer may present his or her ideas in the order of their importance, with the most important ideas first. This, in fact, is the way a newspaper article is written—"from the top down"—in case the reader doesn't have time to finish it all.

If you can determine the organization of a passage, you can zero in on the relationship between the main parts of a passage.

> **CLUES TO FINDING THE RELATIONSHIP BETWEEN THE MAIN PARTS OF A PASSAGE**
>
> **Sequence of ideas** is indicated by such words as:
>
> | | | |
> |---|---|---|
> | first | next | finally |
> | second | further | |
>
> **Additional ideas** are indicated by such words as:
>
> | | | |
> |---|---|---|
> | and | furthermore | likewise |
> | besides | also | in addition |
>
> **Opposing or contrasting ideas** are indicated by such words as:
>
> | | | |
> |---|---|---|
> | on the other hand | but | yet |
> | however | still | although |

DRAWING CONCLUSIONS

Another step involves *drawing conclusions from the material presented.* Conclusions are often indicated by such words as:

thus	accordingly	consequently
therefore	so	as a result

Sometimes, however, the author does not draw the conclusion, but leaves it to you, the reader, to do so. You infer the conclusion from the materials presented; you draw the inference as a result of details you have noted and the relationships you have determined (time sequence, logical order, cause-and-effect, among others). Thus, if an author indicates that a given president vetoed many bills, you might infer that the president and the Congress differed in their thinking about legislation, perhaps because the Congress was controlled by a political party different from that of the president.

To train yourself to **make inferences** properly in order to draw a conclusion, ask yourself these questions:

1. What do I think will happen next? (inference or prediction as to the outcome)
2. Putting these arguments together, what conclusion can I reach?
3. If one result was caused by something, will a similar effect take place in another situation where the same cause is operating?
4. What is the writer suggesting, rather than saying outright?

READING CRITICALLY

In addition to drawing conclusions and making inferences, it is essential in social sciences that you react to what you have read. Often you must judge the material you are reading, not merely understand it. Historians, political scientists, economists, sociologists, and anthropologists often present one side of the story, their side, but there is almost always another side. In otherwords, they may "slant" the material to suit their bias by including only facts and arguments favorable to their own view and omitting everything else. It is essential for you to *read critically*. Do *not* accept everything that is written just because it appears in print.

You must develop the habit of challenging the author by raising questions, judging the completeness and truth of the information presented, and distinguishing fact from opinion.

A *statement of fact* is one that can be proved true by consulting a reliable source of information such as an encyclopedia, an almanac, or an official government document. Here is an example.

EXAMPLE

The federal government spends billions of dollars each year helping states with aid to needy persons: needy through unemployment, disability, or family problems.

This statement can be verified by consulting the official federal budget.

A *statement of opinion or belief* is one that expresses the feelings, thoughts, or beliefs of a person or persons, and that cannot be proved to be true by reference to any reliable source at the present time.

EXAMPLE

It is believed that by the year 2000, population will have outstripped food production and starvation will be widespread.

This is a prediction in the form of a statement or belief attributed to an unidentified source ("It is believed...") that cannot be proved until the year 2000. It is possible that others may have their own beliefs. In any case, the statement is definitely not a fact.

Note that certain words are clues to statements of opinion.

WORDS THAT ARE CLUES TO STATEMENTS OF OPINION

claim	probably
believe	possibly
think	might
consider	should (have)
will be	could (have)
likely	ought

WORDS THAT PROBABLY REFLECT OPINION RATHER THAN FACT

better	undesirable
worse	necessary
desirable	unnecessary

REMEMBER: Always apply the test, "Can this statement be proved by reference to a reliable source?"

It is important to distinguish fact from opinion in the printed word when writers unconsciously allow their opinions or biases to enter into their writing. It is even more important to do so when a writer slants his or her material deliberately.

You can **read critically** if you ask yourself the following questions:

1. Why is the author writing this selection?
2. What is the author trying to get me, the reader, to believe?
3. Is the author presenting a balanced or one-sided view of the situation?
4. Is the author omitting essential information?
5. Is the author appealing to my mind or to my emotions and prejudices?
6. Does the author have some hidden reason for writing what he or she writes?
7. Is the author accurate? Or does he or she deal in half-truths?
8. Does the author use words with specific agreed-upon meanings, or does he or she use words that are "loaded" because they have special meanings?

DETECTING PROPAGANDA AND PROPAGANDA TECHNIQUES

When writers deliberately spread ideas or opinions to benefit themselves or institutions to which they belong or to damage opponents or opposing institutions, they are engaging in propaganda. A propagandist tries to influence your thinking or behavior and to turn your opinions and actions in a certain direction. He or she uses words that appeal to your emotions—your fears, your loves, your hates—rather than to your reason, to your ability to think clearly, in order, ultimately, to make you do things in a way you never ordinarily would do.

Seven common techniques in propaganda are:

1. ***Name-calling.*** The writer tries to influence you by attaching a bad name to an individual, group, nation, race, policy, practice, or belief.

   EXAMPLE

   It would be wise to pay no attention to that loony liberal (or retarded reactionary, depending upon the writer's point of view).

   Certain names are loaded with emotional overtones: Fascist, Red, Nazi, Commie. You must note carefully in what way and for what purpose these terms are used. Name-calling is a common propaganda technique.

2. ***Glittering generalities.*** The writer attaches "good" names to people and policies, in the hope that you will accept them without really looking into the facts.

   EXAMPLE

   The writer appeals to our emotions by using such "good" terms as *forward-looking*, *peace-loving*, *straight-shooting*, and *idealistic*.

   We all love progress, peace, honesty, and idealism so we tend to accept rather than challenge. Always ask the questions "why" and "how" when "good" terms are applied to people and policies.

3. ***Transfer.*** The writer tries to use the approval and prestige of something or some institution we respect to get us to accept something else in which he or she is interested.

   EXAMPLE

   Most Americans are law-abiding and respect their police officers. One who writes on behalf of an athletic league supported by the local police will try to get you to transfer your approval of the police to the athletic league he or she is sponsoring.

   Always examine the person or institution receiving the transfer on its own merits rather than on the merits of the original institution you love and respect.

4. ***Testimonial.*** Advertisements on television and radio make wide use of testimonials. A top athlete endorses a breakfast cereal. A beautiful actress recommends a cosmetic cream. An ex-senator testifies to the value of a credit card. A testimonial is a recommendation made by someone on behalf of a person, a product, or an institution.

   But is the athlete an expert on nutrition? Is the actress an expert on skin care? Is the politician an expert on personal money management? REMEMBER: these people are being paid to make these testimonials. You must ask yourself whether the person making the testimonial is expert enough to do so before you believe what you read or hear.

More subtle is newspaper reporting that is based on *indirect* testimonials.

EXAMPLES

Official circles report...; It was learned from a senior government official...: A reliable source stated...

Always ask *which* circles, *which* official, *which* source. Be careful of any information that comes from a high *unidentified* source.

5. ***Card-stacking.*** The writer attempts to get you to see only one side of a particular issue. To do so, he or she will use half-truths and omit the other side of the argument. Examples occur frequently in "authorized" biographies that present a person's life in glowing terms, including all the good qualities while omitting or toning down the poor ones. When reading about an issue, always note whether both sides have been discussed or whether the cards have been stacked by the writer on one side of the issue only.
6. ***Bandwagon.*** The writer tries to make you go along with the crowd. Since most people like to follow the trend, they will respond favorably to such statements as "Nine out of ten Americans prefer..." or "...sells more... than all other companies put together." In politics, the bandwagon technique is often seen in action in national political conventions. "Join the swing to...."

The bandwagon-approach writer does not want you to think clearly for yourself. You should always ask *why* you should join the others, and not do so because your emotions have gotten the better of you.

REMEMBER:

A critical reader

- does not believe everything he or she reads simply because it is in print;
- accepts as true only statements that can be proved or that are made by reliable authorities;
- separates fact from opinion, recognizes emotional language and bias, and is aware of slanting by omission.

DETERMINING CAUSE AND EFFECT

A reading skill frequently used in social studies involves determining the relationship between events. Events rarely occur in isolation. They are generally the result of other events that happened earlier.

EXAMPLE

The Japanese bombed Pearl Harbor on December 7, 1941. The United States then declared war on Japan.

The bombing of Pearl Harbor was the cause; the declaration of war was the result or effect of the bombing. Always try, when reading of an event, to determine its cause or causes. *Here is a question involving cause and effect:*

QUESTION

1. President Franklin D. Roosevelt's New Deal policy led to numerous government agencies, created in an effort to combat the effects of the Great Depression. One major result of this policy was to

(1) weaken the power of the chief executive
(2) strengthen the policy of laissez-faire
(3) increase the power of the federal government
(4) expand the importance of states' rights
(5) lessen the need for judicial review

ANSWER AND ANALYSIS

The question asks for a result of President Franklin D. Roosevelt's New Deal policy. The opposite results occurred from those listed as Choices 1, 4, and 5; that is, the New Deal strengthened the power of the chief executive; weakened the importance of states' rights, and increased the need for judicial review. Choice 2, the policy of laissez-faire, provides for little or no interference by government in the affairs of business, clearly an incorrect response. Only Choice 3 is correct because the New Deal program called for executive action to advance economic recovery and social welfare.

COMPARING AND CONTRASTING IDEAS AND ORGANIZATIONS

Another frequently needed skill in social studies reading involves the ability to compare and contrast institutions and events. You may be asked to compare American democracy with French democracy, contrast democracy with communism, compare the platforms of the Republicans and Democrats, or contrast the role of women in the eighteenth century with their role in the twentieth.

QUESTION

1. The careers of Theodore Roosevelt and Franklin D. Roosevelt were similar because each man
   (1) was an outstanding military leader before becoming president
   (2) led the cause for international peace, but involved the United States in a war
   (3) succeeded to the presidency upon the death of the preceding president
   (4) believed in a strong presidency and acted accordingly
   (5) represented the same political party

ANSWER AND ANALYSIS

You are asked to compare the careers of two American presidents. Franklin D. Roosevelt was not an outstanding military leader before becoming president. Theodore Roosevelt did not involve the United States in a war. Franklin D. Roosevelt did not succeed to the presidency upon the death of the preceding president. Theodore Roosevelt was a Republican; Franklin D. Roosevelt, a Democrat. Thus Choices 1, 2, 3, and 5 are incorrect. Choice 4 is correct because both Roosevelts were strong presidents: Theodore Roosevelt was a trust buster, had a Square Deal policy, and pursued an expansionist foreign policy; Franklin D. Roosevelt carried out New Deal policies and a Good Neighbor policy with Latin America, and he led the nation for most of World War II.

LEARNING SOCIAL STUDIES VOCABULARY AND DERIVING MEANING FROM CONTEXT

In social studies as in science, vocabulary is of critical importance. Words found in social studies may

- represent complicated ideas, such as *nationalism, referendum, mercantilism;*
- imply a whole set of ideas, such as *feudalism, militarism, bimetallism;*
- have meanings specific to the social studies although they have other meanings as well, such as *Axis, act, shop;*
- come from foreign languages, such as *apartheid, junta, laissez-faire;*
- have meanings that go beyond the usual ones, such as *dove, plank, scab.*

Try to derive the correct meaning from the *context*—the words with which the term appears in a sentence.

You can **check your understanding of the meaning of the vocabulary** in a given selection by asking yourself:

1. What is the key word in the sentence (paragraph, selection)?
2. What is the meaning of the word in *this* sentence (context)?
3. What is the exact meaning (denotation) of the word in this selection?
4. What is the extended meaning (connotation) of the word in this selection? (What does it *suggest* as well as say?)
5. What is the effect of a given word on me?
6. What is the special meaning of this word in social studies?

Practice with Social Studies Readings

A representative selection in each of the social studies follows, together with questions based on it. Read each of the selections and try to answer the questions *without* referring to the answer analyses that follow. Then check your answers by carefully reading the analyses. Each of the sets of questions following the selections contains a question that

- is aimed at testing whether you can *locate the main idea* ("The best title for the selection is...");
- is designed to test your ability to *locate details* ("One difference between ______ and ______ is...");
- requires you to show your *knowledge of social studies vocabulary* ("All of the following words used in economics are correctly paired with their meanings EXCEPT...");
- forces you to *make a conclusion or predict an outcome* ("We can conclude that..." "It is most likely that...").

In addition, there are questions designed to test your ability to

- *find reasons* that the author uses to support an argument;
- *follow the organization* of a selection;
- *identify the position taken by the author* (or any bias he or she may have).

POLITICAL SCIENCE, WITH ANSWERS AND ANSWER ANALYSIS

There are the following four key committees at a political convention.

➤ The *Credentials Committee.* This group decides who is an official delegate entitled to vote.

➤ The permanent *Organization Committee,* which picks the convention's officers, including the chairperson. This official decides who can speak at the convention and who cannot.

➤ The *Rules Committee,* which makes the rules by which the convention and the party organization are run.

➤ The *Resolutions and Platform Committee,* which writes the party platform. Usually, a convention lasts about four days. Typically, a temporary convention chairperson opens the convention with a *keynote address,* which is meant to set the tone of the convention—and quite frequently does. The real business of the day, however, goes on behind the podium, where the Credentials Committee settles disputes over *delegate credentials.*

On the second day the *party platform* is read, debated, and usually voted upon. A *permanent chairperson* is installed, and the convention is asked to approve the reports of its major committees.

On the third day actual *nominations* for presidential candidates are taken. States are called alphabetically at the Republican Convention, by lottery at the Democratic. Each state may nominate one candidate, second a nomination already made, yield (surrender the floor to another state), or pass. After each nomination there is usually a loud demonstration for the nominee.

Balloting begins only after nominations have been closed. A *simple majority*—one more than half the votes—is all that is needed to win. Every Republican presidential candidate since 1948 and every Democratic one since 1952 has won on the first ballot. If no one wins a simple majority on the first ballot, the vote is taken again until a candidate is picked.

By the fourth day a *presidential nominee* has usually emerged. He, in turn, addresses party leaders and tells them whom he prefers for *vice president.* Usually he gets his way.

Finally, the two candidates make their *acceptance speeches,* go through a few ceremonial events, and the *convention ends.*

1. The main idea of the above selection is
   (1) choosing a president and vice president
   (2) four key committees
   (3) how Republican and Democratic conventions differ
   (4) conventions: American political dramas
   (5) how conventions are organized and run

2. The vice-presidential candidate is chosen by the
   (1) party leaders
   (2) roll-call vote
   (3) Rules Committee
   (4) permanent convention chairman
   (5) presidential nominee

3. In the next convention, it is most likely that the party candidates will be nominated by
   (1) simple majority on the second ballot
   (2) plurality on the second ballot
   (3) two-thirds vote on the first ballot
   (4) simple majority on the first ballot
   (5) plurality on the first ballot

4. The INCORRECTLY paired group below is
   (1) Organization Committee—convention chairperson
   (2) permanent chairperson—keynote address
   (3) nominees—acceptance speeches
   (4) states—nominations
   (5) simple majority—choice of nominee

5. One difference between Republican and Democratic conventions is the way in which
   (1) committees are organized
   (2) convention chairpersons are chosen
   (3) nominations for presidential candidates are made
   (4) balloting takes place
   (5) party platforms are decided

6. The writer of this selection has organized the passage
   (1) logically
   (2) psychologically
   (3) chronologically
   (4) argumentatively
   (5) critically

NOTE:

The words in the questions that are defined in the "Glossary of Social Studies Terms" under Political Science (page 282) are *ballot, convention, majority, nominate, party, platform* and *plurality.*

ANSWER KEY

1. **5** 2. **5** 3. **4** 4. **2** 5. **3** 6. **3**

ANSWER ANALYSIS

1. **5** Question 1 calls for the main idea of the selection. The possible answers generally fall into several categories. *One of the choices* will be incorrect or irrelevant; that is, it will have nothing to do with the question. *Other choices* will focus on details and not on the main idea. *Still another choice* will be too general, too vague. *The correct answer* will be broad in scope yet specific enough to indicate the main idea or purpose of the article. Choice 5 is correct because it indicates the main idea of the article, which is to explain how conventions are organized by committees and how they are run to accomplish their purposes, namely, nominating a presidential and a vice-presidential candidate and adopting a party platform. Choice 1, choosing a president and vice president, is incorrect since the convention merely nominates. It chooses the presidential and vice presidential candidates who may become president and vice president if elected. Choices 2 and 3 deal with details—the committee structure and the one point of difference between the Republican and the Democratic conventions. Choice 4 is too broad; conventions may be American political dramas but that is *not* the main idea or purpose of this selection.

2. **5** This question requires you to locate a detail, albeit an important detail, in the passage. Skimming (reading rapidly) through the passage, you will note the term *vice president* for the first time in the next to last paragraph. It is there you will find the correct answer—Choice 5. The presidential nominee tells the party leaders whom he prefers for vice president.

3. **4** Question 3 requires you to predict an outcome because it uses the words "In the next convention, it is most likely...." Since the presidential candidate has won on the first ballot for over twenty

years in both parties' political conventions, and since a simple majority is all that is required to win, it is safe to predict that this will be true of future conventions. Therefore, Choice 4 is correct.

4. **2** Question 4 is somewhat tricky. All of the choices contain correct associations but one. Thus, the Organization Committee chooses the convention chairperson; the nominees make acceptance speeches; the states make nominations; a simple majority results in a nomination. Only Choice 2 is in error; the *temporary* chairperson makes the keynote address.
5. **3** Question 5 pinpoints the one difference between the Republican and the Democratic conventions. Skimming to a point halfway through the selection, looking for the words *Republican* and *Democratic*, you find that the actual nominations are made differently—by alphabet in one and by lottery in the other. The correct choice, therefore, is 3.
6. **3** Question 6 calls your attention to the organization of the article. To find the answer, you note how the various paragraphs in the passage follow one another. In this instance, the second paragraph indicates the length of the convention—four days—and tells how it opens. The third paragraph deals with the second day; the fourth paragraph, with the third day. The next to the last paragraph indicates what has happened by the fourth day. Since the passage follows the time sequence of the convention, it is organized chronologically. Choice 3 is the correct answer.

HISTORY, WITH ANSWERS AND ANSWER ANALYSIS

The United States is often considered a young nation, but in fact it is next to the oldest continuous government in the world. The reason is that its people have always been willing to accommodate themselves to change. We have been dedicated to equality, but have been willing to realize it by flexible means. In the European sense of the term, America's political parties are not parties at all, because they do not divide over basic beliefs. Neither wishes to overturn or replace the existing political and economic order; they merely desire to alter it at slower or faster rates of speed.

One of our proudest achievements has been the creation of a system of controlled capitalism that yields the highest living standards on earth, and has made possible a society as nearly classless as man has ever known. The profit system as it has developed in America shares its benefits with all parts of society: capital, labor, and the consuming masses. Yet even this was the result of trial and error. Unprincipled businessmen had first to be restrained by government, and by the growing power of organized labor, before they came to learn that they must serve the general good in pursuing their own economic interests. Now labor is feeling the restraint.

Even our creed of democracy is not fixed and unchangeable. Thus the statesmen of the early republic, though they strongly believed in private enterprise, chose to make the post office a government monopoly and to give the schools to public ownership. Since then, government has broadened its activities in many ways. Americans hold with Lincoln that "the legitimate object of government is to do for a community of people whatever they need to have done but cannot do at all, or cannot do so well for themselves, in their separate and individual capacities."

NOTE:
The terms in the passage and in the questions that are defined in the "Glossary of Social Studies Terms" are *capitalism, democracy, party, profit, monopoly, republic,* and *standard of living.*

1. The main quality of the United States stressed in this passage is its

(1) youth
(2) equality
(3) high living standards
(4) profit system
(5) flexibility

2. The widely held belief about the United States with which the passage mentions disagreement concerns American

(1) political parties
(2) capitalism
(3) private enterprise
(4) labor
(5) public ownership

3. All of the following are characteristic of the United States, according to the passage, EXCEPT a

(1) dedication to equality
(2) classless society
(3) belief in democracy
(4) profit system
(5) controlled capitalism

4. An agency that performs a function of which Lincoln, according to his quoted words, would most approve is the

(1) U.S. Office of Education
(2) U.S. Chamber of Commerce
(3) National Guard
(4) Public Service Commission
(5) Federal Aviation Administration

5. The creation of the U.S. government post office monopoly is cited as an example of a

(1) replacement of the existing economic order
(2) restraint of unprincipled businesspersons
(3) control of organized labor
(4) flexible view of private enterprise
(5) system of shared profits

6. According to the passage, which of the following statements is true?

(1) Our political parties agree on goals but not on methods.
(2) Business has a larger share of profits than labor.
(3) Government has tended to restrict its role in American life.
(4) Americans are conservative where change is required.
(5) Americans have kept their democratic beliefs intact.

7. The author's view of change in America is

(1) critical
(2) cautious
(3) favorable
(4) qualified
(5) unclear

Answer Key

1. **5** 2. **1** 3. **2** 4. **5** 5. **4** 6. **1** 7. **3**

Answer Analysis

1. **5** This question requires you to determine the author's main purpose in writing this passage. Each of Choices 1 through 4 refers to a quality of the United States, but none of them is central to the selection. Flexibility is mentioned in many ways: "willing to accommodate themselves to change"; "flexible means"; "trial and error"; "not fixed and unchangeable."

2. **1** The question calls for selecting a common belief about the United States that is called into question in the passage. While two exceptions to private enterprise are cited, the belief in private enterprise is not challenged. Three other beliefs are mentioned, but none of them except political parties is called into question. The passage states that Europeans would not consider America's political parties parties at all. So Choice 1 is the correct answer.

3. **2** Here location of a detail in the passage is required. Of the five characteristics mentioned, four are true characteristics of the United States. The fifth, a classless society, is not, although a society "as nearly classless as man has ever known" is a quality of American life.

4. **5** This difficult question involves applying the principle stated by Lincoln to

contemporary American institutions. What is the principle? That government fills a need for a community that the community itself cannot fill or fill well. Choice 1 is incorrect since education is a function the states have traditionally performed. Choice 2 is incorrect since the U.S. Chamber of Commerce is a private organization, not a federal agency. Choice 3 is incorrect since the National Guard is under state jurisdiction in peacetime. Choice 4 is incorrect because Public Service Commissions are generally state agencies. By the process of elimination, Choice 5 is correct. The Federal Aviation Administration regulates air commerce, including a national system of airports and air traffic control, an interstate function that a state ("community") cannot efficiently perform.

5. **4** This question calls for recall of a detail mentioned in the passage. Although the founders of our republic "strongly believed in private enterprise," they "chose to make the post office a government monopoly." This is an example of how flexible they were. The correct answer is 4. The other choices are irrelevant.

6. **1** Involved here are four statements that are false according to the passage and one that is true. Each statement has to be considered in light of what is said in the passage, and four must be discarded. Choices 3, 4, and 5 contradict what is said: government has actually broadened its role; Americans have always been willing to accommodate to change; our creed of democracy is not fixed. Choice 2 is not answerable solely on the evidence given in the passage, since we are not told the size of the shares of profit that capital and labor receive. Only Choice 1 is true: our political parties wish to retain "the existing political and economic order." They differ, however, on the rate of speed at which to change it.

7. **3** This question requires an inference on your part. "From what I have read," you must ask yourself, "what is the author's view of the issue he discusses?" The issue is change and the author obviously applauds it. Choice 3—favorable—is the correct answer. Why? The reason is found in the first two sentences. All the rest of the passage merely gives examples of change. The author cites the fact that the United States is "next to the oldest continuous government in the world." He is proud of that and he attributes that fact, in the next sentence, to our willingness to accommodate ourselves to change. Therefore, change must be good if it enables our government to survive.

Thus far, we have thoroughly analyzed the answers to two passages in political science and history. We have *located the main ideas* of each selection. We have dealt with the problem of *identifying* various kinds of *details*. In each selection, your *knowledge of social studies vocabulary* was tested. Finally, you were required to *draw inferences and predict outcomes*. The remaining four selections will give you further practice in these reading skills. We will analyze only those questions that introduce new reading techniques or that present special problems. Be certain to check your answers against the correct answers that follow the questions. If you made an error, do not hesitate to go back to the selection and read it through once more.

ECONOMICS, WITH ANSWERS AND ANSWER ANALYSIS

Could the United States fall into the depths of another Great Depression?

Economists can't say for sure. Most feel, however, that past depressions have taught us how to avoid economic disaster.

We've learned, for example, of the need for:

- *Government regulation of the stock market.* The Securities Act of 1933 made stock dealings less of a shell game by bringing them out into the open. The Securities Exchange Act of 1934 set up the Securities and Exchange Commission (S.E.C.), which acts as a sort of official consumer watchdog group. One of its jobs is to warn the investing public against the sort of crazy speculating that preceded the 1929 crash.

- ***A permanent Council of Economic Advisers to take the economy's pulse for the government.*** The Employment Act of 1946 created the Council of Economic Advisers. Its recommendations in 1949, 1958, 1969, and 1985 observers feel, helped keep the recessions of these years from becoming depressions.
- ***A Federal Deposit Insurance Corporation (F.D.I.C.) to promise government backing of bank deposits.*** The F.D.I.C. insures certain bank deposits. Such insurance has so far prevented the type of bank runs—panic withdrawals—that forced thousands of banks to close their doors in the early 1930s.
- ***A federal relief system for jobless people.*** State and local governments struggled to provide relief for the poor in the early years of the Great Depression. For the most part, they failed. They, too, ran out of money.

The New Deal introduced Social Security, a government pension plan. Government insurance followed for workers who are laid off or can't work because of injuries. Veterans' benefits and public assistance (welfare) are two other forms of government help in which Washington became involved during the 1930s.

These *transfer funds*, as they are called, don't merely help the recipients. In the long run, they help the whole economy by giving people buying power. This buying power helps keep up the demand for bonds. Thus, it helps keep factories open and factory workers employed.

For these and other reasons, many economists believe that we are now in better control of the U.S. economy, which, in the 1990s, is one of the strongest in the world.

NOTE:
The words *crash, depression, inflation, panic, speculation, welfare,* and *unemployment* are all in the Economics section of the *"Glossary of Social Studies Terms."*

1. The selection emphasizes
   (1) the effects of the Great Depression
   (2) the contributions of the New Deal
   (3) the strength of the U.S. economy
   (4) ways to avoid economic disaster
   (5) the role of people's buying power

2. All of the following are associated with the New Deal EXCEPT
   (1) Social Security
   (2) Council of Economic Advisers
   (3) veterans' benefits
   (4) welfare
   (5) unemployment insurance

3. All of the following were characteristics of the Great Depression that economists sought to correct EXCEPT
   (1) stock market speculation
   (2) bank failures
   (3) unemployment
   (4) soaring inflation
   (5) poverty

4. The federal government stepped in where state and local governments failed in
   (1) regulating the stock market
   (2) backing bank deposits
   (3) providing relief for the jobless
   (4) providing veterans' benefits
   (5) introducing Social Security

5. Which of the following statements is NOT true?
   (1) The United States avoided depressions in each decade following the Great Depression.
   (2) Bank panics have been avoided since the Great Depression.
   (3) The Securities and Exchange Commission alerts investors to the kind of stock market activity that preceded the Great Depression.
   (4) Transfer funds help the unemployed.
   (5) We have learned how to prevent another Great Depression.

6. We can conclude from the author's presentation that he sees another Great Depression as

   (1) inevitable
   (2) likely
   (3) unlikely
   (4) impossible
   (5) predictable

Answer Key

1. **4** 2. **2** 3. **4** 4. **3** 5. **5** 6. **3**

Answer Analysis

Let us look at questions 5 and 6.

5. **5** Question 5 gives you five statements, one of which is false. You have to check each statement against the passage. Choice 1 is true since the passage states that the recommendations of the Council of Economic Advisers helped avoid depressions in 1949, 1958, 1969 and 1985. Choice 2 is true since the passage states the Federal Deposit Insurance Corporation "has so far prevented" bank runs. Choice 3 is also true since the Securities and Exchange Commission has, as one of its responsibilities, warned the public against speculation. Choice 4 is true because unemployment insurance is included in transfer funds. Choice 5 is *not* true since economists are not certain we can avoid another Great Depression, although most of them may feel that way.

6. **3** Question 6 asks you to make an inference, one of the most difficult reading skills. The author concludes the article on an optimistic note—"economists believe that we are now in better control" of our economy, which is "one of the strongest in the world." Therefore, we are safe in inferring or drawing the conclusion that the author sees another Great Depression as unlikely, Choice 3.

GEOGRAPHY, WITH ANSWERS AND ANSWER ANALYSIS

Geography may be subdivided into several areas of study.

Physical Geography In the study of physical (natural) geography, stress is laid upon the natural elements of man's environment. These include topography, soils, earth materials, earth-sun relationships, surface and underground water, weather and climate, and native plant and animal life. Physical geography must also include the impact of man on his physical environment as well as those influences omnipresent in nature.

Cultural Geography In cultural geography emphasis is placed upon the study of observable features resulting from man's occupation of the earth. These features include population distribution and settlement, cities, buildings, roads, airfields, factories, railroads, farm and field patterns, communication facilities, and many other examples of man's work. Cultural geography is one of the very significant fields of geographic inquiry.

Economic Geography In economic geography, the relationship between man's efforts to gain a living and the earth's surface on which they are conducted are correlated. In order to study how man makes a living, the distribution of materials, production, institutions, and human traits and customs are analyzed.

Regional Geography In regional geography the basic concern is with the salient characteristics of areas. Emphasis is placed upon patterns and elements of the natural environment and their relationships to human activities. By using the regional technique in studying geographic phenomena, what otherwise might be a bewildering array of facts is brought into focus as an organized, cohesive pattern.

Systematic Geography It is also feasible to study the geography of a small area or the entire surface of the earth in systematic fashion. Settlement, climates, soils, landforms, minerals, water, or crops, among others, may be observed, described, analyzed, and explained. Research in systematic geography has proved to be very valuable.

1. This passage describes geography's

   (1) growth
   (2) scope
   (3) importance
   (4) role in the social sciences
   (5) principles

2. The difference among the five areas of geography described is one of

   (1) method
   (2) importance
   (3) emphasis
   (4) recency
   (5) objectivity

3. A student interested in the influence of a geographical feature of a region on available jobs would study

   (1) physical geography
   (2) cultural geography
   (3) economic geography
   (4) regional geography
   (5) systematic geography

4. A meteorologist would likely be most interested in

   (1) physical geography
   (2) cultural geography
   (3) economic geography
   (4) regional geography
   (5) systematic geography

5. An urban sociologist would probably study

   (1) physical geography
   (2) cultural geography
   (3) economic geography
   (4) regional geography
   (5) systematic geography

6. A person studying the problems of the Middle East will use the approach found in

   (1) physical geography
   (2) cultural geography
   (3) economic geography
   (4) regional geography
   (5) systematic geography

7. A conservationist studying the effects of such human activities as strip mining and land erosion would turn to

   (1) physical geography
   (2) cultural geography
   (3) economic geography
   (4) regional geography
   (5) systematic geography

8. That aspect of geography that seeks to study in a planned and orderly way the geography of a small area is

   (1) physical geography
   (2) cultural geography
   (3) economic geography
   (4) regional geography
   (5) systematic geography

ANSWER KEY

1. **2** 2. **3** 3. **3** 4. **1** 5. **2** 6. **4**
7. **1** 8. **5**

ANSWER ANALYSIS

Four of the questions—3, 6, 7, and 8—deal with definitions. Two call for knowledge of terms in addition to those defined in the passage.

2. **3** Question 2 is a little tricky, but, if you read closely, you will notice that the author uses the words *stress* and *emphasis* in his definitions of the various areas of geography.

Questions 4 and 5 are, in effect, two-step questions. First, you must define the term in the question. Then, you must recall the definition of the area of geography to which it relates.

4. **1** In question 4, you must know that a meteorologist is concerned with weather. Only then can you identify physical geography as his or her primary interest.
5. **2** In this question, you must know that an urban sociologist studies cities, an area of interest to the cultural geographer.

BEHAVIORAL SCIENCES, WITH ANSWERS AND ANSWER ANALYSIS

PASSAGE 1

Onta, a youth in his middle teens, was led away from his parents by one of the tribal elders. He was taken to a hut on the other side of the village. There he and several other young men went through the ceremony. After they were bound together in a large circle, the chief quizzed each boy on the tribal traditions they had all studied. Then, each had to pass through a line of elders, head covered with ash from a nearby fire. Finally, after two more hours of religious chanting, the binding was cut; and each youth was formally received into the tribe as a man, having left childhood behind forever.

David, a youth in his middle teens, was led away from his parents by one of the officials dressed in a dark uniform. He was taken to a room somewhere on the other side of the building. There he and several other young men began the examination. Seated in neat rows they underwent the examination under the stern eye of another official.

Later they were required to manipulate a giant machine under the watchful eye of still another official. Finally, after waiting at home for a period of up to several weeks, they were welcomed into the community of their brothers.

Onta and David are fictional people, but their rites of passage are not. A rite of passage is a ceremony, usually formal and dictated by custom. It formally marks a person's transition from one stage to another: from childhood to maturity, from being single to being married, from life to death.

Onta's trial is fairly common (there are many variations) among so-called primitive people. Sometimes called a puberty rite, it is usually held around the time a young person achieves sexual maturity. Passing through the rite means that, in his society, Onta is officially a man.

But the practice is hardly limited to primitive tribes. All kinds of rituals, including rites of passage, are common to people everywhere. The Jewish Bar Mitzvah, a religious rite performed when a boy turns 13, is a proclamation that the youth has passed into manhood.

Rites can change, of course, according to the time and temper of the society. In David's case, if you hadn't already guessed, the rite is something vital to great numbers of young people in the United States today.

In a way, David too finally became a member of the tribe after passing through the *rite* of passage: completing his examination, and receiving his driver's license. In motor-minded America, a male teenager who can't pass his driver's test is probably under the same kind of scorn as an Indian boy who flunked his test of manhood.

Getting a driver's license is a popular rite of passage. There are others, some of them regional, some even local. Are there special rites of passage in your community?

One of the first to identify "rites of passage" was a French anthropologist named Arnold van Gennep. Gennep divided rites of passage into three stages: separation, transition, and incorporation. He found that each stage is present in rites everywhere in the world.

"Among the majority of peoples, in all sorts of ceremonies, identical rites are performed for identical purposes....

"Their position may vary, depending on whether the occasion is birth or death, initiation or marriage, but the differences lie only in matter of detail. The underlying arrangement is always the same."

1. This selection deals mainly with

   (1) Onta and David
   (2) rites of passage
   (3) getting a driver's license
   (4) the views of Arnold van Gennep
   (5) the Jewish Bar Mitzvah

2. All of the following are rites of passage referred to in the article EXCEPT

   (1) birth
   (2) initiation
   (3) marriage
   (4) parenthood
   (5) death

3. The author
   (1) deals only with the experiences of Onta and David
   (2) stresses the many differences in rites throughout the world
   (3) points out the essential similarity of rites throughout the world
   (4) emphasizes the unchanging nature of certain rites
   (5) feels that rites are unimportant rituals that must be observed

4. Onta's trial at puberty is an example, as a rite of passage, of
   (1) separation
   (2) separation and transition
   (3) transition
   (4) transition and incorporation
   (5) incorporation

5. Puberty rites are associated in this article with
   (1) proclamations
   (2) driver's licenses
   (3) tribal traditions
   (4) life and death
   (5) religious rites

6. All of the following are true of rites of passage EXCEPT that they
   (1) are milestones on the road of life
   (2) mark the end of a stage of life
   (3) mark the beginning of a stage of life
   (4) are fictional
   (5) are common to people everywhere

ANSWER KEY

1. **2** 2. **4** 3. **3** 4. **4** 5. **2** 6. **4**

ANSWER ANALYSIS

4. **4** The only difficult question here is this one, which deals with a detail in the passage. It refers to the three stages into which rites of passage are divided: separation, transition, and incorporation. You have to think of life as a series of rites of passage. The author mentions death, for example, and that is an example of separation or leaving. Marriage can be considered an example of separation and incorporation—separation from the original family and incorporation into a new family that is being formed. Onta's trial represents a period (transition) during which he is formally received into the tribe (incorporation), so Choice 4 is correct.

PASSAGE 2

Our solid American citizen awakens . . . and puts on clothes whose form originally developed from the skin clothing of the nomads of the Asiatic steppes, puts on shoes made from skins tanned by a process invented in ancient Egypt and cut to a pattern developed in ancient Greece, and ties around his neck a bright-colored cloth which is a survival of the shoulder shawls worn by 17th-century Croatians of Southern Europe. Before going out to breakfast, he glances through a window made of glass developed in Egypt, and, if it is raining, puts on overshoes made of rubber first used by Central American Indians, and takes an umbrella invented in Southeast Asia.

On his way to breakfast, he buys a newspaper and pays for it with coins of ancient Lydian invention. At the restaurant, his plate is made of a form of pottery invented in China. His knife is of steel, an alloy first used in southern India, his fork is a medieval Italian invention, and his spoon comes from a Roman original. He begins breakfast with an orange from the eastern Mediterranean, a cantaloupe from Persia, or perhaps a piece of African watermelon. With this he has coffee, an African plant. He goes on to waffles, cakes made from a Scandinavian technique from wheat first raised in the Near East. He may have eggs, first eaten in eastern Asia, or strips of an animal which has been salted and smoked by a process developed in Northern Europe.

When our friend has finished eating, he reads the news of the day, imprinted in characters invented in Germany. As he absorbs the news of problems that exist in other countries, he will, if he is a good conservative citizen, thank a Hebrew deity in an Indo-European language that he is 100 percent American.

1. The main idea of the selection is
   (1) it is great to be 100 percent American
   (2) the man described is a solid American citizen
   (3) the man described is enjoying home-grown comforts
   (4) Western life is superior to all others
   (5) the cultures of many lands have contributed to American life

2. The tone of the selection is
   (1) straightforward
   (2) sarcastic
   (3) nostalgic
   (4) depressing
   (5) derogatory

3. The things the man uses in the restaurant are
   (1) American
   (2) original
   (3) borrowed
   (4) conservative
   (5) unfamiliar

4. The author indicates that, if the American is a good conservative, he will be
   (1) thankful
   (2) critical
   (3) independent
   (4) creative
   (5) patriotic

5. All of the following items mentioned in the passage are of Asiatic origin EXCEPT
   (1) the man's clothes
   (2) his umbrella
   (3) the eggs he ate
   (4) the pottery from which his plate was made
   (5) the coffee he drank

6. All of the following continents are mentioned directly or indirectly EXCEPT
   (1) North America
   (2) Central America
   (3) Europe
   (4) Africa
   (5) Asia

ANSWER KEY

1. **5** 2. **2** 3. **3** 4. **1** 5. **5** 6. **1**

ANSWER ANALYSIS

1. **5** The main idea is that our solid American citizen benefits from the contributions of many cultures of the world, including those of Asia, Egypt, Central America, and southern Europe.
2. **2** The citizen appears to be unaware of the origins of items mentioned; the author sarcastically implies that the man thinks they are all American, whereas none of them are.
3. **3** The things he faces in the restaurant are borrowed from China, India, and Italy.
4. **1** The author indicates that the man will thank a Hebrew deity.
5. **5** Coffee is an African plant. The man's clothes were developed from the skin clothing of the nomads of the Asiatic steppes. Eggs were first eaten in eastern Asia. The type of pottery he used was invented in China.
6. **1** Only North America, where the "solid American citizen" was born and lives, is *not* mentioned. All the other continents are.

Practice with Interpreting Tables, Graphs, Maps

Since study of the social sciences involves the gathering and interpretation of facts, you will frequently encounter various methods for presenting the facts you need. Most often, these facts will be presented in the form of tables or charts, graphs, or maps. Let us deal with each of these methods in turn.

TABLES

The ability to read tables is an important skill because tables are the most common means of presenting data in the social studies.

What is a table? It is an arrangement of figures, usually in one or more columns, which is intended to show some relationship between the figures. In political science, a table may show the growth of the number of eligible voters in national elections. In economics, a table may show the annual incomes of various groups within the population of a country. A table may also show the relationship between two factors, for example, between the amounts of education of various groups as related to their annual incomes.

First note the title of the table: Sizes, Populations, and Densities of the World's Largest Nations and Regions.

Now, look at the headings of the columns in the table. Six headings are given: Country, Size, Population 1968, Population 1990, People per Square Mile 1968, People per Square Mile 1990.

Next, locate the columns to which each heading is related. In the first column, the different countries or areas of the world are listed. The next column gives their sizes in square miles. The next two columns list population figures for 1968 and 1990, and the last two give the numbers of people per square mile for the same two dates.

Just how do you read a table? First you read the title of the table to determine just what figures are being presented. The title is usually at the top of the column or columns of figures. Let us use the following table as a typical illustration.

SIZES, POPULATIONS, AND DENSITIES OF THE WORLD'S LARGEST NATIONS AND REGIONS

1	2	3	4	5	6
		Population (U.N. Estimate)		People per Square Mile	
Country	Size (sq. mi.)	1968	1990	1968	1990
USSR*	8,600,000	238,000,000	290,122,000	28	33.5
Canada	3,850,000	21,000,000	26,620,000	5	7.5
China	3,700,000	730,000,000	1,133,000,000	197	306.7
United States	3,600,000	200,000,000	251,394,000	57	68.3
Brazil	3,300,000	88,000,000	150,368,000	27	45.8
India	1,200,000	534,000,000	853,373,000	437	698.0
		Other Areas			
Japan	143,000	101,000,000	123,692,000	706	848.0
Southeast Asia	1,692,000	270,000,000	447,000,000	159	262.9
Middle East	3,784,000	261,000,000	306,400,000	69	81.0
Africa— south of the Sahara	8,600,000	254,000,000	500,000,000	30	62.2

Note the great increase of population in the 22 years that separate the two sets of figures. Scientists estimate that the earth's present population will double in the next 50 years.

*Note that "USSR" refers to all the former republics of the former Soviet Union.

Having identified the title, the column headings, and the columns to which they relate, you are now in a position to *locate facts.*

QUESTIONS

1. What is the size of the United States?
2. What was the population of India in 1968? What is the U.N. estimate of the population of India in 1990?
3. What was the number of people per square mile in Japan in 1990?
4. What country's population grew to over 1 billion between 1968 and 1990?

ANSWERS

1. **3,600,000 square miles**
2. **534,000,000   853,373,000**
3. **848.0**
4. **China**

ANSWER ANALYSIS

1. The second column from the left lists sizes. Put your finger at the top of that column, and move it down until you locate the figure on a line with United States—3,600,000.
2. Locate the column for population in 1968. Put your finger at the top of the column, and move it down to the figure on a line with India—534,000,000. Do the same for 1990.
3. Locate the column for people per square mile in 1990. Find the number on a line with Japan—848.0.
4. To answer this question, you have to locate two populations, one in 1968 and one in 1990. You also must locate a figure that is over 1 billion. Scan both columns of population figures. Only one is over 1 billion, that of China in 1990. In the column to the immediate left for 1968, the figure for China's population is 730,000,000, so that figure grew to 1,133,000 in 1990.

Now you are ready to *find relationships between facts.* This type of question requires you to locate one figure and then relate it to at least one other figure.

QUESTIONS

1. What is the basic trend of the world's population?
2. What is the basic trend in the number of people per square mile?
3. From 1968 to 1990, what country or area had the smallest increase in population?
4. In what country or area did the number of people per square mile double?

ANSWERS AND ANALYSIS

1. Compare column 4 (pop. 1990) with column 3 (pop. 1968). In every instance, the population in 1990 is greater. The conclusion can be reached that population is increasing all over the world.
2. Compare column 6 (people per square mile—1990) with column 5 (people per square mile—1968). The conclusion can be reached that the number of people per square mile is increasing all over the world.
3. Subtracting the figures in column 3 (pop. 1968) from those in column 4 (pop. 1990), it is apparent that Canada had the smallest increase, 5,620,000, in population.
4. Comparing the figures in columns 5 and 6 for people per square mile in 1968 and 1990, it is clear that in Africa—south of the Sahara the number of people per square mile more than doubled, from 30 to 62.2.

Now you can proceed to the most difficult skill of all—*inferring conclusions from the facts presented.* Sometimes you can draw a conclusion from the table alone. Other times, you must add facts from your general knowledge.

QUESTIONS

1. What conclusion can you draw from Japan's population figures?
2. What conclusion can you draw about the population in Africa—south of the Sahara?
3. What major problem may exist for Canada's population?
4. What common problems may China, India, and Japan experience?

ANSWERS AND ANALYSIS

1. Japan has the most crowded population in the world, with attendant problems of housing, health, and transportation among others.
2. The half-billion population of Africa—south of the Sahara is spread over 8,600,000 square miles. This fact will result in problems of distribution of goods and services to the countries of the area.
3. A similar problem exists for Canada, with the added possibility that adequate manpower may not be available.
4. The high population density in each country suggests potential difficulty in providing food, shelter, and other essential services to the inhabitants.

SUMMARY OF HOW TO READ A TABLE

1. Note the title.
2. Look at the column headings.
3. Locate the column to which the other columns are related.
4. Locate facts.
5. Find relationships between facts.
6. Infer conclusions from the facts presented.

GRAPHS

THE CIRCLE (PIE) GRAPH

Tables, as you have just seen, are composed of columns of figures selected to show the relationship between facts that the social studies writer considers important. Very often, the author will present these same facts in another way so that you can visualize them more readily and draw conclusions more easily. The writer does this by means of a graph.

Let us look at the following set of facts arranged in a table. They concern the principal religions of the world in the year 1991.

PRINCIPAL RELIGIONS OF THE WORLD, 1991	
Buddhist	6%
Christian	33%
Hindu	13%
Islam	18%
No religion	21%
Other	1%
Para-religions	8%

Looking at these facts in table form, you find it hard to draw any ready conclusions. But when you see them in the form of a circle (pie) graph, you are able to immediately visualize the relationships that exist between them.

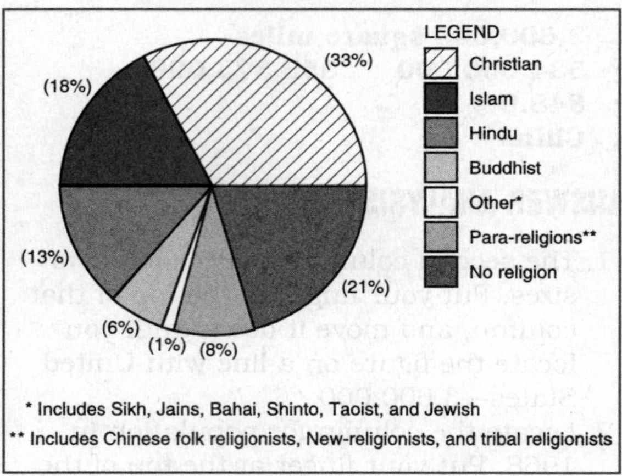

Now use this graph to answer the following questions.

QUESTIONS

1. Which religion has the most followers?
2. Which of the individually named religions has the fewest followers?
3. Which two religions account for more than half of the world's population?
4. Which proportion of the world's people do not practice a religion?

ANSWERS

1. **Christian**
2. **Buddhist**
3. **Islam and Christianity**
4. **21%**

ANSWER ANALYSIS

The answers almost leap up at you from the circle graph. The Christian religion has by far the largest slice of the circle; all of the religions combined under "Other" are hardly visible. By visually combining the various slices of the pie, you can see that the Christian and Islamic religions account for just over half of the total pie. By referring to the legend and then back to the pie, you can see that a large slice of the pie represents people who practice no religion. Just by inspection, you can estimate the number at around one-fifth or 20% of the total. The actual figure (21%) is provided.

The circle graph can also help you to compare visually two sets of facts. Here are a circle graph and a graph of another type (the bar graph).

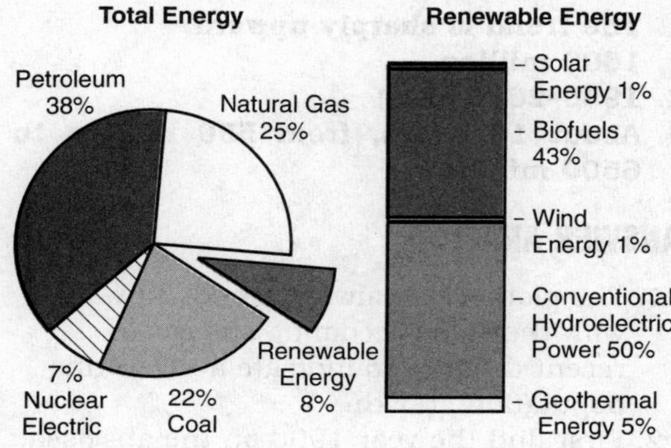

Note the title—Share of Total Energy, 1995
Note the unit used—percent of 100
Note the date—1995
Note the major categories—petroleum, natural gas, renewable energy, coal, nuclear electric

Study both graphs carefully and answer the following questions.

QUESTIONS

1. What are the most important sources of energy?
2. To reduce our dependence on oil imports, the use of which sources would have to be increased?
3. What percent of total energy does conventional hydroelectric power contribute?

ANSWERS AND ANALYSIS

1. **Three sources—petroleum, natural gas, and coal—amount to 70% of total energy.**
2. **The percents of the other sources—natural gas, coal, renewable energy, and nuclear electric—would have to be increased from their current total of 62%.**
3. **The circle graph tells you that renewable energy contributes 8% of the total energy consumed. Now look at the bar graph. Conventional hydroelectric power contributes half of renewal energy, or 4% of total energy.**

THE LINE GRAPH

This common type of graph shows relationships between facts by plotting points on a coordinate plane (two lines are involved) and connecting them with straight lines.

As an example, let us construct a line graph based on the following data about world population growth between 1650 and 2000 (estimated).

Year	World Population in Millions
1650	550
1750	725
1850	1175
1900	1600
1950	2490
1993	5554
2000 (est.)	6500

To construct the graph, draw a horizontal line and, perpendicular to it, a vertical line. Let:

- the horizontal line (technically known as the *abscissa*) represent the period of years from 1650 to 2000 (est.);
- the vertical line (technically known as the *ordinate*) represent world population.

To plot the line graph, start with the first line of data—year 1650, world population 550 million. Go up the ordinate 550, and place a dot there. Then find the next date, 1750, on the abscissa and go up the ordinate and place a dot opposite 725. Next find the date 1850 on the horizontal line and go up to a point opposite 1175. Place a dot there. Continue to do the same thing for each year on the table. Then draw a straight line from dot to dot to complete the graph.

What can you tell or visualize from this line graph?

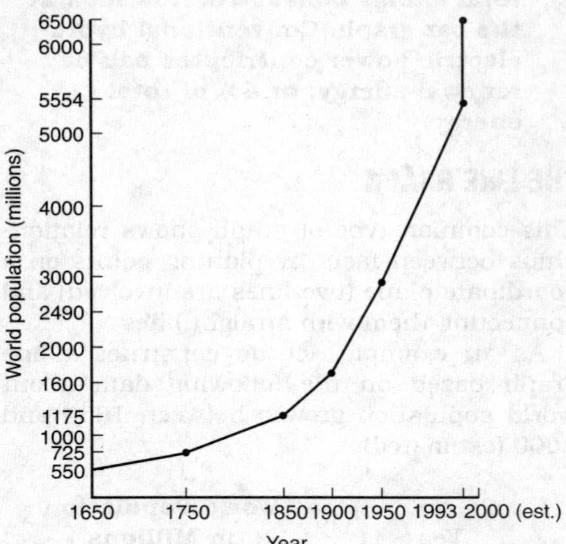

QUESTIONS

1. What is the trend of the world population?
2. What was the world population in 1900?
3. In what 50-year period was the increase the greatest?
4. In the period covered by the graph, approximately how many times did the population grow?

ANSWERS

1. **The trend is sharply upward.**
2. **1600 million**
3. **1950–2000 (est.)**
4. **About 12 times, from 550 million to 6500 million**

ANSWER ANALYSIS

1. The plotted line always trends upward, with the slant becoming steeper in recent decades to indicate accelerating population growth.
2. First find the year 1900 on the abscissa. Then move your finger straight up to the point in line with the ordinate indicating the population. The number is 1600 million.
3. The growth is greatest where the line is steepest—between 1950 and 2000 (est.).
4. The population grew from 550 million to 6500 million, or about 12 times.

THE BAR GRAPH

A bar graph is very much like the line graph we just studied. There is the same visual presentation of one set of facts in relation to another set. There is the same horizontal line (*abscissa*) representing one set of facts. The same vertical line (*ordinate*) represents the other set.

For a bar graph, however, you do not put a dot at the point that represents one fact in relation to another, nor do you connect those points by lines. Instead, you make bars of equal width and of heights that indicate the relationship. Thus you could change the line graph you just studied to a bar graph by making a bar for each point identified.

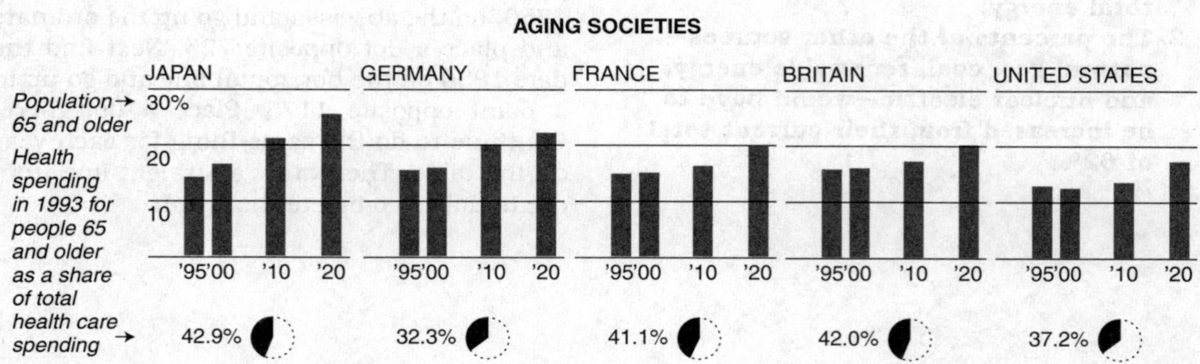

The bar graph on the preceding page is entitled "Aging Societies." It gives the percentages of population 65 and over for five countries at four different times, one past and three projected. It also indicates by small pie graphs the percentages of health spending in 1993, in each country, for people 65 and over as a share of total health care spending.

Use these graphs to answer the following practice questions.

QUESTIONS

1. In what country will the government have to spend the most in the year 2020 for health care for the aging?

   (1) Japan
   (2) Germany
   (3) France
   (4) Britain
   (5) United States

2. Which country will have the greatest population under 65 in 2020?

   (1) Japan
   (2) Germany
   (3) France
   (4) Britain
   (5) United States

3. Which countries have the most similar aging characteristics?

   (1) Japan and Germany
   (2) Germany and France
   (3) France and Britain
   (4) Britain and the United States
   (5) Japan and the United States

4. Which country will have the least stable growth of population over 65 for the rest of this century?

   (1) Japan
   (2) Germany
   (3) France
   (4) Britain
   (5) United States

5. What country was the least responsive to the health-care needs of its aging population in 1993?

   (1) Japan
   (2) Germany
   (3) France
   (4) Britain
   (5) United States

ANSWER KEY

1. **1** 2. **5** 3. **3** 4. **1** 5. **2**

ANSWER ANALYSIS

1. **1** In 2020, 25% of the population of Japan will be 65 or older, at least 4% more than any other country in the graph.
2. **5** In 2020, the United States will be the only country with an over-65 population below 20%.
3. **3** For France and Britain, percents are nearly identical for 1995, 2000, and 2010. The two countries will have the identical percent of population 65 or older in 2020, and in 1995 differed by less than 1% in percent of health care spending for the elderly as a share of total health-care spending.
4. **1** Japan will have an increase in population over 65. The other countries will remain at the same level.
5. **2** The pie graphs show that Germany spent least, approximately 9 to 10% less than France and Britain, for similar numbers of elderly.

MAPS

A map is a visual representation of all or part of the surface of the earth. A map may or may not include a number of aids to help you visualize the surface it is depicting. It will always include a *title*. If the map uses symbols, it will always include a *legend* (or key) to give the meaning of those symbols. It may also include:

- latitude and longitude to indicate direction and help you to find a specific location;
- a scale of miles to indicate what distance on the map equals a specific distance in miles on land;

PER CAPITA INCOME AND UNEMPLOYMENT IN THE UNITED STATES

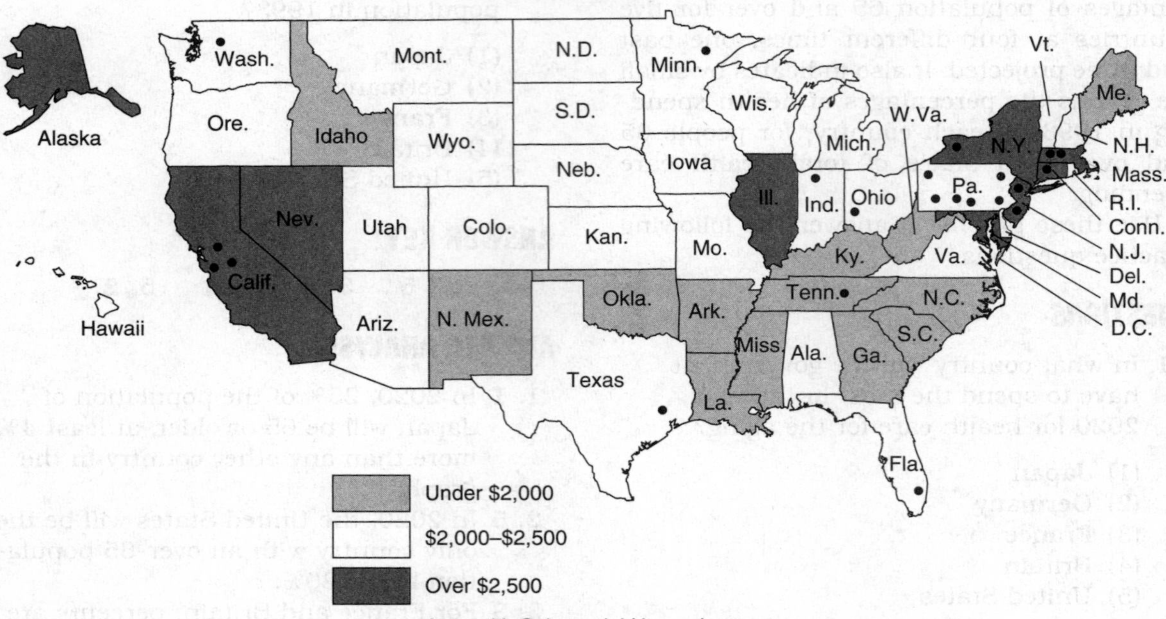

- a grid, or square, usually identified by a set of letters on one axis (vertical or horizontal) and a set of numbers on the other, so that a place can be found in, for example, a grid identified as F 3 or H 7;
- relief or differences in height of land, shown by lines.

The two most important aids that you must learn to use in order to read a map are its *title* and its *legend* (or key). The map above is in many respects typical of the maps you will encounter. The following questions will sharpen your skills in map reading.

QUESTIONS

1. What is the *title* of the map?
2. What three indications make up the *legend?*
3. What does ● mean?
4. What is the average per capita income of the population of the state of New York?
5. What is the average per capita income of the population of the state of New Mexico?
6. What is the average per capita income of the population of the state of Iowa?
7. Which state has a larger per capita income, Alaska or Hawaii?

ANSWERS AND ANALYSIS

1. The title of the map is "Per Capita Income and Unemployment in the United States." See the heading above the map.
2. The dark gray areas indicate per capita income over $2,500; the white areas indicate per capita income between $2,000 and $2,500; the light gray areas indicate per capita income under $2,000.
3. The ● indicates an area with substantial unemployment.
4. Since New York is a dark gray area, its per capita income is over $2,500.
5. Since New Mexico is a light gray area, its per capita income is under $2,000.
6. Since Iowa is a white area, its per capita income is between $2,000 and $2,500.
7. Since Alaska is a dark gray area (per capita income over $2,500) and Hawaii is a white area (per capita income between $2,000 and $2,500), Alaska has a larger per capita income than Hawaii.

This map introduces a complication, the idea of substantial unemployment, a feature that is not typical of most maps. That idea is the topic of questions 3–7 that follow.

ADDITIONAL QUESTIONS

1. Per capita income in Maine is most nearly equal to per capita income in

(1) Washington
(2) Idaho
(3) Utah
(4) Nevada
(5) Missouri

2. Which generalization is best supported by the map?

(1) All New England states have per capita incomes of over $2,000.
(2) All states along the Atlantic seaboard have a high per capita income.
(3) All southern states have incomes below $2,000.
(4) All states along the Pacific coast have per capita incomes of $2,000 or over.
(5) Most states have per capita incomes over $2,500.

3. According to the map, in which state is unemployment a major problem?

(1) Pennsylvania
(2) Florida
(3) Alabama
(4) Texas
(5) Washington

4. Which state has both a per capita income of between $2,000 and $2,500, and an area with substantial unemployment?

(1) Kansas
(2) Ohio
(3) Kentucky
(4) Mississippi
(5) California

5. Which state has a high per capita income and substantial unemployment?

(1) Florida
(2) Louisiana
(3) Minnesota
(4) California
(5) Nevada

6. Unemployment is less of a problem in Indiana than in

(1) Massachusetts
(2) Tennessee
(3) Mississippi
(4) Louisiana
(5) Arizona

7. Which conclusion concerning the state of Tennessee is supported by the map?

(1) It is larger than Montana and richer than Mississippi.
(2) It has more unemployment than Georgia and was richer than Kentucky.
(3) It is as rich as Arkansas and poorer than Nevada.
(4) It had less unemployment than Oklahoma and more unemployment than Georgia.
(5) It is smaller than Minnesota and richer than Illinois.

ANSWER KEY

1. 2 2. 4 3. 1 4. 2 5. 4 6. 1
7. 3

ANSWER ANALYSIS

1. **2** The answer is Choice 2 since both states are light gray areas, with per capita incomes under $2,000.
2. **4** Choice 4 is correct. California had a per capita income of over $2,500; Washington and Oregon had incomes between $2,000 and $2,500; all have incomes of $2,000 or over per capita. Choice 1 is incorrect since Maine has an income of less than $2,000. Choice 2 is wrong since three states—North Carolina, South Carolina, and Georgia—have incomes lower than $2,000. Choice 3 is incorrect since Texas, Florida, and Virginia have incomes above $2,000. Choice 5 is incorrect; only 10 states have per capita incomes over $2,500.
3. **1** On the map, Pennsylvania has six dotted areas with substantial unemployment; Florida, Washington, and Texas have one each and Alabama has none. Choice 1 is correct.
4. **2** You have to find a white area with a dot. Only Ohio, Choice 2, fits these criteria.

5. **4** You have to find a dark gray area with several dots. Only California, Choice 4, fits this description.
6. **1** You need to locate a state with more than one dot since Indiana has one such dot. The correct answer is Choice 1, Massachusetts, which has two dots.
7. **3** The map compares Tennessee with other states with regard to per capita income *and* unemployment. Choice 1 is wrong since Montana is larger. Choice 2 is wrong since Tennessee is not richer than Kentucky but the same. Choice 4 is wrong since Tennessee has more unemployment than both Oklahoma and Georgia. Choice 5 is incorrect since Tennessee is poorer than Illinois. Choice 3 is correct; both Tennessee and Arkansas have per capita incomes of less than $2,000, while Nevada has a per capita income of over $2,500.

Now it is time for further practice. The following practice exercises will give you ample preparation in reading tables, graphs, and maps for the GED Examination.

Additional Practice with Tables, Graphs, and Maps

Read each of the following questions carefully. Select the best answer.

Questions 1–4 are based on the following map.

NEW GOALS FOR REDUCING POLLUTION

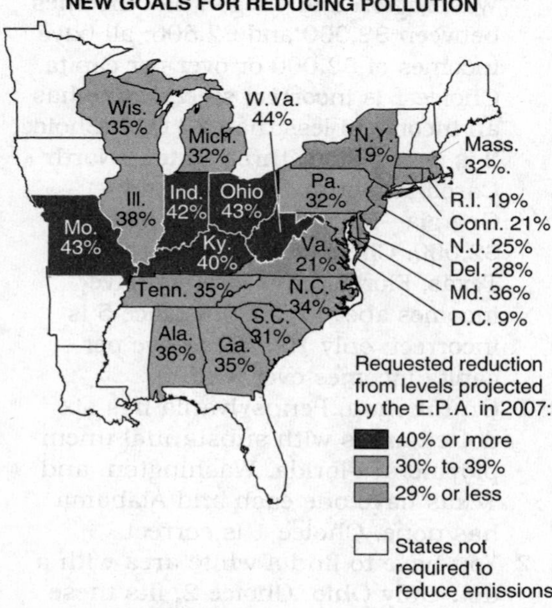

Source: Environmental Protection Agency

1. According to the map, the state that probably will have the most pollution is
   (1) Missouri
   (2) Indiana
   (3) Ohio
   (4) Kentucky
   (5) West Virginia

2. The states that have exactly similar goals in the reduction of pollution are
   (1) Michigan, Pennsylvania, Massachusetts
   (2) Missouri, Indiana, Ohio
   (3) Alabama, Georgia, South Carolina
   (4) Virginia, Connecticut, Maryland
   (5) New York, Rhode Island, New Jersey

3. The area with the lowest requested reduction in pollution is
   (1) Virginia
   (2) District of Columbia
   (3) Rhode Island
   (4) New York
   (5) Connecticut

4. Pollution appears to be lowest in the region of
   (1) the Midwest
   (2) the Great Lakes
   (3) the Southeast
   (4) the Middle Atlantic States
   (5) the Deep South

Questions 5–11 are based on the following graphs.

THE BUDGET DOLLAR OF FEDERAL GOVERNMENT

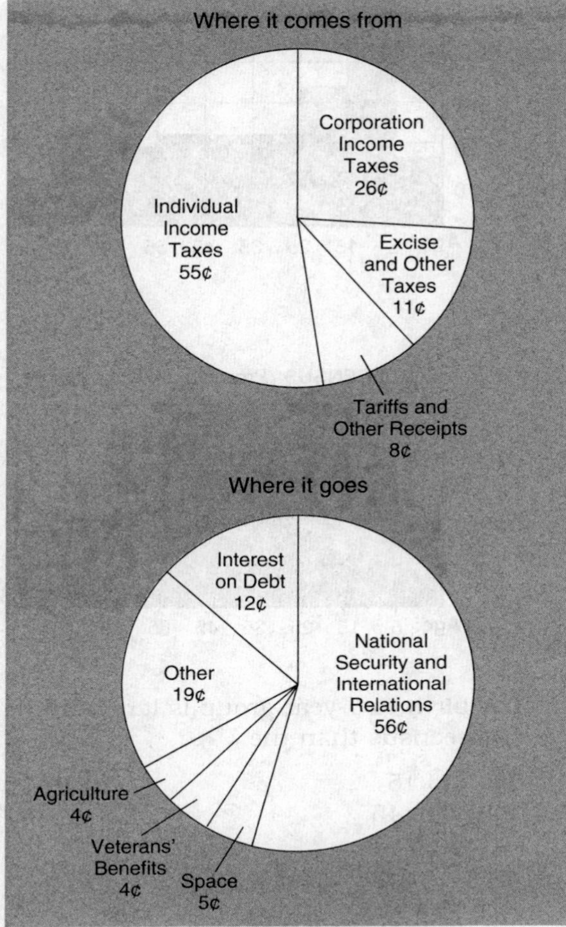

5. Forty-five percent of the national income is derived from
   (1) individual income taxes, excise taxes, and tariffs
   (2) corporation income taxes, excise taxes, and tariffs
   (3) individual income taxes, corporation income taxes, and excise taxes
   (4) individual income taxes, corporation income taxes, and tariffs
   (5) individual income taxes and excise taxes

6. The largest amount of the national income is expended on
   (1) health and welfare
   (2) national security and international relations
   (3) space
   (4) interest on debt
   (5) veterans' benefits

7. The two areas on which equal amounts of the national income are expended are
   (1) agriculture and veterans' benefits
   (2) space and agriculture
   (3) health and welfare and interest on debt
   (4) veterans' benefits and space
   (5) space and all others

8. The amount of income received from the collection of excise and other taxes approximately equals the amount expended for
   (1) interest on debt
   (2) health and welfare
   (3) space
   (4) agriculture
   (5) veterans' benefits

9. What is the biggest source of income for the federal government?
   (1) tariffs
   (2) excise taxes
   (3) corporation taxes
   (4) individual income taxes
   (5) other receipts

10. The combined expenditure for agriculture and veterans' benefits equals that for the income category entitled
   (1) excise and other taxes
   (2) health and welfare
   (3) interest on debt
   (4) tariffs and other receipts
   (5) national security

11. The income from individual income taxes most nearly equals the expenditure for
   (1) national security and international relations
   (2) health and welfare
   (3) space
   (4) veterans' benefits
   (5) all others

Questions 12–15 are based on the following graphs.

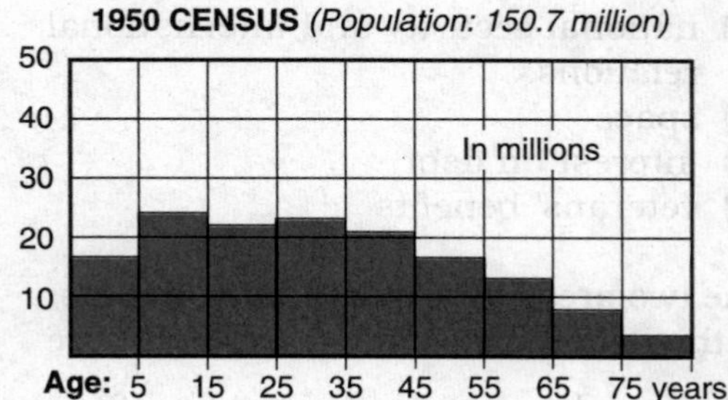

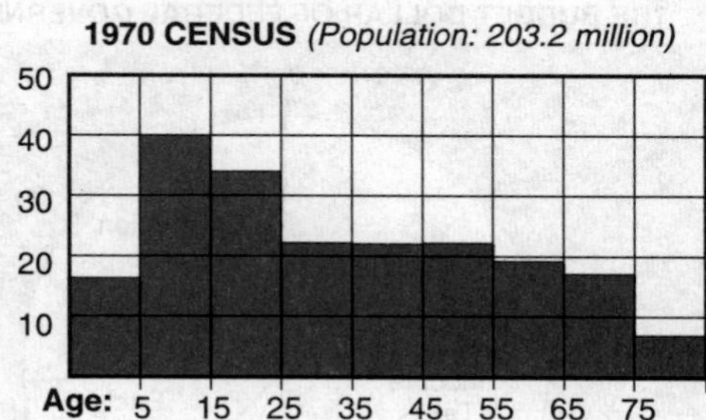

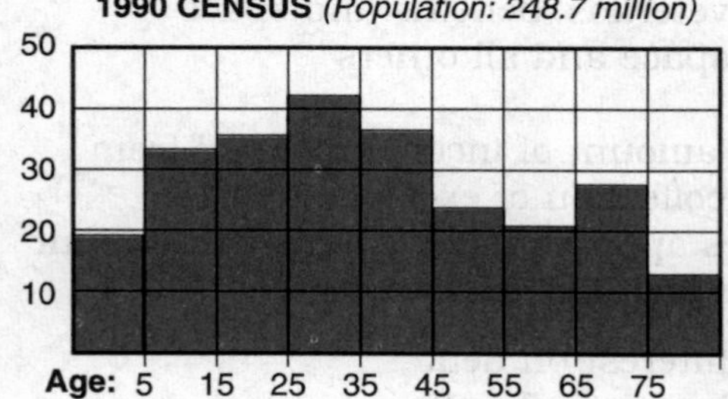

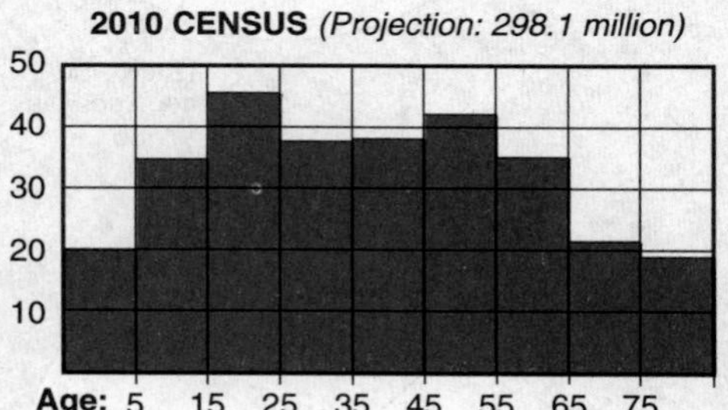

12. According to the graphs, the population census takes place

    (1) every 10 years
    (2) every 20 years
    (3) every 30 years
    (4) every 50 years
    (5) irregularly

13. The 1990 census reveals that the largest age group is that between

    (1) 5 and 15
    (2) 15 and 25
    (3) 25 and 35
    (4) 35 and 45
    (5) 45 and 55

14. The birth to 5-year group is larger in each census than the

    (1) 5 to 15
    (2) 35 to 45
    (3) 45 to 55
    (4) 65 to 75
    (5) over 75

15. The group that will have grown the most in percentage between 1950 and 2010 is the

    (1) 5 to 15
    (2) 15 to 25
    (3) 25 to 35
    (4) 35 to 45
    (5) over 75

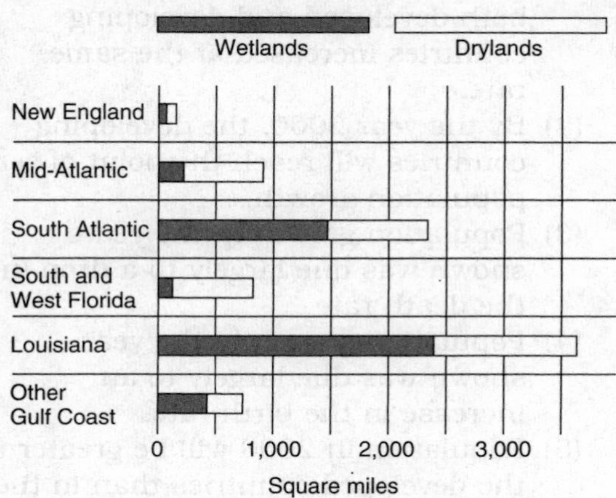

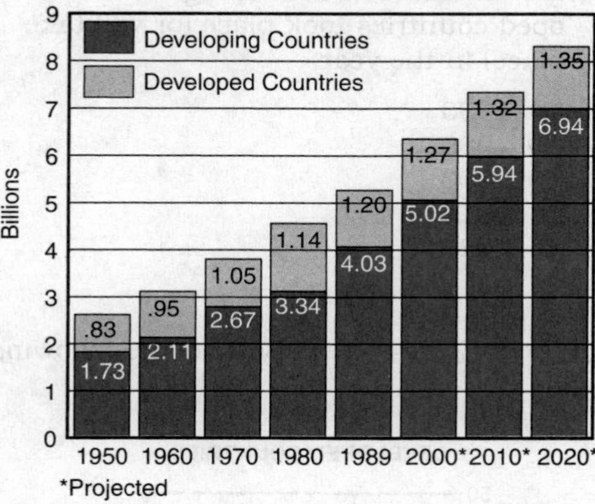

16. According to the graph, if sea levels rose 20 inches by the year 2100, the coastal lands that would be most affected are in
    (1) the South Atlantic
    (2) the Mid-Atlantic
    (3) Louisiana
    (4) Other Gulf Coast
    (5) Florida

17. The coastal drylands that would be most affected are in the
    (1) Mid-Atlantic
    (2) South Atlantic
    (3) South and West Florida
    (4) Other Gulf Coast
    (5) New England

18. Which statement is true, according to the graph?
    (1) The northeast United States would be more affected than the Gulf Coast.
    (2) The east coast would be more affected than the Gulf Coast.
    (3) The Gulf Coast would be the hardest hit.
    (4) Generally the wetlands would be affected more than the drylands.
    (5) The shoreline is greater on the Atlantic than on the gulf.

19. Which statement is best supported by the data in the graph?
    (1) The rate of world population growth has begun to decrease.
    (2) The world's population tripled between 1970 and 1989.
    (3) Most of the world's population lives in economically developing countries.
    (4) The population of economically developed countries consumes most of the world's resources.
    (5) The world is nearing zero population growth.

20. Which factor best accounts for the difference in the growth rate between developing and developed countries as shown in the graph?
    (1) increased family planning in developed countries
    (2) increasing pollution in developed countries
    (3) the breakdown of extended families in developing countries
    (4) the rise of single-parent families throughout the world
    (5) the greater likelihood of wars in developing countries

21. The greatest difference in population growth between developing and developed countries took place (or will take place) in the year

    (1) 1980
    (2) 1989
    (3) 2000
    (4) 2010
    (5) 2020

Questions 22–24 are based on the following graphs.

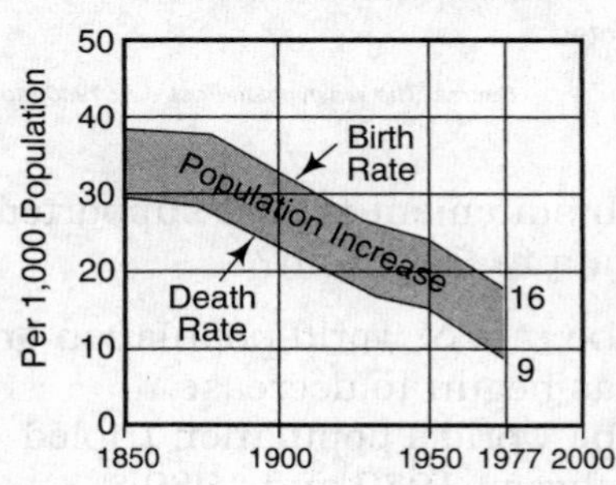

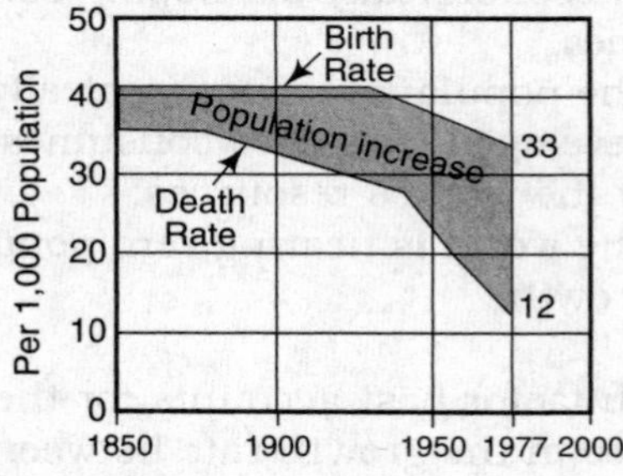

RATE OF POPULATION INCREASE = BIRTH RATE – DEATH RATE
Source: United Nations Population Division

22. Which statement is best supported by the information in the graphs?

    (1) In the years shown, population in both developed and developing countries increased at the same rate.
    (2) By the year 2000, the developing countries will reach the point of zero population growth.
    (3) Population growth in the years shown was due largely to a drop in the death rate.
    (4) Population growth in the years shown was due largely to an increase in the birth rate.
    (5) Population in 2000 will be greater in the developed countries than in the developing countries.

23. According to the graphs, in the developed countries

    (1) the birth rate surpassed the death rate for the years shown
    (2) the death rate surpassed the birth rate for the years shown
    (3) the population is growing at an increased rate
    (4) the birth rate is increasing
    (5) the death rate is increasing

24. According to the graphs, a comparison of developed and developing countries shows that

    (1) the birth rate and the death rate have always been greater in the developing countries
    (2) only the birth rate has been greater in the developing countries
    (3) only the death rate has been greater in the developing countries
    (4) birth and death rates have been similar in both
    (5) population increases have been similar in both

Questions 25–30 are based on the following illustrations.

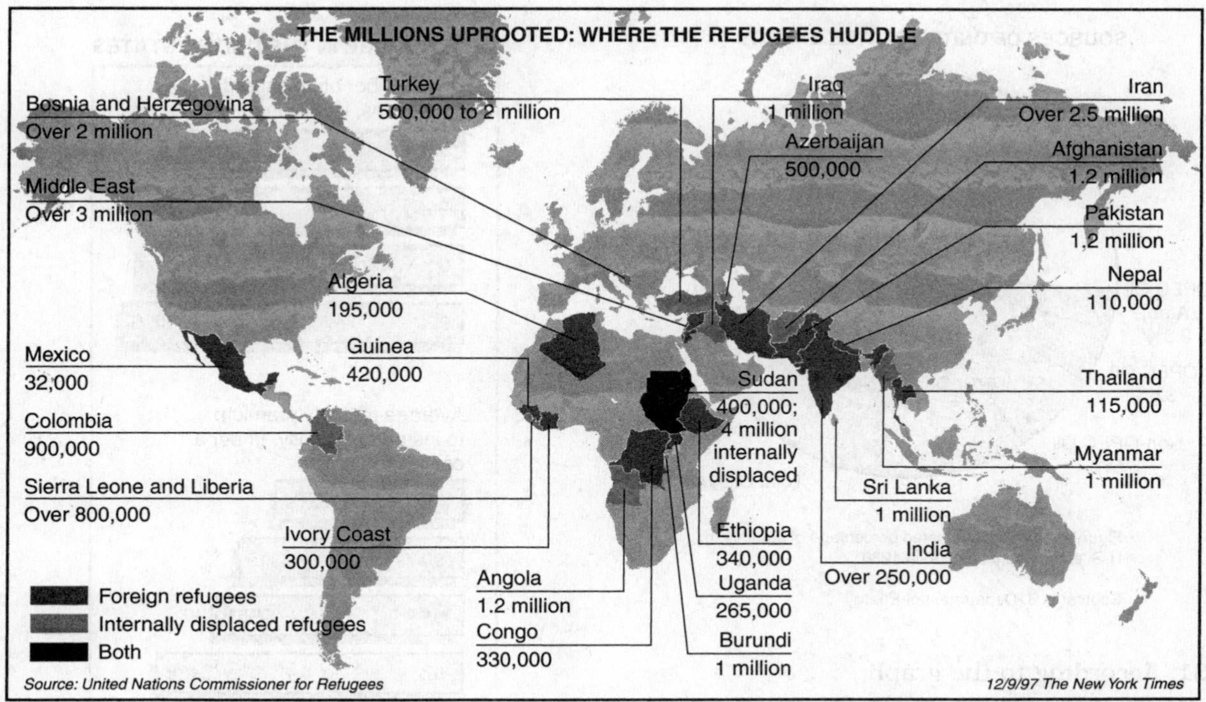

25. According to the map, the country with the largest number of foreign refugees is

(1) Algeria
(2) Congo
(3) Azerbaijan
(4) Uganda
(5) Iran

26. The country with the largest number of internally displaced refugees is

(1) Sudan
(2) Angola
(3) Afghanistan
(4) Pakistan
(5) Myanmar

27. The European country with the largest number of refugees is

(1) Turkey
(2) France
(3) Italy
(4) Bosnia and Herzegovina
(5) Greece

28. The number of countries that have over 1 million refugees is

(1) 3
(2) 5
(3) 6
(4) 8
(5) 10

29. The continent with the fewest number of refugees is

(1) North America
(2) South America
(3) Europe
(4) Africa
(5) Asia

30. The country for which the number of refugees is least precise is

(1) Colombia
(2) Algeria
(3) Turkey
(4) Nepal
(5) Thailand

Questions 31–33 are based on the following graph.

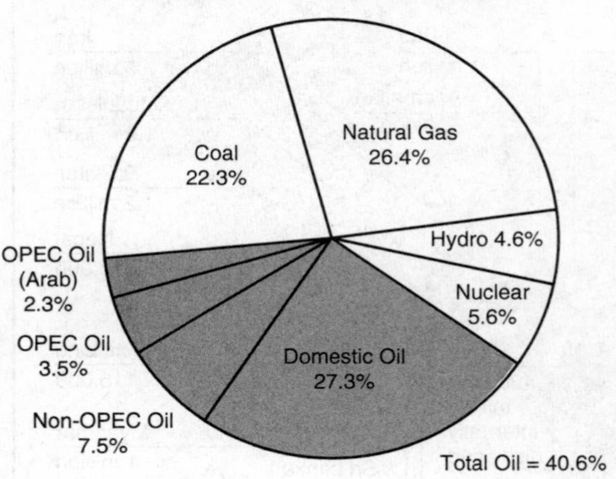

Figures represent estimated percentage of sources for U.S. energy consumption in 1986.

Source: U.S. Department of Energy

31. According to the graph,
    (1) oil contributes more to U.S. energy than coal and natural gas
    (2) OPEC (Arab) oil is the smallest contributor to U.S. energy
    (3) OPEC oil exceeds non-OPEC oil as a source of U.S. energy
    (4) natural gas is the largest single source of U.S. energy
    (6) hydro energy and nuclear energy exceed foreign oil as sources of U.S. energy

32. According to the graph, the largest single source of U.S. energy is
    (1) coal
    (2) natural gas
    (3) domestic oil
    (4) nuclear and hydro
    (5) OPEC and non-OPEC foreign oil

33. It can be inferred from the graph that foreign sources account for what percentage of U.S. energy?
    (1) 27.3%
    (2) 26.4%
    (3) 22.3%
    (4) 13.3%
    (5) 10.2%

Questions 34–35 are based on the following graph.

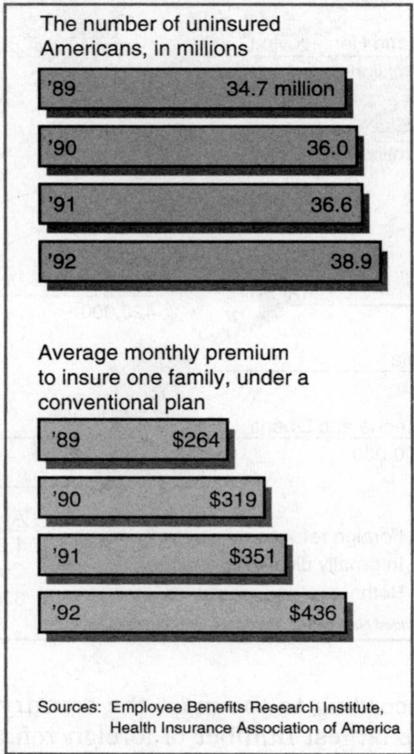

Sources: Employee Benefits Research Institute, Health Insurance Association of America

34. According to the graph, the most valid conclusion that can be drawn is that
    (1) health care is not available for most Americans
    (2) the number of Americans not insured for health has reached a peak
    (3) the premiums for conventional plans for health care cannot be afforded by most Americans
    (4) health care is becoming less available and more costly to American families
    (5) the rate of increases in health care costs is declining

35. The average monthly premium to insure one family
    (1) had its greatest increase from 1989 to 1990
    (2) had its greatest increase from 1990 to 1991
    (3) had its greatest increase from 1991 to 1992
    (4) saw a decrease in the rate of increases
    (5) increased at a rate of 50% in the four-year period 1989–1992

Questions 36–37 are based on the following graph.

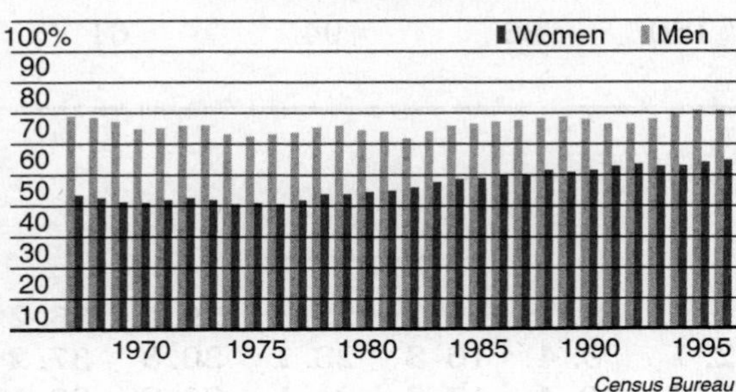

36. According to the graph, during the period shown:
    (1) the number of men working full time increased dramatically.
    (2) the number of women working full time increased dramatically.
    (3) the number of men working full time fell slightly.
    (4) the total number of men and women working full time leveled off.
    (5) the total number of men and women working full time decreased.

37. From the figures given in the graph, there probably was a recession in the years
    (1) 1967–1973
    (2) 1974–1978
    (3) 1979–1985
    (4) 1985–1990
    (5) 1991–1996

Questions 38–40 are based on the following chart.

ECONOMIC AND SOCIAL PROFILES OF SELECTED COUNTRIES—EAST ASIA

	Populations (Millions est.) 1976	1990	Per Capita Income 1989	GNP (billions of dollars) 1989	Literacy Rate (%) 1976	1992	Doubling Population Time (Years)
Japan	113	124	23,730	2,920	99	100	exceeds 100
Korea (South)	36	43.2	4,400	186.5	88.5	96	70
Korea (North)	16	21.8	1,240	28	NA	95	38
China (Peoples Republic)	852	1,150	360	393	40	73	48
Taiwan (Republic of China)	16.3	20.5	7,480	150	86	94	61

Source: *Encyclopedia Britannica Book of the Year 1992*

38. Which of the following is true according to the chart?
    (1) Taiwan leads China in both per capita income and literacy rate.
    (2) Taiwan is the least populated country.
    (3) North Korea is wealthier than South Korea.
    (4) South Korea leads China in GNP.
    (5) The population of North Korea showed the least growth between 1976 and 1990.

39. The country with the greatest increase in population and literacy rate is
    (1) Japan
    (2) North Korea
    (3) South Korea
    (4) China
    (5) Taiwan

40. Individuals are benefiting most from the GNP in
    (1) Japan
    (2) North Korea
    (3) South Korea
    (4) China
    (5) Taiwan

Answer Key

1. 5	8. 1	15. 2	22. 3	29. 1	36. 2
2. 1	9. 4	16. 3	23. 1	30. 3	37. 2
3. 2	10. 4	17. 2	24. 1	31. 2	38. 1
4. 4	11. 1	18. 3	25. 5	32. 3	39. 4
5. 2	12. 2	19. 3	26. 1	33. 4	40. 1
6. 2	13. 3	20. 1	27. 4	34. 4	
7. 1	14. 5	21. 5	28. 5	35. 3	

WHAT'S YOUR SCORE?

______right, ______wrong

Excellent	36–41
Good	32–35
Fair	28–31

If you scored lower, you may need more review. Reread the section, "Practice with Interpreting Tables, Graphs, Maps" (page 241), and try again.

ANSWER ANALYSIS

1. **5** West Virginia has a proposed level of 44%, the highest percentage indicated.
2. **1** All three states have levels of 32%.
3. **2** The District of Columbia, at 9%, has by far the lowest projected level of pollution.
4. **4** The Middle Atlantic states, with the exception of Maryland have projected levels of pollution of less than 30%.
5. **2** These three sources provide 26%, 11%, and 8%, respectively, for a total of 45%.
6. **2** National security and international relations represent 56% of the national expenditure.
7. **1** Four percent is expended on each.
8. **1** Excise and other taxes bring in 11%, 12% is spent on interest on debt.
9. **4** Fifty-five percent of federal income comes from individual income taxes.
10. **4** These add up to 8%, the amount received from tariffs and other receipts.
11. **1** Income from individual income taxes is 55%; expenditure for national security and international relations is 56%.
12. **2** The titles of the bar graphs are the 1950 census, 1970 census, 1990 census, and 2010 census; here is a 20-year gap between them.
13. **3** Over 40 million persons are between 25 and 35.
14. **5** In each census, there are more in the birth to 5-year group than the over-75 group.
15. **2** The 15 to 25 age group will grow from 21% to 46%, more than any other age group.
16. **3** Louisiana would lose about 3600 square miles, at least 1000 square miles more than anywhere else.
17. **2** The loss to South Atlantic drylands would constitute about 900 square miles, hundreds of square miles more than the Mid-Atlantic and South and West Florida.
18. **3** The Gulf Coast and Louisiana would lose about 4300 square miles, the total of all the other areas combined.
19. **3** The graph shows that most of the world's population lives in economically developing nations. In 1989, 4.03 billion, of a total world population of 5.23 billion, or 80% of the total, lived in developing nations.
20. **1** Inspection of the figures shows that the growth rate is higher in developing than in developed nations; people in developing nations have less access to family-planning assistance.
21. **5** In 2020, the gap as shown in the graph is 6.94 minus 1.35 or 5.59 billions, greater than for any other year.
22. **3** While the graph for developed countries shows a steady balance between declining birth and death rates, the graph for developing countries shows a relative population increase that grows from about 1875 to the present because the death rate drops more and more compared with the birth rate.
23. **1** The birth rate line is consistently above the death rate line.
24. **1** The birth rate and the death rate lines for the developing countries have always been higher than those for the developed countries.
25. **5** Iran has over 2.5 million foreign refugees. The other choices all have fewer than half a million.
26. **1** Sudan has 4 million internally displaced persons.
27. **4** Bosnia and Herzegovina has over 2 million internally displaced refugees.
28. **5** The following countries have over 1 million refugees—Angola, Iraq, Burundi, Sudan, Sri Lanka, Iran, Afghanistan, Pakistan, Myanmar, and Bosnia and Herzegovina.
29. **1** Only Mexico in North America has refugees, and they total 32,000.
30. **3** Turkey's refugee population is indicated as having a range between 500,000 to 2 million.
31. **2** OPEC (Arab) oil, contrary to popular belief, is the smallest contributor to United States energy, 2.3%.
32. **3** Domestic oil counts for 27.3% of United States energy.
33. **4** 13.3% is the total of OPEC and non-OPEC contributions.
34. **4** Health care is becoming less available because fewer and fewer people have insurance and each year it gets more costly for a family.

35. **3** The increase was $85 a month per family—$351 to $436.
36. **2** The percentage of women working full time in 1976 was 40%. In 1996, it was 55%, an increase of 15% in 20 years. The percentage of men in the same period of time grew half as much, from 62% to 70%.
37. **2** The percentage of both men and women working dropped visibly in the years 1974–1978, to 62% and 40%, respectively, from consistently higher levels prior to that period, probably because fewer jobs were available.
38. **1** Inspection of the chart shows that per capita income in Taiwan is 7480, many times that in China, 360. Taiwan had literacy rates of 86 in 1976 and 94 in 1992, much higher than those of China for the same dates.
39. **4** The population of China grew from 852 to 1150 and the literacy rate grew from 40% to 73%; these increases were greater than than those of any other country listed.
40. **1** Japan has a per capita income far greater than that of any other country in the chart. The same is true for its gross national product.

Basics in Interpreting Political Cartoons

Political cartoons, as a distinct art form, first became important in the second half of the nineteenth century. Two cartoonists, in particular, achieved great fame during that period.

Thomas Nast, of *Harper's Weekly*, attacked Tammany Hall in 1869, when Boss Tweed and his Ring were in control of New York City. His most famous cartoon, "The Tammany Tiger Loose—'What are you going to do about it?'" led to the voting out of Ring officials and Tweed's conviction and jailing for grand larceny. This cartoon is on page 261.

Joseph Keppler, who founded *Puck*, the first humorous weekly in the United States, used color to powerful effect in his cartoons. A famous cartoon, "Bosses of the Senate," attacked the financial interests represented in the U.S. Senate. This cartoon is on page 261.

1. Most cartoons deal with a single important issue, usually an election campaign issue, questions of peace or war, or corruption in government.
2. The cartoonist frequently uses an exaggerated likeness, or caricature, of some well-known person or institution, for example, Uncle Sam, as the main focus of attention. Or he or she may use or create a familiar symbol to represent an important idea; a dove for peace, a tiger for Tammany Hall.
3. Reading is kept to a minimum so that the appeal is largely visual. A few words at most are used to drive home an idea, so the visual appeal of the political cartoon is universal. Boss Tweed pointed out that, even if his followers could not read, they could "look at the d__n pictures." Thus the cartoonist presents an issue in simplified form, stripped of all relatively unimportant details, in a way that his readers can understand.
4. The cartoonist graphically presents his or her own point of view or that of a newspaper or magazine. The cartoonist is usually openly anticorruption or antiwar, and portrays the object of his or her criticism in the ugliest manner possible.

Because of the visually appealing use of a caricature and/or a symbol focusing critically on a single important issue, the political cartoon is a powerful means of shaping public opinion. Its appeal to the emotions is difficult to equal, and its influence continues to the present day.

How, then, do you interpret a political cartoon when you encounter it on the High School Equivalency Examination?

Here are a few suggestions, using the Nast and Keppler cartoons.

Step 1. *Identify the caricatures or symbols used in the cartoon.* For historical cartoons, you may need some social studies background. In contemporary cartoons, the caricatures and symbols are easier to identify.

In the Nast cartoon, Boss Tweed, sitting in the gallery under the standard reading TAMMANY SPOILS, is a symbol of political power. The tiger represents Tammany Hall, the corrupt political club, and the woman in the tiger's claws is the dead Republic surrounded by the breakdown of law and the destroyed democratic freedom of the ballot.

Step 2. *Identify the issue being exposed or criticized by the cartoonist.* In the case of Nast, it is the undermining of the democratic process by a corrupt political boss and his cronies. In the Keppler cartoon, it is the taking over of the U.S. Senate by monopolies and trusts.

Step 3. *Determine the point of view being expressed by the cartoonist.* In the Nast cartoon, the snarl on the face of the tiger and the exaggerated size of Boss Tweed show how vicious the cartoonist considers the political boss, his organization (the Tweed Ring), and Tammany Hall to be. In the Keppler cartoon, the bloated stomachs of the trusts and their ugly facial expressions convey the cartoonist's disgust.

Now turn to a third cartoon, study it, and try to answer the questions based on it.

QUESTIONS

1. What issue is the subject of this cartoon?
2. What do the elephant and the donkey represent?
3. What is each trying to do?
4. What point of view is the cartoonist expressing?

ANSWERS AND ANALYSIS

1. The issue is campaign-funding abuse, as indicated on the cookie jar.
2. The elephant is the traditional symbol of the Republican party; the donkey, of the Democratic party.
3. Each has a hand in the cookie jar and is trying to extract money for the campaign.
4. The cartoonist finds both parties at fault even though he portrays the equally guilty Republicans expressing disapproval of the Democrats.

Practice with Cartoons

1. The main purpose of Mike Thompson's cartoon is to

   (1) portray the conflict between Republicans and Democrats
   (2) show the superiority of the Republicans over the Democrats
   (3) show the superiority of the Democrats over the Republicans
   (4) show that Republicans and Democrats are both at fault in campaign fund-raising
   (5) show that Democrats do not feel guilty about their campaign fund-raising

2. The cartoonist achieves his purpose by

   (1) exaggerating the conduct of both parties
   (2) arousing our sympathy for both parties
   (3) portraying the humor of the conduct of both parties
   (4) favoring Republicans over Democrats
   (5) showing the irony of the Republicans' conduct

Answer Key

1. **4** 2. **5**

Answer Analysis

1. **4** Choice 4 is correct because the cartoonist indicates that both parties have their hands in the cookie jar and are guilty of campaign fund-raising abuses. Neither party is superior to the other, nor does either feel guilty.
2. **5** The irony arises from the fact that each party has a hand in the jar, yet the Republican elephant is faulting the Democratic donkey for an abuse of which both are equally guilty.

10

Handling Social Studies Skills Questions

The Social Studies test no longer tests your ability to recall information such as dates, isolated facts, or events. It now emphasizes higher level skills. It does so by testing your ability to understand the written word or graphics, to analyze and apply the given information and ideas, and to evaluate the accuracy of the information and the conclusions based on it.

Comprehension Items

Twenty percent of the test, or about 13 items, require you to understand the meaning and purpose of written material, passages or quotations, and information contained in maps, graphs, tables, and political cartoons. These items test your ability to restate information, summarize ideas, and identify incorrectly stated ideas. The question will usually include a quotation and be followed by the words "This most nearly means" or "The best explanation of this statement is" or "The author believes or suggests."

EXAMPLE

A CODE

> Never DO, BE, or SUFFER anything in soul or body, less or more, but what tends to the glory of God.
>
> *Resolved,* never to lose one moment of time; but improve it the most profitable way I possibly can.
>
> *Resolved,* to think much, on all occasions, of my own dying, and of the common circumstances which attend death.
>
> *Resolved,* to maintain the strictest temperance in eating and drinking.

QUESTION

1. The author of the code believes that people should be mainly concerned with

(1) monetary issues
(2) luxuries
(3) patriotism
(4) spiritual matters
(5) politics

ANSWER AND ANALYSIS

The passage reflects the ideas of Puritanism, a code that stresses spiritual concerns.

You can answer this question correctly if you read the passage carefully and decide what is being emphasized. Then, look for the answer that identifies that emphasis. In this question, the emphasis is on living for the glory of God, concern for one's manner of dying, and discipline in such material concerns as eating and drinking. The spiritual is stressed. Indeed, you can answer the question even if you do not know it is the Puritan Code that is being quoted. The correct choice is 4.

Application Items

Thirty percent of the test, or about 19 items, require you to use information and ideas in a situation other than that indicated to you in the question. Applying information and ideas is a high-level skill because you must not only understand the general content, but also be able to transfer it to the context of a particular situation. In other words, you must go from the general information you are given to a specific case.

EXAMPLE

The principle of judicial review provides for the judiciary to determine the constitutionality of both state and federal laws.

QUESTION

1. Which action best illustrates the principle of judicial review?

(1) Congress enacts civil rights legislation.
(2) The Senate approves appointment of federal judges.
(3) An act of Congress is struck down by the Supreme Court.
(4) The states refuse to cooperate with the federal authorities in crime control.
(5) Congress overrides a presidential veto.

ANSWER AND ANALYSIS

The principle of judicial review means the power of the U.S. Supreme Court to rule on the constitutionality of acts of Congress, state legislatures, executive officers, and lower courts. The only choice that involves a court action is Choice 3, a specific application of this principle to an act of Congress. You must apply the principle of judicial or court reexamination to an act of Congress.

The purpose of another form of question or item on the High School Equivalency Examination Social Studies test is to test your ability to apply given information that defines ideas in historical documents, divisions of subject matter in the social studies, systems of government, economics, psychology, and groups of basic concepts in the five areas of the social studies. You will have to

1. understand information that is presented in defined categories, usually five in number;
2. relate a situation, action, or event to those categories;
3. arrive at an application of the information in the categories to the given situation, action, or event.

An illustration will make this clear. In this example, the information presented in defined categories is the central idea of each of five articles of the Bill of Rights, the first ten amendments to the Constitution.

EXAMPLE

The first ten amendments to the Constitution make up the Bill of Rights ratified by Congress in 1791. Parts of five of the amendments read as follows:

(A) Article 1—Congress shall make no law...abridging the freedom of speech or of the press.
(B) Article 2—The right of the people to keep and bear arms shall not be infringed.
(C) Article 5—No person...shall be compelled in any criminal case to be a witness against himself, nor be deprived of life, liberty, or property, without due process of law.
(D) Article 7—The right to trial by jury shall be preserved.
(E) Article 8—Excessive bail shall not be required...nor cruel and unusual punishments inflicted.

The questions that follow deal with three ways in which the given information can be used by three individuals in three different situations.

QUESTIONS

Indicate the amendment (article) most likely to be cited in support of his or her position by

1. an opponent of capital punishment

(1) Article 1
(2) Article 2
(3) Article 5
(4) Article 7
(5) Article 8

2. a member of the National Rifle Association

   (1) Article 1
   (2) Article 2
   (3) Article 5
   (4) Article 7
   (5) Article 8

3. a person accused of a criminal act who is testifying at his or her trial

   (1) Article 1
   (2) Article 2
   (3) Article 5
   (4) Article 7
   (5) Article 8

ANSWERS AND ANALYSIS

You must apply the categorized information to each situation.

The correct answer to question 1 is Choice 5. An opponent of capital punishment will cite Article 8's prohibition against cruel and unusual punishment.

The correct answer to question 2 is Choice 2. A member of the National Rifle Association will cite Article 2, "The right of the people to keep and bear arms shall not be infringed."

The correct answer to question 3 is Choice 3. The person on trial might "take the Fifth," citing the provision of Article 5 that "no person...shall be compelled in any criminal case to be a witness against himself."

Try another item set in this format.

EXAMPLE

Psychology is the science of behavior and of human thought processes. There are a number of closely interrelated branches of human psychology.

(A) Social psychology investigates the effect of the group on the behavior of the individual.
(B) Applied psychology puts to practical use the discoveries and theories of psychology as in industrial psychology.
(C) Clinical psychology diagnoses and treats mental disorders and mental illnesses.
(D) Comparative psychology deals with different behavioral organizations of animals including human beings.
(E) Physiological psychology attempts to understand the effects of body functions on human behavior.

QUESTIONS

Each of the following describes a proposed study. Indicate which branch of psychology is most clearly involved.

1. A company wants to study the effects of music piped into a factory where workers are on an assembly line.

   (1) Social psychology
   (2) Applied psychology
   (3) Clinical psychology
   (4) Comparative psychology
   (5) Physiological psychology

2. A drug rehabilitation center wants to study the role of peer pressure on a teenager in a drug prevention program.

   (1) Social psychology
   (2) Applied psychology
   (3) Clinical psychology
   (4) Comparative psychology
   (5) Physiological psychology

3. A grant is available for a study of schizophrenia, a disorder characterized by hallucinations and delusions.

   (1) Social psychology
   (2) Applied psychology
   (3) Clinical psychology
   (4) Comparative psychology
   (5) Physiological psychology

ANSWERS AND ANALYSIS

The correct answer to question 1 is Choice 2. Applied psychology puts the findings of industrial psychologists to practical use, in this case for people who work on an assembly line.

The correct answer to question 2 is Choice 1. Social psychologists are concerned with the effects of groups, in this case teenagers, who put pressure on their peers to use drugs.

The correct answer to question 3 is Choice 3. Clinical psychologists would apply for the grant because of their interest in schizophrenia, a mental disorder.

Analysis Items

Thirty percent of the test, or about 19 items, require you to break down information into its parts to determine their interrelationships. These items involve the ability to identify cause-and-effect relationships, separate fact from opinion, separate conclusions from supporting statements, and show that you can recognize assumptions on which conclusions are based.

QUESTION

1. Democracy may be defined as government by the people directly or through representatives chosen in free elections. Which quotation from the Declaration of Independence best describes the fundamental principle of democracy in the United States?

   (1) "imposing taxes on us without our consent"
   (2) "governments long established should not be changed for light and transient causes"
   (3) "depriving us, in many cases, of the benefits of trial by jury"
   (4) "deriving their just powers from the consent of the governed"
   (5) "quartering large bodies of armed troops among us"

ANSWER AND ANALYSIS

Not only must you understand the meaning of each possible answer, but you must analyze it to determine which is a *fundamental* principle of government in the United States. First you must understand; then you must analyze.

You have to go through all of the following steps:

Choice 1: imposing taxes without consent—meaning taxation without representation

Choice 2: governments long established should not be changed for light causes—meaning change in government must be for good reason

Choice 3: benefits of trial by jury—meaning the right to trial by jury

Choice 4: deriving powers from consent of the governed—meaning the government gets its power from those it governs, the people

Choice 5: quartering armed troops—meaning compulsion to keep soldiers in homes

Now the test of a *fundamental* principle of government in the United States must be applied to each.

Choice 1 is not fundamental; it is a grievance.

Choice 2 refers not to the government of the United States, but to changing governments in general.

Choice 3, trial by jury, is an important right, but it is not as fundamental as Choice 4, which states that the U.S. government is a democracy in which the people rule through their elected representatives. This is an absolutely fundamental principle.

Choice 4 is the only correct interpretation that can be made.

Choice 5 refers to unauthorized quartering of soldiers—important, but not fundamental.

Evaluation Items

Twenty percent of the test, or about 13 items, are the most difficult. You must make judgments about the soundness or accuracy of information. These questions test your ability to determine whether facts are adequately documented or proved, whether they are appropriately used to support conclusions, and whether they are used correctly or incorrectly in the presentation of opinions or arguments.

QUESTION

1. Which statement is an opinion rather than a fact?

   (1) France was involved in the Vietnam conflict before the United States entered it.
   (2) There are tensions between mainland China and Taiwan.
   (3) Peace will be achieved by regional agreements throughout the world.
   (4) Great Britain has become a full member of the European Common Market.
   (5) The United States is a member of the North Atlantic Treaty Organization.

ANSWER AND ANALYSIS

Five statements are presented. Four are facts that can be proved or verified by evidence—that France was involved in Vietnam; that mainland China and Taiwan have tensions; that Great Britain is a member of the

European Common Market; that the United States is a member of the North Atlantic Treaty Organization. Choice 3, peace will be achieved by regional agreements throughout the world, is an opinion or a hypothesis—not a fact—and it remains to be proved.

Practice with Social Studies Skills Questions

COMPREHENSION

1. During the last 150 years, immigrants were attracted to the United States because manpower needs increased. This occurred when the United States was experiencing periods of

(1) economic expansion
(2) economic depression
(3) war
(4) political change
(5) stability

2. "The privilege to be involved and to conduct a business in any manner that one pleases is not guaranteed by the Constitution. The right to engage in certain businesses may be subject to various conditions. Laws regulating businesses have been found to be valid. We find no justification to reject the state law under question."

Which is best illustrated by the passage?

(1) residual powers
(2) legislative consent
(3) judicial review
(4) executive order
(5) executive privilege

3. Which is a basic assumption of the graduated income tax?

(1) The ability to pay increases as wealth increases.
(2) Each wage earner should contribute to the government the same percentage of his or her income.
(3) The middle class should bear the burden of financing the government.
(4) Citizens should pay the costs of government services in proportion to their use of such services.
(5) Taxes on the wealthy should not be too great.

4. "In a sense the people of the Third World were forced to help pay for the Industrial Revolution in the West."

Which statement most clearly supports this viewpoint?

(1) The colonizing powers encouraged industries in their colonies.
(2) Western nations depended upon raw materials from their colonies.
(3) Financial centers of the world blocked investments in these new nations.
(4) The Third World is now experiencing an Industrial Revolution.
(5) The Third World supplied most of the manpower needed by the West.

5. "Public opinion is of major significance in social control."

The author of this statement most probably means that

(1) the influence of public opinion on government leaders is very limited
(2) problem solving is simplified when public opinion is not known
(3) public opinion may be predicted accurately, especially in the time of national crisis
(4) government officials must pay attention to public opinion in the formulation of policies
(5) polls provide little help to lawmakers

ANALYSIS

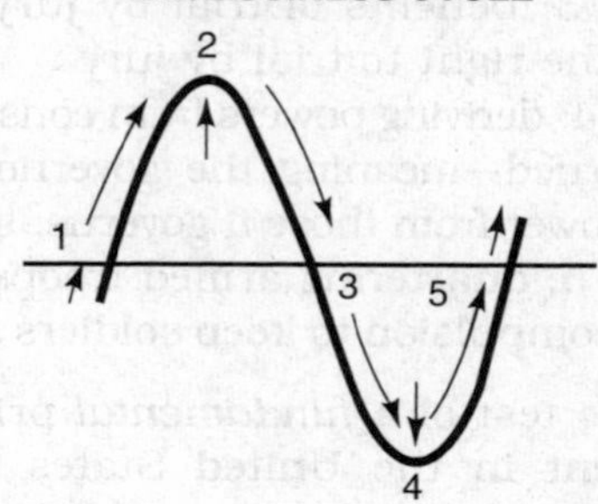

6. If economic indicators place the economy at a point on the cycle between 1 and 2, then the Council of Economic Advisers would most likely suggest which action to the president?
   (1) planned deficit spending
   (2) increasing income tax rates
   (3) lowering interest rates
   (4) increasing government expenditures
   (5) encouraging higher wages

7. "The showpieces are, with rare exceptions, the industries dominated by a handful of large firms. The foreign visitor, brought to the United States...visits the same firms as do the attorneys of the Department of Justice in their search for monopolies."

   The best explanation of this seemingly contradictory behavior is that
   (1) only the largest corporations will allow foreign visitors to inspect their factories
   (2) both State and Justice Department officials oppose the development of monopolies
   (3) the developing countries of the world are interested only in large corporations
   (4) the largest corporations often pioneer in research and production methods
   (5) small firms do not welcome foreign investment

8. "Why, by interweaving our destiny with that of any part of Europe, entangle our peace and prosperity in the toils of European ambition, rivalship, interest, humor, or caprice?"

   Which action by the United States best reflects the philosophy expressed in this quotation?
   (1) passage of legislation restricting immigration
   (2) rejection of the Treaty of Versailles
   (3) enactment of the Lend-Lease Act
   (4) approval of the United Nations Charter
   (5) membership in the North Atlantic Treaty Organization

9. "If a nation expects to be ignorant and free, in a state of civilization, it expects what never was and never will be."

   Which idea is most strongly supported by this statement?
   (1) the government's right to tax
   (2) universal suffrage
   (3) a strong central government
   (4) compulsory education
   (5) abolition of slavery

10. "Ours is a country where people...can attain to the most elevated positions or acquire a large amount of wealth...according to their talents, prudence, and personal exertions."
    This quotation most clearly supports the idea that
    (1) upward social mobility and the work ethic are closely related
    (2) economic collectivism is part of American life
    (3) regulated capitalism reflects private initiative
    (4) the United States has a centrally controlled economic system
    (5) the U.S. economic system favors the wealthy

APPLICATION

11. Which is the most valid statement concerning the problem of balancing human wants with limited resources?
    (1) It exists only in societies with a free enterprise economy.
    (2) It has been solved in nations with strong governmental controls over economic activity.
    (3) It has become less of a problem with the advancements in technology.
    (4) It exists in all societies, no matter what the economic system.
    (5) It will be solved by the year 2000.

12. A "strict constructionist," one who would permit the federal government to exercise only those powers specifically granted by the U.S. Constitution, would favor which of the following actions?

(1) the institution of programs for social reform
(2) annexation of territory by the United States
(3) bypassing constitutional restraints
(4) limiting the power of the federal government
(5) increasing the power of the states

A basic principle of the U.S. Constitution is the division of governmental power in the executive, the legislative, and the judicial branches. Legislative powers are vested in Congress; judicial powers, in the Supreme Court and federal court system; executive powers, in the president and his governmental machinery. Thus, a system of checks and balances exists among the three branches of government.

Each of the following is an example of the system of checks and balances in operation. Identify the one branch that is checking the other by choosing the appropriate response.

13. Congress overrides a presidential veto.

(1) the executive checks the legislative
(2) the executive balances the judicial
(3) the judicial balances the legislative
(4) the legislative checks the executive
(5) the legislative checks the judicial

14. The Senate refuses to confirm a presidential nominee for an ambassadorship.

(1) the executive checks the legislative
(2) the executive balances the judicial
(3) the judicial balances the legislative
(4) the legislative checks the executive
(5) the legislative checks the judicial

15. The president nominates a Supreme Court justice.

(1) the executive checks the legislative
(2) the executive balances the judicial
(3) the judicial balances the legislative
(4) the legislative checks the executive
(5) the legislative checks the judicial

EVALUATION

16. Which statement would be most *difficult* to prove?

(1) Japan's emperors have reigned but have seldom ruled.
(2) The workers of the United States are better workers than those of Japan.
(3) In the post-World War II period, the United States was the source of much cultural borrowing by the Japanese.
(4) Japanese technology in the 1970s was more advanced than it was in the 1940s.
(5) The cost of living in Japan has been rising ever since World War II.

17. Which statement would be most *difficult* to prove?

(1) Popular ideas of third parties in the United States tend to be adopted by the major political parties.
(2) The Articles of Confederation rendered more authority to the state government than to the federal government.
(3) The Sherman Antitrust Act was used to reduce the effectiveness of labor unions.
(4) World War II was necessary in order to end the Great Depression.
(5) The right to vote has been extended in the twentieth century.

18. Which information about country *X* would be most useful to the head of a government establishing a foreign policy toward country *X*?

(1) an analysis of the national resources and goals of country *X*
(2) a file containing the major public statements made by the leaders of country *X* concerning their nation's foreign policies
(3) an analysis by religious leaders of the major religious groups and beliefs of the people of country *X*
(4) a newspaper report summarizing the treaties and international agreements of country *X*
(5) knowledge of the party to which leaders of country *X* belong

19. Which statement expresses an opinion rather than a fact?
    (1) The United States did not join the League of Nations.
    (2) At one time, the United States was on the gold standard.
    (3) President Franklin D. Roosevelt made unnecessary concessions to the Russians at Yalta.
    (4) The Oregon Dispute was settled by extending the 49th parallel to the Pacific Ocean.
    (5) The United States is a member of NATO.

20. "The privilege to be involved and to conduct a business in any manner that one pleases is not guaranteed by the Constitution. The right to engage in certain businesses may be subject to various conditions. Laws regulating businesses have been found to be valid. We find no justification to reject the state law under question."
    Which concept would most likely be REJECTED by the author of this passage?
    (1) laissez-faire
    (2) welfare
    (3) competition
    (4) profit motive
    (5) antitrust legislation

ANSWER KEY

1. **1**	5. **4**	9. **4**	12. **4**	15. **2**	18. **1**
2. **3**	6. **2**	10. **1**	13. **4**	16. **2**	19. **3**
3. **1**	7. **4**	11. **4**	14. **4**	17. **4**	20. **1**
4. **2**	8. **2**				

WHAT'S YOUR SCORE?

______right,	______wrong
Excellent	19–20
Good	15–18
Fair	13–14

If your score was low, the explanation of the correct answers below will help. Analyze your errors. Reread the appropriate sections in this chapter. There are more skills questions in the two full-length practice examinations at the end of this book.

ANSWER ANALYSIS

1. **1** Immigrants have been attracted when there were opportunities for farming on cheap, fertile land; and for jobs in factories and mines and in building transportation lines. Immigration has fallen off during wars, when it was dangerous and difficult to travel, and during depressions, when jobs were not available.
2. **3** Judicial review is the power of the Supreme Court to determine the constitutionality of laws of Congress and the states, and the acts of government executives. The hypothetical decision in the passage is the result of the Supreme Court's being willing to hear a case on appeal from a lower court because a constitutional issue was involved.
3. **1** The graduated income tax raises the *rate* of taxation as one's income increases. For example, a family of four earning $55,000 pays a federal income tax at a higher rate than a similar family having a taxable income of $25,000.
4. **2** From about 1870 on, the growth of European industrialization led to increased demand for African copper, precious woods, diamonds, gold and (later) uranium; and the development of rubber and cocoa plantations by U.S. firms and Western European nations. In Asia, areas such as Malaya and Indonesia furnished rubber, tin, and petroleum to the West.

5. **4** Social controls are composed of two parts. There are, first, the laws against what society defines as criminal actions, such as malicious destruction of property or the sale of narcotics. Those laws are enforced by police and courts to the extent of their ability and efficiency. Then there are the informal controls, based upon the human desire for the good opinion of others, that society exerts upon its members. Teenage fads illustrate the control exerted by group conformity. Public opinion in general is a powerful factor in social control. Political leaders know that they cannot stray too far from public opinion without risking loss of control, for example, with respect to imposing a state sales tax where none exists.
6. **2** A major economic aim of government is to smooth out the extremes of the business cycle in order to avoid "boom and bust." During the period of economic expansion and prosperity indicated in the question, a rise in income tax rates would reduce disposable income, slowing the rate of inflation that can shorten the period of expansion. Another reason for higher tax rates under these conditions is to create a budget surplus to repay part of the national debt.
7. **4** Foreign businesspersons and engineers are interested in both the techniques of large-scale production and the research and development programs that can be afforded only by such large and wealthy firms as Xerox, IBM, Intel, and DuPont. This research is responsible for patents that create monopolies over techniques and products—e.g., xerography, nylon fibers—that may attract the attention of the antitrust division of the Department of Justice.
8. **2** The Treaty of Versailles provided for a League of Nations, but the view expressed in the quotation prevailed. The United States never joined the League of Nations.
9. **4** This statement of Thomas Jefferson strongly supports compulsory education. To implement it, Jefferson designed a system of public education from elementary school through secondary school and then the university.
10. **1** Upward social mobility or movement refers to the potential ability of anyone in America to move up in socioeconomic status. If one has talent, plans carefully ("prudence"), works hard ("personal exertions"), one can advance in American society.
11. **4** The central problem of *all* economic systems is how best to use limited resources to meet unlimited human needs and desires.
12. **4** A *strict construction* would permit the federal government to exercise only the powers specifically delegated in the Constitution, restricting the use of the elastic clause. A *broad construction* would favor more flexibility in the interpretation of the elastic clause, thus leading to more power for the federal government.
13. **4** Legislative powers are vested in Congress, but the president must sign bills enacted by Congress before they become law. The presidential veto is a check of the executive on the legislature. However, Congress may override a president's veto by a two-thirds vote in each house, in which case, as in this item, the legislative branch checks the executive branch.
14. **4** The Constitution provides that a majority vote of the Senate is needed to confirm appointment of ambassadors. In this instance, the legislative branch is exercising a check on the executive.
15. **2** The Constitution grants the president (executive) the power to appoint "judges of the Supreme Court" with the advice and consent of the Senate. The executive branch is given this power over the judicial branch; the Supreme Court cannot choose its own judges.
16. **2** The term *better* involves many factors, and it would be difficult to reach an agreement about *what* was to be measured, let alone *how* to measure the many factors.
17. **4** Each of the other choices can be substantiated by objective, factual evidence, such as examples of minor-party ideas that major parties

have adopted, a restrictive list of the powers the Constitution gives to the national government, and examples of the use of the Sherman Act against labor unions. In the twentieth century women and 18-year-olds have been given the vote. The above facts are generally accepted and agreed upon. That is not true for the controversial statement linking the Great Depression and World War II.

18. 1 One nation should understand the purposes and resources of another in order to carry on intelligent dealings with it. An analysis of those items is particularly valuable.

19. 3 We may define a fact as a statement that can be proved or verified and about which most people agree. An opinion is a personal conclusion that may be based on factual information, one's own biases and background, and even wishful thinking. An opinion is not verifiable, and people tend to disagree about opinions; for example, which team will win next year's World Series or Superbowl game, who is the world's greatest musician, whether a particular presidential action was wise or foolish.

20. 1 The paragraph approves of state laws that regulate business in the public interest. Laissez-faire is an economic policy that provides for little or no interference by government in the affairs of business, so the author of this passage would most likely reject it.

Outline of Study for the Social Studies

Although the Social Studies test does not ask you to recall specific facts, reading passages are based on the topics that are covered in the high school curriculum. The more you know about these topics, therefore, the easier it will be for you to understand the reading passages.

Use the following outline of topics that may appear on the Social Studies test to guide you in your review.

ECONOMICS

I. The meaning of economics

II. How businesses behave
   - A. How business is organized
   - B. Economic markets
   - C. Capitalism
   - D. Supply and demand
   - E. How prices are determined
   - F. Competition and monopoly

III. Production
   - A. Role of production
   - B. Deciding what and how to produce and distribute
   - C. Production of goods and services
   - D. Uses and rewards of factors of production

IV. The individual as a consumer
   - A. Consumer problems and responsibilities
      1. The American standard of living: wages, working conditions, food, shelter, clothing, health care, educational and recreational activities
      2. Factors influencing price and quality of goods: supply and demand (Note: Simple illustrations; e.g., snowstorm in citrus fruit belt, drought, strikes)
      3. Business organizations as they affect the consumer, independent stores, chain stores, cooperatives
      4. Consumer information services: private and government aids
      5. Consumer protection
         - a. Credit associations: origin, functions
         - b. Protective legislation: Bureau of Standards, price controls, Food and Drug Administration, grading and labeling
      6. Installment buying: advantages and disadvantages
      7. Advertising: values, government curbs
      8. Inflation; deflation; effects on the consumer
   - B. Responsibilities of consumers
      1. Saving; budgeting
      2. Economical buying and use of materials and possessions

V. The individual as a worker
   - A. Choice of a vocation

1. Occupational trends
2. Qualifications and preparation
3. Employment opportunities
4. City, state, national, and private employment services

B. Rights and responsibilities as a worker
1. Bargaining individually and collectively
2. Producing efficiently; conserving wisely; consuming intelligently

C. Problems of capital and labor
1. Labor's struggle for economic freedom
   a. Against evils of industrialism; against monopoly
   b. Development of trade unionism
2. Rights and responsibilities of labor and management
3. Recent trends toward labor-management cooperation
4. Problems of increasing centralization: large corporations, large labor unions, government controls, and services

D. Labor and the economy
1. Labor market—union and nonunion labor
2. Distribution of income—profit and wages
3. Collective bargaining, strikes, picketing
4. Productivity

E. Government employees
1. Types of service
2. Means of securing positions: merit system, history of Civil Service
3. Economic status and problems

VI. Economics and financial institutions
A. Money and monetary policy
B. Banking and interest
C. Financial institutions other than banks

VII. Government's role in the economy
A. Taxes and other sources of revenue
B. Government expenditures

VIII. How the overall economy behaves
A. Measuring the economy
B. How the economy grows
C. Problems of growth
D. Economic fluctuations—business cycles
E. Inflation and deflation
F. Policies for stabilization of the economy
G. Formulating modern economic policy

IX. United States and the world economy
A. International trade
B. Foreign exchange and the balance of payments

X. Other economic systems
A. Comparative economics
B. Communism and socialism
C. Economics of underdeveloped nations

XI. Contemporary problems of the American economy
A. Social economic problems—poverty in plenty
B. Economic security
C. Economy problems of agriculture
D. Problems of urbanization

XII. Molders of economic thought (Adam Smith, John Maynard Keynes, John Stuart Mill, Karl Marx, Thomas Malthus, et al.)

HISTORY

I. Beginnings of America
A. Old World backgrounds
B. The new lands
1. The explorers: their motives, achievements, utilization of natural gateways to America
2. Geographic factors and their effects on life in new lands
3. Leaders: Spanish, Portuguese, Dutch, French, English

C. Colonization and growth of settlements
1. Reasons for leaving Europe
2. Diversity of cultural origin; effects on patterns of life in New World
3. Effects of economic and geographic influences: on agricultural development, growth of commerce and industry, transportation and communication, social and cultural life
4. Growth of ideals of religious freedom: the Puritans, Roger Williams, the Quakers and William Penn, the Baltimores and Maryland
5. Characteristic examples of self-government: Virginia,

Massachusetts, New York, Pennsylvania, Rhode Island
6. Conflicting ideals and systems: political, industrial, economic, social

D. French and Indian War, 1754–1763: causes, effects, significance

E. Democracy in colonial times
1. European influences
2. Contributions of immigrants toward shaping American ideal
3. Influence of geographic factors
4. Leaders of early democratic ideals: Patrick Henry, James Otis, Samuel Adams, John Adams, Benjamin Franklin
5. Zenger case: freedom of the press

F. Establishing the new nation: growth of democracy
1. The American Revolution: causes, leaders, events, results
2. The Declaration of Independence: Thomas Jefferson
3. The Articles of Confederation, 1781–1789; weaknesses
4. The Constitution
   a. The Constitutional Convention: main compromises, struggle for adoption
   b. Contributions: James Madison, George Washington, Alexander Hamilton
   c. Adoption; provision for amendment
   d. Study of the Constitution: federal nature of our government; division of powers between federal government and states; separation of powers: executive, legislative, judicial
   e. Bill of Rights: origin, adoption, significance

II. The expansion of the United States

A. Original extent of thirteen states and territories

B. Northwest Ordinance, 1787: foundation of our expansion and colonial policy; its effects on later history

C. Growth of continental United States of America (Louisiana Purchase, Florida Purchase, annexation of Texas, acquisition of Oregon Territory, Mexican Cession)

D. The frontier
1. Meaning: description of frontier life, geographic influences
2. Influence of frontier on American life
3. Leaders: Daniel Boone, Brigham Young, Kit Carson

E. Acquisition of territory beyond continental United States (Alaska, Pacific Islands, Hawaii, Guam, Philippines, Caribbean area, Puerto Rico, Panama Canal Zone, Virgin Islands): how acquired, present status

III. Development of democratic way of life

A. Roots of American democracy in colonial and early American periods
1. European sources; colonial experience; influence on making of Constitution; Bill of Rights
2. Problems confronting new nation: organization of federal government, interpretation of Constitution
3. Federalists vs. Anti-Federalists; beginning of political parties
4. Leaders: Washington, Hamilton, John Adams, Jefferson, Madison

B. Jeffersonian Democracy (Jefferson's ideas on democracy; agrarian versus commercial influences; War of 1812; effects on American life; Era of Good Feeling, 1816–1823)

C. Jacksonian Democracy (meaning; evidences in economic, social, and political life; extension of suffrage; humanitarian reforms—care of sick, criminals, needy; early cooperative movement)

IV. National unity versus sectionalism

A. Factors that promoted nationalism (Monroe Doctrine; Supreme Court decisions; development of an American culture)

B. Factors that promoted sectionalism (differences in ways of earning a living; industrialism of the North; plantation-holding system of the

South; acquisition and settlement of new territory)

C. Major issues of sectionalism (Tariff; the Bank; internal improvement; admission of new states; slavery)

D. Slavery (origin; influence of geographic factors on slavery as an institution; effect of inventions [Eli Whitney's cotton gin]; Missouri Compromise; Abolitionists—Garrison, Stowe; growing tension between North and South)

E. Civil War (election of Abraham Lincoln, 1860; highlights of the war; leaders and events; Emancipation Proclamation; results of war)

F. Reconstruction Period
   1. Problems: the plight of freed slaves; readmission of the seceded states; the rebuilding of the South; contribution of reconstructed states to South; high taxes and corruption; "carpetbaggers," "scalawags," the Ku Klux Klan
   2. Significance of constitutional amendments: XIII, XIV, XV
   3. Effects of Reconstruction

V. The industrial era

A. Geographic background
   1. The physiographic regions of the United States: Atlantic Coastal Plain, Appalachian Highlands, Great Central Plain, Cordilleran Highlands
   2. Geographic study of each region: differences in location, climate, topography, natural resources; man's utilization and control of natural environment; effects on life of people, types of industries, products; interdependence of peoples of different regions
   3. Geographic reasons for location and growth of big cities: New York, Philadelphia, Boston, Chicago, Denver, Seattle, New Orleans, San Francisco, Detroit, Pittsburgh

B. The Industrial Revolution
   1. Meaning
   2. Causes: inventions, wealth of raw materials, abundant labor supply, ready markets, capital
   3. Inventions
      a. European: textile machinery, steam engine
      b. American: cotton gin, steamboat, sewing machine, telegraph, farming machines, newer processes for steel manufacture, later inventions
   4. Effects on social, industrial, and political life
   5. Significance in our lives today

C. Development of our business economy
   1. America's riches: abundant natural resources; energetic, inventive people
   2. Domestic and international trade
      a. Bases of trade: needs of people, climatic variations, unequal distribution of natural resources
      b. Exports; imports; tariffs
   3. Development of industries (geographic basis)
      a. Agriculture: chief agricultural regions of the United States, life and problems of the farmer, chief products
      b. Transportation and communication: significance in our industrial development
      c. Commerce
      d. Mining: coal, iron, oil, copper
      e. Manufacturing industries: steel, oil, textiles, automobiles, machinery, motion pictures, radio and television
      f. The factory system: effects on worker, methods of work, and population movements
      g. Growth of cities

D. Recent trends
   1. Regional developments: Tennessee Valley Authority, Boulder Dam, Grand Coulee, Bonneville, Missouri Valley
   2. Conservation: need for; work of Theodore Roosevelt, Franklin Roosevelt, Gifford Pinchot, Rachel Carson and others

3. Social legislation: Social Security Act; care of aged, dependent, unemployed
4. Increase of government controls
5. Contemporary contacts of the family with the federal and the state government: taxes, draft, education

VI. Our American heritage
- A. Our democratic institutions and ideals
  1. Division of power between the central government and the states
  2. Bill of Rights and Civil Liberties; Four Freedoms
  3. Development of Women's Rights movement; leaders
  4. Extension of democracy to social and economic life; free tax-supported educational system; legislative restrictions against discrimination in employment
- B. Development of an American culture
  1. Influence of American literature
  2. Influence of science
  3. Growth of art, architecture, and music
- C. Education for democracy
  1. Organs of information and opinion: schools and colleges, newspapers, periodicals, radio, movies, pressure groups
  2. Propaganda: its meaning and recognition
- D. Our people
  1. Story of immigration; "Americanizing" the immigrant
  2. Contribution of various peoples to our culture
  3. Problems of groups of diverse racial, religious, and national origins
  4. Intercultural understandings and appreciations
- E. Democracy vs. totalitarianism

VII. Growth of America as a world power
- A. Our foreign policy
  1. Washington's Farewell Address—isolation and neutrality
  2. Jefferson's "no entangling alliance"
  3. The Monroe Doctrine: origin, provisions, importance
  4. Westward Expansion: Louisiana and Florida purchases; Mexican War; Oregon Treaty
  5. Overseas Expansion: Spanish-American War
  6. America's relations with the Far East and Japan: opening of Japan; Open-Door Policy, 1899
  7. Relations of United States with Latin America; life and culture of people; leaders of several Latin American countries; Pan-Americanism; Good Neighbor Policy; present relations
  8. The Panama Canal: acquisition; construction; importance
- B. The United States and World War I
  1. Origin and causes of World War I
  2. Entry of the United States into the war
  3. Peace problems
  4. League of Nations; Woodrow Wilson
- C. The United States and World War II
  1. Origin and causes of World War II
  2. Reason for U.S. participation
  3. Outcomes of World War II
- D. Post World War II
  1. Emergence of new nations
  2. The Cold War
  3. The Truman Doctrine
  4. The Marshall Plan
  5. Regional organizations: OAS, NATO, CENTO, OAU; Benelux, EU, Colombo Plan, GATT
  6. The Korean War
  7. The Civil Rights and Feminist movements
  8. The spread of nuclear weapons and efforts to contain them
  9. Space exploration
  10. The Vietnam War
  11. The Third World

VIII. The United States as a member of the United Nations
- A. Historical background of peace movements
- B. Events leading to formation of the United Nations
- C. Organization
- D. Main current problems
- E. Role of United States in world affairs

GEOGRAPHY

I. The individual in his or her relationships to the earth
  A. The earth as the home of man
    1. The earth as a globe: principal features, size, shape, relation to other heavenly bodies, revolution and rotation, inclination of the axis, great circles, the equator and the measurement of latitude, the prime meridian and the measurement of longitude, relative sizes and positions of land masses and water areas, the atmosphere, effects on human living
    2. Representations of the earth
      a. Maps; globes
      b. Types and uses of map projections; relation of map to globe
    3. Climate
      a. Climatic controls: latitude, altitude, topography, distance from the sea, prevailing winds, ocean currents (study of major climatic regions of world: tropical rain forest, tropical savanna, tropical desert, maritime, humid continental, continental steppe, continental desert, Mediterranean subtropical, humid subtropical, taiga, tundra, polar ice cap)
      b. Effects on human living: on energy and temperament, on natural resources, on occupations and industries, on population movements
    4. Topography
      a. Chief topographical features of earth: plains; plateaus; mountains; valleys; continents; bodies of water—oceans, lakes, seas, rivers
      b. Relation to human living: transportation and communication; population movements
    5. Natural resources: their utilization, conservation, effect on human living
    6. People: cause and effect of population distribution and movements, present trends
    7. The air age: relation of shape of earth to development effects of air age on human living

II. The individual in his or her relationships to the life and culture of peoples of different lands
  A. Latin America, our southern neighbor
    1. Reasons for our interest
    2. Geographic influences: relative location, comparative area, range in latitude, climatic range, topography (mountains—Andes; volcanoes; plateaus—Brazilian highlands, Altiplano; plains—pampas; rivers—Amazon, Orinoco)
    3. Natural regions and countries
    4. People
      a. Composition and distribution of the population, sharp regional differences, effects of racial diversity, economic and social groups; education and culture; role of the church—population trends (fast growth) and movements; contributions to world culture—foods, vocabulary
      b. Utilization of resources for development of industry; mode of life in agricultural, grazing, mining, and limited industrial areas; one-crop countries; big landowners, inadequate food supply; urban centers
    5. Transportation and communication problems (poor topography, lack of roads and railroads)
    6. Trade relations: characteristic products, imports, exports (only raw materials), world markets, port cities
    7. Significance of region in the world community
  B. Canada—our northern neighbor
    1. Reasons for our interest; common bonds

2. Natural regions and provinces
3. Geographic influences: relative location (latitudinal factor), comparative area, climatic range, topography, natural resources, effects on life of people
4. People; size and distribution of population; causes and effects of two national cultures; utilization of resources of land and adjacent waters for development of industries; mode of life in different regions; interdependence of regions; newer trends in industrialization; population movements; urban centers
5. Transportation and communication handicaps; effects of air age
6. Trade: characteristic products; imports, exports (agriculture, wheat, automobiles, forest products, fish, furs, minerals); trade relations with United States, Great Britain, other countries; ports
7. Place in British Commonwealth; in world community

C. Northern and western Europe
1. Reasons for our interest
2. Regions and countries included (23 nations in northwest Europe, southern Europe, middle (central) Europe, Scandinavia)
3. Geographic influences; strategic location; comparative area; climatic factors; bodies of water; nature of coastline; variety and location of resources; effects on life of people
4. People: 300 million, composition, distribution (urbanization); low population growth; diversity of skills; multilingual—60 languages, ethnic minority problems; similarities and contrasts in education and culture; life and work in various regions; maximum use of resources of environment (land and sea) for development of industry and agriculture; locations of agricultural areas and industrial centers; contributions of various national groups to world culture; cultural centers
5. Trade: characteristic products, farming, food surpluses; major industrial products, imports, exports, trade centers; role of European Union (EU), role of European Free Trade Association (EFTA), world markets, port cities
6. Transportation and communication facilities; effects of air age
7. Current problems: colonial policies, regional problems, American relations with European countries, trade barriers, postwar problems.
8. Significance of region in world community

D. Mediterranean region and Near East, including southwest Asia
1. Reasons for our interest
2. Natural regions and countries
3. Strategic points: Suez Canal, Dardanelles, Bosporus, Gibraltar
4. Mediterranean climate (desert areas of little rainfall); topography—great mountain systems (Alps), major rivers, northern European plains; natural resources—two-thirds of world's oil reserves, effects on life of people
5. People: 400 million, distribution of population (small density); diverse cultural backgrounds; methods of utilizing resources for limited agricultural and limited industrial development; mode of life in different regions; population trends and movements; urban centers
6. Transportation and communication
7. Trade: characteristic products; imports, exports (oil), importance of trade route through Suez Canal; trade centers and ports; world markets

E. Eastern Europe
1. Reasons for our interest
2. Natural regions and countries in the area: Poland, Czech Republic, former Yugoslavia, Balkan nations, Russia and CIS

3. Geographic influences; comparative area and extent; climatic range; topography—mountains (Carpathians, Urals), rivers (Volga); natural resources—coal, effects on life of people
4. People: size and distribution of population; diversity of nationalities and cultures; utilization of resources: mode of life in agricultural (Ukraine), forest, and mining areas; industry (in Czech Republic) and in the growing manufacturing centers; effects of government land policies; program of expansion
5. Trade: limited foreign trade; emphasis on internal trade; effects of lack of good ports; characteristic products—coal, oil, agriculture; imports and exports
6. Significance of region in world community

F. The Far East
1. Reasons for our interest
2. Natural and climatic regions; countries—China, Japan, India, southeast Asia, south Asia, the two Koreas, Taiwan, the Philippines, Indonesia
3. Geographic influences: relative location; comparative area and extent (one-third of the earth's surface); types of climate: tundra, taiga, grasslands of steppes, monsoons (southeast Asia), tropical rainforests (Indonesia), humid subtropical (south China), humid continental (north China), desert (Gobi); topography—mountains (Himalayas), plateaus (Mongolia), desert (Gobi), active volcanoes, rivers—Yangtze, Yellow, Indus, Ganges, Mekong, deltas; natural resources—coal, oil, iron ore, tungsten; effects on lives of people
4. People: 60% of total world population; unequal distribution (one-third in urban centers); social classes (India), racial and cultural diversity: Mongoloid, Caucasoid, Negroid; high birth rate
5. Mode of life: adverse climatic conditions; utilization of natural resources; types and methods of agriculture—need for intensive soil cultivation, prevalence of subsistence crops; home industries; factors limiting industrial expansion; trends toward industrialization
6. Transportation and communication problems in greater part of region; topographic handicaps
7. Trade: characteristic products—two-thirds agricultural (wheat, rice, spices), imports, exports (tea, silk), world markets reached mostly by air

G. Australia and New Zealand
1. Reasons for our interest
2. Natural regions: western plateau, Red Heart, Great Barrier Reef
3. Geographic influences: remoteness; comparative area—3 million square miles; mild climate; low population destiny; natural resources (iron ore, gold)
4. People: 17 million, including 200,000 aborigines; population concentrated in coastal cities; effects of remoteness on life and culture; mode of life in different regions (cities, outback); high level of industrialization; agricultural regions; urban centers; effects of progressive government
5. Transportation and communication: importance of internal travel by air because of vast distances
6. Trade: 25% of world's wool (sheep-raising in New Zealand), meat (beef, lamb), wheat as principal exports; imports; trade centers, ports, trade relations with United Kingdom and United States
7. Problems of immigration and multiculturalism
8. Place in British Commonwealth; in world community

H. Africa
1. Natural regions and countries
2. Geographic influences: 10% of

world area, 5000 miles from north to south, 4600 miles from east to west; second largest continent; climatic range—tropical rainforest, grasslands, desert (Sahara), the Rift Valley, rivers (Nile, Zambezi), effects on life of people
3. People: size, distribution (70% black); native and European cultures; effects of exploitation by European powers; mode of life in mining, grazing, agricultural regions; handicaps limiting development of resources; special case of South Africa
4. Transportation and communication problems; no railroads; lack of capital
5. Trade: exports—tropical crops, minerals; imports—machinery, manufactured goods; problem of smooth coastline and few natural harbors; lack of skilled labor
6. Potential for future development

III. World Trade
- A. Bases of world trade (Needs of people; climatic variations; unequal distribution of natural resources)
- B. Importance of trade in our economic, political, and cultural life
- C. Man's role in world trade
  1. Making of goods: raw materials; capital; labor; transportation; inventions and improved processes that make possible better utilization of natural and human resources
  2. Marketing of goods: transportation; land, water, and sky routes; influence of government policies on the flow of goods; effect of trade on group living
  3. Utilization of goods and services; production, consumption, law of supply and demand; surpluses and shortages; effects of prosperity or depression in one region on other regions
  4. Importance of communication and its effect on trade; major agencies of communication; effects of airplane and of computers and other new inventions
- D. Relation of world trade to world peace

IV. Toward a better world
- A. The development of better understanding among peoples; reasons why understanding is essential; factors that tend to foster understanding; factors that tend to foster disunity and conflict; suggested methods of dealing with such problems
- B. Implications of atomic age: peacetime development; atomic energy and war; need for international control of atomic energy
- C. International organization: past efforts to bind people of the world together; creation of the United Nations; functioning of the United Nations; future hopes for world unity

POLITICAL SCIENCE

I. Nature of political systems
- A. Government and society—importance and basic role of government
- B. Types of modern governments
- C. Meaning of democracy

II. American political system
- A. Foundations of American government; modern political and economic systems; heritage
- B. Declaration of Independence and U.S. Constitution
- C. American federalism

III. American political process
- A. Political party system
- B. Right to vote and voter behavior
- C. Nominations and elections
- D. Public opinion and pressure groups (lobbyists)

IV. National executive branch
- A. Office and powers of the president
- B. Functions
- C. Vice president
- D. President's cabinet

V. National legislative branch
- A. Nature, structure, and powers of Congress
- B. Functions
- C. Roles of Congress

VI. National judiciary branch
- A. American system of justice—importance of law and the legal system

B. Federal court system and role of Supreme Court
C. Judicial process and administration of law
D. Civil liberties and civil rights
E. Goal of equal justice for all

VII. State governments
A. Nature and functions of state governments
B. State executive, legislative, and judiciary branches
C. Financing state and local governments

VIII. Local governments
A. Importance
B. Governing the communities—cities, towns, counties
C. Financing

IX. Government and the general welfare
A. Federal revenues and expenditures
B. Money and banking policies
C. Our government and business—capitalism
D. Labor and Social Security
E. Agriculture and conservation

X. The United States in today's world
A. American foreign policy
B. U.S. and international organizations
C. Population explosion; technological revolution; meeting social responsibilities—health, education, welfare, crime, and other social issues

BEHAVIORAL SCIENCES

I. Introduction to behavioral sciences

II. From the psychologist's view
A. What psychology is
B. Humans as individuals
C. Primary needs for survival and well-being
D. Understanding human behavior—measures of personality and intellect
E. Heredity and environment
F. Principles of learning
G. Humans' beliefs, feelings, attitudes—male/female roles

III. From the sociologist's view
A. What sociology is
B. Humans in groups
1. Family
2. Schools
3. Peer groups
4. Behavior in small groups
5. Other social institutions
C. Social stratification
1. Social class
2. Occupational scale
3. Ethnic background—minority, immigrant, and ethnic experiences
4. Norms and values

IV. From the anthropologist's view
A. What anthropology is
B. Humans in culture
1. Social relationships
2. Problems of society
3. When cultures meet
4. Race and prejudice
C. The search for identity

Glossary of Social Studies Terms

In social studies, as in science, vocabulary is of critical importance. The following selected subject-area vocabulary lists consist of words from the five social sciences—history (see below), political science (page 285), economics (page 288), geography (page 292), and behavioral sciences (page 294). The definitions have been simplified, and in the simplification some aspects of the definition have been omitted. If a definition is not clear, be certain to consult a dictionary. In any event, be sure to review the section "Learning Social Studies Vocabulary and Deriving Meaning from Context" in Chapter 9 (page 230).

Don't forget: The glossary defines a number of terms that are likely to be used on the test. Be sure to consult the glossary when you encounter unfamiliar terms in the questions in the next chapter.

HISTORY

ABOLITIONIST one who favored abolishing slavery in the United States prior to the Civil War

AGGRESSION attack by one country on another without any provocation

ANNEXATION addition of territory to an already existing country or state

APARTHEID policy of racial segregation and discrimination against blacks and other non-Europeans practiced by the Republic of South Africa until 1990

APPEASEMENT policy of giving into the demands of an enemy power in an effort to maintain peace

ARMISTICE temporary stopping of war by agreement of both sides before a peace treaty is signed

ARYAN term wrongly used by the Nazis to refer to a person of German or northern European descent

AXIS in World War II, the countries—Nazi Germany, Fascist Italy, and Japan—that fought against the United States and its allies

BLACKLIST list of people or organizations to be avoided in trade or denied employment because of government policy or suspected disloyalty

BLOCKADE action taken to cut off trade and communication with an enemy

BOONDOGGLE spending of public money to create unnecessary jobs

BOURGEOISIE the middle class

BOYCOTT refusal to deal with a country or an organization for political or economic reasons

CHARTER in colonial times, a grant from the English ruler to a person or corporation giving certain rights and privileges of settlement

CIVIL WAR American war between the northern and southern states (1861–1865)

COLD WAR diplomatic and economic conflict between nations short of actual warfare

COLONY settlement in a distant land that remains under control of the country from which its settlers came

COMPROMISE agreement in which each side gives up some things it wanted

CONSERVATION policies and practices that aim at preservation of natural resources such as forests and wildlife

COUP D'ETAT sudden overthrow of a government by force

DECREE order of a government or a church

DESEGREGATION removal of separation of races in public places such as schools

DISARMAMENT reduction in arms and armed forces as a result of agreement between nations

DISCRIMINATION prejudice in the treatment of one group, as compared with another, in such matters as jobs, housing, and admission to schools

DOCTRINE principle or belief or a set of principles or beliefs

DOVE one who espouses the cause of peace and/or pursues a conciliatory policy in foreign affairs

EDICT official proclamation or decree

EMANCIPATION setting free of a slave or anyone else in bondage

EMBARGO official order preventing ships from entering or leaving the ports of a country for the purpose of commerce

EMIGRATION movement of a person or persons from one country to settle in another

EMPIRE group of states, colonies, or territories joined together under the rule of a dominant power

EVOLUTION theory that plants and animals develop from earlier life forms by the passing down, from one generation to the next, of variations that help them to survive

FAIR DEAL continuation and development of the principles of the New Deal by the Truman administration

FEMINISM movement to win for women, rights equal to those of men in political, social, and economic areas

FEUDALISM medieval (9th to 15th centuries) social and economic organization of society in Europe

GENOCIDE systematic killing off of an entire national, racial, or cultural group

HAWK one who advocates an aggressive and warlike approach to foreign policy

HERESY a religious belief opposed to doctrine established by the church

IMMIGRATION movement of a person into a new country to settle there

IMPERIALISM policy of a nation to extend its power by establishing colonies and controlling territories, raw materials, and world markets

INDUSTRIAL REVOLUTION social and economic changes brought about by the development of large-scale industrial production

ISOLATIONISM policy of a country that is based on unwillingness to take part in international affairs

MANDATE authority given by the League of Nations to one nation to administer a territory or geographic region

MANIFESTO public declaration by a government of intention to act or of action taken

MEDIEVAL referring to the period in Europe between the 9th and 15th centuries

MILITARISM belief that the military should dominate the government and that military efficiency is the ideal of the state

MONARCHY government in which supreme power rests with a king, queen, or emperor and where such power may be absolute or limited

MONOTHEISM doctrine that there is only one God

NATIONALISM doctrine that the interests and security of one's own country are more important than those of other nations or international groups

NAZISM system in Germany (1933–1945) that controlled all activities of the people, fostered belief in the supremacy of a Fuhrer (Leader), and promoted the German people as a master race and the establishment of Germany as the dominant world power

NEW DEAL principles and policies of liberal democrats as advocated under the leadership of President Franklin Roosevelt

NONAGGRESSION referring to an agreement between two nations not to attack one another

PACIFISM belief that conflicts between nations should be settled by peaceful means rather than by war

PACT agreement or treaty between nations

PAN-AMERICANISM belief in political, economic, social, and cultural cooperation and understanding between the nations of North, Central, and South America

PARLIAMENT the legislative body of Great Britain, consisting of the House of Lords and the House of Commons

PARTITION division of a geographic area into two or more countries or into areas annexed to already existing countries

PLEBISCITE direct vote of all eligible voters on an important political issue

PROHIBITION in the United States, the period between 1920 and 1933 when the manufacture and sale of alcoholic drinks was forbidden by federal law

PROPAGANDA systematic spread of ideas or doctrines with a view to convincing others of their truth, using repetition and, in some cases, distortion

PROTECTORATE weaker state protected and in some instances controlled by a stronger state

PROVISIONAL referring to a government that functions temporarily until a permanent government is established

PURITAN Protestant in 16th and 17th century England and America who sought greater reform in the Church of England

QUOTA greatest number of persons who may be admitted, as to the United States or to an institution such as a college

RATIFICATION granting of formal approval, as to a constitution or a treaty

REACTIONARY extreme conservative, one who opposes progress or liberalism

RECIPROCAL applying by mutual agreement to both parties or countries concerned, as in trade

RECONSTRUCTION period after the Civil War (1865–1877) during which the Confederate states were controlled by the federal government and recognized prior to readmission to the Union

RENAISSANCE period (14th through 16th centuries) of revival in learning and the arts in Europe

REPARATION payment by a defeated nation for damages done to persons and property of the victorious country in a war

SANCTIONS measures taken by a group of nations to force another to stop a violation of international law that it is considered to have made

SATELLITE a small state that is dependent on a larger, more powerful state and must, as a result, maintain similar policies

SECTIONALISM placing of the interests of a section of a country ahead of those of the nation

SEDITION acts that tend to foment rebellion against the existing government

SELF-DETERMINATION right of a people to determine its own form of government independently

SHARECROPPER farmer who does not own land but works it for a share of the crop

SOVEREIGNTY supreme and independent political authority of a state

STATUS QUO the existing political, social, and economic order

SUFFRAGETTE woman who works actively for the right of women to vote

TOLERATION freedom to hold religious beliefs different from those in authority

TRUSTEESHIP authority from the United Nations to a country to administer a territory or region

WHIG member of a political party that supported limitation of presidential power and opposed the Democrats in the United States (1836–1856); also a person who supported the American Revolution

ZIONIST supporter of the movement to establish a Jewish national state in Palestine; now, a supporter of the State of Israel

POLITICAL SCIENCE

ACT document made into law by a legislative body

ADMINISTRATION term of office of the executive branch of government

AGENCY bureau that administers a governmental function

ALIEN one who owes allegiance to a government or country other than the country in which he resides

ALLEGIANCE duty of a citizen to his or her government

ALLIANCE formal agreement between nations to achieve a common purpose

AMENDMENT change or revision made in a constitution or a law

AMNESTY general pardon to a group of persons, freeing them from punishment for offenses against a government or society

ANARCHY complete absence of government and law with resulting disorder

APPELLATE court that can receive appeals and reverse the decisions of lower courts

APPORTIONMENT allotment of representatives to a group in proportion to their members

APPROPRIATION money made available by formal act of a legislative body for a specific public purpose

AT-LARGE official chosen by all the voters of a particular election district

AUTONOMY self-government

BALLOT (1) the paper on which a vote is recorded (2) the right to vote

BICAMERAL legislature made up of two houses, such as a Senate and an Assembly or a Senate and a House of Representatives

BILL preliminary form of a law proposed to a legislative body

BIPARTISAN representing or composed of members of two parties

BLOC combination of legislators or nations that acts as a unit with a common interest or purpose

BOSS politician who controls a political machine and has influence over legislation and appointments to office

BUREAUCRACY government that functions through departments that follow given rules and have varying degrees of authority in the organization

CABINET group of advisers to the head of a country who usually administer governmental departments

CAMPAIGN program of activities designed to elect a candidate to political office

CAUCUS closed meeting of party members to decide policy or to select candidates for office

CENSURE reprimand voted by a governmental body of one of its members or of the government or its cabinet

CENTER in politics, a party or group that follows policies between the left (which advocates change) and the right (which opposes it)

CHECKS AND BALANCES system of government that provides for each branch (executive, legislative, and judicial) to have some control over the others

CIVIL LIBERTIES rights to think, speak, and act without interference that are guaranteed to the individual by law and custom

CIVIL RIGHTS rights that are guaranteed to the individual by the Constitution and by acts of Congress; e.g., right to vote

CIVIL SERVICE those in the employ of government who got their positions through open competitive examination on the basis of merit

COALITION temporary alliance of countries or parties for action to achieve some purpose

COMMISSION government agency with administrative, judicial, or legislative powers

COMMITTEE group chosen by a legislative body to consider a particular law or topic

CONFERENCE meeting of committees from two branches of a legislature to settle differences in a bill they have enacted

CONFIRMATION approval by a legislative body of an act or appointment by an executive

CONGRESS the legislature of the United States, consisting of the Senate and the House of Representatives

CONSERVATIVE person or party that tends to oppose change in government and its institutions

CONSTITUTION system of fundamental laws and principles, written or unwritten, by which a people is governed

CONVENTION gathering of members or delegates of a political group for a specific purpose, such as choosing a candidate for office

DELEGATE (1) representative to a convention (2) person empowered to act on behalf of those who choose him or her

DEMOCRACY government by the people directly or through representatives chosen in free elections

DICTATORSHIP state ruled by one who has absolute power and authority

ELECTION choosing by vote among candidates for public office

EXECUTIVE the branch of government charged with administering the laws of a nation

FASCISM a system of government characterized by power in the hands of a dictator, suppression of opposition parties, and aggressive nationalism (Italy, 1922–1945)

FEDERAL referring to a system of government in which a constitution divides powers between the central government and such political subdivisions as states

FILIBUSTER tactics, such as nonstop oratory, used by a minority in a legislative body to delay action on a bill

FOREIGN POLICY course of action adopted by a country in its dealings with other nations

FREEDOM civil or political liberty

GOVERNMENT established system of political administration by which a country or its subdivisions is ruled

HEARING session of a legislative committee in which evidence bearing on possible legislation is obtained from witnesses

IMPEACH to bring charges against a public official for wrongdoing prior to possible trial and removal from office if a conviction is obtained; **IMPEACHMENT** the act of bringing such charges

INAUGURATION formal induction into office of a public official

INDICTMENT formal accusation of someone with the commission of a crime, usually after investigation by a grand jury of charges made by a prosecutor

INITIATIVE right of a citizen to bring up a matter for legislation, usually by means of a petition signed by a designated number of voters

INJUNCTION court order preventing a person or group from taking an action that might be in violation of the law

JUDICIAL referring to the courts and their functions or to the judges who administer these functions

JURISDICTION authority of a government or court to interpret and apply the law

LAW bill that has been approved by a legislative body and signed by the chief executive

LEFT members of a legislative body who take more radical and liberal political positions than the other members

LEGISLATION laws made by a legislative body, such as a Senate

LEGISLATURE group of persons having the responsibility and authority to make laws for a nation or a political subdivision of it

LIBERAL individual or political party whose beliefs stress protection of political and civil liberties, progressive reform, and the right of an individual to govern him- or herself

LOBBY to attempt to influence legislators to support bills that favor some special group or interest

MACHINE political organization under the leadership of a boss and his lieutenants that controls party policy and job patronage

MAJORITY (1) number of votes for a candidate that is greater than the votes for all the other candidates put together (2) party in a legislative body that commands the largest number of votes

MINORITY political group that is smaller than the controlling group in a government or legislature and does not have the necessary votes to gain control

MUNICIPAL referring to local government such as that of a city, town, or village

MUNICIPALITY city or town that has the power to govern itself

NATURALIZE to give the rights of citizenship to a noncitizen or alien

NEUTRALITY policy of a government that avoids taking sides directly or indirectly in disputes between other nations

NOMINATE to name a candidate for election to public office

ORDINANCE law enacted by local governmental authority

OVERRIDE action taken by a legislative body to enact a law that has been disapproved (vetoed) by the chief executive of a political unit such as a nation or state

PARDON official release from (continued) legal punishment for an offense

PARTISAN position or vote that follows party policy ("the party line")

PARTY organization of persons who work to elect their candidates to political office to further the governmental philosophy and causes in which they believe

PATRONAGE power of a political organization or its representative to give jobs

PETITION request for specific legal or judicial action that is initiated and signed by an interested individual or group of individuals

PLANK one of the items in a party program or platform

PLATFORM statement of the policies and principles of a political party or its candidate for office

PLURALITY number of votes by which the winning candidate in an election defeats his or her nearest opponent

POLL (1) vote as recorded by a voter (2) count of votes cast (3) questioning of a group of people chosen at random on their views on political and other matters

PRECINCT subdivision of a town or city that serves as an election unit

PRESSURE GROUP group of people who seek to change government law or policy through the use of lobbies, propaganda, and media

PRIMARY vote by members of a political party to choose candidates for political office or for some other political purpose

PROGRESSIVE person or party that stands for moderate political and social change or reform

PUBLIC OPINION views of a people, generally as they influence social and political action

QUORUM minimum number of a legislative body that must be present before the body can legally conduct business

RADICAL person or party that stands for extreme political and social change

RATIFY give formal approval to a document such as a treaty or constitution

RECALL right of or action taken by vote of the people or by petition to remove a public official from office

REFERENDUM practice of submitting to direct popular vote a proposed law or an act that has been passed by a legislative body

REFORM political movement designed to correct abuses in government by changes in the law

REGIME form or manner of government or rule

REGISTRATION signing up of a person in his or her election district to enable that person to vote

REGULATE to control or bring under the control of government or a government agency

REPRESENTATIVE member of a legislative body chosen to act on behalf of those who elected him or her to represent them

REPUBLIC government in which power remains with all the citizens, who are entitled to vote and who elect representatives who act for them and are responsible to them

RESOLUTION formal statement of opinion or intention voted by a legislative or other group

REVIEW reexamination by higher judicial authority of the proceedings or decision of a lower court

REVOLUTION complete overthrow, usually by force, of an established government or political system

RIGHT (1) members of a legislative body who hold more conservative views than the other members (2) that which belongs to an individual by law or tradition, such as the right to free speech

SELF-GOVERNMENT government of a people by its own members or their representatives instead of by some outside power

SENIORITY consideration given to length of service in a legislative body in making assignments to important positions or to membership in committees of that body

SOCIAL SECURITY federal system of old age, unemployment, and disability insurance for employed and dependent persons

SOVEREIGNTY supreme and independent power or authority in government

SPEAKER public official who presides over a law-making body such as the House of Representatives or an assembly

STATE any of the political units that constitute the federal government

STATUTE law passed by a legislative body

SUBPOENA written order to a person to appear in court or before a legislative body to give evidence

SUBVERSIVE referring to an act or a person that would tend to overthrow the existing government

SUFFRAGE right to vote in political elections or on political matters

SUMMONS written order to appear in court, addressed to a person who may be involved in or have knowledge of a crime

SUPREME COURT highest federal court whose decisions are final and take precedence over those of all other courts

TENURE (1) length of time a person holds office (2) an individual's right to hold office until retirement or death

TESTIFY to present evidence in a court under oath

TICKET list of candidates nominated for election by a political party

TOTALITARIAN kind of government in which one political party is in power to the exclusion of all others

TREASON betrayal of one's country by actively helping its enemies in their attempt to overthrow it or defeat it in war

TREATY formal agreement, entered into by two or more nations, dealing with commerce or policies

URBAN having to do with a town or city

VETO act or power of a chief executive to turn down a bill passed by a legislative body by actually rejecting it or refusing to sign it

VOTE to cast a ballot or take any other necessary action to express one's choice in an election of a candidate for office or of any proposal for legislative change

ECONOMICS

ARBITRATION attempt to settle, or settlement of, a dispute by submitting it to a third party designated to decide it after hearing evidence presented by both sides

ASSET property and resources of all kinds of a person or a corporation

AUTOMATION production and distribution of goods automatically by mechanical and electronic, rather than human, means

BALANCE OF PAYMENTS relationship between a nation's outflow of money (imports, foreign aid) and inflow of money (exports, gifts)

BALANCE SHEET financial statement balancing the assets, liabilities and net worth of an individual or a business

BANKING practice of receiving, keeping, lending, or issuing money and making easier the exchange of funds

BANKRUPTCY financial condition in which a person or business is found legally unable to pay creditors

BARTER system of trading in which one good is exchanged for another without the use of money

BUDGET statement of an individual, business, or government in which expected incomes are allocated as expenses in designated necessary areas

BUSINESS buying and selling of commodities and services for a profit

CAPITALISM economic system based on private ownership of the means of production with freedom of private enterprise to earn a profit under free market (competitive) conditions

CARTEL combination of businesses to establish a national or international monopoly by limiting competition

CENSUS official count of the population of a country (required every ten years in the United States by the Constitution)

CERTIFICATE document that shows that a person owns stock and is entitled to the benefits and liabilities of a stockholder

COLLECTIVE BARGAINING negotiation between management and labor regarding wages, hours, working conditions, and other benefits

COMMERCE large-scale buying and selling of goods involving transportation of the goods between cities or countries

COMMODITY any good that is bought or sold in a commercial transaction

COMMUNISM economic system based on ownership of all property by the state and, in Marx's view, on equal distribution of economic goods through revolutionary means

COMPENSATION payment given as recompense for an injury or loss, as to a worker who has been hurt on the job

COMPETITION in a free enterprise system, the attempts by rival businesses to get customers for the goods they manufacture or distribute

CONSUMER one who uses goods or services out of need

CONSUMER PRICE INDEX single number that compares consumer prices in one year with prices paid by consumers in previous years

CONTRACT agreement between two or more people or companies to do something, set forth in writing or orally, and enforceable by law

CORPORATION group of individuals who possess shares and have the privileges and obligations of a single person, with limited liability

COST amount of money, labor, and other expenses involved in producing or obtaining goods or services

CRAFT (members of) trade requiring special skills, such as printing

CRASH sudden decline in market values of shares in a business

CREDIT money, based on a person's economic standing, that he or she is allowed to borrow and repay at a later date

CREDITOR person or institution to whom money is owed

CURRENCY money, such as coin or bank notes, that is in circulation in a country

CUSTOMS duty or tax levied by a government on imported and exported goods

CYCLE in business, a sequence of events that occurs and recurs in a given order and involves boom, downturn, depression or recession, and recovery

DEBT obligation of an individual or corporation to pay something to a creditor

DEFICIT amount by which a corporation's or a government's debts are greater than its credits or assets

DEFLATION fall in prices brought about by a decrease in spending

DEMAND desire and ability to pay for goods and services usually within a given price range at a given time

DEPLETION using up of natural resources such as oil and timber

DEPOSIT money put into a bank or given in partial payment for something purchased

DEPRECIATION decrease in value of business property or equipment through "wear and tear"

DEPRESSION period of low business activity, wide unemployment, and falling prices

DEVALUATION lowering of the exchange value of one currency with respect to another by decreasing the amount of gold backing it

DISCOUNT amount deducted from the original price of something sold

DISTRIBUTION process of making goods and services available to consumers, as well as the promotion of the buying and selling of these goods and services

ECONOMICS science that deals with the production, distribution, and consumption of goods and services

ECONOMIC SYSTEM manner in which a nation's resources are used, and goods and services are produced and distributed

ECONOMY structure and functioning of a nation's economic system

ENTREPRENEUR person who enters into business and risks his or her skills, time, and money in the hope of earning a profit

EQUILIBRIUM market price at which supply equals demand
EXCISE tax on the production, sale or use of certain commodities within a country
EXPORT goods sold by one country to another

FISCAL having to do with taxes, public revenues, or public debt
FOREIGN EXCHANGE currency that can be used to pay international debts
FRINGE benefit given by an employer that, although not paid directly as wages, involves a cost to the employer

GOODS merchandise
GROSS NATIONAL PRODUCT (GNP) total value of a nation's annual output of goods and services

IMPORT goods brought into by one country from another
INCOME money received by a person or business organization for work or services performed or from investment or property
INDUSTRY businesses as a group that are engaged in manufacturing
INFLATION rise in prices caused by an increase in the amount of money in circulation or by an increase in the amount of spending resulting from greater demand than supply
INPUT amount of money and/or manpower invested in a project or process
INSTALLMENT system of credit in which goods purchased are paid for over a period of time by partial payments
INTEREST (1) charge for money borrowed, usually expressed as a percentage of the money lent (2) money paid to a depositor for money left in a bank for a stated period
INVESTMENT money put into a business or property in the hope of receiving income or earning a profit

LABOR economic group of wage-earning workers
LEVY tax imposed or collected by a government or other authority
LIABILITY debt owed by a business, a corporation, or an individual
LOCKOUT prevention by an employer of his or her workers from working during a dispute
LOSS amount by which the cost of an article sold is greater than the selling price

MANAGEMENT those who direct the affairs of a business or industry
MARGIN difference between the cost and the selling price of a product
MARKET buying and selling of goods or property
MEDIATION entry of a third party into a dispute between management and labor, with the intention of settling it fairly
MERGER combination of two or more businesses or corporations in which one of them eventually controls the other(s)
MONETARY having to do with the money of a country
MONEY coin or paper stamped by government authority, used as a medium of exchange and measure of value
MONOPOLY exclusive control of a product or service in a market so that prices for the product or service can be fixed and competition eliminated

NOTE written promise to pay a debt, such as a promissory note

OBSOLESCENCE process by which the plant and equipment of a business become outdated and can no longer be used efficiently to produce the goods needed
OUTPUT work done or amount produced by a person, machine, or assembly line in a given period
OVERHEAD costs involved in running a business, such as those for rent and electricity

PANIC period in which fear of economic collapse results in frenzied attempts to convert property, goods, and securities into cash
PARTNERSHIP form of business organization in which two or more people put money or property into a business and share the profits or losses
POVERTY extreme lack of the things necessary to sustain life, such as food, shelter, and clothing
PRICE amount of money or its equivalent for which anything is bought, sold, or offered for sale
PRODUCTION creation of economic value by making goods and services available to meet the needs of consumers
PRODUCTIVITY degree of ability to produce goods and services of economic value

PROFIT amount by which the selling price of an article sold is greater than the cost

PROPERTY possessions that may be personal (movable), land or real estate, or securities (stocks and bonds)

PROSPERITY condition in which the economy of a country or a business enjoys a state of well-being

RECESSION period of temporarily reduced business activity

RENT income received by a land or property owner for the use of his or her land or property

RESOURCES natural and human assets that can be used to produce economic goods or provide services

REVENUE income from taxes and other sources that is available for use on behalf of the public

SAVINGS total money saved by an individual or a nation

SCAB employee of a business who continues to work during a strike against that business

SCARCITY gap between the supply of goods produced and human needs

SECURITIES documents, usually bonds or stock certificates, that are evidence of either indebtedness (bonds) or ownership (stocks)

SERVICES duties performed or work done for others that has economic value

SHOP if *open*, a business establishment where workers are employed regardless of union membership; if *union*, one in which labor and management agree that all employees must be union members

SLUM highly crowded area in which housing is rundown, sanitary conditions are poor, and poverty is widespread

SOCIALISM ownership and operation of the means of production and distribution by society rather than by private persons, with all members sharing in the work and the products

SPECULATION use of capital to buy and sell stocks, property, commodities, and businesses in situations where above-average risk is taken

STANDARD OF LIVING level of subsistence of a country or an individual that takes into account possession of the necessities and comforts of life

STOCK shares held by an individual in a corporation

STRIKE work stoppage carried out by workers to force the employer to improve working conditions and benefits and/or to increase wages

SUBSIDY sum of money given by a government to a private individual or business in the public interest

SUBSISTENCE lowest level of food, clothing, and shelter needed to sustain life

SUPPLY amount of goods and services available for sale, usually within a given price range at a given time

SURPLUS amount of goods over and above what is needed

SURTAX tax that is added to an already existing tax

TARIFF tax imposed by a country on imported goods

TAX sum that an individual or corporation is required by the government to pay on income or property or an object purchased

TECHNOLOGY use of scientific knowledge in industry and commerce

TRADE buying and selling of economic goods

TRUST combination of corporations in an industry to control prices and eliminate competition

UNDERDEVELOPED NATION country inadequately developed economically and industrially with a relatively low standard of living

UNEMPLOYMENT condition of being out of work

UNION organization of workers that seeks to protect and advance the interests of its members with respect to working conditions and wages, usually through collective bargaining

WAGES money paid to an employee for work done

WEALTH everything having economic value measurable in price

WELFARE referring to a state or nation in which government rather than private organizations assumes the primary responsibility for the well-being of its citizens

WILDCAT referring to a strike that takes place without the permission of the union representing the striking workers

GEOGRAPHY

ALTITUDE elevation of an object above sea level
ANTARCTIC relating to the region near the South Pole
ARCHIPELAGO group of many islands
ARCTIC relating to the region around the North Pole to approximately 65° N

BASIN body of water partly or fully enclosed
BAY inlet of the sea or other body of water, usually smaller than a gulf
BAYOU lake occupying the abandoned part of a stream channel
BLUFF steep rise of ground between bottom land and higher land on the shore of a river, sea, or lake
BUTTE steep-sided, round-topped hill or mountain

CANYON deep, narrow valley with steep sides cut by a river
CLIMATE average weather conditions at a given place over a period of years as evidenced by temperature, precipitation, and winds
CONSERVATION planned management of natural resources to prevent exploitation, destruction, or neglect
CONTINENT one of the great land areas of the earth
CYCLONE violent storm or system of winds rotating about a calm center of low atmospheric pressure, traveling at a speed of 20 to 30 miles per hour and accompanied by rain

DELTA triangular or fan-shaped area of low-lying land formed by deposits at the mouth of a river
DESERT dry, barren expanse of land unable to support normal plant and animal life
DROUGHT prolonged period of lack of rainfall

EARTHQUAKE shaking or trembling of the earth that is volcanic in origin or involves the earth's crust
ECOLOGY science concerned with the interrelationship of organisms and their environments
ELEVATION height above the level of the sea
ENVIRONMENT climatic, soil, and living factors that influence an organism or an ecological community
EQUATOR great circle of the earth that is equidistant from the North and South poles and divides the earth's surface into the Northern and Southern hemispheres
EQUINOX one of two times each year when day and night are everywhere of equal length
EROSION wearing away by the action of water, wind, or glacial ice of the surface features of the earth—mountains, plateaus, valleys, coasts

FAR EAST countries of east Asia, including China, Japan, and Korea, and southeast Asia and the Malay Archipelago
FAULT break in the earth's crust accompanied by a displacement of one side of the break with respect to the other
FAUNA animals or animal life of a region
FJORD narrow inlet of the sea between steep cliffs and extending far into the land
FLORA plants or plant life of a region or special environment
FRONT boundary between differing air masses that differ in temperature

GEYSER hot spring that, from time to time, violently ejects boiling water and steam
GLACIER large mass of ice and snow moving slowly down a mountain or valley
GLOBE spherical model of the earth
GRASSLAND area of grass or grasslike vegetation, such as a prairie
GULF large area of a sea or ocean partially enclosed by land

HABITAT region where a particular plant or animal naturally lives
HIGH center of high atmospheric pressure
HUMIDITY moisture or water vapor in the atmosphere
HURRICANE severe tropical cyclone having winds of over 75 miles per hour and usually involving heavy rains

ISLAND land mass, smaller than a continent, entirely surrounded by water
ISTHMUS narrow strip of land having water at each side and connecting two larger bodies of land

JUNGLE land densely overgrown with tropical vegetation and trees

LAKE relatively large inland body of water, usually fresh
LANDLOCKED surrounded by land, as a bay
LATIN AMERICA part of the Western Hemisphere south of the United States: Mexico, Central America, the West Indies and South America
LATITUDE distance north or south of the equator, measured in degrees
LEGEND title or key accompanying an illustration or map
LONGITUDE distance in degrees east or west of the prime meridian
LOW region of depressed barometric pressure

MAP representation on a flat surface of all or part of the earth
MARITIME on, near, or living near the sea
MEDITERRANEAN CLIMATE climate characterized by warm, dry summers and rainy winters
MERIDIAN any of the lines of longitude
MESA high, broad, and flat plateau bounded by a steep cliff
METROPOLIS any large, important city
MIDDLE EAST lands from the eastern shores of the Mediterranean and Aegean seas to India
MIGRATION movement of people from one region or country to another, with the intention to settle there
MONSOON seasonal wind that blows over the Indian Ocean from Australia to India

NATURAL RESOURCES forms of wealth supplied by nature, such as coal, oil, and water power

OASIS place in a desert that is fertile because of the presence of water
OCEAN any of the five main divisions of the body of salt water that covers over 70 percent of the earth's surface: Atlantic, Pacific, Indian, Arctic, or Antarctic

PARALLEL imaginary line parallel to the equator and representing degrees of latitude on the earth's surface
PENINSULA land area almost entirely surrounded by water and connected to the mainland by a narrow strip of land
PLAIN extent of level country
PLATEAU elevated tract of fairly level land
POLAR ICE CAP mass of glacial ice that spreads slowly out in all directions from the poles
POPULATION DENSITY number of people in a given area
POPULATION EXPLOSION very great and continuing increase in human population in modern times
PRAIRIE large area of level or slightly rolling grassland that occupies the region between the Ohio and the Mississippi-Missouri rivers
PRECIPITATION rain, snow, sleet deposited on the earth
PRIME MERIDIAN great circle on the earth's surface from which longitude is measured both east and west: 0° longitude

RAINFALL amount of water falling in the form of rain, snow, etc., over a given area in a given period of time
RAIN FOREST dense, evergreen forest occupying a tropical region that has abundant rainfall throughout the year
RANGE a series of connected mountains forming a single system
RAW MATERIAL material still in its natural or original state, before processing or manufacture
REGION large, indefinite part of the earth's surface
RELATIVE HUMIDITY amount of moisture in the air, expressed as a percentage, as compared with the maximum amount that the air could contain at the same temperature
REVOLUTION movement of a heavenly body, as a star or planet, in an orbit or circle
ROTATION turning of a body, such as the earth, around a center point or axis

SCALE proportion that the size of a feature on a map bears to the actual size of the feature it represents
SEA large body of salt water wholly or partly enclosed by land
SEASON any of four divisions of the year, characterized chiefly by differences in temperature, precipitation, amount of daylight, and plant growth
SOLSTICE either of two points on the sun's path at which it is farthest north or farthest south of the equator

SOUND wide channel or strait linking two large bodies of water or separating an island from the mainland

STEPPE in Europe and Asia, vast, usually level plain having few trees

STRAIT narrow waterway connecting two large bodies of water

SUBCONTINENT large subdivision of a continent

SUBTROPICAL referring to regions bordering on the tropical zone

TAIGA forests of cone-bearing trees in the far north of Europe, Asia, and North America

TEMPERATE ZONE one of two zones between the tropics and the polar circles

TERRACE any of a series of flat platforms of earth with sloping sides, rising one above the other, as on a hillside

TERRAIN natural or surface features of a tract of land

THUNDERSTORM storm accompanied by thunder and lightning

TIDAL WAVE unusually large wave sent inshore by an earthquake or a very strong wind

TIDES alternating rise and fall of the surfaces of oceans and of waters connected with them, caused by the attraction of the moon and sun and occurring twice in approximately 24 hours

TOPOGRAPHY surface features of a region, including hills, valleys, rivers, lakes, and man-made features: canals, bridges, roads, etc.

TORNADO violently whirling column of air, extending down from a mass of storm clouds, that usually destroys everything in its rapid advance along a narrow path

TORRID ZONE area of the earth's surface lying between the Tropic of Cancer and the Tropic of Capricorn and divided by the equator

TRIBUTARY stream or river flowing into a larger stream or river

TROPICS area between the Tropic of Cancer and and the Tropic of Capricorn, 23½° north and south of the equator

TUNDRA any of the vast, nearly level, treeless, and marshy plains of the arctic and extreme northern regions

TYPHOON violent tropical cyclone originating in the west Pacific, especially in the South China Sea, principally from July to October

VALLEY stretch of low land lying between hills or mountains and usually having a river or stream flowing through it

VOLCANO cone-shaped mountain built up around a vent to form a crater with lava, cinders, ashes, and gases escaping through the vent from the earth's interior when the volcano is active

WEATHER general condition of the atmosphere at a particular time and place with regard to temperature, moisture, cloudiness, etc.

WESTERLIES winds blowing primarily from the west

WIND air naturally in horizontal motion at the earth's surface, coming from any direction, with any degree of velocity

BEHAVIORAL SCIENCES

ACCULTURATION the process of becoming familiar with a culture different from the one in which a person was originally raised

ACHIEVEMENT accomplishment or attainment of a goal

ADAPTIVE BEHAVIOR way in which an organism acts to satisfy its own needs and to meet the demands of its environment

ADJUSTMENT achievement of harmony between an individual and his or her environment

AGGRESSION angry or hostile feelings and behavior

AMBIVALENCE conflicting reactions toward a person or object

ANGER emotion arising from frustration

ANXIETY fear or apprehension

APATHY indifferent and listless behavior

APTITUDE capacity for skillful performance on an as yet unlearned task

ASSIMILATION acceptance of an outsider as a member of a social group

ATTITUDES inclination to respond positively or negatively to particular objects or issues

AVOIDANCE act of fleeing or withdrawing from harmful or potentially harmful stimulation

AWARENESS consciousness; cognizance of one's surroundings

BEHAVIOR any activity of an organism

BEHAVIORAL SCIENCES study of anthropology, psychology, and sociology

CASTE social class or group formed on the basis of birth and wealth, and existing under strict rules within a social system, with little or no movement into or out

CATHARSIS release of tensions through the expression of pent-up emotions

CHRONOLOGICAL AGE age in years

CLASS group of people considered as a unit according to economic, occupational, or social status in the community or society

CLIQUE small, exclusive circle of people

COGNITION knowing or understanding

COMPENSATION counterbalancing failure in one area by excellence in another

COMPULSION irrational and irresistible impulse to perform some act repeatedly

CONFLICT simultaneous arousal of two or more incompatible motives

CONFORMITY response governed by prevailing attitudes and opinions

CREATIVITY seeking and discovering of new relationships and new solutions to problems

CULTURAL ANTHROPOLOGY study of the structure and function of societies

CULTURAL DIFFUSION spreading of culture over additional areas

CULTURE sum of the activities—skills, arts, customs, ideas—of a people at a given time in history

DEFENSE MECHANISM reaction to frustration in which the individual deceives him- or herself about his or her real motives and goals to avoid anxiety

DELINQUENCY, JUVENILE behavior by minors under a given age, usually 18 years, that is antisocial or violates the law

DEMOGRAPHY, SOCIAL distribution, density, and vital statistics of populations within a society

DEVELOPMENT orderly, progressive changes in behavior that accompany the growth of all normal human beings

DEVIANT BEHAVIOR behavior departing from the general norms of society, such as crime and alcoholism

DISCRIMINATION unfavorable treatment of persons based on negative prejudgments made without regard to fact

DIVORCE legal and formal termination of a marriage

EGO that part of personality corresponding most closely to one's idea of self

EMPATHY realization and understanding, of another person's feelings and attitudes

ETHNICITY (1) classification or affiliation with one of the races of mankind distinguished by customs, language, and common history; (2) identification of groups by race, religion, and nationality

EXTENDED FAMILY family that includes other relatives (grandparents, uncles and aunts, cousins, in-laws) beyond the immediate, nuclear family (parents and children)

FAMILY basic unit in society, having as its nucleus two or more adults living together and cooperating in the care and rearing of their children

FRUSTRATION emotional state resulting from the blocking of behavior that is seeking achievement of a goal

GROUP persons classified together because of common characteristics, interests, or needs

GROUP DYNAMICS forces interacting within a human group

GUILT painful feeling of self-reproach resulting from a belief that one has done something wrong or immoral

HABITS actions, occurring in an accustomed set of circumstances, that become virtually automatic

HEREDITY transmission of qualities from parents to offspring

HUMAN RELATIONS interaction between persons or groups of persons

IDENTIFICATION process wherein a person takes over the features of another person and makes them part of his own personality

IDENTITY characteristics or qualities that set one person apart from others

INHIBITION mental or psychological suppression of an action, emotion, or thought

INSIGHT sudden intuitive perception of the solution of a problem after other attempts have failed

INSTINCT unlearned behavior, based on a biological urge

INTEGRATION incorporation of different racial or ethnic groups into free and equal association in a society or an organization

INTELLECT ability to reason, understand, or perceive relationships between ideas and objects
INTELLIGENCE ability to form concepts and to grasp relationships
INTERACTION communication between people through talking, listening, writing, reading, and gestures
INTERGROUP RELATIONS relations between different ethnic or racial groups in a society
I Q (INTELLIGENCE QUOTIENT) index of the rate of mental growth, obtained as a numerical relationship between actual age and score achieved on a test

KINSHIP relationship that includes both the nuclear and the extended family

LEADERSHIP guidance provided by the person or persons who direct a group in its activities
LEARNING modification of behavior resulting from reinforced practice or the effects of experience

MARRIAGE state of, or relation between, a man and woman who have become husband and wife; and whose purpose may be to found and maintain a family
MATRILINEAL referring to a society in which descent is traced through the maternal line
MEMORY body of information that has been learned and retained
MENTAL AGE mental level of a person as determined by a test that enables comparison of his or her score with average scores obtained by others
MINORITY GROUP racial, religious, ethnic, or political group smaller than and differing from the larger, controlling group in a community or nation
MOBILITY movement or shifting of membership between or within social classes, either from place to place within the same class or from one class to another
MOTIVATION factors that arouse and maintain behavior directed toward satisfaction of needs, drives, desires, or wishes

NEED essential or highly desirable requirement that is lacking in a living being
NEUROTIC referring to the behavior of a person suffering from an emotional disorder
NORM standard of achievement as represented by the average achievement of a group
NUCLEAR FAMILY father, mother, and child(ren) living together

OPINIONS, ATTITUDES, AND BELIEFS a person's preferences or positions on matters in the public arena, based on rational and/or emotional judgments; opinions are short-term attitudes, are more lasting, and beliefs deal with the more basic values of life
ORGANIZATION body having a formal set of goals, policies, procedures, and rules governing the behavior of its members

PARANOIA behavior featuring delusions of either grandeur or persecution
PEER GROUP all persons of about the same age and status in a society having a similar system of values
PERCEPTION awareness of the outside world through interpreting sense impressions
PERSONALITY characteristic pattern of behavior of any individual as expressed by physical and mental activities and attitudes
PHOBIA unreasonable, strong fear of a particular thing or situation
PREJUDICE hostile attitude without foundation in fact or knowledge, toward an ethnic group or any member of it
PROJECTION seeing one's own traits and motives in others, especially when they are considered undesirable or cause anxiety
PROPAGANDA systematic spreading and promotion of particular ideas
PSYCHIATRY branch of medicine that specializes in the diagnosis and treatment of mental and emotional illness
PSYCHOANALYSIS treatment of mental and emotional disorders that tries to give the patient insight into his or her unconscious conflicts and motives
PSYCHOLOGY science dealing with the mind and with mental and emotional processes as well as human and animal behavior
PSYCHOSIS severe mental disorder in which the personality is very seriously disorganized, and contact with reality is usually weakened

PSYCHOTHERAPY treatment of mental and emotional disorders by using psychological methods such as suggestion, counseling, and psychoanalysis

RACE one of three primary major divisions of mankind—Caucasian, Negro, and Mongoloid—differing in physical characteristics

RATIONALIZATION justification of impulsive or irrational behavior by presenting false but seemingly acceptable reasons for that behavior

RECIDIVISM relapse into crime or antisocial behavior

REGRESSION return to earlier or more infantile behavior patterns

REINFORCEMENT procedure whereby a response is immediately followed by a consequence that results in the repetition of the behavior that produced it

REPRESSION exclusion of unpleasant memories or impulses from conscious awareness

RESPONSE behavioral result brought about by particular stimuli

ROLE behavior pattern of a person in a particular social situation

ROTE learning by memory alone, without understanding or thought

SCHIZOPHRENIA abnormal behavior in which the patient becomes withdrawn and apathetic, with hallucinations and delusions

SEGREGATION policy or practice of compelling racial or ethnic groups to live apart from each other

SELF-ESTEEM belief in oneself, self-respect

SIBLING RIVALRY competition between persons born of the same parents or having one parent in common

SOCIAL CHANGE broad and basic change in the nature of a society and in the basic institutions and organizations within it

SOCIALIZATION process of learning the values and customs of the culture in which one exists

SOCIETY group of people that is self-sustaining, that has a definite location and a long continuity, and whose members share a way of life

SOCIOECONOMIC STATUS position in society based on social and economic factors

STATUS position or rank with respect to others in society

STEREOTYPE fixed or conventional notion or belief regarding a person, group, or idea that is held by a number of people and allows no individuality or critical judgment

STIGMA mark or sign indicating that something is not considered normal

STIMULUS something that directly influences activity of a living organism

SUBLIMATION process whereby unacceptable impulses are diverted into constructive, acceptable forms

SUBLIMINAL below the level of conscious awareness

TABOO forbidding of an act in order to protect a cultural group against supernatural retaliation

THINKING process of using the mind to form ideas

TRADITION handing down of information, beliefs, and customs by word of mouth from one generation to another

URBANIZATION creation of population areas that include one or more cities and adjoin densely settled urban places

VALUES social principles, goals, or standards held or accepted by an individual, class or society

Social Studies Practice

Political Science

Read each of the following selections carefully. After each selection, there are questions to be answered or statements to be completed. Select the best answer.

Questions 1–3 are based on the following passage.

The American Revolution is the only one in modern history that, rather than devouring the intellectuals who prepared it, carried them to power. Most of the signatories of the Declaration of Independence were intellectuals. This tradition is ingrained in America, whose greatest statesmen have been intellectuals: Jefferson and Lincoln, for example. These statesmen performed their political function, but at the same time they felt a more universal responsibility, and they actively defined this responsibility. Thanks to them there is in America a living school of political science. In fact, it is at the moment the only one perfectly adapted to the emergencies of the contemporary world, and one which can be victoriously opposed to communism. A European who follows American politics will be struck by the constant reference in the press and from the platform to this political philosophy, to the historical events through which it was best expressed, to the great statesmen who were its best representatives.

1. This passage deals chiefly with
   (1) the causes of the American Revolution
   (2) Jefferson and Lincoln as ideal statesmen
   (3) the basis of political philosophy in the United States
   (4) democracy versus communism
   (5) a living school of political science

2. According to this passage, intellectuals who pave the way for revolutions are usually
   (1) honored
   (2) misunderstood
   (3) destroyed
   (4) forgotten
   (5) elected to office

3. Which statement is true according to the passage?
   (1) America is a land of intellectuals.
   (2) The signers of the Declaration of Independence were all well educated.
   (3) Jefferson and Lincoln were revolutionaries.
   (4) Adaptability is a characteristic of American political science.
   (5) Europeans are confused by American politics.

<u>Questions 4–6</u> are based on the following passage.

By the words *public duty* I do not necessarily mean official duty, although it may include that. I mean simply that constant and active practical participation in the details of politics without which, upon the part of the most intelligent citizens, the conduct of public affairs falls under the control of selfish and ignorant or crafty and venal men. I mean that personal attention—which, as it must be incessant, is often wearisome and even repulsive—to the details of politics, attendance at meetings, service upon committees, care and trouble and expense of many kinds; patient endurance of rebuffs, chagrins, ridicules, disappointments, defeats—in a word, all those duties and services which, when selfishly and meanly performed, stigmatize a man as a mere politician; but whose constant, honorable, intelligent, and vigilant performance is the gradual building, stone by stone and layer by layer, of that great temple of self-restrained liberty which all generous souls mean that our government should be.

4. The paragraph is primarily concerned with

   (1) the public duty of intelligent men
   (2) the evils of indifference
   (3) characteristics of the mere politician
   (4) the imaginary democracy
   (5) true patriotism

5. Public duty stresses

   (1) craftiness
   (2) mean performance
   (3) venal acts
   (4) official duty
   (5) attention to details

6. Which one of the following statements best expresses an idea found in the passage?

   (1) Politics has never been under the control of selfish persons.
   (2) Personal attention of officeholders ensures American democratic principles.
   (3) Genuine public spirit demands personal sacrifice.
   (4) Public duty is synonymous with official duty.
   (5) American liberty is based upon constant legislation.

<u>Questions 7–9</u> are based on the following passage.

The average citizen today is knowledgeable about "landmark" court decisions concerning such questions as racial segregation, legislative apportionment, prayers in the public schools, or the right of a defendant to counsel in a criminal prosecution. Too often, however, he thinks that these decisions settle matters once and for all. Actually, of course, these well-publicized court decisions are merely guideposts pointing toward a virtually endless series of vexing legal questions.

For example, this nation could hardly fail to agree that state-compelled racial segregation in the public schools is a denial of the equal protection of the laws guaranteed by the 14th amendment. The real difficulty lies in determining how desegregation shall be accomplished and how to solve the problem of de facto school segregation, perpetuated by the practical if unfortunate realities of residential patterns.

7. According to the author, the effect of many decisions in the courts has been to

   (1) make citizens study the law
   (2) lead to more legal complications
   (3) contradict the Constitution
   (4) deny states' rights
   (5) provide final solutions to many problems

8. The author implies that, so far as important court decisions are concerned, the public today is generally
   (1) disinterested
   (2) mystified
   (3) critical
   (4) well informed
   (5) disapproving

9. As used in the first line of the passage, the word *landmark* most nearly means
   (1) exciting
   (2) just
   (3) significant
   (4) publicized
   (5) legal

Questions 10–12 are based on the following passage.

It was not a governing class that America needed—that ideal cherished by the Federalists and revived by the civil service reformers—but a people intelligent enough to use government to prosper the commonwealth, realistic enough to recognize the economic bases of politics, moderate enough to exercise self-restraint, bold enough to countenance experiments, mature enough to distinguish between statesmanship and demagoguery, far-sighted enough to plan for their children and their children's children. All this was, to be sure, a large order, and only perfectionists could be disappointed that it was not filled. Yet if Americans remained politically immature, they revealed as great a competence in the art and science of politics as any other people, and rather more than most. They were reluctant to modernize their machinery of government, yet though it needed constant care it never wholly broke down as it often did in the Old World.

10. This passage deals mainly with
    (1) America's competence at self-government
    (2) an American governing class
    (3) American political morality
    (4) political maturity
    (5) intelligence in government service

11. The author's attitude toward Americans as politicians is one of
    (1) amusement
    (2) doubt
    (3) suspicion
    (4) approval
    (5) disapproval

12. The author suggests that Americans as politicians have been essentially
    (1) idealistic
    (2) realistic
    (3) selfish
    (4) pessimistic
    (5) hypocritical

Economics

Read each of the following selections carefully. After each selection, there are questions to be answered or statements to be completed. Select the best answer.

Questions 13–15 are based on the following passage.

There are hundreds and thousands of homeless children in this nation—a fivefold increase in the years since 1981. Because they are scattered in a thousand different cities, they are easily unseen. Many of them will never live to tell their stories.

None of these children has committed any crime. They have done nothing wrong. Their only crime is being born poor in a rich nation.

Last year I met a homeless family in Los Angeles. The mother had come there from Ohio to search for rent that she could afford. The father—there was a father, none of these families fit the stereotypes; few people do—the father worked full time, for minimum wage, in a sweatshop making blue jeans, earning $500 a month. The parents couldn't pay their rent and feed their child in Los Angeles on $500. The child was with them in the street—38 days old. I shook my head and asked myself, "Is this the best the United States can do?"

Dr. Martin Luther King, Jr., told us, "I have been to the mountain." But almost every voice that we have heard for 20 years has counseled us to shut that mountain out of mind, and to direct our eyes instead to the attractive flatlands where careers are made, résumés typed, and profits maximized. Our culture heroes have been sleek and agile people; cynical and cold, streamlined for efficient malice, and unweighted by the excess burden of compassion.

"We owe a definite homage to the reality around us," Thomas Merton wrote, "and we are obliged at certain times to say what things are and to give them their right names." The right name for the willingness of a rich nation to leave half a million homeless children in its streets is sheer betrayal of ourselves and our best values.

It has been a long winter. But as with the seasons, so too with a nation: life renews itself.

I like to think another season of compassion is before us. We look to you who graduate this morning to renew this weary earth, to water the soil of the 1990s with the simple but forgotten values of the heart, to heal the ill, house the homeless, feed the hungry, and bring mercy to the frightened mother and her child.

It is not by standing tall, but by bending low—to reach a hand to those who are too frail to stand at all—that good societies are defined.

13. The author focuses on the plight of
    (1) cultural heroes
    (2) sleek people
    (3) homeless children
    (4) cynical and cold leaders
    (5) graduates of a university

14. The many homeless children are unseen because they
    (1) were born poor
    (2) are scattered
    (3) are decreasing in number
    (4) are sleek and agile
    (5) are cynical and cold

15. The author feels that the plight of the homeless is a result of
    (1) betrayal of our values
    (2) national poverty
    (3) obsession with résumés and careers
    (4) propaganda against the poor
    (5) maximized profits

<u>Questions 16–18</u> are based on the following passage.

The term *factory system* is applied to the system of production that developed as a result of the Industrial Revolution. It arose in England at the end of the 18th century. Under this system, goods are produced with the use of machinery rather than by hand as under the domestic system. Special buildings had to be constructed to house the machinery; these became known as factories. Workers from nearby areas gathered each day in these factories. This caused concentration of population around them and led to the rise of cities. Workers were no longer skilled artisans or craftsmen; instead, each became proficient at the particular work done by the machine which he tended. A division of labor was set up for greater speed and efficiency. Various machines were devised, each to be used for turning out some portion of the product for later assembly. No one worker, therefore, turned out the entire product. These were the chief characteristics of the *factory system* as it evolved.

16. The factory system is directly responsible for
    (1) the rise of suburbia in the 17th century
    (2) individual pride in the production of goods
    (3) specialization and division of labor
    (4) the need for skilled craftsmen
    (5) closer employer-employee relationship

17. The factory system replaced the
    (1) Industrial Revolution
    (2) domestic system
    (3) trade union
    (4) small farmer
    (5) machine system

18. The author of this passage would agree with all of the following statements EXCEPT that the
    (1) factory system is responsible for automation
    (2) factory system is a result of the Industrial Revolution
    (3) factory system had its beginnings in England
    (4) factory system encouraged worker versatility
    (5) factory system depended upon inventions of new machinery

Questions 19–21 are based on the following passage.

The American consumer benefits most of all from an increase in foreign trade. Imports give him a wider choice of products at competitive prices. They introduce new ideas and new tastes which often lead to new demands for American production.

Increased imports stimulate our own efforts to increase efficiency, and supplement antitrust and other efforts to assure competition. Many industries of importance to the American consumer and economy are dependent upon imports for raw materials and other supplies. Thus American-made goods can also be made much less expensively for the American consumers if we lower the tariff on the materials that are necessary to their production....

Moreover, we must reduce our own tariffs if we hope to reduce tariffs abroad and thereby increase our exports and export surplus....

It is obvious, therefore, that the warnings against increased imports based upon the lower level of wages paid in other countries are not telling the whole story.

—John F. Kennedy

19. President John F. Kennedy, who wrote this passage, advocated
    (1) increased imports, increased exports, increased tariffs
    (2) decreased imports, increased exports, increased tariffs
    (3) decreased imports, decreased exports, decreased tariffs
    (4) increased imports, decreased exports, decreased tariffs
    (5) increased imports, increased exports, decreased tariffs

20. President Kennedy answered the argument that increased imports
    (1) adversely affect America's highest paid industries
    (2) adversely affect the skill of American workers
    (3) are based on lower wages paid in other countries
    (4) affect total labor costs
    (5) represent higher competitive cost of labor

21. Increased imports offer all the following benefits EXCEPT
    (1) new ideas
    (2) new tastes
    (3) assured competition
    (4) source of raw materials
    (5) more costly American products

Questions 22–25 are based on the following passage.

Most Americans look at the developing areas of the world without having the slightest idea of the difficulties with which they are faced. We must try to understand what life is like for the almost 4 billion human beings who live in developing nations.

Let us imagine how an American family, living in a housing development on a very low yearly income, could be changed into a family of the underdeveloped world.

Our first step is to strip our American home of its furniture. Everything from the living quarters goes—beds, chairs, tables, television set, lamps. Leave a few old blankets, a kitchen table, a wooden chair. For clothing, each member of the family may keep his oldest suit or dress, plus a shirt or blouse. Permit a pair of shoes for the head of the family, but none for the wife. In the kitchen the appliances have already been taken out, the water and the electric power shut off. The box of matches may stay, as well as a small bag of flour and some sugar and salt. We will leave a handful of onions and a dish of dried beans. All the rest must go—the meat, fresh vegetables, canned goods, crackers.

The house itself must go. The family can move into a small shack. It may be crowded, but they are fortunate to have any shelter at all.

Communication must go next—no more newspapers, magazines, books. They will not be missed, since we are not able to read. In our community, there will be only one radio.

Government services must go also. No more mail delivery or fire protection. There is a school, but it is three miles away and consists of two classrooms. It is not overcrowded, since only half the children in the neighborhood go to school. There are no hospitals or doctors nearby. The nearest clinic is ten miles away.

The human body requires a daily input of at least 2300 calories to make up for the energy used by the body. If we do no better than the Latin American peasant, we will average not more than 2000 to 2100 calories per day and our bodies will run down.

So we have brought our American family down to the very bottom of the human scale. When we are told that more half the world's population enjoys a standard of living of less than 100 dollars a year, this is what that figure means.

22. The purpose of the author is to describe

(1) American family life
(2) the comforts of civilization
(3) life in developing nations
(4) the American home
(5) changes in the family

23. Over half the world's population has

(1) a daily input of 2300 calories
(2) crowded classrooms
(3) kitchen appliances
(4) a poor living standard
(5) high-tech machinery

24. The passage implies that Americans

(1) are well informed
(2) lack understanding of life in developing nations
(3) contribute to the problems of developing nations
(4) distort the realities of life
(5) provide help to those less fortunate

25. With which of the following necessities is a family in an underdeveloped nation left?

(1) a house
(2) a local hospital
(3) electric power
(4) government services
(5) food

History

Read each of the following selections carefully. After each selection, there are questions to be answered or statements to be completed. Select the best answer.

<u>Questions 26–28</u> are based on the following passage.

The early Europeans imagined that the natives of the New World were rovers, who lived and hunted at random wherever they pleased. They were mistaken: the tribes had their separate tracts that were marked off by definite boundaries. But the fundamental difference between the European conception of property and that of the Native Americans was that the Native Americans' property was held in common. The Native Americans had no idea of legal title, of the individual ownership of land, and the Europeans were incapable of thinking in any other terms. In 1879, a General Allotment Act was introduced in Congress. The object, or ostensible object, was to encourage the Native Americans to engage in farming by breaking up the reservations. The fragments were to be allotted, a hundred and sixty acres to heads of families and eighty to single persons. The remainder could be bought by the government, and the individual owners, after twenty-five years, were authorized to sell their land.

The bill encountered opposition, but the

act was passed in 1887 and had the effect of depriving the Native Americans of ninety million of their hundred and forty million acres. Few of them had taken to farming. Even if they had been eager to farm, they had no money to invest in equipment or livestock, and since their allotments were held in trust, they were unable to get commercial credit. If they did not dispose of their property, and it was divided among their descendants, there was soon very little left for anybody.

—adapted from Edmund Wilson

26. According to the passage, early Europeans believed natives of the New World to be

(1) agrarian
(2) uncivilized
(3) nomadic
(4) disorganized
(5) unprogressive

27. According to the passage, the essential difference between the Native American and European concepts of property is that Europeans believed in

(1) individual ownership of the land
(2) governmental control of the land
(3) breaking up large tracts of land
(4) farming the land instead of hunting on it
(5) handing it down to descendants

28. The official purpose of the General Allotment Act of 1879 was to

(1) introduce new methods of hunting
(2) encourage Native Americans to pursue a different way of life
(3) allow the Native Americans to move about more freely
(4) sell large tracts of land
(5) consolidate ownership of land

Questions 29–31 are based on the following passage.

Foreign propagandists have a strange misconception of our national character. They believe that we Americans must be hybrid, mongrel, undynamic; and we are called so by the enemies of democracy because, they say, so many races have been fused together in our national life. They believe we are disunited and defenseless because we argue with each other, because we engage in political campaigns, because we recognize the sacred right of the minority to disagree with the majority and to express that disagreement even loudly. It is the very mingling of races, dedicated to common ideals, which creates and recreates our vitality. In every representative American meeting there will be people with names like Jackson and Lincoln and Isaacs and Schultz and Kovacs and Sartori and Jones and Smith. These Americans with varied backgrounds are all immigrants or the descendants of immigrants. All of them are inheritors of the same stalwart tradition of unusual enterprise, of adventurousness, of courage—courage to "pull up stakes and git moving." That has been the great compelling force in our history.

29. According to the paragraph, our national character thrives because we have

(1) few disagreements
(2) majority groups
(3) shared our wealth
(4) common ideals
(5) minority rights

30. Foreign propagandists believe that Americans

(1) are enemies of democracy
(2) lack a common heritage
(3) have a unified national character
(4) refuse to argue with each other
(5) are ashamed of foreign descent

31. Foreign propagandists and the author agree that Americans

(1) are disunited
(2) have no common tradition
(3) come from varied backgrounds
(4) have the courage of their convictions
(5) are deeply religious

Questions 32–34 are based on the following passage.

Underlying historical events which influenced two great American peoples, citizens of Canada and of the United States, to work out their many problems through the years with such harmony and mutual benefit constitute a story which is both colorful and fascinating. It is a story of border disputes, questions and their solutions, for certainly the controversies and wars of the early years of Canada and the northern colonies of what now is the United States, and after 1783 their continuation through the War of 1812, scarcely constituted a sound foundation for international friendship.

Yet it is a fact that solutions were found for every matter of disagreement that arose, and the two nations have been able to work out peaceful results from the many difficulties naturally arising in connection with a long and disputed boundary line, in many cases not delineated by great natural barriers.

32. The title that best expresses the ideas of this passage is
    (1) "A Proud Record"
    (2) "Our Northern Neighbor"
    (3) "Cooperation with Canada"
    (4) "Our Northern Boundary Line"
    (5) "The Role of the Loyalists in Canada"

33. Disagreements between Canada and the United States
    (1) did not occur after 1800
    (2) have been solved in every case
    (3) constituted a basis for friendship
    (4) were solved principally to America's advantage
    (5) resulted from the presence of natural barriers

34. The writer considers the period before 1812
    (1) an insurmountable barrier
    (2) a time of geographical disputes
    (3) the definer of our differences
    (4) a cementer of our Canadian friendship
    (5) the period that settled our northern boundary

Questions 35–37 are based on the following passage.

The gradual loss of Indian tribal authority was suddenly reversed in 1934 with the passage of the Indian Reorganization Act, which addressed the strengthening of tribal life and government with federal assistance. The act, the product of the thinking of John Collier, commissioner of Indian affairs, put Indian communities then nearing political and cultural dissolution on the road to recovery and growth. Collier, struck by the strength and viability of Indian communal societies in the Southwest (e.g., the Hopis) and appalled by the destructive effects on tribal societies of the allotment system, sought to restore tribal structures by making the tribes instrumentalities of the federal government. In this way, he asserted, tribes would be surrounded by the protective guardianship of the federal government and clothed with the authority.

Indian tribal governments, as Collier foresaw, now exist on a government-to-government basis with the states and the federal government. Although they are financially and legally dependent upon the federal government, they have been able to extend their political and judicial authority in areas nineteenth-century politicians would have found unimaginable.

American Indians, now a rapidly growing minority group, possess a unique legal status (based on treaties and constitutional decisions) and are better educated, in better health, and more prosperous than ever before (despite the persistence of high levels of unemployment, poverty, and disease).

35. The Indian Representative Act was the result of
    (1) Indian tribal authority pressure
    (2) the allotment system
    (3) action by the states
    (4) legislation by nineteenth-century politicians
    (5) action by a federal employee

36. The Indian Reorganization Act sought to
    (1) strengthen tribal government
    (2) dissolve Indian communities
    (3) widen the allotment system
    (4) make tribes independent
    (5) give states a more important role

37. Indian tribal governments are now
    (1) stronger politically and judicially
    (2) stronger financially and legally
    (3) weaker communally and culturally
    (4) weaker in tribal structure
    (5) weaker in government relations

Questions 38–40 are based on the following passage.

The Capitol Building in Washington, D.C. is more than just the home of the legislative branch of the federal government. It is an awe-inspiring edifice, symbolizing the strength and majesty of the United States of America.

The actual design of the Capitol evolved as a result of a public competition proposed by President Washington and Secretary of State Jefferson. The winning design, selected by Washington himself, was the work of Dr. William Thornton, an amateur architect. His plans provided for a square central section topped by a low dome and two attached rectangular buildings.

When the Houses soon outgrew their quarters, Congress decided in 1850 to construct two entirely new chambers designed by Thomas Walter, an architect from Philadelphia.

Before work on the new wings had progressed very far, however, it was realized that the two massive marble extensions on either side of the central dome were going to dwarf it, so under Walter's direction, the copper one was removed to make way for the enormous iron dome that is the symbol of the Capitol today.

38. The design for the Capitol was
    (1) suggested by Thomas Jefferson
    (2) selected by George Washington
    (3) rejected by Thomas Walter
    (4) improved by Dr. William Thornton
    (5) ratified by Congress

39. The Capitol is the home of the
    (1) executive branch of the federal government
    (2) judicial branch
    (3) military branch
    (4) secret service branch
    (5) legislative branch

40. The chief symbol of the Capitol is its
    (1) iron dome
    (2) copper dome
    (3) wooden dome capped with copper
    (4) south wing
    (5) north wing

Geography

Read each of the following selections carefully. After each selection, there are questions to be answered or statements to be completed. Select the best answer.

Questions 41–43 are based on the following table.

SIZES, POPULATIONS, AND DENSITIES OF THE WORLD'S LARGEST NATIONS AND REGIONS

Country	Size (sq. mi.)	Population (UN Estimate)* (millions) 1992	Population (UN Estimate)* (millions) 2000	People per Square Mile 1992	People per Square Mile 2000
Canada	3,850,000	27.36	30.42	7.1	7.9
China	3,700,000	1,187.99	1,309.74	321.1	353.98
USA	3,600,000	255.16	257.32	70.88	76.48
Brazil	3,300,000	154.11	172.77	46.7	52.36
India	1,200,000	879.55	1,018.67	732.96	848.89
Japan	143,000	124.49	128.06	870.57	895.57
Southeast Asia	1,692,000	461.5	531.01	272.75	313.83
Western Asia	1,830,817	139.27	171.43	76.07	93.64
Africa	11,700,000	681.69	836.15	58.26	71.47

*(Note the estimated increase of population in the eight years that separate the two sets of figures. Scientists estimate that the earth's population will double in less than 50 years.)

Current annual population growth rates for world regions					
Africa	2.9%	Latin America	2.0%	Oceania	1.6%
Asia	1.9%	Europe	0.4%	World	1.7%
North America	1.0%	Former Soviet Union	0.8%		

41. From the table, it can be inferred that population growth is

    (1) greatest in Europe
    (2) greatest in developed countries
    (3) led by the United States and Japan
    (4) greatest in the Middle East
    (5) greatest in India

42. The country that will have the largest increase in population density by the year 2000 is

    (1) India
    (2) China
    (3) Japan
    (4) Brazil
    (5) the United States

43. It can be inferred from the table that

    (1) Africa is more densely populated than the United States
    (2) Canada has primarily a favorable environment
    (3) Japan is highly industrialized
    (4) India has an unhealthy climate
    (5) the population of North America is growing at a greater rate than that of Latin America

Questions 44–46 are based on the following passage.

The conference members often broke down into two groups. On one side were the 120 developing nations ranging in size from China (population 800 million) to the South Pacific island of Nauru (population 6,500). They saw the conference as a chance to divide the oceans' wealth. To them the idea of "freedom of the seas" gave an unfair advantage to the developed nations. On the other side was a group of 29 modern industrial nations including the U.S., the European nations, Canada, Australia, and Japan. They felt that freedom of the seas and the development of the seas were open only to limited negotiation.

However, the less developed nations were not completely united. The less developed nations who are landlocked and shelf-locked (little sea) did not like the idea of other nations dividing the richest parts of the oceans.

The outcome of this Third World Conference on the Law of the Sea and future conferences on the sea—for it is not expected that agreements will be easily reached—is of great importance to all people.

44. "Freedom of the seas," as used in this passage, refers to freedom

    (1) geographically
    (2) politically
    (3) economically
    (4) legally
    (5) historically

45. It can be inferred from the passage that

    (1) industrial nations outnumber developing nations
    (2) landlocked nations outnumber shelf-locked nations
    (3) industrial nations are largely landlocked
    (4) developing nations are less developed industrially
    (5) all nations see the need to change the current arrangement

46. The evidence presented in the passage indicates an outlook toward future control of the oceans' use that is

    (1) optimistic
    (2) pessimistic
    (3) cooperative
    (4) indifferent
    (5) idealistic

<u>Questions 47–49</u> are based on the following map and passage.

THE MIDDLE EAST AND NORTH AFRICA

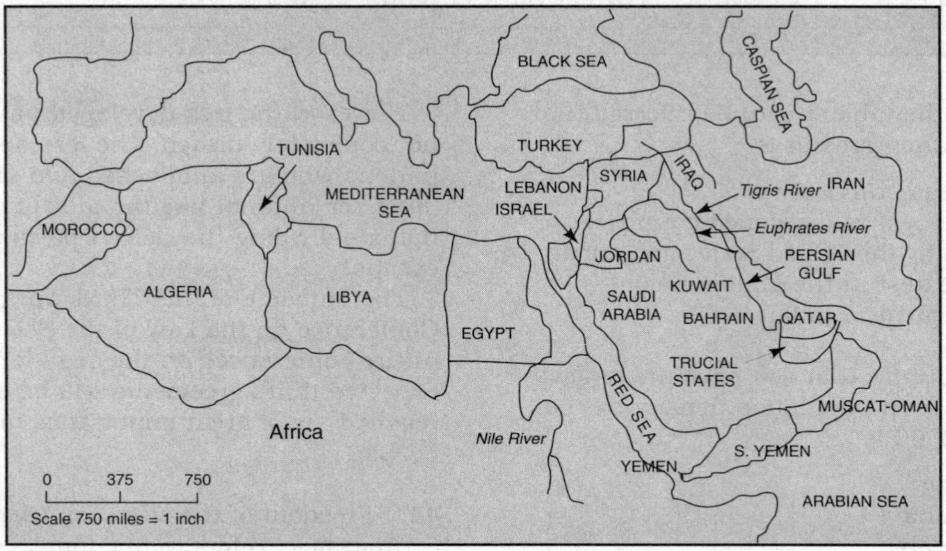

BLACK SEA
CASPIAN SEA
TUNISIA
TURKEY
SYRIA
IRAQ
IRAN
LEBANON
ISRAEL
MEDITERRANEAN SEA
Tigris River
Euphrates River
MOROCCO
JORDAN
PERSIAN GULF
KUWAIT
ALGERIA
LIBYA
SAUDI ARABIA
BAHRAIN
QATAR
EGYPT
TRUCIAL STATES
RED SEA
MUSCAT-OMAN
Africa
Nile River
S. YEMEN
YEMEN
ARABIAN SEA
0 375 750
Scale 750 miles = 1 inch

It is important to know about the Middle East for many reasons.

1. The Middle East is very rich in oil. It is believed that two-thirds of the world's total oil reserves lie in the Middle East. Oil is vital to industry throughout the world.
2. The Middle East has always been of great importance because it is located at the crossroads of three continents. Trade between Asia, Africa and Europe has had to pass through the Middle East, and its waterways have been used as trade routes since the beginning of civilization....
3. Some of the earliest civilizations developed in the Middle East....
4. Three of the world's great religions—Judaism, Christianity, and Islam—began in this part of the world. Many places in Israel, Jordan, and Saudi Arabia are thought of as holy by Christians, Moslems, and Jews.
5. Finally, the Jewish state of Israel stands in the middle of the Arab countries of the area. Israel is a democracy in a part of the world where most people have very little voice in their own government....

47. The map reveals that among the following the country with the smallest area is

(1) Egypt
(2) Saudi Arabia
(3) Iran
(4) Jordan
(5) Israel

48. Of the reasons given for knowing about the Middle East, the most important are

(1) political
(2) economic
(3) historical
(4) religious
(5) cultural

49. According to the map and the text, the bodies of water accessible for trade from the Mediterranean Sea include all of the following EXCEPT the

(1) Black Sea
(2) Caspian Sea
(3) Persian Gulf
(4) Arabian Sea
(5) Red Sea

Questions 50–52 are based on the following passage.

The initial impetus for the environmental movement was the growing interest in outdoor recreation in a more natural environment. This led to the creation of the National Preservation System (1964), the National Trails System (1968), and the National Wild and Scenic Rivers System (1968) and to a public purchase program in the Land and Water Conservation Act (1964). By 1989 the wilderness system, the most dramatic result of these measures, had reached 90 million acres.

These programs set a direction in resource management different from the conservation focus on efficient development of material resources. In wilderness areas, no timber was to be cut and no roads built. Wild and scenic rivers were to remain free-flowing with no dams built in them. The programs meant that resources were now prized for their aesthetic rather than their material value.

The environmental movement gave rise to a new appreciative use of wildlife as an object of observation rather than of hunting. This led to a federal endangered species program, nongame wildlife programs fostered by the states, a heightened interest in habitat for wild plants and animals, and a focus on biological diversity of wild resources.

In the environmental era, a new interest arose in curbing pollution—first air and water pollution in the 1950s and 1960s and then pollution from toxic wastes in the 1970s and thereafter.

50. The environmental movement arose from a desire for

(1) conservation of natural resources
(2) civilizing the wilderness
(3) more hunting and fishing
(4) resource management
(5) outdoor recreation

51. The most recent efforts in the environmental field have focused on

(1) curbing toxic chemical wastes
(2) obtaining profit from natural resources
(3) land and water conservation
(4) reducing air and water pollution
(5) controlling wildlife

52. New appreciation of wildlife has led to

(1) increased hunting
(2) increased profits from the sale of furs
(3) conservation in resource management
(4) efficient development of material resources
(5) a federal endangered species program

Behavioral Sciences

Read each of the following selections carefully. After each selection there are questions to be answered or statements to be completed. Select the best answer.

Questions 53–55 are based on the following passage.

Sparked by the debates of President John F. Kennedy's Commission on the Status of Women and by the birth of a new women's movement, a spate of legislation support women's efforts to overcome job discrimination. In 1963, Congress passed a long-sought Equal Pay Act. The 1964 Civil Rights Act forbade discrimination on the grounds of sex and created an Equal Employment Opportunity Commission that workers could use to bring suit against employers who did not comply with the law. As a result, a small number of women managed to inch their way into better jobs. By the seventies, medical and law schools, corporate and financial institutions, and political bureaucracies had increased equal access for women.

Poor women, however, did not seem to benefit as much. Those who headed the expanding number of single-parent families searched for ways to combine family life with work. Many women found themselves confined to retail sales, clerical, and service jobs where low wages and part-time work carried no benefits. New immigrants could find jobs only in sweatshops. At the same time, the rising cost of living locked many two-parent families into dual wage earning, with the problem of how to integrate work and family life. As attention shifted from workplace conditions, legislators increasingly advocated such reforms as subsidized child care, paid pregnancy and parental leaves, flextime, and more generous health-care coverage. Most experts agreed that resolving these family-related issues would be the key to achieving equality in the workplace of the 21st century.

53. According to the passage, for many families equality for women in the workplace depends most on

 (1) the generosity of corporate and financial institutions
 (2) the Commission on the Status of Women
 (3) the rising cost of living
 (4) the ability to integrate work and family life
 (5) the improvement of workplace conditions

54. It can be inferred from the passage that efforts on behalf of women

 (1) had widely differing effects
 (2) improved the lot of most women
 (3) penalized employers
 (4) had little general effect
 (5) overcame conflict in the workplace

55. The major interest of legislators now is in

 (1) workplace conditions
 (2) family-related issues
 (3) better jobs for women
 (4) equal pay for women
 (5) job discrimination

Questions 56–58 are based on the following passage.

Puerto Rican migration to the city has constituted the largest influx since the great waves of European immigration in the 19th century.

The islander soon found out what early immigrants had learned. Wages were better but prices were higher; houses were dilapidated; crime was rampant; the weather was cold and damp; and the society at large was strange and different.

How to keep one's family together and preserve one's identity were problems faced by every immigrant group, and they are problems faced by New York Puerto Ricans today. Life in the city was not easy, but there was little to return to.

Unlike many other non-English-speaking newcomers to the city, Puerto Ricans are American citizens. As Americans, they have the right to come and go as they please. Also, unlike previous immigrants, Puerto Ricans did not have to sever their ties to the homeland once they arrived in the city. Thus they could maintain, and even constantly renew, contact with their culture.

56. Puerto Rican immigrants differ from other non-English-speaking newcomers to New York City in that they

 (1) have no language problems
 (2) are needed in the factories
 (3) came with high hopes
 (4) are already American citizens
 (5) were unprepared for migration

57. Puerto Ricans faced all the following problems previous immigrant groups faced EXCEPT

 (1) prices outdistancing wages
 (2) inadequate housing
 (3) poor climate
 (4) crime being prevalent
 (5) broken cultural ties

58. The passage implies that, once they immigrated to New York City, Puerto Ricans

 (1) were just like other immigrant groups
 (2) remained outside the normal course of daily life
 (3) had little alternative but to remain
 (4) returned to Puerto Rico in large numbers
 (5) eventually solved the problem of identity

Questions 59–61 are based on the following passage.

Much has sometimes been made of the great importance for human evolution of the hand with its opposable thumb; it was important, certainly, but only as the servant of a growing brain. The hands of the higher monkeys would be perfectly capable of the finest skills had they a mind to set them to work; monkeys could be watchmakers had they ever conceived the notion of time.

A further stimulus to mental growth was given our ancestors when they left the trees and a mainly vegetarian diet and began to adapt themselves to living in relatively open country and eating meat. Undoubtedly meat's nutritive value, so much greater than that of herbs and fruit, relieved them of the necessity of perpetual eating. More important, the need for a creature with a relatively flat muzzle and no sharp claws or canine teeth to kill, skin and break up animal food must have led first to the use and then to the manufacture of tools.

59. Man's beginning to eat meat had as its first direct consequence

(1) a flat muzzle
(2) canine teeth
(3) the use of tools
(4) the manufacture of tools
(5) increased barbarity

60. It can be inferred that, when man learned to eat meat, he

(1) improved his brain
(2) spent less time eating
(3) suffered nutritionally
(4) was equipped to obtain animal food
(5) developed an opposite thumb

61. The most important element in human evolution, according to the author, was

(1) a sharpening of sight
(2) a flexible hand
(3) an opposable thumb
(4) a more varied diet
(5) a growing brain

Questions 62–64 are based on the following passage.

One mnemonic technique...consists simply of searching for or elaborating some vivid connection between...two items. One way to establish a connection is to imagine the two elements interacting in some way....

Consider learning a series of word pairs such as *dog-hat, man-pencil, clock-woman, sofa-floor*, and *pipe-clown*. People usually learn a list such as this by rapidly repeating each pair as often as possible in the allotted time. The method is reasonably satisfactory for short lists and over short retention intervals. Extend either the length of the list or the retention interval, however, and the rehearsal method falters seriously. People who have learned to use mental imagery to relate the items of a pair perform much better. They visualize a dog wearing a hat, a man resting a large pencil on his shoulder like a rifle, a woman wearing a clock on a chain around her neck, a section of floor resting on a sofa, and a clown smoking a pipe.... This procedure can improve recall by as much as 100 to 150 percent.

62. The selection deals mainly with

(1) the value of mental imagery in remembering
(2) the learning of word pairs
(3) improvement of recall
(4) learning rapidly
(5) developing a foreign-language vocabulary

63. It can be inferred from the passage that

(1) mental imagery is inferior to repetition
(2) rehearsal and repetition are essentially similar
(3) learners prefer repetition to rehearsal
(4) repetition is effective in mastering lengthy lists
(5) memorization is an effective technique

64. Retention, as used in this passage, is most similar in meaning to

(1) recall
(2) repetition
(3) rehearsal
(4) image
(5) connection

Answer Key

Political Science

1. **3**	3. **4**	5. **5**	7. **2**	9. **3**	11. **4**
2. **3**	4. **1**	6. **2**	8. **4**	10. **1**	12. **2**

Economics

13. **3**	16. **3**	18. **4**	20. **3**	22. **3**	24. **2**
14. **2**	17. **2**	19. **5**	21. **5**	23. **4**	25. **5**
15. **1**					

History

26. **3**	29. **4**	32. **3**	35. **5**	37. **2**	39. **5**
27. **1**	30. **2**	33. **2**	36. **1**	38. **2**	40. **1**
28. **2**	31. **3**	34. **2**			

Geography

41. **5**	43. **3**	45. **4**	47. **5**	49. **2**	51. **1**
42. **1**	44. **3**	46. **2**	48. **2**	50. **5**	52. **5**

Behavioral Sciences

53. **4**	55. **2**	57. **5**	59. **3**	61. **5**	63. **2**
54. **1**	56. **4**	58. **3**	60. **2**	62. **1**	64. **1**

WHAT'S YOUR SCORE?

_______right,	_______wrong
Excellent	58–64
Good	51–57
Fair	44–50

If your score is low for the "Social Studies Practice," you may need more social studies review. The explanations of the correct answers that follow will help you determine where your weaknesses lie. Analyze your errors. Then reread the chapter "Reading and Interpreting Social Studies Materials" at the beginning of this unit and review the areas in which you had the most trouble.

Answer Analysis

Political Science

1. **3** The theme of the passage is expressed in the fourth sentence. The American statesmen are described as not only performing their political function, but also expressing a more universal responsibility. This is the basis of American political philosophy.
2. **3** The opening words of the passage indicate that intellectuals who lead the way for a revolution are usually devoured, or destroyed, by the forces that are unleashed.
3. **4** The middle part of the passage states that American political science is the only one perfectly adapted to the emergencies of the contemporary world.
4. **1** The paragraph stresses public duty, as opposed to official duty, of persons whose performance is "constant, honorable, intelligent, and vigilant."
5. **5** The paragraph stresses the personal attention to detail that lifts public servants above the level of mere politicians.
6. **2** Personal attention to the details of politics is indicated as the foundation of the "great temple of...liberty" that is our government.
7. **2** The passage states that court decisions often lead to "virtually endless series of vexing legal questions."
8. **4** The opening sentence indicates that the average citizen is knowledgeable about important court decisions.
9. **3** *Landmark* refers to a distinguishing feature that guides someone on his or her way. It is, therefore, "significant."
10. **1** The passage is an evaluation of the use of government by Americans.
11. **4** The author indicates that Americans revealed more competence than most others in politics.
12. **2** The political realism of Americans is illustrated by their ability to "recognize the economic bases of politics."

Economics

13. 3 The author centers his remarks on the "hundreds and thousands of homeless children in this nation."

14. 2 The children are unseen because they are "scattered in a thousand different cities."

15. 1 He calls our leaving a half-million homeless children on our streets a sheer betrayal of ourselves and our best values.

16. 3 The passage indicates, as characteristics of the factory system, that workers became proficient at the particular work done by the machine, that is, specialization, and that a division of labor was set up.

17. 2 The passage implies that hand production of goods, the domestic system, preceded the factory system where goods are produced with the use of machinery.

18. 4 Choice 4 incorrectly states that the factory system encouraged worker versatility, whereas the reverse is true: instead, each worker became proficient at the specialized job performed by the machine he or she tended.

19. 5 The president advocated increased imports (paragraph two), decreased tariffs (paragraph three) and increased exports (paragraph three).

20. 3 The president was replying to warnings against increased imports based on the lower level of wages paid in other countries.

21. 5 The president pointed out that lowered tariffs and, therefore, increased imports will provide raw materials and other supplies that allow American products to be made *less* expensively, not *more* expensively.

22. 3 The author wants the reader to understand what life is like in developing nations. For this purpose he imagines that a poor American family is transformed into "a family of the underdeveloped world."

23. 4 The article states that over half of the world's population has a standard of living of less than $100 a year.

24. 2 The author implies that most Americans do not understand the life of almost 4 billion persons living in underdeveloped nations. To help them do so, he creates an imaginary family.

25. 5 Families in underdeveloped nations lack houses, nearby hospitals, electric power, and government services. They have a daily food input of 2000 to 2100 calories, but that is not enough to sustain health.

History

26. 3 "The early Europeans imagined that the natives of the New World were rovers...."

27. 1 The author states that the Native Americans had "no idea of...the individual ownership of land, and the Europeans were incapable of thinking in any other terms."

28. 2 According to the author, the object of the General Allotment Act was to "encourage the Native Americans to engage in farming by breaking up the reservations."

29. 4 The passage refers to a "the mingling of races, dedicated to common ideals..."

30. 2 The words *hybrid* and *mongrel* indicate the lack of a common heritage.

31. 3 The author concedes that the "mingling of races," which foreign propagandists believe to be true of America, is a fact.

32. 3 The passage emphasizes the fact that Canada and the United States have cooperated to solve many problems.

33. 2 The passage states that solutions have been found for every matter of disagreement.

34. 2 The passage mentions border disputes that occurred through the War of 1812.

35. 5 The passage states that the Indian Reorganization Act was the work of John Collier, the commissioner of Indian affairs.

36. 1 The act sought to restore tribal authority; it "addressed the strengthening of tribal life and government."

37. 2 The passage refers both to the American Indian's unique legal status and his or her being more prosperous than ever before.

38. 2 Although various people were involved in the planning and construction of the Capitol, the design itself was selected by George Washington. See the second paragraph.

39. **5** As the first paragraph indicates, the Capitol is the home of the legislative branch of the federal government, consisting of the House of Representatives and the Senate.

40. **1** The enormous iron dome is the symbol of the Capitol today. The last paragraph describes its appearance and its characteristics.

Geography

41. **5** From 1992 to 2000, population growth in India will be over 139 million. China is second with over 121 million.

42. **1** In 2000, India's density per square mile will have had the largest increase: from 732.96 to 848.89.

43. **3** Since Japan has the largest number of people per square mile and high population densities frequently occur in areas of heavy industrialization, it can be inferred that Japan is highly industrialized.

44. **3** "Freedom of the seas" is equated in the passage with the oceans' wealth, which the developing nations wish to share.

45. **4** Developing nations are "on the other side" from industrial nations, so they must be lacking industry.

46. **2** The evidence includes unsuccessful fishery management, difficulty in reaching agreements, and the possibility that development of ocean resources will not occur.

47. **5** Israel, about the size of the state of New Jersey, is by far the smallest with an area of 7,992 square miles, less than one quarter the size of Jordan, one fiftieth the size of Egypt, one eightieth the size of Iran, and one hundredth the size of Saudi Arabia.

48. **2** Oil and trade are mentioned first.

49. **2** The Caspian Sea is an inland sea.

50. **5** The initial impetus was a "growing interest in outdoor recreation in a more natural environment."

51. **1** In the 1970s and thereafter, a new interest arose in curbing pollution from toxic chemical wastes.

52. **5** Wildlife was seen as existing, not for being hunted, but for observation so a federal endangered species program was created.

Behavioral Sciences

53. **4** The passage refers to the problem, for dual wage-earning parents, of finding ways to integrate work and family life.

54. **1** Poor women did not benefit as much as a small number of more fortunate women who managed to get better jobs.

55. **2** Legislators are now interested in family-related issues such as paid pregnancy, child care, and health care.

56. **4** Unlike other newcomers to New York City, Puerto Ricans are already American citizens when they arrive.

57. **5** The first four responses are problems all newcomers faced. The exception is Choice 5; Puerto Ricans could maintain and renew contact with their culture.

58. **3** The passage states that, while life in the city was difficult, there was little in Puerto Rico for the immigrants to return to.

59. **3** The passage states that the need to break up animal food (i.e., meat), must have first led to the use of tools.

60. **2** Because meat provided greater nutrition than herbs and fruit, human beings did not have to eat as often as previously.

61. **5** The passage mentions that a waxing (growing) brain was even more important than the hand with its opposable thumb.

62. **1** The author states that people who use mental imagery can associate items better.

63. **2** The passage states that rapid repetition (the rehearsal method) is helpful for short lists and time intervals, but that this method falters for long lists and/or intervals.

64. **1** Both mean "remembering" or "memory."

UNIT V

SCIENCE

TEST 3

CHAPTER 12: Reading and Interpreting Science Questions

Science questions on the GED Examination may be based on reading passages, graphs, diagrams, or tables. Test-taking tactics are presented here by means of 31 explained examples and step-by-step explanations.

CHAPTER 13: Handling Science Skills Questions

Comprehension, application, analysis, and evaluation of science material are four skills on which you will be tested when you take the GED Examination. Twenty examples of typical questions are included in this chapter. The answers are briefly analyzed for you. Also, to help you with unfamiliar vocabulary, a handy "Glossary of Scientific Terms" is included.

CHAPTER 14: Science Practice

In this chapter 150 questions are arranged by subject (biology, earth science, chemistry, and physics). Articles, tables, graphs, and diagrams are presented in the actual GED format. Conveniently placed answer keys and full explanations follow the exercises in each subject.

12

Reading and Interpreting Science Questions

There are several types of questions on the Science test, and each calls for a specific plan of attack.

Single-Item Questions

In this type, a short paragraph of one or two sentences is followed by a single question. Your first task in dealing with this kind of question is to identify the main idea or ideas presented, and the best way to do this is to start by reading the paragraph and the question quickly, without stopping to be sure you understand every point. This will give you some sense of the content of the question and of the kind of information you will need to answer it. Fix in your mind the main idea of the paragraph.

Next, reread the question carefully. You may be able to select the correct answer at once. If you have any doubt, go back to the paragraph and reread it carefully, searching for the answer to the question.

Practice this technique on the following question:

QUESTION

Growing plants will not develop their green color, caused by the chlorophyll in their leaves, unless they have both sunlight and the necessary genetic system.

If a seedling growing in dim light turns out to be colorless, what could be done to find out why?

(1) Give it a new set of genes.
(2) Add chlorophyll to the soil.
(3) Graft it onto a green plant.
(4) Move it into the sunlight.
(5) Add fertilizer to the soil.

ANSWER AND ANALYSIS

A quick reading tells you that the main idea deals with the factors involved in the development of a plant's green color. Now go back to the paragraph and read it again. After rereading, you know that the crucial factors are sunlight and genes. This narrows the answer possibilities to Choices 1 and 4. Since there is no way to give the plant a new set of genes, the answer is Choice 4.

Here is another sample of this kind of question:

QUESTION

Carbon dioxide (CO_2) gas is dissolved in soda water, but the bubbles of gas are invisible while the bottle is sealed. When the cap is removed, however, the liquid foams up with the release of bubbles of CO_2 gas. If the soda water is warm, the bubbling is even more violent.

What general rule would explain these observations?

(1) Warm water tends to lower the pressure of the dissolved gas.
(2) CO_2 gas is more soluble at low temperature and high pressure.
(3) CO_2 gas does not dissolve in water when the pressure is too high.
(4) CO_2 gas is not as soluble when the pressure and temperature are too high.
(5) High pressure tends to keep the temperature low.

ANSWER AND ANALYSIS

A quick reading tells you that the main idea concerns the solubility of gases and its dependence on pressure and temperature. Now you have to reread carefully to find out just what this dependence is.

This question introduces a type of difficulty that you may meet often—the *unstated assumption*. To get the answer to this question, you will have to realize that the pressure in a sealed soda bottle is high. This should be obvious: when you remove the cap from the bottle of soda, gas rushes out. You will often be expected to supply, for yourself, bits of information that are commonly and widely known.

Adding this piece of information, you can now go back to the passage to find out how temperature and pressure affect the solubility of the gas in the soda. When you take the cap off, you reduce the pressure and the gas comes out of solution, so it is clear that the gas is more soluble when the pressure is high. Since there is more foaming when the soda is warm, the gas is more soluble at lower temperatures. Thus the answer is Choice 2.

Multiple-Item Questions Based on Readings

Some questions require you to read a passage consisting of several paragraphs and then to answer a number of questions about the material. In this case, you need to study the passage carefully *before* you look at the questions. As you read, note two or three main ideas.

To find the main ideas in the passage, look for key words. These are words such as *aorta* and *nucleus* and *ecosystem* that are normally used in a scientific context. Once you have found these words, they should lead you to one of the main ideas in the passage.

EXAMPLE

The annual migration of birds is a complex process that is only partly understood. Some birds that hatch in the Arctic fly thousands of miles to South America each winter, and then return to the place where they were born. The adults make these trips separately from their offspring. The young birds, however, find their way to the correct wintering grounds even though no adult bird shows them the way. No one knows how they are able to do this.

Biologists do understand, however, that in temperate zones the urge to migrate is prompted by a change in the length of daylight. As days grow shorter in the fall, certain physical changes occur in the birds, such as degeneration of the ovaries or testes. These changes are accompanied by restlessness and the urge to fly south.

There is some evidence that birds navigate using many clues, including the earth's magnetic field, the position of the sun in the sky, visible land forms, and even the pattern of the stars at night. How they know the route, however, is a complete mystery. It can be called instinct, but that is simply a word that explains nothing.

As you read this passage through for the first time, you should identify several key words, such as *migration, degeneration, ovaries, testes, navigate, magnetic field*. Now use these words to locate the main ideas in the passage. They will probably lead you to three main ideas: (1) the changing length of daylight is the signal that prompts migration; (2) birds use a number of clues to navigate; and (3) how they know the route is completely unknown.

Once you have these main ideas firmly fixed in your mind, you are ready to read the questions. Refer to the passage as needed to find the answers.

QUESTION

What is the most probable factor that prompts birds to migrate north in the spring?

(1) depletion of the food supply during the winter
(2) the disappearance of snow from the ground
(3) the coming of warmer weather
(4) the increase in the amount of daylight
(5) the instinct to fly north

ANSWER AND ANALYSIS

One of the main ideas tells you that, in the fall, migration is prompted by the decreasing length of daylight. It is surely reasonable to suppose that the reverse is true in the spring, so the answer is Choice 4. It should not be necessary for you to reread the passage.

QUESTION

In an experiment, the testes are removed from birds in the Arctic in the summertime. It is found that the birds then show the typical restlessness that precedes migration. What hypothesis does this suggest?

(1) Early migration causes the testes to degenerate.
(2) The length of the day has nothing to do with migration.
(3) The immediate physiological factor that initiates migration is degeneration of the testes.
(4) Increasing length of daylight causes the testes to degenerate.
(5) Restlessness is not a sign that migration is about to begin.

ANSWER AND ANALYSIS

This question requires you to analyze a cause-and-effect relationship. Since it deals with the factors that initiate migration, your attention is drawn to the second paragraph, where you find that degeneration of the testes (or ovaries) always precedes migration. The experiment tests whether loss of the testes is an actual cause of the urge to migrate. When it is found that removal of the testes produces premigratory restlessness, the cause-and-effect relationship is established; the answer is Choice 3. Choice 1 is wrong because a cause cannot come after an effect. Choice 2 is wrong because it introduces a factor not tested for in the experiment. Choice 4 is wrong because the length of daylight decreases, not increases, as the summer advances toward fall. Choice 5 is wrong because it violates one of the assumptions on which the experiment was based.

QUESTION

What has the study of migration revealed about how birds know what route to follow?

(1) Young birds learn by following their parents.
(2) Birds are born with an instinct that tells them the route.
(3) Birds use several different means of navigation.
(4) The changing length of daylight gives birds the necessary clues.
(5) So far, investigation has not given any answers to the question.

ANSWER AND ANALYSIS

One of the main ideas, already extracted from the passage, is Choice 5—the answer. The passage says that Choice 1 is not true, and Choice 2 offers a word, *instinct*, but not an explanation. Choices 3 and 4 are true, but irrelevant to this particular question.

QUESTION

In the tropics, some birds migrate for short distances between wet and dry seasons. How do we know that they do not use the same seasonal clues as temperate-zone birds?

(1) There is no marked temperature variation between winter and summer in the tropics.
(2) Food is available all year round in the tropics.
(3) The testes and ovaries of tropical birds do not change cyclically during the year.
(4) In the tropics, the length of daylight is much the same all year.
(5) Since it is always warm in the tropics, the birds have no definite nesting season.

ANSWER AND ANALYSIS

The seasonal clue used by migrating birds in temperate zones is the change in the amount of daylight. Since there are no seasons to change in the tropics, the correct answer is choice 4. Choices 1, 2, and 5 may be correct statements, but the question concerns seasonal changes, not temperature or the availability of food. Choice 3 may also be true, but it is not a valid answer because the statement cannot be verified with information presented in the passage.

Here is another passage for you to practice on:

EXAMPLE

Sicklemia is a hereditary disease of the erythrocytes (red blood cells) that is found chiefly in the people of tropical Africa and their descendants in America. It is characterized by abnormal hemoglobin, the red protein in erythrocytes.

People afflicted with this condition are subject to repeated attacks, brought on by conditions in which the erythrocytes receive insufficient oxygen in their passage through the lungs. This may happen during periods of intense physical exertion, or at high altitudes where the oxygen pressure is low. Under these conditions, the abnormal hemoglobin gels, distorting the erythrocytes into a rigid sickle shape. They are then unable to pass through the capillaries. Blockage of the circulation produces a variety of severe symptoms and may result in death.

The gene that produces the abnormal hemoglobin confers a certain benefit on its carriers. Children of a mating between a person with sicklemia and one with normal hemoglobin have some damaged erythrocytes, but not enough to make them ill except under very severe conditions. They benefit by being immune to malaria, which is a devastating and often fatal disease in tropical Africa.

This is a complex passage containing many key words: *sicklemia, Africa, erythrocyte, hemoglobin, hereditary, oxygen, capillary, malaria*. Some of these words may be unfamiliar, but you should note that three of them are defined for you. You are told that erythrocytes are red blood cells, hemoglobin is the red protein in these cells, and malaria is a devastating disease. Sicklemia is described in detail through the passage. You are expected to know the meaning of *Africa, hereditary, oxygen,* and *capillary*.

Using these words, you should find the following key ideas: (1) sicklemia is hereditary; (2) it occurs in Africa, where malaria is common; (3) it involves abnormal hemoglobin; (4) attacks occur in conditions of low oxygen supply; (5) sicklemia protects against malaria.

Now you are ready to look at the questions.

QUESTION

Which of the following might be an appropriate treatment for a person suffering an acute attack of sicklemia?

(1) Administer antimalarial medication.
(2) Move the person to a high altitude.
(3) Administer oxygen.
(4) Make the person exercise strenuously to open the capillaries.
(5) Remove the sickled erythrocytes.

ANSWER AND ANALYSIS

One of the key ideas tells you that attacks are provoked by shortage of oxygen in the blood, so the answer is Choice 3. It should not be necessary to refer to the passage to get this answer.

QUESTION

Why does sicklemia produce some benefit in Africa, but not in the United States?

(1) There is no malaria in the United States.
(2) The United States has a temperate climate.
(3) There is more oxygen in the air in the United States.
(4) The gene for sicklemia is not found in the United States.
(5) The United States has a lower altitude than Africa.

ANSWER AND ANALYSIS

The last paragraph of the passage details the only benefit of sicklemia: protection against malaria in the carriers of the gene. Where there is no malaria, this benefit disappears, and the answer is Choice 1. Choices 3, 4, and 5 are not true, and Choice 2 is irrelevant.

QUESTION

Of the following, in which group is sicklemia likely to appear most frequently?

(1) Americans living in Africa
(2) Americans of African descent
(3) people who have been exposed to malaria
(4) all people living in the tropics
(5) people who have been in close contact with individuals who have sicklemia

ANSWER AND ANALYSIS

One of the key points is that sicklemia is hereditary; another is that it is common in Africa. It follows that people of African descent are most liable to get it. The answer is Choice 2.

QUESTION

A test is available to determine whether an individual is a carrier of sicklemia. Someone might take such a test to help him or her decide whether to

(1) move to a tropical climate
(2) take an office job
(3) work at manual labor at a high altitude
(4) go to a hospital for treatment
(5) make a will

ANSWER AND ANALYSIS

This is a difficult question, which cannot be answered except by careful reading of the passage. The last paragraph tells you that under severe conditions a carrier may become ill. In the second paragraph you learned that severe conditions mean a limited supply of oxygen, brought on by hard physical exertion or high altitude. The answer is Choice 3, a combination of both these factors.

QUESTION

Natural selection tends to eliminate genes that produce serious illness and no benefit. Which of the following would result in long-range reduction of the amount of sicklemia in the world?

(1) improved sanitation in tropical countries
(2) a new vaccine against the disease
(3) restriction of immigration from Africa
(4) quarantine of affected individuals
(5) complete elimination of malaria in the world

ANSWER AND ANALYSIS

Since the disease is hereditary rather than infectious, Choices 1, 2, and 4 would have no effect. Choice 3 would have no effect in Africa. The only choice left is 5. The question states that natural selection eliminates genes that cause serious illnesses and no benefit. Since the only benefit of sicklemia is immunity to malaria, elimination of malaria should cause the elimination of sicklemia as well.

Questions Based on Graphs, Diagrams, and Data Tables

LINE GRAPHS

A line graph is a common way to show how something changes or to show the relationship between two or more things. This kind of graph uses two scales, one going up the left side of the graph, called the vertical axis, and another along the bottom of the graph, called the horizontal axis.

If you are given a line graph on the GED test, read it carefully. Note the title, the labels on the vertical and horizontal axes, and the legend or key if there is one. Take your time, and pay attention to all of the printed material as well as the lines and the scales. Only then will you be ready to answer questions based on the line graph.

Here is a sample for you to work on:

EXAMPLE

The graph below represents the temperatures of a white sidewalk and a black asphalt driveway on a sunny day. The surfaces are side by side, and the measurements were made during a 24-hour period.

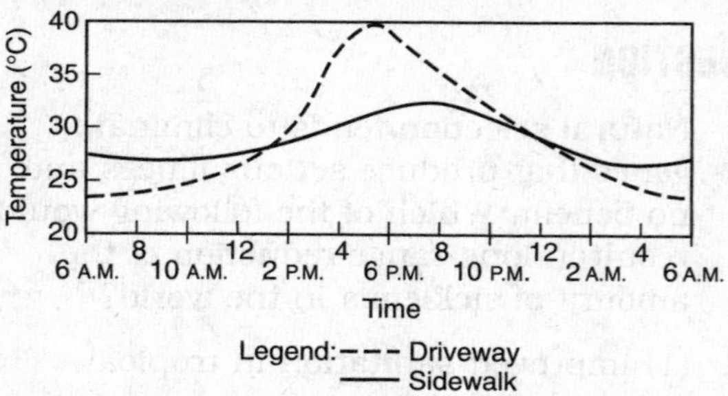

What are the features of this graph? The vertical axis represents temperatures between 20 and 40 degrees Celsius. It does not matter whether you are familiar with the Celsius scale of temperature or not. All you need to be able to do is recognize the changes and the intervals from one temperature to another.

The horizontal axis represents the time of day. It is divided into 4-hour intervals for a 12-hour period.

According to the legend, the solid line on the graph represents the temperature of the sidewalk and the dash lines represents the temperature of the driveway. Note that both temperatures increase during daylight hours and start to decrease in the late afternoon or early evening.

Now you are ready for the questions.

QUESTION

At noon, what was the temperature of the driveway?

(1) 22°C
(2) 26°C
(3) 28°C
(4) 30°C
(5) 32°C

ANSWER AND ANALYSIS

Noon is halfway between 10 A.M. and 2 P.M., so start by placing the point of your pencil halfway between these two points on the horizontal scale. Move it straight up until it meets the dashed line, which represents the driveway. Now move the pencil point to the left; it meets the temperature scale at 26°. The answer is Choice 2.

QUESTION

What is the difference in the times when the two surfaces reach their maximum temperatures?

(1) The driveway reaches its maximum about 4 hours before the sidewalk.
(2) The sidewalk reaches its maximum about 4 hours before the driveway.
(3) The driveway reaches its maximum about 2 hours before the sidewalk.
(4) The sidewalk reaches its maximum about 2 hours before the driveway.
(5) Both surfaces reach their maximums at the same time.

ANSWER AND ANALYSIS

The dashed line (driveway) peaks at about 4 P.M. halfway between 2 P.M. and 6 P.M. The solid line (sidewalk) peaks a little before 8 P.M. The difference is fairly close to 4 hours, so the answer is Choice 1.

QUESTION

Where and when does the temperature increase most rapidly?

(1) the driveway at 4:30 P.M.
(2) the sidewalk at 5 P.M.
(3) the sidewalk at 7:30 P.M.
(4) the driveway at noon
(5) the driveway at 3 P.M.

ANSWER AND ANALYSIS

The most rapid change is shown as the steepest slope of the graph. This occurs on the dashed line at about 3 P.M., so the answer is Choice 5.

QUESTION

How do the temperature patterns of the two surfaces compare?

(1) The driveway is always warmer than the sidewalk.
(2) The sidewalk is warmer than the driveway at night and cooler in the afternoon.
(3) The two surfaces are never at the same temperature.
(4) The sidewalk changes temperature faster than the driveway.
(5) The driveway is always cooler than the sidewalk.

ANSWER AND ANALYSIS

Choices 1 and 5 are wrong by inspection of the graph. Choice 2 is right, because the graph for the driveway rises above the one for the sidewalk at about 1:30 P.M. and falls below it at midnight. Choice 3 is wrong because the two lines coincide at two times. Choice 4 is wrong because the line for the driveway is always steeper than that for the sidewalk.

QUESTION

What hypothesis might be advanced on the basis of this graph?

(1) Radiant heat flows in either direction more easily through a black surface than through a white one.
(2) Black objects tend to retain heat, while white ones lose it more easily.
(3) White objects tend to absorb heat more rapidly than black objects do.
(4) Black objects are always cooler at night than in the daytime.
(5) White objects are usually cooler than black ones.

ANSWER AND ANALYSIS

Since the black surface both warms up and cools down faster than the white one, the answer is Choice 1. Choice 2 is wrong because the black surface cools down faster than the white one. Choice 3 is wrong because the white surface warms up more slowly than the black one. Choices 4 and 5 are wrong because they do not take into account the conditions on which the graph was based, namely, that the two surfaces were in sunlight during the day.

BAR GRAPHS

Whereas a line graph is used to show how something changes, a bar graph is used to compare several quantities. Like a line graph, a bar graph has a vertical axis marked off as a kind of scale. The horizontal axis is used to indicate the different quantities that are being compared.

Look at a bar graph the same way you would a line graph. Read the title and the legend (if any). Then note the information given on the horizontal axis and on the vertical axis.

EXAMPLE

The following bar graphs show the percentages by volume of the sediment sizes found in four different sediment deposits, *A*, *B*, *C*, and *D*.

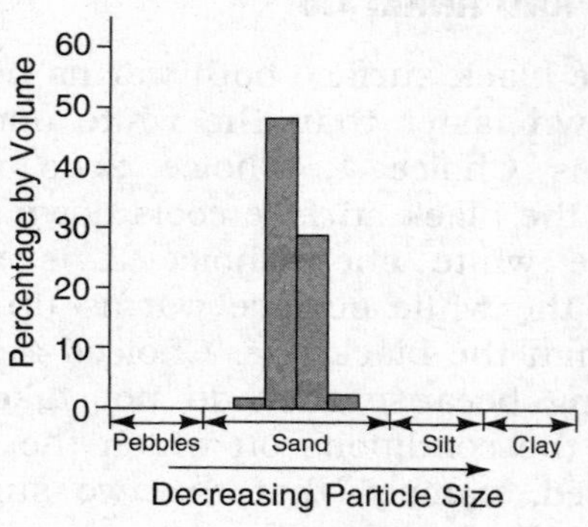

DEPOSIT *A*

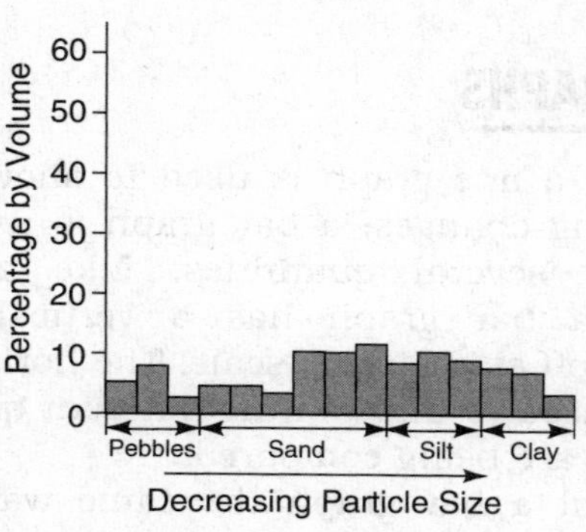

DEPOSIT *B*

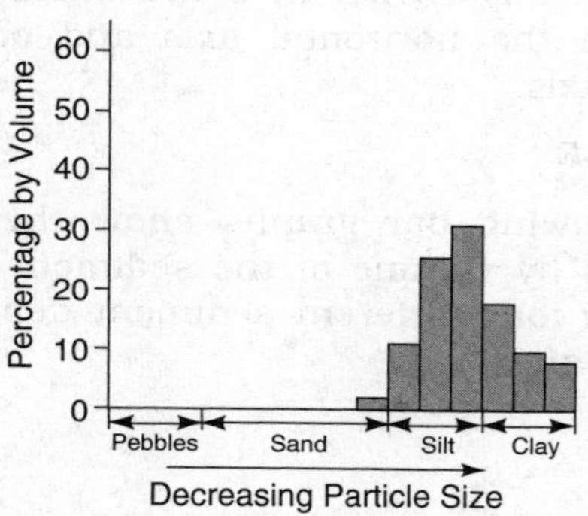

DEPOSIT *C*

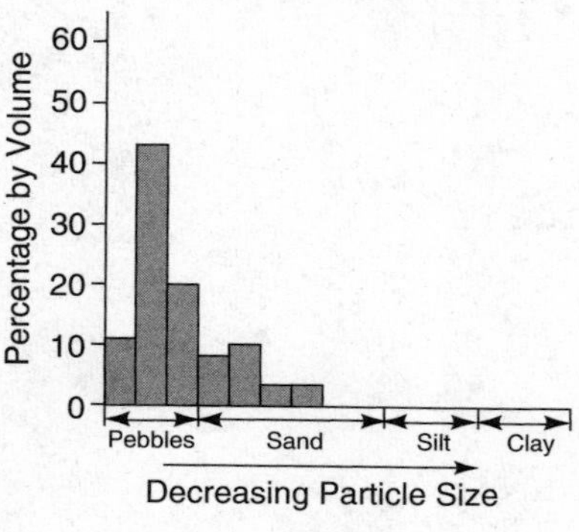

DEPOSIT *D*

QUESTION

What is the total percentage of silt in deposit *B*?

(1) 5%
(2) 9%
(3) 27%
(4) 48%
(5) 54%

ANSWER AND ANALYSIS

In deposit *B* there are three bars representing silt. Each deposit is 10% or slightly less. Adding the three deposits of silt together produces a total of a little less than 30%, Choice 3.

QUESTION

Glaciers carry a wide range of particles. When glacier ice melts, this mixture of material is deposited. In which bar graph(s) is the material most likely deposited by a glacier reflected?

(1) deposit *A*
(2) deposit *B*
(3) deposit *C*
(4) deposit *D*
(5) deposits *A* and *D*

ANSWER AND ANALYSIS

The only graph that reflects the wide range of particles—pebbles, sand, silt, and clay—carried by a glacier is *B*, Choice 2.

QUESTION

Smaller particles tend to remain in suspension. In which deposit(s) is there the highest percentage of sediments that would stay in suspension for the longest time before settling?

(1) deposit *A*
(2) deposit *B*
(3) deposit *C*
(4) deposit *D*
(5) deposits *A* and *D*

ANSWER AND ANALYSIS

Deposit *C* contains mostly silt and clay, which are the smallest particles. The materials in deposit *C* would therefore tend to remain in suspension for the longest period of time. Choice 3 is the answer.

EXAMPLE

The following graph represents the counts of three kinds of leukocytes (white blood cells) in an animal that was administered a standard dose of a drug starting on day 4.

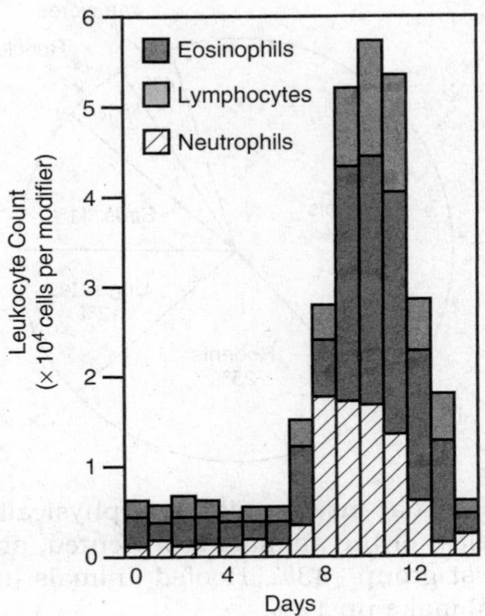

Note that the numbers of the three different kinds of leukocytes are indicated by using different patterns in the bars.

QUESTION

How long did the medication take to produce its maximum effect?

(1) 4 days
(2) 7 days
(3) 10 days
(4) 12 days
(5) 14 days

ANSWER AND ANALYSIS

Remember that the drug was started on day 4. The peak of leukocyte production was reached on day 10. When you subtract the three days during which no medication was given, you have the answer: 7 days, Choice 2.

QUESTION

In regard to amount of increase, how did the three different kinds of leukocytes react to the medication?

(1) All three increased in roughly the same proportion.
(2) The neutrophils increased proportionally more than the others.
(3) The eosinophils increased proportionally more than the others.
(4) There was proportionally less increase in the eosinophils.
(5) There was proportionally less increase in the lymphocytes.

ANSWER AND ANALYSIS

At the peak, the ratios were about 1/4 neutrophils and 1/5 eosinophils, which were not much different from the starting ratios. The answer is Choice 1.

QUESTION

What do the data suggest as to the potential usefulness of this drug?

(1) It might be used to produce an increase in the leukocyte count in someone suffering from a long-time shortage of leukocytes.
(2) It is completely useless because the improvement is temporary.
(3) It is too dangerous because the increase in the leukocyte count is so great.
(4) It might be useful in producing a large, temporary increase in the availability of leukocytes.
(5) It is dangerous because, after the effect wears off, the leukocyte count is extremely low.

ANSWER AND ANALYSIS

In some condition, perhaps a systemic infection, in which the body has a sudden demand for an exceptionally large, temporary supply of leukocytes, this drug might be useful. The answer is Choice 4.

QUESTION

What is the probable reason that the drug was administered from day 4 instead of at the very start of the experiment?

(1) The delay allowed the animal to become used to its cage and the other conditions of its surroundings.
(2) The drug was not available for the first 3 days.
(3) The delay allowed the animal's leukocyte count to rise to normal levels before the experiment was begun.
(4) The experimenter needed this time to determine the correct dosage.
(5) The first three days served as a control to establish the pattern of leukocyte count before the drug was given.

ANSWER AND ANALYSIS

Before beginning the experiment, the scientist had to make sure that any changes in the leukocyte count were the result of the medication, and not some other factor. The answer is Choice 5.

PIE CHARTS

A pie chart is a circular graph in which the circle is divided into sections. Pie charts are useful when a particular item of information is a part, that is, a fraction or percentage, of a whole.

The first thing to notice on a pie chart is the labels, which tell you what the various segments represent. Each label is usually accompanied by a number that indicates what part of the whole this segment represents. Next you should note the sizes of the segments to get some idea of which are largest and which are smallest.

EXAMPLE

The pie chart below indicates the average numbers of macroscopic (large) organisms in one area.

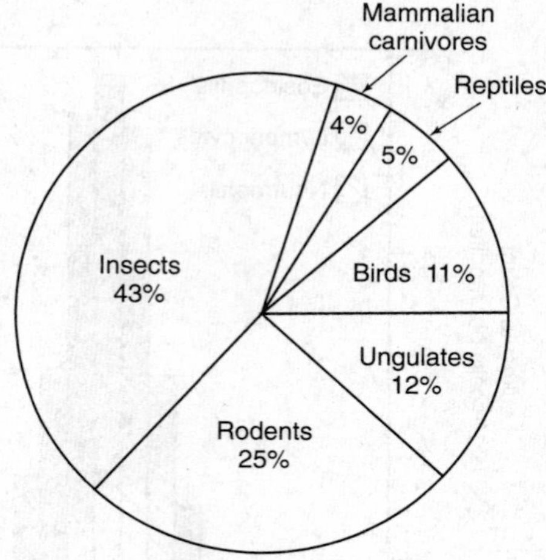

Note that insects, although physically the smallest of the animals represented, are the largest group—43%. Hoofed animals (ungulates) make up 12%.

QUESTION

Which statement is supported by the chart?

(1) Birds eat either insects or seeds.
(2) Most reptiles are carnivores.
(3) Eighty percent of the ecosystem consists of herbivores.
(4) The ecosystem in this study was a savannah.
(5) Insects are important because they are plant pollinators.

ANSWER AND ANALYSIS

Although Choices 1 and 2 are true statements, nothing on the chart indicates what birds or reptiles eat. Choice 4 is an excellent assumption, but noting on the chart proves this statement conclusively. Choice 5 is partly true, but again is not supported by the chart. The best answer is Choice 3. If you know that a great many insects, ungulates (hoofed animals), and rodents eat plants, and if you add up the number represented by their portions of the chart, the total is 80%.

QUESTION

If the population of carnivores increased by 10%, what would be the result?

(1) Rodents would increase.
(2) Ungulates and rodents would decrease, then carnivores would decrease.
(3) Birds and reptiles would increase, then decrease.
(4) Ungulates would decrease.
(5) Ungulates and rodents would increase, then decrease.

ANSWER AND ANALYSIS

There is no reason to suspect that any other population would increase because carnivores did so; therefore Choices 1, 3, and 5 cannot be correct. Choice 4 is a possible answer; however, Choice 2 is more specific and likely as a result of the increase in the population of carnivores. Carnivores feed on ungulates and rodents, and occasionally on some insects. If their population increased, carnivores would need more food, so the number of prey animals would decrease. When the food level dropped to a point where it could not support such a large population of consumers, however, the number of carnivores would also begin to decline.

DIAGRAMS

Diagrams, sometimes called graphics, show the relationships among the various parts of an object. Some parts may be inside others, be connected to others, or even be completely separate. When you see a diagram, the first things to look for are the connections between parts. Be sure to read all of the labels.

EXAMPLE

The following diagram represents the human ear. Empty spaces are shown in black.

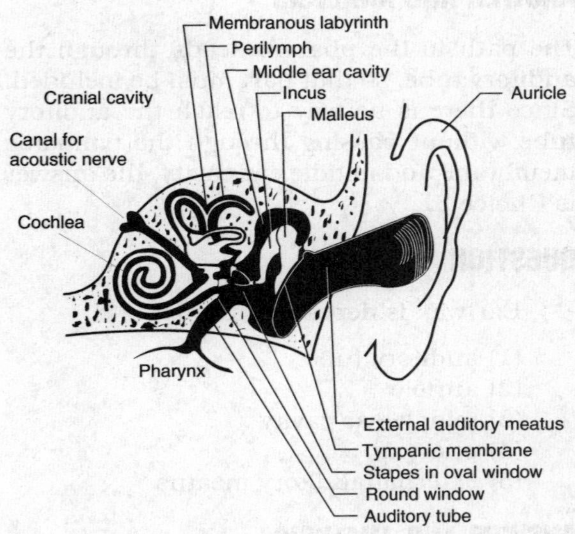

You should see at once that the external auditory meatus is an empty space separated from the middle ear cavity by the tympanic membrane. The middle ear cavity contains three bones.

QUESTION

The incus is inside the

(1) malleus
(2) middle ear cavity
(3) tympanic membrane
(4) round window
(5) auditory tube

ANSWER AND ANALYSIS

The label "Incus" points to something white, a bone. The label "Middle ear cavity" indicates a black area, a cavity. The answer is Choice 2.

QUESTION

For a sound wave to get from the external auditory meatus into the pharynx, it would have to go through

(1) the malleus, incus, and stapes only
(2) the tympanic membrane, malleus, and middle ear cavity only
(3) the tympanic membrane, middle ear cavity, and auditory tube only
(4) the middle ear cavity, round window, and cochlea only
(5) the tympanic membrane and auditory tube only

ANSWER AND ANALYSIS

The path to the pharynx leads through the auditory tube, so that part must be included. Since there is no way to reach the auditory tube without passing through the tympanic membrane and middle ear cavity, the answer is Choice 3.

QUESTION

Ear wax is deposited in the

(1) auditory tube
(2) auricle
(3) middle ear cavity
(4) pharynx
(5) external auditory meatus

ANSWER AND ANALYSIS

The canal from the outside through the auricle leads into the external auditory meatus, where ear wax is found. The answer is Choice 5.

DATA TABLES

When a series of objects or situations, each having a certain value, is under consideration, a data table is used to make comparison easy. The table is in columns, each column headed by a label that tells what the column contains. If there are numerical data, the column head will also indicate the unit of measure, usually in parentheses. There are no special precautions in reading a data table; just be sure you know what the headings mean.

EXAMPLE

The following table gives the symbols, atomic numbers, and average atomic weights of the most common elements in the Earth's crust. The atomic number is the number of protons in the atom.

Element	Symbol	Atomic Number	Average Atomic Weight (daltons)
Aluminum	Al	13	27.0
Calcium	Ca	20	40.1
Carbon	C	6	12.0
Iron	Fe	26	55.8
Magnesium	Ma	12	24.3
Oxygen	O	8	16.0
Potassium	K	13	39.1
Silicon	Si	14	28.1
Sodium	Na	11	23.0

QUESTION

How many protons are there in a molecule of magnesium oxide (MgO)?

(1) 4
(2) 8
(3) 12
(4) 16
(5) 20

ANSWER AND ANALYSIS

Just add the 12 in magnesium to the 8 in oxygen; the answer is Choice 5.

QUESTION

Which of the following groups is arranged in order of increasing atomic weight?

(1) calcium, iron, potassium
(2) carbon, oxygen, silicon
(3) aluminum, carbon, magnesium
(4) iron, silicon, sodium
(5) oxygen, calcium, silicon

ANSWER AND ANALYSIS

Choice 2 gives carbon, at 12.0 daltons (D); oxygen, at 16.0 D; and silicon at 28.1 D, and is the answer.

OTHERS

There is no limit to the inventiveness of a scientist who sets out to present data. You must expect to meet on the GED Examination an unfamiliar form of graph, table, or diagram. Study it carefully, and make sure you understand the information presented before you tackle the questions based on it.

13

Handling Science Skills Questions

The makers of the GED Examination try to test you for a wide range of skills. You can be asked to do something as simple as restating an idea from the passage, or something as complex as evaluating the scientific validity of an experiment. The questions are generally grouped into four levels of skill.

The Four Skills

It is not worth your while to try to determine to which of the four levels any one question belongs, or to develop special strategies for each of the four levels. In taking the test, this sort of approach would consume valuable time and require you to use a part of your thinking ability that is best reserved for answering questions. Nevertheless, it is a good idea to become familiar with the four levels of skill that are investigated in the test.

COMPREHENSION

Comprehension is the simplest level. What it comes down to is this: Do you understand the passage, graph, or diagram? Can you rephrase some of the information in it? Can you summarize it? Can you identify a simple implication of the information given?

Here are some examples of the simple comprehension type of question:

QUESTION

Elements can be either mixed mechanically to form a mixture, or combined chemically to form a compound. In a mixture, the properties of each of the elements present are recognizable. A mixture is rather like a stew in which the carrots, potatoes, and tomatoes are all identifiable. In a compound, however, the original elements are no longer recognizable as themselves, and another form of matter with its own characteristics has been produced.

Which of the following is NOT a mixture?

(1) iron filings in sawdust
(2) sugar water
(3) vegetable soup
(4) fireplace ash
(5) soda water

ANSWER AND ANALYSIS

If you understood the passage, you know that the components of a mixture remain separate and identifiable, while the components of a compound are changed into a new form of matter. The only answer in which the elements have been completely altered is Choice 4, fireplace ash, the result of burning wood. All of the other substances can be separated into their original parts.

QUESTION

The scientific name of an animal is printed in italic type and has two parts. The first word (capitalized) is the name of the genus to which the animal belongs. The second word (lower case) is the name of its species within the genus. Here are the English and scientific names of five birds:

A. American robin, *Turdus migratorius*
B. European robin, *Erithacus rubecula*
C. European blackbird, *Turdus merula*
D. Military macaw, *Ara militaris*
E. Red-breasted blackbird, *Sturnella militaris*

Of the following pairs, which belong to the same genus?

(1) A and B only
(2) D and E only
(3) B and C only
(4) A and C only
(5) C and E only

ANSWER AND ANALYSIS

Since the passage deals only with scientific names, you can ignore the English names. The first word of the scientific name is the same for two birds in the same genus, so the answer is Choice 4. If you understood the passage, you got the answer.

QUESTION

When you place a solution in a test tube and then spin the test tube very rapidly in a machine called a centrifuge, the materials in the solution will separate, with the heaviest ones on the bottom and the lightest ones on top.

The following diagram represents the result of spinning a suspension of broken cells in a centrifuge. Which is the correct conclusion?

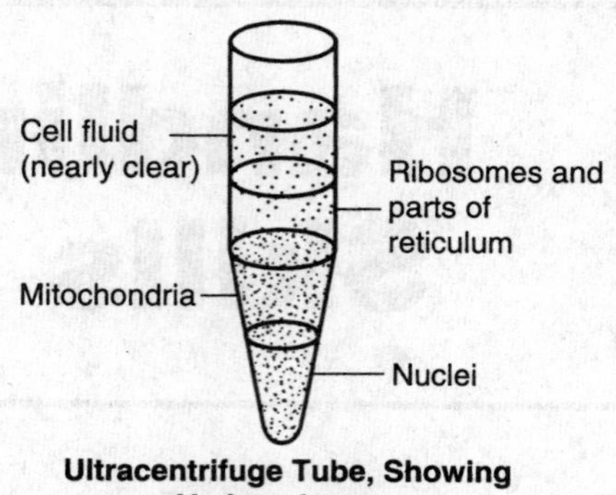

Ultracentrifuge Tube, Showing Various Layers

(1) Ribosomes are more dense than mitochondria.
(2) Nuclei are more dense than mitochondria.
(3) Mitochondria and ribosomes are equal in density.
(4) The cell consists of only solid components.
(5) Nuclei are less dense than mitochondria.

ANSWER AND ANALYSIS

The correct choice is 2 because the most dense particles settle at the bottom after spinning.

QUESTION

The soft body feathers of a bird are useful as insulation, while the stiff feathers of the wings and tail form airfoil surfaces, like those of an airplane wing. If a new species of bird is found that has no stiff feathers, it is safe to assume that it

(1) cannot fly
(2) lives in a tropical country
(3) migrates south in winter
(4) lives mainly in the water
(5) is able to run rapidly

ANSWER AND ANALYSIS

This question calls for you to make a simple deduction. If the stiff feathers are used in flight, a bird without them cannot fly, so the answer is Choice 1.

QUESTION

The table below gives the densities of four kinds of materials found in the Earth:

Substance	Density (g/cm^3)
Water	1.00
Petroleum	0.86
Wood chips	0.75
Sand	2.10

If a mixture of all four materials is placed in a cylinder, shaken, and allowed to stand, the materials will settle out with the most dense on the bottom. What will the cylinder look like?

(1) The sand and wood chips will be mixed together on the bottom, and the water will be on top of the petroleum.
(2) The sand will be on the bottom; above will be the water with the wood chips in the layer between the petroleum and the water.
(3) The wood chips will form a layer above the sand on the bottom, and the water will form a layer over the petroleum.
(4) The sand will be on the bottom; the petroleum will form a layer over the water, with the wood chips floating on top.
(5) The water will be on the bottom, with the wood chips floating on it; the petroleum and sand will be mixed above the water.

ANSWER AND ANALYSIS

The materials, top to bottom must be in the sequence of increasing density—wood chips, petroleum, water, sand—so the answer is Choice 4.

APPLICATION

If you have thoroughly understood the information provided in the passage, graph, diagram, or table, you should be able to apply what you have learned. The application questions ask you to use the general principle contained in the information, but to apply that principle to a different situation.

Here are some examples:

QUESTION

Study the graph below, which shows the percentage distributions of the Earth's surface elevation above, and depth below sea level.

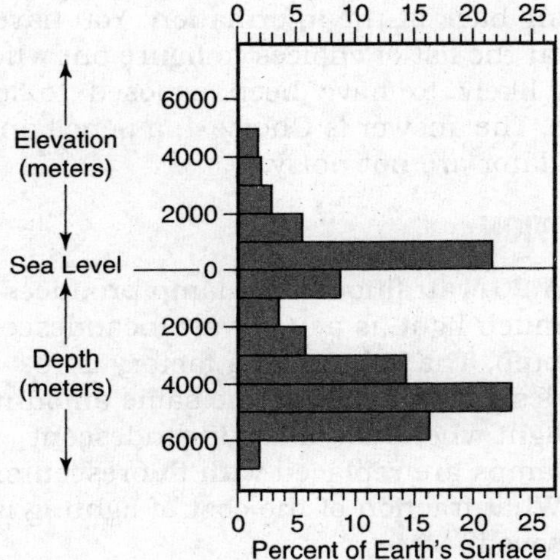

Approximately what total percentage of the Earth's surface is below sea level?

(1) 30%
(2) 50%
(3) 70%
(4) 80%
(5) 90%

ANSWER AND ANALYSIS

There are more shaded bars below than above sea level on the graph. Adding up the lengths of all the shaded bars below sea level yields a total of about 70%. This represents the total percentage of the Earth's surface below sea level. The correct answer is Choice 3.

QUESTION

High-energy sound waves are known to produce long-term damage to the ears, resulting in loss of ability to hear high frequencies. Which of the following individuals is most likely to have good high-frequency hearing after many years of work?

(1) a rock musician
(2) an aircraft mechanic
(3) a riveter
(4) an accountant
(5) a sawmill operator

ANSWER AND ANALYSIS

Again, you cannot get the answer just by looking back at the information. You have to look at the list of choices to figure out who is least likely to have been exposed to loud noise. The answer is Choice 4; a pencil and a calculator are not noisy.

QUESTION

A 20-watt fluorescent lamp produces as much light as a 100-watt incandescent bulb. The lighting in a factory is redesigned to provide the same amount of light when half of the incandescent lamps are replaced with fluorescents. What fraction of the cost of lighting is saved?

(1) 10%
(2) 20%
(3) 25%
(4) 40%
(5) 80%

ANSWER AND ANALYSIS

A complete change to fluorescents would save 80 of every 100 watts. Since only half of the lamps are changed, the saving is half this, 40%; the answer is Choice 4.

QUESTION

When an animal eats another that contains PCB pollutants, the PCB concentrates in the predator's liver. The following food relationships exist in a certain ecosystem:

Big fish eat little fish.
Little fish eat plankton.
Wolves eat otters.
Otters eat big fish.

If the water of a pond contains PCB, which of the following will have the greatest concentration of PCB?

(1) otters
(2) wolves
(3) big fish
(4) plankton
(5) little fish

ANSWER AND ANALYSIS

The concentration of PCB must increase in the sequence plankton, little fish, big fish, otters, wolves, so the answer is Choice 2.

QUESTIONS

Many foods, such as bread, potatoes, and spaghetti, contain a great deal of starch. An enzyme in saliva slowly changes starch to sugar. Which of the following statements is most probably true?

(1) A piece of bread held in the mouth for a long time becomes sweet.
(2) Spaghetti in the mouth causes an increase in the flow of saliva.
(3) If you eat a potato, the enzyme is in your saliva.
(4) If you eat sugar, it can turn to starch in the mouth.
(5) A cookie tastes sweet because it contains starch.

ANSWER AND ANALYSIS

If the saliva in the mouth changes the starch in the bread to sugar, you might expect that the bread would begin to taste sweet. Choice 1 is correct. None of the other choices is suggested by the information given.

ANALYSIS

These questions are more complicated. To answer them, you will have to find the relationships among several different items of information. Some of these items will not be given; you will be expected to know things that are general knowledge. It is possible to identify five somewhat different kinds of skills that belong to the general category of analysis:

- Recognizing unstated assumptions
- Using several related pieces of information
- Distinguishing fact from opinion
- Distinguishing cause from effect
- Drawing conclusions from data

Here are some examples of questions requiring analysis:

QUESTION

A doctor discovers that a patient has blood pressure of 170/110. He tells the patient that medication, accompanied by a reducing diet and limited exercise, will bring the blood pressure down. What has the doctor assumed without actually stating it?

(1) Blood pressure of 170/110 is dangerous to the health of the patient.
(2) Medication can bring down blood pressure.
(3) Medication will reduce the patient's weight.
(4) The patient has not been exercising at all.
(5) Blood pressure varies greatly in the population at large.

ANSWER AND ANALYSIS

Surely the doctor would not bother with the problem if he did not assume that the patient's blood pressure is too high for continued good health, so the answer is Choice 1. Choice 2 is true, but it is not unstated; the doctor told the patient that medication would work. Since there is no reason to believe that the medication is used for weight reduction, Choice 3 is wrong. Choice 4 is wrong because the prescription for limited exercise might just as easily mean that the patient has been exercising too much. Choice 5 is true, but irrelevant.

If you are asked to find an unstated assumption, do *not* select one that is (a) stated in the information given; (b) untrue; (c) ambiguous; or (d) irrelevant.

QUESTION

Corals are tiny animals that obtain their energy from their close association with green algae. Fish that eat corals do not live in deep water because

(1) the pressure is too great in deep water
(2) the fish that live in deep water eat them
(3) sunlight does not penetrate into deep water
(4) there are no currents in deep water to carry nutrients to them
(5) it is too cold in deep water

ANSWER AND ANALYSIS

This is one of the questions in which you are expected to know a few facts and to put some ideas together. You should know that green algae need sunlight to grow, and that corals use energy for growth. The answer is Choice 3. Some of the other answers may be true, but they are irrelevant.

QUESTION

Someone sees a high waterfall on the side of a cliff and comments about it. Which of the following comments is probably based on opinion rather than fact?

(1) The waterfall is about 30 meters high.
(2) The valley into which it falls was carved by a glacier.
(3) The rock in the mountain is a form of granite.
(4) The speed of the water at the bottom of the fall is about 25 meters per second.
(5) A photograph of the fall would be really beautiful.

ANSWER AND ANALYSIS

"Based on fact" is not the same as "factual." A statement is probably based on fact if it can be derived from one or more facts. Choices 1 and 4 could be determined by measurement or calculation—facts. Choices 2 and 3 could be determined from facts by any competent geologist. Since beauty is in the eye of the beholder, Choice 5 is an opinion.

QUESTION

It is found that, when a stream becomes more muddy, the population of catfish increases. Three possible explanations are offered:

A. More catfish tend to make the water muddy.
B. Catfish thrive on invertebrates that live in mud.
C. Other fish cannot live in muddy water, so catfish have less competition.

Which of these explanations is (are) feasible?

(1) A only
(2) B only
(3) C only
(4) A and B only
(5) B and C only

ANSWER AND ANALYSIS

This question requires you to tell the difference between cause and effect. Is it possible that explanation A is true? No; the water became muddy before the catfish population increased, and a cause can never come after its effect. In both explanation B and explanation C, the water is already muddy, and both are reasonable hypotheses, so the answer is Choice 5.

This type of question can be tricky. If one event follows another, the one that occurs first may or may not be the cause of the second, even if the second invariably follows the first. The crowing of the rooster does not make the sun rise. In the example given, the sequence of the two events stated in the question establishes only that B and C are possible explanations, not that they must necessarily be true.

QUESTION

A chemical factory manufacturing a detergent discovers that its product contains a material that is considered a biohazard. Of the following, which can be considered a conclusion based on data?

(1) The amount of reactant *A* is twice as great as that of reactant *B*.
(2) The temperature of the reaction is 140°C.
(3) The pH of the reaction mixture is 5.4.
(4) The problem can be solved by adding an alkali.
(5) There is a contaminant in reactant *A*.

ANSWER AND ANALYSIS

Fact or conclusion? All the statements except Choice 4 are data, testable and presumably confirmed by measurement. Putting all the known facts together, the engineer might use his knowledge of the process to obtain an overall picture of what is happening. He can then draw the conclusion in Choice 4.

A conclusion is a general statement that is not obtained from direct observation. It comes from intelligent application of known principles to measurement data.

EVALUATION

We all have our own beliefs and ideas, and most of our beliefs and general thought processes are not scientific. But then, this is how it should be. Science cannot tell you what career to choose or whom to marry, or whether to go to church on Sunday, or who to vote for, or what kind of music to listen to. What science can do, however, is provide highly reliable and accurate answers to questions.

On the GED Examination, evaluation questions test your ability to apply the rules of scientific analysis to questions. Before you can do this, though, you need to understand a little about some of the many different kinds of statements that you will encounter.

FACT OR DATUM

A fact (datum) is something that can be observed and proved to be true.

EXAMPLE

If you measure a piece of wood and it is precisely 8 feet long, you have established a fact. If, however, someone estimates and tells you that the piece is 8 feet long even though it has not been measured, then you have an estimation, not a fact. Another kind of statement is an opinion, as when someone remarks that the piece of wood is an attractive color. Again, you do not have a fact.

You may be asked to determine whether a statement is a valid fact. Sloppy techniques can produce a statement that looks like a fact, but which cannot be supported by evidence or by the experimental process. You will need to be able to identify such statements.

HYPOTHESIS

A hypothesis is an educated guess, the possible answer to a question. It is a purely tentative statement that may be modified or even disproved when more information becomes available.

EXAMPLE

If you find that a type-A shrub in the sunlight grows better than another type-A shrub in the shade, you might propose the hypothesis that type-A shrubs need sunlight for optimum growth. This hypothesis can be tested by a controlled experiment. The most common mistake that people make is to accept a hypothesis as a fact without realizing the need for an experiment to provide proof.

You may have to distinguish between a fact and a hypothesis.

CONCLUSION

A conclusion may be the result of a controlled experiment. A hypothesis becomes a conclusion when you have tested and verified the initial statement.

EXAMPLE

If the type-A shrub really does grow better in the sunlight during a carefully designed experiment, then it is a reasonable conclusion that this particular plant should be grown in the sun.

You may be asked whether it is reasonable to draw a certain conclusion from a given set of data. You will have to be able to distinguish between a hypothesis and a conclusion.

GENERALIZATION

A generalization is a conclusion that can apply to a wide variety of situations.

EXAMPLE

Many experiments with green plants have indicated that all of them, whether a tiny alga cell or an enormous redwood tree, need some sunlight in order to live.

If you are asked whether a certain generalization is reasonable, look to see if it applies to many situations.

VALUE JUDGMENT

A value judgment is an opinion based on cultural or emotional factors rather than on scientific evidence. Opinions have an important place in our lives, but they cannot be allowed to affect the process of arriving at a scientific conclusion.

EXAMPLE

A certain landowner decided that he should kill every snake on his property because he didn't like snakes. He also killed squirrels and chipmunks for the same reason—he didn't like them.

You will be asked to distinguish value judgments from scientifically valid statements.

LOGICAL FALLACY

A fallacy is a wrong conclusion that results when you use information incorrectly. The most common logical fallacy goes by the imposing name *post hoc ergo propter hoc*, which means "followed by, therefore caused by."

EXAMPLE

I drink a glass of milk for breakfast every morning, and I always get sleepy. Does the milk make me sleepy? Maybe. Or maybe I would become sleepy even if I didn't drink the milk. The way to avoid this kind of fallacy is to perform a controlled experiment and test the possible relationship.

The examples below will give you some idea of the sorts of questions that will test your ability to evaluate scientific statements.

QUESTION

A proposal to build a dam on a river is opposed by a group of citizens, offering various reasons. Which of the following reasons is based on a value judgment rather than scientific information?

(1) The river should be preserved because it is a habitat for much beautiful wildlife.
(2) The cost of the dam will be too high for the amount of electricity it produces.
(3) It is not possible to dam the river at the site selected because of the surface features of the land.
(4) The proposed site is on a fault, and the dam could be destroyed by an earthquake.
(5) The river carries so much silt that the lake formed by it would soon fill up and render the dam useless.

ANSWER AND ANALYSIS

The word *beautiful* in Choice 1 is a giveaway, specifying a value judgment. Whoever makes that argument sees an esthetic value in the preservation of wildlife. All the other objections are based on arguments that can be subjected to rigid testing, using established scientific principles.

QUESTION

The following graph shows the average growths of two groups of rats. The solid line represents a group raised under standard conditions by a supplier of laboratory animals; the dashed line, a group raised in a laboratory and treated with pituitary extract.

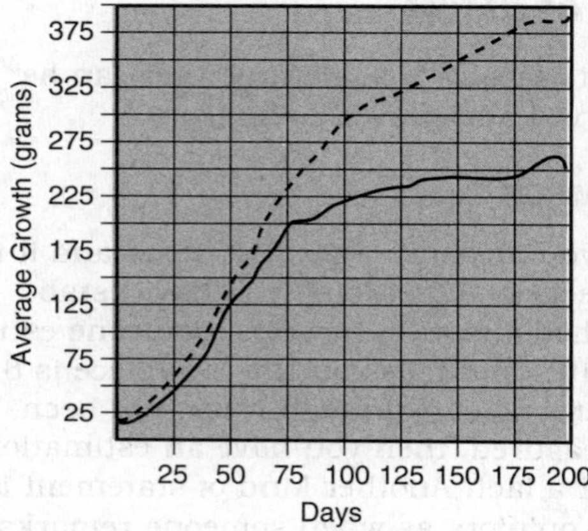

What is a proper conclusion from the experiment?

(1) It is known that pituitary extract stimulates growth, and the experiment confirms it.
(2) The difference between the control group and the experimental group is so clear that it can be concluded that pituitary extract stimulates growth.
(3) The growths of the two groups are too similar to show that there is any difference in average growth.
(4) The experiment is useless because there is no reason to believe that the same result would be obtained with human beings.
(5) The experiment is inconclusive because there was no attempt to control the heredity of the animals or the conditions of their nurture.

ANSWER AND ANALYSIS

Whether an experiment should have some obvious use is a value judgment that is not at issue here, so Choice 4 is wrong. Choice 1 is wrong because it suggests that the outcome of the experiment was prejudiced in advance. At first this looks like a nice, neat experiment; the difference in growth is marked, and so Choice 3 is wrong. However, Choice 2 is wrong because the controls are inadequate. The rats were not necessarily of the same breed, nor were they raised in the same place. They could differ also in their hereditary endowments, their feeding, and any number of other factors. The results of this experiment could lead to a hypothesis, but not a conclusion, so the answer is Choice 5.

QUESTION

Over the last hundred years, people have been burning more and more fossil fuel, which releases carbon dioxide into the atmosphere. This excess CO_2 is a cause of global warming, which, according to ecologists, is one of the most serious problems facing us today. Carbon dioxide in the upper atmosphere traps the Sun's heat, in much the same way that the panes of glass hold heat in a greenhouse.

Which graph best represents what most likely happens to the temperature of the Earth's atmosphere as the amount of carbon dioxide in the atmosphere increases over a period of many years?

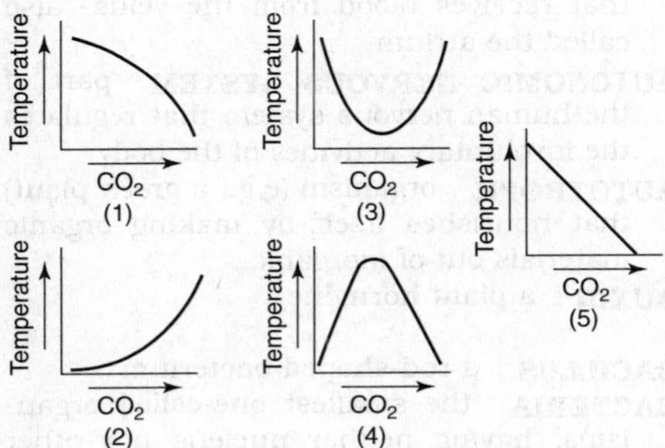

ANSWER AND ANALYSIS

Graph (2) shows that, as the amount of carbon dioxide increases, the average temperature of the atmosphere also increases.

QUESTION

Which of the following advertising claims for a toothpaste cannot be confirmed or contradicted by laboratory tests?

(1) It contains 2% stannous fluoride.
(2) It removes plaque.
(3) It has a fresh taste.
(4) It is not abrasive.
(5) It prevents cavities.

ANSWER AND ANALYSIS

Taste is a highly subjective value judgment, and what is a fresh taste for one person may be revolting to another, so the answer is Choice 3.

QUESTION

A field biologist finds that for three successive winters the beavers in a pond were unusually active and the water in the pond was exceptionally high in the following spring.

Which of the following is an appropriate response?

(1) She concludes that the winter activity of the beavers raises the water level.
(2) She decides to see what happens to the water level in years in which the beavers are less active.
(3) She suggests the possibility that the high water level makes the beavers more active.
(4) She proposes limiting the winter activity of the beavers so as to avoid flooding.
(5) She suggests that there is no connection between the water level and the activity of the beavers.

ANSWER AND ANALYSIS

Choice 1 is wrong because the evidence is insufficient for a conclusion; the fact that the rising water level followed the activity does not prove a cause-and-effect relationship. Choice 3 is wrong because an effect can never come before a cause. Choice 4 is wrong because there has been no suggestion that flooding is a problem, or that limiting the activity of the beavers will prevent it. Choice 5 is wrong because the evidence is sufficient to suggest the hypothesis that winter activity of beavers raises the water level. More investigation is called for, and Choice 2 is a good idea.

Glossary of Scientific Terms

In your preparation for the Science test you may on occasion find a term, an expression, or a reference that is not familiar to you. This handy glossary may save you trips to another source of reference. On some occasions your idea of a term may be hazy; you may have known the meaning of it well in the past but have now forgotten. Make it a habit to turn to this glossary to locate clear, succinct definitions. Some students have also used the glossary as a tool for checking up on science information. Your science background will greatly improve if you can find time to develop this habit.

ABIOGENESIS belief that living things may develop from lifeless matter

ACID a compound that dissociates in water to produce hydrogen ions; usually tastes sour

ACID RAIN rain with an excessively acidic composition that has a bad effect on fish and other animal and plant life

ALLOY substance composed of two or more metals (e.g., bronze)

AMOEBA a type of protozoan that has no permanent shape

AMORPHOUS without definite shape

AMPLITUDE the maximum value of a wave or vibration

ANAEROBIC RESPIRATION fermentation, or respiration in the absence of oxygen

ANEMIA condition in which the blood has insufficient red blood cells

ANODE positive electrode of an electrolytic cell; positive terminal of a battery; plate of a vacuum tube

ANTIBIOTIC substance made by a microorganism that destroys germs

ANTIBODY a substance, usually in the blood of an organism, that serves to counteract the effects of disease-producing bacteria

ANTIDOTE a substance used to counteract the effects of poison

ANTISEPTIC a substance that prevents the growth or activity of germs

ANTITOXIN substance in the body that neutralizes toxins

APPENDIX wormlike, narrow part of the alimentary canal, in the lower right-hand part of the human abdomen

ARMATURE a piece of metal or a coil of wire that moves back and forth, or rotates, in a magnetic field

ARTERY a muscular vessel carrying blood away from the heart to the periphery of the body

ARTHROPODS the phylum consisting of animals with nonliving external skeletons and jointed appendages; insects, spiders, crustaceans

ASCORBIC ACID vitamin C; found in citrus fruits, tomatoes, and green vegetables

ASEPTIC free of live germs

ASEXUAL REPRODUCTION producing offspring without union of individuals or germ cells

ASSIMILATION process by which digested food is utilized by the body to build up or repair cells

ASTEROID one of a group of "minor planets" between Mars and Jupiter, of which about 1,500 are known

ATMOSPHERE the whole mass of air surrounding the Earth

ATOM smallest unit of an element, consisting of a nucleus surrounded by electrons

ATOMIC FISSION the breaking down of an atomic nucleus, into two or more parts, with a great release of energy

ATOMIC FUSION the joining of atomic nuclei to form heavier nuclei, such as deuterium (heavy hydrogen) and tritium (another form of heavy hydrogen) to make helium, resulting in the release of enormous quantities of energy

AURICLE an upper chamber of the heart that receives blood from the veins—also called the atrium

AUTONOMIC NERVOUS SYSTEM part of the human nervous system that regulates the involuntary activities of the body

AUTOTROPH organism (e.g., a green plant) that nourishes itself by making organic materials out of inorganic

AUXIN a plant hormone

BACILLUS a rod-shaped bacterium

BACTERIA the smallest one-celled organisms, having neither nucleus nor other organelles

BALANCE IN NATURE the interdependence of all plants and animals with their environment

BAROMETER an instrument that measures air pressure

BASAL METABOLISM the rate at which the body's activities are carried on when the body is at rest

BASE chemical compound that produces a salt when it reacts with an acid; an alkali

BEDROCK the solid surface of the Earth's crust, often overlaid by soil or sediments

BENIGN TUMOR a growth that, although abnormal, does not spread and does no particular harm unless it presses a vital organ

BILE a fluid that is secreted by the liver and passes into the small intestine, where it aids in the digestion of fats

BINOMIAL NOMENCLATURE double name used to identify a living organism by genus and species

BIOME a community of plants and animals

BIOPSY the removal of a small part of living tissue for microscopic examination to see whether it is malignant

BRAIN main center of the human nervous system, consisting of cerebrum, cerebellum, and medulla

BRONCHIAL TUBE one of the two branches of the windpipe

CALORIE a unit of measure of heat or other forms of energy

CANCER an abnormal growth that, if not detected early and removed or destroyed, will usually, in time, spread widely throughout the body and ultimately cause death

CAPACITOR device that stores electric charge

CAPILLARY a thin-walled tube; one of the tiny blood vessels in the network connecting the arteries and the veins

CARBOHYDRATE a compound consisting of carbon, hydrogen, and oxygen (e.g., starch, sugar)

CARBON DIOXIDE colorless, odorless gas present in the air in small amounts; breathed out from the lungs

CARBON MONOXIDE poisonous gas that prevents oxygen from entering the red blood cells; produced when gasoline is not completely burned

CARCINOMA cancerous growth

CARNIVORE a flesh-eating mammal with long eyeteeth and sharp claws (e.g, cat, lion, dog)

CARTILAGE an elastic, yet hard, tissue composing most of the skeleton of the very young of all vertebrates and the breastbone of adults

CATALYST a substance that affects the rate of a chemical reaction without any change in itself

CATHODE negative electrode of an electrolytic cell; negative terminal of a battery; electron source in a vacuum tube

CELL basic unit of plant and animal life, consisting of a small mass of protoplasm, including a nucleus, surrounded by a semipermeable membrane

CELL MEMBRANE the thin outer layer of cytoplasm acting as a cell boundary

CELLULOSE a complex carbohydrate found in the wall of plant cells

CELL WALL the nonliving, rigid wall surrounding the cells of plants, algae, fungi, and bacteria

CELSIUS temperature scale on which 0° is the freezing point of water and 100° is the boiling point; this term has replaced "centigrade"

CHEMOTHERAPY treatment of illness by the use of chemicals (drugs)

CHITIN material forming the exoskeleton of anthropods

CHLOROPHYLL a green substance that enables green plants to make glucose by the process of photosynthesis

CHLOROPLAST a small green body that contains chlorophyll

CHOLESTEROL crystalline fatty substance found in animal fats

CHROMOSOME one of several small, more or less rod-shaped bodies in the nucleus of a cell; contains the hereditary factors (genes)

CLAY finely ground quartz, feldspar, and mica resulting from the erosion of rocks

CLIMATE a composite of weather conditions over a long period of time

COMET heavenly body having a head and tail and traveling in a long, oval orbit around the Sun

COMPOUND substance composed of two or more chemically united elements

CONDENSATION process by which a liquid or solid is formed from a vapor or gas

CONDUCTOR a material (e.g., copper wire) that carries a flow of electrons (electricity)

CONGLOMERATE sedimentary rock made up of a mixture of rounded fragments cemented together by natural substances such as clay

CONSERVATION wise and careful use of natural resources

CONSTELLATION any of the groups of stars and the area of the sky in the group's vicinity to which a definite name has been given (e.g., Ursa Major, the Great Bear)

CORNEA transparent tissue in front of the iris and the pupil of the eye

CORONARY pertaining to the blood vessels of the heart muscle

CORPUSCLE red or white cell in the blood

CORROSION the wearing away of a metal by chemical action, such as oxidation

CYCLONE storm or system of winds blowing counterclockwise about a nearly circular region of low air pressure in the Northern Hemisphere and extending over an area covering thousands of square miles

CYCLOTRON instrument used to study the properties of atoms by increasing the speed of atomic particles

CYTOPLASM that part of the cell that lies outside the nucleus; carries on all life activities except reproduction

DECIBEL unit for measuring the relative loudness of a sound

DECIDUOUS vegetation that regularly loses its leaves with the change in seasons

DEHYDRATION loss of water

DEOXYRIBONUCLEIC ACID (DNA) nucleic acid that controls the metabolism of the cell and stores the hereditary information of the cell

DESALINATION removal of salt from a solution, as in the purification of seawater

DIABETES a disease in which the body cannot utilize sugar because of lack of insulin

DIAPHRAGM a sheet of muscle that separates the chest cavity from the abdomen and by its movement helps in breathing; also, the vibrating disk of metal in a telephone

DIFFUSION the process whereby the molecules of substances tend to intermingle, as when two gasses or solutions are brought into contact

DIGESTION a process of chemical change that prepares food for absorption by breaking down complex molecules into simpler ones

DISINFECTANT a chemical that kills microbes

DISTILLATION the process of heating a substance until it turns into a gas and then condensing this gas by cooling

EBB TIDE outgoing tide

ECHO a reflected sound wave

ECLIPSE cutting off of light from one celestial body by another

ECOLOGY study of the relationships of living things with each other and with their environment

ELECTRIC CURRENT flow of electric charge (e.g., electrons in a wire, ions in a solution)

ELECTROLYSIS chemical breakdown of a compound due to the passage of an electric current through it

ELEMENT a chemical substance made up of one kind of atom; cannot be decomposed by ordinary means (e.g., hydrogen, sodium)

EMBRYO organism in an early stage of development

EMULSIFIER a substance (e.g., soap) that can break large fat droplets into many smaller droplets suspended in water

ENZYME organic substance that speeds up the reaction of chemicals without change to itself

EROSION wearing away of the Earth's surface by water, ice, and winds

ESOPHAGUS (gullet) tube that connects the mouth with the stomach

ESTROGEN female hormone secreted by the ovaries

EVAPORATION escape of molecules from the surface of liquids or solids

EVOLUTION the process by which living things change into other kinds through the generations

EXCRETION elimination of the wastes of metabolism: carbon dioxide and water

FALLOUT radioactive particles that fall to Earth as the result of an atomic or hydrogen bomb explosion

FARSIGHTEDNESS defect of the eye in which sharper images of objects at a distance are formed than of things nearby

FATTY ACID organic substance whose molecule is a long hydrocarbon chain with a carboxyl group at the end; component of molecules of fats and oils

FAUNA animal life typical of a particular region

FERMENTATION chemical change brought about by enzymes produced by microbes; in the making of beer or wine, yeasts ferment sugars into alcohol and carbon dioxide

FERTILIZATION process that occurs in sexual reproduction when the gametes, a sperm and an egg, unite

FILAMENT fine wire inside an electric light bulb that gives off light and heat when electricity is passed through it

FISSION splitting of the nucleus of an atom with the release of tremendous amounts of energy

FJORD a narrow inlet of the sea between cliffs or steep slopes

FOG a cloud of condensed water vapor formed on or near the ground

FOOD CHAIN pathway of energy through an ecosystem from producers to consumers

FOOD WEB complex feeding relationships within a biological community

FOSSIL remains or impression, in rock or amber, of a plant or animal that lived long ago

FOSSIL FUEL remains of organisms that lived hundreds of millions of years ago; used to release energy on burning (e.g., coal, oil, natural gas)

FRATERNAL TWIN one of two individuals that result from the fertilization of two ova simultaneously by two different sperm

FUNGUS kingdom of plantlike organisms that lack chlorophyll and therefore cannot make their own food

FUSION atomic reaction in which the nuclei of atoms combine and energy is released

GALAXY a large group of billions of stars

GALLBLADDER sac attached to the liver that stores bile

GAMETE one of the two cells that unite in sexual reproduction (e.g., egg or sperm)

GAS phase of matter in which the substance spreads out to fill all the space in its container

GASOHOL a motor fuel that consists of nine parts gasoline and one part ethanol

GASTRIC JUICE acid digestive fluid produced by the glands in the walls of the stomach

GENE a part of a DNA molecule that controls the manufacture of a specific protein. Since it is copied and passed on in every cell division, it forms the unit of heredity

GEOTHERMAL ENERGY great amounts of heat produced in the Earth's interior

GESTATION the period of time necessary for embryo development; pregnancy

GLUCOSE a simple, soluble sugar oxidized in the body to give energy

GROUND WATER water that saturates the soil, filling all the space between particles

HALF-LIFE time required for half of any sample of a radioactive material to undergo transformation into something else

HARD WATER water containing a large quantity of dissolved mineral salts

HEMOGLOBIN an iron-rich chemical, found in the red blood cells, which unites with oxygen

HEMOPHILIA physical condition in which blood fails to clot properly; inherited by sons from mothers who are carriers

HEREDITARY the tendency of offspring to resemble parents due to the passage of genes in the reproduction process

HETEROTROPH organism that cannot synthesize food from inorganic material

HIBERNATION torpid or resting state of an organism throughout some or all of the winter season

HOMEOSTASIS maintenance of a stable internal environment in an organism

HOMOGENIZE to distribute the solute in a solution to form a permanent emulsion

HOMO SAPIENS scientific name for a human being

HORMONE chemical messenger, produced by an endocrine gland, that helps to control and coordinate the activities of the body (e.g., insulin)

HORSEPOWER a unit for measuring the rate of work, equal to 550 foot-pounds per second

HUMIDITY amount of water vapor in the air

HUMUS dead and decaying organic matter found in the soil

HURRICANE a tropical cyclone with winds of at least 74 miles per hour

HYBRID a cross between species; an organism with dissimilar genes for a trait

HYDROCARBON compound containing only hydrogen and carbon atoms

HYDROELECTRIC referring to the generation of electric energy from falling water

HYDROGEN BOMB a bomb consisting of deuterium and tritium (forms of heavy hydrogen), which are fused into helium, releasing a great deal of energy

HYDROPONICS soilless growth of plants

HYPOTHESIS assumption made as a basis for further investigation or research

IDENTICAL TWIN one of two individuals that result from the division of a single fertilized egg

IMMUNITY ability of the body to resist or overcome infection

INERTIA property by which a body at rest remains at rest or a body in motion remains in motion

INFECTIOUS DISEASE illness caused by microorganisms

INGESTION taking in of food

INHALATION phase of breathing in which air is drawn into the lungs

INSTINCT complex inborn pattern of involuntary responses

INSULATION material used to reduce the transfer of heat or to shield a conductor of electricity

INSULIN hormone secreted by the pancreas that enables cells to use glucose

INTERNAL-COMBUSTION ENGINE an engine in which the fuel is burned inside the cylinders

INTESTINE a section of the digestive system below the stomach in which digestion and absorption of substances take place

INVERTEBRATE animal without a backbone

IONOSPHERE the part of the atmosphere 40–300 miles above the Earth

IRIS muscular, colored part of the eye, surrounding the pupil

IRRIGATION supplying of land with water by means of canals and ditches

JET STREAM swift, high-altitude wind at a height of about 35,000 feet

KIDNEY one of a pair of bean-shaped organs in the back part of the abdomen that collect the wastes of metabolism from the blood

KILOMETER unit of distance, equal to about 5/8 mile

KINETIC ENERGY energy possessed by an object because of its motion, depending on its mass and velocity

LACTATION secretion of milk by the mammary glands

LAGOON shallow body of water near or communicating with a larger body of water

LARVA young, usually wormlike stage of an invertebrate

LARYNX the voice box, located in the upper part of the windpipe, in which the vocal cords are found

LASER device in which atoms, when stimulated by focused lightwaves, amplify and condense these waves and then emit them in a narrow, intense beam

LATEX a milky substance from which rubber is made

LATITUDE the distance due north or south from the Equator, measured in degrees and marked by an imaginary line parallel to the equator

LAVA liquid rock material that flows out on the surface of the earth from underground sources

LEGUME a member of the pea family: peas, beans, clover, alfalfa; roots contain nodules with nitrogen-fixing bacteria

LEUKEMIA a disease of the blood-forming organs: bone, lymph glands, spleen, etc.; characterized by uncontrolled multiplication of white blood cells

LEVER a rigid rod turning around a fulcrum to increase the force or distance moved of the work input

LICHEN a complex organism composed of a fungus and an alga in intimate connection, able to live in highly unfavorable conditions

LIGAMENT tissue joining two or more bones

LIGHT-YEAR distance that light, traveling at about 186,000 miles each second, travels in one year

LIMESTONE a type of sedimentary rock, rich in calcium carbonate, that yields lime when burned

LIPID a fat, oil, or wax

LIVER largest gland in the body; makes bile, stores extra sugar as glycogen

LOAM ordinary garden soil; a loose soil made up mainly of clay and sand and a small amount of humus

LODESTONE natural rock magnet occurring in the Earth

LONGITUDE distance on the Earth's surface measured in degrees east or west of the Greenwich meridian

LUNAR ECLIPSE an eclipse that occurs when the full Moon crosses the plane of the Earth's umbra

LYMPH a nearly colorless liquid containing proteins, found in the lymphatic vessels of the body

LYMPHOCYTE type of white blood cell involved in immunity

MAGGOT larva of a fly
MAGMA molten material from which igneous rocks are derived
MALARIA a disease of the blood caused by a protozoan and transmitted by the female *Anopheles* mosquito
MALIGNANT TUMOR a cancerous growth
MAMMAL a vertebrate that suckles its young
MARINE referring to saltwater environments
MARSUPIAL mammal whose young continue development in a pouch after birth
MATTER substance that occupies space
MEMBRANE a thin sheet of tissue; also the outer edge of the cytoplasm of a living cell
METABOLISM sum total of all chemical activity in an organism
METAMORPHOSIS the change from larval to adult form, as in insect and amphibian development
METEOR streak of light in the sky caused by the burning of a meteroid as it enters the Earth's atmosphere
METEOROID a small stony or metallic body in outer space
METEORITE a meteroid that strikes the Earth's surface
METER a unit of length in the metric system, equal to 39.37 inches
MINERAL chemical element or compound occurring free or found in rocks
MIXTURE two or more substances mixed together in no definite proportions and not chemically united
MOLD a filamentous fungus
MOLECULE smallest unit, composed of one or more atoms, of any pure chemical substance
MOLLUSK a soft-bodied invertebrate; usually has a shell outside the body (e.g., snail, octopus, clam)
MOLTING the process by which an animal sheds its shell, skin, feathers, or other outer covering and grows a new one

NATURAL IMMUNITY resistance to disease produced without medical intervention, as by exposure to the causative organism or by passage of antibodies from mother to offspring
NATURAL SELECTION survival of organisms that are best adjusted to the conditions in which they live
NEARSIGHTEDNESS a defect of the eye in which sharper images of things nearby are formed than of things at a distance
NERVE bundle of nerve fibers held together by connective tissue
NIGHT BLINDNESS a condition in which a person does not see well in dim light, sometimes due to a deficiency of vitamin A
NOVA a star that suddenly becomes brighter than normal and then fades again
NUCLEAR FISSION breakup of a nucleus of an atom into two or more smaller nuclei
NUCLEAR FUSION joining of two or more atomic nuclei
NUCLEAR REACTOR device for splitting an atom in order to produce useful energy or valuable radioactive materials
NUCLEUS (BIOLOGY) specialized chromosome-containing portion of the protoplasm of cells; coordinates cell activities
NUCLEUS (PHYSICAL SCIENCE) positively charged, dense part of an atom
NUTRIENT one of a group of substances in food used to nourish and repair body tissue

OPTIC NERVE nerve that carries impulses from the eye to the brain
ORE rock from which one or more minerals can be extracted
ORGAN group of tissues performing a special function in a plant or an animal
ORGANIC COMPOUND compound containing carbon and hydrogen
ORGANISM any individual living animal or plant
OXIDATION union of oxygen with some other substance; reaction involving the loss of electrons from an atom
OXYGEN colorless, odorless gas that makes up 20% of the air; needed by cells to burn food for energy
OZONE a form of oxygen (O_3), usually formed by an electrical charge

PALEONTOLOGY the study of fossils
PANCREAS a dual gland, near the beginning of the small intestine, that makes the pancreatic juice; also produces the hormone insulin in the cells of the islets of Langerhans
PARASITE animal or plant that obtains its food by living inside or on another living thing (e.g., tapeworm, hookworm, louse, ringworm, many harmful bacteria)
PASTEURIZATION process of heating to kill pathogenic microorganisms
PATHOGEN organism that causes an infectious or parasitic disease

PAYLOAD the contents of an earth satellite or rocket useful in gathering information

PENICILLIN antibiotic obtained from a type of mold; used effectively in the treatment of many diseases, such as pneumonia

PETRIFIED referring to plant or animal remains that have become like stone

PHARYNX (THROAT) common passageway for air and food

PHOSPHORESCENCE capacity of a substance to emit visible light when stimulated by electrons

PHOTON particle of light

PHOTOSYNTHESIS process by which, in the presence of light, a green plant makes sugar from water and carbon dioxide

PLACENTA structure by which the young are nourished in the body of a mammal

PLANET one of the nine bodies circling the Sun (e.g., Earth, Mars)

PLANETOID one of the many small bodies between the orbits of the planets Mars and Jupiter

PLANKTON minute floating organisms that live at the surface of the ocean and serve as food for large animals

PLASMA the liquid part of the blood; contains antibodies, hormones, and digested foods

PLASTIC synthetic substance capable of being molded (e.g., cellophane)

POLIO a virus disease that injures the nerve cells in the brain or spinal cord; may result in paralysis of the diaphragm or other muscles

POLLINATION transfer of pollen from the stamen of a flower to a pistil

POLLUTANT substance that contaminates air, water, or soil

POLLUTION accumulation of harmful substances in air, soil, or water

POLYMER giant molecule formed when smaller molecules join together

PRECIPITATION all forms of moisture falling from the sky: hail, snow, rain, and sleet

PREVAILING WIND wind that almost always blows from one direction

PRIMARY LIGHT COLOR one of a group of three colors, usually red, green, and blue, that can be combined to produce all the colors visible to the human eye

PRIMATES order of mammals that includes lemurs, monkeys, apes, and humans

PROGESTRONE hormone produced by the ovaries that regulates the menstrual cycle and the uterus during pregnancy

PROTEIN one of a group of nitrogen-containing organic compounds of large molecular size; important constituent of protoplasm

PROTON positively charged particle found in the nuclei of all atoms

PROTOPLASM all the living substance of a cell

PSYCHIATRIST medical doctor who specializes in mental illness

PSYCHOLOGY the study of behavior and learning

PTOMAINE poisonous substance formed by the action of certain bacteria

PULLEY a wheel with a grooved rim, used with a rope or chain to change direction of a pulling force; simple machine

PULSE beat of an artery, produced by the surging of blood out of the heart

PUS yellowish white matter consisting of dead tissue, white blood cells, and bacteria, present in an abscess or boil

QUARANTINE isolation of an individual carrying a contagious disease

QUININE drug used to prevent and treat malaria

RABIES (HYDROPHOBIA) a dangerous disease of the nervous system caused by a virus; transmitted in the saliva when an infected dog, fox, or similar animal bites a victim

RADAR acronym for ra̲dio d̲etection a̲nd r̲anging; device used for the detection of objects by radio waves

RADIANT ENERGY energy in the form of light or other kinds of radiation

RADIANT HEATING a heating system in which hot water or steam pipes set in floors or walls send out heat into rooms

RADIATION process by which energy is transferred in space

RADIOACTIVITY property of large atomic nuclei that are unstable and break down spontaneously, emitting particles and radiation

RECYCLE to save and return material so that it can be used again

REFLEX an inborn, immediate response to a stimulus, made without thinking

REFRIGERANT a liquid (e.g., ammonia) that evaporates easily and therefore is useful in the cooling coils of a refrigerator

REGENERATION regrowth of lost body parts

RELATIVE HUMIDITY ratio of the amount of water vapor actually present in the air to the greatest amount that would be possible at a given temperature

Rh FACTOR a blood protein present in most people; incompatible Rh factors from the parents cause damage to the blood of newborns

ROTATING CROPS farming method in which different plants are sown in the same soil in succeeding years

ROUGHAGE coarse, fibrous food (e.g., bran) that adds bulk to the diet and prevents constipation

RUNOFF surface water that runs to the sea without entering the underground water supply

RUST a fungus related to the smuts; different forms cause plant diseases, such as wheat rust

SALINITY degree of saltiness

SALIVA a secretion produced by three pairs of glands near the tongue; contains an enzyme that changes starch into sugar

SALT a compound composed of a positive (metallic) ion and a negative ion other than OH^-

SATELLITE natural or artificial body circling the Earth or another planet

SCURVY a disease characterized by weakness of the capillaries, caused by vitamin C deficiency

SEED a developed ovule consisting of a protective coat, stored food, and an embryo plant

SHORT CIRCUIT an accidental direct connection between the two sides of an electric circuit, producing a destructive surge of current

SILT soil particles intermediate in size between clay particles and sand grains

SMOG layer of fog that contains smoke and irritating gases

SOFT WATER water that is relatively free of mineral salts

SOLAR CELL a device that produces electricity from the energy of sunlight

SOLAR SYSTEM the Sun with the group of bodies in space that, held by its attraction, revolve around it

SOLID phase of matter in which the substance has a definite shape and size

SOLSTICE time when the sun seems to reverse its apparent movement north or south of the equator

SOLUBLE capable of being dissolved

SOLUTION a mixture in which molecules or ions of a substance are dispersed in a liquid

SOLVENT liquid part of a solution in which a substance is dissolved

SOUND BARRIER the speed at which an airplane overtakes its own sound waves, resulting in violent vibration

SPAWNING the shedding of eggs and milt into the water during the reproductive process of fish

SPECIES a group of similar organisms, consisting of populations that can interbreed freely

SPECTRUM the array of colors or wavelengths into which light is divided, usually by the action of a prism or diffraction grating

SPONTANEOUS COMBUSTION bursting into flame of a substance because of the accumulated heat of slow oxidation

STATIC ELECTRICITY electric charge accumulated on an object

STERILITY complete absence of microscopic life; also, inability to have offspring

STIMULUS any form of energy to which protoplasm is sensitive

STREPTOMYCIN antibiotic used to combat infections, such as tuberculosis

SUBATOMIC PARTICLE particles that make up the atom

SUBLIMINATION change from solid to gas or gas to solid without going through the liquid phase

SULFA DRUG synthetic drug used to combat certain bacterial infections

SUSPENSION a cloudy mixture composed of a finely divided solid in a liquid

SWEAT GLAND gland in the skin that excretes onto the skin surface a fluid consisting of water, salts, and urea

SYMBIOSIS beneficial relationship between organisms living closely together

SYNTHESIS building up of compounds from simpler compounds or elements

SYSTEM group of organs in an organism that deal with the same function

THEORY scientific principle, more or less acceptable, that is offered in explanation of observed facts

THERMODYNAMICS study of laws governing heat

THERMOMETER instrument for measuring the temperature

THERMONUCLEAR referring to a nuclear reaction that requires heat in order to occur

THERMOSTAT device on a heating system that automatically controls temperature

THUNDER sound following a flash of lightning and caused by the sudden expansion of air in the path of the discharge

THYROID large ductless or endocrine gland in front of and on either side of the trachea in the lower part of the neck

TIDES regular movement of the oceans caused by the gravitational pull of the Moon and Sun

TISSUE group of similar cells and intercellular material that perform similar work

TOPSOIL upper fertile layer of soil, containing humus, that is necessary to plant life

TORNADO one of the most violent of windstorms, noted for its funnel-shaped clouds, high-speed winds, and great destructiveness over a short path and a small area

TOTAL ECLIPSE complete hiding of one heavenly body by another or by the umbra of the shadow cast by another

TOXIN poisonous substance of microbial origin

TRAIT distinguishing quality of a person or thing

TRANSFORMER device for transforming high voltage to low voltage, or low voltage to high voltage

TUBER underground storage stem that produces new plants (e.g., the white potato)

TUMOR an abnormal swelling or enlargement, either benign or malignant

TUNDRA far-northern type of ecological community; water soaked, with permanently frozen ground, bogs, and low plants

TURBINE rotary engine powered by steam, water, or gas

ULTRASONIC SOUND high-pitched sound above the range of human hearing

ULTRAVIOLET RAY electromagnetic radiation with wavelengths too short to be seen

UMBILICAL CORD structure that connects a mammalian embryo with the placenta

URANIUM heavy, radioactive element present in an ore called pitchblende

VACCINATE to inoculate with dead or weakened germs of a disease, such as smallpox, thereby causing a light attack of the disease but conferring future immunity

VACCINE a substance consisting of dead or weakened bacteria or viruses; used to produce immunity

VEIN a blood vessel that drains the other organs of the body and carries blood toward the heart

VELOCITY the time rate to traverse a distance in a particular direction

VENEREAL DISEASE disease transmitted through sexual intercourse (e.g., syphilis)

VENTRICLE one of the two muscular chambers of the heart that pump blood to parts of the body

VERTEBRATE animal having a backbone (e.g., bird, reptile, fish, dog)

VIRUS submicroscopic disease-causing organism, consisting of a DNA or RNA molecule surrounded by a protein coat

VITAMIN chemical found in foods and needed in small quantities for special body functioning

VOLCANO an opening in the Earth's crust from which molten rock and steam are ejected

VOLT unit of electric potential, equal to 1 joule per coulomb

WARM FRONT boundary between a mass of advancing warm air and a retreating mass of relatively cooler air

WATERSHED area from which a river or lake draws its water

WATER TABLE level below which the soil is saturated with water

WATT unit of power, equal to a joule per second

WAVELENGTH the distance between two points in the same phase on a wave, such as from one crest to the next

WEIGHT measure of the pull of gravity on an object

WHITE BLOOD CELL leukocyte; blood cell that helps destroy bacteria and other foreign particles that enter the body

YEAST a single-celled fungus, responsible for many kinds of fermentation and certain infections

14 Science Practice

Biology

Questions 1 to 3 refer to the following article.

Insects enjoy many advantages for survival. Insects reproduce often and in large numbers. Their small size is a very definite advantage. Their food needs are small, and they can easily escape detection, especially with their keen senses of sight and smell. They are not fussy about diet and can adapt to changes, as illustrated by the new forms that have evolved that defy human poisons. Camouflage helps many insects blend with the environment. The names assigned to such insects as the "walking stick" and the "dead leaf" are illustrations. Mimicry is another device used for protection and ultimate survival. Birds often turn down a meal of a viceroy butterfly because it looks just like the unpleasant-tasting monarch butterfly.

Let us bear in mind that we need some members of the insect world. For example, some species of insect transfer pollen from anthers of stamens to the pistils of blossoms. The reason why flowers have bright colors and attractive odors is to lure insect pollinators. Without pollination, fruit formation is impossible. Silk comes from the material of the cocoon of an insect, and a tiny beetle gives us a beautiful red dye. Also, we benefit from the activity of the honeybee.

1. Flowers of grasses consist of stamens and pistils only, with neither petals nor odor. Which of the following is a reasonable assumption about these flowers?

   (1) Insects need excellent eyesight to find these flowers.
   (2) These flowers do not have to be pollinated.
   (3) These flowers are pollinated by wind.
   (4) These flowers do not form seed.
   (5) Grasses reproduce only by asexual means.

2. Which of the following account(s) for the survival of insects through the ages?

   (A) mimicry and camouflage
   (B) ability to pollinate blossoms
   (C) body size

   (1) A and B
   (2) B and C
   (3) C only
   (4) A and C
   (5) A, B, and C

3. Without the insect world, all of the following are possible EXCEPT

   (1) disease
   (2) fruits
   (3) nylon
   (4) beeswax
   (5) natural syrups

Questions 4 to 7 refer to the following information.

Plant hormones (auxins) can be produced in the laboratory. One of these, NAA, is used on blossoms to produce fruit without pollination. These resulting seedless fruits have great economic value. The use of 2,4-D to kill weeds without damaging the grass on lawns is widespread. Botanists classify seed-bearing plants into dicots and monocots. Interestingly enough, it has been found that in certain concentrations 2,4-D is more effective on dicots than on monocots; these doses cause such abnormal growth that the dicot plant dies. Since most weeds are dicots and grass is a monocot, an effective chemical weed killer has been developed from our knowledge of plant hormones and taxonomy.

4. Which of the following is necessary in order for a flower to produce seeds?

   (1) pollination
   (2) hormones
   (3) abnormal growth
   (4) weed killer
   (5) grass

5. Taxonomy (the science of classification) has contributed to agriculture by

   (1) producing new plant hormones
   (2) devising more effective weed killers
   (3) producing grass of better quality
   (4) distinguishing the plants that respond to weed killers
   (5) all of the above

6. How does 2,4-D effectively kill weeds?

   (1) causes abnormal rapid growth of dicots
   (2) causes abnormal rapid growth of monocots
   (3) retards the growth of monocots
   (4) retards the growth of dicots
   (5) retards the growth of leaves

7. A newly introduced plant may or may not be affected by 2,4-D. Which of the following will most probably be destroyed by 2,4-D?

   (1) a weed
   (2) a parasite
   (3) a dicot
   (4) an auxin
   (5) a hormone

Questions 8 to 10 refer to the following information.

When a new individual is produced from a single parent cell or from two parent cells, the process of reproduction occurs. This life function differs from all other life processes in that it preserves the species rather than ensuring the survival of the individual. To understand how a cell divides, one must consider the behavior of the nuclear material and the cytoplasmic division. Mitosis is the process by which the hereditary material of the nucleus is doubled and then distributed into the daughter cells. This is accompanied by the division of the cytoplasmic material so that, as a result of cell division, normally two cells similar to the parent cell are produced. This is the basis of all forms of asexual reproduction, in which a single parent is involved, as is the case in binary fission in single-celled organisms such as amoebas, paramecia, and bacteria, or in the process of budding in yeast cells or sporulation in bread mold.

8. Which life function is more important to the species than the individual?

   (1) growth
   (2) movement
   (3) food manufacture
   (4) reproduction
   (5) protection

9. Which of the following terms does NOT belong with the others?

   (1) fertilization
   (2) budding
   (3) sporulation
   (4) asexual reproduction
   (5) binary fission

10. Which of the following processes is a part of all the others?

   (1) binary fission
   (2) asexual reproduction
   (3) sporulation
   (4) budding
   (5) mitosis

Questions 11 to 13 refer to the following passage.

The basic unit of all living organisms is the cell, a complex organization consisting of many parts. Plant and animal cells are basically the same, but there are two exceptions. A plant cell, unlike an animal cell, has a cell wall, a rigid container of nonliving material. Also, plant cells have organelles called plastids; the most common is the chloroplast, which contains green pigment and is very important in photosynthesis. Another plastid in plant cells is the leucoplast, which contains enzymes that turn sugar into starch. Vacuoles are present in both plant and animals cells. These organelles are primarily storage sacks for water, wastes, and dissolved materials. They also help to maintain the internal pressure in the cell. In plant cells they are usually large; in animal cells they are small. Animal cells have an additional organelle called a centrosome, which functions in cell division.

11. The word *organelle* is used in the passage to describe

(1) a small organ composed of cells
(2) the protoplasmic material in cells
(3) one of the specialized structures within the cell that have various functions
(4) a special kind of cell
(5) a part of the cell that is present in plants but not in animals

12. According to the passage, which of the following structures are present in plant cells but not in animal cells?

(1) cell walls, cell membrane, and chromosomes
(2) cell wall, leucoplasts, and mitochondria
(3) chromosomes, plastids, and vacuoles
(4) cell wall, chloroplasts, and leucoplasts
(5) chloroplasts, vacuoles, and chromosomes

13. Which of the following structures is probably responsible for wood retaining its rigidity after the tree is dead?

(1) chloroplasts
(2) leucoplasts
(3) the cell wall
(4) chromosomes
(5) plastids

Questions 14 and 15 refer to the following passage.

Surprisingly, a fish's caudal fin (tail), is not used for propulsion. Fins are used primarily for stability and steering. In order to swim, a fish needs to be able to flex its body back and forth very rapidly. To create this motion, a fish's muscles are arranged in a series of waves or segments called myomeres.

Fish have two kinds of muscle fibers, white and red. White myomeres are used for short bursts of swimming. Groupers and other slow-moving fish have almost all white myomeres. Open-sea fish, such as the tuna and mackerel, are capable of cruising at high speed for long periods of time. The blood in their red muscle fibers is rich in a pigment called myoglobin, which can carry large amounts of oxygen. The oxygen nourishes muscle cells, enabling them to work harder for longer periods of time.

14. Cellular respiration requires the oxidation of fuel that is in the form of organic molecules. In the fish, which of the following is (are) responsible for carrying large amounts of oxygen?

(1) caudal fins
(2) myomeres
(3) hemoglobin
(4) myoglobin
(5) red muscles

15. On dissecting a fish, a biologist saw that it had large quantities of red muscle fibers. From this observation he can assume that this fish

(1) lived in a coral reef
(2) would be good to eat
(3) came from shallow waters
(4) was usually slow moving
(5) came from the open sea

Questions 16 and 17 refer to the following information.

It is well known that plants tend to grow toward the light, a process known as phototropism. Research with plant hormones, known as auxins, has disclosed the mechanisms at work. One such mechanism results in the bending of a stem toward the light. In the grass family, the tip of the growing stem produces an auxin. When light strikes one side of the tip, the auxin moves to the other side. It then diffuses down the stem, where it promotes the elongation of the cells below the tip. As the cells on the dark side elongate, the stem bends toward the light.

16. What causes a stem to turn toward the light?

    (1) phototropism
    (2) the need for light for photosynthesis
    (3) an auxin that controls cell elongation
    (4) the effect of light in stimulating growth
    (5) a plant hormone produced in the dark

17. Which of the following best describes auxins?

    (1) leaf structures
    (2) stem tips
    (3) tropisms
    (4) plant hormones
    (5) light filters

Questions 18 to 20 refer to the following passage.

If you were to cross two plants, one that carries only genes for tallness and one that carries only genes for shortness, the next generation of plants would be either all tall or all short. For this example let us say that all the second-generation plants were tall. The gene that causes a visible characteristic—here, tallness—is called dominant, and the other gene, for shortness, is called recessive.

A small chart called a Punnett square is a useful way to illustrate how dominant and recessive genes may combine. On the assumption that each parent carries two genes for a certain characteristic, the square shows four possible combinations of the four parent genes.

For example, if a tall plant is crossed with a short plant, the Punnett square may look like this:

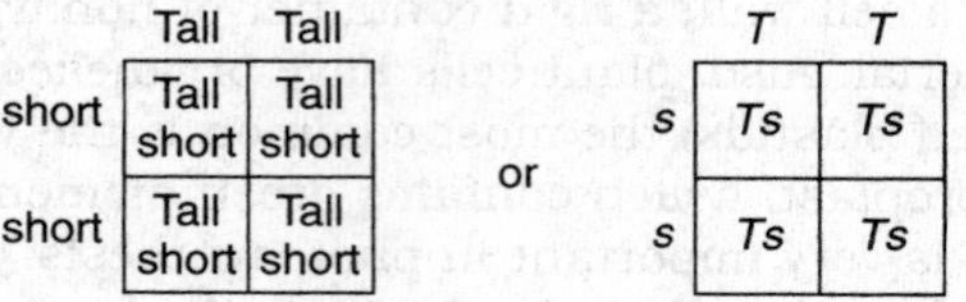

Across the top of the square are one parent's two genes for tallness. Along the side are the other parent's two genes for shortness. Each square displays a possible combination of the four parent genes, one gene from each parent. As the Punnett square shows, the offspring from this breeding will be 100 percent hybrid, each carrying one dominant and one recessive gene.

18. If two of the hybrid offspring are mated, what is the possible combination of offspring?

    (1) 50% pure tall, 50% pure short
    (2) 75% pure tall, 25% hybrid
    (3) 75% pure short, 25% hybrid
    (4) 25% pure tall, 25% pure short, 50% hybrid
    (5) 50% pure tall, 25% pure short, 25% hybrid

19. Brown eyes are dominant over blue. If three of four children have brown eyes and one has blue eyes, what is the possible genetic makeup of the parents?

    (1) pure blue and pure brown
    (2) hybrid blue and pure brown
    (3) hybrid brown and pure blue
    (4) hybrid brown and hybrid blue
    (5) hybrid brown

20. Any one of the brown-eyed children from the family described in question 19 could be

(1) either 100% brown or hybrid
(2) hybrid brown only
(3) 100% brown only
(4) hybrid blue/brown only
(5) either 50% brown or hybrid

Questions 21 to 25 refer to the following article.

The timber wolf occupies an important position in the food chain. Like any other large carnivore, it plays a major role in keeping populations of smaller animals in balance. Its diet includes many rodents. Even as a deer killer, it is more helpfully selective than its rival predator, the human.

The human hunter kills for sport and pride, most often shooting the finest member of the deer herd, but the wolf kills for food alone, picking off the weakest, the oldest, and the sickliest. Thus, humans lower the quality of the herd, but the wolf preserves its health and keeps its numbers geared to the sustaining support of the land. The result is good for the deer, good for the wolf, and good for the browsing area.

Recently a project was launched in Minnesota to extend the range of the wolf. The plan is to trap a small pack of wolves there and then transplant them to a new wild environment in northern Michigan. At one time wolves inhabited this area but are now almost extinct there. The purpose of the project is to have the wolves breed and preserve the species. In this way, Northern Michigan University and several wildlife organizations that are sponsoring the experiment will be doing a service to preserve a creature that is useful in the natural environment. They hope also to explode the myth of the wolf's wickedness.

21. Which deer are killed by the wolf?

(1) weakest
(2) strongest
(3) best specimens
(4) those that eat rodents
(5) fastest

22. In connection with deer population why is the human race more destructive than the wolf?

(1) The wolf destroys only browsing areas.
(2) The hunter preserves the health of the herd.
(3) The hunter shoots deer for food alone.
(4) The hunter shoots the weakest, the oldest, and the sickliest deer.
(5) The hunter shoots the finest members of the herd.

23. What is the purpose of the Northern Michigan University Project?

(1) trap the wolves in Michigan and export them to Minnesota
(2) increase the range of the wolf in Michigan
(3) increase the number of deer in Michigan
(4) keep wolves out of Michigan
(5) prove the wolf's wickedness

24. Which of the following best describes the wolf's position in the food chain?

(1) important because it keeps the population of its prey in balance
(2) unimportant because it preys mostly on rodents
(3) unimportant because it is a large carnivore
(4) unimportant because it leaves healthy deer alone
(5) important because it lives in the midst of tall timber

25. Two examples of predators mentioned in the selection are

(1) wolf and man
(2) wolf and deer
(3) man and deer
(4) wolf and rodent
(5) rodent and deer

Questions 26 to 28 refer to the following information.

The food energy in a food chain may be transferred by predators, scavengers, or symbionts. A *predator* kills prey and then eats it. *Scavengers* consume dead animals or plants. Many bacteria, yeasts, and molds live on dead organic material. They are known as saprophytes, as contrasted with parasites, which live on living things. A *symbiont* is a member of a nutritive relationship (symbiosis) in which neither partner causes harm to the other. The lichen, which grows on a rock and may ultimately erode the rock, is an alga and a fungus. The alga with its chlorophyll carries on photosynthesis, and the fungus absorbs water for itself and the alga. Such a symbiotic relationship is known as mutualism. Where only one member benefits, with no harm to the other member of the symbiotic relationship, the term *commensalism* is applied.

26. Which term describes the type of nutritional relationship in which both symbionts benefit from the association?
    (1) commensalism
    (2) autotrophism
    (3) parasitism
    (4) saprophytism
    (5) mutualism

27. Many orchids live rooted high in trees, where they can receive the effects of sunlight but do not damage the trees. The orchids would be classified as
    (1) parasites
    (2) saprophytes
    (3) commensals
    (4) scavengers
    (5) mutual symbionts

28. In a lichen, why does the fungus need the alga to survive?
    (1) The fungus cannot absorb enough water.
    (2) Neither the alga nor the fungus alone can grow on rock.
    (3) The fungus provides the alga with protection against drying.
    (4) The fungus cannot carry on photosynthesis.
    (5) The fungus cannot absorb nutrients from the soil.

<u>Questions 29 to 33</u> refer to the following information.

The higher forms of plants and animals, such as seed plants and vertebrates, are similar or alike in many respects but decidedly different in others. For example, both of these groups of organisms carry on digestion, respiration, reproduction, conduction, and growth and exhibit sensitivity to various stimuli. On the other hand, a number of basic differences are evident. Plants have no excretory systems comparable to those of animals. Plants have no heart or similar pumping organ. Plants are very limited in their movements. Plants have nothing similar to the animal nervous system. In addition, animals cannot synthesize carbohydrates from inorganic substances. Animals do not have special regions of growth, comparable to terminal and lateral meristems in plants, which persist throughout the life span of the organism. And finally the animal cell has no wall, only a membrane, but plant cell walls are more rigid, usually thicker, and may be composed of such substances as cellulose, lignin, pectin, cutin, and suberin. These characteristics are important to an understanding of living organisms and their functions and should, consequently, be carefully considered in plant and animal studies.

29. Which of the following do animals lack?
    (1) ability to react to stimuli
    (2) ability to conduct substances from one place to another
    (3) reproduction by gametes
    (4) a cell membrane
    (5) a terminal growth region

30. Plants have rigid cell walls, but animals do not. This is probably related to the difference between animals and plants in the function of
    (1) respiration
    (2) photosynthesis
    (3) excretion
    (4) responsiveness
    (5) locomotion

31. Which of these do only plants possess?

(1) specialized organs for circulation
(2) excretory organs
(3) organs of locomotion
(4) the ability to manufacture carbohydrates
(5) specialized nerve tissue

32. Which of the following do plants lack?

(1) rigid cell walls
(2) pumping structures
(3) special regions of growth
(4) structures for reproduction
(5) a digestive process

33. Which of these processes are carried on by plants and animals?

(1) the synthesis of carbohydrates
(2) conduction
(3) the manufacture of cellulose
(4) the production of cutin
(5) excretion through excretory organs

Questions 34 to 36 refer to the following information.

The natural successions of plant and animal communities refer to the changes in animal and plant life of a region as a result of environmental changes. The study of organisms in relation to their environment is known as *ecology*. With changes in environment, the previous animal and plant life disappears and is succeeded by new types, adapted to new conditions. Thus, a bare rock area can support the primitive algae and lichens. Gradually, as the rock decomposes to become soil, the mosses, grasses, and quick-growing weeds appear, followed by small shrubs. As the soil becomes deeper and more porous, the larger evergreens appear, crowding out the grasses and shrubs. If these rocky, shallow soils change to deeper ones of firmer loam, the evergreens are replaced with hardwoods, such as maple and beech.

34. Which of these is the main concern of ecology?

(1) methods of preventing runoff of water
(2) erosion of land
(3) the relationship between the environment and living things
(4) the effect of living things on the environment
(5) changes in plants

35. After a lava flow produces new rock, which of the following will be the first to appear?

(1) insects
(2) grasses
(3) mosses
(4) rodents
(5) lichens

36. Which of the following represents the most probable order of natural succession of plants in a barren rocky area?

(1) mosses, grasses, shrubs, trees
(2) lichens, mosses, grasses, shrubs
(3) lichens, grasses, shrubs, mosses
(4) grasses, shrubs, trees, mosses
(5) mosses, lichens, grasses, shrubs

Questions 37 to 39 refer to the following information.

Chloroplasts take many forms and can vary widely in the number per cell in different plants. In some algae, such as *Spirogyra*, there is only a single chloroplast in each cell. When this cell divides, the chloroplast divides as well, providing each new cell with one chloroplast. In contrast, a single cell in a grass leaf can have 30 to 50 chloroplasts. The chloroplasts of the higher vascular plants consist of two parts: a colorless background material; and grana, small green structures containing chlorophyll.

Although blue-green algae perform photosynthesis, they are classed with bacteria rather than with other plants. Instead of definite chloroplasts, they have loosely arranged membranes within their cytoplasm on which photosynthetic pigments are layered. These photosynthetic membranes are called chromatophores, but we know very little about the molecular arrangement of their light-absorbing pigments. However, if blue-green algae and other photosynthetic bacteria are kept in the dark, they lose their chromatophores and are no longer photosynthetic. The chromatophore behaves like the chloroplasts in a plant and is its functional, if not its structural, equivalent.

37. Chloroplasts are important to the cell because they control

    (1) cell division
    (2) grana
    (3) photosynthesis
    (4) pigmentation
    (5) filamentation

38. Which of the following is a correct statement?

    (1) Brown algae have no chlorophyll.
    (2) No bacteria are photosynthetic.
    (3) All algae have cells with chloroplasts.
    (4) Cells of a grass leaf have chloroplasts.
    (5) All chloroplasts are composed of grana.

39. How are chromatophores and chloroplasts similar?

    A. structure
    B. function
    C. location

    (1) A only
    (2) B only
    (3) C only
    (4) A and B
    (5) A, B, and C

<u>Questions 40 to 46</u> refer to the following article.

Whenever microorganisms have successfully invaded the body and are growing at the expense of the tissues, the process is called an infection. The term *infection* should always imply the existence of an abnormal state or unnatural condition resulting from the harmful action of microorganisms. In other words, the simple presence of an organism is not sufficient to cause disease.

Infection may arise from the admission of microorganisms to the tissues through the gastrointestinal tract, through the upper air passages, through wounds made by the contaminated teeth or claws of animals or by contaminated weapons, and by the bite of suctorial insects. Another type of infection sometimes occurs when for some reason the body has become vulnerable to the pathogenic action of bacteria whose normal habitat is the body.

The reaction of the body to the attack of an invading organism results in the formation of substances of a specific nature. The reaction bodies that circulate mainly in the blood serum are known as antibodies and are classified according to their activities. Some, known as antitoxins, neutralize poisonous substances produced by the infecting organism. Others, called bacteriolysins, destroy bacteria by dissolving them. Opsonins or bacteriotropins prepare the bacteria for destruction by phagocytes; precipitins and agglutinins have the property of grouping the invading agents into small clumps of precipitates. The formation of defensive substances is specific for each organism.

40. Which of the following conditions illustrates an infection?

    (1) A guinea pig is exposed to diphtheria toxin.
    (2) A nurse taking care of a tubercular patient inhales some tuberculosis bacilli.
    (3) A man cuts his finger with a dirty knife. He uses no antiseptic.
    (4) A student examines his saliva with a microscope. Under high power he observes some streptococci.
    (5) Malaria parasites in the blood cause chills and fever.

41. Since each antibody is specific for the invading organism, it follows that

(1) the body can produce only a small number of different kinds of antibodies
(2) the antidiphtheria antibody will not protect against tetanus
(3) there are many kinds of invading organisms that cannot be attacked by antibodies
(4) an individual cannot be immune to more than one kind of disease organism at a time
(5) immunity to some diseases weakens the body's ability to protect itself against others

42. Which of the following statements is true of phagocytes?

(1) Opsonins are also called phagocytes.
(2) Opsonins prepare bacteria for destruction by phagocytes.
(3) Phagocytes destroy opsonins.
(4) Bacteriotropins destroy phagocytes.
(5) Phagocytes prepare bacteria for destruction by opsonins.

43. Which of the following is a correct statement?

(1) The white blood corpuscles help ward off infection by distributing antibodies to all parts of the body.
(2) A disease organism that lives in the body of a person always has a bad effect on the person.
(3) Antibodies are classified according to the type of organism they attack.
(4) Infection is accompanied by an abnormal state of the body.
(5) Antitoxins are formed against every organism that enters the body.

44. All of the following are antibodies EXCEPT

(1) phagocytes
(2) antitoxins
(3) bacteriolysins
(4) opsonins
(5) precipitins

45. All of the following might result in infection EXCEPT

(1) inhalation of dust particles
(2) a drink of contaminated water
(3) a bite from a mosquito
(4) a cut with a knife
(5) a fly landing on the skin

46. By what process do agglutinins destroy invading organisms?

(1) dissolving
(2) neutralizing
(3) clumping
(4) engulfing
(5) digesting

Questions 47 to 49 are based on the following information.

Relationships between organisms are classified according to the way they affect each other. Below are five types of relationships.

(1) parasitism—a relationship in which one organism lives on another organism and harms it
(2) commensalism—a relationship in which one organism is benefited and the other is neither harmed nor benefited
(3) saprophytism—a relationship in which an organism feeds on the dead remains or products of other organisms
(4) mutualism—a relationship between two organisms in which both organisms benefit from the association
(5) cannibalism—a relationship in which an organism feeds on the flesh of its own kind

Each of the following statements describes a relationship that refers to one of the categories just defined. For each item, choose the one category that best describes the relationship.

47. The relationship between athlete's-foot fungus and humans is best classified as

(1) parasitism
(2) commensalism
(3) saprophytism
(4) mutualism
(5) cannibalism

48. Nitrogen-fixing bacteria enrich the soil by producing nitrates beneficial to green plants. The bacteria live in nodules located on the roots of legumes. These nodules provide a favorable environment for the bacteria to grow and reproduce. The relationship between these bacteria and the leguminous plant is an example of

(1) parasitism
(2) commensalism
(3) saprophytism
(4) mutualism
(5) cannibalism

49. Bacteria of decay decompose dead plants and animals, releasing ammonia into the environment. This relationship would best be described as

(1) parasitism
(2) commensalism
(3) saprophytism
(4) mutualism
(5) cannibalism

Questions 50 to 55 refer to the following article.

At the beginning of the nineteenth century, it was generally believed that any features of an individual would be passed on to offspring. Thus, if a man lifted weights and had huge muscles, it was believed his children would have huge muscles as well. Jean Lamarck developed a theory of evolution, called the theory of use and disuse, in which this inheritance of acquired characteristics was considered to be the reason for the change in any organism through the generations.

Although Charles Darwin accepted the concept of inheritance of acquired characteristics, he believed that it played only a minor role. The main driving force of evolution, he said, is natural selection. This means that the only individuals that can survive long enough to reproduce are the ones that are optimally adapted to their environment. These adaptations improve generation after generation because only the best adapted individuals pass on the favorable traits to their offspring.

Later, August Weismann's theory suggests that acquired characteristics cannot be inherited because genes are somehow isolated from the rest of the body. Modern genetics has substantiated this theory; the information in the genes is already coded when the organism is born, and nothing that happens to it thereafter can change this coding. Today the theory of inheritance of acquired characteristics is dead, and Darwin's idea of natural selection remains a cornerstone of all theories of evolution.

50. Why was Darwin able to accept the theory of inheritance of acquired characteristics?

(1) He did not know of Lamarck's work.
(2) He had not gathered enough information.
(3) There was good experimental evidence for it.
(4) There was then no knowledge of the gene.
(5) Weismann had developed a theory to explain it.

51. How would someone using Lamarck's theory of evolution probably explain the development in South American monkeys of a strong prehensile tail?

(1) There was a mutation that made the tails strong.
(2) The gene for a strong tail was dominant.
(3) The monkeys interbred with other kinds.
(4) The tail muscles were strengthened by use.
(5) Strong-tailed monkeys left more offspring.

52. Which of these theories has been discredited by the development of modern genetics?

(1) There is variation within a species.
(2) The best adapted individuals survive.
(3) Inherited features are passed on to offspring.
(4) Acquired characteristics are inherited.
(5) Development is controlled by genes.

53. Why have certain strains of bacteria that were susceptible to penicillin in the past now become resistant?

(1) The mutation rate must have increased naturally.
(2) The strains have become resistant because they needed to do so for survival.
(3) A mutation was retained and passed on to succeeding generations because it had high survival value.
(4) The principal forces influencing the pattern of survival in a population are isolation and mating.
(5) Penicillin strains became less effective.

54. Which of the following statements is a modern expression of the theory of the continuity of the germ plasm?

(1) Acquired characteristics may be inherited.
(2) Genes are not altered to suit environmental demands.
(3) Natural selection is an important factor in evolution.
(4) Evolution produces better adapted forms.
(5) Heredity changes by gene mutation.

55. In any species, which organisms are most likely to survive and reproduce?

(1) the largest
(2) the strongest
(3) the best adapted
(4) the most prolific
(5) the most intelligent

<u>Questions 56 to 60</u> refer to the following information.

Cholesterol is a fatty substance that is manufactured by the liver and has many important functions in the human body. It is found in all animal fats, but not in any plant product. Cholesterol circulates in the blood, combined with proteins, in two forms: HDL and LDL. Research has shown that, if there are high levels of LDL, fatty material is deposited inside the arteries, restricting the flow of blood. This is especially dangerous in the arteries of the heart and the brain. HDL is a form in which the deposits are removed from the arteries. Saturated fats and oils, such as coconut oil and the solid fats of animals, tend to raise the LDL level in the blood. On the other hand, exercise and unsaturated vegetable oils, such as olive oil, tend to raise the HDL level.

56. All of the following foods tend to raise the LDL level in the blood EXCEPT

(1) bacon
(2) coconut candy
(3) corn oil
(4) beefsteak
(5) pepperoni pizza

57. How does exercise benefit the arteries?

(1) It lowers the cholesterol level.
(2) It raises the LDL level.
(3) It strengthens the artery walls.
(4) It strengthens the body muscles.
(5) It raises the HDL level.

58. What is a dangerous result of fatty deposits on arteries?

(1) high cholesterol levels
(2) lipid deposits
(3) dietary deficiencies
(4) heart attacks
(5) obesity

59. What kind of evidence probably led to the conclusion that high blood cholesterol levels are undesirable?

(1) People with high cholesterol levels suffer from indigestion.
(2) The rate of heart attack is greater in people with high cholesterol levels.
(3) Statistics show that people with high cholesterol levels are often overweight.
(4) Cholesterol is a main ingredient of blood clots.
(5) Saturated fats in the diet tend to elevate the blood cholesterol level.

60. According to modern medicine, which of these should most definitely be avoided to prevent heart attacks and strokes?

(1) candy
(2) raisins
(3) animal fats
(4) nuts
(5) all oily foods

---

61. Homologous structures are those that have the same basic structure, but do not necessarily share the same function. They may, however, be indicators of some common ancestor far back on the evolutionary tree. Which of the following are homologous structures?

(1) the foreleg of a horse and the arm of a human
(2) the wings of a bee and the wings of a bird
(3) the legs of a kangaroo and the legs of a grasshopper
(4) the fins of a fish and the flipper of a whale
(5) the wings of a bat and the wings of a butterfly

62. The term *metamorphoses* refers to a series of changes undergone from birth to adult. This is a common process in a number of organisms that change from one shape to another as they grow. Which of the following is NOT considered a metamorphosis?

(1) The eggs of a frog hatch in the water, where the tadpoles must live and go through a series of physical changes before they can move onto the land.
(2) A trout hatches from an egg and lives for a time as fry before growing into a mature fish.
(3) A butterfly emerges from a chrysalis after spending the spring as a caterpillar.
(4) It is much easier to kill flea larvae, with their soft bodies, before they become armored in chitin as adults.
(5) During an early stage in its life, the jellyfish is attached to the ocean floor and looks rather like a plant. Only later does it become a free-swimming medusa.

63. Which assumption is the basis for the use of the fossil record as evidence for evolution?

(1) Fossils have been found to show a complete record of the evolution of all mammals.
(2) In undisturbed layers of the Earth's crust, the oldest fossils are found in the lowest layers.
(3) All fossils can be found embedded in rocks.
(4) All fossils were formed at the same time.
(5) All fossils are found in sedimentary rock.

64. The graph shows the relationship between the number of cases of children with Down syndrome per 1,000 births and maternal age.

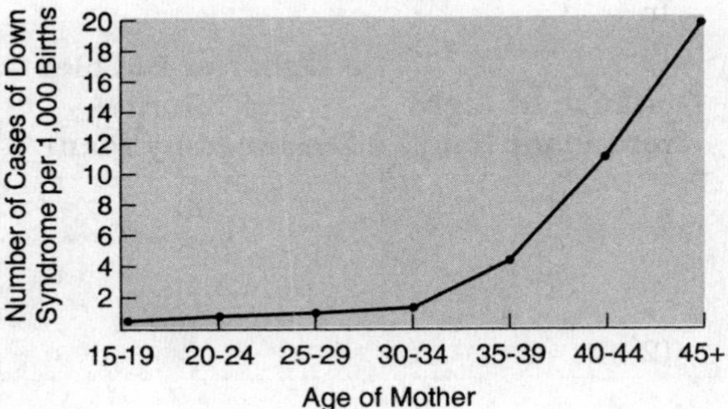

According to the graph, the incidence of Down syndrome

(1) generally decreases as maternal age increases
(2) is about nine times less at age 45 than at age 30
(3) stabilizes at 2 per 1,000 births after age 35
(4) is greater at age 15 than at age 35
(5) is about nine times greater at age 45 than at age 30

65. The data presented in the graph suggest that

(1) women over the age of 34 should not have children
(2) older women should seek genetic counseling before planning a pregnancy
(3) only younger women should have children
(4) genetic counseling may be a good idea if there is reason to suspect that your baby has Down syndrome
(5) children with Down syndrome need special care and training

Questions 66 and 67 are based on the following information.

People who want to stay healthy need to keep themselves well nourished. One important fact to remember is to eat moderate portions from each of the four food groups every day.

BASIC FOOD GROUPS			
Meat	**Dairy**	**Fruits and Vegetables**	**Grains (Cereal, Breads)**
2–3 servings	2 servings for adults 3 for children and pregnant women 4 for nursing mothers	4 servings	3–4 servings
Source of Protein B vitamins Minerals Fats	Source of Calcium Protein Phosphorus Vitamin A	Source of Vitamins A and C Minerals Fiber	Source of Fiber Starch Protein Vitamins Minerals

66. A person wanting to eliminate fats but still eat a high-protein diet might do which of the following?

(1) Eat only from groups 2 and 4 and not from group 1.
(2) Eat all the groups except 1.
(3) Choose from group 4 only.
(4) Choose mostly from groups 2, 3, and 4 and sparingly from group 1.
(5) Eat only from groups 2 and 4.

67. From the information given in the table you can conclude that

(1) citrus fruits are a good source of vitamin C
(2) active people should eat a lot of protein
(3) junk foods contain the most fats
(4) nursing mothers should drink more milk than other adults
(5) spinach is a good source of fiber

Questions 68 to 70 are based on the following graphs.

The graphs show data on some environmental factors acting in a large lake.

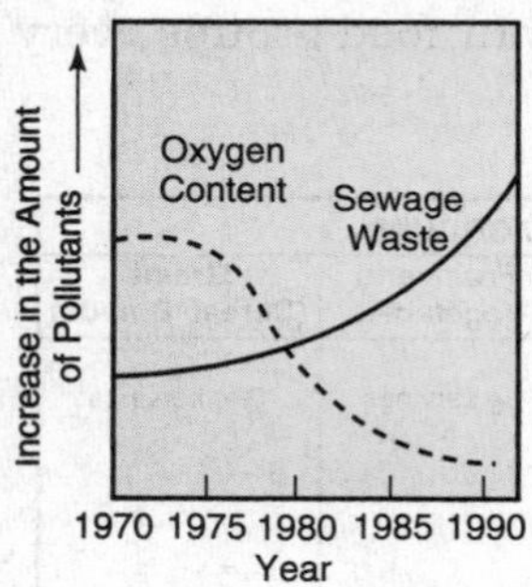

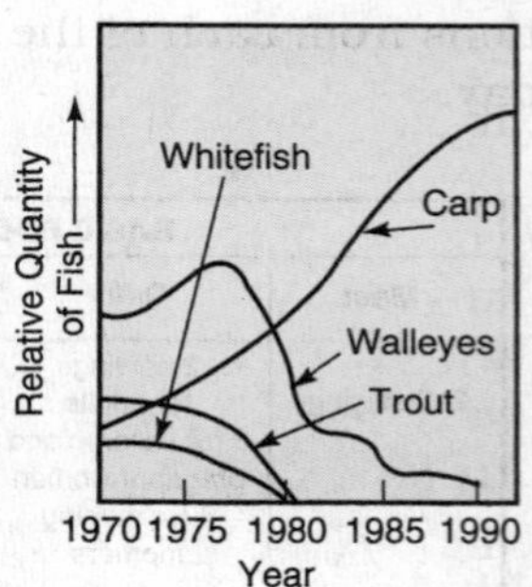

68. Which relationship can be correctly inferred from the data presented?
    (1) As oxygen content decreases, the carp population decreases.
    (2) As oxygen content decreases, the trout population increases.
    (3) Sewage waste and oxygen content are not related.
    (4) As sewage waste increases, oxygen content increases.
    (5) As sewage waste increases, oxygen content decreases.

69. Between what years did the greatest change in the lake's whitefish population occur?
    (1) 1970 and 1975
    (2) 1975 and 1980
    (3) 1980 and 1982
    (4) 1983 and 1985
    (5) 1986 and 1990

70. Which fish species appear(s) able to withstand the greatest degree of oxygen depletion?
    (1) trout
    (2) trout and walleye
    (3) walleye
    (4) whitefish
    (5) carp

Question 71 is based on the following information.

A green plant was placed in a test tube. A light, placed at varying distances from the plant, illuminated the plant. The bubbles of O_2 given off by the plant were counted. The table shows the data collected during this experiment.

Distance of Light from Plant (cm)	Number of Bubbles per Minute Produced by Plant
10	60
20	25
30	10
40	5

71. Which conclusion can be drawn from this investigation?
    (1) As the distance from the light increases, the number of bubbles produced decreases.
    (2) As the distance from the light increases, the number of bubbles produced increases.
    (3) As the distance from the light decreases, the number of bubbles produced decreases.
    (4) As the distance from the light decreases, the number of bubbles produced increases.
    (5) There is no relationship between the number of bubbles produced and the distance of the plant from the light.

Questions 72 and 73 are based on the following passage.

A certain method is used by all scientists to design and conduct an experiment. If the experiment was performed correctly, the system allows any scientist anywhere in the world to duplicate the results. This procedure is called the Scientific Method.

The steps of the Scientific Method are as follows:

1. State the problem or ask a question.
2. Research the subject to see what others have found that might apply to the problem or question.
3. Form a hypothesis; based on the data acquired in step 2, attempt to predict a solution to the problem or an answer to the question.
4. Design and perform an experiment. In most situations, two groups of test sub-

jects are used; an experimental group, which will test the factor in question (called the variable), and a control group, which will provide background information about the experimental group if the members of the control group are not exposed to the variable.

5. Observe, measure, and record as the experiment proceeds.
6. Draw conclusions based on the data from the experiment.
7. Repeat the experiment.

72. A botanist was experimenting with two groups of plants. Group 1 was watered with a solution containing a new plant food. Group 2 received plain water with no plant food of any kind. The plant food received by group 1 was the

(1) control
(2) variable
(3) experimental group
(4) data
(5) hypothesis

73. A drug company tested a new medication before putting it on the commercial market. Pills without the medication were given to 500 test subjects in group *A*, and pills containing the medication were given to 500 test subjects in group *B*. In this experiment, the individuals in group *A* served as the

(1) host
(2) variable
(3) control
(4) hypothesis
(5) generalization

WHAT'S YOUR SCORE?

______right,	______wrong
Excellent	65–73
Good	48–64
Fair	37–47

If your score is low, don't get discouraged. Perhaps biology is a difficult subject for you. Try to find out why you failed. The analysis of correct answers that follows will help you to pinpoint your errors. If your mistake was lack of information, turn to the "Glossary of Scientific Terms" (page 338) and look up the meanings of the words you did not understand. If it was a mistake in interpretation, review the analysis of the question.

Answer Analysis

1. **3** With neither petals nor odor, these flowers do not attract insects, so pollination must be by some other means.
2. **4** Insects can escape enemies by mimicry and camouflage. The small body size of insects permits them to hide from enemies and also reduces food requirements. The ability to pollinate blossoms may help a plant, but has no survival value for an insect.
3. **4** Not all causative agents of disease are carried by insects. Some fruits would develop without insects by wind pollination or self-pollination. Nylon is a synthetic product. Syrups are usually products of sugar.
4. **1** The passage says flowers that are not pollinated produce no seed.
5. **4** Taxonomy distinguishes dicots from monocots, which are immune to the weed killer 2,4-D.
6. **1** The weed killer 2,4-D causes an abnormal growth of the dicot plant.
7. **3** See the answer to question 6.
8. **4** Reproduction preserves the species.
9. **1** Fertilization is a sexual process, while all the others are asexual.
10. **5** All reproductive processes must include the division of cells by mitosis.
11. **3** The passage refers to various special-

ized structures within the cell, calling them organelles.

12. **4** A plant cell contains a cell wall, chloroplasts, and leucoplasts. Chromosomes are found in animal cells; vacuoles are present in both plant and animal cells.
13. **3** Although the passage does not specifically discuss which structure may help a plant retain its shape, the only rigid material mentioned in the passage is the cell wall.
14. **4** According to the passage, a red pigment called myoglobin carries large amounts of oxygen to the muscle cells.
15. **5** Open-sea fish have large quantities of red muscle fibers, which make it possible for these fish to cruise at high speeds for long periods of time.
16. **3** An auxin that controls cell elongation causes the cells on the dark side to elongate, and the stem turns toward the light. Choice 1 is merely the name of the process, not a statement of causation. Choice 2 tells why the bending is useful, but does not explain how it happens.
17. **4** An auxin is a chemical substance that moves through the plant and carries instructions for growth. This is a hormone.
18. **4**

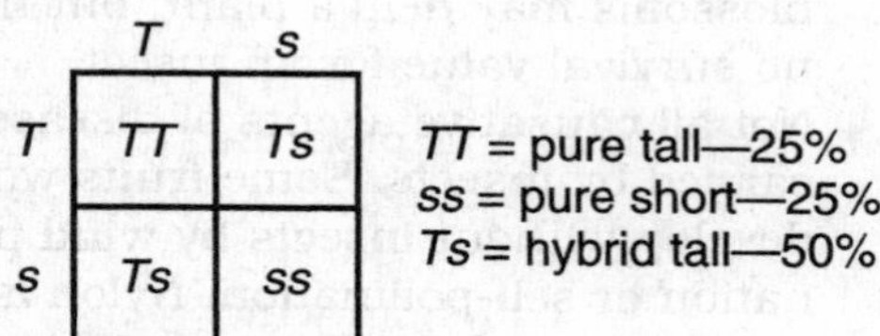

19. **5**

	B	b
B	BB	Bb
b	Bb	bb

B = brown
b = blue
BB = pure brown
Bb = hybrid brown
bb = pure blue
Hybrid blue is not possible.

20. **1** Either pure brown or hybrid. Brown will dominate over the blue gene, so a hybrid child's eyes will be brown even though he or she carries a blue gene.
21. **1** The wolf kills only for food and eliminates the weakest, the oldest, and the sickliest deer.
22. **5** Humans kill for sport and pride and try to pick off the finest specimen of the herd.
23. **2** The project is aimed at exporting wolves from Minnesota into northern Michigan to preserve the species and extend the wolf's range there.
24. **1** The wolf occupies an important position in the food chain by keeping populations of smaller animals in balance. In addition, the wolf keeps the number of deer geared to the sustaining support of the land.
25. **1** The end of the first paragraph compares the wolf to its rival predator, the human. It thus identifies both as predators.
26. **5** Mutualism refers to a type of symbiotic relationship in which both members benefit from the relationship. Commensalism is a relationship wherein only one member benefits, with no harm to the other member of the symbiotic relationship. In parasitism and saprophytism, only one member benefits, but at the expense of the other. An independent organism, such as a green plant, is an example of autotrophism.
27. **3** Orchids benefit from their position in the tree, but do not harm the tree. This is an example of commensalism.
28. **4** The passage says that the alga performs photosynthesis for the benefit of both the fungus and itself.
29. **5** Animals do not have special regions of growth, comparable to terminal and lateral meristems in plants, that persist throughout the life span of the organism.
30. **5** The rigid cell walls severely limit the flexibility of the plant body, so that it is unable to move freely.
31. **4** Green plants have the ability to synthesize carbohydrates from inorganic substances (carbon dioxide and water) in the presence of light.
32. **2** Plants have no heart or similar pumping organ.
33. **2** Food, wastes, and other substances are conducted from one part of a plant or animal to another.
34. **3** Ecology is the study of the relationships of living things with each other and with their environment. The incorrect choices are factors relating to ecology.

35. 5 Only lichens can survive on bare, dry rock.

36. 2 One kind of plant succeeds another when the soil is thick enough to support the newcomer. In Choice 2, the plants are in order of increasing soil depth.

37. 3 Chloroplasts are involved in the process of photosynthesis. Choice 1 is incorrect; the passage mentions the division of chloroplasts as the cell divides. Choice 2 is incorrect; grana are units that make up some chloroplasts. Choice 4 is incorrect; although chloroplasts give the green color to plants, their function is to carry on photosynthesis. Choice 5 is incorrect; *Spirogyra*, a filamentous alga, is mentioned as a cell with a single chloroplast.

38. 4 All higher plants have chloroplasts composed of grana. The passage tells that brown algae have chlorophyll, some bacteria photosynthesize, and some algae have chlorophyll without chloroplasts or chloroplasts without grana.

39. 2 The chromatophore has the same function as the chloroplast, but the two differ in structure. Also, they are not similar in regard to location. Chromatophores are in some bacterial cells; chloroplasts, in the green cells of higher plants.

40. 5 Only in this choice is there evidence that the invading organism has produced a disease process.

41. 2 An antibody is produced in response to a specific invading organism, and will protect only against that one. The body can produce an unlimited variety of antibodies, and the blood usually has many of them.

42. 2 Opsonins prepare bacteria for destruction by phagocytes.

43. 4 Microorganisms that cause an infection produce an abnormal state or unnatural condition.

44. 1 Phagocytes are white blood cells that destroy bacteria by engulfing them.

45. 5 Unbroken skin is an excellent barrier against the invasion of microorganisms. In some cases, microorganisms may enter through normal body openings; in other cases, through wounds or bites.

46. 3 Agglutinins group or clump invading organisms.

47. 1 The relationship between athlete's-foot fungus and humans is known as parasitism. A parasite is an organism that lives in or on another organism and harms it.

48. 4 The relationship between nitrogen-fixing bacteria and the leguminous plant is an example of mutualism. Mutualism is an association between two organisms that benefits both. In this case, the plant gets nitrogen and the bacteria have a place to live.

49. 3 In a saprophytic relationship, an organism feeds on the dead remains of other organisms.

50. 4 After Darwin's day, the work of Weismann and others showed that genes (unknown to Darwin) pass unchanged by environmental influences from generation to generation.

51. 4 The theory of use and disuse said that any organ that is used becomes stronger. Although this is true of some organs, the changes are not hereditary and thus have no effect on evolution.

52. 4 With the discovery that heredity is controlled by genes that are sequestered in the germ cells, it became clear that there is no mechanism by which acquired characteristics can be inherited.

53. 3 Bacteria resistant to penicillin developed as a result of mutation. Organisms that did not receive the mutated gene were killed by the antibiotic. Those in which gene mutation occurred survived and passed the mutation on to succeeding generations.

54. 2 Continuity of the germ plasm occurs because no environmental influence affects the genes.

55. 3 Being larger, stronger, more prolific, or more intelligent may or may not promote survival. The general statement in Choice 3 is the only one that applies universally.

56. 3 All animal fats and coconut oil are saturated fats and tend to raise the LDL level. Most vegetable oils are unsaturated.

57. **5** The passage says that exercise raises the HDL level and that higher HDL tends to clean the arteries.

58. **4** Blood flow is not normal through clogged arteries. If the arteries that feed the heart are affected, heart attacks may result.

59. **2** The crucial evidence is the relationship between high cholesterol level and the state of the arteries, which is a factor in heart disease.

60. **3** Not all oily foods contain cholesterol, but most animal fats are rich in cholesterol.

61. **1** The foreleg of a horse is homologous to the arm of a human. In Choices 2, 3, and 5, a bird or mammal is compared to an insect, which is structurally quite different. In Choice 4, although both a fish and a whale are aquatic, the whale is a mammal.

62. **2** When a trout hatches from an egg, it looks very much like a little trout. All the other answers describe organisms that go through distinct stages as they mature.

63. **2** *Fossils* are the remains of organisms of the past. When an organism dies, it may be covered by sediment. Sediments are deposited in layers. The layers are compacted into rock. The oldest fossils are found in the lowest layers.

64. **5** According to the graph, the maximum number of Down syndrome cases occurs at age 45: 18 cases per 1,000 births. At age 30, there are 2 cases per 1,000 births. Therefore at age 45, there are nine times as many cases as at age 30.

65. **2** Choices 1 and 3 are opinions. Choice 5 is true, but has noting to do with the question. Genetic counseling is useful before planning a pregnancy, not after a baby is born, so Choice 4 is meaningless.

66. **4** According to the passage it is recommended that we eat something from all four groups. Cutting back on fats would mean eating less from group 1 and making up for the lost protein by eating a bit more from groups 2 and 4. The fiber and vitamins from group 3 remain important.

67. **4** The fact that the table does not mention specific foods eliminates Choices 1, 3, and 5. Although it may be true that active people need more protein (Choice 2), there is nothing to support this view in either the passage or the table. The table does say, however, that nursing mothers need more servings of dairy foods than others.

68. **5** According to the graph, oxygen content decreases as sewage waste increases. The organisms that decompose sewage are aerobic organisms, which consume oxygen.

69. **2** There was the greatest change in the whitefish population between 1975 and 1980. The whitefish population disappeared from the lake by 1980.

70. **5** The carp appears to be able to withstand oxygen depletion. The number of carp increased as the oxygen content decreased.

71. **1** According to the table of results, the number of bubbles produced by the plant decreases as the distance from the light increases. The results indicate that there is a relationship between the number of bubbles produced and the distance of the plant from the light.

72. **2** According to the passage, the variable is the part of the experiment that is being tested. In this case, the variable is the plant food.

73. **3** A control is a part of an experiment in which no changes have been made. Group *A* was the control. The individuals in this group received pills that did not contain the medication.

Earth Science

Questions 1 to 3 refer to the following article.

A nonrenewable resource is something that cannot be replaced once it has been used up. Minerals, natural gas, petroleum, and coal are all examples of nonrenewable resources. Minerals form in many different ways, depending on the geological history of the area in which they are found. Some ores are deposited when minerals dissolved in hot water are carried to the surface; others form when magma in the Earth's interior cools. It takes millions of years for natural gas to form from the remains of ancient sea life. According to geologists, petroleum, also known as crude oil, came from the decaying remains of algae and protozoans. Coal was created from the remains of prehistoric plants kept under tremendous pressure for a very long time.

1. Which of the following are the fossile fuels mentioned in the article?
   (1) petroleum, coal, and minerals
   (2) petroleum and oil
   (3) natural gas, ore, and coal
   (4) minerals and petroleum
   (5) coal, natural gas, and petroleum

2. Which of the following statements can be supported by the article?
   (1) Fossils are often found in coal deposits.
   (2) Nonrenewable resources cannot be replaced.
   (3) Coal deposits are found only where there are many forms of animal life.
   (4) Minerals have a wide geographical distribution.
   (5) Protozoans are organisms.

3. The main idea of the article is that
   (1) it takes millions of years for many nonrenewable resources to form
   (2) most nonrenewable resources are inorganic
   (3) petroleum products are vital to our way of life today
   (4) the conservation of renewable resources is of concern to scientists today
   (5) people who have oil wells are usually very wealthy

---

4. The Moon is approximately 240,000 miles from Earth. How long would a spacecraft launched from the Moon and traveling at an average velocity of 24,000 miles per hour, take to reach Earth?
   (1) 10 hours
   (2) 47 hours
   (3) 10 days
   (4) 15 days
   (5) 20 days

Questions 5 to 7 refer to the following information.

The Moon goes through a cycle of four major phases in a period of 4 weeks. As it revolves around the Earth, its orbit takes it first between the Sun and the Earth and then to the other side of the Earth away from the Sun. When the Moon is in the area between the Earth and Sun, the side of the Moon toward us is not lighted directly by the Sun. However, the Moon is slightly visible because of sunlight reflected by the Earth. The light is called earthshine.

APPEARANCE OF THE MOON FROM THE EARTH

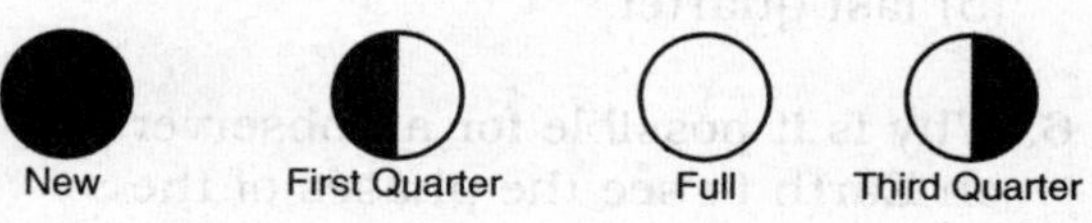

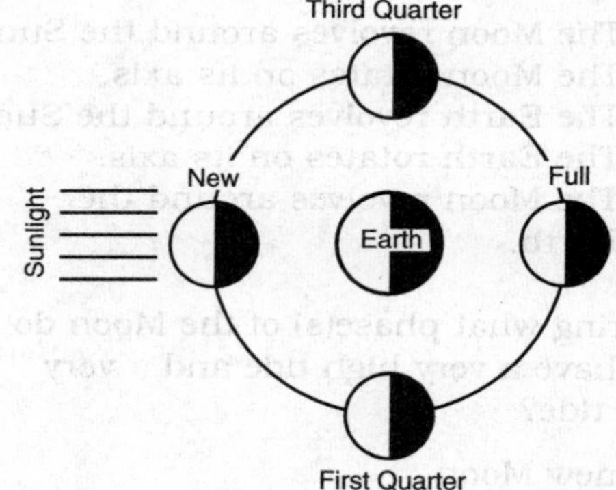

Tides are the result of the gravitational pull of the Moon and the Sun on the freely moving waters of the Earth. Since the Moon is so much closer to the Earth than is the Sun, the Moon has a much greater effect on the tides than does the Sun. The effect is greatest during the periods of the full and new Moon when the Moon and Sun are in direct line with the Earth and exert a pull in the same direction. The result is a *spring tide*, or tide of great range. At the periods of the first and third quarters, the Sun and the Moon pull at right angles and thus oppose each other. Thus the pull of the Moon is lessened, the result being a *neap tide*, or tide of small range.

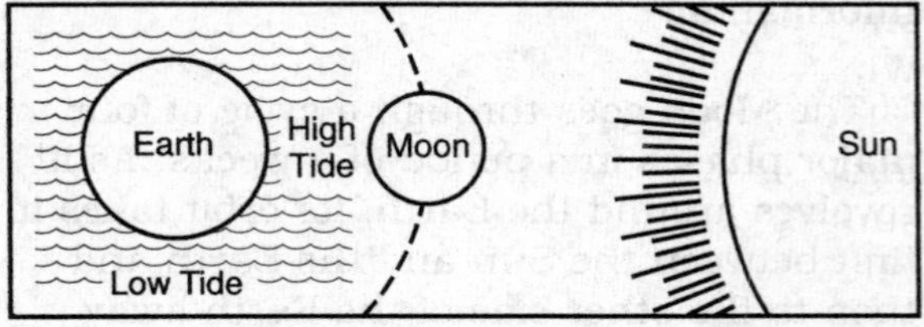

5. Earthshine is illumination seen during which phase of the Moon?

   (1) full
   (2) new
   (3) first quarter
   (4) crescent
   (5) last quarter

6. Why is it possible for an observer on Earth to see the phases of the Moon?

   (1) The Moon revolves around the Sun.
   (2) The Moon rotates on its axis.
   (3) The Earth revolves around the Sun.
   (4) The Earth rotates on its axis.
   (5) The Moon revolves around the Earth.

7. During what phase(s) of the Moon do we have a very high tide and a very low tide?

   A. new Moon
   B. full Moon
   C. first quarter
   D. third quarter

   (1) A only
   (2) B only
   (3) A and B
   (4) C only
   (5) D only

Questions 8 to 10 refer to the following information.

According to geological evidence, Africa was once a continent of ice, while the Antarctic was a tropical jungle. Paleontologists have also found fossil remains from the same organisms on different continents far apart from each other. For example, the fossil of a medium-sized dinosaur called Kannemyerid has been found in North America, South America, Asia, and India.

Attempts to explain such discoveries have led to the theory of continental drift and plate tectonics. This theory states that the continents of Earth once formed one vast landmass, but later broke away from each other and are still drifting farther apart. Sometimes the geological plates carrying landmasses collide with one another, and we have an earthquake.

Evidence for continental drift lies in a chain of undersea mountains circling the globe. When marine geologists took the temperature in a deep valley running through the middle of this mountain range, they discovered that the valley was much warmer than the surrounding sea. Scientists believe that this is where molten rock is pushed up from within the Earth. As this new rock rises, it spreads out the seafloor, pushing the continents farther apart. More evidence to support this theory was discovered when core samples indicated that the rock nearest the mountains was much younger than rock farther away from the mountains.

8. From the evidence in the article we can infer that a paleontologist

   (1) collects rocks
   (2) studies volcanoes
   (3) maps the ocean floor
   (4) studies fossil remains
   (5) studies plate tectonics

9. The theory that the landmasses of Earth ride on huge geological plates is supported by the occurrence of

   (1) hurricanes
   (2) tidal waves
   (3) continental drifts
   (4) volcanoes
   (5) earthquakes

10. A prehistoric species could range over a number of continents with no problem because at that time
    (1) the continents formed one large landmass
    (2) there were land bridges between the continents
    (3) the oceans were much shallower
    (4) the creatures were excellent swimmers
    (5) large numbers of the animals evolved separately on each continent

Questions 11 to 13 refer to the following article.

Toward the end of the year 1973, the comet Kohoutek began to make newspaper headlines as it moved toward the Sun at great speed. Predictions were made that it would be more spectacular than Halley's comet, which was last seen in 1910, as well as Ikeya-Seki of 1965 and Bennett's comet of 1970. Kohoutek was first discovered in March 1973 by a Czech astronomer Dr. Lubos Kohoutek, when it was still more than 500 million miles from the Sun. Astronomers reasoned that if it was visible that far away, it would probably prove to be spectacular when it streaked to within 13 million miles of the Sun on December 28. Thus, it was expected to be the third brightest object in the sky, after the Sun and the Moon.

Measurements indicated that Kohoutek's nucleus was 20–25 miles across, its coma about 10,000 miles in diameter, and its tail about 20 million miles in length. The nucleus of a comet is thought to be composed of a clump of "dirty ice"—dust particles, stony matter, and frozen gases, such as water, methane, and ammonia. The coma is a large, hazy cloud formed when the Sun's heat liberates dust and gases from the nucleus as the comet enters the inner part of the solar system. The tail is a long cloud of ions and molecules that may become fluorescent under the influence of the solar wind.

Despite the predictions made for it, the comet Kohoutek turned out to be of such minimum brightness that few people were actually able to see it. The reason for its disappointing appearance may be traced to the fact that it was not the typical "dirty snowball" astronomers had predicted. Whereas the icy head of Halley's comet released streams of dust particles on melting as it approached the Sun, catching the sunlight and reflecting it in orange and yellow bands, Kohoutek turned out to be a relatively clean, blue-white comet.

Astronomers have identified in Kohoutek the complex molecule methyl cyanide, which is believed essential in star formation; this substance was previously detected only in the vast dust clouds toward the center of the galaxy. Consequently, the conclusion is drawn by some astronomers that comet Kohoutek originated in a dust cloud outside the solar system.

11. What is the composition of the comet Kohoutek?
    (1) a nucleus, a coma, and a tail
    (2) a nucleus, a comet, and a tail
    (3) only a nucleus and a tail
    (4) only a tail
    (5) star dust

12. Why was Kohoutek not as bright as predicted?
    (1) It originated within the solar system.
    (2) It originated outside the solar system.
    (3) It originated in a dust cloud.
    (4) It did not release streams of dust particles on approaching the Sun.
    (5) It contained too much ice.

13. Why was Kohoutek expected to be spectacularly bright?
    (1) Its appearance coincided with the Christmas season.
    (2) It would pass within 13 million miles of the Sun.
    (3) It was first visible when more than 500 million miles from the Sun.
    (4) It was the third brightest object in the sky.
    (5) Its nucleus was very large, about 10,000 miles in diameter.

Questions 14 to 18 refer to the following article.

One of the contributions of the space age has been a new vantage point for viewing the Earth's surface from distant heights. The Earth can now be viewed by remote sensing, which can be defined as detecting an object from afar without direct contact. All our lives could be influenced by the results of the new era of accomplishment that makes possible such activities as immediate observation of natural and human-made disasters; continuous study of the ocean; monitoring and more efficient management of land, food, and water resources; discovery of additional natural resources; identification of pollution; tracing current flow along coastlines; studying the distribution of fish; and mapmaking.

In July 1972, the Earth Resources Technology Satellite (ERTS-1) was launched to make a systematic surveillance of North America and other areas from space. This unmanned satellite follows a near-polar orbit at an altitude of 920 kilometers and circles the Earth 14 times daily. As it passes overhead, images are transmitted through its various cameras to a number of receiver stations. It also collects and relays information dealing with water quality, snow depth, rainfall, and earthquake activity from about 100 stations located in remote parts of the continent.

In addition to the advantages of viewing the Earth's surface from high altitudes is the value of using infrared photography to study features that would not be visible with ordinary photography. These include plant growth, fungus infections of plants, circulation of sewage in lakes, spread of oil slicks, spawning grounds of sea life, identification of bedrock, surveys of mineral deposits, volcanic activity, and temperature differences in warm water currents, such as the Gulf Stream. It is highly probable that the ultimate benefits to be derived from this program will far exceed the original cost.

14. Which of the following best defines the term *remote sensing*?
    (1) study of fish distribution by the use of sensitive currents
    (2) release of a rowboat to see its path in an ocean current
    (3) study of the Earth's features without direct contact
    (4) measurement of the effect of an atom bomb in causing an earthquake
    (5) measurement of the depth of snow without the use of snowshoes

15. The space age has contributed all of the following values of remote sensing in viewing the Earth's surface EXCEPT
    (1) immediate observation of natural disasters
    (2) continuous surveillance of the oceans
    (3) identification of pollution
    (4) monitoring of food resources
    (5) making accurate observations of the land features of the planet Mars

16. Which of the following describes the orbit of ERTS?
    (1) 14 times daily, at an altitude of 920 kilometers
    (2) 14 times daily, at an altitude of 920 miles
    (3) 41 times daily, at an altitude of 290 miles
    (4) 290 times daily, at an altitude of 41 kilometers
    (5) It is an orbit around the Equator.

17. What can be accomplished by infrared photography?
    (1) Fungus infections of plants can be sterilized.
    (2) Circulation of sewage in lakes can be speeded up.
    (3) The spread of oil slicks can be absorbed.
    (4) The location of mineral deposits can be surveyed.
    (5) The direction of the Gulf Stream can be influenced.

18. Which statement gives correct information about the Earth Resources Technology Satellite?

    (1) The Russians were the first to launch their ERTS in 1954.
    (2) The ERTS was launched in 1972 to make a study of North America.
    (3) In 1972, the Soviet Union applied for permission to survey North America with its ERTS.
    (4) The Apollo project to the Moon was equivalent to the use of the ERTS around the Earth.
    (5) The next use of ERTS is to study the surface of the planet Venus.

Questions 19 to 23 are based on the following information.

The diagrams show the general effect of the Earth's atmosphere on solar radiation at middle latitudes during the clear-sky and cloudy-sky conditions. The graph shows the percentage of sunlight reflected by the Earth's surface at different latitudes in the Northern Hemisphere in winter.

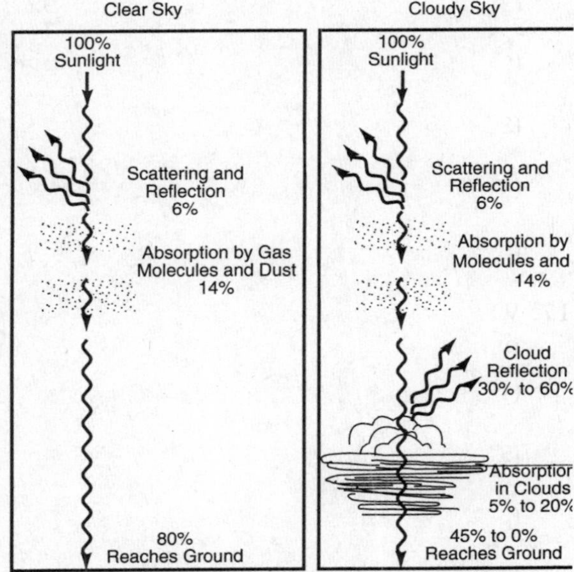

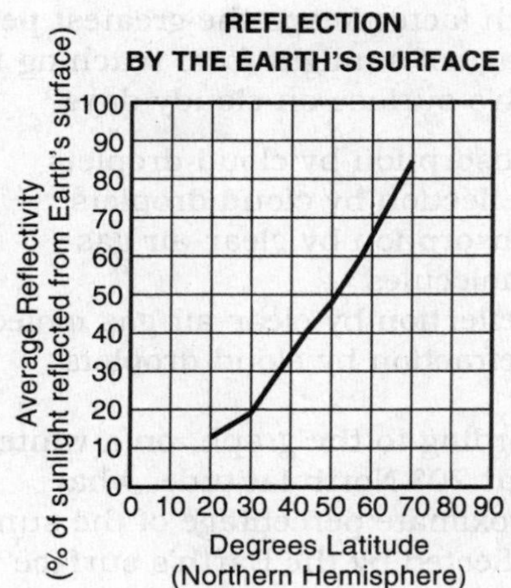

19. Approximately what percentage of the sunlight actually reaches the ground at 45° North latitude on a clear day?

    (1) 100%
    (2) 80%
    (3) 60%
    (4) 45%
    (5) 85%

20. Which factor keeps the greatest percentage of sunlight from reaching the Earth's surface on cloudy days?

    (1) absorption by cloud droplets
    (2) reflection by cloud droplets
    (3) absorption by clear-air gas molecules
    (4) reflection by clear-air gas molecules
    (5) refraction by cloud droplets

21. According to the graph, on a winter day at 70° North latitude, what approximate percentage of the sunlight is reflected by the Earth's surface?

    (1) 50%
    (2) 65%
    (3) 85%
    (4) 100%
    (5) 90%

22. Which statement best explains why, at high latitudes, reflectivity of sunlight is greater in winter than in summer?

    (1) The North Pole is tilted toward the Sun in winter.
    (2) Snow and ice reflect almost all sunlight.
    (3) The colder air holds much more moisture.
    (4) Dust settles quickly in cold air.
    (5) Snow and ice absorb all sunlight.

23. The radiation that passes through the atmosphere and reaches the Earth's surface has the greatest intensity in the form of

    (1) visible-light radiation
    (2) infrared radiation
    (3) ultraviolet radiation
    (4) radio-wave radiation
    (5) invisible light radiation

Questions 24 to 27 are based on the information in the following table, which shows the physical properties and chemical compositions of nine minerals.

Mineral	Color	Luster	Streak	Hardness	Density (g/mL)	Chemical Composition
Biotite mica	black	glassy	white	soft	2.8	$K(Mg,Fe)_3(AlSi_3O_{10})(OH_2)$
Diamond	varies	glassy	colorless	hard	3.5	C
Galena	gray	metallic	gray-black	soft	7.5	PbS
Graphite	black	dull	black	soft	2.3	C
Kaolinite	white	earthy	white	soft	2.6	$Al_4(Si_4O_{10})(OH)_8$
Magnetite	black	metallic	black	hard	5.2	Fe_3O_4
Olivine	green	glassy	white	hard	3.4	$(Fe,Mg)_2SiO_4$
Pyrite	brass yellow	metallic	greenish-black	hard	5.0	FeS_2
Quartz	varies	glassy	colorless	hard	2.7	SiO_2

Definitions

Luster: the way a mineral's surface reflects light
Streak: color of a powdered form of the mineral
Hardness: resistance of a mineral to being scratched
(soft—easily scratched; hard—not easily scratched)

Chemical Symbols

Al – Aluminum	Pb – Lead
C – Carbon	Si – Silicon
Fe – Iron	K – Potassium
H – Hydrogen	S – Sulfur
Mg – Magnesium	
O – Oxygen	

24. Which mineral has a different color in its powdered form than in its original form?

(1) pyrite
(2) graphite
(3) kaolinite
(4) magnetite
(5) galena

25. Which mineral contains iron, has a metallic luster, is hard, and has the same color and steak?

(1) biotite mica
(2) galena
(3) kaolinite
(4) magnetite
(5) graphite

26. Why do diamond and graphite have different physical properties, even though they are both composed entirely of the element carbon?

(1) Only diamond contains radioactive carbon.
(2) Only graphite consists of organic material.
(3) The minerals have different arrangements of carbon atoms.
(4) The minerals have undergone different amounts of weathering.
(5) The minerals have similar arrangements of carbon atoms.

27. Which mineral would most likely be weathered most after being placed in a container and shaken for 10 minutes?

(1) pyrite
(2) quartz
(3) magnetite
(4) kaolinite
(5) olivine

Questions 28 and 29 refer to the following information.

Since land heats up more rapidly than water, the air pressure over the land is lower. As the heated air rises, it moves out to the ocean and is replaced by the cooler air blowing in from the ocean. The diagram represents a coastal region with daytime wind direction as indicated.

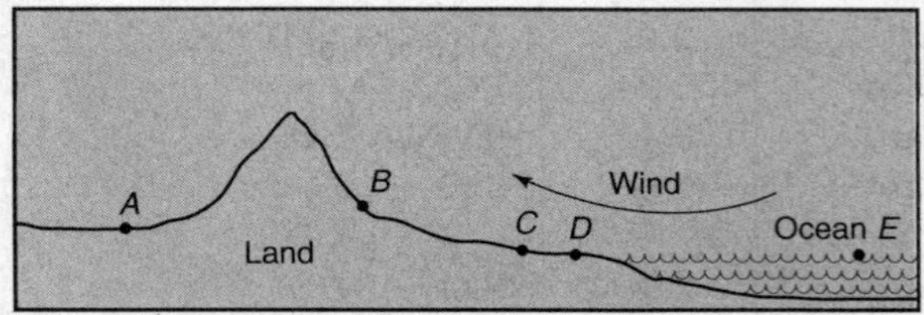

28. Which of the following best explains the direction of the wind?

    (1) the land being cooled during a clear night
    (2) more water vapor in the air over the ocean than in the air over the land
    (3) low pressure over the land and high pressure over the ocean
    (4) warm ocean currents
    (5) high pressure over the land and low pressure over the ocean

29. According to the prevailing wind direction shown in the diagram, which location probably records the highest annual precipitation?

    (1) *A*
    (2) *B*
    (3) *C*
    (4) *D*
    (5) *E*

Questions 30 to 33 are based on the following information.

A cold air mass is more dense than a warm air mass. Since two air masses do not mix, when they meet, the more dense air mass will lift the less dense mass. The boundary between two air masses is called a front.

On Wednesday, the weather service predicted that a cold front was coming and that the warm weather would end by Thursday night. The following graph describes the weather at 6-hour intervals for 3 days.

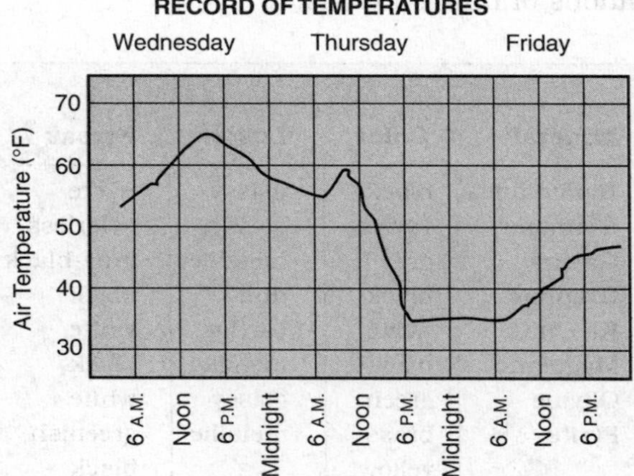

30. What is the lowest temperature indicated on the graph?

    (1) 30°F
    (2) 35°F
    (3) 40°F
    (4) 65°F
    (5) 60°F

31. During which interval of time did the temperature vary LEAST?

    (1) 6 P.M. Wednesday to 6 A.M. Thursday
    (2) 6 A.M. to 6 P.M. Thursday
    (3) 6 P.M. Thursday to 6 A.M. Friday
    (4) 6 A.M. to 6 P.M. Friday
    (5) 6 A.M. to noon on Thursday

32. On Thursday, from 9 A.M. to 6 P.M., the approach of which of the following was most probably responsible for the change in temperature?

    (1) warm front
    (2) cold front
    (3) stationary air
    (4) warm air mass
    (5) combination of any of these

33. On Wednesday what was the difference in the temperature from 3 A.M. to noon?

(1) 1°
(2) 9°
(3) 10°
(4) 19°
(5) 20°

Questions 34 to 37 are based on the following graph.

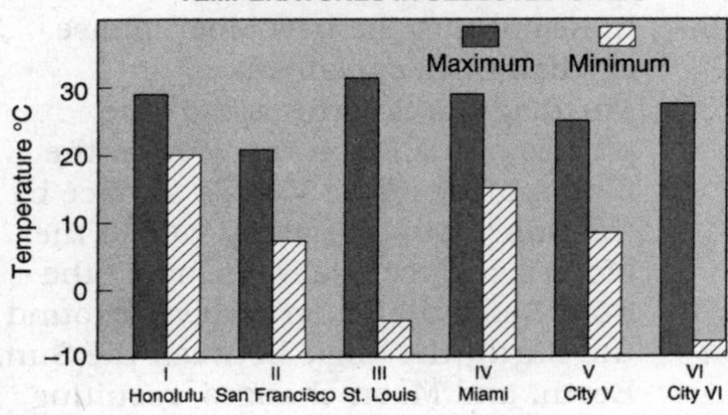

The graph represents data collected from six cities showing the average maximum and the average minimum temperatures for a 12-month period.

34. Of the following, which location has the highest average maximum monthly temperature?

(1) I
(2) II
(3) III
(4) IV
(5) V

35. Of the following, which location has the greatest difference in average monthly temperatures?

(1) I
(2) II
(3) IV
(4) V
(5) VI

36. Between San Francisco and what other city is the variation in temperature extremes greatest?

(1) Honolulu
(2) Miami
(3) St. Louis
(4) city V
(5) any of the above

37. To the climate of which city is the climate of city VI most similar?

(1) I
(2) II
(3) III
(4) IV
(5) V

Questions 38 and 39 are based on the following graph.

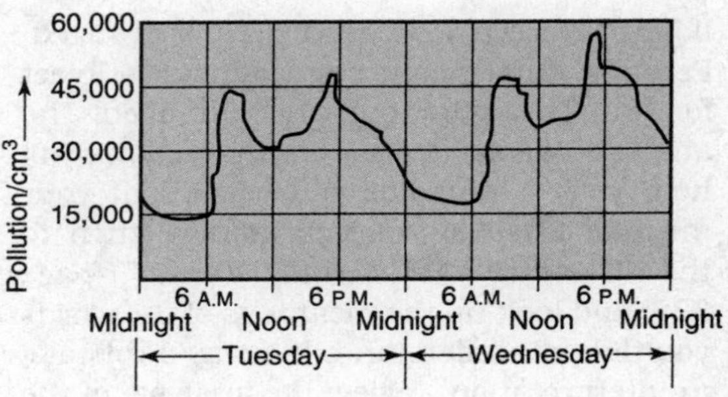

This graph shows the measurements of air pollutants as recorded in a large city for a 2-day period—July 10 and 11.

38. What is a probable cause for the increase in pollutants at 8 A.M. and 5 P.M. on the two days?

(1) change in amount of sunlight
(2) occurrence of precipitation
(3) high wind velocity
(4) heavy automobile traffic
(5) any of the above

39. On the basis of the trends indicated by the graph, at what time on Thursday, July 12, will the greatest amount of pollutants probably be observed?

(1) 12 noon
(2) 5 P.M.
(3) 3 A.M.
(4) 8 A.M.
(5) midnight

40. An explosion occurs at the upper surface of an ocean. The sound returns to the original site of the explosion 4 seconds later, after having been reflected from the ocean bottom. If the speed of sound in ocean water is 4,800 feet per second, how deep is the water?

(1) 4,800 ft.
(2) 9,600 ft.
(3) 14,400 ft.
(4) 19,200 ft.
(5) 96,000 ft.

WHAT'S YOUR SCORE?

______right,	______wrong
Excellent	35–40
Good	25–34
Fair	20–24

If your score is low, don't get discouraged. Perhaps earth science is a difficult subject for you. Try to find out why you failed. The analysis of correct answers that follows will help you to pinpoint your errors. If your mistake was lack of information, turn to the "Glossary of Scientific Terms" (page 338) and look up the meanings of the words you did not understand. If it was a mistake in interpretation, review the analysis of the question.

Answer Analysis

1. **5** Fossil fuels are derived from the fossilized remains of once-living organisms. According to the article, the materials that fit this description are petroleum, coal, and natural gas. Minerals are rock and were never alive.
2. **2** All of the answer choices are more or less true statements; however, only Choice 2 is taken from the passage.
3. **1** The main idea of the passage is that nonrenewable resources, once consumed, cannot be replaced because of the long times involved in their formation. Choice 2 is an idea that is mentioned, but it is not the main idea. Choices 3 and 4 are not mentioned, and Choice 5 has nothing to do with the passage.
4. **1** This question involves a basic mathematical formula:

   distance ÷ rate = time.

   The question tells us that the average distance from the Moon to Earth is 240,000 miles, and that the average velocity of the spacecraft is 24,000 miles per hour (mph). Substitute these values in the formula:

   $$\frac{240{,}000 \text{ miles}}{24{,}000 \text{ mph}} = 10 \text{ hours}$$
5. **2** In discussing the new Moon phase, earthshine is explained.
6. **5** The diagram illustrates that the phases of the Moon result from the illumination of the Moon's surface by the Sun. Note that about half of the Moon's surface is always facing the Sun. Since the Moon revolves around the Earth, the angle between the Sun, Earth, and Moon changes, resulting in the different phases of the Moon.
7. **3** This question refers to the spring tide, when the gravitational pulls of the Moon and the Sun cause tides of great range.
8. **4** The article states that "paoleontologists have found fossil remains," implying that these scientists study fossils.
9. **5** The second paragraph states that occasionally the plates carrying landmasses collide with each other, causing an earthquake.
10. **1** This answer is given in the second paragraph. There is no mention of land bridges (Choice 2), the depth of the ocean (Choice 3), the creatures' swimming ability (Choice 4), or the animals' evolution on separate continents (Choice 5).
11. **1** A comet consists of three parts—a tightly packed nucleus consisting of frozen gases, dust particles, and stony matter, about 20–25 miles across; a hazy coma around the nucleus, composed of dust transformed into a glowing vapor under the Sun's influence, and 10,000 miles or more in diameter; and the tail, composed of ions and molecules, which stretches out millions of miles in length.

12. **4** A comet with lots of dust is spectacularly visible to the naked eye when it is near the Sun. Light and electrified particles from the Sun blast the dust out of the comet's head, and the dusty tail reflects the yellow sunlight. Apparently Kohoutek did not release much dust.

13. **3** Astronomers reasoned that since comet Kohoutek was already visible at such a great distance from the Sun in March, it would be spectacular by the time it streaked to within 13 million miles of the Sun on December 28.

14. **3** *Remote sensing*, the ability to view the Earth's surface from the vantage point of heights, is a contribution of the space age.

15. **5** No mention is made of studying other planets in this project.

16. **1** The ERTS (Earth Resource Technology Satellite) follows a near-polar orbit at an altitude of 920 kilometers and circles the Earth 14 times daily.

17. **4** The use of infrared photography permits the study of features of the Earth's surface that would not be visible with ordinary photography.

18. **2** ERTS was launched to make a systematic surveillance of North America and other areas from space.

19. **2** The left-hand diagram shows that, when there is a clear sky, 80% of the sunlight reaches the ground.

20. **2** The right-hand diagram indicates that, when the sky is cloudy, cloud reflection returns 30% to 60% of the sunlight. This is greater than the percentage scattered and reflected by the atmosphere (6%), absorbed by gas molecules and dust (14%), or absorbed in clouds (5% to 20%).

21. **3** Find 70° North latitude on the horizontal axis of the graph. Trace upward until you reach the curve. The average reflectivity of sunlight (vertical axis) is 85% for this latitude.

22. **2** Compared to other ground surfaces, snow and ice are both very good reflectors of sunlight. This fact explains why surfaces covered with snow or ice do not heat up as quickly.

23. **1** The atmosphere is a better absorber of infrared, ultraviolet, or radio-wave radiation than of visible light. As a result, the greatest intensity of sunlight passing through the atmosphere and reaching the Earth's surface represents the visible part of the electromagnetic spectrum.

24. **1** The streak of a mineral is the color of its powdered form. This property is shown in the table. A sample of pyrite has a brass-yellow color. When pyrite is powdered, however, the color is greenish black. The other minerals have the same or nearly the same color in both crystal and powdered form, according to the table.

25. **4** Biotite mica contains iron (Fe), but it is soft. Galena has a metallic luster, but it does not contain iron and is soft. Kaolinite has the same color in mineral and powdered form, but is earthy and soft and does not contain iron. Magnetite contains iron and is hard. It has a metallic luster, and both the mineral sample and the powdered form are black. Graphite is a form of carbon.

26. **3** The arrangement of the atoms in a mineral can affect the properties of the mineral. The close-knit structure of the atoms of carbon in a diamond makes the diamond very hard and transparent. In graphite the carbon atoms are loosely arranged, so graphite is more brittle and opaque.

27. **4** According to the table, pyrite, quartz, olivine, and magnetite are hard minerals. Hence they are resistant to weathering. Kaolinate, however, is soft and therefore would weather the most over the same period of time.

28. **3** As the air above the land heats up, its pressure becomes lower than that of the air above the water. This difference in pressure explains the direction of wind.

29. **2** As the air blowing in from the ocean reaches the mountainous area, it tends to rise. As it rises, it cools, causing moisture in the air to condense. This condensation would probably cause location *B* to record the highest annual precipitation.

30. **2** The lowest temperature occurred during the period of time between 6 P.M. Thursday and 6 A.M. Friday. At this time, the temperature remained fairly constant (at about 35°F).
31. **3** The temperature remained almost constant from 6 P.M. Thursday to 6 A.M. Friday, as indicated by the horizontal line on the graph.
32. **2** On Thursday from 9 A.M. to 6 P.M. the temperature dropped steadily. This may have been caused by the approach of a cold front. As the cold front approached, it brought cold air to replace the warm air.
33. **2** On Wednesday at 3 A.M., the temperature was 52°F. By noon, the temperature had risen to 61°F. The temperature, therefore, rose 9°F over a period of 9 hours.
34. **3** The solid bar is tallest for St. Louis, indicating that it has the highest average maximum monthly temperature.
35. **5** In city I, the average maximum temperature is about 29° and the average minimum is about 20°: 29° – 20° = 9°. In city II, the average maximum temperature is about 20° and the average minimum is about 7°: 20° – 7 ° = 13°. In city IV, the average maximum temperature is about 30° and the average minimum is about 15°: 30° – 15° = 15°. In city V, the average maximum temperature is about 26° and the average minimum is about 9°: 26° – 9° = 17°. City VI has the greatest difference since the average maximum temperature is about 29° and the average minimum is – 8°: 29° – (– 8°) = 37°.
36. **3** Except for city VI (which is not one of the choices), the difference between the length of the two bars is greatest for St. Louis.
37. **3** Cities III and VI have similar maximum and minimum temperatures and would therefore probably have similar climates. However, since climate also depends upon the amount of moisture, it is possible that the two cities have some differences in climates.
38. **4** Automobile emission adds pollutants to the atmosphere. Traffic is heaviest at 8 A.M. and 5 P.M. in most large cities. Changes in the amount of sunlight generally have little or no effect on pollution levels. Precipitation tends to remove some pollutants, such as particulate matter. High winds decrease pollution levels by blowing away polluted air and replacing it with fresh, clean air.
39. **2** Since the pattern indicates that the highest pollution level occurs at 5 P.M., it is reasonable to assume that the highest level will also be reached at that time on the following day.
40. **2** One-half of the 4 seconds is the time that the sound vibrations took to reach the bottom of the ocean:

    (2 sec) (4,800 ft/sec) = 9,600 ft.

Chemistry

Questions 1 to 4 refer to the following information.

A student floated a lighted candle on a cork in a shallow pan of water. He carefully inverted a bottle over the burning candle and measured the time required for the candle to stop burning. He then removed the bottle, relit the candle, filled the bottle with exhaled air, and again inverted it over the candle. When the candle went out, he repeated this second part of his demonstration, but before filling the bottle with exhaled air, he ran 100 yards at top speed.

1. What was the student attempting to demonstrate?

   (1) Inhaled and exhaled air differ in composition.
   (2) Exhaled air contains less carbon dioxide than inhaled air.
   (3) Combustion releases heat.
   (4) Respiration produces heat.
   (5) Combustion produces carbon dioxide.

2. In regard to the candle going out, what observation would the student make?

(1) The candle stopped burning most quickly in the first trial.
(2) The candle went out most quickly in the last trial.
(3) The candle stopped burning at the same time in all three trials.
(4) Only in the first trial did the candle stop burning.
(5) The candle stopped burning after a long waiting period in all three trials.

3. What conclusion can be reached about exhaled air?

(1) It contains carbon dioxide.
(2) It contains no oxygen.
(3) It has less carbon dioxide than inhaled air.
(4) It has less oxygen than inhaled air.
(5) It contains as much oxygen as inhaled air.

4. Which of the following is a justified conclusion of the demonstration?

(1) Activity results in a higher percentage of oxygen in exhaled air.
(2) Activity results in a higher percentage of carbon dioxide in exhaled air.
(3) Respiration is similar to burning.
(4) Respiration produces more carbon dioxide than burning.
(5) The rate of respiration remains constant.

Questions 5 to 9 are based on the following information.

All matter on Earth is composed of approximately 100 elements. An element is a substance that cannot be changed into anything simpler. A few substances, such as gold, silver, iron, sulfur, lead, and copper, have been known since ancient times. During the Middle Ages and the Renaissance, more elements were discovered. Through the years, scientists have continued to add elements to a growing list, but there are still only 110 elements.

In the Earth's crust are approximately 90 elements. Our atmosphere is composed primarily of oxygen and nitrogen. Water, which covers most of the Earth's surface, consists of hydrogen and oxygen.

An atom is the smallest particle of an element. As shown in the diagram, it consists of a nucleus surrounded by a cloud composed of electrons. Each atom has a unique number of electrons, protons, and neutrons. Two or more atoms combine in either an ionic bond (transferring electrons) or a covalent bond (sharing electrons) to form a molecule.

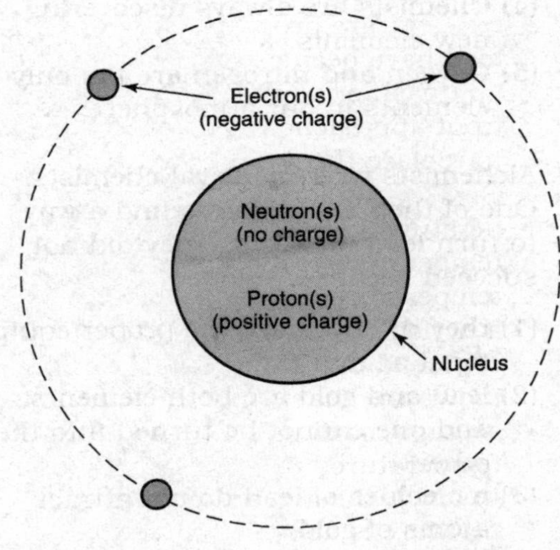

5. Which of the following is NOT an element?

(1) iron
(2) silver
(3) hydrogen
(4) water
(5) sulfur

6. According to the diagram, the nucleus of an atom

(1) contains elements
(2) consists of electrons and protons
(3) has a negative charge
(4) has a positive charge
(5) has no charge

7. An atom, with its cloud of electrons, resembles

(1) a stable configuration of particles
(2) subatomic particles in stasis
(3) a botanical inflorescence
(4) a cell with its nucleus
(5) moons in orbit around a planet

8. Which statement can be supported by the article?
   (1) Atoms share or transfer electrons to form molecules.
   (2) Since there are relatively few elements, matter on Earth is not particularly complex.
   (3) Atoms and elements can combine freely.
   (4) Chemists are always discovering new elements.
   (5) Oxygen and nitrogen are the only elements in our atmosphere.

9. Alchemists wree medieval chemists. One of their goals was to find a way to turn lead into gold. They did not succeed because
   (1) they did not have the proper equipment at that time
   (2) lead and gold are both elements, and one cannot be turned into the other
   (3) moleclues of lead do not attract atoms of gold
   (4) ionic bonding is not possible with gold atoms
   (5) the lead the alchemists used was not pure lead

---

10. The three phases of matter are the three states in which matter can exist—as a solid, a liquid, or a gas. Substances change from one to another phase as their temperatures change. Temperature reflects the rate of molecular movement, slow movement indicating colder temperature, and fast movement warmer temperature. For most substances, the freezing temperature and the melting temperature are the same, as are the boiling point and the condensation point.

    Antifreeze is added to the water-filled cooling system of an automobile engine to protect it from the effects of both overheating and freezing. This is possible because antifreeze
   (1) doesn't freeze
   (2) has a much lower freezing temperature than water and a higher boiling point
   (3) consists of alcohols that resist corrosion and can get to all parts of the car's cooling system
   (4) has slower moving molecules than water
   (5) can be used in various amounts to protect against a variety of temperatures

<u>Questions 11 to 14</u> refer to the following article.

All living things need proper temperature. Our body stays at 98.6°F in good health. To survive in cold or hot climates special protection is required. The same is true for plants and animals. Roses will not grow in the icelands, and polar bears cannot thrive near the Equator.

Temperatures vary. In Antarctica temperatures colder than 100°F below zero have been recorded. A temperature of above 149°F has been recorded in Death Valley, California. Even greater variations have been recorded in the laboratory and in industry. The lowest possible temperature is 459°F below zero.

These low temperatures are of interest to the scientist who specializes in cryogenics. Cryogenic temperatures start at the point where oxygen liquefies (−297°F) and go down to the lowest temperature possible. This point, known as absolute zero, is almost –460°F, or 273° below zero on the Celsius scale. Physicists are approaching this temperature by modern methods of removing most heat from solids. At low temperatures, atoms and molecules move slowly. Microscopic observation is like watching a slow-motion replay of a football game that offers an ideal way of analyzing a specific occurrence. Scientists have thus found many clues to the nature of atoms and molecules. From the physicist's point of view, temperature is a measure of the average kinetic energy, or energy of motion, of these particles.

At high temperatures, atoms and molecules move faster and thus turn into liquids or gases. The human body cannot survive high temperatures, partly because the proteins in our protoplasm would coagulate.

11. What is the lowest temperature recorded outside the laboratory?

(1) –100°F
(2) 149°F
(3) –459°F
(4) –297°F
(5) 100°F

12. Death Valley is not suitable for constant, successful human existence. What does the high temperature affect most?

(1) shape of atoms
(2) number of molecules
(3) protoplasm
(4) sweat glands
(5) liquids

13. What is required in order to liquefy oxygen?

(1) adding heat
(2) adding pressure and heat
(3) reducing pressure and adding heat
(4) decreasing the movement of atoms
(5) removing the heat

14. Which of the following best describes cryogenics?

(1) the supercold world
(2) the science of atomic structure
(3) crystallography
(4) the study of Celsius and Fahrenheit
(5) physical chemistry

Questions 15 to 20 refer to the following article.

Nature has her own ways of purifying water. These methods can be physical, chemical, or biological. As a stream flows, the water becomes cleaner because sediments, for example, are thinned by the addition of more and more water, and they may be deposited here and there along the bank of the stream.

Today, however, in our technologically complex civilization, human activity may cause some dangerous components to remain in stream water. Communities that wish to utilize water from "self-purified" streams have to use precautions, including filtration and chlorination.

Aeration, which may be accomplished in nature by wind action, turbulent flow, and waterfalls, causes an exchange of gases between the atmosphere and the water. In this way hydrogen sulfide, carbon dioxide, and methane are liberated from the water, and oxygen is absorbed from the atmosphere.

Light has an important effect on water. Light stimulates photosynthesis in aquatic plant life, and by this process carbon dioxide is absorbed and oxygen is liberated. Furthermore, the plants remove and use organic material that may be dissolved in the water. Light also has a germicidal effect on the surface of the water, although this effect below the surface is slight.

A process called sedimentation removes organic bacterial food from water. Sedimentation, which is caused by gravity, occurs when the water is filtered through some fine material such as sand. Sedimentation is most effective in quiet waters.

Some bacteria help clean the water by oxidizing organic material, converting it into basic mineral substances. In the absence of oxygen, other organisms, known as anaerobic bacteria, can split organic compounds and prepare the way for subsequent oxidation. These anaerobic bacteria thrive at the bottom of bodies of water where there is a great deal of concentrated pollution.

Biological cycles also purify water. Protozoa, one-celled animals, thrive on bacteria. As the bacteria are reduced in population, green algae appear. They in turn consume carbon dioxide, nitrates, and ammonia and produce oxygen. Large invertebrate animals, such as worms and mollusks, appear and feed on the deposits at the bottom.

15. Which of the following prevents streams from purifying themselves?
    (1) humanity
    (2) evaporation
    (3) condensation
    (4) filtration
    (5) chlorination

16. What is accomplished by aeration of water?
    (1) loss of oxygen
    (2) loss of methane
    (3) gain of carbon dioxide
    (4) gain of hydrogen
    (5) gain of carbon dioxide and loss of oxygen

17. Which of these causes sedimentation?
    (1) wind action
    (2) bacterial residue
    (3) turbulent water
    (4) gravity
    (5) organic material

18. Which of the following statements is correct in regard to the process of photosynthesis?
    (1) It is carried on by all protozoa.
    (2) Oxygen is necessary for this process to occur.
    (3) Light is necessary for this process to occur.
    (4) Carbon dioxide is given off during this process.
    (5) This process has a germicidal effect on deep stagnant water.

19. Which of these would best remove wastes at the bottom of ponds?
    (1) fish
    (2) aerobic bacteria
    (3) green plants
    (4) anaerobic bacteria
    (5) algae

20. All of the following tend to purify water EXCEPT
    (1) sedimentation
    (2) aeration
    (3) light
    (4) aquatic plants
    (5) bacteria

WHAT'S YOUR SCORE?

______right,	______wrong
Excellent	16–20
Good	13–15
Fair	10–12

If your score is low, don't get discouraged. Perhaps chemistry is a difficult subject for you. Try to find out why you failed. The analysis of correct answers that follows will help you to pinpoint your errors. If your mistake was lack of information, turn to the "Glossary of Scientific Terms" (page 338) and look up the meanings of the words you did not understand. If it was a mistake in interpretation, review the analysis of the question.

Answer Analysis

1. **1** In the first trial, the student used ordinary air, which is the same as inhaled air. In the second and third trials, he used exhaled air. He compared the time necessary for the candle to go out in each case. The difference in time was due to the difference in composition of the inhaled and exhaled air.
2. **2** In the last trial, the candle would go out most quickly because the exhaled air would contain the least amount of oxygen. The act of running required the use of more oxygen for the body cells.
3. **4** Since the candle would not burn as long in exhaled air, it is obvious that exhaled air contains less oxygen than inhaled air.
4. **2** As a result of respiration, carbon dioxide is given off. With strenuous exertion, a higher percentage of carbon dioxide is exhaled.

5. **4** Water is a compound made up of hydrogen and oxygen.
6. **4** According to the diagram, the nucleus of an atom contains neutrons, which have no charge, and protons, which have a positive charge.
7. **5** The only thing from the list of choices that the diagram resembles is some kind of satellite, such as a moon, in orbit around a sun or a planet.
8. **1** There is nothing in the article about the complexity of matter on Earth, thus eliminating Choice 2, or the continual discovery of new elements, eliminating Choice 4. The nature of atoms and elements, as discussed in the article, precludes their combining, thus eliminating Choice 3. The article does say that oxygen and nitrogen are elements in the Earth's atmosphere (Choice 5), but it specifies that they are *primary* elements, implying that other elements are also present.
9. **2** The unique nature of an element does not allow one to be changed into another. The other answer choices are nonsense.
10. **2** The answer to this question must be derived by analyzing the information and realizing that, to keep something—in this case, water—from freezing, you have to add a substance that has a much lower freezing point than water. Similarly, to protect the same engine from overheating, you have to add a substance that has a higher boiling point than water. Antifreeze, in combination with water, can accomplish these purposes. Antifreeze and water will freeze at a low enough temperature, so Choice 1 is not valid. Choice 3 is not a good answer because resistance to corrosion is not the subject. If anything, the molecules in antifreeze have to move faster than water molecules, so Choice 4 is incorrect. Choice 5 may or may not be true, but it is not as logical an answer as Choice 2.
11. **1** Observe the temperature recorded for Antarctica.
12. **3** Proteins of protoplasm coagulate at very high temperatures.
13. **5** Removing heat from a substance causes molecules to move more slowly. States of matter (solid, liquid, gas) depend on this factor.
14. **1** Cryogenic temperatures are 297° Fahrenheit below zero.
15. **1** Humans are responsible for many forms of water pollution, including those due to industrial processes.
16. **2** During aeration of water, methane and carbon dioxide are liberated, and oxygen is absorbed from the air.
17. **4** Objects heavier than water will drop to the bottom of the water. This is an effect of gravity.
18. **3** Green plants absorb carbon dioxide and liberate oxygen during photosynthesis. The plants need light in order to carry on the process.
19. **4** Anaerobic bacteria thrive in environments, such as the bottom of ponds, that do not have oxygen.
20. **5** While bacteria of decay may at times decompose organic wastes, in this question the other four choices are definite methods of water purification. Another justification for Choice 5 is that bacteria may be pathogenic.

Physics

Questions 1 and 2 refer to the following information.

As you break a beam of light, in one case you may be operating an automatic door opener and in another case you may be setting off a burglar alarm system. Actually your body is breaking a beam of light that is focused on a photoelectric cell.

That beam has been producing a flow of electrons from the photoelectric cell. When your body interrupts the beam, the current stops. The result is to close a relay that starts a motor.

Almost a hundred years ago Heinrich Hertz found that certain substances give off a weak electric current when struck by a beam of light. This is the basis for the electric eye, in which light energy is changed into electricity.

1. Which of the following illustrates a change from mechanical energy to electrical energy?

   (1) electric iron
   (2) steam engine
   (3) fluorescent lamp
   (4) electric eye
   (5) electric generator

2. A photoelectric cell is a device that

   (1) opens doors
   (2) sets off burglar alarms
   (3) breaks a beam of light
   (4) produces electric energy from light
   (5) starts a motor

Questions 3 to 6 refer to the following information.

Why does a steel ship float? More than 2,000 years ago, Archimedes realized that objects seemed to weigh less in water than they do in the air. After some investigation, he found that the weight of water displaced by a floating object was exactly the amount that the object "lost" when placed in the water. Thus, an object will float in water if it displaces a volume of water greater than its own weight.

A cubic foot of steel weighing about 500 pounds will displace 1 cubic foot of water, weighing 62.4 pounds. This block of steel will sink. If, however, this cubic foot of steel were to be cut into thin strips and fastened together to form a box, the same weight of steel could be made to float. Consider the possible dimensions of the box as 2 feet high, 3 feet wide, and 2 feet long. The box would have a volume of 12 cubic feet and would displace 12 cubic feet of water having a weight of (62.4) (12) or 748.8 pounds. Since this is more than the weight of a cubic foot of steel (500 pounds), the steel box will float.

3. What must be similar for two rock specimens that seem to lose the same weight when a string is attached to each and the specimens are submerged in water?

   (1) weight in air
   (2) weight in water
   (3) weight in salt water
   (4) volume
   (5) chemical and physical properties

4. Because objects seem to weigh less in water than in air, what characteristic do they have?

   (1) The objects displace a volume of water.
   (2) They sink or float.
   (3) They exert pressure against water.
   (4) They are affected by water pressure.
   (5) They are not affected by air pressure.

5. What unit is used to express the pull of gravity?

   (1) kilometers
   (2) miles per hour
   (3) pounds
   (4) quarts
   (5) liters

6. What is the apparent loss of weight of a block of steel 5 feet by 2 feet by 3 feet when it is submerged in water?

   (1) 180 lb.
   (2) 1,000 lb.
   (3) 1,872 lb.
   (4) 3,000 lb.
   (5) 18,000 lb.

Questions 7 and 8 refer to the following information.

Energy can take two forms, potential and kinetic. Potential energy is typically exemplified by an object at rest, its energy ready and waiting to be expressed. Kinetic energy is exemplified by an object in motion. An example of potential energy is a parked car. Kinetic energy is the car in motion.

7. Which of the following is NOT an example of potential energy?
   (1) a runner at the starting point
   (2) a bag of golf balls
   (3) an exercise bicycle
   (4) a sleeping child
   (5) a falling book

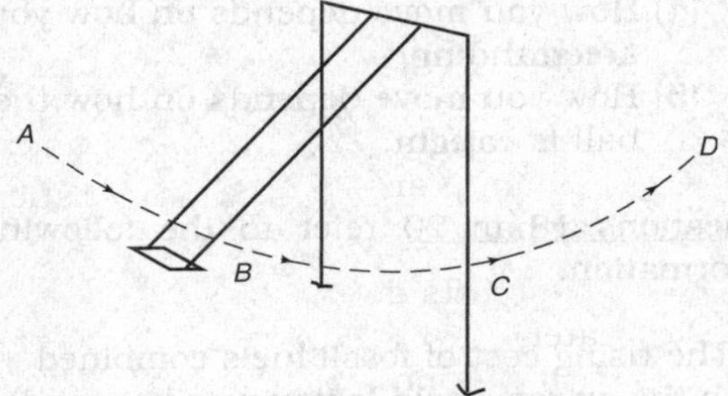

8. As a child on the swing shown in the diagram reaches the highest point (*A*), the swing seems to hesitate an instant before it begins to fall back. This hesitation is repeated at the other end of the arc (*D*). How is the energy of this motion expressed in the diagram at the points marked *A* through *D*?
   (1) potential, kinetic, potential, kinetic
   (2) kinetic, potential, kinetic, potential
   (3) potential, kinetic, potential, potential
   (4) potential, kinetic, kinetic, potential
   (5) kinetic, kinetic, potential, potential

Questions 9 to 11 refer to the following information.

The field of ultrasonics makes use of the sounds you cannot hear. An object must vibrate at least 16 times per second to make sound vibrations that the human ear can detect. The human ear cannot hear sounds made by vibrations of more than 20,000 per second. Sounds beyond the range of our hearing are called ultrasonic sounds. Bats use these sounds to avoid whatever is in the path of flight. The bat sends out a sound, and hearing no echo indicates that the path is clear. An echo makes the bat change the direction of flight.

Sound waves can be absorbed by soft material, but they will reflect when they strike a rigid surface. This principle is used in a device called sonar (sound navigation and ranging), which is used to detect submarines and other underwater objects. Sound waves are sent out. The time the waves take to return gives a measure of the distance of the object that produced the echo.

9. What principle explains why test explosions made underwater can be picked up by instruments hundreds of miles away?
   (1) Sound waves travel through water.
   (2) Special instruments can pick up sound waves out of the range of human hearing.
   (3) Sound waves bounce.
   (4) Echoes can be silenced by acoustics.
   (5) Sonar can find objects beyond the range of ordinary sight and hearing.

10. Of the following, which is the best way to avoid echoes in a busy room?
    (1) Keep all windows closed.
    (2) Use air-conditioning.
    (3) Hang curtains and draperies.
    (4) Lower all ceilings.
    (5) Adjust the sound of rings on the telephone and door bells.

11. Which term describes a reflected sound?
    (1) frequency
    (2) wave
    (3) echo
    (4) pitch
    (5) vibration

Questions 12 to 17 refer to the following information.

Although both a jet engine and a rocket engine operate on the principle of Newton's third law, they differ in that a jet must take in oxygen from the air to burn its fuel, but a rocket must carry its own oxygen. In both engines gases escaping under great pressure in one direction exert a push on the engine in the opposite direction. According to Newton's third law, to each action there is an equal and opposite reaction. You can illustrate the principle by blowing up a rubber balloon and then letting it go as you allow the air to escape. Notice that the balloon moves forward as the air escapes in the opposite direction.

12. Which of the following describes Newton's third law?
    (1) an object at rest
    (2) gravitational force
    (3) objects in uniform motion
    (4) falling bodies
    (5) action equals reaction

13. What characteristic of rocket engines is NOT characteristic of jet engines?
    (1) method of obtaining oxygen
    (2) method of using oxygen
    (3) reaction to the escaping gases
    (4) application of Newton's third law
    (5) methods involved in the burning process

14. Which of the following would be best explained by Newton's third law?
    (1) A balloon with a lower density than air rises.
    (2) A bat strikes a ball and the bat breaks.
    (3) A sled accelerates while sliding downhill.
    (4) A boat slows down when its engines are turned off.
    (5) A rock, thrown horizontally, falls to the ground.

15. Which of the following is (are) NOT found in an airplane with a jet engine?
    (1) ailerons
    (2) a fuselage
    (3) propellers
    (4) rudders
    (5) flaps

16. What propels jet planes?
    (1) the thrust of hot gases
    (2) propeller blades
    (3) rocket motors
    (4) steam turbines
    (5) any of these

17. Imagine that you are standing on a frictionless ice rink, holding a large, heavy ball. What will happen if you throw the ball forward?
    (1) You will move backwards.
    (2) You will move forward, following the ball.
    (3) You will not move at all.
    (4) How you move depends on how you are standing.
    (5) How you move depends on how the ball is caught.

Questions 18 to 20 refer to the following information.

The rising cost of fossil fuels combined with the extreme cold last winter has made us more conscious of the need for heat conservation. Americans have become aware that new fuels should be sought; and, perhaps just as important, new ways of preventing heat loss should be developed.

A number of alternative methods of producing energy and ultimately heat are being explored. Solar energy, wind and water energy, and geothermal energy are all potentials. Solar energy comes from the Sun. Although sunlight is free and plentiful, the equipment necessary to transfer light into heat and electricity is still rather expensive. The same holds true for wind energy. While wind easily drives a small turbine and produces electricity, storing the electricity for nonwindy times remains a problem. Water energy and geothermal energy are useful only on a large scale. Hydroelectric dams produce about 5% of the electricity used in the United States. The problem with these dams, however is their negative impact on the local habitat. The use of geothermal energy requires that wells be tapped into the Earth at certain places where there are subterranean hot springs. These springs can produce enough energy to run an electrical generator.

18. Which of the following is an opinion?

   (1) Solar panels are expensive.
   (2) The use of solar energy can help reduce air pollutants.
   (3) The cost of electricity is high and apparently will continue to rise.
   (4) The supply of fossil fuels is diminishing.
   (5) Solar panels do not contribute to the aesthetic value of a house.

19. Why is geothermal energy not used more widely?

   (1) Most people don't know about this form of energy.
   (2) It's too hard to find geothermal vents.
   (3) Hot springs are located only in certain areas.
   (4) Power companies have a monopoly on electricity.
   (5) Geothermal energy is not an efficient form of electricity.

20. Dams in the Pacific Northwest blocked rivers used by salmon going upstream to spawn. Which of the following was a possible result?

   (1) The fish spawned farther downstream; but salmon populations remained stable.
   (2) The fish spawned farther upstream, and salmon populations declined.
   (3) People near the coast used less water for irrigation projects.
   (4) The dams were abandoned because of the controversy over which was more important, producing electricity or preserving the natural habitat for the salmon.
   (5) Engineers decided to build special openings in the dams with fish "ladders" so that the salmon could still get upstream.

WHAT'S YOUR SCORE?

______right,	______wrong
Excellent	16–20
Good	13–15
Fair	10–12

If your score is low, don't get discouraged. Perhaps physics is a difficult subject for you. Try to find out why you failed. The analysis of correct answers that follows will help you to pinpoint your errors. If your mistake was lack of information, turn to the "Glossary of Scientific Terms" (page 338) and look up the meanings of the words you did not understand. If it was a mistake in interpretation, review the analysis of the question.

Answer Analysis

1. **5** An electric generator is driven by steam or water power. This rotary mechanical energy is converted into electrical energy. In an electric iron (Choice 1), electrical energy is converted into heat energy when electricity passing through the core heats the element. In a steam engine (Choice 2), steam expands and pushes a piston that is attached to a drive shaft. Thus, heat energy is converted into mechanical energy. In a fluorescent lamp (Choice 3), electrical energy is converted into light energy. The electric current vaporizes some mercury in the lamp, and ultraviolet rays are produced. These rays strike the inner coating of the lamp and cause the chemical phosphorus in it to glow. The electric eye (Choice 4) or photoelectric cell and its operation are described in the selection. Light energy is converted into electric energy.
2. **4** All of the events in the choices do occur, but the photoelectric cell does nothing but produce electricity when light strikes it.
3. **4** The apparent loss of weight is equal to the weight of the displaced water. Since the two specimens displace equal weights of water, they must have equal volumes.

4. **1** The apparent loss of weight is due to the weight of the liquid (in this case, water) that is displaced by the submerged object.
5. **3** Kilometers (Choice 1) are used to measure linear distances. Speed is expressed in miles per hour (Choice 2). Quarts and liters (Choices 4 and 5) are units to measure liquids. A pound is the amount of matter that will exert a pound of force as a result of the attraction between it and the Earth, that is, the pull of gravity.
6. **3** The volume of this block of steel is (5 ft.) (2 ft.) (3 ft.), or 30 cu. ft. Since it will displace 30 cu. ft. of water, it will lose (30) (62.4) or 1,872 lb.
7. **5** The only moving object among the choices is the falling book. All the other objects mentioned are stationary; therefore they are examples of potential energy.
8. **4** The passage mentions that the swing pauses at the highest points, *A* and *D*, where it changes direction. At those times the energy is potential energy. At the other points, *B* and *C*, the energy is kinetic.
9. **1** Some liquids carry sound waves better than air. At normal room temperature sound travels at 1,130 ft./sec. in air and at 4,800 ft./sec. in water.
10. **3** To catch sound waves before they can become echoes, curtains and draperies can be used to absorb the sound waves.
11. **3** In sound, the frequency (Choice 1) of the wave is the number of complete vibrations back and forth per second. A wave (Choice 2) is a disturbance in a medium as a result of transfer of energy. An echo is a reflected sound. Pitch (Choice 4) is one of the basic characteristics of musical sounds. Vibration (Choice 5) is a rapid movement to and fro.
12. **5** To each action there is an equal and opposite reaction.
13. **1** The passage mentions that a rocket must carry its own oxygen supply, but the jet uses the oxygen of the air.
14. **2** When the bat strikes the ball, the ball strikes the bat, causing it to break.
15. **3** In jet engines the force of hot, expanding gases provides the energy that drives the plane forward. In other engines, the blades of the propeller pull against the air as they whirl. Ailerons (Choice 1) are flaps on the rear edge of the wing of the plane that help change the direction of the plane in flight. The fuselage (Choice 2) is the body of the plane. Rudders (Choice 4) are the part used to swing the nose of the plane and prevent it from slipping when making a turn. The flaps (Choice 5) act as brakes in the air and slow down the motion for a smooth landing.
16. **1** According to Newton's third law, the action of the ejected gases produces a reaction that thrusts the plane forward.
17. **1** If you push the ball forward, the ball will push you backward.
18. **5** This statement mentions aesthetics, which is always based on personal preference.
19. **3** Geothermal energy can be used only where there are pockets of hot water near the surface of the Earth.
20. **5** This answer is based on logic and on prior knowledge. To have the energy produced by the dam and to minimize the negative impact on the environment, engineers build dams with special fish ladders so that the fish can still get upstream to spawn. This is not a perfect solution, but it is considered better than doing nothing to help the salmon.

UNIT VI

LITERATURE AND THE ARTS

TEST 4

CHAPTER 15: Reading and Interpreting Literature and the Arts

The three basic reading skills, presented here, are finding the main idea, finding details, and making inferences. Basic reading skills are applied to reading of prose, poetry, and drama selections. Reading commentary on the arts is also treated. The Glossary of Literary Terms is a mini-dictionary with definitions and illustrations of each.

CHAPTER 16: Literature and the Arts Practice

There are 120 questions on interpreting literature and the arts. All of the arts are tested—literature, art, music, theater, dance, film, and television.

15

Reading and Interpreting Literature and the Arts

Basic Reading Skills

Reading consists of a complex combination of skills. The writer sets forth his or her ideas using the medium of language consisting of printed words. If the writer has stated the ideas clearly, they have been well organized and well developed. You, the reader, must draw meaning from the ideas expressed on the printed page. In addition, there may be ideas that are implied rather than openly stated. For example, a woman dressed in black is described as *grieving*. The implication is that she has lost a loved one, even if this fact is not stated in so many words.

Reading requires the use of a number of skills so you can decode or derive from the language used the meaning intended by the writer, whether it is explicitly stated or suggested by implication.

These skills are basically three in number.

You read to find the main idea of the selection.

You find the main idea in a variety of places. It may be stated directly in the first sentence (easy to find). It may be stated in the final sentence to which the others build up (a bit harder to find). It may have to be discovered within the passage (most difficult); an example (note the underscored words) occurs in the following paragraph:

> Several students were seriously injured in football games last Saturday. The week before, several more were hospitalized. Football has become a dangerous sport. The piling up of players in a scrimmage often leads to serious injury. Perhaps some rule changes would lessen the number who are hurt.

You may also find that the main idea is not directly expressed, but can only be inferred from the selection as a whole.

> The plane landed at 4 P.M. As the door opened, the crowd burst into a long, noisy demonstration. The waiting mob surged against the police guard lines. Women were screaming. Teenagers were yelling for autographs or souvenirs. The visitor smiled and waved at his fans.

The main idea of the paragraph is not expressed, but it is clear that some popular hero, movie or rock star is being welcomed enthusiastically at the airport.

To find the main idea of a passage, ask yourself any or all of these questions:

1. What is the *main idea* of the passage? (Why did the author write it?)
2. What is the *topic sentence* of the paragraph or paragraphs (the sentence that the other sentences build on or flow from)?
3. What *title* would I give this selection?

You read to find the details that explain or develop the main idea.

How do you do this? You must determine how the writer develops the main idea. He or she may give examples to illustrate that idea, or may give reasons why the statement that is the main idea is true, or may give arguments for or against a position stated as the main idea. The writer may define a complex term and give a number of aspects of a complicated belief (such as democracy). He or she may also classify a number of objects within a larger category. Finally, the writer may compare two ideas or objects (show how they are similar) or contrast them (show how they are different).

In the paragraph immediately above, you can see that the sentence "You must determine how the writer develops the main idea" *is* the main idea. Six ways in which the writer can develop the main idea follow. These are the details that actually develop the main idea of the paragraph.

To find the main details of a passage, the questions to ask yourself are these:

1. What examples illustrate the main point?
2. What reasons or proof support the main idea?
3. What arguments are presented for or against the main idea?
4. What specific qualities are offered about the idea or subject being defined?
5. Into what classifications is a larger group broken down?
6. What are the similarities and differences between two ideas or subjects being compared or contrasted?

You read to make inferences by putting together ideas that are expressed to arrive at other ideas that are not.

In other words, you draw conclusions from the information presented by the author. You do this by locating relevant details and determining their relationships (time sequence, place sequence, cause and effect).

How do you do this? You can put one fact together with a second to arrive at a third that is not stated. You can apply a given fact to a different situation. You can predict an outcome based on the facts given.

To make inferences from a passage, ask yourself the following questions:

1. From the facts presented, what conclusions can I draw?
2. What is being suggested, in addition to what is being stated?
3. What will be the effect of something that is described?
4. What will happen next (after what is being described)?
5. What applications does the principle or idea presented have?

READING POPULAR LITERATURE

The basic reading skills apply to popular and classical literature alike. Popular literature is easier to read. The content presents fewer problems since you are more likely to have shared the same experiences as the writer. Also, you are generally more familiar with the language of the writer. Since the selections are drawn from sources that you read quite frequently—newspapers and magazines, for example—they should be no more difficult than the usual materials geared to the high school graduate.

READING CLASSICAL LITERATURE

Classical literature differs from popular literature in a number of ways. The settings are certainly different because they go back at least fifty to two hundred years. Also, the style of writing is different; sentences are longer and more complicated. The vocabulary is less familiar. Some of the subject matter may be dated for today's reader. On the other hand, fine classical literature deals with the eternal emotions of love, hate, greed, loyalty, self-sacrifice, joy, fear, among others. And many themes are eternal—the relationship of man to his fellow man and woman, of man to God, of man to nature, of man to his family, of man to his country.

Reading classical literature requires patience but it can be greatly rewarding. Try to imagine the unfamiliar setting. Reread the difficult sentences. Get the meaning of the unfamiliar word from its context. Find the application to life today of the theme of the selection. Continued practice will make these worthwhile tasks easier and the literature more satisfying.

Reading Prose, Poetry, and Drama

In addition to the reading skills required in general reading, to read literary material, whether popular or classical, additional special skills are necessary, namely the ability to: recognize the mood of the selection and the purpose for which it was written; deal with involved sentences and sentence structure; figure out unusual word meanings from the sentences in which they appear; interpret figures of speech. (See the Glossary of Literary Terms beginning on page 411.)

Read carefully the following treatment of these special skills and then go to the sample reading passages and the questions and analyzed answers based on them to get a feeling for these special, and necessary, skills.

LOCATING THE MAIN IDEA

Depending upon the type of passage—poetry, fiction, essay, drama—the technique of finding the main idea may vary. In the essay, for example, the main idea may very well appear as a straightforward statement, usually expressed in the topic sentence. In this particular case, the trick is to find the topic sentence. In works of fiction, poetry, or drama, the main idea might be found in a line of dialogue or exposition, or within a long, flowing line of verse.

PROSE

In reading *prose*, the main unit is the paragraph. Since all the paragraphs you will encounter on the GED examination have been chosen for their "loaded" content—that is, because they contain a number of ideas offering possibilities for questions—it is important that you learn how to locate the main idea. This, in turn, will enable you to understand many of the subordinate (less important) elements of the paragraph—all of which may also be the basis for examination questions.

The topic sentence containing the main idea is used in five standard patterns:

1. The topic sentence, expressing the main idea, may introduce the paragraph and be followed by sentences containing details that explain, exemplify, prove, or support the idea, or add interest.

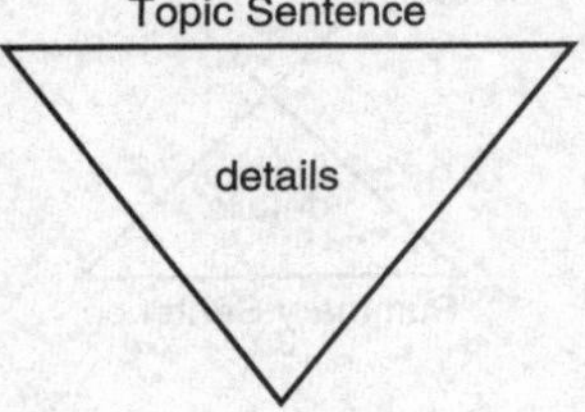

EXAMPLE

In *Alice in Wonderland*, Lewis Carroll created a world of fantasy out of essentially real creatures, transformed into whimsy by the odd patterns of a dream. Sitting with her sister by a stream, Alice sees a rabbit; as she dozes off, the rabbit becomes larger, dons a waistcoat and a pocket watch, and acquires human speech.

2. The topic sentence may appear at the end of the paragraph, with a series of details leading to the main idea.

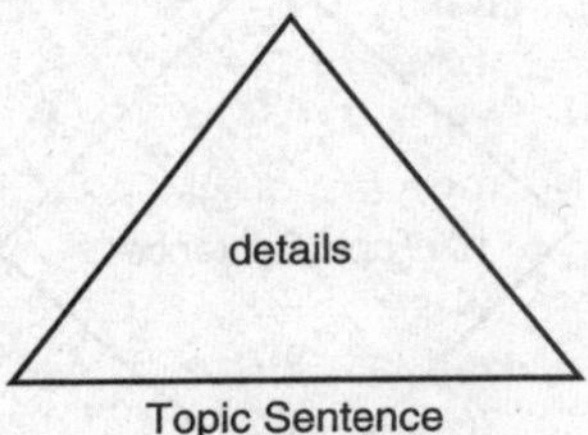

EXAMPLE

The small, darting rabbit on the riverbank becomes a huge White Rabbit, complete with waistcoat and pocket watch. The cards in a discarded deck become the Queen of Hearts and her court. <u>The real world of Alice Liddell becomes, through the odd patterns of the dream, the fantasy world of *Alice in Wonderland*.</u>

3. The selection may begin with a broad generalization (topic sentence) followed by details that support the main idea and lead to another broad generalization that is called the "summary sentence" (conclusion).

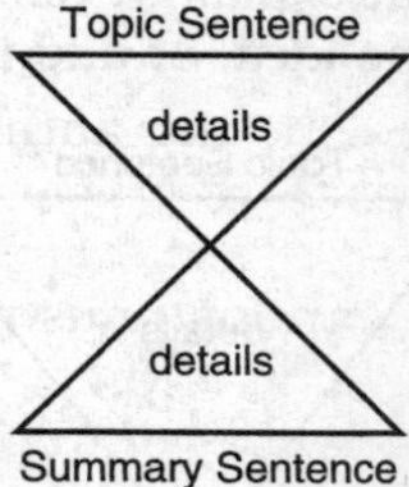

EXAMPLE

<u>The elements of the real world become, through the strange, shifting patterns of the dream, objects and creatures of curiosity and whimsy.</u> A scurrying rabbit becomes a humanized White Rabbit; a deck of cards becomes the court of the Queen of Hearts; a kitten becomes a chess Queen. In *Alice in Wonderland* reality becomes fantasy and, for a while, fantasy becomes reality.

4. The topic sentence may appear in the body of the paragraph.

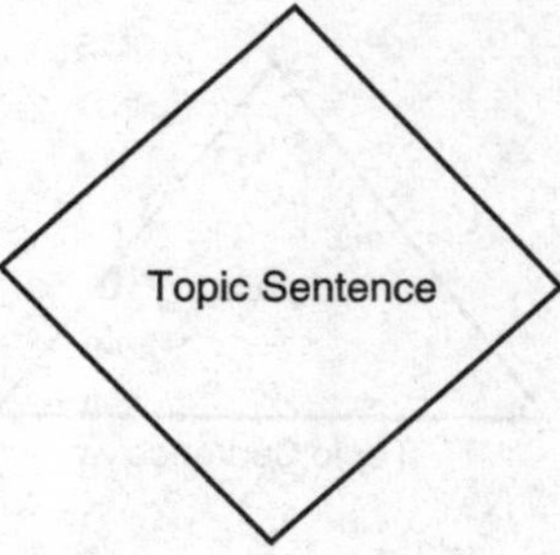

EXAMPLE

When Alice goes through the looking glass, she enters a garden where the flowers speak. In a dark forest, a fawn befriends her. <u>The dream world reverses the events of the real world.</u> The Lion and the Unicorn come off their shield and do battle. The Red Queen, originally a kitten of Alice's pet cat Dinah, gives Alice instructions in etiquette.

5. The selection may contain *no expressed topic sentence* but consist of a series of sentences giving details and implying a central thought.

EXAMPLE

A deck of cards becomes a royal court. A kitten becomes a chess Queen. A scurrying wild creature becomes a sophisticated courtier, a White Rabbit in vest and pocket watch. A proper Victorian tea party becomes the setting for rude remarks and outrageous behavior.

POETRY

Poetry is a form of literature that is difficult to define. Dictionary definitions are very complicated. One states that a poem is a rhythmical composition, sometimes rhymed, expressing experiences, ideas, or emotions in a style more concentrated, imaginative, and powerful than that of ordinary speech or prose. Another dictionary defines poetry as writing that formulates a concentrated imaginative awareness in language chosen and arranged to create a specific emotional response through meaning, sound, and rhythm. A desk encyclopedia defines poetry as a meaningful arrangement of words into an imaginative emotional discourse, always with a strong rhythmic pattern.

All these definitions stress certain common elements.

1. The content is an experience of the poet, usually emotional, filtered through the poet's imagination.
2. The poet uses a special language that is concentrated, using words that suggest more than their exact meaning.
3. The poet creates rhythmic and sound patterns that contribute to the experience described. He or she frequently, but not necessarily, uses rhyme.

With these elements in mind, let us analyze the poem "Ozymandias" by Percy Bysshe Shelley.

WHAT REMAINS OF A ONCE POWERFUL KING

I met a traveler from an antique land
Who said: "Two vast and trunkless legs of stone
Stand in the desert... Near them, on the sand,
Half sunk, a shattered visage lies, whose frown
And wrinkled lip, and sneer of cold command,
Tell that its sculptor well those passions read
Which yet survive, stamped on these lifeless things,
The hand that mocked them, and the heart that fed;
And on the pedestal these words appear:
'My name is Ozymandias, king of kings:
Look on my works, ye Mighty, And despair!'
Nothing beside remains. Round the decay
Of that colossal wreck, boundless and bare
The lone and level sands stretch far away."

The poet meets someone who describes something seen in a desert. It is the colossal wreck of a statue of a powerful king that has decayed over time. The remains consist of several parts—two legs, a shattered face, and the pedestal on which the statue once stood. The poet wants to portray a scene of utter desolation. Only the shattered statue survives amidst the emptiness of the boundless, bare desert sands. The poem gains its power by means of irony—the opposite of what we expect for a powerful king, not a royal palace but a broken statue of a king, is described. The poet creates, in a few words, the character of the king—his frown, his wrinkled lip, his sneer of authority. All of these details lead to the lesson the poet wishes to teach the Mighty: life is brief; human desires are vain; power leads to despair. He does this in 14 lines and 111 words.

Technically the poem has faulty rhyme—*stone* and *frown*, *appear* and *despair*, and the word order in "Nothing beside remains" is unusual. Nevertheless, an emotional response from us results by the picture the poet creates and the message engraved on the pedestal: nothing lasts forever, not even the power of a mighty king.

FINDING DETAILS

Very often questions on reading passages will test your ability to locate relevant details. In a descriptive passage, the author may give a general impression of a scene. Take, as an example, Edgar Allan Poe's famous short story, "The Fall of the House of Usher." The narrator conveys his reaction on seeing the house with these words: "I know not how it was, but, with the first glimpse of the building, a sense of insufferable gloom pervaded my spirit." Two sentences later you learn the details that made him feel that way.

Or, in a passage dealing with the character of the subject of a biography, details will document the point the author is making. Sandburg's biography of Abraham Lincoln contains many passages that follow this pattern. To show the industriousness of Lincoln, Sandburg writes: "Abe knew the sleep that comes after long hours of work outdoors...." You feel almost certain that the "work" that is mentioned will be described in detail, and it is. Among the jobs listed are "clearing timberland," "splitting rails," "harrowing," "planting," "pulling fodder," "helping...house raisings, log-rollings, corn-huskings."

Details are also used to move the plot or story interestingly and smoothly along the way. In Hawthorne's "The Ambitious Guest," there is the sentence, "The simplest words must intimate, but not portray, the unutterable horror of the catastrophe." Immediately there follow the details that tell just how horrible the catastrophe was.

Finally, details are often used to provide reasons for a conclusion that has been reached. Sherlock Holmes, in talking to Dr. Watson about his solution of the case entitled, "The Adventure of the Speckled Band," says, "I had come to these conclusions before ever I had entered his room." Then Holmes proceeds to give the details of why he reached the conclusions.

How do you locate a detail? It may be necessary for you to return to the reading passage many times to dig out the particular detail required to answer a given question. In your search, a number of clues may help you. These involve what are called ***transitional words***, words that point out the purpose of the details presented.

TRANSITIONAL WORDS

These words may indicate *illustrations* of a general idea or impression:

for example	in such cases	
for instance	in the same manner	
in other words	just as	

Or they may signal *additional items*:

again	another	second
also	as well as	third
and	besides	

Or they may point to *opposite evidence*:

but	nevertheless	although
however	otherwise	despite

Sometimes they *identify an important detail*:

don't overlook	notice that	most important

Finally, they may announce a helpful *conclusion* that the details document:

accordingly	finally	in conclusion
as a result	hence	in short

DETERMINING TONE AND MOOD

Tone is the aspect of the author's style that reveals attitude toward the subject. *Mood* is the atmosphere, or emotional effect, created by the manner in which the author presents the material.

To determine the tone or mood of a passage, consider the feelings or attitudes that are expressed. Examine, for example, the following passages:

EXAMPLE

> The room was dark—so dark that even after giving her eyes a while to accustom themselves to the blackness, she could still see nothing. Something soft—she hoped it was only a cobweb—brushed her lip. And the throbbing sound, attuned to her own heavy heartbeat, became stronger and faster.

EXAMPLE

> The room was dark—not dark as it is when your eyes are just not used to blackness, but really *dark* dark. Then some soft creepy thing brushed her lip, and she found herself hoping very hard that it was only a cobweb. And then there was that sound—baBoom, baBoom, baBoom—getting faster and louder all the time like her own heart going thump, thump, thump.

Consider the contrasting moods of the two passages above. The first passage presents a sustained mood of suspense and fear. The woman in the room can see nothing; something strange touches her; she hears a heavy and mysterious sound. We have the feeling that something is going to happen; the indication is that what will happen is dangerous, evil, or deadly.

The second paragraph relates essentially the same event. But we are distracted somewhat from what is happening by several devices. First, we are brought informally into the story—we know what a room is like when it's *really* dark. And the quality of darkness is also expressed informally—it is not pitch dark, or night dark, but "dark dark." "Then something creepy" is felt, and the sounds of the noise and the woman's heart are described—baBoom. The feeling conveyed by these devices is somehow made less frightening by the familiarity of the language, and the general impression is less one of total fear than of "scariness"—an easier emotion to deal with. Thus we have the impression from this second passage that whatever happens will probably not be all that bad or, if it is, it will somehow be easier to overcome.

INFERRING CHARACTER

Character is often implied by a person's words or actions, rather than by direct description. This has always been particularly true of drama, where the reader of a play is often called upon to interpret a character's personality without benefit of stage directions or other descriptive material. In the modern novel, too, the trend has been away from utilizing long descriptive passages and more toward allowing the characters' actions, speech, or thoughts (often called "inner dialogue") to reveal their personalities. The reader must rely, therefore, on the hints offered by the playwright or novelist to interpret character—and even then, a wide range of interpretation may be possible.

The following scene, from Oscar Wilde's comedy *The Importance of Being Earnest*, offers a good sketch of two minor characters. They are Miss Prism, a governess, and Canon (or Doctor) Chasuble, a clergyman.

EXAMPLE

MISS PRISM: You are too much alone, dear Dr. Chasuble. You should get married. A misanthrope, who hates everyone, I can understand—a womanthrope, never!

CANON CHASUBLE: Believe me, I do not deserve such a new-fangled phrase. The teaching as well as the practice of the early church was distinctly against marriage.

MISS PRISM: That is obviously the reason why the early church has not lasted up to the present day. And you do not seem to realize, dear Doctor, that by persistently remaining single, a man converts himself into a permanent public temptation. Men should be more careful; this very condition of remaining unmarried leads weaker persons astray.

CANON CHASUBLE: But is a man not equally attractive when married?

MISS PRISM: No married man is ever attractive except to his wife.

CANON CHASUBLE: And often, I've been told, not even to her.

MISS PR1SM: That depends on the intellectual sympathies of the woman. Maturity can always be depended on. Ripeness can be trusted. Young women are green. [Canon Chasuble shows surprise.] I spoke horticulturally. My metaphor was drawn from fruits.

What do we learn about Miss Prism? First, she is quickwitted. She quickly demolishes the Canon's argument about the teachings and practices of the Church. Then, we are given an example of her intellectual prowess. Her argument that bachelors become a permanent temptation to weaker women is a brilliant comment; also, when Chasuble questions it, she disposes of his observation that a married man may also be attractive. Finally, she marshals all the arguments on her own behalf since she is an intelligent and mature woman. She stresses "intellectual sympathies"; she mentions her doubts about the trustworthiness of young wives—only maturity and ripeness can really be trusted; young women do not make dependable wives. The conclusion: Miss Prism, who is no longer in the first flush of her youth, thinks she would make an ideal wife.

What has been revealed of Canon Chasuble? First, he is obviously something of a stuffed shirt; his first response to Miss Prism's unusual word—*womanthrope*—is to scold her for it. He then launches into a speech on the practices of the ancient Church regarding marriage of the clergy. Finally, Miss Prism manages to draw from him a more human response to the idea of marriage: the Canon sadly remarks that married men are not often attractive even to their wives. We can conclude from this remark that he is also somewhat shy, or frightened, by the idea of marriage, although not from personal experience; when a man like Dr. Chasuble says "I've been told," he means it. He is a man who speaks, and who must be spoken to, quite precisely; thus, when Miss Prism says "Young women are green," she feels obliged to explain that she is using the word *green* in a special sense.

Briefly, we may draw the following inferences from this passage: (1) the two characters are no longer youthful; (2) they have known each other for a long time; (3) Miss Prism is determined to marry Dr. Chasuble; (4) she understands his personality and has apparently made up her mind that she can adjust to it; and (5) the Canon is a stuffy, somewhat impractical man who is probably no match for a woman of Miss Prism's determination. If asked to draw any conclusions, we might well decide that Miss Prism will probably have her way, and that the two will probably make the necessary adjustments to a married life of limited happiness and total respectability.

Obviously, some ways of portraying character are easier to understand than others, and the personalities described may be more or less complex. The GED Examination questions, however, do not delve too deeply into the characters discussed; the answers can readily be found in the reading passages. You merely have to pick up the author's clues.

INFERRING SETTING

A number of factors are involved in the setting of a selection. These include not only *place* (physical location, type of locale—noisy, crowded, tranquil, etc.), but *time* (of day, of season, of historical period). See what clues to the setting you can find in the following passage.

EXAMPLE

He knew she would be late, but he could not keep himself from hurrying, pushing his way impatiently through the strolling, multilingual crowd. The Germans, their sunburned necks garlanded with camera straps, bargained gutturally with the indifferent women at their stalls, thinking to strike a sharp bargain on the price of a straw handbag or a painted box. The women let them struggle with the unfamiliar numbers, knowing exactly how much they would ultimately settle for. Three American girls, distinguishable by their short hair and madras skirts above sandalled feet and bare legs, dawdled along, giggling at the pleadings of two persistent *pappagalli* who seemed determined to improve international relations at all costs.

The sidestreet leading to the Signoria was hardly less busy, and he found it easier to dodge the small motorbikes bouncing noisily along the cobbled roadway than to struggle against the crowds pouring out of the great museum and onto the narrow sidewalks. He hated these annual floods of holiday-makers and culture-seekers who jammed the streets, the hotels, and the small restaurants so that the year-round residents found it necessary to retreat more than ever to the interiors of their cool, stone houses and their small, closed social circles. The more fortunate natives, of course, headed for Viareggio or the beaches of the South or the Riviera.

He finally found a table at the back of the cafe—a little too close to the bar but partially screened by a box hedge—and ordered a drink. The ancient *piazza* was mostly in shade now, except for the very tops of the towers which had been turned by the sun from the faded buff of the old stone to a rich gold against the blue sky.

What can we tell of the setting described?

Place: We can immediately pick up a number of clues. Obviously the setting is a city (crowds, sidewalks, a market, a museum). It is also not in the United States, since American girls are particularly distinguishable. By the mention of the Riviera as a nearby vacation spot, we know that we are somewhere in western Europe—but not Germany (the Germans are not familiar with the language). We can narrow the location down even further (although you are not expected to have all this extra information): two foreign words, *pappagalli* and *piazza*, might lead to the educated guess that the country is Italy.

Time: (1) Period—although the city itself is old (cobbled streets, narrow sidewalks, towers in an ancient piazza), the period is more recent. Motorbikes, barelegged girls, camera-carrying tourists all indicate the modern era. (2) Season—we can assume by the dress of the tourists, and by the fact that the natives usually head for the beach during this season, that it is summer. (3) Time of day—The piazza is in shade, except for the tops of the towers. It is unlikely, therefore, to be midday. Since the main character orders a drink in a cafe-bar, and since we have nowhere been given to understand that he has a drinking problem, we can assume it is late afternoon (cocktail time) and he has an appointment with someone for a predinner drink.

You should be made aware that the above passage was prepared solely to give you practice in inferring setting, and that you are not likely to find too many passages on the actual examination that concentrate on such description. However, you should learn to pick up small clues here and there that will give you an idea of the setting in a descriptive passage. Remember that, more often than not, the locale will be inferred rather than actually stated.

READING PROSE

Now let us turn to two representative passages from prose literature. Read these carefully; answer the six questions based on each; compare your answers with those in the answer key; then study the analysis of the answers, particularly for questions those that you answered incorrectly.

PRACTICE IN READING POPULAR AND CLASSICAL PROSE

WHAT IS ABOUT TO HAPPEN TO BORIS?

The light carriage swished through the layers of fallen leaves upon the terrace. In places, they lay so thick that they half covered the stone balusters and reached the knees of Diana's stag. But the trees were bare; only here and there a single golden leaf trembled high upon the black twigs. Following the curve of the road, Boris's carriage came straight upon the main terrace and the house, majestic as the Sphinx herself in the sunset. The light of the setting sun seemed to have soaked into the dull masses of stone. They reddened and glowed with it until the whole place became a mysterious, a glorified abode, in which the tall windows shone like a row of evening stars.

Boris got out of the britska in front of the mighty stone stairs and walked toward them, feeling for his letter. Nothing stirred in the house. It was like walking into a cathedral. "And," he thought, "by the time that I get into that carriage once more, what will everything be like to me?"

1. The title that expresses the main idea of this passage is
   (1) "The Lure of Autumn"
   (2) "Sphinx in the Sunset"
   (3) "A Mysterious Cathedral"
   (4) "A Terrifying Surprise"
   (5) "An Important Visit"

2. From the description of the house, we may most safely conclude that the house
   (1) is sometimes used as a place of worship
   (2) is owned by a wealthy family
   (3) was designed by Egyptian architects
   (4) is constructed of modern brick
   (5) is a dark, cold-looking structure

3. This story probably takes place in
   (1) the British Isles
   (2) the Far East
   (3) eastern Europe
   (4) southern United States
   (5) the Mediterranean

4. We may most safely conclude that Boris has come to the house in order to
   (1) secure a job
   (2) find out about his future
   (3) join his friends for the holidays
   (4) attend a hunting party
   (5) visit his old family home

5. In this passage, which atmosphere does the author attempt to create?
   (1) pleasant anticipation
   (2) quiet peace
   (3) carefree gaiety
   (4) unrelieved despair
   (5) vague uncertainty

6. From this passage, which inference can most safely be drawn?
   (1) The house was topped by a lofty tower.
   (2) Boris is tired from his journey.
   (3) There is only one terrace before the house is reached.
   (4) The most imposing feature of the house is the door.
   (5) Boris intends to stay at the house for only a short time.

ANSWER KEY

1. 5 **2. 2** **3. 3** **4. 2** **5. 5** **6. 5**

ANSWER ANALYSIS

1. 5 Boris has come to the house and as he enters, he wonders what changes may take place for him as a result of his visit. To Boris, this will be "an important visit." Choice 1 cannot be correct. Going back to the passage, we find "the trees were bare; only here and there a single golden leaf trembled high upon the black twigs." This and a reference to "layers of fallen leaves" in line 2 are the only indications of season, and "the lure" of the season is not even mentioned.

We reject this choice because it states only the setting for the main idea of the selection and background detail at best. It is not the *main* idea. Choices 2 and 3 are incorrect for similar reasons. In each case, a *detail* has been picked out of the selection and offered as the *main* idea. Choice 2 refers to the house, compared in majesty to the Sphinx. Choice 3 also involves a comparison—this time of the house with a cathedral. Choice 4 is completely incorrect. There is no surprise, nor is the selection's mood one of terror. There is anticipation of something about to happen, rather than something surprising that has happened.

2. **2** We can conclude that the house is owned by a wealthy family because there are several terraces, the stone stairs are "mighty," the windows are tall, and there are "masses of stone." Of the possibilities offered, this is the one we may most safely conclude is correct. Choices 1 and 3 are both incorrect, for similar reasons. Each is based on a figure of speech used in the passage, an implied comparison between the house and a cathedral and the stated comparison of the house to the sphinx. These are comparisons in the mind of the writer. Choice 4 is incorrect because it flatly contradicts the passage; the house is built of stone. Choice 5 is incorrect because it, too, contradicts the selection. The stone is not dark; it glows with the light of the setting sun.

3. **3** This question calls on you to draw an inference. The chief character has a Russian name, Boris. He gets out of a britska, and, even if you don't know that this is a kind of open carriage used in eastern Europe, the word suggests a conveyance that immediately eliminates "the British Isles" and "southern United States." It is safe to conclude, because of the name Boris, that the story "probably takes place in eastern Europe."

4. **2** The purpose of the question is to see whether you can determine the purpose of Boris's visit from the *evidence given*. While Choices 1, 3, and 4 may possibly be correct, there is no evidence in the passage to support them. Choice 5 must be considered along with Choice 2. If the selection ended just before the final sentence, the two choices would be equally plausible. But Boris is not merely making a visit. The question he asks himself in the final sentence makes it clear that the visit promises to change his future. Therefore, Choice 2 is the better of the two.

5. **5** Usually this type of question can be quite difficult. It involves not only locating details but also deciding what feeling the author wishes these details to create in you, the reader. Choices 5 and 2 remain possibilities. While "quiet peace" could describe the atmosphere, "vague uncertainty," Choice 5, is clearly superior as the answer. The whole place became "mysterious." Boris feels for his letter, the contents of which we are forced to guess. The uncertainty is climaxed by Boris's question, which asks, in effect, "What will become of me?" Choices 1, 3 and 4 involve some indication of Boris' feelings—of pleasure, of gaiety, of despair, but the passage contains no such indications.

6. **5** This question again calls for an inference, a conclusion that you, the reader, must draw from the facts that are presented. Choice 5 is correct because it represents the inference that "can most safely be drawn." Boris mentions getting back into the carriage. From this *fact* in the passage, we can *infer* that he intends to stay at the house for only a short time. Choices 1, 2, and 4 are not based on any facts in the passage: no tower is mentioned, nor is the door, and Boris's feelings are not described. Choice 3 contradicts the facts in the passage; one terrace is mentioned at the beginning and a main terrace is mentioned later. Clearly there are two terraces.

WHAT IS A CAMP OF WAR-WOUNDED LIKE?

Then the camps of the wounded—O heavens, what scene is this?—is this indeed humanity—these butchers' shambles? There are several of them. There they lie, in the largest, in an open space in the woods, from 200 to 300 poor fellows—the groans and the screams—the odor of blood, mixed with the fresh scent of the night, the grass, the trees—that slaughter-house! O well is it their mothers, their sisters cannot see them—cannot conceive, and never conceiv'd these things. One man is shot by a shell, both in the arm and leg—both are amputated—there lie the rejected members. Some have their legs blown off—some bullets through the breast—some indescribably horrid wounds in the face or head, all mutilated, sickening, torn, gouged out—some in the abdomen—some mere boys—many rebels, badly hurt—they take their regular turns with the rest, just the same as any—the surgeons use them just the same. Such is the camp of the wounded—such a fragment, a reflection afar off of the bloody scene—while all over the clear, large moon comes out at times softly, quietly shining. Amid the woods, that scene of flitting souls—amid the crack and crash and yelling sounds—the impalpable perfume of the woods—and yet the pungent, stifling smoke—the radiance of the moon, looking from heaven at intervals so placid—the sky so heavenly—the clear-obscure up there, those buoyant upper oceans—a few large placid stars beyond, coming silently and languidly out, and then disappearing—the melancholy, draperied night above, around. And there, upon the roads, the fields, and in those woods, that contest, never one more desperate in any age or land—both parties now in force—masses—no fancy battle, no semi-play, but fierce and savage demons fighting there—courage and scorn of death the rule, exceptions almost none.

—Walt Whitman

1. The author's main purpose in writing this selection is to

(1) express his sympathy for the wounded
(2) point out the brutal treatment of the rebels
(3) praise the courage of the fighters
(4) deplore the horrors of war
(5) describe the camps of the wounded

2. The author shows his emotions in all of the following ways EXCEPT by

(1) asking unanswerable questions
(2) effective use of epithets
(3) contrasting the battle with its peaceful setting
(4) including gruesome details
(5) sympathizing with the surgeons

3. All of the following relate to our sense of smell EXCEPT

(1) "fresh scent of the night"
(2) "the odor of blood"
(3) "the radiance of the moon"
(4) "the pungent, stifling smoke"
(5) "the impalpable perfume of the woods"

4. The soldiers are referred to by all of the following EXCEPT

(1) butchers
(2) poor fellows
(3) mere boys
(4) flitting souls
(5) savage demons

5. The reader can infer from the final sentence that, for the soldiers, the author has a feeling of

(1) pity
(2) contempt
(3) indifference
(4) admiration
(5) resignation

6. That the author is also a poet may be inferred from his

(1) description of the wounded
(2) comments on the camps
(3) conclusions about war
(4) awareness of the night's beauty
(5) indignation at what he sees

Answer Key

1. **4** 2. **5** 3. **3** 4. **1** 5. **4** 6. **4**

ANSWER ANALYSIS

1. **4** The key word in the question is *main.* The question calls for you to identify the "main purpose" of the author. Although it is true that the author expresses his sympathy for the wounded ("poor fellows") and he does describe the camps of the wounded, his main purpose is to use these camps as "a reflection" of the "bloody scene" to express his disgust at the horrors of war. Therefore, Choices (1) and (5) are incorrect. Choice 2 is obviously wrong since the author indicates that the rebel soldiers got the same treatment as the rest. He mentions the courage of the fighters almost incidentally in the last sentence of the selection, so Choice 3 cannot be the main purpose of the author.
2. **5** This question requires you to go back to the selection and to ferret out the details that the possible answers identify. Choice 5 is correct because the one thing the author does *not* do is sympathize with the surgeons, although he does refer to the impartiality with which they treat soldiers on both sides. In the first two lines, the author asks unanswerable questions.

   Epithets describe significant qualities of the nouns they modify. We find "horrid" wounds and "desperate" contest, "fierce and savage" demons, as well as such poetic epithets as "melancholy, draperied" night. The bloody battle is indeed contrasted with the "placid," moon and "heavenly" sky. Gruesome detail abounds in the selection.
3. **3** This relatively easy question contains many clues to the answer. *Scent* and *odor* are synonyms of *smell.* While *pungent* may refer to both taste and smell, it is the smell of smoke, rather than its taste, that is obviously referred to here. Perfume, of course, is something that is smelled. The correct choice is 3 because "the radiance of the moon" refers to the sense of sight, not the sense of smell.
4. **1** Careful attention to the details of the passage reveals that the soldiers are referred to as "poor fellows," "some mere boys," "flitting souls," and "fierce and savage demons." The term *butchers' shambles* compares the camp of the wounded with a butchers' slaughterhouse and does not refer at all to the soldiers.
5. **4** The question identifies the specific place where the answer may be found—the final sentence. Study of that sentence gives us two clues to the author's feeling for the soldiers. They are "fierce and savage demons." "Courage and scorn of death" is typical of their fighting. The author does not pity the soldiers in this sentence, nor does he show any indifference to their "desperate" plight. There is no evidence that he is resigned to their having to continue the battle. While he does allude to their ferocity and savagery, he does not show contempt or scorn for the soldiers. Rather, he emphasizes their courage, since it is true that almost all display this quality in the fierce battle. Therefore, his feeling is one of admiration.
6. **4** What details would lead you, the reader, to conclude that any writer has the qualities of a poet? The "Glossary of Literary Terms" beginning on page 411 defines a poem as literature that has "deep emotion; highly imaginative language with figures of speech; distinctive rhythm;... words that mean more than they apparently say" among others. Mere description, comment, and conclusion are not poetic qualities. The writing of a good reporter has all of these features. Anger, while it is a deep emotion, is not as good a clue to the fact that the author is a poet as is his unusual sensitivity to the night's beauty: "the radiance of the moon," "those buoyant upper oceans" (referring to the sky), "the melancholy, draperied night above." The scene is viewed by the light of the moon, the sky is compared to a sea, and the night is compared to a hanging curtain in a way that only a poet could succeed in doing.

SUMMARY OF PROSE INTERPRETATION

Thus far, what have you learned, with respect to skills of interpretation, from the study of prose?

You should:

1. *Read the selection carefully.*
2. *In* ***selecting a title*** *that expresses the main idea, go back to the selection constantly. Arrive at the correct answer by a process of elimination.* Eliminate the one or more possibilities that are clearly incorrect. Eliminate the possibilities that are based on minor details; there will be one or two of these. From the remaining choices, you must select the one that expresses the main rather than the subordinate idea.
3. *In* ***drawing inferences****, find the clues in the passage from which you can draw the proper conclusion.* The clue may be a name, a place, an adjective, an object, an unusual word. You may have to reread the selection a few times before you locate the clue or the two details that can be linked to make a clue.
4. *In* ***determining purpose****, ask yourself why the author wrote the passage; what he or she wanted you, the reader, to understand or feel.* After you have read the passage several times, try to define the *total impression* you get from your reading. The purposes of authors at various times may be to inform, to arouse anger, to poke fun at, to evoke pity, to amuse, and to urge to action, among others. Which of these predominates?
5. *In* ***determining mood****, try to find words that either create an atmosphere or evoke an emotion.* This is related to the author's purpose but may not necessarily be his or her main purpose. *There are two main guides to determining atmosphere: selection of details and use of adjectives and adverbs.*

READING POETRY

Reading poetry requires a special set of skills because the poet uses both a special language and special writing techniques.

In poetry, words are not used in their normal, literal senses. Rather, they are used in such a way that you, the reader, must call on your imagination to fully understand them. Let's consider an example.

"I almost blew my top."

Here the words *blew* and *top* do not have their regular meanings, but are used figuratively to express the idea "I almost went crazy."

Skill One. In poetry, words are often used in a figurative sense. Do not take these words literally. Use your imagination in order to understand them as the poet uses them.

In poetry, meaning is frequently compressed into a few words by the use of figures of speech such as metaphors. (See the "Glossary of Literary Terms," page 411.)

"The road was a ribbon of moonlight."

In seven words, the poet Walter de la Mare tells us that the time is night, the moon was shining, and the road is a lighted area surrounded by darker ones.

"The moon was a ghostly galleon."

In six words, the poet tells us that the moon is like a ship, the sky is like an ocean, and the moon creates an eerie, supernatural feeling as it moves across the sky.

Skill Two In poetry, words often compress or condense extended meanings and pictures into a few words, usually by the use of figures of speech such as metaphors. Add to the words you read the implied meanings and pictures they create.

In poetry, meaning is closely related to rhythm. For this reason it helps to read poetry aloud.

> ***Skill Three.*** Read the poem aloud paying attention to the rhythm, because the rhythm of the poem will help you understand its meaning.

In poetry, in addition to rhythm, which is always present, you will frequently encounter rhyme. Rhyme, too, often helps to convey meaning. In Edgar Allan Poe's poem "The Raven," the rhyme is repeated in *door, more, Lenore, forevermore,* and *nevermore.*

"'Tis some visitor,' I muttered, 'tapping at my chamber door: Only this and nothing more.'"

The sound itself adds to the atmosphere of mystery.

> ***Skill Four.*** As you read the poem aloud, note the rhyme as well as the rhythm, since both add to the meaning and feelings expressed.

In poetry, the poet uses sounds in addition to rhyme to help convey meaning. The poet John Masefield describes the effect of the wind with a series of "w" and "wh" sounds. He wants to return

"To the gull's *w*ay and the *wh*ales's *w*ay
*wh*ere the *w*ind's like a *wh*etted knife."

This technique is known as alliteration. (See the "Glossary of Literary Terms," page 411.)

Another technique is the use of words whose sounds correspond to their meaning. Here is the way one poet describes the movement of the waters of a river:

"And rushing and flushing and brushing and gushing,
And flapping and rapping and clapping and slapping..."

> ***Skill Five.*** As you read the poem aloud, note the sounds of the words as well as their rhyme and their rhythm, since each adds to the meaning and feelings expressed by the poet.

In poetry, the poem itself has a certain shape or form. The poem can be in a very definite form, such as the sonnet, or in a very loose form. "The New Colossus," by Emma Lazarus, which follows below, is a sonnet with a definite rhythm and a definite rhyme scheme. The form of "The New Colossus" is appropriate because it lends itself to the main ideas expressed in each of the two stanzas of the poem.

> ***Skill Six.*** As you read the poem, study its form and structure. If it is divided into stanzas or paragraph units, try to determine what each stanza adds to the meaning of the poem. The poem's form is another aid to your understanding its meaning. Consult the "Glossary of Literary Terms," page 411, for *sonnet* and *stanza*, terms that relate to poetic form and structure.

Read the following poem carefully and answer the questions based on it. Compare your answers with the answer key: then study the analysis of the answers, particularly for questions that you have answered incorrectly.

Practice in Reading Poetry

WHAT DOES THE NEW STATUE REPRESENT?

The New Colossus

Not like the brazen giant of Greek fame,
With conquering limbs astride from land to land;
Here at our sea-washed, sunset gates shall stand
A mighty woman with a torch, whose flame
Is the imprisoned lightning, and her name
Mother of Exiles. From her beacon-hand
Glows world-wide welcome; her mild eyes command
The air-bridged harbor that twin cities frame.

"Keep, ancient lands, your storied
pomp!" cries she
with silent lips. "Give me your tired,
your poor,
Your huddled masses yearning to
breathe free,
The wretched refuse of your teeming
shore.
Send these, the homeless, tempest-
tost, to me.
I lift my lamp beside the golden
door!"

—Emma Lazarus

1. The main idea of the poem is that
   (1) the ancient lands of Europe should serve as a beacon to America
   (2) the Greek statue serves as a model for the American statue
   (3) the mighty are asked to come to these shores
   (4) America welcomes all persecuted freedom-lovers
   (5) the lamp guides those who come to the golden door

2. In the choices below, the incorrectly paired words are
   (1) brazen—of brass
   (2) sunset—east
   (3) beacon—guiding light
   (4) refuse—trash
   (5) pomp—splendor

3. The "mighty woman" and "Mother of Exiles" is the
   (1) United States of America
   (2) city of New York
   (3) Statue of Liberty
   (4) Plymouth Rock
   (5) Golden Gate

4. The title of this poem, "The New Colossus," implies
   (1) similarity to the old
   (2) replacement of the old
   (3) difference from the old
   (4) inferiority to the old
   (5) acceptance of the old

5. The *incorrectly* matched phrase from the poem with the figure of speech or poetic device it demonstrates is
   (1) "Her mild eyes"—epithet
   (2) "Keep, ancient lands, your storied pomp!" cries she—personification
   (3) "shall stand a mighty woman"—inversion
   (4) "world-wide welcome"—alliteration
   (5) "flame is the imprisoned lightning"—simile

6. The form of the poem is that of
   (1) a ballad
   (2) an octet
   (3) an ode
   (4) a sestet
   (5) a sonnet

ANSWER KEY

1. 4 2. 2 3. 3 4. 3 5. 5 6. 5

ANSWER ANALYSIS

1. 4 Choice 1 is not correct because the reverse is actually true; America's "beacon-hand" as represented in the statue is a beacon to the exiles from the ancient lands of Europe. Nor is Choice 2 correct since the opening line begins "Not like" the Greek statue is the American statue. Choice 3 is incorrect; it is the "tired," "poor," and "homeless" who are welcomed to these shores. While Choice 5 is true as far as it goes, it is not the main idea. Choice A is correct.

REMEMBER: You must read the selection carefully. ***In selecting the main idea,*** *you must go back to the selection several times. Arrive at the correct answer by a process of elimination.*

2. **2** While this question is seemingly a vocabulary question that requires you to recall the meanings of the words in the five possible answers, the poem does provide hints or context clues to the meanings of several of the words. "From her *beacon*-hand glows world-wide welcome" indicates that light is going forth. The *refuse* is described as *wretched*. Pomp is contrasted with the *poor* and the *refuse*. Therefore, you can conclude that these words are correctly paired. If you deduce from the first verse that an ancient statue is being described, the meaning of *brass* for *brazen* seems logical. But even if you can't, "our"—meaning America's—"sunset gates" must be located in the west, where the sun sets. Choice 2 is the correct answer because sunset is always associated with the west rather than the east.

> *REMEMBER: Never give up on a question.* ***Where the meaning of words is involved****, carefully study the clues to their meaning given by other nearby words in the passage.*

3. **3** To answer this question, you must draw an inference or conclusion from what is stated indirectly in the poem. What does the poem tell us about the "mighty woman" and "Mother of Exiles"? We learn that she stands "with a torch"; we also learn that "her mild eyes command the...harbor." These facts rule out all possible answers except Choice 3. The United States of America and the city of New York do not, even symbolically, stand "with a torch." Neither Plymouth Rock (a rock) nor the Golden Gate (a bridge) fits the clues contained in the poem.

> *REMEMBER:* ***In drawing inferences or making deductions*** *from the text, find the clues that can help you. You may have to reread the selection a few times before you find them.*

4. **3** This is not a difficult question if you read the poem with care from the very beginning. The new colossus is "not like" the old, according to the very first verse, so Choices 1 and 2 are immediately ruled out. To find the correct answer, you must determine how the poet feels about this new colossus. Since she is "mighty" and since her eyes are "mild," it is obvious that the poet admires the new colossus and finds it superior to the old (which the poet rejects). Therefore, Choices 4 and 5 are also incorrect. It is the "difference" and the fact that the new is "not like" the old that are stressed. Therefore, Choice 3 is correct.
5. **5** It is important for you to refer to the "Glossary of Literary Terms" on page 411 if you haven't mastered the definitions already because all five possible answers are defined in that vocabulary. *Epithet*, an adjective or phrase that identifies a significant quality of the noun it describes, is exemplified by her *mild* eyes, so Choice 1 contains a correctly matched pair. *Personification*, the act of attributing human qualities to a "thing" (in this case the power of speech to a statue), is correctly paired with the quotation from the poem. *Inversion*, reversal of normal word order, applies to "shall stand a mighty woman" because the normal order is "a mighty woman shall stand." "Worldwide welcome" is a perfect example of *alliteration* since the same consonant sound, "w," is repeated at the beginning of two words that follow one another. By elimination, Choice 5 is correct since *simile* is *incorrectly* paired with "flame is the imprisoned lightning." *Like* or *as* is *not* used to make the comparison, so "flame is the imprisoned lightning" is properly called a *metaphor*.
6. **5** Where the form of a poem is required to answer a question, first count the number of lines. Then figure out the rhyme scheme. Here there are 14 lines with a rhyme scheme as follows:

fame	—*a*
land	—*b*
stand	—*b*
flame	—*a*
name	—*a*
hand	—*b*
command	—*b*
frame	—*a*
she	—*c*
poor	—*d*
free	—*c*
shore	—*d*
me	—*c*
door	—*d*

If you consult the "Glossary of Literary Terms" beginning on page 411, you will find that this form cannot fit the definitions of a ballad (which deals with a simple story) or an ode (which is a lengthy lyric poem). Since the poem has 14 lines, it cannot be an octet (eight lines) or a sestet (six lines). The correct answer must be Choice 5, a sonnet. This poem is actually only a fairly good example of an Italian sonnet. The octet or first eight lines present the main idea—the contrast between the new colossus, which represents a welcome to the exiles, and the old colossus, which symbolized conquest—and is in the exact rhyme scheme required. The sestet or second six lines expands the idea by stressing the freedom and opportunity offered to the exiles in contrast to their rejection by the countries from which they came. The rhyme scheme, instead of rigidly following the *c d e c d e* of the Italian sonnet, confines itself to *c d c d c d*, one of the possible combinations.

It should be noted that the sestet of this famous sonnet is inscribed on the base of the Statue of Liberty and is one of the most frequently quoted American poems.

SUMMARY OF INTERPRETATION OF POETRY

The skills needed in reading and interpreting poetry call for you to:

1. Try to get the extended meaning of words used figuratively by using your imagination to add to the usual meanings of the words.
2. Since poetry compresses meaning and description into a few words, fill in the suggested meanings and pictures they create by studying the figures of speech used, such as similes and metaphors.
3. Read the poem aloud, since the rhythm will help you determine its meaning.
4. Note the rhymes used, since they will also help you get meaning and feeling from the poem.
5. Note the sounds of the words, since they reinforce meaning.
6. Study the form of the poem, since its subdivisions (stanzas) can help you understand it better.

Note: First, read the poem through quickly to get an overall idea of its meaning and feeling. Then read it more slowly and carefully after you have read the questions based on it.

READING DRAMA

Earlier, we indicated how character can be inferred from words or actions, since in drama, direct description, as in prose, is not possible. It is true that, of all the forms of literature, plays are among the most difficult to read. The playwright does not speak directly to the reader in modern drama, as do the novelist and short story writer. Sometimes the playwright sets the scene for those who produce or read the play, and sometimes he or she includes instructions to the actors about mood or action. For the most part, however, the playwright leaves it to the actor and the reader to figure out appearance, character, actions, and feelings. The only real help the playwright should and must give is through the dialogue, the conversation between the characters. From this dialogue alone, you must *imagine the setting, visualize the action*, including "hearing" the speech of the actors, and *draw conclusions about their character and motives*. In addition, you must understand the nature of the essence of drama, which is conflict between ideas or characters. This is made clear only through the dialogue. A final point: you may also be asked to predict what is likely to happen on the basis of what you have read.

An analysis of the following scene from a modern American play will illustrate the skills you need to read and understand drama. Reading it aloud will help.

PRACTICE IN READING DRAMA

HOW ARE OLSON'S DREAMS DESTROYED?

OLSON: [*After a pause—worriedly*] I tank I should go after dem. Cocky iss very drunk, too, and Drisc—

FREDA: Aar! The big Irish is all right. Don't yer 'ear 'im say as 'ow they'd surely come back 'ere, an' fur you to wait fur 'em?

OLSON: Yes; but if dey don't come soon I tank I go see if dey are in boarding house all right.

FREDA: Where is the boardin' 'ouse?

OLSON: Yust little way back from street here.

FREDA: You stayin' there, too?

OLSON: Yes—until steamer sail for Stockholm—in two day.

FREDA: [*She is alternatingly looking at* JOE *and feverishly trying to keep* OLSON *talking so he will forget about going away after the others.*] Yer mother won't be arf glad to see yer agen, will she? [OLSON *smiles.*] Does she know yer comin'?

OLSON: No. I tought I would yust give her surprise. I write to her from Bonos Eres but I don't tell her I come home.

FREDA: Must be old, ain't she, yer ole lady?

OLSON: She iss eighty-two. [*He smiles reminiscently.*] You know, Miss Freda, I don't see my mother or my brother in—let me tank—[*He counts laboriously on his fingers.*] must be more than ten year. I write once in while and she write many time; and my brother he write me, too. My mother say in all letter I should come home right away. My brother he write same ting, too. He want me to help him on farm. I write back always I come soon; and I mean all time to go back home at end of voyage. But I come ashore, I take one drink, I take many drinks, I get drunk, I spend all money, I have to ship away for other voyage. So dis time I say to myself; Don't drink one drink, Ollie, or, sure, you don't get home. And I want go home dis time. I feel homesick for farm and to see my people again. [*He smiles.*] Yust like little boy, I feel homesick. Dat's why I don't drink noting tonight but dis—bellywash! [*He roars with childish laughter, then suddenly becomes serious.*] You know, Miss Freda, my mother get very old, and I want see her. She might die and I would never—

FREDA: [*Moved a lot in spite of herself*] Ow, don't talk like that! I jest 'ates to 'ear any one speakin' abaht dyin'. [*The door to the street is opened and* NICK *enters, followed by two rough-looking, shabbily dressed men, wearing mufflers, with caps pulled down over their eyes. They sit at the table nearest to the door.* JOE *brings them three beers, and there is a whispered consultation, with many glances in the direction of* OLSON.]

OLSON: [*Starting to get up—worriedly*] I tank I go around to boarding house. I tank something go wrong with Drisc and Cocky.

FREDA: Ow, down't go. They kin take care of theyselves. They ain't babies. Wait 'arf a mo'. You ain't 'ad yer drink yet.

JOE: [*Coming hastily over to the table, indicates the men in the rear with a jerk of his thumb*] One of them blokes wants yer to 'ave a wet wiv 'im.

FREDA: Righto! [*To* OLSON] Let's drink this. [*She raises her glass. He does the same.*] 'Ere's a toast fur yer: Success to yer bloomin' farm an' may yer live long an' 'appy on it. Skoal! [*She tosses down her brandy. He swallows half his glass of ginger beer and makes a wry face.*]

OLSON: Skoal! [*He puts down his glass.*]

FREDA: [*With feigned indignation*] Down't yer like my toast?

OLSON: [*Grinning*] Yes. It iss very kind, Miss Freda.

FREDA: Then drink it all like I done.

OLSON: Well—[*He gulps down the rest.*] Dere! [*He laughs.*]

FREDA: Done like a sport!

ONE OF THE ROUGHS: [*With a laugh*] Amindra, ahoy!

NICK: [*Warningly*] Sssshh!
OLSON: [*Turns around in his chair*] Amindra? Iss she in port? I sail on her once long time ago—three mast, full rig, skys'l yarder? Iss dat ship you mean?
THE ROUGH: [*Grinning*] Yus; right you are.
OLSON: [*Angrily*] I know dat damn ship—worst ship dat sail to sea. Rotten grub and dey make you work all time—and the Captain and Mate wus Bluenose devils. No sailor who know anything ever ship on her. Where iss she bound from here?
THE ROUGH: Round Cape 'Orn—sails at daybreak.
OLSON: Py yingo, I pity poor fallers make dat trip round Cape Stiff dis time year. I bet you some of dem never see port once again. [*He passes his hand over his eyes in a dazed way. His voice grows weaker.*] Py golly, I feel dizzy. All the room go round and round like I was drunk. [*He gets weakly to his feet.*] Good night, Miss Freda. I bane feeling sick. Tell Drisc—I go home. [*He takes a step forward and suddenly collapses over a chair, rolls to the floor, and lies there unconscious.*]
JOE: [*From behind the bar*] Quick, nawh! [NICK *darts forward with* JOE *following.* FREDA *is already beside the unconscious man and has taken the roll of money from his inside pocket. She strips off a note furtively and shoves it into her bosom, trying to conceal her action, but* JOE *sees her. She hands the roll to* JOE, *who pockets it.* NICK *goes through all the other pockets and lays a handful of change on the table.*]
JOE: [*Impatiently*] 'Urry, 'urry, can't yer? The other blokes'll be 'ere in 'arf a mo'. [*The two roughs come forward.*] 'Ere, you two, tike 'im in under the arms like 'e was drunk. [*They do so.*] Tike 'im to the Amindra—yer knows that, don't yer?—two docks above. Nick'll show yer. An' you, Nick, down't yer leave the bleedin' ship till the capt'n guvs yer this bloke's advance—full month's pay—five quid, d'yer 'ear?
NICK: I knows me bizness, ole bird. [*They support* OLSON *to the door.*]
THE ROUGH: [*As they are going out*] This silly bloke'll 'ave the s'prise of 'is life when 'e wakes up on board of 'er. [*They laugh. The door closes behind them.*]

—Eugene O'Neill

1. The playwright creates mood by his effective use of all of the following EXCEPT

(1) stage directions
(2) names of characters
(3) dialogue
(4) dialect
(5) humor

2. The main purpose of the playwright is to describe

(1) a sailor's life in port
(2) the frustrated longings of a sailor
(3) the weakness of character of a sailor
(4) how a sailor is exploited
(5) his admiration for sailors

3. Olson's mood is best described as one of

(1) bitterness
(2) nostalgia
(3) happiness
(4) resignation
(5) despair

4. Sympathy for Olson is created by the playwright by all of the following EXCEPT his

(1) devotion to his family
(2) abandonment by his shipmates
(3) resolution to stay sober
(4) courtesy to Freda
(5) description of the *Amindra*

5. The reader can correctly infer from the incident all of the following EXCEPT

(1) Joe, Nick, Freda, and the two roughs plotted against Olson
(2) Olson may never get to see his mother
(3) Olson's life on board the *Amindra* will be difficult
(4) Olson's drink was spiked
(5) Freda regretted her role in the incident

6. Suspense is created by all the following EXCEPT
   (1) Drisc and Cocky's departure
   (2) Freda's encouraging Olson to stay
   (3) the entry of Nick and the roughs
   (4) Olson's reluctance to take a drink
   (5) Olson's talk about the *Amindra*

7. The playwright
   (1) feels sorry for Olson
   (2) criticizes the habitual drinking of the sailors
   (3) despises Joe, Nick, Freda, and the roughs
   (4) describes the action with no comment
   (5) feels life is unfair

Answer Key

1. **5** 2. **2** 3. **2** 4. **2** 5. **5** 6. **1** 7. **4**

Answer Analysis

1. 5 The playwright uses stage directions to help create a mood of impending trouble in a waterfront saloon: "Nick enters, followed by two rough-looking, shabbily dressed men, wearing mufflers, with caps pulled down over their eyes." The names of the characters add to the mood: Cocky, Drisc, Big Irish, and The Rough. The dialogue, too, contributes: "I know dat damn ship—worst ship dat sail to sea...." The dialect of the waterfront is most effective: "... down't yer leave the bleedin' ship till the capt'n guvs yer this bloke's advance." Choice 5 is correct because it is the exception among the five choices. There is no humor in the selection.

2. 2 The key word in this question is *main*, since the question calls for the *main* purpose of the playwright. Only Choice 2 describes the main theme of the scene—how Olson's longing to return home is thwarted. "I feel homesick for farm," says Olson and his plan to go back is made to fail. Choice 5 is obviously wrong since no admiration for sailors is present. Choices 1, 3, and 4 are partially correct—a brief period in a sailor's life in port is depicted; Olson's weakness of character is shown, since he cannot resist a drink; Olson is exploited, as are others on the *Amindra*.

3. 2 Choice 2 is correct because nostalgia best describes the homesickness Olson feels. He isn't bitter or despairing. "He smiles reminiscently" and has plans to return to see his mother. He isn't resigned either. Although he roars with laughter, he can't be considered happy.

4. 2 A great playwright succeeds in getting the viewer or the reader involved with the characters he creates. We cannot help sympathizing with Olson because he is a decent person, one who is courteous ("Miss Freda"), devoted to his family (he wants to see his mother and help his brother), full of good intentions to stay sober ("Dat's why I don't drink noting tonight"). The playwright cleverly lets us in on the fate awaiting Olson on the "worst ship dat sail to sea." Only Choice 2 doesn't contribute to our sympathy since the reason for his shipmates' leaving isn't given.

5. 5 This question calls for a number of inferences. There is evidence that the five plotted against Olson ("...there is a whispered consultation, with many glances in the direction of Olson"); since voyages lasted many months and Olson's mother is 82, Olson may never get to see her; from his description of life on the *Amindra* ("rotten grub and dey make you work all time"), we know Olson's life will be difficult; after the drink, Olson falls unconscious, so it must have been spiked. Only Choice 5 isn't true; Freda stole money from the unconscious Olson.

6. 1 The incident is concerned with Olson's future, and suspense begins with Freda's encouraging Olson to stay. It continues with Nick's entrance with the others, and with Olson's reactions to Freda and the mention of the *Amindra*. Only Choice 1 does not build suspense in the scene.

7. 4 Since every effort is made by the playwright to be realistic, he carefully refrains from injecting his own views.

SUMMARY OF INTERPRETATION OF DRAMA READING

The skills needed in reading and interpreting drama call for you to:

1. Try to imagine the setting. If no stage directions are given, deduce from the speech and dialogue of the characters where the action is taking place.
2. Visualize the action. As the characters speak, figure out *what they are doing* while they are speaking.
3. Determine their motives. Why are the characters speaking as they do? *Why are they doing what they do?*
4. Determine their character and personality. What sort of person talks and acts the way he does? Why?
5. Determine the conflict that is taking place. Since the essence of drama is conflict, who or what is in conflict with whom or what? Is the conflict physical? Is it emotional? Is it a conflict of ideas?
6. Try to predict on the basis of all of the above what is most likely to happen next.
7. Read the scene aloud, trying to project yourself into the character of each of the roles.

Reading Commentary on the Arts

Selections that fall under the term *commentary* are limited to the aspects of contemporary writing that deal with the arts—music, art, theater, movies, television, literature, and dance. They are further limited to selections in which the author comments critically on the arts, discussing the value of the content and the style of these means of expression.

In reading commentaries, try to determine the point of view of the writer and whether his or her evaluation of the artist, the musician, the author, the playwright, the film, the television program, or the dancer is favorable or unfavorable. Also look for the insights of the critic into the meaning and emotion conveyed by the artist or the medium.

The writing style will be that of the author of a piece of popular literature, so sentence structure and vocabulary will be relatively simple. *Here is a helpful hint.* Since critics who comment on the arts are describing their reactions, they resort to many adjectives that express their judgment. Here are a couple of dozen of such adjectives: *adept, authentic, candid, credible, dynamic, eloquent, exquisite, graphic, inane, inept, laudable, lucid, naive, poignant, prosaic, spontaneous, superb, superlative, tedious, timeless, tiresome, trite, vivacious, witty.*

Practice in Reading Commentary on the Arts

WHAT DID THE CREATOR OF THE MUPPETS CONTRIBUTE TO CHILDREN'S TELEVISION?

He built an empire on a discarded green coat and a Ping-Pong ball. Jim Henson, creator of Kermit the Frog and a menagerie of other furry creatures known as the Muppets, revolutionized puppetry and reinvented children's television.

The Muppets charmed audiences of all ages on *Sesame Street*, possibly the most influential children's show ever, and later on *The Muppet Show*, which became the mostly widely watched TV program in the world, attracting 135 million viewers in 100 countries.

Henson succeeded with craftsmanship and showmanship and salesmanship. But above all, he constantly challenged the status quo.

Henson was one of the first producers to use television not merely as a medium but as a tool to enhance his performances.

While earlier puppet programs, such as *Kukla, Fran, and Ollie*, simply plunked a camera in front of a traditional stage, Henson used a variety of camera lenses to create illusions which made his Muppets more agile and antic.

He also taught his puppeteers to work while using a TV monitor. For the first time, they could see not only their performances as they were unfolding, but also what the viewers could see.

That insight led Henson to create a new, softer-looking style of puppet that was extremely expressive in TV closeups.

Henson's unconventional approach to life came through in his Muppets—a word he coined for the crossbreed of marionettes and puppets he developed in the mid-50s.

While companies like Disney were creating model characters that lived up to the era's model of perfection, such as Bambi, Henson's creatures, such as the proud Miss Piggy, the grumpy Oscar the Grouch, and the uncontrollable Animal, were wildly irreverent.

Henson also applied this irreverent approach to his work. He promoted productivity, not by demanding results, but by encouraging his associates to have fun. He promoted silliness, even chaos, on the set. In fact, he was most satisfied with a scene when it had grown so funny that no one could perform it without busting up, former associates say.

Despite his childlike enthusiasm, Henson was also a pragmatist who tackled situations by approaching them from new angles. He was a problem solver and had a knack for sidestepping complexity and finding a simpler, purer way of doing things.

1. The contributions of Jim Henson, according to the article,

   (1) retained earlier approaches
   (2) added little to current programming
   (3) climbed on the bandwagon of children's television
   (4) imitated Kukla, Fran, and Ollie
   (5) broke new ground in puppetry

2. The reinventing of children's TV was exemplified by the worldwide success of

   (1) *Sesame Street*
   (2) *The Muppet Show*
   (3) *Kukla, Fran, and Ollie*
   (4) Kermit the Frog
   (5) the status quo

3. The most important reason for the success of Jim Henson was

   (1) his craftsmanship
   (2) his showmanship
   (3) his salesmanship
   (4) his unconventional approach
   (5) his charm

4. Henson pioneered in using television

   (1) as a medium
   (2) to improve performance
   (3) as a traditional stage
   (4) to teach tried-and-true methods
   (5) to preserve the familiar puppets

5. Henson's Muppets

   (1) sought perfection
   (2) imitated Disney's creations
   (3) were disrespectful
   (4) were ideal role models
   (5) were static and serious

6. Jim Henson was all of the following EXCEPT

   (1) a man of childlike enthusiasm
   (2) a searcher for simple solutions
   (3) a pragmatist
   (4) an irreverent innovator
   (5) a conformist

Answer Key

1. **5** 2. **2** 3. **4** 4. **2** 5. **3** 6. **5**

Answer Analysis

1. **5** The author stresses Henson's challenging of the status quo and his revolutionizing of puppetry. Since Henson rejected earlier approaches, Choice 1 is wrong. Being dissatisfied with current programming, he searched for something new and came up with Kermit the Frog, adding much to current programs. He didn't climb on the children's TV bandwagon (Choice 3); he reinvented children's TV. Whereas the progam *Kukla, Fran, and Ollie* was static and traditional, Henson injected movement into his characters by new uses of the camera.

2. 2 The audience for Choice 1 is not identified; but for Choice 2, *The Muppet Show*, its worldwide success is mentioned and its domination by the numbers of millions of viewers in a hundred countries. None of the other choices deals directly with the *success* of the Muppets.

3. 4 While Henson's craftsmanship, showmanship, and salesmanship are mentioned, his unconventional approach and unusual characters are stressed. The charm of the Muppets is subordinate to their unusual character.

4. 2 Henson used television not only as a medium but also as a tool to enhance performance. He opposed the tradtional, the tried and true, and the familiar.

5. 3 Henson's Muppets were unlike Disney's characters because they were not perfect, not ideal. They were proud, grumpy, and disrespectful.

6. 5 Henson's childlike enthusiasm, his search for simple solutions, and his irreverence are mentioned, but the major point of the article is Henson's nonconformism, his *not* acting in traditional ways.

Glossary of Literary Terms

This list includes words used frequently in discussing literature.

ACCENT emphasis given to a syllable or to syllables of a word; used primarily with reference to poetry and also used for the mark (′) that shows this emphasis

ALLITERATION repetition of the same consonant sound at the beginning of two or more words in close proximity ("The fair *b*reeze *b*lew, the white *f*oam *f*lew...")

ALLUSION offhand reference to a famous figure or event in literature or history ("He opened a Pandora's box.")

AUTOBIOGRAPHY story of a person's life written by him- or herself (Franklin's *Autobiography*)

BALLAD verse form that presents in simple story form a single dramatic or exciting episode and stresses such feelings as love, courage, patriotism, and loyalty ("Sir Patrick Spens")

BIOGRAPHY story of a person's life written by someone else (Boswell's *Life of Johnson*)

CLIMAX high point in the telling of a story, be it in fictional, poetic, or dramatic form (the appearance of Banquo's ghost in *Macbeth*)

COMEDY light form of drama that aims to amuse and/or instruct us and that ends happily (*All's Well That Ends Well*)

DIALOGUE conversation between people in a play

ELEGY lyric poem expressing a poet's ideas concerning death (Gray's "Elegy Written in a Country Churchyard")

EPIC long poem that tells a story about noble people and their adventures centering around one character who is the hero

EPITHET word, such as an adjective, or phrase that effectively identifies a significant quality of the noun it describes (Alexander the *Great*)

ESSAY prose writing that can be recognized by its treatment of any topic, no matter how unimportant, and by its approach—*formal* (containing an analysis with a moral) or *informal* (revealing the personality of the author through his or her humor, bias, and style)

FIGURE OF SPEECH expression used to appeal to the reader's emotions and imagination by presenting words in unusual meaning or context ("My love's like a red, red rose...")

FOOT certain number of syllables making up a unit in a verse of poetry

IMAGE figure of speech, especially a simile or a metaphor

INVERSION reversal of the normal order of words in a sentence ("A king of men am I.")

IRONY figure of speech in which the writer or speaker uses words meaning the exact opposite of what he really thinks (In *Julius Caesar*, Antony attacks Brutus with the words, "Brutus is an honorable man.")

LIMERICK jingle in verse containing five lines, with lines 1, 2, and 5 rhyming and lines 3 and 4 rhyming

LYRIC short poem expressing deep emotion in highly melodic and imaginative verse ("The Daffodils")

METAPHOR figure of speech that compares two things, or a person and a thing, by using a quality of one applied to the other. *Like* or *as* is omitted. ("All the world's a stage.")

METER rhythm patterns in verse

MYTH story of unknown origin, religious in character, that tries to interpret the natural world, usually in terms of supernatural events (the story of Atlas)

NARRATIVE story of events or experiences, true or fictitious. A poem may be narrative, as "The Rime of the Ancient Mariner."

NOVEL lengthy prose story dealing with imaginary characters and settings that creates the illusion of real life (Scott's *Ivanhoe*)

ODE lyric poem of particularly serious purpose written in language that is dignified and inspired (Keats' "Ode on a Grecian Urn")

ONOMATOPOEIA use of words whose sounds resemble and/or suggest their meanings (*buzz, hiss*)

PARADOX statement that seems contradictory, but that may, in fact, be true (In *The Pirates of Penzance*, the hero had only five birthdays although he was 21 years old. He was born on February 29th of a leap year!)

PARODY writing that pokes fun at a serious work by using exaggeration or broad humor in imitation of the serious work

PERSONIFICATION figure of speech wherein an idea or a thing is given human qualities ("Death, be not proud...")

POEM literature that has any or all of the following qualities to a high degree: deep emotion; highly imaginative language with figures of speech; distinctive rhythm; compression of thought; use of the familiar in a symbolic sense; rhyme scheme; words that mean more than they apparently say

REFRAIN word or group of words repeated regularly in a poem, usually at the end of a stanza (*nevermore* in "The Raven")

REPETITION restating of a phrase or line for emphasis
("And miles to go before I sleep
And miles to go before I sleep.")

RHYME in poetry, agreement in the final sounds of two or more words at the ends of lines (*June, moon*)

RHYTHM in poetry and certain kinds of prose, patterns of stress or accent in the units that make up the verse or sentence.

SARCASM figure of speech that is harsh in tone and expresses meaning by use of the opposite ("Excellent" said when a mistake is made.)

SATIRE work that makes fun of a person, an idea, or a social custom or institution by stressing its foolishness or lack of reasonableness (Swift's *Gulliver's Travels*)

SHORT STORY short prose narrative dealing with imaginary characters usually in a single setting, often relating a single incident, and striving for a single effect (Poe's "The Pit and the Pendulum")

SIMILE figure of speech in which two things essentially unlike are compared, with *like* or *as* being used to make the comparison ("...a poem lovely as a tree")

SOLILOQUY speech of a character in a play, uttered when alone on the stage, in which the speaker informs the audience of his or her thoughts or of knowledge the audience needs to follow the action of the play. (Hamlet's "To be or not to be...")

SONNET form of poetry consisting of fourteen verses in which two aspects of an idea are presented

In the *Italian* or *Petrarchan sonnet*, the first aspect of the idea or theme is presented in the first eight lines, which rhyme *a b b a a b b a*; the second aspect of the idea or commentary on the theme is presented in the second six lines, which rhyme (in various combinations) *c d e c d e*. The first eight lines are the *octet*; the second six lines the *sestet*.

In the *Shakespearean sonnet*, the first aspect is presented in the first twelve lines, which rhyme *a b a b c d c d e f e f;* the second aspect is presented in the last two lines, which rhyme *g g*.

STANZA unit in a poem, similar to a paragraph in prose writing, usually consisting of four or more lines

SYMBOL object that represents an idea, either psychological, philosophical, social, or religious (The cross represents Christianity; the Star of David is the symbol of Judaism.)

TRAGEDY form of drama that has any or all of the following qualities: conflict of character that ends unhappily; a person of great and noble character who meets with a sudden fall because of his or her own weakness; a theme that appeals to our emotions of pity and fear (*Othello*)

VERSE single line of poetry

16

Literature and the Arts Practice

The Interpreting Literature and the Arts test consists of excerpts from classical and popular literature and articles about literature or the arts. Each excerpt is followed by multiple-choice questions about the reading material. Read each excerpt first and then answer the questions following it. Refer to the reading material as often as necessary to answer the questions.

Each excerpt is preceded by a "purpose question," which gives a reason for reading the material. Use these purpose questions to help focus your reading. You are not required to answer these purpose questions. They are given only to help you concentrate on the main idea presented in a particular selection.

Popular Literature (Prose, Poetry, and Drama)

Questions 1 to 5 refer to the following selection.

WHAT DO WE LEARN ABOUT SWANS?

On Lake Budi some years ago, they were hunting down the swans without mercy. The procedure was to approach them stealthily in little boats and then rapidly—very rapidly—row into their midst. Swans have difficulty in flying; they must skim the surface of the water at a run. In the first phase of their flight they raise their big wings with great effort. It is then that they can be seized; a few blows with a bludgeon finish them off.

Someone made me a present of a swan: more dead than alive. It was of a marvelous species I have never seen anywhere else in the world: a black-throated swan—a snow boat with a neck packed, as it were, into a tight stocking of black silk. Orange-beaked, red-eyed.

They brought it to me half-dead. I bathed its wounds and pressed little pellets of bread and fish into its throat; but nothing stayed down. Nevertheless the wounds slowly healed, and the swan came to regard me as a friend. At the same time, it was apparent to me that the bird was wasting away with nostalgia. So, cradling the heavy burden in my arms through the streets, I carried it to the river. It paddled a few strokes, very close to me. I had hoped it might learn how to fish for itself, and pointed to some pebbles far below, where they flashed in the sand like silvery fish. The swan looked at them remotely, sad-eyed.

For the next 20 days I carried the bird to the river and toiled back with it to my house. One afternoon it seemed more abstracted than usual, swimming very close and ignoring the lure of insects with which I tried vainly to tempt it to fish again. It became very quiet; so I lifted it into my arms to carry it home again. It was breast high, when I suddenly felt a great ribbon unfurl, like a black arm encircling my face: it was the big coil of the neck, dropping down.

It was then that I learned swans do not sing at their death, if they die of grief.

—Pablo Neruda

1. The swan's wounds healed in spite of its lack of

   (1) courage
   (2) nourishment
   (3) intelligence
   (4) shelter
   (5) companionship

2. The narrator implies that the swan's feeling toward him was one of

   (1) apprehension
   (2) trust
   (3) indifference
   (4) compassion
   (5) skepticism

3. The narrator realized that the swan was

   (1) eager to recover its strength
   (2) suspicious of human contact
   (3) angry at its imprisonment
   (4) homesick for its former life
   (5) devoid of feeling

4. What was the swan's reaction to the narrator's attempts to teach it to fish?

   (1) fear
   (2) antagonism
   (3) apathy
   (4) stubbornness
   (5) eagerness

5. According to the narrator, the swan songs of legends do not apply to death caused by

   (1) bludgeoning
   (2) starvation
   (3) heartbreak
   (4) neglect
   (5) exposure

<u>Questions 6 to 10</u> refer to the following selection.

WHAT IS THE TRUTH ABOUT FOOTBALL?

The football is oval in shape, usually thrown in a spiral, and when kicked end over end may prove difficult to catch. If not caught on the fly, it bounces around erratically.

The apparent intent of the game is to deposit the ball across the opponent's goal line. Any child with a ball of his own might do it, six days a week and most of Sunday morning, but the rules of the game specify it must be done with members of both teams present and on the field. Owing to large-scale substitutions this is often difficult.

In the old days people went crazy trying to follow the ball. The players still do, but the viewing public, who are watching the game on TV, can relax and wait for the replay. If anything happens, that's where you'll see it. The disentanglement of bodies on the goal line is one of the finer visual moments available to sports fans. The tight knot bursts open, the arms and legs miraculously return to the point of rest, before the ball is snapped. Some find it unsettling. Is this what it means to be born again?

All ball games feature hitting and socking, chopping and slicing, smashing, slamming, stroking, and whacking, but only in football are these blows diverted from the ball to the opponent. And the more the players are helped or carried from the field, the more attendance soars. This truly male game is also enjoyed by women who find group therapy less rewarding. The sacking of the passer by the front four is especially gratifying. Charges that a criminal element threatens the game are a characteristic, but hopeful, exaggeration. What to do with big, mean, boyish-hearted men, long accustomed to horsing around in good clean dormitories, unaccustomed to the rigors of life in the Alaska oilfields, was, until football, a serious national dilemma.

6. Which audience would most likely find the greatest enjoyment in this passage?
   (1) young boys who plan to play football
   (2) women who love sports
   (3) nonathletic Americans
   (4) professional football players
   (5) newspaper reporters

7. The purpose of the second paragraph is to suggest that football
   (1) has very strict rules
   (2) is made unnecessarily complicated
   (3) can be played anywhere and any time
   (4) is best played on a regulation field
   (5) is best played by the young

8. According to this selection, football is unlike other sports in that it
   (1) is played with a ball that is difficult to catch
   (2) is being infiltrated by criminals
   (3) relies on instant replay as a vital part of the game
   (4) directs violence at the players rather than at the ball
   (5) is losing attendance

9. One of the ironies of football is that
   (1) the players cannot follow the ball as well as the viewers can
   (2) children can play the game
   (3) the game is played by men acting as children
   (4) both men and women love the game
   (5) women like the game more than men do

10. The tone of this passage can best be described as
   (1) argumentative
   (2) questioning
   (3) offensive
   (4) factual
   (5) satiric

<u>Questions 11 to 15</u> refer to the following selection.

WHAT ARE SOME OF THE EFFECTS OF THE HOLOCAUST?

She walked along the river until a policeman stopped her. It was one o'clock, he said. Not the best time to be walking alone by the side of a half-frozen river. He smiled at her, then offered to walk her home. It was the first day of the new year, 1946, eight and a half months after the British tanks had rumbled into Bergen-Belsen.

That February, my mother turned twenty-six. It was difficult for strangers to believe that she had ever been a concentration camp inmate. Her face was smooth and round. She wore lipstick and applied mascara to her large dark eyes. She dressed fashionably. But when she looked into the mirror in the mornings before leaving for work, my mother saw a shell, a mannequin who moved and spoke but who bore only a superficial resemblance to her real self. The people closest to her had vanished. She had no proof that they were truly dead. No eyewitnesses had survived to vouch for her husband's death. There was no one living who had seen her parents die. The lack of confirmation haunted her. At night before she went to sleep and during the day as she stood pinning dresses she wondered if, by some chance, her parents had gotten past the Germans or had crawled out of the mass grave into which they had been shot and were living, old and helpless, somewhere in Poland. What if only one of them had died? What if they had survived and had died of cold or hunger after she had been liberated, while she was in Celle dancing with British officers?

She did not talk to anyone about these things. No one, she thought, wanted to hear them. She woke up in the mornings, went to work, bought groceries, went to the Jewish Community Center and to the housing office like a robot.

11. The policeman stopped the author's mother from walking along the river because
    (1) the river was dangerous
    (2) it was the wrong time of day
    (3) it was still wartime
    (4) it was too cold
    (5) it was forbidden to do so

12. The author states that her mother thought about her parents when she
    (1) walked along the river
    (2) thought about death
    (3) danced with the officers
    (4) was at work
    (5) looked into the mirror

13. When the author mentions her mother's dancing with British officers, she implies that her mother
    (1) compared her dancing to the suffering of her parents
    (2) had clearly put her troubles behind her
    (3) felt it was her duty to dance with the officers
    (4) felt guilty about dancing
    (5) wanted to escape from her past

14. The mother did not discuss her concerns about her loved ones with anyone because she
    (1) thought no one was interested
    (2) felt it was no one's business
    (3) was too shy
    (4) did not know anyone
    (5) didn't want to hurt anyone

15. The author's purpose in writing this selection is most likely to
    (1) inform people about atrocities in the concentration camp
    (2) explain the long-range effects of a traumatic emotional experience
    (3) enlist active participation in refugee affairs
    (4) encourage people to prosecute former concentration camp guards
    (5) gain sympathy from her readers

<u>Questions 16 to 20</u> refer to the following selection.

HOW HAVE HUMAN BEINGS CORRUPTED THEIR ENVIRONMENT?

I turned on my back and floated, looking up at the sky, nothing around me but cool clear Pacific, nothing in my eyes but long blue space. It was as close as I ever got to cleanliness and freedom, as far as I ever got from all the people. They had jerrybuilt the beaches from San Diego to the Golden Gate, bulldozed superhighways through the mountains, cut down a thousand years of redwood growth, and built an urban wilderness in the desert. They couldn't touch the ocean. They poured their sewage into it, but it couldn't be tainted.

There was nothing wrong with Southern California that a rise in the ocean level wouldn't cure. The sky was flat and empty, and the water was chilling me. I swam to the kelp-bed and plunged down through it. It was cold and clammy like the bowels of fear. I came up gasping and sprinted to shore with a barracuda terror nipping at my heels.

I was still chilly a half-hour later, crossing the pass to Nopal Valley. Even at its summit, the highway was wide and new, rebuilt with somebody's money. I could smell the source of the money when I slid down into the valley on the other side. It stank like rotten eggs.

The oil wells from which the sulphur gas rose crowded the slopes on both sides of the town. I could see them from the highway as I drove in: the latticed triangles of the derricks where trees had grown, the oil-pumps nodding and clanking where cattle had grazed. Since 'thirty-nine or 'forty, when I had seen it last, the town had grown enormously, like a tumor.

16. In the first paragraph, the ocean is a symbol of nature's

(1) inability to adapt
(2) resistance to humanity's endeavors
(3) submission to a mechanized society
(4) attack on technology
(5) constant change

17. What are the dominant images in lines 19–23?

(1) light and dark
(2) cold and heat
(3) terror and fear
(4) death and defeat
(5) ugliness and hopelessness

18. In this passage, the narrator apparently is trying to

(1) appeal to legislators for environmental action
(2) inform readers of what Southern California looks like
(3) indicate his disapproval of what has been done
(4) show the potential beauty of the area
(5) celebrate human progress

19. In the last paragraph, the main idea is developed through the use of

(1) cause and effect
(2) contrast
(3) analogy
(4) incident
(5) comparison

20. In the last paragraph, the narrator feels that the growth of the town is

(1) detrimental
(2) inevitable
(3) progressive
(4) hasty
(5) necessary

Questions 21 to 25 refer to the following selection.

HOW DOES THE HAWK'S JOYOUS CRY AFFECT THE WRITER?

I saw him look that last look away beyond me into the sky so full of light that I could not follow his gaze. The little breeze flowed over me again, and nearby a mountain aspen shook all its tiny leaves. I suppose I must have had an idea then of what I was going to do, but I never let it come up into consciousness. I just reached over and laid the hawk on the grass.

He lay there a long minute without hope, unmoving, his eyes still fixed on that blue vault above him. It must have been that he was already so far away in heart that he never felt the release from my hand. He never even stood. He just lay with his breast against the grass.

In the next second after the long minute he was gone. Like a flicker of light, the head vanished with my eyes full on him, but without actually seeing even a premonitory wing beat. He was gone straight into that towering emptiness of light and crystal that my eyes could scarcely bear to penetrate. For another long moment there was silence. I could not see him. The light was too intense. Then from far up somewhere a cry came ringing down.

I was young then and had seen little of the world, but when I heard that cry my heart turned over. It was not a cry of the hawk I had captured; for, by shifting my position against the sun, I was now seeing further up. Straight out of the sun's eye where she must have been soaring restlessly above us for untold hours hurtled his mate. And from far up, ringing from peak to peak of the summits over us, came a cry of such unutterable and ecstatic joy that it sounds down across the years and tingles among the cups of my quiet breakfast table.

21. In line 1, "that last look" suggests that the hawk

(1) has been blinded
(2) expects to be rescued
(3) believes that his death is near
(4) cannot understand what is happening
(5) is looking for sympathy

22. In line 8, the clause "I never let it come up into consciousness" suggests that the freeing of the hawk is

(1) premeditated
(2) impulsive
(3) impossible
(4) accidental
(5) an afterthought

23. In line 12, the minute is "long" to the narrator because he

(1) is thinking of changing his mind
(2) is young and inexperienced
(3) regrets the action he is taking
(4) is not sure what the hawk will do
(5) is impatient

24. In this selection, the natural phenomenon the narrator seems most impressed by is the

(1) deathlike silence
(2) intense light
(3) steady breeze
(4) blue sky
(5) quaking aspen

25. The narrator's most lasting memory is of the

(1) hawk's eyes
(2) bright light
(3) complete stillness
(4) joyous call of the hawk
(5) beauty of the soaring hawk

Questions 26 to 30 refer to the following selection.

WHAT DANGEROUS MISTAKE WAS NEARLY MADE?

I was vainly trying to go to sleep that evening when I became aware of unfamiliar sounds. Sitting bolt upright, I listened intently.

The sounds were coming from just across the river, and they were a weird medley of whines, whimpers and small howls. My grip on the rifle slowly relaxed. If there is one thing at which scientists are adept, it is learning from experience; I was not to be fooled twice. The cries were obviously those of a husky, probably a young one, and I deduced that it must be one of Mike's dogs (he owned three half-grown pups not yet trained to harness, which ran loose after the team) that had got lost, retraced its way to the cabin, and was now begging for someone to come and be nice to it.

I was delighted. If that pup needed a friend, a chum, I was its man! I climbed hastily into my clothes, ran down to the riverbank, launched the canoe, and paddled lustily for the far bank.

The pup had never ceased its mournful plaint, and I was about to call out reassuringly when it occurred to me that an unfamiliar human voice might frighten it. I decided to stalk it instead, and to betray my presence only when I was close enough for soothing murmurs.

I had assumed the dog was only a few yards away from the far bank, but as I made my way over boulders and gravel ridges, the sounds seemed to remain at the same volume while I appeared to be getting no closer. I assumed the pup was retreating, perhaps out of shyness. In my anxiety not to startle it away, I kept quiet, even when the whimpering stopped, leaving me uncertain about the direction to pursue. However, I saw a steep ridge looming ahead of me and I suspected that, once I gained its summit, I would have a clear enough view to enable me to locate the lost animal. I got down on my stomach (practicing the fieldcraft I had learned in the Boy Scouts) and cautiously inched my way the last few feet.

My head came slowly over the crest — and there was my quarry. He was lying down, evidently resting after his mournful singsong, and his nose was about six feet from mine. We stared at one another in silence. I do not know what went on in his massive skull, but my head was full of the most disturbing thoughts. I was peering straight into the amber gaze of a fully grown arctic wolf, who probably weighed more than I did, and who was certainly a lot better versed in close-combat techniques than I would ever be.

—Farley Mowat

26. What made the sounds so unusual?
    (1) They were very loud.
    (2) They were a strange mixture.
    (3) They were inhuman.
    (4) They were coming from across water.
    (5) They were persistent.

27. The expression "not to be fooled twice" (lines 11–12) implies that the
    (1) narrator was annoyed by a previous mistake
    (2) sounds were made by an echo
    (3) sounds were a trick
    (4) narrator had dealt with canines before
    (5) narrator was stubborn

28. The inference in the second paragraph is that Mike is
    (1) a forest ranger
    (2) a hunter
    (3) a dogsled owner
    (4) a child
    (5) a wildlife biologist

29. What do lines 22 and 23 suggest about the narrator?
    (1) He is an animal lover.
    (2) He is a clever man.
    (3) He is an excellent athlete.
    (4) He is a nervous individual.
    (5) He is restless.

30. What caused the narrator to lose track of the pup?
    (1) the terrain
    (2) the darkness
    (3) the silence
    (4) the distance
    (5) the lack of experience

Questions 31 to 35 refer to the following selection.

WHAT CAN A PERSON DO TO FIGHT OFF LONELINESS?

Leventhal's apartment was spacious. In a better neighborhood, or three stories lower, it would have rented for twice the amount he paid. But the staircase was narrow and stifling and full of turns. Though he went up slowly, he was out of breath when he reached the fourth floor, and his heart beat thickly. He rested before unlocking the door. Entering, he threw down his raincoat and flung himself on the bed in the front room. Mary had moved some of the chairs into the corners and covered them with sheets. She could not depend on him to keep the windows shut and the shades and curtains drawn during the day. He got up and opened a window. The curtains waved once and then were as motionless as before. There was a movie house strung with lights across the street; on its roof a water tank sat heavily uneven on its timbers; the cowls of the chimneys, which rattled in the slightest stir of air, were still.

The motor of the refrigerator began to run. There was nothing inside except a few lemons and some milk. He drank a glass of milk and it refreshed him. He had already taken off his shirt and was sitting on the bed unlacing his shoes when there was a short ring of the bell. Eagerly he pulled open the door and shouted, "Who is it?" The flat was unbearably empty. He hoped someone had remembered that Mary was away and had come to keep him company. There was no response below. He called out again, impatiently. It was very probable that someone had pushed the wrong button, but he heard no other doors opening. Could it be a prank? This was not the season for it. Nothing moved in the stairwell, and it only added to his depression to discover how he longed for a visitor. He stretched out on the bed. He thought he would doze off. But a little later he found himself standing at the window, holding the curtains with both hands. He was under the impression that he had slept. It was only eight-thirty by the whirring electric clock on the night table, however. Only five minutes had passed.

—Saul Bellow

31. What does the author suggest about Leventhal's apartment?
    (1) Its location is excellent.
    (2) Its security is admirable.
    (3) Its cost is attractive.
    (4) Its convenience is evident.
    (5) Its furnishings are comfortable.

32. What does the author suggest by the statement "The curtains waved once and then were as motionless as before" (line 19)?
    (1) the stagnation of the surroundings
    (2) the emptiness of the flat
    (3) the depth of Leventhal's emotions
    (4) the carefulness of Mary's housekeeping
    (5) the heat of the day

33. The contents of the refrigerator (lines 28 and 29) suggest that
    (1) Leventhal could not afford food.
    (2) Mary had been in charge of the groceries.
    (3) Leventhal could not eat because Mary was away.
    (4) Mary and Leventhal had just moved in.
    (5) Leventhal was economical.

34. What does the statement "This was not the season for it" (line 44) seem to reveal about Leventhal?
    (1) He expected things to occur at their proper times.
    (2) He had forgotten that it was April Fool's Day.
    (3) He would be angry if someone tried to trick him.
    (4) He was quite affected by seasonal changes.
    (5) He was explaining away his feelings.

35. What effect did the lack of movement in the stairwell (line 45) have upon Leventhal?
    (1) He became very frightened.
    (2) He gained a better understanding of his state of mind.
    (3) He became bitter because he had been tricked.
    (4) He suddenly became very tired.
    (5) He realized he needed a change.

<u>Questions 36 to 40</u> refer to the following selection.

WHAT ARE THE POET'S THOUGHTS ABOUT LIFE?

Alone

Lying, thinking
Last night
How to find my soul a home
Where water is not thirsty
And bread loaf is not stone
I came up with one thing
And I don't believe I'm wrong
That nobody,
But nobody
Can make it out here alone.

Alone, all alone
Nobody, but nobody
Can make it out here alone.

There are some millionaires
With money they can't use
Their wives run round like banshees
Their children sing the blues
They've got expensive doctors
To cure their hearts of stone.
But nobody
No nobody
Can make it out here alone.

Alone, all alone
Nobody, but nobody
Can make it out here alone.

Now if you listen closely
I'll tell you what I know
Storm clouds are gathering
The wind is gonna blow
The race of man is suffering
And I can hear the moan,

Cause nobody,
But nobody
Can make it out here alone.

Alone, all alone
Nobody, but nobody
Can make it out here alone.

—Maya Angelou

36. The main idea of the poem is that

(1) a soul needs a home
(2) a person needs bread and water
(3) any individual can achieve success
(4) people need people
(5) no one need be lonely

37. The poet comes to her conclusion out of her

(1) bitter experience
(2) thoughts
(3) need for recognition
(4) envy of others
(5) fear of loneliness

38. The poet's idea of some wealthy persons is that

(1) they spend money wastefully
(2) their families live well
(3) they are unfeeling
(4) they are well adjusted
(5) they have physical ailments

39. The poet mentions "storm clouds" and "the wind" because

(1) she foresees conflict
(2) some people are wealthy
(3) people are impatient
(4) the future is uncertain
(5) nature is unfriendly

40. The poem derives its power from effective use of

(1) metaphor
(2) rhyme
(3) rhythm
(4) repetition
(5) irony

Questions 41 to 45 refer to the following selection.

HOW DOES A CHILD REACT TO AN OLD PHOTOGRAPH?

Old Photograph of the Future

That center of attention—an infantile face
That long years ago showed, no doubt, pink and white—
Now faded, and in the photograph only a trace
Of grays, not much expression in sight.

That center of attention, swathed in a sort of white dress,
Is precious to the woman who, pretty and young,
Leans with a look of surprised blessedness
At the mysterious miracle forth-sprung.

In the background somewhat, the masculine figure
Looms, face agleam with achievement and pride.
In black coat, derby at breast, he is quick to assure
You the world's in good hands—lay your worries aside.

The picture is badly faded. Why not?
Most things show wear around seventy-five,
And that's the age this picture has got.
The man and woman no longer, of course, live.

They lie side by side in whatever love survives
Under green turf, or snow, and that child, years later, stands there
While old landscapes blur and he in guilt grieves
Over nameless promises unkept, in undefinable despair.

—Robert Penn Warren

41. In the first stanza, what does the narrator say is "now faded"

(1) the light
(2) the memory
(3) the face of a baby
(4) the past
(5) the nameless promise

42. In the old photograph, repetition serves to emphasize

(1) the woman
(2) the masculine figure
(3) the man and the woman
(4) the infant
(5) the old landscapes

43. The poet, at 75, experiences

(1) nostalgia
(2) love
(3) pride
(4) wonder
(5) regret

44. What does the poet intend the reader to infer about the photograph?
    (1) It is a photograph from an advertisement.
    (2) Everyone in the photograph is dead.
    (3) It is a photograph of his family.
    (4) He has just discovered the photograph.
    (5) It exists only in his imagination.

45. The title of the poem is intended to suggest that
    (1) memories can be inaccurate
    (2) love is important
    (3) patience is a virtue
    (4) life is cyclical
    (5) nothing lasts forever

<u>Questions 46 to 50</u> refer to the following passage from a play.

HOW DOES ONE COPE WITH THE LOSS OF A BROTHER?

BERGER'S OFFICE.
CONRAD (*barely audible*): Thanks.
BERGER: What happened?
CONRAD (*looks up at him; ready to cry*): I need something.
BERGER: Tell me.
CONRAD: I can't! I can't get through this. It's all hanging over my head.
BERGER: What's hanging over your head?
CONRAD (*sobbing*): I don't know! I need something.
BERGER: What do you need?
CONRAD: I need to, I need to get, get off the hook.
BERGER: What hook?
CONRAD: (*suddenly fiercely angry through the tears*): YOU KNOW WHAT HOOK! (*afraid*) I'm sorry, I'm sorry, I didn't mean to be angry.
BERGER: You were on opposite sides of the boat, you couldn't even see each other. He was a better swimmer than you. He was stronger. He had more endurance. There's no hook.
CONRAD: That's what I don't understand.
BERGER: What do you think you were supposed to have done?
CONRAD: I don't know, something. Why'd he let go?
BERGER: He got tired maybe.
CONRAD: Buck never got tired, not before me. He told me not to get tired—he told me to hang on and then he let go.
BERGER: Maybe you just wanted to hang on longer than he did, maybe he was *always* more tired than you were.
CONRAD: That's crazy, he had more to hold on for; that doesn't make sense.
BERGER: How do you know what makes sense for somebody else? The point is it happened.
CONRAD: No, that's not it, that's too simple.
BERGER: You want simple, let me tell you a story. A very simple story about this perfect kid who had a younger brother. A not-so-perfect kid, and all the time they were growing up this not-so-perfect kid tried to model himself after his brother, the perfect kid. It worked, too. After all, they were a lot alike, and the not-so-perfect kid was a very good actor, listen to me! Then, along came this sailing accident, are you hearing me?
CONRAD: Yes.
BERGER: And the impossible happened. The not-so-perfect kid makes it. The other kid, the one he's patterned his whole life after, isn't so lucky. So, where is the sense in that, huh? Where is the justice?
CONRAD: There isn't any.
BERGER: The justice, obviously, is for the not-so-perfect kid to become the other, perfect kid. For everybody. For his parents, for his grandparents, his friends, and most of all, himself. Only, that's one heck of a burden, see? So, finally, he decides he can't carry it. But how to set it down? No way. A problem without a solution. And so, because he can't figure out how to solve the problem, he decides to destroy it. (*pauses, leans forward*) Doesn't any of this make sense to you?
CONRAD: I don't know, nothing makes sense. I'm scared.
BERGER: A very far-out act of self-preservation—Conrad, do you get that? And do you see the truth that it's okay to be just you?

46. The dialogue is apparently between
    (1) two friends
    (2) two sons
    (3) a father and son
    (4) two children
    (5) a brother and a psychiatrist

47. "Get off the hook" refers to
    (1) a crime Conrad committed
    (2) Conrad's feelings of guilt
    (3) Conrad's failure to be loyal
    (4) Conrad's lapse of memory
    (5) Buck's advice

48. It can be inferred from the dialogue that
    (1) Buck got tired
    (2) Buck had no reason to hang on
    (3) Buck lacked endurance
    (4) Buck let go for no apparent reason
    (5) Buck was let down by Conrad

49. Conrad
    (1) looked up to his brother
    (2) surpassed his brother
    (3) resented his brother
    (4) was older than his brother
    (5) rivaled his brother

50. The burden Conrad is asked to carry is
    (1) his own perfection
    (2) his memories
    (3) his need for self-preservation
    (4) his good acting
    (5) his replacing his brother properly

Questions 51 to 55 refer to the following passage from a play.

WHY DO POOR PEOPLE CHOOSE SUCH EXPENSIVE FUNERALS?

SALESMAN: [*Chewing*] I really don't understand...wherever you look, in all the newspapers, you read the most horrible stories about conditions among the weavers, and you get the impression that all the people here are half-starved. And then you see such a funeral! Just as I came into the village, there were brass bands, schoolteachers, children, the pastor, and a whole string of people; my God, you'd think the Emperor of China was being buried. If these people can pay for that...! [*He drinks his beer. Then he puts his glass down and suddenly speaks in a frivolous tone.*] Isn't that so, Miss? Don't you agree with me?

[ANNA *smiles, embarrased, and continues busily with her embroidery.*]

SALESMAN: Those must be slippers for Papa.

WELZEL: Oh, I don't like to wear them things.

SALESMAN: Just listen to that! I'd give half my fortune if those slippers were for me.

MRS. WELZEL: He just don't appreciate such things.

WIEGAND: [*After he has coughed several times and moved his chair about, as if he wanted to speak*] The gentleman has expressed himself mighty well about the funeral. Now tell us, young lady, isn't that just a small funeral?

SALESMAN: Yes, I must say...That must cost a tremendous amount of money. Where do these people get the money for it?

WIEGAND: You'll forgive me for saying it, sir, there is no such folly among the poorer classes hereabouts. If you don't mind my sayin' so, they have such exaggerated ideas of the dutiful respect and the obligations that's due the deceased and the blessed dead. And when it's a matter of deceased parents, they are so superstitious that the descendants and the next of kin scrape together their last penny. And what the children can't raise, they borrow from the nearest moneylender. And then they're in debts up to their necks; they'll be owing His Reverence the Pastor, the sexton, and everybody else in the neighborhood. And drinks and victuals and all the other necessary things. Oh, yes, I approve of respectful duty on the part of children toward their parents, but not so that the mourners are burdened down the rest of their lives by such obligations.

SALESMAN: I beg your pardon, but I should think the pastor would talk them out of it.

WIEGAND: Beggin' your pardon, sir, but there I would like to interpose that every little congregation has its ecclesiastical house of worship and must support its reverend pastor. The high clergy get a wonderful revenue and profit from such a big funeral. The more elaborate such a funeral can be arranged, the more profitable is the offeratory that flows from it. Whoever knows the conditions of the workers hereabouts can, with unauthoritative certainty, affirm that the pastors only with reluctance tolerate small and quiet funerals.

51. Which character in the passage seems to see things most clearly?
    (1) the salesman
    (2) Mrs. Welzel
    (3) Welzel
    (4) Wiegand
    (5) Anna

52. What do the italicized portions in the passage signify?
    (1) directions to the actors
    (2) asides to the actors
    (3) directions to the cameraperson
    (4) important parts of the dialogue
    (5) comments by the playwright

53. Why do the townspeople apparently have such elaborate funerals?
    (1) They have more money than the public has been led to believe.
    (2) They have strong ideas of the respect due to the dead.
    (3) They look upon the funerals as holiday occasions.
    (4) They wish to impress their neighbors.
    (5) They wish to defy the advice of their parents.

54. Wiegand's speech about the church suggests that he views it as an institution that is
    (1) sympathetic to the weavers' needs
    (2) interested only in formal worship
    (3) in favor of small and quiet, rather than large and boisterous, funerals
    (4) organized to do God's work on earth
    (5) interested in making money from the people

55. From this passage, the reader can most safely conclude that Anna is
    (1) Wiegand's wife
    (2) Welzel's daughter
    (3) the salesman's friend
    (4) a worker in the weaving mills
    (5) a servant

Classical Literature

Questions 56 to 60 refer to the following selection.

HOW DID RIP VAN WINKLE SEEK COMFORT?

Rip Van Winkle was one of those happy mortals, of foolish, well-oiled dispositions, who take the world easy, eat white bread or brown, which ever can be got with least thought or trouble, and would rather starve on a penny than work for a pound. If left to himself, he would have whistled life away, in perfect contentment; but his wife kept continually dinning in his ears about his idleness, his carelessness, and the ruin he was bringing on his family. Morning, noon, and night, her tongue was incessantly going, and everything he said or did was sure to produce a torrent of household eloquence. Rip had but one way of replying to all lectures of the kind, and that, by frequent use, had grown into a habit. He shrugged his shoulders, shook his head, cast up his eyes, but said nothing. This, however, always provoked a fresh volley from his wife, so that he was fain to draw off his forces, and take to the outside of the house—the only side which, in truth, belongs to a henpecked husband.

Rip's sole domestic adherent was his dog Wolf, who was as much henpecked as his master; for Dame Van Winkle regarded them as companions in idleness, and even looked upon Wolf with an evil eye as the cause of his master's going so often astray....

...For a long while he used to console himself, when driven from home, by frequenting a kind of perpetual club of the sages, philosophers, and other idle personages of the village, which held its sessions on a bench before a small inn, designated by a rubicund portrait of His Majesty George the Third. Here they used to sit in the shade through a long, lazy summer's day, talking listlessly over village gossip, or telling endless, sleepy stories about nothing....How solemnly they would listen to...Derrick Van Brummel, the schoolmaster.

—Washington Irving

56. The story takes place about

(1) 1660
(2) 1770
(3) 1800
(4) 1812
(5) 1848

57. An example of the author's sense of humor may be found in sentences

(1) 2
(2) 3
(3) 4
(4) 5
(5) 6

58. The blame for Rip's conduct was placed by Dame Van Winkle on

(1) Wolf
(2) George the Third
(3) Derrick Van Brummel
(4) the club of sages
(5) other idle villagers

59. Rip may be described by *all* of the following adjectives EXCEPT

(1) henpecked
(2) easygoing
(3) happy
(4) complaining
(5) resigned

60. Rip's only problem was his

(1) poverty
(2) idleness
(3) wife's nagging
(4) wife's evil eye
(5) village companions

Questions 61 to 65 refer to the following selection.

WHY DID THE AUTHOR GO TO THE WOODS?

I went to the woods because I wished to live deliberately, to front only the essential facts of life, and see if I could not learn what it had to teach, and not, when I came to die, discover that I had not lived. I did not wish to live what was not life, living is so dear; nor did I wish to practise resignation, unless it was quite necessary. I wanted to live deep and suck out all the marrow of life, to live so sturdily and Spartan-like as to put to rout all that was not life, to cut a broad swath and shave close, to drive life into a corner, and reduce it to its lowest terms, and, if it proved to be mean, why then to get the whole and genuine meanness of it, and publish its meanness to the world; or if it were sublime, to know it by experience, and be able to give a true account of it in my next excursion. For most men, it appears to me, are in a strange uncertainty about it, whether it is of the devil or of God, and have *somewhat hastily* concluded that it is the chief end of man here to 'glorify God and enjoy him forever.'

Still we live meanly, like ants; though the fable tells us that we were long ago changed into men; like pygmies we fight with cranes; it is error upon error, and clout upon clout, and our best virtue has for its occasion a superfluous and evitable wretchedness. Our life is frittered away by detail. An honest man has hardly need to count more than his ten fingers, or in extreme cases he may add his ten toes, and lump the rest. Simplicity, simplicity, simplicity! I say, let your affairs be as two or three, and not a hundred or a thousand; instead of a million count half a dozen, and keep your accounts on your thumb-nail.

—Henry D. Thoreau

61. The best statement of why the author went to the woods is that he went to

 (1) discover that he had not lived
 (2) live meanly, like ants
 (3) practice resignation
 (4) reduce life to its simplest terms
 (5) glorify God

62. The author thinks that life should be *all* of the following EXCEPT

 (1) Spartan-like
 (2) complicated
 (3) creative
 (4) noble
 (5) moral

63. All of the following words as used in this selection are correctly defined EXCEPT

 (1) *deliberately*—unhurriedly
 (2) *front*—confront
 (3) *swath*—space
 (4) *mean*—nasty
 (5) *frittered*—wasted

64. The tone of the selection is

 (1) bitter cynicism
 (2) moral indignation
 (3) flippant humor
 (4) quiet resignation
 (5) self-congratulation

65. The author

 (1) wishes to learn from nature
 (2) is afraid of death
 (3) has little regard for life
 (4) seeks reconciliation with God
 (5) celebrates the human life-style

Questions 66 to 70 refer to the following selection.

WHY DID THE GIRL CLIMB THE TREE?

There was the huge tree asleep yet in the paling moonlight, and small and hopeful Sylvia began with utmost bravery to mount to the top of it, with tingling, eager blood coursing the channels of her whole frame, with her bare feet and fingers that pinched and held like bird's claws to the monstrous ladder reaching up, up, almost to the sky itself. First she must mount the white oak tree that grew alongside, where she was almost lost among the dark branches and the green leaves heavy and wet with dew; a bird fluttered off its nest, and a red squirrel ran to and fro and scolded pettishly at the harmless housebreaker. Sylvia felt her way easily. She had often climbed there and knew that higher still one of the oak's upper branches chafed against the pine trunk, just where its lower boughs were set close together. There, when she made the dangerous pass from one tree to the other, the great enterprise would really begin.

She crept out along the swaying oak limb at last and took the daring step across into the old pine tree. The way was harder than she thought; she must reach far and hold fast. The sharp dry twigs caught and held her and scratched her like angry talons; the pitch made her thin little fingers clumsy and stiff as she went round and round the tree's great stem, higher and higher upward. The sparrows and robins in the woods below were beginning to wake and twitter to the dawn, yet it seemed much lighter there aloft in the pine tree, and the child knew that she must hurry if her project were to be of any use.

The tree seemed to lengthen itself out as she went up and to reach farther and farther upward. It was like a great mainmast to the voyaging earth; it must truly have been amazed that morning through all its ponderous frame as it felt this determined spark of human spirit creeping and climbing from higher branch to branch. Who knows how steadily the least twigs held themselves to advantage this light, weak creature on her way! The old pine must have loved his new dependent. More than all the hawks and bats and moths and even the sweet-voiced thrushes was the brave, beating heart of the solitary gray-eyed child. And the tree stood still and held away the winds that June morning while the dawn grew bright in the east.

—Sarah Orne Jewett

66. The girl's blood was tingling (line 5) because she was
   (1) cold
   (2) frightened
   (3) excited
   (4) ill
   (5) clumsy

67. Why did Sylvia climb the oak tree?
   (1) to observe the birds
   (2) to get closer to the pine tree
   (3) to get to the ladder
   (4) to chase a squirrel
   (5) to observe the sunset

68. Why was the first part of Sylvia's climb easy for her?
   (1) The branches were close together.
   (2) It was almost daylight.
   (3) There was a ladder nearby.
   (4) She had climbed the tree before.
   (5) She was in good physical shape.

69. In line 45, the tree is compared to
   (1) a giant's hand
   (2) the earth's axis
   (3) a part of a ship
   (4) a space shuttle
   (5) a monument

70. In lines 55 through 63, the pine tree is portrayed as a
   (1) kindly protector
   (2) solitary sentinel
   (3) stern parent
   (4) brave soldier
   (5) human spirit

Questions 71 to 75 refer to the following selection.

WHAT ARE FEUDS?

"Don't you know what a feud is?"

"Never heard of it before—tell me about it."

"Well," says Buck, "a feud is this way: A man has a quarrel with another man, and kills him; then that other man's brother kills *him*; then the other brothers, on both sides, goes for one another; then the *cousins* chip in—and by and by everybody's killed off, and there ain't no more feud. But it's kind of slow, and takes a long time."

"Has this one been going on long, Buck?"

"Well, I should *reckon*! It started thirty years ago, or some'ers along there. There was trouble 'bout something, and then a lawsuit to settle it; and the suit went agin one of the men, and so he up and shot the man that won the suit—which he would naturally do, of course. Anybody would."

"What was the trouble about, Buck—land?"

"I reckon maybe—I don't know."

"Well, who done the shooting? Was it a Grangerford or a Shepherdson?"

"Laws, how do *I* know? It was so long ago."

"Don't anybody know?"

"Oh, yes, pa knows, I reckon, and some of the other old people: but they don't know now what the row was about in the first place."...

"Has anybody been killed this year, Buck?"

"Yes; we got one and they got one. 'Bout three months ago my cousin Bud, fourteen year old, was riding through the woods...and sees old Baldy Shepherdson a-linkin' after him with his gun in his hand and his white hair a-flying in the wind;...so at last Bud seen it warn't any use, so he stopped and faced around so as to have the bulletholes in front, you know, and the old man he rode up and shot him down. But he didn't git much chance to enjoy his luck, for inside of a week our folks laid *him* out."

Next Sunday we all went to church, about three mile, everybody a-horseback. The men took their guns along, so did Buck, and kept them between their knees or stood them handy against the wall. The Shepherdsons done the same. It was pretty ornery preaching—all about brotherly love...

—Mark Twain

71. The main purpose of this selection is to

(1) write humorously of Southern mountainfolk
(2) tell the story of the Grangerfords and the Shepherdsons
(3) preach the importance of brotherly love
(4) extol the courage of the narrator
(5) satirize feuds

72. All of the following are true of the Grangerford-Shepherdson quarrel EXCEPT that it

(1) was of long duration
(2) was started by a Grangerford
(3) had an unknown cause
(4) involved courageous people
(5) involved children as well as adults

73. Buck is

(1) the author
(2) a stranger
(3) a Grangerford
(4) a Shepherdson
(5) an impartial observer

74. The church incident is mentioned to

(1) bring out the importance of brotherly love
(2) reaffirm the author's faith
(3) place the blame on neither the Grangerfords nor the Shepherdsons
(4) point up the hypocrisy of those who attended
(5) present the author's view on grace and predestination

75. The attitude of Buck toward feuds is

(1) impartial
(2) critical
(3) unquestioning
(4) regretful
(5) bitter

Poetry

Questions 76 to 80 refer to the following poem.

WHAT CAN WE LEARN ABOUT OPPORTUNITY?

Opportunity

This I beheld, or dreamed it in a dream:—
There spread a cloud of dust along a plain;
And underneath the cloud, or in it, raged
A furious battle, and men yelled, and swords
Shocked upon swords and shields. A prince's banner
Wavered, then staggered backward, hemmed by foes.
A craven hung along the battle's edge,
And thought, "Had I a sword of keener steel—
That blue blade that the king's son bears—but this
Blunt thing!" he snapped and flung it from his hand,
And lowering crept away and left the field.
Then came the king's son, wounded, sore bestead,
And weaponless, and saw the broken sword,
Hilt-buried in the dry and trodden sand,
And ran and snatched it, and with battle-shout
Lifted afresh he hewed his enemy down,
And saved a great cause that heroic day.

—Edward Roland Sill

76. The main purpose of the poem is to

(1) tell what happened in a dream
(2) relate an act of cowardice
(3) applaud an act of bravery
(4) teach a lesson in conduct
(5) tell an interesting story

77. The most logical words to continue the quotation that begins on line 14 are

(1) "...I could defend myself better."
(2) "...but I cannot have the blue blade."
(3) "...I could safely escape."
(4) "...I could help defeat the enemy."
(5) "...but what good would it do."

78. The word *craven* as used in this poem means a person who is best described as

(1) envious
(2) desirous
(3) cowardly
(4) traitorous
(5) angry

79. Lines 8 and 9 are an example of

(1) personification
(2) irony
(3) metaphor
(4) simile
(5) alliteration

80. The poem derives its power by presenting

(1) a graphic picture of nature
(2) a stark contrast in behavior
(3) a description of battle
(4) an effective use of rhyme
(5) a human tragedy

<u>Questions 81 to 85</u> refer to the following poem.

HOW IS GRIEF AT THE LOSS OF A LOVED ONE EXPRESSED?

Stop All the Clocks

Stop all the clocks, cut off the telephone,
Prevent the dog from barking with a juicy bone,
Silence the pianos and with muffled drum
Bring out the coffin, let the mourners come.

Let aeroplanes circle moaning overhead
Scribbling on the sky the message He Is Dead,
Put crepe bows round the white necks of the public doves,
Let the traffic policemen wear black cotton gloves.

He was my North, my South, my East and West,
My working week, and my Sunday rest,
My noon, my midnight, my talk, my song:
I thought that love would last for ever: I was wrong.

The stars are not wanted now; put out every one:
Pack up the moon and dismantle the sun;
Pour away the ocean and sweep up the woods;
For nothing now can ever come to any good.

—W.H. Auden

81. In line 1, the effect of using the one-syllable words *stop* and *cut* is to

(1) conceal the speaker's grief
(2) create an instant picture for the reader
(3) fill the reader with similar suffering
(4) emphasize the shock the speaker has suffered
(5) simplify a complex feeling

82. In line 10, which poetic device is used in the phrase "Scribbling on the sky"?

(1) onomatopoeia
(2) pun
(3) alliteration
(4) simile
(5) metaphor

83. Which statement best summarizes the third stanza?

(1) He was everything to me, but I lost him.
(2) He was with me everywhere I went.
(3) He was always talking or singing.
(4) He was my life, my everything.
(5) He was place and time for me.

84. In which line(s) does the climax of the poem occur?

(1) lines 8 and 9
(2) lines 14 and 15
(3) lines 19 and 20
(4) lines 21 and 22
(5) lines 25 and 26

85. Although the title of the poem is "Stop All the Clocks," the speaker really wants to stop everything that

    (1) records time
    (2) reflects love
    (3) causes grief
    (4) continues life
    (5) makes sounds

Drama

Questions 86 to 90 refer to this excerpt from a play.

HOW DO MOTHER AND DAUGHTER DIFFER?

DAUGHTER (*gently*): Ma, you worked all your life. Why don't you take it easy?
OLD LADY: I don't want to take it easy. Now that your father's dead and in the grave I don't know what to do with myself.
DAUGHTER: Why don't you go out, sit in the park, get a little sun like the other old women?
OLD LADY: I sit around here sometimes, going crazy. We had a lot of fights in our time, your father and I, but I must admit I miss him badly. You can't live with someone 41 years and not miss him when he's dead. I'm glad that he died, for his own sake—it may sound hard of me to say that—but I am glad. He was in nothing but pain the last few months, and he was a man who could never stand pain. But I do miss him.
DAUGHTER (*gently*): Ma, why don't you come live with George and me?
OLD LADY: No, no, Annie, you're a good daughter.
DAUGHTER: We'll move Tommy into the baby's room, and you can have Tommy's room. It's the nicest room in the apartment. It gets all the sun.
OLD LADY: I have wonderful children. I thank God every night for that. I...
DAUGHTER: Ma, I don't like you living here alone...
OLD LADY: Annie, I been living in this house for eight years, and I know all the neighbors and the store people, and if I lived with you, I'd be a stranger.
DAUGHTER: There's plenty of old people in my neighborhood. You'll make friends.
OLD LADY: Annie, you're a good daughter, but I want to keep my own home. I want to pay my own rent. I don't want to be some old lady living with her children. If I can't take care of myself, I'd just as soon be in the grave with your father. I don't want to be a burden on my children.

86. The daughter's attitude toward the mother is one of

    (1) indifference
    (2) antagonism
    (3) caring
    (4) disrespect
    (5) conciliation

87. The mother's attitude toward the daughter is one of

    (1) antagonism
    (2) disrespect
    (3) indifference
    (4) bitterness
    (5) appreciation

88. The mother wants to

    (1) enjoy her leisure
    (2) forget her past life
    (3) retain her independence
    (4) criticize her children
    (5) forget her husband

89. The mother wants to live alone because

    (1) she wants an easy life
    (2) she doesn't get on well with her children
    (3) she is undecided what to do
    (4) she knows the neighborhood
    (5) she can't take care of herself

90. The daughter offers the mother all of the following EXCEPT
    (1) a sunny room
    (2) a friendly neighborhood
    (3) potential friends of the same age
    (4) independence
    (5) old companions

Commentary on the Arts

Questions 91 to 95 deal with the following selection on the theater.

WHAT IS THE ROLE OF SETTING IN A PLAY'S SUCCESS?

Rain pounds the cobblestone streets—empty except for a handful of urchins hovering around an enormous and imposing mansion. Then come the sounds of laughter and the clinking of champagne glasses. Cut to a shadowy figure in trench coat and snap-brim hat.

This may sound like *film noir*—in fact, *Vertigo*-like music fills the theater—but instead, the scene is from Broadway's latest and most intriguing hit. And it's not so much *An Inspector Calls*'s competent 50-year-old script or the solid acting that has excited critics and audiences. It's the remarkably inventive and surprising set designed by 34-year-old Ian MacNeil, who with director Stephen Daldry, 33, has transformed J.B. Priestly's sometimes preachy whodunit into first-rate theater.

MacNeil attributes the triumph of British set design not to artistic superiority but to the art-comes-first atmosphere of England's state-subsidized theaters. "At home, if you want to do *Medea* with a steel set," he says, "you do it. There aren't producers around who second-guess whether audiences want to pay to see it." He also adds that "while I'm not union-bashing, the restrictions are rather elaborate here."

Priestly's potboiler—a pretty working-class girl commits suicide, and an inspector interrogates members of the upper-crust Birling family—has always been popular among British community theaters, but up until now, more serious theatergoers have been dismissive.

Daldry and MacNeil say they experimented "with setting the play in Algiers at the end of World War II, with tanks and all, as a play-within-a-play; we tinkered with other ideas as well." Instead, they settled for a grand Edwardian mansion in the north of England. "It's amazing how long it takes to arrive at the obvious," MacNeil says now.

The play's most powerful moment is actually a set change: the fall, quite literally, of the house of Birling. Not everyone is happy with the fact that the set, not the play, is the thing. From an actor's point of view, says one cast member, "these sets are disturbing and a hindrance. It's not my particular cup of tea."

91. The review indicates that *An Inspector Calls* is good theater because of its
    (1) script
    (2) acting
    (3) direction
    (4) sound effects
    (5) set

92. *An Inspector Calls* is
    (1) a *film noir*
    (2) musical theater
    (3) a new play
    (4) a mystery
    (5) an American play

93. J.B. Priestly is the
    (1) author
    (2) director
    (3) set designer
    (4) producer
    (5) featured actor

94. The success of the set design for the play is due to
    (1) artistic superiority
    (2) British producers
    (3) union regulations
    (4) government assistance
    (5) experimentation

95. The reaction of some cast members to the set is
    (1) enthusiastic
    (2) indifferent
    (3) negative
    (4) dismissive
    (5) predictable

Questions 96 to 100 refer to the following selection on literature.

WHAT IS THE NATURE OF SHAKESPEARE'S GENIUS?

Given Shakespeare's popularity as an actor and a playwright, and his conspicuous financial success (he was getting a percentage of the profits of the Globe Theater, in whose ownership he was a partner), it was not surprising that jealous rivals began to snipe at his work. In later centuries, a common charge was that Shakespeare did not invent many of his plots, but took his basic stories from Plutarch, Ovid, well-known English history and old legends.

Quite true; these sources were used by *all* English dramatists. But what Shakespeare *did* to the common facts is wholly remarkable: he invented new characters, transformed old ones, created a gallery of kings, maidens, courtiers, warriors and clowns of startling psychological depth. He rearranged familiar tales with an extraordinary gift for drama, comedy, fantasy. And over all this work, so rich with soaring language and glistening poetry, he cast an unprecedented mood of grandeur and glory. Never had the theater been showered with such lyricism and passion, such insight and profundity.

In *Macbeth*, for instance, Shakespeare converted a folk tale about a petty, ambitious king into a riveting drama about *two* murderers, husband and wife, locked in their evil and intertwining guilts. The monologues are so dazzling, the poetry so brilliant, that they make the story of the real Macbeth seem a shallow episode laden with clichés.

Othello was a tired murder story until Shakespeare's monumental vision invested it with intellectual and moral range far beyond the bounds of the original.

Hamlet is based in part on an antiquated melodrama that had often been performed by the Lord Chamberlain's Men. Shakespeare gave the tale a wholly new interpretation; he made Hamlet a paralyzed victim of warring internal forces—contemptuous of custom, scornful of sex, steeped in indecision, mourning the hollowness of love. To have produced the immortal tale of Hamlet from the histrionics of a tenth-rate melodrama is one small measure of Shakespeare's genius.

Or consider *Romeo and Juliet*, transformed by Shakespeare from a poem into a torrent of passion, a celebration of young love and a damnation of hate. To the pristine character of Juliet, Shakespeare added a bawdy sideshow; a ribald Mercutio and the Nurse brimming with sensual fantasies.

96. The major purpose of the author is to
    (1) explain Shakespeare's popularity
    (2) praise his acting ability
    (3) emphasize his financial success
    (4) praise his handling of plots
    (5) describe his lack of originality

97. Shakespeare was remarkable in all of the following EXCEPT
    (1) his characters
    (2) his language
    (3) his grandeur
    (4) his psychology
    (5) his originality

98. Shakespeare took his plots from all of the following EXCEPT
    (1) legends
    (2) history
    (3) Ovid
    (4) Plutarch
    (5) jealous rivals

99. The play that was derived from a folk tale is
    (1) *Macbeth*
    (2) *Othello*
    (3) *Hamlet*
    (4) *Romeo and Juliet*
    (5) *The Merchant of Venice*

100. The source of *Romeo and Juliet* was
    (1) a sideshow
    (2) a fantasy
    (3) a Greek myth
    (4) a medieval ballad
    (5) a poem

Questions 101 to 105 refer to the following passage on film.

WHAT IS HOLLYWOOD REALLY LIKE?

Like other forms of American popular culture, Hollywood is a little world in itself—a subculture of the larger society, but with marked mirror distortions. It has strata of prestige and power, narrowing to a small top group who sit at the peak of the pyramid. They are the studio executives in charge of production. A mass of legendry clings to each of them, and what passes for conversation in Hollywood is likely to be anecdotes, gossip, and malice about them. Their royal position casts a deep shadow on Hollywood, for independent critical judgment is impossible where the employee must also be a courtier. A Hollywood "big shot" is surrounded by yes-men whose function is to give Number One the heady sense of being right. Where one man has the power of life and death there can be none of that responsibility which must mean taking risks in order to make independent choices. No one feels secure in his tenure—not even the top executives, who fear the intrigues of their rivals and the power of the bankers, and these in turn fear the whims and hostility of the movie audience.

The final decisions that affect creativeness are made in the "front office" with an eye on picture budgets that may run into millions of dollars. Everyone connected with a picture, including the director and script writers, knows that two or three million dollars may be at stake: as a result, no one takes risks with ideas, theme, treatment. The phrase "venture capital" has an ironic meaning when applied to Hollywood: since the capital being ventured is big, nothing else can be ventured. This is the nub of Hollywood's timidity. And timidity joins with bureacracy and the money yardstick to form Hollywood's deadly trinity.

The movie colony is always in feverish motion, always coming up with "terrific" ideas for "colossal" successes; yet for all its febrile quality, it is always in danger of becoming stagnant. It isn't a metropolis, yet it feels too important to be content with the life of a small town—nor could it even if it wished, since it is torn away from all the normal activities of a town. Thus Hollywood is one of the loneliest places in the world.

101. The attitude of the author to Hollywood is
(1) objective
(2) critical
(3) admiring
(4) even-handed
(5) traditional

102. The structure of Hollywood society
(1) makes for security
(2) stifles independent thinking
(3) encourages risk-taking
(4) results in group tensions
(5) reflects the larger society

103. The author implies that the ultimate authority rests with
(1) the studio executive
(2) the Hollywood employee
(3) rivals of the top executives
(4) the bankers
(5) the movie audience

104. The word that best describes Hollywood movie-making is
(1) legendary
(2) responsible
(3) venturesome
(4) independent
(5) fearful

105. The author points up a contradiction in Hollywood's
(1) size
(2) bureaucracy
(3) success
(4) creativeness
(5) conversation

Questions 106 to 110 refer to the following passage.

WHAT IS THE SECRET OF A MOVIE DIRECTOR'S SUCCESS?

Orson Welles was once asked which director's work he admired. Welles, who had himself made cinematic history on a few occasions, responded: "The old masters, by which I mean John Ford, John Ford, and John Ford."

Welles wasn't alone in his admiration of Ford. His fellow directors awarded Ford Oscars for best director on four different occasions. While a few directors have produced individual films that equal, or perhaps even surpass, Ford's best, no one can match his total body of work.

Over a career spanning five decades, Ford directed 112 feature films, with only a couple of outright failures. Dozens of his films are recognized by critics as classics. The vast majority of the rest remain eminently watchable. *Stagecoach, Young Mr. Lincoln, The Grapes of Wrath, How Green Was My Valley, The Searchers, The Quiet Man, She Wore a Yellow Ribbon*—these are just a few of the classics he made.

Ford, who always protested that he did not aspire to make great art, only entertaining films, shrugged off the praise. He told anyone that would listen that he filled the set with mist and kept the actors in shadows because he didn't have a budget big enough for good sets.

This frugality was a trait that Ford did not abandon even at the height of his success. Another trait that distinguished Ford's filmmaking was his speed. The cavalry film, *She Wore a Yellow Ribbon*, for example, was shot in just 28 days. Most films have a shooting schedule of at least 60 days. His speed and frugality grew out of his character. Ford believed in hard work and was tight with a buck even in his private life. But these traits also seemed to be part of a deliberate strategy on Ford's part.

Because his films were so inexpensive, few of them failed to at least break even. Because he was so prolific, Ford could be certain that, even when one of his films was less-than-successful, he would be back in theaters just a few months later with one that would likely be a hit.

106. Ford's honors came from

(1) his audiences
(2) his actors
(3) his choice of subjects
(4) his critics
(5) his fellow directors

107. The reader can infer from his reaction to praise that Ford was

(1) hungry for recognition
(2) antisocial
(3) egocentric
(4) proud
(5) modest

108. The reader can infer from Ford's filling the set with mist that he

(1) didn't have good actors
(2) didn't have an adequate budget
(3) had a love for the mysterious
(4) valued a good set
(5) was lavish in his direction

109. Ford's speed and frugality were a result of

(1) necessity
(2) poor planning
(3) pressure to succeed
(4) a purposeful plan
(5) an unfortunate inefficiency

110. Ford's films were profitable because they were

(1) made inexpensively
(2) produced on lavish sets
(3) made in foreign countries
(4) notable for artistic quality
(5) based on classics

Questions 111 to 115 refer to the following selection on the theater.

HOW DO PLAY, PLAYWRIGHT, AND AUDIENCE INTERREACT?

The theater is a jungle in which the playwright, the actor, and the director struggle for supremacy. Sometimes the fight goes one way and then, for a time, another. I have lived through the reign of each in turn and now it seems to me the playwright is once more supreme. Pinter, Stoppard, and Gray stalk unchallenged by Olivier and Peter Brook. Once more the audience is invited not only to look and listen but to think as they once thought with Shaw and Galsworthy. There is a rich heritage in the British theater, but it is not, alas, the heritage of the actor, still less of the director. The playwright must in the final battle always prove the winner. His work, imperishable; his fame, enduring. I write "alas" because although I have tried my hand at both directing and playwriting, I am in essence one of those of whom Shakespeare wrote that we were destined to strut and fret an hour upon the stage and then be heard no more.

My generation of actors were trained to entice our prey. We kept an eye open, a claw sharpened, even when we professed to slumber. However deep the tragedy or shallow the farce, we never forgot to face front. Nowadays, the relation between player and public tends to be more sophisticated. Together they share a mutual experience of pain and sorrow. Sometimes the actor seems able to dispense with his audience—to no longer need them. He may choose or chance to perfect his performance on a wet afternoon in Shrewsbury, with hardly anyone watching, and thereafter the repetition for him may stale. For me this never happens. I never perfect a performance, though obviously I am sometimes better or worse, but I have learned that without a perfect audience, my struggle to the summit is impossible. I am aware as the curtain rises of the texture of the house.

—Robert Morley

111. According to this passage, Pinter, Stoppard, and Gray are involved with the theater as

(1) theater owners
(2) actors
(3) playwrights
(4) directors
(5) theatergoers

112. Which image is presented in lines 1 through 16?

(1) Producing a play is like a battle.
(2) The playwright is like a god.
(3) The director is a hunter who attempts to capture and tame the actors.
(4) Actors are like murderers and directors are their victims.
(5) Each participant is a king.

113. What reason does the author give for using the word "alas" in line 19?

(1) He believes that playwrights have too much power.
(2) He believes that directors have too much power.
(3) He feels he has been ignored.
(4) He realizes he has limited abilities.
(5) He would prefer to be a director.

114. What relationship usually exists between the modern actor and his audience?

(1) The actor ignores the audience completely.
(2) The actor merely presents the playwright's ideas to the audience.
(3) The audience enters into the experience with the actor.
(4) The audience must be perfect or the actor will not be successful.
(5) The audience expects perfection.

115. In lines 26 through 31, the actors of the author's generation are pictured as

(1) hypocrites
(2) predators
(3) perfectionists
(4) sophisticates
(5) strugglers

Questions 116 to 120 refer to the following selection on art.

WHAT WERE LEONARDO DA VINCI'S TALENTS?

Leonardo carried on his studies in mathematics and physics, botany and anatomy, not in addition to his art but as a part of it. To him there was no essential difference between art and science. Both are ways of describing God's one universe. He poured scorn on artists who wish to improve on Nature. Let them improve on themselves; Nature can't be wrong!

But when he came to paint, Leonardo flung over chill, naked fact the glowing cloak of beauty. His knowledge, his technique, his peerless draftsmanship, were concealed like a conjuror's sleight, and he painted like a man in love with life. How he loved it can be seen by turning over his sketchbooks' pages—hundreds of them. Here on one sheet may be seen the dimples and creases in a baby's knee, together with the contorted features of soldiers dying and killing. Here are naked laborers straining, there is a young woman kneeling in prayer. Now he draws the nervous anxiety in the neck tendons of an old pauper, and here he has captured the gaiety of a playing child. It is said that he would follow beautiful or grotesque people around all day to study them. He visited the hospitals to watch old men die, and hastened to see a criminal hanged. Conspicuous for his golden locks topped with a little round black cap, and for his rose-colored cloak streaming like an anemone in the gusty streets, he loitered to watch the innocent greed of a baby at its mother's breast; then secretly, for it was frowned on, he hurried and dissected a human body that his brush might accurately paint "the divine proportion."

Indeed on no science did Leonardo spend so much time as on anatomy. Our muscles he demonstrated to be the levers they are, and he revealed the eye to be a lens. The heart he proved to be a hydraulic pump, and showed that the pulse is synchronized with the heart beat. He was the first discoverer, too, of the moderator bands involved in the contraction of the heart muscles. His many observations in the hospitals led him to the discovery of hardening of the arteries as a cause of death in old age.

116. According to the article, Leonardo da Vinci's life combined interests in
(1) nature and science
(2) technique and inspiration
(3) God and art
(4) science and art
(5) nature and the universe

117. The contradiction in Leonardo implied by the writer found expression in his
(1) scorn of artists
(2) painting
(3) distrust of nature
(4) morbid curiosity
(5) conspicuous clothing

118. The writer admires all of the following about Leonardo EXCEPT his
(1) improvements on nature
(2) technique
(3) knowledge
(4) draftsmanship
(5) painting

119. His sketches of babies, soldiers, and laborers are cited as examples of Leonardo's
(1) concealed technique
(2) love of life
(3) versatility
(4) curiosity
(5) realism

120. Leonardo's scientific studies led to discoveries regarding all of the following EXCEPT the
(1) muscles
(2) eye
(3) heart
(4) pulse
(5) blood

ANSWER KEY

Popular Literature/Page 414

1. **2**	11. **2**	20. **1**	29. **1**	38. **3**	47. **2**
2. **2**	12. **4**	21. **3**	30. **3**	39. **1**	48. **4**
3. **4**	13. **4**	22. **2**	31. **3**	40. **4**	49. **1**
4. **3**	14. **1**	23. **4**	32. **1**	41. **3**	50. **5**
5. **3**	15. **2**	24. **2**	33. **2**	42. **4**	51. **4**
6. **3**	16. **2**	25. **4**	34. **1**	43. **5**	52. **1**
7. **2**	17. **3**	26. **2**	35. **2**	44. **3**	53. **2**
8. **4**	18. **3**	27. **4**	36. **4**	45. **4**	54. **5**
9. **1**	19. **2**	28. **3**	37. **2**	46. **5**	55. **2**
10. **5**					

Classical Literature/Page 425

56. **2**	60. **3**	64. **2**	67. **2**	70. **1**	73. **3**
57. **5**	61. **4**	65. **1**	68. **4**	71. **5**	74. **4**
58. **1**	62. **2**	66. **3**	69. **3**	72. **2**	75. **3**
59. **4**	63. **4**				

Poetry and Drama/Page 429/431

76. **4**	79. **5**	82. **3**	85. **4**	87. **5**	89. **4**
77. **4**	80. **2**	83. **1**	86. **3**	88. **3**	90. **4**
78. **3**	81. **4**	84. **4**			

Commentary on the Arts/Page 432

91. **5**	96. **4**	101. **2**	106. **5**	111. **3**	116. **4**
92. **4**	97. **5**	102. **2**	107. **5**	112. **1**	117. **2**
93. **1**	98. **5**	103. **5**	108. **2**	113. **4**	118. **1**
94. **4**	99. **1**	104. **5**	109. **4**	114. **3**	119. **2**
95. **3**	100. **5**	105. **1**	110. **1**	115. **2**	120. **5**

WHAT'S YOUR SCORE?

______right,	______wrong
Excellent	108–120
Good	96–107
Fair	84–95

If your score was low, the explanation of the correct answers that follows will help you. Analyze your errors. Then, reread the section on Basic Reading Skills (beginning on page 389) and Reading Prose, Poetry, and Drama (page 391).

ANSWER ANALYSIS

Popular Literature/Page 414

1. **2** The passage states that, despite the fact that no food stayed down, "the wounds slowly healed."
2. **2** The swan "came to regard me as a friend."
3. **4** The narrator felt "the bird was wasting away with nostalgia."
4. **3** The swan looked at the pebbles (fish) "remotely."
5. **3** In the last sentence, the narrator says, "Swans do not sing at their death if they die of grief."
6. **3** The writer is making fun of the sport and the people who like it, so the audience most likely to enjoy the passage is nonathletic individuals.
7. **2** We learn first that any child could "deposit the ball across the opponent's goal line." Apparently the game is simple, but the rules make it complicated.
8. **4** The selection states that "only in football are these blows diverted from the ball to the opponent."
9. **1** The first two sentences of the third paragraph that lead to this conclusion: "If anything happens, that's where [on TV] you'll see it."
10. **5** Satire is a technique that pokes fun at a person, an institution, or an idea. The writer is directing his satire at football.
11. **2** The selection states it was "not the best time to be walking alone by the side of a half-frozen river."
12. **4** The words "during the day as she stood pinning dresses" indicate that this activity took place regularly. Pinning dresses, therefore, must have been her work.
13. **4** The sentence "What if they...had died of cold or hunger...while she was...dancing with British officers?" communicates a sense of guilt.
14. **1** The sentence "No one, she thought, wanted to hear them" indicates that the woman believed others were not interested, not that she did not want to tell them. The fact that she continued to go to the Jewish Community Center proves that answer Choices 3 and 4 are incorrect.

15. 2 The last paragraph describes the long-range effects of the Holocaust. That is what the reader is meant to remember and to understand.

16. 2 The fact that "They poured their sewage into it, but it couldn't be tainted" means that, no matter what else happened around the ocean, nothing could taint it.

17. 3 Terror and fear are indicated by such words and phrases as *chilling*, *clammy*, and *bowels of fear*.

18. 3 The narrator wishes to show how the area has been ruined by the changes he describes.

19. 2 The contrasts are derricks instead of trees and oil-pumps instead of cattle.

20. 1 The clue is found in the last phrase, "like a tumor."

21. 3 "Taking a last look" is an expression that is often used in relation to death or a catastrophic event.

22. 2 To do something "consciously" is to do it "with deliberate thought or awareness." That the speaker did not let the freeing of the hawk "come into consciousness" would mean that it was never planned.

23. 4 The passage states that "He lay there a long minute without hope...his eyes still fixed on that blue vault above him." A minute may seem longer than a minute if it is filled with suspense and uncertainty.

24. 2 We are told the sky is "so full of light that I could not follow his gaze." Later, we are told that the "light was too intense."

25. 4 The passage refers to "a cry of such unutterable and ecstatic joy that it sounds down across the years and tingles...."

26. 2 The sounds were unusual because "...they were a weird medley of whines, whimpers and small howls."

27. 4 The narrator has learned "from experience.... The cries were obviously those of a husky."

28. 3 Mike "owned three half-grown pups not yet trained to harness..."

29. 1 The narrator states, "If that pup needed a friend...I was its man!"

30. 3 In the fifth paragraph, the narrator "kept quiet, even when the whimpering stopped, leaving me uncertain about the direction...."

31. 3 The author claims that the apartment, if in a better neighborhood or on a lower floor, "would have rented for twice the amount he paid."

32. 1 This stagnation is reinforced by "the cowls of the chimneys, which rattled in the slightest stir of air, were still."

33. 2 It is likely that Mary was responsible for running the household since "she could not depend on him [even] to keep the windows shut...."

34. 1 If it were April first or Halloween, he would not have been surprised. He would have expected some sort of trick. This suggests his sense of the proper order of events.

35. 2 "...it only added to his depression to discover how he longed for a visitor." This longing indicates a state of mind.

36. 4 The poet says repeatedly that "nobody can make it out here alone."

37. 2 The poet writes that "thinking last night" she came to her conclusion.

38. 3 The poet states that some millionaires have "hearts of stone."

39. 1 The poet says "Storm clouds are gathering" and "The wind is gonna blow" because "the race of man is suffering."

40. 4 Line 10 is repeated in lines 22 and 34.

41. 3 The center of attention is an "infantile face...now faded."

42. 4 The second stanza again refers to an infant, "swathed in a sort of white dress," as the "center of attraction."

43. 5 The poet [he] regrets "promises unkept."

44. 3 The man and the woman, the poet's father and mother, no longer live, but "that child, years later, stands there" filled with emotion.

45. 4 The child is now over 75, so his picture in the photograph, with his young parents, now dead, is a portent of his own future.

46. 5 It can be inferred that Conrad, the younger brother, is seeking help from Berger, a psychiatrist, in coping with his problem.

47. 2 Conrad feels guilty because Buck, his older brother, drowned.

48. Berger and Conrad cannot agree on an explanation, Buck never got tired, did have a reason to hang on, and had endurance, and Conrad was not responsible.

49. **1** Conrad tried to model himself on his brother.
50. **5** The burden is "to become the other, perfect kid," that is, his brother Buck.
51. **4** Wiegand is the only character who can clarify matters for the salesman. The others hardly talk.
52. **1** These portions call for actions by the actors.
53. **2** Wiegand refers to their "exaggerated ideas of the dutiful respect" for the dead.
54. **5** Wiegand mentions that the clergy get revenue and profit from big funerals.
55. **2** Anna is embroidering slippers for Papa, and Welzel says he doesn't like to wear them.

Classical Literature/Page 425

56. **2** See the section "Inferring Setting" (page 396). The reference to the portrait of George III, the reigning monarch at the time just prior to the American Revolution, implies a date of about 1770.
57. **5** The author refers to the outside of the house as "the only side which, in truth, belongs to a henpecked husband."
58. **1** Dame Van Winkle looked upon Wolf with "an evil eye as the cause of his master's going so often astray."
59. **4** The author says that Rip never said anything in response to his wife's nagging.
60. **3** He would be content were it not for his wife's "dinning in his ear."
61. **4** The author states "I went to the woods...to front only the essential facts of life...."
62. **2** The author says, "Our life is frittered away by detail... "Simplicity, simplicity, simplicity!... keep your accounts on your thumb-nail."
63. **4** *Mean* is used here to imply the opposite of *sublime* (used in the next clause), that is, as in the sentence "Still we live meanly, like ants."
64. **2** The author implies that people do not know how to live properly, but they should learn.
65. **1** The author went to the woods to see if he "could not learn what it had had to teach."
66. **3** "Small and hopeful Sylvia" climbed the tree with "tingling, eager blood coursing" through her body.
67. **2** Sylvia "knew that higher still one of the oak's upper branches chafed against the pine trunk...."
68. **4** The first part of Sylvia's climb was easy because "She had often climbed there...."
69. **3** "It was like a great mainmast...." A ship's mast supports its sails.
70. **1** "The old pine must have loved his new dependent."
71. **5** The feud has been going on for years and nobody knows what it is about. The author implies that a trivial event has been blown out of proportion.
72. **2** Buck doesn't know, so we aren't told, who started the feud; only a few old men remember.
73. **3** Buck talks of his cousin Bud's being ambushed by Baldy Shepherdson; we can, therefore, assume that Buck is a Grangerford.
74. **4** To hear a sermon about brotherly love, all the men arrive armed.
75. **3** Buck states, in answer to two questions, "I don't know" and "how do *I* know?"

Poetry and Drama/Page 429/431

76. **4** The main purpose of the poem is to teach us a lesson in conduct—that, regardless of our station in life, we must make our own opportunities with the resources we have at hand.
77. **4** "I could help defeat the enemy" follows logically from the incomplete thought, "Had I a sword of keener steel."
78. **3** The "craven" hangs along the edge of the battle and creeps away, both actions of a cowardly person.
79. **5** The words "...swords shocked upon swords and shields" provide an example of alliteration, that is, repetition of the same sound.
80. **2** The bravery of the king's son is contrasted with the cowardly behavior of the craven soldier.
81. **4** *Stop* and *cut* are short, sharp words, just as *shock* is, both in sound and meaning.

82. 3 See the "Glossary of Literary Terms" (page 411) for a definition of alliteration. Here the letter *s* is repeated at the beginning of two or more words in close proximity—"scribbling" and "sky."

83. 1 The first three verses establish the importance of the poet's love. The last verse stresses the effects of the loss of that love.

84. 4 All of the emotion that follows from the loss of a loved one is indicated in lines 21 and 22.

85. 4 To the poet, none of the elements mentioned in the final stanza that represent life serve any purpose.

86. 3 The daughter cares; she doesn't like her mother living alone.

87. 5 The mother appreciates her daughter's caring and says, "Annie, you're a good daughter."

88. 3 The mother wants to be independent. She says, "I want to keep my own home."

89. 4 The mother wants to stay where she knows "all the neighbors and the store people."

90. 4 The daughter mentions everything except independence. Her mother doesn't want to be "some old lady living with her children."

Commentary on the Arts/Page 432

91. 5 The review refers to "the remarkably inventive and surprising set."

92. 4 The play is referred to as a who-dunit," that is, a mystery.

93. 1 The play's author is J.B. Priestly.

94. 4 The success of the set design is attributed to "the art-comes-first atmosphere of England's state-subsidized theaters."

95. 3 One cast member says the sets are not his "particular cup of tea."

96. 4 The author says that what Shakespeare did to common facts is wholly remarkable.

97. 5 The author repeats the charge that Shakespeare was not original in that he "did not invent many of his plots."

98. 5 "Jealous rivals" are not mentioned as sources. The others choices are.

99. 1 The article states that Shakespeare, in *Macbeth*, "converted a folk tale" into a "riveting drama."

100. 5 According to the article, *Romeo and Juliet* was "transformed by Shakespeare from a poem into a torrent of passion."

101. 2 The author refers to Hollywood's "marked mirror distortions" of society and its timidity, among other criticisms.

102. 2 It is stated that the position of the studio executives at the top of a pyramid makes independent critical judgment impossible.

103. 5 Executives fear rivals and bankers, who, in turn, fear the movie audience.

104. 5 The author refers to Hollywood's timidity or fearfulness.

105. 1 Hollywood, according to the article, isn't a metropolis nor is it a small town.

106. 5 Ford's fellow directors awarded him Oscars for best director.

107. 5 Ford shrugged off praise (fourth paragraph).

108. 2 Ford filled the set with mist "because he didn't have a budget big enough for good sets."

109. 4 Ford's speed and frugality were "part of a deliberate strategy on [his] part."

110. 1 The author of the article claims that, "Because his films were so inexpensive, few of them failed to at least break even."

111. 3 Pinter, Stoppard, and Gray are cited as playwrights who are "once more supreme" and "stalk unchallenged" by actors such as Olivier and Brook.

112. 1 The theater is pictured as a "jungle" in which participants "struggle for supremacy," as in a battle.

113. 4 The author says "alas" because he is, "in essence," not a playwright but an actor, described by Shakespeare as one who is "destined to strut and fret an hour upon the stage and then be heard no more."

114. 3 Morley states that audience and actor "share a mutual experience of pain and sorrow."

115. 2 Actors are referred to as predators "trained to entice [their] prey."

116. 4 Leonardo saw no essential difference between art and science.

117. 2 His painting resulted in the contradiction of art disguising reality (nature).

118. 1 Da Vinci hated artists who tried to improve on nature.

119. 2 These sketchbooks' pages show how Leonardo loved life.

120. 5 All are mentioned *except* circulation of the blood, which was discovered later.

UNIT VII

MATHEMATICS

TEST 5

CHAPTER 17: Handling Mathematics Questions

Five sequential steps explain how to read and solve word problems. Test-taking tactics for mathematics give practical hints for achieving a maximum score on the GED Mathematics test.

CHAPTER 18: Arithmetic: Worked-Out Examples and Practice

Basic operations, fractions, decimals, and percents are reviewed. Business applications such as profit and loss, interest, sales tax, and investments receive attention.

CHAPTER 19: Algebra: Worked-Out Examples and Practice

Fundamental concepts of algebra, including scientific notation, probability, and the mean (average) and the median are presented.

CHAPTER 20: Geometry: Worked-Out Examples and Practice

This chapter includes problems that provide extensive experience with geometric concepts.

CHAPTER 21: Graphs: Worked-Out Examples and Practice

Pictographs and bar, line, and formula graphs are presented.

CHAPTER 22: Measures: Worked-Out Examples and Practice

Measures of length, time, and weight, liquid measure, and the metric system are discussed.

CHAPTER 23: Three Practice Mathematics Tests

Each test has the standard 56 questions with explained answers. You are referred to other chapters in this unit to refresh your understanding of questions answered incorrectly.

17 Handling Mathematics Questions

How to Read and Solve Word Problems

Some mathematics questions on the GED Examination require only that you perform simple arithmetic calculations, solve an easy equation, or interpret data in a graph. Most of the mathematics questions, however, are presented as word problems. Therefore, before beginning a review of all of the mathematics that you need to know for the GED, a simple five-step procedure that will help you set up and solve word problems correctly will be presented.

PLAN FOR SOLVING WORD PROBLEMS

1. Read the problem carefully.
2. Collect the information that is given in the problem.
3. Decide what must be found.
4. Develop a plan to solve the problem.
5. Use your plan as a guide to complete the solution of the problem.

When you do the practice exercises in this book, you should follow these steps. The following examples show how this systematic method is used in arithmetic, algebra, and geometry.

ARITHMETIC PROBLEM

1. ***Read the problem carefully.***
   At John's Clothing Store, all items were on sale. Jackets were reduced by 50% off the marked price, and all other items by 25%. Mr. Bates bought a jacket that was marked \$80 and a shirt that was marked \$16. How much did Mr. Bates save by buying at the sale?
2. ***Collect the information that is given in the problem.***

	Marked Price	Discount Percent
Jacket	\$80	50%
Shirt	\$16	25%

3. ***Decide what must be found.***
   Find the amount of money saved.
4. ***Develop a plan to solve the problem.***
   Find the amount saved on the jacket. Then find the amount saved on the shirt. Finally, add the two savings.
5. ***Use your plan as a guide to complete the solution of the problem.***
   Saving on jacket = 50% of \$80 = \$40
   Saving on shirt = 25% of \$16 = \$4
   Total amount saved = \$40 + \$4 = \$44

ALGEBRA PROBLEM

1. ***Read the problem carefully.***
   A father is 15 years more than twice the age of his daughter. If the sum of the ages of the father and daughter is 48 years, what is the age of the daughter?
2. ***Collect the information that is given in the problem.***
   Age of father = twice age of daughter + 15
   Age of father + age of daughter = 48
3. ***Decide what must be found.***
   Find the age of the daughter.
4. ***Develop a plan to solve the problem.***
   Set up an equation using the given facts. Then solve the equation.
5. ***Use your plan as a guide to complete the solution of the problem.***

Let n = age of daughter, and $2n + 15$ = age of father

$$\begin{aligned} \text{Age of daughter} + \text{age of father} &= 48 \\ n + (2n + 15) &= 48 \\ 3n + 15 &= 48 \\ 3n &= 33 \\ n &= \frac{33}{3} \\ &= 11 \end{aligned}$$

The daughter's age is 11 years.

GEOMETRY PROBLEM

1. ***Read the problem carefully.***
   A room is 22 feet long, 14 feet wide, and 9 feet high. If the walls and ceiling of the room are to be painted, how many square feet must be covered by paint?
2. ***Collect the information that is given in the problem.***
   For geometry problems always draw a diagram.

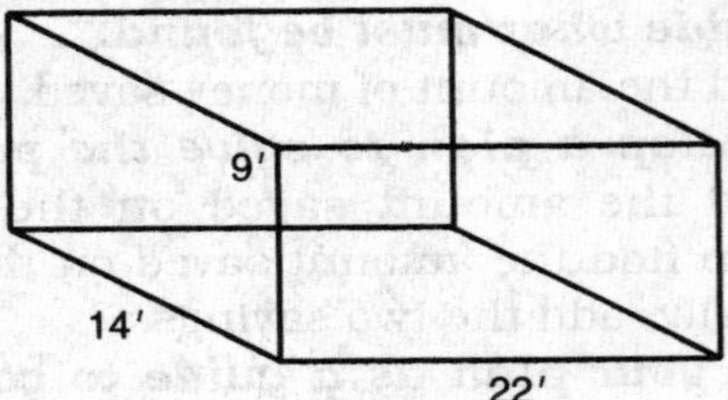

3. ***Decide what must be found.***
   Find the sum of the areas of the front and back, the two sides, and the ceiling of the room.
4. ***Develop a plan to solve the problem.***
   Since all the walls and the ceiling are rectangles, use the formula $A = lw$ to find each area and then add.
5. ***Use your plan as a guide to complete the solution of the problem.***

$$\begin{aligned} \text{Area of front} &= 9 \times 22 = 198 \text{ sq. ft.} \\ + \text{ area of back} &= 9 \times 22 = 198 \text{ sq. ft.} \\ + \text{ area of side} &= 9 \times 14 = 126 \text{ sq. ft.} \\ + \text{ area of second side} &= 9 \times 14 = 126 \text{ sq. ft.} \\ + \text{ area of ceiling} &= 14 \times 22 = \underline{308 \text{ sq. ft.}} \\ \text{Total area} &= 956 \text{ sq. ft.} \end{aligned}$$

Test-Taking Tactics for Mathematics

TACTIC 1:

Be sure that you are answering the question that is asked.

In the excitement of taking the test you may neglect to complete a problem and thus will receive no credit on a question that is easy for you. Consider the following problem:

EXAMPLE

A mechanic and his helper earned a total of \$30. The mechanic earned \$6 more than his helper. How much did the mechanic earn?

Let x = amount helper earned, and $x + 6$ = amount mechanic earned.

$$\begin{aligned} x + x + 6 &= 30 \\ 2x + 6 &= 30 \\ 2x &= 24 \\ x &= 12 \end{aligned}$$

The choices are:

(1) \$12
(2) \$15
(3) \$16
(4) \$18
(5) \$24

You may carelessly choose (1), which is the value of x, and which would be correct if the question were "How much did the helper earn?" However, (4) is the correct choice, because the mechanic earned $x + 6$ dollars, and \$12 + \$6 = \$18.

EXAMPLE

The senior class at Ridgemont High School has 350 members. If 60% of the class consists of girls, how many boys are in the senior class?

(1) 210
(2) 220
(3) 230
(4) 140
(5) 150

A careless reading of the problem may lead to choice (1): (0.60)(350) = 210. However, this is the number of girls in the class. The correct solution, (4), can be found either by subtracting 210 from 350 to obtain 140 as the number of boys, or by taking 40% of 350: $350 \times 0.40 = 140$.

TACTIC 2:

Do not assume any fact that is not specifically stated.

If two lines on a geometric figure appear to be perpendicular, do not assume that they are perpendicular unless this fact is given. Consider the following problem:

EXAMPLE

Find the area of the triangle in the figure.

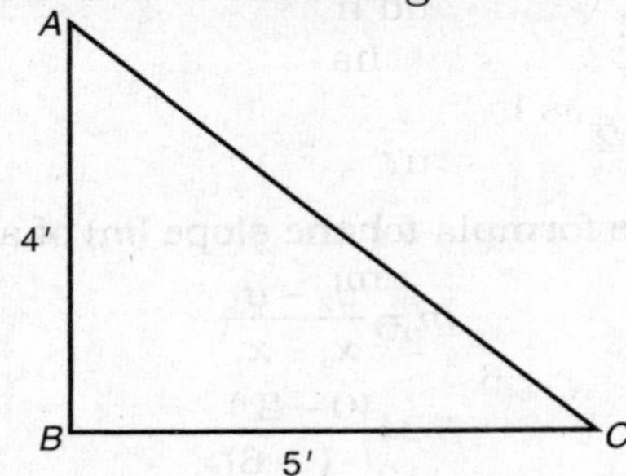

(1) 20 sq. ft.
(2) 16 sq. ft.
(3) 10 sq. ft.
(4) 9 sq. ft.
(5) Not enough information is given.

If you assumed that *AB* is perpendicular to *BC*, and you used the formula $A = \left(\frac{1}{2}\right) bh$, you would determine that the area of the triangle is 10 sq. ft. (3). Since, however, you do not know that *AB* is perpendicular to *BC*, the correct answer is (5).

A second example illustrates the fact that you cannot assume that prices are the same in two different time periods.

EXAMPLE

Stephen sold 5 suits costing $225 each on his first day as a clothing salesman. The next day he sold 8 suits. What was the total value of the suits Stephen sold during the 2 days?

(1) $292.50
(2) $2,925.00
(3) $29.25
(4) $2,250.00
(5) Not enough information is given.

If you assumed that the suits Stephen sold on the second day were also priced at $225, you would arrive at choice (2) by multiplying $\$225 \times 13 = \$2,925$. Since, however, the problem doesn't state the prices of the suits sold on the second day, the correct answer is (5).

TACTIC 3:

On any geometry problem, if a diagram is not provided, draw one. Consider the following problem:

EXAMPLE

A tree casts a shadow that is 15 feet long at the same time of day that a person who is 6 feet tall casts a shadow 3 feet long. About how tall is the tree?

(1) 9 ft.
(2) 15 ft.
(3) 18 ft.
(4) 21 ft.
(5) 30 ft.

Drawing a diagram will help you to visualize the problem and to see that the lengths of the objects (the tree and the person) and of their shadows are in proportion:

$$\frac{x}{15} = \frac{6}{3}$$

$$3x = 6 \times 15 = 90$$
$$x = 30 \text{ ft.}$$

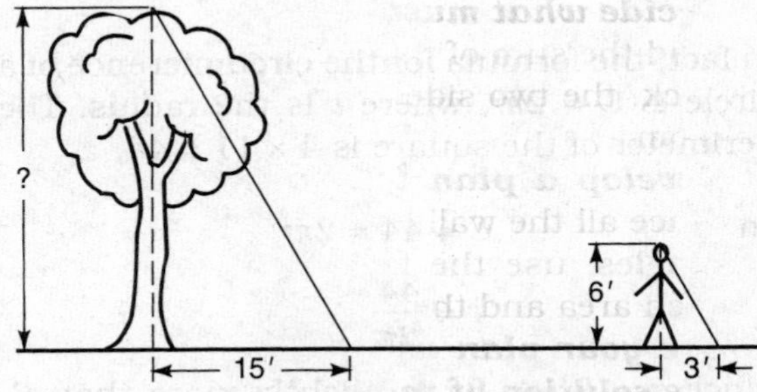

Note: You don't have to draw a tree or a person; in fact, you shouldn't waste the time. Each can be represented by a single line segment.

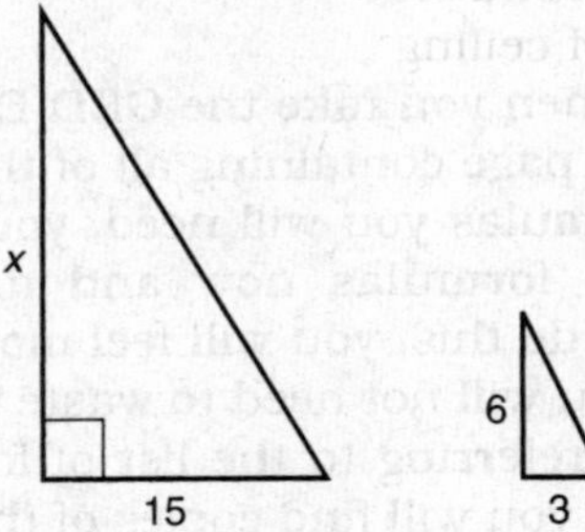

Consider another example:

EXAMPLE

The circumference of a circle and the perimeter of a square are equal. One side of the square measures 11 inches. Which of the following is the radius of the circle, in inches, rounded to the nearest whole number?

(1) 3
(2) 6
(3) 7
(4) 12
(5) 14

First, draw a square, and label each side 11". Then draw, on the square, a circle whose circumference is approximately the same as the perimeter of the square. From the diagram, it is clear that the radius of the circle is about 7 in.

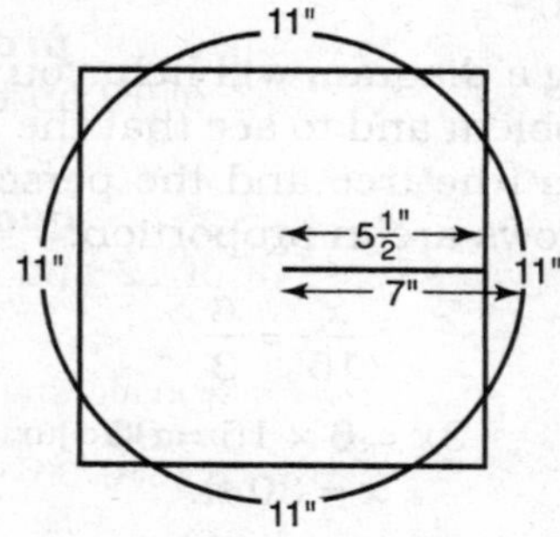

In fact, the formula for the circumference of a circle is $C = 2\pi r$, where r is the radius. The perimeter of the square is $4 \times 11 = 44$,

so $$C = 44 = 2\pi r$$

$$r = \frac{44}{2\pi}$$

Since $\pi \approx 3.14$, 2π is slightly more than 6, and so r is approximately 7.

TACTIC 4:

Although, when you take the GED Examination, given a page containing all of the mathematical formulas you will need, you should study these formulas now and memorize them. If you do this, you will feel more confident, and you will not need to waste valuable test time in referring to the list of formulas. In this book, you will find copies of the list on the first page of Chapter 23 and at the beginning of the Mathematics sections of the Diagnostic Test and the Practice Examinations. Consider this example:

EXAMPLE

Find the slope of a line through points (6,2) and (–1,0).

(1) 2
(2) $\frac{1}{2}$
(3) $\frac{7}{2}$
(4) $\frac{2}{7}$
(5) –2

Use the formula for the slope (m) of a line:

$$m = \frac{y_2 - y_1}{x_2 - x_1} = \frac{(0-2)}{(-1-6)} = \frac{-2}{-7} = \frac{2}{7}$$

Consider another example:

EXAMPLE

A shoebox has dimensions 15 inches by 7 inches by 5 inches. What is the volume, in cubic inches, of the box?

(1) 525
(2) 82
(3) 27
(4) 50
(5) 110

Use the formula $V = lwh$.
$V = 15 \times 7 \times 5 = 525$ cu. in.

18

Arithmetic: Worked-Out Examples and Practice

Basic Operations

To do well on the GED Mathematics test, you need to feel comfortable with most topics of basic arithmetic. This chapter reviews the basic arithmetic operations, divisors and prime numbers, fractions, decimals, and percents. A few other topics in arithmetic, such as ratios and averages, are covered in Chapter 19 on algebra.

On the GED Examination the word *number* always means *real number*, a number that can be represented by a point on the number line.

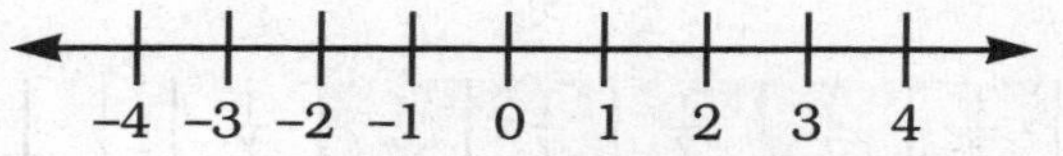

On the line above, we have indicated only the *integers* (positive, negative, and 0), but every number corresponds to a point on the line. For example, $\frac{1}{2}$ is exactly midway between 0 and 1, and 2.01 is slightly to the right of 2. In this chapter, we will concern ourselves only with 0 and positive numbers; we will discuss negative numbers Chapter 19.

In arithmetic we are basically concerned with the addition, subtraction, multiplication, and division of numbers. The correct terms for the results of these operations follow.

Operation	Symbol	Result
addition	+	***sum***
16 is the sum of 12 and 4. $16 = 12 + 4$		
subtraction	−	***difference***
8 is the difference of 12 and 4. $8 = 12 - 4$		
multiplication*	×	***product***
48 is the product of 12 and 4. $48 = 12 \times 4$		
division	÷	***quotient***
3 is the quotient of 12 and 4. $3 = 12 \div 4$		

Note: Multiplication, especially in algebra, can also be indicated by a dot, parentheses, or the juxtaposition of symbols without any sign: $2^2 \cdot 2^4$, $3(4)$, $3(x + 2)$, $3a$, $4abc$.

EXAMPLE

What is the sum of the product and quotient of 10 and 5?

Product: $10 \times 5 = 50$ Quotient: $10 \div 5 = 2$
Sum: $50 + 2 = 52$

The sum, difference, and product of two integers is *always* an integer; the quotient of two integers may be, but is not necessarily, an integer. When 23 is divided by 10, the quotient can be expressed as $\frac{23}{10}$ or $2\frac{3}{10}$ or 2.3. If the quotient is to be an integer, we can also say that the quotient is 2 and there is a *remainder* of 3. It depends upon the items with which we are dealing. For example, if 23 dollars is to be divided among 10 people, each one will get \$2.30 (2.3 dollars); but if 23 books are to be divided among 10 people, each one will get 2 books and 3 (the remainder) will be left over.

Divisors and Prime Numbers

Every whole number greater than 1 has at least two positive divisors, 1 and itself—and possibly many more. For example, 6 is divisible by 1 and 6, as well as by 2 and 3; whereas 7 is divisible only by 1 and 7. Whole numbers, such as 7, that have exactly two positive divisors are called *prime numbers* or *primes*.

Here are the first few primes:

2, 3, 5, 7, 11, 13, 17, 19, 23

Memorize this list—it will come in handy. Note that 1 is *not* a prime.

The *even numbers* are all the multiples of 2:

{..., –4, –2, 0, 2, 4, 6, ...}

The *odd numbers* are the integers that are not divisible by 2:

{..., –5, –3, –1, 1, 3, 5, ...}

Practice

1. What is the largest prime divisor of 24?
2. How many even numbers are there between 25 and 35?
3. How many primes are less than 10?
4. What number is a divisor of every even number?
5. What is the smallest prime greater than 20?

Answers

1. **3** 2. **10** 3. **4** 4. **2** 5. **23**

Fractions

Several questions on the GED Mathematics test involve fractions. In this section all of the important facts you need to know will be reviewed.

WORKING WITH FRACTIONS

When a whole is *divided* into *n* equal parts, each part is called *one nth* of the whole, written as $\frac{1}{n}$. For example:

- If a pizza is cut *(divided)* into 8 equal slices, each slice is one eighth $\left(\frac{1}{8}\right)$ of the pizza.

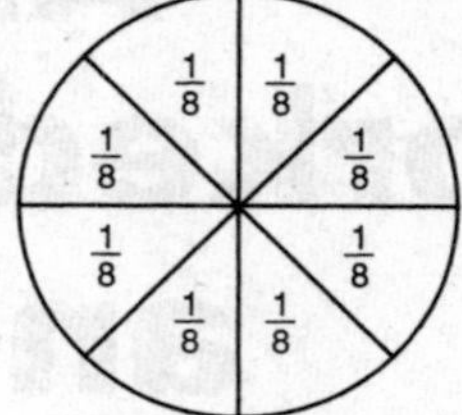

- A week is *divided* into 7 days, so a day is one seventh $\left(\frac{1}{7}\right)$ of a week.

$\frac{1}{7}$	$\frac{1}{7}$	$\frac{1}{7}$	$\frac{1}{7}$	$\frac{1}{7}$	$\frac{1}{7}$	$\frac{1}{7}$
Sun.	Mon.	Tues.	Wed.	Thurs.	Fri.	Sat.

- An inch is one twelfth $\left(\frac{1}{12}\right)$ of a foot.

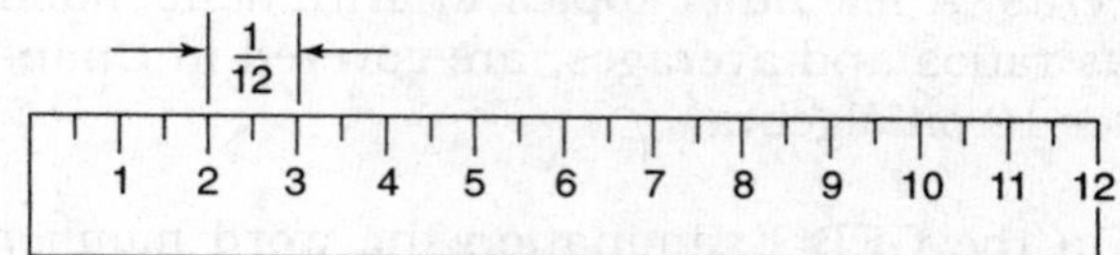

- If Sam went to Paris for 5 days, he was there for five sevenths $\left(\frac{5}{7}\right)$ of a week.

$\frac{1}{7}$	$\frac{1}{7}$	$\frac{1}{7}$	$\frac{1}{7}$	$\frac{1}{7}$	$\frac{1}{7}$	$\frac{1}{7}$	
Sun.	Mon.	Tues.	Wed.	Thurs.	Fri.	Sat.	$\frac{5}{7}$

- If Tara's paint brush is 12 inches long, it measures twelve twelfths $\left(\frac{12}{12}\right)$ of a foot.

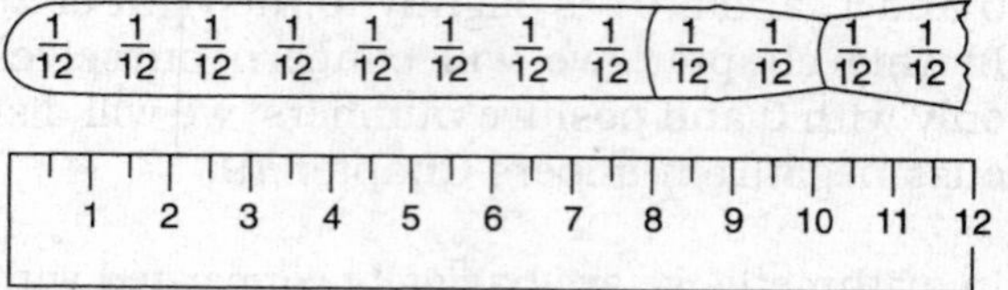

- If Tom bought 10 slices of pizza, he bought ten eighths $\left(\frac{10}{8}\right)$ of a pie.

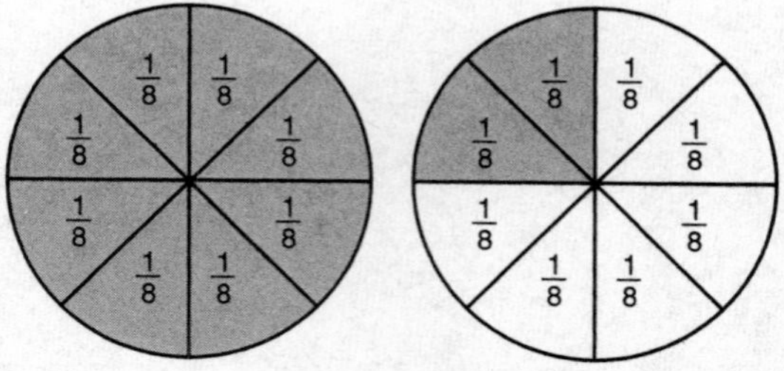

Numbers such as $\frac{5}{7}$, $\frac{12}{12}$, and $\frac{10}{8}$, in which one integer is written over a second integer, are called *fractions*. The center line is called the *fraction bar*. The number above the bar is called the *numerator*, and the number below the bar is the *denominator*.

CAUTION: The denominator of a fraction can *never* be 0.

It is useful to think of the fraction bar as a symbol for division. If 3 pizzas are divided equally among 8 people, each person gets $\frac{3}{8}$ of a pizza.

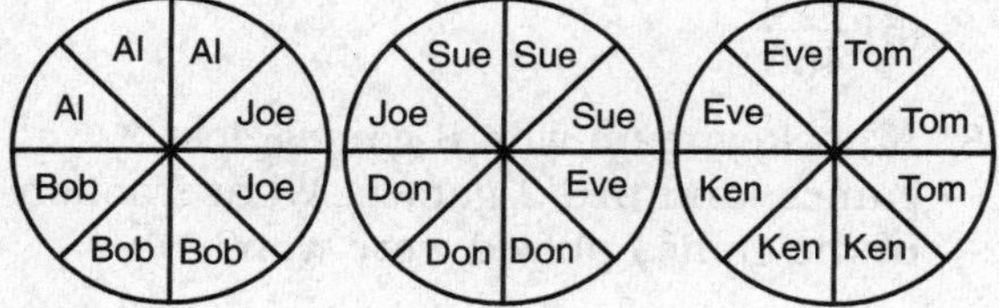

EXAMPLE

A baseball team won 37 games and lost 15 games. What fraction of the games played did the team win?

The required fraction is

$$\frac{\text{number of games won}}{\text{total number of games played}}$$

$$= \frac{37}{37 + 15} + \frac{37}{52}$$

EXAMPLE

A certain school has an enrollment of 500 students. Of these students, 255 are girls. The boys are what fraction of the total enrollment?

Since the total enrollment is 500 and 255 students are girls, the number of boys is obtained by subtracting 255 from 500. Thus, the number of boys enrolled in the school is 500 – 255 = 245.

The required fraction is

$$\frac{\text{number of boys}}{\text{total enrollment}} = \frac{245}{500}$$

PRACTICE

1. The Star Movie Theater has 650 seats. At one performance 67 seats were not occupied. What fractional part of the theater seats were occupied?

(1) $\frac{67}{650}$

(2) $\frac{583}{650}$

(3) $\frac{67}{588}$

(4) $\frac{67}{717}$

(5) $\frac{583}{717}$

2. Mr. Davis parked his car at 2:45 P.M. in a 1-hour parking zone. If he drove away at 3:08 P.M., during what fractional part of an hour was his car parked?

(1) $\frac{63}{100}$

(2) $\frac{53}{60}$

(3) $\frac{45}{60}$

(4) $\frac{8}{60}$

(5) $\frac{23}{60}$

3. Mr. Barnes spent \$10 for a jacket and \$18 for a pair of slacks. The money he spent for the jacket was what fraction of the total money he spent?

(1) $\frac{10}{18}$

(2) $\frac{18}{10}$

(3) $\frac{18}{28}$

(4) $\frac{10}{28}$

(5) $\frac{28}{10}$

4. On a test taken by 80 students, 17 students failed. What fraction of the students passed the test?

(1) $\frac{63}{80}$

(2) $\frac{17}{80}$

(3) $\frac{80}{7}$

(4) $\frac{17}{63}$

(5) $\frac{80}{63}$

5. A carpenter cut strips 2 inches wide from a board 16 inches wide. After he had cut 5 strips, what fraction of the board was left? (Do not allow for waste.)

(1) $\frac{10}{16}$

(2) $\frac{6}{16}$

(3) $\frac{5}{14}$

(4) $\frac{5}{32}$

(5) $\frac{5}{16}$

6. A class has 35 students. If 6 pupils were absent, what fraction of the class was present?

(1) $\frac{6}{35}$

(2) $\frac{35}{6}$

(3) $\frac{29}{35}$

(4) $\frac{35}{29}$

(5) $\frac{29}{41}$

7. A family spent 100 dollars for food, 200 dollars for rent, and 150 dollars for all other expenses. What fraction of the money spent was spent for food?

(1) $\frac{450}{100}$

(2) $\frac{100}{450}$

(3) $\frac{100}{300}$

(4) $\frac{200}{250}$

(5) $\frac{250}{450}$

8. A hockey team won 8 games, lost 3 games, and tied 2 games. What fraction of the games played were won?

(1) $\frac{8}{13}$

(2) $\frac{8}{11}$

(3) $\frac{10}{13}$

(4) $\frac{8}{5}$

(5) $\frac{11}{13}$

ANSWER KEY

1. **2** 2. **5** 3. **4** 4. **1** 5. **2** 6. **3** 7. **2** 8. **1**

Improper Fractions and Mixed Numbers

A fraction, such as $\frac{5}{24}$, whose numerator is less than its denominator, is called a *proper fraction*. Its value is less than 1.

A fraction, such as $\frac{30}{12}$, whose numerator is greater than its denominator, is called an *improper fraction*. Its value is greater than 1.

A fraction, such as $\frac{8}{8}$, whose numerator and denominator are the same, is also an *improper fraction*. Its value is 1.

A *mixed number* is a number, such as $5\frac{1}{2}$, that consists of a whole number followed by a fraction. It is an abbreviation for the *sum* of the integer and the fraction; thus, $5\frac{1}{2}$ is an abbreviation for $5 + \frac{1}{2}$.

Changing an Improper Fraction to a Mixed Number

To change an improper fraction to a mixed number, divide the numerator by the denominator; the quotient is the whole number and the remainder is placed over the denominator to form the fractional part.

EXAMPLE

Change $\frac{17}{5}$ to a mixed number. When 17 is divided by 5, the quotient is 3 and the remainder is 2, so

$$\frac{17}{5} = 3 + \frac{2}{5} = 3\frac{2}{5}$$

Changing a Mixed Number to an Improper Fraction

To change a mixed number to an improper fraction, multiply the whole number by the denominator and add the numerator; then write that sum over the denominator.

EXAMPLE

Change $2\frac{3}{7}$ to an improper fraction.

$2 \times 7 = 14$ and $14 + 3 = 17$, so

$$2\frac{3}{7} = \frac{17}{7}$$

Equivalent Fractions

If Bob and Joe shared a pizza, and Bob ate $\frac{1}{2}$ of the pizza and Joe ate $\frac{4}{8}$, they had exactly the same amount. We express this idea by saying that $\frac{1}{2}$ and $\frac{4}{8}$ are *equivalent fractions*; that is, they have the exact same value.

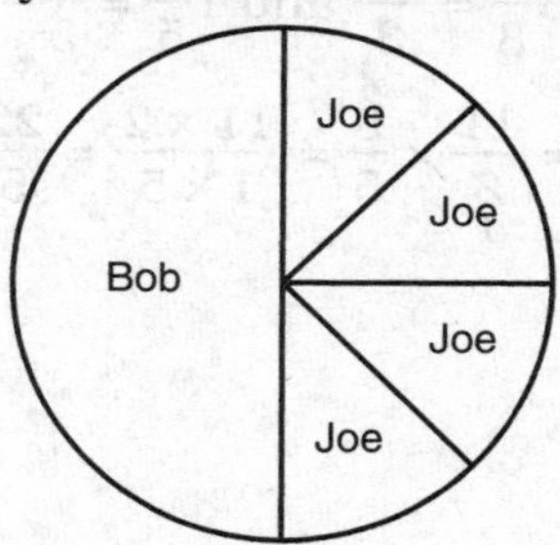

Two fractions are equivalent if multiplying or dividing both the numerator and the denominator of the first fraction *by the same number* gives the second fraction.

EXAMPLES

Are $\frac{3}{8}$ and $\frac{45}{120}$ equivalent?

Since $3 \times 15 = 45$ and $8 \times 15 = 120$, the fractions are equivalent.

Are $\frac{2}{3}$ and $\frac{28}{45}$ equivalent?

Since $2 \times 14 = 28$, the fractions will be equivalent if $3 \times 14 = 45$; but $3 \times 14 \neq 45$. Therefore, the fractions are *not* equivalent.

Reducing a Fraction to Lowest Terms

A fraction is in *lowest terms* if no positive integer greater than 1 divides evenly into both the numerator and denominator.

For example, $\frac{9}{20}$ is in lowest terms, since no integer greater than 1 is a divisor of both 9 and 20; but $\frac{9}{24}$ is not in lowest terms, since 3 is a divisor of both 9 and 24.

Every fraction is equivalent to a fraction in lowest terms. To *reduce* a fraction to lowest terms, divide the numerator and the denominator by their greatest common divisor, which is also called their greatest common factor.

EXAMPLES

Reduce $\frac{21}{28}$ to lowest terms.

The largest integer that is a divisor of both 21 and 28 is 7: $21 \div 7 = 3$ and $28 \div 7 = 4$.

Thus $\frac{21}{28} = \frac{3}{4}$, which is in lowest terms.

Reduce $\frac{42}{63}$ to lowest terms.

42 and 63 are each divisible by 7:

$$42 \div 7 = 6 \text{ and } 63 \div 7 = 9$$

Thus $\frac{42}{63} = \frac{6}{9}$. But $\frac{6}{9}$ is *not* in lowest terms, since both 6 and 9 are divisible by 3:

$$6 \div 3 = 2 \text{ and } 9 \div 3 = 3$$

Thus $\frac{42}{63} = \frac{6}{9} = \frac{2}{3}$, and $\frac{2}{3}$ *is* in lowest terms.

PRACTICE

Change the following improper fractions to mixed numbers:

1. $\frac{8}{5}$

2. $\frac{9}{8}$

3. $\frac{22}{7}$

4. $\frac{26}{9}$

5. $\frac{17}{3}$

Change the following mixed numbers to improper fractions:

6. $1\frac{2}{3}$

7. $5\frac{3}{7}$

8. $2\frac{7}{10}$

9. $3\frac{5}{7}$

10. $3\frac{1}{2}$

Reduce the following fractions to lowest terms:

11. $\frac{4}{6}$

12. $\frac{16}{18}$

13. $\frac{12}{32}$

14. $\frac{36}{64}$

15. $\frac{56}{84}$

ANSWERS

1. $1\frac{3}{5}$	4. $2\frac{8}{9}$	7. $\frac{38}{7}$	10. $\frac{7}{2}$	13. $\frac{3}{8}$
2. $1\frac{1}{8}$	5. $5\frac{2}{3}$	8. $\frac{27}{10}$	11. $\frac{2}{3}$	14. $\frac{9}{16}$
3. $3\frac{1}{7}$	6. $\frac{5}{3}$	9. $\frac{26}{7}$	12. $\frac{8}{9}$	15. $\frac{2}{3}$

Multiplying Fractions

To multiply two or more fractions, multiply the numerators to obtain the numerator of the product. Then, multiply the denominators to obtain the denominator of the product.

EXAMPLE

Multiply $\frac{4}{7}$ by $\frac{3}{5}$.

$$\frac{4}{7} \times \frac{3}{5} = \frac{4 \times 3}{7 \times 5} = \frac{12}{35}$$

The process of multiplying fractions can be simplified by reducing each fraction to lowest terms before performing the multiplication.

EXAMPLE

Multiply $\frac{8}{15}$ by $\frac{5}{12}$.

$$\frac{8}{15} \times \frac{5}{12}$$

Since 8 and 12 are both divisible by 4, and 5 and 15 are both divisible by 5,

$$\frac{\overset{2}{\cancel{8}}}{\underset{3}{\cancel{15}}} \times \frac{\overset{1}{\cancel{5}}}{\underset{3}{\cancel{12}}} = \frac{2 \times 1}{3 \times 3} = \frac{2}{9}$$

If you are required to multiply a whole number by a fraction, write the whole number in fractional form, with 1 as the denominator, and proceed as before.

EXAMPLE

Multiply 12 by $\frac{5}{9}$.

$$12 \times \frac{5}{9} = \frac{12}{1} \times \frac{5}{9} = \frac{\overset{4}{\cancel{12}}}{1} \times \frac{5}{\underset{3}{\cancel{9}}} = \frac{4 \times 5}{1 \times 3} = \frac{20}{3}$$

If you are required to multiply two mixed numbers, convert them to improper fractions, and proceed as before. The product will be an improper fraction, which can be changed to a mixed number.

EXAMPLE

Multiply $3\frac{2}{3}$ by $1\frac{1}{5}$.

$$3\frac{2}{3} = \frac{11}{3} \text{ and } 1\frac{1}{5} = \frac{6}{5}$$

$$\frac{11}{3} \times \frac{6}{5} = \frac{11}{\underset{1}{\cancel{3}}} \times \frac{\overset{2}{\cancel{6}}}{5} = \frac{11 \times 2}{1 \times 5} = \frac{22}{5} = 4\frac{2}{5}$$

Practice

1. $\frac{2}{3} \times \frac{5}{7}$

2. $\frac{1}{4} \times \frac{3}{10}$

3. $\frac{1}{6} \times \frac{4}{5}$

4. $15 \times \frac{2}{3}$

5. $\frac{5}{6} \times \frac{9}{10}$

6. $12 \times \frac{5}{6}$

7. $3 \times 2\frac{2}{5}$

8. $8 \times 1\frac{3}{4}$

Answers

1. $\mathbf{\frac{10}{21}}$ 3. $\mathbf{\frac{2}{15}}$ 5. $\mathbf{\frac{3}{4}}$ 7. $\mathbf{\frac{36}{5}}$

2. $\mathbf{\frac{3}{40}}$ 4. **10** 6. **10** 8. **14**

Dividing Fractions

To divide one fraction by another fraction, invert the divisor and multiply the resulting fractions.

EXAMPLES

Divide $\frac{2}{3}$ by $\frac{5}{6}$.

$$\frac{2}{3} \div \frac{5}{6} = \frac{2}{3} \times \frac{6}{5} = \frac{2}{\cancel{3}_1} \times \frac{\cancel{6}^2}{5} = \frac{4}{5}$$

Divide 8 by $\frac{6}{7}$.

Write 8 in fractional form, as $\frac{8}{1}$, and proceed as before:

$$8 \div \frac{6}{7} = \frac{8}{1} \times \frac{7}{6} = \frac{\cancel{8}^4}{1} \times \frac{7}{\cancel{6}_3} = \frac{28}{3} = 9\frac{1}{3}$$

Divide $3\frac{3}{5}$ by $2\frac{1}{10}$.

$$3\frac{3}{5} = \frac{18}{5} \text{ and } 2\frac{1}{10} = \frac{21}{10}$$

$$\frac{18}{5} \div \frac{21}{10} = \frac{18}{5} \times \frac{10}{21} = \frac{\cancel{18}^6}{\cancel{5}_1} \times \frac{\cancel{10}^2}{\cancel{21}_7} = \frac{12}{7} = 1\frac{5}{7}$$

Practice

1. $\frac{1}{3} \div \frac{1}{2}$

2. $\frac{2}{7} \div \frac{2}{3}$

3. $\frac{3}{4} \div \frac{5}{8}$

4. $\frac{7}{10} \div \frac{1}{5}$

5. $4 \div \frac{2}{5}$

6. $1\frac{1}{8} \div \frac{9}{20}$

7. $\frac{5}{6} \div 1\frac{1}{4}$

8. $\frac{7}{8} \div 5\frac{1}{4}$

Answers

1. $\mathbf{\frac{2}{3}}$ 3. $\mathbf{\frac{6}{5}}$ 5. **10** 7. $\mathbf{\frac{2}{3}}$

2. $\mathbf{\frac{3}{7}}$ 4. $\mathbf{\frac{7}{2}}$ 6. $\mathbf{\frac{5}{2}}$ 8. $\mathbf{\frac{1}{6}}$

Adding and Subtracting Fractions

In the same way that $5 plus $2 is $7, and 5 boys plus 2 boys is 7 boys, five ninths plus two ninths is seven ninths. This example illustrates the following rule: To add or subtract fractions with the same denominator, add or subtract the numerators and keep the denominator:

$$\frac{5}{9} + \frac{2}{9} = \frac{7}{9} \text{ and } \frac{5}{9} - \frac{2}{9} = \frac{3}{9} = \frac{1}{3}$$

To add or subtract fractions with different denominators, first rewrite the fractions as equivalent fractions with the same denominators. For example,

$$\frac{1}{6}+\frac{3}{4}=\frac{2}{12}+\frac{9}{12}=\frac{11}{12}$$

Note that the *easiest* denominator to get is the product of the two denominators ($6 \times 4 = 24$, in this case), but the *best* denominator to use is the *least common denominator* (L.C.D.), which is the smallest integer (12 in this case) that is a multiple of each of the denominators. Using the least common denominator minimizes the amount of reducing necessary to express the answer in lowest terms.

EXAMPLE

Add $\frac{2}{3}$ and $\frac{5}{7}$.

The multiples of 7 are 7, 14, 21, 28, ... The smallest one that is also a multiple of 3 is 21, so that is the L.C.D. Now form equivalent fractions by multiplying the numerator and denominator of $\frac{2}{3}$ by 7 and the numerator and denominator of $\frac{5}{7}$ by 3:

$$\frac{2}{3}\times\frac{7}{7}=\frac{14}{21} \text{ and } \frac{5}{7}\times\frac{3}{3}=\frac{15}{21}$$

$$\frac{2}{3}+\frac{5}{7}=\frac{14}{21}+\frac{15}{21}=\frac{29}{21}=1\frac{8}{21}$$

EXAMPLE

Subtract $\frac{1}{10}$ from $\frac{2}{15}$.

For a common denominator you *could* use $15 \times 10 = 150$, but using the L.C.D., which is 30, makes the problem easier.

$$\frac{2}{15}-\frac{1}{10}=\frac{4}{30}-\frac{3}{30}=\frac{1}{30}$$

To add mixed numbers, add the whole numbers and the fractions separately, and then combine the results.

EXAMPLE

Add $3\frac{5}{6}$ and $2\frac{3}{4}$.

The L.C.D. is 12.

$$3+2=5 \text{ and } \frac{5}{6}+\frac{3}{4}=\frac{10}{12}+\frac{9}{12}=\frac{19}{12}=1\frac{7}{12}$$

$$5+1\frac{7}{12}=6\frac{7}{12}$$

When mixed numbers are subtracted, it is sometimes necessary to borrow, as in the following example.

EXAMPLE

Subtract $1\frac{5}{12}$ from $4\frac{1}{8}$.

The L.C.D. is 24.

$$4\frac{1}{8}=4\frac{3}{24} \text{ and } 1\frac{5}{12}=1\frac{10}{24}$$

Since $\frac{10}{24}$ cannot be subtracted from $\frac{3}{24}$, borrow 1, in the form of $\frac{24}{24}$, from the 4. Then

$$4\frac{3}{24}=3+1+\frac{3}{24}=3+\frac{24}{24}+\frac{3}{24}=3\frac{27}{24}$$

$$\begin{array}{r} 3\frac{27}{24} \\ -\,1\frac{10}{24} \\ \hline 2\frac{17}{24} \end{array}$$

PRACTICE

Express the answer to each addition and subtraction in lowest terms.

1. $\frac{1}{12}+\frac{5}{12}$
2. $\frac{3}{10}+\frac{1}{2}$
3. $\frac{7}{8}+\frac{2}{3}$
4. $\frac{3}{4}+\frac{1}{6}$
5. $\frac{3}{7}+\frac{1}{2}$
6. $1\frac{4}{9}+\frac{5}{6}$
7. $2\frac{3}{8}+3\frac{1}{2}$
8. $2\frac{7}{10}+\frac{1}{6}$
9. $\frac{5}{9}-\frac{1}{9}$
10. $\frac{2}{3}-\frac{1}{6}$
11. $\frac{3}{4}-\frac{1}{3}$
12. $\frac{5}{6}-\frac{1}{4}$
13. $\frac{5}{8}-\frac{1}{6}$
14. $5\frac{2}{3}-3\frac{1}{6}$
15. $3\frac{1}{3}-1\frac{1}{2}$
16. $5\frac{3}{10}-2\frac{5}{6}$

Answers

1. $\frac{6}{12} = \frac{1}{2}$	5. $\frac{13}{14}$	9. $\frac{4}{9}$	13. $\frac{11}{24}$
2. $\frac{8}{10} = \frac{4}{5}$	6. $2\frac{5}{18}$	10. $\frac{3}{6} = \frac{1}{2}$	14. $2\frac{1}{2}$
3. $\frac{37}{24} = 1\frac{13}{24}$	7. $5\frac{7}{8}$	11. $\frac{5}{12}$	15. $1\frac{5}{6}$
4. $\frac{11}{12}$	8. $2\frac{26}{30} = 2\frac{13}{15}$	12. $\frac{7}{12}$	16. $2\frac{7}{15}$

Problems Involving Fractions

In general, there are two types of problems involving fractions.

1. To find a number that is a fractional part of a number.

EXAMPLE

A dealer sold 70 television sets in September. If $\frac{2}{5}$ of the sets were color sets, how many color sets were sold?

The word *of* indicates that you need to multiply 70 by $\frac{2}{5}$.

$$\frac{70}{1} \times \frac{2}{5} = \frac{\overset{14}{\cancel{70}}}{1} \times \frac{2}{\underset{1}{\cancel{5}}} = 28$$

The dealer sold 28 color television sets.

2. To find a number when a fractional part of the number is known.

EXAMPLE

In a package of stamps, 78 are French. If $\frac{3}{5}$ of the stamps are French, how many stamps are in the package?

To visualize this problem, imagine that the stamps are divided into 5 equal piles, each containing $\frac{1}{5}$ of the stamps.

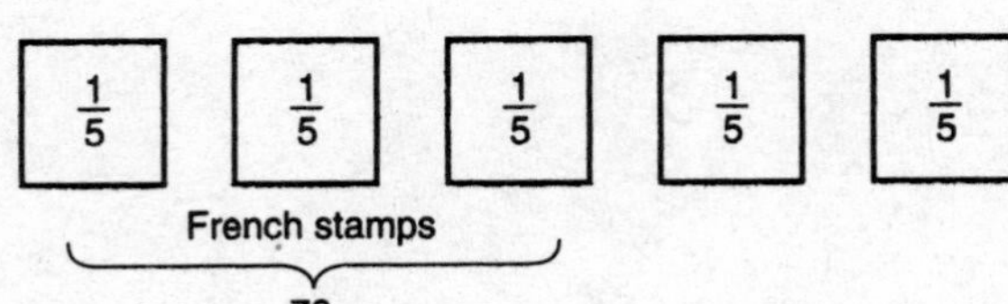

Assume that the first 3 piles contain the French stamps. Since the total number in those 3 piles is 78, each pile contains 78 ÷ 3 = 26 stamps. Finally, there are 5 piles, so there are

$$5 \times 26 = 130 \text{ stamps in all.}$$

Note that what you did was to divide 78 by 3 and then multiply by 5. This is exactly the same as multiplying 78 by $\frac{5}{3}$, which is equivalent to dividing by $\frac{3}{5}$:

$$78 \div \frac{3}{5} = 78 \times \frac{5}{3} = 130$$

Practice

1. The Globe Theater has 600 seats. At one showing, $\frac{4}{5}$ of the seats were taken. How many seats were taken?
   (1) 400
   (2) 420
   (3) 450
   (4) 480
   (5) 750

2. At a sale, Mr. Rodriguez bought a coat for \$96. This was $\frac{3}{4}$ of the regular price of the coat. The regular price of the coat was
   (1) \$72
   (2) \$128
   (3) \$120
   (4) \$125
   (5) \$80

3. An oil tank holds 640 gallons. When the tank is $\frac{3}{8}$ full, the number of gallons of oil in the tank is
   (1) 240
   (2) 320
   (3) 350
   (4) 400
   (5) 450

4. A football team scored 35 points in a game. If the team scored 21 points in the first half, the fraction of the total scored in the second half was

(1) $\frac{3}{5}$

(2) $\frac{7}{12}$

(3) $\frac{1}{5}$

(4) $\frac{2}{5}$

(5) $\frac{3}{7}$

5. A plane contains 5 times as many second-class seats as first-class seats. Second-class seats make up what fraction of the total seats on the plane?

(1) $\frac{1}{6}$

(2) $\frac{1}{5}$

(3) $\frac{5}{6}$

(4) $\frac{3}{5}$

(5) $\frac{1}{3}$

6. A baseball player hit 90 singles in one season. If this was $\frac{3}{5}$ of his total number of hits, the number of hits the player made that season was

(1) 54
(2) 150
(3) 540
(4) 144
(5) 154

7. During a sale on radio sets, $\frac{1}{4}$ of the stock was sold the first day. The next day, $\frac{2}{3}$ of the remaining sets were sold. What fraction of the total stock was sold on the second day?

(1) $\frac{2}{3}$

(2) $\frac{1}{4}$

(3) $\frac{1}{6}$

(4) $\frac{1}{2}$

(5) $\frac{1}{12}$

8. On a motor trip Mr. Anderson covers $\frac{3}{8}$ of the distance during the first day by driving 300 miles. The total distance to be covered by Mr. Anderson is

(1) 624 mi.
(2) 640 mi.
(3) 720 mi.
(4) 750 mi.
(5) 800 mi.

9. An auditorium contains 540 seats and is $\frac{4}{9}$ filled. The number of unoccupied seats is

(1) 240
(2) 60
(3) 120
(4) 200
(5) 300

10. In his will, Mr. Mason left $\frac{1}{2}$ of his estate to his wife, $\frac{1}{3}$ to his daughter, and the balance, consisting of \$12,000, to his son. The value of Mr. Mason's estate was

(1) \$24,000
(2) \$60,000
(3) \$14,400
(4) \$65,000
(5) \$72,000

11. An oil tank is $\frac{3}{10}$ full. To fill the tank, 420 gallons more are needed. The number of gallons the tank holds is

(1) 600
(2) 480
(3) 840
(4) 1,260
(5) 1,000

12. A family spends $\frac{1}{4}$ of its income for rent and $\frac{1}{5}$ for food. What fraction of its income is left?

(1) $\frac{9}{20}$

(2) $\frac{19}{20}$

(3) $\frac{11}{20}$

(4) $\frac{4}{5}$

(5) $\frac{8}{9}$

ANSWER KEY

1. **4**	5. **3**	9. **5**
2. **2**	6. **2**	10. **5**
3. **1**	7. **4**	11. **1**
4. **4**	8. **5**	12. **3**

Arranging Fractions in Order

To compare two fractions, cross-multiply as indicated below. Multiply each denominator by the opposite numerator (as indicated by the arrows), and write the products above the numerators (by the tips of the arrows).

If the two products are equal, the fractions are equivalent. If the products are unequal, the fraction with the larger product written next to it is greater. The symbol > means *is greater than*, and the symbol < means *is less than*.

$\overset{6}{\frac{1}{2}} \times \overset{6}{\frac{3}{6}}$	$\overset{15}{\frac{3}{4}} \times \overset{8}{\frac{2}{5}}$	$\overset{18}{\frac{3}{7}} \times \overset{35}{\frac{5}{6}}$
$1 \times 6 = 2 \times 3$	$3 \times 5 > 4 \times 2$	$3 \times 6 < 7 \times 5$
$\frac{1}{2} = \frac{3}{6}$	$\frac{3}{4} > \frac{2}{5}$	$\frac{3}{7} < \frac{5}{6}$

PRACTICE

In each case, use the symbol =, >, or < to show the relationship between the given fractions:

1. $\frac{3}{4} \quad \frac{7}{10}$
2. $\frac{6}{9} \quad \frac{40}{60}$
3. $\frac{2}{3} \quad \frac{11}{16}$
4. $\frac{5}{8} \quad \frac{4}{7}$
5. $\frac{4}{9} \quad \frac{7}{15}$
6. $\frac{12}{20} \quad \frac{3}{5}$
7. $\frac{21}{28} \quad \frac{24}{32}$
8. $\frac{18}{13} \quad \frac{15}{8}$

ANSWERS

1. $\mathbf{\frac{3}{4} > \frac{7}{10}}$
2. $\mathbf{\frac{6}{9} = \frac{40}{60}}$
3. $\mathbf{\frac{2}{3} < \frac{11}{16}}$
4. $\mathbf{\frac{5}{8} > \frac{4}{7}}$
5. $\mathbf{\frac{4}{9} < \frac{7}{15}}$
6. $\mathbf{\frac{12}{20} = \frac{3}{5}}$
7. $\mathbf{\frac{21}{28} = \frac{24}{32}}$
8. $\mathbf{\frac{18}{13} < \frac{15}{8}}$

Sometimes, three fractions must be arranged in order of size, such as $\frac{1}{4}$, $\frac{1}{2}$, and $\frac{5}{6}$.

You may write $\frac{1}{4} < \frac{1}{2}$ and $\frac{1}{2} < \frac{5}{6}$. However, these two comparisons can be combined and written as $\frac{1}{4} < \frac{1}{2} < \frac{5}{6}$. This is read as "$\frac{1}{4}$ is less than $\frac{1}{2}$ *and* $\frac{1}{2}$ is less than $\frac{5}{6}$."

Instead, you may write $\frac{5}{6} > \frac{1}{2} > \frac{1}{4}$, which is read as "$\frac{5}{6}$ is greater than $\frac{1}{2}$ *and* $\frac{1}{2}$ is greater than $\frac{1}{4}$."

EXAMPLE

Use symbols to write "$\frac{9}{10}$ is greater than $\frac{3}{5}$ and $\frac{3}{5}$ is greater than $\frac{2}{7}$."

$$\frac{9}{10} > \frac{3}{5} > \frac{2}{7}$$

EXAMPLE

Use the symbol < to arrange the fractions $\frac{5}{8}$, $\frac{3}{4}$, and $\frac{1}{6}$ in order of magnitude.

$$\frac{1}{6} < \frac{5}{8} \text{ since } 8 \times 1 < 5 \times 6$$

$$\frac{5}{8} < \frac{3}{4} \text{ since } 5 \times 4 < 3 \times 8$$

You may write this result as $\frac{1}{6} < \frac{5}{8} < \frac{3}{4}$.

PRACTICE

Use the symbol > to arrange the following sets of fractions in order of magnitude:

1. $\frac{1}{3}, \frac{6}{7}, \frac{3}{5}$
2. $\frac{3}{7}, \frac{7}{9}, \frac{1}{4}$
3. $\frac{7}{10}, \frac{3}{8}, \frac{5}{6}$

Use the symbol < to arrange the following sets of fractions in order of magnitude:

4. $\frac{2}{3}, \frac{1}{6}, \frac{3}{5}$
5. $\frac{4}{7}, \frac{8}{9}, \frac{5}{8}$
6. $\frac{7}{10}, \frac{2}{9}, \frac{1}{2}$

ANSWERS

1. $\frac{6}{7} > \frac{3}{5} > \frac{1}{3}$
2. $\frac{7}{9} > \frac{3}{7} > \frac{1}{4}$
3. $\frac{5}{6} > \frac{7}{10} > \frac{3}{8}$
4. $\frac{1}{6} < \frac{3}{5} < \frac{2}{3}$
5. $\frac{4}{7} < \frac{5}{8} < \frac{8}{9}$
6. $\frac{2}{9} < \frac{1}{2} < \frac{7}{10}$

Decimals

A *decimal number* is equivalent to a fraction whose denominator is a power of 10 (10, 100, 1,000, etc.), but the number is not written in fractional form; rather, it is written with a decimal point. In writing a decimal number, be sure that there are the same number of digits to the right of the decimal point as there are zeros in the denominator. If necessary, insert zeros after the decimal point to have the correct number of digits. For example:

Written as Common Fractions	Written as Decimals
$\frac{3}{10}$	0.3
$\frac{5}{100}$	0.05
$\frac{7}{1,000}$	0.007
$\frac{163}{10,000}$	0.0163

To express a mixed number as a decimal number, write the whole number to the left of the decimal point, and the fractional part to the right. For example:

$$8\frac{3}{10} = 8.3$$

$$9\frac{7}{1,000} = 9.007$$

Note: The value of a decimal is *not* changed by annexing zeros after the last digit to the right of the decimal point. For example,

$$\frac{1}{2} = 0.5 = 0.50 = 0.500 = 0.5000$$

One reason to use decimals is that they are convenient to write and to work with. For example, it is more convenient to write that a shirt costs \$8.25 than that it costs $\$8\frac{1}{4}$.

Addition of Decimals

In adding decimal numbers, always line up the decimal points. It is useful to add zeros at the ends of some numbers so that each number has the same number of digits.

EXAMPLE

Add 2.3, 0.789, 5, and 1.08.

```
2.300
0.789
5.000
1.080
-----
9.169
```

Subtraction of Decimals

Use the same procedure for subtraction as for addition: line up the decimal points and add zeros if necessary.

EXAMPLE

Subtract 9.7 from 15.58.

```
 15.58
 -9.70
 -----
  5.88
```

Multiplication of Decimals

In multiplying decimals, the number of decimal places in the product is the sum of the number of decimal places in the numbers being multiplied.

EXAMPLES

Multiply 0.02 by 0.3.

```
  0.02  (2 decimal places)
 × 0.3  (1 decimal place)
 -------------------------
 0.006  (3 decimal places)
```

Multiply 1.02 by 0.004.

```
    1.02  (2 decimal places)
 × 0.004  (3 decimal places)
 ---------------------------
 0.00408  (5 decimal places)
```

Division of Decimals

In dividing decimals, move the decimal point in the divisor all the way to the right, and then move the decimal point in the dividend the same number of places to the right. The decimal point in the quotient is always in the same place as in the new dividend.

EXAMPLES

Divide: 6.93 ÷ 0.3.

```
       23.1
 0.3.)6.9.3
```

Divide: 35.75 ÷ 0.05.

```
         715.
 0.05.)35.75.
```

Divide: 0.08136 ÷ 0.006.

```
          13.56
 0.006.)0.081.36
```

Sometimes, there is a remainder and you are told to find the answer to the nearest tenth, nearest hundredth, and so on. In such cases, carry out the division to one more place than is called for. *Regarding remainders*: If the digit just to the right of the desired decimal place is 5 or greater, add 1 to the desired decimal place number. Otherwise, drop the digit to the right of the desired decimal place.

EXAMPLES

Divide 3.734 by 0.9, and express the answer to the nearest tenth.

```
       4.15
 0.9.)3.7.38   The answer is 4.2.
```

Divide 2.4873 by 0.7, and express the answer to the nearest hundredth.

$$0.7.\overline{)2.4.873}\quad = 3.553$$

The answer is 3.55.

Conversion of Fractions to Decimals

It is sometimes necessary to change a fraction to a decimal. To do this, divide the numerator by the denominator, annexing zeros after the decimal point in the numerator when they are needed.

EXAMPLES

Change $\frac{3}{8}$ to a decimal.

$$8\overline{)3.000} = 0.375$$

$$\frac{3}{8} = 0.375$$

Change $\frac{5}{12}$ to a decimal.

$$12\overline{)5.0000} = 0.4166\tfrac{2}{3}$$

To the nearest tenth, $\frac{5}{12} = 0.4$.

To the nearest hundredth, $\frac{5}{12} = 0.42$.

To the nearest thousandth, $\frac{5}{12} = 0.417$.

PRACTICE

1. Add 38.5 + 7.09 + 92.78 + 0.84.
2. Add 2.806 + 0.93 + 4.037 + 65 + 0.029.
3. From 1.907 subtract 0.02.
4. Take 3.79 from 12.82.
5. Multiply 5.68 by 2.9.
6. Multiply 3.14 by 0.015.
7. Divide 1.6357 by 0.37 and express the result to the nearest hundredth.
8. Divide 0.32277 by 5.3.
9. Convert $\frac{17}{20}$ to a decimal.
10. Convert $\frac{8}{15}$ to a decimal to the nearest hundredth.

ANSWERS

1. **139.21**	5. **16.472**	8. **0.0609**
2. **72.802**	6. **0.04710**	9. **0.85**
3. **1.887**	7. **4.42**	10. **0.53**
4. **9.03**		

Percent

You have seen that fractions may be expressed as decimals. A fraction may also be expressed as a percent. In this section, you will learn how to work with percents.

On a motor trip of 100 miles, 73 miles were on a parkway. To indicate this part of the trip, you may say that $\frac{73}{100}$ of the trip was on a parkway. Another way of stating the same fact is to say that 0.73 of the trip was on a parkway. A third way to express the same idea is to say that 73% of the trip was on a parkway. *Percent is just another way of writing a fraction in which the denominator is 100.* The % sign is used instead of writing the denominator 100. In short, 73% means $\frac{73}{100}$ or 0.73. It is a simple matter to change a percent to a fraction or to a decimal.

EXAMPLE

Change 45%: (a) to a decimal

$$45\% = 0.45$$

(b) to a fraction

$$45\% = \frac{45}{100} = \frac{9}{20}$$

EXAMPLES

Change 0.37 to a percent.

$$0.37 = \frac{37}{100} = 37\%$$

Change 0.025 to a percent.

$$0.025 = \frac{25}{1{,}000} = \frac{2.5}{100} = 2.5\% \text{ or } 2\tfrac{1}{2}\%$$

EXAMPLES

Change $\frac{3}{4}$ to a percent.

Change $\frac{3}{4}$ first to a decimal and then to a percent.

$$4\overline{)3.00}\quad = 0.75$$

$$\frac{3}{4} = 0.75 = 75\%$$

Change $\frac{5}{19}$ first to a decimal and then to a percent.

$$\begin{array}{r} 0.26 \\ 19\overline{)5.00} \\ 3\ 8 \\ \hline 1\ 20 \\ 1\ 14 \\ \hline 6 \end{array}$$

$$\frac{5}{19} = 0.26\frac{6}{19} = 26\frac{6}{19}\%$$

PRACTICE

Fill in the blanks in each of the following.

	Fraction	Decimal	Percent
1.	$\frac{1}{2}$	0.5	50%
2.	$\frac{7}{20}$	0.35	35%
3.	$\frac{9}{25}$	0.36	36%
4.	$\frac{3}{7}$	$0.42\frac{6}{7}$	$42\frac{6}{7}\%$
5.	$\frac{6}{25}$	0.24	24%

ANSWERS

	Fraction	Decimal	Percent
1.	$\frac{1}{2}$	0.50	50%
2.	$\frac{35}{100} = \frac{7}{20}$	0.35	35%
3.	$\frac{36}{100} = \frac{9}{25}$	0.36	36%
4.	$\frac{3}{7}$	$0.42\frac{6}{7}$	$42\frac{6}{7}\%$
5.	$\frac{6}{25}$	0.24	24%

Certain fractions and their equivalent percents are used frequently.

HELPFUL EQUIVALENTS TO MEMORIZE

$\frac{1}{2} = 50\%$	$\frac{3}{4} = 75\%$	$\frac{4}{5} = 80\%$	$\frac{3}{8} = 37\frac{1}{2}\%$
$\frac{1}{3} = 33\frac{1}{3}\%$	$\frac{1}{5} = 20\%$	$\frac{1}{6} = 16\frac{2}{3}\%$	$\frac{5}{8} = 62\frac{1}{2}\%$
$\frac{2}{3} = 66\frac{1}{3}\%$	$\frac{2}{5} = 40\%$	$\frac{5}{6} = 83\frac{1}{3}\%$	$\frac{7}{8} = 87\frac{1}{2}\%$
$\frac{1}{4} = 25\%$	$\frac{3}{5} = 60\%$	$\frac{1}{8} = 12\frac{1}{2}\%$	

PROBLEMS INVOLVING PERCENTS

Since percents are fractions in another form, problems involving percents are similar to problems involving fractions.

1. To find a percent of a given number.

EXAMPLE

In a factory, 4,775 machine parts were manufactured. When these were tested, 4% were found to be defective. How many machine parts were defective?

In this case, the word *of* indicates that you are to multiply 4,775 by 4%. Since 4% = 0.04:

4775	parts manufactured
× 0.04	percent defective
191.00	number of defective parts

191 machine parts were defective.

2. To find what percent one number is of another.

EXAMPLE

During the season, a professional basketball player tried 108 foul shots, and made 81 of them. What percent of the shots tried were made?

Form a fraction:

$$\frac{\text{number of shots made}}{\text{total number of shots tried}} = \frac{81}{108}$$

This fraction may be expressed as a percent by changing $\frac{81}{108}$ to a decimal and then to a percent:

$$\begin{array}{r} 0.75 \\ 108\overline{)81.00} \\ \underline{75\ 6} \\ 5\ 40 \\ \underline{5\ 40} \end{array}$$

$$\frac{81}{108} = 0.75 = 75\%$$

The player made 75% of his shots.

3. To find a number when a percent of it is given.

EXAMPLE

A businessman decided to spend 16% of his expense budget for advertising. If he spent $2,400, what was his total expense?

You know that 16%, or $\frac{16}{100}$, of his expenses amounted to $2,400.

To find the total expense, divide by $\frac{16}{100}$ $\left(\text{which means mutiply by } \frac{100}{16}\right)$:

$$\$2{,}400 \times \frac{100}{16} = \frac{\$240{,}000}{16} = \$15{,}000$$

PERCENT INCREASE AND DECREASE

The *percent increase* of a quantity is

$$\frac{\text{actual increase}}{\text{original amount}} \times 100\%$$

and the *percent decrease* of a quantity is

$$\frac{\text{actual decrease}}{\text{original amount}} \times 100\%.$$

If the price of a chair rises from $80 to $100, the actual increase is $20, and the percent increase is

$$\frac{20}{80} \times 100\% = \frac{1}{4} \times 100\% = 25\%$$

If a $100 chair is on sale for $80, the actual decrease in price is $20, and the percent decrease is

$$\frac{20}{100} \times 100\% = 20\%$$

Note that the percent increase in going from 80 to 100 is not the same as the percent decrease in going from 100 to 80. Sometimes you will need to work with percents greater than 100%.

EXAMPLE

Mr. Fowler bought some stock at $40 per share. Three years later he sold the stock at $90 per share. What percent of profit did he make?

$90	selling price of stock per share
– 40	cost of stock per share
$50	profit per share

$$\frac{50}{40} = \frac{\text{profit per share}}{\text{original cost per share}}$$

$$\begin{array}{r} 1.25 \\ 40\overline{)50.00} \\ \underline{40} \\ 100 \\ \underline{80} \\ 200 \\ \underline{200} \end{array}$$

Mr. Fowler made a profit of 125%.

PRACTICE

1. Of $500 spent by the Moreno family one month, $150 was spent for clothing. The percent spent for clothing was

(1) $33\frac{1}{3}\%$
(2) 40%
(3) 30%
(4) 12%
(5) 20%

2. Mr. Frank bought a jacket for $48 and a pair of slacks for $20.60. If a sales tax of 3% was added to his bill, the amount of the tax was

(1) $2.05
(2) $2.06
(3) $20.60
(4) $2.16
(5) $2.15

3. A TV dealer made 20% of her annual sales during the month before Christmas. If she sold 130 sets during this month, the number of sets she sold during the year was

(1) 650
(2) 260
(3) 1,300
(4) 520
(5) 390

4. Of 600 students in a high school graduating class, 85% plan to go on to college. The number of students planning to go on to college is

(1) 5,100
(2) 51
(3) 540
(4) 500
(5) 510

5. A motorist planned a trip covering 720 miles. After he had covered 600 miles, what percent of the trip was completed?

(1) 80%
(2) $83\frac{1}{3}\%$
(3) 60%
(4) $16\frac{2}{3}\%$
(5) 85%

6. A school library contained 3,200 books. Of these, 48% were books of fiction. The number of books of fiction that the library contained was

(1) 1,200
(2) 1,208
(3) 1,536
(4) 1,380
(5) 1,300

7. A homeowner figured that 60% of his expenses were taxes. If his tax bill was $900, the total expense of running his house was

(1) $540
(2) $5,400
(3) $1,800
(4) $1,500
(5) $2,000

8. The value of a new car decreases 35% during the first year. Ms. Ames paid $15,600 for a new car. The value of the car at the end of the first year was

(1) $5,460
(2) $10,040
(3) $9,140
(4) $14,520
(5) $10,140

9. In a large housing development there are 1,250 apartments. Of these, 250 are three-room apartments. The percent of three-room apartments in the development is

(1) $16\frac{2}{3}\%$
(2) 25%
(3) 20%
(4) 24%
(5) 30%

10. When Mrs. Chan had paid $600 for her computer, she had paid 40% of the total cost. The total cost of the computer was

(1) $1,000
(2) $1,200
(3) $1,500
(4) $2,400
(5) $1,800

11. Mrs. Miller received a bill for electricity for $24.50. She was allowed a discount of 2% for early payment. If Mrs. Miller paid promptly, her payment was

(1) $0.49
(2) $19.60
(3) $24.45
(4) $24.01
(5) $4.90

12. A certain type of table usually sells for $72. Because it was slightly shopworn, it sold for $60. The percent of reduction was

(1) 20%
(2) $16\frac{2}{3}\%$
(3) 80%
(4) 30%
(5) $12\frac{1}{2}\%$

13. The sales tax on a lawn mower was $4.80. If the tax rate is 4%, the selling price of the mower was

(1) $19.20
(2) $192
(3) $124.80
(4) $120
(5) $115.20

14. From 1985 to 1995 the number of girls playing varsity sports at City High increased from 240 to 300. What was the percent increase in the number of girls playing varsity sports?

(1) 20%
(2) 25%
(3) 30%
(4) 60%
(5) 80%

15. In 1980 the population of Hadleyville was 1200. In 1990 it was 960. What was the percent decrease in the population of Hadleyville during this time?

(1) 15%
(2) 20%
(3) 24%
(4) 25%
(5) 80%

16. A man bought a house for $80,000. Eight years later he sold the house for $128,000. What percent of profit did he make?

(1) 40%
(2) $37\frac{1}{2}$%
(3) 50%
(4) 60%
(5) 75%

17. During a sale an overcoat was reduced from $120 to $102. What was the percent of reduction?

(1) 18%
(2) 15%
(3) 50%
(4) 12%
(5) 16%

18. A dealer sold a watch at 130% of her cost. If the sale price was $39, how much did the watch cost the dealer?

(1) $5.70
(2) $11.70
(3) $16.50
(4) $30
(5) $89.70

ANSWER KEY

1. **3**	5. **2**	9. **3**	13. **4**	17. **2**
2. **2**	6. **3**	10. **3**	14. **2**	18. **4**
3. **1**	7. **4**	11. **4**	15. **2**	
4. **5**	8. **5**	12. **2**	16. **4**	

Applications of Percents

Manufacturers will frequently suggest a price, called the *list price*, for which an article is to be sold. Dealers will sometimes reduce the list price, however, in order to meet competition. The amount by which the list price is reduced is called the *discount*, and the reduced price is called the *net price*, or *selling price*.

EXAMPLE

In a department store, a chair was marked as follows: "List price $44. For sale at $33." What was the rate of discount?

The rate of discount is just the percent decrease in the price. The actual discount was

$$\$44.00 - \$33.00 = \$11.00$$

and the percent discount was

$$\frac{\text{actual decrease in price}}{\text{original price}} \times 100\%$$

$$= \frac{11}{44} \times 100\% = \frac{1}{4} \times 100\% = 25\%$$

Sometimes one discount is followed by another; such discounts are called *successive discounts*. You must be careful not to add these discounts, but rather to take them one after another.

EXAMPLE

The list price of a VCR is $200. Appliance City, which normally sells all VCR's at 20% off the list price, is having a special sale in which all merchandise is reduced an additional 15%. How much does the VCR cost during this sale?

Adding 20% and 15% and taking 35% off the $200 list price would result in a sale price of $130. This is *not* correct. You must first take 20% off the $200 list price:

$$\$200 - 0.20 \times \$200 = \$200 - \$40 = \$160$$

You then take 15% off the $160 price:

$$\$160 - 0.15 \times \$160 = \$160 - \$24 = \$136$$

During the sale the VCR costs $136.

The same principle holds for *successive percent increases*.

EXAMPLE

Meghan's salary was $400 per week. In June, she received a 10% increase, and in October received another 10% increase. What was her salary after the second increase?

Do *not* add the increases and take 20% of $400. In June, Meghan received a $40 increase (10% of $400), bringing her salary to $440. In October, her 10% increase was based on $440, so her salary was increased $44 to $484.

PRACTICE

1. The list price of a coat was $120. Mr. Stern bought the coat at a discount of 10%. The net price of the coat was

   (1) $132
   (2) $12
   (3) $108
   (4) $118
   (5) $100

2. A men's store advertises a shirt that usually sells for $32.00 at a special price of $24.00. The rate of discount is

   (1) $33\frac{1}{3}\%$
   (2) 25%
   (3) 20%
   (4) 40%
   (5) 35%

3. An electric toaster has a list price of $21. If it is sold at a discount of $33\frac{1}{3}\%$, the net price is

   (1) $7
   (2) $28
   (3) $14
   (4) $25
   (5) $16

4. The net price of a watch was $40 after a discount of 20%. The list price of the watch was

   (1) $50
   (2) $30
   (3) $48
   (4) $35.20
   (5) $45

5. Ms. Natali bought a television set. The list price was $400. She was allowed successive discounts of 10% and 5%. How much did Ms. Natali actually pay for the set?

   (1) $340.00
   (2) $350.00
   (3) $352.00
   (4) $342.00
   (5) $324.00

ANSWER KEY

1. **3** 2. **2** 3. **3** 4. **1** 5. **4**

Investments

In the most common type of investment, money is placed in a savings bank, where it draws interest. To compute interest, use the following formula:

> Interest = Principal × Rate × Time
> $I = PRT$

The principal is the amount invested, the rate is the percent of the principal given to the investor each year, and the time is stated in years.

EXAMPLE

What is the interest on $1,200 at 6% for 9 months?

$$I = PRT$$

In this case
$$\begin{cases} P = \$1{,}200 \\ R = \dfrac{6}{100} \\ T = \dfrac{9}{12} \text{ or } \dfrac{3}{4} \end{cases}$$

Therefore, $I = 1{,}\overset{3}{\cancel{12}}00 \times \dfrac{6}{\underset{1}{\cancel{100}}} \times \dfrac{3}{\underset{1}{\cancel{4}}} = 54$

The interest is $54.00.

Add the interest to the principal to obtain the new *amount*.

In this case, the amount is $1,200 + $54.00 = $1,254.00.

A corporation may borrow money by selling *bonds* to the public. Bonds carry a fixed rate of interest and are issued for a certain number of years. At the *maturity date* of the bond the corporation pays back the borrowed amount to the bondholder.

EXAMPLE

Mr. Glenn owns six $1,000 bonds that pay 7% interest each year. How much does Mr. Glenn receive in interest each year?

This is a problem in computing simple interest. The principal is 6 × $1,000 or $6,000, the rate is 7%, and the period is 1 year.

$$\text{Interest} = 6{,}000 \times \frac{7}{100} \times 1$$

$$= \overset{60}{\cancel{6{,}000}} \times \frac{7}{\underset{1}{\cancel{100}}} \times 1 = 420$$

Mr. Glenn receives $420 in interest.

PRACTICE

1. Simple interest on $2,400 at $4\frac{1}{2}$% for 3 years is

   (1) $288
   (2) $32.40
   (3) $3,240
   (4) $324
   (5) $314

2. Mr. Payne borrowed $5,200 from a friend for 1 year and 3 months. He agreed to pay $5\frac{1}{2}$% simple interest on the loan. The amount of money that he paid back at the end of the loan period was

   (1) $5,553.50
   (2) $357.50
   (3) $5,557.50
   (4) $4,842.50
   (5) $5,000

3. Lee Holden kept $3,800 in a savings bank for 9 months at $5\frac{1}{2}$% simple interest. The interest on her money was

   (1) $156.75
   (2) $156.50
   (3) $140.75
   (4) $157.75
   (5) $160.50

4. Ms. Fernandez purchased five $2,000 bonds that pay 6% interest. If the bonds mature in 4 years, what is the total amount of interest she will receive?

   (1) $240
   (2) $480
   (3) $1,200
   (4) $2,400
   (5) $4,800

ANSWER KEY

1. **4** 2. **3** 3. **1** 4. **4**

Sales Tax

Many states in the United States have a *sales tax* on articles bought at retail. This may be 3%, 4%, 5% or a higher percent of the retail price of an article.

EXAMPLE

Mrs. Horn buys a small rug for $39.95. If she has to pay a sales tax of 3%, what is the total cost of the rug?

3% of $39.95 = 0.03 × $39.95 = $1.1985

In a case such as this, the amount of tax is rounded off to the nearest penny. Since the tax is $1.20, Mrs. Horn must pay $39.95 + $1.20, or $41.15.

PRACTICE

1. Jason buys sneakers for $137.50. If he must pay a sales tax of 3%, the total cost of the sneakers is

   (1) $178.80
   (2) $141.63
   (3) $137.92
   (4) $133.37
   (5) $141.03

2. On a purchase of a table for $64, Mrs. Morton paid a sales tax of $2.56. The rate of sales tax was

   (1) 3%
   (2) $3\frac{1}{2}$%
   (3) 2%
   (4) $2\frac{1}{2}$%
   (5) 4%

3. A sweater that normally sells for $80 is on sale at 20% off. What is the cost of the sweater including sales tax of 5%?

   (1) $63.00
   (2) $67.20
   (3) $69.00
   (4) $84.00
   (5) $105.00

4. John bought a book that had a list price of $25.00. He was entitled to a 5% student discount, but had to pay 5% sales tax. What was the total cost of the book?

   (1) $22.00
   (2) $24.94
   (3) $25.00
   (4) $26.25
   (5) $27.50

Answer Key

1. **2** 2. **5** 3. **2** 4. **2**

Properties of Operations

You know that

$$7 + 2 = 9$$
$$\text{and} \quad 2 + 7 = 9.$$

In fact, the order in which two numbers are added does not matter as far as obtaining the correct sum is concerned. This mathematical principle is called the *commutative law of addition*, stated as follows:

> COMMUTATIVE LAW OF ADDITION
> If a and b are numbers, then
> $a + b = b + a$.

You also know that

$$4 \times 6 = 24$$
$$\text{and} \quad 6 \times 4 = 24.$$

In fact, the order in which two numbers are multiplied does not matter as far as obtaining the correct product is concerned. This mathematical principle is called the *commutative law of multiplication*, stated as follows:

> COMMUTATIVE LAW OF MULTIPLICATION
> If a and b are numbers, then
> $ab = ba$.

To find the sum of 3, 6, and 5, you add 3 + 6 to obtain 9 and then add 5 to the result to obtain 14. This process is indicated by using parentheses to group 3 and 6 for addition before adding 5 to the result:

$$(3 + 6) + 5 = 9 + 5 = 14$$

Could the grouping be arranged differently? If 6 and 5 are grouped for addition before 3 is added to the result, you have

$$3 + (6 + 5) = 3 + 11 = 14$$

Thus,

$$(3 + 6) + 5 = 3 + (6 + 5)$$

This freedom in grouping is called the *associative law of addition*, stated as follows:

> ASSOCIATIVE LAW OF ADDITION
> If a, b, and c are numbers, then
> $(a + b) + c = a + (b + c)$.

To multiply the numbers 4, 5, and 7, you multiply 4×5 to obtain 20 and then multiply the result by 7 to obtain $20 \times 7 = 140$. This process is indicated by using parentheses to group 4 and 5 for multiplication before multiplying the result by 7:

$$(4 \times 5) \times 7 = 20 \times 7 = 140$$

Could the grouping be arranged differently? If 5 and 7 are grouped for multiplication before multiplying by 4, you have

$$4 \times (5 \times 7) = 4 \times 35 = 140$$

Thus,

$$(4 \times 5) \times 7 = 4 \times (5 \times 7)$$

This freedom in grouping is called the *associative law of multiplication*, stated as follows:

> ASSOCIATIVE LAW OF MULTIPLICATION
> If a, b, and c are numbers, then
> $(ab)c = a(bc)$.

EXAMPLE

A sales clerk earns \$8.00 per hour. He works 7 hours on Friday and 4 hours on Saturday. How much does he earn on these 2 days?

You can compute his earnings as follows:

$8 \times 7 = \$56$ for Friday
$8 \times 4 = \underline{\$32}$ for Saturday
Total: \$88

You can compute the earnings more simply in this way:

$7 + 4 = 11$ (total hours worked)
$8 \times (7 + 4) = 8 \times 11 = \$88$ (total earnings)

Thus,

$$8 \times (7 + 4) = 8 \times 7 + 8 \times 4$$

The principle described above is called the *distributive law of multiplication with respect to addition*. It is usually called simply the *distributive law*, stated as follows:

> DISTRIBUTIVE LAW
> If a, b, and c are numbers, then
> $a(b + c) = ab + ac$.

PRACTICE

In each case, identify the law illustrated:

1. $(8 \times 5) \times 2 = 8 \times (5 \times 2)$
2. $3 \times 7 = 7 \times 3$
3. $(5 + 6) + 9 = 5 + (6 + 9)$
4. $7(6 + 8) = 7 \times 6 + 7 \times 8$
5. $4 + 5 = 5 + 4$
6. $6 \times (3 \times 7) = (6 \times 3) \times 7$
7. $3 \times 5 + 3 \times 7 = 3(5 + 7)$
8. $6 \times 9 = 9 \times 6$

In each case, indicate whether the statement is true or false:

9. $4 \times 6 = 6 + 4$
10. $7(5 + 2) = 7 \times 5 + 2$
11. $6 \times (8 \times 9) = (6 \times 8) \times 9$
12. $8 + 3 = 3 + 8$
13. $2 + (7 + 9) = (2 + 7) + 9$
14. $(6 \times 8) + 4 = 6 \times 8 + 6 \times 4$
15. $3 \times 8 + 3 \times 7 = 3(8 + 7)$
16. $5 + 9 = 9 \times 5$

17. Which expression is equal to $67(83 + 59)$?
 (1) $67 \times 83 + 59$
 (2) $67 + 83 + 67 \times 59$
 (3) $83 + 67 \times 59$
 (4) $67 \times 83 + 67 \times 59$
 (5) $67 \times (83 \times 59)$

18. A motorist drove at an average speed of 45 miles per hour for 3 hours before lunch. After lunch he continued at 45 miles per hour for another 5 hours. Which expression gives the number of miles covered by the motorist?
 (1) $45 + 3 \times 5$
 (2) $45 \times 3 + 5$
 (3) $3 \times 45 + 5 \times 45$
 (4) $3 + 5 \times 45$
 (5) $5 \times 45 + 3$

ANSWERS

1. **Associative law of multiplication**
2. **Commutative law of multiplication**
3. **Associative law of addition**
4. **Distributive law**
5. **Commutative law of addition**
6. **Associative law of multiplication**
7. **Distributive law**
8. **Commutative law of multiplication**
9. **False**
10. **False**
11. **True**
12. **True**
13. **True**
14. **False**
15. **True**
16. **False**
17. **4**
18. **3**

19

Algebra: Worked-Out Examples and Practice

Fundamentals

Chapter 18 on arithmetic dealt only with numbers. Now, as we start this chapter on algebra, we must review the use of letters as *variables*. If we let J = Judy's age, and A = Adam's age, we can express the statement "Judy is 8 years older than Adam" by the algebraic equation

$$J = A + 8$$

Then we can use this equation to answer each of the following questions:

If Adam is 21, how old is Judy?
Replace A by 21 and get:

$$J = 21 + 8 = 29$$

When Adam was 7, how old was Judy?
Replace A by 7 and get:

$$J = 7 + 8 = 15$$

When Adam is 55, how old will Judy be?
Replace A by 55 and get:

$$J = 55 + 8 = 63$$

In algebraic expressions, we express addition and subtraction by using the same signs as in arithmetic: + and − . To express division, we can use the division symbol, ÷, but more often we use the fraction bar; instead of writing $n \div 3$, we usually write $\frac{n}{3}$. To express multiplication, we *never* use the multiplication sign, ×. The most common letter we use as a variable is x, and writing $3 \times x \times y$ to express "3 times x times y" would be very confusing. Instead, we have three other ways to express multiplication in algebraic expressions.

1. Write the numbers or letters with no symbol between them: $3xy$.
2. Use a raised dot between the numbers or letters: $3 \cdot x \cdot y$.
3. Write the numbers or letters in parentheses, with no symbol between the parentheses: $(3)(x)(y)$.

Most of the time, we use method 1, but often we must use parentheses to avoid confusion. If we want to multiply the sum of x and y by 6, we *cannot* write $6 \cdot x + y$ or $6x + y$, because in those expressions only the x is being multiplied by 6. We must write $6(x + y)$.

To use algebra effectively, we must learn how to translate from ordinary English into symbols and letters.

EXAMPLES

John is x years old. How old will he be 7 years from now?

ANSWER:
$x + 7$

One apple costs a cents. What is the cost of 6 apples?

ANSWER:
$6a$

Alice weighed y pounds a year ago. Since then she has lost 9 pounds. What is her present weight?

ANSWER:
$y - 9$

Take a number z. Increase it by 2. Multiply the result by 6.

ANSWER:
$6(z + 2)$. Note that this *must* be written with parentheses.

PRACTICE

1. A sweater costs $18. The cost of c sweaters is

(1) $18 + c$
(2) $18 \div c$
(3) $c \div 18$
(4) $18c$
(5) $c - 18$

2. Fred is x years old. Bill is 4 years younger. Bill's age is

(1) $x + 4$
(2) $x - 4$
(3) $4 - x$
(4) $4x$
(5) $4x - 4$

3. The perimeter, P, of a rectangle is found by adding the length, l, to the width, w, and doubling the result. $P =$

(1) $l + w \times 2$
(2) $2 \times l + w$
(3) $2 + l + w$
(4) $2(l + w)$
(5) $(2 + l)(2 + w)$

4. Bob had $15 and spent x dollars. The amount he had left was

(1) $x - 15$
(2) $15x$
(3) $15 \div x$
(4) $x \div 15$
(5) $15 - x$

5. If 12 eggs cost a cents, the cost of one egg is

(1) $12a$
(2) $\frac{12}{a}$
(3) $\frac{a}{12}$
(4) $12 + a$
(5) $a - 12$

ANSWER KEY

1. **4** 2. **2** 3. **4** 4. **5** 5. **3**

Exponents and Evaluations

There are times when we wish to multiply a number by itself. Of course, if we wish to multiply 7 by itself, we can write 7×7. However, in modern science, where we may have occasion to multiply a number by itself many times, it becomes awkward to write such numbers as $7 \times 7 \times 7 \times 7 \times 7 \times 7 \times 7 \times 7 \times 7$. Instead, we use a shortcut and write the product of nine 7's as 7^9. In this case 9 is called the *exponent* and 7 is the *base*.

EXAMPLES

5^1 means 5.
6^3 means $6 \times 6 \times 6$
a^5 means $a \cdot a \cdot a \cdot a \cdot a$
$3b^4$ means $3 \cdot b \cdot b \cdot b \cdot b$
$(3b)^4$ means $(3b)(3b)(3b)(3b)$

We often wish to find the numerical value of an algebraic expression when we know the numerical value assigned to each letter of the expression.

When a calculation requires more than one operation, it is critical that the operations be carried out in the correct order. For decades students have memorized the sentence "Please Excuse My Dear Aunt Sally," or just the first letters, PEMDAS, to remember the proper order of operations. The letters stand for:

1. Parentheses: first do whatever appears in parentheses, following PEMDAS within the parentheses if necessary.

2. Exponents: next evaluate all terms with exponents.

3. Multiplication and Division: next do all multiplications and divisions *in order from left to right*—do not multiply first and then divide.

4. Addition and Subtraction: finally do all additions and subtractions *in order from left to right*—do not add first and then subtract.

EXAMPLES

Evaluate $3b^3$ and $(3b)^3$ when $b = 2$.

$3b^3 = 3 \times 2^3 = 3 \times 8 = 24$

$(3b)^3 = (3 \times 2)^3 = (6)^3 = 216$

Notice that, in evaluating $(3b)^3$, we first evaluated what was in Parentheses ($3 \times 2 = 6$) and then took the Exponent ($6^3 = 216$). In evaluating $3b^3$, we first evaluated the Exponent ($2^3 = 8$) and then Multiplied by 3 ($3 \times 8 = 24$). The order matters!

Evaluate $5x + 3y \div 6z$ when $x = 6$, $y = 4$, and $z = 1$.

$$\begin{aligned} 5x + 3y \div 6z &= (5 \cdot 6) + (3 \cdot 4) \div (6 \cdot 1) \\ &= 30 + 12 \div 6 \\ &= 30 + 2 = 32 \end{aligned}$$

Find the value of $4a^3 - 9c^2 \div 4b$ when $a = 5$, $b = 3$, and $c = 2$.

$$\begin{aligned} 4a^3 - 9c^2 \div 4b &= (4 \cdot 5^3) - (9 \cdot 2^2) \div (4 \cdot 3) \\ &= (4 \cdot 125) - (9 \cdot 4) \div (4 \cdot 3) \\ &= 500 - 36 \div 12 \\ &= 500 - 3 = 497 \end{aligned}$$

Find the value of $5(x^3 - 2y^2)$ when $x = 4$ and $y = 3$.

$$\begin{aligned} 5(x^3 - 2y^2) &= 5(4^3 - 2 \cdot 3^2) = 5(64 - 18) \\ &= 5 \cdot 46 \\ &= 230 \end{aligned}$$

PRACTICE

Evaluate each of the following expressions when $x = 5$, $y = 4$, $z = 3$, $a = 2$, and $b = 1$.

1. $2x^3 + 3y$

(1) 112
(2) 32
(3) 47
(4) 262
(5) 98

2. $3x + 5a - 7b$

(1) 18
(2) 17
(3) 15
(4) 20
(5) 37

3. $3ab + x^2y$

(1) 9
(2) 32
(3) 11
(4) 15
(5) 106

4. $2x^2 - y^2 + 5ab$

(1) 54
(2) 94
(3) 44
(4) 92
(5) 78

5. $x(a^3 + b)^2$

(1) 245
(2) 320
(3) 405
(4) 2,025
(5) 1,002,001

ANSWER KEY

1. **4** **2.** **1** **3.** **5** **4.** **3** **5.** **3**

Operations with Exponents and Scientific Notation

Multiplication with Exponents

Since $2^3 = 2 \cdot 2 \cdot 2$ and $2^4 = 2 \cdot 2 \cdot 2 \cdot 2$,

$$2^3 \cdot 2^4 = (2 \cdot 2 \cdot 2) \cdot (2 \cdot 2 \cdot 2 \cdot 2) = 2^7 = 2^{3+4}.$$

This is a special case of the following law:

> For any numbers a, m, and n:
> $a^m \cdot a^n = a^{m+n}$

PRACTICE

Find the following products:

1. $c^5 \cdot c^3$
2. $y^2 \times y^5$
3. $a^4 \times a$
4. $b \times b^3$
5. $x^3 \cdot x^7$

ANSWERS

1. $\mathbf{c^8}$ 2. $\mathbf{y^7}$ 3. $\mathbf{a^5}$ 4. $\mathbf{b^4}$ 5. $\mathbf{x^{10}}$

Expressing Large Numbers in Scientific Notation

Scientists such as astronomers and space engineers frequently deal with very large numbers in their work. In order for scientists to be able to write these numbers conveniently and to use them effectively, the *scientific notation* system was developed. The definition of scientific notation for writing a number is given below.

> **DEFINITION:** When a number is written in scientific notation it is written as the product of two numbers:
>
> a. a number greater than or equal to 1, but less than 10
> b. a power of 10

EXAMPLE

The distance between two planets is 460,000,000,000 miles. Write this number in scientific notation.

The number between 1 and 10 is 4.6. When you go from 4.6 to 460,000,000,000, you move the decimal point 11 places to the right. Each move of the decimal point to the right represents multiplication by 10. Thus, a move of the decimal point 11 places to the right is equivalent to multiplication by 10^{11}.

Therefore, $460{,}000{,}000{,}000 = 4.6 \times 10^{11}$.

EXAMPLE

Express 875,000,000 in scientific notation.

The number between 1 and 10 is 8.75. When you go from 8.75 to 875,000,000, you move the decimal point 8 places to the right.

Therefore, $875{,}000{,}000 = 8.75 \times 10^8$.

EXAMPLE

Express 3.35×10^5 as an integer.

To multiply by 10^5, move the decimal point 5 places to the right, filling in 0's once the decimal point is all the way to the right.

Therefore, $3.35 \times 10^5 = 335{,}000$.

PRACTICE

Write each of the following in ordinary extended form:

1. 6×10^5
2. 3.2×10^7
3. 5.89×10^9
4. 4.75×10^6
5. 3.14×10^3
6. 6.5×10^8

Write each of the following in scientific notation:

7. 8,200,000,000
8. 76,000,000,000
9. 45,800,000,000,000
10. 7,000,000
11. 9,020,000,000,000
12. 86,000,000,000

ANSWERS

1. **600,000**
2. **32,000,000**
3. **5,890,000,000**
4. **4,750,000**
5. **3,140**
6. **650,000,000**
7. $\mathbf{8.2 \times 10^9}$
8. $\mathbf{7.6 \times 10^{10}}$
9. $\mathbf{4.58 \times 10^{13}}$
10. $\mathbf{7 \times 10^6}$
11. $\mathbf{9.02 \times 10^{12}}$
12. $\mathbf{8.6 \times 10^{10}}$

Expressing Small Numbers in Scientific Notation

Atomic scientists and other physicists have occasion to work with very small numbers. The ability to express these small numbers in scientific notation is a great convenience. The definition of scientific notation previously given applies to very small, as well as to very large, numbers.

EXAMPLE

The length of a wave of violet light is 0.000016 inch. Express this number in scientific notation.

The number between 1 and 10 is 1.6.

When you go from 1.6 to 0.000016, you move the decimal point 5 places to the left. Each move of the decimal point to the left represents division by 10, which we express as multiplication by 10^{-1}. Thus, a move of the decimal point 5 places to the left is equivalent to division by 10^5 or multiplication by 10^{-5}.

Therefore, $0.000016 = 1.6 \times 10^{-5}$.

EXAMPLE

Express 7.9×10^{-4} as an ordinary decimal number.

To multiply by 10^{-4}, move the decimal point 4 places to the left, filling in 0's once the decimal point is all the way to the left.

Therefore, $7.9 \times 10^{-4} = 0.00079$.

PRACTICE

Write each of the following as an ordinary decimal number:

1. 3×10^{-4}
2. 8.5×10^{-6}
3. 650×10^{-2}
4. 79×10^{-5}
5. 3.14×10^{-3}
6. 6.78×10^{-1}

Write each of the following in scientific notation.

7. 0.0069
8. 0.00000037
9. 0.00085
10. 0.0000076
11. 0.0000000057
12. 0.000045

ANSWERS

1. **0.0003**	7. $\mathbf{6.9 \times 10^{-3}}$
2. **0.0000085**	8. $\mathbf{3.7 \times 10^{-7}}$
3. **6.5**	9. $\mathbf{8.5 \times 10^{-4}}$
4. **0.00079**	10. $\mathbf{7.6 \times 10^{-6}}$
5. **0.00314**	11. $\mathbf{5.7 \times 10^{-9}}$
6. **0.678**	12. $\mathbf{4.5 \times 10^{-5}}$

The following set of practice exercises is a review of the entire topic of operations with exponents and scientific notation.

PRACTICE

Find the following products:

1. $x^2 \cdot x^3$
2. $y \cdot y^2$
3. $z^5 \cdot z^2$
4. $b^4 \cdot b^4$
5. $x^6 \cdot x^2$
6. $y^3 \cdot y$
7. $z^2 \cdot z^2$
8. $a^{14} \cdot a^4$
9. During 1 year the U.S. government collected $587,000,000,000 in taxes. Write this number in scientific notation.
10. The diameter of a particle is 0.000032 inch. Express this number in scientific notation.

Express each of the following numbers in scientific notation:

11. 640,000
12. 59,000,000,000
13. 0.000375

ANSWERS

1. $\mathbf{x^5}$	8. $\mathbf{a^{18}}$
2. $\mathbf{y^3}$	9. $\mathbf{5.87 \times 10^{11}}$
3. $\mathbf{z^7}$	10. $\mathbf{3.2 \times 10^{-5}}$
4. $\mathbf{b^8}$	11. $\mathbf{6.4 \times 10^5}$
5. $\mathbf{x^8}$	12. $\mathbf{5.9 \times 10^{10}}$
6. $\mathbf{y^4}$	13. $\mathbf{3.75 \times 10^{-4}}$
7. $\mathbf{z^4}$	

Formulas

Temperature readings given in weather reports use the *Fahrenheit* scale, on which the freezing point of water is 32° and the boiling point of water is 212°. However, in the science laboratory and in many European countries the *Celsius* scale is used. On the Celsius scale, the freezing point of water is 0° and the boiling point of water is 100°. The relationship between the Fahrenheit scale and the Celsius scale is given by the formula

$$F = \frac{9}{5}C + 32$$

where F represents the Fahrenheit temperature and C represents the Celsius temperature.

EXAMPLE

On a certain day the noon temperature in Paris is recorded as 20° Celsius. What is the corresponding Fahrenheit temperature?

Use the formula

$$F = \frac{9}{5}C + 32$$

In this case $C = 20$.

$$F = \frac{9}{\not{5}_1} \times \overset{4}{\not{20}} + 32$$

$$= 9 \times 4 + 32 = 36 + 32 = 68°$$

PRACTICE

1. On an early spring day the temperature recorded in Atlanta was 10° Celsius. Use the formula $F = \frac{9}{5}C + 32$ to find the corresponding Fahrenheit reading.

   (1) 40°
   (2) 43°
   (3) 70°
   (4) 50°
   (5) 45°

2. The formula $A = \frac{a + b + c}{3}$ is used to find the average, A, of three numbers, a, b, and c. The average of 95, 119, and 104 is

   (1) 108
   (2) 106
   (3) 160
   (4) $104\frac{2}{3}$
   (5) 110

3. The formula $C = 80 + 15(n - 4)$ is used to find the cost, C, of a taxi ride, where n represents the number of $\frac{1}{4}$ miles of the ride.

   The cost of a taxi ride of $2\frac{3}{4}$ miles is

   (1) $0.95
   (2) $3
   (3) $1.65
   (4) $1.85
   (5) $2

4. The formula $C = 72m + 32h$ is used to find the daily labor cost, in dollars, of a job in carpentry, where m represents the number of master carpenters and h represents the number of helpers. On a certain job, 6 master carpenters and 4 helpers are used. The daily labor cost is

   (1) $480
   (2) $550
   (3) $650
   (4) $600
   (5) $560

5. The formula for the relationship between the length, l, and width, w, of a certain flag is $l = 1.8w$. A flag has a width of 5 feet. Its length is

   (1) 2.3 ft.
   (2) 9 ft.
   (3) 90 ft.
   (4) 1.3 ft.
   (5) 8 ft.

ANSWER KEY

1. **4** 2. **2** 3. **4** 4. **5** 5. **2**

Solving Equations

The ability to solve equations is important because it enables us to solve many different types of problems. In this section, you will learn how to solve some of the simpler kinds of equations. In a later section you will apply these skills in problem solving.

An equation states that two quantities are equal.

For example, the equation

$$3x + 2 = 20$$

tells us that $3x + 2$ and 20 are different names for the same number. If this is so, then $3x$ must represent the number 18, since 18 is the only number that can be added to 2 to get 20. Then, since 3 times x equals 18, x must be equal to 6.

A number that yields a true statement when it replaces the variable in an equation is called a *solution* of that equation. To *solve* an equation means to find its solution. In the preceding paragraph, when we solved the equation $3x + 2 = 20$, we determined that the solution was $x = 6$.

On the GED Mathematics test, many of the equations that you will have to solve can be reasoned out in the same way. Try to use this method on the following eight practice problems.

PRACTICE

Solve each of the following equations for *x*.

1. $x + 2 = 9$
   (1) 5
   (2) 9
   (3) 7
   (4) 3
   (5) 10

2. $x - 3 = 5$
   (1) 5
   (2) 3
   (3) 2
   (4) 10
   (5) 8

3. $2x = 10$
   (1) 8
   (2) 5
   (3) 20
   (4) $\frac{1}{5}$
   (5) 9

4. $\frac{x}{3} = 4$
   (1) 12
   (2) $\frac{4}{3}$
   (3) $\frac{3}{4}$
   (4) 1
   (5) 6

5. $2x + 1 = 7$
   (1) 4
   (2) $3\frac{1}{2}$
   (3) 5
   (4) 3
   (5) 6

6. $2x - 1 = 9$
   (1) 10
   (2) 8
   (3) 5
   (4) 4
   (5) 3

7. $\frac{x}{2} + 3 = 7$
   (1) 4
   (2) 8
   (3) $1\frac{1}{2}$
   (4) $2\frac{1}{2}$
   (5) 20

8. $\frac{x}{3} - 1 = 5$
   (1) 18
   (2) 12
   (3) 2
   (4) 6
   (5) 15

ANSWER KEY

1. **3**	3. **2**	5. **4**	7. **2**
2. **5**	4. **1**	6. **3**	8. **1**

You will now learn a systematic method of finding the solution of an equation. The basic principle is this: *do exactly the same thing to each side of the equation.* For example, you may always add the same number to each side, subtract the same number from each side, or multiply or divide each side by the same number (except 0).

Virtually every equation that you will have to solve on the GED Examination has only one variable and no exponents. The simple six-step method shown in the following example can be used on all of these equations.

EXAMPLE

If $\frac{1}{2}x + 3x - 3 = 2(x + 1) + 4$, what is the value of x?

STEP	WHAT TO DO	EXAMPLE
1	Get rid of fractions by multiplying both sides by the LCD (Least Common Denominator).	Multiply each term by 2: $x + 6x - 6 = 4(x + 1) + 4$
2	Use the distributive law to get rid of all parentheses.	$x + 6x - 6 = 4x + 4 + 8$
3	Combine like terms on each side.	$7x - 6 = 4x + 12$
4	By adding or subtracting, get all the variables on one side.	Subtract $4x$ from each side: $3x - 6 = 12$
5	By adding or subtracting, get all the plain numbers on the other side.	Add 6 to each side $3x = 18$
6	Divide both sides by the number in front of the variable.	Divide both sides by 3: $x = 6$

This example is actually harder than any equation on the GED Examination, because it requires all six steps. On the GED that never happens.

Think of the six steps as a list of questions that must be answered. Ask yourself whether each step is necessary. If it isn't, move on to the next one; if it is, do it.

Now let's look at some equations that require only a few steps to solve. We'll start with the equation we solved at the beginning of this section.

EXAMPLES

Solve the equation $3x + 2 = 20$.

There are no fractions or parentheses, there are no like terms, and the variable is on only one side of the equation, so skip steps 1 through 4.

Subtract 2 from each side: $3x = 18$

Divide each side by 3: $x = 6$

Solve the equation $\frac{x}{3} = 20$.

There is a fraction, so do step 1. Multiply both sides by the denominator, 3:

$$3\left(\frac{x}{3}\right) = 3(20)$$
$$x = 60$$

Solve the equation $\frac{3}{5}x - 1 = 8$.

There is a fraction, so do step 1. Multiply each side by the denominator, 5:

$$5\left(\frac{3}{5}x\right) - 5(1) = 5(8)$$
$$3x - 5 = 40$$

Skip to step 5. Add 5 to each side:

$$3x = 45$$

Do step 6. Divide each side by 3:

$$x = 15$$

PRACTICE

Solve each of the following equations for *x*.

1. $x + 1 = 3$
2. $x - 2 = 4$
3. $3x = 12$
4. $\frac{x}{2} = 5$

5. $x + 5 = 7$
6. $x - 3 = 4$
7. $5x = 10$
8. $\frac{x}{4} = 2$
9. $x + 2 = 9$
10. $5x = 15$
11. $x - 2 = 9$
12. $x + 4 = 7$
13. $\frac{x}{5} = 2$
14. $3x = 18$
15. $x + 9 = 11$
16. $2x + 3x = 40$
17. $\frac{2}{3}x = 12$
18. $4x - 1 = 27$
19. $\frac{x}{5} + 4 = 6$
20. $3x - 5 = 16$
21. $3x + 7 = 37$
22. $4x - 2 = 22$
23. $\frac{x}{2} - 3 = 5$
24. $2(x + 5) = 3(x - 1)$
25. $3(x + 4) + 2 = 4(x + 1) + x$

ANSWERS

1. **2**	6. **7**	11. **11**	16. **8**	21. **10**
2. **6**	7. **2**	12. **3**	17. **18**	22. **6**
3. **4**	8. **8**	13. **10**	18. **7**	23. **16**
4. **10**	9. **7**	14. **6**	19. **10**	24. **13**
5. **2**	10. **3**	15. **2**	20. **7**	25. **5**

Solving Problems

We may use equations to solve problems such as the following.

EXAMPLE

A plumber must cut a pipe 50 inches long into two pieces so that one piece will be 12 inches longer than the other piece. Find the length of each piece.

Let x = length of the shorter piece.
Then $x + 12$ = length of the longer piece.
Since the sum of the two pieces is 50 inches:

$$x + (x + 12) = 50$$

Combine like terms: $2x + 12 = 50$
Subtract 12 from each side: $2x = 38$
Divide each side by 2: $x = 19$

The shorter piece is 19 in. long, and the longer piece is 19 + 12 = 31 in. long.

EXAMPLE

Divide an estate of $46,000 among three sons so that the second son gets $6,000 more than the youngest, and the eldest son gets 3 times as much as the youngest.

Let x = amount the youngest son gets.
then $x + 6{,}000$ = amount the second son gets,
and $3x$ = amount the eldest son gets.

$$x + (x + 6000) + 3x = 46{,}000$$

Combine like terms: $5x + 6000 = 46{,}000$
Subtract 6,000 from each side: $5x = 40{,}000$
Divide each side by 5: $x = 8{,}000$

The youngest son gets $8,000; the second son gets 8,000 + 6,000 = $14,000; and the eldest son gets 3(8,000) = $24,000.

Algebra problems are sometimes more easily understood and analyzed when approached through analogous problems in arithmetic.

EXAMPLE

Arithmetic Problem: If 1 pencil costs 10 cents, then 6 pencils cost _______cents.

Algebra Problem: If 1 pencil costs y cents, then 6 pencils cost _______ cents.

To solve the arithmetic problem, you need to multiply 6 times 10 cents, to arrive at 60 cents as the answer. In the algebra problem, you use the same procedure: multiply 6 times y cents to get the answer, $6y$.

Here is a more complicated example:

EXAMPLE

Arithmetic Problem: George has 50 dollars. He buys 5 articles for 8 dollars each. The number of dollars George has left is _______.

Algebra Problem: George has x dollars. He buys y articles for z dollars each. The number of dollars George has left is _______.

To solve the arithmetic problem, you need to multiply 5 times 8 and subtract the result from 50, to get $50 - (5)(8) = 50 - 40 = 10$ as the answer. In the algebra problem, you use the same procedure: multiply y times z, and subtract the result from x, to get $x - yz$ as the answer.

EXAMPLE

Eighteen coins, consisting of nickels and dimes, have a total value of $1.25. How many dimes are there?

Let x = number of dimes,
and $18 - x$ = number of nickels.

Since each dime is worth 10 cents, and each nickel is worth 5 cents, the value of all the dimes is $10x$ cents, and the value of all the nickels is $5(18 - x)$ cents. Then, since the total value of the coins is $1.25 or 125 cents:

	$10x + 5(18 - x) = 125$
Get rid of parentheses:	$10x + 90 - 5x = 125$
Combine like terms:	$5x + 90 = 125$
Subtract 90 from each side:	$5x = 35$
Divide each side by 5:	$x = 7$

There are 7 dimes.

EXAMPLE

At a track meet the total score for each event was 20 points. First place counted twice as much as second place, and third place counted 4 points less than second place. How many points did first place count?

Let x = number of points for second place.
Then $2x$ = number of points for first place, and
$x - 4$ = number of points for third place.

	$x + 2x + (x - 4) = 20$
Combine like terms:	$4x - 4 = 20$
Add 4 to each side:	$4x = 24$
Divide each side by 4:	$x = 6$

First place counted for $2(6) = 12$ points.

EXAMPLE

Two cars start at the same time from two cities that are 480 miles apart and travel toward each other. One car averages 35 miles per hour, and the other car averages 45 miles per hour. In how many hours will the two cars meet?

Let x = number of hours the two cars take to meet.

In problems involving motion, it is convenient to collect the information in a box, as shown below, with the formula

Rate × Time = Distance.

	Rate	**× Time**	**= Distance**
First car	35	x	$35x$
Second car	45	x	$45x$

Since the sum of the two distances covered is 480 miles:

	$35x + 45x = 480$
Combine like terms:	$80x = 480$
Divide each side by 80:	$x = 6$

The cars will meet in 6 hr.

PRACTICE

1. Two partners in a business earn $60,000 one year. If the senior partner's share is 3 times that of the junior partner, what is the junior partner's share? $15,000
2. A wooden beam is 58 inches long. A carpenter must cut the beam so that the longer part is 8 inches longer than the shorter part. How long is the shorter part? 25 in
3. The length of a rectangular field is 3 times its width. If the perimeter of the field is 312 feet, what is the width of the field? 39ft
4. A master carpenter earns $5 more per hour than his helper. Together they earn $119 for a 7-hour job. How much does the helper earn per hour? $6
5. A boy has $3.75 in nickels and dimes. If he has 6 more dimes than nickels, how many dimes does he have? 27
6. Mr. Dale asked his son to deposit $495 in the bank. There were exactly 70 bills, consisting of 10-dollar bills and 5-dollar bills. Find the number of 10-dollar bills the son had to deposit. 29
7. The perimeter of a triangle is 27 inches. One side is 3 inches longer than the shortest side, and the longest side is twice the length of the shortest side. What is the length of the shorter side? 6in

8. Frank had $\frac{1}{4}$ as much money as Angel. Together they had \$125. How much money did Frank have?
9. The Rivera family has an annual income of \$48,000. Of this, \$45,000 consists of salaries and the balance is obtained by an investment that pays 8% annually. How much is invested at 8%?
10. At a sale, some radio sets were sold for \$50 each and the rest for \$35 each. If 175 sets were sold and the receipts were \$7,250, how many \$50 sets were sold?
11. On a fishing trip José caught 8 more fish than Joe. Together they caught 32 fish. Which of the following equations may be used to find how many fish José caught?
    (1) $x + 8x = 32$
    (2) $x + 32 = 8x$
    (3) $x + x + 8 = 32$
    (4) $8x - x = 32$
    (5) $x + 32 + x = 8$
12. A sofa was marked \$270. This was a discount of 25% off the original price. What was the original price?
13. Beth has \$4.35 in nickels and dimes. If she has 12 more dimes than nickels, how many nickels does she have?
14. A college football squad of 50 players consisted of seniors, juniors, and sophomores. If there were twice as many seniors as sophomores, and 14 more juniors than sophomores, which of the following equations may be used to find how many sophomores were on the squad?
    (1) $x + 2x + 14 = 50$
    (2) $x + 2x - 14 = 50$
    (3) $x + 2x + 14x = 50$
    (4) $x + 2x + x + 14 = 50$
    (5) $x + x + 14 + x = 50$
15. Two trains are 800 miles apart. At 9:00 A.M. they start traveling toward each other. One train travels at an average rate of 45 miles per hour, and the other train travels at an average rate of 55 miles per hour. At what time do the trains meet?

ANSWERS

1. **\$15,000**	9. **\$37,500**
2. **25 inches**	10. **75**
3. **39 feet**	11. **(3)**
4. **\$6.00**	12. **\$360**
5. **27**	13. **21**
6. **29**	14. **(4)**
7. **6 inches**	15. **5:00 P.M.**
8. **\$25**	

Solving Inequalities

We recall that the symbol > means *is greater than* and that the symbol < means *is less than*. For example, $9 > 5$ and $3 < 8$.

An inequality is a statement in which two quantities are unequal. The inequality

$$3x + 2 > 20$$

tells us that $3x + 2$ names a number that is greater than 20. To solve such an inequality, we use the exact same six-step method that we use for solving equations.

	$3x + 2 > 20$
Subtract 2 from each side:	$3x > 18$
Divide each side by 3:	$x > 6$

Since *any number* greater than 6 is a solution, the inequality $3x + 2 > 20$ has infinitely many solutions. Of course, 7, 8, 9, 10, . . . are all solutions, but solutions do not have to be integers—6.4, $117\frac{1}{2}$, and $\sqrt{55}$ are also solutions. For example,

$3(6.4) + 2 = 19.2 + 2 = 21.2$,

which is greater than 20.

The symbol ≥ means *is greater than or equal to*, and the symbol ≤ means *is less than or equal to*. For example, $x \geq 5$ means that $x > 5$ or $x = 5$.

EXAMPLES

The positive integers that satisfy the inequality $x \geq 3$ are 3, 4, 5, ...

The positive integers that satisfy the inequality $x \leq 3$ are 1, 2, and 3. Of course, 0 and all of the negative integers also satisfy this inequality.

PRACTICE

In exercises 1–4, which choice is a solution to the given inequality?

1. $2x + 3 > 11$

   (1) 4
   (2) 1
   (3) $2\frac{1}{2}$
   (4) 5
   (5) 3

2. $2x - 3 < 5$

   (1) 2
   (2) 5
   (3) 7
   (4) 6
   (5) 4

3. $x + 2 \geq 5$

   (1) 2
   (2) 0
   (3) 2.5
   (4) 3
   (5) 1

4. $3x - 2 \leq 10$

   (1) 2
   (2) 5
   (3) 7
   (4) 6.5
   (5) 8

In exercises 5–8, find the complete solution to the given inequality.

5. $\frac{y}{3} - 4 > 1$
6. $5y + 1 \leq 6$
7. $7y - 2 \geq 19$
8. $\frac{y}{4} + 3 > 5$

ANSWERS

1. **4**	3. **4**	5. $y > 15$	7. $y \geq 3$
2. **1**	4. **1**	6. $y \leq 1$	8. $y > 8$

Ratio and Proportion

A ***ratio*** is a fraction that compares two quantities that are measured in the same units. The first quantity is the numerator, and the second quantity is the denominator.

For example, if Mr. Carson earns $48 per day and Mr. Burns earns $16 per day, we may say that the ratio of Mr. Carson's earnings per day to Mr. Burns's earnings per day is $\frac{48}{16}$. We may reduce $\frac{48}{16}$ to $\frac{3}{1}$ or 3, which indicates that Mr. Carson earns 3 times as much per day as Mr. Burns.

The comparison of the two pay rates may be written as $\frac{48}{16}$ or as 48 : 16, which is read as "48 to 16." In general, the ratio of number a to number b is $\frac{a}{b}$, or $a:b$.

EXAMPLES

At a party there are 12 men and 8 women. What is the ratio of men to women?

The ratio is $\frac{12}{8}$, or 12 : 8. In simplest form, this is $\frac{3}{2}$, or 3 : 2.

At the same party, what is the ratio of women to men?

The ratio is $\frac{8}{12}$ or 8 : 12. In simplest form, this is $\frac{2}{3}$, or 2 : 3.

At the same party, what is the ratio of men to the number of people at the party?

Since there are 8 + 12 = 20 people at the party, the ratio is $\frac{12}{20}$, or 12 : 20. In simplest form this is $\frac{3}{5}$, or 3 : 5.

If two numbers are in the ratio of a:b, then, for some number x, the first number is ax and the second number is bx. Therefore, in any ratio problem, you should write the letter x after each number and use some given information to solve for x.

EXAMPLE

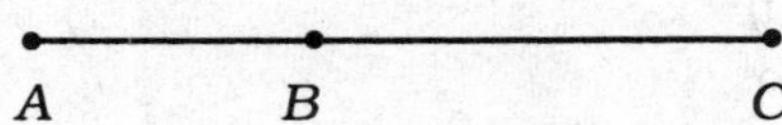

If $AB:BC = 2:3$, and if $AC = 30$ inches, what is the length of AB?

Let $AB = 2x$ and $BC = 3x$. Since
$AB + BC = AC$
then $2x + 3x = 30$
$5x = 30$
$x = 6$
Therefore, $AB = 2x = 2(6) = 12$.

EXAMPLE

If the number of children at a picnic is between 40 and 50, and the ratio of boys to girls is 5:4, how many girls are at the picnic?

If $5x$ and $4x$ are the numbers of boys and girls, respectively, at the picnic, then the number of children present is $5x + 4x = 9x$. Therefore, the number of children must be a multiple of 9. The only multiple of 9 between 40 and 50 is 45, so $9x = 45$ and $x = 5$. Since the number of girls is $4x$, there are $4(5) = 20$ girls.

A ***proportion*** is an equation that states that two ratios are equivalent. Since ratios are just fractions, any equation such as $\frac{4}{6} = \frac{10}{15}$ in which each side is a single fraction is a proportion.

The easiest way to solve a proportion is to cross-multiply: if $\frac{a}{b} = \frac{c}{d}$, then $ad = bc$

EXAMPLE

If $\frac{3}{7} = \frac{x}{84}$ what is the value of x?

Cross-multiply: $3(84) = 7x$, so $252 = 7x$ and $x = 36$.

EXAMPLE

If a tank contains 24 quarts of alcohol, how many quarts of water must be added to make an antifreeze mixture in which the ratio of alcohol to water is 3 : 4?

Set up a proportion.

Let x = number of quarts of water needed.

$$\frac{\text{alcohol}}{\text{water}} = \frac{3}{4} = \frac{24}{x}$$

Now, cross multiply.

$$\frac{3}{4} \times \frac{24}{x}$$

$$3x = 4 \times 24$$
$$= 96$$
$$x = 32$$

A ***rate*** is a fraction that compares two quantities measured in different units. The word *per* often appears in rate problems: miles per hour, dollars per week, cents per ounce, children per classroom, and so on.

The following examples will indicate how ratios and proportions can be used to solve problems.

EXAMPLE

Sharon read 24 pages of her book in 15 minutes. At this rate, how many pages can she read in 40 minutes?

Handle this rate problem exactly as you do a ratio problem. Set up a proportion and cross-multiply:

$$\frac{\text{pages}}{\text{minutes}} = \frac{24}{15} = \frac{x}{40}$$
$$15x = 40 \times 24 = 960 \text{ and}$$
$$x = 64$$

EXAMPLE

The scale on a map is 1 inch to 60 miles.

If the distance between two cities is $2\frac{3}{4}$ inches on the map, what is the actual distance between the two cities?

Let d = distance between the cities.
Set up a proportion and cross-multiply:

$$\frac{\text{inches}}{\text{miles}} = \frac{1}{60} = \frac{2.75}{d}$$
$$d = 60(2.75) = 165 \text{ mi.}$$

EXAMPLE

Two numbers are in the ratio 9 : 5. Their difference is 28. Find the numbers.

Let $9x$ = larger number,
and $5x$ = smaller number.

Then $28 = 9x - 5x = 4x$ and $x = 7$.
The larger number is $9x$, or $9 \cdot 7 = 63$.
The smaller number is $5x$, or $5 \cdot 7 = 35$.

EXAMPLE

The numerator and denominator of a fraction are in the ratio 3 : 7. If 2 is added to both the numerator and the denominator, the ratio becomes 1 : 2. Find the original fraction.

Let $3n$ = numerator of the fraction, and $7n$ = denominator of the fraction.

Add 2 to both the numerator and the denominator; the numerator becomes $3n + 2$ and the denominator becomes $7n + 2$. Thus:

$$\frac{3n+2}{7n+2} = \frac{1}{2}$$

Cross multiply

$$1(7n + 2) = 2(3n + 2)$$
$$7n + 2 = 6n + 4$$
$$n + 2 = 4$$
$$n = 2$$

The original denominator was $3n$, or 6.
The original numerator was $7n$, or 14.

The original fraction was $\frac{6}{14}$.

PRACTICE

1. At a dance, the ratio of the number of boys to the number of girls is 4 : 3. If 32 boys are present, the number of girls present is

(1) 36
(2) 40
(3) 20
(4) 24
(5) 28

2. John earned $150 one week and spent $120. The ratio of the amount John saved to the amount John spent is

(1) 1 : 5
(2) 1 : 4
(3) 4 : 1
(4) 4 : 5
(5) 5 : 4

3. On a trip, a motorist drove x miles on a local road and y miles on a parkway. The ratio of the number of miles driven on the parkway to the total number of miles driven was

(1) $\frac{y}{x}$

(2) $\frac{x}{y}$

(3) $\frac{y}{x+y}$

(4) $\frac{x}{x+y}$

(5) $\frac{x+y}{y}$

4. The ratio of a father's age to his son's age is 9 : 2. If the son's age is 12 years, the age of the father, in years, is

(1) 45
(2) 36
(3) 63
(4) 50
(5) 54

5. On line segment $\overline{RS}$, $RT = 4$ and $RT : TS = 2 : 5$. The length of $\overline{RS}$ is

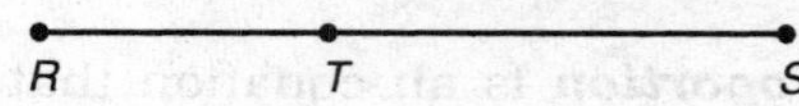

(1) 10
(2) 12
(3) 7
(4) 9
(5) 14

6. If three shirts cost $53, the cost of a dozen shirts at the same rate is

(1) $159
(2) $75
(3) $65
(4) $212
(5) $250

7. On a map, the scale is 1 inch to 80 miles. The actual distance between two cities is 200 miles. The distance between the cities, on the map, is

(1) 2 in.
(2) 3 in.
(3) $2\frac{1}{2}$ in.
(4) $3\frac{1}{2}$ in.
(5) 4 in.

8. A certain recipe that will yield 4 portions calls for $1\frac{1}{2}$ ounces of sugar. If the recipe is used to yield 6 portions, the amount of sugar needed is

(1) $2\frac{1}{2}$ oz.
(2) $2\frac{1}{4}$ oz.
(3) $2\frac{3}{4}$ oz.
(4) 2 oz.
(5) 3 oz.

9. A family consumes q quarts of milk each week. The number of quarts this family consumes in 10 days is

(1) $\frac{7q}{10}$
(2) $\frac{10q}{7}$
(3) $\frac{70}{q}$
(4) $\frac{10}{7q}$
(5) $\frac{q}{70}$

10. In making a certain type of concrete, the ratio of cement to sand used is 1:4. In making x barrels of this concrete, the number of barrels of cement used is

(1) $\frac{x}{5}$
(2) $\frac{x}{4}$
(3) x
(4) $4x$
(5) $\frac{1}{5x}$

ANSWER KEY

1. **4**	3. **3**	5. **5**	7. **3**	9. **2**
2. **2**	4. **5**	6. **4**	8. **2**	10. **1**

Signed Numbers

On the GED Examination the word *number* always means *real number*, a number that can be represented by a point on the number line.

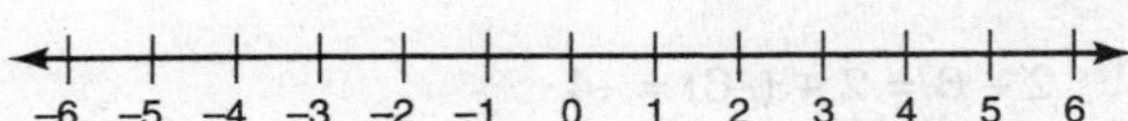

The numbers to the right of 0 on the number line are called ***positive***, and those to the left of 0 are called ***negative***. Negative numbers must be written with a *negative sign* (−2); positive numbers may be written with a *plus sign* (+2) but are usually written without a sign (2). All numbers can be called ***signed numbers.***

The ***absolute value*** of a number, ***a***, denoted as $|a|$, is the distance between a and 0 on the number line. For example, since 3 is 3 units to the right of 0 on the number line and −3 is 3 units to the left of 0, both have an absolute value of 3:

$$|3| = 3 \quad \text{and} \quad |-3| = 3$$

Multiplying and dividing signed numbers is easy as long as you know when the result is positive and when it is negative. The product and quotient of two positive numbers or two negative numbers are positive; the product and quotient of a positive number and a negative number are negative. For example,

$6 \times 3 = 18$ $\quad$ $6 \div 3 = 2$
$(-6) \times (-3) = 18$ $\quad$ $(-6) \div (-3) = 2$
$6 \times (-3) = -18$ $\quad$ $6 \div (-3) = -2$
$(-6) \times 3 = -18$ $\quad$ $(-6) \div 3 = -2$

Adding and subtracting signed numbers requires a little more care. The sum of two positive numbers is positive, and the sum of two negative numbers is negative. To find the sum of a positive and a negative number, find the difference of their absolute values and use the sign of the number with the larger absolute value. For example:

$6 + 2 = 8$ $\quad$ $(-6) + (-2) = -8$

To calculate $6 + (-2)$ or $(-6) + 2$, take the *difference*, $6 - 2 = 4$, and use the sign of the number whose absolute value is 6.

$6 + (-2) = 4$ $\quad$ $(-6) + 2 = -4$

To subtract signed numbers, change the problem to an addition problem by changing the sign of the number that is being subtracted. For example:

$2 - 6 = 2 + (-6) = -4$
$2 - (-6) = 2 + (6) = 8$
$(-2) - (-6) = (-2) + (6) = 4$
$(-2) - 6 = (-2) + (-6) = -8$

In each case, the minus sign was changed to a plus sign, and either the 6 was changed to -6 or the -6 was changed to 6.

EXAMPLE

What is the product of the odd integers between -6 and 4?

The product of the odd integers between -6 and 4 is $(-5)(-3)(-1)(1)(3)$. To evaluate, just multiply from left to right: $(-5)(-3) = 15$, $15(-1) = -15$, $-15(1) = -15$, $-15(3) = -45$.

EXAMPLE

Solve for x and check: $-3x + 5 = -10$.

$-3x = -10 - 5 = -15$
$x = (-15) \div (-3) = 5$
Check: $-3(5) + 5 = -15 + 5 = -10$

PRACTICE

1. $-2 + (-3) - (-4) =$
2. $-2(-3)(-4) =$
3. $(-1)^4 - (-1)^5 =$
4. $6 + 4 \div (-2) =$
5. $6 \times 4 \div (-2) =$
6. $(-12) \div (-6) \times (-2) - (-1)$
7. What is the sum of all of the integers that are greater than -4 and less than 5?
8. What is the product of all of the integers that are greater than -4 and less than 5?
9. Solve for x: $3x - 10 = -28$.
10. Solve for x: $-3(x - 10) = 42$.

ANSWERS

1. **−1**	3. **2**	5. **−12**	7. **4**	9. **−6**
2. **−24**	4. **4**	6. **−3**	8. **0**	10. **−4**

Factoring and the Solution of Quadratic Equations

The Meaning of Factoring

When two numbers or two polynomials are multiplied, each one is called a *factor* of their product. For example, since
$1 \times 12 = 12$, $2 \times 6 = 12$, and $3 \times 4 = 12$, 1, 2, 3, 4, 6, and 12 are all factors of 12.

Similarly, 1, 2, 3, 5, 6, 10, 15, and 30 are all factors of 30.

Note that 1, 2, 3, and 6 are factors of both 12 and 30; they are the *common factors* of 12 and 30, and 6, the largest, is the *greatest common factor* (GCF) of 12 and 30.

These terms apply to algebraic expressions, as well.

Since $(3xy)(2x) = 6x^2y$, then $3xy$ and $2x$ are each factors of $6x^2y$.

Some, but not all, of the factors of $6x^2y$, are also factors of $9x^3y^2$. To find the greatest common factor of $6x^2y$, and $9x^3y^2$, take the product of 3 (the GCF of 6 and 9), and x^2y (the highest powers of x and y that are factors of each of them). The GCF is $3x^2y$.

EXAMPLE

Find the greatest common factor of $42a^2b^3$ and $28a^5b^2$.

$42 = 6 \times 7 = 2 \times 3 \times 7$
$28 = 4 \times 7 = 2 \times 2 \times 7$

The greatest common factor of 42 and 28 is 2×7, or 14.

The greatest common factor of a^2b^3 and a^5b^2 is a^2b^2.

The greatest common factor of $42a^2b^3$ and $28a^5b^2$ is $14a^2b^2$.

PRACTICE

Find the greatest common factor of each of the following:

1. 6 and 9
2. 12 and 15
3. 18 and 30
4. 75 and 45
5. 48 and 80
6. x^3y^4 and x^2y^3
7. $8a^2b^2$ and $20a^2b$
8. $15c^3$ and $10c$

ANSWERS

1. **3**	3. **6**	5. **16**	7. $\mathbf{4a^2b}$
2. **3**	4. **15**	6. $\mathbf{x^2y^3}$	8. **5c**

Factoring Polynomials That Have a Common Factor

In factoring a polynomial, first find the greatest common factor of the terms of the polynomial and then divide each term of the polynomial by this GCF to find the other factor.

EXAMPLES

Factor $7x + 7y$.

The greatest common factor of $7x$ and $7y$ is 7. Divide each term of $7x + 7y$ by 7:

$$7x + 7y = 7(x + y)$$

$7(x + y)$ is called the factored form of $7x + 7y$.

Factor $24a^2 - 16a$.

The greatest common factor of $24a^2$ and $16a$ is $8a$. Divide each term of $24a^2 - 16a$ by $8a$:

$$24a^2 - 16a = 8a\,(3a - 2)$$

PRACTICE

Factor each of the following expressions:

1. $5a + 5b$
2. $6x - 6y$
3. $4c + 8d$
4. $6a + 12b$
5. $x^2 - xy$
6. $3ab^2 + 6a^2b$
7. $p + prt$
8. $4a^2 + 4y^2$
9. $3xy - 12y^2$
10. $8ab - 12a^2$

ANSWERS

1. $\mathbf{5(a + b)}$	6. $\mathbf{3ab(b + 2a)}$
2. $\mathbf{6(x - y)}$	7. $\mathbf{p(1 + rt)}$
3. $\mathbf{4(c + 2)}$	8. $\mathbf{4(a^2 + y^2)}$
4. $\mathbf{6(a + 2b)}$	9. $\mathbf{3y(x - 4y)}$
5. $\mathbf{x(x - y)}$	10. $\mathbf{4a(2b - 3a)}$

Factoring the Difference of Two Squares

Consider $(x + y)(x - y)$, the product of $(x + y)$ and $(x - y)$. To complete the multiplication first multiply $x - y$ by x and then by y, and combine the results. Use the following arrangement to carry out the multiplication:

$$\begin{array}{r} x - y \\ x + y \\ \hline x^2 - xy \quad\;\; \\ + xy - y^2 \\ \hline x^2 \qquad - y^2 \end{array}$$

That is, $(x + y)\,(x - y) = x^2 - y^2$.

If the sum of any two terms is multiplied by the difference of the same two terms, the result will always be the difference of the squares of the two terms. For example, $(2c + 3d)\,(2c - 3d) = (2c)^2 - (3d)^2 = 4c^2 - 9d^2$.

In effect, you have a method of factoring an expression that is the difference of two squares. For example:

$$a^2 - b^2 = (a + b)\,(a - b)$$
$$x^2 - 4 = (x + 2)\,(x - 2)$$
$$25 - z^2 = (5 + z)\,(5 - z)$$
$$9c^2 - 16 = (3c + 4)\,(3c - 4)$$

A polynomial with two terms is called a *binomial*. Each of the polynomials in the preceding set of practice exercises is a binomial. If the two terms of a binomial do not have a common factor, you can factor the binomial *only* if it is the difference of two squares.

PRACTICE

In each case, factor the expression:

1. $c^2 - d^2$
2. $y^2 - 9$
3. $x^2 - 100$
4. $36 - b^2$
5. $9a^2 - 16$
6. $49 - 4x^2$
7. $b^2 - 64$
8. $x^2 - 16y^2$

ANSWERS

1. $(c + d)(c - d)$	5. $(3a + 4)(3a - 4)$
2. $(y + 3)(y - 3)$	6. $(7 + 2x)(7 - 2x)$
3. $(x + 10)(x - 10)$	7. $(b + 8)(b - 8)$
4. $(6 + b)(6 - b)$	8. $(x + 4y)(x - 4y)$

Factoring Trinomials

A polynomial with three terms is called a *trinomial*. Some trinomials can be factored as the product of two binomials. To see how this is done, we will start by multiplying two binomials and writing the product as a trinomial. Let us consider the product of the binomials $(y + 2)$ and $(y + 3)$. We arrange our work as follows:

$$\begin{array}{r} y+3 \\ y+2 \\ \hline y^2+3y \\ +2y+6 \\ \hline y^2+5y+6 \end{array}$$

In obtaining this trinomial result, we note that:

1. The first term of the product (y^2) is obtained by multiplying the first terms of the two binomials, $(y)(y)$.
2. The last term in the product $(+6)$ is obtained by multiplying the second terms of the binomials, $(+3)(+2)$.
3. The middle term of the product $(+ 5y)$ is the sum of the two cross-products:

$$(y)(+3) + (y)(+2) = 3y + 2y = 5y.$$

If the binomials are written horizontally, the middle term can be found mentally by obtaining the algebraic sum of the products of the terms shown by the arrows.

$$(y + 2)\,(y + 3) = y^2 + 3y + 2y + 6 = y^2 + 5y + 6$$

EXAMPLES

Find the product $(x + 5)\,(x - 2)$.

$$(x + 5)\,(x - 2) = x^2 - 2x + 5x - 10 = x^2 + 3x - 10$$

Find the product $(2y + 3)\,(y - 5)$.

$$(2y + 3)\,(y - 5) = 2y^2 - 10y + 3y - 15 =$$

$$2y^2 - 7y - 15$$

PRACTICE

Find the following products:

1. $(y + 2)\,(y + 1)$
2. $(a + 3)\,(a + 4)$
3. $(x - 3)\,(x - 1)$
4. $(y + 4)\,(y - 3)$
5. $(a - 7)\,(a + 2)$

ANSWERS

1. $y^2 + 3y + 2$
2. $a^2 + 7a + 12$
3. $x^2 - 4x + 3$
4. $y^2 + y - 12$
5. $a^2 - 5a - 14$

We have noticed that the product of two binomials may be a trinomial. For example, $(x + 5)\,(x + 7) = x^2 + 12x + 35$. In solving some equations it is necessary to write a trinomial as the product of two binomials. For example, $y^2 + 7y + 10 = (y + 5)\,(y + 2)$. This process of writing a trinomial as the product of two binomials is called *factoring the trinomial*. The following examples will illustrate the method of factoring a trinomial.

EXAMPLES

Factor the trinomial $y^2 + 8y + 15$.

The product of the first terms of the two binomials must be y^2. Therefore, each first term must be y. Thus, we may write

$$y^2 + 8y + 15 = (y \quad)\,(y \quad)$$

where the second term of each binomial is still to be determined.

The product of the last two terms of the binomials must be +15. Thus, these last two terms must both be positive or both negative. The possible pairs of factors are (+15)(+1) or (+5)(+3) or (−15)(−1) or (−5)(−3). We may test the pairs to select the pair that will yield the correct middle term as follows:

$(y + 15)(y + 1) : 15y + y =$
$16y$ for the middle term

This is rejected.

$(y + 5)(y + 3) : 5y + 3y =$
$8y$ for the middle term

This is the correct choice.
Thus, $y^2 + 8y + 15 = (y + 5)(y + 3)$.

Factor the trinomial $a^2 - 3a + 2$.

The possible choices are $(a + 2)(a + 1)$ and $(a - 2)(a - 1)$
If we check these choices, we have

$(a + 2)(a + 1) : 2a + a =$
$+3a$ for the middle term

This choice is rejected.

$(a - 2)(a - 1) : -2a - a =$
$-3a$ for the middle term

This is the correct choice.

Thus, $a^2 - 3a + 2 = (a - 2)(a - 1)$.

Factor the trinomial $y^2 - 3y - 10$.

The possible choices are:

$(y - 10)(y + 1) : -10y + y = -9y$, reject

$(y + 10)(y - 1) : 10y - y = +9y$, reject

$(y + 5)(y - 2) : 5y - 2y = +3y$, reject

$(y - 5)(y + 2)$: $-5y + 2y = -3y$, correct

Thus, $y^2 - 3y - 10 = (y - 5)(y + 2)$.

Factor the trinomial $2a^2 - 9a - 5$.

The possible choices are:

$(2a - 1)(a + 5) : -a + 10a = +9a$, reject

$(2a + 5)(a - 1) : 5a - 2a = +3a$, reject

$(2a - 5)(a + 1) : -5a + 2a = -3a$, reject

$(2a + 1)$: $(a - 5) : a - 10a = -9a$, correct

Thus, $2a^2 - 9a - 5 = (2a + 1)(a - 5)$.

PRACTICE

Factor the following trinomials:

1. $y^2 + 3y + 2$
2. $a^2 + 4a + 3$
3. $x^2 + 5x + 6$
4. $y^2 + 7y + 6$
5. $b^2 - 4b + 3$
6. $z^2 - 6z + 5$
7. $x^2 - x - 2$
8. $y^2 - 3y - 4$
9. $a^2 - a - 6$
10. $x^2 - 2x - 15$
11. $a^2 + 6a + 9$
12. $y^2 - 2y - 8$

ANSWERS

1. **$(y + 2)(y + 1)$**	7. **$(x - 2)(x + 1)$**
2. **$(a + 3)(a + 1)$**	8. **$(y - 4)(y + 1)$**
3. **$(x + 3)(x + 2)$**	9. **$(a - 3)(a + 2)$**
4. **$(y + 6)(y + 1)$**	10. **$(x - 5)(x + 3)$**
5. **$(b - 3)(b - 1)$**	11. **$(a + 3)(a + 3)$**
6. **$(z - 5)(z - 1)$**	12. **$(y - 4)(y + 2)$**

Solving Quadratic Equations by Factoring

A quadratic equation is an equation that can be written in the form $ax^2 + bx + c = 0$, where a, b, and c are constants and $c \neq 0$.
For example:

1. $x^2 - 6x + 8 = 0$
2. $3x^2 - x - 2 = 0$
3. $x^2 = 4x + 5$, which becomes $x^2 - 4x - 5 = 0$ when written in the form $ax^2 + bx + c = 0$
4. $x^2 - 9 = 0$, which is in the required form but has $b = 0$.

If a quadratic equation is written in the form $ax^2 + bx + c = 0$ and the left side of the equation can be factored, then the equation can readily be solved. In solving quadratic equations by factoring, we make use of the following properties of 0:

1. The product of 0 and any real number is 0. For example, $7 \times 0 = 0$, and $0 \times 0.3 = 0$. This property is called the *multiplication property of 0.*
2. If the product of two real numbers is 0, then at least one of these real numbers must be 0. For example, if $ab = 0$, then either $a = 0$ or $b = 0$, possibly both.

The method of solving quadratic equations by factoring is illustrated by the examples below.

EXAMPLES

If $x(x-3) = 0$, then $x = 0$ or $x - 3 = 0$. In the latter case, $x = 3$, so $x = 0$ or $x = 3$.

If $(x + 4)(x - 2) = 0$, then $x + 4 = 0$ (in which case $x = -4$) or $x - 2 = 0$ (in which case $x = 2$).

EXAMPLES

Solve the equation $x^2 - 2x - 15 = 0$.

When we factor the left side of this equation, we have $(x - 5)(x + 3) = 0$.

Since the product $(x - 5)(x + 3)$ is 0, at least one of the factors must be 0.

If $x - 5 = 0$, then $x = 5$.

If $x + 3 = 0$, then $x = -3$.

The solutions of the equation are 5 and -3. This is checked as follows.

Check for $x = 5$	Check for $x = -3$
$x^2 - 2x - 15 = 0$	$x^2 - 2x - 15 = 0$
$5^2 - 2(5) - 15 = 0$	$(-3)^2 - 2(-3) - 15 = 0$
$25 - 10 - 15 = 0$	$9 + 6 - 15 = 0$
$0 = 0$	$0 = 0$

Solve the equation $2x^2 + 7x - 4 = 0$.

When we factor the left side of the equation, we have $(2x - 1)(x + 4) = 0$.

If $2x - 1 = 0$	If $x + 4 = 0$
$2x = 1$	$x = -4$
$x = \frac{1}{2}$	

The solutions are $\frac{1}{2}$ and -4.

Check for $x = \frac{1}{2}$	Check for $x = -4$
	$2x^2 + 7x - 4 = 0$
$2x^2 + 7x - 4 = 0$	$2(-4)^2 + 7(-4) - 4 = 0$
$2\left(\frac{1}{2}\right)^2 + 7\left(\frac{1}{2}\right) - 4 = 0$	$2(16) - 28 - 4 = 0$
	$32 - 28 - 4 = 0$
$2\left(\frac{1}{4}\right) + \frac{7}{2} - 4 = 0$	$0 = 0$
$\frac{1}{2} + \frac{7}{2} - 4 = 0$	
$4 - 4 = 0$	

If $b = 0$, no factoring is necessary. We just solve the equation for x^2 as though x^2 were the variable; the solutions will then be the square root of the number or the negative of that square root.

EXAMPLES

$x^2 - 9 = 0$

If 9 is added to both sides, the result is $x^2 = 9$. Since the square root of 9 is 3, $x = 3$ or $x = -3$.

$3x^2 - 1 = 47$

Two steps are required to solve for x^2:

$$3x^2 - 1 = 47$$
$$3x^2 = 47 + 1 = 48$$
$$\frac{3x^2}{3} = \frac{48}{3}$$
$$x^2 = 16$$
$$x = 4 \text{ or } -4$$

PRACTICE

Solve and check each of the following equations:

1. $y^2 - 3y + 2 = 0$ y=1,2
2. $x^2 - 4x + 3 = 0$ x=1,3
3. $a^2 + 5a + 4 = 0$ a=-1,-4
4. $z^2 + 4z + 3 = 0$ z=-1,-3

5. $c^2 - 5c + 6 = 0$
6. $x^2 + x - 6 = 0$
7. $y^2 + 2y - 8 = 0$
8. $a^2 - a - 12 = 0$
9. $x^2 - 4x - 12 = 0$
10. $z^2 - z - 20 = 0$
11. $y^2 + 2y - 15 = 0$
12. $x^2 - 5x + 4 = 0$

ANSWERS

1. **2, 1**	7. **−4, 2**
2. **3, 1**	8. **4, −3**
3. **−4, −1**	9. **6, −2**
4. **−3, −1**	10. **5, −4**
5. **3, 2**	11. **−5, 3**
6. **−3, 2**	12. **4, 1**

Using Quadratic Equations to Solve Problems

Quadratic equations may be used to solve problems.

EXAMPLE

A room, rectangular in shape, is 5 feet longer than it is wide. If the area of the room is 300 square feet, find the dimensions of the room.

x — Area = 300 — $x + 5$

Let x = width, in feet, of the room.
Then $x + 5$ = length, in feet, of the room.

$$x(x + 5) = 300$$
$$x^2 + 5x = 300$$
$$x^2 + 5x - 300 = 0$$
$$(x - 15)(x + 20) = 0$$

If $x - 15 = 0$, $x = 15$
If $x + 20 = 0$, $x = -20$, which we must reject, since a length cannot be negative.

Thus, the width of the room is 15 ft., and the length is 15 + 5 = 20 ft.

Check: If the room is 20 ft. long and 15 ft. wide, the area of the room is 20 × 15 = 300 sq. ft.

PRACTICE

Solve the following problems:

1. A rectangular garden plot is 4 feet longer than it is wide. If the area of the garden plot is 96 square feet, what are the dimensions of the garden plot?
2. When the square of a positive number is added to the number, the result is 42. Find the number.
3. An auditorium has 192 seats. The number of seats in each row is 4 less than the number of rows. Find the number of seats in each row.
4. A sail is triangular in shape and has an area of 24 square feet. If the base of the sail is 2 feet greater than the altitude of the sail what is the altitude of the sail?
5. Take a positive whole number and square it. To this square add twice the original number. If the result is 99, find the original number.

ANSWERS

1. **12 ft. long, 8 ft. wide**
2. **6**
3. **12 seats in each row**
4. **6 ft.**
5. **9**

Probability

The *probability* that an event will occur is a number between 0 and 1, usually written as a fraction, which indicates how likely it is that the event will happen. For example, if a person spins the spinner pictured below, there are 4 possible outcomes and it is equally likely that the spinner will stop in any of the 4 regions.

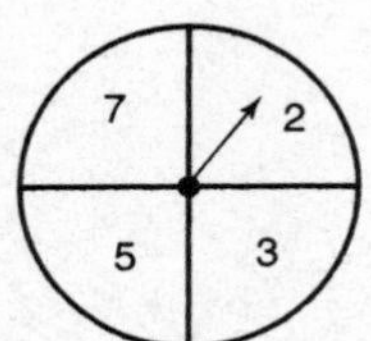

There is 1 chance in 4 that it will stop in the region marked 2, so we say that the probability of spinning a 2 is one-fourth and write $P(2) = \frac{1}{4}$. Since 2 is the only even number on the spinner, we can also say $P(\text{even}) = \frac{1}{4}$. There are 3 chances in 4 that the spinner will land in a region with an odd number in it, so $P(\text{odd}) = \frac{3}{4}$.

If *E* is any event, the probability that *E* will occur is given by

$$P(E) = \frac{\text{number of favorable outcomes}}{\text{total number of possible outcomes}},$$

assuming that all the possible outcomes are equally likely.

For the spinner shown above, each of the 4 regions is the same size, so it is equally likely that the spinner will land on the 2, 3, 5, or 7. Therefore,

$$P(\text{odd}) = \frac{\text{number of ways to get odd number}}{\text{number of possible outcomes}} = \frac{3}{4}.$$

We note that the probability of *not* getting an odd number is 1 minus the probability of getting an odd number: $1 - \frac{3}{4} = \frac{1}{4}$.

Let's look at some other probabilities associated with spinning this spinner once.

$$P(\text{number} > 10) = \frac{\text{number of ways to get a number} > 10}{\text{number of possible outcomes}} = \frac{0}{4} = 0$$

$$P(\text{prime number}) = \frac{\text{number of ways to get prime}}{\text{total number of possible outcomes}} = \frac{4}{4} = 1$$

$$P(\text{number} < 4) = \frac{\text{number of ways to get a number} < 4}{\text{total number of possible outcomes}} = \frac{2}{4} = \frac{1}{2}$$

The following box contains six important facts about probabilities.

FACTS ABOUT PROBABILITY

1. If event *E* is *impossible* (such as getting a number greater than 10), $P(E) = 0$.
2. If it is certain that event *E* will occur (such as getting a prime number), $P(E) = 1$.
3. In all cases $0 \le P(E) \le 1$.
4. The probability that event *E* will *not* occur is $1 - P(E)$.
5. If 2 or more events constitute all the outcomes, the sum of their probabilities is 1; for example:
$$P(\text{even}) + P(\text{odd}) = \frac{1}{4} + \frac{3}{4} = 1.$$
6. The more likely it is that an event will occur, the higher (the closer to 1) is its probability; the less likely it is that an event will occur, the lower (the closer to 0) its probability is.

Even though probability is defined as a fraction, we can also write probabilities as decimals or percents. Thus, instead of writing $P(E) = \frac{1}{2}$, we can write $P(E) = .50$ or $P(E) = 50\%$.

EXAMPLE

John has a blue tie, a red tie, a brown tie, and a gray tie. If John selects a tie at random, what is the probability that he selects a blue tie?

In selecting a tie John may select any 1 of 4 colors. Therefore, the probability that John selects a blue tie is $\frac{1}{4}$.

EXAMPLE

A football squad consists of 29 linemen and 15 backfield men. If 1 man on the squad is chosen to be captain, what is the probability that the man chosen is a lineman?

In all, there are 29 + 15, or 44 men on the squad. Of the 44 men, 29 are linemen. Therefore, the probability that the choice is a lineman is $\frac{29}{44}$.

EXAMPLE

Joan had 3 dimes and 2 quarters in her purse. If she selected a coin at random from her purse, what is the probability that the coin chosen was a nickel?

Since Joan did not have a nickel in her purse, it was impossible for her to have withdrawn a nickel. Therefore, the probability is 0.

EXAMPLE

A group of 8 senators are having a committee meeting. During the meeting 1 of them is called to the telephone. What is the probability that the person called to the telephone is a senator?

In this case, the 1 called to the telephone is part of the group of 8 senators. Thus it is certain that the person called to the telephone is a senator. The probability is 1.

PRACTICE

Solve the following problems:

1. Mr. Andrews had 2 blue suits, 3 gray suits, and 2 brown suits. If he selects a suit at random, what is the probability that
   a. he selects a gray suit?
   b. he selects a brown suit?
2. A purse contains 4 quarters, 3 dimes, and 5 pennies. If a coin is drawn at random from the purse, what is the probability that it is a penny?
3. A class has 17 boys and 15 girls. If the teacher calls on a member of the class to recite, what is the probability that the teacher calls on a girl?
4. There are ten digits in our system of numeration: 0, 1, 2, 3, 4, 5, 6, 7 8, 9. If we select a digit without looking, what is the probability that
   a. the digit is 7?
   b. the digit is an odd number?
   c. the digit is less than 10?
   d. the digit is greater than 12?
5. A jar contains 10 blue marbles, 9 red marbles, and 7 yellow marbles. If a marble is selected at random from the jar, what is the probability that the marble is
   a. red?
   b. yellow?
   c. not red?
6. A jar contains 15 green marbles. If 1 marble is drawn at random from the jar, what is the probability that the marble chosen is green?
7. A man has 5 white shirts, 4 blue shirts, and 3 gray shirts. One white shirt cannot be worn because it needs laundering. If the man chooses 1 of the other shirts what is the probability that he chooses a blue shirt?

   (1) $\frac{1}{5}$

   (2) $\frac{1}{4}$

   (3) $\frac{4}{7}$

   (4) $\frac{4}{11}$

   (5) $\frac{3}{11}$

8. A class consists of 16 boys and 12 girls. If a boy and a girl are absent, what is the probability that a girl is called upon to recite?

   (1) $\frac{12}{27}$

   (2) $\frac{11}{27}$

   (3) $\frac{11}{26}$

   (4) $\frac{12}{26}$

   (5) $\frac{11}{28}$

ANSWERS

1a. $\frac{3}{7}$	4a. $\frac{1}{10}$	5a. $\frac{9}{26}$	7. **(4)**
b. $\frac{2}{7}$	b. $\frac{1}{2}$	b. $\frac{7}{26}$	8. **(3)**
2. $\frac{5}{12}$	c. **1**	c. $\frac{17}{26}$	
3. $\frac{15}{32}$	c. **0**	6. **1**	

The Mean and the Median

The Mean (Average)

The ***average***, A, of a set of n numbers is the sum of those numbers divided by n:

$$A = \frac{\text{sum of the } n \text{ numbers}}{n}$$

Although the technical name for this quantity is the *mean* or *arithmetic mean*, you will almost always hear it referred to as the average.

EXAMPLE

Mary's grades on a series of tests in history were 75, 90, 80, 65, and 70. What was the average, or mean, of Mary's grades?

To find the average, first add the scores:

$$75 + 90 + 80 + 65 + 70 = 380$$

Then divide this sum by the number of scores, namely, 5:

$$380 \div 5 = 76$$

The average of Mary's grades was 76.

Often on the GED Examination, you are *not* asked to find an average: rather, you are given the average of a set of numbers and asked for some other information. The key to solving such problems is to first find the sum of the numbers. Since $A = \frac{\text{sum}}{n}$, multiplying both sides by n yields

$$\text{sum} = nA$$

EXAMPLE

One day a truck driver picked up 20 packages whose average weight was 14.3 pounds. What was the total weight of all the packages?

Just multiply: $20 \times 14.3 = 286$ lb.

Note: You are not told how much any individual package weighed or how many packages weighed more or less than 14.3 pounds. All you know is the total weight.

EXAMPLE

In its first 5 games the Cardinal Basketball Team scored 58, 49, 62, 53, and 41 points. How many points must the team score in its sixth game to achieve an average score of 56 points per game?

To average 56 points per game, the team needs a total of $6 \times 56 = 336$ points. In its first 5 games it earned

$$58 + 49 + 62 + 53 + 41 = 263 \text{ points.}$$

Therefore, in the sixth game the team needs to score $336 - 263 = 73$ points.

EXAMPLE

John took 5 English tests during the first marking period, and his average was 85. If his average after the first 3 tests was 83, what was the average of his fourth and fifth tests?

On his 5 tests John earned $5 \times 85 = 425$ points. On his first 3 tests he earned $3 \times 83 = 249$ points. Therefore, on his last 2 tests, John earned $425 - 249 = 176$ points. His average on those last 2 tests was $176 \div 2 = 88$ points.

EXAMPLE

In an office there are four clerks, each of whom receives a salary of $300 per week, and an office manager who receives a salary of $950 per week. What is the mean salary earned by this office staff?

To find the mean of the salaries, find the sum and divide it by 5.

$$(300 + 300 + 300 + 300 + 950) \div 5 = 2{,}150 \div 5 = 430$$

Thus, the mean salary of the staff is $430.

In the above example, the mean salary does not fairly represent the situation. Only one person receives a salary above the mean of $430, whereas four people receive salaries well below the mean. To avoid having one or two extreme scores creating a misleading impression about a set of data, we often use another measure, called the *median*.

The Median

When we arrange a set of numbers in increasing or decreasing order, the number in the middle is the *median*.

EXAMPLE

The weights, in pounds, of the starting team of the Madison football team are 186, 195, 207, 173, 192, 201, 236, 228, 198, 215, and 179. What is the median weight of the members of this team?

Arrange the weights in decreasing order, starting with the heaviest.

236, 228, 215, 207, 201, 198, 195, 192, 186, 179, 173

median

Listing the weights in increasing order, starting with the lightest, will yield the same result.

Note: In all cases where there is an even number of scores, there will be two middle scores. To find the median, take the average of the two middle scores.

EXAMPLE

Find the median of the following set of numbers:

47, 56, 79, 83, 45, 64, 72, 53

First, arrange the numbers in order:

83, 79, 72, 64, 56, 53, 47, 45

In this case, there are two middle numbers (64 and 56). To find the median, take the average of these numbers:

$(64 + 56) \div 2 = 120 \div 2 = 60.$

The median is 60.

PRACTICE

1. David's marks on six science tests were 85, 70, 75, 90, 95, and 65. Find his test average.
2. Mr. Woods is a salesman working on a commission basis. His daily earnings for one week were $79, $86, $94, $81, and $70. Find the average of Mr. Woods's daily earnings.
3. The heights of the members of a professional basketball squad, in inches, were 75, 78, 82, 81, 76, 80, and 77. Find the median height of the members of this team.
4. During a special sale on TV sets the number of sales for six days were 124, 96, 87, 91, 58, and 47. Find the median number of sales.
5. Andrea's marks on six mathematics tests were 83, 74, 68, 85, 91, and 78. What mark must she get on a seventh test in order to obtain an average of 80 for the seven tests?
6. Find the mean for each of the following sets of numbers:
   a. 102, 86, 79, 115, 94, 82
   b. 17, 29, 43, 38, 51, 31, 49, 30
   c. 41, 52, 39, 68, 27, 59, 46, 53, 38
7. Find the median for each of the following sets of numbers:
   a. 63, 42, 59, 37, 64, 87, 51
   b. 105, 69, 94, 38, 112, 96, 83, 97, 38
   c. 24, 36, 29, 18, 31, 37, 27, 35
8. The average weekly earnings of John, Frank, and Fred are $360. If John earns $375 per week, and Frank earns $350 per week, what are Fred's weekly earnings?

ANSWERS

1. **80**	4. **89**	6b. **36**	7b. **94**
2. **$82**	5. **81**	6c. **47**	7c. **30**
3. **78**	6a. **93**	7a. **59**	8. **$355**

20 Geometry: Worked-Out Examples and Practice

Points, Lines, and Space

By a *point* in geometry we mean a definite location in space. A point has no length, width, or thickness. We usually name a point with a capital letter.

When we use the word *line* in geometry, we always mean a straight line. Moreover, a line extends infinitely, in either direction. For this reason, arrows are frequently shown on a line, as follows:

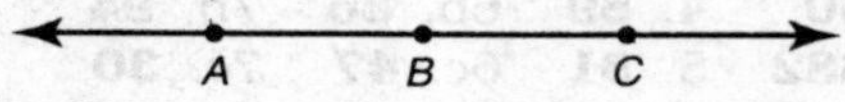

We can think of a line as a special set of points. A line is usually named by indicating two points on the line and adding an overhead double-arrowed symbol. For example, the line above could be named $\overleftrightarrow{AB}$, or $\overleftrightarrow{BA}$ or, $\overleftrightarrow{AC}$, and so on.

A *segment*, or *line segment*, consists of two points on a line, together with points between those two points. The two points are called the *endpoints* of the segment. We usually name a segment by indicating the endpoints and placing a bar above. For example, the segment below could be called $\overline{CD}$ or $\overline{DC}$.

In geometry, a *ray* consists of a point, *A*, on a line, together with all of the points on that line that are on the same side of *A*. Point *A* is called the *endpoint* of the ray. We name a ray by indicating its endpoint and another point on the ray with an overhead arrow symbol. For example, the ray shown below is called $\overrightarrow{AE}$ or $\overrightarrow{AF}$.

We can think of a *plane* in geometry as a set of points making up a perfectly flat surface. A plane is suggested by the floor of a room or the cover of a book.

By *space*, in geometry we mean the set of all points in three dimensions.

Geometric Figures

Geometric figures may be classified in two groups, plane figures and solid figures. *If all the points of a figure lie in the same plane, it is called a plane figure. If the points of a figure lie in more than one plane, the figure is called a solid figure.* Below are diagrams of some important plane and solid figures.

PLANE FIGURES

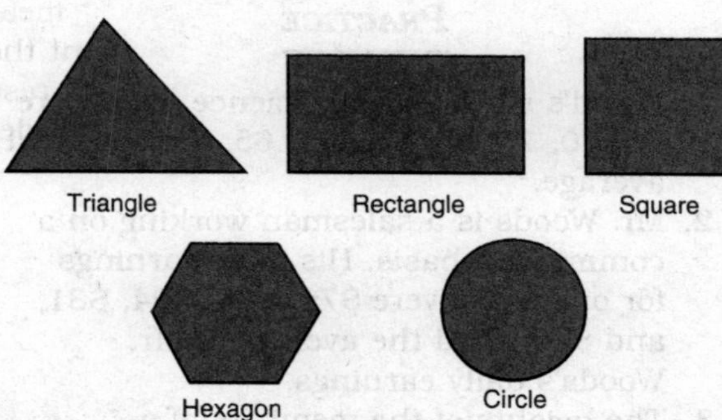

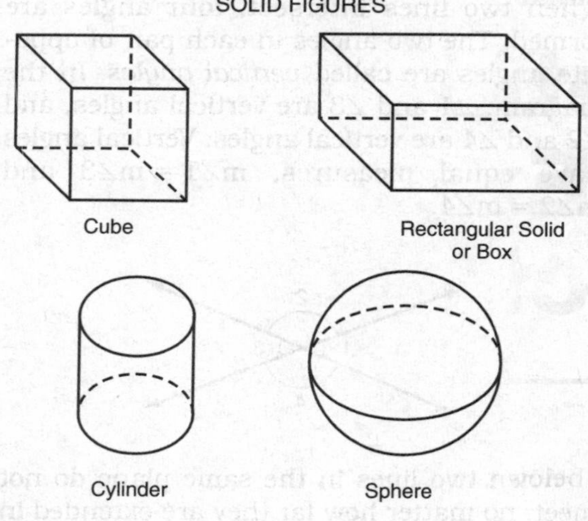

Geometric Concepts and Relationships

Angles

An *angle* is a set of points consisting of two rays having the same endpoint. For example, rays $\overrightarrow{AB}$ and $\overrightarrow{AC}$ having the same endpoint, *A*, form the angle shown below. We name an angle by indicating a point on one ray, then the common endpoint, and finally a point on the other ray. The symbol for angle is ∠. The angle shown may be called ∠*BAC* or ∠*CAB*. When there is no ambiguity in meaning, an angle may be named by indicating only its *vertex*, the endpoint of the two rays that form its sides. Thus, ∠*BAC* may be called ∠*A*.

On the GED Mathematics test, angles are always measured in degrees. As shown in the box headed "Basics on Angles," angles are classified according to their degree of measures. We use the letter "m" to represent the measure of an angle; for example, to express the fact that the measure of ∠*BAC* is 45 degrees, we write m∠*BAC* = 45°.

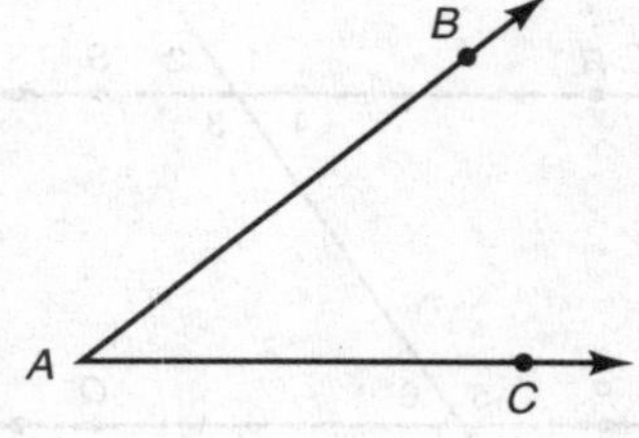

BASICS ON ANGLES

An *acute angle* is an angle whose measure is less than 90°. ∠*RST* is an acute angle: m∠*RST* < 90°.

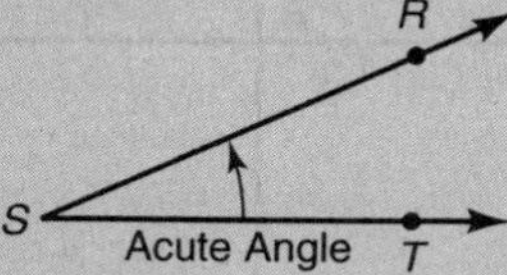

A *right angle* is an angle whose measure is 90°. ∠*VWX* is a right angle: m∠*VWX* = 90°. A small square drawn in an angle *always* means that the angle is a right angle.

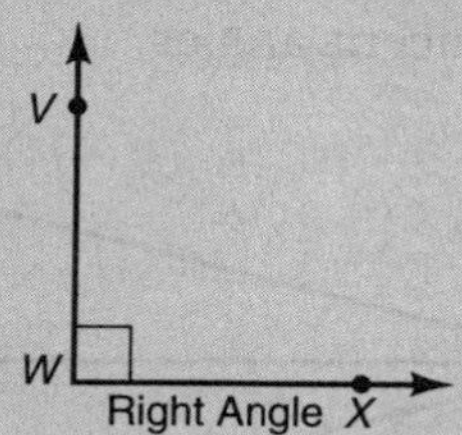

An *obtuse angle* is an angle whose measure is greater than 90° and less than 180°. ∠*OFG* is an obtuse angle: 90° < m∠*OFG*<180°

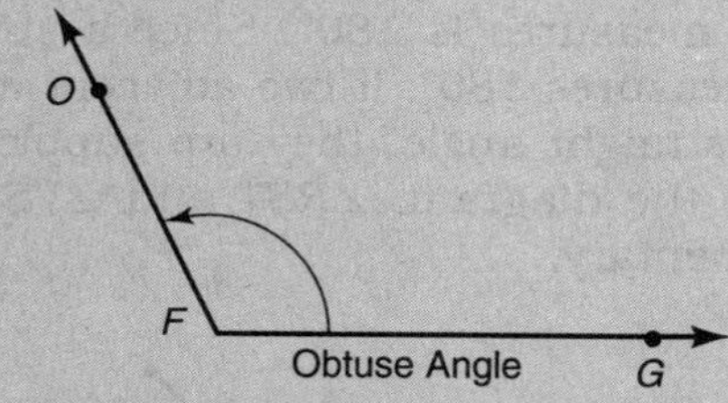

A *straight angle* is an angle whose measure is 180°. ∠*LOC* is a straight angle: m∠*LOC* = 180°

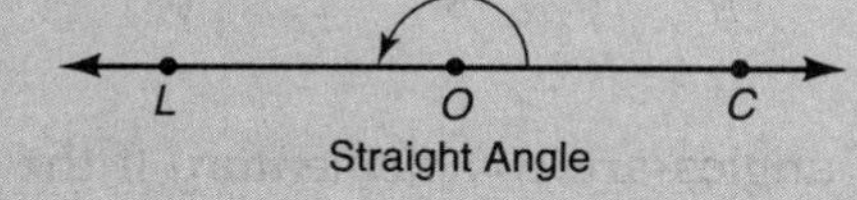

When two lines meet to form right angles, we say that the lines are *perpendicular* to each other. The symbol ⊥ is used to indicate perpendicular lines. In the diagram, $\overleftrightarrow{DE}$ is perpendicular to $\overleftrightarrow{BC}$; this may be expressed as $\overleftrightarrow{DE} \perp \overleftrightarrow{BC}$. The four right angles formed are ∠*DAB*, ∠*DAC*, ∠*EAB*, and ∠*EAC*.

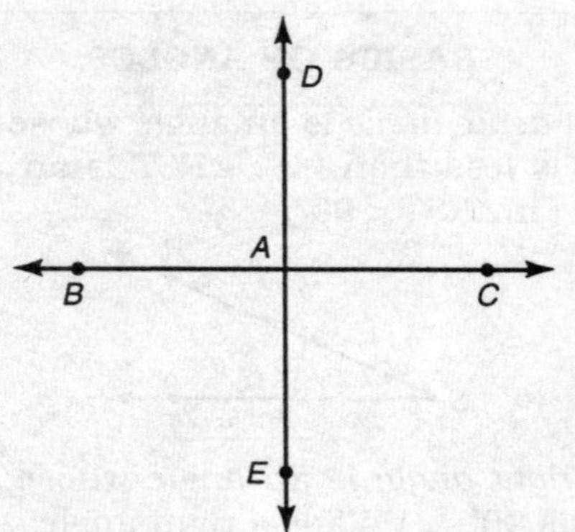

Two angles are *adjacent* if they have the same vertex and have a common side between them. In the diagram, ∠*ABC* and ∠*DBC* are adjacent angles.

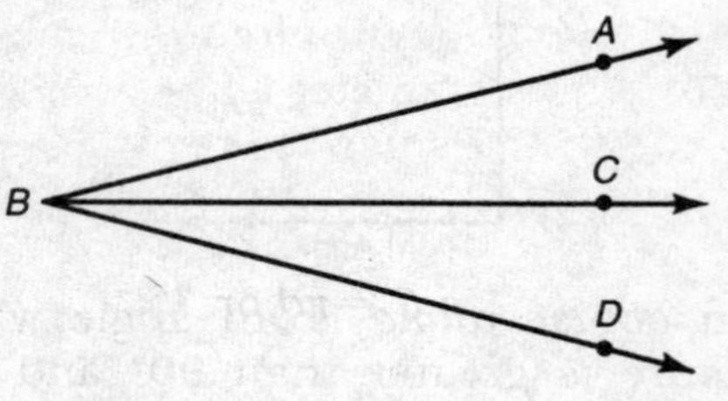

Two angles are *supplementary* if the sum of their measures is 180°. Since a straight angle measures 180°, if two adjacent angles form a straight angle, they are supplementary. In the diagram, ∠*RST* and ∠*VST* are supplementary.

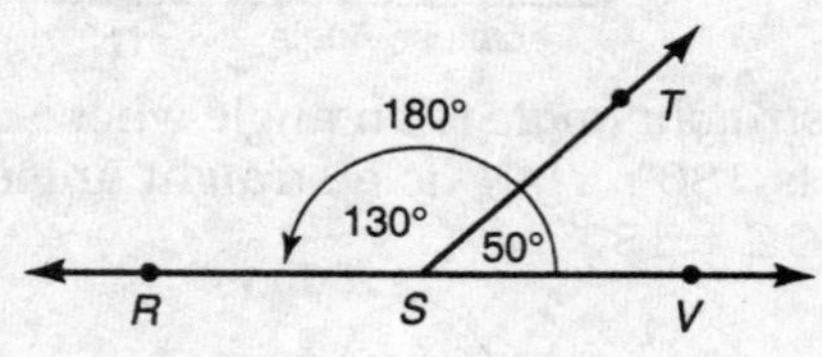

Two angles are *complementary* if the sum of their measures is 90°. In the diagram, since m∠*ABC* = 90°, ∠*ABE* and ∠*CBE* are complementary.

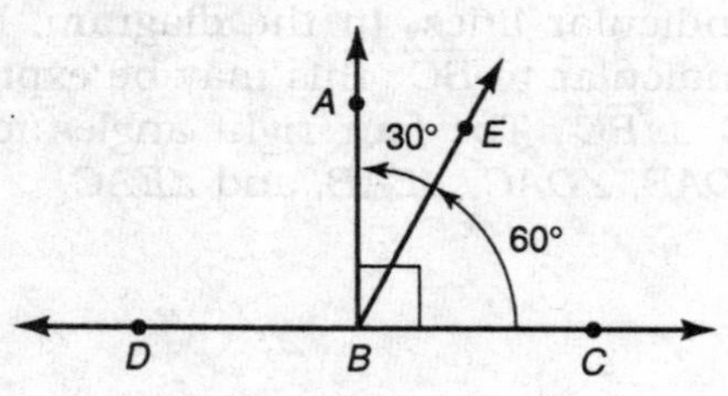

When two lines intersect, four angles are formed. The two angles in each pair of opposite angles are called *vertical angles*. In the diagram, ∠1 and ∠3 are vertical angles, and ∠2 and ∠4 are vertical angles. Vertical angles have equal measures, m∠1 = m∠3 and m∠2 = m∠4.

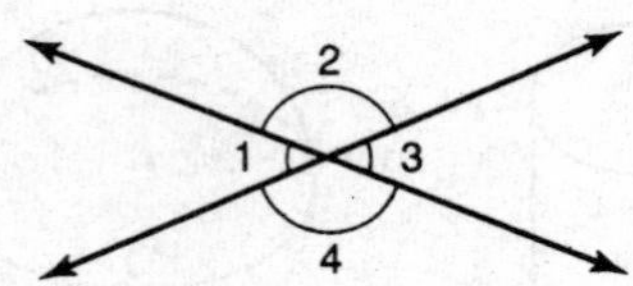

When two lines in the same plane do not meet, no matter how far they are extended in either direction, the lines are said to be *parallel* to each other. The symbol || is used to indicate parallel lines.

In the diagram below, $\overleftrightarrow{RS} \parallel \overleftrightarrow{PQ}$.

Since parallel lines don't intersect, they form no angles. However, if a third line, called a *transversal*, intersects a pair of parallel lines, eight angles are formed, and the relationships between these angles are very important.

If the transversal is perpendicular to the parallel lines, all eight angles are right angles, and so, of course, have the same measure: 90°. If, however, the transversal is not perpendicular to the parallel lines, as in the diagram below, four of the angles are acute and four are obtuse; and the following important relationships hold:

1. All four acute angles are equal: m∠2 = m∠4 = m∠6 = m∠8
2. All four obtuse angles are equal: m∠1 = m∠3 = m∠5 = m∠7
3. The sum of the measures of any acute angle and any obtuse angle is 180°: for example, m∠6 + m∠5 = 180° and m∠3 + m∠8 = 180°.

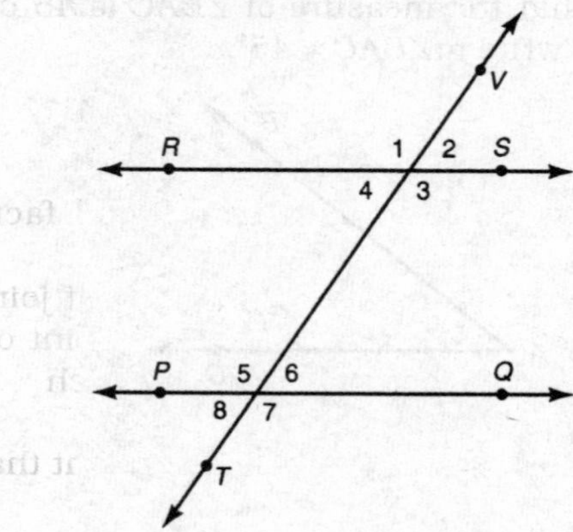

EXAMPLE

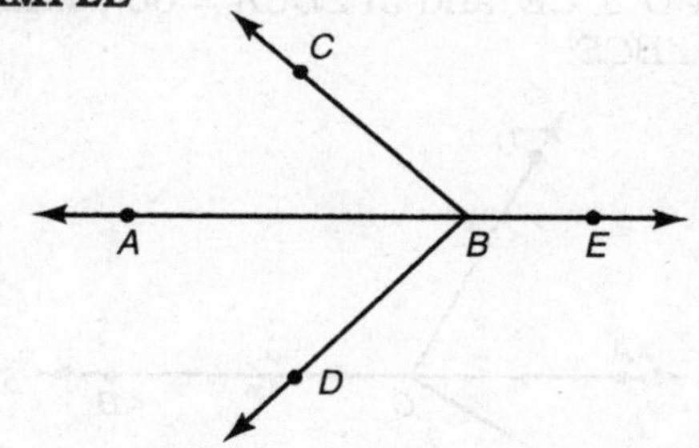

If $\overleftrightarrow{CB} \perp \overleftrightarrow{BD}$ and the measure of $\angle CBA$ = 38°, find the measure of $\angle DBE$.

Since $\overleftrightarrow{CB} \perp \overleftrightarrow{BD}$, $m\angle CBA + m\angle ABD = 90°$.
Then $38° + m\angle ABD = 90°$,
and $m\angle ABD = 90° - 38° = 52°$.
$m\angle ABD + m\angle DBE = 180°$
Then $52° + m\angle DBE = 180°$,
and $m\angle DBE = 180° - 52° = 128°$.

EXAMPLE

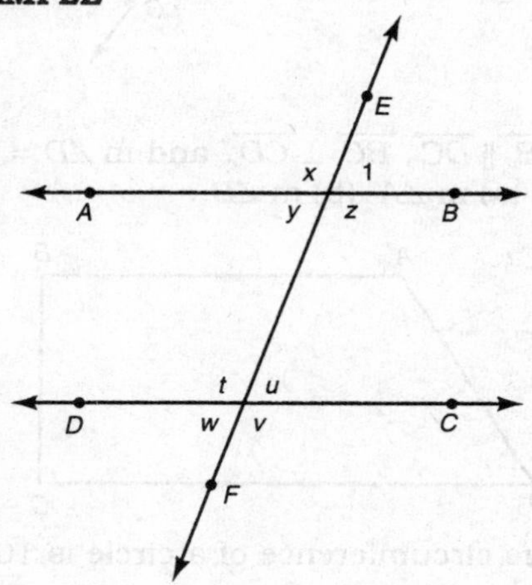

If $\overleftrightarrow{AB} \parallel \overleftrightarrow{CD}$ and $m\angle 1 = 70°$, find $m\angle x$, $m\angle y$, $m\angle z$, $m\angle v$, and $m\angle w$.

Since $m\angle x + m\angle 1 = 180°$,
$m\angle x = 180 - 70° = 110°$.
The measure of each acute angle is 70°:
$m\angle 1 = m\angle y = m\angle u = m\angle w = 70°$,
and the measure of each obtuse angle is 110°:
$m\angle x = m\angle z = m\angle t = m\angle v = 110°$.

Circles

Here are some important terms and facts that you need to know about circles.

A *radius* of a circle is a line segment joining the center of the circle and any point on the circle. In the following diagram, each of $\overline{OA}$, $\overline{OC}$, and $\overline{OD}$ is a radius.

A *diameter* of a circle is a line segment that passes through the center of the circle and has its two endpoints on the circle. $\overline{CD}$ is a diameter. The length of the diameter is twice the length of the radius: $d = 2r$.

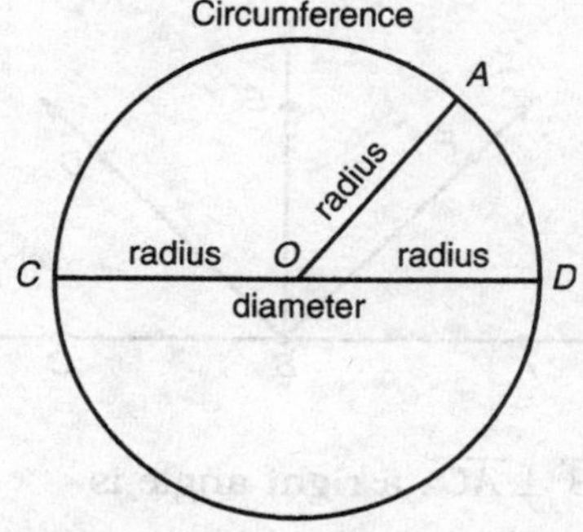

The *circumference* of a circle is the distance around the circle. In all circles, the ratio of the length of the circumference to the length of the diameter is the same. The Greek letter π (pi) is used to represent this ratio: $\pi = \frac{C}{d}$. Multiplying both sides of this equation by d gives $C = \pi d$ or, since $d = 2r$, $C = \pi(2r) = 2\pi r$.

The approximate value of π is 3.14; a slightly less accurate approximation is $\frac{22}{7}$.

BASICS ON CIRCLES

Let r, d, and C represent the radius, diameter and circumference of a circle. Then

$$\mathbf{d = 2r}$$

$$\pi = \frac{C}{d}$$

$$C = \pi d = 2\pi r$$

EXAMPLE

If the diameter of a circle is 12 inches, what is its circumference, in inches?

Use the formula $C = \pi d$:

$$C = \pi(12) = 12\pi \text{ in.}$$

This is approximately 12(3.14) = 37.68 in.

PRACTICE

Questions 1 and 2 refer to the following diagram.

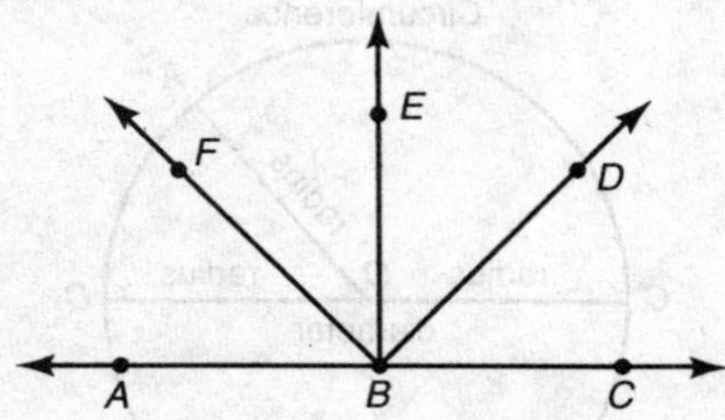

1. If $\overleftrightarrow{EB} \perp \overleftrightarrow{AC}$, a right angle is

   (1) ∠FBA
   (2) ∠DBF
   (3) ∠CBE
   (4) ∠EBD
   (5) ∠ABC

2. An obtuse angle is

   (1) ∠EBA
   (2) ∠DBE
   (3) ∠CBA
   (4) ∠FBC
   (5) ∠EBC

3. The diameter of a circle is 30 inches in length. The length of the radius of the same circle is

   (1) 60 in.
   (2) 60π in.
   (3) 15 in.
   (4) 15π in.
   (5) $7\frac{1}{2}$ in.

4. The diameter of a circle is 20 inches. If π = 3.14, the circumference of the circle, in inches, is

   (1) 3.14
   (2) 62.8
   (3) 3.4
   (4) 6.28
   (5) 31.4

5. If $\overleftrightarrow{CD} \perp \overleftrightarrow{CE}$ and m ∠DCA = 60°, find m ∠BCE.

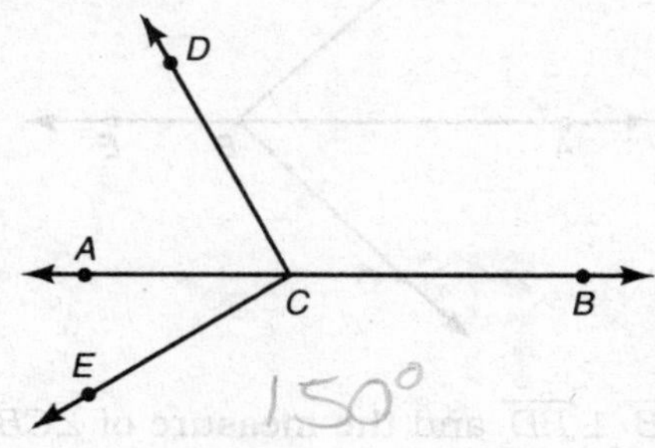

6. If $\overleftrightarrow{AB} \parallel \overleftrightarrow{DE}$, BC bisects ∠ABD, and m ∠ABC = 62°, find m∠BDE.

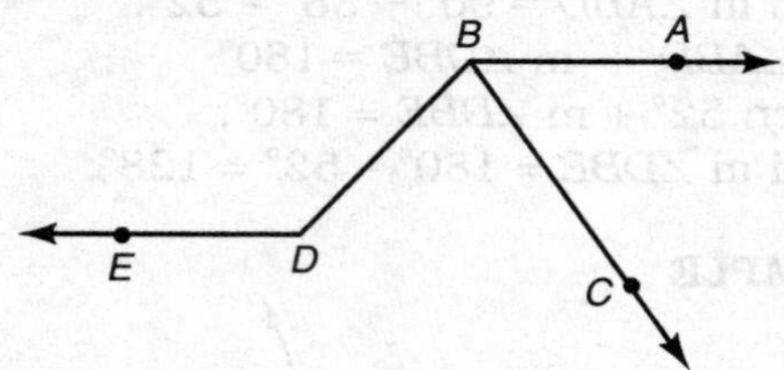

7. If $\overleftrightarrow{AB} \parallel \overleftrightarrow{DC}$, $\overleftrightarrow{BC} \perp \overleftrightarrow{CD}$, and m ∠D = 68°, find (a) m ∠A (b) m ∠B.

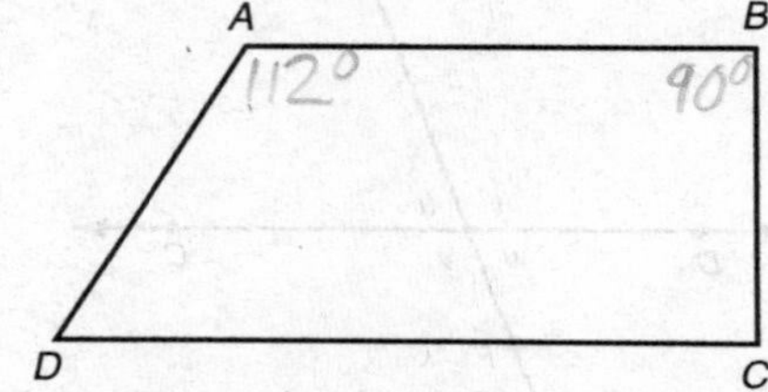

8. If the circumference of a circle is 10, what is its radius? $\frac{5}{\pi}$

ANSWERS

1. **3**	4. **2**	7. **112°, 90°**
2. **4**	5. **150°**	8. $\mathbf{\frac{5}{\pi}}$
3. **3**	6. **124°**	

Triangles

More geometry questions on the GED Mathematics test concern triangles than any other figure. The following box contains several important facts about triangles.

BASICS ON TRIANGLES

The sum of the measures of the three angles in any triangle is 180°.

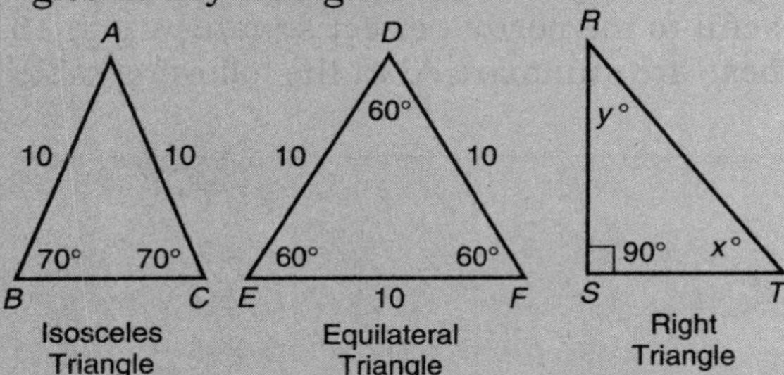

A triangle that has two sides of equal length is called an *isosceles triangle.* The two angles opposite the equal sides are called *base* angles; their measures are equal. The third angle is called a *vertex* angle. $\triangle ABC$ is isosceles.

A triangle in which all three sides have the same length is called an *equilateral triangle*. Each of the three angles measures 60°. $\triangle DEF$ is equilateral.

A *right triangle* is a triangle that has one right angle. $\triangle RST$ is a right triangle; $\angle RST$ is the right angle. The other two angles are acute, and the sum of their measures is 90°: $x + y = 90$. The longest side (RT), which is opposite the 90° angle, is called the *hypotenuse*; the other two sides (RS and ST) are *legs*.

EXAMPLE

If each base angle of an isosceles triangle measures $x°$, what is an expression for the measure of the third angle?

Let x = measure of each base angle,
and y = measure of the third angle.
Then $180° = x + x + y = 2x + y$
and $y = (180 - 2x)°$.

PRACTICE

1. If two angles of a triangle measure 65° and 79°, the measure of the third angle is

(1) 56°
(2) 144°
(3) 115°
(4) 36°
(5) 101°

2. One acute angle of a right triangle measures $n°$. The other acute angle measures

(1) $2n°$
(2) $(90 - n)°$
(3) 90°
(4) $(90 + n)°$
(5) $(180 - n)°$

3. If the vertex angle of an isosceles triangle measures 102°, what is the measure of each base angle?

(1) 78°
(2) 34°
(3) 39°
(4) 49°
(5) 35°

4. The measures of the two acute angles of a right triangle are in the ratio 2 : 3. The smallest angle of the triangle measures

(1) 36°
(2) 54°
(3) 30°
(4) 70°
(5) 24°

ANSWER KEY

1. **4** 2. **2** 3. **3** 4. **1**

Indirect Measurement

If we wish to measure a length, we ordinarily use a ruler. However, this is not practicable if we wish to find the height of a mountain or the distance across a river. Such measurements are made indirectly. In this section, we will discuss one very important method of indirect measurement.

EXAMPLE

A nature group hikes 8 miles east and then 6 miles north. How many miles is the group from its starting point?

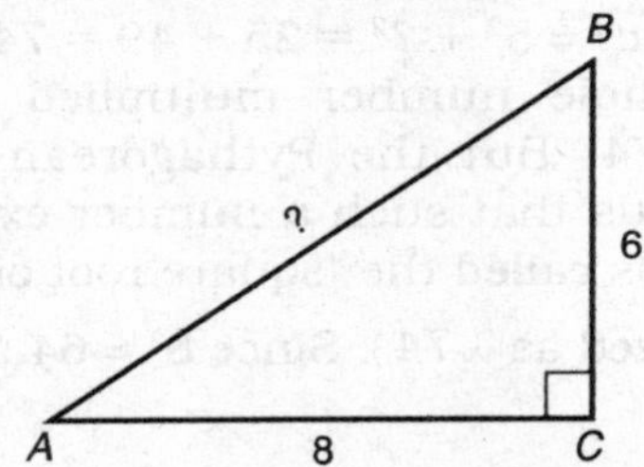

If you look at the diagram, you see that the triangle formed by the hikers is a right triangle. To solve the problem, you may make use of a well-known property of right triangles that is stated in the *Pythagorean theorem.*

Pythagorean Theorem

Let *a*, *b*, and *c* be the sides of $\triangle ABC$, with $a \le b \le c$. If $\triangle ABC$ is a right triangle, then $a^2 + b^2 = c^2$; conversely if $a^2 + b^2 = c^2$, then $\triangle ABC$ is a right triangle.

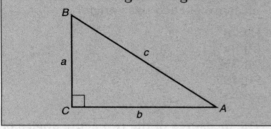

To solve the problem about the hikers, let c = the length of the side opposite $\angle c$, and use the Pythagorean theorem:

$$c^2 = 6^2 + 8^2 = 36 + 64 = 100$$

The equation $c^2 = 100$ asks the question, "What number multiplied by itself is equal to 100?" The number that makes this statement true is $c = 10$. Thus, the nature group is 10 mi. from its starting point.

EXAMPLE

Next, suppose that the nature group had hiked 7 miles east and then 5 miles north. How many miles would the group be from the starting point?

Draw a diagram, and use the Pythagorean theorem.

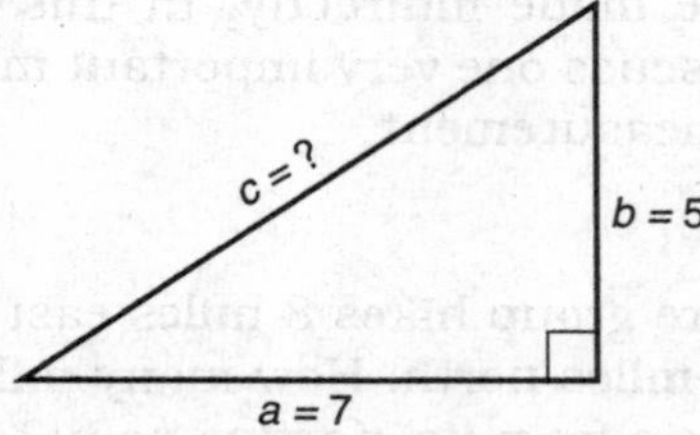

$$c^2 = 5^2 + 7^2 = 25 + 49 = 74$$

No whole number multiplied by itself equals 74. But the Pythagorean theorem assures us that such a number exists. This number is called the "square root of 74" (symbolized as $\sqrt{74}$). Since $8^2 = 64$ and $9^2 = 81$, $\sqrt{74}$ is a number between 8 and 9.

A whole number multiplied by itself is called a *perfect square.* Thus the square roots of perfect squares are whole numbers. It is useful to memorize perfect squares up to 15. These are summarized in the following table:

$1^2 = 1$	$\sqrt{1} = 1$
$2^2 = 4$	$\sqrt{4} = 2$
$3^2 = 9$	$\sqrt{9} = 3$
$4^2 = 16$	$\sqrt{16} = 4$
$5^2 = 25$	$\sqrt{25} = 5$
$6^2 = 36$	$\sqrt{36} = 6$
$7^2 = 49$	$\sqrt{49} = 7$
$8^2 = 64$	$\sqrt{64} = 8$
$9^2 = 81$	$\sqrt{81} = 9$
$10^2 = 100$	$\sqrt{100} = 10$
$11^2 = 121$	$\sqrt{121} = 11$
$12^2 = 144$	$\sqrt{144} = 12$
$13^2 = 169$	$\sqrt{169} = 13$
$14^2 = 196$	$\sqrt{196} = 14$
$15^2 = 225$	$\sqrt{225} = 15$

There are special right triangles, called *Pythagorean triples*, in which the lengths of all three sides are whole numbers. Two of these triangles appear frequently in problems and, therefore, should be memorized:

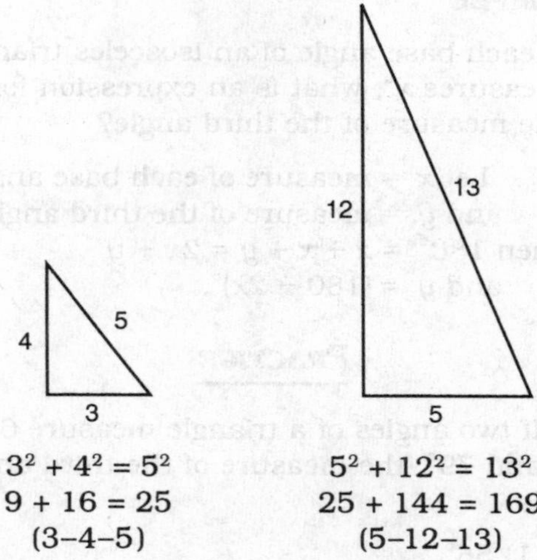

$3^2 + 4^2 = 5^2$
$9 + 16 = 25$
(3–4–5)

$5^2 + 12^2 = 13^2$
$25 + 144 = 169$
(5–12–13)

Multiples of these are also Pythagorean triples. For example, a triangle with side lengths 6, 8, and 10, or 10, 24, and 26, is also a right triangle.

EXAMPLE

A ladder 13 feet long leans against a building and reaches the ledge of a window. If the foot of the ladder is 5 feet from the foot of the building, how high, in feet, is the window ledge?

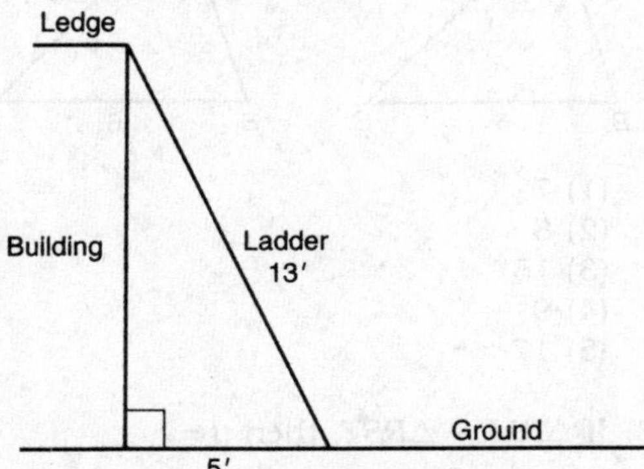

You can see that the ladder, the side of the building, and the ground form a right triangle. Two sides of the right triangle are known: 5 and 13. Therefore the third side—the height of the ledge—is 12.

EXAMPLE

A farmer is making a rectangular gate 6 feet high and 8 feet wide. How long, in feet, is the diagonal piece that he uses to strengthen the gate?

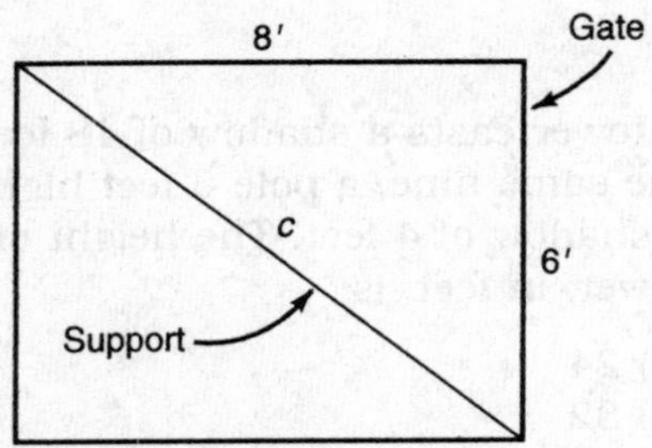

A right triangle is formed by the supporting piece and two of the sides having lengths of 6 ft. and 8 ft. Therefore, the length of the third side of this right triangle is 10 ft. because 6, 8, and 10 are twice 3, 4, and 5. If you don't immediately recognize the 6–8–10 right triangle, use the Pythagorean theorem: $c^2 = 6^2 + 8^2 = 36 + 64 = 100$, so $c = 10$.

Congruence and Similarity

Two geometric figures are said to be *congruent* if they have exactly the same size and the same shape. The symbol for congruence is ≅. The two triangles shown in the diagram below are congruent; that is, $\triangle ABC \cong \triangle DEF$. Since congruent triangles can be made to fit if one is placed on top of the other, corresponding sides have the same length. Also, corresponding angles of congruent triangles have the same measure. For example, in the diagram $AB = DE$, $AC = DF$, $BC = EF$, $m\angle A = m\angle D$, $m\angle B = m\angle E$, and $m\angle C = m\angle F$. Congruent triangles can be used to make measurements indirectly.

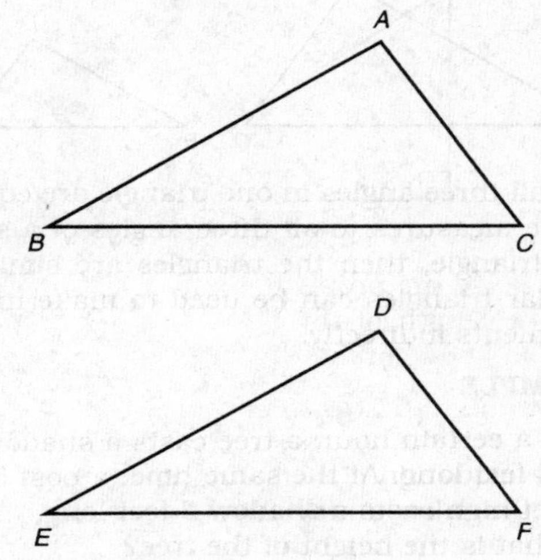

EXAMPLE

Find the distance *(DE)* across the river shown in the diagram.

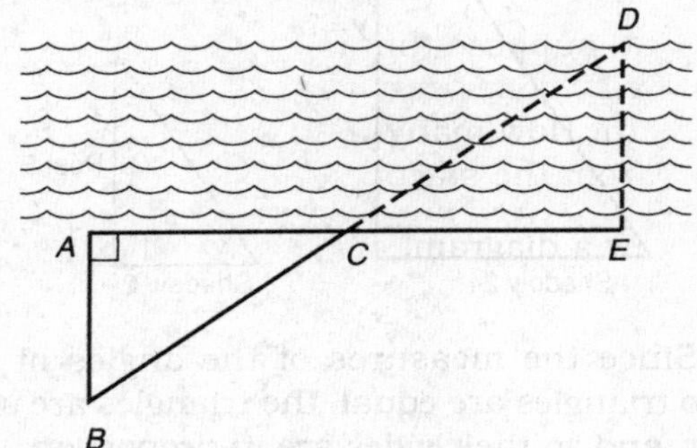

At point *E*, sight a point, *D*, on the other bank of the river. Measure *EA* at right angles to *ED*. At *C*, the midpoint of *EA*, set a stake. Then mark off distance *AB* so that $\angle A$ is a right angle and point *B* lines up with points *C* and *D*. It can be shown that $\triangle BAC \cong \triangle DEC$ and that *AB* and *DE* are corresponding sides. Thus, distance *AB*, which can be measured, is equal to *DE*, the distance across the river.

Two geometric figures are said to be *similar* if they have the same shape. Because similar figures have the same shape, their corresponding angles have equal measures and the lengths of their corresponding sides are in proportion. The symbol for similarity is ~. The two triangles shown in the following diagram are similar; that is, $\triangle ABC \sim \triangle DEF$. Since the lengths of corresponding sides of similar triangles are in proportion:

$$\frac{AB}{DC} = \frac{AC}{DF} = \frac{BC}{EF}$$

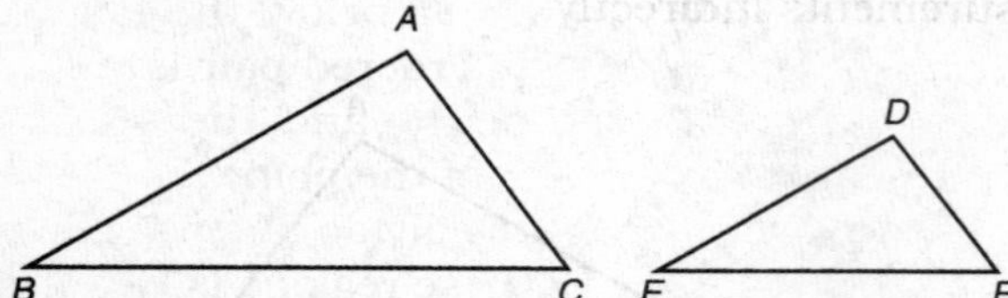

If all three angles in one triangle are equal to the measures to all three angles of a second triangle, then the triangles are similar. Similar triangles can be used to make measurements indirectly.

EXAMPLE

At a certain hour, a tree casts a shadow 24 feet long. At the same time, a post 5 feet high casts a shadow 2 feet long. What is the height of the tree?

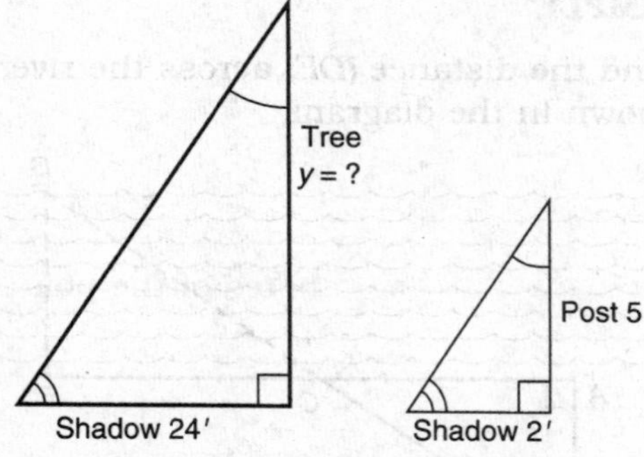

Since the measures of the angles of the two triangles are equal, the triangles are similar, and so their sides are in proportion.

$$\frac{y}{5} = \frac{24}{2}$$

$$2y = 120$$

$$y = \frac{120}{2} = 60$$

The tree is 60 ft. high.

PRACTICE

1. If $\triangle ABC \cong \triangle DEF$, then $x =$

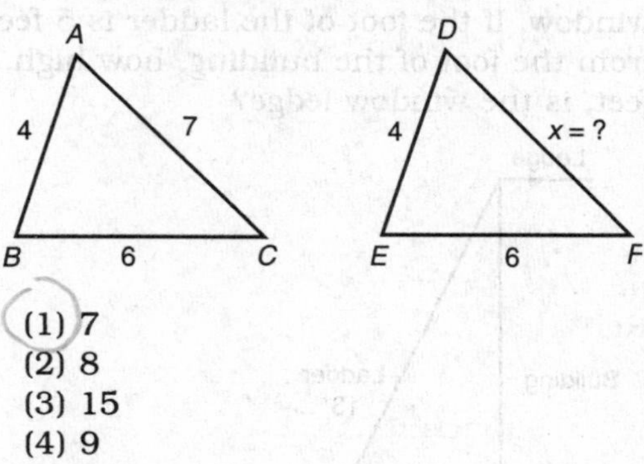

(1) 7
(2) 8
(3) 15
(4) 9
(5) 17

2. If $\triangle KLP \sim \triangle RST$, then $y =$

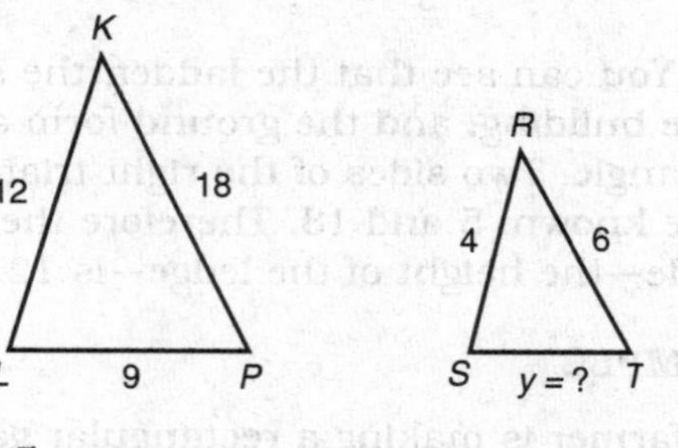

(1) 5
(2) 7
(3) 8
(4) 12
(5) 3

3. A tower casts a shadow of 48 feet. At the same time, a pole 6 feet high casts a shadow of 4 feet. The height of the tower, in feet, is

(1) 24
(2) 32
(3) 96
(4) 72
(5) 64

ANSWER KEY

1. **1** 2. **5** 3. **4**

Coordinate Geometry

There are times when we find it convenient to use pairs of numbers to locate points. For example, suppose you make an appointment to meet a friend. We might say, "Meet me at the corner of 5th Avenue and 3rd Street." We write this number pair as (5,3), where it is understood that the first number (5) indicates the avenue and the second number (3) locates the street of the meeting. On the other hand, if we wrote (3,5), we would mean that the meeting place is the corner of 3rd Avenue and 5th Street. The order in which the numbers are written is important. For this reason, such pairs of numbers are called *ordered number pairs*.

Recall that we can locate points on the number line. For example:

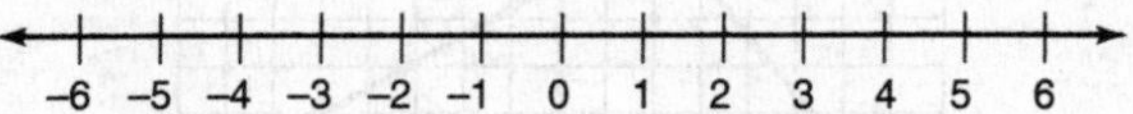

However, we may wish to locate points in the plane that are *not* on the number line. To do this, we use two number lines that are perpendicular to each other as shown below:

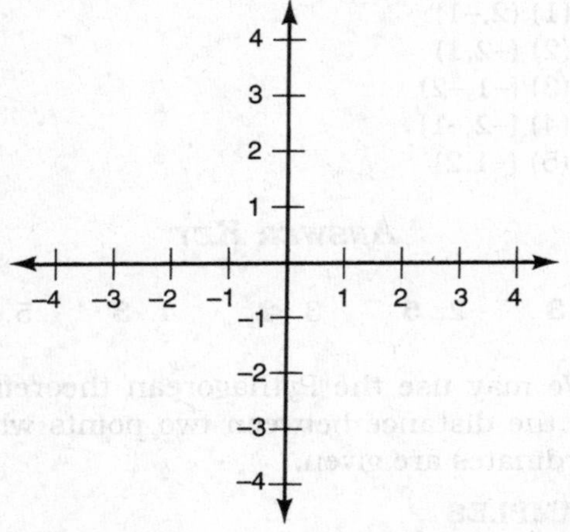

In this case, the horizontal number line is called the *x*-axis, and the vertical number line is the *y*-axis. For convenience in locating points, we draw lines parallel to the axes to form a graph chart as shown:

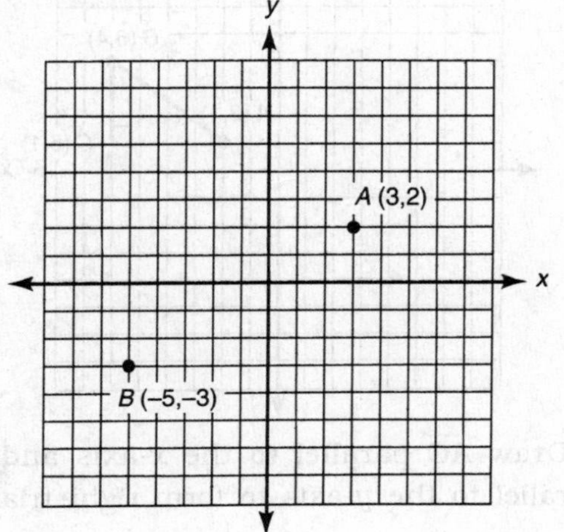

Consider point *A*. We locate point *A* in the plane by using the number pair (3,2). This indicates that point *A* is 3 units to the right of the *y*-axis and 2 units above the *x*-axis.

Consider point *B*. Point *B* is 5 units to the left of the *y*-axis and 3 units below the *x*-axis. Its number pair is (–5,–3).

To avoid confusion, we agree that the first number of the ordered pair will indicate the number of units to the right or left of the *y*-axis and the second number will indicate the number of units above or below the *x*-axis. The first number of the ordered pair is called the *abscissa* of the point, and the second number is the *ordinate* of the point.

Note that the two axes divide the plane into four regions. Each of these regions is called a *quadrant*. The quadrants are numbered I, II, III, and IV. The point where the coordinate axes meet is called the *origin*. The coordinates, or number pair, of the origin are (0,0).

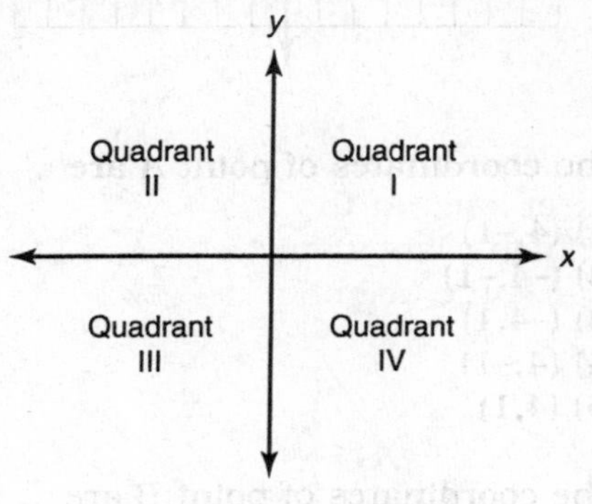

EXAMPLE

What are the coordinates of the points shown on the graph?

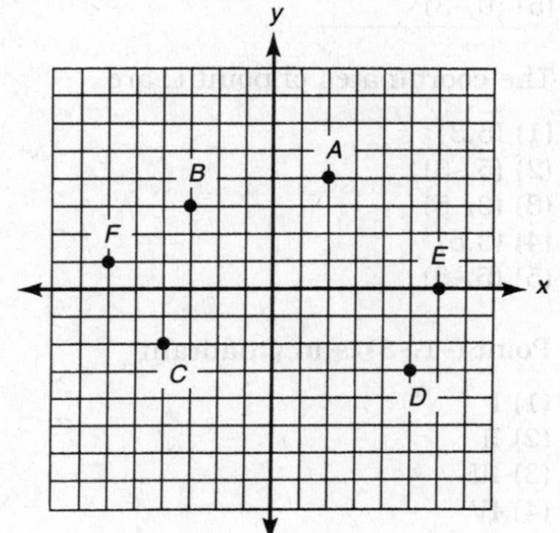

Point A (2,4), point B (−3,3), point C (−4,−2), point D (5,−3), point E (6,0), point F (−6,1)

PRACTICE

Questions 1–4 refer to the following graph.

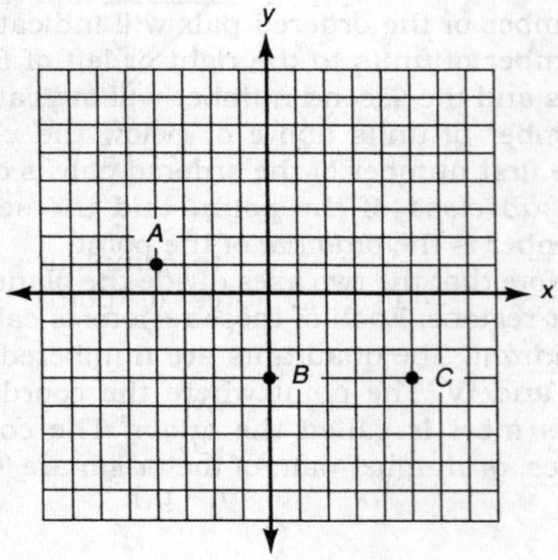

1. The coordinates of point A are

(1) (4,−1)
(2) (−4,−1)
(3) (−4,1)
(4) (4,−1)
(5) (4,1)

2. The coordinates of point B are

(1) (0,3)
(2) (−3,0)
(3) (0,3)
(4) (0,0)
(5) (0,−3)

3. The coordinates of point C are

(1) (5,3)
(2) (5,−3)
(3) (3,−5)
(4) (3,5)
(5) (5,−5)

4. Point (−1,−3) is in Quadrant

(1) I
(2) II
(3) III
(4) IV
(5) O

5. The point at which $\overleftrightarrow{AB}$ and $\overleftrightarrow{CD}$ meet, called the *point of intersection* of the two lines, is

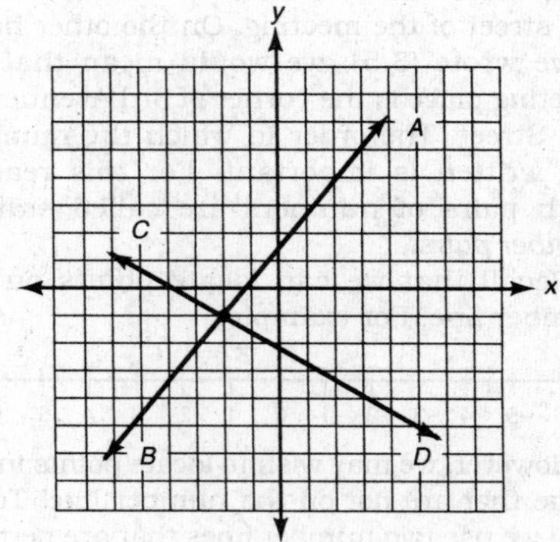

(1) (2,−1)
(2) (−2,1)
(3) (−1,−2)
(4) (−2,−1)
(5) (−1,2)

ANSWER KEY

1. 3 **2. 5** **3. 2** **4. 3** **5. 4**

We may use the Pythagorean theorem to find the distance between two points whose coordinates are given.

EXAMPLES

Find the distance between points A (2,1) and B (6,4).

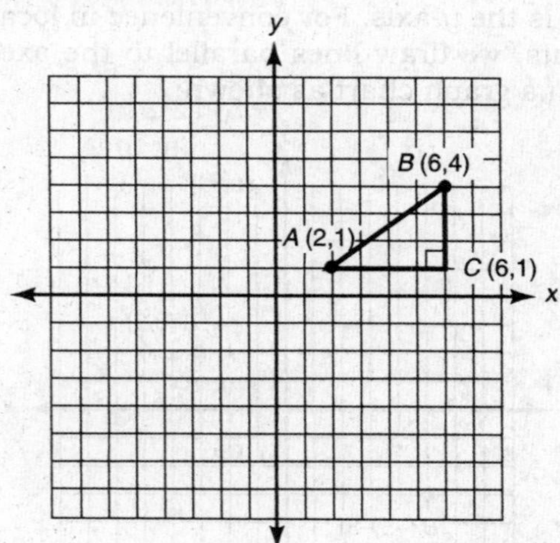

Draw $\overline{AC}$ parallel to the x-axis and $\overline{BC}$ parallel to the y-axis to form right triangle

ACB with hypotenuse $\overline{AB}$.

In right triangle ACB,

$$(AB)^2 = (AC)^2 + (BC)^2$$

The coordinates of C are (6,1). To find the length of horizontal line segment $\overline{AC}$, count the number of boxes from A to C to discover that $AC = 4$. To find the length of vertical line segment $\overline{BC}$, count the number of boxes from B to C to discover that $BC = 3$.

$$(AB)^2 = (3)^2 + (4)^2 = 9 + 16 = 25$$
$$AB = \sqrt{25} = 5$$

Find the distance between points A (–3,4) and B (2,–8).

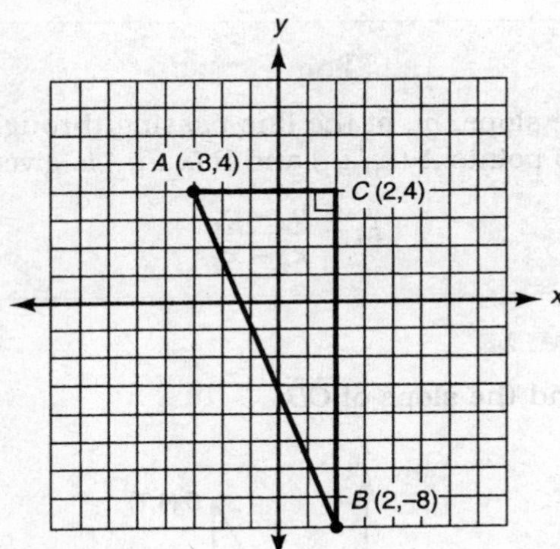

Draw $\overline{AC}$ parallel to the x-axis and $\overline{BC}$ parallel to the y-axis to form right triangle ACB with hypotenuse $\overline{AB}$. The coordinates of point C are (2,4).

Count boxes to see that $AC = 5$ and $BC = 12$. If you remember the 5–12–13 right triangle, you will know immediately that $AB = 13$. If you don't, you must use the Pythagorean theorem.

$$(AB)^2 = (5)^2 + (12)^2 = 25 + 144 = 169$$
$$AB = \sqrt{169} = 13$$

We may use the Pythagorean theorem to derive a formula for finding the distance between two points A (x_1,y_1) and B (x_2,y_2).

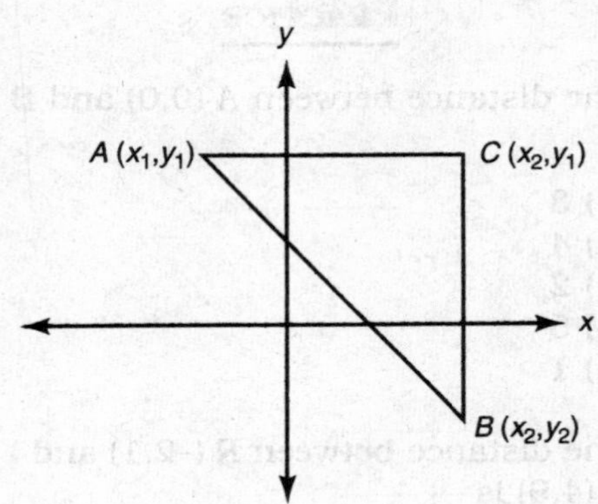

We draw $\overline{AC}$ and $\overline{BC}$ to complete a right triangle. The coordinates of point C are (x_2,y_1).

$$AC = x_2 - x_1$$
$$BC = y_1 - y_2$$

Note that $(y_1 - y_2) = -(y_2 - y_1)$, so $(y_1 - y_2)^2 = (y_2 - y_1)^2$

Since $(AB)^2 = (BC)^2 + (AC)^2$,

$$(AB)^2 = (x_2 - x_1)^2 + (y_2 - y_1)^2$$

If we let $AB = d$, we have

$$d^2 = (x_2 - x_1)^2 + (y_2 - y_1)^2$$
$$d = \sqrt{(x_2 - x_1)^2 + (y_2 - y_1)^2}$$

The Distance Formula

The distance, d, between two points A (x_1, y_1) and B (x_2, y_2) is given by

$$\mathbf{d = \sqrt{(x_2 - x_1)^2 + (y_2 - y_1)^2}}$$

EXAMPLE

Find the distance between P (10,9) and Q (2,3).

Use the formula $d = \sqrt{(x_2 - x_1)^2 + (y_2 - y_1)^2}$. In this case, $x_2 = 10$, $x_1 = 2$, $y_2 = 9$, and $y_1 = 3$.

$$d = \sqrt{(10 - 2)^2 + (9 - 3)^2}$$
$$= \sqrt{8^2 + 6^2} = \sqrt{64 + 36}$$
$$= \sqrt{100} = 10$$

PRACTICE

1. The distance between A (0,0) and B (3,4) is

   (1) 3
   (2) 4
   (3) 2
   (4) 5
   (5) 1

2. The distance between R (−2,1) and S (4,9) is

   (1) 7
   (2) 10
   (3) 5
   (4) 9
   (5) 4

3. The distance between C (5,7) and D (5,1) is

   (1) 6
   (2) 0
   (3) 5
   (4) 8
   (5) 10

4. The distance between P (−5,−3) and Q (7,6) is

   (1) 10
   (2) 15
   (3) 12
   (4) 14
   (5) 20

ANSWER KEY

1. **4** 2. **2** 3. **1** 4. **2**

The Slope of a Line

In designing a road, engineers are concerned with the steepness, or slope, of the road. In this section, we will discuss the meaning and the measurement of the slope of a line.

The *slope of a line* between two points on the line is defined as the distance that the line rises between the points divided by the horizontal distance between the two points. For example, in the following diagram

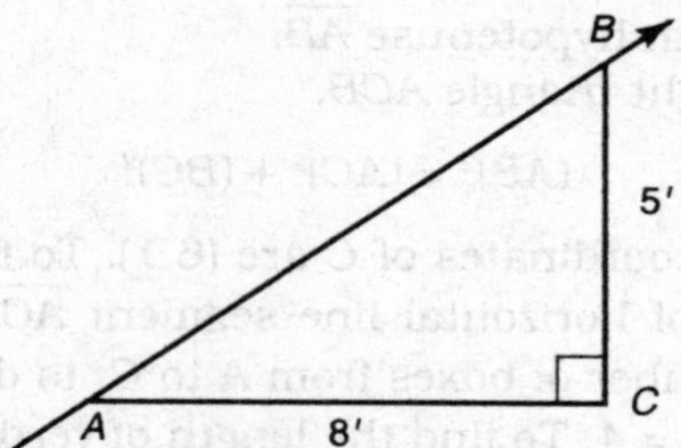

if BC represents the distance the line rises between points A and B, and AC represents the horizontal distance between points A and B, then the slope of $\overline{AB}$ is $\frac{5}{8}$.

In general, we can define the slope of a line as the change in the y-coordinates divided by the change in the x-coordinates of the two points.

> **The Slope Formula**
>
> The slope, m, of the line passing through two points A (x_1, y_1) and B (x_2, y_2) is given by
>
> $$m = \frac{y_2 - y_1}{x_2 - x_1}$$

EXAMPLE

Find the slope of $\overline{OB}$.

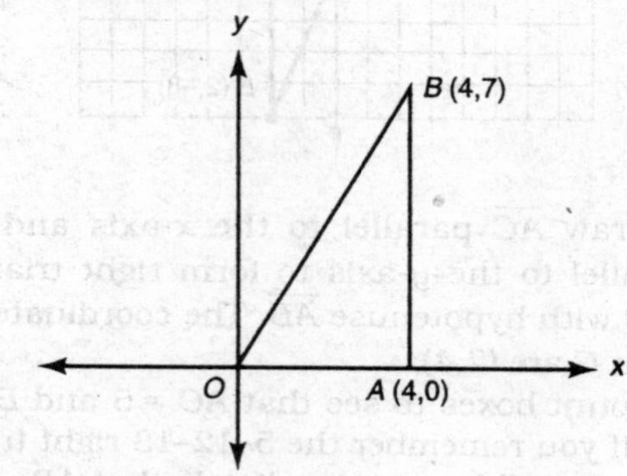

In this case,

$$\frac{\text{change in y-coordinates}}{\text{change in x-coordinates}} = \frac{7-0}{4-0} = \frac{7}{4}$$

EXAMPLE

Find the slope of the line joining points A (2,1) and B (5,8).

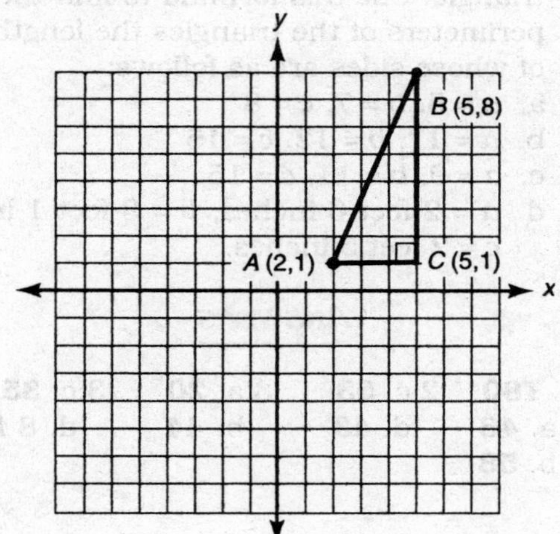

Of course, you should just use the slope formula:

$$m = \frac{8-1}{5-2} = \frac{7}{3}.$$

If you forget the formula, however, you can proceed as follows:

Draw $\overline{AC}$ parallel to the x-axis and $\overline{BC}$ parallel to the y-axis.

Slope of $\overline{AB}$ =

$$\frac{\text{change in } y\text{-coordinates}}{\text{change in } x\text{-coordinates}} = \frac{CB}{AC}$$

By counting, you find that $CB = 7$ and that $AC = 3$.

The slope of $\overline{AB} = \frac{CB}{AC} = \frac{7}{3}$.

PRACTICE

1. **The slope of the line joining A (0,0) and B (5,6) is**
   (1) 5
   (2) 6
   (3) $\frac{5}{6}$
   (4) $\frac{6}{5}$
   (5) 0

2. **The slope of the line joining C (3,2) and D (6,7) is**
   (1) $\frac{3}{5}$
   (2) $\frac{5}{3}$
   (3) $\frac{7}{5}$
   (4) $\frac{5}{7}$
   (5) $\frac{7}{6}$

3. **The slope of the line joining R (−1,5) and S (4,7) is**
   (1) $\frac{5}{2}$
   (2) $\frac{2}{3}$
   (3) $\frac{2}{5}$
   (4) 5
   (5) $\frac{3}{2}$

4. **The slope of the line joining P (5,−3) and Q (7,5) is**
   (1) 4
   (2) $\frac{1}{4}$
   (3) 1
   (4) $\frac{2}{7}$
   (5) $\frac{5}{2}$

5. **The slope of the line joining K (−2,−1) and L (2,3) is**
   (1) 3
   (2) 1
   (3) $\frac{1}{3}$
   (4) $\frac{2}{3}$
   (5) $\frac{3}{2}$

ANSWER KEY

1. **4** 2. **2** 3. **3** 4. **1** 5. **2**

Perimeters

Mr. Wells had a garden 60 feet long and 40 feet wide. He wished to fence in the garden. How many feet of fencing did he need?

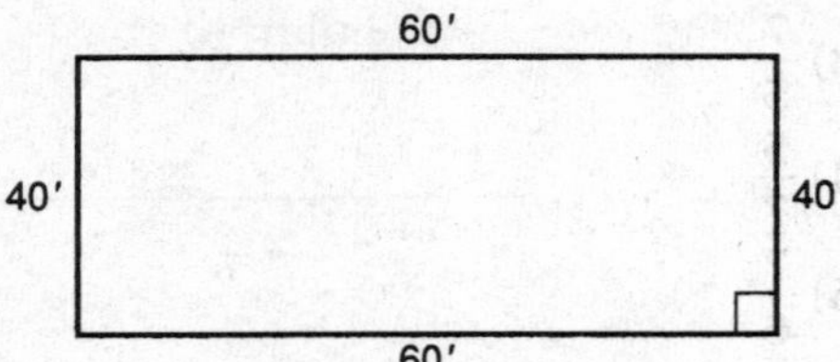

We can see that Mr. Wells needed two lengths of 60 feet each and two widths of 40 feet each. Thus, he needed $(2 \times 60) + (2 \times 40)$, or $120 + 80 = 200$ feet.

The *perimeter* of any plane geometric figure is a measure of its outside boundary. For a circle, the perimeter is the circumference; for a polygon, the perimeter is the sum of the lengths of all of the sides. For example, the perimeter of a 3–4–5 right triangle is $3 + 4 + 5 = 12$, and the perimeter of a square each of whose sides is 5 is $5 + 5 + 5 + 5 = 4(5) = 20$.

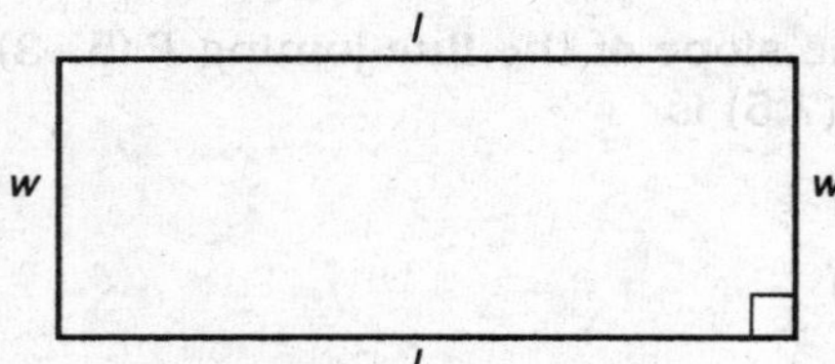

Perimeter of a Rectangle

If the length and width of a rectangle are denoted by l and w, and its perimeter by P, then

$$P = l + w + l + w = 2l + 2w = 2(l + w)$$

PRACTICE

1. Mr. Dale wishes to fence in a rectangular lawn 60 feet long and 30 feet wide. How many feet of fence does he need? 180
2. Use the formula $P = 2(l + w)$ to find the perimeters (P) of rectangles whose lengths (l) and widths (w) are as follows:
   a. $l = 15$, $w = 8$ 46
   b. $l = 17$, $w = 12$ 58
   c. $l = 19.5$, $w = 7$ 52
   d. $l = 16.4$, $w = 5.1$ 53
3. If a, b, and c represent the lengths of the sides of a triangle, the formula $P = a + b + c$ gives the perimeter of the triangle. Use this formula to find the perimeters of the triangles the lengths of whose sides are as follows:
   a. $a = 5$, $b = 7$, $c = 8$ 20
   b. $a = 17$, $b = 12$, $c = 15$ 44
   c. $a = 9$, $b = 11$, $c = 15$ 35
   d. $a = 2$ feet 6 inches, $b = 3$ feet 1 inch, $c = 2$ feet 5 inches. 8ft.

ANSWERS

1. **180** 2.a. **46** b. **58** 2.c. **53** d. **43** 3.a. **20** b. **44** 3.c. **35** d. **8 ft.**

Areas

If we wish to find the amount of carpeting needed to cover a floor, we have the problem of finding the surface *area* of the floor. In finding a length, we use units such as 1 foot, 1 yard, or 1 mile. To find the area of a floor, our unit of measure is 1 square foot or 1 square yard. Below are diagrams of 1 square foot and 1 square yard.

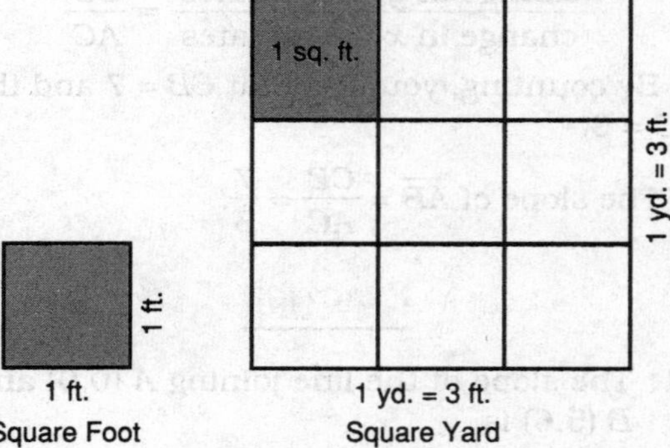

If we wish to find the number of square feet in a floor, we must find the number of square feet units that will cover the floor. Similarly, if we wish to find the number of square yards in the floor, we must find the number of square yard units that will cover the floor. Let us see how this works in the following example.

EXAMPLE

The wooden board shown below measures 6 feet by 9 feet. What is the area of the board (a) in square feet, (b) in square yards?

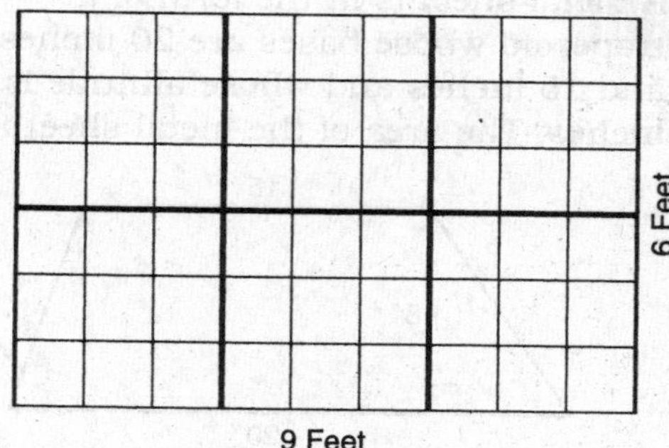

(a) Since there are 9-ft. units along the length and 6-ft. units along the width, the area of the board is 54 sq. ft.

(b) Since there are 3-yd. units along the length and 2-yd. units along the width, the area of the board is 6 sq. yd. As the diagram indicates, there are 9 sq. ft. in 1 sq. yd.

The following box contains all of the area formulas that you need to know for the GED Mathematics test.

AREA FORMULAS

Rectangle

The area of a rectangle is the product of its length (l) and width (w): $\mathbf{A = lw}$.

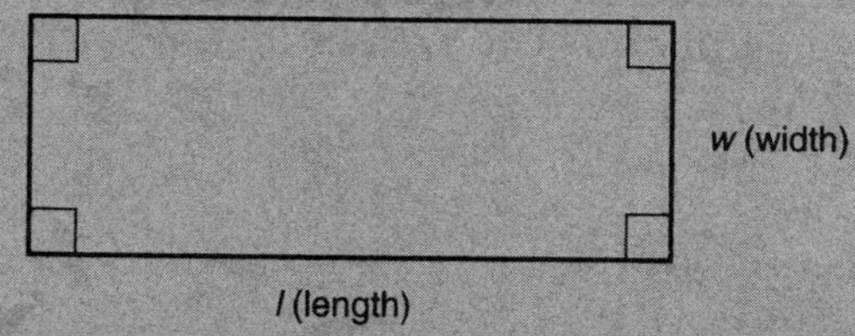

Square

Since a square is a rectangle, its area is also given by $\mathbf{A = lw}$. In a square, however, the length and width are equal and each is usually called a side (s), so $A = s^2$.

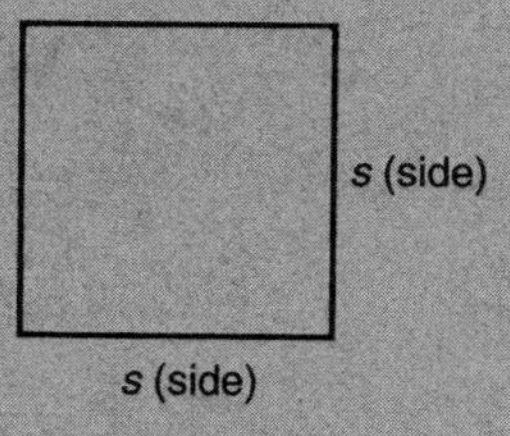

Parallelogram

The area of a parallelogram is the product of its base (b) and height (h). Note in the diagram below that the base is a side of the parallelogram, but the height is not—the height is perpendicular to the base: $\mathbf{A = bh}$.

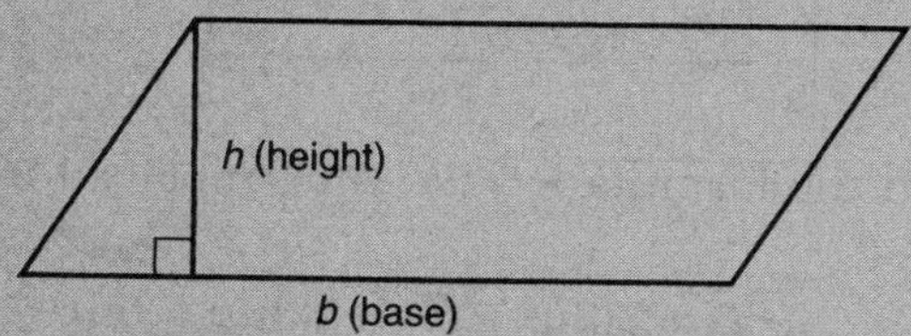

Triangle

Since a triangle is half a parallelogram, its area is given by the formula: $\mathbf{A = \frac{1}{2}bh}$.

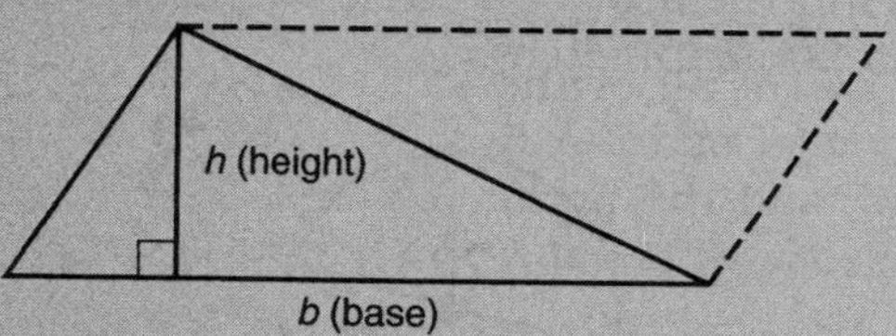

Trapezoid

The two parallel sides of a trapezoid are called bases (b_1 and b_2). The area of a trapezoid is the product of the height and the average of the two bases:

$$\mathbf{A = h\left(\frac{b_1 + b_2}{2}\right)} \quad \text{or} \quad \mathbf{A = \frac{1}{2}h(b_1 + b_2)}.$$

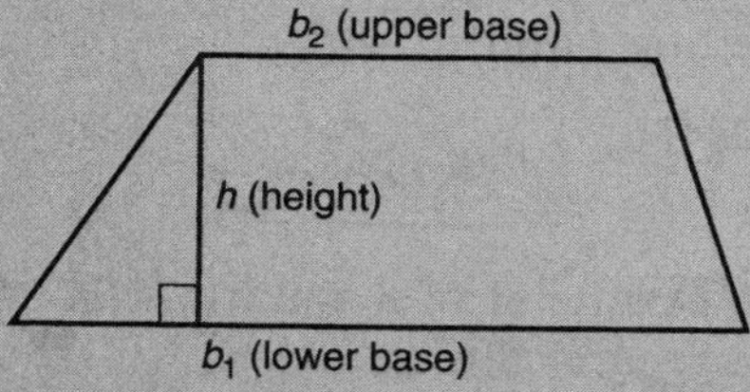

Circle

The area of a circle is given by the formula $\mathbf{A = \pi r^2}$.

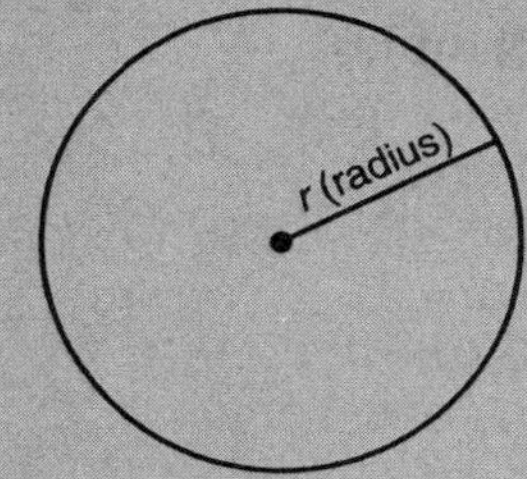

EXAMPLE

Find the area of a rectangle whose length is twice its width and whose perimeter is 60 inches.

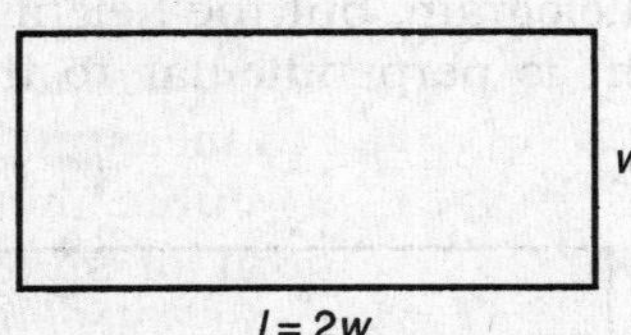

In the formula $P = 2(l + w)$, replace l by $2w$:

$$60 = 2(2w + w) = 2(3w) = 6w$$

Then $w =$ 10 in. and $l =$ 20 in., so

$$A = 20(10) = 200 \text{ sq. in.}$$

EXAMPLE

Find the area of a circle whose diameter is 20 centimeters.

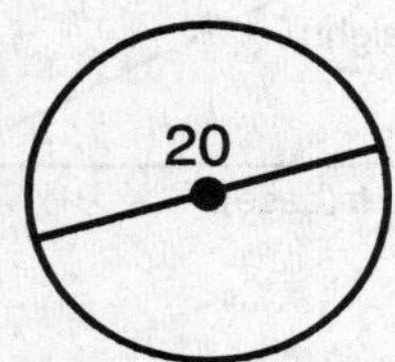

Since the radius is one-half of the diameter, $r = 10$ cm, and $A = \pi(10)^2 = 100\pi$ sq. cm.

You can get a more useful answer, however, by approximating π by 3.14:

$$A \approx 100(3.14) = 314 \text{ sq. cm}$$

PRACTICE

1. The perimeter of a square is 24 inches. The area of the square is

   (1) 576 sq. in.
   (2) 16 sq. in.
   (3) 64 sq. in.
   (4) 36 sq. in.
   (5) 100 sq. in.

2. A metal sheet is in the form of a trapezoid whose bases are 20 inches and 15 inches and whose altitude is 8 inches. The area of the metal sheet is

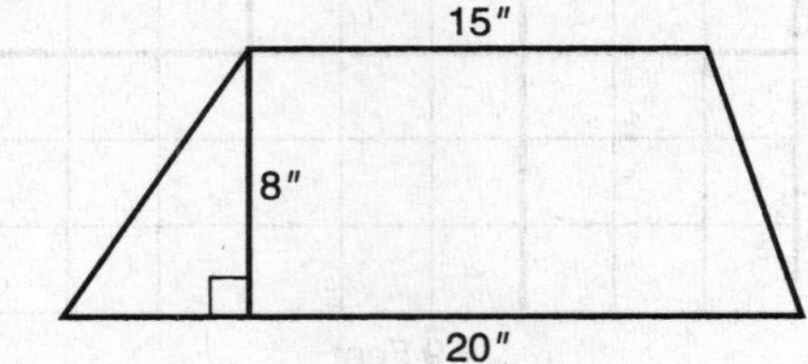

   (1) 420 sq. in.
   (2) 270 sq. in.
   (3) 140 sq. in.
   (4) 110 sq. in.
   (5) 47 sq. in.

3. A rectangle and a square have equal areas. The length of the rectangle is 20 inches, and its width is 5 inches. A side of the square measures

   (1) 100 in.
   (2) 10 in.
   (3) 20 in.
   (4) 40 in.
   (5) 12 in.

4. A circular mirror has a diameter of 14 inches. The area of the mirror is [Use $\pi = \frac{22}{7}$.]

   (1) 154 sq. in.
   (2) 144 sq. in.
   (3) 616 sq. in.
   (4) 308 sq. in.
   (5) 88 sq. in.

5. The diagram below represents an L-shaped room. The cost of carpeting this room at $10.50 per square yard is

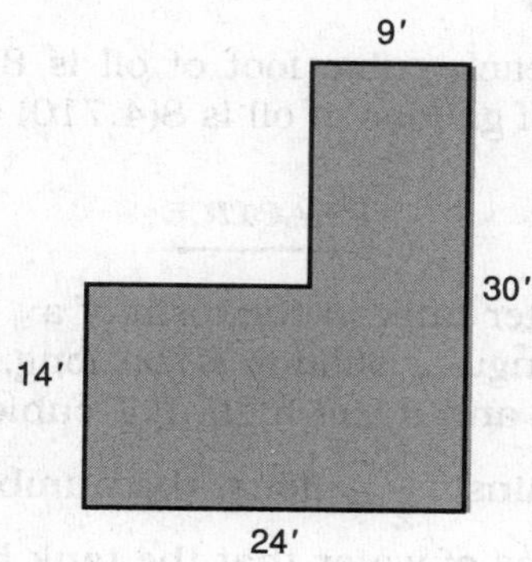

(1) $5,040
(2) $864
(3) $720
(4) $650
(5) $560

6. The diagram below represents a cross section of a pipe. If the radius of the outer circle is 10 inches and the radius of the inner circle is 6 inches, the area of the cross-section is [Use $\pi = 3.14$.]

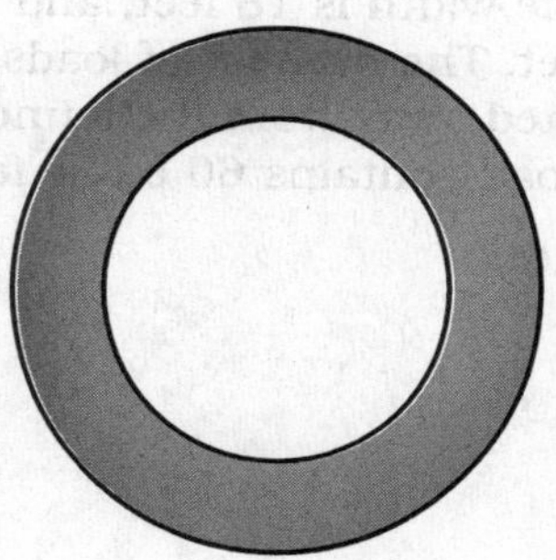

(1) 314 sq. in.
(2) 200.96 sq. in.
(3) 110.04 sq. in.
(4) 157 sq. in.
(5) 220.08 sq. in.

ANSWER KEY

1. **4**	3. **2**	5. **5**
2. **3**	4. **1**	6. **2**

Volumes

If we want to know the amount of space that a box occupies, we must determine its *volume*. Just as length is measured in units such as inches, feet, and meters, and area is measured in square inches, square feet, and square meters, volume is measured in cubic inches, cubic feet, and cubic meters. One cubic inch is the amount of space that is taken up by a cube each of whose edges is 1 inch long.

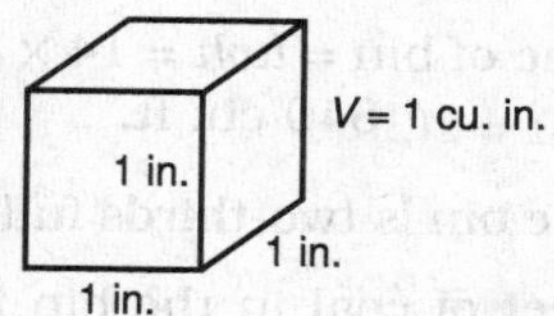

Thus, if we want to find the volume of a box that is 4 inches long, 3 inches wide, and 2 inches high, we have to determine how many 1-inch cubes can fit in the box. From the following figure, we can see that we can fit 4 cubes along the length and 3 cubes along the width. We can therefore fit 12 cubes in one layer. Since we can place 2 layers in the box, the volume of the box is $2 \times 12 = 24$ cubic inches. In general, the volume of a box (called a *rectangular solid*) is obtained by multiplying the number of units in the length by the number of units in the width by the number of units in the height. In this case, $V = 4 \times 3 \times 2 = 24$ cubic inches.

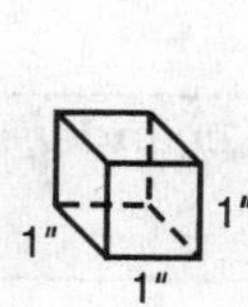

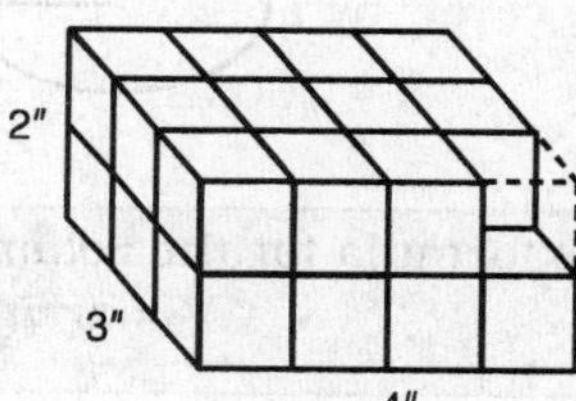

The formula for the *volume of a rectangular solid* is

$$V = lwh$$

If we wish to find the volume of a cube, we note that, in a cube, the length, width, and height are equal. If we represent each dimension of a cube by *s*, then:

> The formula for the *volume of a cube* is
>
> $V = s^3$

EXAMPLE

A coal bin is in the form of a rectangular solid. The bin is 14 feet long, 10 feet wide, and 6 feet high. If 1 ton of coal occupies 35 cubic feet of space, and the bin is two-thirds full, how many tons of coal are in the bin?

Volume of bin = $lwh = 14 \times 10 \times 6 =$ 840 cu. ft.

Since the bin is two-thirds full, the number of cubic feet of coal in the bin is $\frac{2}{3} \times 840 =$ 560. To find the number of tons in the bin, divide: $560 \div 35 = 16$.

An important solid figure that we encounter frequently is the cylinder. In a cylinder, the upper and lower bases are circles that lie in parallel planes. The volume of a cylinder is obtained by multiplying the area of one base by the height.

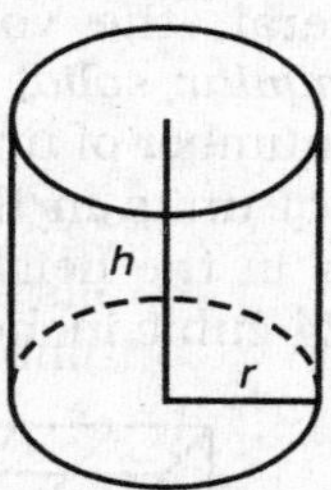

> The formula for the *volume of a cylinder* is
> $V = \pi r^2 h$

EXAMPLE

A storage oil tank in the form of a cylinder is three-fourths full. The radius of the base of the tank is 10 feet, and the height of the tank is 20 feet. Find the number of gallons of oil in the tank if each cubic foot of space holds 8 gallons of oil. [Approximate π by 3.14.]

Volume of cylinder $= \pi r^2 h$
$= 3.14(10)(10)(20)$
$= 6,280$ cu. ft.

Since the tank is $\frac{3}{4}$ full, it contains $\frac{3}{4} \times 6,280 = 4,710$ cu. ft. of oil.

Since each cubic foot of oil is 8 gal., the number of gallons of oil is $8(4,710) = 37,680$.

PRACTICE

1. A water tank in the form of a rectangular solid is 8 feet long, 6 feet wide, and 9 feet high. If 1 cubic foot contains $7\frac{1}{2}$ gallons, the number of gallons of water that the tank holds when it is two-thirds full is

   (1) $38\frac{2}{5}$
   (2) 2,060
   (3) 412
   (4) 2,160
   (5) 824

2. The foundation of a house that is to be built is in the form of a rectangular solid. The length of the foundation is 20 feet, the width is 18 feet, and the height is 6 feet. The number of loads of soil to be carted away from the foundation if each load contains 60 cubic feet is

   (1) 57,600
   (2) 36
   (3) 27
   (4) 30
   (5) 48

3. A food can in the form of a cylinder has a base radius of 5 inches and a height of 7 inches. The number of cubic inches in the can is [Use $\pi = \frac{22}{7}$.]

   (1) 550
   (2) 280
   (3) 2,200
   (4) 320
   (5) 575

ANSWER KEY

1. **4** 2. **2** 3. **1**

Areas of Surfaces of Solids

We are sometimes interested in the area of the surface of a solid figure. For example, a room is in the form of a rectangular solid. If we wish to paint the room, we will be interested in the area of the walls and ceiling.

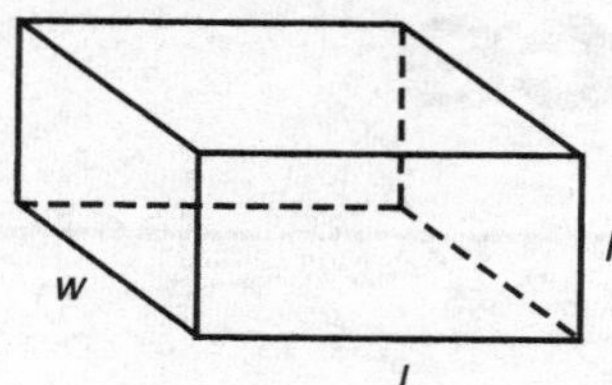

We can see that the area of the surface of the rectangular solid in the diagram is obtained by adding lw (bottom) + lw (top) + wh (side) + wh (side) + lh (front) + lh (back).

A formula for the area of the *surface of a rectangular solid* is

$$A = 2lw + 2wh + 2lh$$

As another example, the label on a cylindrical can (or *cylinder*) covers only the area on the side of the can.

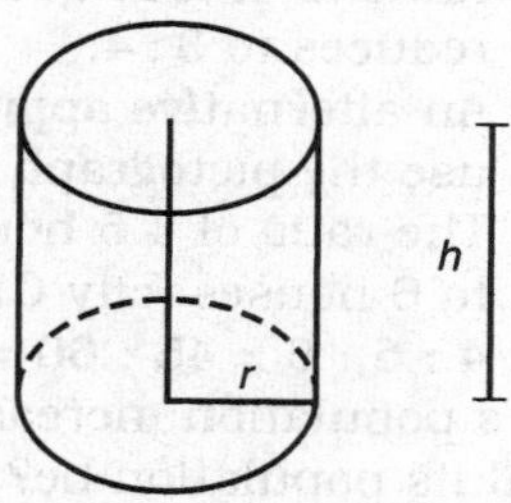

The formula for the *side area of a cylinder*, called the *lateral area*, is

$$A = 2\pi rh$$

EXAMPLE

Find the number of square feet of cardboard used to make a carton 4 feet long, 3 feet wide, and 2 feet high.

Use the formula

$A = 2lw + 2wh + 2lh$

In this case, $l = 4$, $w = 3$, and $h = 2$:

$A = 2 \times 4 \times 3 + 2 \times 3 \times 2 + 2 \times 4 \times 2$
$A = 24 + 12 + 16 = 52$

EXAMPLE

A can has a radius of $3\frac{1}{2}$ inches and is 5 inches high. What is the area of the label used on the can? [Use $\pi = \frac{22}{7}$.]

Lateral area of cylinder $= 2\pi rh$
$= 2 \times \frac{22}{7} \times \frac{7}{2} \times 5$
$= 110$

The area of the label is 110 sq. in.

PRACTICE

1. A room is 20 feet long, 12 feet wide, and 8 feet high. The number of square feet of wallpaper needed to paper the walls of this room is

Hint: Do not include the floor and the ceiling. Thus, the formula to use is $A = 2wh + 2lh$.

(1) 992
(2) 800
(3) 1,824
(4) 512
(5) 1,920

2. A room is 24 feet long, 15 feet wide, and 9 feet high. If the walls and ceiling are to be painted, the number of square feet to be covered is

(1) 1,062
(2) 1,422
(3) 3,240
(4) 1,186
(5) 1,132

3. A cylindrical stovepipe has a radius of 7 inches and is 48 inches long. Its area is [Use $\pi = \frac{22}{7}$.]

(1) 2,002 sq. in.
(2) 1,056 sq. in.
(3) 956 sq. in.
(4) 2,112 sq. in.
(5) 1,006 sq. in.

ANSWER KEY

1. **4** 2. **1** 3. **4**

21 Graphs: Worked-Out Examples and Practice

Pictures or graphs are often used in reports, magazines, and newspapers to present a set of numerical facts. These visual devices enable the viewer to make comparisons and to draw quick conclusions. In this section, we will learn how to interpret *pictographs*, *bar graphs*, *line graphs*, *circle graphs*, and *formula graphs*.

Pictographs

A *pictograph* is a graph in which objects are used to represent numbers.

EXAMPLE

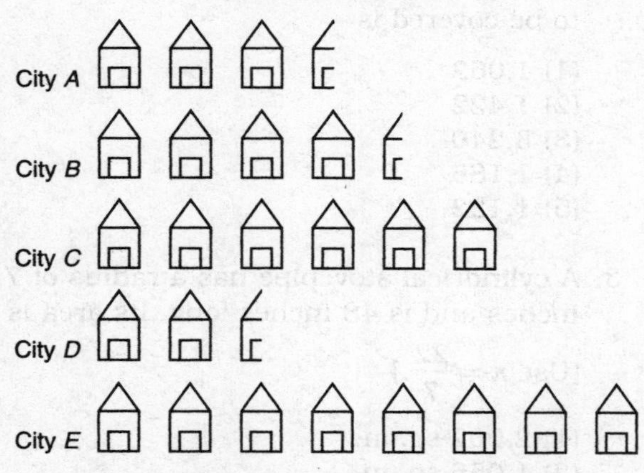

1. Which city has the largest population?

   ANSWER: City E

2. By how many people does the population of the largest city exceed the population of the next largest city?

   ANSWER: City E has 80,000 people.
   City C has 60,000 people.
   City E has 20,000 more people than city C.

3. What is the ratio of the population of city B to city C?

   ANSWER: City B has 45,000 people.
   City C has 60,000 people.
   Ratio is 45,000 : 60,000, which reduces to 3 : 4.
   An alternative approach is to use the pictograph symbols. The ratio of 4.5 houses (city B) to 6 houses (city C) is 4 : 5 : 6 = 45 : 60 = 3 : 4.

4. If city D's population increases by 40%, what will its population be?

   ANSWER: City D has a population of 25,000. Since 40% of 25,000 = 0.4 × 25,000 = 10,000, city D's population will grow to 35,000.

Bar Graphs

A *bar graph* is used to show relationships among a set of quantities. Here, bars are used as opposed to the pictures in a pictograph.

EXAMPLE

In a recent year, a large industrial concern used each dollar of its sales income as shown in the following graph.

Number of Cents Spent: 0 5 10 15 20 25 30 35 40

Wages Materials Taxes Depreciation Dividends Use in Business

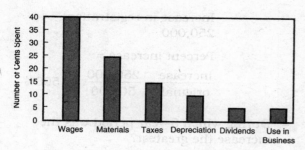

1. **How many cents of each dollar of sales income did the company use to pay wages?**

   ANSWER: 40

2. **How many more cents of each sales dollar were spent on wages than on materials?**

   ANSWER: 40 − 25 = 15

3. **What percent of the sales dollar was spent for depreciation and dividends?**

   ANSWER: 15% (15¢ is 15% of $1.00)

4. **The amount of money the company paid in taxes was how many times the amount of money it paid in dividends?**

   ANSWER: 15 ÷ 5 = 3

5. **What percent of the sales dollar was spent on wages, materials and taxes?**

   ANSWER: 40% + 25% + 15% = 80%

PRACTICE

Use the graph on the bottom of this page to answer the following questions.

1. **Which stock had the greatest percent increase in price during any year?**

   (1) B
   (2) H
   (3) D
   (4) G
   (5) A

2. **Which of the following pairs of stocks gained in price during each of the years 1988, 1989, and 1990?**

   (1) H and I
   (2) A and D
   (3) B and E
   (4) C and G
   (5) F and I

3. **Of the following stocks, which one had the smallest average percent change in the years 1988, 1989, and 1990?**

   (1) A
   (2) C
   (3) D
   (4) E
   (5) F

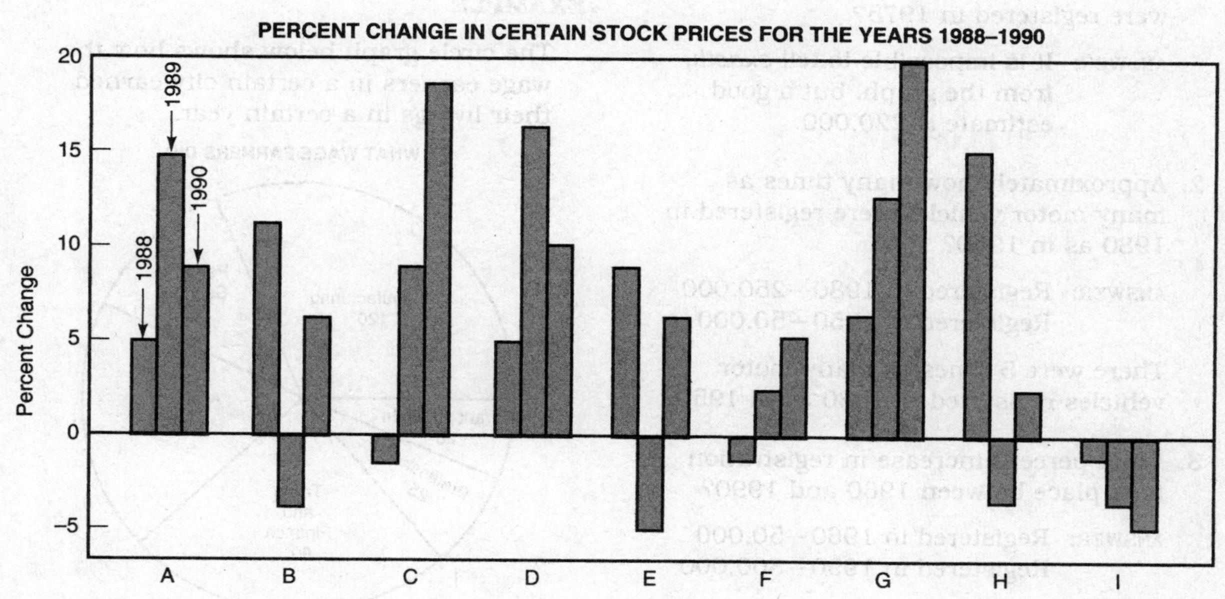

4. If the value of stock D was $200 at the beginning of 1988, which of the following is the closest approximation to its value at the end of 1990?

(1) $230
(2) $250
(3) $270
(4) $300
(5) $320

Answer Key

1. **4** 2. **2** 3. **5** 4. **3**

Line Graphs

A *line graph* is especially helpful in showing changes over a period of time.

EXAMPLE

The graph below shows the growth in motor vehicle registration in a certain state.

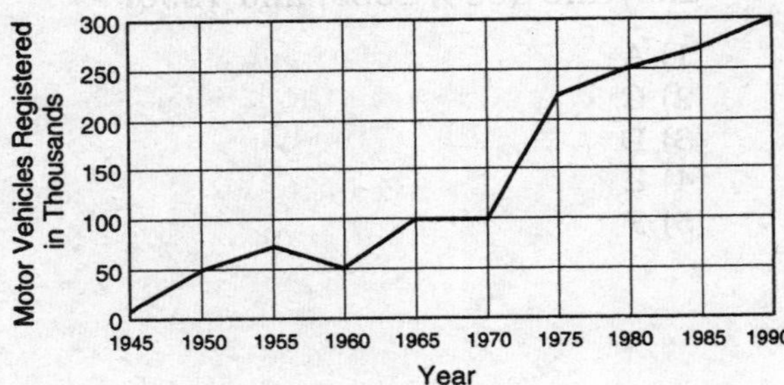

1. Approximately how many motor vehicles were registered in 1975?

ANSWER: It is impossible to tell *exactly* from the graph, but a good estimate is 220,000.

2. Approximately how many times as many motor vehicles were registered in 1980 as in 1950?

ANSWER: Registered in 1980—250,000
Registered in 1950—50,000

There were 5 times as many motor vehicles registered in 1980 as in 1950.

3. What percent increase in registration took place between 1960 and 1990?

ANSWER: Registered in 1960—50,000
Registered in 1990—300,000

Increase in registration—250,000

Percent increase =

$$\frac{\text{increase}}{\text{original}} = \frac{250{,}000}{50{,}000}, \text{ or } 500\%$$

4. During which 5-year period was the increase the greatest?

ANSWER: Between 1970 and 1975. This is shown on the graph by the sharpest rise in the line between these years.

5. During which 5-year period was there no increase?

ANSWER: Between 1965 and 1970. This is shown by the horizontal line between these years.

Circle Graphs

A *circle graph* is used when a quantity is divided into parts, and we wish to make a comparison of the parts. Recall that a circle can be divided into 360°. Thus, if we wish to mark off one-quarter of the circle, the angle at the center must be $\frac{1}{4} \times 360°$, or 90°. For the same reason, a part of the circle with an angle at the center of 60° will be $\frac{60}{360}$, or $\frac{1}{6}$ of the circle.

EXAMPLE

The circle graph below shows how the wage earners in a certain city earned their livings in a certain year.

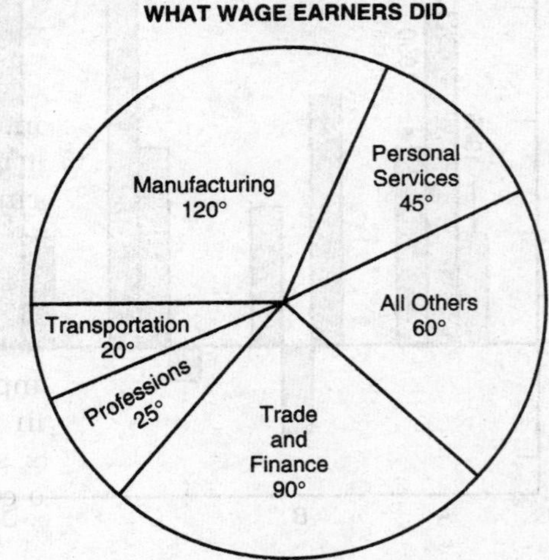

1. What fractional part of the labor force worked in professions?

ANSWER: $\frac{25}{360} = \frac{5}{72}$

2. What fractional part of the labor force worked in personal services?

ANSWER: $\frac{45}{360} = \frac{1}{8}$

3. If there were 180,000 workers in the city, how many were engaged in manufacturing?

ANSWER: The fractional part of the workers engaged in manufacturing was $\frac{120}{360} = \frac{1}{3}$.

$\frac{1}{3}$ of 180,000 = 60,000

4. What was the ratio of the number of workers in transportation to the number of workers in personal services?

ANSWER: The ratio was 20 : 45, or 4 : 9.

5. What percent of the workers were in trade and finance?

ANSWER: The fractional part of the total number of workers in trade and finance was $\frac{90}{360} = \frac{1}{4}$,

and $\frac{1}{4}$ = 25%.

Formula Graphs

In working with a formula, we may need to obtain a number of items of information. Instead of using the formula each time it may be easier to work from a graph of the formula (a *formula graph*).

EXAMPLE

In most parts of Europe and in all scientific work, the scale used to measure temperature is the Celsius scale. However, in the United States, the Fahrenheit scale is still used. We sometimes find it necessary to convert from one scale to the other. The graph below shows how the two scales are related.

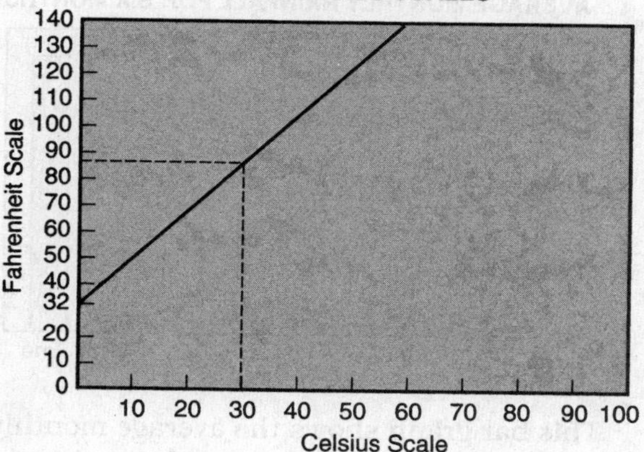

1. A weather report in Paris indicated that the temperature was 30° Celsius. What was the corresponding Fahrenheit temperature?

ANSWER: Locate 30° on the Celsius scale (the horizontal scale). At this point draw a line perpendicular to the Celsius scale line and intersecting the heavy line as shown in the diagram.

You can read the corresponding Fahrenheit temperature by drawing a line perpendicular to the Fahrenheit scale line from the point where the first line you drew intersects the graph. You cannot read the *exact* value, but it appears to be about 86°.

2. What Celsius reading corresponds to a Fahrenheit reading of 77?

ANSWER: 25°

3. During 1 day the temperature rose from 41° to 68° Fahrenheit. What was the corresponding rise in temperature on the Celsius scale?

ANSWER: The Celsius temperature rose about 15°, from 5° to 20°.

PRACTICE

Questions 1–3 refer to the following graph.

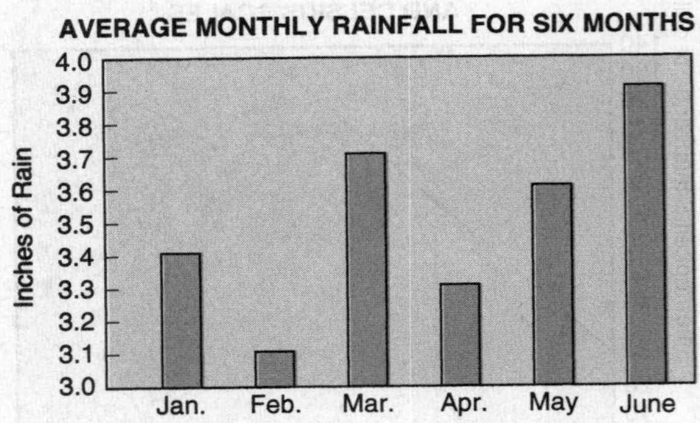

This bar graph shows the average monthly rainfalls, in inches, for the first 6 months of a year in a certain city.

1. The month with the greatest rainfall was

   (1) February
   (2) March
   (3) May
   (4) June
   (5) January

2. The total rainfall for the 6 months was

   (1) 10 in.
   (2) 19 in.
   (3) 19.6 in.
   (4) 21 in.
   (5) 18.5 in.

3. The average monthly rainfall for the 6-month period was

   (1) 3 in.
   (2) 3.2 in.
   (3) 3.3 in.
   (4) 3.5 in.
   (5) 3.8 in.

Questions 4–6 refer to the following graph.

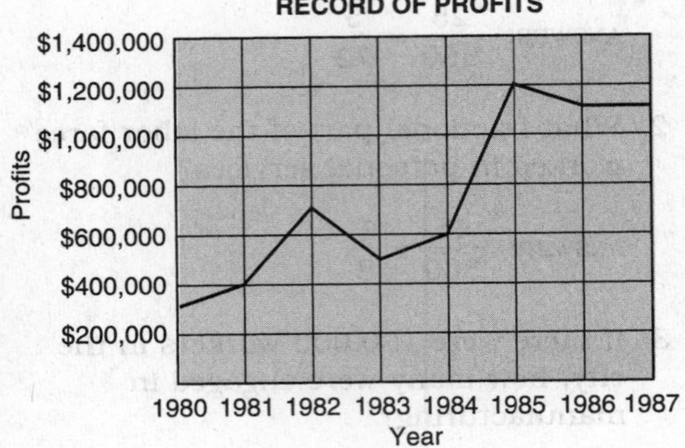

This graph shows the record of profits of the Beacon Co. for a period of 8 years.

4. The profits of the Beacon Co. rose most sharply between the years

   (1) 1981 and 1982
   (2) 1984 and 1985
   (3) 1985 and 1986
   (4) 1982 and 1983
   (5) 1980 and 1981

5. The year when the profits of the Beacon Co. were about $700,000 was

   (1) 1984
   (2) 1987
   (3) 1983
   (4) 1982
   (5) 1985

6. The profits of the Beacon Co. dropped most sharply between the years

   (1) 1986 and 1987
   (2) 1983 and 1984
   (3) 1982 and 1983
   (4) 1980 and 1981
   (5) 1985 and 1986

Questions 7–10 refer to the following graph.

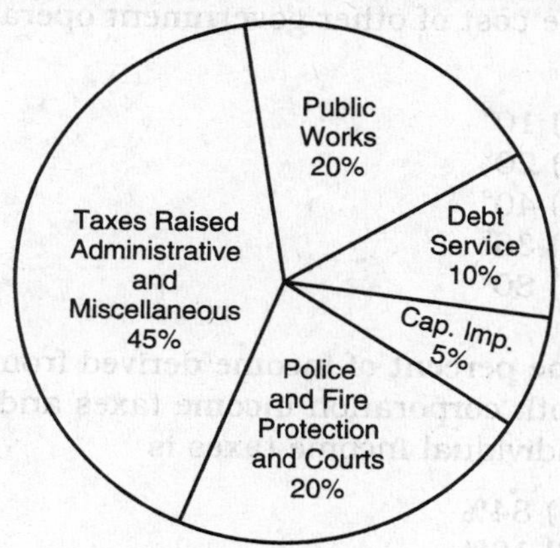

In a large city, the breakdown of the $30,000,000 raised by means of real estate taxes is shown in the graph.

7. The angle at the center for the public works sector measures

(1) 90°
(2) 72°
(3) 100°
(4) 80°
(5) 75°

8. If 10% of the public works budget is shifted to capital improvements, what percent of the tax revenue will be spent on capital improvements?

(1) 5.5%
(2) 7%
(3) 10%
(4) 15%
(5) 50%

9. The amount of money spent for public works is

(1) $5,000,000
(2) $1,500,000
(3) $6,000,000
(4) $3,000,000
(5) $2,500,000

10. The ratio of money spent for administrative and miscellaneous to the money spent for public works is

(1) 9 : 4
(2) 4 : 9
(3) 9 : 5
(4) 5 : 9
(5) 2 : 1

Questions 11–13 refer to the following graph.

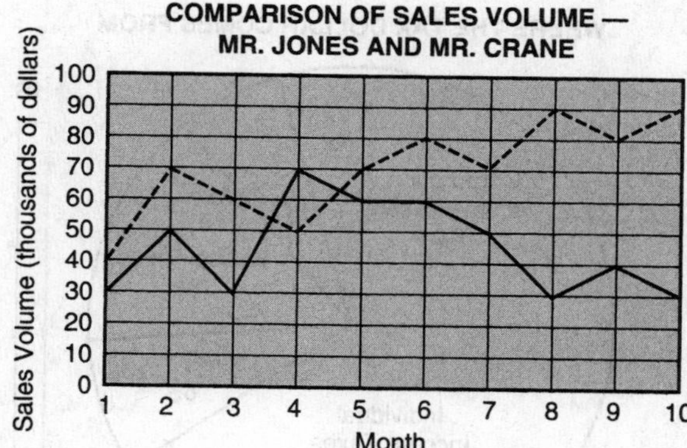

Mr. Jones and Mr. Crane are salesmen. They kept a record of their sales over a 10-month period. The solid line on the graph above represents Mr. Jones's volume of sales, and the broken line represents Mr. Crane's volume of sales.

11. Mr. Jones's greatest sales volume for the 10-month period occurred in the month numbered

(1) 3
(2) 4
(3) 7
(4) 6
(5) 9

12. By how much greater volume, in thousands of dollars, did Mr. Crane's best month exceed Mr. Jones's best month?

(1) 10
(2) 30
(3) 50
(4) 90
(5) 20

13. In what percent of the months covered in the graph did Mr. Jones's volume of sales exceed that of Mr. Smith?

(1) 10%
(2) 20%
(3) 50%
(4) 80%
(5) 90%

Questions 14–17 refer to the following graphs.

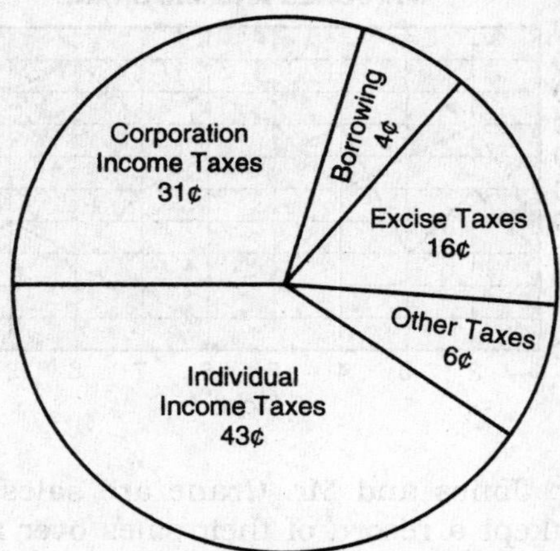

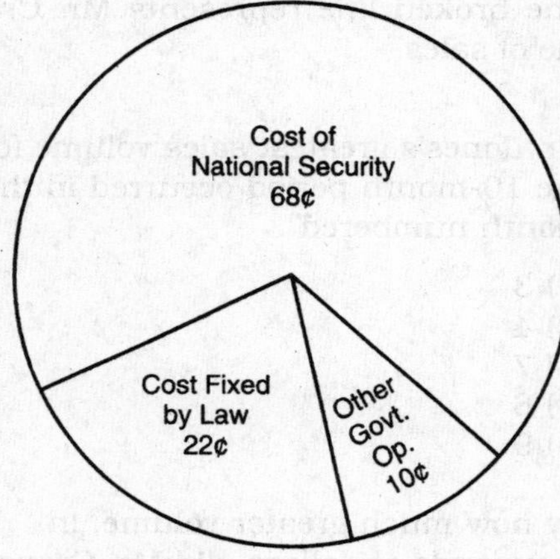

These graphs were published by the federal government to show how the tax dollar is obtained and how it is spent.

14. The percent spent on national security is

(1) 78%
(2) 90%
(3) 68%
(4) 10%
(5) 32%

15. By what percent is the money obtained from the excise taxes greater than the money obtained by borrowing?

(1) 12%
(2) 20%
(3) 64%
(4) 300%
(5) 400%

16. The angle at the center of the sector for the cost of other government operations is

(1) 10°
(2) 20°
(3) 40°
(4) 36°
(5) 80°

17. The percent of income derived from both corporation income taxes and individual income taxes is

(1) 84%
(2) 12%
(3) 75%
(4) 82%
(5) 74%

Questions 18–20 refer to the following pictograph.

The Blue Sox professional baseball team opens its season at the beginning of May and closes its season at the end of September. The pictograph below shows the total attendance for each month of last season.

Each ⚾ represents 4,000 fans.

May ⚾⚾⚾⚾ ◖
June ⚾⚾⚾⚾⚾ ◺
July ⚾⚾⚾⚾⚾⚾
August ⚾⚾⚾⚾⚾ ◖
September ⚾⚾⚾⚾ ◔

18. What was the attendance in May?

(1) 4,500
(2) 16,000
(3) 18,000
(4) 19,000
(5) 22,000

19. What was the attendance in September?

(1) 16,000
(2) 18,000
(3) 18,500
(4) 19,000
(5) 23,000

20. By how many fans did the August attendance exceed the June attendance?

(1) 250
(2) 500
(3) 750
(4) 800
(5) 1,000

ANSWER KEY

1. **4**	5. **4**	9. **3**	13. **1**	17. **5**
2. **4**	6. **3**	10. **1**	14. **3**	18. **3**
3. **4**	7. **2**	11. **2**	15. **4**	19. **4**
4. **2**	8. **2**	12. **5**	16. **4**	20. **5**

22 Measures: Worked-Out Examples and Practice

Length

The most *common measures of length* are

12 inches = 1 foot
3 feet = 1 yard
5,280 feet = 1 mile

We often use the following abbreviations: *in.* for inches, *ft.* for feet, and *yd.* for yards.

EXAMPLE

A plumber has a pipe $\frac{3}{4}$ yard in length. If he cuts off a piece 23 inches long, how much pipe does he have left?

1 yd. = 3 ft. = 3(12 in.) = 36 in.

$\frac{3}{4}$ yd. = $\frac{3}{4}$ (36 in.) = 27 in.

There are 27 − 23 = 4 in. of pipe left.

PRACTICE

1. A plane flies at a height of 23,760 feet. In miles, this height is

(1) 4
(2) $4\frac{2}{3}$
(3) $4\frac{1}{4}$
(4) $4\frac{1}{2}$
(5) $4\frac{3}{4}$

2. Mrs. Bryant buys 6 yards of linen. The number of towels each 27 inches in length that she can cut is

(1) 8
(2) 6
(3) 12
(4) 9
(5) 15

3. A lecture room is 50 feet wide. On each side of the room is an aisle 40 inches wide. The number of seats, 20 inches wide, that can be fitted across the room is

(1) 20
(2) 26
(3) 40
(4) 30
(5) 35

ANSWER KEY

1. **4** 2. **1** 3. **2**

Time

The most *common measures of time* are

60 seconds = 1 minute
60 minutes = 1 hour

24 hours = 1 day
7 days = 1 week

12 months = 1 year
365 days = 1 year

EXAMPLE

A man works from 9:45 A.M. until 1:30 P.M. How many hours does he work?

From 9:45 A.M. to 10:00 A.M. is 15 min.

$15 \text{ min.} = \frac{15}{60} \text{ hr.} = \frac{1}{4} \text{ hr.}$

From 10:00 A.M. to 1:00 P.M. is 3 hrs.

From 1:00 P.M. to 1:30 P.M. is 30 min.

$30 \text{ min.} = \frac{30}{60} \text{ hr.} = \frac{1}{2} \text{ hr.}$

The man works $\frac{1}{4} + 3 + \frac{1}{2} = 3\frac{3}{4}$ hr.

PRACTICE

1. Nicole is paid $6.50 per hour. She works from 10:45 A.M. until 3:15 P.M. She earns

(1) $30.50
(2) $16.25
(3) $29.25
(4) $27.75
(5) $22.75

2. A man leaves New York on a plane at 10:40 A.M. bound for Los Angeles. If he gains 3 hours in time and the trip takes 5 hours and 50 minutes, he arrives in Los Angeles at

(1) 1:30 P.M.
(2) 2:30 P.M.
(3) 3:30 P.M.
(4) 3:10 P.M.
(5) 2:50 P.M.

3. In flight, a plane covers 1 mile in 10 seconds. At the same rate of speed, the number of miles the plane covers in 1 hour is

(1) 100
(2) 200
(3) 720
(4) 300
(5) 360

ANSWER KEY

1. 3 2. 1 3. 5

Weight

The most *commonly used measures of weight* are

16 ounces = 1 pound
2,000 pounds = 1 ton

We often use the following abbreviations: *lb.* for pound and *oz.* for ounce.

EXAMPLE

How many 2-ounce portions of candy can be obtained from a 10-pound box?

Since there are 16 oz. in 1 lb., each lb. of candy will yield $\frac{16}{2}$, or 8 portions. Therefore, 10 lbs. of candy will yield 8 × 10, or 80, portions.

PRACTICE

1. Potatoes sell for $0.32 per pound. The cost of a bag of potatoes weighing 3 pounds 6 ounces is

(1) $0.98
(2) $1.08
(3) $1.12
(4) $0.78
(5) $1.15

2. A 12-ounce package of cheese costs $1.38. What is the cost of 1 pound of the same cheese?

   (1) $1.56
   (2) $1.90
   (3) $1.92
   (4) $1.84
   (5) $2.08

3. A shipment of coal weighs 9,500 pounds. What is the cost of the shipment if 1 ton of coal costs $52.80?

   (1) $250.80
   (2) $213.70
   (3) $221.40
   (4) $209.10
   (5) $225.20

ANSWER KEY

1. **2**   2. **4**   3. **1**

Liquid Measure

The most *commonly used liquid measures* are

8 ounces = 1 cup
2 cups = 1 pint
2 pints = 1 quart
4 quarts = 1 gallon

We often use the following abbreviations: *pt.* for pint, *qt.* for quart, and *gal.* for gallon.

CAUTION: The word *ounce* is used as both a unit of weight and a unit of liquid measure, but the two are unrelated. For example, 1 ounce of water does *not* weigh 1 ounce.

EXAMPLE

A snack bar sells milk in half-pint containers for 15 cents. If 3 gallons of milk are sold one morning, how much money is taken in?

Since a half-pint container sells for 15 cents, a full pint sells for 30 cents. Thus, 1 qt. sells for 60 cents, 1 gal. sells for $2.40, and 3 gal. sell for $3 \times \$2.40 = \$7.20$.

PRACTICE

1. The number of cups of milk in a 5-gallon can is

   (1) 40
   (2) 60
   (3) 80
   (4) 100
   (5) 160

2. A can of orange juice contains 36 ounces. The number of pints of orange juice is

   (1) 2
   (2) $2\frac{1}{2}$
   (3) $1\frac{1}{4}$
   (4) $2\frac{1}{4}$
   (5) 3

3. The number of fluid ounces in 1 gallon is

   (1) 64
   (2) 48
   (3) 100
   (4) 96
   (5) 128

ANSWER KEY

1. **3**   2. **4**   3. **5**

The Metric System

The *metric system* of measures is used in most scientific work and for all purposes in most foreign countries. The metric system is also used to some degree in the United States for nonscientific measurements, and it may be used more extensively in the future. It is especially useful because its units are related by powers of 10. In this section we will consider the most frequently used metric measures and will cover the aspects of the metric system that may appear on the GED Examination.

In the metric system, the basic unit of length is the *meter*, the basic unit of weight is the *gram*, and the basic unit of liquid measure is the *liter*. To name units that are larger or smaller than these, we use prefixes. The most common prefixes are:

- *kilo-*, which means 1,000
- *centi-*, which means $\frac{1}{100}$
- *milli-*, which means $\frac{1}{1,000}$

Metric Units of Length

One *meter* (m) is slightly more than 1 yard (approximately 39 inches) and is useful for measuring distances between a few feet and a mile.

Large distances, such as the distance between cities or the distance from the Earth to the Sun, are measured in *kilometers* (km).

One kilometer is approximately $\frac{5}{8}$ mile.

$$1 \text{ kilometer} = 1,000 \text{ meters}$$

$$1 \text{ meter} = \frac{1}{1,000} \text{ kilometer}$$

For measuring short distances, such as the dimensions of a piece of paper or the length of a pencil, the *centimeter* (cm) is used. One centimeter is slightly less than $\frac{1}{2}$ inch.

$$1 \text{ centimeter} = \frac{1}{100} \text{ meter}$$

$$1 \text{ meter} = 100 \text{ centimeters}$$

For even smaller lengths, such as the width of a human hair or the thickness of a piece of paper, the *millimeter* (mm) is used.

$$1 \text{ millimeter} = \frac{1}{1,000} \text{ meter}$$

$$1 \text{ meter} = 1,000 \text{ millimeters}$$

EXAMPLES

How many meters are there in 5 kilometers?

Since 1 km = 1,000 m, 5 km = 5 × 1,000, = 5,000 m.

How many centimeters are there in 8,000 millimeters?

$$8,000 \text{ mm} = 8,000\left(\frac{1}{1,000}\right) \text{ m} = 8 \text{ m}$$

$$8 \text{ m} = 8\ (100 \text{ cm}) = 800 \text{ cm}$$

PRACTICE

In each case, replace the blank space with a number that makes the statement true:

1. 1 kilometer = ______ meter(s)
2. 1 millimeter = ______ meter(s)
3. 1 meter = ______ centimeter(s)
4. 1 centimeter = ______ millimeter(s)
5. 1 kilometer = ______ centimeter(s)
6. 500 millimeters = ______ centimeter(s)

ANSWERS

1. **1,000**
2. $\mathbf{\frac{1}{1,000}}$
3. **100**
4. **10**
5. **100,000**
6. **50**

Metric Units of Weight

A *gram* (g) is a light weight. There are approximately 28 grams in 1 ounce, or 454 grams in 1 pound. For example, a pat of butter weighs about 3 grams, and an apple may weigh 150 or 200 grams. Heavier weights, such as the weight of a person, a truck, or even the Earth, are measured in *kilograms* (kg). A kilogram is approximately 2.2 pounds.

$$1 \text{ kilogram} = 1,000 \text{ grams}$$

$$1 \text{ gram} = \frac{1}{1,000} \text{ kilogram}$$

For measuring very light objects, like the small quantities of drugs that a pharmacist uses, the *milligram* (mg) is used.

$$1 \text{ milligram} = \frac{1}{1,000} \text{ gram}$$

$$1 \text{ gram} = 1,000 \text{ milligrams}$$

EXAMPLE

A cake weighs 250 grams. How many kilograms does the cake weigh?

$$250\text{g} = 250\left(\frac{1}{1,000} \text{ kg}\right) = \frac{1}{4} \text{ kg} = 0.25 \text{ kg}$$

Metric Units of Liquid Measure

In the metric system, the basic unit of liquid measure is the *liter*. One liter contains a little more than 1 quart. In countries where the metric system is used, it is convenient to sell milk and gasoline in liter units.

For measuring large liquid quantities, the *kiloliter* may be used.

$$1 \text{ kiloliter} = 1{,}000 \text{ liters}$$

$$1 \text{ liter} = \frac{1}{1{,}000} \text{ kiloliter}$$

Small quantities of liquid, in a pharmacy or a laboratory, for example, are measured in *milliliters*.

$$1 \text{ milliliter} = \frac{1}{1{,}000} \text{ liter}$$

$$1 \text{ liter} = 1{,}000 \text{ milliliters}$$

EXAMPLE

A glass contains 0.5 liter of milk. How many milliliters is this?

0.5 liter = 0.5(1,000) = 500 milliliters

PRACTICE

In each case, replace the blank space with a number that makes the statement true:

1. 1 kilogram = ______ gram(s)
2. 1 gram = ______ milligram(s)
3. 1 milliliter = ______ liter(s)
4. 500 grams = ______ kilogram(s)
5. 1 milligram= ______ gram(s)
6. 1 liter = ______ milliliter(s)

ANSWERS

1. **1,000**
2. **1,000**
3. $\frac{1}{1{,}000}$
4. **0.5**
5. $\frac{1}{1{,}000}$
6. **1,000**

The following set of practice exercises is a review of metric units of length, weight, and liquid measure.

PRACTICE

In each case, replace the blank space with a suitable metric unit of measure:

1. Each day John drinks 1 ______ of milk.
2. The speed limit on roads in the United States is 88 ______ per hour.
3. Mrs. Jones takes a pill that weighs 80 ______.
4. Frank Sloan is the center on his basketball team. His height is 2 ______.
5. Jane Morris bought a chicken that weighed 1½ ______.
6. The distance between New York and Los Angeles is approximately 4,000 ______.
7. A bunch of grapes weighed 200 ______.
8. The length of my pencil is 14 ______.

ANSWERS

1. **liter**
2. **kilometers**
3. **milligrams**
4. **meters**
5. **kilograms**
6. **kilometers**
7. **grams**
8. **centimeters**

Area and Volume in the Metric System

In the English system, common measures of area include the square inch, the square foot, and the square mile. Similarly, in the metric system, measures of area include the square millimeter, the square centimeter, and the square meter. The square kilometer is used as a measure of large tracts of land.

In the English system, common measures of volume are the cubic inch, the cubic foot, and the cubic yard. Similarly, in the metric system, measures of volume include the cubic millimeter, the cubic centimeter, and the cubic meter.

PRACTICE

1. What is the area of a rectangle whose length is 6 centimeters and whose width is 8 centimeters?
2. What is the volume of a cube whose sides are 2 meters long?
3. What is the area of a circle whose diameter is 10 meters?
4. What is the volume of a rectangular box whose length is 1 meter, whose width is 50 centimeters, and whose height is 80 centimeters?

ANSWERS

1. **48 square centimeters**
2. **8 cubic meters**
3. **25π square meters**
4. **0.4 cubic meters = 400,000 cubic centimeters**

Operations with Measures

It is often necessary to add, subtract, multiply, and divide with measures. The examples below indicate how this is done.

EXAMPLE

A woman bought a steak weighing 2 pounds 14 ounces and another steak weighing 3 pounds 6 ounces.

How many pounds of steak did she buy?

```
 2 lb. 14 oz.
 3 lb.  6 oz.
 ------------
 5 lb. 20 oz.
```

Since there are 16 oz. in 1 lb.,
20 oz. = 1 lb. 4 oz.

5 lb. 20 oz. = 5 lb. + 1 lb. + 4 oz. = 6 lb. 4 oz.

Note: Since 4 oz. = $\frac{4}{16}$ lb. = $\frac{1}{4}$ lb., this answer may also be expressed as $6\frac{1}{4}$ lb. or 6.25 lb.

EXAMPLE

A plumber had a piece of pipe 6 feet 3 inches long. If he cut off a piece 2 feet 7 inches in length, what was the length of the pipe that was left?

Since you cannot subtract 7 in. from 3 in., "borrow" 1 ft. from the 6 ft. and add it (as 12 in.) to the 3 in.:

```
  6 ft. 3 in.        5 ft.15 in.
– 2 ft. 7 in.      – 2 ft.  7 in.
                     3 ft.  8 in.
```

The piece of pipe that was left was 3 ft. 8 in.

Note: An alternative method is to convert both quantities to inches, and then convert back.

6 ft. 3 in. = 6(12) in. = 3 in. = 75 in.
2 ft. 7 in. = 2(12) in. + 7 in. = 31 inc.
75 in. – 31 in. = 44 in. = 3 ft. 8 in.

EXAMPLE

A butcher cuts steaks each of which weighs 1 pound 9 ounces. What is the weight of 5 such steaks?

```
 1 lb. 9 oz.
         × 5
 ------------
 5 lb. 45 oz.
```

When 45 is divided by 16, the quotient is 2 and the remainder is 13: 45 = 2(16) = 13. Then 5 lb. 4 oz. = 5 lb. + (2 lb. + 13 oz.) = 7 lb. 13 oz.

EXAMPLE

Mrs. Gordon buys a bolt of cloth 25 feet 8 inches in length. She cuts the bolt into 4 equal pieces to make drapes. What is the length of each piece?

```
      6 ft. 5 in.
  4 )25 ft. 8in.
     24 ft.
     ------
      1 ft. 8 in.   (crossed out)
      20 in.
```

The length of each piece is 6 ft. 5 in.

Note: An alternative method is to convert both quantities to inches, and then convert back.

25 ft. 8 in. = 25(12) in. + 8 in. = 308 in.
308 in. + 4 = 77 in. = 6 ft. 5 in.

PRACTICE

1. A picture frame is 2 feet 6 inches long and 1 foot 8 inches wide. The perimeter of the frame is

(1) 4 ft. 2 in.
(2) 8 ft. 8 in.
(3) 8 ft. 6 in.
(4) 8 ft.
(5) 8 ft. 4 in.

2. On a certain day the sun rises at 6:48 A.M. and sets at 7:03 P.M. The time from sunrise to sunset is

(1) 12 hr. 15 min.
(2) 12 hr. 5 min.
(3) 11 hr. 45 min.
(4) 12 hr. 25 min.
(5) 10 hr. 15 min.

3. If 6 cans of orange juice weigh 15 pounds 6 ounces, the weight of 1 can of orange juice is

(1) 2 lb. 6 oz.
(2) 2 lb. 7 oz.
(3) 2 lb. 1 oz.
(4) 2 lb. 9 oz.
(5) 2 lb. 3 oz.

4. A jug contains 2 gallons, 3 quarts of milk. The number of 8-ounce glasses that can be filled from this jug is

(1) 24
(2) 32
(3) 44
(4) 36
(5) 40

5. A carpenter has a board 5 feet 3 inches in length. He cuts off a piece 2 feet 7 inches in length. The length of the piece that is left is

(1) 3 ft. 6 in.
(2) 2 ft. 6 in.
(3) 2 ft. 3 in.
(4) 2 ft. 8 in.
(5) 2 ft. 5 in.

6. A set of books weighs 7 pounds 10 ounces. The weight of 4 such sets is

(1) 28 lb. 4 oz.
(2) 30 lb. 8 oz.
(3) 29 lb. 8 oz.
(4) 29 lb. 10 oz.
(5) 29 lb. 11 oz.

ANSWER KEY

1. **5**	3. **4**	5. **4**
2. **1**	4. **3**	6. **2**

23 Three Practice Mathematics Tests

This section is designed to give you practice in taking the Mathematics test of the High School Equivalency Examination. In taking each of these practice tests, give yourself the benefit of good working conditions. Select a quiet place and allow yourself 90 minutes for each test. If you finish in less time, use the remaining time to check your work.

After you have completed a test, use the answer key to find your score and then study the solutions and explanations. You may discover new ways to attack problems. Also you will obtain help on the questions that you could not answer, and you will be able to correct any errors that you have made.

Remember that you do not have to get a perfect score to pass the test. If you find that you are weak on a certain topic, review the material in the text on that topic.

FORMULAS

Description	Formula
AREA (A) of a:	
square	$A = s^2$; where s = side
rectangle	$A = lw$; where l = length, w = width
parallelogram	$A = bh$; where b = base, h = height
triangle	$A = \frac{1}{2}bh$; where b = base, h = height
circle	$A = \pi r^2$; where $\pi = 3.14$, r = radius
PERIMETER (P) of a:	
square	$P = 4s$; where s = side
rectangle	$P = 2l + 2w$; where l = length, w = width
triangle	$P = a + b + c$; where a, b, and c are the sides
circumference (C) of a circle	$C = \pi d$; where $\pi = 3.14$, d = diameter
VOLUME (V) of a:	
cube	$V = s^3$; where s = side
rectangular container	$V = lwh$; where l = length, w = width, h = height
cylinder	$V = \pi r^2 h$; where $\pi = 3.14$, r = radius, h = height
Pythagorean relationship	$c^2 = a^2 + b^2$; where c = hypotenuse, a and b are legs of a right triangle
distance (d) between two points in a plane	$d = \sqrt{(x_2 - x_1)^2 + (y_2 - y_1)^2}$; where (x_1,y_1) and (x_2,y_2) are two points in a plane
slope of a line (m)	$m = \frac{y_2 - y_1}{x_2 - x_1}$, where (x_1,y_1) and (x_2,y_2) are two points in a plane

FORMULAS (continued)

Description	Formula
mean	mean = $\frac{x_1 + x_2 + \ldots + x_n}{n}$ where the x's are the values for which a mean is desired, and n = number of values in the series
median	median = the point in an ordered set of numbers at which half of the numbers are above and half of the numbers are below this value
simple interest (i)	$i = prt$; where p = principal, r = rate, t = time
distance (d) as function of rate and time	$d = rt$; where r = rate, t = time
total cost (c)	$c = nr$; where n = number of units, r = cost per unit

Practice Test One

1. In a theater audience of 650 people, 80% were adults. How many children were in the audience?

(1) 130
(2) 150
(3) 450
(4) 500
(5) 520

2. On a certain map 1 inch represents 60 miles. If two towns are 255 miles apart, what is the distance, in inches, between the towns on the map?

(1) 4
(2) $4\frac{1}{4}$
(3) $4\frac{1}{2}$
(4) $4\frac{5}{6}$
(5) $4\frac{7}{8}$

3. A carpenter has a board 4 feet 3 inches in length. He cuts off a piece 2 feet 8 inches in length. The length of the piece that is left is

(1) 1 ft. 5 in.
(2) 2 ft. 7 in.
(3) 2 ft. 5 in.
(4) 1 ft. 7 in.
(5) 2 ft. 3 in.

4. How many square feet of cardboard are used in making a closed carton 5 feet long, 3 feet wide, and 2 feet high?

(1) 40
(2) 50
(3) 54
(4) 60
(5) 62

5. A suitable metric unit to use in stating a man's weight is the

(1) liter
(2) millimeter
(3) kilogram
(4) cubic meter
(5) centimeter

6. If O is the center of the circle and m $\angle B = 52°$, find m $\angle O$.

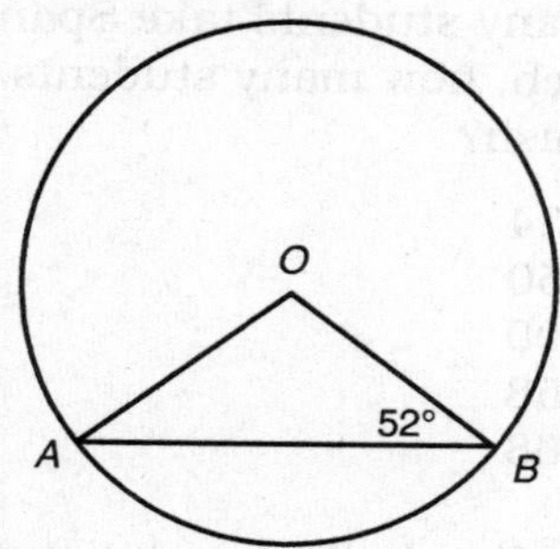

(1) 52°
(2) 76°
(3) 80°
(4) 94°
(5) Not enough information is given.

7. On line segment $\overline{AC}$, $AB : BC = 3 : 5$ and $BC = 20$ inches.

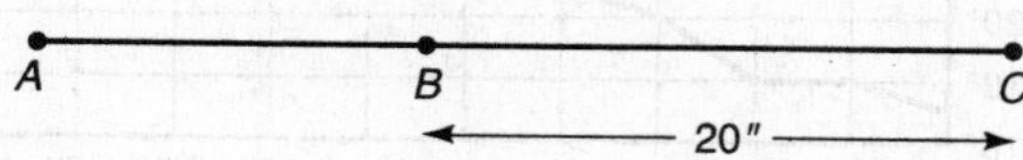

The length, in inches, of $\overline{AB}$ is
(1) 3
(2) 10
(3) 12
(4) 15
(5) 16

8. The diagram below represents a cross section of a pipe. If the diameter of the outer circle is $7\frac{1}{2}$ inches and the diameter of the inner circle is $4\frac{1}{2}$ inches, what is the thickness of the pipe?

(1) 1 in.
(2) $1\frac{1}{4}$ in.
(3) $1\frac{1}{2}$ in.
(4) 2 in.
(5) 3 in.

9. Mr. Gray's weekly salary was increased from $400 per week to $500 per week. The percent increase in his salary was
(1) 20%
(2) 25%
(3) 80%
(4) 100%
(5) 125%

10. A shopper buys a loaf of bread at x cents and 2 pounds of coffee at y cents per pound. If she pays with a $5.00 bill, the number of cents she receives in change is

(1) $500 - x - y$
(2) $500 - (x - y)$
(3) $500 - x + y$
(4) $500 - x - 2y$
(5) $x + y - 500$

11. The area of a rectangular living room is 240 square feet. If the length of the room is 20 feet, what is the perimeter, in feet, of the room?
(1) 12
(2) 32
(3) 50
(4) 64
(5) Not enough information is given.

12. The Center Movie House charges $2 for matinee performances and $4 for evening performances. On 1 day 267 matinee tickets and 329 evening tickets were sold. An expression that represents the total receipts, in dollars, for that day is
(1) 4(267) + 2(329)
(2) 2(267) + 4(329)
(3) 6(267 + 329)
(4) 2(267 + 329) + 4(267 + 329)
(5) 4(267 + 329)

13. A crew of painters can paint an apartment in $4\frac{1}{2}$ hours. What part of the apartment can they paint in $2\frac{1}{2}$ hours?

(1) $\frac{5}{9}$
(2) $\frac{5}{7}$
(3) $\frac{2}{3}$
(4) $\frac{5}{6}$
(5) $\frac{7}{8}$

14. Which of the following expresses 2,347,516 in scientific notation?

(1) 2.347516×10^5
(2) 23.47516×10^5
(3) 234.7516×10^4
(4) 23.47516×10^6
(5) 2.347516×10^6

15. The expression $x^2 - 5x + 6$ may be written as

(1) $(x + 3)(x + 2)$
(2) $(x + 3)(x - 2)$
(3) $(x - 3)(x - 2)$
(4) $(x - 3)(x + 2)$
(5) $x(5x + 6)$

16. A class has 32 students. On a certain day x students are absent. What fractional part of the class is present on that day?

(1) $\frac{x}{32}$
(2) $\frac{32 - x}{x}$
(3) $\frac{x}{32 - x}$
(4) $\frac{32 - x}{32}$
(5) $\frac{32 - x}{32 + x}$

17. At the Adams High School 402 students are taking Spanish and French. If twice as many students take Spanish as take French, how many students take Spanish?

(1) 134
(2) 150
(3) 200
(4) 258
(5) 268

18. According to the graph below, which of the following statements is correct?

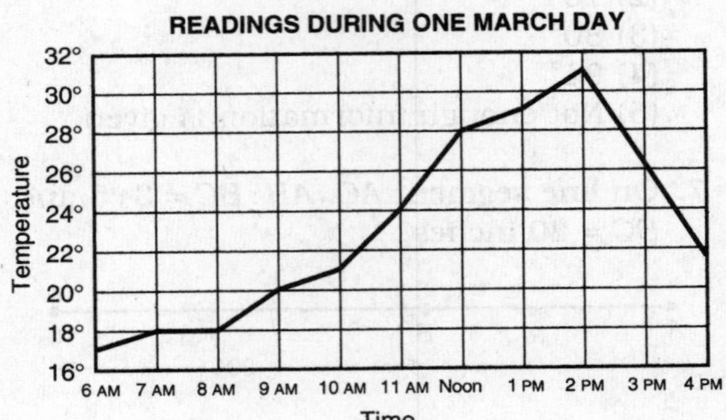

(1) The change in temperature between 7 A.M. and noon was 8°.
(2) The highest temperature reached during the day was 32°.
(3) The change in temperature between 8 A.M. and noon was −10°.
(4) The temperature did not change between 7 A.M. and 8 A.M.
(5) The temperature at noon was 30°.

19. A shipment of 2,200 pounds of sugar is packed in 40-ounce bags. How many bags are needed for the shipment?

(1) 640
(2) 750
(3) 780
(4) 800
(5) 880

20. A ship sails 8 miles due east and then 15 miles due north. At this point, how many miles is the ship from its starting point?

(1) 17
(2) 19
(3) 20
(4) 24
(5) 25

21. A book salesman earns 12% commission on sales. Last month he sold a set of 300 textbooks at $20 per book, a group of 20 art books at $50 per book, and a shipment of 400 novels at $25 per book. What was his commission for the month?

(1) $204
(2) $1,700
(3) $2,040
(4) $17,000
(5) $20,400

22. Mrs. Alvin bought 120 shares of RST Corporation at $32.75 per share and sold these shares a year later at $36.50 per share. Her profit before paying commission and taxes was

(1) $400
(2) $450
(3) $480
(4) $520
(5) $560

23. Mr. and Mrs. Donato went on a vacation motor trip. When the trip started, the odometer reading in their car was 8,947 miles. When the trip was completed the odometer reading was 9,907 miles. How many gallons of gas, to the nearest gallon, were used on the trip?

(1) 36
(2) 38
(3) 40
(4) 41
(5) Not enough information is given.

24. In a class of 34 students, there are 6 more girls than boys. How many girls are in the class?

(1) 14
(2) 15
(3) 18
(4) 20
(5) 22

25. The number of miles per hour needed to cover 120 miles in x hours may be expressed as

(1) $\frac{120}{x}$
(2) $\frac{x}{120}$
(3) $120x$
(4) $120 + x$
(5) $x - 120$

26. In 5 years the population of a town decreased from 3,500 to 2,800. The percent of decrease was

(1) 20%
(2) 25%
(3) 30%
(4) 40%
(5) 70%

27. Mr. Fox's will provided that his wife receive $\frac{1}{2}$ of his estate, and his three sons divide the rest equally. If each son's share was $8,000, what was the value of the estate?

(1) $24,000
(2) $32,000
(3) $40,000
(4) $48,000
(5) $50,000

28. Joshua earns $72 for typing 20 pages. At the same rate, how much does he earn for typing 15 pages?

(1) $48
(2) $54
(3) $60
(4) $72
(5) $84

29. A woman buys a Thanksgiving Day turkey weighing 19 pounds 6 ounces. If the turkey sells for $0.88 per pound, how much change does the woman receive from a $20 bill?

(1) $1.95
(2) $2.05
(3) $2.95
(4) $3.95
(5) $4.15

30. Frank had x dollars. He bought y articles for z dollars each. The number of dollars Frank had left was

(1) $yz - x$
(2) $yx - z$
(3) $x - yz$
(4) $x + yz$
(5) $xy + z$

Questions 31 and 32 are based on the following information.

The fare schedule for Checker Taxi is shown below:

First one-fifth mile 1 dollar
Each one-fifth mile after the first 20 cents

31. How much would a 3-mile trip cost (not including tip)?

(1) \$2.00
(2) \$2.50
(3) \$3.00
(4) \$3.80
(5) \$5.00

32. If a passenger has exactly \$10.00, how many miles can she ride and still be able to give the driver a tip of \$1.00?

(1) 7 or less
(2) more than 7 but no more than 8
(3) more than 8 but no more than 9
(4) more than 9 but no more than 10
(5) more than 10

33. In the diagram below, a semicircle surmounts a rectangle whose length is $2a$ and whose width is a. A formula for finding A, the area of the whole figure, is

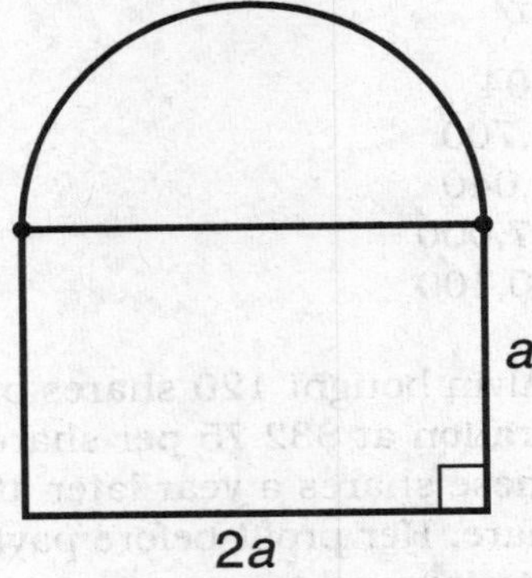

(1) $A = 2a^2 + \frac{1}{2}\pi a^2$
(2) $A = 2\pi a^2$
(3) $A = 3\pi a^2$
(4) $A = 2a^2 + \pi a^2$
(5) Not enough information is given.

34. The graph indicates the way a certain man spends his day. Which one of the following statements is correct?

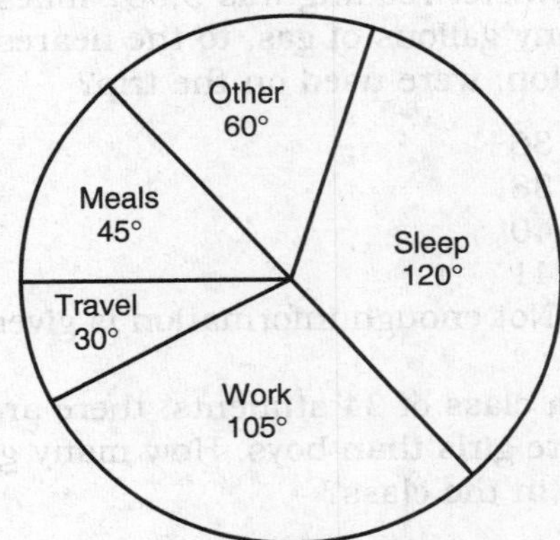

(1) The man works 8 hr. per day.
(2) The man spends 1 hr. more on meals than he does on travel.
(3) The man sleeps 7 hr. per day.
(4) The man spends half his time on work and travel.
(5) The man spends 4 hr. on meals.

35. A storage oil tank in the form of a cylinder is full of oil. The radius of the base of the tank is 7 feet and the height of the tank is 6 feet. Find the number of gallons of oil in the tank if each cubic foot of space holds 7 gallons of oil.

[Use $\pi = \frac{22}{7}$.]

(1) 924
(2) 3,234
(3) 5,000
(4) 6,468
(5) 7,200

36. If $y = 2x^2(z - 3)$, find the value of y if $x = 5$ and $z = 7$.

(1) 54
(2) 150
(3) 180
(4) 200
(5) 400

37. On a motor trip Mr. Shore covered $\frac{2}{7}$ of his total trip distance during the first day by driving 384 miles. The total distance to be covered, in miles, was

(1) 98
(2) 1,244
(3) 1,306
(4) 1,344
(5) 1,500

38. The table below gives the annual premiums for a life insurance policy taken out at various ages.

AGE IN YEARS	PREMIUM PER $1,000
22	$18
30	$22
38	$28
46	$38

If the policy is fully paid up after 20 years, how much is saved by taking out a $10,000 policy at age 30 rather than at age 46?

(1) $160
(2) $320
(3) $400
(4) $3,200
(5) $4,000

39. In a right triangle, the ratio of the two acute angles is 3 : 2. The number of degrees in the larger acute angle is

(1) 36
(2) 54
(3) 72
(4) 90
(5) Not enough information is given.

40. If $3x - 1 < 5$, then x must be

(1) greater than 2
(2) less than 2
(3) greater than 3
(4) less than 0
(5) greater than 5

41. If $\overleftrightarrow{AB} \parallel \overleftrightarrow{GH}$, m $\angle BDE = 100°$, $\overrightarrow{DJ}$ bisects $\angle BDE$, $\overrightarrow{EJ}$ bisects $\angle DEH$, find m $\angle J$.

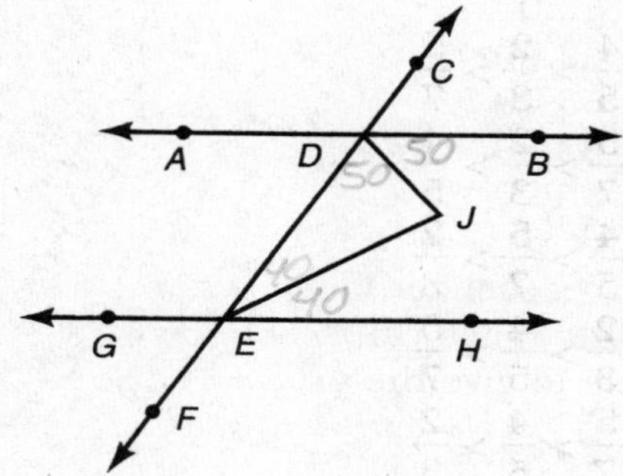

(1) 40°
(2) 60°
(3) 65°
(4) 75°
(5) 90°

42. A chair was marked for sale at $315. This was a discount of 25% off the original price. What was the original price of the chair?

(1) $236.50
(2) $390
(3) $420
(4) $450
(5) $520

43. There are 48 couples at a dance. Each couple consists of 1 male and 1 female. Mr. Fowler selects a female dancing partner for the next dance at random. What is the probability that Mr. Fowler selects his wife?

(1) $\frac{1}{50}$
(2) $\frac{1}{48}$
(3) $\frac{2}{48}$
(4) $\frac{1}{2}$
(5) $\frac{2}{3}$

44. Which inequality is true?

(1) $\frac{4}{5} > \frac{2}{3} > \frac{5}{7}$
(2) $\frac{5}{7} > \frac{2}{3} > \frac{4}{5}$
(3) $\frac{4}{5} > \frac{5}{7} > \frac{2}{3}$
(4) $\frac{2}{3} > \frac{4}{5} > \frac{5}{7}$
(5) $\frac{5}{7} > \frac{4}{5} > \frac{2}{3}$

45. If p pounds of oranges can be bought for c cents, how many pounds can be bought for 98 cents?

(1) $\frac{98c}{p}$
(2) $98cp$
(3) $\frac{cp}{98}$
(4) $\frac{98p}{c}$
(5) $\frac{p}{98c}$

46. A man invests $6,000 in a stock that pays dividends amounting to 5% annually on his investment. How much more must he invest in a stock that pays 6% annually in dividends so that his annual income from both investments will be $900?

(1) $3,000
(2) $5,000
(3) $8,000
(4) $10,000
(5) $12,000

47. A tree is 24 feet tall and casts a shadow of 10 feet. At the same time a tower casts a shadow of 25 feet. What is the height, in feet, of the tower?

(1) 45
(2) 60
(3) 75
(4) 80
(5) 84

48. Mr. Capiello is on a diet. For breakfast and lunch together, he consumes 40% of his allowable number of calories. If he still has 1,200 calories left for the day, his daily calorie allowance is

(1) 2,000
(2) 2,200
(3) 2,400
(4) 2,500
(5) 2,800

49. If $3x - y = 11$ and $2y = 8$, then $x =$

(1) 3
(2) 4
(3) $4\frac{1}{2}$
(4) 5
(5) 6

50. Ms. Ruiz pays $4,800 in income taxes. If this is 15% of her annual income, what is her annual income?

(1) $25,000
(2) $30,000
(3) $32,000
(4) $36,000
(5) $40,000

51. A side of a square is n feet in length. Each side of the square is increased by 2 feet, thus creating a new square whose area exceeds that of the original square by 48 square feet. An equation that expresses the relationship between the areas of the two squares is

(1) $n^2 = (n + 2)^2 + 48$
(2) $(n + 2)^2 = n^2 + 48$
(3) $n^2 + (n + 2)^2 = 48$
(4) $n^2 - (n + 2)^2 = 48$
(5) $(n + 4)^2 - n^2 = 48$

52. A man invests part of $10,000 at 6% and the rest at 8%. His annual income from both investments is $720. If x represents the amount invested at 6%, which one of the following equations may be used to find the value of x?

(1) $0.06x + 0.08(10{,}000 - x) = 720$
(2) $6x + 8(10{,}000 - x) = 720$
(3) $0.06x + 0.08x + 720 = 10{,}000$
(4) $0.06x + 0.08(x - 10{,}000) = 720$
(5) $0.06(x - 10{,}000) + 0.08x = 720$

53. A family spent $\frac{1}{4}$ of its income for rent and $\frac{1}{5}$ of its income for food. What percent of its income remains?

(1) 40%
(2) 45%
(3) 50%
(4) 52%
(5) 55%

54. The perimeter of a triangle is 42 inches. If one side of the triangle is 6 inches longer than the first side and the third side is double the size of the first side, find the length of the first side.

(1) 8 in.
(2) 9 in.
(3) 10 in.
(4) 12 in.
(5) 15 in.

55. On the number line below, $\sqrt{7}$ is located at point

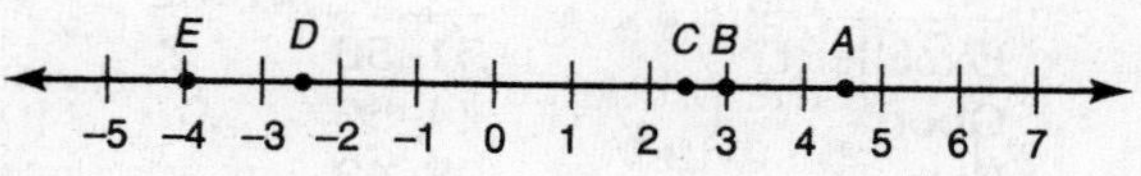

(1) A
(2) B
(3) C
(4) D
(5) E

56. A certain recipe that will yield 4 portions calls for $1\frac{1}{2}$ cups of sugar. If the recipe is used to yield 10 portions, the amount of sugar needed, in cups, is

(1) $3\frac{1}{2}$
(2) $3\frac{3}{4}$
(3) 4
(4) $4\frac{1}{4}$
(5) $4\frac{3}{4}$

ANSWER KEY

1. 1	13. 1	24. 4	35. 4	46. 4
2. 2	14. 5	25. 1	36. 4	47. 2
3. 4	15. 3	26. 1	37. 4	48. 1
4. 5	16. 4	27. 4	38. 4	49. 4
5. 3	17. 5	28. 2	39. 2	50. 3
6. 2	18. 4	29. 3	40. 2	51. 2
7. 3	19. 5	30. 3	41. 5	52. 1
8. 3	20. 1	31. 4	42. 3	53. 5
9. 2	21. 3	32. 3	43. 2	54. 2
10. 4	22. 2	33. 1	44. 3	55. 3
11. 4	23. 5	34. 2	45. 4	56. 2
12. 2				

WHAT'S YOUR SCORE?

55 right	1 wrong
Excellent	51–56
Good	44–50
Fair	38–43

If your score was low, the explanation of the correct answers that follows will help you. You may obtain additional help and practice by referring to the review material in Unit VII.

ANSWER ANALYSIS

Following the correct answer are the chapter and section containing the material covered in the question.

1. 1 Chapter 18 (Arithmetic, Percent)
If 80% of the audience were adults, 100% – 80% = 20% were children.
20% = 0.20, and 0.20(650) = 130

2. 2 Chapter 19 (Algebra, Ratio and Proportion)
Let x = number of inches between the towns on the map.
Set up a proportion:

$$\frac{1 \text{ in.}}{60 \text{ mi.}} = \frac{x \text{ in.}}{225 \text{ mi.}}$$

$$60x = 255$$

$$x = \frac{255}{60} = 4\frac{1}{4}$$

3. 4 Chapter 22 (Measures, Operations with Measures)

$$\begin{array}{r} 4 \text{ ft. } 3 \text{ in.} \\ -2 \text{ ft. } 8 \text{ in.} \end{array} = \begin{array}{r} 3 \text{ ft. } 15 \text{ in.} \\ -2 \text{ ft } \ \ 8 \text{ in.} \\ \hline 1 \text{ ft. } \ \ 7 \text{ in.} \end{array}$$

4. 5 Chapter 20 (Geometry, Areas)
To find the amount of cardboard needed, add up the areas of all six sides of the carton.

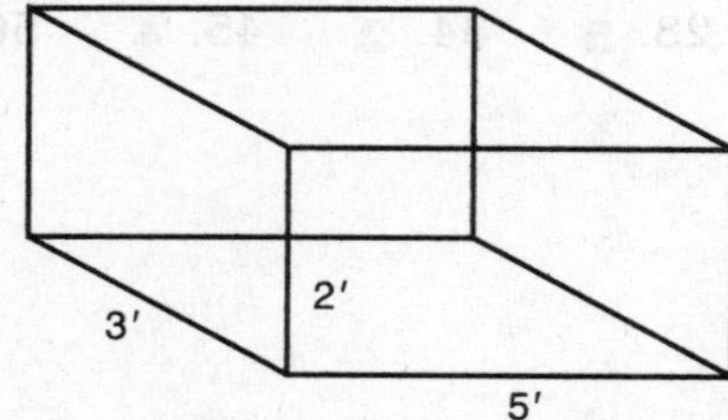

Area of bottom = 5 × 3 = 15 sq. ft.
Area of top = 15 sq. ft.
Area of front = 5 × 2 = 10 sq. ft.
Area of back = 10 sq. ft.
Area of side = 3 × 2 = 6 sq. ft.
Area of other side = 6 sq. ft.
Total area = 15 + 15 + 10 + 10 + 6 + 6 = 62 sq. ft.

5. 3 Chapter 22 (Measures, The Metric System)
Of the metric units listed, only the kilogram is a unit of weight.

6. 2 Chapter 20 (Geometry, Geometric Concepts and Relationships)

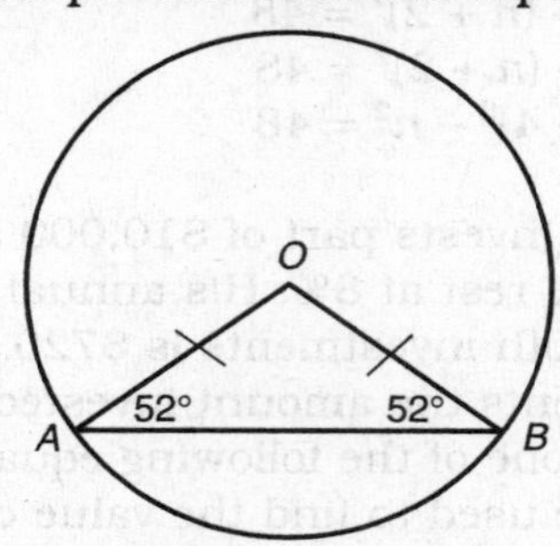

$OA = OB$, since each is a radius.
$m\angle A = m\angle B = 52°$
$m\angle A + m\angle B + m\angle O = 180°$
$52 + 52 + m\angle O = 180$
$104 + m\angle O = 180$
$m\angle O = 180 - 104 = 76°$

7. 3 Chapter 19 (Algebra, Ratio and Proportion)

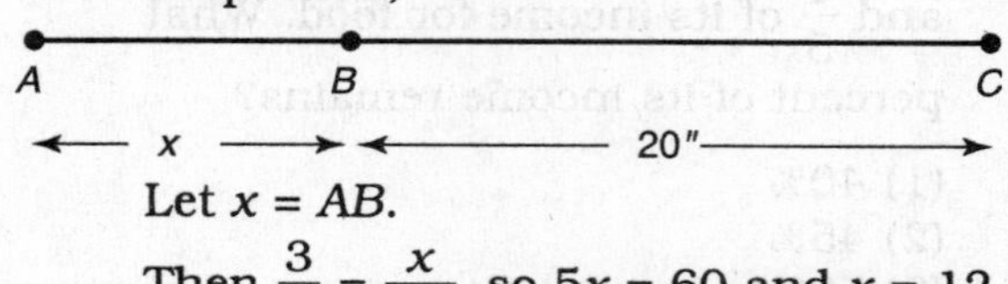

Let $x = AB$.
Then $\frac{3}{5} = \frac{x}{20}$, so $5x = 60$ and $x = 12$.

8. 3 Chapter 20 (Geometry, Areas)

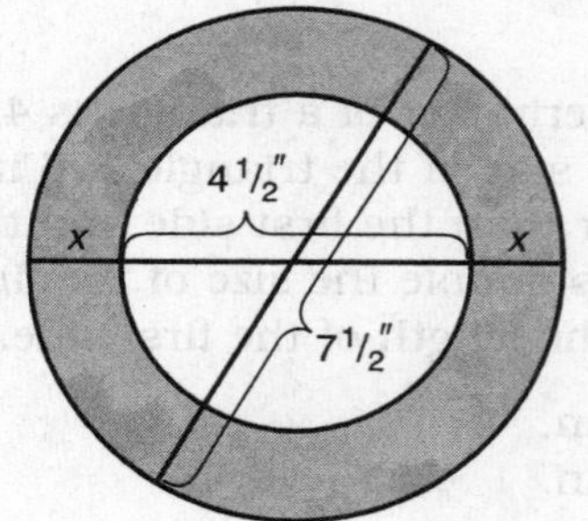

Let x = thickness of the pipe.
Then $x + x + 4\frac{1}{2} = 7\frac{1}{2}$
so $2x = 3$ and $x = 1\frac{1}{2}$ in.

9. 2 Chapter 18 (Arithmetic, Percent)

$$\text{Percent increase} = \frac{\text{actual increase}}{\text{original amount}}$$

Actual increase: \$500 – \$400 = \$100

Percent increase: $\frac{100}{400} = \frac{1}{4} = 25\%$

10. 4 Chapter 19 (Algebra, Fundamentals)
The shopper gives the storekeeper \$5.00, or 500 cents. From this amount the storekeeper takes out x cents for the bread and $2y$ cents for the coffee.
The result is $500 - x - 2y$.

11. 4 Chapter 20 (Geometry, Areas)
Draw a diagram:

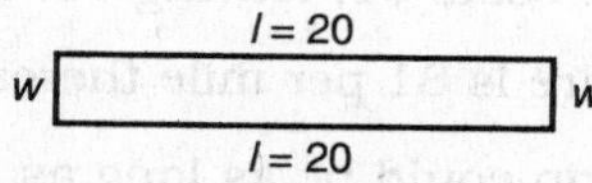

Since $A = lw = 240$, then $20w = 240$, and $w = 12$. Then
$P = 2(l + w) = 2(20 + 12) = 2(32) = 64$.

12. 2 Chapter 18 (Arithmetic)
To find the total receipts, find the receipts of the matinee performances and add to these the receipts of the evening performances.
$2(267) + 4(329) =$ total receipts

13. 1 Chapter 18 (Arithmetic, Fractions)
The part of the apartment painted in $2\frac{1}{2}$ hours =

$$\frac{2\frac{1}{2}}{4\frac{1}{2}} = \frac{5}{2} \div \frac{9}{2} = \frac{5}{2} \times \frac{2}{9} = \frac{5}{9}$$

14. 5 Chapter 19 (Algebra, Exponents and Scientific Notation)
To write a number in scientific notation, write it as the product of a number between 1 and 10 and a power of 10.
In this case, the number between 1 and 10 is 2.347516. In going from 2.347516 to 2,347,516, move the decimal point 6 places to the right. Therefore,
$2,347,516 = 2.347516 \times 10^6$

15. 3 Chapter 19 (Algebra, Factoring and the Solution of Quadratic Equations)
The expression $x^2 - 5x + 6$ factors as $(x - 3)(x - 2)$. If you can't factor, check each choice by multiplying out.

16. 4 Chapter 19 (Algebra, Fundamentals)
If there are 32 students in the class and x students are absent, then $32 - x$ students are present.
The fractional part of the students present is $\frac{32 - x}{32}$.

17. 5 Chapter 19 (Algebra, Solving Problems)
Let x = number of students taking French,
and $2x$ = number of students taking Spanish.

$$x + 2x = 402$$
$$3x = 402$$
$$x = 402 \div 3 = 134$$
$$2x = 2(134) = 268$$

18. 4 Chapter 21 (Graphs, Line Graphs)
Note on the graph that the temperature neither rose nor fell, that is, it did not change, between 7 A.M. and 8 A.M.

19. 5 Chapter 22 (Measures, Operations with Measures)
Since there are 16 oz. in 1 lb.
2,200 lb. = 2,200 × 16 = 35,200 oz.
35,200 ÷ 40 = 880

20. 1 Chapter 20 (Geometry, Indirect Measurement)
Use the Pythagorean theorem.

$$x^2 = 8^2 + 15^2$$
$$= 64 + 225$$
$$= 289$$
$$x = \sqrt{289} = 17$$

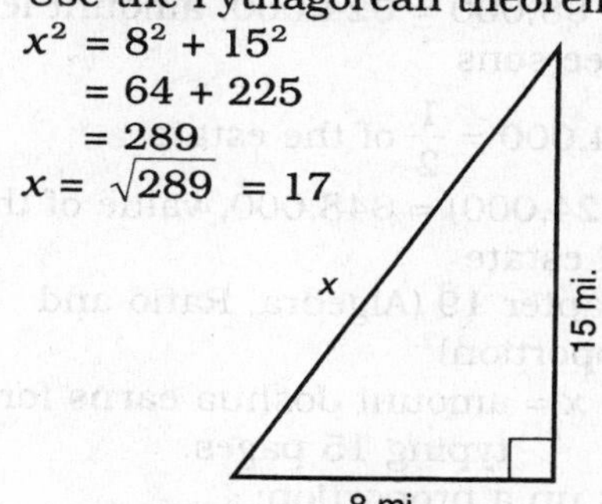

21. 3 Chapter 18 (Arithmetic, Percent)
Textbook sales: 300 × \$20 = \$6,000
Art book sales: 20 × \$50 = \$1,000
Novel sales: 400 × \$25 = \$10,000
Total sales = \$17,000
Commission: 12% of \$17,000 = \$2,040

22. 2 Chapter 18 (Arithmetic, Fractions)
Profit per share:
\$36.50 − \$32.75 = \$3.75
Total profit: 120 × \$3.75 = \$450

23. 5 Chapter 18 (Arithmetic)
You could subtract to find the number of miles driven, but since the number of miles per gallon is not given, the problem cannot be solved.

24. 4 Chapter 19 (Algebra, Solving Problems)
Let x = number of boys,
and $x + 6$ = number of girls.
$x + x + 6 = 34$

$2x + 6 = 34$
$2x = 34 - 6 = 28$
$x = 28 \div 2 = 14$
$x + 6 = 14 + 6 = 20$ girls

25. **1** Chapter 19 (Algebra, Fundamentals)
Use the relationship
Rate × Time = Distance
or Rate = $\frac{\text{Distance}}{\text{Time}}$
In this case, distance = 120 mi. and time = x
Therefore, the number of miles per hour is $\frac{120}{x}$.

26. **1** Chapter 18 (Arithmetic, Percent)
Percent decrease = $\frac{\text{actual decrease}}{\text{original number}}$
Actual decrease: 3,500 – 2,800 = 700
Percent decrease: $\frac{700}{3{,}500} = \frac{1}{5} = 20\%$

27. **4** Chapter 18 (Arithmetic, Fractions)
\$8,000 = 1 son's share
3 × \$8,000 = \$24,000, amount left to three sons
\$24,000 = $\frac{1}{2}$ of the estate
2(\$24,000) = \$48,000, value of the full estate

28. **2** Chapter 19 (Algebra, Ratio and Proportion)
Let x = amount Joshua earns for typing 15 pages.
Set up a proportion:
$\frac{\text{pages typed}}{\text{dollars earned}}: \frac{20}{72} = \frac{15}{x}$
$20x = 15 \times 72 = 1{,}080$, and
$x = 1{,}080 \div 20 = \$54$.

29. **3** Chapter 18 (Arithmetic, Decimals)
6 oz. = $\frac{6}{16} = \frac{3}{8}$ lb.
19 lb. costs 19(\$0.88) = \$16.72
$\frac{3}{8}$ lb. costs $\frac{3}{8}$(\$0.88) = \$0.33 (0.11 / 1 after cancelling)
$19\frac{3}{8}$ lb. costs \$16.72 + \$.33 = \$17.05
Change = \$20.00 – \$17.05 = \$2.95

30. **3** Chapter 19 (Algebra, Fundamentals)
Frank spent yz dollars.
Subtract yz from x. The result is $x - yz$.

31. **4** Chapter 18 (Arithmetic, Decimals)
Note that, after the first $\frac{1}{5}$ mi., the fare amounts to \$1 per mile.
Therefore, a 3-mi. trip would cost \$2 for the second and third miles. The first $\frac{1}{5}$ mi. would cost \$1, and each of the next $\frac{4}{5}$'s would cost 20 cents each, for a total of \$1.80. The entire 3-mi. trip would cost \$2.00 + \$1.80 = \$3.80.

32. **3** Chapter 18 (Arithmetic)
Taking \$1 tip from the \$10 available leaves \$9 for the actual travel. The first $\frac{1}{5}$ mi. costs \$1, leaving \$8. Since the fare is \$1 per mile thereafter, the trip could be as long as $8\frac{1}{5}$ mi.

33. **1** Chapter 20 (Geometry, Areas)
Area of rectangle = $(2a)(a) = 2a^2$.
Radius of semicircle = $\frac{1}{2}(2a) = a$.
The formula for the area of a circle is $A = \pi r^2$.
Area of semicircle = $\frac{1}{2}(\pi a^2)$.
Area of whole figure =
$2a^2 + \frac{1}{2}\pi a^2$.

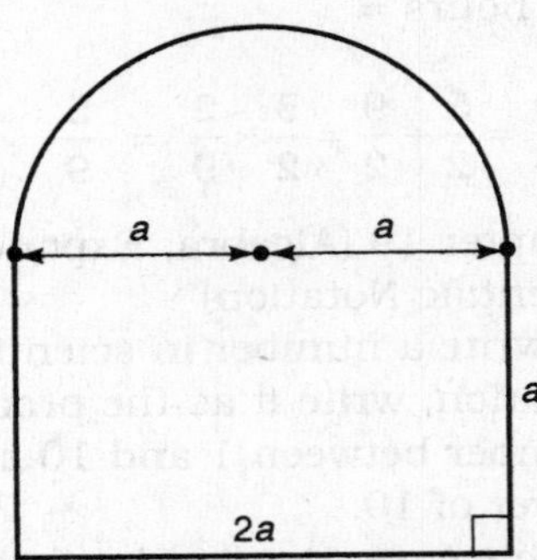

34. **2** Chapter 21 (Graphs, Circle Graphs)
The man spends $\frac{45}{360} = \frac{1}{8}$ day on meals. $\frac{1}{8}$ day = $\frac{1}{8} \times 24 = 3$ hr.
The man spends $\frac{30}{360} = \frac{1}{12}$ day on travel. $\frac{1}{12}$ day = $\frac{1}{12} \times 24 = 2$ hr.
The man spends 1 hr. more on meals than on travel. Each of the other statements is incorrect. For example, consider statement (1).
$\frac{105°}{360°} = \frac{7}{24}$, $\frac{7}{24} \times 24 = 7$
Each day, the man works 7 hr., not 8 hr.

35. 4 Chapter 20 (Geometry, Points, Lines, and Space)
Use the formula for the volume of a cylinder: $V = \pi r^2 h$.

In this case, $\pi = \frac{22}{7}$, $r = 7$, and $h = 6$.

$$V = \frac{22}{7} \times 7 \times 7 \times 6$$
$$= 924 \text{ cu. ft.}$$

$924 \times 7 = 6{,}468$

36. 4 Chapter 19 (Algebra, Exponents and Evaluations)

$y = 2x^2(z - 3)$
$= 2(5)(5)(7 - 3)$
$= 2(5)(5)(4)$
$= 200$

37. 4 Chapter 18 (Arithmetic, Fractions)
Let x = total distance to be covered.

$\frac{2}{7}x = 384$
$2x = 7(384) = 2{,}688$
$x = 2{,}688 \div 2 = 1{,}344$

38. 4 Chapter 18 (Arithmetic)
At age 30, the policy costs 22(10) = \$220 per year.
At age 46, the policy costs 38(10) = \$380 per year.
Thus, \$380 – \$220 = \$160 saved per year.
In 20 years, the savings is 160(20) = \$3,200.

39. 2 Chapter 20 (Geometry, Geometric Concepts and Relationships)

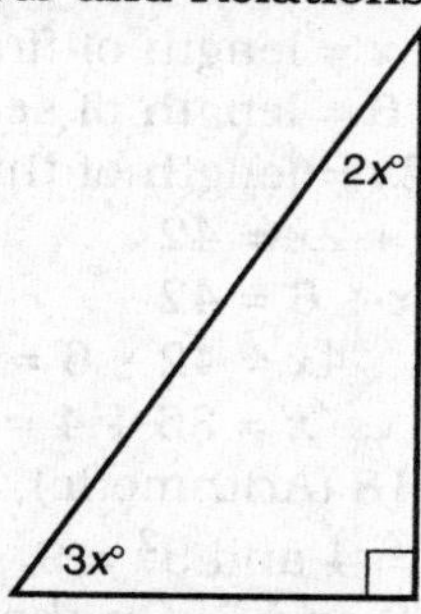

Let $3x$ = measure of the larger angle, and $2x$ = measure of the smaller angle
$3x + 2x = 90$
$5x = 90$
$x = 90 \div 5 = 18$
$3x = 3(18) = 54°$

40. 2 Chapter 19 (Algebra, Solving Inequalities)
$3x - 1 < 5$
$3x < 6$
$x < 2$
x must be less than 2.

41. 5 Chapter 20 (Geometry, Geometric Concepts and Relationships)

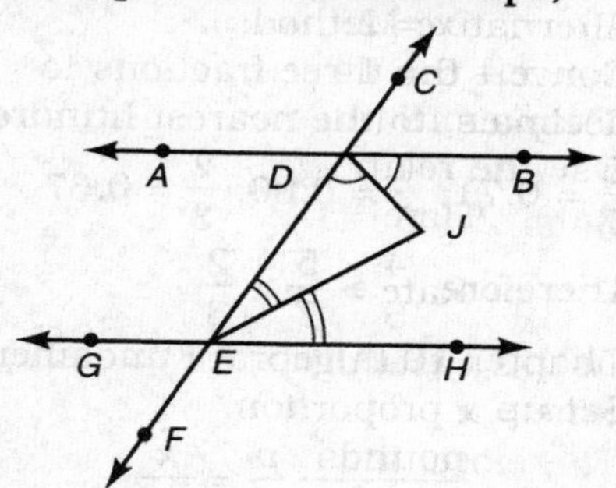

$m\angle BDE = 100°$
Since $\overleftrightarrow{AB} \parallel \overleftrightarrow{GH}$, $m\angle BDE + m\angle DEH = 180°$
$100 + m\angle DEH = 180$
$m\angle DEH = 180 - 100 = 80°$
$m\angle JDE = \frac{1}{2} m\angle BDE = 50°$
$m\angle DEJ = \frac{1}{2} m\angle DEH = 40°$
$m\angle J + 50 + 40 = 180$
$m\angle J = 180 - 50 - 40 = 90°$

42. 3 Chapter 18 (Arithmetic, Percent)

$25\% = \frac{1}{4}$. Selling price of chair

was $\frac{3}{4}$ of original selling price.

Let x = original selling price.

$\frac{3}{4}x = \$315$

$x = \$315 \div \frac{3}{4} = \$315 \times \frac{4}{3} = \$420$

43. 2 Chapter 19 (Algebra, Probability)
Probability =
$$\frac{\text{number of successful outcomes}}{\text{number of possible outcomes}}$$

In this case, the number of successful outcomes is 1 since, of the 48 women present, only 1 woman is Mr. Fowler's wife. The number of possible outcomes is 48 since there are 48 possible women partners.
Probability = $\frac{1}{48}$

44. 3 Chapter 18 (Arithmetic, Fractions)
$\frac{4}{5} > \frac{5}{7}$ because $4 \times 7 > 5 \times 5$

$\frac{5}{7} > \frac{2}{3}$ because $5 \times 3 > 7 \times 2$

Thus, $\frac{4}{5} > \frac{5}{7} > \frac{2}{3}$ is correct.
Alternative Method:
Convert the three fractions to decimals, to the nearest hundredth.
$\frac{5}{7} = 0.71$, $\frac{4}{5} = 0.80$, $\frac{2}{3} = 0.67$
Therefore, $\frac{4}{5} > \frac{5}{7} > \frac{2}{3}$

45. 4 Chapter 19 (Algebra, Fundamentals)
Set up a proportion.
$$\frac{\text{pounds}}{\text{cents}}: \frac{p}{c} = \frac{x}{98}$$
Then $98p = cx$, and $x = \frac{98p}{c}$.

46. 4 Chapter 18 (Arithmetic)
\$6,000 at 5% = \$6,000 × 0.05 = \$300 income
The man needs \$900 − \$300 = \$600 more in income.
6% of the new amount needed = \$600
Let x = new amount needed.
$0.06x = 600$
$x = 600 \div 0.06 = \$10,000$

47. 2 Chapter 20 (Geometry, Congruence and Similarity)

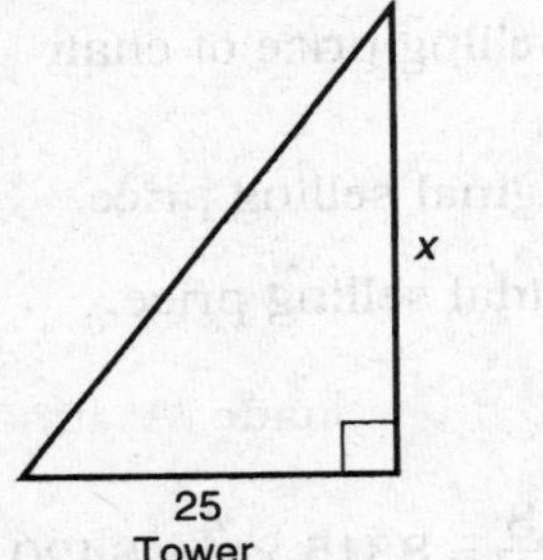

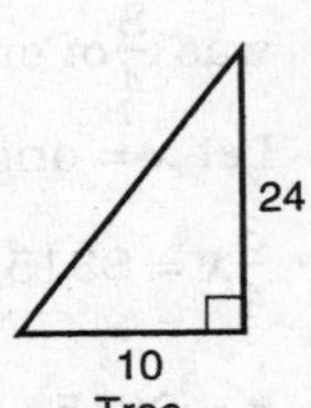

Let x = height of tower.
Set up a proportion.
$$\frac{\text{height of object}}{\text{length of shadow}}: \frac{x}{25} = \frac{24}{10}$$
$10x = 25(24) = 600$
$x = 600 \div 10 = 60$

48. 1 Chapter 18 (Arithmetic, Percent)
If Mr. Capiello has consumed 40% of his allowable calories, he has 60% left.
Let x = his daily allowance of calories
$0.60x = 1,200$
$x = 1,200 \div 0.60 = 2,000$

49. 4 Chapter 19 (Algebra, Solving Equations)
Since $2y = 8$, then $y = 4$.
$3x - y = 11$
$3x - 4 = 11$
$3x = 15$ and $x = 5$

50. 3 Chapter 18 (Arithmetic, Decimals)
Let x = Ms. Ruiz's annual income.
$15x = \$4,800$
$x = \frac{\$4,800}{0.15} = \frac{\$480,000}{15}$
$= \$32,000$

51. 2 Chapter 19 (Algebra, Solving Problems)
Area of enlarged square = $(n + 2)(n + 2)$
Area of original square = n^2
Use this relationship:
Enlarged square area = original square area + 48
$(n + 2)^2 = n^2 + 48$

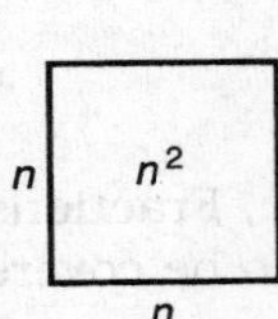

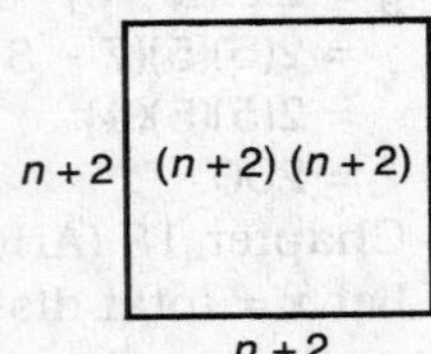

52. 1 Chapter 18 (Arithmetic, Percent)
$0.06x$ = income on 6% investment
$0.08(10,000 - x)$ = income on 8% investment
Then $0.06x + 0.08(10,000 - x) = 720$

53. 5 Chapter 18 (Arithmetic, Fractions)
Fractional part of income spent on rent and food: $\frac{1}{4} + \frac{1}{5} = \frac{5}{20} + \frac{4}{20} = \frac{9}{20}$
$1 - \frac{9}{20} = \frac{11}{20}$, remaining income
$\frac{11}{20} = 0.55 = 55\%$

54. 2 Chapter 19 (Algebra, Solving Problems)
Let x = length of first side.
Then $x + 6$ = length of second side, and $2x$ = length of third side.
$x + x + 6 + 2x = 42$
$4x + 6 = 42$
$4x = 42 - 6 = 36$
$x = 36 \div 4 = 9$ in.

55. 3 Chapter 18 (Arithmetic)
Since $2^2 = 4$ and $3^2 = 9$, $\sqrt{7}$ is between 2 and 3. On the number line, only point C lies between 2 and 3.

56. 2 Chapter 19 (Algebra, Ratio and Proportion)
Let x = number of cups of sugar needed. Set up a proportion:
$$\frac{\text{number of portions}}{\text{cups of sugar}}: \frac{4}{1.5} = \frac{10}{x}$$
Then $4x = 10(1.5) = 15$, and
$x = \frac{15}{4} = 3\frac{3}{4}$

Practice Test Two

1. An oil tank contained 480 gallons of oil. After 180 gallons were used, the percent of oil left in the tank was

(1) $37\frac{1}{2}\%$
(2) 62%
(3) $62\frac{1}{2}\%$
(4) 65%
(5) $83\frac{1}{3}\%$

2. A man is planning to remake his lawn next fall. The lawn, which is level and is in the shape of a rectangle 90 feet long and 30 feet wide, is to be covered with topsoil to a depth of 4 inches. The man carts the topsoil in a small truck that holds 15 cubic feet. How many full loads will he need?

(1) 30
(2) 40
(3) 45
(4) 50
(5) 60

3. The drawing below is part of a bar graph showing the population of a small town. How many people lived in the town in 1988?

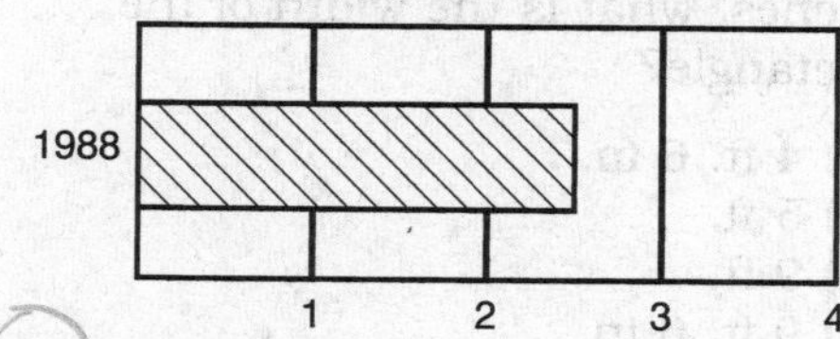

(1) 2,500
(2) 2,800
(3) 3,000
(4) 3,500
(5) 250,000

4. If 1 pound 12 ounces of beef costs \$4.97, what is the cost of beef per pound?

(1) \$1.24
(2) \$1.56
(3) \$2.79
(4) \$2.84
(5) \$3.32

5. A bookcase has 3 shelves. Each of 2 shelves has x books on it. The third shelf holds y books. What is the total number of books in the bookcase?

(1) $2xy$
(2) $x + 2y$
(3) $2(x + y)$
(4) $2x + y$
(5) $2 + x + y$

6. A front lawn measures 25 feet in length and 15 feet in width. The back lawn of the same house measures 50 feet in length and 35 feet in width. What is the ratio of the area of the front lawn to the area of the back lawn?

(1) 1:14
(2) 1:5
(3) 3:14
(4) 7:10
(5) 7:9

7. A bottle is full of lemonade. At lunch, $\frac{1}{3}$ of the bottle is emptied. At dinner, $\frac{3}{4}$ of the rest is used. What fractional part of the lemonade is left?

(1) none
(2) $\frac{1}{12}$
(3) $\frac{1}{6}$
(4) $\frac{1}{5}$
(5) Not enough information is given.

8. A farmer is making a rectangular gate 5 feet high and 12 feet wide as shown in the diagram below. How long is the diagonal piece that she uses to strengthen the gate?

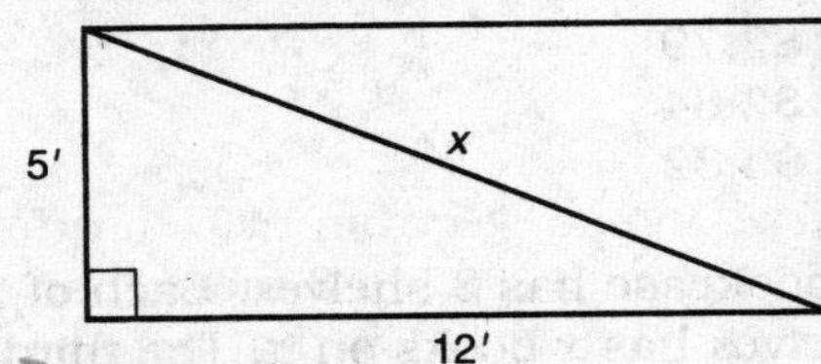

(1) 13 ft.
(2) 14 ft.
(3) 15 ft.
(4) 16 ft.
(5) 17 ft.

9. A television set priced at $400 was reduced 25% in price just before a new model came out. In addition, a 2% discount is allowed for cash. What was the actual cash price a buyer paid for this television set?

(1) $196
(2) $292
(3) $294
(4) $298
(5) $373

10. The circle graph below shows the budget of the James family. Which one of the following statements is correct?

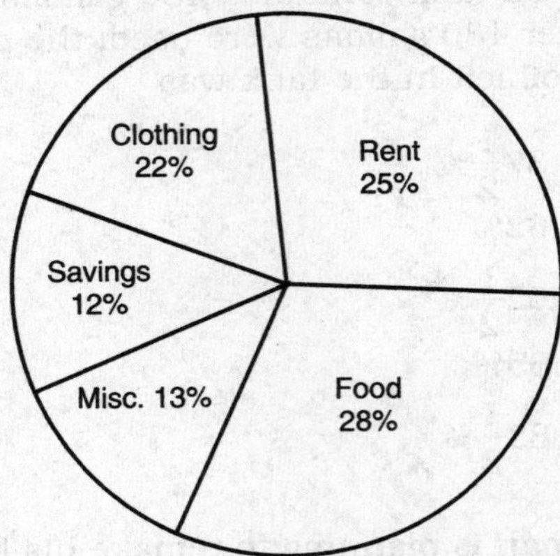

(1) If the monthly income of the James family is $2,500, their allowance for rent is $650.
(2) The angle at the center of the savings sector is 45°.
(3) More than one-half of the James family budget is spent on food and rent.
(4) If the monthly income is $2,500 the James family saves more than $5,000 per year.
(5) Less than $\frac{1}{3}$ of the James family income is spent on clothing and savings.

11. The perimeter of a rectangle is 40 feet. If the length of the rectangle is 15 feet 6 inches, what is the width of the rectangle?

(1) 4 ft. 6 in.
(2) 5 ft.
(3) 9 ft.
(4) 9 ft. 6 in.
(5) 5 ft. 6 in.

12. It takes Rosita x hours to complete a job. What part of the job can Rosita complete in 5 hours?

(1) $\frac{5}{x}$
(2) $5x$
(3) $5 + x$
(4) $(x - 5)$
(5) Not enough information is given.

13. The length of a small particle is 0.0000017 millimeter. Express this number in scientific notation.

(1) 1.7×10^{-5}
(2) 1.7×10^{-6}
(3) 17×10^{-4}
(4) 1.7×10^{6}
(5) 1.7×10^{3}

14. A rectangular solid is 5 feet in length, 4 feet in width, and x feet high. The volume of the solid is 50 cubic feet. Which of the following equations may be used to find the height of the rectangular solid?

(1) $5 + 4 + x = 50$
(2) $4x + 5 = 50$
(3) $5x + 4 = 50$
(4) $50x = 20$
(5) $20x = 50$

15. In the diagram below, if $AC = 24$ and $AB = 6$, the ratio $AB : BC$ is

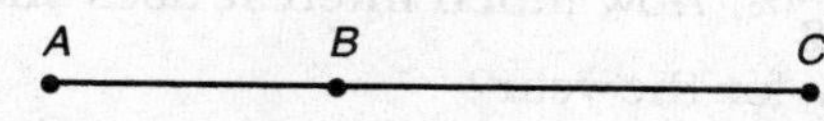

(1) 1 : 4
(2) 1 : 3
(3) 1 : 2
(4) 2 : 1
(5) 3 : 1

16. *ABCD*, shown in the diagram below, is a rectangle. The ratio of the area of $\triangle EDC$ to the area of the rectangle *ABCD* is

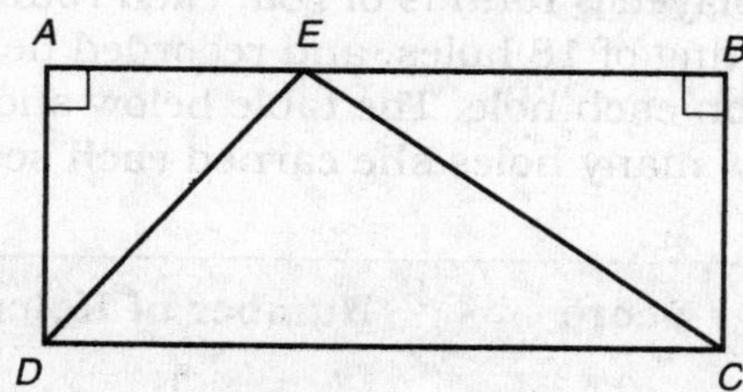

(1) 1 : 4
(2) 1 : 3
(3) 1 : 2
(4) 3 : 5
(5) 3 : 4

17. The cost of 3 pounds 10 ounces of chicken at $0.72 per pound is

(1) $2.61
(2) $2.65
(3) $2.73
(4) $2.79
(5) $2.85

18. If 5 is subtracted from twice a number, the result is equal to 3 more than the number. An equation that may be used to find this number is

(1) $5 - 2x = x + 3$
(2) $2x - 5 = x - 3$
(3) $2x - 5 = x + 3$
(4) $x = 5 - 2x + 3$
(5) $x = 2x - 5 + 3$

19. A businessman spends $\frac{1}{5}$ of his income for rent and $\frac{3}{8}$ of the remainder of his income for salaries. What part of his income does he spend for salaries?

(1) $\frac{3}{10}$
(2) $\frac{1}{2}$
(3) $\frac{23}{40}$
(4) $\frac{3}{4}$
(5) $\frac{4}{5}$

20. On a transatlantic flight of 3,200 miles a plane averages 480 miles per hour. How long does the plane take to make the trip?

(1) 6 hr.
(2) $6\frac{1}{2}$ hr.
(3) 6 hr. 40 min.
(4) 6 hr. 45 min.
(5) $6\frac{5}{6}$ hr.

21. José earns \$8 per hour whenever he works 40 or fewer hours in a week. When he works overtime, he receives $1\frac{1}{2}$ times his regular hourly rate for each hour in excess of 40 hours. If José works 49 hours in 1 week, an expression that states his total pay, in dollars, for that week is

(1) $8(40) + 4\frac{1}{2}(8)$

(2) $8(40) + 4\frac{1}{2}(12)$

(3) 8(60) + 9(12)
(4) 8(40) + 9(12)
(5) Not enough information is given.

22. Janet spent twice as much on a jacket as on a pair of slacks. In all, she spent \$81. How much did she pay for the jacket?

(1) \$27
(2) \$31
(3) \$35
(4) \$48
(5) \$54

23. In right triangle *ABC*, *AC* = *BC*. The measure of ∠*A* is

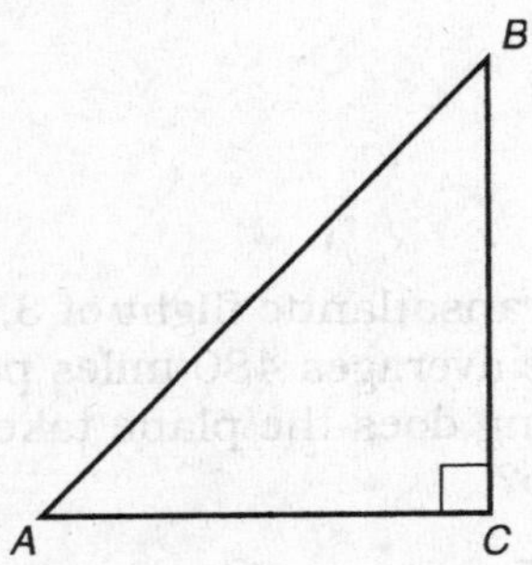

(1) 30°
(2) 35°
(3) 45°
(4) 50°
(5) 60°

24. Mr. Page and his wife have dinner at a restaurant. The bill is \$28. To this is added 5% sales tax. If Mr. Page leaves a tip of 15% based on the \$28 bill, what was the total cost of the dinner?

(1) \$33.60
(2) \$34.41
(3) \$35.00
(4) \$38.50
(5) \$38.70

25. It takes 20 men 36 days to do a construction job. How long will it take 24 men to do the same job?

(1) 25 days
(2) 30 days
(3) 32 days
(4) 40 days
(5) 44 days

26. Ms. Rivera borrows \$8,500 from her bank at an annual interest rate of $12\frac{1}{2}$%. How much interest does she pay for the year?

(1) \$106.25
(2) \$1,062.50
(3) \$1,065.00
(4) \$1,075.00
(5) \$1,650.20

<u>Questions 27–29</u> are based on the following information.

Beth played 5 rounds of golf, each round consisting of 18 holes, and recorded her score on each hole. The table below shows on how many holes she earned each score.

Score	Number of Holes
2	1
3	8
4	13
5	25
6	29
7	5
8	3
more than 8	4

27. On how many holes did she have a score of 4?

(1) 4
(2) 13
(3) 22
(4) 25
(5) more than 25

28. On how many holes was her score greater than 6?

(1) 3
(2) 12
(3) 29
(4) 41
(5) Not enough information is given.

29. What was her median score per hole?

(1) 3
(2) 4
(3) 5
(4) 6
(5) 7

---

30. At State College last year, the entering class numbered 840. If 65% of the entering class were men, how many were women?

(1) 280
(2) 290
(3) 294
(4) 350
(5) 546

31. What is the value of $3a^2 + a(2a^3 - 5)$ when $a = 4$?

(1) 450
(2) 540
(3) 2096
(4) 2196
(5) Not enough information is given.

32. In the figure below, a circle is inscribed in a square. If the diameter of the circle is 6 inches, what is the area, in square inches, of the shaded portion?

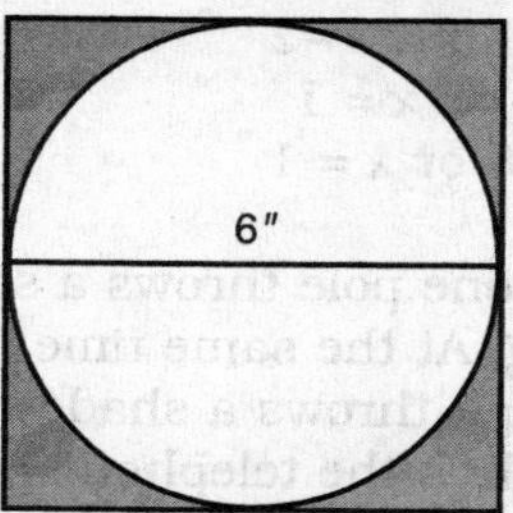

(1) 9π
(2) $36 - 9\pi$
(3) $36 + 9\pi$
(4) $36 - 36\pi$
(5) $9\pi - 36$

33. If 5 is subtracted from 3 times a certain number, the result is 16. What is the number?

(1) –4
(2) 3
(3) 0
(4) 7
(5) 9

34. Justin's average on 4 tests is 80. What grade does he need on his fifth test to raise his average to 84?

(1) 82
(2) 84
(3) 92
(4) 96
(5) 100

35. During a fund-raising drive, an organization collected \$105,000, which amounted to 105% of its goal. What was the goal?

(1) \$90,000
(2) \$95,000
(3) \$100,000
(4) \$110,000
(5) \$120,000

36. If $x^2 - 2x - 8 = 0$, which of the following must be true?

(1) $x = 2$ or $x = -4$
(2) $x = -2$ or $x = -4$
(3) $x = 4$ or $x = -2$
(4) $x = 8$ or $x = 1$
(5) $x = -8$ or $x = 1$

37. A telephone pole throws a shadow 48 feet long. At the same time, a fence post 3 feet high throws a shadow 4 feet long. How high is the telephone pole?

(1) 30 ft.
(2) 36 ft.
(3) 50 ft.
(4) 60 ft.
(5) 64 ft.

38. In a triangle, the measure of the largest angle is 3 times the measure of the smallest, and the measure of the other angle is twice the measure of the smallest. What is the measure of the largest angle of the triangle?

(1) 60°
(2) 65°
(3) 75°
(4) 80°
(5) 90°

39. The diagram below shows a rectangle after a semicircle was cut out of each end. What is the area, in square inches, of the remaining shaded region?

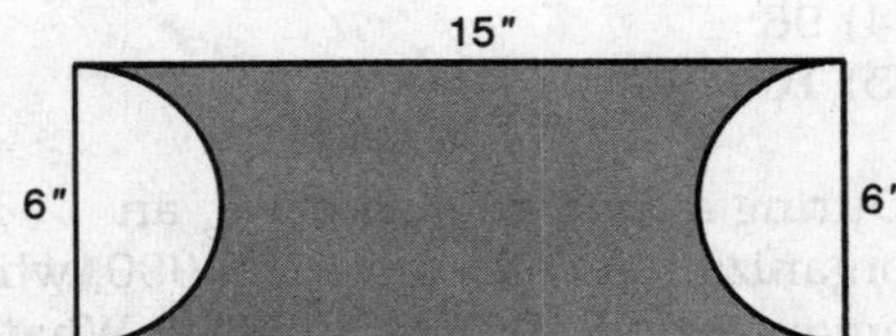

(1) $42 - 6\pi$
(2) $42 - 9\pi$
(3) $90 - 4.5\pi$
(4) $90 - 9\pi$
(5) $90 - 36\pi$

40. A chair was sold on sale for $240. This was a discount of 25% off the original price. What was the original price?

(1) $280
(2) $290
(3) $300
(4) $315
(5) $320

41. To raise funds, the Atlas Club is conducting a raffle. The club is selling tickets at $5 each and is awarding one prize. Mrs. Allen, a member of the club, buys 7 tickets. What is the probability that Mrs. Allen will win the prize?

(1) $\frac{7}{500}$
(2) $\frac{5}{7}$
(3) $\frac{5}{500}$
(4) $\frac{500}{7}$
(5) Not enough information is given.

42. Of the following numbers, the one that is closest to $\sqrt{7}$ is

(1) 2
(2) 2.4
(3) 2.6
(4) 3.1
(5) 3.4

43. The slope of the line joining points $(4,y)$ and $(2,3)$ is 2. What is the value of y?

(1) 3
(2) 4
(3) 5
(4) 6
(5) 7

44. There are 7 employees working in a small business firm. The average (mean) weekly salary of these workers is $584. If each of 3 of the workers earns $450 per week and 3 others earns $600 per week, how much does the seventh worker earn?

(1) $450
(2) $525
(3) $850
(4) $908
(5) $938

45. Mr. Barr invested $12,000 at 7% annual interest. How much more must he invest at 8% so that his total annual income is $1,560?

(1) $6,000
(2) $8,000
(3) $9,000
(4) $10,000
(5) $15,000

46. At a concert, orchestra seats sell for $15 each and balcony seats sell for $10 each. If 324 orchestra seats were sold and the box office collected $7,540, how many balcony seats were sold?

(1) 249
(2) 268
(3) 275
(4) 279
(5) Not enough information is given.

47. In a triangle, the length of the altitude is equal to one-half the length of the base. If n represents the length of the altitude and the area of the triangle is 50 square inches, an equation that expresses this relationship is

(1) $n(2n) = 50$
(2) $\frac{1}{2}(n)(2n) = 50$
(3) $\frac{n^2}{2} = 50$
(4) $2n(4n) = 50$
(5) $2n(n + 1) = 50$

48. John has x dollars. He spends $5 each for 2 movie tickets and y dollars at a cafe. Which of the following expresses the number of dollars he has left?

(1) $2x - 10 + y$
(2) $x - 10 + y$
(3) $x - (10 - y)$
(4) $x - 10 - y$
(5) $x + y + 10$

49. In which of the following pairs of numbers are both numbers solutions of the inequality $2x + 3 \geq 11$?

(1) 0, 3
(2) 1, 2
(3) 2, 5
(4) 3, 6
(5) 4, 10

50. If, in the diagram below, $\overleftrightarrow{AB} \parallel \overleftrightarrow{CD}$ and the ratio of $m\angle D$ to $m\angle A$ is 3 : 2, then $m\angle D =$

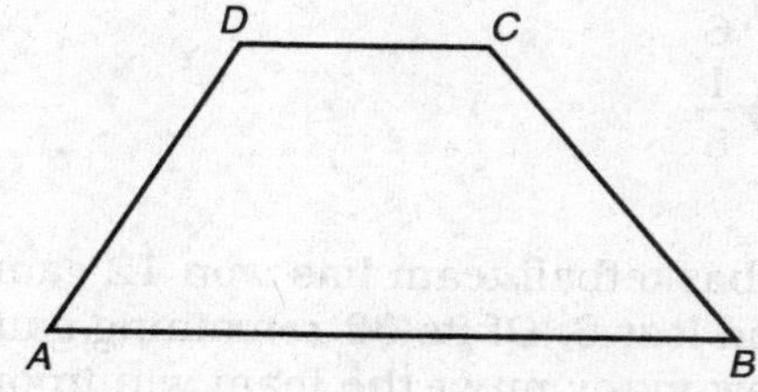

(1) 72°
(2) 90°
(3) 108°
(4) 120°
(5) Not enough information is given

51. Kelly drives a distance of 290 miles in 6 hours. During the first 2 hours she averages 45 miles per hour. What is her average speed for the remaining 4 hours?

(1) 30 mph
(2) 35 mph
(3) 40 mph
(4) 45 mph
(5) 50 mph

52. Ben has $35 more than Joe. If Ben gives Joe $5, Ben will have twice as much as Joe. How much does Joe have?

(1) $10
(2) $15
(3) $18
(4) $20
(5) $25

53. If $2x + 3y = 15$ and $4y = 20$, then $x =$

(1) 0
(2) −2
(3) 1
(4) 3
(5) 5

54. A man left $\frac{1}{3}$ of his estate to his wife and divided the balance of the estate equally among his 4 children. What part of the estate does each child inherit?

(1) $\frac{1}{4}$

(2) $\frac{1}{5}$

(3) $\frac{1}{3}$

(4) $\frac{1}{6}$

(5) $\frac{1}{8}$

55. A basketball team has won 12 games and lost 6. Of its 32 remaining games, how many must the team win in order to have a winning percentage of 64%?

(1) 12
(2) 20
(3) 22
(4) 24
(5) 25

56. Robert earns x dollars per month and his brother, Tom, earns y dollars per month. The total number of dollars the men earn in 1 year is

(1) $x + y$
(2) $12x + y$
(3) $x + 12y$
(4) $12(x + y)$
(5) $x - y$

ANSWER KEY

1. 3	13. 2	24. 1	35. 3	46. 2
2. 5	14. 5	25. 2	36. 3	47. 2
3. 1	15. 2	26. 2	37. 2	48. 4
4. 4	16. 3	27. 2	38. 5	49. 5
5. 4	17. 1	28. 2	39. 2	50. 3
6. 3	18. 3	29. 3	40. 5	51. 5
7. 3	19. 1	30. 3	41. 5	52. 4
8. 1	20. 3	31. 2	42. 3	53. 1
9. 3	21. 4	32. 2	43. 5	54. 4
10. 3	22. 5	33. 4	44. 5	55. 2
11. 1	23. 3	34. 5	45. 3	56. 4
12. 1				

WHAT'S YOUR SCORE?

56 right	0 wrong
Excellent	51–56
Good	44–50
Fair	38–43

If your score was low, the explanation of the correct answers that follows will help you. You may obtain additional help and practice by referring to the review material in Unit VII.

ANSWER ANALYSIS

Following the correct answer are the chapter and section containing the material covered in the question.

1. 3 Chapter 18 (Arithmetic, Percent)
There are 480 – 180 = 300 gal. left in the tank.

$\frac{300}{480} = \frac{5}{8} = 0.625 = 62\frac{1}{2}\%$

2. 5 Chapter 20 (Geometry, Points, Lines, and Space)

4 in. $= \frac{4}{12} = \frac{1}{3}$ ft.

The volume of topsoil to be carted is

$90 \times 30 \times \frac{1}{3} = 900$ cu. ft.

The number of full loads is
$900 \div 15 = 60$

3. 1 Chapter 21 (Graphs, Bar Graphs)
Note that the solid bar ends midway between 2 and 3.
Therefore, the population was 2.5 thousand, or 2,500.

4. 4 Chapter 22 (Operations with Measures)

12 oz. $= \frac{12}{16} = \frac{3}{4}$ lb.

$1\frac{3}{4}$ or $\frac{7}{4}$ lb. costs \$4.97.

$\frac{1}{4}$ lb. costs $\frac{\$4.97}{7} = \$0.71$.

$\frac{4}{4}$, or 1 lb., costs 4(\$0.71) = \$2.84.

5. 4 Chapter 19 (Algebra, Fundamentals)
Each of 2 shelves has x books for a total of $2x$ books.

The third shelf has y books.
The total is $2x + y$ books.

6. 3 Chapter 20 (Geometry, Areas)
Area of front lawn = $25 \times 15 = 375$ sq. ft.
Area of back lawn = $50 \times 35 = 1{,}750$ sq. ft.
Ratio of front lawn to back lawn = $375:1{,}750 = 3:14$

7. 3 Chapter 18 (Arithmetic, Fractions)
At lunch, $\frac{1}{3}$ of the lemonade was used, so $\frac{2}{3}$ was left.
At dinner $\frac{3}{4} \times \frac{2}{3} = \frac{1}{2}$ of the lemonade was used. In all,
$\frac{1}{3} + \frac{1}{2} = \frac{2}{6} + \frac{3}{6} = \frac{5}{6}$ of the lemonade was used, and $\frac{1}{6}$ remained.

8. 1 Chapter 20 (Geometry, Indirect Measurement)

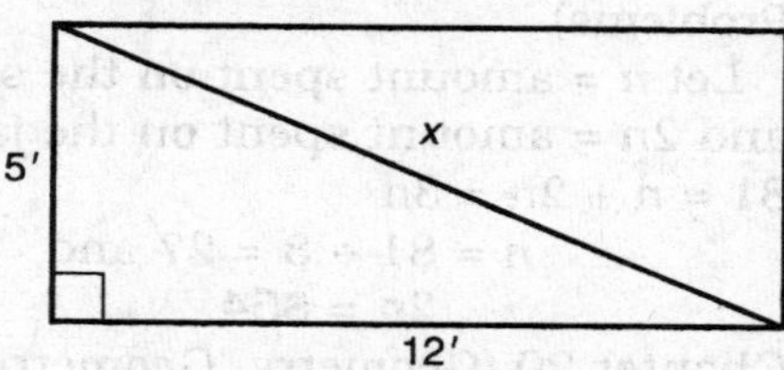

Use the Pythagorean theorem.

$$x^2 = 5^2 + 12^2$$
$$x = 25 + 144 = 169$$
$$= \sqrt{169}$$
$$= 13 \text{ ft.}$$

9. 3 Chapter 18 (Arithmetic, Percent)
$25\% = \frac{1}{4}$,
$\frac{1}{4}$ of \$400 = \$100 reduction
\$400 − \$100 = \$300 sale price
\$300(0.02) = \$6 reduction for cash
\$300 − \$6 = \$294, price paid

10. 3 Chapter 21 (Graphs, Circle Graphs)
Cost of food is 28% of budget.
Cost of rent is 25% of budget.
28% + 25% = 53%, which is more than half of the budget.
None of the other statements is true.

11. 1 Chapter 20 (Geometry, Perimeters)
Let x = width of rectangle

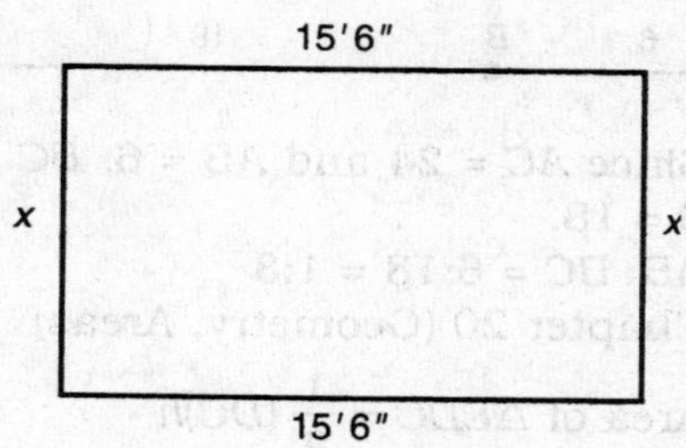

$$6 \text{ in.} = \frac{6}{12} = \frac{1}{2} \text{ ft.}$$
$$x + 15\frac{1}{2} + x + 15\frac{1}{2} = 40$$
$$2x + 31 = 40$$
$$2x = 40 - 31 = 9$$
$$x = \frac{9}{2} = 4\frac{1}{2} \text{ ft.}$$
$$4\frac{1}{2} \text{ ft.} = 4 \text{ ft. } 6 \text{ in.}$$

12. 1 Chapter 19 (Algebra, Fundamentals)
If Rosita takes x hr. to complete a job, she can do $\frac{1}{x}$ of the job in 1 hr.
Then she can do $5\left(\frac{1}{x}\right) = \frac{5}{x}$ in 5 hr.

13. 2 Chapter 19 (Algebra, Exponents and Scientific Notation)
To write a number in scientific notation, write it as the product of a number between 1 and 10 and a power of 10.
In this case, the number between 1 and 10 is 1.7. In going from 1.7 to 0.0000017, the decimal point is moved 6 places to the left. Therefore, $0.0000017 = 1.7 \times 10^{-6}$.

14. 5 Chapter 20 (Geometry, Volumes)

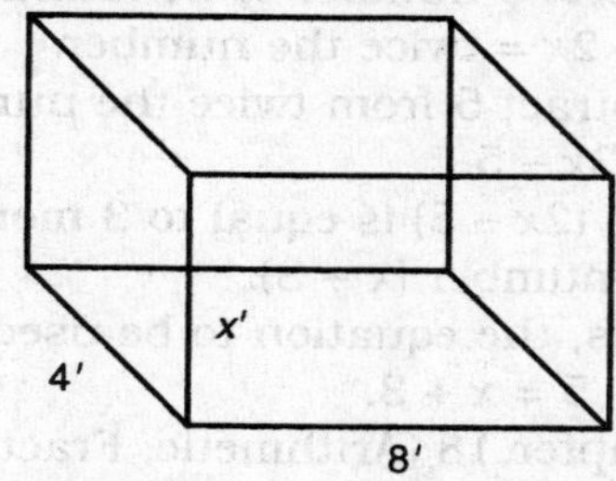

Let x = height of solid.
Use the formula $V = lwh$.
In this case, $V = 50$, $l = 5$, $w = 4$, and $h = x$.
$50 = 5(4)x$
$50 = 20x$, or $20x = 50$

15. 2 Chapter 19 (Algebra, Ratio and Proportion)

A 6 B 18 C

Since $AC = 24$ and $AB = 6$, $BC = 24 - 6 = 18$.

$AB:BC = 6:18 = 1:3$

16. 3 Chapter 20 (Geometry, Areas)

Area of $\Delta EDC = \frac{1}{2}(DC)h$

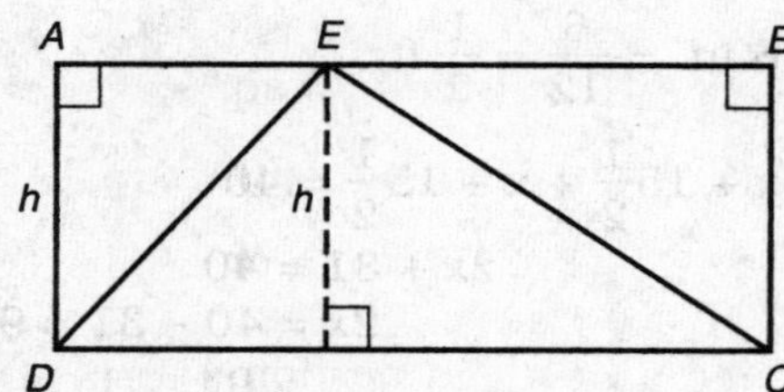

Area of rectangle $ABCD = (DC)h$.
Thus, area of ΔEDC is equal to one-half area of rectangle $ABCD$. Ratio of area of ΔEDC to area of rectangle $ABCD = 1:2$.

17. 1 Chapter 22 (Measures, Operations with Measures)

Since there are 16 oz. in 1 lb.,

$10 \text{ oz.} = \frac{10}{16} = \frac{5}{8} \text{ lb.}$

Thus, you must find the cost of $3\frac{5}{8}$ lb. of chicken at \$0.72 per pound.

3 lb. cost 3(\$0.72) = \$2.16

$\frac{5}{8}$ lb. costs $\frac{5}{8}(\$0.72) = \$0.45$ (0.72 cancelled to 0.09, 8 cancelled to 1)

Total = \$2.16 + \$0.45 = \$2.61

18. 3 Chapter 19 (Algebra, Solving Problems)

Let x = number to be found, and $2x$ = twice the number.
Subtract 5 from twice the number to get $2x - 5$.
This $(2x - 5)$ is equal to 3 more than the number $(x + 3)$.
Thus, the equation to be used is $2x - 5 = x + 3$.

19. 1 Chapter 18 (Arithmetic, Fractions)

If the businessman spends $\frac{1}{5}$ of his income for rent, he has $\frac{4}{5}$ of his income left.

$\frac{3}{8}$ of the remainder $= \frac{3}{8} \times \frac{4}{5} = \frac{3}{10}$

$\frac{3}{10}$ of the income is spent for salaries.

20. 3 Chapter 18 (Arithmetic)

To find the number of hours the plane takes to make the trip, divide the distance covered (3,200 mi.) by the rate of speed (480 mph).

$3{,}200 \div 480 = 6\frac{2}{3}$

$\frac{2}{3} \text{ hr.} = \frac{2}{3} \times 60 = 40 \text{ min.}$

$6\frac{2}{3}$ hr. = 6 hr. and 40 min.

21. 4 Chapter 18 (Arithmetic, Properties of Operations)

José works 40 or fewer hours at \$8 per hour. Thus, his salary for regular working time = 8(40).
José works 9 hours at
$(1\frac{1}{2} \times 8) = \frac{3}{2} \times 8 = \$12$ per hour.
Thus, his overtime salary is 9(12).
His total salary = 8(40) + 9(12) dollars.

22. 5 Chapter 19 (Algebra, Solving Problems)

Let n = amount spent on the slacks, and $2n$ = amount spent on the jacket.

$81 = n + 2n = 3n$

$n = 81 \div 3 = 27$ and

$2n = \$54$

23. 3 Chapter 20 (Geometry, Geometric Concepts and Relationships)

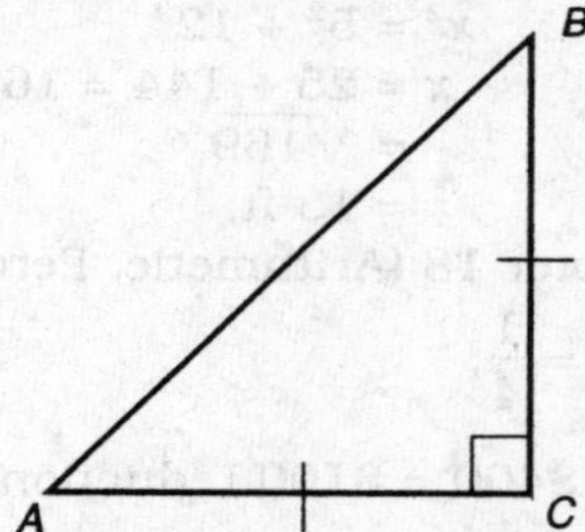

Since $AC = BC$, $m\angle A = m\angle B$

$m\angle A + m\angle B + m\angle C = 180$

$m\angle A + m\angle B + 90 = 180$

$m\angle A + m\angle B = 180 - 90 = 90$

Since $m\angle A = m\angle B$, $m\angle A = \frac{1}{2}(90) = 45°$

24. 1 Chapter 18 (Arithmetic, Percent)

To the \$28 bill, Mr. Page must add 5% tax and a 15% tip, a total addition of 20%.

20% of \$28 = 0.20 × \$28 = \$5.60.

Total cost was \$28.00 + \$5.60 = \$33.60.

25. **2** Chapter 18 (Arithmetic)
$20 \times 36 = 720$ man-days are needed to do the job
Let x = number of days 24 men take to do the job.
Then $24x = 720$, and $x = 30$.

26. **2** Chapter 20 (Arithmetic, Interest)
$12\frac{1}{2}\% = 12.5\% = 0.125$
$0.125(\$8{,}500) = \$1{,}062.50$

27. **2** Chapter 21 (Graphs, Pictographs)
A correct interpretation of the table is required to answer this question. The numbers in the right column represent the *frequency* with which each score in the left column is achieved. In other words, Beth earned a score of 4 on 13 of the $90 = (5)(18)$ holes she played in 5 rounds.

28. **2** Chapter 21 (Graphs, Pictographs)
The last three rows of the table represent scores greater than 6 (7, 8, and more than 8). Beth scored more than 6 on $5 + 3 + 4 = 12$ holes.

29. **3** Chapter 19 (Algebra, The Mean and the Median)
To find Beth's median score, you could list all 90 scores in increasing order and look for the middle scores, but that's too much work. The list would start with one 2, followed by eight 3's, and thirteen 4's. That would bring you to the 22nd number in the list. Adding twenty-five 5's gets you to the 47th number, so both the 45th and 46th numbers are 5, which is the median.

30. **3** Chapter 18 (Arithmetic, Percent)
$100\% - 65\% = 35\%$ of the entering class were women.
$(0.35)(840) = 294$ women

31. **2** Chapter 19 (Algebra, Exponents and Evaluations)
$3a^2 + a(2a^3 - 5)$
$= 3(4)^2 + 4(2 \cdot 4^3 - 5)$
$= 3(16) + 4(128 - 5)$
$= 48 + 4(123) = 48 + 492$
$= 540$

32. **2** Chapter 20 (Geometry, Areas)

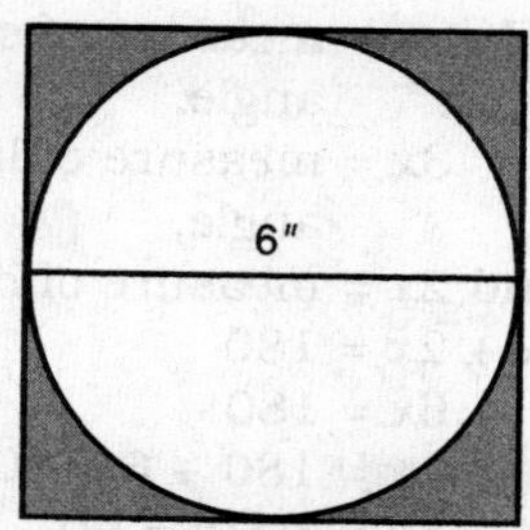

Each side of square is 6 in. in length.
Area of square is 36 sq. in.
Radius of circle is $\frac{1}{2}(6) = 3$ in.
Area of circle $= \pi r^2 =$ or $\pi \cdot 3 \cdot 3 = 9\pi$ sq. in.
Area of shaded portion = Area of square – Area of circle
Area of shaded portion $= 36 - 9\pi$

33. **4** Chapter 19 (Algebra, Solving Problems)
Let x = number.
$3x - 5 = 16$
$3x = 16 + 5 = 21$
$x = 21 \div 3 = 7$

34. **5** Chapter 21 (Algebra, The Mean and the Median)
Since Justin's average is 80, he has earned a total of $4 \times 80 = 320$ points. For his average to be 84 after 5 tests, he needs a total of $5 \times 84 = 420$ points. Justin needs a grade of $420 - 320 = 100$.

35. **3** Chapter 18 (Arithmetic, Percent)
Let x = goal.
$1.05x = 105{,}000$
$x = \$105{,}000 \div 1.05 = \$100{,}000$

36. **3** Chapter 19 (Algebra, Solving Equations)
$x^2 - 2x - 8 = 0$
$(x - 4)(x + 2) = 0$
$x - 4 = 0$ or $x + 2 = 0$
$x = 4$ or $x = -2$
The roots of the equation are 4,–2.

37. **2** Chapter 20 (Geometry, Indirect Measurement)
The ratio of the height of the telephone pole to its shadow is equal to the ratio of the length of the post to its shadow.
Let x = height of the telephone pole.
$\frac{x}{48} = \frac{3}{4}$
$4x = 3(48) = 144$
$x = 144 \div 4 = 36$ ft.

38. **5** Chapter 20 (Geometry, Geometric Concepts and Relationships)

Let x = measure of smallest angle,
$3x$ = measure of largest angle,
and $2x$ = measure of other angle.

$x + 3x + 2x = 180$
$6x = 180$
$x = 180 \div 6 = 30$
$3x = 3(30) = 90°$

39. 2 Chapter 20 (Geometry, Areas)
Area of rectangle is $6 \times 15 = 90$. Together the two white semicircles form a circle of radius 6, whose area is $\pi(6)^2 = 36\pi$. Area of shaded region is $90 - 36\pi$.

40. 5 Chapter 18 (Arithmetic, Percent)
Let x = original price of the chair. Then the sale price was $100\% - 25\% = 75\%$ of x: $\$240 = 0.75x$, so $x = \$240 \div 0.75 = \$320$.

41. 5 Chapter 19 (Algebra, Solving Equations)
Probability = $\dfrac{\text{number of successful events}}{\text{number of possible events}}$
In this case, the number of successful events is 7 since Mrs. Allen bought 7 tickets. However, the total number of tickets sold is not known. Therefore, the probability cannot be determined.

42. 3 Chapter 19 (Algebra, Formulas)
Since $2^2 = 4$ and $3^2 = 9$, $\sqrt{7}$ is between 2 and 3. In fact, $(2.5)^2 = 6.25$, so $2.5 < \sqrt{7} < 3$. The only choice that works is 2.6.

43. 5 Chapter 20 (Geometry, Coordinate Geometry)

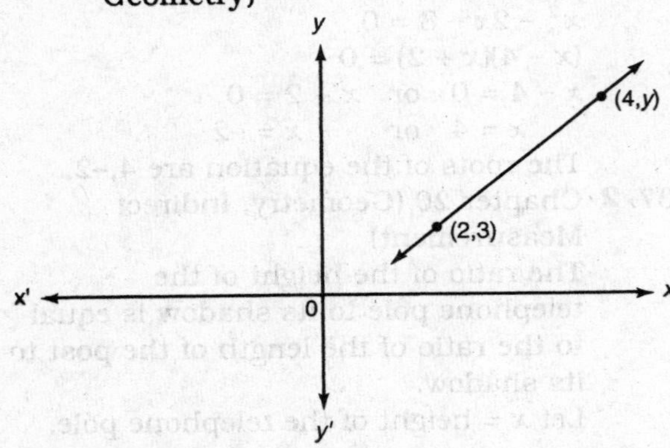

Slope of line = $\dfrac{\text{change in } y\text{-coordinates}}{\text{change in } x\text{-coordinates}} = \dfrac{y_1 - y_2}{x_1 - x_2}$

In this case, $y_1 = y$, $y_2 = 3$, $x_1 = 4$, and $x_2 = 2$.

Slope = $\dfrac{y-3}{4-2} = \dfrac{y-3}{2}$

Since the slope of the line is 2, then $\dfrac{y-3}{2} = 2$.

Therefore, $y - 3 = 4$ and $y = 7$.

44. 5 Chapter 19 (Algebra, The Mean and the Median)
The weekly payroll of the business firm is $7 \times \$584 = \$4{,}088$.
3 workers earn
$3 \times \$450 = \$1{,}350$ weekly.
3 other workers earn
$3 \times \$600 = \$1{,}800$ weekly.
6 of the 7 workers earn
$\$1{,}350 + \$1{,}800 = \$3{,}150$.
The seventh worker earns
$\$4{,}088 - \$3{,}150 = \$938$.

45. 3 Chapter 18 (Arithmetic, Percent)
On his 7% investment Mr. Barr gets $\$12{,}000 \times 0.07 = \$840$ per year. He wishes to get \$1,560, or \$720 more.
Let x = amount to be invested at 8%.
Then $0.08x = 720$,
so $x = 720 \div 0.08 = \$9{,}000$

46. 2 Chapter 18 (Arithmetic)
324 orchestra seats at \$15 each = \$4,860
\$7,540 − \$4,860 = \$2,680 collected for balcony seats
2,680 ÷ 10 = 268 balcony seats sold

47. 2 Chapter 19 (Algebra, Solving Problems)
Since the length (n) of the altitude is equal to one-half the length of the base, the length of the base is $2n$.

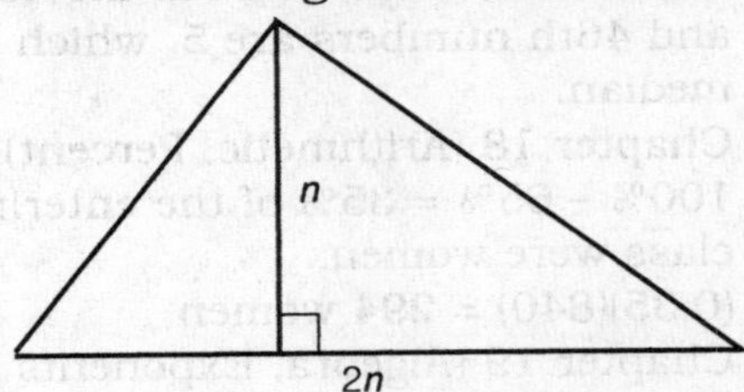

Area of triangle $= \frac{1}{2}bh$
$= \frac{1}{2}(2n)(n)$
$= \frac{1}{2}(n)(2n)$.

Since the area is 50, $\frac{1}{2}(n)(2n) = 50$.

48. **4** Chapter 18 (Arithmetic)
To find the number of dollars John has left, subtract the amount he spent from x dollars.
$5 \times 2 = \$10$, spent for movie tickets
$\$y$, spent at cafe
Amount left $= x - 10 - y$

49. **5** Chapter 19 (Algebra, Solving Inequalities)
$2x + 33 \geq 11$
$2x \geq 11 - 3 = 8$
$x \geq 4$
Of the pairs of numbers given, only 4 and 10 satisfy the inequality.

50. **3** Chapter 20 (Geometry, Geometric Concepts and Relationships)
Since $\overleftrightarrow{AB} \parallel \overleftrightarrow{CD}$, $m\angle A + m\angle D = 180°$.
Let $3x = m\angle D$ and $2x = m\angle A$.
$180 = 3x + 2x = 5x$
$x = 180 \div 5 = 36°$
$3x = 3(36) = 108°$

51. **5** Chapter 18 (Arithmetic)
Kelly covered $2 \times 45 = 90$ mi. during the first 2 hr.
This left $290 - 90 = 200$ mi. for the remaining 4 hr.
$200 \div 4 = 50$ mph.

52. **4** Chapter 19 (Algebra, Solving Problems)
Let x = number of dollars Joe has
And $x + 35$ = number of dollars Ben has
$x + 35 - 5 = x + 30$ = number of dollars Ben has after giving Joe \$5
$x + 5$ = number of dollars Joe has after receiving \$5 from Ben
Ben will have twice as much as Joe
↓ ↓ ↓
$x + 30 \quad = \quad 2 \quad x + 5$
$x + 30 = 2x + 10$
$30 - 10 = 2x - x$
$20 = x$, or $x = \$20$,

53. **1** Chapter 19 (Algebra, Solving Equations)
If $4y = 20$, then $y = 20 \div 4 = 5$.
$2x + 3y = 15$
$2x + 3(5) = 15$
$2x + 15 = 15$
$2x = 15 - 15 = 0$
$x = 0$

54. **4** Chapter 18 (Arithmetic, Fractions)
$1 - \frac{1}{3} = \frac{2}{3}$ of the estate is left to the 4 children.
$\frac{2}{3} \div 4 = \frac{2}{3} \times \frac{1}{4} = \frac{1}{6}$

55. **2** Chapter 18 (Arithmetic, Percent)
The team plays a total of $18 + 32 = 50$ games.
64% of 50 = 32 games the team must win.
Since the team has already won 12 games, it must win $32 - 12 = 20$ of the remaining games.

56. **4** Chapter 19 (Algebra, Fundamentals)
Robert earns x dollars per month, and Tom earns y dollars per month. Together, Robert and Tom earn $x + y$ dollars per month.
In 1 year, Robert and Tom earn $12(x + y)$ dollars.

Practice Test Three

1. On November 1, Janice's heating oil tank was $\frac{7}{8}$ full. On December 1, the tank was $\frac{1}{4}$ full. The tank holds 320 gallons when full. At \$1.06 per gallon, what was the cost of the oil Janice used during the month of November?

(1) \$192.00
(2) \$198.40
(3) \$202.00
(4) \$212.00
(5) \$2,120.00

2. The circle below represents a family's total income. The shaded section shows the part of the income spent for rent. If the family income is $32,400.00 per year, the amount spent for rent is

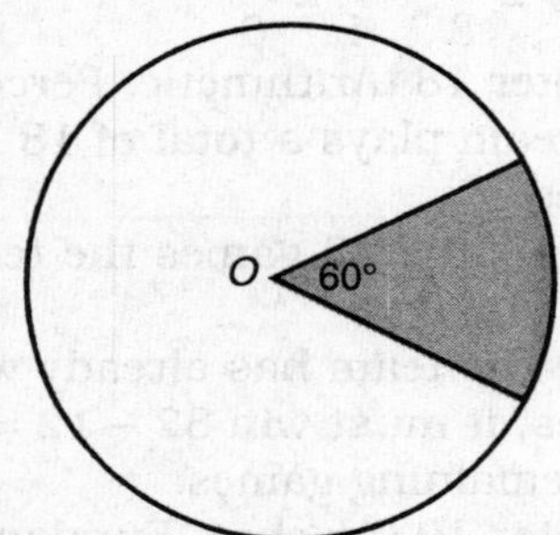

(1) $5,400
(2) $5,500
(3) $6,400
(4) $7,200
(5) $10,800

3. A man drove for 2 hours at an average rate of 45 miles per hour. During the next 3 hours he covered 140 miles. His average speed, in miles per hour, for the entire trip, was

(1) 45
(2) 46
(3) 48
(4) 56
(5) Not enough information is given.

4. The graph below shows the population of Springville (in thousands) for each 5-year period between 1965 and 1985. During which 5 year period did the population of Springville remain the same?

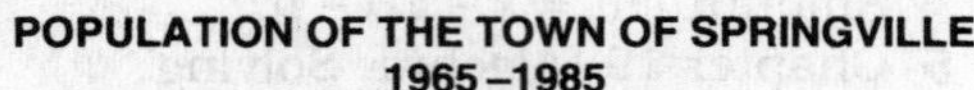

POPULATION OF THE TOWN OF SPRINGVILLE
1965–1985

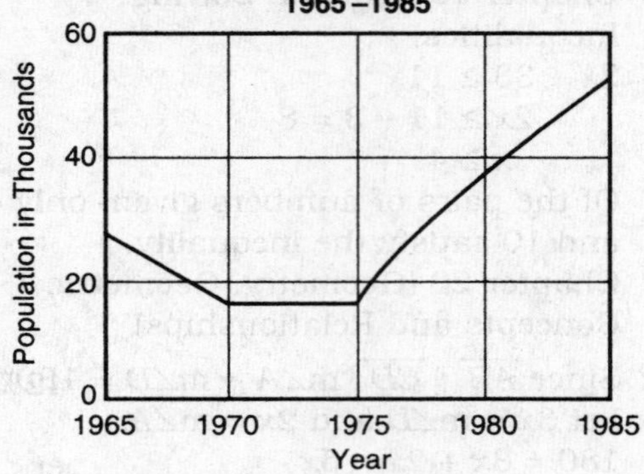

(1) 1965–1970
(2) 1970–1975
(3) 1975–1980
(4) 1980–1985
(5) none of these

5. If the measures of two angles of a triangle are 40° and 70°, the triangle is

(1) equilateral
(2) right
(3) isosceles
(4) obtuse
(5) equiangular

6. A man wishes to buy a set of tools for his workshop. Dealer *A* lists the tools at $440 and offers a 25% discount. Dealer *B* lists the same set of tools at $400. Dealer *B* always offers a discount of 10%, but during a sale offers a 5% saving off his already reduced price. How much does the man save by taking the better offer?

(1) $10
(2) $12
(3) $15
(4) $16
(5) $18

7. A drawing of a building plot has a scale of 1 inch to 40 feet. How many inches on the drawing represent a distance of 175 feet on the plot?

(1) $4\frac{1}{8}$
(2) $4\frac{3}{8}$
(3) $4\frac{1}{2}$
(4) $4\frac{5}{8}$
(5) $4\frac{3}{4}$

8. A family spends 20% of its monthly income on rent, 23% on food, and 42% on other expenses, and saves the balance. If the family saves $300 per month, what is its monthly income?

(1) $200
(2) $2,000
(3) $2,400
(4) $3,000
(5) $20,000

9. Find the value of $8y^2 - y(7y - 1)$ if $y = 5$.

(1) 10
(2) 15
(3) 18
(4) 25
(5) 30

10. If $2x + 7 = 19$, the value of x is

(1) 3
(2) 5
(3) 6
(4) 7
(5) 10

11. A rectangular swimming pool is 80 feet long and 60 feet wide. What is the diagonal distance across the pool?

(1) 70 ft.
(2) 75 ft.
(3) 90 ft.
(4) 100 ft.
(5) 140 ft.

12. The perimeter of rectangle *ABCD*, shown below, is

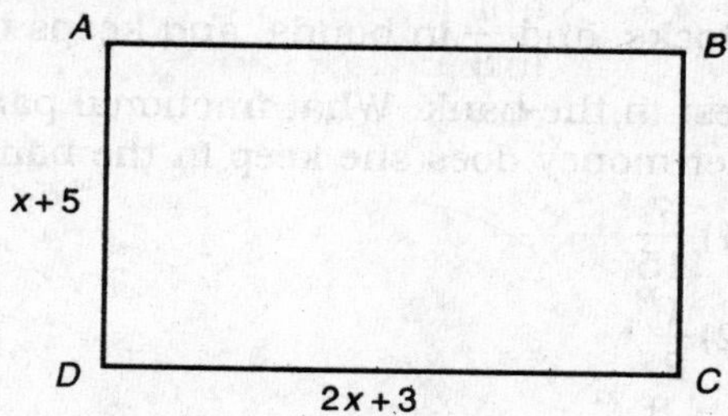

(1) $(x + 5) + (2x + 3)$
(2) $2(2x + 3) + (x + 5)$
(3) $(2x + 3) + 2(x + 5)$
(4) $2(2x + 3) + 2(x + 5)$
(5) $3x + 8$

13. A hotel has single and double rooms. The number of double rooms in the hotel is 3 times the number of single rooms. Which of the following cannot be the number of rooms in the hotel?

(1) 40
(2) 50
(3) 100
(4) 200
(5) Not enough information is given.

14. A shopper buys 1 pound 10 ounces of cheese at $2.40 per pound. How much change does the shopper receive from a $5 bill?

(1) $.90
(2) $1.00
(3) $1.10
(4) $2.60
(5) $3.90

15. Ms. Riley invests $\frac{1}{5}$ of her money in stocks, and $\frac{1}{3}$ in bonds, and keeps the rest in the bank. What fractional part of her money does she keep in the bank?

(1) $\frac{7}{15}$
(2) $\frac{1}{2}$
(3) $\frac{8}{15}$
(4) $\frac{5}{6}$
(5) $\frac{14}{15}$

16. On a bar graph, a bar $3\frac{1}{2}$ units high represents \$840. On the same graph, a bar $5\frac{1}{2}$ units high represents

(1) \$240
(2) \$480
(3) \$960
(4) \$1,320
(5) \$1,500

17. The number of points scored this season by each of the 10 players on a basketball team is listed below.

Grant	189	Bell	179
Weber	214	Carlin	191
Albert	197	Mason	223
Grimes	203	Damon	193
Hanson	219	Garry	215

What was the median number of points scored?

(1) 197
(2) 200
(3) 203
(4) 204
(5) 205

18. The cost of 6 shirts and 5 ties is \$136. If the average cost of a tie is \$8, what is the average cost of a shirt?

(1) \$12
(2) \$13
(3) \$14
(4) \$15
(5) \$16

19. In the figure below, the radius of the large circle is R and the radius of each small circle is r. Write a formula that may be used to find the area (A) of the shaded portion.

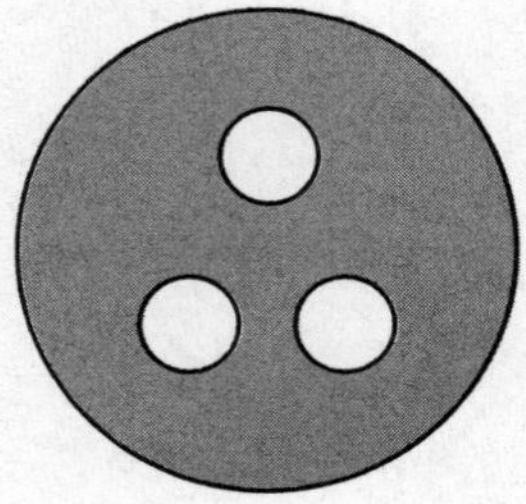

(1) $A = \pi R^2 - \pi r^2$
(2) $A = 2\pi R - 2\pi r$
(3) $A = \pi R^2 - 3\pi r^2$
(4) $A = \pi R - \pi r$
(5) $A = 3\pi R^2 - \pi r$

Questions 20 and 21 are based on the following pie chart.

The pie chart shows the sources of funding for the political campaign of a candidate.

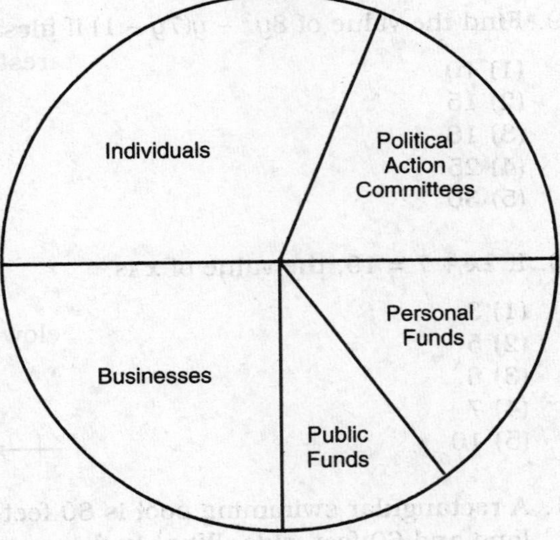

20. Which of the following statements is **FALSE**?

    (1) Excluding the candidate, individuals accounted for less than half of total contributions.
    (2) About a quarter of the contributions came from businesses.
    (3) Political Action Committees contributed more than businesses.
    (4) The smallest contribution came from public funds.
    (5) Individuals and businesses accounted for more than half the contributions.

21. If Political Action Committees contributed one-sixth of the total, what size angle should be allotted for that slice of the pie?

    (1) 30°
    (2) 45°
    (3) 60°
    (4) 75°
    (5) 90°

22. Mrs. Leach buys a refrigerator for $619.79. In addition, she pays a sales tax of 6%. Her total bill, to the nearest cent, is

    (1) $646.98
    (2) $656.97
    (3) $656.98
    (4) $660.98
    (5) $665.38

23. Which letter on the number line below corresponds to −4?

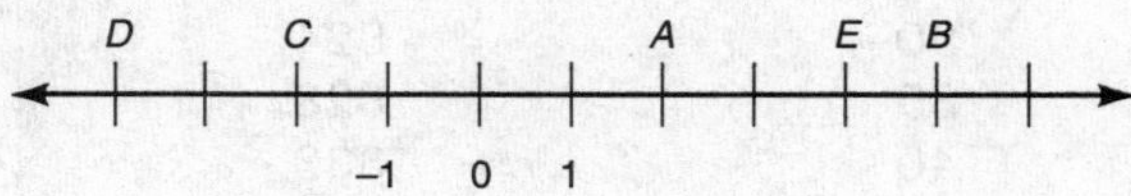

    (1) *A*
    (2) *B*
    (3) *C*
    (4) *D*
    (5) *E*

24. John leaves home at noon to drive to a friend's home 150 miles away. If John averages 45 miles per hour at about what time will he reach his friend's home?

    (1) 3:00 P.M.
    (2) 3:20 P.M.
    (3) 3:30 P.M.
    (4) 3:33 P.M.
    (5) 4:20 P.M.

25. $a + b + 2c + 2b - a - c =$

    (1) $3b + c$
    (2) $2b + c$
    (3) $2a + b$
    (4) $a + b + c$
    (5) $a + 2b - c$

26. Evaluate $3x^2 - 5y$ if $x = 4$ and $y = -2$.

    (1) 28
    (2) 38
    (3) 48
    (4) 58
    (5) 62

27. If all of the angles in the figure below are right angles, which of the following is an expression for the total area?

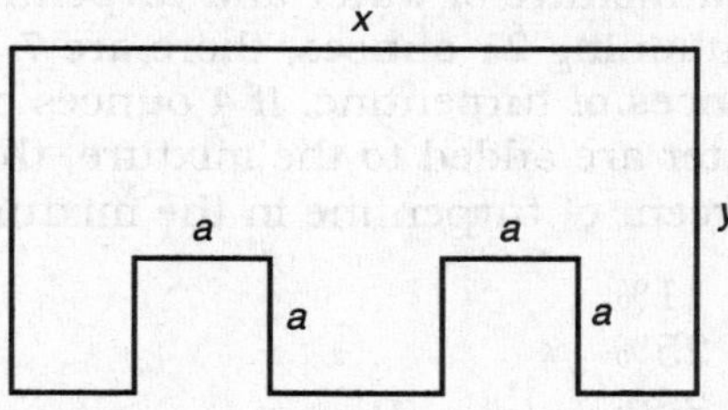

    (1) $xy + 2a^2$
    (2) $xy + a^2$
    (3) $xy - 2a^2$
    (4) $xy - a^2$
    (5) $xy - 4a$

28. In basketball, a foul shot counts 1 point and a field goal counts 2 points. A team scored 103 points, making 8 more field goals than foul shots. How many field goals did the team make?

    (1) 29
    (2) 32
    (3) 36
    (4) 37
    (5) 39

29. A brick wall is 50 feet long, 6 feet high, and 6 inches thick. What is the weight of the wall if 1 cubic foot of brick weighs 120 pounds?

(1) 9 tons
(2) $9\frac{1}{2}$ tons
(3) 12 tons
(4) 15 tons
(5) 18 tons

30. Find the cost of 5 feet 3 inches of slipcover material at $8 per foot.

(1) $14
(2) $24
(3) $40
(4) $42
(5) $48

31. An auditorium contains x rows, with y seats in each row. The number of seats in the auditorium is

(1) $x + y$
(2) xy
(3) $x - y$
(4) $x \div y$
(5) $y - x$

32. In a mixture of water and turpentine containing 21 ounces, there are 7 ounces of turpentine. If 4 ounces of water are added to the mixture, the percent of turpentine in the mixture is

(1) 11%
(2) 25%
(3) 28%
(4) 30%
(5) $33\frac{1}{3}$%

33. A rectangle and a square have the same perimeter. The length of the rectangle is 2 feet greater than a side of the square. Which statement is true?

(1) The rectangle and the square have the same area.
(2) The area of the rectangle is greater than the area of the square.
(3) The area of the square is 4 sq. ft. greater than the area of the rectangle.
(4) The area of the rectangle is twice the area of the square.
(5) The area of the square is 16 sq. ft. greater than the area of the rectangle.

34. Ms. Martino was offered a monthly salary of $1,500 or a commission of 10% on sales. She accepted the commission basis and sold $198,000 worth of goods for the year. How much did she gain that year by taking the commission basis over the salary basis?

(1) $800
(2) $1,000
(3) $1,500
(4) $1,600
(5) $1,800

35. Below is a table for premiums on ordinary life insurance.

If Taken Out At Age	Annual Premium per $1,000 of Insurance
20	$18
25	$20
30	$24
35	$28
40	$33

A man took out four of these insurance policies as follows: $1,000 at age 20; $2,000 at age 25; $2,000 at age 30; $5,000 at age 35.

Find the total premium he pays per year on the four policies.

(1) $246
(2) $248
(3) $256
(4) $268
(5) $276

36. If 2 apples cost 29 cents, what is the cost of 2 dozen apples at the same rate?

(1) \$1.74
(2) \$2.61
(3) \$2.76
(4) \$3.24
(5) \$3.48

37. The roof of a house is a square measuring 40 feet on a side. It costs \$1,400 to replace this roof. At the same rate, the cost of replacing a square roof measuring 80 feet on a side is

(1) \$2,800
(2) \$3,500
(3) \$4,000
(4) \$5,600
(5) \$6,400

38. The value of a car decreases 35% the first year and 20% the second year. If a new car costs \$12,000, what is its value at the end of 2 years?

(1) \$5,400
(2) \$5,800
(3) \$6,080
(4) \$6,240
(5) \$6,440

39. The measure of the smallest angle of a triangle is 20° less than the measure of the second angle, and 40° less than the measure of the third angle of the triangle. What is the measure of the smallest angle of the triangle?

(1) 40°
(2) 42°
(3) 45°
(4) 50°
(5) 55°

40. A solution of the inequality $2x + 1 < 3$ is

(1) 0
(2) 4
(3) 5
(4) 7
(5) 10

41. At a certain hour, a tree casts a shadow 32 feet long. At the same time, a post 5 feet high casts a shadow 4 feet long. What is the height of the tree?

(1) $25\frac{3}{5}$ ft.
(2) 30 ft.
(3) 36 ft.
(4) 40 ft.
(5) 60 ft.

42. A family has an income of \$2,500 per month. Each month the family spends x dollars for food and rent and y dollars for other expenses. How many dollars does the family save per month?

(1) $2,500 - x + y$
(2) $2,500 + x - y$
(3) $2,500 - (x + y)$
(4) $x + y - 2,500$
(5) Not enough information is given.

43. A college club meeting was attended by 7 sophomores, 5 juniors, and 11 seniors. One student was selected as chairperson of the meeting. What is the probability that the student chosen was a senior?

(1) $\frac{1}{11}$
(2) $\frac{11}{23}$
(3) $\frac{7}{16}$
(4) $\frac{10}{23}$
(5) $\frac{11}{12}$

44. 50 kilometers =

(1) 5,000 miles
(2) 50,000 centimeters
(3) 50,000 meters
(4) 500,000 millimeters
(5) 1,000 kilograms

45. The population of the Earth is approximately 6,000,000,000. This number, written in scientific notation, is

(1) 6×10^9
(2) 60×10^8
(3) $.6 \times 10^8$
(4) $.6 \times 10^{10}$
(5) 600×10^7

46. A line segment connects two points whose coordinates are (5,6) and (−3,6). What is the length of the line segment?

(1) 2
(2) 3
(3) 5
(4) 8
(5) 12

47. If $C = \frac{5}{9}(F - 32)$, the value of C when $F = 50$ is

(1) 0
(2) 10
(3) 18
(4) 40
(5) 90

48. A sailboat travels 8 miles due east. Then it travels 15 miles due north. How far, in miles, is the sailboat from its starting point?

(1) 16
(2) 17
(3) 18
(4) 19
(5) 20

49. When a certain number is divided by 15, the quotient is 8 and the remainder is 7. The number is

(1) 71
(2) 113
(3) 123
(4) 127
(5) Not enough information is given.

50. The ratio of two numbers is 8:5. If the difference of the numbers is 21, what is the larger number?

(1) 35
(2) 39
(3) 56
(4) 85
(5) 91

51. Two cash prizes totaling $1,000 were awarded in a radio game show. If the first prize was $200 less than 3 times as much as the second prize, what was the first prize?

(1) $300
(2) $400
(3) $600
(4) $700
(5) $800

52. The water tank shown below is in the form of a cylinder. The diameter of the circular base is 12 feet, and the height of the tank is 10 feet. An expression that gives the approximate value of the volume of the tank is

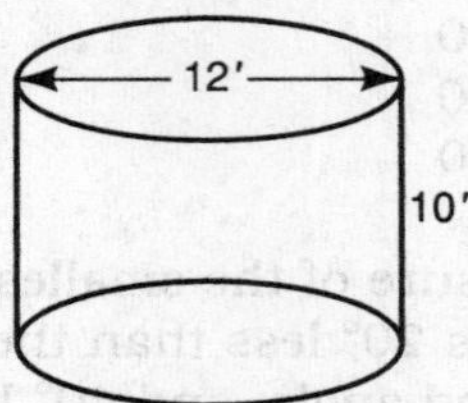

(1) $(3.14)(12)^2(10)$
(2) $(3.14)(6)^2(10)$
(3) $(3.14)(6)(10)$
(4) $(3.14)(6)(10)^2$
(5) $(3.14)(12)(10)^2$

53. The numbers that satisfy the equation $x^2 - 5x + 6 = 0$ are

(1) 3, 2
(2) −3, −2
(3) 3, −2
(4) −3, 2
(5) 1, 6

54. If O is the center of the circle shown below and $m\angle BOC = 86°$, what is $m\angle A$?

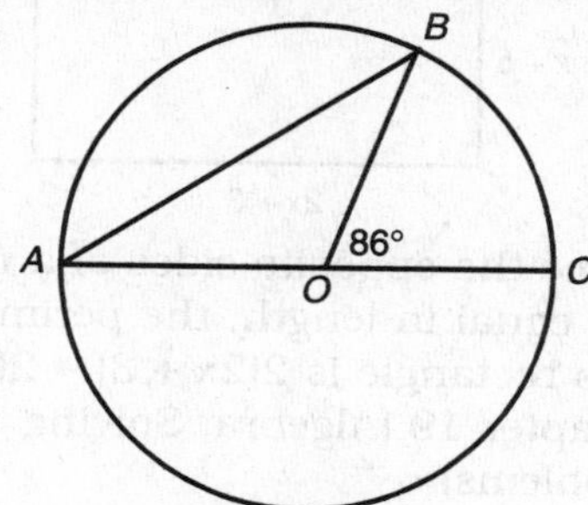

(1) 24°
(2) 43°
(3) 45°
(4) 50°
(5) Not enough information is given.

55. A team has played 104 games. It has won 8 more games than it has lost. How many games has the team won?

(1) 40
(2) 42
(3) 50
(4) 54
(5) 56

56. Jack has twice as much money as Fred. If Jack gives Fred $12, the two boys will have equal amounts of money. How much did Jack have before he gave money to Fred?

(1) $24
(2) $28
(3) $30
(4) $36
(5) $48

ANSWER KEY

1. 4	13. 2	24. 2	35. 1	46. 4
2. 1	14. 3	25. 1	36. 5	47. 2
3. 2	15. 1	26. 4	37. 4	48. 2
4. 2	16. 4	27. 3	38. 4	49. 4
5. 3	17. 2	28. 4	39. 1	50. 3
6. 2	18. 5	29. 1	40. 1	51. 4
7. 2	19. 3	30. 4	41. 4	52. 2
8. 2	20. 3	31. 2	42. 3	53. 1
9. 5	21. 3	32. 3	43. 2	54. 2
10. 3	22. 3	33. 3	44. 3	55. 5
11. 4	23. 4	34. 5	45. 1	56. 5
12. 4				

WHAT'S YOUR SCORE?

______right	______wrong
Excellent	51–56
Good	44–50
Fair	38–43

If your score was low, the explanation of the correct answers that follows will help you. You may obtain additional help and practice by referring to the review material in Unit VII.

ANSWER ANALYSIS

Following the correct answer are the chapter and section containing the material covered in the question.

1. **4** Chapter 18 (Arithmetic, Fractions)
Janice used $\frac{7}{8} - \frac{1}{4} = \frac{7}{8} - \frac{2}{8} = \frac{5}{8}$ of a tank of oil.
$\frac{5}{8} \times 320 = 200$ gal. of oil
$\$200 \times 1.06 = \$212.00$ cost of oil

2. **1** Chapter 20 (Geometry, Geometric Concepts and Relationships)
The sum of the measures of the angles around point O is 360°. Thus, the sector of the circle containing an angle whose measure is 60° is $\frac{60}{360} = \frac{1}{6}$ of the circle.
The amount spent for rent is $\frac{1}{6}$ of ($32,400.00) = $5,400.

3. **2** Chapter 18 (Arithmetic)
To obtain the average speed, divide the total distance by the total time.
Distance = $2 \times 45 + 140 =$
$90 + 140 = 230$ mi.
Total time = 5 hr.
$230 \div 5 = 46$ mph

4. **2** Chapter 21 (Graphs, Line Graphs)
Between 1970 and 1975 there was no change in population. On the graph the line for that period is parallel to the base line.

5. **3** Chapter 20 (Geometry, Geometric Concepts and Relationships)
Since the sum of the measures of the three angles of a triangle = 180°, the measure of the third angle =

$180° - (40 + 70) = 180 - 110 = 70°$.
Since the triangle has two angles whose measures are 70°, the triangle is isosceles.

6. 2 Chapter 18 (Arithmetic, Percent)
Dealer *A* offers a 25% discount:
25% of \$440 = $\frac{1}{4}$(\$440) = \$110, and \$440 – \$100 = \$330.
Dealer *B* normally sells the tools for \$400 – \$40 = \$360, but is now offering a further reduction of 5%: 5% of \$360 = 0.05(\$360) = \$18, and \$360 – \$18 = \$342.
Finally, \$342 – \$330 = \$12.

7. 2 Chapter 19 (Algebra, Ratio and Proportion)
On the drawing, 1 in. represents 40 ft.
$175 \div 40 = 4\frac{15}{40} = 4\frac{3}{8}$ in.

8. 2 Chapter 18 (Arithmetic, Percent)
20% + 23% + 42% = 85%
Thus, the family saves 100% – 85% = 15% of its monthly income.
Let x = family's monthly income
$0.15x = 300$
$x = 300 \div 0.15 = \$2{,}000$

9. 5 Chapter 19 (Algebra, Exponents and Evaluations)
$8y^2 - y(7y - 1)$
$8(5)^2 - 5(7 \times 5 - 1)$
$8(25) - 5(35 - 1) = 200 - 5(34)$
$= 200 - 170 = 30$

10. 3 Chapter 19 (Algebra, Solving Equations)
$2x + 7 = 19$
$2x = 19 - 7 = 12$
$x = 12 \div 2 = 6$

11. 4 Chapter 20 (Geometry, Indirect Measurement)

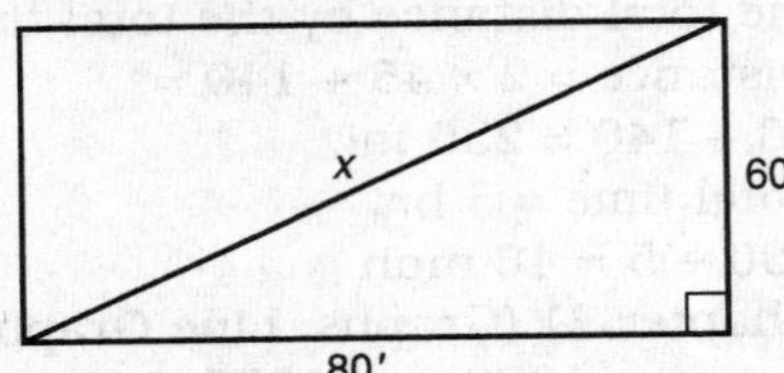

Use the Pythagorean theorem.
$x^2 = 80^2 + 60^2$
$= 6400 + 3600$
$= 10{,}000$
$x = \sqrt{10{,}000}$
$= 100$ ft

12. 4 Chapter 20 (Geometry, Perimeters)

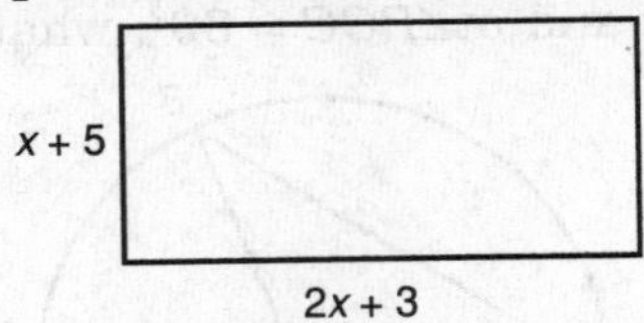

Since the opposite sides of a rectangle are equal in length, the perimeter of this rectangle is $2(2x + 3) + 2(x + 5)$.

13. 2 Chapter 19 (Algebra, Solving Problems)
Let x = number of single rooms. Then $3x$ = number of double rooms, and total number of rooms = $4x$. Since the number of rooms must be a multiple of 4, the hotel cannot have 50 rooms.

14. 3 Chapter 22 (Measures, Operations with Measures)
Since there are 16 oz. in 1 lb., 10 oz. is $\frac{10}{16}$, or $\frac{5}{8}$ lb.
Since 1 lb. of cheese costs \$2.40, $\frac{5}{8}$ lb. costs $\frac{5}{8} \times \$2.40 = \$1.50$.
\$2.40 + \$1.50 = \$3.90, total cost of cheese
Change: \$5.00 – \$3.90 = \$1.10

15. 1 Chapter 18 (Arithmetic, Fractions)
$\frac{1}{5} + \frac{1}{3} = \frac{3}{15} + \frac{5}{15} = \frac{8}{15}$ invested in stocks and bonds
$\frac{15}{15}$ (total) $- \frac{8}{15} = \frac{7}{15}$ kept in bank

16. 4 Chapter 21 (Graphs, Bar Graphs)
Let x = amount of money represented by a $5\frac{1}{2}$-unit bar, and set up a proportion:
$\frac{\text{height of bar}}{\text{amount of money}} = \frac{3.5}{840} = \frac{5.5}{x}$
$3.5x = 5.5(840) = 4620$
$x = 4620 \div 3.5 = \$1{,}320$

17. 2 Chapter 19 (Algebra, The Mean and the Median)
To find the median score, arrange the scores in increasing order:
179, 189, 191, 193, 197, 203, 214, 215, 219, 223

Since there are 10 scores, the median score is the average of the 5th and 6th scores:

$\frac{203 + 197}{2} = \frac{400}{2} = 200$, median score

18. 5 Chapter 18 (Arithmetic)
Total cost of the ties = $5 \times \$8 = \$40$.
Therefore, total cost of the shirts = $\$136 - \$40 = \$96$, and average cost per shirt = $\$96 \div 6 = \$16$.

19. 3 Chapter 22 (Geometry, Perimeters)
To find a formula for the area of the shaded portion, find the area of the large circle and subtract from this result the sum of the areas of the small circles.

Area of large circle = πR^2
Area of each small circle = πr^2
Sum of areas of 3 small circles = $3\pi r^2$
Therefore, area (A) of shaded portion = $\pi R^2 - 3\pi r^2$

20. 3 Chapter 21 (Graphs, Circle Graphs)
Businesses account for just about one quarter of the circle, while Political Action Committees account for less than a quarter. Therefore, statement (3) is false.

21. 3 Chapter 21 (Graphs, Circle Graphs)
The measure of a whole circle is 360°, one-sixth of which is $\frac{360}{6} = 60°$.

22. 3 Chapter 18 (Arithmetic, Percent)
6% of \$619.79 = $0.06 \times \$619.79$ = \$37.19, to the nearest cent
\$619.79 + \$37.19 = \$656.98

23. 4 Chapter 18 (Arithmetic)

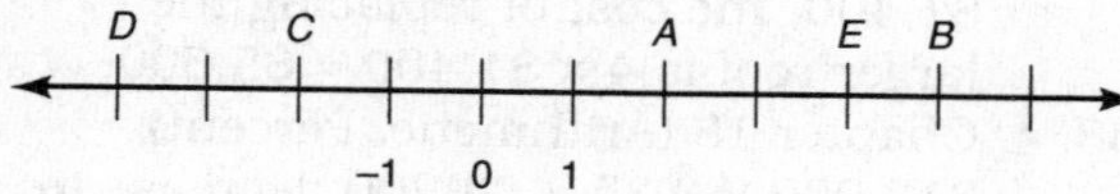

To locate –4 on the number line, start at the *0* point and count 4 spaces to the left. This takes you to point *D*.

24. 2 Chapter 18 (Arithmetic, Fractions)
To find the number of hours John takes to drive 150 mi. we divide 150 by 45.

$\frac{150}{45} = \frac{10}{3} = 3\frac{1}{3}$ hr.

$\frac{1}{3}$ hr. = $\frac{1}{3}(60) = 20$ min.,

so John takes 3 hr. and 20 minutes to complete the trip.
John arrives at 3:20 P.M.

25. 1 Chapter 19 (Algebra, Fundamentals)
$a + b + 2c + 2b - a - c$
$= a - a + b + 2b + 2c - c$
$= 0 + 3b + c$
$= 3b + c$

26. 4 Chapter 19 (Algebra, Exponents and Evaluations)
$3x^2 - 5y$
$= 3(4)^2 - 5(-2)$
$= 3(16) + 10$
$= 48 + 10 = 58$

27. 3 Chapter 20 (Geometry, Areas)
The figure is a large rectangle x units long and y units wide, from which two squares are cut out, each square having a side of length a.
Area of large rectangle = xy.
Area of each small square = a^2.
Total area = $xy - 2a^2$.

28. 4 Chapter 19 (Algebra, Solving Problems)
Let x = number of foul shots,
and $x + 8$ = number of field goals.
Also, x = number of foul-shot points.
and $2(x + 8)$ = number of field-goal points.

$x + 2(x + 8) = 103$
$x + 2x + 16 = 103$
$3x + 16 = 103$
$3x = 103 - 16 = 87$
$x = 87 \div 3 = 29$
$x + 8 = 29 + 8 = 37$

There were 37 field goals.

29. 1 Chapter 20 (Geometry, Points, Lines, and Space)
6 in. = $\frac{1}{2}$ ft.
Use the formula $V = lwh$, with $l = 50$, $h = 6$, and $w = \frac{1}{2}$.
Volume of wall = $50 \times \frac{1}{2} \times 6 = 150$ cu. ft.
$150 \times 120 = 18{,}000$ lb.
$18{,}000 \div 2{,}000 = 9$ tons

30. 4 Chapter 22 (Measures, Operations with Measures)

3 in. = $\frac{3}{12}$ ft. = $\frac{1}{4}$ ft.

Since 5 ft. cost 5($8) = $40 and $\frac{1}{4}$ ft. costs $\frac{1}{4}$($8) = $2, then $5\frac{1}{4}$ ft. cost $42.

31. 2 Chapter 19 (Algebra, Fundamentals)

To find the number of seats in the auditorium, multiply the number of rows (x) by the number of seats (y) in each row. The result is xy.

32. 3 Chapter 18 (Arithmetic, Percent)

The number of ounces of turpentine is 7.

The number of ounces in the mixture is 21 + 4 = 25

The fractional part of the mixture that is turpentine is $\frac{7}{25}$, and $\frac{7}{25} = \frac{28}{100}$ = 28%.

33. 3 Chapter 20 (Geometry, Areas)

Let x = length of each side of the square.

Then the perimeter is $4x$, and the area is x^2.

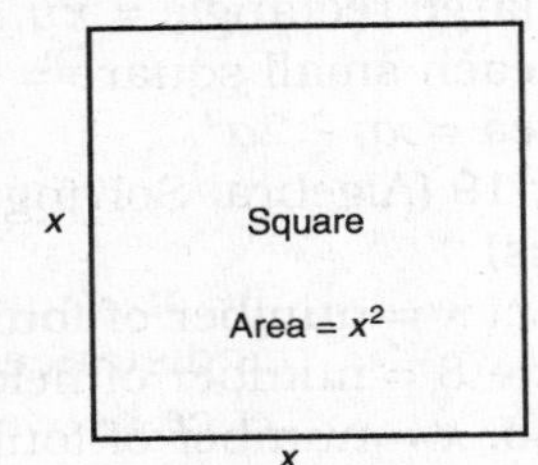

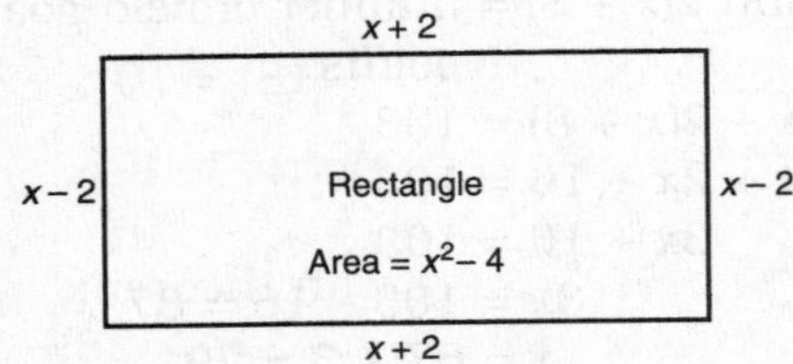

Since the rectangle and the square have equal perimeters and the length of the rectangle is 2 ft. greater than a side of the square, the width of the rectangle must be 2 ft. less than a side of the square.

Thus, the area of the rectangle = $(x + 2)(x - 2) = x^2 - 4$.

Since the area of the square is x^2 and the area of the rectangle is $x^2 - 4$, the area of the square is 4 sq. ft. greater than the area of the rectangle.

34. 5 Chapter 19 (Algebra, Exponents and Evaluations)

At $1,500 per month Ms. Martino would earn 12 × $1,500 = $18,000 per year.

At 10% of sales, she earned 0.1 × $198,000 = $19,800 for the year.

She gained $19,800 − $18,000 = $1,800 by taking the commission basis.

35. 1 Chapter 18 (Arithmetic)

$1,000 policy at age 20 costs $18.

$2,000 policy at age 25 costs 2($20) = $40.

$2,000 policy at age 30 costs 2($24) = $48.

$5,000 policy at age 35 costs 5($28) = $140

Total = $246

36. 5 Chapter 18 (Arithmetic, Decimals)

Two dozen (24) apples cost 12 times as much as 2 apples:

12 × 29¢ = 348¢ = $3.48.

37. 4 Chapter 20 (Geometry, Areas)

Area of smaller square is 40 × 40 = 1,600 sq. ft.

Area of larger square is 80 × 80 = 6,400 sq. ft.

$\frac{6,400}{1,600} = \frac{4}{1}$

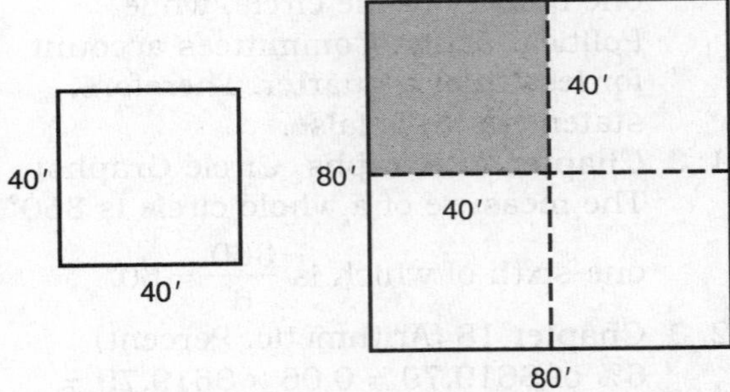

Thus, area of larger square is 4 times area of smaller square. Since the cost of replacing the smaller roof is $1,400, the cost of replacing the larger roof is 4 × $1,400 = $5,600.

38. 4 Chapter 18 (Arithmetic, Percent)

$12,000 × 0.35 = $4,200 decrease in value the first year

$12,000 − $4,200 = $7,800 value after the first year

$7,800 × 0.20 = $1,560 decrease in value the second year

$7,800 − $1,560 = $6,240 value after the second year

39. 1 Chapter 19 (Algebra, Solving Problems)
Let x = measure of the smallest angle,
$x + 20$ = measure of the second angle,
and $x + 40$ = measure of the third angle.

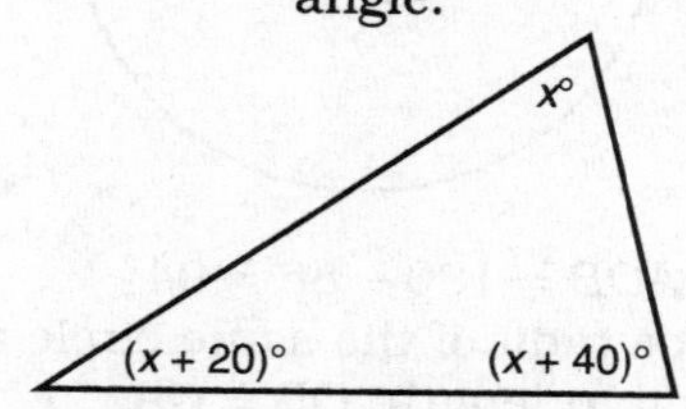

$$x + (x + 20) + (x + 40) = 180$$
$$3x + 60 = 180$$
$$3x = 180 - 60 = 120$$
$$x = 120 \div 3 = 40$$

40. 1 Chapter 19 (Algebra, Solving Inequalities)
$2x + 1 < 3$
$2x < 3 - 1 = 2$
$x < 1$
The only choice less than 1 is 0.

41. 4 Chapter 20 (Geometry, Indirect Measurement)
At any given time of the day the ratio of the height of a tree to the length of the tree's shadow is the same as the height of a post to the length of the post's shadow.

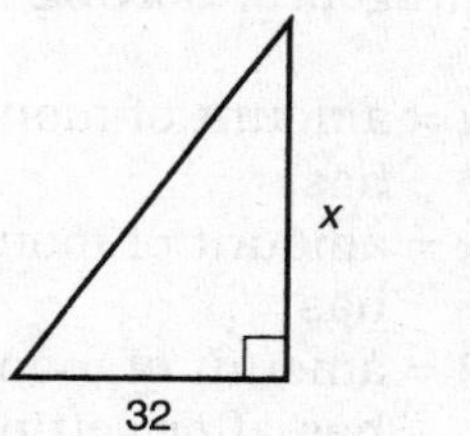

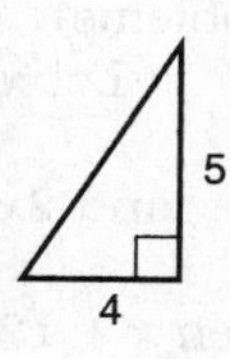

Let x = height of the tree.
Set up a proportion:
$$\frac{x}{32} = \frac{5}{4}$$
$$4x = 5(32) = 160$$
$$x = 160 \div 4 = 40 \text{ ft.}$$

42. 3 Chapter 19 (Algebra, Fundamentals)
Since each month the family spends $x + y$ dollars, it saves $2{,}500 - (x + y)$ = dollars.

43. 2 Chapter 19 (Algebra, Probability)
Of the 23 students present, 11 were seniors. Thus, the probability of selecting a senior is 11 out of 23, or $\frac{11}{23}$.

44. 3 Chapter 22 (Measures, The Metric System)
Since 1 km = 1,000 m,
50 km = 50,000 m.

45. 1 Chapter 19 (Algebra, Solving Inequalities)
To write a number in scientific notation, write it as the product of a number between 1 and 10 and a power of 10.
In the case of 6,000,000,000, the number between 10 and 10 is 6.
In going from 6 to 6,000,000,000 you move the decimal point 9 places to the right; that is, you multiply 6 by 10^9.
Thus, $6{,}000{,}000{,}000 = 6 \times 10^9$.

46. 4 Chapter 20 (Geometry, Coordinate Geometry)

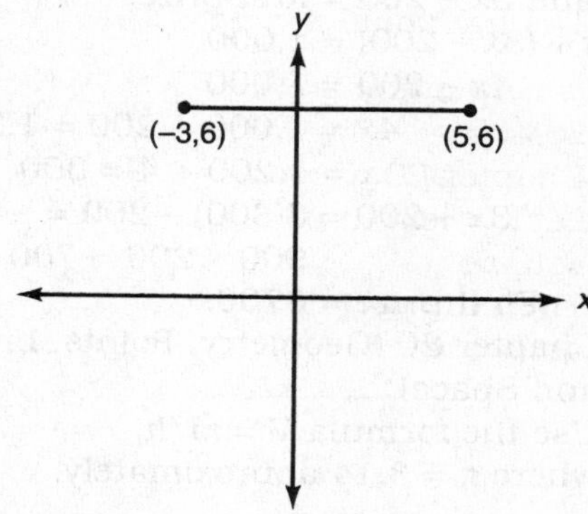

When two points lie on the same horizontal line, the distance between them is the difference between their x-coordinates: $5 - (-3) = 5 + 3 = 8$.

47. 2 Chapter 19 (Algebra, Formulas)
$$C = \frac{5}{9}(50 - 32) = \frac{5}{9}(18) = 10$$

48. 2 Chapter 20 (Geometry, Indirect Measurement)
Use the Pythagorean theorem.
$$x^2 = 8^2 + 15^2 = 64 + 225 = 289$$
$$x = \sqrt{289} = 17$$

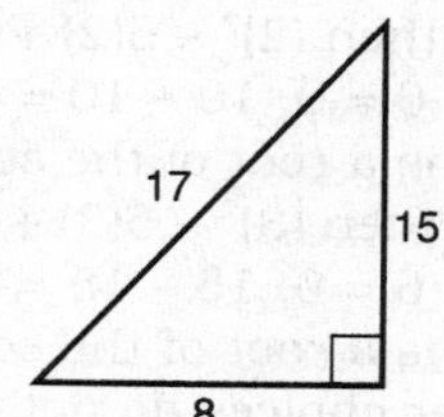

49. 4 Chapter 19 (Algebra, Solving Problems)

Let x = the number.

$$\begin{array}{r} 8 \\ 15\,\overline{)\,x} \\ \underline{120} \\ 7 \end{array}$$

Thus $x - 120 = 7$ and $x = 127$.

50. 3 Chapter 19 (Algebra, Ratio and Proportion)

Let $8x$ = larger number,
and $5x$ = smaller number.

$21 = 8x - 5x = 3x$
$x = 21 \div 3 = 7$
$8x = 8(7) = 56$

51. 4 Chapter 19 (Algebra, Solving Problems)

Let x = second prize,
and $3x - 200$ = first prize.

$x + (3x - 200) = 1{,}000$
$4x - 200 = 1{,}000$
$4x = 1{,}000 + 200 = 1{,}200$
$x = 1{,}200 \div 4 = 300$
$3x - 200 = 3(300) - 200 =$
$900 - 200 = 700$

First prize = $700.

52. 2 Chapter 20 (Geometry, Points, Lines, and Space)

Use the formula $V = \pi r^2 h$,
where $\pi = 3.14$ approximately.

In this case $r = \frac{1}{2}(12) = 6$ and $h = 10$.

Thus, $V = 3.14(6)^2(10)$

53. 1 Chapter 19 (Algebra, Solving Equations)

$x^2 - 5x + 6 = 0$

Factor the left side of the equation:

$(x - 3)(x - 2) = 0$
$x - 3 = 0$ or $x - 2 = 0$
$x = 3$ or $x = 2$

Alternative Solution:

Determine the roots by substituting the choices and determining which numbers satisfy the equation.

If $x = 2$, then $(2)^2 - 5(2) + 6 = 0$.
$4 - 10 + 6 = 0$, $10 - 10 = 0$
Thus, 2 is a root of the equation.
If $x = 3$, then $(3)^2 - 5(3) + 6 = 0$
$9 - 15 + 6 = 0$, $15 - 15 = 0$
Thus, 3 is a root of the equation.
The other choices do not satisfy the equation.

54. 2 Chapter 20 (Geometry, Geometric Concepts and Relationships)

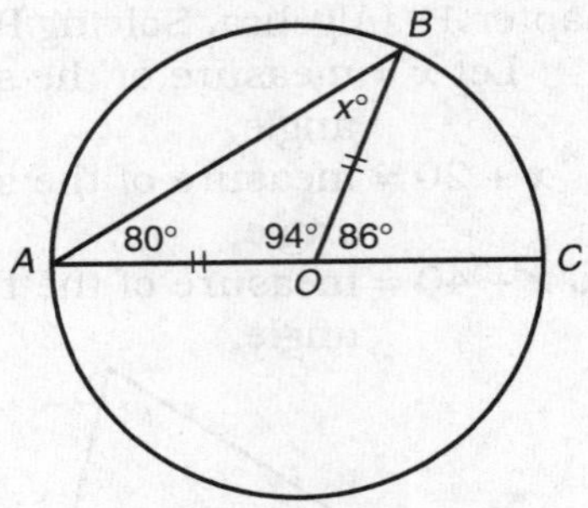

$m\angle AOB = 180 - 86 = 94°$

Since radii of the same circle are equal in length, $OB = OA$.
$\triangle OAB$ is isosceles, and the base angles have equal measures; that is, $m\angle A = m\angle B$.

$m\angle A + m\angle B = 180 - 94 = 86$

Let $m\angle A = x$. Then $m\angle B = x$.

$x + x = 86$
$2x = 86$
$x = 86 \div 2 = 43°$

55. 5 Chapter 19 (Algebra, Solving Problems)

Let x = number of games lost,
and $x + 8$ = number of games won.

$x + x + 8 = 104$
$2x + 8 = 104$
$2x = 104 - 8 = 96$
$x = 96 \div 2 = 48$
$x + 8 = 48 + 8 = 56$

56. 5 Chapter 19 (Algebra, Solving Problems)

Let x = amount of money Fred has,
and $2x$ = amount of money Jack has.
Then $x + 12$ = amount of money Fred has after getting $12 from Jack,
and $2x - 12$ = amount of money Jack has after giving $12 to Fred.

$2x - 12 = x + 12$
$2x - x = 12 + 12$
$x = 24$
$2x = 2(24) = \$48$

UNIT VIII

TWO PRACTICE EXAMINATIONS

Answer Sheet for the Practice Examination

TEST 1: WRITING SKILLS, PART I

1. ① ② ③ ④ ⑤
2. ① ② ③ ④ ⑤
3. ① ② ③ ④ ⑤
4. ① ② ③ ④ ⑤
5. ① ② ③ ④ ⑤
6. ① ② ③ ④ ⑤
7. ① ② ③ ④ ⑤
8. ① ② ③ ④ ⑤
9. ① ② ③ ④ ⑤
10. ① ② ③ ④ ⑤
11. ① ② ③ ④ ⑤
12. ① ② ③ ④ ⑤
13. ① ② ③ ④ ⑤
14. ① ② ③ ④ ⑤
15. ① ② ③ ④ ⑤
16. ① ② ③ ④ ⑤
17. ① ② ③ ④ ⑤
18. ① ② ③ ④ ⑤
19. ① ② ③ ④ ⑤
20. ① ② ③ ④ ⑤
21. ① ② ③ ④ ⑤
22. ① ② ③ ④ ⑤
23. ① ② ③ ④ ⑤
24. ① ② ③ ④ ⑤
25. ① ② ③ ④ ⑤
26. ① ② ③ ④ ⑤
27. ① ② ③ ④ ⑤
28. ① ② ③ ④ ⑤
29. ① ② ③ ④ ⑤
30. ① ② ③ ④ ⑤
31. ① ② ③ ④ ⑤
32. ① ② ③ ④ ⑤
33. ① ② ③ ④ ⑤
34. ① ② ③ ④ ⑤
35. ① ② ③ ④ ⑤
36. ① ② ③ ④ ⑤
37. ① ② ③ ④ ⑤
38. ① ② ③ ④ ⑤
39. ① ② ③ ④ ⑤
40. ① ② ③ ④ ⑤
41. ① ② ③ ④ ⑤
42. ① ② ③ ④ ⑤
43. ① ② ③ ④ ⑤
44. ① ② ③ ④ ⑤
45. ① ② ③ ④ ⑤
46. ① ② ③ ④ ⑤
47. ① ② ③ ④ ⑤
48. ① ② ③ ④ ⑤
49. ① ② ③ ④ ⑤
50. ① ② ③ ④ ⑤
51. ① ② ③ ④ ⑤
52. ① ② ③ ④ ⑤
53. ① ② ③ ④ ⑤
54. ① ② ③ ④ ⑤
55. ① ② ③ ④ ⑤

TEST 2: SOCIAL STUDIES

1. ① ② ③ ④ ⑤
2. ① ② ③ ④ ⑤
3. ① ② ③ ④ ⑤
4. ① ② ③ ④ ⑤
5. ① ② ③ ④ ⑤
6. ① ② ③ ④ ⑤
7. ① ② ③ ④ ⑤
8. ① ② ③ ④ ⑤
9. ① ② ③ ④ ⑤
10. ① ② ③ ④ ⑤
11. ① ② ③ ④ ⑤
12. ① ② ③ ④ ⑤
13. ① ② ③ ④ ⑤
14. ① ② ③ ④ ⑤
15. ① ② ③ ④ ⑤
16. ① ② ③ ④ ⑤
17. ① ② ③ ④ ⑤
18. ① ② ③ ④ ⑤
19. ① ② ③ ④ ⑤
20. ① ② ③ ④ ⑤
21. ① ② ③ ④ ⑤
22. ① ② ③ ④ ⑤
23. ① ② ③ ④ ⑤
24. ① ② ③ ④ ⑤
25. ① ② ③ ④ ⑤
26. ① ② ③ ④ ⑤
27. ① ② ③ ④ ⑤
28. ① ② ③ ④ ⑤
29. ① ② ③ ④ ⑤
30. ① ② ③ ④ ⑤
31. ① ② ③ ④ ⑤
32. ① ② ③ ④ ⑤
33. ① ② ③ ④ ⑤
34. ① ② ③ ④ ⑤
35. ① ② ③ ④ ⑤
36. ① ② ③ ④ ⑤
37. ① ② ③ ④ ⑤
38. ① ② ③ ④ ⑤
39. ① ② ③ ④ ⑤
40. ① ② ③ ④ ⑤
41. ① ② ③ ④ ⑤
42. ① ② ③ ④ ⑤
43. ① ② ③ ④ ⑤
44. ① ② ③ ④ ⑤
45. ① ② ③ ④ ⑤
46. ① ② ③ ④ ⑤
47. ① ② ③ ④ ⑤
48. ① ② ③ ④ ⑤
49. ① ② ③ ④ ⑤
50. ① ② ③ ④ ⑤
51. ① ② ③ ④ ⑤
52. ① ② ③ ④ ⑤
53. ① ② ③ ④ ⑤
54. ① ② ③ ④ ⑤
55. ① ② ③ ④ ⑤
56. ① ② ③ ④ ⑤
57. ① ② ③ ④ ⑤
58. ① ② ③ ④ ⑤
59. ① ② ③ ④ ⑤
60. ① ② ③ ④ ⑤
61. ① ② ③ ④ ⑤
62. ① ② ③ ④ ⑤
63. ① ② ③ ④ ⑤
64. ① ② ③ ④ ⑤

TEST 3: SCIENCE

1. ① ② ③ ④ ⑤
2. ① ② ③ ④ ⑤
3. ① ② ③ ④ ⑤
4. ① ② ③ ④ ⑤
5. ① ② ③ ④ ⑤
6. ① ② ③ ④ ⑤
7. ① ② ③ ④ ⑤
8. ① ② ③ ④ ⑤
9. ① ② ③ ④ ⑤
10. ① ② ③ ④ ⑤
11. ① ② ③ ④ ⑤
12. ① ② ③ ④ ⑤
13. ① ② ③ ④ ⑤
14. ① ② ③ ④ ⑤
15. ① ② ③ ④ ⑤
16. ① ② ③ ④ ⑤
17. ① ② ③ ④ ⑤
18. ① ② ③ ④ ⑤
19. ① ② ③ ④ ⑤
20. ① ② ③ ④ ⑤
21. ① ② ③ ④ ⑤
22. ① ② ③ ④ ⑤
23. ① ② ③ ④ ⑤
24. ① ② ③ ④ ⑤
25. ① ② ③ ④ ⑤
26. ① ② ③ ④ ⑤
27. ① ② ③ ④ ⑤
28. ① ② ③ ④ ⑤
29. ① ② ③ ④ ⑤
30. ① ② ③ ④ ⑤
31. ① ② ③ ④ ⑤
32. ① ② ③ ④ ⑤
33. ① ② ③ ④ ⑤
34. ① ② ③ ④ ⑤
35. ① ② ③ ④ ⑤
36. ① ② ③ ④ ⑤
37. ① ② ③ ④ ⑤
38. ① ② ③ ④ ⑤
39. ① ② ③ ④ ⑤
40. ① ② ③ ④ ⑤
41. ① ② ③ ④ ⑤
42. ① ② ③ ④ ⑤
43. ① ② ③ ④ ⑤
44. ① ② ③ ④ ⑤
45. ① ② ③ ④ ⑤
46. ① ② ③ ④ ⑤
47. ① ② ③ ④ ⑤
48. ① ② ③ ④ ⑤
49. ① ② ③ ④ ⑤
50. ① ② ③ ④ ⑤
51. ① ② ③ ④ ⑤
52. ① ② ③ ④ ⑤
53. ① ② ③ ④ ⑤
54. ① ② ③ ④ ⑤
55. ① ② ③ ④ ⑤
56. ① ② ③ ④ ⑤
57. ① ② ③ ④ ⑤
58. ① ② ③ ④ ⑤
59. ① ② ③ ④ ⑤
60. ① ② ③ ④ ⑤
61. ① ② ③ ④ ⑤
62. ① ② ③ ④ ⑤
63. ① ② ③ ④ ⑤
64. ① ② ③ ④ ⑤
65. ① ② ③ ④ ⑤
66. ① ② ③ ④ ⑤

TEST 4: INTERPRETING LITERATURE AND THE ARTS

1. ① ② ③ ④ ⑤
2. ① ② ③ ④ ⑤
3. ① ② ③ ④ ⑤
4. ① ② ③ ④ ⑤
5. ① ② ③ ④ ⑤
6. ① ② ③ ④ ⑤
7. ① ② ③ ④ ⑤
8. ① ② ③ ④ ⑤
9. ① ② ③ ④ ⑤
10. ① ② ③ ④ ⑤
11. ① ② ③ ④ ⑤
12. ① ② ③ ④ ⑤
13. ① ② ③ ④ ⑤
14. ① ② ③ ④ ⑤
15. ① ② ③ ④ ⑤
16. ① ② ③ ④ ⑤
17. ① ② ③ ④ ⑤
18. ① ② ③ ④ ⑤
19. ① ② ③ ④ ⑤
20. ① ② ③ ④ ⑤
21. ① ② ③ ④ ⑤
22. ① ② ③ ④ ⑤
23. ① ② ③ ④ ⑤
24. ① ② ③ ④ ⑤
25. ① ② ③ ④ ⑤
26. ① ② ③ ④ ⑤
27. ① ② ③ ④ ⑤
28. ① ② ③ ④ ⑤
29. ① ② ③ ④ ⑤
30. ① ② ③ ④ ⑤
31. ① ② ③ ④ ⑤
32. ① ② ③ ④ ⑤
33. ① ② ③ ④ ⑤
34. ① ② ③ ④ ⑤
35. ① ② ③ ④ ⑤
36. ① ② ③ ④ ⑤
37. ① ② ③ ④ ⑤
38. ① ② ③ ④ ⑤
39. ① ② ③ ④ ⑤
40. ① ② ③ ④ ⑤
41. ① ② ③ ④ ⑤
42. ① ② ③ ④ ⑤
43. ① ② ③ ④ ⑤
44. ① ② ③ ④ ⑤
45. ① ② ③ ④ ⑤

TEST 5: MATHEMATICS

1. ① ② ③ ④ ⑤
2. ① ② ③ ④ ⑤
3. ① ② ③ ④ ⑤
4. ① ② ③ ④ ⑤
5. ① ② ③ ④ ⑤
6. ① ② ③ ④ ⑤
7. ① ② ③ ④ ⑤
8. ① ② ③ ④ ⑤
9. ① ② ③ ④ ⑤
10. ① ② ③ ④ ⑤
11. ① ② ③ ④ ⑤
12. ① ② ③ ④ ⑤
13. ① ② ③ ④ ⑤
14. ① ② ③ ④ ⑤
15. ① ② ③ ④ ⑤
16. ① ② ③ ④ ⑤
17. ① ② ③ ④ ⑤
18. ① ② ③ ④ ⑤
19. ① ② ③ ④ ⑤
20. ① ② ③ ④ ⑤
21. ① ② ③ ④ ⑤
22. ① ② ③ ④ ⑤
23. ① ② ③ ④ ⑤
24. ① ② ③ ④ ⑤
25. ① ② ③ ④ ⑤
26. ① ② ③ ④ ⑤
27. ① ② ③ ④ ⑤
28. ① ② ③ ④ ⑤
29. ① ② ③ ④ ⑤
30. ① ② ③ ④ ⑤
31. ① ② ③ ④ ⑤
32. ① ② ③ ④ ⑤
33. ① ② ③ ④ ⑤
34. ① ② ③ ④ ⑤
35. ① ② ③ ④ ⑤
36. ① ② ③ ④ ⑤
37. ① ② ③ ④ ⑤
38. ① ② ③ ④ ⑤
39. ① ② ③ ④ ⑤
40. ① ② ③ ④ ⑤
41. ① ② ③ ④ ⑤
42. ① ② ③ ④ ⑤
43. ① ② ③ ④ ⑤
44. ① ② ③ ④ ⑤
45. ① ② ③ ④ ⑤
46. ① ② ③ ④ ⑤
47. ① ② ③ ④ ⑤
48. ① ② ③ ④ ⑤
49. ① ② ③ ④ ⑤
50. ① ② ③ ④ ⑤
51. ① ② ③ ④ ⑤
52. ① ② ③ ④ ⑤
53. ① ② ③ ④ ⑤
54. ① ② ③ ④ ⑤
55. ① ② ③ ④ ⑤
56. ① ② ③ ④ ⑤

PRACTICE EXAMINATION ONE

TEST 1: WRITING SKILLS, PART I

Directions

The Writing Skills test is intended to measure your ability to use clear and effective English. It is a test of English as it should be written, not as it might be spoken. This test includes both multiple-choice questions and an essay. These directions apply only to the multiple-choice section; a separate set of directions is given for the essay.

The multiple-choice section consists of paragraphs with numbered sentences. Some of the sentences contain errors in sentence structure, usage, or mechanics (spelling, punctuation, and capitalization). After reading the numbered sentences, answer the multiple-choice questions that follow. Some questions refer to sentences that are correct as written. The best answer for these questions is the one that leaves the sentence as originally written. The best answer for some questions is the one that produces a sentence that is consistent with the verb tense and point of view used throughout the paragraph.

You should spend no more than 75 minutes on the multiple-choice questions and 45 minutes on your essay. Work carefully, but do not spend too much time on any one question. You may begin working on the essay part of this test as soon as you complete the multiple-choice section.

To record your answers, mark one numbered space on the answer sheet beside the number that corresponds to the question in the test.

FOR EXAMPLE:

Sentence 1: **We were all honored to meet governor Phillips.**

What correction should be made to this sentence?

(1) insert a comma after honored
(2) change the spelling of honored to honered
(3) change governor to Governor
(4) replace were with was
(5) no correction is necessary

① ② ● ④ ⑤

In this example, the word "governor" should be capitalized; therefore, answer space 3 would be marked on the answer sheet.

GO ON TO THE NEXT PAGE

TEST 1: WRITING SKILLS, PART I

Questions 1 to 9 refer to the following paragraphs.

(1) Safe food must be planned and not left to chance, for the consumer, food safety begins in the marketplace. (2) All cooperative efforts made by states and the U.S. department of agriculture to make available a clean, safe, wholesome food supply will be in vain unless the consumer takes certain precautions to keep it that way. (3) The precautions to be taken by the consumer include care in buying, storing, handling, and cooking food.

(4) Shop for groceries last after all other errands have been run. (5) Take foods home immediately and don't leave them unattended for a long period of time. (6) Suficient light in grocery stores is necessary to enable you to adequately view foods for proper selection. (7) Store personnel should make sure that foods are replaced frequently in order to keep them as fresh as possible.

(8) Under no circumstances buy swollen or leaking cans. (9) The food in a swollen or leaking can may be dangerous to eat or even to taste.

(10) Ask the checkout clerk to bag cold foods together so that they keep cold longer; interspersed with room-temperature foods, they may warm up quickly.

1. Sentence 1: **Safe food must be planned and not left to chance, for the consumer, food safety begins in the marketplace.**

   Which of the following is the best way to write the underlined portion of this sentence? If you think the original is the best way, choose option (1).

   (1) chance, for
   (2) chance: for
   (3) chance; for
   (4) chance, For
   (5) chance. For

2. Sentence 2: **All cooperative efforts made by states and the U.S. department of agriculture to make available a clean, safe, wholesome food supply will be in vain unless the consumer takes certain precautions to keep it that way.**

   What correction should be made to this sentence?

   (1) insert a hyphen in cooperative
   (2) capitalize department and agriculture
   (3) remove the comma after clean
   (4) change it to them
   (5) no correction is necessary

3. Sentence 3. **The precautions to be taken by the consumer include care in buying, storing, handling, and cooking food.**

   If you rewrote sentence 3 beginning with

   Care in buying, storing, handling and cooking food

   the next words should be

   (1) include
   (2) is
   (3) is among
   (4) would be among
   (5) will be among

4. Sentence 4: **Shop for groceries last after all other errands have been run.**

   What correction should be made to this sentence?

   (1) insert a comma after last
   (2) remove the word other
   (3) change have been to will have been
   (4) change run to ran
   (5) no correction is necessary

GO ON TO THE NEXT PAGE

TEST 1: WRITING SKILLS, PART I

5. Sentence 5: **Take foods home immediately <u>and don't</u> leave them unattended for a long period of time.**

   Which of the following is the best way to write the underlined portion of this sentence? If you think the original is the best way, choose option (1).

   (1) and don't
   (2) also don't
   (3) but don't
   (4) however don't
   (5) nevertheless don't

6. Sentence 6: **Suficient light in grocery stores is necessary to enable you to adequately view foods for proper selection.**

   What correction should be made to this sentence?

   (1) change the spelling of <u>suficient</u> to <u>sufficient</u>
   (2) insert a comma after <u>stores</u>
   (3) change the spelling of <u>necessary</u> to <u>necessery</u>
   (4) insert a comma after <u>foods</u>
   (5) no correction is necessary

7. Sentence 7: **Store personnel should make sure that foods are replaced frequently in order to keep them as fresh as possible.**

   What correction should be made to this sentence?

   (1) change the spelling of <u>personnel</u> to <u>personal</u>
   (2) change <u>should</u> to <u>might</u>
   (3) change <u>them</u> to <u>it</u>
   (4) change <u>fresh</u> to <u>freshly</u>
   (5) no change is necessary

8. Sentences 8 and 9: **Under no circumstances buy swollen or leaking cans. The food in a swollen or leaking can may be dangerous to eat or even to taste.**

   The most effective combination of sentences 8 and 9 would include which of the following groups of words?

   (1) which contain food that may be
   (2) and the food in a swollen can
   (3) since the food in a swollen can
   (4) being dangerous to eat
   (5) that may be dangerous to eat

9. Sentence 10: **Ask the checkout clerk to bag cold foods together so that they keep cold <u>longer; interspersed</u> with room-temperature foods, they may warm up quickly.**

   Which of the following is the best way to write the underlined portion of this sentence? If you think the original is the best way, choose option (1).

   (1) longer; interspersed
   (2) longer. interspersed
   (3) longer: interspersed
   (4) longer, interspersed
   (5) longer, Interspersed

<u>Questions 10 to 18</u> refer to the following paragraphs.

(1) The traditional family grouping will remain dominant, although the people in the family may change because of divorce, separation, and remarriage.

(2) The family with dual careers, both husband and wife working, will increase—particularly among the young. (3) The husband and wife family with no children will also increase.

(4) Some couples will choose to remain childless, others will spend the major part of their lifetime with no children present because of the possibilities for spacing and limiting family size.

GO ON TO THE NEXT PAGE

TEST 1: WRITING SKILLS, PART I

(5) An increasing number of single-parent families will be formed as a result of divorce, death, abandonment, or the choice of the unwed to rear their children alone. (6) In most cases, the single-parent family will have an employed woman at its head.

(7) Because of increased acceptability, more individuals may remain unmarried and establish single households. (8) The single adult living alone will establish close kin or simulated kin networks, relying upon and sharing with others economic and emotional resources to fulfill parentlike roles in an "aunt-uncle" capacity.

(9) These family forms, will present different issues and problems for family members.

(10) Families will need information to select wisely the family pattern they want to pursue.

10. Sentence 1: **The traditional family grouping will remain <u>dominant, although</u> the people in the family may change because of divorce, separation, and remarriage.**

    Which of the following is the best way to write the underlined portion of this sentence? If you think the original is the best way, choose option (1).

    (1) dominant, although
    (2) dominant, indeed
    (3) dominant, so
    (4) dominant, therefore
    (5) dominant, nevertheless

11. Sentences 2 and 3: **The family with dual careers, both husband and wife working, will increase—particularly among the young. The husband and wife family with no children will also increase.**

    The most effective combination of sentences 2 and 3 would include which of the following groups of words?

    (1) as well as
    (2) but
    (3) although
    (4) nevertheless
    (5) therefore

12. Sentence 4: **Some couples will choose to remain <u>childless, others</u> will spend the major part of their lifetime with no children present because of the possibilities for spacing and limiting family size.**

    Which of the following is the best way to write the underlined portion of this sentence? If you think the original is the best way, choose option (1).

    (1) childless, others
    (2) childless. others
    (3) childless. Others
    (4) childless; Others
    (5) childless: others

13. Sentence 5: **An increasing number of single-parent families will be formed as a result of divorce, death, abandonment, or the choice of the unwed to rear their children alone.**

    If you rewrote sentence 5 beginning with

    <u>As a result of</u> . . . <u>alone</u>

    the next words should be

    (1) an increasing number
    (2) single-parent families
    (3) divorce, death, abandonment
    (4) the choice of the unwed
    (5) to rear their children

14. Sentence 6: **In most cases, the single-parent family will have an employed woman as its head.**

    What correction should be made to this sentence?

    (1) remove the comma after <u>cases</u>
    (2) remove the hyphen in <u>single-parent</u>
    (3) change <u>will have</u> to <u>has</u>
    (4) change <u>its</u> to <u>it's</u>
    (5) no change is necessary

GO ON TO THE NEXT PAGE

TEST 1: WRITING SKILLS, PART I

15. Sentence 7: **Because of increased acceptability, more individuals may remain unmarried and establish single households.**

    What correction should be made to this sentence?

    (1) change the spelling of acceptability to acceptibility
    (2) remove the comma after acceptability
    (3) change may remain to will remain
    (4) insert a comma after unmarried
    (5) no correction is necessary

16. Sentence 8: **The single adult living alone will establish close kin or simulated kin networks, relying upon and sharing with others economic and emotional resources to fulfill parentlike roles in an "aunt-uncle" capacity.**

    What correction should be made to this sentence?

    (1) add a comma after close kin
    (2) remove the comma after networks
    (3) change the spelling of resources to resourses
    (4) change to fulfill to fulfilling
    (5) no correction is necessary

17. Sentence 9: **These family forms, will present different issues and problems for family members.**

    What correction should be made to this sentence?

    (1) remove the comma after forms
    (2) change will present to will have presented
    (3) insert a comma after issues
    (4) insert a comma after problems
    (5) no correction is necessary

18. Sentence 10: **Families will need information to select wisely the family pattern they want to pursue.**

    What correction should be made to this sentence?

    (1) change will need to will be needing
    (2) change select wisely to wisely select
    (3) change the spelling of pattern to pattren
    (4) change the spelling of pursue to persue
    (5) no correction is necessary

GO ON TO THE NEXT PAGE

TEST 1: WRITING SKILLS, PART I

Questions 19 to 27 refer to the following paragraphs.

(1) Drug abuse is like a communicable disease. (2) It spreads—by example, by word of mouth, and by imitation. (3) Drug abuse is certainly increasing, but so is the number of young people who have tried drugs and want out. (4) As we provide treatment services for them, these young people become able to tell other youth that the drug scene is not as great as they thought it was before they got hooked. (5) And, of greater importance, they are beleived by their contemporaries before experimentation becomes habit.

(6) Parents can help prevent drug usage by setting an example, by knowledge, and by understanding. (7) If they are to talk to their children about drugs they must be informed. (8) usually they know far less about drugs than do their children. (9) Ideally, before their child is tempted to experiment, they will be able to explain to him the undesirability of the drugged life. (10) What is even more convincing to young people, they will have been able to communicate to him the actual damage that a drug abuser does to their body.

19. Sentences 1 and 2: **Drug abuse is like a communicable disease. It spreads—by example, by word of mouth, and by imitation.**

    The most effective combination of sentences 1 and 2 would include which of the following groups of words?

    (1) disease. it spreads
    (2) disease although it spreads
    (3) disease yet it spreads
    (4) disease that spreads
    (5) disease having spread

20. Sentence 3: **Drug abuse is certainly increasing, but so is the number of young people who have tried drugs and want out.**

    What correction should be made to this sentence?

    (1) remove the comma after increasing
    (2) change but to and
    (3) change number to amount
    (4) insert a comma after people
    (5) no correction is necessary

21. Sentence 4: **As we provide treatment services for them, these young people become able to tell other youth that the drug scene is not as great as they thought it was before they got hooked.**

    What correction should be made to this sentence?

    (1) change As to Although
    (2) remove the comma after them
    (3) change become to became
    (4) change thought to think
    (5) no correction is necessary

22. Sentence 5: **And, of greater importance, they are beleived by their contemporaries before experimentation becomes habit.**

    What correction should be made to this sentence?

    (1) remove the commas before of and after importance
    (2) change beleived to believed
    (3) insert commas before by and after contemporaries
    (4) change becomes to will become
    (5) no correction is necessary

GO ON TO THE NEXT PAGE

TEST 1: WRITING SKILLS, PART I

23. Sentence 6: **Parents can help prevent drug usage by setting an example, by knowledge, and by understanding.**

    What correction should be made to this sentence?

    (1) change can to could
    (2) change by setting an example to by example
    (3) change the spelling of knowledge to knowlege
    (4) remove the comma before and
    (5) no correction is necessary

24. Sentence 7: **If they are to talk to their children about drugs they must be informed.**

    What correction should be made to this sentence?

    (1) change are to to would
    (2) change their to they're
    (3) insert a comma after drugs
    (4) change informed to informative
    (5) no correction is necessary

25. Sentences 7 and 8: **If they are to talk to their children about drugs they must be informed. usually they know far less about drugs than do their children.**

    Which of the following is the best way to write the underlined portion of this sentence? If you think the original is the best way, choose option (1).

    (1) informed. usually
    (2) informed usually
    (3) informed: usually
    (4) informed—Usually
    (5) informed. Usually

26. Sentence 9: **Ideally, before their child is tempted to experiment, they will be able to explain to him the undesirability of the drugged life.**

    What correction should be made to this sentence?

    (1) change the spelling of ideally to idealy
    (2) remove the comma before before
    (3) change be able to have been able
    (4) change the spelling of undesirability to undesireability
    (5) no correction is necessary

27. Sentence 10: **What is even more convincing to young people, they will have been able to communicate to him the actual damage that a drug abuser does to their body.**

    What correction should be made to this sentence?

    (1) move even to after convincing
    (2) remove the comma after people
    (3) change the spelling of communicate to comunicate
    (4) change their to his
    (5) no change is necessary

GO ON TO THE NEXT PAGE

TEST 1: WRITING SKILLS, PART I

Questions 28 to 37 refer to the following paragraphs.

(1) Statistically, by far the most common type of home accidents are falls. (2) Each year thousands of americans meet death in this way, within the four walls of their home or in yards around their house. (3) Nine out of ten of the victims are over 65 but people of all ages experience serious injuries as a result of home falls. (4) It is impossable to estimate how many injuries result from falls, but they must run into the millions.

(5) Falls can be a problem for all ages. (6) In the process of growing up, children or teenagers often will fall. (7) Fortunately their bodies are supple, so they may suffer only skinned knees bumps, and bruises. (8) In an older person, however, the same fall may cause a broken arm, leg, or hip, or other injury that requires hospitalization or medical care. (9) As you get older, you may not fall any more often, but the results usually are more serious and may even be fatal.

(10) Adults fall because they don't look where they're going, are in a hurry, are careless, or thinking about something else.

(11) A few inexpensive items such as a suction-type rubber mat or safety strips in the tub, a non-slip mat on the floor, and bathtub handholds can go a long way toward eliminating falls in the bathroom.

28. Sentence 1: **Statistically, by far the most common type of home accidents are falls.**

What correction should be made to this sentence?

(1) change the spelling of Statistically to Statisticly
(2) remove the comma before by
(3) insert a comma after accidents
(4) change are to is
(5) no correction is necessary

29. Sentence 2: **Each year thousands of americans meet death in this way, within the four walls of their home or in yards around their house.**

What correction should be made to this sentence?

(1) change americans to Americans
(2) remove the comma after way
(3) change within to in
(4) insert a comma after home
(5) no correction is necessary

30. Sentence 3: **Nine out of ten of the victims are over 65 but people of all ages experience serious injuries as a result of home falls.**

What correction should be made to this sentence?

(1) change are to is
(2) insert a comma after 65
(3) change but to and
(4) change experience to experiance
(5) no correction is necessary

31. Sentence 4: **It is impossable to estimate how many injuries result from falls, but they must run into the millions.**

What correction should be made to this sentence?

(1) change the spelling of impossable to impossible
(2) change result to results
(3) remove the comma after falls
(4) change but to since
(5) no correction is necessary

GO ON TO THE NEXT PAGE

TEST 1: WRITING SKILLS, PART I

32. Sentences 5 and 6: **Falls can be a problem for all ages. In the process of growing up, children or teenagers often will fall.**

    Which of the following is the best way to write the underlined portion of this sentence? If you think the original is the best way, choose option (1).

    (1) ages. In
    (2) ages. in
    (3) ages: In
    (4) ages: in
    (5) ages; In

33. Sentence 7: **Fortunately their bodies are supple, so they may suffer only skinned knees bumps, and bruises.**

    What correction should be made to this sentence?

    (1) change the spelling of Fortunately to Fortunitely
    (2) remove the comma after supple
    (3) change suffer only to only suffer
    (4) insert a comma after knees
    (5) no correction is necessary

34. Sentence 8: **In an older person, however, the same fall may cause a broken arm, leg, hip, or other injury that requires hospitalization or medical care.**

    What correction should be made to this sentence?

    (1) remove the commas around however
    (2) insert a colon after cause
    (3) insert a comma after injury
    (4) change requires to require
    (5) no correction is necessary

35. Sentence 9: **As you get older, you may not fall any more often, but the results usually are more serious and may even be fatal.**

    What correction should be made to this sentence?

    (1) change As to When
    (2) change get to will get
    (3) change but to and
    (4) change more to most
    (5) no correction is necessary

36. Sentence 10: **Adults fall because they don't look where they're going, are in a hurry, are careless, or thinking about something else.**

    What correction should be made to this sentence?

    (1) change don't to doesn't
    (2) change they're to there
    (3) remove the comma after hurry
    (4) insert are before thinking
    (5) no correction is necessary

37. Sentence 11: **A few inexpensive items such as a suction-type rubber mat or safety strips in the tub, a non-slip mat on the floor, and bathtub handholds can go a long way toward eliminating falls in the bathroom.**

    If you rewrote sentence 11 beginning with

    To eliminate falls in the bathroom

    the next words should be

    (1) a few inexpensive items
    (2) a suction-type rubber mat
    (3) safety strips
    (4) a non-slip mat
    (5) bathtub handles

GO ON TO THE NEXT PAGE

TEST 1: WRITING SKILLS, PART I

Questions 38 to 46 refer to the following paragraphs.

(1) The only known cure for bikomania, a highly contagious fever, sweeping the country from coast to coast, is to ride a bike. (2) Nearly 100 million happy victims, including mom and pop and the kids, now are taking this delightful treatment and pedaling their two-wheelers into an exciting new world of fun and adventure.

(3) Why buy a bike? Partly because riding a bike benefits both you and your enviroment. (4) A bike doesn't foul up the air, makes no noise, keeps you in top physical shape, takes up little room on the road. and is easy to park in a small space. (5) With apropriate accessories—such as saddle bags, luggage racks, or baskets—a bike can be used on shopping missions, picnic excursions, or bicycle tours.

(6) What kind of bike should you get? (7) Bewildered by the tantalizing display of racing models with 10-speed gearshifts and lots of fancy gimmicks, your apt to plunge into something you really don't need. (8) Best advice: buy the simplest model that meets your transportation requirements. (9) You need not invest in dropped handlebars, multigear ratios, and special frames that may be too complicated for your purposes.

(10) Try renting a bike before you buy one. (11) Spend a couple of weekends pedaling various makes over typical terrain in your area; this tryout will answer many of your questions.

38. Sentence 1: **The only known cure for bikomania, a highly contagious fever, sweeping the country from coast to coast, is to ride a bike.**

What correction should be made to this sentence?

(1) remove the comma after bikomania
(2) change the spelling of contagious to contageous
(3) remove the comma after fever
(4) remove the comma after coast
(5) no correction is necessary

39. Sentence 2: **Nearly 100 million happy victims, including mom and pop and the kids, now are taking this delightful treatment and pedaling their two-wheelers into an exciting new world of fun and adventure.**

What correction should be made to this sentence?

(1) remove the comma after victims
(2) capitalize mom, pop
(3) capitalize kids
(4) change the spelling of exciting to exsiting
(5) no correction is necessary

40. Sentence 3: **Why buy a bike? Partly because riding a bike benefits both you and your enviroment.**

What correction should be made to this sentence?

(1) remove the question mark after bike
(2) change the spelling of benefits to benifits
(3) change your to you're
(4) change the spelling of enviroment to environment
(5) no correction is necessary

41. Sentence 4: **A bike doesn't foul up the air, makes no noise, keeps you in top physical shape, takes up little room on the road. and is easy to park in a small space.**

Which of the following is the best way to write the underlined portion of this sentence? If you think the original is the best way, choose option (1).

(1) road. and
(2) road. And
(3) road, and
(4) road, And
(5) road: and

GO ON TO THE NEXT PAGE

TEST 1: WRITING SKILLS, PART I

42. Sentence 5: **With apropriate accessories—such as saddle bags, luggage racks, or baskets—a bike can be used on shopping missions, picnic excursions, or bicycle tours.**

What correction should be made to this sentence?

(1) change the spelling of aproriate to appropriate
(2) remove the dashes before such and after baskets
(3) remove the comma after bags
(4) change the spelling of excursions to excurshuns
(5) no change is necessary

43. Sentence 7: **Bewildered by the tantalizing display of racing models with 10-speed gearshifts and lots of fancy gimmicks, your apt to plunge into something you really don't need.**

What correction should be made to this sentence?

(1) insert commas before with and after gearshifts
(2) remove the comma after gimmicks
(3) change the spelling of your to you're
(4) change the spelling of really to realy
(5) no correction is necessary

44. Sentence 8: **Best advice: buy the simplest model that meets your transportation requirements.**

Which of the following is the best way to write the underlined portion of this sentence? If you think the original is the best way, choose option (1).

(1) Best advice: buy
(2) Best advice; Buy
(3) Best advice; buy
(4) Best advice, Buy
(5) Best advice, buy

45. Sentence 9: **You need not invest in dropped handlebars, multigear ratios, and special frames that may be too complicated for your purposes.**

If you rewrote sentence 9 beginning with

Nor need you

the next words should be

(1) invest in
(2) dropped handlebars
(3) multigear ratios
(4) that may be
(5) for your purposes

46. Sentence 11: **Spend a couple of weekends pedaling various makes over typical terrain in your area; this tryout will answer many of your questions.**

Which of the following is the best way to write the underlined portion of this sentence? If you think the original is the best way, choose option (1).

(1) area; this
(2) area: this
(3) area, this
(4) area. this
(5) area this

GO ON TO THE NEXT PAGE

TEST 1: WRITING SKILLS, PART I

Questions 47 to 55 refer to the following paragraphs.

(1) At every stage of development, clothes can help establish a person's identity for himself and for those with who he interacts. (2) The childhood game of "dressing up" in parents' clothes provides an opportunity for the child to practise the roles he will be expected to play in adult life.

(3) The degree to which a person choses clothes that fit the roles will affect his performance in those roles.

(4) Clothes are an important factor in developing feelings of self-confidence and self-respect. (5) When you look good, you feel good. (6) For most people, clothes are often a source of positive reaction from others, since in our culture we are more apt to compliment a person on his appearance than on other aspects of the "self."

(7) Most Americans also recognize that a proper appearance and proper dress are the keys to association with the right crowd, which in turn opens the door to job advancement increased income, and greater prestige.

(8) Our clothing needs are influenced by a multitude of circumstances. (9) Buying motives are seldom simple.

(10) The first step in the decision-making process is to make a conscious ordering of the things that are important to us. (11) If a person recognizes and accepts the priorities of his values—for example, that his status and prestige may be more important than his physical comfort—his choice of clothing is not only simplified, but more likely to bring him greater satisfaction.

47. Sentence 1: **At every stage of development, clothes can help establish a person's identity for himself and for those with who he interacts.**

What correction should be made to this sentence?

(1) change the spelling of development to developement
(2) remove the comma after development
(3) insert a comma after himself
(4) change who to whom
(5) no correction is necessary

48. Sentence 2: **The childhood game of "dressing up" in parents' clothes provides an opportunity for the child to practise the roles he will be expected to play in adult life.**

What correction should be made to this sentence?

(1) remove the quotation marks around "dressing up"
(2) change parents' to parent's
(3) change provides to provide
(4) change the spelling of practise to practice
(5) no correction is necessary

49. Sentence 3: **The degree to which a person choses clothes that fit the roles will affect his performance in those roles.**

What correction should be made to this sentence?

(1) remove the word to
(2) change the spelling of choses to chooses
(3) insert a comma after roles
(4) change the spelling of affect to effect
(5) no correction is necessary

50. Sentences 4 and 5: **Clothes are an important factor in developing feelings of self-confidence and self-respect. When you look good, you feel good.**

The most effective combination of sentences 4 and 5 would include which of the following groups of words?

(1) self-respect, moreover, when
(2) self-respect, although, when
(3) self-respect, nevertheless, when
(4) self-respect, therefore, when
(5) self-respect, since, when

GO ON TO THE NEXT PAGE

TEST 1: WRITING SKILLS, PART I

51. Sentence 6: **For most people, clothes are often a source of positive reaction from others, since in our culture we are more apt to compliment a person on his appearance than on other aspects of the "self."**

What correction should be made to this sentence?

(1) remove the comma after people
(2) change the spelling of compliment to complement
(3) change the spelling of appearance to appearence
(4) change than to then
(5) no correction is necessary

52. Sentence 7: **Most Americans also recognize that a proper appearance and proper dress are the keys to association with the right crowd, which in turn opens the doors to job advancement increased income, and greater prestige.**

What correction should be made to this sentence?

(1) change Americans to americans
(2) change the spelling of recognize to reconize
(3) remove the comma after crowd
(4) insert a comma after advancement
(5) no correction is necessary

53. Sentences 8 and 9: **Our clothing needs are influenced by a multitude of circumstances. Buying motives are seldom simple.**

The most effective combination of sentences 8 and 9 would include which of the following groups of words?

(1) circumstances, although buying
(2) circumstances, because buying
(3) circumstances, but buying
(4) circumstances, that is, buying
(5) circumstances, however, buying

54. Sentence 10: **The first step in the decision-making process is to make a conscious ordering of the things that are important to us.**

If you rewrote sentence 10 beginning with

Making a conscious ordering . . .to us

the next word(s) should be

(1) the first step
(2) in the decision-making process
(3) is
(4) are
(5) things that are

55. Sentence 11: **If a person recognizes and accepts the priorities of his values—for example, that his status and prestige may be more important than his physical comfort—his choice of clothing is not only simplified, but more likely to bring him greater satisfaction.**

What correction should be made to this sentence?

(1) change the spelling of accepts to excepts
(2) remove the comma after for example
(3) change may to might
(4) remove the comma after simplified
(5) no correction is necessary

GO ON TO THE NEXT PAGE

TEST 1: WRITING SKILLS TEST, PART II

Directions

This part of the Writing Skills test is intended to determine how well you write. You are asked to write an essay that explains something or presents an opinion on an issue. In preparing your essay, you should take the following steps:

1. Read carefully the directions and the essay topic given below.
2. Plan your essay carefully before you write.
3. Use scratch paper to make any notes.
4. Write your essay on the lined pages of a separate answer sheet.
5. Read carefully what you have written and make any changes that will improve your essay.
6. Check your paragraphs, sentence structure, spelling, punctuation, capitalization, and usage, and make any necessary corrections.

You will have 45 minutes to write on the topic below.

The computer is one of the most important technological developments in the twentieth century. Our lives have been vastly affected by computers, from the giant supercomputer to the small personal computer.

There exist widely differing views about the computer's contribution to the quality of our life. Some regard it as indispensable; others consider it a liability. Write a composition of about 200 words in which you present your view on this issue, giving reasons and examples to support your position.

END OF EXAMINATION

TEST 2: SOCIAL STUDIES

Directions

The Social Studies test consists of multiple-choice questions intended to measure general social studies concepts. The questions are based on short readings that often include a graph, chart, or figure. Study the information given and then answer the question(s) following it. Refer to the information as often as necessary in answering the questions.

You should spend no more than 85 minutes answering the questions. Work carefully, but do not spend too much time on any one question. Be sure you answer every question. You will not be penalized for incorrect answers.

To record your answers, mark the numbered space on the answer sheet beside the number that corresponds to the question in the test.

FOR EXAMPLE:

Early colonists of North America looked for settlement sites that had adequate water supplies and were accessible by ship. For this reason, many early towns were built near

(1) mountains
(2) prairies
(3) rivers
(4) glaciers
(5) plateaus

① ② ● ④ ⑤

The correct answer is "rivers"; therefore, answer space 3 would be marked on the answer sheet.

GO ON TO THE NEXT PAGE

TEST 2: SOCIAL STUDIES

Questions 1 to 3 are based on the following passage.

The term *genocide*, a joining of the Greek *genos*, meaning race or tribe, and the Latin suffix *-cide*, or killing, was coined in 1946 by a distinguished international legal scholar, Professor Raphael Lemkin.

The mass murder of six million Jews by the Nazis was the most vivid, violent, and tragic expression of genocide. But this century alone has seen others—Armenians, Gypsies, Chinese, Slavs. Some 20 million people have been slaughtered because of their racial, religious, or ethnic backgrounds.

In the language of the United Nations Convention on the Prevention and Punishment of the Crime of Genocide, *genocide* means certain specifically defined acts "*committed with intent to destroy, in whole or in part, a national, ethnical, racial or religious group, as such*."

1. The word *genocide* literally means

   (1) mass murder
   (2) race killing
   (3) slaughter
   (4) convention
   (5) ratification

2. According to this passage, genocide involves intent to destroy *all* of the following EXCEPT

   (1) nations
   (2) races
   (3) ethnic groups
   (4) political groups
   (5) religious groups

3. All of the following have been subjected to genocide EXCEPT

   (1) Jews
   (2) Nazis
   (3) Slavs
   (4) Gypsies
   (5) Chinese

Questions 4 to 6 are based on the following passage.

We come then to the question presented: Does segregation of children in public schools solely on the basis of race, even though the physical facilities and other "tangible" factors may be equal, deprive the children of the minority group of equal educational opportunities? We believe that it does.

"Segregation of white and colored children in public schools has a detrimental effect upon the colored children. A sense of inferiority affects the motivation of a child to learn. Segregation with the sanction of law, therefore, has a tendency to [retard] the educational and mental development of Negro children and to deprive them of some of the benefits they would receive in a racial[ly] integrated school system."

Whatever may have been the extent of psychological knowledge at the time of *Plessy v. Ferguson*, this finding of the Kansas court is amply supported by modern authority. Any language in *Plessy v. Ferguson* contrary to this finding is rejected. We conclude that in the field of public education the doctrine of "separate but equal" has no place.

4. "We" (first paragraph) refers to

   (1) the plaintiff
   (2) the defendant
   (3) the Congress
   (4) the Supreme Court
   (5) Plessy and Ferguson

5. Segregation of children in grade or high school is rejected for

   (1) historical reasons
   (2) political reasons
   (3) physical reasons
   (4) psychological reasons
   (5) economic reasons

GO ON TO THE NEXT PAGE

TEST 2: SOCIAL STUDIES

6. The passage implies that *Plessy v. Ferguson*
   (1) called for integration
   (2) stated that separate facilities were unequal
   (3) was based on outmoded psychology
   (4) was constitutional
   (5) applied only to private schools

---

7. The most useful indicator of the degree of democracy reached by a particular society is whether it has a
   (1) formal method whereby people can effect changes in government policy
   (2) system of government checks and balances
   (3) two-house legislature
   (4) system of liberal and humane courts
   (5) civilian government

8. "Without our two great political parties cutting across economic and geographic interests, democracy as we know it could never have been made to function." The author of this statement probably meant to suggest that
   (1) political parties in the United States tend to represent sectional interests
   (2) each political party appeals to a different social class
   (3) there is no significant difference between the Democratic and Republican parties
   (4) an important feature of the U.S. political system is the broadly based appeal of the two political parties
   (5) only a two-party system can function in a democracy

Question 9 is based on the following cartoon.

9. What is the main idea of this 1994 cartoon?
   (1) White South Africans can no longer vote in their own country.
   (2) Free elections are the key to true democracy in South Africa.
   (3) People who fail to vote in South Africa's elections may be arrested.
   (4) Black can control elections by casting multiple votes.
   (5) Slavery has been abolished in South Africa.

GO ON TO THE NEXT PAGE

TEST 2: SOCIAL STUDIES

<u>Questions 10 and 11</u> are based on the following passage.

Increased growth by acquisition by our largest corporations has resulted in a situation where the American economy will be dominated by virtually independent economic giants. Growth of these vast corporate structures, even though accompanied by an increase in the number of much smaller and less powerful companies that operate under their control, foretells the creation of monopoly-like structures throughout American business.

In general, the major acquisitions by the sample companies were corporate organizations that were profitable and successful before acquisition. The main effect of the merger or acquisition was to transfer control and management of an already successful enterprise to a new group. For some of the major acquired companies, profitability ratios, which provide a measure of management performance, for the year immediately preceding acquisition, as compared to the years after acquisition, indicate that, in most instances, the acquired companies operated less efficiently after acquisition.

10. Where mergers took place, the companies that were added had

    (1) low profitability ratios
    (2) inferior corporate values
    (3) achieved success
    (4) poor productivity
    (5) management difficulties

11. According to the passage, one measure of management performance is a corporation's

    (1) geographic market
    (2) available capital
    (3) corporate values
    (4) profitability ratio
    (5) cartel-like structure

<u>Questions 12 and 13</u> are based on the following graph.

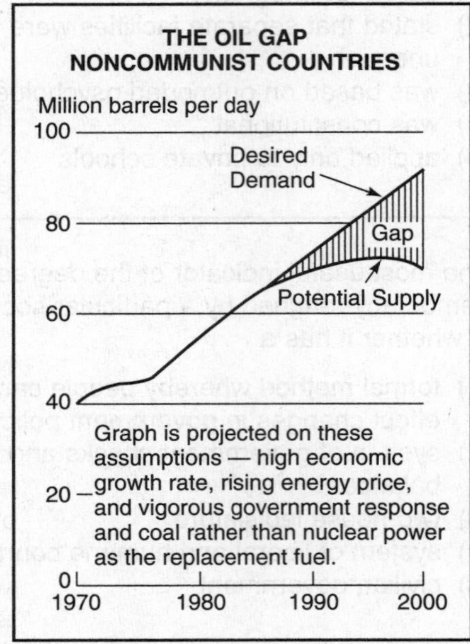

12. Based on the information in the graph, the demand of noncommunist countries for oil will begin to exceed the supply of oil in about the year

    (1) 1980
    (2) 1985
    (3) 1990
    (4) 1995
    (5) 2000

13. A valid conclusion that can be drawn from the data in the graph is that the noncommunist countries (western Europe and Japan) would

    (1) have serious economic problems if alternative sources of energy are not developed
    (2) avoid any gap between oil supply and demand by increasing oil production
    (3) have until the year 2000 to make major changes in energy policies
    (4) be unable to solve their energy problems
    (5) use less oil because of its high price

GO ON TO THE NEXT PAGE

TEST 2: SOCIAL STUDIES

14. A study of the causes of the American Revolution of 1776, the French Revolution of 1789, and the Russian Revolution of 1917 best supports the generalization that revolution is most likely to occur when
    (1) those in power are resistant to change
    (2) a society has a lower standard of living than those around it
    (3) a society has become industrialized
    (4) stable governments are in power
    (5) people are given too much voice in their government

<u>Questions 15 to 17</u> are based on the following statements by four historians.

<u>Speaker *A*:</u> American history is a series of conflicts between the haves and have-nots. Those in control of our society have always tried to maintain their wealth and power and prevent the lower classes and oppressed peoples from getting justice.

<u>Speaker *B*:</u> The American experience is unique in the story of nations. Due especially to the presence of a large, unused frontier during most of our history, we have been spared many of the problems and conflicts found in the rest of the world.

<u>Speaker *C*:</u> American history is a series of compromises between groups who have disagreed, but never over basic issues. From the writing of the Constitution to the decision to withdraw from Vietnam, extremists have represented only a minority view; the majority of the American people have usually favored compromise and moderate solutions to problems.

<u>Speaker *D*:</u> In every crisis of American history a great person, often a president, has risen above party politics and personal interest to lead the nation in the direction of greatness. We owe everything to those famous Americans who have governed us in the past.

15. Which speakers would be most likely to agree that the American Revolution cannot be compared with the French Revolution because the American Revolution did not involve a basic class struggle?
    (1) *A* and *D*
    (2) *B* and *C*
    (3) *B* and *D*
    (4) *C* and *D*
    (5) *A* and *C*

16. With which statement about the United States would Speaker *B* most likely agree?
    (1) The United States has one of the highest crime rates in the world.
    (2) The United States has not experienced some of the problems of other nations, mainly because of the availability of space.
    (3) Large cities in the United States tend to have more progressive social policies than small towns.
    (4) Many of the social institutions found in the United States originated in Europe.
    (5) The United States has few social problems.

17. The most valid inference to be drawn from the statements of the four speakers is that
    (1) all the facts should be known before a conclusion is drawn
    (2) historians must be free of personal bias
    (3) a study of history enables people to predict future events
    (4) historians disagree over interpretation of events
    (5) only one of the speakers is correct in his views

GO ON TO THE NEXT PAGE

TEST 2: SOCIAL STUDIES

Question 18 is based on the following chart.

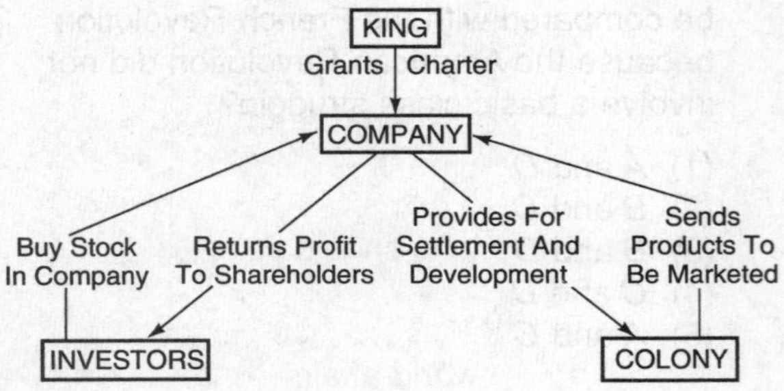

18. Which is a valid conclusion that can be drawn from the information in the chart?
    (1) The main purpose of the system illustrated was to benefit the colonies.
    (2) Nationalism was the motivating factor in English colonization.
    (3) The profit motive was a strong force in colonization.
    (4) The opportunity to own land attracted many settlers to the colonies.
    (5) Inducements were offered to prospective settlers.

Questions 19 and 20 are based on the following passage.

The task of economic policy is to create a prosperous America. The *unfinished task of prosperous Americans is to build a Great Society.*

Our accomplishments have been many; these tasks remain unfinished:
—to achieve full employment without inflation;
—to restore external equilibrium and defend the dollar;
—to enhance the efficiency and flexibility of our private and public economies;
—to widen the benefits of prosperity;
—to improve the quality of American life . . .

—Lyndon B. Johnson

19. Former President Lyndon B. Johnson felt that the most important first step in the war against poverty is
    (1) full employment
    (2) a sound dollar
    (3) private and public economics
    (4) our natural defense
    (5) efficiency in government

20. The speech implies that America's prosperity
    (1) is threatened
    (2) is at its peak
    (3) must be retained
    (4) must be broadened
    (5) threatened Johnson's war against poverty

Questions 21 and 22 are based on the following cartoon.

A GOOD TIME FOR REFLECTION

Source: Library of Congress

GO ON TO THE NEXT PAGE

TEST 2: SOCIAL STUDIES

21. The cartoon encourages the American public to
    (1) exercise caution regarding involvement in European conflicts
    (2) demand repayment of World War II debts owed by European nations
    (3) support countries resisting communist aggression
    (4) provide food to eastern Europe
    (5) support the United Nations

22. The cartoon implies that
    (1) membership in organizations such as the North Atlantic Treaty Organization is worthwhile
    (2) economic prosperity is an effective response to the threat of war
    (3) a strong defense is a deterrent to war
    (4) creditor nations should collect their debts
    (5) the United States should become involved in world affairs

Questions 23 to 25 are based on the following chart.

Nations	Birthrate (per 1000 females)	Infant Mortality Rate (per 1000 births)
Uganda	51	104
Somalia	50	122
Angola	47	137
Cambodia	46	112
Ethiopia	46	110
Pakistan	40	109
Canada	14	6.8
France	13	6.7
Denmark	13	6.6
Italy	10	8.3
Germany	10	5.9
Japan	10	4.4

Source: Information Please Almanac, 1995 (est. mid-1994)

23. Which is a valid generalization based on the information in the chart?
    (1) In developing nations, the infant mortality rate decreases as the birthrate increases.
    (2) Industrialized nations have lower birthrates and infant mortality rates than developing nations.
    (3) Decreasing the infant mortality rate will limit population growth in developing nations.
    (4) Industrialized nations have higher population densities than developing nations.
    (5) Developing nations have ten times the infant mortality of industrialized nations.

24. Accord to the chart, the lowest birthrates are found mostly in
    (1) western Europe
    (2) Southeast Asia
    (3) North America
    (4) Africa
    (5) Latin America

GO ON TO THE NEXT PAGE

TEST 2: SOCIAL STUDIES

25. According to the chart, the highest infant mortality rates are in
    (1) western Europe
    (2) Southeast Asia
    (3) North America
    (4) Africa
    (5) Latin America

---

26. From the point of view of an environmentalist, which is probably the most significant argument against offshore drilling for oil?
    (1) There is little need to take such natural resources from the ocean waters.
    (2) Oil corporations are falsely advertising an oil shortage in order to expand their drilling operations.
    (3) The potential oil to be found is not worth the capital investment needed to extract it.
    (4) The possible harm to the balance of nature is more important than a gain in energy.
    (5) Coal is a preferable resource to oil.

27. Topography deals with surface features of a region, including its landforms and rivers, lakes, etc., and with man-made features such as canals, bridges, and roads. According to this definition, the topography of a region includes its
    (1) climate
    (2) plants
    (3) animals
    (4) mountains
    (5) inhabitants

<u>Questions 28 to 30</u> are based on the following passage.

A Continental army and Congress composed of men from all the states, by freely mixing together, were assimilated into one mass. Individuals of both, mingling with the citizens, spread principles of union among them. Local prejudices lessened. By frequent contact, a foundation was laid for the establishment of a nation out of varied materials. Intermarriages between men and women of different states were much more common than before the war, and became an additional cement to the Union. Unreasonable jealousies had existed between the inhabitants of the eastern and of the southern states; but on becoming better acquainted with each other, these in a great measure subsided. A wiser policy prevailed. Men of liberal minds led the way in discouraging local differences, and the great body of the people, as soon as reason got the better of prejudice, found that their best interests would be best promoted by union.

28. The passage deals principally with the
    (1) prejudices in America at the time of the Revolution
    (2) frictions between the sections during the Revolution
    (3) positive social and political results of the Revolution
    (4) triumph of union over local differences
    (5) fear of the Church of England

29. Prior to the Revolution
    (1) a spirit of cooperation existed in the colonies
    (2) reason prevailed over prejudice
    (3) regional rivalry was present
    (4) most Americans knew one another
    (5) religious freedom was the general rule

GO ON TO THE NEXT PAGE

TEST 2: SOCIAL STUDIES

30. The passage implies that
    (1) self-interest has little to do with prejudice
    (2) social contact helps do away with prejudice
    (3) Americans were generally very much alike
    (4) trade discourages social contact
    (5) Congress was a divisive instrument

Questions 31 to 33 are based on the following passage.

Since the days when the fleet of Columbus sailed into the waters of the New World, America has been another name for opportunity, and the people of the United States have taken their tone from the possibilities of expansion open to them. But never again will such gifts of free land offer themselves. Each frontier did indeed furnish a new field of opportunity, a gate of escape from the bondage of the past. What the Mediterranean Sea was to the Greeks, breaking the bond of custom, offering new experiences, calling out new institutions and activities, that, and more, the ever-retreating frontier has been to the United States. And now, four centuries from the discovery of America, at the end of a hundred years of life under the Constitution, the frontier has gone, and with its going has closed the first period of American history.

31. The term *frontier* as used in this passage means
    (1) the New World
    (2) American energy
    (3) movement
    (4) the expansive nature of American life
    (5) the availability of free land

32. The attitude of the author to the frontier is one of
    (1) admiration
    (2) regret
    (3) indifference
    (4) restraint
    (5) suspicion

33. References in the passage lead to the conclusion that it was written approximately in the year
    (1) 1865
    (2) 1875
    (3) 1890
    (4) 1900
    (5) 1920

GO ON TO THE NEXT PAGE

TEST 2: SOCIAL STUDIES

Questions 34 and 35 are based on the following cartoon.

LOOKS LIKE THE REMAINS OF A GIANT LUMBERING CREATURE THAT COULDN'T ADAPT TO THE CHANGING ENVIRONMENT.

34. Which political system is referred to in the cartoon?
    (1) feudalism
    (2) monarchy
    (3) democracy
    (4) communism
    (5) fascism

35. The "giant lumbering creature" symbolized by the hammer and sickle is
    (1) NATO
    (2) OPEC
    (3) the USSR
    (4) OAS
    (5) the UN

36. Which statement best illustrates the principle of multiple causation of human behavior?
    (1) To each according to his or her needs.
    (2) Environment and heredity are constantly interacting.
    (3) Geographic differences account for variations in civilizations.
    (4) Wealth and power go together.
    (5) Habit results from repeated acts.

Questions 37 and 38 are based on the following passage.

Since 1750, about the beginning of the Age of Steam, the earth's population has more than tripled. This increase has not been an evolutionary phenomenon with biological causes. Yet there was an evolution—it took place in the world's economic organization. Thus 1,500,000,000 more human beings can now remain alive on the earth's surface, can support themselves by working for others who in turn work for them. This extraordinary tripling of human population in six short generations is explained by the speeded-up economic unification that took place during the same period. Thus most of us are now kept alive by this vast cooperative unified world society.

GO ON TO THE NEXT PAGE

TEST 2: SOCIAL STUDIES

37. The writer considers trade necessary for
    (1) travel
    (2) democracy
    (3) political unity
    (4) self-preservation
    (5) the theory of evolution

38. The basic change that led to the greatly increased population involves
    (1) new explorations
    (2) economic factors
    (3) biological factors
    (4) an increase in travel
    (5) the growth of world government

---

39. The number of Native American men and women in professional life has multiplied remarkably in the past generation. Movement back and forth from the Native American to the white world has become freer. At the same time, the long-standing conviction that sooner or later all Indians would become totally assimilated into the standardized stream of American life has steadily lost ground. Most experts today feel that Native American tribes and communities will retain separate identities for a long, long time into the future—and most experts believe that is good, not bad.

    There is a difference of opinion regarding Native Americans'
    (1) status as wards of the United States
    (2) status as citizens
    (3) assimilation into American life
    (4) property holdings
    (5) tribes and communities

40. "The parties agree that an armed attack against one or more of them in Europe or North America shall be considered an attack against them all. . . ."

    This quotation is most closely associated with which concept?
    (1) collective security
    (2) intervention
    (3) ultimatum
    (4) appeasement
    (5) aggression

41. Social mobility refers to a society in which an individual can and often does change in social status. Which best illustrates social mobility in the United States?
    (1) A midwestern farm family buys a farm in California.
    (2) The son of a president of a large manufacturing plant becomes a company executive.
    (3) The daughter of an unskilled immigrant worker becomes a teacher.
    (4) A woman whose parents are both college professors receives a graduate degree.
    (5) A New Yorker moves to Boston.

42. Cultural diversity, a variety of cultural patterns, is generally the result of
    (1) actions by the government of the area
    (2) the desire of the inhabitants to develop original ideas and styles
    (3) competition among the people for control of food sources
    (4) migrations to the area by various groups
    (5) reciprocal regional agreements

43. Culture shock is the confusion experienced by someone encountering unfamiliar surroundings, a strange community, or a different culture. Which situation is the best example of culture shock?
    (1) the refusal of the Amish to drive motor vehicles
    (2) the hippies' rejection of the "Establishment" in the 1960s
    (3) the difference in lifestyles between European and western American Indian tribal groups
    (4) the initial reaction of a U.S. Peace Corps participant arriving in a developing nation
    (5) the generation gap

GO ON TO THE NEXT PAGE

TEST 2: SOCIAL STUDIES

44. An extended family is a group of relatives by blood, marriage, or adoption living in close proximity or together, especially if three generations are involved.

    Which is usually a characteristic of societies that have the extended family as their basic unit?

    (1) The society tends to be highly industrialized.
    (2) The roles of the family members are economically and socially interdependent.
    (3) The government usually provides incentives to increase family size.
    (4) The functions of the family unit are defined mainly by the government.
    (5) The family becomes widely dispersed geographically.

45. Pluralism is the existence within a society of groups distinctive in ethnic origin, cultural patterns, or religion. Maintaining stability in a pluralistic society is difficult because

    (1) individuals are often forced to deal with the views of others that may challenge their own ideas
    (2) there is usually no well-defined order of governmental authority
    (3) new members in the society are often unwilling to obey established laws of the society
    (4) the wide variety of citizens' abilities hinders the management of labor resources
    (5) there are differing degrees of respect for authority

Questions 46 and 47 refer to the following passage.

The secret of getting along with people is to recognize how they feel, and to let them know you know. When someone is rude or quarrelsome, it's often a way of saying, "Pay attention to my feelings." When we say of someone, "He understands me," we're really saying, "He knows how I feel." Awareness of feelings in others comes naturally, if only you let it.

In difficult situations, the "right thing to do" is not hard to find if you let people's feelings come through to you and acknowledge your own. . . .

You can share money, food or sex with another and still remain perfect strangers. In the end, the *only way* you can mean anything to another human being is to share his feelings.

46. The author regards feelings as

    (1) deceptive
    (2) unhealthy
    (3) reliable
    (4) private
    (5) conflicting

47. Misbehavior, according to the author, is

    (1) often a call to recognize feelings
    (2) an unnatural action
    (3) a cause for concern
    (4) a basis for an apology
    (5) sometimes the right thing to do

---

48. Mountains and coasts have served to restrict settlements; rivers and plains, to extend them. Each of these natural features has placed a characteristic imprint on the society that it dominated, largely fashioning its mode of life, its customs, morals, and temperament.

    The passage implies that

    (1) mountains and coasts are unfriendly to human beings
    (2) mountains and rivers exert equal influences on society
    (3) mountains and plains have similar effects on settlement
    (4) natural features result from the society that evolves within them
    (5) geographic features influence the society that develops

GO ON TO THE NEXT PAGE

TEST 2: SOCIAL STUDIES

Questions 49 and 50 are based on the following tables.

TABLE *A*

Question: "Here are two suggestions that people have made to improve stability and order in this country. For each, would you favor or oppose such a step being taken?"

Suggestions	**Percent of Public**		
	Favor	**Oppose**	**Not Sure**
A law should be passed allowing police officers to search a home without a warrant in an emergency, as when they are looking for drugs.	32	65	3
The government should be given authority to use wiretaps and other electronic surveillance to gather evidence against citizens suspected of criminal activity, even if a court does not authorize such activity	27	68	5

TABLE *B*

Question: "Do you feel the federal government should be allowed to engage in wiretapping and electronic surveillance if, in each case, it had to go to court beforehand to obtain court permission, or don't you feel the federal government should ever be allowed to engage in wiretapping or electronic surveillance?"

Response	**Percent of Public**
Should be allowed	63
Should not be allowed	28
Not sure	9

49. The information in Table *A* indicates that most people questioned
    (1) were undecided on the issues in question
    (2) supported the idea of a search without a warrant only in an emergency
    (3) favored protecting their privacy
    (4) favored permitting the government to investigate their lives
    (5) favored electronic eavesdropping over searches

50. A valid conclusion based on both tables is that the results of opinion surveys
    (1) tend to obscure the issues
    (2) are purposely biased by the pollsters
    (3) can vary according to the way the issue is presented
    (4) show that public attitudes are generally consistent
    (5) tend to be inconclusive

GO ON TO THE NEXT PAGE

TEST 2: SOCIAL STUDIES

<u>Questions 51 and 52</u> are based on the following graph.

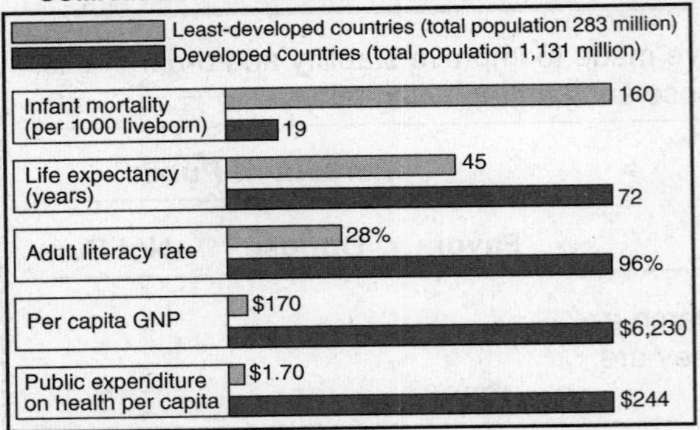

Note: The figures are weighted averages based on data for 1980 or latest available year.
Source: United Nations Children's Fund (UNICEF)

51. A valid conclusion that can be made from the chart is that nations with low per capita GNP's have

    (1) greater life expectancies
    (2) greater public expenditures on health per capita
    (3) high infant mortality rates
    (4) high adult literacy rates
    (5) larger populations

52. The gap between the least developed nations and the developed nations is greatest in

    (1) Infant mortality
    (2) life expectancy
    (3) adult literacy rate
    (4) per capita GNP
    (5) public expenditure on health per capita

<u>Questions 53 and 54</u> are based on the following time line.

1905–1915	1915–1945	1945–1975	1975–1985	1985–1995
A	*B*	*C*	*D*	*E*

53. The rise of aggressive fascist governments in Europe occurred during the period represented by the letter

    (1) *A*
    (2) *B*
    (3) *C*
    (4) *D*
    (5) *E*

54. Independence was achieved by most African and Asian nations during the period represented by the letter

    (1) *A*
    (2) *B*
    (3) *C*
    (4) *D*
    (5) *E*

GO ON TO THE NEXT PAGE

TEST 2: SOCIAL STUDIES

Questions 55 and 56 are based on the following map.

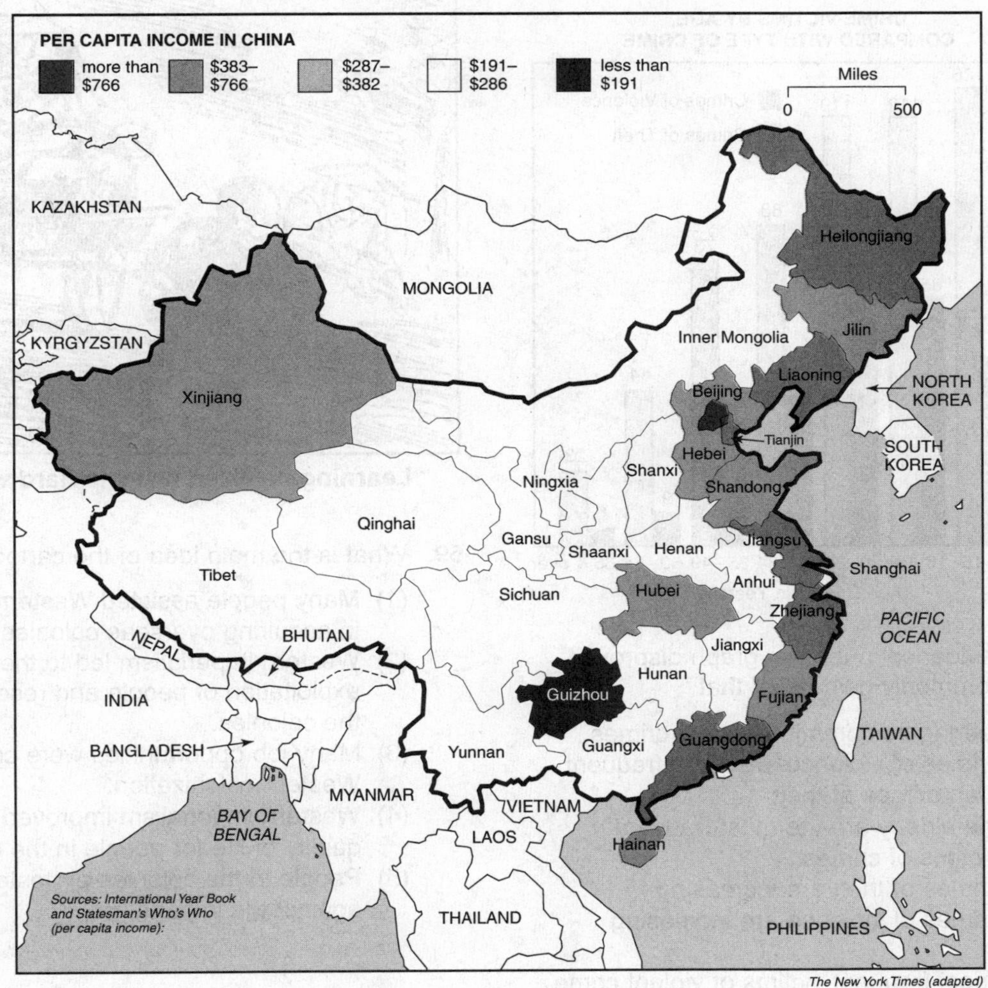

55. The map shows that the

(1) economies of all the regions of China are developing at the same rate
(2) distribution of income in China is unequal
(3) economies of the interior provinces of China are developing faster than those of the coastal provinces
(4) economic development in China is dependent upon the cash crops of Xinjiang and Tibet
(5) larger regions have more per capita income than the smaller regions

56. Most regions fall into the per capita income range of

(1) more than \$766
(2) \$383–\$766
(3) \$287–\$382
(4) \$191–\$286
(5) less than \$191

GO ON TO THE NEXT PAGE

TEST 2: SOCIAL STUDIES

Questions 57 and 58 are based on the following graph.

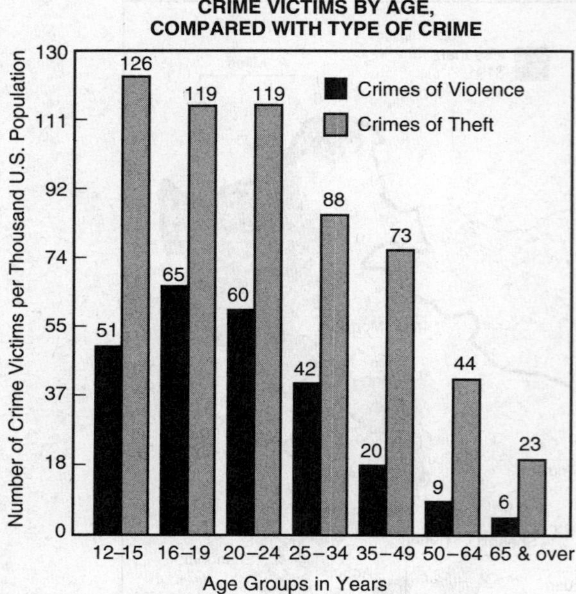

57. The evidence in the bar graph disproves the commonly held belief that
    (1) teenagers commit the most crimes
    (2) crimes of violence are more frequent than crimes of theft
    (3) the elderly are the most frequent victims of crimes
    (4) crimes of theft are increasing
    (5) crimes of violence are increasing

58. The most frequent victims of violent crime are people aged
    (1) 12–15
    (2) 16–19
    (3) 20–24
    (4) 25–34
    (5) 35–49

Question 59 is based on the following cartoon.

"Learning civilized ways is hard work!"

59. What is the main idea of the cartoon?
    (1) Many people assisted Western nations in acquiring overseas colonies.
    (2) Western imperialism led to the exploitation of people and resources in the colonies.
    (3) Many job opportunities were created by Western colonization.
    (4) Western imperialism improved the quality of life for people in the colonies.
    (5) People in the colonies protested against the imperialists.

Questions 60 to 62 are based on the following passage.

Geography is a group of sciences dealing with the earth's surface, its physical structures, and the distribution of life on earth.

Among the many branches of geography are:

(1) physical geography, which deals with the physical features of the earth and includes climatology and oceanography

(2) political geography, which deals with the world as divided into nations

(3) regional geography, which deals with the world in terms of regions separated by physical rather than national boundaries

GO ON TO THE NEXT PAGE

TEST 2: SOCIAL STUDIES

(4) economic geography, which deals with the patterns of the world's commerce in terms of production, trade, and transportation

(5) biogeography, which is concerned with the distribution of life, both plant and animal (including human), around the world

For each of the following concerns, identify the branch of geography involved.

60. The number of endangered species is increasing.

(1) physical geography
(2) political geography
(3) regional geography
(4) economic geography
(5) biogeography

61. The warming or "greenhouse effect" is causing major changes in climatic patterns and a rise in sea level as polar ice melts.

(1) physical geography
(2) political geography
(3) regional geography
(4) economic geography
(5) biogeography

62. Drought conditions have caused malnutrition in East Africa.

(1) physical geography
(2) political geography
(3) regional geography
(4) economic geography
(5) biogeography

<u>Questions 63 and 64</u> are based on the following map.

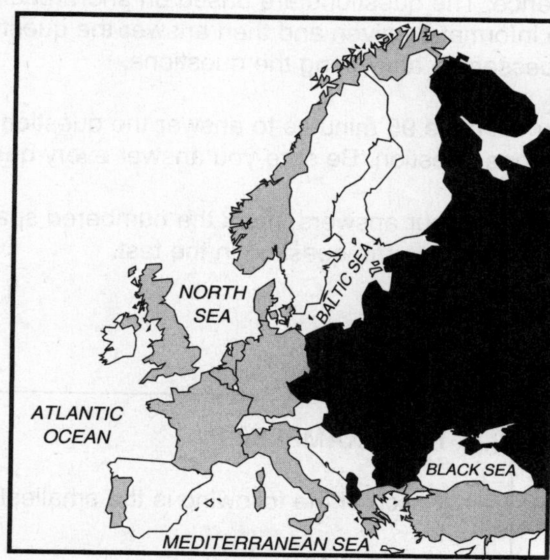

63. The map illustrates a division of Europe that led to the creation of the

(1) Axis and the Allied powers
(2) North Atlantic Treaty Organization (NATO) and the Warsaw Pact
(3) Triple Alliance and the Triple Entente
(4) United Nations and the League of Nations
(5) European Economic Community and GATT (General Agreement for Tariffs and Trade)

64. The lightly shaded countries are members of NATO, the North Atlantic Treaty Organization. Which of these countries is <u>not</u> a member of NATO?

(1) Great Britain
(2) France
(3) Italy
(4) Portugal
(5) Spain

END OF EXAMINATION

TEST 3: SCIENCE

Directions

The Science test consists of multiple-choice questions intended to measure the general concepts in science. The questions are based on short readings that often include a graph, chart, or figure. Study the information given and then answer the question(s) following it. Refer to the information as often as necessary in answering the questions.

You will have 95 minutes to answer the questions. Work carefully, but do not spend too much time on any one question. Be sure you answer every question. You will not be penalized for incorrect answers.

To record your answers, mark the numbered space on the answer sheet beside the number that corresponds to the question in the test.

FOR EXAMPLE:

Which of the following is the smallest unit?

(1) solution
(2) element
(3) atom
(4) compound
(5) mixture

① ② ● ④ ⑤

The correct answer is "atom"; therefore, space 3 would be marked on the answer sheet.

GO ON TO THE NEXT PAGE

TEST 3: SCIENCE

<u>Questions 1 to 6</u> are based on the following article.

The study of ecology, the branch of biology that deals with the interrelations between living things and their environment, is most important today. The environment of living things must be considered from the point of view of the physical factors, such as temperature, soil, and water, and the biotic factors, which are the living organisms.

Ecologists organize groups of living things into populations, communities, ecological systems, and the biosphere. A *population* consists of organisms of the same species living together in a given location, such as all the oak trees in a forest or all the frogs of the same species in a pond. A *community* consists of populations of different species, living together and interacting with each other.

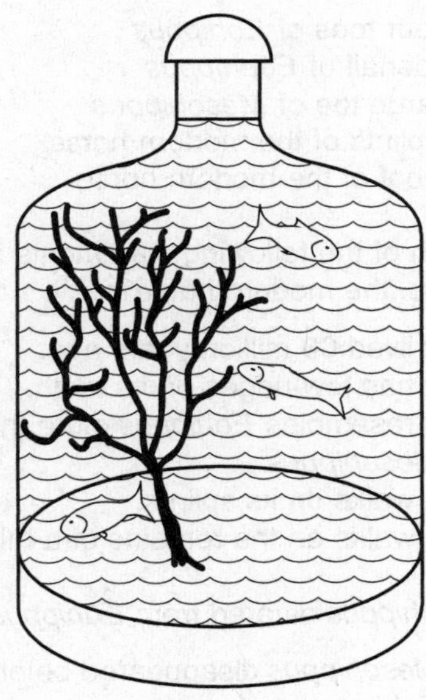

The accompanying diagram illustrates a simple community. It pictures a large bottle with a layer of mud on the bottom. The bottle was filled with pond water, and several fish and some green plants were added. The bottle was then made airtight. The members of this community will thrive as long as the balance is maintained.

1. Which of the following consists of a single species?

   (1) biosphere
   (2) community
   (3) ecosystem
   (4) biome
   (5) population

2. The fact that living things can survive in an airtight bottle illustrates the

   (1) need for green plants in our environment
   (2) need for physical factors in a community
   (3) balance within a population
   (4) need for biotic factors in a community
   (5) interrelations between living things and the physical and biotic factors of the environment

3. When species of plants and animals are introduced into a new habitat, they often become pests there, even though they were not pests in their native habitats. The most probable reason for this is that in the new habitat they

   (1) have fewer natural enemies
   (2) have a much lower mutation rate
   (3) develop better resistance to the new climate
   (4) learn to use different foods
   (5) have more predators

4. If the airtight container and its contents were weighed each day for several days, it would be found that the total weight would

   (1) increase gradually
   (2) remain the same
   (3) decrease gradually
   (4) decrease for the first few days and then increase
   (5) increase for the first few days and then decrease

GO ON TO THE NEXT PAGE

TEST 3: SCIENCE

5. All of the following are biotic factors affecting the balance of the airtight container EXCEPT

(1) the concentration of minerals in solution
(2) the number of fishes
(3) the kinds of protozoa in the water
(4) the kinds of plants
(5) the presence of crustaceans in the mud

6. Many different species of organisms interacting in a particular environment is an example of a

(1) population
(2) biosphere
(3) community
(4) biome
(5) species

Questions 7 to 10 refer to the following article.

Even though scientists have different ways of explaining how evolution occurs, they all agree that living things evolved from a few common ancestors. For example, there are fossil records that trace the horse through a complete series of prehistoric protohorses. The first of these was called the Dawn Horse, or *Eohippus*. This animal lived about 60 million years ago and stood approximately 1 foot high. *Eohippus* had four toes on each front foot and three on each back foot. Each of these toes had a toenail, a primitive hoof. The teeth of this little horse were small and had few if any ridges, indicating that it browsed on leaves rather than eating grass. It had a short neck and a small skull.

Descendants of *Eohippus* include the slightly larger *Mesohippus*. This animal had only three toes on each foot, and the middle toe was large enough to carry most of its weight. The teeth of this primitive horse had well-developed ridges; the animal was probably a grass eater. An even later horse, *Hypohippus*, was smaller than the modern horse, but it had a definite hoof. It also had two small, very obvious toes. Unlike the toes of *Mesohippus*, these toes did not touch the ground.

The modern horse, *Equus*, has one toe, called a hoof, that carries all its weight. If you were to carefully feel or X-ray this horse's legs, however, you would feel two bones, called splints, on either side of its lower legs. These are all that remains of *Eohippus*'s toes.

7. The author draws the facts in the article from a study of

(1) toes
(2) fossils
(3) teeth
(4) splints
(5) body size

8. Organisms often possess structures that are useless to the individual but are thought to have been functional in their remote ancestors. Such structures are called vestigial. An example of a vestigial structure is the

(1) four toes of *Eohippus*
(2) toenail of *Eophippus*
(3) large toe of *Mesohippus*
(4) splints of the modern horse
(5) hoof of the modern horse

9. Which of the following statements is true of *Equus*, the modern horse?

(1) It lived 60 million years ago.
(2) It has few ridges on its teeth.
(3) It resembles *Eohippus* more than *Mesohippus*.
(4) It walks on its splints.
(5) It walks on the remains of a middle toe.

10. *Mesohippus* differed from *Eohippus* in that

(1) *Mesohippus* disappeared before *Eohippus* evolved.
(2) *Eohippus* had three toes on each foot.
(3) *Mesohippus* had two small side toes that didn't touch the ground.
(4) *Mesohippus* had a more highly developed tooth structure.
(5) *Eohippus* had a larger middle toe.

GO ON TO THE NEXT PAGE

TEST 3: SCIENCE

Questions 11 to 15 refer to the following article.

A marvelous thing is the human brain. It is the command center of the body; it controls movement and growth. We use it to store memories, to think, and to "feel." The brain interprets all of the stimuli that we receive through sense organs such as the eyes, ears, skin, and tongue. The brain enables us to build a bomb or to write a poem, and all of this is accomplished by 3 pounds of tissue consisting of approximately 10 billion cells called neurons. The neurons are arranged in interconnecting pathways that conduct electrical and chemical messages to and from various parts of the body.

You may have heard someone described as left-brained or right-brained, but what exactly does this mean? If you were to look down at the top of a human brain, you would see that it looks much like a shelled walnut. There are two distinct sides, joined in the middle by a bundle of nerve fibers called the *corpus callosum*.

Scientists believe that each side of the brain is responsible for specific functions. We do know that each side controls a specific side of the body. It is interesting that the left hemisphere of the brain controls the right side of the body, while the right hemisphere controls the left. The *corpus callosum* connects the two halves, and this nerve tissue provides a way for information to pass from one side to the other.

The chart below lists some of the specific functions attributed to each side of the human brain.

11. An injury to the left side of the brain would probably affect which of the following abilities?
    (1) musical talent
    (2) speech
    (3) artistic ability
    (4) motion of the left hand and the left foot
    (5) depth perception

12. The cells that make up the brain are called
    (1) hemispheres
    (2) spindle fibers
    (3) dominant cells
    (4) neurons
    (5) brain fibers

13. The right side of the brain controls which of the following functions?
    (1) insight, imagination, and spatial relations
    (2) artistic ability, music, and numbers
    (3) the right side of the body and intuition
    (4) holistic skills, reasoning, and written language
    (5) linked ideas, spatial relationships, and time

LEFT HEMISPHERE	RIGHT HEMISPHERE
Controls right side of the body: spoken language, written language, number skills, keeping track of time, scientific skills, linking ideas, i.e., one idea leading to another (linear thinking), reasoning skills—logic	Controls left side of the body: nonverbal communication, synthesis, imagination, awareness, insight, perceiving relationships between things, intuitive, musical/artistic, spatial—perceives in three dimensions— holistic ability—sees the whole thing at one time

GO ON TO THE NEXT PAGE

TEST 3: SCIENCE

14. Studies have indicated that the *corpus callosum* of a woman is slightly larger than the *corpus callosum* of a man. Which of the following statements might be supported by this information?

    (1) Women tend to be better at right-brain functions, while men excel at left-brain functions.
    (2) Left-handed male dyslexics have more trouble learning to read than right-handed female dyslexics have.
    (3) A woman has a better chance of recovering completely from a stroke because her nervous system is more likely to transfer the functions of the damaged half of the brain to the undamaged half.
    (4) Young girls are better at learning to play the piano and draw pictures than young boys are.
    (5) Since a woman scientist did the research on the *corpus callosum*, the data may be compromised.

15. According to the passage, which of the following may state a fact?

    (1) Brain function is electrical and chemical.
    (2) The brain is the most important part of the body.
    (3) Writing and speaking skills are much more important than intuitive and spatial skills.
    (4) Brainy people have split personalities.
    (5) The human brain is much bigger than an ape's brain.

---

16. Scientists admit that they still have a great deal to learn about the human brain. What they do know so far is that the nervous system is composed of neurons that carry signals throughout the body. The junction between neurons is called a synapse. A long, thin part of the neuron, called an axon, actually carries the signal. Unlike the wires in an electrical circuit, which sends signals by movement of electrons, the biological circuit of the nervous system dispatches information by means of ions of potassium and sodium, called neurotransmitters.

    In the biological circuit of the nervous system, a signal passes from

    (1) transmitter to neuron to synapse
    (2) neuron to axon to synapse
    (3) axon across synapse to axon
    (4) neuron to neuron across axon
    (5) axon to synapse by way of neuron

Questions 17 and 18 refer to the following article.

A question puzzling humans is: How did life originate? We agree that all life comes from preexisting life, but to answer this question we must consider a time when there was no life. In particular, we must seek an explanation of the origin of complex organic compounds, since we know that our present-day complex organic compounds are the results of life processes.

Any consideration of the origin of life must be concerned with the element carbon since organic substances are carbon compounds. We must also consider amino acids, the building blocks of protein and protoplasm—the living substance. One explanation tells us that simple chemical elements of the atmosphere were combined to form an amino acid that later may have been synthesized into a more complex bit of "stuff" that we now call protoplasm. The energy needed to cause this chemical synthesis, it is thought, may have been provided by lightning or by the ultraviolet energy of the Sun.

17. All living matter contains the chemical element

    (1) water
    (2) phosphorus
    (3) carbon
    (4) carbon dioxide
    (5) protein

18. The problem of explaining the origin of life on Earth involves an answer to the question of the origin of

    (1) ultraviolet rays
    (2) proteins
    (3) atoms
    (4) molecules
    (5) organic compounds

GO ON TO THE NEXT PAGE

TEST 3: SCIENCE

Questions 19 to 22 refer to the following information.

Scientists performed an experiment to determine whether there is a connection between learning ability and food. They took two groups of 20 mice each, all from the same purebred strain. The mice were deprived of food for 3 days and then given a standard learning session in running through a maze. They were trained by giving them a mild electric shock whenever they took a wrong turn. Immediately after each learning session, one group of mice was fed, but the other was not. A week later, all of the mice were tested to see whether they could still run the maze correctly. The group that had been fed had retained this ability, but the other group had not.

19. The probable reason that the scientists used only mice from the same pure-bred strain is so that
    (1) the mice would all be the same size
    (2) the mice would all be the same color
    (3) the experiment could be repeated with the same mice
    (4) genetic differences would not affect the outcome of the test
    (5) the experiment wouldn't cost as much

20. A finding is a proved result obtained as part of an experiment. Which of the following could be considered a valid finding?
    (1) Mice remember better if they are fed immediately after each training session.
    (2) Mice remember better if they are fed and then allowed some time to think about the training.
    (3) Experiments with mice have nothing to do with human learning processes.
    (4) Mice used in experiments have to be from the same purebred strain.
    (5) Mice do not need to be fed in order to learn.

21. The use of an electric shock in the teaching process is
    (1) necessary to keep the mice alert
    (2) cruel and should not be allowed
    (3) a way to show the mice that they have taken a wrong turn in the maze
    (4) designed to elicit a predetermined response
    (5) part of the variable

22. It was noted that the mice could learn to run the maze more readily if it was well illuminated. This information is
    (1) an irrelevant detail
    (2) vital to the experiment
    (3) an assumption made by someone who observed the experiment
    (4) a result of the experiment
    (5) an important finding

Questions 23 to 25 are based on the following article.

There are a number of problems to be solved before humans can live safely and comfortably in space. Maintaining air pressure, purifying air for breathing, providing protection from radiation, solving the problems of weightlessness, and providing for the basic needs of daily living are only a few of the solutions that must be found.

Air pressure can obviously be handled with an airtight habitat. Entrance is gained through air locks, small rooms or chambers with one door opening to space and the other door opening into the station.

Purifying air for breathing is a more difficult task. Probably the best solution thus far is the use of green plants. As well as consuming carbon dioxide in photosynthesis, these plants could provide some fresh food.

On Earth, our atmosphere, especially the ozone layer, protects us from dangerous ultraviolet radiation. In space, however, this security blanket of air is missing. Space suits for astronauts and the outer skin of the space station will provide some protection from radiation. However, we need to learn more

GO ON TO THE NEXT PAGE

TEST 3: SCIENCE

about the different kinds of radiation in space and their potential danger to humankind.

A prolonged stay in a weightless environment has a definite physical effect on humans. As well as leaching calcium from the bones, weightlessness produces a marked change in blood and blood vessels and a distinct atrophy of the muscles from disuse. Some people also experience space sickness: nausea and a general malaise. Disorientation and a loss of balance occur because of the absence of the distinct gravity based up and down to which we are accustomed. With the development of artificial gravity, however, these problems can be overcome.

The last and most important problem faced by space pioneers is a way to provide for their basic physical needs. In addition to approximately 2.2 pounds of oxygen per day, each space dweller will need about a pound of food concentrates and 4.5 pounds of water. It would be easy to haul from Earth enough supplies for a couple of people for a month or so, but supplying a space colony would require solutions that would allow the station itself to provide for its inhabitants—that is, to be self-sustaining. The only way the astronauts might do this is by recycling resources and finding ways to produce even more on the station.

23. The main problems that must be addressed in order to create a working space station involve

(1) food, air, and oxygen
(2) water, weightlessness, and calcium loss
(3) radiation, oxygen, and weightlessness
(4) air pressure, food, and water
(5) food, water, air, and lack of gravity

24. To supply five people for 2 weeks, a space station would have to provide

(1) 30.8 x 5 pounds of oxygen
(2) 308 x 5 pounds of oxygen
(3) 6 x 5 pounds of food
(4) 84 x 5 pounds of food
(5) 22 x 5 pounds of water

25. If 1 gallon of water weighs 8.33 pounds, how much water would be needed to supply one person for 1 day?

(1) 2.5 gallons
(2) 2.5 pounds
(3) 4.5 gallons
(4) 4.5 pounds
(5) 8.33 pounds

<u>Questions 26 to 31</u> refer to the following article.

Acid deposition, commonly called acid rain, is a complex and serious environmental problem. It can mean either of two things: (1) sulfur and nitrogen pollutants in the atmosphere react with water in the air and form acid precipitation, or (2) sulfur and nitrogen pollutants are directly deposited on the surface of the Earth, where they react with water, forming acid substances.

Either way, the increased acidity changes the chemistry of both land and water environments. Two main causes of acid deposition are the burning of fossil fuels, such as coal, oil, and gasoline, and natural sources, such as volcanoes and bacterial decay.

Water in pollution-free environments is actually slightly acidic. It has an average pH of 5.6, so a pH of 5.6 is a standard that may be used to judge whether water in the environment (rain, lakes, etc.) is truly more acidic than usual.

In cases of acid deposition, pH values from 3 to 5 are common, with some as low as 1.5. An important factor is *where* the acid deposition occurs. Other substances in the environment can neutralize the acid. For example, in one area the acid may be neutralized by the presence of calcium compounds or ammonia.

Evidence shows that acid deposition has an adverse effect on the environment. In lakes with increasing acidity, scientists have observed a decrease in the fish population. The acidity appears to reduce the ability of the fish to reproduce and the ability of the young fish to survive. It also seems to decrease the productivity of the plankton (free-floating, usually microscopic, organisms found near the surface of the water) and to encourage the growth of more acid-resistant types of plants. On land, increased acidity can damage trees and change the chemistry of the soil.

GO ON TO THE NEXT PAGE

TEST 3: SCIENCE

26. Which substance may neutralize acidic conditions in the environment?
    (1) carbon dioxide
    (2) nitrogen
    (3) sulfur
    (4) carbon
    (5) calcium carbonate

27. Which of the following is NOT a possible source of acid deposition?
    (1) gasoline exhaust
    (2) diesel exhaust
    (3) a water-powered electric-generating plant
    (4) a volcanic eruption
    (5) burning of coal in industry

28. Acid deposition can serve as
    (1) a promoter of growth for algae
    (2) a growth accelerator for fish
    (3) an agent to produce alkaline soil
    (4) a biotic factor in the environment
    (5) a selective agent in the environment

29. Which of the following is an abiotic factor that relates to the acid deposition problem?
    (1) plankton
    (2) sulfur
    (3) fish
    (4) tree
    (5) alga

30. Which of the following represents a rational, direct approach to reducing acid deposition?
    (1) allowing lakes to continue to acidify indefinitely
    (2) restocking the lakes where affected species exist
    (3) altering weather patterns to prevent precipitation
    (4) controlling air pollution at the source
    (5) seeding the clouds to produce rain artificially

31. The accompanying scale shows the pH values of five substances. Acid rain has a pH closest to that of which of these substances?

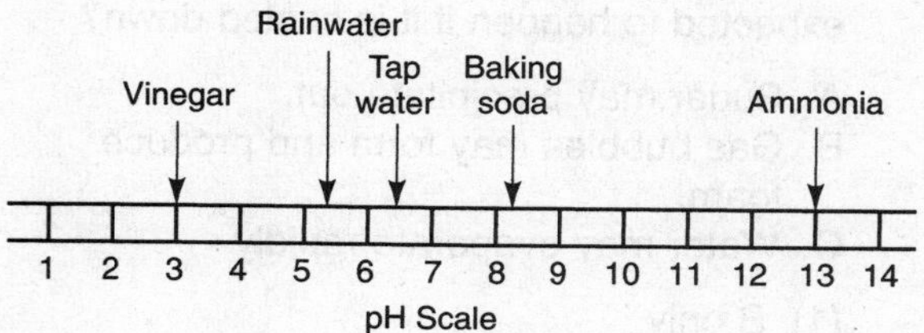

    (1) ammonia
    (2) tap water
    (3) baking soda
    (4) vinegar
    (5) rainwater

---

32. Chemical fertilizers stimulate plant growth; but if the concentration is too high, they may damage roots. What precautions concerning chemical fertilizers must a gardener take?
    (1) Use them only on some of his or her plants.
    (2) Use only the amount recommended.
    (3) Do not apply chemical fertilizers.
    (4) Apply as much as possible without damaging roots.
    (5) Give the plants only tiny amounts.

33. Amniote vertebrates are generally classified into three orders: Reptilia, Aves (birds), and Mammalia. Of the following, which group of three animals contains one member of each order?
    (1) ostrich, American robin, Norway rat
    (2) Beluga whale, black-footed ferret, box turtle
    (3) timber rattlesnake, fence lizard, leopard
    (4) African lion, sea otter, herring gull
    (5) house sparrow, garter snake, African elephant

GO ON TO THE NEXT PAGE

TEST 3: SCIENCE

34. As temperature rises, solids become more soluble in water, but gases become less soluble. If a soft drink contains high concentrations of sugar and carbon dioxide, which of the following may be expected to happen if it is cooled down?

A. Sugar may precipitate out.
B. Gas bubbles may form and produce foam.
C. Water may evaporate rapidly.

(1) B only
(2) B and A only
(3) A only
(4) C and B only
(5) A and C only

Question 35 is based on the following graph.

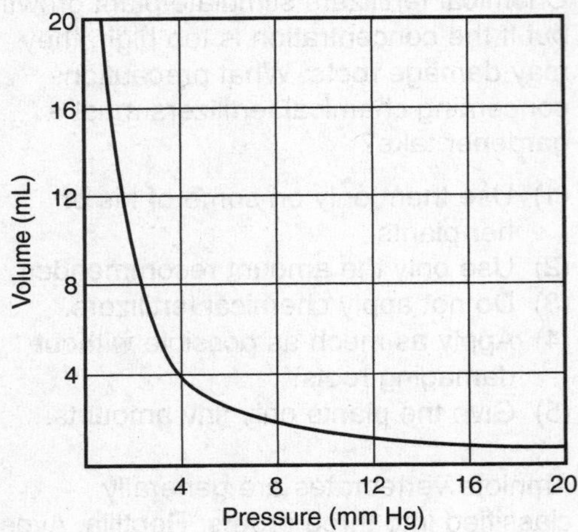

35. This graph represents the relationship of the pressure and volume of a given mass of a gas at constant temperature. When the pressure equals 8 millimeters of mercury (mmHg), what is the volume, in milliliters (mL)?

(1) 1
(2) 2
(3) 4
(4) 8
(5) 16

36. Which of the following is a nonelectrolyte?

(1) HNO_3 (nitric acid)
(2) HCl (hydrochloric acid)
(3) H_2SO_4 (sulfuric acid)
(4) C_2H_8 (propane gas)
(5) NaCl (table salt)

Ions are electrically charged particles that are formed when certain compounds are dissolved in water. These solutions will conduct electricity. The Swedish scientist Svante Arrhenius coined the term *ion* (which means wanderer) to explain why solutions of electrolytes will conduct an electric current. When an electrolyte is made into a solution, it dissolves or dissociates into ions, a process called ionizing. If a substance does not ionize, it will not conduct an electric current.

Electrolytes include acids, bases, and salts. Some conductors include hydrogen and sodium chloride, copper sulfate, and potassium nitrate. Substances that are not electrolytes are distilled water, sugar water, and glycerine.

37. Which of the following compounds in the liquid phase can be considered an electrolyte?

(1) H_2O (distilled water)
(2) CO_2 (carbon dioxide)
(3) NaCl (sodium chloride)
(4) CuO (rusted copper)
(5) H_2O_2 (hydrogen peroxide)

GO ON TO THE NEXT PAGE

TEST 3: SCIENCE

38. An object accelerates (changes its speed) only if the forces acting on it in one direction are greater than the forces in the opposite direction. All of the following objects will accelerate EXCEPT
    (1) a gas balloon in which the buoyant force is greater than its weight and air resistance
    (2) a man in a parachute when the air resistance is less than his weight
    (3) an airplane in horizontal flight when the thrust of the engine is equal to the drag of the air
    (4) a ball striking a wall, in which the force of the ball on the wall is equal to the force of the wall on the ball
    (5) a rocket fired straight up, when the engine thrust is equal to the air resistance

39. The four giant planets, Jupiter, Saturn, Uranus, and Neptune (in that order), are very far from the Sun; only the small planet Pluto is farther. The *Voyager* space explorer found that Neptune and Uranus are surrounded by rings like those of Saturn. What hypothesis would be suggested by the discovery that Pluto has no rings?
    (1) All large planets have rings, and small ones do not.
    (2) Rings are present around any planet that is far from the Sun.
    (3) Rings are distributed at random, regardless of the size or position of the planet.
    (4) Large planets may have rings, but small ones do not.
    (5) Pluto has lost its rings because it is so far from the Sun.

40. Wind can carry dry sand, blowing it against bedrock and eroding the rock into fantastic shapes. What kind of ecosystem is most likely to have wind-eroded rocks?
    (1) seashore
    (2) desert
    (3) prairie
    (4) tundra
    (5) deciduous forest

41. In a tank with water contaminated with bacteria, a surgical wound in a frog's skin heals much more rapidly than a similar wound on a fish. Any of the following might be a possible explanation EXCEPT
    (1) The bacteria in the tank are not harmful to frogs.
    (2) Some chemical in the frog's skin defends against bacteria.
    (3) The frog's immune system responds efficiently to the bacteria.
    (4) Frog skin has a much better ability to regenerate than the skin of a fish.
    (5) The water contains some chemical substance that promotes healing.

Questions 42 and 43 are based on the following table.

Mass of Sample (g)	Heating time (min)
5.0	0.0
4.1	5.0
3.1	10.
3.0	15.
3.0	30.
3.0	60.

The table shows the data collected during the heating of a 5.0-gram sample of salt water.

42. After 60 minutes, how many grams of water appear to remain in the salt?
    (1) 0.00
    (2) 0.9
    (3) 1.9
    (4) 2.0
    (5) 3.0

43. What is the percentage of water in the original sample?
    (1) 30%
    (2) 40%
    (3) 50%
    (4) 60%
    (5) 82%

GO ON TO THE NEXT PAGE

TEST 3: SCIENCE

44. In a reflex, an impulse starts at a sense organ, passes through sensory neurons to the brain or spinal cord, then goes through motor neurons to a muscle or a gland. What is the sequence of organs in the reflex that causes tears to flow when the cornea of the eye is irritated?

    (1) cornea–tear gland–brain–sensory neuron–motor neuron
    (2) cornea–brain–motor neuron–sensory neuron–tear gland
    (3) cornea–sensory neuron–brain–motor neuron–tear gland
    (4) tear gland–cornea–motor neuron–brain–sensory neuron
    (5) brain–cornea–sensory neuron–motor neuron–tear gland

45. In a certain area, DDT-resistant mosquitoes now exist in greater numbers than 10 years ago. What is the most probable explanation for this increase in numbers?

    (1) DDT causes sterility in mosquitoes.
    (2) Mosquito eggs were most likely to have been fertilized when exposed to DDT.
    (3) DDT acted as a reproductive hormone for previous generations of mosquitoes.
    (4) DDT serves as a new source of nutrition.
    (5) Genetic differences permitted some mosquitoes to survive DDT use.

46. A scientist studying fossils in undisturbed layers of rock identified a species that, he concluded, had changed little over the years. Which observation probably would have led him to this conclusion?

    (1) The simplest fossil organisms appeared only in the oldest rocks.
    (2) The simplest fossil organisms appeared only in the newest rocks.
    (3) The same kind of fossil organisms appeared in old and new rocks.
    (4) No fossil organisms of any kind appeared in the newest rocks.
    (5) Few fossil organisms appeared in the oldest rock.

47. In sexual reproduction, the original chromosome number must be reduced in order that members of the next generation will have the same chromosome number as their parents. For this reason, each reproductive cell—egg or sperm—has only half as many chromosomes as the other cells in the organism. The pollen grain of a wheat plant produces a sperm nucleus with 14 chromosomes. How many chromosomes will there be in the egg nucleus and in a leaf cell?

    (1) 14 in the egg nucleus, 28 in a leaf cell
    (2) 14 in both the egg nucleus and leaf cells
    (3) 28 in both the egg nucleus and leaf cells
    (4) 7 in the egg nucleus, 14 in a leaf cell
    (5) 7 in the egg nucleus, 28 in a leaf cell

48. A salmon will die after laying thousands of eggs, depositing them in the open water. A robin lays about 4 eggs and cares for the young when they hatch. It is reasonable to assume that

    (1) there are far more salmon than robins in the world
    (2) far more salmon than robins die before reaching adulthood
    (3) more food is available for growing salmon than for young robins
    (4) salmon do not reproduce until they are much older than adult robins
    (5) robins are better parents than salmon

49. Corn plants that are grown in the dark will be white and usually much taller than genetically identical corn plants grown in light, which will be green. The most probable explanation for this finding is that the

    (1) corn plants grown in the dark are all mutants for color and height
    (2) expression of a gene may be dependent on the environment
    (3) plants grown in the dark will always be genetically albino
    (4) phenotype of a plant is independent of its genotype
    (5) genotype is independent of its phenotype

GO ON TO THE NEXT PAGE

TEST 3: SCIENCE

50. Potatoes can be reproduced either by cuttings of the tubers or by seed formed sexually. Why would an agriculture specialist decide to go to the trouble of growing potatoes from seed?

(1) to produce the largest possible crop
(2) to try out a new fertilizer
(3) to reduce the difficulty of planting
(4) to produce new varieties
(5) to protect the new plants from insects

51. Element *A* and element *B* chemically combine to form substance *C*. Substance *C* must be

(1) a solution
(2) a compound
(3) an element
(4) a mixture
(5) an isotope

<u>Questions 52 to 54</u> refer to the following article.

Perhaps if it weren't for Joseph Priestley's work about 200 years ago, we would have no ice-cream sodas today. It was he who experimented with the gas carbon dioxide that the chemist Joseph Black had prepared by pouring acid on chalk. By dissolving this gas in water, Priestley was the first to make carbonated water. His interest in the properties of gases led him to his famous experiment of heating mercuric oxide. This resulted in the formation of a silvery film deposited on the inside of the glass container and the liberation of a gas that we now call oxygen.

52. In addition to releasing oxygen, heating mercuric oxide yields

(1) nitrogen
(2) silver
(3) charcoal
(4) mercury
(5) carbon dioxide

53. Which of the following is formed when carbon dioxide is dissolved in water?

(1) chalk
(2) acid
(3) sodium
(4) carbonated water
(5) heavy water

54. When acid is poured on chalk, the fizz is due to the presence of

(1) carbon dioxide
(2) mercuric oxide
(3) oxygen
(4) water
(5) mercury

---

55. A flask at 25°C is partially filled with water and stoppered. After a period of time the water level is found to have remained constant. Which relationship best explains this observation?

(1) The rate of condensation exceeds the rate of evaporation.
(2) The rates of condensation and evaporation are both zero.
(3) The rate of evaporation exceeds the rate of condensation.
(4) The rate of evaporation equals the rate of condensation.
(5) The rate of evaporation is less than the rate of condensation.

GO ON TO THE NEXT PAGE

TEST 3: SCIENCE

Questions 56 and 57 are based on the following information.

The diagram below represents a closed glass greenhouse. The data table shows the air temperatures inside and outside the greenhouse from 6 A.M. to 6 P.M. on a particular day.

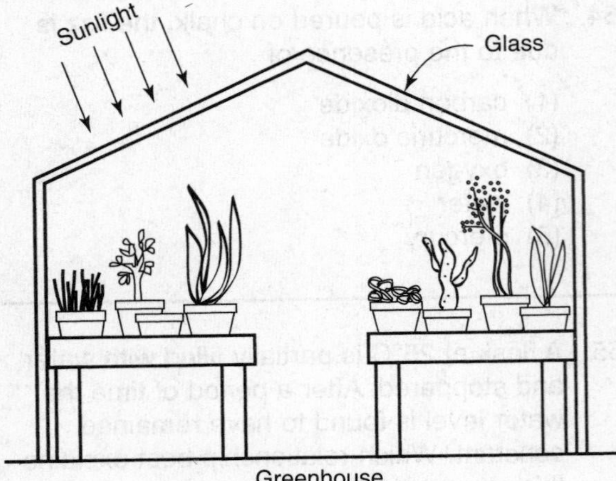

AIR TEMPERATURE

Time	Average Outside Temperature (°C)	Average Inside Temperature (°C)
6 A.M.	10	13
8 A.M.	11	14
10 A.M.	12	16
12 noon	15	20
2 P.M.	19	25
4 P.M.	17	24
6 P.M.	15	23

56. The highest temperature was recorded at

(1) 12 noon outside the greenhouse
(2) 2 P.M. outside the greenhouse
(3) 12 noon inside the greenhouse
(4) 2 P.M. inside the greenhouse
(5) 6 P.M. inside the greenhouse

57. If the temperature continues to drop at the same rate, what temperature can we expect inside the greenhouse at 12 midnight?

(1) 22°C
(2) 20°C
(3) 18°C
(4) 17°C
(5) 16°C

Questions 58 to 61 refer to the following article.

Recent findings by psychologists seem to indicate that exposure to different colors of light as well as different sources of light affect one's well-being. What are light rays? Light rays are forms of electromagnetic radiation—wave motion in ether—differing from one another in wavelength and frequency. For example, violet has the shortest wavelength, measured in angstrom units (Å), violet has a wavelength of less than 4500Å. Red has the longest wavelength of more than 6000Å. The colors in between, that is from about 4000Å in deep violet to the 7500Å in the deep red is the visible spectrum. Light with wavelengths shorter than violet is called ultraviolet light. A great deal of this light comes to us from the Sun and is responsible for human sunburn. Light with wavelengths longer than red is called infrared light, which we cannot see, but we can feel its warmth. Much of the Sun's warmth comes to us in this form.

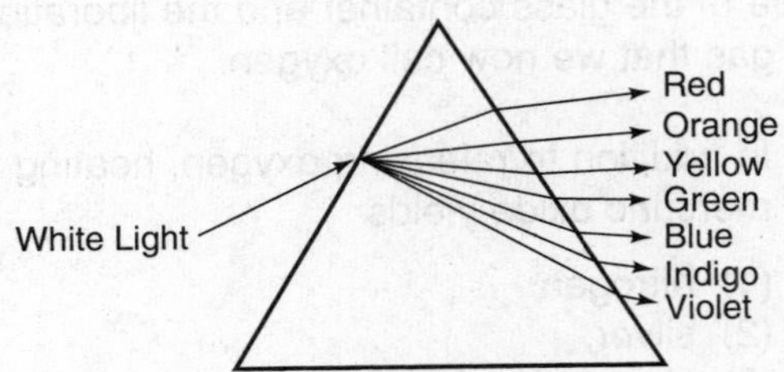

GO ON TO THE NEXT PAGE

TEST 3: SCIENCE

When a beam of white light is passed through a prism, it is split up into its components, forming a band having all the colors of the rainbow. Each of these colors, according to psychologists, has a particular effect on living things. Photography is also concerned with this phenomenon as it uses different filters to absorb certain colors of the spectrum, while allowing other colors to pass. Thus a filter that absorbs blue and red is green but one that absorbs only blue appears yellow because it transmits the combination of green and red.

58. Which of the following is the wavelength of red light?
    (1) less than 4500Å
    (2) 4500Å
    (3) more than 6000Å
    (4) 7500Å
    (5) more than 7500Å

59. A photographer would use a blue filter to
    (1) form a prism
    (2) absorb blue light
    (3) transmit green light
    (4) absorb green light
    (5) transmit blue light

60. Yellow glass to be used as a filter must
    (1) absorb yellow light
    (2) transmit all light colors but yellow
    (3) transmit blue light
    (4) absorb blue light
    (5) absorb red light

61. Which of the following is the wavelength of infrared rays?
    (1) less than 4500Å
    (2) 4500Å
    (3) less than 6000Å
    (4) 6000Å
    (5) more than 7500Å

---

62. Electric power, the energy converted per second, is found by multiplying potential difference (in volts) by current (in amperes).

    Volts x Amperes = Power

    Of the following, which consumes the LEAST amount of electric power?
    (1) a starter motor using 50 amperes at 12 volts for 10 seconds
    (2) a clock using 0.002 ampere at 120 volts for 1 year
    (3) a TV set using 2.5 amperes at 120 volts for 6 hours
    (4) an air conditioner using 3 amperes at 240 volts for an hour
    (5) a flashlight bulb using 0.20 ampere at 3 volts for ½ hour.

63. A ringing electric bell is placed inside a bell jar, and the air in the jar is evacuated. As the air is removed, the sound heard gets softer, and eventually the ringing cannot be heard at all. What is the most reasonable explanation?
    (1) Electricity cannot travel through a vacuum.
    (2) The clapper of the bell cannot vibrate without air.
    (3) The glass of the bell jar blocks the passage of sound.
    (4) The ability to hear depends on the presence of air.
    (5) Sound waves need air in which to travel.

GO ON TO THE NEXT PAGE

TEST 3: SCIENCE

Questions 64 and 65 refer to the table below.

Planet	Diameter (miles)	Period of Rotation	Approximate Distance from the Sun (miles)	Time to Orbit the Sun (days)	Number of Moons
Mercury	3,100	25 days	43,000,000	88.0	0
Venus	7,700	58 days	67,000,000	224.7	0
Earth	7,927	243 days	94,000,000	365.3	1
Mars	4,220	24 hrs	155,000,000	687.0	2
Jupiter	88,600	10 hrs	507,000,000	4,332.1	12
Saturn	75,000	10 hrs	937,000,000	10,825.9	10
Uranus	29,600	11 hrs	185,900,000	30,685.1	5
Neptune	27,700	16 hrs	2,821,000,000	59,911.1	2
Pluto	about 3,600	6 days, 9 hours	4,551 000,000	90,824.2	0

64. The planet that takes the longest to travel around the Sun is

(1) Mars
(2) Saturn
(3) Uranus
(4) Neptune
(5) Pluto

65. Which statement can be supported by information in the table?

(1) The distant planets take less time to rotate than those near the Sun.
(2) Smaller planets take longer to rotate than larger ones do.
(3) Earth takes twice as long as Mars to orbit the Sun.
(4) Only the planets near the Sun have no natural satellites.
(5) The atmosphere of Venus is dense with clouds.

66. The world of quantum mechanics is the world of the ultrasmall. It deals with particles that are smaller than atoms. Particles in this world do not obey any of the physical laws as we know them. For example, if we want to see something in this world, we look at it—our eye receives light bouncing off the object, and the light is translated into nervous impulses that are then received and analyzed by the brain. The only way we can "see" a subatomic particle, however, is to do something to it—smack it with another subatomic particle, for example. Unfortunately, this action disrupts the particle we wanted to examine, changing it in some way—a bit of a quandary that has led to something called the Heisenberg uncertainty principle.

Examining a subatomic particle is rather like

(1) looking at atoms with an electron microscope
(2) learning the taste of a pineapple by eating it
(3) measuring ingredients for a cake into a bowl
(4) driving a car
(5) looking at a picture in a museum

END OF EXAMINATION

TEST 4: INTERPRETING LITERATURE AND THE ARTS

Directions

The Interpreting Literature and the Arts test consists of excerpts from classical and popular literature and articles about literature or the arts. Each excerpt is followed by multiple-choice questions about the reading material.

Read each excerpt first and then answer the questions following it. Refer to the reading material as often as necessary in answering the questions.

Each excerpt is preceded by a "purpose question." The purpose question gives a reason for reading the material. Use these purpose questions to help focus your reading. You are not required to answer these purpose questions. They are given only to help you concentrate on the ideas presented in the reading materials.

You should spend no more than 65 minutes answering the questions. Work carefully, but do not spend too much time on any one question. Be sure you answer every question. You will not be penalized for incorrect answers.

To record your answers, mark the numbered space on the answer sheet beside the number that corresponds to the question in the test.

FOR EXAMPLE:

It was Susan's dream machine. The metallic blue paint gleamed, and the sporty wheels were highly polished. Under the hood, the engine was no less carefully cleaned. Inside, flashy lights illuminated the instruments on the dashboard, and the seats were covered by rich leather upholstery.

The subject ("It") of this excerpt is most likely

(1) an airplane
(2) a stereo system
(3) an automobile
(4) a boat
(5) a motorcycle

① ② ● ④ ⑤

The correct answer is "an automobile"; therefore, answer space 3 would be marked on the answer sheet.

GO ON TO THE NEXT PAGE

TEST 4: INTERPRETING LITERATURE AND THE ARTS

Questions 1 to 5 refer to the following passage.

HOW DID A CHILD REACT TO AUGUST WEATHER?

I grew up near the Atlantic Ocean among marshes and estuaries, only a few miles back from a low-lying coast. I remember the month of August with a special kind of pleasure. At this time of year, mainland, marshland, and ocean would blend together into a grey, hot, humid haze. My mother would open all the windows, pull all the blinds, and hope to catch a sea breeze, but no breeze stirred. The dogs lay under the tables and panted; the cats lurked in the cool tunnels of the earth cellar. August was a time to do nothing and be proud of it.

But I also remember August with a bit of anxiety. August was the time of hurricanes and polio. Hurricanes and polio were different in many ways but were alike in that both were very bad things that usually happened to other people. During my childhood, I was lucky enough never to get polio. But we had bad hurricanes three times.

The hurricanes were pretty scary for the adults, but for a child, they were mostly a lot of fun. First, there was all the getting ready: buying candles and flashlight batteries and food, filling the car with gasoline, helping neighbors board up the only plate-glass window in the neighborhood, and making sure the buildings were closed up snug and everything loose was stashed away.

Then there was watching for the storm. I remember my father pointing out to me the eerie sky with its banners of cirrus clouds radiating out of the south, and I remember the strange feel of the air. The first breezes of the hurricane were so mild, so moist, so soft as to be barely distinguishable from the feel of one's own skin.

The storm itself wasn't so bad, except I had to stay indoors. I remember peering through windows watching the water sheet down outside, the ocean tide creep up in the back marsh, and the trees lash back and forth. Every time the wind let up I would say, "Is this the eye of the hurricane? Can I go outside and see the eye?"

—Calvin Simonds

1. The mood in lines 1 through 13 is expressed chiefly through the use of

(1) descriptive details
(2) sequential order
(3) figurative language
(4) simple sentences
(5) objective observation

2. Why was the narrator "proud" (line 13) to do nothing in August?

(1) He was lazy.
(2) It was easier to keep cool.
(3) He was observing animals' actions.
(4) It was proper August behavior.
(5) He was afraid of hurricanes.

3. The narrator characterizes hurricanes and polio as reasons for

(1) fearing the weather
(2) being concerned in August
(3) discussing misfortunes
(4) helping the neighbors
(5) staying indoors

4. In the fourth paragraph, the narrator suggests that the early stages of a hurricane are

(1) unpredictable
(2) obvious to the eye only
(3) apparent in the atmosphere
(4) felt before they are seen
(5) frightening for children

5. Which words best describe the narrator's memories of August?

(1) confusing events
(2) conflict and danger
(3) contrasting feelings
(4) freedom and relaxation
(5) expectancy and fulfillment

GO ON TO THE NEXT PAGE

TEST 4: INTERPRETING LITERATURE AND THE ARTS

Questions 6 to 10 refer to the following passage.

WHO ARE THE MOST RECENT SEEKERS AFTER THE AMERICAN DREAM?

New immigrants are trying all over to integrate themselves into the system. They have the same hunger. On any given day, there are millions throughout the world who are applying to come to the United States and share the American Dream. The same battles.

Sometimes the whole family saves up and gives the bright young man or the bright young woman the family savings. It even goes in hock for a year or two. They pin all their hopes on this one kid, put him on a bus, let him go a thousand miles. He doesn't speak a word of English. He's only seventeen, eighteen years old, but he's gonna save that family. A lot rides on that kid, who's a busboy in some hotel.

He's gonna be the first hook, the first pioneer coming into an alien society, the United States. He might be in Chicago. He works as a busboy all night long. They pay him minimum or less, and work him hard. He'll never complain. If he makes a hundred a week, he will manage to send back twenty-five.

After the kid learns a bit, because he's healthy and young and energetic, he'll probably get another job as a busboy. He'll work at another place as soon as the shift is over. He'll try to work his way up to be a waiter. He'll work incredible hours. He doesn't care about union scale. He doesn't care about conditions, about humiliations. He accepts all this as his fate.

He's burning underneath with this energy and ambition. He outworks the U.S. busboys and eventually becomes the waiter. Where he can maneuver, he tries to become the owner and gives a lot of competition to the locals.

The only thing that helps me is remembering the history of this country. We've always managed, despite our worst, unbelievably nativist actions, to rejuvenate ourselves, to bring in new people. Every new group is scared of being in the welfare line or in the unemployment office. They go to night school. They learn about America. We'd be lost without them.

I see all kinds of new immigrants starting out all over again, trying to work their way into the system. They're going through new battles, yet they're old battles. They want to share in the American Dream. The stream never ends.

6. The attitude of the author toward the new immigrant is

(1) critical
(2) skeptical
(3) cautious
(4) enthusiastic
(5) cynical

7. The approach to immigration by the immigrant family is to

(1) come as a unified family
(2) send a promising youth
(3) borrow from relatives
(4) expect the worst
(5) bank on a senior member

8. From the passage, it can be inferred that

(1) other family members will follow the pioneer
(2) the family will be abandoned
(3) the family will despair of achieving the American Dream
(4) the family will give up their efforts
(5) the family will be frightened by feeling alien

9. The American Dream, as illustrated in this article, allows newcomers to

(1) make a lot of money
(2) be exploited
(3) move upward in society
(4) be welcomed enthusiastically
(5) be victims of exclusion

10. The history of America indicates that immigrants

(1) benefit the United States
(2) are losing faith
(3) are easily discouraged
(4) expect help
(5) seek welfare

GO ON TO THE NEXT PAGE

TEST 4: INTERPRETING LITERATURE AND THE ARTS

Questions 11 to 15 refer to the following passage.

HOW DOES A NATURALIST VIEW THE SEQUOIA?

The Big Tree (*Sequoia gigantea*) is nature's forest masterpiece and, as far as I know, the greatest of living things. It belongs to an ancient stock, as its remains in old rocks show, and has a strange air of other days about it, a thoroughbred look inherited from the long ago, the *auld lang syne* of trees. Once the genus was common, and with many species flourished in the now-desolate Arctic regions, in the interior of North America, and in Europe; but in long eventful wanderings from climate to climate only two species have survived the hardships they had to encounter, the *gigantea* and *sempervirens*: the former now restricted to the western slopes of the Sierra, the other to the Coast Mountains, and both to California, excepting a few groves of redwood which extend into Oregon.

The Pacific coast in general is the paradise of conifers. Here nearly all of them are giants and display a beauty and magnificence unknown elsewhere. The climate is mild, the ground never freezes, and moisture and sunshine abound all the year. Nevertheless, it is not easy to account for the colossal size of the sequoias. The largest are about three hundred feet high and thirty feet in diameter. Who of all the dwellers of the plains and prairies and fertile home forests of round-headed oak and maple, hickory and elm, ever dreamed earth could bear such growths? Sequoias are trees that the familiar pines and firs seem to know nothing about, lonely, silent, serene, with an appearance almost godlike, and so old that thousands of them still living had already counted their years by tens of centuries when Columbus set sail from Spain, and were in the vigor of youth or middle age at the time of the birth of Jesus of Nazareth. As far as humanity is concerned, they are the same yesterday, today, and forever, emblems of permanence.

—John Muir

11. The use of the phrase "ancient stock" in line 4 suggests that the sequoia
    (1) has a firmly established heritage
    (2) had no natural enemies
    (3) was originally imported
    (4) was probably planted by Native Americans
    (5) is a newcomer

12. The author suggests that survival of the sequoia was greatly affected by
    (1) environmental difficulties
    (2) industrial expansion
    (3) cosmic forces
    (4) human settlements
    (5) old rocks

13. The author characterizes the Pacific coast as being
    (1) rich in history
    (2) varied in climate
    (3) abundant in animal life
    (4) nurturing to some plants
    (5) lacking in moisture

14. The author characterizes the sequoias' exceptional growth as
    (1) mysterious
    (2) seasonal
    (3) completed
    (4) uncontrollable
    (5) familiar

15. The author suggests that the most probable reaction to seeing a giant sequoia is
    (1) fear
    (2) disbelief
    (3) indifference
    (4) envy
    (5) reverence

GO ON TO THE NEXT PAGE

TEST 4: INTERPRETING LITERATURE AND THE ARTS

Questions 16 to 20 refer to the following poem.

HOW DOES THE POET FEEL ABOUT TELEVISION?

The crooked crosses overhead proclaim
High homage to the god-of-living-rooms;
As silently as Pharaohs in their tombs
Men sit before the sacrificial flame.
The incense from the king-size cigarettes
Is wafted idly toward the altar box
Where current ministers harangue their flocks
With tired wit and lively murder threats.
Tonight I shall not play the pious role
Nor join the dead who once had been so quick;
But I shall try to walk, strange heretic,
Among neglected precincts of my soul.

16. The "crooked crosses" (line 1) are
    (1) church towers
    (2) ceiling beams
    (3) telephone poles
    (4) television antennae
    (5) altar decorations

17. The poet criticizes television programs in
    (1) line 4
    (2) line 6
    (3) line 8
    (4) line 10
    (5) line 12

18. The poet has decided not to watch television, but to devote the evening to
    (1) prayer
    (2) repentance
    (3) self-education
    (4) self-contemplation
    (5) physical conditioning

19. In line 3, there is an example of
    (1) a simile
    (2) a metaphor
    (3) an epithet
    (4) alliteration
    (5) onomatopoeia

20. In lines 6 and 12, there are examples of
    (1) similes
    (2) metaphors
    (3) epithets
    (4) alliteration
    (5) onomatopoeia

Questions 21 to 25 refer to the following poem.

WHY DOES THE POET OBJECT TO A PHOTOGRAPH?

To a Photographer

I have known love and hate and work and fight;
I have lived largely, I have dreamed and planned,
And Time, the Sculptor, with a master hand
Has graven on my face for all men's sight
Deep lines of joy and sorrow, growth and blight,
Of labor and of service and command
—And now you show me this, this waxen, bland
And placid face, unlined, unwrinkled, white.
This is not I—this fatuous thing you show,
Retouched and smoothed and prettified to please.
Put back the wrinkles and the lines I know;
I have spent blood and tears achieving these,
Out of the pain, the struggle and the wrack
These are my scars of battle—put them back!

—Berton Braley

21. It can be assumed from the poet that
    (1) the poet has taken a photograph
    (2) the poet has been shown a photograph of himself
    (3) a faithful photograph has been taken of him
    (4) the poet is still young
    (5) the poet is a dreamer

GO ON TO THE NEXT PAGE

TEST 4: INTERPRETING LITERATURE AND THE ARTS

22. The poet wishes everyone to know that he has
    (1) led a quiet life
    (2) experienced hardships
    (3) been unsuccessful
    (4) maintains a youthful appearance
    (5) aged gracefully

23. The passage of time has left the poet with a face that is
    (1) lined
    (2) placid
    (3) ashen
    (4) smooth
    (5) bland

24. The poet is
    (1) content with his lot
    (2) resentful of time
    (3) proud of his scars
    (4) desirous of youth
    (5) untrue to himself

25. The poem is written in the form of a
    (1) ballad
    (2) dialogue
    (3) lyric
    (4) limerick
    (5) sonnet

Questions 26 to 30 refer to the following excerpt from a play.

WHY DOES A CANDIDATE DECIDE NOT TO RUN FOR OFFICE?

GRANT: I'm not going to kid anybody along. I never have.

KAY *(pleadingly)*: Grant, everybody here tonight was thinking of the future—which is how to get you elected. It's stupid right now to think in any other terms.

(Grant unbuttons his coat and takes it off. Kay turns to Conover in alarm.)

CONOVER *(going to Grant)*: I've got to talk to these people, and that means you've got to talk to me.

GRANT: I'm talking to a lot of people in my speech Thursday night. You'll be one of them. I promised myself when I went into this that I'd appeal to the best in the American people. The only advice I've ever had from any of you was to appeal to their worst. And that's what both parties are starting to do today. Let's end rationing. Who cares if Europe starves? Let's lift price ceilings—suppose it does bring inflation. Let's lower taxes and all get rich.

CONOVER: I see. You're the only honest man in politics.

GRANT: No, Jim! We have some good men. There are some wonderful men in the Senate and in the House, too—Democrats and Republicans. But, Jim, there aren't enough of them to shape party policies, so, to get votes, both parties are out to buy the American public. I can't do that, Jim. So I'm afraid I can't be of any use to you.

KAY: Well, Grant, I won't accept that decision. Oh, Grant, we've always talked these things out together. All right, we won't discuss it any more tonight. You're upset. I'll be in touch with you tomorrow. Come on, Jim. *(She exits.)*

CONOVER: I think Kay's right, Grant. You'd better sleep on it. I can stay over another day.

GRANT: No, Jim, I've made up my mind.

CONOVER: Grant, in this country we play politics—and to play politics you have to play ball . . . .*(He exits.)*

GRANT: Thank God that's settled. I hope they're all listening in Thursday night because I'm going to burn their ears off. Any candidate for any office who threatens world peace for a few votes—there's the international criminal for you. I'll take care of them Thursday night—and from now on.

26. You can deduce from what Kay and Conover are saying that
    (1) they disagree with each other
    (2) they agree with Grant
    (3) they agree with the American people
    (4) they disagree with Grant
    (5) they think well of Grant

GO ON TO THE NEXT PAGE

TEST 4: INTERPRETING LITERATURE AND THE ARTS

27. Grant is implying
    (1) he won't play politics
    (2) he will lift price ceilings
    (3) he will lower taxes
    (4) he will buy the American public
    (5) he'll get rich

28. Grant is critical of
    (1) all Republicans
    (2) all Democrats
    (3) Congress
    (4) the American public
    (5) both political parties

29. Grant feels that the American public
    (1) can be bought
    (2) can be fooled
    (3) can be appealed to
    (4) plays politics
    (5) is cynical about politicians

30. Grant will
    (1) be a candidate for public office
    (2) compromise his principles
    (3) attack dishonest candidates
    (4) go along with Kay and Conover
    (5) drop out of politics

Questions 31 to 35 refer to the following passage.

WHAT IS THE MEANING OF THE FATHER'S ACT?

So it was with a heart full of longing and hope that my father led us to school on that first day. He took long strides in his eagerness, the rest of us running and hopping to keep up.

At last the four of us stood around the teacher's desk; and my father, in his impossible English, gave us over in her charge. . . . I venture to say that Miss Nixon was struck by something uncommon in the group we made. . . . My little sister was pretty as a doll, with her clear pink-and-white face, short golden curls, and eyes like blue violets when you caught them looking up. My brother . . . stood up straight and uncringing before the American teacher, his cap respectfully doffed. Next to him stood a starved-looking girl with eyes ready to pop out, and short dark curls that would not have made much of a wig for a Jewish bride.

All three children carried themselves rather better than the common run of "green" pupils that were brought to Miss Nixon. But the figure that challenged attention to the group was the tall, straight father, with his earnest face and fine forehead, nervous hands eloquent in gesture, and a voice full of feeling. This foreigner, who brought his children to school as if it were an act of consecration, was not like other aliens, who brought their children in dull obedience to the law; was not like the native fathers, who brought their unmanageable boys, glad to be relieved of their care. I think Miss Nixon guessed what my father's best English could not convey. I think she divined that by the simple act of delivering our school certificates to her he took possession of America.

—Mary Antin

31. The best title for this selection is
    (1) "Our First Day at School"
    (2) "America: Land of Opportunity"
    (3) "We Were Different"
    (4) "A Father's Faith in Education"
    (5) "Americanization of the Alien"

GO ON TO THE NEXT PAGE

TEST 4: INTERPRETING LITERATURE AND THE ARTS

32. From their use in the passage, all of the following words are correctly paired EXCEPT

(1) *charge*—care
(2) *uncommon*—unusual
(3) *doffed*—removed
(4) *consecration*—dedication
(5) *divined*—heavenly

33. The author's father regarded school in the United States as all of the following EXCEPT

(1) an act of dedication
(2) a parental responsibility
(3) a legal obligation
(4) a source of hope
(5) a stake in America

34. The incorrect group of words describing the persons in the passage is

(1) the author's sister—blonde and beautiful
(2) the author's brother—erect and respectful
(3) the author's father—calm and sincere
(4) the author—observant and plain-looking
(5) Miss Nixon—sensitive and understanding

35. As used in this passage, *green* means

(1) inexperienced
(2) frightened
(3) disobedient
(4) sallow-complexioned
(5) immigrant

Questions 36 to 40 refer to the following passage on music.

WHAT IS THE DIFFERENCE BETWEEN CLASSICAL AND POPULAR MUSIC?

There is another way to divide music into two categories that usually creates more problems than it solves. This is the division into popular or light music and classical or serious music. Most people have some idea of what is meant by these terms and could probably decide, for example, that a rock tune in the "top 40" or a theme song from a current film would belong in the first category, while a piano concerto by Tchaikovsky or a symphony by Haydn would belong in the second. However, no adequate terms to describe these categories have yet been found. If we measure popularity by the total number of enthusiastic listeners through the years and not just during one year, then the Tchaikovsky *Concerto No. 1 for Piano* would be more "popular" than the rock song. A theme song from a movie might be quite serious and a Haydn symphony may be light in character. The term "classical" is probably best reserved for a specific period of music history (roughly from 1750 to 1825); for a general stylistic tendency marked by such characteristics as balance, clarity, stability, or restraint; or for a notable accomplishment as when a symphony is called a classic example of colorful orchestration.

Above all, the distinction between popular and classical music, as well as a similar dichotomy between folk music and art music, all too often has implications and connotations of value, integrity, and level of technical achievement that are highly inappropriate. No single type of music has a monopoly on worth, sincerity, or craftsmanship, and no single type of music can be dismissed categorically as inferior, insincere, or incompetent. Like Sir Donald Tovey, the perceptive British music critic, we are not sure if there is such a thing as bad music, but if there is, then we prefer "good bad music" to "bad good music."

36. According to the article, the difference between classical and popular music is

(1) important
(2) clear
(3) well understood
(4) confusing
(5) helpful

GO ON TO THE NEXT PAGE

TEST 4: INTERPRETING LITERATURE AND THE ARTS

37. According to the passage,
    (1) only popular music can be popular
    (2) only classical music can be classic
    (3) classical music can be popular
    (4) popular music is best confined to a single era
    (5) both popular and classical music have balance and restraint

38. The passage implies that most people, in their views of classical and popular music,
    (1) use imprecise terms
    (2) can distinguish between popular and classical
    (3) prefer light music to serious music
    (4) are limited by experience
    (5) make mistakes in their classification

39. The author feels that
    (1) classical music is preferable to popular
    (2) popular music is preferable to classical
    (3) the two types are similar
    (4) any music can be worthwhile
    (5) some music is inferior to other music

40. The passage states that distinctions between folk music and art music lead to
    (1) greater integrity
    (2) higher technical achievement
    (3) inferior music
    (4) monopolies
    (5) invalid judgments

Questions 41 to 45 refer to the following passage on the theater.

WHAT IS THE PLACE OF THEATER AMONG THE ENTERTAINMENT MEDIA?

The fact that the theater is closely linked with TV and the movies is not in itself an element of weakness. It is true that Hollywood and Madison Avenue exploit Broadway by buying its plays and offering jackpots to the successful playwrights, hiring them much as the Roman conquerors hired the Greek intellectuals to teach them philosophy and art. But despite the swagger and brashness of the Hollywood money one may question which is the main stream and which the tributary. There is a wholeness in a play which neither the movies nor TV offers—a wholeness of experience for playwright, actor, and audience alike.

When several arts are linked together, as is true of the theater, the movies, and TV, they may fertilize one another, and each of them may profit from the connection. The era of dramatic creativeness in America coincides curiously with the emergence of the movies and TV. I do not say that these are the only forces at work, but they help. The knowledge of a playwright that his play, while first produced on Broadway for a limited audience, may ultimately reach millions of people, must prove a stimulus to his imagination. Some of the people he ultimately reaches may lack sensibility, but this will not be true of all of them. The fact is that an Elizabethan audience showed a sense of excitement even when the crowd in the pit applauded and derided at the wrong passages. They sensed that new things were happening in their world, and the theater gave a concrete dramatic form to this awareness. The Americans too have an awareness of new things happening: And although millions of them flock to the movies and watch TV, while only the thousands go to the theater, the fact is that, for writers and actors alike, the prestige attaches to the theater and not to the big media. No great theater is possible in any culture unless the people consider it a great art—a place of great writing, poetry, and mime, and a place for the enactment of ideas and passions.

41. The author feels that the artistic medium that offers the audience the most rewarding experience is
    (1) television
    (2) movies
    (3) theater
    (4) philosophy
    (5) art

GO ON TO THE NEXT PAGE

TEST 4: INTERPRETING LITERATURE AND THE ARTS

42. The author feels that television, movies, and theater

    (1) compete with one another
    (2) harm one another
    (3) benefit one another
    (4) are viewed by equal numbers of people
    (5) are equally creative

43. The author implies that

    (1) the movies give inspiration to the theater
    (2) television gives inspiration to the movies
    (3) the movies give inspiration to television
    (4) the movies and television give inspiration to the theater
    (5) the theater gives inspiration to the movies and television

44. The author is critical of

    (1) the emergence of movies and television
    (2) dramatic creativeness in America
    (3) the Broadway playwright
    (4) movie and television audiences
    (5) theater audiences

45. The most important factor in the greatness of theater, according to the passage, is

    (1) Hollywood and Madison Avenue
    (2) successful playwrights
    (3) intellectuals
    (4) money
    (5) the audience

END OF EXAMINATION

TEST 5: MATHEMATICS

Directions

The Mathematics test consists of multiple-choice questions intended to measure general mathematics skills and problem-solving ability. The questions are based on short readings that often include a graph, chart, or figure.

You should spend no more than 90 minutes answering the questions. Work carefully, but do not spend too much time on any one question. Be sure you answer every question. You will not be penalized for incorrect answers.

Formulas you may need are given on page 632. Only some of the questions will require you to use a formula. Not all the formulas given will be needed.

Some questions contain more information than you will need to solve the problem. Other questions do not give enough information to solve the problem. If the question does not give enough information to solve the problem, the correct answer choice is "Not enough information is given."

The use of calculators is not allowed.

To record your answers, mark the numbered space on the answer sheet beside the number that corresponds to the question in the test.

FOR EXAMPLE:

If a grocery bill totaling $15.75 is paid with a $20.00 bill, how much change should be returned?

(1) $5.26
(2) $4.75
(3) $4.25
(4) $3.75
(5) $3.25

① ② ● ④ ⑤

The correct answer is "$4.25"; therefore, answer space 3 would be marked on the answer sheet.

GO ON TO THE NEXT PAGE

TEST 5: MATHEMATICS

FORMULAS

Description	Formula
AREA (A) of a:	
square	$A = s^2$; where s = side
rectangle	$A = lw$; where l = length, w = width
parallelogram	$A = bh$; where b = base, h = height
triangle	$A = \frac{1}{2}bh$; where b = base, h = height
circle	$A = \pi r^2$; where $\pi = 3.14$, r = radius
PERIMETER (P) of a:	
square	$P = 4s$; where s = side
rectangle	$P = 2l + 2w$; where l = length, w = width
triangle	$P = a + b + c$; where a, b, and c are the sides
circumference (C) of a circle	$C = \pi d$; where $\pi = 3.14$, d = diameter
VOLUME (V) of a:	
cube	$V = s^3$; where s = side
rectangular container	$V = lwh$; where l = length, w = width, h = height
cylinder	$V = \pi r^2 h$; where $\pi = 3.14$, r = radius, h = height
Pythagorean relationship	$c^2 = a^2 + b^2$; where c = hypotenuse, a and b are legs of a right triangle
distance (d) between two points in a plane	$d = \sqrt{(x_2 - x_1)^2 + (y_2 - y_1)^2}$; where (x_1,y_1) and (x_2,y_2) are two points in a plane
slope of a line (m)	$m = \frac{y_2 - y_1}{x_2 - x_1}$; where (x_1,y_1) and (x_2,y_2) are two points in a plane
mean	mean = $\frac{x_1 + x_2 + \ldots + x_n}{n}$; where the x's are the values for which a mean is desired, and n = number of values in the series
median	median = the point in an ordered set of numbers at which half of the numbers are above and half of the numbers are below this value
simple interest (i)	$i = prt$; where p = principal, r = rate, t = time
distance (d) as function of rate and time	$d = rt$; where r = rate, t = time
total cost (c)	$c = nr$; where n = number of units, r = cost per unit

GO ON TO THE NEXT PAGE

TEST 5: MATHEMATICS

1. Luisa worked 40 hours and earned \$6.30 per hour. Her friend Joan earned \$8.40 per hour at her job. How many hours did Joan have to work in order to equal Luisa's earnings for 40 hours?
   (1) 20
   (2) 25
   (3) 30
   (4) 252
   (5) Not enough information is given.

Question 2 is based on the following figure.

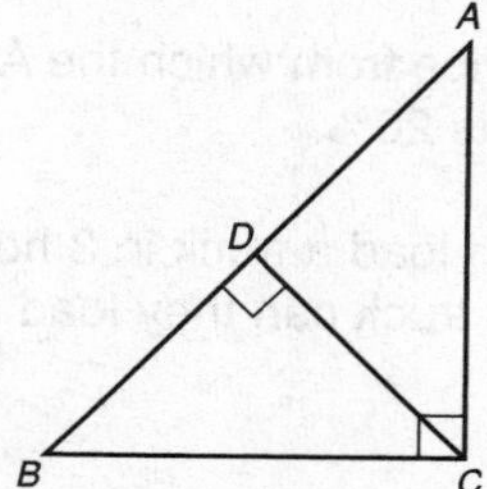

2. $\triangle ABC$ is a right triangle, and $\overline{CD} \perp \overline{AB}$. If the measure of $\angle CAD = 40°$, what is the measure of $\angle DCB$?
   (1) 10°
   (2) 20°
   (3) 40°
   (4) 50°
   (5) 90°

3. The number of students in a class is x. One day 5 students were absent. What fractional part of the class was present?
   (1) $\frac{x}{5}$
   (2) $\frac{5}{x}$
   (3) $\frac{5}{x-5}$
   (4) $\frac{x+5}{5}$
   (5) $\frac{x-5}{x}$

4. The gasoline gauge shows that a gasoline tank is $\frac{1}{3}$ full. In order to fill the tank, 16 gallons of gasoline are added. How many gallons of gasoline does the tank hold when full?
   (1) 20
   (2) 24
   (3) 30
   (4) 32
   (5) 48

Question 5 is based on the following figure.

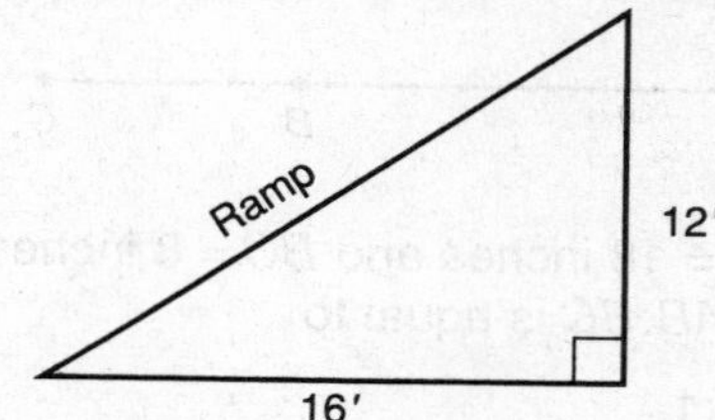

5. What is the length in feet, of the ramp?
   (1) 13
   (2) 17
   (3) 20
   (4) 24
   (5) Not enough information is given.

6. At a luncheon, 48 half-pints of fruit juice are served. What is the cost, at \$3.50 per gallon, of these servings of fruit juice?
   (1) \$6.00
   (2) \$7.00
   (3) \$10.50
   (4) \$12.50
   (5) \$15.00

GO ON TO THE NEXT PAGE

TEST 5: MATHEMATICS

7. If $5x - 1 = 34$, then $2\frac{1}{2}x$ is equal to

(1) 7
(2) 14
(3) $16\frac{2}{3}$
(4) 17
(5) $17\frac{1}{2}$

<u>Question 8</u> is based on the following figure.

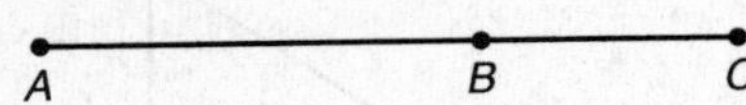

8. If $AC = 18$ inches and $BC = 8$ inches, the ratio $AB{:}BC$ is equal to

(1) 2:1
(2) 4:5
(3) 3:2
(4) 5:4
(5) Not enough information is given.

---

9. A rectangular living room has a floor area of 322 square feet. If the length of the room is 23 feet, what is the perimeter?

(1) 28 ft.
(2) 37 ft.
(3) 45 ft.
(4) 60 ft.
(5) 74 ft.

10. Don Brown saw a TV set priced at $280 at the Triangle Store. He then saw an advertisement for the same TV set at the ABC Store, announcing 20% off on all merchandise. What additional information does Don need in order to make a wise buying decision?

(1) The Triangle Store has a better reputation than the ABC Store.
(2) The sales tax on TV purchases is 5%.
(3) Both stores have a $5 delivery charge.
(4) The name of the manufacturer of the TV set.
(5) The price from which the ABC Store deducts 20%.

11. A crew can load a truck in 3 hours. What part of the truck can they load in 45 minutes?

(1) $\frac{1}{8}$
(2) $\frac{1}{4}$
(3) $\frac{1}{3}$
(4) $\frac{1}{2}$
(5) Not enough information is given.

12. Given the equation $x^2 + x - 6 = 0$, which of the following give(s) a complete solution of the equation?

(1) 2
(2) 2 and −3
(3) −2 and 3
(4) 2 and 3
(5) 3 and −3

GO ON TO THE NEXT PAGE

TEST 5: MATHEMATICS

Question 13 is based on the following figure.

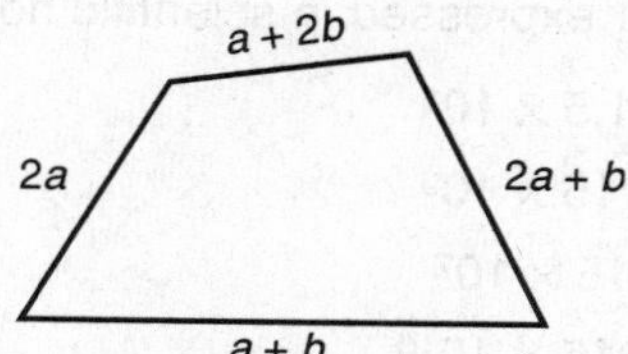

13. What is the perimeter of the figure?

(1) $6a + b$
(2) $5a + 5b$
(3) $6a + 4b$
(4) $4a + 4b$
(5) $3a + 5b$

---

14. Henry has $5 more than Bob, who has the same amount of money as Tom. Together, they have $65. How much money does Bob have?

(1) $10
(2) $12
(3) $15
(4) $20
(5) Not enough information is given.

15. A motel charges $48.00 per day for a double room. In addition, there is a 5% tax. How much does a couple pay for several days' stay?

(1) $144.00
(2) $151.20
(3) $156.20
(4) $158.40
(5) Not enough information is given.

16. If the square of a number is added to the number increased by 4, the result is 60. If n represents the number, which equation can be used to find n?

(1) $n^2 + 4 = 60$
(2) $n^2 + 4n = 60$
(3) $n^2 + n + 4 = 60$
(4) $n^2 + 60 = 4n + 4$
(5) $n^2 + n = 64$

17. A box of cereal is priced at x cents per box. A customer has a 15-cents-off coupon. If the store reduces prices by doubling the value of each coupon, how much, in cents, does the customer pay for the box of cereal?

(1) $x - 15$
(2) $x - 30$
(3) $x + 15$
(4) $x + 30$
(5) Not enough information is given.

18. The measures of the angles of a triangle are in the ratio 3:2:1. What is the measure of the largest angle of the triangle?

(1) 65°
(2) 70°
(3) 72°
(4) 80°
(5) 90°

GO ON TO THE NEXT PAGE

TEST 5: MATHEMATICS

<u>Question 19</u> is based on the following figure.

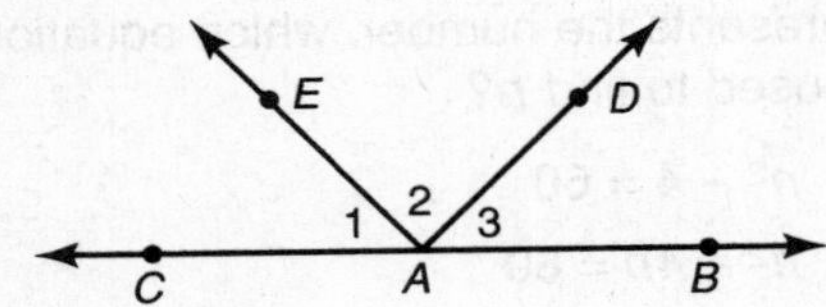

19. If m∠1 = 36° and m∠2 = 2(m∠3), then m∠3 equals

(1) 36°

(2) 40°

(3) 44°

(4) 48°

(5) Not enough information is given.

---

20. Mrs. Adams bought 4 pounds of beef and $3\frac{1}{2}$ pounds of chicken for $13.98. If the beef costs $2.76 per pound, what was the cost of the chicken per pound?

(1) $0.72

(2) $0.80

(3) $0.84

(4) $0.87

(5) $0.92

21. A carpenter earns $16 per hour, and his assistant earns half as much. Which of the following expressions represents how many dollars both men earned on a job that took 9 hours?

(1) $9(16) + 9(\frac{1}{2})$

(2) $9(16) + 9(10)$

(3) $16(8) + 9(9)$

(4) $16(\frac{1}{2}) + 9(\frac{1}{2})$

(5) $9(16) + 9(8)$

22. The distance between two heavenly bodies is 63,150,000,000 miles. What is this number expressed in scientific notation?

(1) 631.5×10^8

(2) 63.15×10^9

(3) 6315×10^7

(4) 6.315×10^{10}

(5) 6.315×10^{-10}

23. An English class has an enrollment of 14 boys and 12 girls. On a rainy day 4 boys and 3 girls are absent. If a student is called at random to recite, what is the probability that the student called is a girl?

(1) $\frac{9}{19}$

(2) $\frac{10}{19}$

(3) $\frac{12}{26}$

(4) $\frac{9}{14}$

(5) Not enough information is given.

24. Mr. Barnes has invested $12,000 in bonds that pay interest at the rate of 9% annually. What is Mr. Barnes's annual income from this investment?

(1) $108

(2) $180

(3) $1,080

(4) $10,800

(5) $12,000

25. Which of the following numbers is a solution of the inequality $3x + 2 < 14$?

(1) 3

(2) 4

(3) 5

(4) 6

(5) 7

GO ON TO THE NEXT PAGE

TEST 5: MATHEMATICS

Question 26 is based on the following graph.

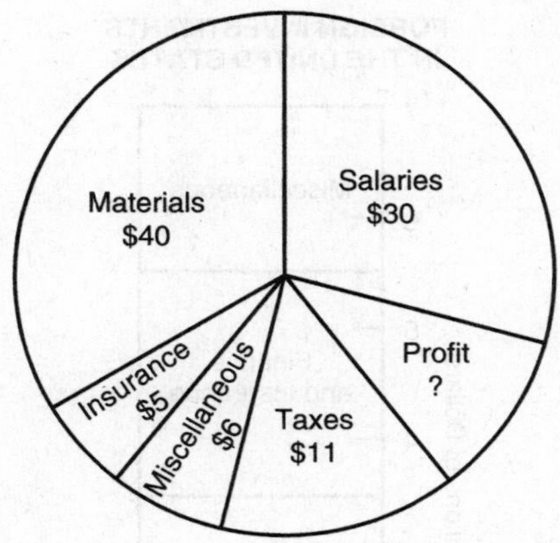

26. The graph shows what happens to each \$100 taken in by a small business firm. How many dollars out of each \$100 taken in represent profit?

(1) \$5

(2) \$6

(3) \$7

(4) \$7.5

(5) \$8

---

27. Over a period of 5 months John saved \$659. At the same rate of saving, how many dollars will he save over a period of 9 months?

(1) 9(659)

(2) $\frac{5(659)}{9}$

(3) 5(659)

(4) $\frac{9(659)}{5}$

(5) 5(9) (659)

28. Ben scored 7 more points than Jack in a basketball game. Paul scored 2 points less than Jack in the same game. If the three boys scored a total of 38 points, how many points did Jack score?

(1) 5

(2) 9

(3) 11

(4) 14

(5) 15

29. A box in the form of a rectangular solid has a square base 5 feet in length and a height of h feet. If the volume of the rectangular solid is 200 cubic feet, which of the following equations may be used to find h?

(1) $5h = 200$

(2) $5h^2 = 200$

(3) $25h = 200$

(4) $h = 200 \div 5$

(5) $h = 5(200)$

Question 30 is based on the following figure.

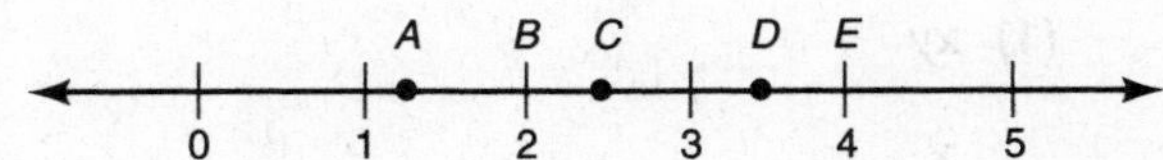

30. Which point on the number line represents the closest approximation to the square root of 12?

(1) *A*

(2) *B*

(3) *C*

(4) *D*

(5) *E*

GO ON TO THE NEXT PAGE

TEST 5: MATHEMATICS

Question 31 is based on the following figure.

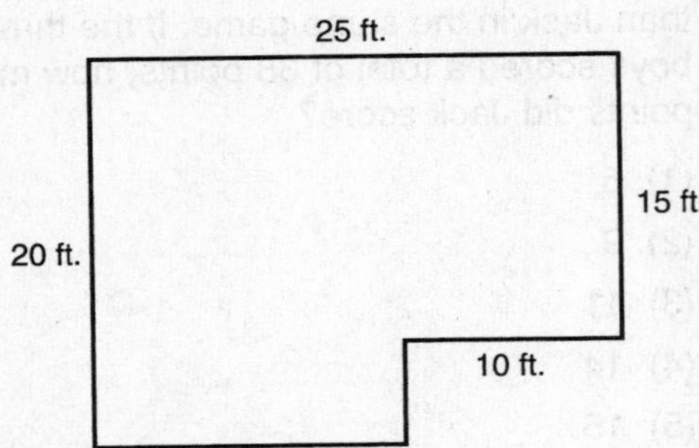

31. The diagram represents a large living room. What is the area, in square yards, of the room?
    (1) 16.6
    (2) 33.3
    (3) 45
    (4) 50
    (5) 450

---

32. If 1 dollar is worth x French francs, what is the value, in dollars, of y French francs?
    (1) xy
    (2) $\frac{x}{y}$
    (3) $\frac{y}{x}$
    (4) $\frac{1}{xy}$
    (5) $x + y$

Question 33 is based on the following graph.

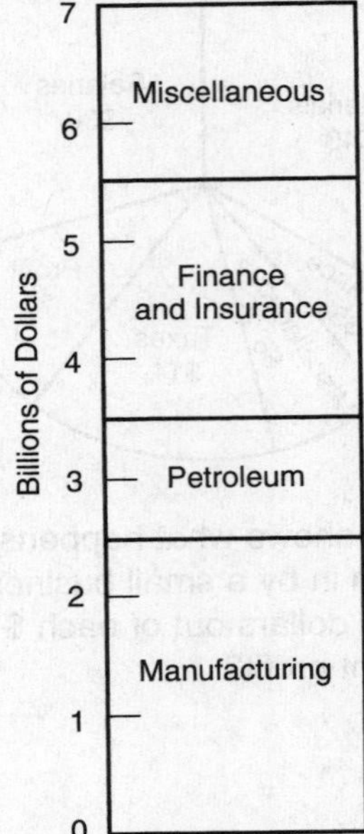

33. By what amount does the investment in manufacturing exceed the amount invested in petroleum?
    (1) $\$1\frac{1}{2}$ million
    (2) $\$3\frac{1}{2}$ million
    (3) $0.5 billion
    (4) $\$1\frac{1}{2}$ billion
    (5) $\$3\frac{1}{2}$ billion

GO ON TO THE NEXT PAGE

TEST 5: MATHEMATICS

34. If point $(x,3)$ is on the graph of the equation $x + y = 7$, what is the value of x?
    (1) 0
    (2) 1
    (3) 3
    (4) 4
    (5) 7

35. On a road map, $\frac{1}{4}$ inch represents 8 miles of actual road distance. The towns of Alton and Waverly are represented by points $2\frac{1}{8}$ inches apart on the map. What is the actual distance, in miles, between Alton and Waverly?
    (1) 17
    (2) 32
    (3) 40
    (4) 60
    (5) 68

36. At a certain time of day, a man 6 feet tall casts a shadow 4 feet in length. At the same time, a church steeple casts a shadow 28 feet in length. How high, in feet, is the church steeple?
    (1) 30
    (2) 32
    (3) 42
    (4) 48
    (5) 56

37. A dealer sells books at 40% above cost. How much does the dealer pay for a shipment of 6 dozen books that she sells for $7 per book?
    (1) $360
    (2) $380
    (3) $450
    (4) $504
    (5) $520

Question 38 is based on the following figure.

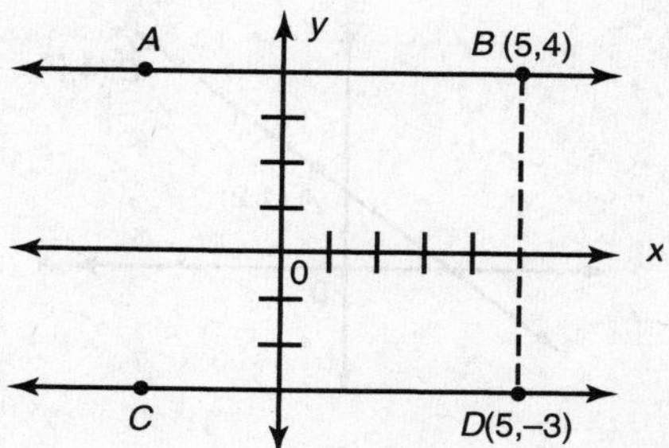

38. In the figure $\overleftrightarrow{AB}$ and $\overleftrightarrow{CD}$ are both parallel to the x-axis. The coordinates of B are (5,4) and the coordinates of D are (5,–3). The perpendicular distance between $\overleftrightarrow{AB}$ and $\overleftrightarrow{CD}$ is
    (1) –2
    (2) 5
    (3) 6
    (4) 7
    (5) 10

39. Evaluate $(6 \times 10^5) \div (4 \times 10^3)$.
    (1) 20
    (2) 100
    (3) 150
    (4) 1,500
    (5) 2,000

GO ON TO THE NEXT PAGE

TEST 5: MATHEMATICS

Question 40 is based on the following graph.

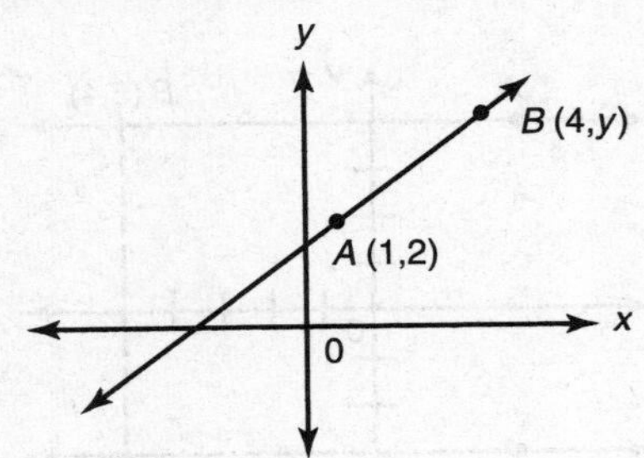

40. If the slope of $\overleftrightarrow{AB}$ is 1, what is the value of y?
    (1) 1
    (2) 2
    (3) 3
    (4) 4
    (5) 5

Questions 41–43 are based on the following graph.

The graph shows the number of gallons of paint sold by a local hardware store in 1 week.

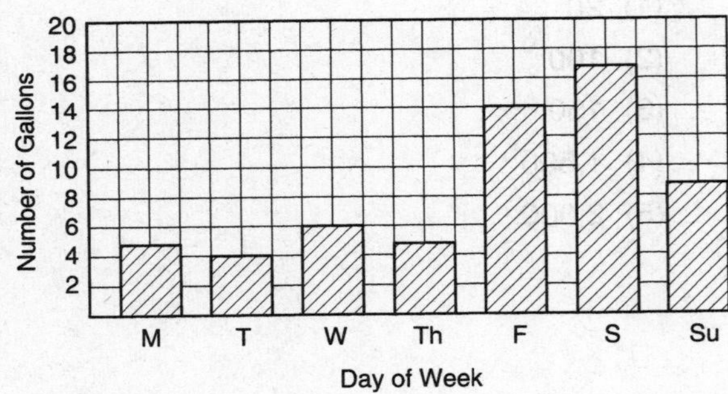

41. How many gallons of paint were sold on Wednesday?
    (1) 3
    (2) 4
    (3) 5
    (4) 6
    (5) 7

42. How much more paint was sold on Saturday than on Monday?
    (1) 6 gal.
    (2) 8 gal.
    (3) 10 gal.
    (4) 11 gal.
    (5) 12 gal.

43. What was the total amount, in gallons, of paint sold by the store that week?
    (1) 20
    (2) 25
    (3) 30
    (4) 60
    (5) Not enough information is given.

Question 44 is based on the following figure.

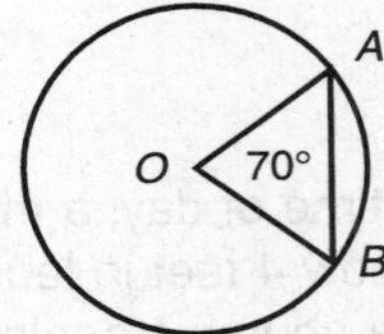

44. O is the center of the circle, and the measure of $\angle O$ is 70°. What is the measure of $\angle OAB$?
    (1) 55°
    (2) 60°
    (3) 65°
    (4) 70°
    (5) 75°

Question 45 is based on the following table.

Time	3:00 P.M.	4:00 P.M.	5:00 P.M.
Distance covered (miles)	80	124	168

GO ON TO THE NEXT PAGE

TEST 5: MATHEMATICS

45. Sylvia took an automobile trip. The table shows the mileage she covered during one afternoon. If she drove at a steady rate, how many miles had she covered at 4:15 P.M.?

(1) 30
(2) 132
(3) 135
(4) 140
(5) Not enough information is given.

---

46. The following is a list of ingredients used in making cornmeal crisps:

1 cup of yellow cornmeal
$\frac{1}{2}$ cup of sifted flour
$\frac{2}{3}$ teaspoon of salt
$\frac{1}{4}$ teaspoon of baking powder
2 tablespoons of melted shortening
$\frac{1}{3}$ cup of milk

If Joan decides to make a larger batch of cookies by using a full cup of milk, she will have to use

(1) 1 cup of sifted flour
(2) 2 teaspoons of salt
(3) 3 teaspoons of baking powder
(4) 3 tablespoons of melted shortening
(5) $2\frac{1}{2}$ cups of yellow cornmeal

<u>Question 47</u> is based on the following graph.

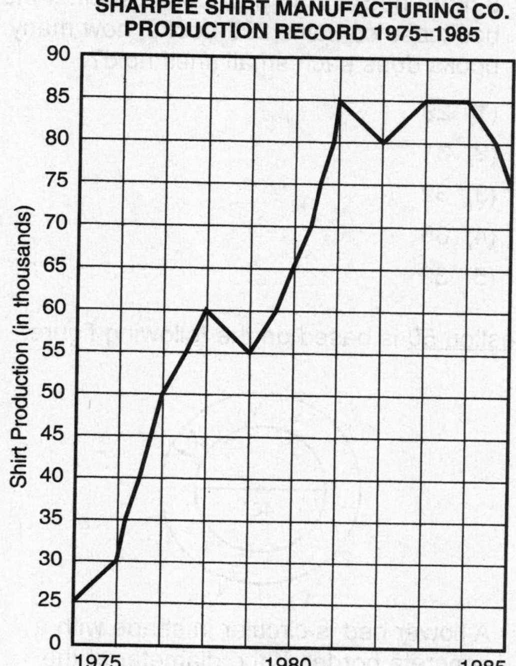

47. What was the number of shirts produced in 1980?

(1) 2,500
(2) 6,500
(3) 25,000
(4) 65,000
(5) 70,000

---

48. A house and a lot cost $120,000. If the house cost 3 times as much as the lot, how much did the house cost?

(1) $30,000
(2) $40,000
(3) $60,000
(4) $90,000
(5) $100,000

GO ON TO THE NEXT PAGE

TEST 5: MATHEMATICS

49. A bookcase has 3 large shelves and 4 small shelves. Each large shelf contains 8 more books than each small shelf. If the bookcase contains 297 books, how many books does each small shelf hold?

(1) 29
(2) 31
(3) 32
(4) 35
(5) 39

Question 50 is based on the following figure.

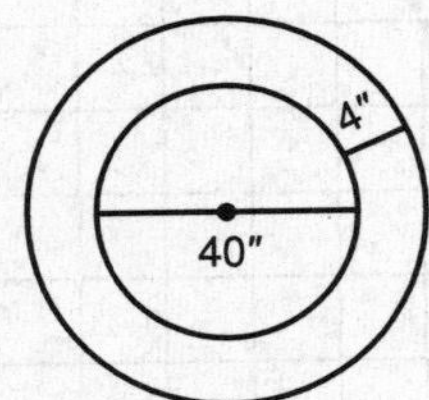

50. A flower bed is circular in shape with a concrete border. If the diameter of the flower section is 40 inches and the width of the concrete border is 4 inches, what is the area, in square inches, of the border? (Leave your answer in terms of π.)

(1) 16π
(2) 176π
(3) 180π
(4) 200π
(5) 240π

51. Mrs. Edwards buys 40 feet of woolen material to use for scarfs. How many scarfs each 3 feet 4 inches in length can she cut from this material?

(1) 12
(2) 15
(3) 16
(4) 18
(5) 120

52. In the figure, the length of each side of the square is 10 inches. The curves are quarter circles. What is the area of the shaded portion?

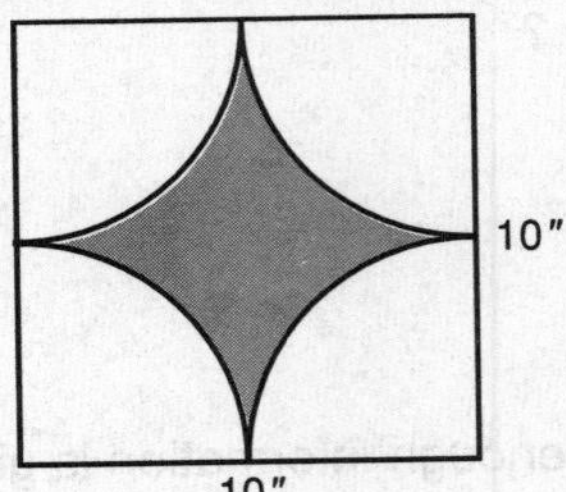

(1) $100 - 100\pi$
(2) $100 - 50\pi$
(3) $100 - 25\pi$
(4) $100 - 10\pi$
(5) Not enough information is given.

Question 53 is based on the following figure.

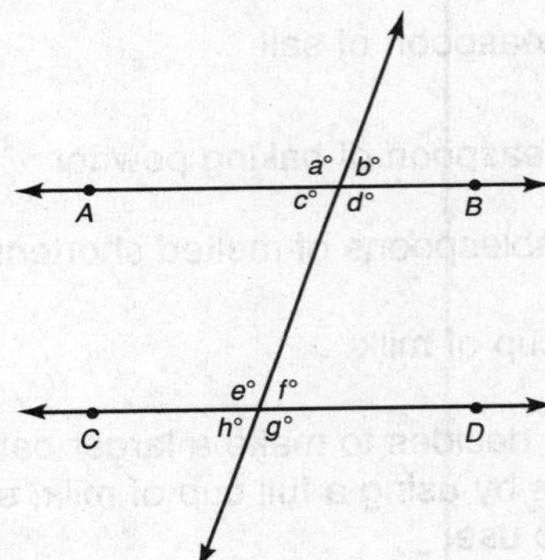

53. If $\overleftrightarrow{AB}$ is parallel to $\overleftrightarrow{CD}$, each of the following is true **EXCEPT**

(1) $a = d$
(2) $b = f$
(3) $c = b$
(4) $f = c$
(5) $b = g$

GO ON TO THE NEXT PAGE

TEST 5: MATHEMATICS

54. $A + B + C = 180$. If $A = B$ and $B = 2C$, then the value of C is

(1) 36
(2) 45
(3) 60
(4) 72
(5) 90

55. Mrs. Evans buys 2 pounds 6 ounces of apples at $0.72 per pound and 3 pounds 4 ounces of peaches at $0.56 per pound. How much change does she receive from a $5 bill?

(1) $1.35
(2) $1.47
(3) $1.82
(4) $3.53
(5) Not enough information is given.

56. A dealer buys ties that are priced at 6 for $39. How much does a shipment of 15 dozen ties cost?

(1) $234
(2) $585
(3) $785
(4) $1,070
(5) $1,170

END OF EXAMINATION

Answer Keys, Summaries of Results, and Self-Appraisal Charts

TEST 1: WRITING SKILLS, PART I/PAGE 575

I. CHECK YOUR ANSWERS, using the following answer key:

1. **5**	12. **3**	23. **2**	34. **5**	45. **1**
2. **2**	13. **1**	24. **3**	35. **5**	46. **1**
3. **3**	14. **5**	25. **5**	36. **4**	47. **4**
4. **5**	15. **5**	26. **3**	37. **1**	48. **4**
5. **1**	16. **5**	27. **4**	38. **3**	49. **2**
6. **1**	17. **1**	28. **4**	39. **2**	50. **5**
7. **5**	18. **5**	29. **1**	40. **4**	51. **5**
8. **1**	19. **4**	30. **2**	41. **3**	52. **4**
9. **1**	20. **5**	31. **1**	42. **1**	53. **2**
10. **1**	21. **5**	32. **1**	43. **3**	54. **3**
11. **1**	22. **2**	33. **4**	44. **1**	55. **5**

II. SCORE YOURSELF:

	Number correct:
Excellent	54 50–55
Good	________ 44–49
Fair	________ 38–43

III. EVALUATE YOUR SCORE: Did you get at least 38 correct answers? If not, you need more practice for the Writing Skills, Part I test. In any event, you can improve your performance to Excellent or Good by analyzing your errors.

IV. ANALYZE YOUR ERRORS: To determine your areas of weakness, list the number of correct answers you had under each of the following categories (which correspond to the content areas of the Writing Skills, Part I test), and compare your score with the average scores in the right-hand column. Review the answer analysis beginning on page 651 for each of the questions you got wrong, and give yourself more practice in your weak areas with the appropriate material in Unit II before attempting Practice Examination Two.

Content Areas	Items	Your Score	Average Score
Sentence Structure	1, 3, 5, 8, 10–13, 19, 25, 32, 37, 45, 50, 53–54	16	11
Usage	16, 23, 26–28, 36, 43, 47	8	6
Mechanics			
Spelling	6, 22, 31, 40, 42, 48–49	7	5
Punctuation	9, 17, 24, 30, 33, 38, 41, 44, 46, 52	10	7
Capitalization	2, 29, 39	3	2
No correction	4, 7, 14–15, 18, 20–21, 34–35, 51, 55	10	8

Total 54

TEST 2: SOCIAL STUDIES/PAGE 589

I. CHECK YOUR ANSWERS, using the following answer key:

1. **2**
2. **4**
3. **2**
4. **4**
5. **4**
6. **3**
7. **1**
8. **4**
9. **2**
10. **3**
11. **4**
12. **3**
13. **1**
14. **1**
15. **2**
16. **2**
17. **4**
18. **3**
19. **1**
20. **4**
21. **1**
22. **2**
23. **2**
24. **1**
25. **4**
26. **4**
27. **4**
28. **4**
29. **3**
30. **2**
31. **5**
32. **1**
33. **3**
34. **4**
35. **3**
36. **2**
37. **4**
38. **2**
39. **3**
40. **1**
41. **3**
42. **4**
43. **4**
44. **2**
45. **1**
46. **3**
47. **1**
48. **5**
49. **3**
50. **3**
51. **3**
52. **5**
53. **2**
54. **3**
55. **2**
56. **4**
57. **3**
58. **2**
59. **2**
60. **5**
61. **1**
62. **3**
63. **2**
64. **5**

II. SCORE YOURSELF:

Number correct:

Excellent ________ 57–64

Good ________ 51–56

Fair ________ 45–50

III. EVALUATE YOUR SCORE: Did you get at least 45 correct answers? If not, you need more practice for the Social Studies test. In any event, you can improve your performance to Excellent or Good by analyzing your errors.

IV. ANALYZE YOUR ERRORS: To determine your specific weaknesses, list the number of correct answers you had under each of the following categories (which correspond to the content areas of the Social Studies test), and compare your score with the average scores specified in the right-hand column. Review the answer analysis section beginning on page 653 for each of the questions you got wrong, and give yourself more practice in your weak areas with the appropriate material in Unit IV (including the "Glossary of Social Studies Terms"), before attempting Practice Examination Two.

Content Areas	Items	Your Score	Average Score
Political Science	1–9, 34–35, 49–50		9
Economics	10–13, 19–20, 34–35		5
History	14–18, 21–22, 28–33, 40, 53–54, 59, 63–64		12
Geography	23–27, 37–38, 48, 51–52, 55–56, 60–62		10
Behavioral Science	36, 39, 41–47, 57–58		8

Total ______

TEST 3: SCIENCE/PAGE 606

I. CHECK YOUR ANSWERS, using the following answer key:

1. 5	15. 1	29. 2	43. 2	57. 2
2. 5	16. 3	30. 4	44. 3	58. 3
3. 1	17. 3	31. 4	45. 5	59. 5
4. 2	18. 2	32. 2	46. 3	60. 4
5. 1	19. 4	33. 5	47. 1	61. 5
6. 3	20. 1	34. 3	48. 2	62. 2
7. 2	21. 3	35. 2	49. 2	63. 4
8. 4	22. 1	36. 4	50. 4	64. 5
9. 5	23. 5	37. 3	51. 2	65. 1
10. 4	24. 1	38. 3	52. 4	66. 2
11. 2	25. 4	39. 4	53. 4	
12. 4	26. 5	40. 2	54. 1	
13. 1	27. 3	41. 5	55. 4	
14. 3	28. 5	42. 1	56. 4	

II. SCORE YOURSELF:

Number correct:

Excellent ______
60–66

Good ______
49–59

Fair ______
40–48

III. EVALUATE YOUR SCORE: Did you get at least 40 correct answers? If not, you need more practice for the Science test. In any event, you can improve your performance to Excellent or Good by analyzing your errors.

IV. ANALYZE YOUR ERRORS: To determine your specific weaknesses, encircle the number of each question you got wrong. This will reveal the specific science area that needs emphasis in planning your study program. After studying the answer analysis section beginning on page 656 for each of the questions you got wrong, list the terms that you feel need further explanation and study them in the "Glossary of Scientific Terms" beginning on page 388. Then give yourself more practice in your weak areas with the appropriate material in Unit V before attempting Practice Examination Two.

Content Areas	Items	Your Score	Average Score
Biology	1–22, 32, 33, 41, 44, 45, 47–50		22
Earth Science	23–25, 37, 39, 40, 46, 64, 65		3
Chemistry	26–31, 34, 36, 37, 42, 43, 51–57		12
Physics	35, 38, 58–63, 66		9

Total ______

TEST 4: INTERPRETING LITERATURE AND THE ARTS/PAGE 621

I. CHECK YOUR ANSWERS, using the following answer key:

1. **1**	10. **1**	19. **1**	28. **5**	37. **3**
2. **4**	11. **1**	20. **2**	29. **3**	38. **1**
3. **2**	12. **1**	21. **2**	30. **3**	39. **4**
4. **3**	13. **4**	22. **2**	31. **4**	40. **5**
5. **3**	14. **1**	23. **1**	32. **5**	41. **3**
6. **4**	15. **2**	24. **3**	33. **3**	42. **3**
7. **2**	16. **4**	25. **5**	34. **3**	43. **5**
8. **1**	17. **3**	26. **4**	35. **5**	44. **4**
9. **3**	18. **4**	27. **1**	36. **4**	45. **5**

II. SCORE YOURSELF:

Number correct: 43

Excellent ________ 41–45

Good ________ 36–40

Fair ________ 31–35

III. EVALUATE YOUR SCORE: Did you get at least 31 correct answers? If not, you need more practice for the Interpreting Literature and the Arts test. You can improve your performance to Excellent or Good by analyzing your errors.

IV. ANALYZE YOUR ERRORS: To determine your specific weaknesses, first list the number of correct answers you had under each of the following categories and compare your score with the average scores in the right-hand column. After studying the Answer Analysis section beginning on page 660 for each of the questions you answered incorrectly, study the material in the sections "Basic Reading Skills" and "Reading Prose, Poetry, and Drama" in Unit VI as well as the "Glossary of Literary Terms" (page 411) to strengthen your weak areas before attempting Practice Examination Two.

Reading Skills	Items	Your Score	Average Score
Locating the Main Idea	6, 26, 28, 31		3
Finding Details	2–3, 7, 11, 13–14, 19–20, 25, 27–29, 33–34, 36–37, 40–42, 44–45		14
Inferring Meaning	4–5, 16, 18, 22–23, 32, 35		5
Making Inferences	8–10, 17, 21, 24, 26–27, 38–39, 43		8
Determining Tone and Mood	1, 13–14		2
Inferring Character	5		1

Total ________

Now to see how your scores in the content areas of Interpreting Literature and the Arts test compare with the average scores in the right-hand column, list your score for each of the following:

Content Areas	Items	Your Score	Average Score
Popular Literature	1–25		17
Classical Literature	26–35		7
Commentary	36–45		7

Total _______

Literary Forms	Items	Your Score	Average Score
Prose Nonfiction	1–15, 31–35		14
Prose Nonfiction (Commentary)	36–45		7
Poetry	16–25		7
Drama	26–30		3

Total _______

Note: While Commentary on the Arts is a content area in itself, the commentary, as written, is in the form of prose nonfiction.

TEST 5: MATHEMATICS/PAGE 631

I. CHECK YOUR ANSWERS, using the following answer key:

1. **3**	13. **3**	25. **1**	37. **1**	49. **5**
2. **3**	14. **4**	26. **5**	38. **4**	50. **2**
3. **5**	15. **5**	27. **4**	39. **3**	51. **1**
4. **2**	16. **3**	28. **3**	40. **5**	52. **3**
5. **3**	17. **2**	29. **3**	41. **4**	53. **5**
6. **3**	18. **5**	30. **4**	42. **5**	54. **1**
7. **5**	19. **4**	31. **4**	43. **4**	55. **2**
8. **4**	20. **3**	32. **3**	44. **1**	56. **5**
9. **5**	21. **5**	33. **4**	45. **3**	
10. **5**	22. **4**	34. **4**	46. **2**	
11. **2**	23. **1**	35. **5**	47. **4**	
12. **2**	24. **3**	36. **3**	48. **4**	

II. SCORE YOURSELF:

Number correct:

Excellent ______ 51–56

Good ______ 44–50

Fair ______ 38–43

III. EVALUATE YOUR SCORE: Did you get at least 38 correct answers? If not, you need more practice for the Mathematics test. In any event, you can improve your performance to Excellent or Good by analyzing your errors.

IV. ANALYZE YOUR ERRORS: To determine your specific weaknesses, list the number of correct answers you had under each of the following categories, and compare your score with the average scores specified in the right-hand column. After studying the Answer Analysis section beginning on page 661 for each of the questions you got wrong, give yourself more practice in your weak areas with the appropriate material in Unit VII before attempting Practice Examination Two.

Content Areas	Items	Your Score	Average Score
Arithmetic	1, 4, 6, 8, 10–11, 15, 18, 20–24, 26–27, 30, 33, 35, 37, 39, 41–43, 45–47, 51–52, 55–56		19
Algebra	3, 7, 12–14, 16–17, 25, 28, 32, 34, 48–49, 54		10
Geometry	2, 5, 9, 19, 29, 31, 36, 38, 40, 44, 50, 53		8

Total ______

YOUR TOTAL GED SCORE

The Writing Skills Test ______

The Social Studies Test ______

The Science Test ______

The Interpreting Literature and the Arts Test ______

The Mathematics Test ______

Total ______

Answer Analysis

TEST 1: WRITING SKILLS, PART I/PAGE 575

1. **5** This change is necessary to correct the run-on sentence.
2. **2** *Department of Agriculture* must be capitalized.
3. **3** The singular subject *Care* requires the singular verb *is*. *Among* is necessary because the verb *include* implies other precautions that are not mentioned.
4. **5** No correction is necessary.
5. **1** The original is correct because two equally important ideas require two independent clauses connected by a coordinate conjunction. Since the clauses express similar, not opposing, ideas, *and*, rather than *but*, is the correct conjunction.
6. **1** The correct spelling is *sufficient*.
7. **5** No correction is necessary.
8. **1** The use of the two adjective clauses *which contain food that may be* avoids the repetition of *swollen or leaking can*.
9. **1** The original is correct because the semicolon separates two independent clauses in the same sentence.
10. **1** The original is correct. The second idea, "the people in the family may change," is in opposition to the first, so *although* is necessary. The comma after *dominant* must be retained.
11. **1** This combination eliminates repetition of the words *will also increase*.
12. **3** This is necessary to avoid the run-on sentence.
13. **1** Following the rewritten sentence's introductory clause should come the subject of the main clause, *an increasing number*.
14. **5** No correction is necessary.
15. **5** No correction is necessary.
16. **5** No correction is necessary.
17. **1** A comma is never used immediately after the subject and before the verb.
18. **5** No correction is necessary.
19. **4** The sentences are best combined by an adjective clause, *that spreads*, which modifies *disease*.
20. **5** No correction is necessary.
21. **5** No correction is necessary.
22. **2** The correct spelling is *believed*.
23. **2** To achieve parallelism with *knowledge* and *understanding*, a noun, *example*, must be used.
24. **3** A comma is needed after a lengthy introductory clause.
25. **5** This change is necessary to prevent a run-on sentence.
26. **3** The proper sequence of tenses requires the future perfect tense *will have been* since this action precedes *is tempted*.
27. **4** The pronoun, *his*, must agree in number with its antecedent, *drug abuser*.
28. **4** The verb, *is*, must be singular because its subject, *type*, is singular.
29. **1** *Americans* should be capitalized.
30. **2** A comma is used to separate independent clauses in a compound sentence that are joined by a conjunction, in this case *but*.
31. **1** The correct spelling is *impossible*.
32. **1** The original is correct because two distinctly different sentences are involved.
33. **4** A comma is used to separate items in a series.
34. **5** No correction is necessary.
35. **5** No correction is necessary.
36. **4** The insertion of *are* is necessary to parallel *are in a hurry* and *are careless*.
37. **1** The subject of the sentence, a few inexpensive items, should follow the introductory clause.
38. **3** No comma is necessary between *fever* and *sweeping*.
39. **2** *Mom* and *Pop* should be capitalized since they are proper nouns.
40. **4** The correct spelling is *environment*.
41. **3** A comma, not a period, is necessary before the final verb in the series, which cannot be a separate sentence.
42. **1** The correct spelling is *appropriate*.
43. **3** *You're*, which is a contraction of *you are*, is required in this sentence.
44. **1** The original is the best way. The colon is used because it introduces the advice.
45. **1** *Invest in* is required by the sense of the sentence.

46. **1** The original is correct; the semicolon is used to separate independent clauses in the same sentence.
47. **4** *Whom* is necessary since this word is the object of the preposition *with* and must be in the objective case.
48. **4** The correct spelling is *practice*.
49. **2** The correct spelling is *chooses*.
50. **5** *Since* would be required because the second idea is the result of the first.
51. **5** No correction is necessary.
52. **4** A comma is needed to separate items in a series.
53. **2** *Because* would be needed since the second idea gives a cause (reason) for the first.
54. **3** *Is* is the verb that must follow the new subject, *Making a conscious ordering . . . to us*.
55. **5** No correction is necessary.

TEST 1: WRITING SKILLS, PART II/PAGE 588

SAMPLE ESSAYS

For the computer

The advent of the computer has vastly improved life in the twentieth century.

Thanks to the computer, it is now possible to do away with much of the drudgery of data handling. The combination of computer, printer, copier saves many hours of routine typing since it is now easy to obtain from a one-time input of data as many copies as one needs.

Thanks to the computer, it is now possible to store important data and to summon the data up when necessary. Files can be set up for hundreds of subjects, and the stored data are instantly available.

Thanks to the computer, it is possible to have endless hours of enjoyment from entertaining and educational games. Learning becomes a joy with computer-aided instruction.

Thanks to the computer, engineers and architects can work out their problems more efficiently using computer-assisted design programs.

Thanks to the computer, families can monitor their budgets and keep financial and family records.

Thanks to the computer's word-processing capabilities, authors can avoid much monotony in editing and revising works in progress.

Thanks to the computer built-in spelling and dictionary programs, computers make letter writing much less burdensome.

Thanks to the computer and an almost infinite variety of software programs, data can be structured to meet nearly every conceivable need.

These are only a few of the many ways the computer has made the world a better place in which to live.

Summary of reasons for the computer:

The computer

1. makes data handling less burdensome;
2. stores and makes data readily available;
3. aids instruction and provides entertainment;
4. aids engineers and architects in their designs;
5. aids families in keeping personal records;
6. aids authors through word processing;
7. makes letter writing more efficient;
8. makes data available in varied ways by means of software programs.

Against the computer

> ***The computer has brought nothing but problems to the world of the twentieth century.***
>
> ***Chief among these problems has been the dehumanization of society. People are no longer human. Each of us is a series of numbers, numbers to be fed into computers. There are our credit card numbers, our bank account numbers, our Social Security numbers, our telephone and electricity numbers—the computer number game is endless.***
>
> ***What happens to these computerized numbers? They are distributed to a network of government agencies and businesses that can use them to invade our privacy. The Internal Revenue Service stores millions of facts about every citizen. Credit agencies exchange information on the spending and saving practices of nearly every American adult. Mailing lists are made available by computers to dozens of organizations, public and private, who bombard us with unwanted mail.***
>
> ***Just let the computer that stores data concerning our accounts, let us say with a credit card company, make an error, and it is almost impossible to straighten things out. The result is an avalanche of bills, threats, and loss of credit standing.***
>
> ***The computer has thrown thousands of people out of work. The gamut of computer-generated unemployed runs from highly skilled technicians to typists.***
>
> ***These are some of the reasons why I feel that the advent of the computer has been detrimental to the quality of our life in the twentieth century.***

Summary of reasons <u>against</u> the computer:

1. The computer has dehumanized society.
2. The computer has invaded our privacy in many ways.
3. Computer errors have caused great hardship to many unfortunate individuals.
4. The computer has thrown many people out of work.

TEST 2: SOCIAL STUDIES/PAGE 589

1. **2** As indicated in the first paragraph, the word *genocide* is the joining of the Greek *genos*, meaning race or tribe, and the Latin suffix *-cide*, meaning killing.
2. **4** The third paragraph gives the scope of the term *genocide* as including the intent to destroy a national, ethnical, racial, or religious group. It does not refer to political groups, as such.
3. **2** Genocide was practiced on a large scale by the Nazis in the destruction of six million Jews. Other groups that have been subjected to genocide, as mentioned in the second paragraph, are Armenians, Gypsies, and Chinese.
4. **4** This obviously is a ruling of a court. Therefore of the choices given, only Choice 4, the Supreme Court, could be correct. Incidentally, this selection is part of the important decision of the Supreme Court on the subject of desegregation of schools.
5. **4** The passage indicates that to separate children in grade and high schools solely because of race is to generate a feeling of inferiority in minority children. This is a psychological reason for rejecting segregation.
6. **3** The first sentence of the final paragraph indicates that modern psychological knowledge does not support the *Plessy* v. *Ferguson* decision and, by implication, indicates that psychological knowledge at the time of *Plessy* v. *Ferguson* no longer applies.
7. **1** Some of these methods include frequent elections, an impartial judiciary (court) system, the right to a free press, the right to petition for a hearing of grievances, the right to introduce legislation by *initiative*, the right to ratify proposed changes in state constitutions, and the right to oust corrupt officials by impeachment or *recall*.

8. **4** Both the Democrats and Republicans include supporters from all sections of the nation and from various social and ethnic backgrounds. Each contains leaders and members whose political views range from conservative to moderate to liberal. To gain control of the government, a political party needs the support of a majority of the American voters, and thus must have broad appeal. The Democrats have usually drawn support from labor and minority groups; the Republicans, from businesspeople and wealthier farmers. Party differences have been greater on domestic issues (e.g., tax cuts and spending for social programs) than on foreign policy.
9. **2** The cartoon refers to the first free elections in South Africa, which took place in 1994, when a new constitution provided equal rights to vote for all South Africans. The shackle falling from the arm of the black voter symbolizes the freedom that came with the right to vote.
10. **3** The added companies are described as already successful enterprises.
11. **4** The passage states that profitability ratios provide a measure of management performance.
12. **3** The gap between the fast-rising "desired demand" and the "potential supply," which levels off, is first noticeable on the graph at about 1990.
13. **1** Western European countries and Japan would lack fuel for their industries, and production would drop, with resultant unemployment and depression.
14. **1** Such resistance is often expressed by *denying* the formal methods for peaceful change. Failure to permit evolutionary change may result in revolution.
15. **2** Speaker *B* holds that the frontier made U.S. history unique; he would see only dissimilarities between the French and American revolutions. Speaker *C* stresses historical compromise between conflicting American groups.
16. **2** Speaker *B* would most likely agree that the existence of the American frontier provided a *safety valve* for those who wanted to leave the more crowded East. Such space was unavailable in the European countries from which most Americans or their forebears had come.
17. **4** The different historical perspective of each historian will assign differing causes and results to the same major events.
18. **3** The company's charter gave it a monopoly over colonization and trade in an area, with profits being shared by the shareholders and the King.
19. **1** President Johnson mentioned full employment as the first of America's unfinished tasks and the first goal that must be achieved in the national interest.
20. **4** President Johnson listed the widening of the benefits of prosperity as one of the tasks that remained unfinished.
21. **1** The cartoon encourages the American public to be cautious about becoming involved in European conflicts, reminding it of the consequences of war.
22. **2** One of the World War reminders that Uncle Sam is holding in the cartoon is economic collapse. Economic prosperity would remove that threat to peace.
23. **2** A valid generalization from the chart is that industrialized nations have lower birth rates and infant mortality rates than developing nations. The first six nations of the chart are developing nations, whereas the last six are industrialized nations. The average birth rate of the developing nations is four times greater than that of the industrialized nations. The difference between infant mortality rates is even greater, from Uganda's, which is 12 times greater than Italy's, to Angola's, which is 31 times greater than Japan's.
24. **1** According to the chart, the lowest birthrates are found mostly in western Europe. Four of the six industrialized nations with low birthrates are in western Europe.
25. **4** Uganda, Somalia, Angola, and Ethiopia, four of the six countries with the highest infant mortality, are in Africa.
26. **4** Oil spills have repeatedly ruined the recreational value of beaches and destroyed fish and birdlife, causing both economic and ecological damage.
27. **4** The definition states that topography deals with the surface features of a region.
28. **4** The passage alludes to "principles of union," "cement to the Union," and "their best interests would be best promoted by union."

29. 3 The passage refers to "reasonable jealousies" between the people of the eastern and the southern states.

30. 2 Jealousies "subsided" when inhabitants of different states became better acquainted.

31. 5 The frontier's passing coincides with the end of gifts of free land.

32. 1 The author lists all the contributions of the frontier—escape from the past and opportunity for new experiences, among others.

33. 3 It was written one hundred years after the Constitution (1789) and four hundred years after the discovery of America (1492).

34. 4 The cartoon refers to the collapse of communism in the early 1990s. The hammer and sickle is a symbol of the Soviet Union. A series of symbols is arranged to look like the rib cage of the skeleton of a dinosaur, and the wording in the cartoon implies that communism, like the dinosaur, could not adapt to change.

35. 3 The hammer and sickle is the symbol of the former Union of Socialist Soviet Republics (USSR).

36. 2 Heredity and environment each represents various factors contributing to the behavior of individuals and groups. No *single* factor can be isolated and identified as determining human actions.

37. 4 It is trade that keeps us alive.

38. 2 Increased population was due to speeded-up economic unification.

39. 3 Two views regarding assimilation of Native Americans into American life are mentioned—a belief that total assimilation is inevitable, and a belief that Native Americans will keep separate identities for a long time into the future.

40. 1 Collective security calls for nations to coordinate their military strength to protect one another from aggression.

41. 3 Social mobility is the movement of individuals up or down in social and economic status in society, largely on ability and effort. Choice 3 is an example of social mobility.

42. 4 Cultural diversity, a variety of cultural patterns, exists where different peoples come together frequently and intermingle. Migration is a principal means of bringing this diversity about.

43. 4 Culture shock results from rapid social change—movement to a more developed society or movement to a less developed one. Choice 4 is an example of the latter.

44. 2 An extended family includes grandparents, uncles, aunts, and cousins. Out of economic necessity, they may live together and survive because of their dependence on one another.

45. 1 A pluralistic society encourages coexistence of peoples of various ethnic heritages, usually holding differing views on important issues.

46. 3 The author says that the right thing to do is not hard to find if you let people's feelings come through to you.

47. 1 The author states that rude or quarrelsome behavior is often a way of calling attention to one's feelings.

48. 5 The passage states that geographic natural features leave their imprint on society.

49. 3 In Table *A*, 65% opposed home searches without a specific warrant; 68% opposed electronic surveillance of citizens without a court order.

50. 3 Table *B* shows that 63% would allow the federal government to eavesdrop with specific court permission. When the same question was asked negatively in Table *A*, 68% opposed electronic eavesdropping without such permission.

51. 3 The graph shows that the nations with low per capita GNPs (the gray bar) have infant mortality rates that are greater by far—160 versus 19 per 1000 liveborn—than nations with high GNPs.

52. 5 The gray bar is smallest, and the black bar is fully extended, for public expenditure on health per capita.

53. 2 The Italian Fascists came to power in 1922. Hitler's Nazi party took over in Germany in 1933. Franco's Spanish Falangists overthrew the previous government in 1936. These dates are all represented on the time line by the letter *B*.

54. 3 Most of the former African and Asian colonies of European nations such as England and France demanded and received their independence during the first twenty years following World War II.

This time period is represented on the time line by the letter *C*.

55. **2** The map shows unequal distribution of income in China. Income per person is four times greater in Beijing and Shanghai than in the Guizhou region.

56. **4** There are more white regions, representing the \$191–\$286 range, than there are shaded areas.

57. **3** The graph shows that people age 65 and over are the victims of the fewest crimes of violence and theft.

58. **2** The 16–19 group has the highest numbers—65 and 119, for a total of 184—of crime victims in the graph. The 12–15 group has 177; the 20–24 group, 179.

59. **2** The main idea of the cartoon is that the people in the colonies, who worked long hours for low pay, were exploited by Western imperialists. The cartoon refers to China, whose coastal cities came under the control of Britain, France, Germany, and Russia in the 19th century.

60. **5** Biogeography is concerned with the distribution of plant and animal life on earth, and the increasing number of endangered species is of concern to the biogeographer.

61. **1** Physical geography deals with climatology, the study of climate and climatic phenomena, and with oceanography, the study of the environment in the oceans. The "greenhouse effect" is of importance to the physical geographer.

62. **3** Drought conditions in East Africa falls into the domain of the regional geographer since it involves a region and a number of the countries in it, Ethiopia and the Sudan, for example.

63. **2** During most of the post-World War II years, the cold war divided Europe into two armed camps—the North Atlantic Treaty Organization (NATO) and the Warsaw Pact. The lightly shaded areas show the nations of Europe in the NATO military alliance. The darker shaded areas represent the Communist nations that formed the Warsaw Pact. The white nations were not aligned with either military treaty organization.

64. **5** Spain. All the other countries mentioned as choices are lightly shaded on the map.

TEST 3: SCIENCE/PAGE 606

1. **5** The article defines population as a group of organisms of the same species living together in a given location. An ecosystem (or ecological system) consists of the living community of a region and its nonliving environment. The biosphere is that portion of the earth in which ecosystems function. A community consists of populations of different species.

2. **5** The diagram illustrates a simple community consisting of populations of different species living together and interacting with each other.

3. **1** The factor that helps to keep a population in check is natural *predators*. Both predators and prey are adapted to each other and to the environment. If an organism is introduced into a new habitat, it will have few natural enemies or predators. Its population increases.

4. **2** In this simple community the plants carry on photosynthesis, whereby they give off oxygen and make food for themselves and the fish. The fish breathe and supply carbon dioxide to the plants, which they need for the process of photosynthesis. The wastes produced by the fish are acted upon by bacteria in the mud and produce nitrates for the plant. As long as these interrelationships are maintained, the total weight of the container and its contents will remain the same.

5. **1** A biotic factor is one concerned with living things. Minerals are not living.

6. **3** A *community* is a particular environment in which organisms of different species live and interact. A community is a self-maintaining unit in which energy and food materials are recycled.

7. **2** Since these ancestors of *Equus* (the modern horse) disappeared long ago, the only evidence of their structures comes from fossils.
8. **4** Refer to the last sentence of this passage.
9. **5** The horse's hoof is the toenail of what was once a middle toe.
10. **4** *Eohippus* had teeth without ridges. *Mesohippus* had teeth with well-developed ridges.
11. **2** According to the chart, speech is the only left-brain function among the answer choices.
12. **4** This information is given in the second paragraph. The other answers make no sense.
13. **1** Each of the other choices includes at least one function attributed to the left hemisphere.
14. **3** The purpose of the *corpus callosum* is to connect the two halves of the brain and provide a means for information to pass from one side to the other. Choices 1, 4, and 5 are all opinions. Choice 2 concerns dyslexia, which is off topic.
15. **1** The importance of the brain and its parts is subjective, eliminating Choices 2 and 3. There is nothing about split personalities in the passage, nor anything about the comparative sizes of the human and ape brains. The article does state that brain functions are chemical and electrical, making Choice 1 the correct answer.
16. **3** The passage says that the axon is the part of the neuron that carries the signal from neuron to neuron, and that the synapse is the junction between neurons. Each of the other choices contains an error.
17. **3** Water, carbon dioxide, and protein are chemical compounds. Not all living things contain the chemical element phosphorus.
18. **2** Protoplasm is a complex protein.
19. **4** Neither size nor color was a factor in this experiment, nor was the cost an issue. The same mice could not be reused; the variable in this experiment is learning, and the mice had already been influenced. Choice 4 is the best answer.
20. **1** This choice is a conclusion that can be drawn from the experiment. All the other choices are irrelevant or erroneous.
21. **3** This answer is given in the passage.
22. **1** The issue of illumination was not part of the experiment and is therefore irrelevant.
23. **5** Although all of the other choices list valid concerns, Choice 5 is more comprehensive.
24. **1** According to the passage, one person requires 2.2 lb. of oxygen per day:

    2.2 x 2 weeks (14 days) = 30.8 lb.

    You have to multiply 30.8 by 5 (the number of people) to obtain the answer.
25. **4** According to the passage, each person requires 4.5 lb. of water per day. The question contains irrelevant information (1 gal. of water weighs 8.33 lbs.), which should be ignored.
26. **5** Since calcium compounds neutralize acids, calcium carbonate is the only correct choice.
27. **3** Pollutants are the sources of acid deposition. Water is a natural part of the environment. No polluting gases are produced by the use of water power to generate electricity.
28. **5** Selective agents work for or against living organisms in the environment. Acid deposition works against fish and plankton and favors the growth of more acid-loving types of plants.
29. **2** Abiotic factors are nonliving factors in the environment. Sulfur is the abiotic factor related to the acid deposition problem.
30. **4** Since acid deposition results from pollutants that come from burning fossil fuels, the best approach to reducing acid deposition is to control air pollution at the source.
31. **4** Household vinegar, which is about 2% acetic acid, has a pH of 3.
32. **2** The only way the gardener can know how much to use is to follow the instructions given.
33. **5** Reptilia: garter snake; Aves: house sparrow; Mammalia: African elephant.
34. **3** The sugar becomes less soluble, and may come out of solution as a solid. The gas becomes more soluble and will remain in solution. If anything, the water will evaporate more slowly at lower temperatures.

35. **2** Locate the given pressure, 8 mm, along the horizontal axis. Move up the 8 mm line until the graph curve is reached. On the vertical axis at the left, you will find that the volume at this point is approximately 2 mL.

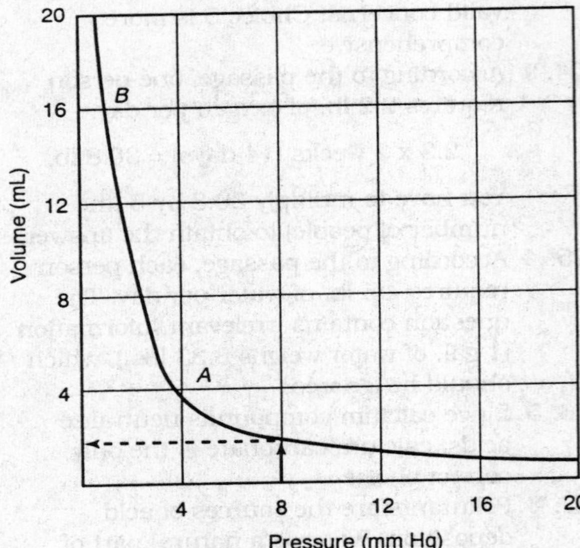

36. **4** Propane (C_2H_8) is an organic compound. HNO_3, H_2SO_4, and HCl are acids. NaCl is a salt.

37. **3** The only solution among the answers that is specifically identified in the passage as an electrolyte is sodium chloride.

38. **3** In horizontal flight, the engine thrust pushes the plane forward and air drag holds it back; if they are equal, there will be no change in speed. In Choices 1 and 2 one of the vertical forces is greater than the other. Choice 4 is wrong because the force acting on the wall has nothing to do with the speed of the ball. Choice 5 is wrong because it takes no account of the pull of gravity.

39. **4** No small planets have rings, but all the large planets except Jupiter have them. Choice 1 is wrong because Jupiter has no rings. Choice 2 is wrong because Pluto has no rings. Choice 3 is wrong because a definite trend is apparent. Choice 5 is wrong because there is no reason to believe that Pluto ever had rings.

40. **2** Only in deserts is dry sand on the surface, where it can be picked up and carried by the wind.

41. **5** If some such substance is present, there is no reason to suppose that it would affect frogs differently from fish.

42. **1** Hydrated salt is a salt that contains water attached to its molecules. This water is easily removed by heating, leaving only the pure salt. The original 5.0 g of this hydrated salt contained pure salt and water. As heating proceeds, the sample loses weight as the water is driven out. After 15 min. the sample weighs 3.0 g. After this there is no further loss of weight, even after heating for a whole hour. We must assume all the water has been driven out of the material. By 15 min., by 30 min., certainly by 60 min. of heating, 0.00 g of water is left in the hydrated salt.

43. **2**

Mass of hydrated salt	= 5.0 g
Mass of dried salt	= 3.0 g
Mass of water removed from salt	= 2.0 g

$$\% \text{ Water} = \frac{\text{mass of water in hydrated salt}}{\text{mass of hydrated salt sample}} \times 100$$

$$= \frac{2.0 \text{ g of } H_2O \text{ in sample}}{5.0 \text{ g of sample taken}} \times 100$$

$$= 0.40 \times 100 = 40\%$$

44. **3** The impulse starts with irritation of the cornea, goes through a sensory neuron to the brain, and then passes through a motor neuron to the tear gland.

45. **5** That DDT-resistant mosquitoes now exist in greater numbers than 10 years ago means that genetic differences permitted some mosquitoes to survive DDT use. Mosquitoes that did not survive DDT use died off. Those with survival power lived and reproduced others with similar survival power. The result was an increase in the numbers of DDT-resistant mosquitoes in the species.

46. **3** Fossils are found in sedimentary rocks, which are laid down in layers. The oldest layers are closest to the Earth's crust, and the youngest layers are near the surface. To conclude that a species had not changed very much over the years, the unchanged fossils of that species must have been distributed throughout the layers.

47. **1** Gametes—eggs and sperms—have half as many chromosomes as somatic cells,

such as leaf cells. The somatic cell number is produced at fertilization.

48. 2 Under normal circumstances, the total number of adult robins or of adult salmon does not change rapidly. Each adult pair, on the average, produces enough eggs to replace itself, so only two eggs survive to adulthood for each adult pair.

49. 2 Corn plants grown in the dark are white. The most probable explanation is that the expression of the gene for color may depend on the environment. That these plants have the genetic information for chlorophyll production can be assumed because they are genetically identical to the plants grown in the light. Light is needed to activate the chlorophyll gene.

50. 4 In sexual reproduction, new properties can be produced by recombination of the genes of the two parents.

51. 2 When two or more elements "chemically combine," they produce a compound. The term *chemically combine* means that the individual properties of the original elements are lost when these elements combine. The substance that is formed has new, different properties and is called a compound. In solutions and mixtures, the various components have not lost their individual properties nor have they formed new substances.

52. 4 Heating mercuric oxide yields oxygen and mercury, the silvery film mentioned in the passage.

53. 4 The production of the carbonated water mentioned in the passage can be explained by the equation $CO_2 + H_2O \rightarrow H_2CO_3$.

54. 1 As mentioned in the passage, chalk ($CaCO_3$) plus acid, in this case hydrochloric acid (HCl), yields the gas carbon dioxide. In the chemical reaction of Choice 1, the initial product is H_2CO_3 (carbonic acid), but this unstable substance quickly breaks up into CO_2, which causes the fizz, and H_2O.

55. 4 Even inside a closed container, water will evaporate. Molecules will leave the liquid phase and enter the gas phase. At the same time molecules in the gas phase will condense and reenter the liquid phase. This process does not stop just because the phases are enclosed in a stoppered flask. The rates of evaporation and condensation do not become zero.

When the moisture level of the air above the water is just right, the rates of evaporation and condensation will be exactly equal. This is called *equilibrium.*

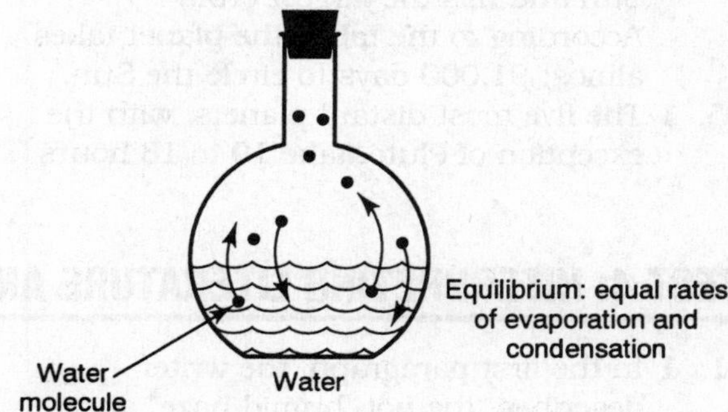

56. 4 At 2 P.M. the temperature inside the greenhouse was 25°C.

57. 2 The temperature inside the greenhouse is dropping at a rate of 1° every 2 hrs. At 8 P.M. it will be 22°C; at 10 P.M., 21°C; and at midnight, 20°C.

58. 3 The selection mentions that red light has a wavelength of more than 6000Å.

59. 5 In order for a particular color to be transmitted, the other colors of the spectrum (here, green and red) must be absorbed.

60. 4 Since the blue rays are absorbed, the green and red rays are transmitted. This gives the yellow appearance mentioned in the closing sentence of the selection.

61. 5 The diagram shows how white light is broken up into its components by a prism. The passage states that red light has the longest wavelength, more than 6000Å. Infrared rays are even longer and, therefore, are not visible to the human eye.

62. 2 The time is irrelevant because power expresses only the rate at which energy is used, not the total amount of energy consumed. Of the choices given, the smallest power consumption is

$$(0.002\text{ A})\ (120\text{ V}) = 0.24\text{ W (watts)}$$

63. 5 Choice 1 is wrong because the electricity is traveling to the bell in wires; air is irrelevant. The movement of the clapper is independent of the air, so Choice 2 is wrong. Choice 3 is wrong because the bell was heard through the glass as long as there was air in the jar. Choice 4 is wrong because the observer's ears are still in air. This leaves only Choice (5), which is the correct explanation.

64. **5** Pluto is the farthest planet from the Sun and has the largest orbit. According to the table, the planet takes almost 91,000 days to circle the Sun.
65. **1** The five most distant planets, with the exception of Pluto, take 10 to 16 hours to rotate on their axes. The four innermost planets take from 24 hrs. to 243 days to rotate once.
66. **2** According to the passage, in order to examine a subatomic particle, you have to change it in some way. The only answer choice that involves a change of that nature is eating a pineapple to learn its taste.

TEST 4: INTERPRETING LITERATURE AND THE ARTS/PAGE 621

1. **1** In the first paragraph, the writer describes "the hot, humid haze" and other details of August in his surroundings.
2. **4** The writer states that "August was a time to do nothing and be proud of it."
3. **2** The writer remembers August "with a bit of anxiety because it "was the time of hurricanes and polio."
4. **3** ". . . I remember the strange feel of the air. The first breezes of the hurricane were so mild, so moist, so soft as to be barely distinguishable from the feel of one's own skin."
5. **3** August is remembered as a time of both pleasure and anxiety. The hurricanes were scary for adults, but they were "a lot of fun" for the narrator.
6. **4** The author states "we'd be lost without" new groups.
7. **2** The family sends a bright young man or woman.
8. **1** Other family members will come with the money the youth is sending back.
9. **3** The newcomer progresses from busboy to waiter and then tries to become the owner.
10. **1** The United States rejuvenates itself by bringing in new people.
11. **1** The heritage of the sequoia can be traced through "its remains in old rocks."
12. **1** Sequoias "have survived the hardships they had to encounter" in their wanderings "from climate to climate."
13. **4** "The Pacific coast in general is the paradise of conifers," and therefore nurturing.
14. **1** "Nevertheless, it is not easy to account for the colossal size of the sequoias." This growth is mysterious.
15. **2** "Who . . . ever dreamed that earth could bear such growths?"
16. **4** The crooked crosses are the poet's metaphorical depiction of television antennas.
17. **3** The poet calls television humor "tired" and criticizes the violence of its programs.
18. **4** The poet will "walk.. /Among neglected precincts of my soul"; that is, he will commune with his own spirit.
19. **1** "As silently as Pharoahs" is a simile.
20. **2** Reference to the television set as "the altar box" and to personal spiritual matters as "precincts of my soul" are metaphors.
21. **2** The poet is reacting to a "fatuous thing" (a photograph of himself) that he has been shown by a photographer.
22. **2** The poet has "spent blood and tears" and experienced "pain, the struggle and the wrack."
23. **1** Time "has graven . . . deep lines of joy and sorrow" on his face.
24. **3** The poet wants his "scars of battle" to be put back into the photograph.
25. **5** The 14-line poem is a sonnet with the rhyme scheme ***a b b a a b b a c d c d e e.***
26. **4** Kay says to Grant, "I won't accept that." Conover says, "I think Kay's right."
27. **1** Grant implies that he won't play ball and states that he will go ahead with his speech.
28. **5** Grant says that "to get votes, both parties are out to buy the American people."

29. 3 Grant promises himself that he would appeal to the best in the American people.

30. 3 Grant says he'll take care of any candidate who threatens peace from now on.

31. 4 See the section "Locating the Main Idea" (page 391). The opening and closing lines refer to the father's devotion to education.

32. 5 *Divined* means "guessed," not "heavenly."

33. 3 The father is described as "not like other aliens, who brought their children in dull obedience to the law . . . ."

34. 3 The author's father is described as "eager," with "nervous hands eloquent in gesture, and a voice full of feeling." He is evidently sincere, but not in the least calm.

35. 5 Here *green* means immigrant, new to the United States.

36. 4 The article states that "no adequate terms to describe these categories [classical and popular] have yet been found."

37. 3 The article cites the Tchaikovsky *Piano Concerto No. 1 for Piano* as having enjoyed great popularity.

38. 1 Besides indicating the inadequacy of the terminology, the article mentions the problems that division into classical and popular creates.

39. 4 The author states that "no single type of music has a monopoly on worth."

40. 5 The passage says that distinctions between classical and popular music leads to inappropriate implications of value.

41. 3 The author states that "there is a wholeness in a play which neither the movies nor TV offers."

42. 3 The author states that the three media "may fertilize one another."

43. 5 The author states that Hollywood (the movies) and Madison (TV) Avenue exploit Broadway (the theater).

44. 4 The author feels that "some of the people" reached by the movies and TV "may lack sensibility."

45. 5 The author concludes that "no great theater is possible . . . unless the people consider it a great art."

TEST 5: MATHEMATICS/PAGE 631

1. 3 Luisa earned a total of 40($6.30) = $252. To find the number of hours Joan would take to earn $252, divide $252 by $8.40:
$252.00 \div 8.40 = 30$

2. 3 Since $m\angle ACB = 90°$ and $m\angle CAD = 40°$, then $m\angle B = 180° - 90° - 40° = 50°$.
In $\triangle BCD$, $m\angle CDB = 90°$ and $m\angle B = 50°$.
Therefore,
$m\angle DCB = 180° - 90° - 50° = 40°$.

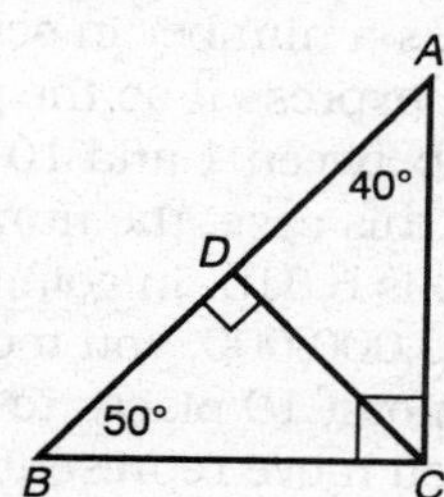

3. 5 If the class has x students and 5 students are absent, then $x - 5$ students are present:
$\frac{x-5}{x}$

4. 2 If the tank is $\frac{1}{3}$ full, it is $\frac{2}{3}$ empty.
Let x = capacity of tank.
$\frac{2}{3}x = 16$, so $x = 16 \div \frac{2}{3} = 16 \times \frac{3}{2} = 24$.

5. 3 Let x = length of ramp.
Use the Pythagorean theorem to obtain the equation:
$x^2 = 12^2 + 16^2 = 144 + 256 = 400$
$x = \sqrt{400} = 20$

6. **3** 48 half-pints = 24 pt.
Since 2 pt. = 1 qt.,
24 pt. = 12 qt.
Since 4 qt. = 1 gal.,
12 qt. = 3 gal.
3($3.50) = $10.50

7. **5** You do not need the value of x, you need the value of $2\frac{1}{2}x = \frac{5}{2}x = \frac{5x}{2}$.
Since $5x - 1 = 34$, then $5x = 35$, and
$\frac{5x}{2} = \frac{35}{2} = 17\frac{1}{2}$.

8. **4** If $AC = 18$ and $BC = 8$ then
$AB = 18 - 8 = 10$.
The ratio $AB{:}BC = 10{:}8$, or $5{:}4$.

A 10 B 8 C

9. **5** Let x = width of room.
$23x = 322$
$x = 332 \div 23 = 14$
Perimeter =
$23 + 14 + 23 + 14 = 74$ ft.

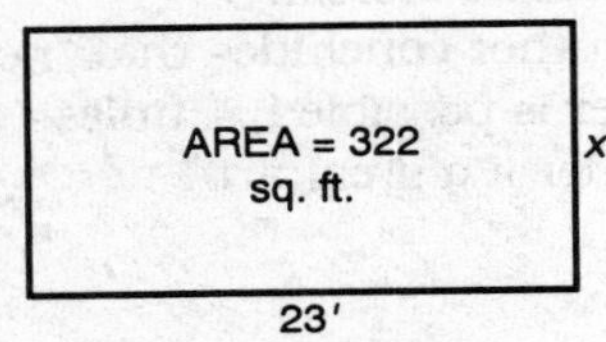

10. **5** To determine the price that the ABC Store charges for the TV set, Don must know the price from which the store deducts 20%.

11. **2** If a crew can load a truck in 3 hr., it can load $\frac{1}{3}$ of the truck in 1 hr. In 45 min., or $\frac{3}{4}$ hr., the crew can load $\frac{3}{4} \times \frac{1}{3} = \frac{1}{4}$ of the truck.

12. **2** $x^2 + x - 6 = 0$
$(x + 3)(x - 2) = 0$
$x + 3 = 0$ or $x - 2 = 0$
$x = -3$ or $x = 2$
The correct choice is (2).

13. **3** To find the perimeter of the figure, find the sum of the lengths of its sides.
$2a + a + b + 2a + b + a + 2b = 6a + 4b$

14. **4** Let x = amount of money Bob has. Then x is also the amount that Tom has, and $x + 5$ = amount that Henry has.
Since $65 = x + x + x + 5 = 3x + 5$,
then $3x = 60$, and $x = \$20$.

15. **5** You cannot compute the cost unless you are told the number of days that the couple stays at the motel. This information is not given.

16. **3** Let n = number.
Then n^2 = square of number,
and $n + 4$ = number increased by 4.
The equation is $n^2 + n + 4 = 60$.

17. **2** Because the coupon has double value, the reduction is 2(15¢) = 30 cents.
The cost of the cereal is $x - 30$.

18. **5** Let x, $2x$, and $3x$ be the measures of the three angles. Then
$3x + 2x + x = 180$
$6x = 180$
$x = 180 \div 6 = 30$
$3x = 3(30) = 90°$

19. **4** Let $x = m\angle 3$,
and $2x = m\angle 2$.
$m\angle 1 + m\angle 2 + m\angle 3 = 180°$
$36 + 2x + x = 180$
$3x + 36 = 180$
$3x = 180 - 36 = 144$
$x = 144 \div 3 = 48°$

20. **3** The beef costs 4($2.76) = $11.04.
The chicken costs $13.98 – $11.04 = $2.94.
To find the cost per pound of chicken, divide $2.94 by $3\frac{1}{2}$, or by $\frac{7}{2}$.
$2.94 \div \frac{7}{2} = 2.94 \times \frac{2}{7} = 0.84$
The chicken cost $0.84 per pound.

21. **5** The carpenter earns $16 per hour or 9(16) dollars for 9 hrs. of work.
The assistant earns $8 per hour or 9(8) for 9 hrs. of work.
Together they earned 9(16) + 9(8) dollars.

22. **4** To express a number in scientific notation, express it as the product of a number between 1 and 10 and a power of 10. In this case, the number between 1 and 10 is 6.315. In going from 6.315 to 63,150,000,000, you move the decimal point 10 places to the right. Each such move represents a multiplication by 10. Thus, the entire movement of the decimal point

represents multiplication by 10^{10}, and, $63{,}150{,}000{,}000 = 6.315 \times 10^{10}$.

23. **1** Of the 26 students in the class, 7 are absent and 19 are present. Of those present, 9 are girls, so the probability that a girl is called is $\frac{9}{19}$.

24. **3** $\$12{,}000 \times 0.09 = \$1{,}080$

25. **1** $3x + 2 < 14$
$3x < 12$
$x < 4$
The only choice less than 4 is 3.

26. **5** Add the amounts given:
$11 + 6 + 5 + 40 + 30 = \$92$
$\$100 - \$92$ leaves $8 for profit.

27. **4** Let y = amount John saves in 9 months, and set up a proportion:
$\frac{5}{659} = \frac{9}{y}$
$5y = 9(659)$ and $y = \frac{9(659)}{5}$

28. **3** Let x = number of points scored by Jack,
$x + 7$ = number of points scored by Ben, and
$x - 2$ = number of points scored by Paul.
$x + x + 7 + x - 2 = 38$
$3x + 5 = 38$
$3x = 38 - 5 = 33$
$x = 33 \div 3 = 11$

29. **3** Use the formula $V = lwh$.
In this case, $l = 5$, $w = 5$, and $h = h$.
Therefore, $V = 5 \times 5 \times h = 25h$ and $25h = 200$.

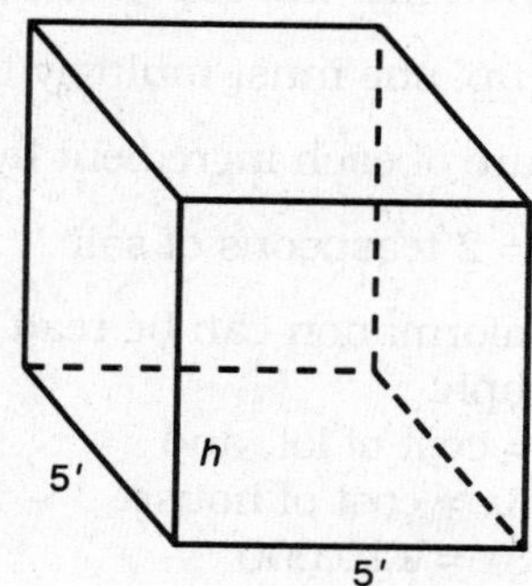

30. **4** Since $3^2 = 9$ and $4^2 = 16$, $\sqrt{12}$ is between 3 and 4. Only point D lies between 3 and 4.

31. **4** Divide the floor space into 2 rectangles by drawing line segment NM.
Area of a rectangle = lw
Area of large rectangle =
$20 \times 15 = 300$ sq. ft.
Area of small rectangle =
$10 \times 15 = 150$ sq. ft.
Total area of floor space =
$150 + 300 = 450$ sq. ft.
Since 9 sq. ft. = 1 sq. yd.,
450 sq. ft. = $450 \div 9 = 50$ sq. yd.

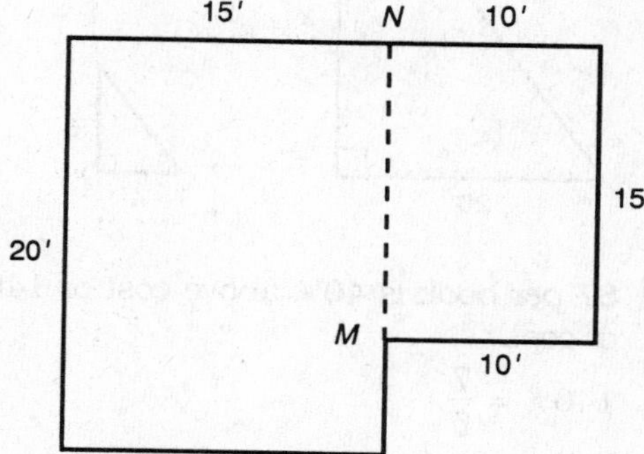

32. **3** If you don't see that you need to divide y by x, set up a proportion.
Let z = number of dollars needed to purchase y francs. Then:
$\frac{\text{dollars}}{\text{francs}}: \frac{1}{x} = \frac{z}{y}$.
Multiply both sides by y to get $z = \frac{y}{x}$.

33. **4** Foreign investment in manufacturing = $\$2\frac{1}{2}$ billion
Foreign investment in petroleum = $1 billion
Difference = $\$1\frac{1}{2}$ billion

34. **4** The equation $x + y = 7$ states that the sum of two numbers is 7. Since the value of y is 3, then $x + 3 = 7$ and $x = 4$.

35. **5** Since $\frac{1}{4}$ in. represents 8 mi., 1 in., represents $4 \times 8 = 32$ mi., and 2 in. represents $2 \times 32 = 64$ mi. $\frac{1}{8}$ in. $= \frac{1}{2}$ of $\frac{1}{4}$ in., so $\frac{1}{8}$ in. represents 4 mi. Then $2\frac{1}{8}$ in. represent $64 + 4 = 68$ mi.

36. 3 Let x = height of steeple. Set up a proportion:

$$\frac{\text{height of object}}{\text{length of shadow}}: \frac{x}{28} = \frac{6}{4}$$

$4x = 6(28) = 168$

$x = 168 \div 4 = 42$ ft.

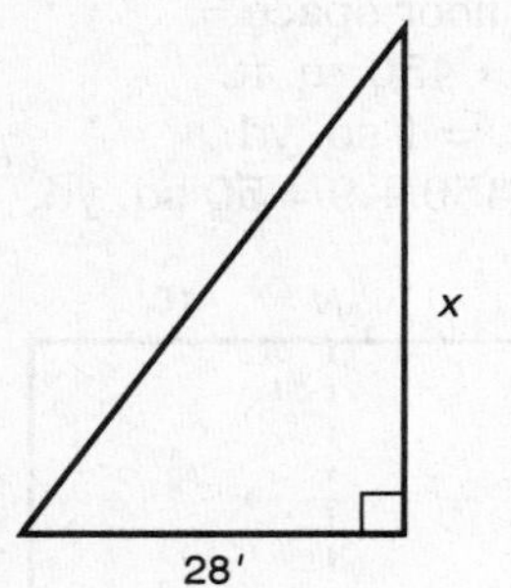

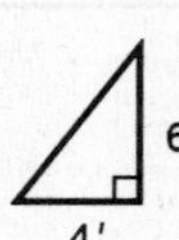

37. 1 $7 per book is 40% above cost or 140% of cost.

$140\% = \frac{7}{5}$.

Let x = dealer's cost per book.

$\frac{7}{5}x = 7$

$7x = 7(5) = 35$

$x = 35 \div 7 = 5$

Dealer's cost is $5 per book.

Six dozen books = $6 \times 12 = 72$ books

$\$5 \times 72 = \$360$, cost of books

38. 4 To find the distance between two points on the same vertical line, subtract their y-coordinates: $4 - (-3) = 4 + 3 = 7$.

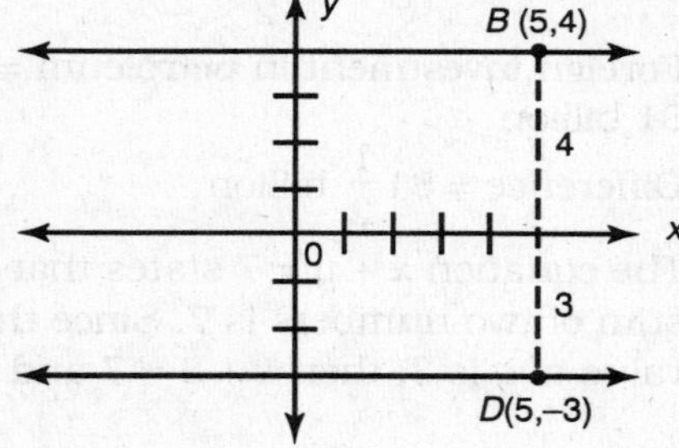

39. 3 $6 \times 10^5 = 600{,}000$

$4 \times 10^3 = 4{,}000$

$600{,}000 \div 4{,}000 = 600 \div 4 = 150$

40. 5 Slope = $\frac{y_1 - y_2}{x_1 - x_2}$

In this case, $y_1 = y$, $y_2 = 2$, $x_1 = 4$, and $x_2 = 1$.

Therefore, $\frac{y-2}{4-1} = 1$

$\frac{y-2}{3} = 1$

$y - 2 = 3$

$y = 3 + 2 = 5$

41. 4 The top of the bar for Wednesday is at 6 on the vertical scale.

42. 5 The top of the bar for Monday is halfway between 4 and 6, so 5 gal. were sold on Monday. The top of the bar for Saturday is halfway between 16 and 18, so 17 gal. were sold on Saturday. The difference between 17 gal. and 5 gal. is 12 gal.

43. 4 The tops of the bars for Monday through Sunday are at 5, 4, 6, 5, 14, 17, and 9. These add up to 60.

44. 1 Let $x = m\angle OAB$

$OA = OB$ since radii of the same circle have equal measures.

Therefore, $m\angle OAB = m\angle OBA$:

$x + x + 70 = 180$

$2x + 70 = 180$

$2x = 180 - 70 = 110$

$x = 110 \div 2 = 55$

45. 3 Between 3:00 P.M. and 4:00 P.M., Sylvia drove $124 - 80 = 44$ mi. Since she was driving at a steady rate for the entire trip, in the $\frac{1}{4}$ hr. from 4:00 to 4:15 she drove another $\frac{1}{4}(44) = 11$ mi.

Therefore, at 4:15 P.M. she had driven $124 + 11 = 135$ mi.

46. 2 If Joan uses a full cup of milk instead of $\frac{1}{3}$ cup, she must multiply the measure of each ingredient by 3.

$3\left(\frac{2}{3}\right) = 2$ teaspoons of salt

47. 4 This information can be read directly on the graph.

48. 4 Let x = cost of lot, and

$3x$ = cost of house.

$x + 3x = 120{,}000$

$4x = 120{,}000$

$x = 120{,}000 \div 4 = 30{,}000$

$3x = 3(30{,}000) = \$90{,}000$

49. **5** Let x = number of books on small shelf, and $x + 8$ = number of books on large shelf. Then $4x$ = number of books on 4 small shelves; and $3(x + 8)$ = number of books on 3 large shelves.

$$4x + 3(x + 8) = 297$$
$$4x + 3x + 24 = 297$$
$$7x + 24 = 297$$
$$7x = 297 - 24 = 273$$
$$x = 273 \div 7 = 39$$

50. **2** Radius of outer circle = $\frac{1}{2}(48) = 24$ in.
Radius of inner circle = 20 in.
Use the formula $A = \pi r^2$.
Area of outer circle =
$\pi \times 24 \times 24 = 576\pi$
Area of inner circle =
$\pi \times 20 \times 20 = 400\pi$
Area of border = $576\pi - 400\pi = 176\pi$

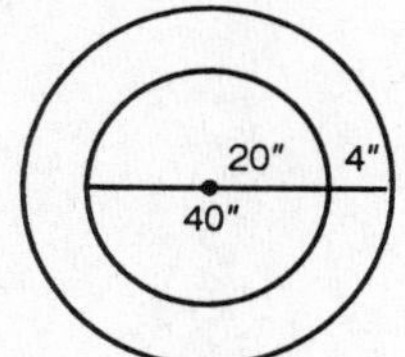

51. **1** 40 ft. = $40 \times 12 = 480$ in.
3 ft. 4 in. = $3(12) + 4 = 36 + 4 = 40$ in.
$480 \div 40 = 12$ scarfs

52. **3** Chapter 20 (Geometry, Areas)
To obtain the area of the shaded portion, find the area of the square and subtract from it the sum of the areas of the 4 quarter circles.

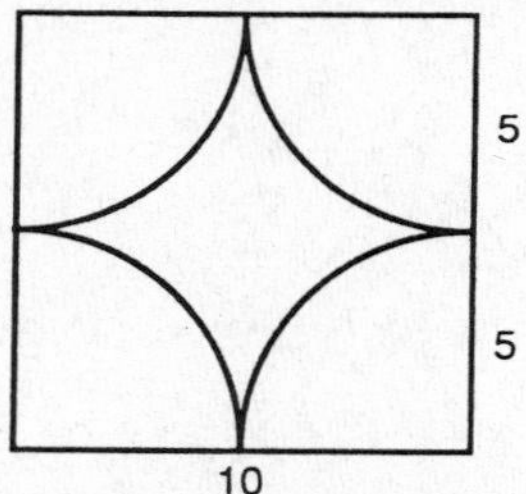

Area of the square = $10 \times 10 = 100$
Area of 4 quarter circles is equal to area of 1 complete circle of radius 5.
$\pi \times 5 \times 5 = 25\pi$.
Area of the shaded portion is
$100 - 25\pi$.

53. **5** In the figure below, the four obtuse angles all have the same measure, and the four acute angles also have the same measure:

$$a = d = e = g \quad b = c = f = h$$

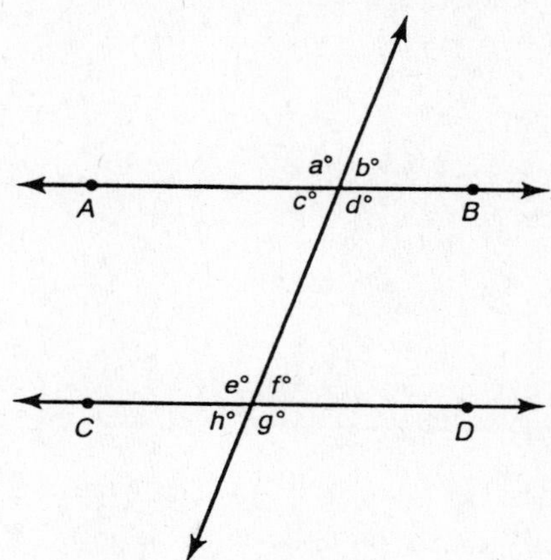

Checking the choices, you see that they are all correct except (5): $b \neq g$

54. **1** $A + B + C = 180$
Since $A = B$, you may write
$B + B + C = 180$
Since $B = 2C$, you may write
$$2C + 2C + C = 180$$
$$5C = 180$$
$$C = 180 \div 5 = 36$$

55. **2** 6 oz. = $\frac{6}{16} = \frac{3}{8}$ lb.

4 oz. = $\frac{4}{16} = \frac{1}{4}$ lb.

2 lb. of apples cost 2($0.72)	= $1.44
$\frac{3}{8}$ lb. of apples cost $\frac{3}{8}$($0.72)	= $0.27
3 lb. of peaches cost 3($0.56)	= $1.68
$\frac{1}{4}$ lb. of peaches costs $\frac{1}{4}$($0.56)	= $0.14
Total cost	$3.53
Change: $5.00 – $3.53	= $1.47

56. **5** 15 dozen = $15 \times 12 = 180$
Form the proportion:
$$\frac{6}{180} = \frac{39}{x}$$
$$6x = 39(180) = 7{,}020$$
$$x = 7{,}020 \div 6 = \$1{,}170$$

Answer Sheet for the Practice Examination

TEST 1: WRITING SKILLS, PART I

1. ① ② ③ ④ ⑤
2. ① ② ③ ④ ⑤
3. ① ② ③ ④ ⑤
4. ① ② ③ ④ ⑤
5. ① ② ③ ④ ⑤
6. ① ② ③ ④ ⑤
7. ① ② ③ ④ ⑤
8. ① ② ③ ④ ⑤
9. ① ② ③ ④ ⑤
10. ① ② ③ ④ ⑤
11. ① ② ③ ④ ⑤
12. ① ② ③ ④ ⑤
13. ① ② ③ ④ ⑤
14. ① ② ③ ④ ⑤
15. ① ② ③ ④ ⑤
16. ① ② ③ ④ ⑤
17. ① ② ③ ④ ⑤
18. ① ② ③ ④ ⑤
19. ① ② ③ ④ ⑤
20. ① ② ③ ④ ⑤
21. ① ② ③ ④ ⑤
22. ① ② ③ ④ ⑤
23. ① ② ③ ④ ⑤
24. ① ② ③ ④ ⑤
25. ① ② ③ ④ ⑤
26. ① ② ③ ④ ⑤
27. ① ② ③ ④ ⑤
28. ① ② ③ ④ ⑤
29. ① ② ③ ④ ⑤
30. ① ② ③ ④ ⑤
31. ① ② ③ ④ ⑤
32. ① ② ③ ④ ⑤
33. ① ② ③ ④ ⑤
34. ① ② ③ ④ ⑤
35. ① ② ③ ④ ⑤
36. ① ② ③ ④ ⑤
37. ① ② ③ ④ ⑤
38. ① ② ③ ④ ⑤
39. ① ② ③ ④ ⑤
40. ① ② ③ ④ ⑤
41. ① ② ③ ④ ⑤
42. ① ② ③ ④ ⑤
43. ① ② ③ ④ ⑤
44. ① ② ③ ④ ⑤
45. ① ② ③ ④ ⑤
46. ① ② ③ ④ ⑤
47. ① ② ③ ④ ⑤
48. ① ② ③ ④ ⑤
49. ① ② ③ ④ ⑤
50. ① ② ③ ④ ⑤
51. ① ② ③ ④ ⑤
52. ① ② ③ ④ ⑤
53. ① ② ③ ④ ⑤
54. ① ② ③ ④ ⑤
55. ① ② ③ ④ ⑤

TEST 2: SOCIAL STUDIES

1. ① ② ③ ④ ⑤
2. ① ② ③ ④ ⑤
3. ① ② ③ ④ ⑤
4. ① ② ③ ④ ⑤
5. ① ② ③ ④ ⑤
6. ① ② ③ ④ ⑤
7. ① ② ③ ④ ⑤
8. ① ② ③ ④ ⑤
9. ① ② ③ ④ ⑤
10. ① ② ③ ④ ⑤
11. ① ② ③ ④ ⑤
12. ① ② ③ ④ ⑤
13. ① ② ③ ④ ⑤
14. ① ② ③ ④ ⑤
15. ① ② ③ ④ ⑤
16. ① ② ③ ④ ⑤
17. ① ② ③ ④ ⑤
18. ① ② ③ ④ ⑤
19. ① ② ③ ④ ⑤
20. ① ② ③ ④ ⑤
21. ① ② ③ ④ ⑤
22. ① ② ③ ④ ⑤
23. ① ② ③ ④ ⑤
24. ① ② ③ ④ ⑤
25. ① ② ③ ④ ⑤
26. ① ② ③ ④ ⑤
27. ① ② ③ ④ ⑤
28. ① ② ③ ④ ⑤
29. ① ② ③ ④ ⑤
30. ① ② ③ ④ ⑤
31. ① ② ③ ④ ⑤
32. ① ② ③ ④ ⑤
33. ① ② ③ ④ ⑤
34. ① ② ③ ④ ⑤
35. ① ② ③ ④ ⑤
36. ① ② ③ ④ ⑤
37. ① ② ③ ④ ⑤
38. ① ② ③ ④ ⑤
39. ① ② ③ ④ ⑤
40. ① ② ③ ④ ⑤
41. ① ② ③ ④ ⑤
42. ① ② ③ ④ ⑤
43. ① ② ③ ④ ⑤
44. ① ② ③ ④ ⑤
45. ① ② ③ ④ ⑤
46. ① ② ③ ④ ⑤
47. ① ② ③ ④ ⑤
48. ① ② ③ ④ ⑤
49. ① ② ③ ④ ⑤
50. ① ② ③ ④ ⑤
51. ① ② ③ ④ ⑤
52. ① ② ③ ④ ⑤
53. ① ② ③ ④ ⑤
54. ① ② ③ ④ ⑤
55. ① ② ③ ④ ⑤
56. ① ② ③ ④ ⑤
57. ① ② ③ ④ ⑤
58. ① ② ③ ④ ⑤
59. ① ② ③ ④ ⑤
60. ① ② ③ ④ ⑤
61. ① ② ③ ④ ⑤
62. ① ② ③ ④ ⑤
63. ① ② ③ ④ ⑤
64. ① ② ③ ④ ⑤

TEST 3: SCIENCE

1. ① ② ③ ④ ⑤
2. ① ② ③ ④ ⑤
3. ① ② ③ ④ ⑤
4. ① ② ③ ④ ⑤
5. ① ② ③ ④ ⑤
6. ① ② ③ ④ ⑤
7. ① ② ③ ④ ⑤
8. ① ② ③ ④ ⑤
9. ① ② ③ ④ ⑤
10. ① ② ③ ④ ⑤
11. ① ② ③ ④ ⑤
12. ① ② ③ ④ ⑤
13. ① ② ③ ④ ⑤
14. ① ② ③ ④ ⑤
15. ① ② ③ ④ ⑤
16. ① ② ③ ④ ⑤
17. ① ② ③ ④ ⑤
18. ① ② ③ ④ ⑤
19. ① ② ③ ④ ⑤
20. ① ② ③ ④ ⑤
21. ① ② ③ ④ ⑤
22. ① ② ③ ④ ⑤
23. ① ② ③ ④ ⑤
24. ① ② ③ ④ ⑤
25. ① ② ③ ④ ⑤
26. ① ② ③ ④ ⑤
27. ① ② ③ ④ ⑤
28. ① ② ③ ④ ⑤
29. ① ② ③ ④ ⑤
30. ① ② ③ ④ ⑤
31. ① ② ③ ④ ⑤
32. ① ② ③ ④ ⑤
33. ① ② ③ ④ ⑤
34. ① ② ③ ④ ⑤
35. ① ② ③ ④ ⑤
36. ① ② ③ ④ ⑤
37. ① ② ③ ④ ⑤
38. ① ② ③ ④ ⑤
39. ① ② ③ ④ ⑤
40. ① ② ③ ④ ⑤
41. ① ② ③ ④ ⑤
42. ① ② ③ ④ ⑤
43. ① ② ③ ④ ⑤
44. ① ② ③ ④ ⑤
45. ① ② ③ ④ ⑤
46. ① ② ③ ④ ⑤
47. ① ② ③ ④ ⑤
48. ① ② ③ ④ ⑤
49. ① ② ③ ④ ⑤
50. ① ② ③ ④ ⑤
51. ① ② ③ ④ ⑤
52. ① ② ③ ④ ⑤
53. ① ② ③ ④ ⑤
54. ① ② ③ ④ ⑤
55. ① ② ③ ④ ⑤
56. ① ② ③ ④ ⑤
57. ① ② ③ ④ ⑤
58. ① ② ③ ④ ⑤
59. ① ② ③ ④ ⑤
60. ① ② ③ ④ ⑤
61. ① ② ③ ④ ⑤
62. ① ② ③ ④ ⑤
63. ① ② ③ ④ ⑤
64. ① ② ③ ④ ⑤
65. ① ② ③ ④ ⑤
66. ① ② ③ ④ ⑤

TEST 4: INTERPRETING LITERATURE AND THE ARTS

1. ① ② ③ ④ ⑤
2. ① ② ③ ④ ⑤
3. ① ② ③ ④ ⑤
4. ① ② ③ ④ ⑤
5. ① ② ③ ④ ⑤
6. ① ② ③ ④ ⑤
7. ① ② ③ ④ ⑤
8. ① ② ③ ④ ⑤
9. ① ② ③ ④ ⑤
10. ① ② ③ ④ ⑤
11. ① ② ③ ④ ⑤
12. ① ② ③ ④ ⑤
13. ① ② ③ ④ ⑤
14. ① ② ③ ④ ⑤
15. ① ② ③ ④ ⑤
16. ① ② ③ ④ ⑤
17. ① ② ③ ④ ⑤
18. ① ② ③ ④ ⑤
19. ① ② ③ ④ ⑤
20. ① ② ③ ④ ⑤
21. ① ② ③ ④ ⑤
22. ① ② ③ ④ ⑤
23. ① ② ③ ④ ⑤
24. ① ② ③ ④ ⑤
25. ① ② ③ ④ ⑤
26. ① ② ③ ④ ⑤
27. ① ② ③ ④ ⑤
28. ① ② ③ ④ ⑤
29. ① ② ③ ④ ⑤
30. ① ② ③ ④ ⑤
31. ① ② ③ ④ ⑤
32. ① ② ③ ④ ⑤
33. ① ② ③ ④ ⑤
34. ① ② ③ ④ ⑤
35. ① ② ③ ④ ⑤
36. ① ② ③ ④ ⑤
37. ① ② ③ ④ ⑤
38. ① ② ③ ④ ⑤
39. ① ② ③ ④ ⑤
40. ① ② ③ ④ ⑤
41. ① ② ③ ④ ⑤
42. ① ② ③ ④ ⑤
43. ① ② ③ ④ ⑤
44. ① ② ③ ④ ⑤
45. ① ② ③ ④ ⑤

TEST 5: MATHEMATICS

1. ① ② ③ ④ ⑤
2. ① ② ③ ④ ⑤
3. ① ② ③ ④ ⑤
4. ① ② ③ ④ ⑤
5. ① ② ③ ④ ⑤
6. ① ② ③ ④ ⑤
7. ① ② ③ ④ ⑤
8. ① ② ③ ④ ⑤
9. ① ② ③ ④ ⑤
10. ① ② ③ ④ ⑤
11. ① ② ③ ④ ⑤
12. ① ② ③ ④ ⑤
13. ① ② ③ ④ ⑤
14. ① ② ③ ④ ⑤
15. ① ② ③ ④ ⑤
16. ① ② ③ ④ ⑤
17. ① ② ③ ④ ⑤
18. ① ② ③ ④ ⑤
19. ① ② ③ ④ ⑤
20. ① ② ③ ④ ⑤
21. ① ② ③ ④ ⑤
22. ① ② ③ ④ ⑤
23. ① ② ③ ④ ⑤
24. ① ② ③ ④ ⑤
25. ① ② ③ ④ ⑤
26. ① ② ③ ④ ⑤
27. ① ② ③ ④ ⑤
28. ① ② ③ ④ ⑤
29. ① ② ③ ④ ⑤
30. ① ② ③ ④ ⑤
31. ① ② ③ ④ ⑤
32. ① ② ③ ④ ⑤
33. ① ② ③ ④ ⑤
34. ① ② ③ ④ ⑤
35. ① ② ③ ④ ⑤
36. ① ② ③ ④ ⑤
37. ① ② ③ ④ ⑤
38. ① ② ③ ④ ⑤
39. ① ② ③ ④ ⑤
40. ① ② ③ ④ ⑤
41. ① ② ③ ④ ⑤
42. ① ② ③ ④ ⑤
43. ① ② ③ ④ ⑤
44. ① ② ③ ④ ⑤
45. ① ② ③ ④ ⑤
46. ① ② ③ ④ ⑤
47. ① ② ③ ④ ⑤
48. ① ② ③ ④ ⑤
49. ① ② ③ ④ ⑤
50. ① ② ③ ④ ⑤
51. ① ② ③ ④ ⑤
52. ① ② ③ ④ ⑤
53. ① ② ③ ④ ⑤
54. ① ② ③ ④ ⑤
55. ① ② ③ ④ ⑤
56. ① ② ③ ④ ⑤

PRACTICE EXAMINATION TWO

TEST 1: WRITING SKILLS, PART I

Directions

The Writing Skills test is intended to measure your ability to use clear and effective English. It is a test of English as it should be written, not as it might be spoken. This test includes both multiple-choice questions and an essay. These directions apply only to the multiple-choice section; a separate set of directions is given for the essay.

The multiple-choice section consists of paragraphs with numbered sentences. Some of the sentences contain errors in sentence structure, usage, or mechanics (spelling, punctuation, and capitalization). After reading the numbered sentences, answer the multiple-choice questions that follow. Some questions refer to sentences that are correct as written. The best answer for these questions is the one that leaves the sentence as originally written. The best answer for some questions is the one that produces a sentence that is consistent with the verb tense and point of view used throughout the paragraph.

You should spend no more than 75 minutes on the multiple-choice questions and 45 minutes on your essay. Work carefully, but do not spend too much time on any one question. You may begin working on the essay part of this test as soon as you complete the multiple-choice section.

To record your answers, mark the numbered space on the answer sheet beside the number that corresponds to the question in the test.

FOR EXAMPLE:

Sentence 1: **We were all honored to meet governor Phillips.**

What correction should be made to this sentence?

(1) insert a comma after honored
(2) change the spelling of honored to honered
(3) change governor to Governor
(4) replace were with was
(5) no correction is necessary

① ② ● ④ ⑤

In this example, the word "governor" should be capitalized; therefore, answer space 3 would be marked on the answer sheet.

GO ON TO THE NEXT PAGE

TEST 1: WRITING SKILLS, PART I

Questions 1–10 refer to the following paragraphs.

(1) Each year more young men and young women are recognizing the rewards in nursing and enroll in nursing programs, but the demand for nurses continues to outstrip the supply.

(2) If you join the personnel of a hospital you can choose among absorbing fields. (3) You can concentrate on work with children, in obstetrics, in surgery, or on the fascinating new techniques of orthopedics, which calls so heavily for a nurse's skill and imagination.

(4) Since Florence Nightingale went to the crimea over a hundred years ago, nurses have been an enormously mobile group. (5) If one wants to travel, many posts are open to you, both in this country and abroad. (6) You can choose foreign service with the World Health Organization, with our own goverment's foreign operations or with one of our armed services.

(7) Schools need nurses. (8) Many married nurses who want time in the afternoon with their own children find part-time positions ideal and easy to get. (9) Private practice brings its special rewards in choice of hours and cases.

(10) Opportunities in community and public health programs that require a bachelor's degree from an accredited school are growing rapidly. (11) A visiting nurse has a fascinating career, moving through many homes each day and leaving order and comfort behind.

1. Sentence 1: **Each year more young men and young women are recognizing the rewards in nursing and enroll in nursing programs, but the demand for nurses continues to outstrip the supply.**

   What correction should be made to this sentence?

   (1) change the spelling of recognizing to reconizing
   (2) change enroll to are enrolling
   (3) remove the comma before but
   (4) change but to and
   (5) no correction is necessary

2. Sentence 2: **If you join the personnel of a hospital you can choose among absorbing fields.**

   What correction should be made to this sentence?

   (1) change join to will join
   (2) change the spelling of personnel to personel
   (3) insert a comma after hospital
   (4) change the spelling of choose to chose
   (5) no correction is necessary

3. Sentence 3: **You can concentrate on work with children, in obstetrics, in surgery, or on the fascinating new techniques of orthopedics, which calls so heavily for a nurse's skill and imagination.**

   What correction should be made to this sentence?

   (1) change the spelling of concentrate to consentrate
   (2) change the spelling of children to childern
   (3) remove the comma after surgery
   (4) change calls to call
   (5) no correction is necessary

4. Sentence 4: **Since Florence Nightingale went to the crimea over a hundred years ago, nurses have been an enormously mobile group.**

   What correction should be made to this sentence?

   (1) change went to had gone
   (2) capitalize crimea
   (3) remove the comma after ago
   (4) change the spelling of enormously to enormusly
   (5) no correction is necessary

GO ON TO THE NEXT PAGE

TEST 1: WRITING SKILLS, PART I

5. Sentence 5: **If one wants to travel, many posts are available to you, both in this country and abroad.**

What correction should be made to this sentence?

(1) change one wants to you want
(2) remove the comma after travel
(3) change the spelling of available to availible
(4) remove the comma after you
(5) no correction is necessary

6. Sentence 6: **You can choose foreign service with the World Health Organization, with our own goverment's foreign operations, or with one of our armed services.**

What correction should be made to this sentence?

(1) change the spelling of foreign to forign
(2) remove the capitals from World Health Organization
(3) remove the comma after Organization
(4) change the spelling of goverment's to government's
(5) no correction is necessary

7. Sentences 7 and 8: **Schools need nurses. Many married nurses who want time in the afternoon with their own children find part-time positions ideal and easy to get.**

The most effective combination of sentences 7 and 8 would include which of the following groups of words?

(1) nurses although many
(2) nurses because many
(3) nurses if many
(4) nurses since many
(5) nurses, so many

8. Sentence 9: **Private practice brings its special rewards in choice of hours and cases.**

What correction should be made to this sentence?

(1) change the spelling of practice to practise
(2) change its to it's
(3) change the spelling of special to speshal
(4) insert a comma after rewards
(5) no correction is necessary

9. Sentence 10: **Opportunities in community and public health programs that require a bachelor's degree from an accredited school are growing rapidly.**

Which of the following is the best way to write the underlined portion of this sentence? If you think the original is the best way, choose option (1).

(1) programs that require
(2) programs who require
(3) programs that do require
(4) programs that are requiring
(5) programs that will require

10. Sentence 11: **A visiting nurse has a fascinating career, moving through many homes each day and leaving order and comfort behind.**

What correction should be made to this sentence?

(1) change the spelling of fascinating to fasinating
(2) remove the comma after career
(3) change the spelling of through to thorough
(4) insert a comma after order
(5) no correction is necessary

GO ON TO THE NEXT PAGE

TEST 1: WRITING SKILLS, PART I

Questions 11 to 19 refer to the following paragraphs.

(1) Nutritional food buying emphasizes the "Basic Four". (2) Backpacking also has its basic four, these being, in order of importance, hiking shoes, the backpack, sleeping gear, and shelter.

(3) Selection of hiking shoes should be your first concern. (4) Even a one-day hike can be misery without comfortable shoes.

(5) Today's hikers prefer a shoe that is six inches high, is made of leather, and thick sturdy composition soles. (6) Break the shoes in thoroughly on short walks before going on any extended hike.

(7) When purchasing a backpack, you will find an almost bewildering array of makes, styles, and materiels to choose from. (8) The backpacking frame must have both shoulder straps and a waist strap. The latter strap being of such design as to permit much of the weight of the pack to rest on the sturdy hip bones rather than on the more fragile shoulder bones.

(9) The sleeping bag and its two accessories (ground cloth and mattress) are next on the list of basics.

(10) The fourth and last of the basic four is the tent or other emergency shelter. (11) An inexpensive shelter is the plastic tube tent.

11. Sentence 1: **Nutritional food buying emphasizes the "Basic Four".**

    What correction should be made to this sentence?

    (1) insert a hyphen in food buying
    (2) change emphasizes to emphasize
    (3) remove the capital from Four
    (4) place the period within the quotation marks
    (5) no correction is necessary

12. Sentence 2: **Backpacking also has its basic four, these being, in order of importance, hiking shoes, the backpack, sleeping gear, and shelter.**

    What correction should be made to this sentence?

    (1) change its to it's
    (2) change the colon to a semicolon
    (3) change being to are
    (4) remove the comma after gear
    (5) no correction is necessary

13. Sentences 3 and 4: **Selection of hiking shoes should be your first concern. Even a one-day hike can be misery without comfortable shoes.**

    The most effective combination of sentences 3 and 4 would include which of the following groups of words?

    (1) concern, also even
    (2) concern, although even
    (3) concern, because even
    (4) concern, if even
    (5) concern, whereas even

14. Sentence 5: **Today's hikers prefer a shoe that is six inches high, is made of leather, and thick sturdy composition soles.**

    What correction should be made to this sentence?

    (1) remove the apostrophe from today's
    (2) insert a comma after shoe
    (3) remove the comma after high
    (4) insert has before thick
    (5) no correction is necessary

GO ON TO THE NEXT PAGE

TEST 1: WRITING SKILLS, PART I

15. Sentence 6: **Break the shoes in thoroughly on short walks before going on any extended hike.**

    Which of the following is the best way to write the underlined portion of this sentence? If you think the original is the best way, choose option (1).

    (1) walks before
    (2) walks, before
    (3) walks: before
    (4) walks. before
    (5) walks. Before

16. Sentence 7: **When purchasing a backpack, you will find an almost bewildering array of makes, styles, and materiels to choose from.**

    What correction should be made to this sentence?

    (1) remove the comma after backpack
    (2) change the spelling of almost to allmost
    (3) remove the comma after makes
    (4) change the spelling of materiels to materials
    (5) no correction is necessary

17. Sentence 8: **The backpacking frame must have both shoulder straps and a waist strap. The latter strap being of such design as to permit much of the weight of the pack to rest on the sturdy hip bones rather than on the more fragile shoulder bones.**

    Which of the following is the best way to write the underlined portion of these sentences? If you think the original is the best way, choose option (1).

    (1) strap. The
    (2) strap. the
    (3) strap, The
    (4) strap, the
    (5) strap: the

18. Sentence 9: **The sleeping bag and its two accessories (ground cloth and mattress) are next on the list of basics.**

    If you rewrote sentence 9 beginning with

    Next on the list of basics

    the next word(s) should be

    (1) the sleeping bag
    (2) its two accessories
    (3) ground cloth and mattress
    (4) are
    (5) is

19. Sentences 10 and 11: **The fourth and last of the basic four is the tent or other emergency shelter. An inexpensive shelter is the plastic tube tent.**

    The most effective combination of sentences 10 and 11 would include which of the following groups of words?

    (1) shelter of which an inexpensive shelter is
    (2) shelter such as the inexpensive plastic tube tent
    (3) shelter whose inexpensive shelter is
    (4) shelter: an inexpensive shelter is
    (5) shelter; an inexpensive shelter is

Questions 20 to 27 refer to the following paragraphs.

(1) We were born to be creative in a world rich in creative design rich in natural resources rich with innovative people who consider creativity fun and a responsibility, in a world of rich endowments from nature and man's creative urge. (2) Crafts are one of the rich heritages of our nation. (3) In pioneer days the itinerant craftsman traveled from home to home, selling his wares and earning his bed and board by weaving fabric or a coverlet or handcarving wooden items for the kitchen or barn.

GO ON TO THE NEXT PAGE

TEST 1: WRITING SKILLS, PART I

(4) If people become involved in these early crafts, they may become interested in "trying their hands." (5) They have not only all the rich natural resources and related contemporary subject matter, but they also have man-made materials and efficient, fast equipment to aid them in their creativity. (6) Their products are limited only by their imagination, skill, and knowledge of design.

(7) If they live in a wooded area and like to collect the unusual from nature's wonders, they may begin to reproduce the pine and nut "kissing balls" and christmas wreaths. (8) If the male member of their family loves to hunt, they may create with feathers. (9) Feather wreaths were made at an early date.

20. Sentence 1: **We were born to be creative in a world rich in creative design rich in natural resources rich with innovative people who consider creativity fun and a responsibility, in a world of rich endowments from nature and man's creative urge.**

    What correction should be made to this sentence?

    (1) insert commas after design and resources
    (2) change the spelling of innovative to inovative
    (3) remove the comma after responsibility
    (4) insert a comma after nature
    (5) no correction is necessary

21. Sentences 2 and 3: **Crafts are one of the rich heritages of our nation. In pioneer days the itinerant craftsman traveled from home to home, selling his wares and earning his bed and board by weaving fabric or a coverlet or handcarving wooden items for the kitchen or barn.**

    Which of the following is the best way to write the underlined portion of this sentence? If you think the original is the best way, choose option (1).

    (1) nation. In
    (2) nation: in
    (3) nation: In
    (4) nation, In
    (5) nation, in

22. Sentence 3: **In pioneer days the itinerant craftsman traveled from home to home, selling his wares and earning his bed and board by weaving fabric or a coverlet or handcarving wooden items for the kitchen or barn.**

    What correction should be made to this sentence?

    (1) insert a comma after craftsman
    (2) change the spelling of traveled to travelled
    (3) change wares to wears
    (4) insert a comma after fabric
    (5) no correction is necessary

23. Sentence 4: **If people become involved in these early crafts, they may become interested in "trying their hands."**

    What correction should be made to this sentence?

    (1) change become to became
    (2) change they to one
    (3) change may to might
    (4) change hands." to hands".
    (5) no correction is necessary

24. Sentence 5: **They have not only all the rich natural resources and related contemporary subject matter, but they also have man-made materials and efficient, fast equipment to aid them in their creativity.**

    What correction should be made to this sentence?

    (1) place not only before have
    (2) change the spelling of contemporary to contemperary
    (3) change but to although
    (4) change the spelling of equipment to equiptment
    (5) no correction is necessary

GO ON TO THE NEXT PAGE

TEST 1: WRITING SKILLS, PART I

25. Sentences 5 and 6: **They have not only all the rich natural resources and related contemporary subject matter, but they also have man-made materials and efficient, fast equipment to aid them in their creativity Their products are limited only by their imagination, skill, and knowledge of design.**

Which of the following is the best way to write the underlined portion of this sentence? If you think the original is the best way, choose option (1).

(1) creativity Their
(2) creativity, their
(3) creativity. their
(4) creativity. Their
(5) creativity: Their

26. Sentence 7: **If they live in a wooded area and like to collect the unusual from nature's wonders, they may begin to reproduce the pine and nut "kissing balls" and christmas wreaths.**

What correction should be made to this sentence?

(1) change live to lived
(2) change like to would like
(3) remove the comma after wonders
(4) capitalize christmas
(5) no correction is necessary

27. Sentences 8 and 9: **If the male member of the family loves to hunt, they may create with feathers. Feather wreaths were made at an early date.**

The most effective combination of sentences 8 and 9 would include which of the following groups of words?

(1) feather and feather wreaths
(2) feathers because feather wreaths
(3) feathers although feather wreaths
(4) feathers, which were made into wreaths
(5) feathers made at an early date

Questions 28 to 36 refer to the following paragraphs.

(1) Housing is the hub of the family's private world, the nature of housing has a direct effect on the quality of family life. (2) It effects the health, time, and energy required to rear a family and care for its members, self-related attitudes, morale, and satisfaction with one's station in life. (3) It also affects the way in which one family relates to another, to the neighborhood, and to the community.

(4) Families do not want, expect, or require dwellings that is identical. (5) Families with limited means are more interested in securing clean, safe, and reasonably comfortable housing than to find quarters that are especially psychologically stimulating. (6) At the same time many families having greater incomes can take basic shelter for granted and proceed to satisfy higher level needs in housing.

(7) Nevertheless, as a nation we are being more and more concerned with housing that does far more than support physical survival. (8) In other words, essentially all American families are upgrading their housing goals and expectations. (9) And the dominant housing image remains the single-family house.

(10) Only when families are more articulate in identifying their needs and when builders and public policy become more sensitive to human needs will the nation have a variety of good housing designed, built, and serviced in line with family purposes.

28. Sentence 1: **Housing is the hub of the family's private world, the nature of housing has a direct effect on the quality of family life.**

Which of the following is the best way to write the underlined portion of this sentence? If you think the original is the best way, choose option (1).

(1) world, the
(2) world. the
(3) world; The
(4) world: The
(5) world. The

GO ON TO THE NEXT PAGE

TEST 1: WRITING SKILLS, PART I

29. Sentence 2: **It effects the health, time, and energy required to rear a family and care for its members, self-related attitudes, morale, and satisfaction with one's station in life.**

    What correction should be made to this sentence?

    (1) change the spelling of effects to affects
    (2) change the spelling of its to it's
    (3) remove the comma after members
    (4) change the spelling of morale to moral
    (5) no correction is necessary

30. Sentence 3: **It also affects the way in which one family relates to another, to the neighborhood, and to the community.**

    What correction should be made to this sentence?

    (1) change also to nevertheless
    (2) insert a comma after way
    (3) remove the comma after another
    (4) change the spelling of neighborhood to nieghborhood
    (5) no correction is necessary

31. Sentence 4: **Families do not want, expect, or require dwellings that is identical.**

    What correction should be made to this sentence?

    (1) change the spelling of families to family's
    (2) remove the comma after want
    (3) change is to are
    (4) change the spelling of identical to identicle
    (5) no correction is necessary

32. Sentence 5: **Families with limited means are more interested in securing clean, safe, and reasonably comfortable housing than to find quarters that are especially psychologically stimulating.**

    What correction should be made to this sentence?

    (1) remove the comma after clean
    (2) change to find to in finding
    (3) change the spelling of especially to especialy
    (4) change the spelling of psychologically to phsycologically
    (5) no correction is necessary

33. Sentence 6: **At the same time many families having greater incomes can take basic shelter for granted and proceed to satisfy higher level needs in housing.**

    What correction should be made to this sentence?

    (1) insert a comma after incomes
    (2) change can to must
    (3) insert a comma after granted
    (4) change the spelling of proceed to procede
    (5) no correction is necessary

34. Sentence 7: **Nevertheless, as a nation we are being more and more concerned with housing that does far more than support physical survival.**

    If you rewrote sentence 7 beginning with

    Housing that does far more than support physical survival

    the next words would be

    (1) as a nation
    (2) we are being
    (3) we, as a nation,
    (4) concerns us, as a nation,
    (5) we are concerned

GO ON TO THE NEXT PAGE

TEST 1: WRITING SKILLS, PART I

35. Sentences 8 and 9: **In other words, essentially all American families are upgrading their housing goals and expectations. And the dominant housing image remains the single-family house.**

    The most effective combination of sentences 8 and 9 would include which of the following groups of words?

    (1) expectations but the single-family house remains
    (2) expectations since the single-family house remains
    (3) expectations although the single-family house remains
    (4) expectations with the single-family house remaining
    (5) expectations despite the single-famiy house remaining

36. Sentence 10: **Only when families are more articulate in identiying their needs and when builders and pubic policy become more sensitive to human needs will the nation have a variety of good housing designed, built, and serviced in line with family purposes.**

    If you rewrote sentence 10 beginning with

    <u>The nation</u>

    the next words should be

    (1) are more articulate
    (2) identifying their needs
    (3) become more sensitive
    (4) will have
    (5) serviced in line

<u>Questions 37 to 45</u> refer to the following paragraphs.

(1) Auto insurance can be bought in the form of a bundle of coverage, or each section in the bundle can be bought seperately.

(2) Liability the core of an auto policy pays for bodily injury and property damage to others when you are legally responsible for the accident. (3) Liability coverage, stated separately for bodily injury and property damage, pays for other people's injuries—not yours.

(4) Medical payments cover you and your passengers medical fees regardless of who was to blame for the accident.

(5) The uninsured motorist coverage offers protection to you, your spouse, and resident children if you are struck by an uninsured motorist or a hit and run driver while driving or walking.

(6) Collision pays for damage to your car when you hit another vehicle or an object like a tree, telephone pole etc. (7) Collision coverage is usually sold in the form of a deductible. (8) The larger the amount of the deductible, the less the premium.

(9) Losses caused by fire, wind, theft, vandalism, collision with animals, explosions, flood, and lightning are covered by the comprehensive coverage feature.

(10) Accidental death and dismemberment coverage pays a lump sum for death in a car accident, loss of a limb, blindness, fractures, and dislocations, plus a disability benifit each week.

37. Sentence 1: **Auto insurance can be bought in the form of a bundle of coverage, or each section in the bundle can be bought seperately.**

    What correction should be made to this sentence?

    (1) change the spelling of <u>insurance</u> to <u>insurence</u>
    (2) insert a comma after <u>bought</u>
    (3) change <u>or</u> to <u>and</u>
    (4) change the spelling of <u>seperately</u> to <u>separately</u>
    (5) no correction is necessary

GO ON TO THE NEXT PAGE

TEST 1: WRITING SKILLS, PART I

38. Sentence 2: **Liability the core of an auto policy pays for bodily injury and property damage to others when you are legally responsible for the accident.**

    What correction should be made to this sentence?

    (1) insert commas before the and after policy
    (2) insert a comma after injury
    (3) change the spelling of legally to legaly
    (4) change the spelling of responsible to responsable
    (5) no correction is necessary

39. Sentence 3: **Liability coverage, stated separately for bodily injury and property damage, pays for other people's injuries—not yours.**

    What correction should be made to this sentence?

    (1) remove the comma before stated and after damage
    (2) change pays to pay
    (3) change people's to peoples'
    (4) change yours to your's
    (5) no correction is necessary

40. Sentence 4: **Medical payments cover you and your passengers medical fees regardless of who was to blame for the accident.**

    What correction should be made to this sentence?

    (1) change cover to covers
    (2) change your to you're
    (3) add an apostrophe after passengers
    (4) change who to whom
    (5) no correction is necessary

41. Sentence 5: **The uninsured motorist coverage offers protection to you, your spouse, and resident children if you are struck by an uninsured motorist or a hit and run driver while driving or walking.**

    What correction should be made to this sentence?

    (1) insert a hyphen in uninsured
    (2) remove the comma after you
    (3) change struck to stricken
    (4) insert hyphens into hit and run
    (5) no correction is necessary

42. Sentence 6: **Collision pays for damage to your car when you hit another vehicle or an object like a tree, telephone pole etc.**

    What correction should be made to this sentence?

    (1) change the spelling of vehicle to vehical
    (2) change like to as
    (3) insert a comma after pole
    (4) remove the period after etc.
    (5) no correction is necessary

43. Sentences 7 and 8: **Collision coverage is usually sold in the form of a <u>deductible. The</u> larger the amount of the deductible, the less the premium.**

    Which of the following is the best way to write the underlined portion of this sentence? If you think the original is the best way, choose option (1).

    (1) deductible. The
    (2) deductible. the
    (3) deductible; The
    (4) deductible; the
    (5) deductible, The

GO ON TO THE NEXT PAGE

TEST 1: WRITING SKILLS, PART I

44. Sentence 9: **Losses caused by fire, wind, theft, vandalism, collision with animals, explosions, flood, and lightning are covered by the comprehensive coverage feature.**

    If you rewrote sentence 9 beginning with

    The comprehensive coverage feature

    the next word(s) would be

    (1) losses caused
    (2) causes losses
    (3) collision
    (4) explosions
    (5) covers

45. Sentence 10: **Accidental death and dismemberment coverage pays a lump sum for death in a car accident, loss of a limb, blindness, fractures, and dislocations, plus a disability benifit each week.**

    What correction should be made to this sentence?

    (1) change the spelling of accidental to acidental
    (2) change pays to pay
    (3) remove the comma after dislocations
    (4) change the spelling of benifit to benefit
    (5) no correction is necessary

Questions 46 to 55 refer to the following paragraphs.

(1) How do you find help, when you require it, in your community, assuming that you or your family just cannot meet your own needs or solve your own problems.

(2) It's not easy, but it can be done. (3) Most Americans, in most communities, can find most of the kinds of help they may need within their local area.

(4) In just about every city in the Nation, there is a classified phone directory called the Yellow Pages and, if any public, voluntary, or private (for profit) services agencies exist, they will be listed under the heading: "Social Services Organizations."

(5) In the Washington, D.C., directory, for example, the organizations under this heading number in the hundreds and range from Big Brothers through Family Service to Young Adult Rehabilitation Council. (6) In your phone book there may be only four agencies listed where you can call for help, or there may be 400. (7) The longer the list, unfortunately, the more difficult it is to decide from organization names which one can help you with your particular problem.

(8) Strangely enough, the best place to call or see is your county or local public welfare office (in some areas called social services or public assistence), whether you can or cannot afford to pay for the help you need. (9) Under the Social Security Act, all Federally funded local welfare agencies provide information and referral services without regard for welfare eligibility by reason of poverty, etc.

(10) Just a word about a very special problem: the problem of where a non-English-speaking person can be sent for help. (11) Because of the increasing awareness of this problem, a number of self-help organizations have recently come into existence in communities where there are significant numbers of ethnic minorities.

46. Sentence 1: **How do you find help, when you require it, in your community, assuming that you or your family just cannot meet your own needs or solve your own problems.**

    What correction should be made to this sentence?

    (1) remove the comma after help
    (2) remove the comma after it
    (3) remove the comma after community
    (4) place a question mark after problems
    (5) no correction is necessary

GO ON TO THE NEXT PAGE

TEST 1: WRITING SKILLS, PART I

47. Sentences 2 and 3: **It's not easy, but it can be done. Most Americans, in most communities, can find most of the kinds of help they may need within their local area.**

The most effective combination of sentences 2 and 3 would include which of the following groups of words?

(1) done, most
(2) done, although most
(3) done, but most
(4) done, nevertheless, most
(5) done, since most

48. Sentence 4: **In just about every city in the Nation, there is a classified phone directory called the Yellow Pages and, if any public, voluntary, or private (for profit) services agencies exist, they will be listed under the heading: "Social Services Organizations."**

What correction should be made to this sentence?

(1) remove the capital in Nation
(2) change the spelling of directory to directry
(3) remove the capitals in Yellow Pages
(4) change the colon to a semicolon after heading
(5) no correction is necessary

49. Sentence 5: **In the Washington, D.C., directory, for example, the organizations under this heading number in the hundreds and range from Big Brothers through Family Service to Young Adult Rehabilitation Council.**

What correction should be made to this sentence?

(1) remove the comma after Washington
(2) remove the comma after D.C.
(3) remove the comma after example
(4) remove the capital from Brothers
(5) no correction is necessary

50. Sentence 6: **In your phone book there may be only four agencies listed where you can call for help, or there may be 400.**

If you rewrote sentence 6 beginning with

Only four agencies

the next words would be

(1) in your phone book
(2) may be
(3) there may be
(4) or there may be
(5) to where you can call

51. Sentence 7: **The longer the list, unfortunately, the more difficult it is to decide from organization names which one can help you with your particular problem.**

What correction should be made to this sentence?

(1) remove the comma after list
(2) remove the comma after unfortunately
(3) change the spelling of difficult to dificult
(4) insert a comma after names
(5) no correction is necessary

52. Sentence 8: **Strangely enough, the best place to call or see is your county or local public welfare office (in some areas called social services or public assistence), whether you can or cannot afford to pay for the help you need.**

What correction should be made to this sentence?

(1) capitalize county
(2) capitalize local public welfare
(3) remove the parentheses before in and before whether
(4) change the spelling of assistence to assistance
(5) no correction is necessary

GO ON TO THE NEXT PAGE

TEST 1: WRITING SKILLS, PART I

53. Sentence 9: **Under the Social Security Act, all Federally funded local welfare agencies provide information and referral services without regard for welfare eligibility by reason of poverty, etc.**

    What correction should be made to this sentence?

    (1) remove the capital from Act
    (2) capitalize funded
    (3) remove the capital from Federally
    (4) add and before etc.
    (5) no correction is necessary

54. Sentence 10: **Just a word about a very special problem: the problem of where a non-English-speaking person can be sent for help.**

    What correction should be made to this sentence?

    (1) add Here is before Just
    (2) remove the colon after problem
    (3) remove the hyphens in non-English-speaking
    (4) remove the capital from English
    (5) no correction is necessary

55. Sentence 11: **Because of the increasing awareness of this problem, a number of self-help organizations have recently come into existence in communities where there are significant numbers of ethnic minorities.**

    What correction should be made to this sentence?

    (1) change Because of to Despite
    (2) remove the comma after problem
    (3) remove the hyphen in self-help
    (4) change the spelling of existence to existance
    (5) no correction is necessary

GO ON TO THE NEXT PAGE

TEST 1: WRITING SKILLS, PART II

Directions

This part of the Writing Skills test is intended to determine how well you write. You are asked to write an essay that explains something or presents an opinion on an issue. In preparing your essay, you should take the following steps:

1. Read carefully the directions and the essay topic given below.
2. Plan your essay carefully before you write.
3. Use scratch paper to make any notes.
4. Write your essay on the lined pages of a separate answer sheet.
5. Read carefully what you have written and make any changes that will improve your essay.
6. Check your paragraphs, sentence structure, spelling, punctuation, capitalization, and usage, and make any necessary corrections.

You will have 45 minutes to write on the topic below.

America's youth has always been a major concern of the American people.

Opinions on the youth of our nation differ widely. Some have a high regard for America's young. Others wonder "what the youth of America is coming to."

In an essay of about 200 words, present your views on America's youth today. Your evaluation may include positive or negative arguments or both. Support your views with appropriate reasons and examples.

END OF EXAMINATION

TEST 2: SOCIAL STUDIES

Directions

The Social Studies test consists of multiple-choice questions intended to measure general social studies concepts. The questions are based on short readings that often include a graph, chart, or figure. Study the information given and then answer the question(s) following it. Refer to the information as often as necessary in answering the questions.

You should spend no more than 85 minutes answering the questions. Work carefully, but do not spend too much time on any one question. Be sure you answer every question. You will not be penalized for incorrect answers.

To record your answers, mark the numbered space on the answer sheet beside the number that corresponds to the question in the test.

FOR EXAMPLE:

Early colonists of North America looked for settlement sites that had adequate water supplies and were accessible by ship. For this reason, many early towns were built near

(1) mountains
(2) prairies
(3) rivers
(4) glaciers
(5) plateaus

① ② ● ④ ⑤

The correct answer is "rivers"; therefore, answer space 3 would be marked on the answer sheet.

GO ON TO THE NEXT PAGE

TEST 2: SOCIAL STUDIES

Questions 1 to 3 are based on the following passage.

The true principle of a republic is that the people should choose whom they please to govern them. . . . This great source of free government, popular election, should be perfectly pure, and the most unbounded liberty allowed. Where this principle is adhered to; where, in the organization of the government, the legislative, executive, and judicial branches are rendered distinct; where, again, the legislature is divided into separate houses, and the operations of each are controlled by various checks and balances, and, above all, by the vigilance and weight of the state governments, —to talk of tyranny, and the subversion of our liberties, is to speak the language of enthusiasm. This balance between the national and state governments . . . is of the utmost importance. . . . I am persuaded that a firm union is as necessary to perpetuate our liberties as it is to make us respectable. . . .

—Alexander Hamilton

1. According to the passage, which one of the following did Mr. Hamilton believe?
   (1) States should determine voting qualifications.
   (2) Suffrage should be granted to all adult males.
   (3) Suffrage should be limited.
   (4) Suffrage should be unrestricted.
   (5) United States senators should be appointed by the state legislatures.

2. Hamilton considered all of the following as safeguards of free government EXCEPT
   (1) popular elections
   (2) separation of the branches of government
   (3) separate legislative houses
   (4) checks and balances
   (5) sovereignty of state governments

3. Hamilton believed that the most important characteristic of a republic is
   (1) popular election
   (2) states' rights
   (3) national militia
   (4) federal taxation
   (5) checks and balances

Questions 4 to 6 are based on the following passage.

The political party organization is designed to influence voters to support its candidates. Its base of direct operations is, therefore, the voting district, where approximately 700 citizens cast their ballots.

Ordinarily, the enrolled party members choose two committeepersons at the annual fall primary in September, but in presidential election years this action is taken at the spring primary in June. This county committee may by rule, however, set the term at two years; it may demand equal representation of the sexes so that there will be one committeeman and one committeewoman in each district; it can provide for as many as four committee members from a large district as long as the representation is proportional. The important point is that the primary is, for each party, an election for its own officers.

4. All of the following statements about committeepersons are true EXCEPT that
   (1) two are chosen at the September primary
   (2) the elections take place at the June primary during a presidential election year
   (3) the term of office may be set at two years by the county committee
   (4) a large district may have four committee members
   (5) women may not serve on the committee

GO ON TO THE NEXT PAGE

TEST 2: SOCIAL STUDIES

5. The purpose of the primary election is
   (1) to designate the primary candidate
   (2) to ensure proportional representation
   (3) to equalize the vote of the sexes
   (4) for each party to elect its own officers
   (5) for the nomination of four committeepersons per district

6. It can be inferred from the passage that
   (1) the role of committeepersons is relatively unimportant
   (2) each committeeperson represents about 350 voters
   (3) committeepersons serve for two years
   (4) the county committees consist of equal numbers of men and women
   (5) all candidates for committeeperson have equal chances for election

Questions 7 and 8 are based on the following cartoon.

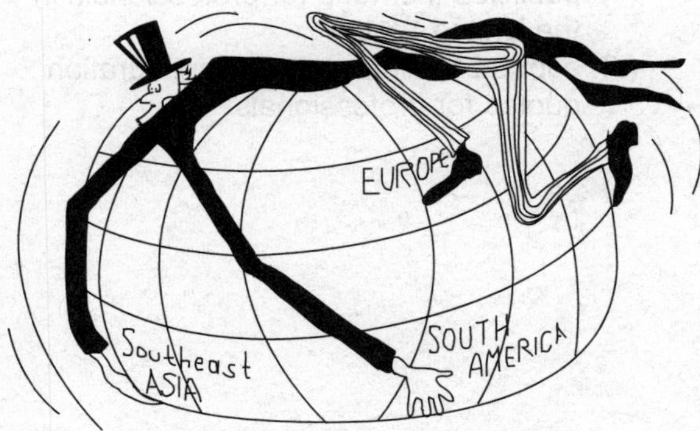

7. The U.S. involvement in Europe indicated in the cartoon most probably refers to the role of the United States in the
   (1) Alliance for Progress
   (2) Common Market
   (3) Nuclear Test-Ban Agreement
   (4) North Atlantic Treaty Organization
   (5) Helsinki Agreement

8. On the basis of the cartoon, it can be concluded that the cartoonist
   (1) questions the U.S. role of "world policeman"
   (2) favors U.S. imperialism
   (3) supports the foreign policy of the United States
   (4) opposes a return to an isolationist policy
   (5) is expressing concern for world survival

9. "To accept passively an unjust system is to cooperate with that system. . . . Noncooperation with evil is as much an obligation as is cooperation with good. But [violence] solves no social problem: it merely creates new and more complicated ones."

   The author of this statement is expressing a belief in
   (1) religious toleration
   (2) civil disobedience
   (3) situational ethics
   (4) anarchy
   (5) socialism

GO ON TO THE NEXT PAGE

TEST 2: SOCIAL STUDIES

Questions 10 to 12 refer to the following graph.

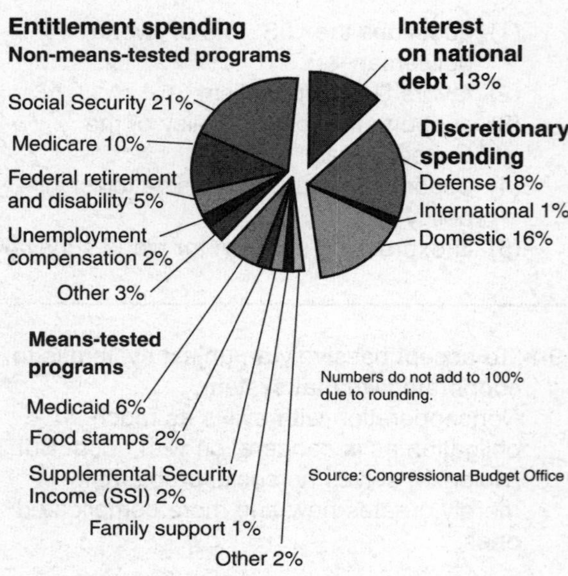

10. Entitlements are government programs providing benefits to members of certain groups. Members of some groups have to be examined (means test) before they can receive benefits. According to the graph, the largest single item of federal spending is

    (1) Social Security
    (2) defense
    (3) interest on the national debt
    (4) Medicare
    (5) Medicaid

11. Of the means-tested programs, the largest is

    (1) Medicaid
    (2) Social Security
    (3) food stamps
    (4) family support
    (5) other

12. The percentage of federal spending going to entitlements is

    (1) 87%
    (2) 54%
    (3) 41%
    (4) 35%
    (5) 13%

Question 13 is based on the following cartoon.

Give me
your scientists,
your doctors,
your teachers,
but keep your
huddled masses
to yourselves.

Adapted from *World Press Review*. November 1980

13. The above cartoon, which appeared in a newspaper published in India, is using the statement attributed to the Statue of Liberty to

    (1) convince the reader of the value of education in the United States
    (2) criticize the United States for not accepting poor immigrants
    (3) deplore the immigration policies in less developed countries
    (4) publicize the need for professionals in the United States
    (5) support the imposition of immigration quotas for professionals

GO ON TO THE NEXT PAGE

TEST 2: SOCIAL STUDIES

Questions 14 to 16 are based on the following passage.

It is said that growth by merger adds nothing to the economy in the way of new investment, whereas so-called "grass roots" growth does. This, too, is not necessarily so. In many cases, a company has the available capital and several other ingredients of success for a new venture, but can only get some missing ingredient—such as qualified technical manpower—by acquiring another company. In such a case the merging of two companies means a new investment which would not have taken place by the "grass roots" method.

Actually, corporate diversification in the past has served to enhance competition, and it will continue to do so. No company today can confidently look upon its established competitors as being its only future competitors. Tomorrow their ranks may be joined by others now in wholly unrelated industries. If new competitors do enter by acquisition or otherwise, it will be only because they think in the long run they can market a better product, or sell at a lower price, and make a profit by doing so.

14. A reason that is offered for the need to merge is to

    (1) meet new competition
    (2) increase diversification
    (3) increase available capital
    (4) provide for "grass roots" growth
    (5) extend consumer choice

15. The author maintains that growth by merger is sometimes necessary to

    (1) acquire capital
    (2) reduce competition
    (3) make a new investment
    (4) gain technically qualified personnel
    (5) add to the economy

16. Motivations for merger mentioned in this passage include all of the following EXCEPT

    (1) marketing a better product
    (2) selling at a lower price
    (3) making a profit
    (4) getting a missing ingredient
    (5) meeting current competition

Questions 17 to 19 are based on the following passage.

Americans are the western pilgrims, who are carrying along with them the great mass of arts, sciences, vigor, and industry which began long since in the East. They will finish the great circle. The Americans were once scattered all over Europe. Here they are incorporated into one of the finest systems of population which has ever appeared and which will hereafter become distinct by the power of the different climates they inhabit. The American ought therefore to love this country much better than that in which either he or his forefathers were born. Here the rewards of his industry follow with equal steps the progress of his labor. His labor is founded on the basis of nature, *self-interest*. Can it want a stronger allurement?

17. The attitude of the author toward the American is one of

    (1) caution
    (2) inquiry
    (3) enthusiastic approval
    (4) self-interest
    (5) prejudice

18. The author predicts that Americans will be unique because of

    (1) a new way of life
    (2) a new government
    (3) a different environment
    (4) their own labors
    (5) self-interest

GO ON TO THE NEXT PAGE

TEST 2: SOCIAL STUDIES

19. The American should be loyal to his new country, according to this passage, because he

(1) is a new man
(2) has a new alma mater
(3) is a western pilgrim
(4) fled Europe
(5) benefits from his own labors

---

20. Which has been an important result of improved means of communication and travel?

(1) Changes in one part of the world can greatly affect other parts of the world.
(2) Countries have become more nationalistic.
(3) Barriers to international trade have been abolished.
(4) There is less need for international organizations.
(5) Isolationism has been eradicated.

21. An extended family is a group of relatives by blood, marriage, or adoption living in close proximity or together, especially if three generations are involved. A nuclear family as the basic social unit consists of parents and their children living in one household.

A major difference between the two types of family is that in the extended family

(1) age and sex roles are not clearly defined
(2) the family ties are weak
(3) intermarriage among close relatives is allowed
(4) there is a sharing of residence and income among several generations
(5) the mother is the dominant figure

<u>Questions 22 and 23</u> are based on the following graph.

DISTRIBUTION OF WORLD POPULATION BY MAJOR REGIONS 1990 AND 2025 (PROJECTED)

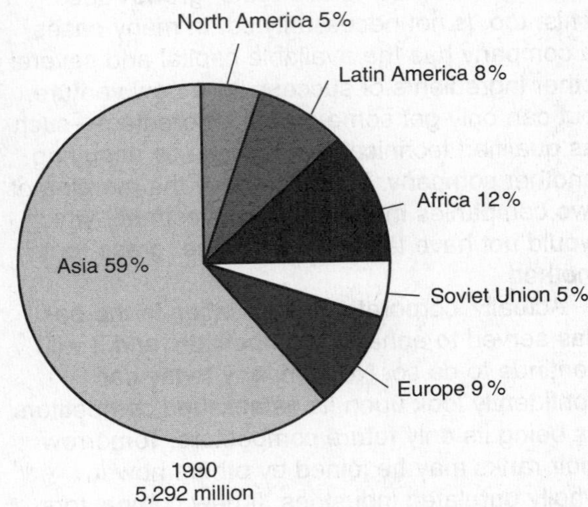

1990
5,292 million

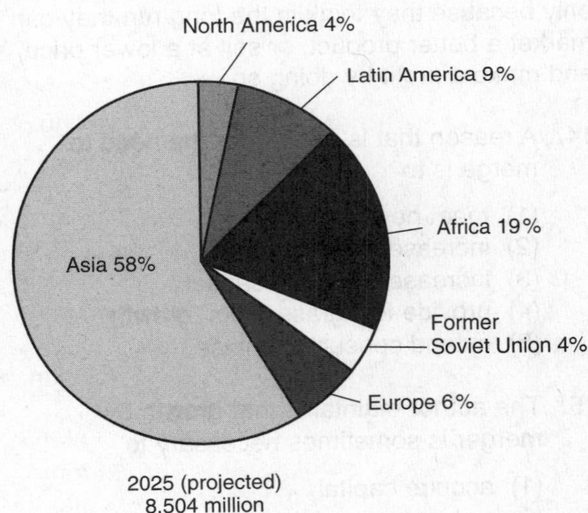

2025 (projected)
8,504 million

GO ON TO THE NEXT PAGE

TEST 2: SOCIAL STUDIES

22. According to the graph, which of the following statements is correct?

    (1) The population of the world will double between 1990 and 2025.
    (2) The distribution of the world's population by regions will remain the same between 1990 and 2025.
    (3) By 2025, there will be a major shift in population from the former Soviet Union to Europe.
    (4) By 2025, Africa's percentage of the world's population will increase more than any other region's percentage.
    (5) By 2025, the former Soviet Union's population will lose the most.

23. The greatest decrease in population from 1990 to 2025 will be in

    (1) North America
    (2) Latin America
    (3) Asia
    (4) the former Soviet Union
    (5) Europe

<u>Questions 24 to 26</u> are based on the following quotation.

It is proper that you should understand what I deem the essential principles of our government. . . .

a jealous care of the right of election by the people—a mild and safe corrective of abuses which are lopped by the sword of the revolution where peaceable remedies are unprovided;

absolute acquiescence in the decisions of the majority — the vital principle of republics, from which there is no appeal but to force, the vital principle and immediate parent of despotism;

a well-disciplined militia—our best reliance in peace and for the first moments of war, till regulars may relieve them;

the supremacy of the civil over the military authority;

economy in the public expense, that labor might be lightly burdened;

the honest payment of our debts and sacred preservation of the public faith;

. . . freedom of religion;

freedom of the press;

freedom of person under the protection of the *habeas corpus*;

and trial by jury impartially selected. . . .

—Thomas Jefferson, Inaugural Address

24. All of the following principles mentioned by Jefferson are found in the Bill of Rights EXCEPT

    (1) freedom of religion
    (2) freedom of the press
    (3) the right of election by the people
    (4) a well-disciplined militia
    (5) trial by jury

25. An example of the "supremacy of the civil over the military authority" is the

    (1) operation of the National Guard
    (2) Pentagon
    (3) President as Commander-in-Chief
    (4) National Security Agency
    (5) National Security Council

26. The alternative to the "right of election by the people," according to the passage, is

    (1) force
    (2) despotism
    (3) war
    (4) peaceable remedies
    (5) revolution

GO ON TO THE NEXT PAGE

TEST 2: SOCIAL STUDIES

Questions 27 and 28 are based on the following passage.

A map is a presentation on flat surface of all, or a part of, the earth's surface, drawn to scale. A map, in order to accomplish fully the objectives for which it was intended, should generally possess certain essentials. These are a title, a legend, direction, scale, latitude and longitude, and a date. . . .

A legend should define the symbols used on a map to explain the colors or patterns employed.... Since a legend unlocks map details, key is probably an appropriate synonym.

Scale may be defined as the ratio between map distance and earth distance. Scale may be shown as a fraction, for example, $\frac{1}{62,500}$, that is, one unit on the map represents 62,500 units on the earth's surface . . . .

A compass rose showing direction is a desirable feature on every map. This directional feature can be eliminated on certain maps where both parallels indicating latitude and meridians indicating longitude are straight lines at right angles to each other.

27. "Drawn to scale" as used in this passage means

(1) the direction of the parallels and meridians
(2) the relationship between map distance and earth distance
(3) linear scales
(4) verbal scales
(5) latitude and longitude

28. A compass rose is associated with

(1) a map title
(2) a legend
(3) scale
(4) direction
(5) latitude and longitude

29. Which statement best supports the argument for expansion of federal power at the expense of state power in the United States?

(1) The economic interdependency of all sections of the United States has increased the number and complexity of national problems.
(2) A uniform penal code is needed in order to insure equal enforcement of the law.
(3) The federal government with its system of checks and balances is a better guarantee of individual freedom than state governments.
(4) Increases in population have made it almost impossible for state governments to function efficiently.
(5) Corruption is more likely to take place at the state governmental level.

30. ". . . the words used are used in such circumstances and are of such a nature as to create a clear and present danger that they will bring about the substantive evils that Congress has a right to prevent . . . . The most stringent protection of free speech would not protect a man in falsely shouting 'fire' in a theatre and causing a panic."

This quotation best reflects the view that freedom of speech is

(1) guaranteed by the Constitution
(2) subject to limitations
(3) clearly dangerous and evil
(4) likely to cause panic
(5) impossible to protect

GO ON TO THE NEXT PAGE

TEST 2: SOCIAL STUDIES

31. ". . . it necessarily became the great object of political economy to diminish as much as possible the importation of foreign goods for home consumption and to increase as much as possible the exportation of the produce of domestic industry."

    Although these words were written in 1776, they apply as well to current U.S. efforts to deal with the problem of the

    (1) decline in the gross national product
    (2) increase in the tariff rates
    (3) surplus in the federal budget
    (4) deficit in the balance of payments
    (5) cost of living

Question 32 is based on the following cartoon.

32. According to the cartoonist, which is a likely result of permitting the Energy Mobilization Board to determine government policy?

    (1) a massive rebuilding program to aid urban areas
    (2) nullification of the benefits of current environmental laws
    (3) an increase in off-shore drilling to lessen our dependence on foreign oil
    (4) land-clearing and home building projects to relieve unemployment among construction workers
    (5) government-sponsored work projects to combat inflation

Questions 33 and 34 are based on the following graph, which shows the relationship of supply and demand for consumer goods and services in five model economies.

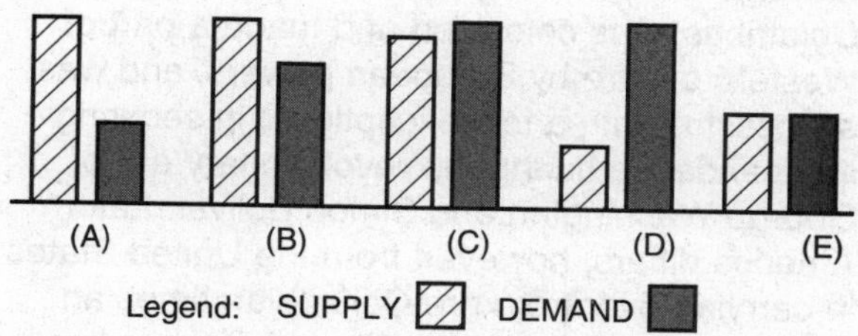

33. If model B were representative of the economy of the United States, which government action would most likely lead to a balance between supply and demand?

    (1) freeze on wages
    (2) limits on consumer credit
    (3) decrease in income tax rates
    (4) increase in sales taxes
    (5) increase in interest rates

34. Which model economy is most similar to the economic situation in the United States during the years 1929–1939?

    (1) A
    (2) B
    (3) C
    (4) D
    (5) E

TEST 2: SOCIAL STUDIES

Questions 35 and 36 refer to the following passage.

Latin America has a rich and varied cultural heritage. It was brought into world history by Columbus, was colonized and made a part of Western culture by European powers, and was successful (with a few exceptions) in securing independence during the revolutionary era of George Washington and Simon Bolivar. Latin America differs, however, from the United States in carrying over from pre-Columbian times an Indian population whose cultural influence has intermingled with that of the European. Latin America was colonized primarily by Spanish and Portuguese. They brought to the area a Catholic religious tradition, an agricultural way of life with a land-owning wealthy class, and an influential military class. Independence resulted in twenty separate countries, the Spanish-speaking portion alone being divided into eighteen states, the Portuguese portion being represented by Brazil, and Haiti, which emerged from a long period of French rule.

35. The countries that colonized Latin America brought with them all of the following EXCEPT
   (1) a religious tradition
   (2) an agricultural way of life
   (3) a military class
   (4) a largely Spanish-speaking population
   (5) an Indian population

36. All of the following peoples are represented in the population of Latin America EXCEPT
   (1) Spanish
   (2) Portuguese
   (3) United States
   (4) French
   (5) Indian

Questions 37 to 39 refer to the following passage.

The main conclusion arrived at in this work, namely, that man is descended from some lowly organized form, will, I regret to think, be highly distasteful to many persons. The astonishment which I felt on first seeing a party of Fuegians, South American Indians, on a wild and broken shore will never be forgotten by me, for the thought at once rushed into my mind—such were our ancestors. He who has seen a savage in his native land will not feel much shame if forced to acknowledge that the blood of some more humble creatures flows in his veins.

Man may be excused for feeling some pride at having risen, though not through his own exertions, to the very summit of the organic scale; and the fact of his having thus risen, instead of having been originally placed there, may give him hopes for a still higher destiny in the distant future. But we are not here concerned with hopes or fears, only with the truth as far as our reason allows us to discover it. I have given the evidence to the best of my ability; and we must acknowledge, as it seems to me, that man, with all his noble qualities, still bears in his bodily frame the indelible stamp of his lowly origin.

37. The author is aware that his conclusions about human beings are
   (1) unscientific
   (2) pessimistic
   (3) unpleasant
   (4) astonishing
   (5) regretful

38. The author states that his conclusions are based on
   (1) religious faith
   (2) personal intuition
   (3) hope
   (4) fear
   (5) reason

GO ON TO THE NEXT PAGE

TEST 2: SOCIAL STUDIES

39. With regard to the future, the author of the selection feels that human beings should be

(1) optimistic
(2) noncommittal
(3) anxious
(4) depressed
(5) concerned

40. Which situation in the United States is an illustration of lobbying, that is, attempting to influence legislators to support bills that favor a special group?

(1) A defeated candidate for the Senate is appointed a member of the president's cabinet.
(2) A corporation hires a person to present its views to certain members of Congress.
(3) Federal public works projects are awarded to a state in return for certain political actions by that state's senators.
(4) Two members of Congress agree to support each other's bills.
(5) A member of Congress prevents a bill from coming to a vote.

41. The Monroe Doctrine states that any attempt by European powers to interfere with their old colonies or with the independence of a republic in the Western Hemisphere would not be tolerated by the United States, nor would any attempt by them "to extend their system to any portion of this hemisphere."

Which event best illustrates the application of the Monroe Doctrine in United States foreign policy?

(1) the United States joining the North Atlantic Treaty Organization (NATO)
(2) President Truman's involving the United States in the Berlin airlift
(3) President Kennedy's response to the Cuban missile crisis
(4) Congress' declaration of war against Germany in World War II
(5) the sale by the United States of AWACs to Saudi Arabia

42. In the United States, changes in occupational titles from busboy to dining room attendant and stewardess to flight attendant illustrate an attempt to deal with the problem of

(1) racism
(2) ethnocentrism
(3) sexism
(4) age bias
(5) unionism

Question 43 is based on the following chart.

Income and Management Level of Men and Women Managers*

Income	**Men**	**Women**
Income in early career	$ 68,480	$57,210
Income in midcareer	102,540	83,370
Management level		
Top level management	23%	9%
Upper-middle management	33	43
Lower-middle management	21	22
Supervisory management	8	10
Nonmanagement	15	16

Source: "The Impact of Gender as Managerial Careers Unfold," by Joy A. Schneer, Rider University, and Frieda Reitman, Pace University, *Journal of Vocational Behavior.*
*Excludes self-employed.

43. The data in the table show that

(1) women earn less than men at every managerial level
(2) men outnumber women on every managerial level
(3) income in midcareer is comparable for men and women
(4) fewer women than men become supervisors
(5) fewer women than men become top-level managers

GO ON TO THE NEXT PAGE

TEST 2: SOCIAL STUDIES

Questions 44 to 46 are based on the following passage.

As psychologists and anthropologists have recently been discovering, human beings instinctively mark out territories or zones which they use and react to in various ways. Edward T. Hall, professor of anthropology at Northwestern University, has identified four separate distances at which most people operate: intimate, personal, social, and public.

Not everyone is capable of handling all four distances with equal ease. Some people feel uncomfortable in public spaces (the stage, a lecture platform) or social situations (a large dinner party); others cannot endure being close to people, including quite often, those who have the right to expect such closeness—their husbands or wives. In such cases, says New York psychiatrist Dr. Frederic F. Flach, "the husband or wife who wants to remain aloof inevitably sends out signals; they're as unmistakable as a KEEP OUT sign."

44. The author discusses husband-wife relations as a problem in

(1) intimate distance
(2) personal distance
(3) social distance
(4) public distance
(5) four different kinds of distance

45. Conflict between husband and wife arises, according to the author, from

(1) their desire for aloofness
(2) need for ritual
(3) too little time together
(4) varying needs or expectations for intimate distance
(5) KEEP OUT signs

46. An example of a situation requiring adaptability to social distance is a

(1) married life
(2) wedding
(3) lecture
(4) stage performance
(5) baseball game

Question 47 is based on the following table.

TAX TABLE

Income	Tax Percentage Rate
$0– 3,000	0
3,001– 8,000	10
8,001–14,000	20
14,001–20,000	25

47. The income tax shown in the table above is best described as

(1) graduated
(2) negative
(3) proportional
(4) regressive
(5) universal

48. "We must bring the benefits of Western civilization and Christianity to the less fortunate."

This idea has been used to justify

(1) imperialism
(2) nationalism
(3) socialism
(4) feudalism
(5) regionalism

49. "Nations strive to prevent any one country from becoming all-powerful and domineering."

Which concept is referred to by this statement?

(1) militarism
(2) imperialism
(3) national sovereignty
(4) balance of power
(5) appeasement

GO ON TO THE NEXT PAGE

TEST 2: SOCIAL STUDIES

Questions 50 and 51 are based on the following chart.

ACTUAL AND PROJECTED POPULATIONS OF WORLD REGIONS

Region	1980	1990	2000 (est.)
Asia	2,583,477,000	3,112,695,000	3,712,542,000
Africa	477,231,000	642,111,000	866,585,000
Europe*	749,973,000	786,966,000	818,378,000
Latin America**	362,685,000	448,076,000	538,439,000
North America	251,909,000	275,866,000	294,712,000
Oceania	22,800,000	26,481,000	30,144,000
World	4,448,048,000	5,292,195,000	6,260,800,000

*Includes the former USSR
**Includes Mexico, Central America, and the Caribbean

50. The chart reveals that

(1) over half of the 1990 population and of the projected world population in 2000 lives in Asia
(2) most of the world's population lives in the Americas
(3) the largest population growth is in North America
(4) the smallest population growth is in Latin America
(5) the population growth is steadiest in Africa

51. By 2000 (est.)

(1) Latin America will have passed Europe in population growth
(2) Africa will have passed Europe in population
(3) North America will have gained on Latin America
(4) Europe will have made the largest gains
(5) the world population will have doubled since 1980

Questions 52 to 54 are based on the following statements:

Speaker *A:* It is in our best interest to steer clear of involvement with other countries. They are continually arguing over things that do not concern us.

Speaker *B:* If we wish to survive, the only way is to participate and learn the ways of other nations. That way, we can try to head off trouble before it gets out of hand.

Speaker *C:* I believe that it is the moral mission of this nation to help others create democratic ways of life. We have to get involved in order to spread democratic reforms.

Speaker *D:* A show of force is necessary now and then to warn other nations of how far we are ready to go to keep the peace on our terms.

GO ON TO THE NEXT PAGE

TEST 2: SOCIAL STUDIES

52. Which presidential action was most consistent with the foreign policy advocated by speaker *A*?

    (1) George Washington's refusal to form an alliance with France against Britain.
    (2) Woodrow Wilson's proposal of the Fourteen Points as the basis of world peace after World War I.
    (3) Harry Truman's support of the United Nations action in Korea.
    (4) Jimmy Carter's call for a boycott of the 1980 Olympics.
    (5) Ronald Reagan's policies in Central America.

53. On which principle of diplomacy would Speakers *B* and *C* most likely agree?

    (1) Success in foreign relations is based on respect for the neutral rights of all nations.
    (2) Only through strong defense alliances can a small nation survive.
    (3) Active diplomacy is critical to achieve national goals in today's world.
    (4) Diplomacy loses its power without military backing.
    (5) Human rights in other nations are none of our concern.

54. If the four speakers were on a television news program, the moderator would probably introduce the topic of their discussion as

    (1) New Paths to Isolationism
    (2) How to Live with Your Allies
    (3) Capitalism vs. Communism in Today's World
    (4) A Classic Problem in Foreign Affairs
    (5) The Moral Mission of the United States

Question 55 is based on the following cartoon.

"Miss Jones, weren't there any founding MOTHERS?"

55. Which statement best expresses the main idea of the cartoon?

    (1) Women have increasingly difficult choices in a modern society.
    (2) More emphasis should be placed on the role of women in U.S. history.
    (3) Women made few significant contributions to society until the 20th century.
    (4) Free public education in the United States was established primarily by women.
    (5) Women are the dominant force in American education today.

GO ON TO THE NEXT PAGE

TEST 2: SOCIAL STUDIES

<u>Questions 56 and 57</u> are based on the following table.

ECONOMIC CONDITIONS IN LATIN AMERICA

Nation	Population (millions)	Per capita GNP (dollars)	Infant Mortality (per 1000)	Literacy (percent)	Years Until Population Doubles	Urban Population (percent)	Life Expectancy (years)
Bolivia	6.9	1,217	142	75	25	46	51
Brazil	144.4	2,002	75	74	30	68	63
Costa Rica	2.9	1,400	38	90	27	48	73
Haiti	6.3	290	107	23	30	28	53
Mexico	83.5	2,590	54	74	27	70	66
Venezuela	18.8	3,726	36	86	25	76	69

56. According to the table, which nation has the greatest problem in regard to public health?
    (1) Bolivia
    (2) Brazil
    (3) Costa Rica
    (4) Mexico
    (5) Venezuela

57. Based on the information in the table, which statement is most accurate?
    (1) Mexico has the largest population in Latin America.
    (2) Brazil has the highest literacy rate in Latin America.
    (3) Most of the people of Venezuela live in cities.
    (4) Costa Rica has the highest per capita GNP in Latin America.
    (5) All the most populous countries have the highest life expectancy.

<u>Question 58</u> is based on the following cartoon.

(adapted)

58. Which statement best describes the main idea of this 1989 cartoon?
    (1) Agricultural development depends on the progress of the nuclear arms race.
    (2) World peace cannot be assured by limiting the nuclear capabilities of only the United States and the former Soviet Union.
    (3) Permanent world peace has come with agreements between the United States and the former Soviet Union to reduce nuclear arms.
    (4) Most nations are eliminating their nuclear weapons programs.
    (5) The threat of nuclear war is diminishing.

GO ON TO THE NEXT PAGE

TEST 2: SOCIAL STUDIES

Questions 59 and 60 are based on the following graph.

PERSONS AGE 65 AND OVER AS A PERCENT OF TOTAL UNITED STATES POPULATION

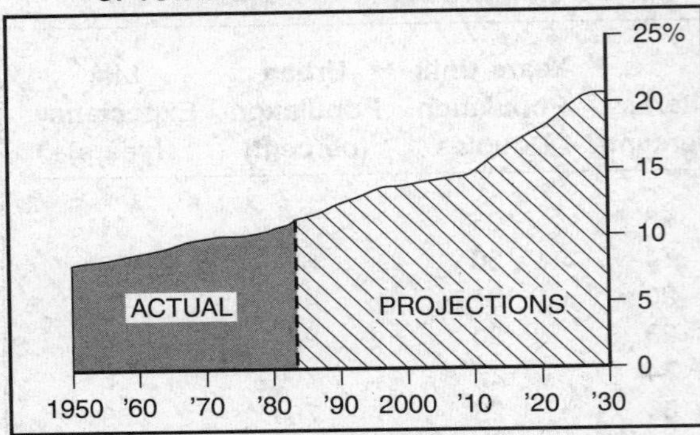

U.S. Census Bureau and Social Security Administration

59. Which statement is supported by the data in the graph?
    (1) The birth rate increased steadily between 1950 and 1980.
    (2) While the percentage of elderly is increasing, the total population is actually decreasing.
    (3) Policies concerning the elderly will have to be reviewed and revised.
    (4) Voters under age 30 will have proportionately more political power during the next 40 years.
    (5) The rate of increase in the percentage of persons aged 65 and over is slowing.

60. If the projection in the graph is correct, a probable consequence will be a decrease in the percentage of
    (1) marriages ending in divorce
    (2) individuals living alone
    (3) Americans below the poverty level
    (4) full-time workers
    (5) welfare cases

Questions 61 to 63 are based on the following passage.

In its Preamble, the Constitution set forth the goals by which the United States was to be governed.

"We the people of the United States, in order to form a more perfect union, establish justice, insure domestic tranquility, provide for the common defense, promote the general welfare, and to secure the blessings of liberty to ourselves and our posterity, do ordain and establish this Constitution for the United States of America."

Each of the following statements sets forth an action taken by the government of the United States to achieve these goals. Choose the specific goal this action was directed to achieve. Goals may be used more than once if they apply to more than one action.

61. The Thirteenth and Fifteenth amendments to the Constitution prohibited slavery and granted suffrage to all citizens regardless of race, color, or previous condition of servitude. These actions sought primarily to
    (1) establish justice
    (2) insure domestic tranquility
    (3) provide for the common defense
    (4) promote the general welfare
    (5) secure the blessings of liberty

62. The Social Security Act of 1935 provided an Old Age and Survivor's Insurance Program. This action sought primarily to
    (1) establish justice
    (2) insure domestic tranquility
    (3) provide for the common defense
    (4) promote the general welfare
    (5) secure the blessings of liberty

GO ON TO THE NEXT PAGE

TEST 2: SOCIAL STUDIES

63. The Sherman Anti-Trust Act of 1890 made illegal combinations in restraint of trade and suppressed the power of corporations to enlarge profits at the expense of the public. This action sought primarily to

(1) establish justice
(2) insure domestic tranquility
(3) provide for the common defense
(4) promote the general welfare
(5) secure the blessings of liberty

Question 64 is based on the following cartoon.

64. What is the main idea of this cartoon from the early 1990s?

(1) The Bolshevik revolutions devastated Russia.
(2) The international community ignored the destruction of cities in the former Yugoslavia.
(3) Self-determination resulted in the creation of Yugoslavia.
(4) The North Atlantic Treaty Organization (NATO) troops forced refugees to leave Yugoslavia.
(5) The nations of the world acted properly in the former Yugoslavia.

END OF EXAMINATION

TEST 3: SCIENCE

Directions

The Science test consists of multiple-choice questions intended to measure the general concepts in science. The questions are based on short readings that often include a graph, chart, or figure. Study the information given and then answer the question(s) following it. Refer to the information as often as necessary in answering the questions.

You will have 95 minutes to answer the questions. Work carefully, but do not spend too much time on any one question. Be sure you answer every question. You will not be penalized for incorrect answers.

To record your answers, mark one numbered space on the answer sheet beside the number that corresponds to the question in the test.

FOR EXAMPLE:

Which of the following is the smallest unit?

(1) solution
(2) element
(3) atom
(4) compound
(5) mixture

① ② ● ④ ⑤

The correct answer is "atom"; therefore, space 3 would be marked on the answer sheet.

TEST 3: SCIENCE

<u>Questions 1 to 3</u> refer to the following article.

In the mammal, the fertilized egg becomes implanted in the wall of the uterus. As the embryo develops, it becomes surrounded by several protective membranes. It obtains its food and oxygen from the mother's bloodstream through the placenta. This structure is well supplied with many blood vessels that carry blood from the mother's circulation in close proximity to the embryo's bloodstream. Wastes diffuse into the parent's blood from the embryo's bloodstream.

1. The process by which materials are exchanged between mother and embryo is known as

   (1) circulation
   (2) adsorption
   (3) secretion
   (4) diffusion
   (5) excretion

2. The human embryo develops in the

   (1) egg
   (2) zygote
   (3) placenta
   (4) uterus
   (5) protective membrane

3. Which of the following passes from the embryo to the mother's bloodstream?

   (1) wastes
   (2) digested food
   (3) oxygen
   (4) blood
   (5) all of these

<u>Questions 4 to 7</u> refer to the following article.

Vertebrate blood, which consists of red and white blood cells and plasma, can be broken down even further into its chemical constituents. The largest mineral ingredient of blood is sodium chloride or salt. This mineral is important because it regulates water exchanges within the organism. This exchange, as some scientists have emphasized, is more extensive and more important than may at first been thought. Cannon points out that "there are a number of circulations of the fluid out of the body and back again without loss."

For example, it is estimated that from a quart to a quart and one-half of water daily "leaves the body" when it enters the mouth as saliva. Another one or two quarts are passed out as gastric juice, and perhaps the same amount is contained in bile and the secretions of the pancreas and the intestinal wall.

This large volume of water enters the digestive processes, and practically all of it is reabsorbed through the intestinal wall, where it performs the equally important function of carrying in the digested foodstuffs. These and other instances of what Cannon calls "the conservative use of water in our bodies" involve essentially osmotic pressure relationships in which the concentration of sodium chloride plays an important part.

4. This passage implies that

   (1) substances can pass through the intestinal wall in only one direction
   (2) water cannot be absorbed by the body unless it contains sodium choloride
   (3) every particle of water ingested is used over and over again
   (4) sodium chloride does not actually enter the body
   (5) regulation of water exchanges in the organism is controlled by the concentration of sodium chloride

5. The main point of this passage is that

   (1) we should drink large quantities of water daily
   (2) water is needed to digest our food completely
   (3) we need to consume large amounts of salt
   (4) salt is important in the regulation of water
   (5) the reuse of body water is an automatic function

GO ON TO THE NEXT PAGE

TEST 3: SCIENCE

6. Sodium chloride is an important constituent of

(1) gastric juice
(2) bile
(3) pancreatic juice
(4) intestinal juice
(5) blood

7. Water is important in the intestine because of its ability to

(1) form saliva
(2) dilute the gastric juice
(3) form bile
(4) act as a vehicle for digested food
(5) dissolve sodium chloride

Questions 8 to 11 refer to the following article.

The process of mitosis has been studied very carefully. Scientists hope some light will be shed on the abnormal cell division that occurs in cancer by observing the normal process of cell division. Also, research in mitosis is important to the science of genetics. The chromosomes—long, thin strands—are carriers of nucleoprotein, which is made up of DNA molecules. Chromosomes are visible only when the cell is undergoing division.

Biologists have observed that the number of chromosomes counted during mitosis is characteristic of the species. For example, in the fruit fly, this number is eight except in the sex cells or gametes. Only four chromosomes are found in the egg cell or sperm cell of the fruit fly. However, during the union of these cells in fertilization, the normal, characteristic number is restored.

Scientists may be guilty of errors; but they are constantly checking, and they make revisions where necessary. For example, it was long believed that the normal number of human chromosomes in body cells is 48. Research on tissue culture has made it necessary to revise the figure to 46.

8. The number of chromosomes normally found in the human egg cell is

(1) 8
(2) 23
(3) 24
(4) 46
(5) 48

9. The number of chromosomes in the body cells is how many times that of the reproductive cells?

(1) $\frac{1}{2}$
(2) $\frac{1}{8}$
(3) $\frac{1}{4}$
(4) 2
(5) the same

10. The process by which cells normally divide is called

(1) mitosis
(2) fertilization
(3) gamete formation
(4) tissue culture
(5) chromosomes

11. Abnormal cell division is most important for research in

(1) plants
(2) chromosome composition
(3) cancer
(4) guinea pigs
(5) fruit flies

GO ON TO THE NEXT PAGE

TEST 3: SCIENCE

Questions 12 to 14 refer to the following article.

What was the Earth's climate like half a million years ago? Fossil studies of radiolaria, a group of one-celled animals characterized by silicon-containing shells, have given scientists a fairly accurate picture of climatic conditions in the distant past. Geologists found these micro-organisms preserved in cores of sediment taken beneath the floor of the Indian Ocean. The cores penetrated deep enough to provide a record going back about 450,000 years.

The cycles of climatic changes were determined by the alternating layers of species of warm and cold-preferring radiolaria. These climatic changes were compared with cycles of changes in the shape, tilt, and seasonal positions of the Earth's orbit, which other scientists studied by investigating past changes in global ice volume. We now have confirmation of a theory that changes in the Earth's orbital geometry caused the ice ages.

12. Fossil studies of radiolaria are possible because these animals

    (1) live in the depths of the ocean
    (2) are one-celled
    (3) have survived through the ages
    (4) have a shell surrounding the cell
    (5) react to cold and warmth

13. The scientists mentioned in this passage were most probably climatologists, oceanographers, and

    (1) anthropologists
    (2) protozoologists
    (3) geologists
    (4) archaeologists
    (5) zoologists

14. The fundamental cause of the ice ages is

    (1) periodic changes in the Earth's orbit around the Sun
    (2) fossil remains of one-celled animals
    (3) accumulation of global ice
    (4) alternating cold and warm seasons
    (5) changes in distance of the Earth from the Sun

Questions 15 to 17 refer to the following information.

Water will change from one phase to another as its temperature changes. In its gaseous form, steam, water has its highest temperature. Water in this form will not change into liquid unless a certain amount of heat is removed. An example is the condensation of water on a bathroom mirror while someone takes a shower. The surface of the mirror is a lot cooler than the warm, steamy bathroom. Water vapor in the air turns into drops of liquid when it touches the cold surface of the mirror. This occurs because the cool mirror cools the air, and cool air cannot hold as much water as warm air.

The diagram represents a sealed plastic container with two Celsius thermometers, one of which is in a glass cup containing ice and water. The purpose of this demonstration is to study the behavior of water vapor and the temperature at which air becomes saturated by water (the dew point).

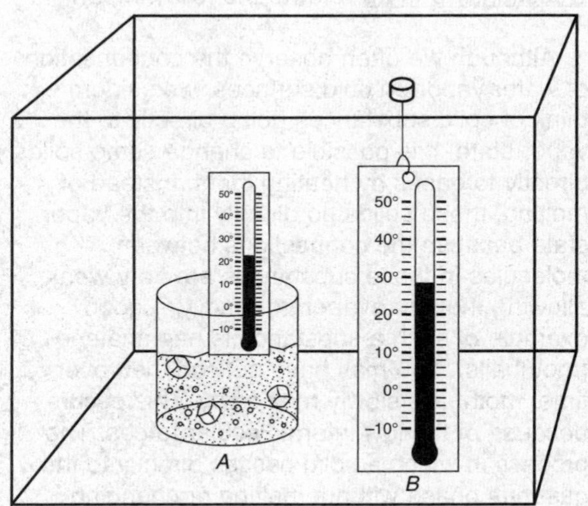

15. What is the temperature of the air in the box?

    (1) 23.0°C
    (2) 25.0°C
    (3) 26.0°C
    (4) 28.0°C
    (5) 29.0°C

GO ON TO THE NEXT PAGE

TEST 3: SCIENCE

16. Why have droplets of water formed on the outside of the glass cup?
    (1) Glass cups always accumulate water droplets on the outside when they are filled with water.
    (2) The air near the glass cup has become saturated with water.
    (3) Water has seeped through the pore spaces in the glass cup.
    (4) The relative humidity of the air near the glass cup is approaching 0 percent.
    (5) The dew point temperature was not reached.

17. If the water droplets have just appeared on the glass cup, what is the dew point temperature?
    (1) 6.5°C
    (2) 23.0°C
    (3) 28.0°C
    (4) 29.0°C
    (5) 50°C

<u>Questions 18 to 20</u> refer to the following article.

Although we often observe the condensation of water vapor on cold surfaces, we seldom think of solid substances going directly to the vapor state. It is possible to change some solids directly to gases by heating them. Instead of melting, these solids go directly into the vapor state because the connections between molecules in these substances are very weak, allowing them to evaporate readily. A good example of such a substance is naphthalene (mothballs). You may have noticed that, over time, mothballs slowly melt away. This occurs because of the low intermolecular forces. The process in which a solid passes directly to the gaseous phase without melting or changing back to the solid state is called sublimation.

18. Condensation is a change from the
    (1) gaseous phase to the solid phase
    (2) gaseous phase to the liquid phase
    (3) liquid phase to the gaseous phase
    (4) liquid phase to the solid phase
    (5) solid phase to the liquid phase

19. Some substances evaporate more easily than others because they
    (1) condense on cold surfaces
    (2) can be heated at atmospheric pressure
    (3) do not change from solid to liquid
    (4) pass from solid state to vapor state
    (5) have weak intermolecular forces

20. Sublimation is a change directly from the
    (1) solid phase to the gaseous phase
    (2) solid phase to the liquid phase
    (3) liquid phase to the gaseous phase
    (4) gaseous phase to the liquid phase
    (5) liquid phase to the solid phase

<u>Questions 21 to 23</u> refer to the following article.

Without Archimedes' principle, the invention of the submarine would have been impossible. According to this principle, when an object is submerged, it is buoyed up by a force equal to the weight of the volume of liquid it displaces. Therefore, when a body sinks, its weight is greater than the buoyant force or weight of the liquid that it displaces.

For a submarine to rise to the surface, water is pumped out of the ballast tanks until the weight of the submarine is less than the upward buoyant force exerted by the water outside. To submerge a submarine the ballast tanks are filled with water until the weight of the submarine is greater than the buoyant forces.

21. This article illustrates the principle of
    (1) Newton
    (2) Archimedes
    (3) Einstein
    (4) Galileo
    (5) Boyle

GO ON TO THE NEXT PAGE

TEST 3: SCIENCE

22. One purpose of filling ballast tanks with water is to ensure that

    (1) a submarine will float
    (2) a submarine will sink
    (3) the buoyant force is less than the mass of the object
    (4) the buoyant force is the same as the volume of the submarine
    (5) liquid is displaced in the reverse proportions

23. Water wings and lifesaving jackets are useful in times of danger in water because they

    (1) act as fins for nonswimmers
    (2) protect from excess wetting and soaking
    (3) increase one's volume
    (4) increase one's weight
    (5) decrease one's volume

Questions 24 to 26 refer to the following article.

Water is a good conductor of sound waves. If you were swimming under water while someone struck two rocks together under water 10 feet away, you would be surprised at how loud the sound was. The U.S. Navy makes use of this knowledge in detecting enemy submarines. During World War II, it was discovered that the sound of propellers or of a hammer being dropped inside a submarine could be heard hundreds of yards away with the use of sensitive listening devices.

Sound waves under water can be used to measure the depth of the water beneath a ship. This is done by sending a sound wave downward from the bottom of a ship. It is known that sound travels 4,800 feet a second through water. When the sound reaches the sea floor, it is reflected back up. Careful measurements are made of the time required for the echo to return to the ship. The longer the time, the deeper is the water. The depth of water under the ship is read directly on a gauge.

In a similar way, a sonar device can measure the distance to underwater objects. A high-frequency sound signal is sent out, and a measurement is made of the return time for the echo. Since many fish make sounds in water, a fishing fleet can detect, by sonar, the presence of a school of fish.

24. Of the following, which can best be concluded from this selection?

    (1) Fish cannot hear ordinary sounds.
    (2) Submarines cannot detect sound waves.
    (3) The propeller of a submarine distorts sound waves.
    (4) Sound waves become compressed in very deep water.
    (5) Water is a good conductor of sound waves.

25. Underwater objects can be detected by sonar, which uses

    (1) high-frequency sounds
    (2) low-frequency sounds
    (3) radar
    (4) high-intensity light waves
    (5) ultrahigh-frequency television

26. A sound wave is sent downward from the bottom of a ship; an echo is received 6 seconds later. The depth of the water is most likely

    (1) 4,800 ft.
    (2) 9,600 ft.
    (3) 12,000 ft.
    (4) 14,400 ft.
    (5) 15,600 ft.

GO ON TO THE NEXT PAGE

TEST 3: SCIENCE

Questions 27 and 28 refer to the following table.

APPROXIMATE SWIMMING SPEEDS OF SOME COMMON FISH

Common Name	Scientific Name	Length (in.)	Speed (mph)
Barracuda	*Sphyraena barracuda*	73	30
Cod	*Gadus callarius*	22	4.2
Eel	*Anguilla vulgaris*	24	2.8
Flounder	*Pleuronectes flesus*	11	2.4
Goldfish	*Carassius aurataus*	5	3.6
Lemon shark	*Negaprion brevirostris*	75	6
Lemon sole	*Pleuronectes microcephalus*	3.5	.26
Mackerel	*Scomber scombrus*	14	5.4
Rainbow trout	*Salmo irideus*	8	3.4
Sea trout	*Salmo trutta*	14	5.4

27. Which of the following statements is supported by information in the table?
    (1) The larger the fish, the faster it swims.
    (2) Some small fish can swim faster than larger fish.
    (3) Sharks are predators and have to swim fast.
    (4) The size of a fish is not related to its speed.
    (5) Saltwater fish are faster than freshwater fish.

28. Other than the two species of trout, which of the following fish are probably related?
    (1) flounder and mackerel
    (2) goldfish and mackerel
    (3) flounder and lemon sole
    (4) lemon shark and lemon sole
    (5) cod and mackerel

29. Commercial fishermen have all the advantages of technology to help them increase their catch. They use locators to find the largest schools and miles of nets to scoop the fish out of the water. Because of overfishing, among other reasons, fish populations all over the world are declining, and the average size of fish that are caught is smaller. This statement is also true of game fish. There are no longer spectacular swordfish of over 1,000 pounds, or giant sea bass weighing 500 pounds. Also, some other fish that were once quite common have become rare.

    All of the statements below are opinions EXCEPT
    (1) no one should be allowed to fish American waters except Americans
    (2) there has to be some other explanation for the decline in game fish; no one could possibly catch enough of them to cause the populations to decline
    (3) the oceans are big enough for everybody to take all the fish he or she wants
    (4) if fishermen would allow enough larger breeder fish to go free, the populations might increase
    (5) the U.S. Department of Fish and Game needs to tell fishermen how many fish they can catch

GO ON TO THE NEXT PAGE

TEST 3: SCIENCE

Questions 30 to 32 are based on the following graphs.

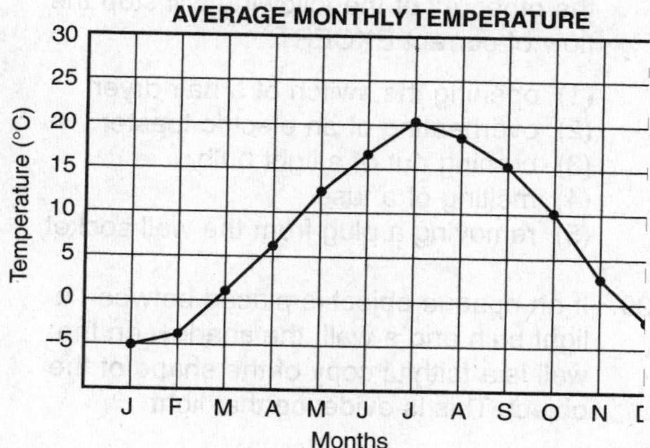

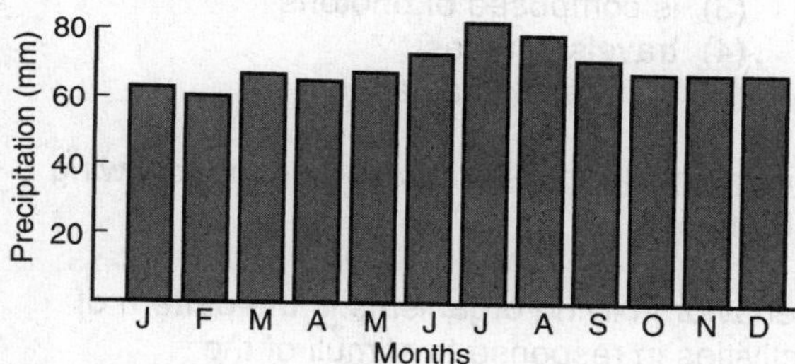

The two graphs represent average monthly temperature and total monthly precipitation from January through December for a city located near the center of a continent.

30. Between which two consecutive months is there the least change in the average temperature?

(1) January and February
(2) February and March
(3) May and June
(4) October and November
(5) December and January

31. The average temperature and the total precipitation during the month of September (S on the horizontal axis of the graphs) were

(1) 7°C; 60 mm
(2) 15°C; 50 mm
(3) 16°C; 68 mm
(4) 21°C; 68 mm
(5) 21°C; 80 mm

32. Which best describes the climate pattern of this location?

(1) hotter and wetter in summer than in winter
(2) hotter in summer than in winter, with no pronounced wet or dry season
(3) wetter in summer than in winter, with fairly constant temperature throughout the year
(4) dry and cold during the winter months
(5) dry and warm during the summer months

33. In temperate climates, flowers are pollinated either by insects or by the wind. The bright colors and strong odors of many flowers are forms of advertising to attract insects. Oak trees bear flowers that have no brightly colored petals. It is reasonable to assume that the oak flowers

(1) can be pollinated either by insects or by wind
(2) have a strong odor
(3) do not have to be pollinated
(4) are wind-pollinated
(5) cannot be wind-pollinated

34. Green plants absorb carbon dioxide from the air and release oxygen; animals use oxygen and produce carbon dioxide. In a completely sealed aquarium, it is found that the oxygen level drops. Of the following causes:

A. too many plants
B. not enough plants
C. too many fish
D. not enough fish

which is the most likely?

(1) B only
(2) D only
(3) B or D
(4) B or C
(5) A or C

GO ON TO THE NEXT PAGE

TEST 3: SCIENCE

35. Pure water has a pH of 7. Acids have pH values lower than 7, and alkalis have values higher than 7. A gardener knows that the plants she grows need soil with a pH of 7.5. If the pH of the soil is 6.5, what action might she take?
    (1) Use only pure water in watering the plants.
    (2) Add a mild acid to the soil.
    (3) Add a mild alkali to the soil.
    (4) Use tap water, which has a pH of 6.5.
    (5) Use an organic fertilizer that becomes acid when it decays.

Question 36 is based on the following diagram.

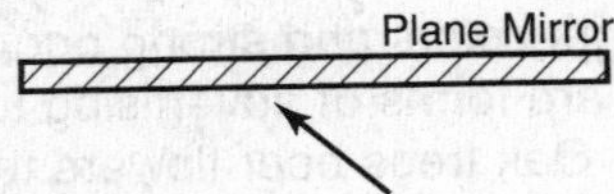

36. The arrow in the diagram represents an object in front of a plane mirror. The image formed in a plane mirror must obey the rule that every point on the image is just as far behind the mirror as the corresponding point on the object. Which of the following arrows represents the image?

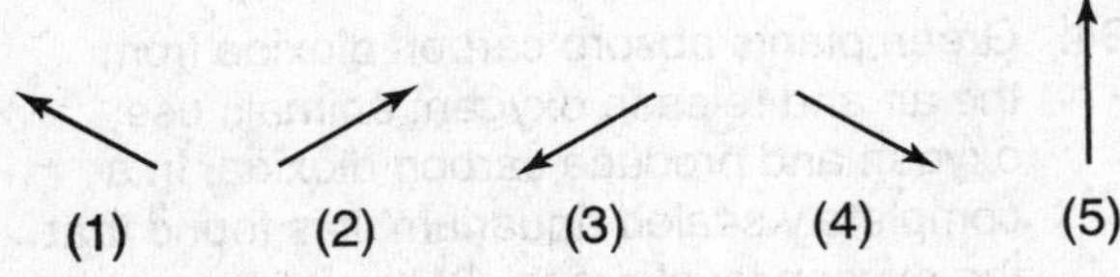

37. An object will not change the speed or direction of its motion unless acted on by an unbalanced force. In which of the following cases can it be assumed that there is no unbalanced force?
    (1) A rock breaks from the side of a cliff and falls.
    (2) A hot-air balloon is released and starts to rise.
    (3) A car with its engine on climbs a hill at 50 miles an hour.
    (4) A car going 50 miles an hour turns a corner.
    (5) A car on a level road shifts to neutral and coasts.

38. In a household circuit, an electric current will flow only if there is a complete circuit going from one terminal of the wall outlet to the other. All of the following will stop the flow of current EXCEPT
    (1) opening the switch of a hair dryer
    (2) overheating of an electric toaster
    (3) burning out of a light bulb
    (4) melting of a fuse
    (5) removing a plug from the wall socket

39. If an opaque object is placed between a light bulb and a wall, the shadow on the wall is a faithful copy of the shape of the object. This is evidence that light
    (1) is a type of wave
    (2) travels in straight lines
    (3) is composed of photons
    (4) travels very fast
    (5) can travel in a vacuum

Questions 40 to 49 are based on the following information.

Behavior in living organisms is the pattern of activities in response to stimuli of the environment. Below are five types of behavior.

(1) reflex act—a simple, inborn, automatic response
(2) instinct—a complex behavior pattern performed without extensive learning
(3) conditioned behavior—a changed stimulus produces the original response
(4) habit—a conscious response becomes automatic after constant repetition
(5) learned behavior—a complex process involving reasoning and insight

Each of the following items refers to one of these types of behavior. For each item choose the category that best describes the one type of behavior. A category may be used more than once in answering the following questions.

GO ON TO THE NEXT PAGE

TEST 3: SCIENCE

40. In January, I find myself dating checks with the old calendar year. This type of behavior is best described as

(1) reflex act
(2) instinct
(3) conditioned behavior
(4) habit
(5) learned behavior

41. Pupils are asked to write their names as many times as they can in 2 minutes. Then they are asked to do the same using the other hand. Comparisons are made regarding quality of performance and number of copies made. This type of behavior is best described as

(1) reflex act
(2) instinct
(3) conditioned behavior
(4) habit
(5) learned behavior

42. The brain of a frog is destroyed in a painless fashion. Some absorbent cotton is dipped in vinegar (two percent acetic acid) and then placed on the frog's thigh. The leg reacts. This type of behavior is best described as

(1) reflex act
(2) instinct
(3) conditioned behavior
(4) habit
(5) learned behavior

43. Joan holds a square of wire mesh closely to her face. Although Martin warns her that he is about to throw a wad of paper at her, when he throws the ball of paper she blinks. This type of behavior is best described as

(1) reflex act
(2) instinct
(3) conditioned behavior
(4) habit
(5) learned behavior

44. Stanley and Lynda finish a difficult crossword puzzle in 60 minutes. Florence and Regina need more time to do the same puzzle. This type of behavior is best described as

(1) reflex act
(2) instinct
(3) conditioned behavior
(4) habit
(5) learned behavior

45. A robin raised in an incubator builds a nest much like those of wild robins. This type of behavior is best described as

(1) reflex act
(2) instinct
(3) conditioned behavior
(4) habit
(5) learned behavior

46. A newborn baby cries when it is uncomfortable, but an older baby will cry just to get attention. This type of behavior is best described as

(1) reflex act
(2) instinct
(3) conditioned behavior
(4) habit
(5) learned behavior

47. A dolphin is rewarded with extra food each time it performs a trick. This type of behavior is best described as

(1) reflex act
(2) instinct
(3) conditioned behavior
(4) habit
(5) learned behavior

GO ON TO THE NEXT PAGE

TEST 3: SCIENCE

48. After a passage is read to a class very slowly, it is read so that the class could copy what they hear but they are told NOT to cross the t's and NOT to dot the i's. Then the number of errors are reported. What is the kind of behavior that causes the errors?

(1) reflex act
(2) instinct
(3) conditioned behavior
(4) habit
(5) learned behavior

49. Persons who have used this book to prepare for the GED have attained satisfactory scores on the test. This type of behavior is best described as

(1) reflex act
(2) instinct
(3) conditioned behavior
(4) habit
(5) learned behavior

<u>Questions 50 to 56</u> refer to the following information.

About 100 years ago, two German scientists studying the function of the pancreas as an organ of digestion removed the entire pancreas from several dogs. A short time later some assistants observed that swarms of flies hovered around the cages that housed these dogs. Many regard this as the initial, but accidental, step in diabetes research. However, it was not until 1922 that Banting and Best showed that the pancreas produces the hormone insulin, which is essential for the proper use by the body of sugar. They concluded that if insulin is lacking, diabetes results.

50. The cages around the group of dogs not given the pancreas surgery did not seem to attract as many flies. This statement should be classified as

(1) the problem statement
(2) a hypothesis
(3) an observation
(4) an assumption
(5) irrelevant information

51. The urine of all dogs was tested for the presence of sugar. The dogs that had the pancreas removed produced urine that gave a positive test for sugar. This statement should be classified as

(1) a hypothesis
(2) the experimental design
(3) an experimental finding
(4) an assumption
(5) a law of nature

52. The dogs in both groups were approximately of the same age, weight, and breed. This statement should be classified as

(1) irrelevant information
(2) the experimental design
(3) a theory
(4) a problem statement
(5) a fact proved by experiment

53. The two German scientists whose work with the pancreas is described in the passage should have shared the honors with Banting and Best for discovering the cure for diabetes. This statement should be classified as

(1) an experimental design
(2) an experimental finding
(3) a hypothesis
(4) an assumption
(5) irrelevant information

54. Before removing the entire pancreas from the dogs, the German researchers experimented several times by removing a segment of this gland. This statement should be classified as

(1) a theory of physiology
(2) the experimental design
(3) an observation
(4) an assumption
(5) irrelevant information

GO ON TO THE NEXT PAGE

TEST 3: SCIENCE

55. The number and nature of the secretions of the pancreas have puzzled scientists for many years. This statement should be classified as

(1) an area for research
(2) an experiment
(3) a theory
(4) an assumption
(5) irrelevant information

56. After completing the experiments on dogs, the German scientists suggested that human diabetes may be the result of a deficiency of the pancreas. This was an

(1) experimental finding
(2) irrelevant statement
(3) observation
(4) assumption
(5) experimental design

---

57. Clouds block the passage of radiant heat, which comes from the Sun to the Earth in the daytime and passes from the Earth into outer space at night. How does cloud cover affect the surface temperature?

(A) It makes days warmer.
(B) It makes days cooler.
(C) It makes nights warmer.
(D) It makes nights cooler.

(1) B only
(2) D only
(3) A and C only
(4) B and D only
(5) B and C only

<u>Questions 58 and 59</u> are based on the following information.

Atoms are the basic units of matter, and groups of atoms make up the elements. An element is a substance that cannot be broken down further by ordinary means. There are approximately 36 common elements, each of which is represented by a chemical symbol. The following table lists a few of the common elements.

Element	Symbol	Atomic Weight*	Atomic Number
Aluminum	Al	27	13
Calcium	Ca	40	20
Carbon	C	12	6
Chlorine	Cl	36	17
Iron	Fe	56	26
Magnesium	Mg	24	12
Oxygen	O	16	8
Potassium	K	31	19
Sulfur	S	32	16
Zinc	Zn	65	30

*Approximate—rounded off

58. In which of the following are the elements arranged in the correct order of increasing atomic weight?

(1) chlorine, magnesium, zinc
(2) iron, oxygen, carbon
(3) sulfur, oxygen, zinc
(4) potassium, sulfur, chlorine
(5) aluminum, chlorine, sulfur

GO ON TO THE NEXT PAGE

TEST 3: SCIENCE

59. An atom consists of a nucleus of neutrons and protons surrounded by electrons in orbit. These electrons account for less than 0.0005% of an atom's weight, and we don't need to consider them here. The atomic number of an element corresponds to the number of protons or electrons in one atom of that element. The number of neutrons can be found by subtracting the number of protons from the atomic weight. How many neutrons are in an atom of potassium?

(1) 20
(2) 12
(3) 19
(4) 39
(5) 59

---

60. The chemical formula represents the number of atoms of each element in a compound and shows how the elements react with one another. The equation

$$Fe + S \rightarrow FeS$$

describes how iron and sulfur combine to form iron sulfide. In the equation

$$2Mg + O_2 \rightarrow 2MgO$$

two atoms of magnesium burn (combine with oxygen) to produce two molecules of magnesium oxide.

When the number of atoms on the right side of a formula is equal to the number of atoms on the left side, the formula is said to be balanced. Which of the following is a balanced equation?

(1) $HgO \rightarrow Hg + O_2$
(2) $Al_2(SO_4)_3 + Ca(OH)_2 \rightarrow 2Al(OH)_2 + CaSO_4$
(3) $S + O_2 \rightarrow SO_2$
(4) $Zn + HCl \rightarrow ZnCl_2 + H_2$
(5) $H_2O + SO_3 \rightarrow 2H_2SO_4$

61. A chemist uses a formula to show what happens during a chemical reaction. As in some kind of esoteric shorthand, symbols are used to indicate the various elements. The molecules that the chemist begins with are called reactants, and the end results are called products. In the chemical formula

$$MgO + 2HCl \rightarrow MgCl_2 + H_2O$$

magnesium oxide (MgO) is treated with hydrochloric acid (HCl) to form magnesium chloride ($MgCl_2$) and water (H_2O).

Which of the following statements is true?

(1) Magnesium oxide is a product of this reaction.
(2) Acids can be dangerous in this combination.
(3) The products in this formula are water and magnesium chloride.
(4) The water molecule comes from the reactant side of the formula.
(5) Hydrochloric acid is a product.

Questions 62 to 65 refer to the following article.

Weather changes daily, but in any given region it follows certain definite patterns that we call the climate of the region. Regions far north and south of the Equator have colder weather than those of low latitude. The reason is that the Earth is warmed by the radiant energy received from the Sun. Near the Equator, these rays arrive nearly vertically most of the year. At higher latitudes, the rays strike the surface at a high angle, and thus their energy is spread out over wider areas. For this reason it is warmer in the middle of the day, when the Sun is nearly overhead, than in the morning or evening.

Proximity to large bodies of water has a strong influence on climate. Water has a high specific heat, so that it warms up and cools down much more slowly than land areas. As a result, places near the ocean have much more uniform temperatures than inland regions. The oceans have another important influence on climate. Cold currents in the ocean lower the temperatures of adjacent land areas, and warm

TEST 3: SCIENCE

currents have the opposite effect.

Accidental phenomena may also have far-reaching effects on climate. A volcanic explosion may put so much dust in the air that the Sun's rays are partially blocked for years. There is reason to believe that nuclear explosions can do the same. In the Amazon rain forest, burning has already produced enough smoke to alter the climate of the region.

62. Climate can best be defined as
    (1) the state of the atmosphere at any given time
    (2) atmospheric conditions at a given location
    (3) weather conditions over a long period of time
    (4) insolation
    (5) nearness to bodies of water

63. As compared with coastal regions in the same latitude, regions that are located at great distances from oceans are likely to have
    (1) hotter summers and colder winters
    (2) hotter summers and warmer winters
    (3) cooler summers and warmer winters
    (4) cooler summers and colder winters
    (5) any of these combinations, depending upon weather conditions

64. The process by which heat is transmitted from the Sun to the Earth is
    (1) conduction
    (2) convection
    (3) radiation
    (4) weathering
    (5) cosmic disturbances

65. Humans can interfere with nature in creating changes in climate by influencing
    (1) topography
    (2) altitude
    (3) winds and storms
    (4) radiation by atomic experimentation
    (5) direction of ocean currents

Question 66 is based on the following graph.

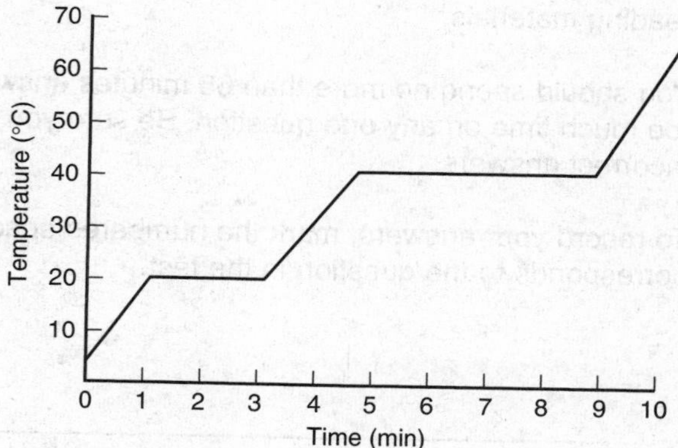

66. While a substance is absorbing heat and undergoing a change of state, its temperature remains constant. The graph above shows the temperature of a substance during a period of time in which heat is being added at a steady rate. The material melts and then boils. What is its boiling temperature?
    (1) 0°C
    (2) 20°C
    (3) 70°C
    (4) 40°C
    (5) 30°C

END OF EXAMINATION

TEST 4: INTERPRETING LITERATURE AND THE ARTS

Directions

The Interpreting Literature and the Arts test consists of excerpts from classical and popular literature and articles about literature or the arts. Each excerpt is followed by multiple-choice questions about the reading material.

Read each excerpt first and then answer the questions following it. Refer to the reading material as often as necessary in answering the questions.

Each excerpt is preceded by a "purpose question." The purpose question gives a reason for reading the material. Use these purpose questions to help focus your reading. You are not required to answer these purpose questions. They are given only to help you concentrate on the ideas presented in the reading materials.

You should spend no more than 65 minutes answering the questions. Work carefully, but do not spend too much time on any one question. Be sure you answer every question. You will not be penalized for incorrect answers.

To record your answers, mark the numbered space on the answer sheet beside the number that corresponds to the question in the test.

FOR EXAMPLE:

It was Susan's dream machine. The metallic blue paint gleamed, and the sporty wheels were highly polished. Under the hood, the engine was no less carefully cleaned. Inside, flashy lights illuminated the instruments on the dashboard, and the seats were covered by rich leather upholstery.

The subject ("It") of this excerpt is most likely

(1) an airplane
(2) a stereo system
(3) an automobile
(4) a boat
(5) a motorcycle

① ② ● ④ ⑤

The correct answer is "an automobile"; therefore, answer space 3 would be marked on the answer sheet.

TEST 4: INTERPRETING LITERATURE AND THE ARTS

Questions 1 to 5 refer to the following passage.

WHAT DOES A VISIT TO KYKUIT, THE ROCKEFELLER FAMILY ESTATE, REVEAL?

The tour takes visitors through the main rooms of the first floor, moving in and out of the building to encompass the surrounding gardens. It is the gardens, mostly laid out by Bosworth, that are the truly spectacular thing here. In many ways, the land has it all over the architecture, since the site is so full of grand gestures, and the house, whatever its virtues, is so empty of them. The one room that tries to do something spectacular, the so-called music room at the heart of the structure, which has an elliptical opening to the floor above, sums up the problem of this house: it is too tall, too tight, too unwilling to let itself go.

Yet how like the generation of Rockefellers who built Kykuit! John D. Rockefeller disapproved of drinking, dancing, and other pleasures; the music room was designed to hold a pipe organ, and Sunday afternoon organ music was the elder Rockefeller's favored entertainment. His son, John D. Rockefeller, Jr., was more comfortable with grand architectural gestures, but even for him, a sense of duty always came first. He envisioned Kykuit not as a palace of pleasure but as the serious expression of the stature of a great family. If this freed Kykuit from the vulgar excesses of Newport and Fifth Avenue, it also gave the estate more than a whiff of dry formality.

It's no accident, then, that Kykuit lacks such showy symbols as a grand staircase; the second floor (which is not included in the public tour) is reached by a stair that is not much larger than the one you would find in a suburban house, tucked behind the partition that once contained the pipe organ. The main public rooms are hardly small, but neither do they approach the institutional scale of the ballrooms and reception rooms of so many American palaces of this period; indeed, these rooms always feel domestic, which was presumably the intention. They are furnished conservatively, with a mix of antiques and plain upholstered pieces, and have a number of paintings of note, including a Gilbert Stuart portrait of George Washington in the library and John Singer Sargent's portrait of the senior Rockefeller in the dining room, as well as numerous examples of Chinese ceramics.

1. The visitor finds that the most positive feature of Kykuit is
   (1) the music room
   (2) its staircase
   (3) the second floor
   (4) the public rooms
   (5) the gardens

2. The visitor is critical of Kykuit's
   (1) vulgar excesses
   (2) formality
   (3) showy symbols
   (4) institutional scale
   (5) site

3. The visitor states that John D. Rockefeller, Jr., had a desire to
   (1) imitate Newport and Fifth Avenue
   (2) create a pleasure palace
   (3) avoid architectural gestures
   (4) reflect a distinguished family
   (5) present favored entertainment

4. The visitor implies that the intent of the Rockefellers was to be
   (1) showy
   (2) homey
   (3) grand
   (4) impressive
   (5) innovative

5. The portraits are mentioned as examples of
   (1) plain pieces
   (2) modern art
   (3) antiques
   (4) radical taste
   (5) famous paintings

GO ON TO THE NEXT PAGE

TEST 4: INTERPRETING LITERATURE AND THE ARTS

Questions 6 to 10 refer to the following passage.

WHAT IS GREEN SEAL'S ROLE IN ENVIRONMENTAL PROTECTION?

Green Seal, a nonprofit organization based in the nation's capital, helps shoppers single out honest environmental claims. The organization develops stringent environmental standards for products ranging from toilet tissue to re-refined motor oil, and then invites companies to let Green Seal test their products. Goods that equal or exceed the standards can print Green Seal's logo–a blue globe overlaid with a green check-mark–on product packaging. Dean says green labeling rewards companies that make environmentally sound products by giving them a presumed competitive edge and encourages more companies to jump on the green wagon.

Launched in 1990, Green Seal is modeled after eco-labeling programs in Germany, Canada, Japan and nearly 15 other nations. However, most of these programs are government run, while money from foundations and individual donors bankrolls Green Seal. Dean, formerly director of the National Wildlife Federation's Environmental Quality Division, says that private financing frees Green Seal from the political problems that would arise with federal funding: "The 80 percent of the companies that aren't getting certified would be placing pressure on their members of Congress to squeeze the organization to become more lenient."

Green Seal develops technical standards for various categories of products. The staff considers how raw materials used to manufacture a product are obtained and monitors the product's role in the environment throughout its use and disposal. "We ask, where are the key impacts, and what can be done in these areas to make the product less damaging?" explains Dean.

For products such as bathroom and facial tissue, impacts include logging to get the wood used in paper pulp, discharge of chlorine and other toxic chemicals from paper mills into rivers, dumping of waste paper in landfills and air pollution from paper incineration.

Green Seal has set standards for roughly 40 categories of consumer products and has put its label on 23 products from eight companies.

6. Green Seal's logo would be most likely influential with shoppers who are

   (1) seeking bargains
   (2) honest
   (3) interested in politics
   (4) concerned about the environment
   (5) influenced by packaging

7. According to the passage,

   (1) companies seek out Green Seal
   (2) Green Seal is generous in its testing
   (3) Green Seal sets standards for products
   (4) environmental claims are honest
   (5) Green Seal profits from its services

8. Green Seal's program is different from that in other nations in that it

   (1) is government run
   (2) collects fees
   (3) is more lenient
   (4) is federally funded
   (5) is privately financed

9. Green Seal's staff is most concerned with a product's

   (1) environmental impact
   (2) profitability
   (3) utility
   (4) performance
   (5) cost

10. From the example of bathroom and facial tissue, it can be concluded that Green Seal is concerned with

    (1) raw materials
    (2) efficient production
    (3) rivers
    (4) landfills
    (5) proper disposal

GO ON TO THE NEXT PAGE

TEST 4: INTERPRETING LITERATURE AND THE ARTS

Questions 11 to 15 refer to the following passage.

HOW DID ONE VILLAGE BRING DISASTER ON ITSELF?

On a morning in early spring, 1873, the people of Oberfest left their houses and took refuge in the town hall. No one knows why, precisely. A number of rumors had raced through the town during recent weeks, were passed on and converted to news; predictions became certainties. On this particular morning, fear turned into terror, and people rushed through the narrow streets, carrying their most precious possessions, pulling their children and dashing into the great hall. The doors were nailed shut, and men took their turns watching out the window. Two days passed. When no disaster came, the fear grew worse, because the people began to suspect that the danger was already in the hall, locked inside. No one spoke to anybody else; people watched each other, looking for signs. It was the children who rang the great bell in the first bell tower—a small band of bored children found the bell rope and swung on it—set the bell clanging. This was the traditional signal of alarm, and in a moment the elders were dashing in panic to all the other bell towers and ringing the bells. For nearly an hour, the valley reverberated with the wild clangor—and then, a thousand feet above, the snow began to crack, and the avalanche began; a massive cataract of ice and snow thundered down and buried the town, silencing the bells. There is no trace of Oberfest today, not even a spire, because the snow is so deep; and, in the shadow of the mountains, it is very cold.

11. Which element is especially significant in this passage?

(1) dialogue
(2) setting
(3) illustrations
(4) levels of usage
(5) rhythm

12. Which is the most valid conclusion regarding the theme of the passage?

(1) It is a minor feature of the passage.
(2) It is not related to the plot.
(3) It is related to the topic sentence.
(4) It is stated, rather than implied.
(5) It is implied, but not stated.

13. That the alarm, traditionally sounded to avert danger, became the apparent cause of the avalanche is an example of

(1) irony
(2) simile
(3) satire
(4) personification
(5) exaggeration

14. The effect of the last phrase of the passage, "it is very cold," depends mainly on

(1) rhythm
(2) rhyme
(3) comparison
(4) connotation
(5) sound

15. Which word best expresses the main idea of the passage?

(1) faith
(2) suspicion
(3) nostalgia
(4) disaster
(5) rumors

Questions 16 to 20 refer to the following poem.

HOW DOES THIS POET FEEL ABOUT HIMSELF?

EVERY GOOD BOY DOES FINE

I practiced my cornet in a cold garage
Where I could blast it till the oil in drums
Boomed back; tossed free-throws till I
couldn't move my thumbs;

GO ON TO THE NEXT PAGE

TEST 4: INTERPRETING LITERATURE AND THE ARTS

Sprinted through tires, tackling a headless dummy.
In my first contest, playing a wobbly solo,
I blew up in the coda, alone on stage,
And twisting like my hand-tied necktie, saw the judge
Letting my silence dwindle down his scale.

At my first basketball game, gangling away from home
A hundred miles by bus to a dressing room,
Under the showering voice of the coach, I stood in a towel,
Having forgotten shoes, socks, uniform.

In my first football game, the first play under the lights
I intercepted a pass. For seventy yards, I ran
Through music and squeals, surging, lifting my cleats,
Only to be brought down by the safety man.
I took my second chances with less care, but in dreams
I saw the bald judge slumped in the front row,
The coach and team at the doorway, the safety man
Galloping loud at my heels. They watch me
now.

You who have always horned your way through passages,
Sat safe on the bench while some came naked to court,
Slipped out of arms to win in the long run,
Consider this poem a failure, sprawling flat on a page.

16. The "I," or speaking voice of the poem, probably regards himself mainly as

(1) an athlete
(2) a musician
(3) a loser
(4) a wit
(5) a critic

17. In relation to the content of the poem, its title is an example of

(1) personification
(2) allegory
(3) sensory language
(4) irony
(5) an epithet

18. In the final stanza, the reader is asked to

(1) make an improper judgment
(2) feel sorry for the poet
(3) feel superior to the poet
(4) agree with the poet
(5) admire the poet

19. In line 9, "twisting like my hand-tied necktie" is an example of

(1) a striking contrast
(2) a vague reference
(3) an implied meaning
(4) an overused symbol
(5) a vivid comparison

20. With which group of words does the poet address the reader directly?

(1) "I practiced my cornet" (line 1)
(2) "In my first contest" (line 7)
(3) "in dreams I saw the bald judge" (lines 28 and 29)
(4) "some came naked to court" (lines 37 and 38)
(5) "Consider this poem a failure" (line 40)

GO ON TO THE NEXT PAGE

TEST 4: INTERPRETING LITERATURE AND THE ARTS

Questions 21 to 25 refer to the following poem.

HOW SHOULD WE LIVE OUR LIVES?

BARTER

Life has loveliness to sell—
All beautiful and splendid things,
Blue waves whitened on a cliff,
Climbing fire that sways and sings,
And children's faces looking up
Holding wonder like a cup.

Life has loveliness to sell—
Music like a curve of gold,
Scent of pine trees in the rain,
Eyes that love you, arms that hold,
And for your spirit's still delight,
Holy thoughts that star the night.

Spend all you have for loveliness,
Buy it and never count the cost.
For one white singing hour of peace
Count many a year of strife well lost,
And for a breath of ecstasy
Give all you have been or could be.

—Sara Teasdale

21. The main idea of the poem is to urge us
    (1) to be cautious in life
    (2) to avoid strife
    (3) to despise the ugly part of life
    (4) to enjoy life's treasures
    (5) not to become involved

22. The beauty of nature is indicated in line
    (1) 3
    (2) 6
    (3) 10
    (4) 12
    (5) 16

23. There is a simile (comparison) in line
    (1) 2
    (2) 4
    (3) 7
    (4) 10
    (5) 16

24. The poet includes the spiritual in life with the words
    (1) "climbing fire"
    (2) "children's faces"
    (3) "arms that hold"
    (4) "holy thoughts"
    (5) "year of strife"

25. The word *barter* means exchange by trade without money. In the poem the exchange is
    (1) personal commitment for life's beauty
    (2) a year of strife for ecstasy
    (3) spirit's delight for peace
    (4) children's faces for wonder
    (5) music for a curve of gold

GO ON TO THE NEXT PAGE

TEST 4: INTERPRETING LITERATURE AND THE ARTS

Questions 26 to 30 refer to this excerpt from a play.

HOW DOES HIS FAMILY REACT TO WILLY LOMAN'S SUICIDE?

REQUIEM

CHARLEY: It's getting dark, Linda.
(Linda doesn't react. She stares at the grave.)
BIFF: How about it, Mom? Better get some rest, heh! They'll be closing the gate soon.
(Linda makes no move. Pause.)
HAPPY *(deeply angered)*: He had no right to do that. There was no necessity for it. We would've helped him.
BIFF: Come along, Mom.
LINDA: Why didn't anybody come?
CHARLEY: It was a very nice funeral.
LINDA: But where are all the people he knew? Maybe they blame him.
CHARLEY: Naa. It's a rough world, Linda. They wouldn't blame him.
LINDA: I can't understand it. At this time especially. First time in thirty-five years we were just about free and clear. He only needed a little salary. He was even finished with the dentist.
CHARLEY: No man only needs a little salary.
LINDA: I can't understand it.
BIFF: There were a lot of nice days. When he'd come home from a trip, or on Sundays, making the stoop, finishing the cellar, when he built the extra bathroom, and put up the garage. You know something, Charley, there's more of him in that front stoop than in all the sales he ever made.
CHARLEY: Yeah, he was a happy man with a batch a cement.
LINDA: He was so wonderful with his hands.
BIFF: He had the wrong dreams. All, all, wrong.
HAPPY: *(almost ready to fight Biff)*: Don't say that.
BIFF: He never knew who he was.
CHARLEY *(stopping Happy's movement and reply. To Biff)*: Nobody dast blame this man. You don't understand. Willy was a salesman. And for a salesman, there is no rock bottom to the life. He don't put a bolt to a nut, he don't tell you the law or give you medicine. He's the man way out there in the blue riding on a smile and a shoeshine. And when they start not smiling back—that's an earthquake. And then you get yourself a couple of spots on your hat, and you're finished. Nobody dast blame this man. A salesman has got to dream, boy. It comes with the territory.
BIFF: Charley, the man didn't know who he was.
HAPPY *(infuriated)*: Don't say that.
BIFF: Why don't you come with me, Happy?
HAPPY: I'm not licked that easily. I'm staying right here in this city, and I'm gonna beat this racket! *(He looks at Biff, his chin set.)* The Loman Brothers!
BIFF: I know who I am, kid.
HAPPY: All right, boy. I'm gonna show you and everybody else that Willy Loman did not die in vain. He had a good dream. It's the only dream you can have—to come out number-one man. He fought it out here, and this is where I'm gonna win it for him.

26. You can deduce from Happy's remarks that he is angry with
    (1) Charley
    (2) Linda
    (3) Biff
    (4) himself
    (5) Willy Loman

27. Biff differs with
    (1) Linda
    (2) Linda and Charley
    (3) Linda and Happy
    (4) Happy and Charley
    (5) Willy Loman

28. Charley
    (1) defends Willy
    (2) attacks salespersons
    (3) agrees with Biff
    (4) thinks Willy was a loser
    (5) thinks people don't need much money

GO ON TO THE NEXT PAGE

TEST 4: INTERPRETING LITERATURE AND THE ARTS

29. Happy is
    (1) disrespectful to Linda
    (2) resentful of Charley
    (3) sympathetic to Biff
    (4) loyal to Willy's dream
    (5) beaten and discouraged

30. The irony in the situation is that, at the time of Willy's suicide, the family is
    (1) splitting up
    (2) united in tragedy
    (3) appreciative of Willy
    (4) in good shape financially
    (5) mutually supportive

Questions 31 to 35 refer to the following passage.

HOW DOES THE AUTHOR FEEL ABOUT PRIZE FIGHT CROWDS?

The fight crowd is a beast that lurks in the darkness behind the fringe of white light shed over the first six rows by the incandescents atop the ring, and is not to be trusted with pop bottles or other hardware.

People who go to prize fights are sadistic.

When two prominent pugilists are scheduled to pummel one another in public on a summer's evening, men and women file into the stadium in the guise of human beings, and thereafter become a part of a gray thing that squats in the dark until, at the conclusion of the bloodletting, they may be seen leaving the arena in the same guise they wore when they entered....

As a rule, the mob that gathers to see men fight is unjust, vindictive, swept by intense unreasoning hatreds, proud of its swift recognition of what it believes to be sportsmanship. It is quick to greet the purely phony move of the boxer who extends his gloves to his rival, who has slipped or been pushed to the floor, and to reward this stimulating but still baloney gesture with a pattering of hands which indicates the following: "You are a good sport. We recognize that you are a good sport, and we know a sporting gesture when we see one. Therefore we are all good sports, too. Hurrah for us!"

The same crowd doesn't see the same boxer stick his thumb in his opponent's eye or try to cut him with the laces of his glove, butt him or dig him a low one when the referee isn't in a position to see. It roots consistently for the smaller man, and never for a moment considers the desperate psychological dilemma of the larger of the two. It howls with glee at a good finisher making his kill. The Roman hordes were more civilized. Their gladiators asked them whether the final blow should be administered or not. The main attraction at the modern prize fight is the spectacle of a man clubbing a helpless and vanquished opponent into complete insensibility. The referee who stops a bout to save a slugged and punch-drunken man from the final ignominy is hissed by the assembled sportsmen.

31. The writer of this passage is
    (1) disgusted
    (2) jovial
    (3) matter-of-fact
    (4) satiric
    (5) optimistic

32. As used in line 25, which action is referred to as a "baloney gesture"?
    (1) pushing the opponent to the floor
    (2) shaking hands with the opponent
    (3) touching gloves with the downed opponent
    (4) smiling at the opponent
    (5) digging the opponent a low blow

GO ON TO THE NEXT PAGE

TEST 4: INTERPRETING LITERATURE AND THE ARTS

33. The "desperate psychological dilemma" of the bigger man (line 39) is caused by the crowd's
    (1) rooting for the smaller man, but cheering a good finisher
    (2) cheering a good finisher, but hissing at the referee
    (3) applauding a friendly gesture, but rooting for the smaller man
    (4) hissing at the referee, but howling at a good finisher
    (5) applauding a friendly gesture, but cheering a helpless opponent

34. Which group of words best indicates the author's opinion?
    (1) *referee, opponent, finisher*
    (2) *gladiators, slugged, sporting gesture*
    (3) *stimulating, hissing, pattering*
    (4) *beast, lurks, gray thing*
    (5) *spectacle, psychological dilemma, sportsmen*

35. The author states that the prize fight audience is
    (1) sportsmanlike
    (2) fair
    (3) civilized
    (4) uninvolved
    (5) vengeful

Questions 36 to 40 refer to the following commentary on literature.

WHAT HERITAGE DID WILLA CATHER LEAVE TO US?

Willa Cather (1873–1947) grew up to be a major American writer, but today many people still do not know her face. Critics rank her with our great modern novelists—Faulkner, Hemingway, Fitzgerald—and she was certainly esteemed in her own time. Supreme Court Justice Oliver Wendell Holmes praised *My Antonia* as a book that "makes the reader love his country more."

Miss Cather wrote that novel and 11 others. Her books still have this effect on readers, for she had the power to elevate ordinary people and places. No one has described the American West with more passion and clarity. In every sentence, her feeling for the earth surges beneath a strong, disciplined prose. This is from *My Antonia:*

We were talking about what it is like to spend one's childhood in little towns like these, buried in wheat and corn, under stimulating extremes of climate: burning summers when the world lies green and billowy beneath a brilliant sky, when one is fairly stifled in vegetation, in the colour and smell of strong weeds and heavy harvests; blustery winters with little snow, when the whole country is stripped bare and grey as sheet-iron. We agreed that no one who had not grown up in a little prairie town could know anything about it. It was a kind of freemasonry, we said.

Willa Cather became the voice of an unsung people, the generation of immigrants who settled our western frontier. Today many writers regard that history as tragic, a paradise lost through careless greed. Cather believed that America's promise would endure: *We come and go, but the land is always here. And the people who love it and understand it are the people who own it—for a little while.*

36. The author implies impatience with
    (1) lack of modern recognition of Cather's work
    (2) lack of critical acclaim for Cather's work
    (3) lack of appreciation by her contemporaries
    (4) Cather's stature as a writer
    (5) Cather's patriotism

37. The author admires Cather's
    (1) huge output
    (2) popular success
    (3) unusual subject matter
    (4) objectivity
    (5) earthiness

GO ON TO THE NEXT PAGE

TEST 4: INTERPRETING LITERATURE AND THE ARTS

38. In the excerpt from *My Antonia*, Cather stresses a childhood rooted in a small town's

    (1) repression
    (2) activity
    (3) passion
    (4) natural characteristics
    (5) brutal hardships

39. The author implies praise for all of the following characteristics of Cather's work EXCEPT her

    (1) style
    (2) passion
    (3) clarity
    (4) effect on her readers
    (5) unusual subjects

40. Cather's view of America was

    (1) cynical
    (2) resigned
    (3) tragic
    (4) optimistic
    (5) regional

Questions 41 to 45 refer to the following commentary on film.

HOW DID THE OSCAR COME TO BE?

The Academy of Motion Picture Arts and Sciences was founded in 1927 after a dinner of film notables at the beach house of M.G.M.'s powerful studio chief, Louis B. Mayer. The organization's professed purpose was to represent the industry as a whole. Actually, it was set up, at least in part, to circumvent the rise of the industry's trade and craft unions. Yet, today, members of Hollywood's guilds and unions are strongly represented in the running of the Academy.

Before the award ceremonies were televised in the 1950s, most of the costs were underwritten by the studios, and they had been known to pressure employees to vote for pictures they produced. But in 1952, when several major film companies refused to come up with their share of the expenses, NBC-RCA made a $100,000 bid for the radio and TV rights. The show has been paid for by a television network ever after—since 1976, by ABC-TV.

The Academy is divided into 13 voting branches, and a member must have gained prominence in his or her field before being invited to join. Each branch for which there is an award nominates achievements in its own field. For example, for the 1986 awards, 107 cinematographers nominated for photography; for best song and score, 243 members of the music branch nominated; and 1207 actors nominated for the four acting awards. But all 4244 voting members of the Academy nominated for Best Picture and were eligible to vote in all but a few categories.

The statuette was first given two years after the Academy's founding. Art director Cedric Gibbons sketched on a tablecloth the naked man who would be Oscar. Molded by sculptor George Stanley, this then-nameless 24K gold-plated statuette was 13½ inches tall and weighed 8 pounds. Today the statuette is mass-produced and costs an estimated $200.

Where did the name Oscar come from? In 1931 Margaret Herrick, longtime executive director of the Academy, was its librarian. She saw the statuette for the first time and exclaimed, "Why, it looks like my Uncle Oscar!" Columnist Sidney Skolsky reportedly overheard Academy members calling the statuette Oscar and began using the nickname. It wasn't long before the word was in the dictionary.

41. The author of the passage is

    (1) objective
    (2) critical
    (3) laudatory
    (4) humorous
    (5) pro-Hollywood

GO ON TO THE NEXT PAGE

TEST 4: INTERPRETING LITERATURE AND THE ARTS

42. The Academy of Motion Picture Arts and Sciences, according to the passage, has
    (1) failed in its purpose
    (2) held to its purpose
    (3) changed its purpose
    (4) achieved its original purpose
    (5) had no specific purpose

43. According to the passage, a change has taken place in
    (1) the selection of Oscar winners
    (2) the composition of the Academy
    (3) the purpose of the Oscar
    (4) the major film companies
    (5) the financing of the award ceremonies

44. The name Oscar became popular after
    (1) careful planning by the Academy
    (2) work by Cedric Gibbons
    (3) work by George Stanley
    (4) use by Sidney Skolsky
    (5) research by Margaret Herrick

45. The author implies that the Oscar awards are now
    (1) subject to studio pressure
    (2) influenced by television networks
    (3) made by qualified experts
    (4) subject to union influence
    (5) granted by the major film companies

END OF EXAMINATION

TEST 5: MATHEMATICS

Directions

The Mathematics test consists of multiple-choice questions intended to measure general mathematics skills and problem-solving ability. The questions are based on short readings that often include a graph, chart, or figure.

You should spend no more than 90 minutes answering the questions. Work carefully, but do not spend too much time on any one question. Be sure you answer every question. You will not be penalized for incorrect answers.

Formulas you may need are given on page 726. Only some of the questions will require you to use a formula. Not all the formulas given will be needed.

Some questions contain more information than you will need to solve the problem. Other questions do not give enough information to solve the problem. If the question does not give enough information to solve the problem, the correct answer choice is "Not enough information is given."

The use of calculators is not allowed.

To record your answers, mark the numbered space on the answer sheet beside the number that corresponds to the question in the test.

FOR EXAMPLE:

If a grocery bill totaling $15.75 is paid with a $20.00 bill, how much change should be returned?

(1) $5.26
(2) $4.75
(3) $4.25
(4) $3.75
(5) $3.25

① ② ● ④ ⑤

The correct answer is "$4.25"; therefore, answer space 3 would be marked on the answer sheet.

GO ON TO THE NEXT PAGE

TEST 5: MATHEMATICS

FORMULAS

Description	Formula
AREA (A) of a:	
square	$A = s^2$; where s = side
rectangle	$A = lw$; where l = length, w = width
parallelogram	$A = bh$; where b = base, h = height
triangle	$A = \frac{1}{2}bh$; where b = base, h = height
circle	$A = \pi r^2$; where $\pi = 3.14$, r = radius
PERIMETER (P) of a:	
square	$P = 4s$; where s = side
rectangle	$P = 2l + 2w$; where l = length, w = width
triangle	$P = a + b + c$; where a, b, and c are the sides
circumference (C) of a circle	$C = \pi d$; where $\pi = 3.14$, d = diameter
VOLUME (V) of a:	
cube	$V = s^3$; where s = side
rectangular container	$V = lwh$; where l = length, w = width, h = height
cylinder	$V = \pi r^2 h$; where $\pi = 3.14$, r = radius, h = height
Pythagorean relationship	$c^2 = a^2 + b^2$; where c = hypotenuse, a and b are legs of a right triangle
distance (d) between two points in a plane	$d = \sqrt{(x_2 - x_1)^2 + (y_2 - y_1)^2}$; where (x_1,y_1) and (x_2,y_2) are two points in a plane
slope of a line (m)	$m = \frac{y_2 - y_1}{x_2 - x_1}$; where (x_1,y_1) and (x_2,y_2) are two points in a plane
mean	mean = $\frac{x_1 + x_2 + \ldots + x_n}{n}$; where the x's are the values for which a mean is desired, and n = number of values in the series
median	median = the point in an ordered set of numbers at which half of the numbers are above and half of the numbers are below this value
simple interest (i)	$i = prt$; where p = principal, r = rate, t = time
distance (d) as function of rate and time	$d = rt$; where r = rate, t = time
total cost (c)	$c = nr$; where n = number of units, r = cost per unit

GO ON TO THE NEXT PAGE

TEST 5: MATHEMATICS

1. A salesman earns $200 per week plus a 5% commission on all sales over $8,000. One week, his sales amounted to $15,000. What were his earnings that week?

   (1) $200
   (2) $350
   (3) $500
   (4) $550
   (5) $600

2. How much does Jane pay for 1 pound 12 ounces of apples at $0.84 per pound?

   (1) $1.36
   (2) $1.47
   (3) $1.57
   (4) $1.65
   (5) $1.75

3. One morning Martin drove 80 miles in 2 hours. After lunch, he covered 100 miles more in 3 hours. What was his average rate of speed, in miles per hour, for the entire trip?

   (1) 35
   (2) 36
   (3) 37
   (4) 45
   (5) Not enough information is given.

4. A picture 8 inches long and 6 inches wide is to be enlarged so that its length will be 12 inches. What is the width, in inches, of the enlarged picture?

   (1) 9
   (2) 10
   (3) 12
   (4) 14
   (5) 16

5. A man bought ABC stock at $\$19\frac{5}{8}$ per share and sold it at $\$23\frac{1}{4}$ per share. What was his profit on 80 shares before deductions for commission and taxes?

   (1) $29
   (2) $240
   (3) $255
   (4) $290
   (5) $358

6. A solution of the inequality $3x - 1 < 5$ is

   (1) 3
   (2) 2
   (3) 1
   (4) 5
   (5) $2\frac{1}{2}$

7. A theater has 850 seats, 60% of which are in the orchestra. How many seats are **NOT** in the orchestra?

   (1) 240
   (2) 260
   (3) 320
   (4) 340
   (5) 510

8. In a right triangle, the ratio of the measures of the two acute angles is 4 : 1. What is the measure, in degrees, of the larger acute angle?

   (1) 50
   (2) 54
   (3) 70
   (4) 72
   (5) Not enough information is given.

GO ON TO THE NEXT PAGE

TEST 5: MATHEMATICS

9. If 18 feet 10 inches is cut from a wire that is 25 feet 8 inches long, what is the length of the wire that is left?

   (1) 6 ft. 1 in.
   (2) 6 ft. 2 in.
   (3) 6 ft. 9 in.
   (4) 6 ft. 10 in.
   (5) 7 ft. 2 in.

10. Bill earns m dollars per month, and Angelo earns n dollars per month. How many dollars do both men earn in 1 year?

   (1) $12mn$
   (2) $12m + n$
   (3) $12(m + n)$
   (4) $12n + m$
   (5) $12n - m$

Question 11 is based on the following figure.

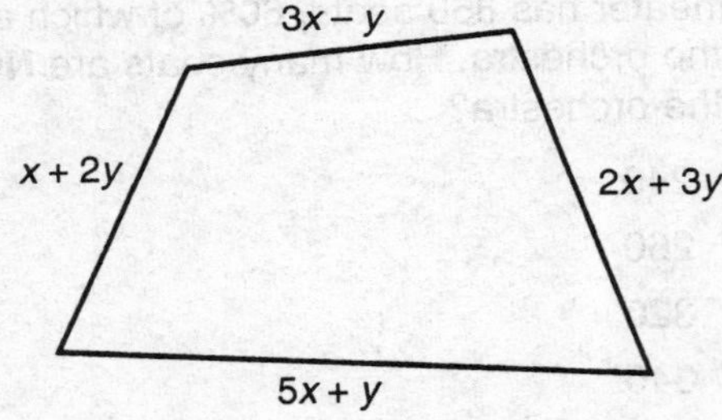

11. What is the perimeter of the figure?

   (1) $11x + 5y$
   (2) $10x + 5y$
   (3) $11x + 4y$
   (4) $9x - y$
   (5) $8x + 3y$

12. Joan and Maria earn money by babysitting. If Joan earns twice as much as Maria and the two girls earn a total of $42, how much does Maria earn?

   (1) $8
   (2) $10
   (3) $12
   (4) $14
   (5) Not enough information is given.

Question 13 is based on the following table.

The table gives the instructions that accompany an income tax form.

If your taxable income is:

At least	But not more than	Your tax is
0	$3,499	2% of the amount
$3,500	$4,499	$70 plus 3% of any amount above $3,500
$4,500	$7,499	$100 plus 5% of any amount above $4,500
$7,500		$250 plus 7% of any amount above $7,500

13. How much tax is due on a taxable income of $5,800?

   (1) $120
   (2) $135
   (3) $150
   (4) $165
   (5) $175

GO ON TO THE NEXT PAGE

TEST 5: MATHEMATICS

14. Given the formula $x = 2a(b + 7)$, find x if $a = 3$ and $b = 5$.

(1) 13
(2) 72
(3) 108
(4) 120
(5) 210

15. The weights of the 11 men on the Panthers football team are 201,197,193, 212, 205, 207, 195, 214, 198, 203, and 184 pounds. What is the median weight, in pounds, of a player on this team?

(1) 199
(2) 200
(3) 201
(4) 203
(5) 205

16. A committee consists of 7 women and 4 men. If a member of the committee is chosen at random to act as chairperson, what is the probability that the choice is a woman?

(1) $\frac{1}{11}$

(2) $\frac{1}{7}$

(3) $\frac{4}{7}$

(4) $\frac{7}{11}$

(5) $\frac{10}{11}$

17. A bag of potatoes weighing 5 pounds 12 ounces costs $2.07. What is the cost of 1 pound of potatoes?

(1) $0.36
(2) $0.38
(3) $0.40
(4) $0.45
(5) $0.48

Question 18 is based on the following figure.

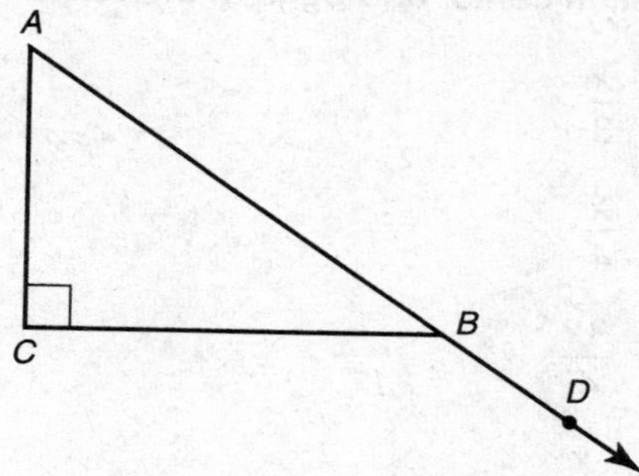

18. If $\overleftrightarrow{AC}$ is perpendicular to $\overleftrightarrow{CB}$ and $m\angle CBD = 125°$ then $m\angle A$ equals

(1) 15°
(2) 20°
(3) 35°
(4) 45°
(5) Not enough information is given.

---

19. In a large class 80 students took a test. When the test papers were rated, it was found that 10% of the students had A papers, 25% had B papers, 30% had C papers, 15% had D papers, and the rest failed. How many students failed the test?

(1) 10
(2) 12
(3) 15
(4) 16
(5) Not enough information is given.

20. A man invests $20,000 at an annual interest rate of 7%, and $12,000 at an annual interest rate of $7\frac{1}{2}$%. What was his annual income on the two investments?

(1) $1,400
(2) $1,500
(3) $2,000
(4) $2,300
(5) $2,800

GO ON TO THE NEXT PAGE

TEST 5: MATHEMATICS

21. A dozen eggs cost x cents. What is the cost, in cents, of 3 eggs at the same rate?

(1) $\frac{x}{3}$

(2) $\frac{x}{4}$

(3) $\frac{3x}{4}$

(4) $\frac{x}{12}$

(5) $3x$

22. Pete Rossini has just graduated from college with honors. He has been offered four jobs with the following pay provisions:

A. $27,000 for the first year
B. $570 per week for the first year
C. $2,250 per month for the first year
D. $2,000 per month for the first 6 months and an increase of 10% for the last 6 months

Which of the above offers will give Pete Rossini the greatest income for the first year?

(1) A
(2) B
(3) C
(4) D
(5) Not enough information is given.

23. A dealer bought two dozen jackets at $48 each. The next month she bought 15 more jackets at $48 each. Which of the following expressions gives the total number of dollars the dealer spent for the jackets?

(1) $24 \times 48 + 15$
(2) $(24 \times 48) \times 15$
(3) $24 + 48 \times 15$
(4) $48(24 + 15)$
(5) $24 + (48 + 15)$

24. One car travels at an average speed of 48 miles per hour. A slower car travels at an average speed of 36 miles per hour. In 45 minutes how many more miles does the faster car travel than the slower car?

(1) 9
(2) 10
(3) 12
(4) 27
(5) 36

<u>Question 25</u> is based on the following graph.

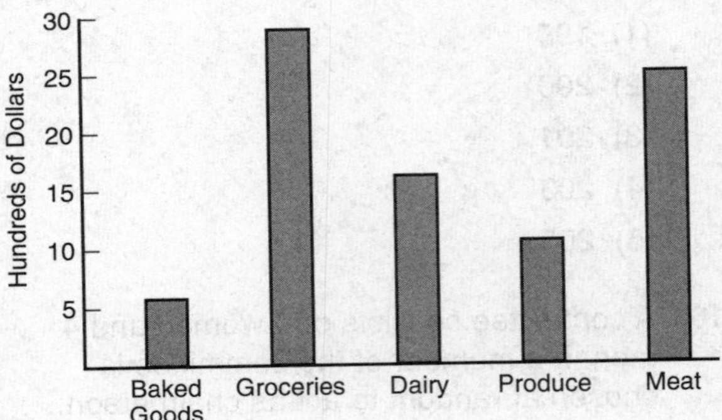

25. By how many dollars do the sales in the meat department exceed the sales in the dairy department?

(1) $100
(2) $1,000
(3) $1,500
(4) $1,800
(5) $10,000

26. A boat travels due east for a distance of 15 miles. It then travels due north for a distance of 20 miles, at which point it drops anchor. How many miles is the boat from its starting point?

(1) 23
(2) 25
(3) 29
(4) 30
(5) 35

GO ON TO THE NEXT PAGE

TEST 5: MATHEMATICS

27. On January 1, a 280-gallon oil tank was $\frac{7}{8}$ full; on January 31 it was $\frac{1}{4}$ full. How many gallons of oil were used during the month?
    (1) 70
    (2) 105
    (3) 175
    (4) 210
    (5) Not enough information is given.

28. Express 2,750,389 in scientific notation.
    (1) 27.50389×10^5
    (2) 275.0389×10^3
    (3) 27.50389×10^6
    (4) 0.2750389×10^7
    (5) 2.750389×10^6

29. A basketball team has won 50 games of 75 played. The team still has 45 games to play. How many of the remaining games must the team win in order to win 60% of all games played during the season?
    (1) 20
    (2) 21
    (3) 22
    (4) 25
    (5) 30

30. A rectangle and a triangle have equal areas. The length of the rectangle is 12 inches, and its width is 8 inches. If the base of the triangle is 32 inches, what is the length, in inches, of the altitude drawn to the base?
    (1) 6
    (2) 8
    (3) 9
    (4) 12
    (5) 16

31. A school has 18 classes with 35 students in each class. In order to reduce class size to 30, how many new classes must be formed?
    (1) 2
    (2) 3
    (3) 5
    (4) 6
    (5) 8

Question 32 is based on the following graph.

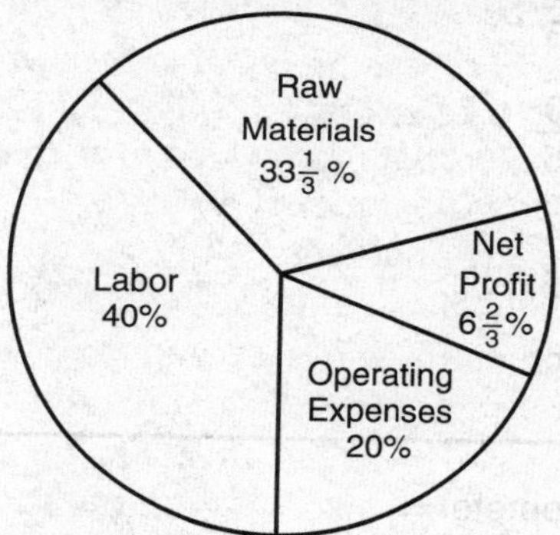

32. How many dollars were spent for labor?
    (1) $4,800
    (2) $9,600
    (3) $48,000
    (4) $96,000
    (5) $960,000

GO ON TO THE NEXT PAGE

TEST 5: MATHEMATICS

Question 33 is based on the following graph.

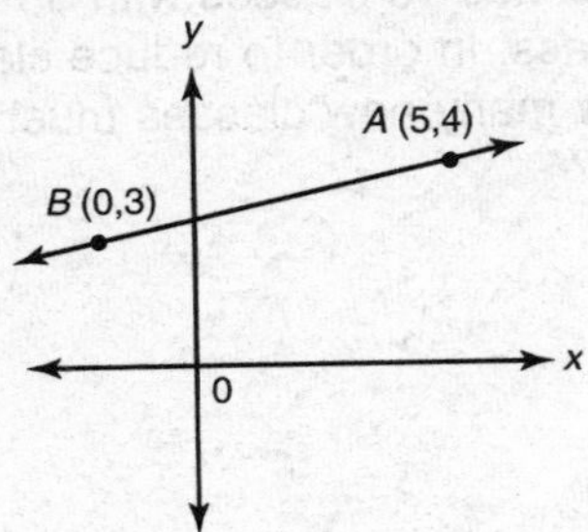

33. What is the slope of the line passing through points *A* (5,4) and *B* (0,3)?

(1) $\frac{1}{10}$

(2) $\frac{1}{5}$

(3) $\frac{3}{5}$

(4) $\frac{4}{5}$

(5) 5

34. 1 kilometer =

(1) 10 meters
(2) 100 meters
(3) 1,000 centimeters
(4) 10,000 centimeters
(5) 1,000,000 millimeters

35. Which of the following pairs of points both lie on the line whose equation is $3x - y = 2$?

(1) (3,–2) and (1,5)
(2) (2,4) and (3,7)
(3) (2,4) and (1,5)
(4) (2,–2) and (1,5)
(5) (3,7) and (3,–2)

36. If $3x - 1 = 11$, what is the value of $x^2 + x$?

(1) 12
(2) 15
(3) 16
(4) 18
(5) 20

37. A bell rings every 2 hours, a second bell rings every 3 hours, and a third bell rings every 4 hours. If all 3 bells ring at 9:00 A.M., at what time will all 3 bells next ring?

(1) noon
(2) 6:00 P.M.
(3) 9:00 P.M.
(4) 10:00 P.M.
(5) Not enough information is given.

38. A family spends 20% of its monthly income on food, 23% on rent, and 42% on other expenses and saves the balance. If the family saves $360 per month, what is its monthly income?

(1) $2,000
(2) $2,200
(3) $2,400
(4) $2,500
(5) $28,800

Question 39 is based on the following figure.

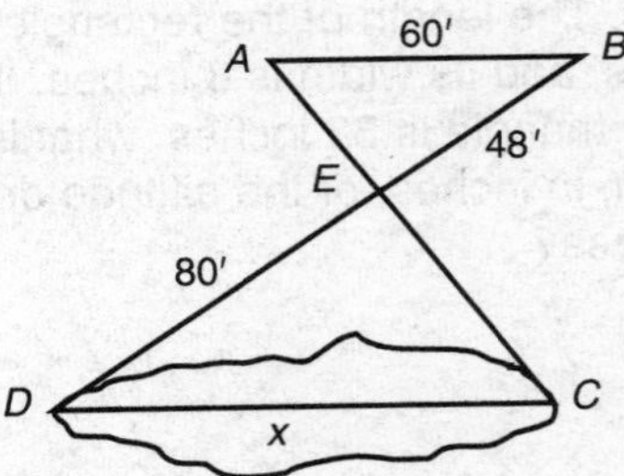

GO ON TO THE NEXT PAGE

TEST 5: MATHEMATICS

39. To measure the distance (DC) across a pond, a surveyor takes points A and B so that $\overleftrightarrow{AB}$ is parallel to $\overleftrightarrow{DC}$. If $AB = 60$ feet, $EB = 48$ feet, and $ED = 80$ feet, find DC.
    (1) 72 ft.
    (2) 84 ft.
    (3) 96 ft.
    (4) 100 ft.
    (5) Not enough information is given.

---

40. How many 4-inch by 8-inch bricks are needed to build a walk 6 feet wide and 24 feet long?
    (1) 54
    (2) 600
    (3) 648
    (4) 840
    (5) 1,000

41. Each of the numbers below is a solution of the inequality $2x + 3 > 7$ **EXCEPT**
    (1) 10
    (2) 5
    (3) 4
    (4) 3
    (5) 0

Question 42 is based on the following figure.

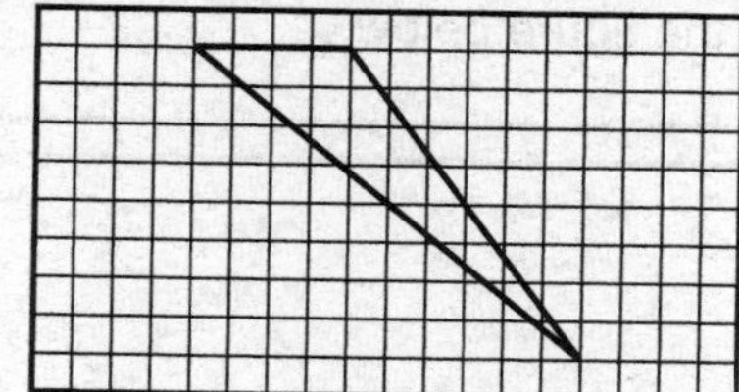

42. What is the area, in square graph units, of the triangle?
    (1) 8
    (2) 10
    (3) 16
    (4) 32
    (5) 48

43. David Gordon is a bright high school senior planning to go to college. He has narrowed his choice to two colleges that he favors equally. He has decided to select the college that will be less costly and is using the following facts to help him arrive at a decision.

    COLLEGE *A*
    Tuition — \$9,480, Board and lodging — \$6,320. Books and incidentals — \$1,200. David has been offered a scholarship of \$4,200 per year.

    COLLEGE *B*
    Tuition — \$9,200, Board and lodging — \$6,150. Books and incidentals — \$1,200. David has been offered a scholarship of \$3,200 per year.
    David has also been offered a part-time job working in the college library.

    What additional information does David need in order to make a choice?
    (1) how many miles he lives from each college
    (2) which college has the better reputation
    (3) how many scholarships each college grants
    (4) how much he can earn by working in the library at College *B*
    (5) which college has better athletic facilities

44. A room is 24 feet long, 18 feet wide, and 9 feet high. How many square yards of wallpaper are needed to paper the four walls of the room?
    (1) 72
    (2) 84
    (3) 96
    (4) 180
    (5) 756

GO ON TO THE NEXT PAGE

TEST 5: MATHEMATICS

45. A man drives x miles the first day, y miles the second day, and z miles the third day. The average mileage covered per day is

(1) $\frac{xyz}{3}$

(2) $\frac{xy + z}{3}$

(3) $x + y + z$

(4) $\frac{x + y + z}{3}$

(5) $3xyz$

46. The diameter of a bicycle wheel is 28 inches. How many inches does the bicycle move when the wheel makes 10 complete revolutions? (Use $\frac{22}{7}$ for π.)

(1) 88
(2) 440
(3) 540
(4) 750
(5) 880

47. After working 4 hours, Frank has made 21 machine parts. At the same rate, how many parts can he make in 7 hours?

(1) $\frac{7(21)}{4}$

(2) $\frac{7(4)}{21}$

(3) $7(21)$

(4) $\frac{4(21)}{7}$

(5) $7(4)(21)$

48. A storage box in a form of a rectangular solid has a square base. If V represents the volume of the box, x represents the length of a side of the base, and y represents the height of the box, which of the following equations expresses the relationship among V, x, and y?

(1) $V = 2xy$
(2) $V = xy^2$
(3) $V = 2xy^2$
(4) $V = x^2y$
(5) $V = x + xy$

49. In his will, Mr. Adams left $\frac{1}{4}$ of his estate to his wife and divided the balance between his son and his daughter. If the son received $36,000 as his share, what was the total value of the estate?

(1) $45,000
(2) $72,000
(3) $80,000
(4) $90,000
(5) Not enough information is given.

<u>Questions 50–52</u> are based on the following information.

A 3-foot-wide walkway is built around a swimming pool that is 20 feet by 30 feet, as shown in the figure below.

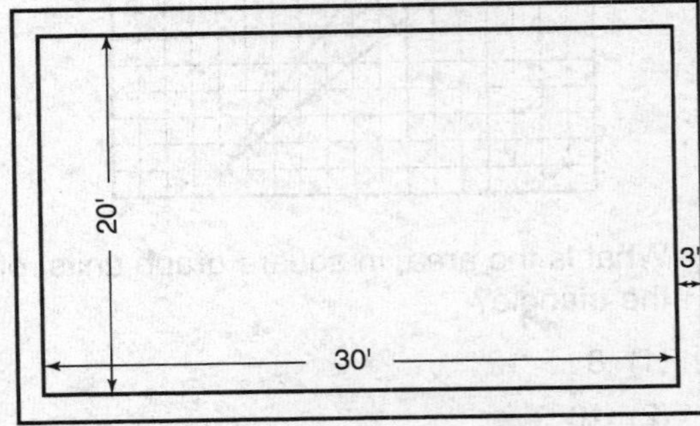

50. In order to determine how much flagstone to buy, the homeowner needs to know the total area, in square feet, of the walkway.

GO ON TO THE NEXT PAGE

TEST 5: MATHEMATICS

Which of the following expressions represents this area?

(1) (23)(33)
(2) (26)(36)
(3) (23)(33) – (20)(30)
(4) (26)(36) – (20)(30)
(5) (26)(36) – (23)(33)

51. If the average depth of the pool is 6 feet, what volume of water, in cubic feet, is needed to fill the pool?

(1) 56
(2) 300
(3) 600
(4) 3,000
(5) 3,600

52. What is the total area, in square feet, of the pool and the walkway?

(1) 50
(2) 62
(3) 759
(4) 936
(5) Not enough information is given.

---

53. A map has a scale of 1 inch = 80 miles. Lakeville and Fulton are $3\frac{5}{8}$ inches apart on the map. What is the actual distance, in miles, between Lakeville and Fulton?

(1) 190
(2) 290
(3) 310
(4) 325
(5) 350

54. The regular price of a pair of slacks is y dollars. If the price is reduced by 20%, which of the following expressions indicates the current cost of 3 pairs of slacks?

(1) $\frac{4}{5}y$
(2) $\frac{3}{5}y$
(3) $3\left(\frac{4}{5}y\right)$
(4) $3\left(\frac{3}{4}y\right)$
(5) $3\left(\frac{1}{5}y\right)$

55. Mr. Perez is on a diet. For breakfast and lunch he consumes 45% of his allowable number of calories. If he still has 1,100 calories left for the rest of the day, what is his daily allowance of calories?

(1) 495
(2) 605
(3) 1,200
(4) 2,000
(5) 2,444

56. A plumber must cut a pipe 64 inches long into two parts so that one part is 8 inches longer than the other part. Find the length, in inches, of the larger part.

(1) 28
(2) 30
(3) 36
(4) 40
(5) Not enough information is given.

END OF EXAMINATION

Answer Keys, Summaries of Results, and Self-Appraisal Charts

TEST 1: WRITING SKILLS, PART I/PAGE 669

I. CHECK YOUR ANSWERS, using the following answer key:

1. **2**	12. **5**	23. **5**	34. **4**	45. **4**
2. **3**	13. **3**	24. **1**	35. **4**	46. **4**
3. **4**	14. **4**	25. **4**	36. **4**	47. **5**
4. **2**	15. **1**	26. **4**	37. **4**	48. **1**
5. **1**	16. **4**	27. **4**	38. **1**	49. **5**
6. **4**	17. **4**	28. **5**	39. **5**	50. **2**
7. **5**	18. **4**	29. **1**	40. **3**	51. **5**
8. **5**	19. **2**	30. **5**	41. **4**	52. **4**
9. **1**	20. **1**	31. **3**	42. **3**	53. **3**
10. **5**	21. **1**	32. **2**	43. **4**	54. **1**
11. **4**	22. **5**	33. **5**	44. **5**	55. **5**

II. SCORE YOURSELF:

	Number correct:
Excellent	50–55
Good	44–49
Fair	38–43

III. EVALUATE YOUR SCORE: Did you get at least 38 correct answers? If not, you need more practice for the Writing Skills, Part I test. In any event, you can improve your performance to Excellent or Good by analyzing your errors.

IV. ANALYZE YOUR ERRORS: To determine your areas of weakness, list the number of correct answers you had under each of the following categories (which correspond to the content areas of the Writing Skills, Part I test), and compare your score with the average scores in the right-hand column. Review the answer analysis beginning on page 743 for each of the questions you got wrong, and give yourself more practice in your weak areas with the appropriate material in Unit II before attempting to take the actual GED Examination.

Content Areas	Items	Your Score	Average Score
Sentence Structure	7, 9, 13, 15, 17–19, 21, 25, 27–28, 34–36, 43–44, 47, 50, 54		13
Usage	1, 3, 5, 14, 24, 31–32		5
Spelling	6, 16, 29, 37, 45, 52		4
Punctuation	2, 11, 20, 22, 33, 38, 40–42, 46		7
Capitalization	4, 26, 48, 53		3
No correction	8, 10, 12, 23, 30, 39, 49, 51, 55		6

Total ______

TEST 2: SOCIAL STUDIES/PAGE 683

I. CHECK YOUR ANSWERS, using the following answer key:

1. **4**
2. **5**
3. **1**
4. **5**
5. **4**
6. **2**
7. **4**
8. **1**
9. **2**
10. **1**
11. **1**
12. **2**
13. **2**
14. **1**
15. **4**
16. **5**
17. **3**
18. **3**
19. **5**
20. **1**
21. **4**
22. **4**
23. **5**
24. **3**
25. **3**
26. **5**
27. **2**
28. **4**
29. **1**
30. **2**
31. **4**
32. **2**
33. **3**
34. **1**
35. **5**
36. **3**
37. **3**
38. **5**
39. **1**
40. **2**
41. **3**
42. **3**
43. **5**
44. **1**
45. **4**
46. **2**
47. **1**
48. **1**
49. **4**
50. **1**
51. **2**
52. **1**
53. **3**
54. **4**
55. **2**
56. **1**
57. **3**
58. **2**
59. **3**
60. **4**
61. **5**
62. **4**
63. **4**
64. **2**

II. SCORE YOURSELF:

Number correct:

Excellent	______ 57–64
Good	______ 51–56
Fair	______ 45–50

III. EVALUATE YOUR SCORE: Did you get at least 45 correct answers? If not, you need more practice for the Social Studies test. In any event, you can improve your performance to Excellent or Good by analyzing your errors.

IV. ANALYZE YOUR ERRORS: To determine your specific weaknesses, list the number of correct answers you had under each of the following categories (which correspond to the content areas of the Social Studies test), and compare your score with the average scores specified in the right-hand column. Review the answer analysis section beginning on page 745 for each of the questions you got wrong, and give yourself more practice in your weak areas with the appropriate material in Unit IV (including the "Glossary of Social Studies Terms"), before taking the actual GED Examination.

Content Areas	Items	Your Score	Average Score
Political Science	1–6, 9, 24–26, 29–30, 40, 52–54, 61–63		13
Economics	10–12, 14–16, 31, 33–34, 43, 47, 56–57		9
History	7–8, 13, 17–19, 41, 48–49, 55, 58, 64		9
Geography	20, 22–23, 27–28, 32, 50–51, 59–60		7
Behavioral Science	21, 35–39, 42, 44–46		8

Total ______

TEST 3: SCIENCE/PAGE 700

I. CHECK YOUR ANSWERS, using the following answer key:

1. **4**
2. **4**
3. **1**
4. **5**
5. **4**
6. **5**
7. **4**
8. **2**
9. **4**
10. **1**
11. **3**
12. **4**
13. **3**
14. **1**
15. **4**
16. **2**
17. **2**
18. **2**
19. **5**
20. **1**
21. **2**
22. **2**
23. **3**
24. **5**
25. **1**
26. **4**
27. **1**
28. **3**
29. **4**
30. **1**
31. **3**
32. **2**
33. **4**
34. **4**
35. **3**
36. **3**
37. **3**
38. **2**
39. **2**
40. **4**
41. **4**
42. **1**
43. **1**
44. **5**
45. **2**
46. **3**
47. **3**
48. **4**
49. **5**
50. **3**
51. **3**
52. **2**
53. **5**
54. **2**
55. **1**
56. **4**
57. **5**
58. **3**
59. **4**
60. **2**
61. **3**
62. **3**
63. **1**
64. **3**
65. **4**
66. **4**

II. SCORE YOURSELF:

Number correct:

Excellent	______ 60–66
Good	______ 49–59
Fair	______ 40–48

III. EVALUATE YOUR SCORE: Did you get at least 40 correct answers? If not, you need more practice for the Science test. In any event, you can improve your performance to Excellent or Good by analyzing your errors.

IV. ANALYZE YOUR ERRORS: To determine your specific weaknesses, circle the number of each question you got wrong. This will reveal the specific science area that needs emphasis in planning your study program. After studying the Answer Analysis section beginning on page 748 for each of the questions you got wrong, list the terms that you feel need further explanation and study them in the "Glossary of Scientific Terms" beginning on page 338. Then give yourself more practice in your weak areas with the appropriate material in Unit V before taking the actual GED Examination.

Content Areas	Items	Your Score	Average Score
Biology	1–11, 27–29, 33, 34, 40–56		23
Earth Science	12–17, 30–32, 57, 62–65		9
Chemistry	18–20, 35, 60, 66		3
Physics	21–26, 36–39, 58, 59, 61		10

Total ______

TEST 4: INTERPRETING LITERATURE AND THE ARTS/PAGE 714

I. CHECK YOUR ANSWERS, using the following answer key:

1. **5**	10. **5**	19. **5**	28. **1**	37. **5**
2. **2**	11. **2**	20. **5**	29. **4**	38. **4**
3. **4**	12. **5**	21. **4**	30. **4**	39. **5**
4. **2**	13. **1**	22. **1**	31. **1**	40. **4**
5. **5**	14. **4**	23. **3**	32. **3**	41. **1**
6. **4**	15. **4**	24. **4**	33. **1**	42. **4**
7. **3**	16. **3**	25. **1**	34. **4**	43. **5**
8. **5**	17. **4**	26. **5**	35. **5**	44. **4**
9. **1**	18. **1**	27. **4**	36. **1**	45. **3**

II. SCORE YOURSELF:

Number correct:

Excellent	______ 41–45
Good	______ 36–40
Fair	______ 31–35

III. EVALUATE YOUR SCORE: Did you get at least 31 correct answers? If not, you need more practice for the Interpreting Literature and the Arts test. You can improve your performance to Excellent or Good by analyzing your errors.

IV. ANALYZE YOUR ERRORS: To determine your specific weaknesses, first list the number of correct answers you had under each of the following categories and compare your score with the average scores in the right-hand column. After studying the answer analysis section beginning on page 751 for each of the questions you answered incorrectly, study the material in the section "Basic Reading Skills" and "Reading Prose, Poetry, and Drama" in Unit VI as well as the "Glossary of Literary Terms" (page 411) to strengthen your weak areas before taking the actual GED Examination.

Reading Skills	Items	Your Score	Average Score
Locating the Main Idea	12, 15, 21, 25, 30		4
Finding Details	1–2, 5, 7, 20, 22–24, 28, 32–33, 35, 37–39, 42–44		12
Inferring Meaning	3, 8, 14, 19, 27–29		4
Making Inferences	4, 6, 9–10, 13, 17–18, 26, 29–30, 34, 36, 40, 45		10
Determining Tone and Mood	31, 41		1
Inferring Character	16		1
Inferring Setting	11		1

Total ______

Now to see how your scores in the content areas of Interpreting Literature and the Arts test compare with the average scores in the right-hand column, list your score for each of the following:

Content Areas	Items	Your Score	Average Score
Popular Literature	11–25, 31–35		14
Classical Literature	26–30		3
Commentary	1–10, 36–45		14

Total ______

Literary Forms	Items	Your Score	Average Score
Prose Fiction	11–15		3
Prose Nonfiction	1–10, 31–35		11
Prose Nonfiction (Commentary)	36–45		7
Poetry	16–25		7
Drama	26–30		3

Total ______

Note: While Commentary on the Arts is a content area in itself, the commentary, as written, is in the form of prose nonfiction.

TEST 5: MATHEMATICS/PAGE 725

I. CHECK YOUR ANSWERS, using the following answer key:

1. **4**
2. **2**
3. **2**
4. **1**
5. **4**
6. **3**
7. **4**
8. **4**
9. **4**
10. **3**
11. **1**
12. **4**
13. **4**
14. **2**
15. **3**
16. **4**
17. **1**
18. **3**
19. **4**
20. **4**
21. **2**
22. **2**
23. **4**
24. **1**
25. **2**
26. **2**
27. **3**
28. **5**
29. **3**
30. **1**
31. **2**
32. **4**
33. **2**
34. **5**
35. **2**
36. **5**
37. **3**
38. **3**
39. **4**
40. **3**
41. **5**
42. **3**
43. **4**
44. **2**
45. **4**
46. **5**
47. **1**
48. **4**
49. **5**
50. **4**
51. **5**
52. **4**
53. **2**
54. **3**
55. **4**
56. **3**

II. SCORE YOURSELF:

Number correct:

Excellent	______ 51–56
Good	______ 44–50
Fair	______ 38–43

III. EVALUATE YOUR SCORE: Did you get at least 38 correct answers? If not, you need more practice for the Mathematics test. In any event, you can improve your performance to Excellent or Good by analyzing your errors.

IV. ANALYZE YOUR ERRORS: To determine your specific weaknesses, list the number of correct answers you had under each of the following categories and compare your score with the average scores specified in the right-hand column. After studying the answer analysis section beginning on page 753 for each of the questions you got wrong, give yourself more practice in your weak areas with the appropriate material in Unit VII before attempting Practice Examination Two.

Content Areas	Items	Your Score	Average Score
Arithmetic	1–3, 5, 7, 9, 12–13, 15–17, 19–20, 22–25, 27–29, 31–32, 34, 37–38, 43, 49, 53, 55		18
Algebra	6, 10–12, 14, 21, 29, 35, 36, 41, 45, 47–48, 54, 56		8
Geometry	4, 8, 18, 26, 30, 33, 39, 40, 42, 44, 46, 50–52		11

Total ______

YOUR TOTAL GED SCORE

The Writing Skills Test	______
The Social Studies Test	______
The Science Test	______
The Interpreting Literature and the Arts Test	______
The Mathematics Test	______
Total	______

Answer Analysis

TEST 1: WRITING SKILLS, PART I/PAGE 669

1. **2** *Are enrolling* is necessary to parallel *are recognizing*.
2. **3** A comma is used after an introductory clause.
3. **4** The plural verb *call* must be used to agree with the plural subject *techniques*.
4. **2** The name of a specific place such as Crimea is capitalized.
5. **1** You cannot shift pronouns that refer to the same person in the same sentence. Use either *you* or *one* throughout the sentence.
6. **4** The correct spelling is *government's*.
7. **5** Since the second sentence is a result of the first, the conjunction *so* must be used.
8. **5** No correction is necessary.
9. **1** The original is the best way.
10. **5** No correction is necessary.
11. **4** The period should be placed within the quotation marks.
12. **5** No correction is necessary.
13. **3** *Because* is correct since the second sentence states the reason for the first.
14. **4** *Has* must be inserted for parallel structure with *is six inches high, is made of leather*.
15. **1** The original is the best way.
16. **4** The correct spelling is *materials*.
17. **4** The comma is necessary to avoid the sentence fragment beginning with the *waist strap*.
18. **4** A plural verb is needed since the new subject, *the sleeping bag and its two accessories*, is plural.
19. **2** The second sentence names an example of the *tent* mentioned in the first sentence, so *such as* is used.
20. **1** Commas are used to separate items in a series.
21. **1** The original is the best way.
22. **5** No correction is necessary.
23. **5** No correction is necessary.
24. **1** The correlatives *not only* and *but also* must be followed by parallel elements.
25. **4** The period is necessary to prevent a run-on sentence.
26. **4** Holidays, such as Christmas, are capitalized.
27. **4** The second sentence becomes an adjective clause modifying *feathers*.
28. **5** The period and capital are necessary to avoid a run-on sentence.
29. **1** The correct spelling in this sentence is *affects*.
30. **5** No correction is necessary.
31. **3** The plural verb *are* is needed to agree in number with *dwellings*, the antecedent of *that*.
32. **2** *In finding* is necessary for parallel structure with *in securing*.
33. **5** No correction is necessary.
34. **4** *Concerns* must follow since the new subject, *housing*, requires a verb.
35. **4** A participial phrase is used to describe *are upgrading*.
36. **4** The sense of the sentence requires the verb *will have* after the new subject, *nation*.
37. **4** The correct spelling is *separately*.
38. **1** Commas are used to set off an appositive.
39. **5** No correction is necessary.
40. **3** An apostrophe is needed to show possession.
41. **4** Hyphens are needed to join the parts of the compound adjective *hit-and-run*.
42. **3** A comma is used to set off items in a series; here, *etc.* is the last item.
43. **4** The semicolon is needed to prevent a sentence fragment starting with *The larger*.
44. **5** The new subject *feature* requires the verb *covers*.
45. **4** The correct spelling is *benefit*.
46. **4** A question mark is used after a sentence that asks a question.
47. **5** The second sentence follows as a reason for the first.
48. **1** Only the names of specific countries are capitalized; *nation* is a common noun.
49. **5** No correction is necessary.
50. **2** The new subject, *four agencies*, is followed by the verb *may be*.
51. **5** No correction is necessary.
52. **4** The correct spelling is *assistance*.
53. **3** *Federally funded* is not a proper adjective.

54. **1** *Here is* is needed to change the fragment into a sentence.

55. **5** No correction is necessary.

TEST 1: WRITING SKILLS, PART II/PAGE 682

SAMPLE ESSAYS
For American youth

America can well take pride in its youth.

Never have young Americans achieved more than they are achieving now. On the high school level, National Merit Scholarships are being awarded to the elite of young high school graduates. Westinghouse awards are made to those young scientists and mathematicians who hold great promise of being tomorrow's leaders in science and technology. Competition for entry into the nation's finest colleges is intense. Most college graduates go on to graduate study.

In addition to educational achievement, today's youth is in the forefront of programs designed to improve the quality of life around the world. There are the scout movements, the 4 H clubs, and the Future Farmers, among many others. Peace Corps volunteers are serving in Third World countries. Youth is in the vanguard of movements that seek to advance peace. Young America is idealistic.

In business and technology, young Americans are being given increasingly important positions as managers and executives. They are, in the best sense of the term, young upwardly mobile professionals (yuppies).

In sports, the prowess of our young athletes is constantly being demonstrated, particularly in the Olympic games. In recent years, teenagers have set records in baseball's major leagues.

In the entertainment media, leaders are more and more youthful, witness the success of Matt Dillon.

Young Americans are serving proudly in our volunteer armed services.

Yes, indeed, America can well take pride in its youth.

Summary of reasons for American youth:

1. American youth is achieving at a high educational level.
2. American youth is in the forefront of groups that seek to improve the quality of life in the United States and abroad.
3. American youth is succeeding in business and technology.
4. American youth is outstanding in sports.
5. American youth leads in the field of entertainment.
6. American youth is serving in our armed forces.

Against American youth:

> *America has good reason to be concerned about its youth.*
>
> *Never before have juveniles been guilty of such heinous crimes. The term "youthful offender" has become part of our daily language, and the courts are deliberating the circumstances in which youthful offenders who have committed capital offenses can be prosecuted as adults.*
>
> *Thousands of young Americans have fallen prey to drugs, from marijuana to crack, from "coke" to heroin. With addiction comes the need to turn to crime to support the habit.*
>
> *In education, high school dropout rates have reached 30 to 40% in urban areas and special programs have proved inadequate to keep the potential dropouts in school.*
>
> *Even among the more privileged of our youth there has been a decline in the work ethic. Youth today seeks instant gratification in all its activities, from its spending habits to its penchant for instant-on television.*
>
> *Traditional values have been flouted by sexual mores that allow for cohabitation without marriage and a casual approach that results in severe health problems and soaring rates of illegitimacy.*
>
> *This generation has been called "laid back," the "now" generation, and deservedly so. In times of plenty, it has chosen to abandon traditional values to pursue its own selfish goals.*
>
> *Indeed, America has good reason to be concerned for the future of its youth.*

Summary of reasons against American youth:

1. Younger and younger Americans are engaged in crime.
2. Thousands of young Americans are drug addicts.
3. Many young Americans are school dropouts.
4. Privileged young Americans seek instant gratification.
5. Traditional sexual mores have been flouted.
6. Traditional values have been abandoned.

TEST 2: SOCIAL STUDIES/PAGE 683

1. **4** Hamilton believed in unrestricted suffrage, that is, right of voting, on the part of the people, as stated in his opening sentence.
2. **5** Rather than sovereignty of governments, Hamilton emphasized "balance between the national and state governments."
3. **1** Hamilton mentioned popular election as "this great source of free government" to be kept "perfectly pure."
4. **5** Women are permitted to serve. In fact, as stated in the middle of the second paragraph, the county committee may require equal representation of the sexes in each district.
5. **4** The end of the second paragraph contains the statement giving the purpose of the primary.
6. **2** If about 700 citizens cast their ballots in a voting district for two committeepersons, the inference can be drawn that each committeeperson represents half of the voters, or about 350.
7. **4** Of the choices given, the United States has direct involvement with Europe only in NATO, a military alliance created in 1949 as a shield against further Communist expansion or aggression. Under the North Atlantic Pact, a mutual defense agreement, an attack on any NATO member is considered an attack on all.
8. **1** The exaggerated, uncomfortable, and desperate position of Uncle Sam is meant to be critical. Note the arms stretched to reach Southeast Asia and South America, the left leg raised to touch Europe, and the outer lines beyond the globe and human figure, showing both to be unstable. The implication is that the United States cannot continue in this position.
9. **2** Henry David Thoreau expressed these ideas in opposition to the Mexican War (1846–1848). The Reverend Martin Luther King, Jr., expressed similar views in violating (what were later

declared to be unconstitutional) state laws imposing racial segregation against African Americans in the 1950s and 1960s. Civil disobedience or passive resistance implies a willingness to risk imprisonment for opposing unjust laws, while challenging those laws in the courts. Both of the above-named Americans were imprisoned for their actions, not for their ideas.

10. **1** Social Security accounts for 21%, 3% more than defense, which is the second largest program.
11. **1** Of the means-tested programs, the largest is Medicaid, three times more in percentage than either food stamps or Supplemental Security Income.
12. **2** The total of entitlement spending, both means-tested and non-means tested, is 54%, slightly more than the interest on the national debt and discretionary spending combined.
13. **2** The quotation is a perversion of the original poem, which reads "Give me your tired, your poor, your huddled masses," that is inscribed on the Statue of Liberty. By changing it to welcome only the educated, the cartoonist is criticizing the United States for not accepting poor immigrants.
14. **1** The second paragraph points out that corporate diversification (by merger) will continue to be necessary to meet new competitors.
15. **4** The third sentence mentions that a company can sometimes get qualified technical manpower only by acquiring another company.
16. **5** The passage emphasizes future, rather than established, competitors as creating a motivation to merge.
17. **3** The author uses such terms as *finest* to describe the American population.
18. **3** He predicts that Americans will become "distinct" because of the "different climates" they inhabit.
19. **5** In America, the rewards of work are readily available.
20. **1** The world is becoming a "global village" according to Marshall McLuhan, as a result of this aspect of the Industrial Revolution.
21. **4** The nuclear family, typical in the modern industrial city, consists only of the parents and their unmarried children. The extended family of more traditional, agricultural societies includes grandparents, parents, children (both married and unmarried), and often such dependents as the wife's sister *all* under one roof. In the extended family, each member has clearly defined roles, and family ties are usually much stronger than in the nuclear one.
22. **4** The graphs project that, by 2025, Africa's percentage of the world's population will increase by 7%, from 12% in 1990 to 19% in 2025 which is more than any other region's percentage.
23. **5** North America, the former Soviet Union, and Asia will each decrease by 1%; Latin America will increase by 1%; Europe will have the largest decrease—3%.
24. **3** All of the others are mentioned in the Bill of Rights: freedom of religion—Amendment 1; freedom of the press—Amendment 1; a well-disciplined militia—Amendment 2; trial by jury—Amendment 7.
25. **3** "The President shall be Commander-in-Chief of the Army and Navy . . . and of the Militia" according to the United States Constitution.
26. **5** Elections by the people correct abuses that otherwise would have to be "lopped by the sword of revolution."
27. **2** Scale is the ratio between distance as shown on a map and the actual distance on the earth.
28. **4** The passage states that a compass rose shows direction.
29. **1** Problems like those of inflation, recession, and shortages of fuel or fertilizer cannot possibly be handled by individual state governments.
30. **2** This is the famous "clear and present danger" doctrine stated by Justice Oliver Wendell Holmes in the case of Schenck v. U.S. (1919). When the right to free speech endangers the common good, the common good prevails and free speech must be limited.
31. **4** The balance of payments involves all the economic transactions that a nation and its people have with the rest of the world, including the trade and investments of businesses, the tourism of citizens, and the economic and military grants and loans of

government. A deficit in the balance of payments reflects a net cash flow out of a nation as a result of all the above exchanges. The quotation says that such a deficit might be minimized or reversed by increasing exports and decreasing imports.

32. **2** Those who favor development of new energy sources tend to give a low priority to the need to protect our environment and to conserve our natural resources.
33. **3** Model *B* shows an economy that could lead to depression if supply and demand were not brought into balance. A balance could result from a decrease in income tax rates, which would increase consumer demand.
34. **1** In 1929–1939, the great depression in the United States was characterized by huge supply and little demand because of high unemployment. This situation is depicted in model *A*.
35. **5** The Indian population was carried over from the time before Columbus discovered the Americas.
36. **3** The United States had no role in settling or colonizing Latin America.
37. **3** In the first sentence, the author acknowledges that his findings will be "highly distasteful to many persons."
38. **5** The author states his concern for truth as discovered through reason.
39. **1** The author states that man may be hopeful for a "still higher destiny" because he has already risen to the top of the organic scale.
40. **2** Lobbying is the use of politically experienced persons to influence lawmakers by providing financial support, testifying at hearings, supplying information, and drafting legislation on behalf of interested parties.
41. **3** The Monroe Doctrine, a statement that any attempt by European powers to intervene in the Western Hemisphere would be regarded as dangerous to the peace and safety of the United States, was applied by President Kennedy to Russia's attempt in 1962 to establish a missile base in Cuba.
42. **3** Sexism, the exploitation and domination of one sex by the other, more traditionally of women by men, has been countered by the Women's Liberation Movement and by legislation. Women, on the basis of preference and ability, now enter occupations, previously closed to them.
43. **5** Top-level management has 23% men and only 9% women.
44. **1** The author gives advice to couples as to how they can improve intimacy in their marriage.
45. **4** The author refers to some who "cannot endure being close to people" and others who "have the right to expect such closeness."
46. **2** A wedding is a social situation. The other situations refer to intimate or public distance.
47. **1** The tax is graduated because it divides the taxed population into income groups with increasing tax percentage rates by stages for groups with increasing incomes.
48. **1** Imperialism is the policy of acquiring colonies or of establishing political and economic control of foreign areas.
49. **4** The cooperation of nations to prevent any one country from becoming dominant is a definition of the term *balance of power*.
50. **1** In 1990, Asia has approximately 31/53 of the world's population. In 2000 (est.), it is projected to have 37/63. Both are over 50%.
51. **2** Africa's projected population is 866,585,000, while that of Europe is 818,378,000.
52. **1** George Washington's policy of avoiding entangling alliances is consistent with the policy of Speaker *A*, who would steer clear of involvement with other countries.
53. **3** Speakers *B* and *C* speak of participation and getting involved. In other words, they advocate active diplomacy to achieve our nation's goals.
54. **4** The statements of all four speakers deal with the foreign affairs of the United States. The "classic problem" involves isolation versus involvement.
55. **2** The point of the pupil's question is the role of women in the founding of the United States, indicating that more attention should be given the role of women in U.S. history.
56. **1** The nation with the greatest public health problem is Bolivia. As the column labeled Infant Mortality indicates, 142 infants die out of each

1,000 born. The Life Expectancy column indicates that Bolivians, of the six nations on the chart, have the lowest odds for a long life (51 years to Costa Rica's 73).

57. **3** According to the Urban Population column in the table, 76% of Venezuelans reside in cities, the highest urban population of the six countries listed in the graph.
58. **2** The danger of nuclear war continues because other nations besides the United States and the former Soviet Union, such as those "growing" small bombs in the forefront of the cartoon, already have some nuclear weapons or have the technical capacity to build them.
59. **3** The projections show that the percentage of persons aged 65 and over as a percent of the total U.S. population will more than double by 2030. Therefore, much greater attention must be paid to this segment of the population, including a review of policies concerning the elderly.
60. **4** Since most people retire or continue as part-time workers after age 65, there will be a decrease in the percentage of full-time workers.
61. **5** Liberty includes freedom from slavery or captivity, plus the rights held in common by the people of a community, including the franchise, the right to vote. The Thirteenth and Fifteenth amendments accomplished the goal of securing the blessings of liberty.
62. **4** Social Security's Old Age and Survivor's Insurance Program was designed to help the elderly and various categories of employed and dependent persons. As such, it promoted the general welfare.
63. **4** By making "every contract, combination in the form of trust or otherwise, or conspiracy in restraint of trade" illegal, the act reflected the government's concern for the public welfare as affected by the actions of private business.
64. **2** The cartoon shows that the international community (the "peace-loving nations of the world") ignored the destruction of cities and the loss of human life in former Yugoslavia and did nothing to end the war that began there in 1992.

TEST 3: SCIENCE/PAGE 700

1. **4** Diffusion is the process whereby molecules of substances tend to intermingle—in this case, as they pass through the placenta.
2. **4** Refer to the statement in the opening sentence of the passage.
3. **1** Digested food and oxygen pass to the embryo from the mother's bloodstream. No blood as such is exchanged. Wastes from the metabolic activities of the embryo are passed into the mother's bloodstream.
4. **5** The first sentence indicates that sodium chloride assumes special significance in the regulation of water exchange in the organism.
5. **4** According to the passage, the largest mineral component of blood is sodium chloride (salt); the purpose of this salt is the regulation of water within the organism.
6. **5** The opening sentence of the passage states that sodium chloride is the largest constituent of the mineral matter of the blood.
7. **4** The digested food is dissolved in water and is absorbed through the intestinal wall.
8. **2** Since the normal number of chromosomes in human body cells is now known to be 46, the number of chromosomes in the sperms and eggs is one-half that number or 23.
9. **4** Body cells have 2 times the number of chromosomes in sex cells. In fertilization (union of sex cells) the normal number of chromosomes is restored.
10. **1** By definition.
11. **3** The passage refers to cancer as an illustration of abnormal cell division.

12. **4** Most protozoa do not lend themselves to fossilization. Only those with silicon-containing shells surrounding the cell will fossilize. Other protozoa have shells of calcium carbonate.
13. **3** Anthropologists deal with the origin, development, ethnic groups, customs, and beliefs of humanity. Protozoologists are mainly interested in live, one-celled animals. Archaeologists study the people, customs, and life of ancient times. Geologists deal with the Earth's crust, the layers of which it is composed, and their history. Zoologists are biologists concerned with the animal kingdom.
14. **1** The closing sentence of the passage summarizes the basic cause of the ice ages.
15. **4** The temperature of the air is indicated on the thermometer marked *B*. The scale is marked in units of 10°, and the mercury has risen to the fourth subdivision between 20° and 30°. Therefore the reading is 28°.
16. **2** The temperature of the ice-water mixture (23°) is lower than the temperature of the air in the box (28°). Therefore, the air near the glass cup will be cooled below the temperature of the surrounding air. At this lower temperature, the amount of moisture the air can hold decreases. The droplets of water represent the excess moisture that has condensed out of the air.
17. **2** The dew point temperature is the temperature at which the air becomes saturated (as shown by the water droplets). Since the temperature of the air near the cup is the same as that of the ice-water mixture, the reading of 23°C on thermometer *A* is the dew point temperature.
18. **2** A change from the gaseous phase to the liquid phase is called condensation. A change from the liquid phase to the gaseous phase is called evaporation. A change from the solid phase to the liquid phase is called melting or fusion.
19. **5** The passage says that naphthalane, for example, vaporizes easily because of weak intermolecular forces.
20. **1** The definition of sublimation is given in the closing sentence of the passage.
21. **2** Newton's laws pertain to bodies in motion. According to Archimedes' principle, as stated in the article, when a body sinks, its weight is greater than the buoyant force or weight of liquid that it displaces. Einstein's law expresses mathematically the relationship between matter and energy. Galileo experimented with falling bodies. Boyle's law deals with the relationship between the volume of a gas and the pressure exerted on it.
22. **2** The purpose of filling the ballast tanks is to ensure that the submarine will sink in the water.
23. **3** The weight of water wings or lifesaving jackets is negligible compared with the increase in the volume of the wearer. According to Archimedes' principle, we can increase the tendency to float either by decreasing the weight of the body or by increasing its volume.
24. **5** The passage opens with the statement that water is a good conductor of sound.
25. **1** Sonar makes use of high-frequency sounds, which are sent out and then reflected from underwater objects.
26. **4** It takes half of the total time, or 3 secs., for the sound wave from the ship to reach the sea floor. Since sound travels at the rate of 4,800 ft./sec. through water, it will travel a distance of 4,800 × 3, or 14,400 ft. to the bottom of the sea before its echoes will start to return.
27. **1** The largest fish on the chart swim faster than the smaller fish. In fact, the slowest fish, the lemon sole, is also the smallest. While size and speed may not actually be connected in this way, from the figures on the chart one may hypothesize that they are.
28. **3** The scientific names of the flounder and the lemon sole indicate that they belong to the same genus, *Pleuronectes*, and therefore are probably related.
29. **4** Being careful that enough breeders survive to replace the fish taken is a logical solution to the problem of declining populations. The other answer choices are opinions.
30. **1** Observe that there is almost no change in temperature between the months of January and February. The temperature in January is –5°C, and in February it is just above –5°C.
31. **3** In September the average temperature was just above 15°C and can be

estimated to be 16°C. The precipitation for September was between 60 mm and 80 mm and can be estimated to be 68 mm.

32. **2** The graph for temperature shows a pronounced rise in the summer months, while the bars for moisture are all about the same size.
33. **4** Without bright petals or a strong odor, the oak flowers could not attract insects and could be pollinated only by wind.
34. **4** Since plants produce oxygen, the level may drop because there are not enough plants. However, animals use oxygen, so too many fish will also lower the oxygen level.
35. **3** Since alkalis have a high pH, adding an alkali will raise the pH of the soil. Choices 2 and 5 add acid, thus lowering the pH. Pure water could raise the pH, but never higher than pH 7. The tap water has the same pH as the soil, so it would make no change at all.
36. **3** For a plane mirror, every point of the image is as far behind the mirror as the corresponding point of the object is in front. This is indicated in the following sketch. Note that Choice 3 closely points in the same direction as the image.

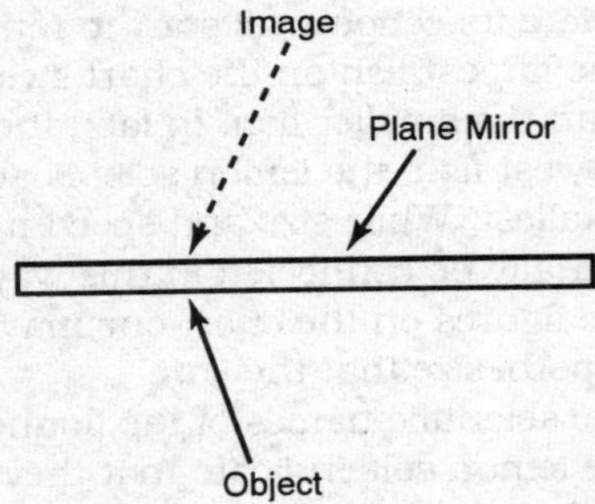

37. **3** The car is going at constant speed in a straight line, so no unbalanced force is acting on it. In Choices 1 and 2, the object starts at rest and picks up speed. Choice 4 involves a change in direction, which requires an unbalanced force. Choice 5 is wrong because a car in neutral will surely slow down.
38. **2** While overheating a device is probably not good, the current continues to flow through it and the circuit is not broken.
39. **2** All of the listed properties of light are true, but only one explains why the shadow conforms to the shape of the object. Straight lines from the lamp to the wall are blocked by the object to form the shadow.
40. **4** After the calendar year has been written on various documents for 365 days, writing these dates becomes automatic, and so, without thinking, the error is made in the early days of the new year.
41. **4** Habit formation leads to efficiency. This explains why the names were written more neatly and in greater number with the hand normally used.
42. **1** The brain is not involved in reflex acts. A reflex is a simple, quick, automatic act that involves the neurons and the spinal cord.
43. **1** See explanation for question 42.
44. **5** Solving a crossword puzzle involves the higher senses of memory and reasoning.
45. **2** Nest building is a complex activity, involving finding materials and constructing the nest. Through instinct, the incubator robin does things right the first time, even though it has never seen a nest.
46. **3** On previous occasions when the baby cried, adult attention was forthcoming. The infant cried in response to pain, but for the older baby crying was conditioned behavior.
47. **3** All training of animals is the result of conditioning. The dolphin associates the reward (food) with the performance of the trick.
48. **4** Dotting *i*'s and crossing *t*'s has been learned by extensive practice, forming a habit that is hard to disobey.
49. **5** The higher senses are involved in the studying and remembering necessary for satisfactory GED scores.
50. **3** This is an important observation that led to further research.
51. **3** This finding established that there was a connection between removal of the pancreas and the presence of sugar in the urine.
52. **2** This similarity provided a control group for the experiment.
53. **5** This suggestion, which is open to question, is unrelated to this problem.
54. **2** This is a good description of the method used.

55. 1 A great many questions are associated with the secretions of the pancreas, and could be answered only by a long series of experiments.

56. 4 There is no direct evidence that human diabetes is related to the results of the experiments on dogs, but the finding of sugar in the urine points strongly in that direction.

57. 5 The clouds block the entry of radiant heat in the daytime, so the days will be cooler. Also, since the clouds block the escape of radiant heat at night, the nights will be warmer.

58. 4 Potassium = 31, sulfur = 32, chlorine = 36.

59. 2 Subtract the number of protons from the atomic weight of an element to find the number of neutrons. For potassium: 31 − 19 = 12.

60. 3 Choice 1 has 1 atom of oxygen on the left side and 2 atoms on the right. Choice 2 has 2 hydroxide (OH) ions on the left side and 4 on the right. Choice 4 has too many chloride and too many hydrogen atoms on the right side. Choice 5 has twice as many atoms of each element on the right side as on the left.

61. 3 Products are on the right side of the equation. In this equation the products are water and magnesium oxide.

62. 3 In the passage, weather is defined as the state of the atmosphere at any given time. Insolation is the amount of solar energy received at the Earth's surface. Nearness to bodies of water may affect climate. Climate is the composite of weather conditions over a long period of time.

63. 1 Bodies of water are stabilizers of temperature. As a result the atmospheric conditions are more uniform over water than over land areas. Regions far from bodies of water do not enjoy the stabilizing effects and have hotter summers and colder winters.

64. 3 Radiation is heat in the form of solar rays. Conduction is the transfer of heat by direct conduct between two bodies. Convection is the transfer of heat by the motion of a gas. Weathering is the process of disintegration or decomposition of rocks at or near the surface of the Earth.

65. 4 Topography is the general configuration of the Earth's surface. Altitude refers to elevation. Humans cannot control winds, storms, or the direction of ocean currents. Radiation from atomic experimentation, however, may affect the atmosphere and climatic conditions.

66. 4 During a phase change, the constant temperature is represented by a horizontal line on the graph. Melting occurs at the lower of the two constant temperatures (20°C), and boiling at the higher one (40°C).

TEST 4: INTERPRETING LITERATURE AND THE ARTS/PAGE 714

1. 5 The author says, "It is the gardens . . . that are the truly spectacular thing here."

2. 2 The author mentions the estate's "dry formality."

3. 4 The article says that John D. Rockefeller, Jr. "envisioned Kykuit as the serious expression of the stature of a great family."

4. 2 He says, "These rooms always feel domestic, which was presumably the intention."

5. 5 "A number of paintings of note" are cited.

6. 4 Since Green Seal "helps shoppers single out honest environmental claims," it would influence shoppers who are concerned about the environment.

7. 3 The article indicates that "the organization develops stringent environmental standards for products."

8. 5 Unlike other nations' programs, Green Seal gets its "money from foundations and individual donors."

9. 1 The staff "monitors the product's role in the environment."

10. 5 Green Seal is concerned with the "dumping of waste paper," among other factors.

11. 2 The setting of Oberfest at the foot of the snow-covered mountains is especially significant because of its contribution to the tragic ending.

12. 5 Nowhere is any theme (the essential subject) of the incident stated. The theme—that people, through actions based on rumor and fear, bring about their own destruction—is left to the reader to deduce from the evidence presented by the author.

13. 1 In addition to the meaning given in the "Glossary of Literary Terms" on page 411, irony also refers to a combination of circumstances that results in the opposite of what might be expected to happen. That is true of this selection; the alarm, which should summon help, brings the opposite—destruction.

14. 4 The word *cold* has two meanings in this context: a literal or denotative meaning of very chilly as applied to climate, and an extended or connotative meaning, lifeless.

15. 4 Oberfest was buried beneath the snow without a trace.

16. 3 "I" failed as a cornetist, a basketball player, and a football player.

17. 4 The title, a way of remembering E, G, B, D, F—the notes of the musical staff, describes the opposite of what happened to the poet.

18. 1 The reader is asked to consider the poem a failure, which it definitely is not.

19. 5 The poet compares his physical posture on stage to his "hand-tied necktie."

20. 5 The poet says to the reader, "Consider this poem a failure."

21. 4 Lines 2–6 and 8–12 list life's treasures, which the poet urges us to enjoy.

22. 1 Line 3 refers to "blue waves whitened on a cliff."

23. 3 In line 7, music is compared to a curve of gold. Since the word *like* is used, this comparison is a simile.

24. 4 The poet indicates that "holy thoughts" will delight the spirit.

25. 1 The poet urges the reader to "give all you have been or could be" for life's loveliness.

26. 5 Happy says Willy "had no right to do that. There was no necessity for it."

27. 4 Happy says to Biff, "Don't say that!" when Biff says Willy "had the wrong dreams." Charley says to Biff, "You don't understand."

28. 1 Charley says, "Nobody dast blame this man. A salesman has got to dream, boy."

29. 4 Happy states that Willy "had a good dream" and he's gonna "win it for him."

30. 4 Linda says, "At this time especially. First time in thirty-five years we were just about free and clear."

31. 1 The author's negative feelings are indicated by the use of such words as *beast* and *sadistic*, and *vindictive*.

32. 3 The action referred to is "the purely phony move of the boxer who extends his gloves to his rival" on the floor.

33. 1 The passage states that the mob "roots consistently for the smaller man" and "howls with glee at a good finisher making his kill."

34. 4 The author's opinion is evident in the use of such words as *beast*, *lurks*, and *gray thing*.

35. 5 The author describes the mob (audience) as "vindictive."

36. 1 The word *still* indicates the author is surprised that many do not know this major American writer.

37. 5 The author refers to Cather's "feeling for the earth."

38. 4 The excerpt refers to the town's "burning summers" and "blustery winters."

39. 5 Cather "had the power to elevate ordinary people and places."

40. 4 "Cather believed that America's promise would endure," states the passage.

41. 1 The author presents a factual account of how the Oscar came to be.

42. 4 The organization now represents the industry as a whole, its professed purpose, since "Hollywood's guilds and unions are strongly represented."

43. 5 The awards are now financed by a television network instead of by the studios.

44. 4 The columnist Sidney Skolsky overheard the name being used and popularized it in his columns.

45. 3 The voting branches are composed of members who "must have gained prominence" in their fields.

TEST 5: MATHEMATICS/PAGE 725

1. **4** \$15,000 – \$8,000 = \$7,000 sales over \$8,000
$0.05 \times \$7,000 = \$350$ commission
\$200 + \$350 = \$550 total salary

2. **2** 12 oz. = $\frac{12}{16}$ lb. = $\frac{3}{4}$ lb.
Cost of $\frac{3}{4}$ lb. of apples: $\frac{3}{4}$(\$0.84) = \$.63
Cost of 1 lb. of apples: \$.84
Total cost: \$1.47

3. **2** To obtain the average rate of speed, divide the total distance covered by the total driving time.
Total distance = 80 + 100 = 180 mi.
Total time = 2 + 3 = 5 hr.
$180 \div 5 = 36$ mph.

4. **1** Let x = width of enlarged picture.
Set up a proportion:
$\frac{\text{length of picture}}{\text{width of picture}}: \frac{8}{6} = \frac{12}{x}$
$8x = 6(12) = 72$
$x = 72 \div 8 = 9$ in.

5. **4** $23\frac{1}{4} = 23\frac{2}{8} = 22\frac{10}{8}$
$22\frac{10}{8} - 19\frac{5}{8} = 3\frac{5}{8}$
$3\frac{5}{8} = \frac{29}{8}$
$\frac{29}{8} \times \$80 = \$290$

6. **3** $3x - 1 < 5$
$3x < 6$
$x < 2$
Of the choices given, the only choice less than 2 is 1.

7. **4** $850 \times 0.60 = 510$ seats in orchestra
$850 - 510 = 340$ seats not in orchestra

8. **4** Let $4x$ = measure of larger acute angle, and x = measure of smaller acute angle.
$4x + x = 90$
$5x = 90$
$x = 90 \div 5 = 18$
$4x = 4(18) = 72°$.

9. **4** 25 ft. 8 in. = 24 ft. + 12 in. + 8 in.
= 24 ft. 20 in.

  24 ft. 20 in.
– 18 ft. 10 in.
  6 ft. 10 in.

10. **3** Bill earns m dollars per month.
Angelo earns n dollars per month.
Together Bill and Angelo earn $(m + n)$ dollars per month.
In 1 year, Bill and Angelo earn $12(m + n)$ dollars.

11. **1** Perimeter of figure is
$x + 2y + 3x - y + 2x + 3y + 5x + y = 11x + 5y$.

12. **4** Let x = Maria's earnings, and $2x$ = Joan's earnings.
$x + 2x = 42$
$3x = 42$
$x = 42 \div 3 = \$14$

13. **4** \$5,800 – \$4,500 = \$1,300
Tax is \$100 + 5% of \$1,300 =
100 + 0.05(1,300) = 100 + 65 = \$165

14. **2** $x = 2a(b + 7)$
$= 2(3)(5 + 7)$
$= 2(3)(12)$
$= 72$

15. **3** To find the median weight, arrange the weights in increasing order and identify the middle weight. In order of increasing size, the weights are as follows:
184, 193, 195, 197, 198, 201, 203, 205, 207, 212, 214 lb.
The median (sixth) weight is 201 lb.

16. **4** Since there are 7 women among the 11 committee members, the probability of choosing a woman is $\frac{7}{11}$.

17. **1** 12 oz. = $\frac{12}{16} = \frac{3}{4}$ lb.
5 lb. 12 oz. = $5\frac{3}{4} = \frac{23}{4}$ lb.
If $\frac{23}{4}$ lb. cost \$2.07, then 1 lb. costs $\$2.07 \div \frac{23}{4}$.
$2.07 \div \frac{23}{4} = 2.07 \times \frac{4}{23} = \$0.36$

18. **3** $m\angle CBD = 125°$
$m\angle ABC = 180° - 125° = 55°$
$m\angle A + m\angle ABC = 90°$
$m\angle A + 55° = 90°$
$m\angle A = 90° - 55° = 35°$

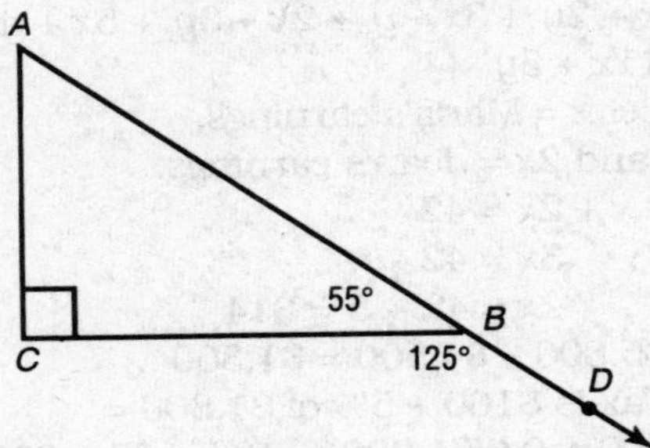

19. **4** 10% + 25% + 30% + 15% = 80%, so 80% passed, and 20% failed.
20% of 80 = 0.20(80) = 16

20. **4** $20,000 × 0.07 = $1,400
$12,000 × 0.075 = $900
$1,400 + $900 = $2,300

21. **2** Since 12 eggs cost x cents, 3 eggs cost $\frac{3}{12}$, or $\frac{1}{4}$, as much: $\frac{1}{4}x = \frac{x}{4}$.

22. **2** Calculate the yearly income for each choice.
A. $27,000
B. $570 × 52 = $29,000
C. $2,250 × 12 = $27,000
D. 6 × $2,000 = $12,000 for the first half-year
10% of $2,000 = $200
$2,000 + $200 = $2,200 each month for the second 6 months
6 × $2,200 = $13,200 for the second half-year
$12,000 + $13,200 = $25,200 for the first year

The correct choice is (2).

23. **4** First, the dealer bought 2(12) or 24 jackets at $48 each. The following month, she bought 15 jackets at $48. In all, she bought (24 + 15) jackets at $48, spending a total of 48(24 + 15) dollars.

24. **1** 45 min. = $\frac{45}{60}$, or $\frac{3}{4}$ hr.
At 48 mph, the faster car covers $\frac{3}{4} \times 48$, or 36 mi.
At 36 mph, the slower car covers $\frac{3}{4} \times 36$, or 27 mi.
36 − 27 = 9 mi.

25. **2** Meat department sales = $2,500
Dairy department sales = $1,500
Difference = $1,000

26. **2** Use the Pythagorean theorem.
$x^2 = (15)^2 + (20)^2$
$= 225 + 400 = 625$
$x = \sqrt{625} = 25$ mi.

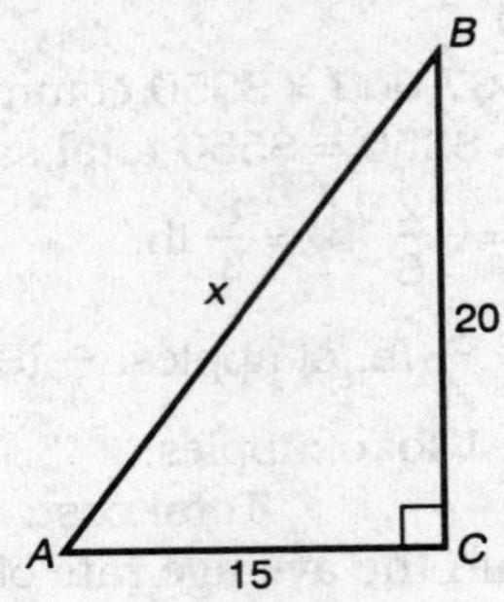

27. **3** $\frac{7}{8} - \frac{1}{4} = \frac{7}{8} - \frac{2}{8} = \frac{5}{8}$
$\frac{5}{8} \times 280 = 175$ gal. used

28. **5** To express a number in scientific notation, express it as the product of a number between 1 and 10 and a power of 10. In this case, the number between 1 and 10 is 2.750389. In going from 2.750389 to 2,750,389, you move the decimal point 6 places to the right. Each move represents a multiplication by 10 and 6 moves represents a multiplication by 10^6.
Thus, 2,750,389 = 2.750389 × 10^6.

29. **3** The team has played 75 games and will play 45 more games.
75 + 45 = 120
60% of 120 = 0.6 × 120 = 72
The team must win 72 games, and it has already won 50 games.
Therefore, the team must win 72 − 50 = 22 more games.

30. **1** Area of rectangle = length × width = 12 × 8 = 96 sq. in.
Area of triangle = $\frac{1}{2}$ base × altitude = $\frac{1}{2}(32)(x) = 16x$
$16x = 96$
$x = 6$ in.

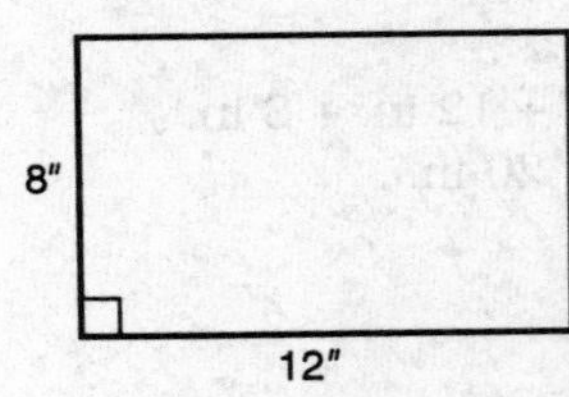

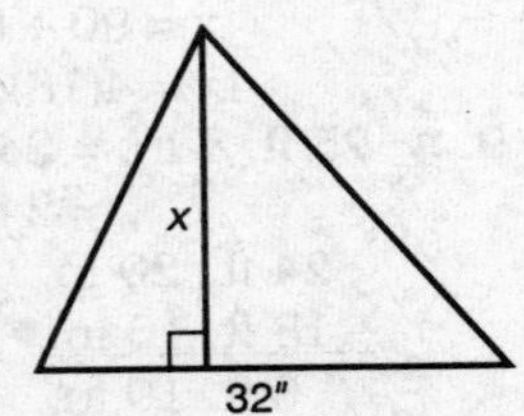

31. **2** The number of students in the school is $18 \times 35 = 630$. If there are to be 30 students in a class, the number of classes needed is $630 \div 30 = 21$. Therefore, the number of new classes needed is $21 - 18 = 3$.

32. **4** 40% of the total expenses of $240,000 went for labor.
$0.40(\$240{,}000) = \$96{,}000$

33. **2** Slope $= \dfrac{y_1 - y_2}{x_1 - x_2}$
In this case $y_1 = 4$, $y_2 = 3$, $x_1 = 5$, and $x_2 = 0$.
Slope $= \dfrac{4-3}{5-0} = \dfrac{1}{5}$

34. **5** 1 km = 1,000 m
1 m = 100 cm, so
1 km = 100,000 cm
1 m = 1,000 mm, so
1 km = 1,000,000 mm.
Only choice (5) is correct.

35. **2** Test each pair: Only (2, 4) and (3, 7) satisfy the equation.
$3(2) - 4 = 6 - 4 = 2$, and
$3(3) - 7 = 9 - 7 = 2$.
None of the other pairs works.

36. **5** $3x - 1 = 11$
$3x = 11 + 1 = 12$
$x = 12 \div 3 = 4$
$x^2 + x = (4)^2 + 4 = 16 + 4 = 20$

37. **3** The first bell rings at 9:00 A.M., 11:00 A.M., 1:00 P.M., 3:00 P.M., 5:00 P.M., 7:00 P.M., 9:00 P.M.
The second bell rings at 9:00 A.M., 12:00 noon, 3:00 P.M., 6:00 P.M., 9:00 P.M.
The third bell rings at 9:00 A.M., 1:00 P.M., 5:00 P.M., 9:00 P.M.
All 3 bells will ring again at 9:00 P.M.

38. **3** Expenditures: 20% + 23% + 42% = 85%
Savings: 100% − 85% = 15%
Let x = family's monthly income. Then $0.15x = \$360$, so $x = \$360 \div 0.15 = \$2{,}400$

39. **4** Let $x = DC$.
Since $\triangle ABE$ is similar to $\triangle CED$, the lengths of their corresponding sides are in proportion.
$\dfrac{x}{60} = \dfrac{80}{48}$
$48x = 80(60) = 4800$
$x = 4800 \div 48 = 100$ ft.

40. **3** Width of walk is 6 ft., or $6 \times 12 = 72$ in. Width of each brick is 4 in. Number of bricks that can be fitted along the width is $72 \div 4 = 18$.
Length of walk is 24 ft., or $24 \times 12 = 288$ in. Length of each brick is 8 in. Number of bricks that can be fitted along the length is $288 \div 8 = 36$.
$18 \times 36 = 648$

41. **5** Since $2x + 3 > 7$, then $2x > 4$, and $x > 2$. Of the choices listed, only 0 is *not* greater than 2.

42. **3** Use the formula for the area of a triangle:
$A = \dfrac{1}{2}bh$.
In this case, $b = 4$ and $h = 8$.
Area $= \dfrac{1}{2}(4)(8) = 16$

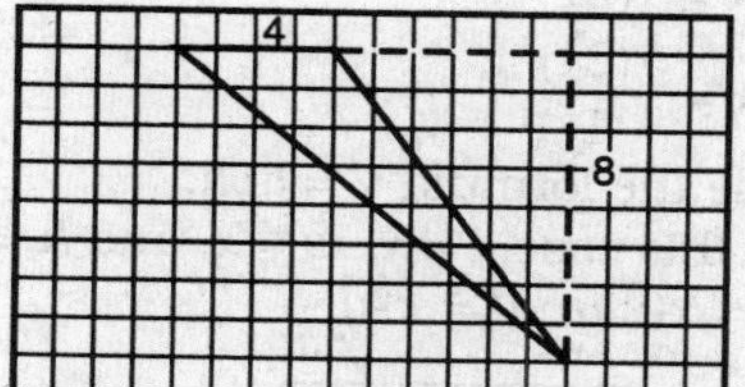

43. **4** To make a sound financial decision, David must know how much he can earn by working in the College *B* library.

44. **2** Area of front wall =
$9 \times 24 = 216$ sq. ft.
Area of back wall =
$9 \times 24 = 216$ sq. ft.
Area of side wall =
$9 \times 18 = 162$ sq. ft.
Area of other side wall =
$9 \times 18 = 162$ sq. ft.
Total area of walls =
$216 + 216 + 162 + 162 = 756$ sq. ft.
$756 \div 9 = 84$ sq. yd.

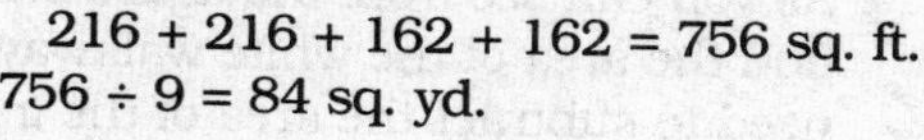

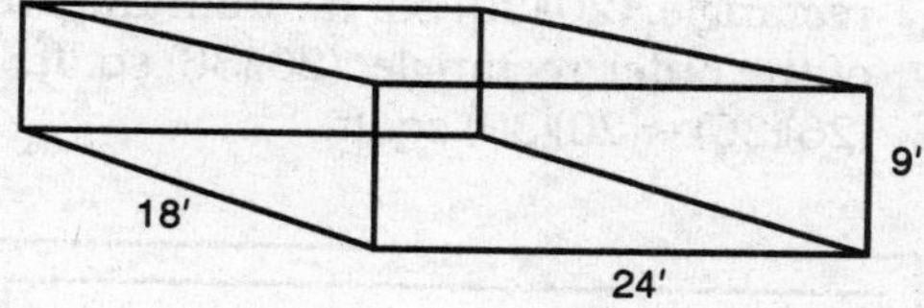

45. **4** To find the average, divide the total mileage by the total time.
Total distance $= x + y + z$
Total time = 3 days
Average $= \dfrac{x + y + z}{3}$

46. **5** To find the circumference of the wheel, use the formula $C = \pi d$.

In this case, $\pi = \frac{22}{7}$ and $d = 28$.

$C = \frac{22}{7} \times 28 = 88$ in.

Every time the wheel makes a complete revolution, the bicycle moves the distance of the circumference, or 88 in. In 10 complete revolutions, the bicycle moves $10 \times 88 = 880$ in.

47. **1** Let x = number of machine parts Frank can make in 7 hr.

Set up a proportion:

$\frac{4}{21} = \frac{7}{x}$

$4x = 7(21)$

$x = \frac{7(21)}{4}$

48. **4** Use the formula $V = lwh$.

In this case, $l = x$, $w = x$, and $h = y$

$V = x(x)y \quad V = x^2y$

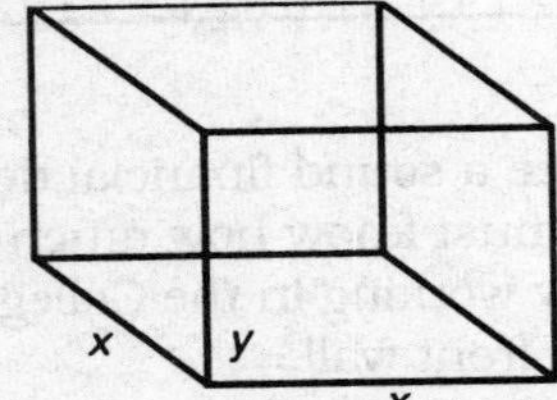

49. **5** To find the value of the estate, you need to know either the daughter's share or the fractional part of the estate received by the son. Neither item of information is given.

50. **4** As you can see from the figure below, to find the area of the white walkway, you need to subtract the area of the inner rectangle, (20)(30) sq. ft., from the area of the outer rectangle, (26)(36) sq. ft.:

(26)(36) – (20)(30) sq. ft.

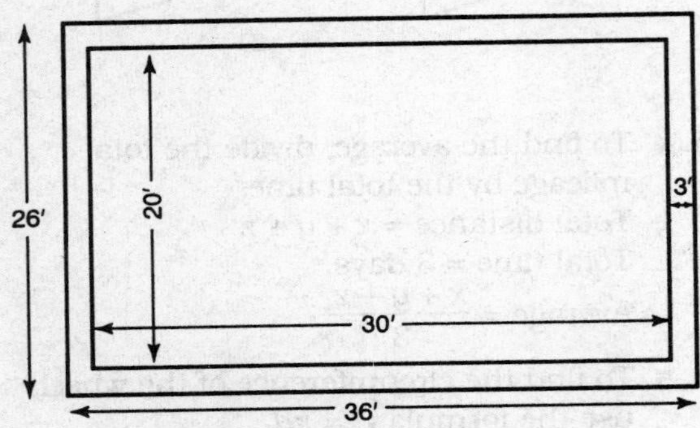

51. **5** Since the average depth of the pool is 6 ft., the water forms a rectangular solid with dimensions 30 by 20 by 6. The volume of the water is the product of these three numbers:

(30)(20)(6) = 3,600 cu. ft.

52. **4** Taken together, the pool and the walkway form a rectangle with dimensions 36 by 26. The total area is the product of these numbers:

(36)(26) = 936 sq. ft.

53. **2** Since 1 in. = 80 mi.,

3 in. = 3(80) = 240 mi., and

$\frac{5}{8}$ in. $= \frac{5}{8}(80) = 50$ mi.

240 + 50 = 290 mi.

54. **3** Since the price of a pair of slacks has been reduced by 20%, or $\frac{1}{5}$, the current price is $\frac{4}{5}$ of the original price: $\frac{4}{5}y$. The current price of 3 pairs of slacks is $3\left(\frac{4}{5}y\right)$.

55. **4** For breakfast and lunch Mr. Perez consumes 45% of his allowable number of calories and has 55% left for the rest of the day.

Let x = number of allowable calories per day.

$0.55x = 1{,}100$

$x = 1{,}100 \div 0.55 = 2{,}000$

56. **3** Let x = length of shorter part, and $x + 8$ = length of longer part.

$x + x + 8 = 64$

$2x + 8 = 64$

$2x = 64 - 8 = 56$

$x = 56 \div 2 = 28$

$x + 8 = 28 + 8 = 36$